Principles and Practice of Lifespan Developmental Neuropsychology

Principles and Practice of Lifespan Developmental Neuropsychology

Jacobus Donders
Scott J. Hunter

2010

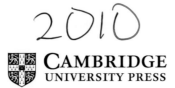

CAMBRIDGE
UNIVERSITY PRESS

CAMBRIDGE UNIVERSITY PRESS
Cambridge, New York, Melbourne, Madrid, Cape Town, Singapore,
São Paulo, Delhi, Dubai, Tokyo

Cambridge University Press
The Edinburgh Building, Cambridge CB2 8RU, UK

Published in the United States of America by
Cambridge University Press, New York

www.cambridge.org
Information on this title: www.cambridge.org/9780521896221

First published 2010

Printed in the United Kingdom at the University Press, Cambridge

A catalogue record for this publication is available from the British Library

ISBN 978-0-521-89622-1 Hardback

Additional resources for this publication at www.cambridge.org/9780521896221

Contents

The color plates are to be found between pp. 276 and 277

Contact information for authors

Vicki Anderson, Ph.D.
Department of Psychology
Royal Children's Hospital
Parkville, Victoria, Australia

Deborah K. Attix, Ph.D.
Department of Psychiatry and Behavioral Sciences
Duke University Medical Center
Durham, NC

James Baños, Ph.D., ABPP-Cn
Department of Physical Medicine & Rehabilitation
University of Alabama, Birmingham
Birmingham, AL

Marcia Barnes, Ph.D.
Children's Learning Institute
University of Texas Health Science Center at Houston
Houston, TX

Marianne Barton, Ph.D.
Department of Psychology
University of Connecticut
Storrs, CT

Miriam Beauchamp, Ph.D.
Department of Psychology
Royal Children's Hospital
Parkville, Victoria, Australia

Anne-Claude V. Bedard, Ph.D.
Department of Psychiatry
Mount Sinai Medical Center
New York, NY

Jane Holmes Bernstein, Ph.D.
Neuropsychology Program
Children's Hospital Boston
Department of Psychiatry
Harvard Medical School
Boston, MA

Olga G. Berwid, Ph.D.
Department of Psychiatry
Mount Sinai Medical Center
New York, NY

Anil Chako, Ph.D.
Department of Psychiatry
Mount Sinai Medical Center
New York, NY

Colby Chlebowski, M.A.
Department of Psychology
University of Connecticut
Storrs, CT

Jamila Cunningham, M.A.
Department of Psychology
Loyola University
Chicago, IL

Jennifer Duncan Davis, Ph.D.
Department of Psychiatry and Human Behavior
Warren Alpert School of Medicine of Brown University
Providence, RI

Jacobus Donders, Ph.D.
Department of Psychology
Mary Free Bed Rehabilitation Hospital
Grand Rapids, MI

Julian Dooley, Ph.D.
Murdoch Childrens Research Institute
Melbourne, Australia

Lianne English
Department of Psychology
University of Guelph
Guelph, Ontario, Canada

Thomas Farmer, Psy.D.
The Chicago School of Professional Psychology
Chicago, IL

Deborah Fein, Ph.D.
Department of Psychology
University of Connecticut
Storrs, CT

Lindsey Felix, Ph.D.
Alexian Brothers
Neuroscience Institute
Chicago, IL

Jodene Goldenring Fine, Ph.D.
Department of Psychiatry
Michigan State University
East Lansing, MI

Felicia C. Goldstein, Ph.D.
Department of Neurology
Emory University School of Medicine and Wesley
Woods Center on Aging
Atlanta, GA

Ilana Gonik, Ph.D
Department of Psychiatry
Loyola University Medical Center
Maywood, IL

Jeffrey M. Halperin, Ph.D
Department of Psychology
Queens College, CUNY
Flushing, NY

Lana L. Harder, Ph.D.
Department of Psychiatry
University of Texas Southwestern Medical School
Children's Medical Centre

Bruce Hermann, Ph.D.
Department of Neurology
University of Wisconsin Madison School of Medicine
Madison, WI

Grayson N. Holmbeck, Ph.D.
Department of Psychology
Loyola University of Chicago
Chicago, IL

Scott J. Hunter, Ph.D.
Departments of Psychiatry & Pediatrics
University of Chicago
Chicago, IL

Peter Isquith, Ph.D.
Department of Psychiatry
Dartmouth Medical School
Hanover, NH

Neelam Jain, Ph.D.
Department of Epidemiology and Cancer Control
St. Jude Children's Research Hospital
Memphis, TN

Kelly Janke, M.A.
Department of Psychology
University of Wisconsin, Milwaukee
Milwaukee, WI

Betsy Kammerer, Ph.D.
Deaf and Hard of Hearing Program
Children's Hospital Boston
Waltham, MA

Michael W. Kirkwood, Ph.D.
Department of Physical Medicine & Rehabilitation
The Children's Hospital
Aurora, CO

Bonnie Klein-Tasman, Ph.D.
Department of Psychology
University of Wisconsin, Milwaukee
Milwaukee, WI

Kevin R. Krull, Ph.D.
Department of Epidemiology and Cancer Control
St. Jude Children's Research Hospital
Memphis, TN

Elizabeth Kunchandy, Ph.D.
Rehabilitation Care Service
VA – Pudget Sound
Seattle, WA

Maureen Lacy, Ph.D.
Department of Psychiatry
University of Chicago
Chicago, IL

Susan H. Landry, Ph.D.
The University of Texas Health Science Center
Department of Pediatrics
Children's Learning Institute
Houston, TX

Harvey S. Levin, Ph.D.
Cognitive Neuroscience Laboratory
Departments of Physical Medicine and Rehabilitation, Neurosurgery and Psychiatry
Baylor College of Medicine
Houston, TX

David Marks, Ph.D.
Department of Psychiatry
Mount Sinai Medical Center
New York, NY

Brenna C. McDonald, PsyD
Departments of Radiology and Neurology
Indiana University School of Medicine
Indianapolis, IN

Lisa M. Noll, Ph.D.
Learning Support Center for Child Psychology
Texas Children's Hospital
Houston, TX

Thomas Novack, Ph.D.
Department of Physical Medicine & Rehabilitation
University of Alabama, Birmingham
Birmingham, AL

Sarah J. Paterson, Ph.D.
Department of Pediatrics
Children's Hospital of Philadelphia
Philadelphia, PA

Celiane Rey-Casserly, Ph.D.
Department of Psychiatry
Children's Hospital and Harvard Medical School, Boston
Boston, MA

Tresa Roebuck-Spencer, Ph.D., ABPP-Cn
Department of Psychology
National Rehabilitation Hospital
Washington DC

Anthony C. Ruocco, Ph.D.
Department of Psychiatry
University of Illinois at Chicago
Chicago, IL

Andrew J. Saykin, PsyD
Departments of Radiology, Neurology, and Psychiatry
Indiana University School of Medicine
Indianapolis, IN

Michael Seidenberg, Ph.D.
Department of Psychology
Rosalind Franklin University of Medicine and Science
North Chicago, IL

Margaret Semrud-Clikeman, Ph.D.
Departments of Psychology & Psychiatry
Michigan State University
East Lansing, MI

Elsa Shapiro, Ph.D.
Pediatric Clinical Neuroscience
University of Minnesota Medical Center
Minneapolis, MN

Mark Sherer, Ph.D., ABPP-Cn
TIRR Memorial Hermann
Baylor College of Medicine
Houston, TX

Abigail B. Sivan, Ph.D.
Department of Psychiatry & Behavioral Science
Feinberg School of Medicine
Northwestern University
Chicago, IL

Elizabeth P. Sparrow, Ph.D.
Sparrow Neuropsychology, P.A.
Durham, NC

Gregory M. Stasi, Ph.D.
Rush Neurobehavioral Center
Skokie, IL

Tyler J. Story, Ph.D.
Division of Neurology
Duke University Medical Center
Durham, NC

H. Lee Swanson, Ph.D.
Graduate School of Education
University of California-Riverside
Riverside, CA

Amy Szarkowski, Ph.D.
Deaf and Hard of Hearing Program
Children's Hospital Boston
Waltham, MA

Lori G. Tall, PsyD
Rush Neurobehavioral Center
Skokie, IL

Heather B. Taylor, Ph.D.
The University of Texas Health Science Center
Department of Pediatrics
Children's Learning Institute
Houston, TX

Joey Trampush, M.A.
Department of Psychology
CUNY Graduate Center
New York, NY

Christine Trask, Ph.D.
Department of Psychiatry and Human Behavior
Warren Alpert School of Medicine of Brown University
Providence, RI

Geoffrey Tremont, Ph.D.
Neuropsychology Program, Rhode Island Hospital
Providence, RI

Marie Van Tubbergen, Ph.D.
Department of Physical Medicine and
Rehabilitation
University of Michigan
Ann Arbor, MI

Clemente Vega
Yale University School of Medicine
Department of Neurosurgery
New Haven, CT

Seth Warschausky, Ph.D.
Department of Physical Medicine and
Rehabilitation
University of Michigan
Ann Arbor, MI

Desiree White, Ph.D.
Department of Psychology
Washington University
St. Louis, MO

John Williamson, Ph.D.
Department of Neurology and
Rehabilitation
University of Illinois at Chicago
Chicago, IL

Julie M. Wolf, Ph.D.
Yale Child Study Center
New Haven, CT

Keith Owen Yeates, Ph.D.
The Research Institute at Nationwide Children's
Hospital
Columbus, OH

Michael Zaccariello, Ph.D.
Department of Psychiatry and Psychology
Mayo Clinic

Alexandra Zagoloff, M.S.
Department of Psychology
Illinois Institute of Technology
Chicago, IL

Kathy Zebracki, Ph.D.
Department of Behavioral Sciences,
Rush University Medical Center,
Pediatric Psychologist,
Shriners Hospital for Children,
Chicago, IL

Frank Zelko, Ph.D.
Neuropsychology Service, Children's Memorial Hospital
Department of Psychiatry and Behavioral Science
Feinberg School of Medicine, Northwestern University
Chicago, IL

Richard Ziegler, Ph.D.
Pediatric Clinical Neuroscience
University of Minnesota Medical Center
Minneapolis, MN

Biography for Jacobus Donders

Jacobus Donders obtained his PhD from the University of Windsor in 1988. He completed his internship at Henry Ford Hospital in Detroit, MI, and his residency at the University of Michigan in Ann Arbor, MI. He is currently the Chief Psychologist at Mary Free Bed Rehabilitation Hospital in Grand Rapids, MI. Dr. Donders is board-certified by the American Board of Professional Psychology in both Clinical Neuropsychology and Rehabilitation Psychology. He has served on multiple editorial and professional executive boards, has authored or co-authored more than 100 publications in peer-reviewed journals, and has co-edited two books about neuropsychological intervention. He is a Fellow of the National Academy of Neuropsychology and of Divisions 40 (Clinical Neuropsychology) and 22 (Rehabilitation Psychology) of the American Psychological Association. His main research interests include construct and criterion validity of neuropsychological test instruments and prediction of outcome in congenital disorders and acquired brain injury.

Biography for Scott J. Hunter

Scott J. Hunter is an Associate Professor of Psychiatry, Behavioral Neuroscience, and Pediatrics in the Pritzker School of Medicine at the University of Chicago, where he serves as the Director of Pediatric Neuropsychology and Coordinator for Child Psychology training. Dr. Hunter obtained his PhD in Clinical and Developmental Psychology from the University of Illinois at Chicago in 1996. He completed his internship at Northwestern University School of Medicine's Stone Institute of Psychiatry, and residencies in Pediatric Neuropsychology and Developmental Disabilities in the Departments of Pediatrics and Neurology at the University of Rochester. He serves as an ad-hoc editor for a number of peer-reviewed publications, and has authored or co-authored multiple peer-reviewed articles, presentations, and book chapters. He co-edited *Pediatric Neuropsychological Intervention* (CUP, 2007) with Jacobus Donders. Both clinically and in his research, Dr. Hunter specializes in identifying and characterizing neurocognitive and behavioral dysfunction in children with complex medical and neurodevelopmental disorders.

To Harry van der Vlugt, my original mentor, for sharing his lifespan wisdom and support.

Jacobus Donders

This book is dedicated to the memory of Arthur Benton and Rathe Karrer, who each mentored my professional development, and to Richard Renfro, for his ongoing support and understanding during the development and completion of this project.

Scott J. Hunter

Introduction

Jacobus Donders and Scott J. Hunter

Neuropsychology is the science and practice of evaluating and understanding brain–behavior relationships and providing recommendations for intervention that can be implemented in the daily lives of persons when brain dysfunction compromises functioning at home or school, on the job, or in the community at large. The associated target behaviors and skills can range from specific cognitive abilities to emotional and psychosocial functioning. This specialty has advanced significantly over the past several years, but recent well-respected published works about common neuropsychological disorders have tended to focus primarily or exclusively on either children or adults, or have provided separate discussions of conditions that are traditionally seen more commonly at either end of the age spectrum (e.g. Morgan and Ricker [1], Snyder et al. [2]). Similarly, there is a dearth of comprehensive discussions in the available literature to date of various neuropsychological syndromes in their different manifestations across the lifespan, and the longitudinal development and longer-term outcomes of such conditions. This has contributed to a sometimes unwarranted bifurcation within the field, where developmental course has been left out of the diagnostic and treatment equation. In response, the primary goal of this volume is to provide an integrated review of neuropsychological function and dysfunction from early childhood through adulthood and, where possible, old age, to support the understanding and consideration of the role development plays in the presentation and outcome of neuropsychological disorders across the lifespan.

Each chapter in this volume is intended as an empirical review of the current state of knowledge concerning the manifestation and evaluation of common neuropsychological disorders as well as their intervention, with additional consideration of what still needs to be done to improve efficacy of practice and research. The first section provides a review of the general principles behind lifespan developmental neuropsychology. The second section examines a number of commonly encountered neurodevelopmental, behavioral, and cognitive disorders. For many of the disorders, there is one chapter focusing on pediatric aspects of the condition, one emphasizing adult and/or geriatric concerns, and a summary commentary chapter that consolidates and synthesizes the knowledge shared across the age-specific review chapters, with a focus on identifying and guiding areas of further research and practice in the domain. For some conditions (e.g. cerebral palsy) there are currently simply not enough data about outcomes into adulthood to warrant a separate chapter, whereas for other diagnostic groups (especially some of the neurodegenerative ones, which are often associated with death prior to adulthood), the emphasis is placed on the time frame in which they most commonly occur. However, for several other disorders (e.g. traumatic brain injury), there is a wealth of information about the correlates of new-onset cases of the condition at different ages, as well as longitudinal outcomes.

Each of the chapters in this volume was written by one or more authors who specialize in clinical practice as well as research with the disorder being discussed. As a result, these experts give the reader an up-to-date account of the state of the art of the field at this time, and make suggestions for improvement in approaches toward assessment, intervention, and empirical investigation of the disorders as they present across the lifespan. We hope that this book will provide a vantage point from which to explore lifespan developmental aspects of a wide range of commonly encountered neuropsychological disorders. We anticipate that it will be of interest not only to pediatric neuropsychologists but also to professionals in rehabilitation, neurology, and various allied health fields.

References

1. Morgan JE, Ricker JH. *Textbook of Clinical Neuropsychology*. New York: Taylor & Francis; 2008.
2. Snyder PJ, Nussbaum PD, Robins, DL. *Clinical Neuropsychology: A Pocket Handbook for Assessment*, 2nd edn. Washington DC: American Psychological Association; 2006.

Theory and models

A lifespan review of developmental neuroanatomy

John Williamson

On the development of functional neural systems

The structure of the brain is in constant flux from the moment of its conception to the firing of its final nerve impulse in death. As the brain develops, functional networks are created that underlie our cognitive and emotional capacities. Our technologies for evaluating these functional systems have changed over time as well, evolving from lesion-based case studies, neuropathological analyses, in vivo neurophysiological techniques (e.g. electroencephalography), and in vivo structural evaluation (CT scan, magnetic resonance imaging (MRI), diffusion tensor imaging (DTI)), to in vivo functional methodologies (functional magnetic resonance imaging (fMRI), positron emission tomography (PET)). And with these rapidly developing technologies, we are able to more thoroughly test some of the earlier hypotheses that were developed about the nature and function of the brain.

Although attempts to localize mental processes to the brain may be traced to antiquity, the phrenologists Gall and Spurtzheim may have initiated the first modern attempt, by hypothesizing that language is confined to the frontal lobes [1]. While these early hypotheses were largely ignored as phrenology fell in ill-repute, they were resurrected in the early 1860s by Paul Broca, who, inspired by a discussion of the phrenologists' work, sparked a renewed interest in localization of brain function with his seminal case studies on aphasia [2]. Broca's explorations were among the earliest examples of lateralized language dominance.

Recently, high-resolution structural MRI was applied to preserved specimens taken from two of Broca's patients, to examine the localization of damage on the surface and interior of the brains. This modern technology revealed extensive damage in the medial regions of the brain and highlighted inconsistencies with previous hypotheses in the area of the brain identified by Broca, which is now identified as Broca's area [3]. This is interesting, both from a historical perspective and also

with respect to our current understandings of the brain systems involved in the behavioral presentations Broca described (beyond the articulatory functions of the inferior frontal gyrus); specifically the extent of behavioral changes identified by Broca is now more accurately reflected by the apparent neuropathology.

A contemporary of Broca's, John Hughlings Jackson, offered a different perspective regarding localization. While Jackson had no problem with the notion of probabilistic behavior profiles with specific brain lesions (e.g. a left inferior frontal lesion most likely will affect expressive speech), he did not agree with the prevailing idea at the time that these lesion/behavior observations represented a confined center of function [4]. Jackson proposed a vertical organization of brain functions, with each level (e.g. brain stem, motor and sensory cortex, and prefrontal cortex) containing a representation, or component of the function of interest. Though this idea was at the periphery of opinion at the time, when strict localizationist theory was gaining momentum, it has come to form the basis of modern thought regarding the mechanisms of brain and behavior relationships.

Holes and gaps in the models of strict localization of behaviors to specific, contained brain regions became more salient to the mainstream neuroscience community over time (cf. the disrepute of phrenology and conflicting findings from lesion/behavior studies). In response, Karl Lashley's search for the memory engram typified another era in the exploration of brain–behavior relationships. Using an experimental approach rather than the classic case study method, Lashley, famously unable to localize memory function in rats (through progressive brain ablation), introduced the constructs of equipotentiality and mass action [5]. Equipotentiality is the concept that all brain tissue is equally capable of taking over the function of any other brain tissue (demonstrated in the visual cortex) and, relatedly, mass action references the idea that the behavioral impact of a lesion is dependent on its size, not its location. Also, although less popularized, he suggested that, at any given time, the pattern of neural activity is more important than location when understanding higher cognitive functions [6]. Although plasticity in the human brain does not conform to notions of equipotentiality, recent research on stem-cell treatments in neurodegenerative diseases has reinvigorated the construct in an albeit new form. Guillame and Zhang [7] review the use of embryonic stem cells as a neural cell replacement technique and strides in functional integration, axonal growth, and neurotransmitter release (e.g. the development of dopamine-producing cells in mouse brains after stem cell implantation).

Historically, political and social influences on the philosophy of science trended Western societies away from the study of brain structures in the understanding of behavior after World War I [8]. In contrast, researchers in the former Soviet Union continued that approach. For example, while in opposition to the idea of equipotentiality, Filimonov (cited in Luria, 1966 [9, 10]), a Soviet neurologist, presented the concepts of functional pluripotentialism and graded localization of functions. Specifically, he postulated that no cerebral formation is responsible for one unique task, and that the same tissue is involved in multiple tasks, given the right conditions. These concepts signaled a move from strict localization approaches to understanding brain–behavior relationships to a dynamic functional systems approach (i.e. back to a Jacksonian view), most notably attributed to Alexandr Romanovich Luria. His approach to neuropsychological investigation stood in contrast to Western psychometric methods, by instead focusing on the effect of specific brain lesions on localized/adjacent functional systems (syndrome analysis) [10].

Luria stated that simple to more complex behavioral operations are not localized to a particular brain region, but instead managed by an "elaborate apparatus consisting of various brain structures" [11]. Though other definitions of functional systems, or even neural networks, have since been posited, this early view eloquently described the construct. Luria proposed that all functional systems must involve three core blocks including (1) the arousal block, (2) the sensory input block, and (3) the output/planning unit. Structurally, the arousal unit referenced reticular formation and related structures that impact cortical arousal; the sensory input unit referenced post central-fissure structures and the integration of cross-modal sensory data; and the output/planning unit referenced primarily the frontal lobes and involved planning and execution of behavior [12].

Luria presented a theory of functional systems development based on these three functional units. He suggested that the three functional units develop hierarchically in the form of increasingly complex cortical zones. These zones correspond to primary, secondary, and tertiary motor and sensory areas, which develop in order of complexity, with the tertiary planning unit (anatomically demarcated by prefrontal areas) appearing last [12]. Luria's developmental theory mirrors Jackson's proposal that neuro-anatomical development proceeds upward from the spinal cord to neocortex and from the posterior to anterior [4].

Functional systems, of course, are organized within a far more complicated web than Luria's original three-tiered theory. Still, modern brain researchers have "run" with the idea of the functional system. Recent research has explored questions of the nature of top-down control (vertical integration), with some investigators arguing for specific areas within the stream as primary originators (e.g. lateral prefrontal cortex [13]), while others argue for different cortical systems as top-down controllers (e.g. fronto-parietal and cingulo-opercular control networks [14]).

Functional neuroanatomy is the basis of our understanding of the human condition, as is an understanding of how that anatomy interacts with the body and its environment; a complex dance. What we do know is that almost any behavior, even a slight deviation in heartbeat interval, may be influenced by myriad factors within the nervous system. A deviation of heartbeat interval can be influenced by fluctuations in physical activity, thinking, and emotional status [15, 16]. Our exploration of brain–behavior relationships is further complicated by language, and more specifically the definition of constructs that are chosen to define these relationships. Take, for example, our understanding of a change in heartbeat interval and its relationship to emotion. Constructs such as fear, anger, sadness, and happiness describe rather large subsets of behavior. In order to capture these emotions at a brain level, Arne Ohman has suggested that emotion is a "flexibly organized ensemble of responses, which uses whatever environmental support is available to fulfill its biological function" [17].

This is a noticeably loose definition. It has to be with constructs such as emotional memory [18], expressive aprosodia and receptive aprosodia [19], emotional intelligence [20], approach and withdrawal [21], and terms such as melancholy, wistfulness, euphoria, mirth, and doldrums floating around in the collective consciousness of researchers and the lay public. To understand that minute shift in heartbeat interval, we need to understand the emotional state of our subject. To evaluate the functional systems involved in that heartbeat shift, we need to understand the interconnecting pathways involved in vagal (cranial nerve X) control of the heart (direct parasympathetic nervous system influence is necessary in a beat-to-beat change in heart rate). What structures connect to the vagus? What structures connect to those structures? Are there afferent feedback loops? How do these control systems develop? The so-called "decade of the brain" has extended and we have an ever-developing complexity in our understanding of the brain's role in defining what it means to be human. It is an exciting time to be a neuropsychologist.

The development of functional neuroanatomy across the lifespan is a complicated topic. This chapter, necessarily, is not a comprehensive review of the subject, but is instead a detailed introduction. As such, the purpose of the following sections is to discuss current research and our current knowledge regarding the neuroanatomical structures that are of particular interest with regard to understanding cognitive and emotional development. The chapter is therefore organized as follows: (1) *Brain structure*. In this section, we cover cellular structures and brain areas in their prototypical forms, discussing general associated functions. (2) *Brain development across the lifespan*. This section covers the mechanism of brain development and notable changes over time in anatomy and function.

Brain structure

The nervous system is composed of central (CNS), peripheral (PNS), and enteric branches. The brain and spinal cord form the CNS. Nerves that connect the spinal cord and brain to peripheral structures such as the heart compose the PNS. The enteric nervous system controls the gastrointestinal system primarily via communication with the parasympathetic and sympathetic nervous systems.

Brain cells

The brain has two classes of cells, neurons and glia. There are many different types of cells within each class, although they all share characteristics that distinguish these nervous system cells from other cells in the body. Generally stated, neurons are specialized electro-chemical signal transmitters and receivers. Glia serve a supporting role in the brain (e.g. nutritional and scavenger functions, growth factors, blood–brain barrier components, and

myelin–white matter creation) and have a role in neurogenesis during development (e.g. radial glia as neuron progenitors [22]).

Neurons

Within the adult neocortex, there are billions of neurons and 10 to 50 times more glia. The total number of synapses is estimated to be approximately 0.15 quadrillion. Myelinated white matter is estimated to span between 150 000 and 180 000 kilometers in the young adult [23, 24].

Neurons are composed of a cell body, axon, and dendritic fields. The cell body contains less than a tenth of the cell's entire volume, with the remainder contained within the axon and dendrites [25]. Synapses are interaction points between neurons. An individual neuron communicates via action potential. Action potentials are all-or-none electrical events which are excited (promoted) or inhibited (prevented) based on the nature of synaptic stimulation (e.g. the nature of chemical and electrical stimulation via neurotransmitters and graded potentials). A single neuron may be in direct contact (via synapse) with thousands of other neurons. The firing rate of a neuron is influenced by the summation of inhibitory and excitatory events along the axon and dendritic–synaptic interactions among the numerous connections. Speed of transmission is a function of white matter width and myelination.

White matter may be myelinated or unmyelinated. Myelination increases transmission speed. Myelin sheaths (covering axons) are generated by specialized glial cells in the brain called *oligodendroglia*, and in the periphery by cells called *Schwann cells*.

Neurons may be classified as unipolar, pseudounipolar, or bipolar depending on the cell body form and number and arrangement of processes. Functional characteristics are also used in classification (e.g. afferent neurons that conduct signals from the periphery to the CNS are also called sensory neurons, and efferent neurons that conduct signals from the CNS to the periphery are also called motor neurons). Further, neurotransmitter receptor types are also used to describe neurons. For example, neurons containing serotonin or glutamate are referenced as serotonergic or glutaminergic neurons [26].

Neurotransmitters

Neurotransmitters are chemical agents that bind to specialized receptors on neurons. Neurotransmitters specifically relevant to neuropsychology include, but are not limited to, serotonin (e.g. depression/anxiety), acetylcholine (e.g. memory), dopamine (e.g. motor), norepinephrine (e.g. depression), glutamate (e.g. memory), and gamma-aminobutyric acid (e.g. anxiety). The effect of a particular neurotransmitter on a functional system is largely determined by receptor types. Each neurotransmitter can bind to multiple receptor types. The distribution of receptor types is not even throughout the brain and may influence emotional state/traits, disease outcomes in mental health, and response to psychopharmacologically active medications. For example, protein expression of serotonin receptors in the prefrontal cortex differentiates successful suicidal patients and controls [27]. Asymmetry in serotonin receptors is found in depressed patients with greater right prefrontal receptor density than left compared with controls [28]. Moreover, higher baseline binding potential in chronic depression pharmacological treatment is associated with worse outcomes [29]. For a more comprehensive review of neuronal structure and function, see Levitan and Kaczmarek [30].

Cranial nerves

There are 12 cranial nerves. A solid understanding of the effects of cranial nerve lesions, or the effects of upstream lesions on cranial nerve activity, is an important tool for neuropsychologists in evaluating patient presentation. Cranial nerves have both sensory and motor functions. For example, cranial nerve level control of the muscles of the eye is distributed across three nerves (the oculomotor, trochlear, and abducens nerves), whereas sensory information from the eye is transmitted via the optic nerve. The optic nerve projects from the retina, to the thalamus, through the temporal and parietal cortices, and to the calcerine cortex in the occipital lobe. Processing is not performed at the level of the cranial nerves, which only serve to connect/transmit information from processing centers. Testing cranial nerve function can, however, give clues as to the nature of a lesion. For example, the optic radiations of the optic nerve travel close to the surface of the cortex of the temporal lobe. A unilateral lesion of the temporal lobe can cause a contralateral visual field cut. Examining associated behavioral changes can suggest a location for a functional lesion. For a more detailed review of cranial nerve functions and assessment see Monkhouse [31].

Rhombencephalon

The rhombencephalon, or hindbrain, is composed of the medulla oblongata, the pons, and the cerebellum. Functionally, the hindbrain contains several structures involved in neural networks regulating autonomic nervous system (ANS) function and arousal. Cranial nerves regulating the ANS (vagus), and movements of the mouth, throat, neck, and shoulders (glossopharyngeal, hypoglossal, trigeminal, spinal accessory) are found in the hindbrain. Additional structures include the reticular formation (basic autonomic functions, respiration), nucleus of the solitary tract (in actuality, this refers to several structures) and the nucleus ambiguus. The nucleus ambiguus and the nucleus of the solitary tract are the primary interface junctions for the vagus nerve, which enervates the viscera. In thinking about the development of brain structures and functional systems relevant to emotional and cognitive behaviors, it may be helpful to consider phylogeny and lessons from comparative neuroscience.

Transitioning from reptiles to mammals, we see the emergence of myelinated vagus. Returning to our earlier example of emotion and changes in heartbeat intervals, Porges [32, 33] discusses the impact of this system and its development on social engagement behaviors in humans with his polyvagal perspective, contrasting and elucidating the interactions of brainstem structures, peripheral afferents, cortical and subcortical top-down control, and myelinated and unmyelinated vagal efferents. Regulation of the autonomic nervous system is a complex component of social behaviors and emotional response. Cortical, subcortical, and other brain structures such as the amygdala, hypothalamus, orbitofrontal cortex, and temporal cortex all interact via direct and indirect pathways with these hindbrain structures to influence parasympathetic and sympathetic nervous system response. Further, the nucleus of the solitary tract receives afferent input from the periphery (e.g. baroreceptors, which monitor and relay changes in blood pressure), which is in turn distributed to subcortical and cortical structures for processing.

These hindbrain structures should be considered as output and input nuclei for a range of supportive behavioral features in the human (e.g. facilitating appropriate arousal levels for performing cognitive, exertional, and social functions). Also contained within the rhombencephalon are the pons and cerebellum. Functionally, these structures contribute to fine motor control via postural and kinesthetic feedback to volitional areas (e.g. premotor and motor cortex). This includes facilitating motor movements in speech.

In addition to fine motor control, lesions of the cerebellum have a wide range of behavioral and cognitive consequences. The cerebellum has reciprocal connections to brainstem nuclei, hypothalamus, and prefrontal and parietal cortices (among other areas). Behavioral effects of cerebellar lesions observed in the literature include autonomic disregulation [34], flattening of affect, distractibility, impulsiveness, stereotyped behaviors, depression [35], memory and learning dysfunction, language problems, and visuospatial effects [36]. Though these problems in cognition and behavior are clearly less severe than lesions in associated areas of neocortex and some reported issues have not been replicated, the variety of impacts suggests an important role for the cerebellum in some of these functional systems. There are some interesting clues as to what that role may be.

Recent research has shown additional roles of the cerebellum in speech with lesion effects beyond dystaxic motor impairments in speech formation. Ackerman et al. [37] review recent clinical and functional imaging data as they pertain to speech syndromes and potential connections to other cognitive functions following cerebellar lesions. They argue that connections to language areas in the cortex function as conduits to subvocalization (self speech) which is involved in verbal working memory (a right cerebellar/left frontal interaction). This subvocalization argument is also present in other modalities (e.g. imagined movements). These connections, along with the hypotheses of planning and rehearsal components attributed to cerebellar activity, may explain the increasing evidence of wide-reaching cognitive and behavioral effects with cerebellar lesions.

Mesencephalon

The midbrain includes the substantia nigra (linked to dopamine production and Parkinson disease), the superior and inferior colliculi (visual and auditory system actions), and a large portion of the reticular activating system (RAS). The reticular activating system, formed in part by nuclei in the midbrain tegmentum, plays a role in consciousness. The discovery of the RAS was critical for understanding coma. It serves as a modulator of sleep and wakefulness via connections to the diencephalic structures, the thalamus (thalamic reticular nucleus) and hypothalamus. These connections ascending from the reticular formation are part of the ascending reticular activating system. Also nested within the midbrain are projections from the dorsal raphe nucleus (from the hindbrain structure, the pons). The raphe is a source of serotonin and is also involved in the regulation of sleep cycles.

The substantia nigra is functionally linked to the basal ganglia, specifically the caudate nucleus and the putamen (referred to collectively as the striatum). It is divided into two sections, the pars compacta and the pars reticulata. The pars compacta projects to the striatum and the pars reticulata projects to the superior colliculus and thalamus. The substantia nigra provides dopamine to the basal ganglia and it is part of the extrapyramidal motor system. Lack of dopamine in the striatum leads to parkinsonian symptoms (rigidity, tremor, slowing); the system still functions without the substantia nigra as long as the level of dopamine is regulated properly.

The superior and inferior colliculi are interconnected small structures in the midbrain that are involved in visual and auditory orientation and attention. The superior colliculus receives projections from the frontal eyefields (premotor cortex) and controls saccadic movements. The interconnection and functional relationship to the prefrontal cortex has led to the use of saccadic eye movement models in evaluating the neural circuitry of schizophrenia and other psychiatric illnesses thought to involve prefrontal cortical systems [38].

Telencephalon

The telencephalon includes the entirety of the cerebral hemispheres including the diencephalon, limbic system, basal ganglia, and other structures. We will continue working our way through the brain from the ventral to the dorsal and the caudal to the rostral. We begin the discussion of the telencephalon with the thalamus and hypothalamus.

Thalamus and hypothalamus

The thalamus and hypothalamus, among other structures, compose the diencephalon. The thalamus is a complex bilateral structure with extensive reciprocal connections to major structures throughout the brain, including efferent fibers to cortical regions (thalamocortical axons) and afferent fibers from cortical regions (corticothalamic axons). There are 11 thalamic nuclei that are classified as either relay or association nuclei based on their target projections. These are specific nuclei. There are also nonspecific nuclei, stimulation of which yields activations along a large area of cortex. The thalamus has nuclei with projections to all major sensory areas except for olfaction. Further, it is a projection site for the RAS (important role for arousal and sleep; logical, given the sensory connections). For a comprehensive review of thalamic nuclei and function, please see Jones [39].

Because of the heterogeneity of nuclei, associated functional systems, and projections of the thalamus, it can be difficult to understand which systems are involved in the neuropsychological sequelae of thalamic lesions. One approach is to use functional imaging technologies, such as PET scan, to evaluate diaschesis effects of a localized thalamic lesion [40].

The thalamus is the most likely location for a strategic infarct (e.g. from a stroke) to cause a dementia. This is probably a consequence of the role of the thalamus in regulating higher-brain activity. As a subcortical structure with dense connections throughout both hemispheres, the thalamus reflects the lateralization of function of involved cortical areas. For example, contralateral attentional neglect occurs with right-sided thalamic lesions. A similar presentation is also evident with right parieto-temporal lesions [41].

Developmentally, abnormalities in thalamic nuclei (e.g. massa intermedia), have been associated with future manifestations of psychiatric conditions such as schizophrenia. The massa intermedia is detectable early in development, within 13 to 14 weeks of gestation [42]. There is some evidence that the medial dorsonuclei reduces in volume as schizophrenia progresses, an area rich in connections to prefrontal cortex (an area implicated in the expression of schizophrenia) [43]. Shimizu et al. [44] find evidence of a developmental interaction between the massa intermedia and mediodorsonuclei in schizophrenic patients.

The hypothalamus is primarily involved in visceromotor, viscerosensory, and endocrine (oxytocin and vasopressin) functions. It directly modulates autonomic nervous system activity. It functions as one connection point for limbic structures (involved in emotional regulation) to control of the autonomic nervous system. The stria terminalis, an afferent white matter tract, connects the amygdaloid bodies to the hypothalamus. The hypothalamus then has direct efferent connections to brainstem nuclei, including the output nuclei for vagal control (nucleus ambiguus) and sympathetic neurons in the spinal cord. These connections make the hypothalamus a critical component in functional systems involved in rage and fear responses.

The interaction of three structures, the hypothalamus, pituitary gland, and adrenal gland, is important in the regulation of mood, sexuality, stress, and energy usage. The so-called hypothalamic-pituitary-adrenal (HPA) axis has been implicated in social bonding and mate-pairing in comparative neuroscience and human research. Developmentally, it has been found in prairie voles that exposure to oxytocin (a hormone produced in the HPA) early on is associated with capacity for social bonding in adult animals [45, 46].

Further connections also involve the hypothalamus in memory functions (e.g. the hippocampus and mammillary bodies are connected via the fornix). Lesions to the mammillary bodies, a hypothalamic structure, can cause severe anterograde memory deficits. Deterioration of this system is associated with the development of Alzheimer's disease.

Basal ganglia

The basal ganglia are a set of subcortical grey matter structures most often associated with aspects of motor control, though recent research demonstrates additional roles in functional systems, including cognitive domains such as attention. Unlike primary motor cortex lesions, paralysis does not occur with basal ganglia damage. Instead, abnormal voluntary movements at rest, and initiation and inertia deficits are typical.

The structures included in the basal ganglia vary by nomenclature, but commonly reference the caudate and putamen (i.e. dorsal striatum or neo-striatum), globus pallidus (internal and external segments), substantia nigra, and subthalamic nucleus. Other nomenclatures include the amygdala (discussed here with limbic system structures), and the nucleus accumbens and olfactory tubercle (ventral striatum).

There are two pathways of activity in the basal ganglia with opposing behavioral outcomes, the indirect and the direct pathways. These pathways facilitate and inhibit the flow of information through the thalamus and operate simultaneously (the overall effect is a function of the current balance of activation pattern between the pathways). Activation of the direct pathway increases thalamic activity and activity of the cortex. Activation of the indirect pathway decreases thalamic activity and activity of the cortex. Damage to the basal ganglia can either decrease or increase movement depending on which structures/neurotransmitters are impacted within the direct and indirect pathways.

Several neurodegenerative disorders are associated with basal ganglia structures including Parkinson disease, Huntington disease, Wilson disease, and various multisystem atrophies (MSAs). Psychiatric disorders that appear in childhood including attention deficit hyperactivity disorder (ADHD) and Tourette syndrome are also associated with abnormalities in the basal ganglia. Recent studies have shown reduced overall caudate volumes and lateralized differences in caudate and globus pallidus volumes (left greater than right) in children diagnosed with ADHD [47]. Further, fractional anisotropy, a measure of apparent white matter integrity using a structural imaging technique called diffusion tensor imaging (DTI), is reduced in ventral prefrontal to caudate pathways in children with ADHD [48]. Behaviorally, this prefrontal/caudal circuit is thought to relate to inhibitory control (e.g. a go–no go task). As for etiological factors, there is recent evidence that early diet can influence future caudate volumes and intellectual aptitude [49], suggesting a potential avenue for environmental factors such as nutrition on neural structure and cognitive/behavioral outcome.

The role of basal ganglia structures in cognitive processes is multi-factorial. Aron et al. [50] present converging evidence on the role of a fronto-basal ganglia network in inhibiting both action and cognition. They review both comparative and human data using go–no go tasks and conclude that the fronto-basal ganglia systems are critical in determining individual differences in a variety of human behaviors, stating, "Variation to key nodes in this circuitry (or to their connections) could produce important individual differences, for example, in aspects of personality, in the response to therapy for eating disorders, and in liability toward and recovery from addiction. Developmental, traumatic, or experimentally induced alterations to key nodes in the control circuit lead to psychiatric symptoms such as inattention, perseveration, obsessional thinking and mania, and could also have relevance for movement and stuttering."

Limbic system

The limbic system is a network of structures involving subcortical, cortical, and brainstem regions that play a role in emotional behaviors including emotionally related memory/learning and social interactions. Important subcortical gray matter structures of the limbic system include the amygdala, nucleus accumbens, and hypothalamic nuclei (as illustrated above in the HPA), among others. Cortical structures include aspects of the prefrontal cortex (orbitofrontal), cingulate gyrus, and the hippocampus.

The amygdala, probably the most central structure (conceptually) of the limbic system, is almond-shaped

and located deep in the anterior temporal lobe. There are multiple nuclei which can be divided into two groups, a basolateral group and a corticomedial group. The amygdala is rich with connections to cortical areas including the orbitofrontal cortex and temporoparietal cortex, subcortical structures including the basal ganglia, thalamus, hypothalamus, brainstem structures including autonomic output nuclei, and the hippocampus (a phylogenetically older area of cortex involved in memory consolidation).

The amygdala is involved in functional systems of emotion, reward, learning, memory, attention, and motivation. Though researchers have strongly focused on fear conditioning and negative emotions in the amygdala (the role of the amygdala in fear startle reflex), it also has a role in positive emotion. For a review of the role of the amygdala in positive affect see Murray [51]. Direct stimulation of the amygdala via electrodes has been shown to most probably elicit fear or anger responses. In rats, electrical stimulation of the amygdala elicits aggressive vocalizations [52]. In humans, in a study of 74 patients undergoing presurgical screening for epilepsy, fear responses were most frequent with amygdala stimulation (higher rate for women than men) [53].

Functionally, in addition to a central role in emotional processing, the amygdala has a role in olfaction (the corticomedial cell group is directly connected to the olfactory bulbs), though there are also interconnections to other sensory areas. The amygdala appears to respond to threatening sensory stimuli via mobilization of fight or flight responses [54], but it also responds to positive sensory stimuli. The key is not the modality of the sensory input or the valence, the amygdala will respond to all, but whether the sensory data contain affective content. The amygdala also enhances cognitive performance in the context of emotional stimuli (e.g. emotional memory formation via linkages to the hippocampus) [55].

Developmental disorders such as autism have been linked to abnormal changes over time in the amygdala. In addition to increased white matter volumes and overall head size early in autism, in a study of young children with autism (36–56 months of age), the amygdala was enlarged by 13–16%. Amygdala volume differences, both larger and smaller, are found in many psychiatric conditions, including schizophrenia, depression, bipolar disorder, generalized anxiety disorder, and borderline personality disorder. Sometimes, conflicts appear with one study showing increased amygdala volume in depression and another showing decreased amygdala volume. Tebartz et al. [56] suggest a resolution to such conflicting results may be a function of the "dominant mode of emotional informational processing." They hypothesize that an enlarged amygdala may relate to depressed mood, anhedonia, phobic anxiety, and rumination and that a smaller amygdala may relate to emotional instability, aggression, and psychotic anxiety.

Another limbic structure, the hippocampus, is located ventrally and medially in the temporal lobe, and can be divided into four regions, designated CA1, CA2, CA3, and CA4. CA stands for cornu ammonis. A major input pathway to the hippocampus stems from the entorhinal cortex and the main output pathway from the fornix. The hippocampus is a critical structure to learning new information. Damage to the hippocampus can cause severe anterograde learning deficits such as in Korsakoff's syndrome, a condition caused by vitamin deficiencies in chronic alcohol abuse that damages hippocampal structures. Classically, the role of the hippocampus in memory was brought to the attention of the scientific community via a case study in 1957 [57] of a patient who underwent bilateral temporal lobe resections, referred to as HM. HM had intact remote and autobiographical memory until the surgical procedure, but was unable to learn new information subsequently. Corkin [58] reviews 45 years of research on HM.

Laterality and extent of peripheral involvement determine the type and severity of memory impairment with hippocampal lesions. Involvement of projection areas such as the entorhinal cortex increases the severity of anterograde deficit. This is the system that deteriorates in cortical dementias such as Alzheimer's disease. Bilateral lesions produce dense anterograde memory deficits. A unilateral left or right hemisphere lesion will produce verbal or spatial memory deficits, respectively.

Normal development of the hippocampus can be interrupted by environmental factors. Hippocampal volumes are reduced in victims of childhood abuse [59]. Pediatric temporal lobe epilepsy can also have a significant impact on hippocampal development. Hippocampal atrophy in children with epilepsy has been shown to relate to reduced neuropsychological performance [60].

Cerebral cortex

The cortex is divided into four lobes, the frontal, temporal, parietal, and occipital. As was discussed earlier in the chapter on top-down control and the organization of functional systems, the cortex is the most highly organized and complex aspect of brain

management. The cortex is thought to be necessary for conscious behaviors (thalamo-cortical relationships), though recent research suggests that some level of consciousness can exist without the cortex [61]. There are two hemispheres divided by a large fissure called the longitudinal fissure. They are generally superficially symmetrical and structures are mirrored across the two. Though there are individual differences in brain structure, on average it is known that the right frontal lobe tends to be wider than the left and the left planum temporale of the superior temporal cortex is larger than the right (thought to be related to language development). Recent neuroimaging research has also demonstrated substantial differences in white matter connectivity; for example, in systems underlying language functions between the left and right hemisphere using diffusion tensor imaging [62].

Several helpful mapping systems have been created to identify various brain regions. Brodmann's map is one of the best-known systems and it is based on cellular architecture (see Fig. 1.1).

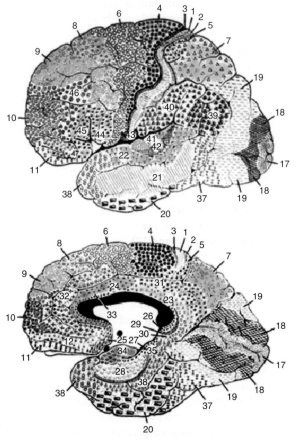

Fig. 1.1. Brodmann's map.

The motor and sensory areas of cortex are divided by a large fissure called the central sulcus (also known as the Rolandic fissure and cruciate fissure). This divides frontal and parietal areas and represents a steep functional boundary. The regions on either side of the fissure are the primary motor cortex (Brodmann's area 4, anterior of the fissure) and primary somatosensory cortex (Brodmann's areas 3, 1, and 2, posterior of the fissure). Organizationally, it is helpful to think in terms of primary, secondary, and tertiary association cortex. Functions progress from simple to complex, from unimodal to multi-modal.

Each sensory system is composed of a primary projection area and secondary and tertiary association areas. Functionally, the primary projection areas are the first area of cortex to receive information from a specific sensory system. Sensory data reaching the primary projection area are necessary for conscious perception. Lesion of primary sensory cortex can result in a loss of awareness of the affected modality; however, the individual may still respond reflexively to the modality (e.g. blindsight). Further sensory processing occurs in secondary association cortex, but it is still limited to one modality. Finally, tertiary association cortex (e.g. Brodmann's area 7 in the parietal lobe) integrates data from multiple sensory modalities.

The primary sensory projection areas are as follows: (1) vision = occipital cortex (calcerine cortex, Brodmann's area 17), (2) audition = superior temporal gyrus, temporal lobe (Brodmann's areas 41 and 42), (3) somatosensation = postcentral gyrus, parietal cortex (Brodmann's areas 3, 1, and 2), (4) gustation = parietal operculum (Brodmann's area 43), (5) olfaction = anterior tip of the temporal lobe (Brodmann's area 38). The secondary and tertiary association cortices surround and extend from the primary projection areas (e.g. visual association areas roughly correspond to Brodmann's areas 18 and 19).

In a normally organized brain, the left hemisphere is dominant for language functions. Around 90% of the population is estimated to be right-handed. Sinistrality is a clue that a brain is not normally organized. Recent neuroimaging studies have demonstrated different activation patterns in left-handers when processing language, with greater bilateral activations and shifts towards right-hemisphere language processing [63]. Assumptions about localization and lateralization of function should be treated with greater caution in these cases. The occurrence of sinistrality appears to be a combination of genetic and environmental factors. Sinistrality is over-represented in several neurological/psychiatric conditions such as epilepsy, autism, and schizophrenia. A recent study demonstrates a potential genetic link between sinistrality and schizophrenia [64].

The hemispheres are functionally specialized to deal both with different kinds of information and the same information in different ways. Although an in-depth review of laterality is well beyond the scope of this chapter, a few common areas of study include language, neglect (attentional space), memory (non-verbal versus verbal), and emotion.

In a normally organized brain, different aspects of language functions are divided across the hemispheres with semantic content, production, and rhythm localized to the left hemisphere, and expressive and receptive prosody/melody localized to the right hemisphere. Further, there is evidence that the right superior temporal lobe is instrumental in the identification of individual voices [65]. Lesions, depending on laterality and position relative to the central sulcus (anterior or posterior), will have expressive or receptive consequences, or both (e.g. a right frontal lesion may produce an expressive aprosodia, or inability to modulate the tone of speech output in a meaningful way, whereas a left frontal lesion may produce an expressive aphasia, inability to produce speech fluently).

In emotion, laterality is not a simple matter. For example, a model of aspects of emotional experience that has been applied across the lifespan is proposed by Fox and Davidson [66]. They present a view of emotional expression with emphasis on right and left frontal modulation. Much of Fox's work has consisted of developmental EEG research. Specifically, Fox infers right and left frontal activation from localized alpha bandwidth (~8–12 Hz) suppression. Two constructs are proffered as indicative of left versus right frontal activation respectively, approach and withdrawal.

Approach and withdrawal behaviors as recently conceptualized refer to social interactions. Approach behaviors are associated with positive affect and withdrawal behaviors are associated with negative affect. These behaviors are evident, at least in some form, as early as infancy. In one study, with a group selection criterion of motor reactivity and a disposition component (assessed through parent report and observation) infants with high motor reactivity and a disposition towards negative affect were found to be more likely to evidence greater right frontal EEG asymmetry, supporting the notion of right frontal mediation of negative emotion [67].

In another study, with implications for the extent of behavioral generalization of Fox's constructs from EEG records, it is demonstrated that resting frontal EEG asymmetry and social behavior during peer play were related to the occurrence of maladaptive behavior in preschool-aged children. Fox et al. [68] assert that resting frontal asymmetry within the alpha band may be a marker for certain temperamental dispositions.

Brain development

Higher-order cognitive and emotional development in humans is in part a byproduct of consciousness. Human consciousness and cognitive and emotional characteristics develop through the integration of increasingly complex functional systems starting early in life. The process of neural development begins simply (cell division). Brain weight increases from the heft of a few dozen cells to about 800 g at birth (males > females), to 1200 g at six years old, to around 1500 g and back down again to 1100–1300 g in the very elderly [69].

Among the very first markers of neural development, prenatally, is the appearance of the neural groove. The neural groove progresses to form the neural plate and then the neural tube. Progenitor cells along the various zones (ventricular, intermediate, and marginal in order of appearance) of the early developing nervous system develop into neurons and glial cells, forming the basic context of spinal and brain systems. The neural tube eventually forms into the central nervous system and it evolves from posterior to anterior with modifications to accommodate specialized brain regions along the rostral–caudal stream through a process called neurulation.

Neural tube defects are a leading cause of infant mortality in the USA and a mechanism of future disability in live births (5.59 per 10 000 live births) [70]. Ingestion of folic acid supplements drastically reduces risk. Neural tube defects, often manifesting as incomplete closure, can present in different ways depending on the etiology and the extent of malformation. The most common defects include spina bifida and anencephaly. Anencephaly results in incomplete formation of the brain and skull. Consciousness cannot occur and neonates generally die within a few days of birth.

Spina bifida malformations occur in three variations, occulta, meningocele, and cystic. The most severe condition is spina bifida meningocele, which can result in significant disability. The symptoms are primarily physical (degree of paralysis, bowel and bladder control problems, and scoliosis), though cognitive issues also occur, especially with co-occurrence of hydrocephalus (15–25% of meningocele cases). Neuropsychological impairments tend to center on delayed/absent development of executive functions over time [71], and memory deficits including prospective and episodic memories [72].

A related condition, the Arnold-Chiari malformation, occurs in almost all children born with spina bifida meningocele, though it also occurs independently. The Arnold-Chiari formation is the etiology of hydrocephalus in spina bifida meningocele. The cerebellum is herniated through the foramen magnum in the base of the skull, blocking the ventricular system. Severity is graded from one to four (four is the most severe). It is often undetected and symptoms, if they occur, can manifest later in life and include deficits associated with hindbrain functions (cranial nerves) and the cerebellum.

By ten weeks after conception, all of the major structures of the central nervous system are recognizable by their appearance. Functional capacity is not achieved until much later. The earliest detection of "normal" EEG patterns in neonates has been evidenced as young as 24 weeks after conception [73]. This is about the time that production of neurons halts. At this point, there can be as many as twice the number of neurons present as in the mature adult brain. After this, there is programmed cell death. Sleep stages, such as REM, can be matched behaviorally and via EEG as early as 25 weeks post-conception age [74]. The earliest detection of auditory response (auditory evoked potentials) is at a post-conception age of 27 weeks. Evoked potentials change over time, even after birth, shifting temporally [75], as do EEG patterns in general (e.g. infant alpha).

There are several cellular processes that are important to understand in the developing brain. Among them apoptosis, synaptogenesis, and myelination occur throughout the lifespan and are critical in brain plasticity and processes such as learning. Apoptosis, or programmed cell death, is an active process in brain development. It plays a prominent role in eliminating the excess neuronal growth produced prenatally and in shaping synaptic connections.

Synaptogenesis is, as one might expect, the formation of synapses. It is a dynamic process and occurs throughout the lifespan. Synapses form and are replaced if they are not reciprocated properly by the target cell. The process is called synaptic stabilization. Not all synapses are equally susceptible to replacement.

For a variety of reasons, synaptic plasticity is necessary throughout the lifespan, e.g. in the case of learning. A vexing problem in literatures on cellular processes in learning is the formation and strengthening of new synapses. A hypothesis that has received increasing support is that of synaptic tagging and capture (STC) proposed by Frey and Morris in 1997 [76]. Barco et al. review ten years of subsequent research and conclude that the model remains the most compelling hypothesis to explain synapse-specific plasticity processes [77]. The concept stipulates that, "the persistence of changes in synaptic strength is mediated by the generation of a transient local synaptic tag at recently activated synapses and by the production of plasticity-related proteins that can be used or captured only at those synapses marked by the tag." This is a necessary factor for selection of synaptic modification at the cellular level. In other words, this is the process by which synapses are identified and strengthened in facilitation of long-term structural change in learning.

In the development of higher-level primates including humans, it becomes apparent that connectivity is a major discriminating factor in the evolution of cognitive functions. There is a disproportionate increase in white matter volume throughout primate evolution, with prefrontal white matter differentiating humans [78]. There is both myelinated and unmyelinated white matter in the brain. Myelin is created by oligodendrocytes (specialized glia) in the central nervous system. This process is called myelination. It begins around the 24th week post conception and increases dramatically through adolescence, with a slow increase through as late as the fourth decade of life [79].

With the development of diffusion tensor imaging over a decade ago [80], due to its sensitivity to changes in white matter structure, there have been several valuable studies of normal development of white matter from childhood through adulthood. The trend is that maturation is associated with increased fractional anisotropy. Fractional anisotropy values increase with greater myelin presence. More recently, efforts have been made to quantify regionally specific changes in white matter integrity and association with cognitive development. In a cross-sectional design, Qui et al. [81] find increased FA in cerebellar, right temporal, superior frontal, and parietal white matter with age.

In the elderly, neuropathological studies have suggested a faster rate of white matter loss than grey matter loss. Neuroimaging results with conventional structural methods have been less clear with respect to changes in white matter as both significant and non-significant results have been reported. Diffusion tensor imaging consistently shows a decline in fractional anisotropy with age [82]. Regionally, the areas that appear to be most affected include prefrontal white matter, the splenium, and periventricular white matter.

Disorders of white matter tend to preferentially impact fronto-subcortical functional systems. Damage to white matter anywhere in the brain results in hypoperfusion of frontal cortex [83]. We see in disorders of white matter such as multiple sclerosis, small vessel ischemic disease, and dementia due to HIV among others, a fronto-subcortical syndrome with characteristic behavioral and cognitive features such as executive functioning deficits, bradyphrenia, abulia, apathy, and encoding problems.

Among gray matter structures, the prefrontal cortex is the latest to fully develop, extending into young adulthood, and the first to decline heading into to old age. John Hughlings Jackson termed this pattern of functional decline "dissolution", namely, those functions which appear last in evolutionary terms, and which emerge later in human development, are the most fragile and are among the first lost.

This late development of prefrontal-related functional systems coincides behaviorally with rapid changes in social behaviors, decision-making, risk-taking behaviors, and the transition from child to adult in terms of responsibility. Comparisons of frontal activity with functional imaging between childhood and adolescence show gender-specific increases in processing affective faces, for example (right frontal increases for boys and bilateral increases for girls) [84]. This activity tends to decrease and become more focal in adults [85]. Cognitive tasks show similar developmental curves, with decreased and more focal frontal activity in well-performing adults. With aging, increased frontal lobe activity to cognitive demand is shown with decreased efficiency in performance, suggesting more effort/resources are necessary to achieve performance results [86]. Clearly, consideration of neuroanatomical development across the lifespan is a critical emphasis in driving our understanding of the behavior of life. Integrating our rapidly advancing ability to analyze structural and functional changes in neural network activity into theories of lifespan development is the future of our field.

References

1. Gall FJ, Spurtzheim G. *Recherches sur le système nerveux en général et sur celui de cerveau en particulier*. Paris: F. Schoell; 1809.

2. Broca P. Nouvelle observation d'aphémie produite par une lésion de la troisième circonvolution frontale. *Bull Soc Anat* (Paris), 2e serie 1861a;**6**:398–407.

3. Dronkers NF, Plaisant O, Iba-Zizen MT, Cabanis EA. Paul Broca's historic cases: high resolution MR imaging of the brains of Leborgne and Lelong. *Brain* 2007;**130**:1432–41.

4. Taylor J, ed. *Selected Wrtitings of John Hughlings Jackson*. London: Hodder and Stoughton, 1931.

5. Lashley KS. Factors limiting recovery after central nervous lesions. *J Nerv Ment Dis* 1938;**888**:733–55.

6. Lashley KS. *Brain Mechanisms and Intelligence*. Chicago: University of Chicago Press, 1929.

7. Guillame DJ, Zhang SC. Human embryonic stem cells: a potential source of transplantable neural progenitor cells. *Neurosurg Focus* 2008;**24**:E3.

8. Heilman K, Valenstein E. *Clinical Neuropsychology*, 3rd edn. Oxford: Oxford University Press; 1993.

9. Filimonov IN. Localization of functions in the cerebral cortex. *Nevropat I Psikhiat* 1940;**9**.

10. Luria AR, Teuber HL, Pribram KH. *Higher Cortical Functions in Man*. New York: Consultants Bureau; 1966, 1980.

11. Luria AR. The functional organization of the brain. *Sci Am* 1970;**222**;66–78.

12. Luria AR. *The Working Brain*. New York: Basic Books; 1973.

13. Miller EK, Cohen JD. An integrative theory of prefrontal cortex function. *Annu Rev Neurosci* 2001;**24**:167–202.

14. Dosenbach N, Fair DA, Cohen AL, Schlaggar BL, Peterson SE. A dual-networks architecture of top-down control. *Trends Cogn Sci* 2008;**12**:99–105.

15. James W. What is an Emotion? *Mind* 1884;**9**:188–205.

16. Rand B. *The Classical Psychologists*. Boston: Houghton Mifflin; 1912: 672–84.

17. Ohman, A. Presidential Address, 1985. Face the beast and fear the face: animal and social fears as prototypes for evolutionary analyses of emotion. *Psychophysiology* 1986;**23**:123–45.

18. Fornari RV, Moreira KM, Oliveira MG. Effects of selective M1 muscarinic receptor antagonist dicyclomine on emotional memory. *Learn Mem* 2000;**7**:287–92.

19. Ross ED. The aprosodias: functional anatomic organization of the affective components of language in the right hemisphere. *Arch Neurol* 1981;**38**:561–8.

20. Golemen D. *Emotional Intelligence*. New York: Bantam Books; 1995.

21. Davidson RJ. Affective style and affective disorders: perspectives from affective neuroscience. Neuropsychological perspectives on affective and anxiety disorder. *Cogn Emot* 1998;**12**:307–30.

22. Mo Z, Moore AR, Filipovic R, Ogawa Y, Kazuhiro I, Antic SD, Zecevic N. Human cortical neurons originate from radial glia and neuron-restricted progenitors. *J Neurosci* 2007;**27**:4132–45.

23. Pakkenberg B, Pelvig D, Marner L, Bundgaard MJ, Jorgen H, Gunderson G, Nyenhgaard JR, Regeur L. Aging and the human neocortex. *Exp Gerontol* 2003;**38**:95–9.

24. Braendgaard H, Evan SM, Howard CV, Gunderson HJ G. The total number of neurons in the human neocortex unbiasedly estimated using optical dissectors. *J. Microsc* 1990;**157**:285–304.

25. Kandel ER, Schwartz JM, Jessel TM. *Principles of Neural Science*. Stanford, CT: Appleton & Lange; 1991.

26. Haines DE. *Fundamental neuroscience for basic and clinical applications*. Oxford: Churchill Livingstone; 2006.

27. Pandey GN, Dwivedi Y, Ren X, Rizavi HS, Faludi G, Sorpso A, Palkovits M. Regional distribution and relative abundance of serotonin (2c) receptors in human brain: effects of suicide. *Neurochem Res* 2006;**31**:167–76.

28. D'haenen H, Bossuyt A, Mertens J, Bossuyt-Piron C, Gijsemans M, Kaufman L. SPECT imaging of serotonin2 receptors in depression. *Psychiatry Res* 1992;**45**:227–37.

29. Moses-Kolko EL, Price JC, Thase ME, Meltzer CC, Kupfer DJ, Mathis CA, Bogers WD, Berman SR, Houck PR, Schneider TN, Drevets WC. Measurement of 5-HT1A receptor binding in depressed adults before and after antidepressant drug treatment using positron emission tomography and [11C]WAY-100635. *Synapse* 2007;**61**:523–30.

30. Levitan IB, Kaczmarek LK. *The Neuron: Cell and Molecular Biology*. Oxford: Oxford University Press; 2002.

31. Monkhouse S. *Cranial Nerves: Functional Anatomy*. Cambridge: Cambridge University Press; 2006.

32. Porges SW. The polyvagal perspective. *Biol Psychol* 2007;**74**;116–43.

33. Porges SW. Social engagement and attachment: a phylogenetic perspective. *Ann NY Acad Sci* 2003;**1008**:31–47.

34. Annoni JM, Ptak R, Caldara-Schnetzer AS, Khateb A, Pollerman BZ. Decoupling of autonomic and cognitive emotional reactions after cerebellar stroke. *Ann Neurology* 2003;**53**:654–8.

35. Schmahmann JD, Weilburg JB, Sherman JC. The neuropsychiatry of the cerebellum: insights from the clinic. *Cerebellum* 2007;**6**:254–67.

36. Timmann D, Daum I. Cerebellar contributions to cognitive functions: a progress report after two decades of research. *Cerebellum* 2007;**6**:159–62.

37. Ackerman H, Mathiak K, Riecker A. The contribution of the cerebellum to speech production and speech perception: clinical and functional imaging data. *Cerebellum* 2007;**6**:202–13.

38. Winograd-Gurvich C, Fitzgerald PB, Georgiou-Karistianis N, Millist L, White O. Inhibitory control and spatial working memory: a saccadic eye movement study of negative symptoms in schizophrenia. *Psychiatry Res* 2008;**157**:9–19.

39. Jones EG. *The Thalamus*, 2nd edn. Cambridge: Cambridge University Press; 2007.

40. Shim YS, Kim JS, Shon YM, Chung YA, Ahn KJ, Yang DW. A serial study of regional cerebral blood flow deficits in patients with left anterior thalamic infarction: anatomical and neuropsychological correlates. *J Neurol Sci* 2008;**266**:84–91.

41. Valenstein E, Heilman KM, Watson RT, Van Den Abell T. Nonsensory neglect from parietotemporal lesions in monkeys. *Neurology* 1982;**32**:1198–201.

42. Rosales RK, Lemay MJ, Yakovlev PI. The development and involution of massa intermedia with regard to age and sex. *J Neuropath Exp Neuro* 1968;**27**:166.

43. Preuss UW, Zetzsche T, Jager M, Groll C, Frodl T, Bottlender R, Leinsinger G, Hegerl U, Hahn K, Moller HJ, Meisenzahl EM. Thalamic volume in first-episode and chronic schizophrenic subjects: a volumetric MRI study. *Schizophr Res* 2005;**73**:91–101.

44. Shimizu M, Fujiwara H, Hiraol K, Namiki C, Fukuyama H, Hayashi Y, Murai T. Structural abnormalities of the adhesion interthalamica and mediodorsal nuclei of the thalamus in schizophrenia. *Schizophr Res* 2008 [Epub ahead of print].

45. Carter CS. Developmental consequences of oxytocin. *Physiol Behav* 2003;**79**:383–97.

46. Grippo AJ, Cushing BS, Carter CS. Depression-like behavior and stressor-induced neuroendocrine activation in female prairie voles exposed to chronic social isolation. *Psychosom Med* 2007;**69**:149–57.

47. Uhikova P, Paclt I, Vaneckova M, Morcinek T, Seidel Z, Krasensky J, Danes J. Asymmetry of basal ganglia in children with attention deficit hyperactivity disorder. *Neuro Endocrinol Lett* 2007;**28**:604–9.

48. Casey BJ, Epstein JN, Buhle J, Liston C, Davidson MC, Tonev ST, Spicer J, Niogi S, Millner AJ, Reiss A, Garrett A, Hinshaw SP, Greenhill LL, Shafritz KM, Vitolo A, Kotler LA, Jarrett MA, Glover G. Frontostriatal connectivity and its role in parent-child dyads with ADHD. *Am J Psychiatry* 2007;**164**:1729–36.

49. Isaacs EB, Gadian DG, Sabatini S, Chong WK, Quinn BT, Fischl BR, Lucas A. The effect of early human diet on caudate volumes and IQ. *Pediatr Res* 2008;**63**:308–14.

50. Aron AR, Durston S, Eagle DM, Logan GD, Stinear CM, Stuphorn V. Converging evidence for a fronto-basal-ganglia network for inhibitory control of action and cognition. *J Neurosci* 2007;**27**:11860–4.

51. Murray EA. The amygdala, reward and emotion. *Trends Cogn Sci* 2007;**11**:489–97.

52. Blanchard DC, Blanchard RJ. Innate and conditioned reactions to threat in rats with amygdaloid lesions. *Annu Rev Psychol* 1972;**39**:43–68.

53. Meletti S, Tassi L, Mai R, Fini N, Tassinari CA, Russo GL. Emotions induced by intracerbral electrical stimulation of the temporal lobe. *Epilepsia* 2006;**47**: 47–51.

54. Chen SW, Shemyakin A, Wiedenmayer CP. The role of the amygdala and olfaction in unconditioned fear in developing rats. *J Neurosci* **26**:233–40.

55. Packard MG, Teather LA. Amygdala modulation of multiple memory systems: hippocampus and caudate-putamen. *Neurobiol Learn Mem* 1998;**69**:163–203.

56. Tebartz L, Ebert D, Hesslinger B. Amygdala volume status might reflect dominant mode of emotional information processing. *Arch Gen Psychiatry* 2007; **64**:251.

57. Scoville WB, Milner B. Loss of recent memory after bilateral hippocampal lesions. *J Neurol Neurosurg Psychiatry* 1957;**20**:11–21.

58. Corkin S. What's new with the amnesic patient H.M.? *Nat Rev Neurosci* 2002;**3**:153–60.

59. Grassi-Oliveira R, Ashy M, Stein LM. Psychobiology of childhood maltreatment: effects of allostatic load? *Rev Bras Psiquitr* 2008;**30**:60–8.

60. Guimaraes CA, Bonilha L, Franzon RC, Li LM, Gendes F, Guerreiro MM. Distribution of regional gray matter abnormalities in a pediatric population with temporal lobe epilepsy and correlation with neuropsychological performance. *Epilepsy Behav* 2007;**11**:558–66.

61. Merker B. Consciousness without a cerebral cortex: a challenge for neuroscience and medicine. *Behav Brain Sci* 2007;**30**:63–81.

62. Glasser MF, Rilling JK. DTI tractography of the human brain's language pathways. *Cereb Cortex* 2008 [Epub ahead of print].

63. Jorgens S, Kleiser R, Indefrey P, Seitz RJ. Handedness and functional MRI activation patterns in sentence processing. *Neuroreport* 2007; **18**: 1339–443.

64. Francks C, Maegawa S, Laurèn J, Abrahams BS, Velayos-Baeza A, Medland SE, Colella S, Groszer M, McAuley EZ, Caffrey TM, Timmusk T, Pruunsild P, Koppel I, Lind PA, Matsumoto-Itaba N, Nicod J, Xiong L, Joober R, Enard W, Krinsky B, Nanba E, Richardson AJ, Riley BP, Martin NG, Strittmatter SM, Möller HJ, Rujescu D, St Clair D, Muglia P, Roos JL, Fisher SE, Wade-Martins R, Rouleau GA, Stein JF, Karayiorgou M, Geschwind DH, Ragoussis J, Kendler KS, Airaksinen MS, Oshimura M, DeLisi LE, Monaco AP. LRRTM1 on chromosome 2p12 is a maternally suppressed gene that is associated paternally with handedness and schizophrenia. *Mol Psychiatry* 2007;**12**:1129–39.

65. Belin P, Zatorre RJ. Adaptation to speaker's voice in right anterior temporal lobe. *Neuroreport* 2003;**14**:2105–9.

66. Fox NA, Davidson RJ. Hemispheric substrates for affect: a developmental model. In Fox NA, Davidson RJ, eds. *The Psychobiology of Affective Development.* Hillsdale, NJ: Erlbaum; 1984.

67. Fox NA, Schmidt LA, Calkins SD, Rubin KH, Coplan RJ. The role of frontal activation in the regulation and dysregulation of social behavior during the preschool years. *Dev Psychopathol* 1996;**8**:89–102.

68. Fox NA, Calkins SD, Porges SW, Rubin KH. Frontal activation asymmetry and social competence at four years of age. *Child Dev* 1995;**66**:1770–84.

69. Dekaban AS, Sadowsky D. Changes in brain weights during the span of human life: relation of brain weights to body heights and body weights *Ann Neurol* 1978; **4**:345–56.

70. Williams LJ, Rasmussen SA, Flores A, Kirby RS, Edmonds LD. Decline in the prevalence of spina bifida and anecephaly by race/ethnicity: 1995–2002. *Pediatrics* 2005;**116**:580–6.

71. Tarazi RA, Zabel TA, Mahone EM. Age-related differences in executive function among children with spina bifida/hydrocephalus based on parent behavior ratings. *Clin Neuropsychol* 2007 [Epub ahead of print].

72. Dennis M, Jewell D, Drake J, Misakyan T, Spiegler B, Hetherington R, Gentili F, Barnes M. Prospective, declarative, and nondeclarative memory in young adults with spina bifida. *J Int Neuropsychol Soc* 2007;**13**:312–23.

73. Clancy RR, Bergqvist AGC, Dlugos DJ. Neonatal electroencephalography. In Ebersol JS, Pedley TA, eds. *Current Practice of Clinical Electroencephalography,* 3rd edn. Philadelphia, PA: Lippincott Williams & Williams; 2003:160–234.

74. Scher MS, Johnson MW, Holditch-Davis D. Cyclicity of neonatal sleep behaviors at 25 to 30 weeks postconceptional age. *Pediatr Res* 2005;**57**:879–82.

75. Schleussner E, Schneider U. Developmental changes of auditory-evoked fields in fetuses. *Exp Neurol* 2004;**190**:59–64.

76. Frey U, Morris RG. Synaptic tagging and long-term potentiation. *Nature* 1997;**385**:533–6.

77. Barco A, Lopez de Armentia M, Alarcon JM. Synapse-specific stabilization of plasticity processes: the synaptic tagging and capture hypothesis revisited 10 years later. *Neurosci Biobehav Rev* 2008;**32**:831–51.

78. Schoenemann PT, Sheehan MJ, Glotzer LD. Prefrontal white matter volume is disproportionately larger in humans than in other primates. *Nat Neurosci* 2005;**8**: 242–52.

79. Courchesne E, Chisum HJ, Townsend J, Cowles A, Covington J, Egaas B, Harwood M, Hinds S, Press GA. Normal brain development and aging: quantitative analysis at in vivo MR imaging in healthy volunteers. *Radiology* 2000;**216**:672–82.

80. Basser PJ, Matiello J, LeBihan D. MR diffusion tensor spectroscopy and imaging. *Biophys J* 1994; **66**:259–67.

81. Qiu D, Tan LH, Zhou K, Khong PL. Diffusion tensor imaging of normal white matter maturation from late childhood to young adulthood: voxel-wise evaluation of mean diffusivity, fractional anisotropy, radial and axial diffusivities, and correlation with reading development. *Neuroimage* 2008 [Epub ahead of press].

82. Abe O, Aoki S, Hayashi N, Yamada H, Kunimatsu A, Mori H, Youikawa T, Okubo T, Ohtomo K. Normal aging in the central nervous system: quantitative MR diffusion-tensor analysis. *Neurobiol Aging* 2002;**23**: 433–41.

83. Tullberg M, Fletcher E, DeCarlie C, Mungas D, Reed BR, Harvey DJ, Weiner MW, Chui HC, Jagust WJ. White matter lesions impair frontal lobe function regardless of their location. *Neurology* 2004;**63**:246–53.

84. Yurgelun-Todd DA, Killgore WD. Fear-related activity in the prefrontal cortex increases with age during adolescence: a preliminary fMRI study. *Neurosci Lett* 2006;**406**:194–9.

85. Monk CS, McClure EB, Nelson EE, Zarahn E, Bilder RM, Leibenluft E, Charney DS, Ernst M, Pine DS. Adolescent immaturity in attention-related brain engagement to emotional facial expressions. *Neuroimage* 2003;**20**:420–8.

86. Velanova K, Lustiq C, Jacoby LL, Buckner RL. Evidence for frontally mediated controlled processing differences in older adults. *Cerebral Cortex* 2007;**17**:1033–46.

Developmental models in pediatric neuropsychology

Jane Holmes Bernstein

"A single good model is worth a thousand empirical studies"
James Heckman (Nobel Prize, Economics, 2000)
quoted by David Kirp [1]

"Good models are like good tools: they do a certain job reasonably well … simple models that work well for a wide variety of jobs are especially valuable … (they yield) islands of conceptual clarity in the midst of otherwise mind-numbing complexity and diversity"
Richerson and Boyd [2]

Introduction

On what grounds does a hard-nosed number-crunching economist make such a claim? What does he mean? What are the implications for the elaboration of the knowledge base? For clinical practice?

A model is a tool for thinking, for organizing a body of data into a theoretically coherent construct whose validity can be tested. Thinking in both research and clinical arenas is based on a constant interaction between models and evidence. The challenge of empirical data (evidence) is that at any one point there may be much to make sense of. Data are not always internally consistent; and, until established by multiple replications across data sets, evidence is constantly subject to discussion, argument, and change. Models may not be subject to as rapid change as the evidence base. They cannot, nonetheless, be static: as evidence accumulates, models must be scrutinized and reformulated.

There are two major sources of change in science. One is the shift in the zeitgeist, the way in which people view the world, to which scientific developments contribute, but do not solely define; the second derives from developments in technology. Both of these are shaped by the modeling⇆evidence transactions that are critical to the advancement of knowledge and influence them in turn.

Change in the zeitgeist and the advent of new technologies have had major implications for the behavioral neurosciences. In the modern era, behavioral neurology and neuropsychology got their start in the observations of language breakdown made by Dax, Broca, and Wernicke in the late nineteenth century, and the nature of language has remained a focus of intense scrutiny. This is easy to understand: our language capacities are central to our existence, and until recently their believed uniqueness reinforced habits of thought that put human beings at the pinnacle of a hierarchical view of life. However, in the wake of the "Modern Synthesis" of evolutionary theory and genetics, the intellectual context in which we view our position in the natural world has changed dramatically, and the implications of the modern synthesis have gained traction in scientific thinking. What is perhaps the most important – and hard-won – impact is the recognition that humans do not represent some sort of pinnacle of life on earth. This change in viewpoint has opened the floodgates for cross-species comparisons of behavior and adaptation, which allow us to explore in greater detail (and with much greater humility) what we share with other organisms, and how we as a species were shaped by natural forces that adapted us to our environments over time. The range of models available to extend our thinking has accordingly expanded many-fold. The inclusion of an evolutionary framework has great potential for integrating multiple disciplines [3].

The advent of modern neuroimaging technology has in the last several decades also changed the investigative landscape significantly and promoted progress in behavioral neuroscience at a rapid rate. Multiple forms of neurodiagnostic imaging have been introduced, assessing structure and function at the anatomical level (computed tomography (CT), positron emission tomography (PET), magnetic resonance imaging (MRI)); the physiological level (single photon emission computed tomography (SPECT), quantitative electroencephalography (qEEG) and transcranial magnetic stimulation (TMS)); and the functional level (functional magnetic resonance imaging (fMRI), diffuse tensor imaging (DTI)). The ability to image the brain in action via fMRI, tractography and TMS has led to a remarkable rapprochement of neuroscience and experimental psychology – and to the new cognitive neurosciences (developmental, social cognitive, affective). Other developments that augur well to advance our understanding of behavior come from such different disciplines as genetics and computer modeling. Microarray technologies that support multivariate genetic analysis and gene expression mapping are being used to determine the role of genes and epigenetic processes in the risk for and manifestation of diseases and disorders, both medical and psychiatric [4]. Computer models range from the cellular level to that of cognition and behavior [5].

The technology-supported paradigms that are increasingly available to support the testing of proposed models also bring their own constraints. Computer modeling is a powerful technique that can answer questions of how things may work, but it does not necessarily address what actually works or why. Similarly, functional neurodiagnostic imaging may provide detailed information about discrete components of complex behavior, but it is not easy to extrapolate from behavior that occurs "in the tube" to behavior that is elicited in response to the meaning, goals, and intentions of the individual in the world. There are considerable hurdles to be overcome in fully understanding the data obtained from these new technologies, both methodologically (*what, in the neural substrate, is being indexed – exactly?*); and practically (*what is the relationship between behavior observed in the specific technology setting and behavior observed in the real world?*). Nonetheless, these paradigms allow us to ask questions that we have not been able to ask before, and, in so doing, further our understanding of brain–behavior and structure–function relationships.

Modeling in development

The core concept of development is that of dynamic change over time in response to experience. Developmental models have to incorporate concepts of change – but also of continuity/stability. The genetic processes that facilitate selection allow organisms to change more or less rapidly to meet changing conditions in their environments. Absent such external change, however, genetic processes function to maintain the match between the organism and its niche.

Concepts of development imply a "start-state" to change from and an "end-state" to change to [6]. The start-state for the human organism is the information

in the genome. This represents the end-state of the macro-developmental processes of evolution. Model building in development thus addresses two questions: one – at the species level – considers the evolution of the brain to this point, asking what changes over time have shaped the brain – and the behavior – of the species. The other – at the individual level – asks how and when species-specific brain organization and behavior is acquired by the individual.

These questions cannot be addressed without reference to the contexts that have constrained and canalized developmental trajectories over time. Models of development – both evolutionary and ontogenetic – entail an environment in which the organism acts. At the evolutionary level, the environment has shaped the species' behavioral repertoire, providing biologically prepared capacities that must be activated in response to particular environmental demands. At the individual level, it is experience with this particular environment that shapes the neural architecture supporting the individual's behavior. Over time and under specific environmental forces, the individual acting in concert with others in a population has the potential for rerouting the trajectory of the species.

The long history of chronic polarization around the nature–nurture debate has been rendered moot in many aspects by the findings of modern neuroscience. Since the formulation of the modern synthesis – and in spite of constant critique from both within and outside science – our understanding of the relationship of intrinsic neurobiological characteristics and extrinsic environmental influences is that it is one of vital interdependence. Both nature and nurture must operate together and questioning must be guided by the two queries offered by Mayr [7]: *how does the organism work?* and *why is it advantageous to work that way?*

The concept of development is one that has not been easy to integrate at the behavioral level where humans are the focus of investigation. Developmental thinking runs counter to long-prevailing concepts of the nature of cognition. Psychological theory in the Western tradition has been dominated by the idea of the autonomous individual as the center of knowledge and cognition [8]. The fundamental assumption is that "the boundaries of the individual provide the proper framework within which psychological processes can be adequately analyzed" [9]. Cognition is thus conceptualized as a set of processes that are internal and accessible only to the person to whom they belong. Furthermore, in Western thought, scientific investigations have been strongly shaped by the Platonic *essence* tradition and conducted in terms of *dichotomous-sources-of-variation* strategies. The former is simply not a developmental concept; the other requires careful evaluation of the appropriateness of its application to developmentally framed questions.

In neuropsychology, a major challenge to the construction of developmental models is the specialization of the adult human brain. This view was derived from observation of the selective disruptive effects of brain lesions in parsing behavioral capacities in the neurology tradition and from investigative paradigms that parse target behavioral capacities into subcomponents in the experimental psychology tradition. These two investigative approaches quickly merged into what is now known as cognitive neuroscience. The primary strategy has been one of dissociation. As behavior was subject to more and more dissection, brain organization was revealed to be highly specialized – and interpreted as mediated by special-purpose modules that function more or less independently, although the nature of the modules and the degree of their independence remain the subject of debate.

When the focus is on brain development and organization in children, however, there is a problem: the modules of the adult cognitive architecture cannot be presumed to be present. They have to emerge in some process of modularization that takes place over time. Thus, models based on a view of adult modular architecture cannot be correct as a description of the child's developing capacities. Nonetheless, such models have proved over and over again to be very seductive, and have been utilized on numerous occasions to attempt to make sense of pediatric brain function.

It has been unfortunate – though not surprising – for the developmental behavioral sciences that the neural specialization model of the adult brain meshed perfectly with the (up to recently) dominant "cognitive" paradigm in modern Western psychology and led to the "downward extension" of adult models – both of brain organization and behavioral measurement – into the pediatric arena. However, it did so because the model as it applied to behavioral measurement meshed perfectly with what was already "on the ground". Measurement tools for children were constructed in the shape and form of those derived for adults in the cognitive tradition.

The influence of the modern synthesis on thinking across all branches of scientific endeavor has, however, paved the way for a re-evaluation of brain functioning and organization. Developmental thinking in particular benefits from this, and is starting to act as a powerful antidote to the influence that has existed to date from both cognitive models of neural organization and behavioral measurement tools that are constructed in an older cognitive tradition.

Models in clinical practice

The increased influence and application of developmental modes of thinking in understanding behavior is particularly exciting for the clinician. The guiding questions at the level of the organism are those that the pediatric clinician wrestles with on a daily basis in working with an individual: how does an organism achieve adaptive success? What is an optimal outcome? What is needed to facilitate this? What factors could constrain the individual from reaching the expected end-state? What is the role of the individual's unique experiences to date and opportunities in the future? And for the clinician specifically: how can I best intervene to maximize the outcome?

Until relatively recently, clinicians have been poorly served by the neuropsychological knowledge base. The "*individual-as-cognizer*" model and "*dichotomous-sources-of-variation*" methodologies do not enrich the portrait of a real person in the real world, and so fail to meet the mandate of clinicians – to match the person more effectively to the demands of his or her world. This mismatch is one source of the failure of clinicians to respond enthusiastically to evidence-based practice thinking and guidelines.

Nonetheless, in the modern era, clinical practice must be evidence-based. Such a statement hardly seems controversial: with the welfare and lives of people at issue, clinicians can hardly go around making up treatments on an ad hoc basis. However, calls for evidence-based medicine and clinical psychological practice are all too often resisted by clinicians; clinical practice guidelines may be treated as nonrelevant to an individual's practice; and long lags can occur between the identification of new successful treatments and their application. This gap between practice guidelines derived from research knowledge and the actual behavior of clinicians is of concern. Arguably, mental health clinicians are even more vulnerable than physicians to resisting standardized guidelines, inasmuch as the focus of treatment/intervention is behavior and an individual's behavioral repertoire is highly individual, constantly influenced by transactions with the full range of intrapersonal and interpersonal environmental variables that are more or less unique to him or her.

One reason for the resistance seems to be a lack of consensus about the nature of evidence-based practice (EBP). EBP is widely viewed as emphasizing data (evidence) collected under research conditions, with the randomized clinical trial all too often being held up as the gold standard, in spite of the availability of detailed analyses of a range of relevant data sources (effectiveness studies, single-subject designs, process-outcome studies, qualitative analyses, hypothesis generation/evaluation, metaanalyses and the like). The label "evidence-based" has focused the discussion on research knowledge even though the Institute of Medicine's defining report *Crossing the Quality Chasm* [10] provided a much more nuanced view of the endeavor, one that requires the *integration* of "the best available research evidence, clinical expertise, client values and available resources". The contribution of practice-based evidence has also been outlined. Nonetheless, in spite of this clear recognition of their critical role in EBP, many clinicians continue to resist evidence-based clinical practice guidelines, arguing that they are not responsive to the experience of the individual patients they actually see in the office, and thus cannot be a substitute for the practitioner's knowledge and experience with individual patients. There are reasons for this attitude among clinicians that need to be examined – and taken seriously by both research teams and clinical practitioners.

One very substantial problem for the application to clinical settings of the data collected in research investigations is the mismatch between the two modes of thinking. Research investigations seek universals, are variable-centered and aim to maximize internal validity. Clinical investigations deal with individuals, are person-centered and have as a primary goal the maximization of external validity. The products of the one cannot simply be transferred wholesale to the other. Standards for research investigations (especially in the behavioral or mental health domains) are often too rigorous to be useful in real conditions, a situation that easily provokes resistance to standards-based care. How is this tension resolved? How is research-obtained knowledge applied to the individual person who seeks care?

The interpretation of the research product to the real world setting of the individual who seeks care requires that thoughtful clinicians build coherent models of their clinical behavior. Indeed, clinicians are master makers of models. Like everyone else, they do it all the time. As clinicians, however, they have a responsibility to know that they are modeling and generating hypotheses whenever observing behavior. Modeling does not await the evaluation of systematically collected data in the clinical interview. Clinicians generate hypotheses on first meeting the patient/client – or reading the medical record. Failing to recognize that they are doing so means that they also fail to evaluate the many sources of bias (social/interpersonal, methodological) that can potentially undermine their "judgment under uncertainty" [11].

Model-building – rigorous, systematic and principled – is at the core of clinical expertise. In evidence-based practice, the "big E" of Evidence must be complemented by the "big E" of Expertise. Research evidence is useless if the practitioner does not know how to use it – which data to select, when and how to apply them. Indeed, clinicians typically organize their thinking within a theoretical framework to do just this [12]. The core of the clinician's expertise then is a theory-based "good (working) model" as advocated by Heckman and it is the need for a thinking structure that guides both the selection and the application of relevant knowledge that is the emphasis of his bold statement.

Both of the "big Es" must be subjected to the same intensity of methodological scrutiny. The latter is, however, frequently given short shrift in this regard. Training in clinical neuropsychology in particular can be very vulnerable, on the one hand, to an overemphasis on exciting developments in neuroimaging techniques and cognitive neuroscience and, on the other hand, to a more or less rigid application of the psychological test batteries preferred by a training site – with at times less, or even no, comprehensive instruction in the nature of clinical work itself. True, it is hard to encompass in a few years of training all of the information currently available in an exciting field like neuropsychology, but clinical neuropsychologists training the next generation of professionals need to provide students with a firm theoretical foundation of the assessment process itself that will guide their thinking as the knowledge base with which they work grows, changes, and is refined.

The good working model guides clinical practice. The model is "working" to the extent that it is not fixed in stone but must be subject to ongoing scrutiny and revised as new knowledge becomes available. In the clinical setting, the model that you use guides, but can also seriously limit, what you look for, what you see and how you interpret your observations. Clinically, the utility of a model depends on its ability to account both for normal behavioral functioning and for different patterns of behavioral breakdown, to be implemented in assessment strategies, and to provide a principled approach to management and intervention.

Actually, however, for the clinician "the good working model" is a misnomer. The clinician typically works within a theoretical framework in which more than one working model is required to encompass the range of activity. As a clinical neuropsychologist working with children, I parse the domain in which I am working into three primary components: the *organism*, the potential *threats to development* to which the organism is subject (including the impact of diseases/disorders and that of adverse environmental experience), and the *assessment strategy*. The model of the organism – how the organism works – is central, shaping the understanding of how threats to development have their impact, and determining how the assessment of behavior proceeds. The organism is viewed through the lens of the *brain-context-development* matrix [13]. The model of the organism necessarily incorporates models of brain, models of context (physical, psychological) and models of development.

Modeling the organism. The primary model guiding the clinician is the model of the organism in question. How does this organism work? All assessment is based on current views of the expected capacities of the individuals under study. There is little point in trying to evaluate behavior in the absence of a sense of what behavior the organism is capable of, nor can the impact of a given disorder be assessed without a sense of the organism's capacities under typical conditions. Models of *neuro* psychological functioning must be based on *brain*; an understanding of *brain* cannot be achieved – as I have argued elsewhere – without an analysis of *context*; models of the neurobehavioral capacities of the child must reflect its developing status and thus must incorporate *development*.

Within this larger *brain-context-development* matrix for modeling the organism, there are two other strands of investigation in which specific models are invoked to help organize the available data and set up the questions that will lead to greater understanding of the concepts involved. One set of models attempts to specify how brain is related to behavior (brain–behavior relationships). Another seeks to account for the nature of specific behavioral capacities such as language, spatial cognition, social behavior, executive capacities and so forth. As previously noted, these models draw from neurology and neuroscience on the one hand and from experimental psychology on the other. Currently, "neuropsychology" has given way to "neuroscience" and modeling of specific behavioral capacities rarely takes place without reference to the potential neural substrates that support the behavior in question. Indeed, the cross-fertilization provided by these two sources of models is what has given the field its power as a source of new insights. In the clinical setting the contribution of these models is further extended by models drawn from clinical psychology. All are brought together under the umbrella of the model of the assessment process itself with the goal of making as comprehensive and nuanced a description of the individual as possible as the basis for acting to promote his or her optimal adaptation in the future.

Modeling the disorders. The disorders that threaten the lives and the optimal development of children are different from those that affect adults. Structural anomalies, genetic syndromes, and prematurity change the course of development from the beginning. Different types of brain tumor and seizure disorder are seen at different ages, require different treatments and having different consequences for behavior. Even the conditions that seem comparable across ages – stroke, head injury – have different types of outcomes when they occur in a developing brain (see the chapters concerning traumatic brain injury in this volume). The core principle is that the neuropathologies of childhood occur in the context of dynamic change over the course of development and thus the pathology becomes part of the developmental course. Behavioral development can be derailed and behavioral outcomes changed. Genetic and structural disorders set up conditions for alternative developmental trajectories; later acquired derailments have potential for resulting in so-called "late effects". Models of brain–behavior relationships that derive their data from neuropathology must address the altered dynamics of the brain–experience interactions of the child with changed neural capacity. Determination of such relationships in the child cannot proceed without reference to developmental processes, both typical and atypical.

The knowledge base of developmental models

In neuropsychology, developmental modeling calls on an extended knowledge base that can be roughly parsed by the so-called "*wh*" questions: what, where, when, how. The knowledge bases that address the *what* question are those of the behavioral sciences, psychology and cognitive neuroscience. The findings of these disciplines are central to the discipline of neuropsychology and have been extensively outlined in a variety of texts, both comprehensive and focused on specific domains. In recent years, as neuropsychological investigations of children's behavior have increased, relevant texts have focused on neuropsychological development in the child. To date, these have largely been the work of clinicians and have focused on the behavioral impact of threats to normal development in the presence of disease or disorder and/or the strategies needed to evaluate and treat children who present for clinical services. The *where* question is answered by the neurosciences, embracing biology, physiology, and chemistry; neuroanatomy and embryology; neuropathology; and behavioral neurology. Again, the range of texts available is extensive and specific systems warrant their own extended descriptions. Neuropsychologists gain familiarity with the *what* and the *where* knowledge bases as part of their training – and develop models for future research investigations or for clinical practice based on this emphasis. However, when the goal is modeling of developmental processes, the *what* and *where* data require supplementation, by data addressing *when* and *how*.

Addressing **when** in developmental modeling

The *when* question is addressed through the knowledge bases of the evolutionary sciences, developmental psychology and the developmental neurosciences. These disciplines all seek to understand the dynamic processes that have created and continue to shape biological organisms. The *when* question is concerned with time passing. It deals in start-states and end-states and the nature of the journey between them.

The start-state of the individual's journey is the end-state of the macrodevelopmental processes of evolution. Evolution is affected by changes in developmental mechanisms over time. Successful adaptation at any point in a species' or an individual's developmental trajectory entails both flexibility and stability. The understanding of development in both its phylogenetic (evolutionary) and its ontogenetic (individual) manifestations requires appreciation of this dramatic tension at the core of the construct: change and continuity. Development proceeds via processes that maintain and reinforce existing structures, as well as setting up the conditions for the formation of new ones – with the latter always constrained by what pre-exists. At the 'macro' level of evolutionary development, selection acts to maintain those morphologies and behaviors that support successful adaptation to a given niche by removing fitness-reducing alleles – constraining variability for stable functioning in current contexts, as well as to facilitate new responsivity to changed environmental conditions – providing adaptive flexibility in future contexts. At the individual level, this involves the products of biological evolution – already evolved proclivities or preparedness to learn – and of epigenesis – the expression of the potentiality in response to the actual – and unique – experience of the individual.

Across evolutionary time, behavior is selected to solve problems that are species-relevant and to promote optimal adaptation to the setting in which the animal finds itself. The potent force is that of survival – of the species and of the individual. Protection, nutrition and reproduction are central – and the structures, both neural and behavioral, selected to support them are critical substrates for all of our subsequently acquired behavioral capacities. Acquisition of the species-specific behavioral repertoire will be the developmental task of the individual.

Optimal adaptation for any organism is defined by the environment in which it lives. Both the larger planetary environment with its specific physical properties and more specific ecological niches shape the evolution of species. For humans, for example, the anthropological record reveals a relationship between the inhospitableness of the environment and the size of the human brain and paleoclimatological data reveal that periods of harsh environmental conditions are correlated with rapid changes in human brain [14, 15]. Climate variation demands behavioral flexibility for success – and brain power to facilitate it. This highly flexible adaptive repertoire of humans means that they can respond not only to different physical conditions, but also to highly complex, non-physical environments of their own making, those that are shaped by social organization and language. The acquisition of culture that these facilitated then shaped the modern human brain-mind, an impact that cannot easily be overstated. The point at which genes and culture became intertwined in a mutual relationship can be considered a major transition in human evolution [2].

The evolution of culture – the shared meanings (knowledge, beliefs, values) embedded in systems of kinship, cosmology, law and ritual – itself depends on Darwinian principles operating within and between populations. Human beings transmit large amounts of information by imitation, by instruction, and by verbal communication. This leads to an extraordinary range of behavioral variation, even in the same environment, on which selection processes can work. Indeed, the ability both to transmit and to receive this information shapes the brain to be more responsive to the information itself. Cultural evolutionary processes in specific environments lead to the evolution of uniquely human social instincts, and the ways in which we learn, feel and think shape the culture in which we live. Those cultural variants that are most easily learned, remembered and/or taught then tend to persist and spread. The rate of cultural change is constrained by evolved rate of brain development and rate at which culture can be acquired by learning. Broadly speaking, at this point in our social and economic evolution, it takes 15 to 25 years to complete physical development and cultural learning, with the years from twenty to fifty being the window for fully realized cultural transmission (allowing for the erosion of cognitive capacity with greater age). The importance of the cultural environment to the evolution of the human species is echoed in the development of the individual. Family environment and resources, parenting/caretaking style and beliefs, personal and societal beliefs and values, all shape the acquisition of thinking, social, and regulatory capacities in the individual, and can influence in significant ways the response to disease or adversity. These effects can be seen at a basic biological level – the impact of stress on fundamental neuroendocrine systems [16] or of adverse conditions on the development of neuropeptide systems critical for social behavior [17]. They can be seen at the level of acquisition of the behavioral repertoire, for example early adversity on subsequent neurobehavioral development [18] and the impact of socioeconomic variables on the acquisition of basic skills in young children [19]. They can also influence,

both positively and negatively, outcomes post-injury, i.e., family variables have bidirectional influence on behavioral outcomes in pediatric head injury [20].

The end-state of the evolutionary journey then is the start-state of the individual. Evolution prepares the biological organism for its role as a member of the species to which it belongs. The individual's developmental trajectory is the journey from biological preparedness to the end-state of the adult in the particular environment obtaining at the time. Modeling this journey requires consideration both of models of the end-state to be achieved and of models of the journey itself – and of the interaction between them. Constraints imposed by the end-state shape the understanding of the nature of the architecture on arrival – and potentially redefine the end-state given its expression across time, within a particular environment. As new knowledge is acquired in the biological neurosciences, the realities of how biological mechanisms and processes constrain and reshape models of the overall system and its construction are more deeply appreciated. In this way developmental thinking influences cognitive science.

Developmental psychology has actively generated models to account for the development of cognition. These range from *nativist*, innate specification of behavioral capacities/maturation of genetically specified forms; to *associationist*, experience with properties of objects in the world leads to mental associations of those properties; to *constructivist*, integration of intellect and senses to create constructed representations. For many theorists, the acquisition of new knowledge within a social context is preeminent – and needs to be explained. As a result, sociocognitive models that aim to integrate the social dimension into the other models are the focus of ongoing research [21]. With the advent of new modes of thought and new technologies in the post-modern synthesis era, such model-building is now the province of the "developmental neurosciences" and, as such, models are being tested and reformulated in the light of new findings in the wider brain sciences. In this context, combined models seem likely to have a better fit with the workings of other principles that are widely applicable to the building of brain and behavior. The combination of nativist and constructivist models as explicated most fully by Karmiloff-Smith et al. [22] appears to align most comfortably with the "gene + plasticity" story.

The nativist + constructivist position is, however, being further extended to integrate the role of experience and context even more fully into a model of the individual actually behaving. The observation that the sea squirt, one of the workhorses of neural science research, only has neural cells during the time it is moving around, which it then digests once it enters its stationary life stage, invites consideration of the brain as a system not for cognizing but for action [23] and has provided a rationale for the development of ecologically framed dynamic systems models of the mind. This perspective argues against the inherent reductionism of the cognitive neurosciences paradigm, explicitly resists the decontextualized representations of mind that derive from the classical understanding, and proposes that the mind is "an emergent property of interactions of brain, body and world" [24], prompting systematic study of the dynamics of trans-actions between them. Without reference to the contexts in which behavior – and the processes that support it – has been forged (from the biological neurosciences), the cognitive neurosciences fail to sit-uate their findings in a model of how the organism actually behaves, a powerful constraint on any theory of human behavior. Integrating evolutionary thinking with cognitive and dynamic systems modeling holds promise to achieve a more comprehensive account [3].

Addressing **how** in developmental modeling

The *how* question accesses two major mechanisms critical for the building of the neural and cognitive architecture: *genes and epigenetics* and *plasticity*. Answering the *how* question also requires some sense of the framework within which these processes are assumed to work. A discussion of developmental mod-els cannot proceed without reference to a concept that has polarized much debate – that of modularity. How one understands this concept shapes the theoretical framework within which models are generated – and how specific processes are deemed to contribute. In 1983, Fodor [25] used this concept in making a dis-tinction between perception and cognition – between input systems that are encapsulated, mandatory, fast operating, and hardwired, and central systems that are unencapsulated and domain-neutral. The former he described as modular in architecture. The concept proved enticing: its match with the specialization models of brain–behavior relationships in the adult human brain derived from neuropsychology, and behavioral neurology investigations led to it being

extended well beyond Fodor's initial formulation to characterize "cognitive" domains such as language, spatial processing, and social processing, in addition to basic sensory inputs. Modularity in the sense of committed processing units is widely accepted as a core feature of the cognitive architecture of the adult human brain. Fodor's "cognition" has been replaced by a modular concept of executive functions or processes at the behavioral level (Baddeley's central executive) that itself has been subject to modular fractionation at the neural level.

The concept – and its cognitive tradition – has also been adopted into the evolutionary context, being used in the evolutionary psychology sense of biological preparedness, the end-state of macro (evolutionary) development. The innate proclivities, the products of our evolutionary history that prepare us to meet species-specific behavioral expectations, are considered modules. The evolutionary psychologists Cosmides and Tooby have proposed a multiplicity of mental modules, arguing that the modern human mind evolved under selection pressure in Pleistocene envi-ronments and is made up of a wide range of modules that address specific adaptive challenges in that setting [26]. The modules are now not only not restricted to sensory inputs, but are "content-rich" in that they provide both rules for solving problems and the infor-mation needed to do so. In this view the developmental model proposes that the modules come on line at different times in ontogenetic development.

It is not clear that the concept of modularity will continue to prove an optimal description of adult brain organization as greater knowledge of neural functioning emerges. The behavioral modules of cognition – linguistic, spatial, social – are no longer thought to be supported in some sort of modular fashion at the neural level: network models wherein behavioral functions are supported by transactions among systems with nodes in different networks are now being widely explored. The same 'nodes' may participate in more than one network; given networks may support a range of different behavioral functions.

Other data available now, however, significantly constrain the "promiscuous modularity" mindset [27] and provide further reason for strong influence exerted on the thinking of neuropsychologists by the observations of specialization of function manifest in adult behavior to be resisted. At deeper levels of anal-ysis this specialization is not the rule. At the gene level, for example, essential genes encoding hub proteins (as opposed to disease genes) are expressed widely in tissues of different types. At the neural level, all areas of cortex initially send outputs to nearly all types of cortical targets (via extra branching of axons). With experience, these are pruned back so that visual areas project to subcortical visual processors, auditory to auditory, and the like [28]. What must be explicated by the developmental scholar is how the organism goes from a brain that is widely interconnected and undifferentiated to one that can be described in terms of specialized modules.

The current data support the position that developmentally the gradient is from global to local processing mechanisms. The overall logic of development is one of association, rather than dissociation: from interactivity to competition to compensation to redundancy to specialization to localization to modularization [29]. Development in this view is a modularizing process that takes place over the lifespan of an individual and is dependent on the developmental transactions between brain and context over time (see Johnson et al.'s interactive specialization model [30]). For one mechanism in support of this general framework, Elman and his colleagues [31] have argued that the logic instantiated in the work on gene expression and cortical sprouting also obtains at the behavioral development level: the availability of domain-relevant learning algorithms (the biologically prepared end-states of evolutionary processes) "jumpstart" the infant brain. Initially all algorithms attempt to process all inputs. Eventually, however, one becomes the winner (probably the most domain-relevant one), leading to domain specificity that becomes even more narrowly specified (modularized) and efficient with continued experience over time.

Biological proclivities, the end-state of evolutionary development, are the foundations of subsequent cognitive capacities; they are encoded in the genome and provide the start-state for individual development. Behavior will emerge and be continually elaborated as the individual experiences the world; processes of plasticity will sculpt and re-sculpt the neural architecture in response to the brain–environment interaction as it is experienced by the individual over time. The precise nature of the steps from biological proclivity to adult modularity may be debated for some time to come but the outline seems clear.

More complete models will need to take into account both evolutionary and ontogenetic perspectives. At the one end, different brain systems are more or less conserved, and dedicated information-processing units (modules?) that provide information about the environment that "cannot be obtained by thought in an ecologically useful timeframe" [32] are crucial for survival. At the other end, within behavioral domains, different functions can be parsed into those that are relatively "focal" in representation and those that depend on widespread activations across networks. Processes of elaboration also appear to reflect both increasing specialization of and increasingly sophisticated interactions among brain systems/networks – among other things, to maximize the efficiency of resource utilization in the adult brain [33].

Genes and epigenetics

The gene story involves genomic information and epigenetic processes. The genome is the end-state of evolutionary development, providing the infant with a basic species-specific plan with which to begin to map the actual world in which it finds itself. Epigenetic processes control gene activity over time, regulating the turning-on and turning-off of gene expression [34]. Gene action is inherently developmental, inherently contextually embedded [35]. The expression of genetic information from the individual's genome lays out the body plan and the large-scale neural structures related by tissue organization and cell type. Epigenetic processes in dynamic transactions with experience in the environment permit the brain to "learn" the nature of itself in a given setting and sculpt and fine-tune the specialized networks needed for mature function. The laying down of structures and circuits begins in utero. Postnatally, the dance between structure and experience speeds up exponentially as the infant has greater and greater access to stimulation: not only sensory, but now social, communicative, cognitive – and rapidly develops the capacity to engage with all the stimuli of the world on his or her own recognizance.

The application of genetically informed models to the understanding of the child's behavior will require clear differentiation of the role of single genes and of multiple genes in the elaboration of complex behaviors and appreciation of the difference in genetic contributions to normal function and to disease. It is unlikely that the complexity of processes underlying a behavioral skill such as reading, for example, could be orchestrated by a single gene or even gene family. However, by the same token, it is entirely plausible that the uncomplicated acquisition of such a complexly orchestrated skill could easily be derailed by the action or inaction of a few genes. Genetically informed modeling will also require close analysis of the biology–environment interaction. Kovas and Plomin [36] argue, for example, that pleiotropy (one gene influences many traits) and polygenicity (many genes influence one trait) mean that the impact of genes on brain and behavior is "generalist" and not modular. In their analysis of the genetic contributions to learning abilities and disabilities, for example, they conclude that discrepancies in children's profiles of performance are largely due to "specialist" environments. But, as the genetic revolution in neuroscience bears more and more fruit, it appears that the range of variables that both researchers and clinicians will need to consider in the brain–behavior analysis only grows – and that gene–environment interactions will have to be considered in light of very specific genetic characteristics of the individual. Thus, adverse environments, that – generally speaking – can be so detrimental to neurobehavioral development may not be so maladaptive for everyone, but may vary as, for example, a function of serotonin gene structure in the individual [37].

Plasticity

Plasticity is "an obligatory consequence of neural activity in response to environmental pressures, functional significance and experience" [38], a "baseline property of the brain" [39]. It is neutral with respect to outcome, being the fundamental mechanism for learning and development, but also the cause of pathology and subsequent clinical disorders. It is not a process that builds a brain and then stops, but an inherent property of the nervous system that is always present. Alternative connectivity is held in check by normal functioning in the world. In parallel to the forces operating at the evolutionary level, as long as the individual keeps acting within his/her repertoire, that is, in an environment with specific parameters, then the attained brain organization remains stable. Should the individual's repertoire change, then plastic responses will re-shape the system to adapt to the new status. Thus, losing sight results in allocation of receptive fields previously committed to visual cortical inputs to auditory and/or tactile inputs [40]; constraining or losing a digit or limb leads to reshaping of the receptive fields [41]. Such resculpting of connections may not work to a patient's advantage, as when an undermined body plan leads to secondary "phantom" experiences including severe and (to date) largely intractable pain [42]. It may, however, be the basis for therapeutic strategies that after injury change outcomes for the better, as in constraint-induced therapy [43]. But disease or injury is not the only way the individual's repertoire may change. Plastic responses are recruited when an individual commits to a demanding musical or motor discipline. The brains of musicians [44], of chess players [45], and of expert golfers [46] are resculpted as they achieve the amount of practice needed for expert performance. Of note is the fact that the increased skill the individuals gain seems to be specific to the domain of practice.

There are two major components of plasticity: expression of normal physiological responses that are subject to inhibitory control when the relevant stimuli are present, and cross modal plasticity de novo in response to severe sensory deprivation [47]. Processes involve unmasking of existing connections (shifts of strength in existing connections) and establishment of new connections. The meaning of stimuli to the organism is crucial – and is reflected in the range of activation elicited. For example, phonemic word generation elicits focal brain activity associated with auditory processing; semantic word representation activates multiple sites, including visual.

Other mechanisms are integral to the workings of plasticity. Competition for connectivity is salient and specific processes of apoptosis with their own trajectories and time lines are crucial sculptors of architecture in the developing brain [48]. The balance between excitatory and inhibitory processes is also dynamic [49], and has important implications for pharmacological interventions in pediatric epilepsy, for example.

Additional themes related to **how**

Two additional themes are central to the *how* of development – timing and white matter. Issues of timing are critical to all models of developmental change and stability. Both genes + epigenes and plasticity are dependent on the timing of expectable inputs. Critical and/or sensitive periods are those during which exposure to relevant stimulation is optimal. Both the onset and the offset of such periods can be biologically specified: gene activity both switches on and switches off a developmental process. The classic demonstration of this principle was provided by Hubel and Wiesel, who showed that development of the columnar organization of the visual receptive fields in the cat depended on visual experience within a particular time frame. The practical application is seen in children with amblyopia: therapeutic occlusion of the non-amblyopic eye has been used to provoke activity-dependent visual development in the "bad" eye and must take place within a given time to be most effective in the long term. A critical or sensitive period can also depend on gene activity for its onset but be terminated "behaviorally" as the onset of new behavioral capacities recruits brain networks for alternative purposes; the development of other functions dependent on the same or adjoining networks effectively closes the window for further gene–environment interaction [50].

For hard-wired systems that are minimally, if at all, responsive to plastic change, the timing of expected inputs may indeed be critical. For skills dependent on more complexly interconnected systems that mature later, failure to acquire a skill because a window of opportunity has passed is not a necessary outcome. Experience (practice) can recruit neural networks to subserve alternate pathways to effect the same end. Differential timing of the brain–experience interaction can result in different cortical territories for the same cultural product: for example, when children learn two languages at the same time the cortical territories in Broca's area overlap; when the two languages are learned later their cortical territories are spatially separate.

In adult behavioral neurology/neuropsychology, white matter (myelinated fiber tracts) has historically taken a back seat to the grey matter (neuronal assemblies) that supports the functional capacities of interest primarily at the cortical level [51]. In contrast, for investigations in developmental neurology and developmental neuroscience, consideration of white matter is central: the laying down of myelin serves to index the increase in neural connectivity that results from the interaction between the brain and its environment (both internal and external) over time. The progress of myelination through childhood and adolescence [52] provides a window into developmental change. Models of neurobehavioral development can be tested against changing patterns of myelin deposition as reflected in, for example, studies of the ratio of grey matter to white matter [53, 54], complemented by the information provided by new techniques of tractography [55].

Examples of developmental models

The following examples illustrate several of the wide range of issues that are part and parcel of developmental thinking – and the applications of developmental models in the quest to understand behavioral development in the child.

Modeling in evolution

From the perspective of the adult end-state and in the context of adult neurological diseases, a horizontal analysis [13] of more or less autonomous functional capacities has seemed eminently reasonable. Brain–behavior relationships for a number of conditions (e.g. the aphasias, agnosias, visual-spatial deficits) and processes (e.g. hemispheric mechanisms) have been outlined and refined. The frontal lobe–executive function connection has proved particularly exciting, both to adult and to pediatric neuropsychologists, and has driven much thinking regarding the development of cognition and behavior. For the pediatric community, this interest has derived specifically from the myelination data of Yakovlev and Lecours [52], which showed how the development of the underlying neural substrate, as indexed by myelination schedules, proceeds over time. Their data prompted the proposal of a model of "late" development of executive functions in the adolescent period – to explain both what was observed, with regard to myelination patterning, and the growth in executive capabilities that as noted over time.

However, the proposed underlying model associated with Yakovlev and Lecours's findings has remained linear, and the individual-as-cognizer model has significantly shaped its interpretation. Consideration of the frontal-executive findings did not take into account the requisite principles of dynamic change and experiential driving of behavioral progress, and so this model did not make sense developmentally, in either evolutionary or ontogenetic frames.

From the logic of an evolutionary perspective, executive functions do not (in fact, cannot) develop "late" in any organism; and they cannot "just develop" in adolescence, as sometimes suggested. Systems supporting executive capacities are critical for survival and, as such, must be part and parcel of a complex system like the brain, and have evolved as an integral component thereof [56]. In order to adapt flexibly to changing environments, all animals must have the capacity for coordination, integration and control (executive processes) of all the complex mechanisms supporting their behavioral repertoire, and the flexibility to deploy them in varying ways across development. Indeed, the neural systems of the frontal lobes are neither new – in evolutionary terms – nor special to humans: they have been part of the neural apparatus of the mammalian line for 176 million years [57]. The goal-oriented behavior that they support is not only common to all mammals, but critical to their survival and to the evolutionary success of the whole mammalian enterprise. Such control processes are – indeed, must be – inextricably embedded in the total package of biological systems that all animals need in order to obtain food, reproductive partners and other critical resources.

Executive processes and the neural systems that support them have been bundled with motivational drives, sensory capacities, and motor outputs from the beginning of the differentiation of the mammalian line. For humans, as sophisticated social capacities have evolved, increased executive "power" has simultaneously developed, to drive the now more complex system. Ever more "power" has been recruited as language was added to the executive toolbox of the human behavioral repertoire; and even more needed to drive the interactions with the new environment of culture that was created by ongoing social and linguistic interchange within and between groups. The amount of neural tissue allotted to executive control processes (ECP) has increased, in response. The driving force has been the acquisition of social and communicative capacities – and the "new world" of experience that they opened up for humans (see Fig. 2a.1).

The association of executive capacities with the frontal lobes, the 'frontal metaphor" of Pennington [58], can also be queried. As with our emotional tie to language being unique to us, so it goes with the frontal lobes. The belief that "since our foreheads bulge more than those of apes, they therefore must house more brain tissue (and more intelligence)" is an easy one to hold (and, indeed, seems self-evident) in the context of a belief in a hierarchical view of life. However, as the zeitgeist changes and we are more willing to interpret human behavior in a comparative framework, it turns out that the "big frontal lobes" of humans are, in reality, no bigger than those of other animals when examined in the context of brain–body ratios, encephalization, or cortical convolutions [57, 59]. Instead, the difference between us and other animals seems likely to be one of how we have used our brains, and the number and complexity of neural connections that we have recruited to manage the social, language and cultural environments that we have created for ourselves in response. Recent work

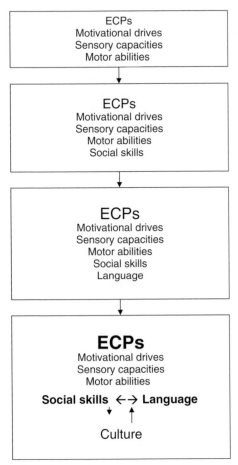

Figure 2a.1. Increasing ECP power to manage more complex systems.

in the comparative tradition suggests that this follows from an up-regulation of gene expression in humans as compared to nonhuman primates [4].

Interpreted from the perspective of the start-state of the organism, Yakovlev and Lecours's myelination data tell us a great deal about what evolution has prepared the brain to do; to support increasingly massive amounts of interaction with both internal and external environmental inputs through "intracortical neuropil association areas" [52]. Specifically, there are two major association areas of the primate brain, both supporting association by means of heteromodal cortex receiving inputs from multiple cell types and modalities [60]. Both of these are critical substrates for adaptive success in humans – which depends heavily on our social skills. The availability of the comparative tradition as a source of new knowledge and new models for understanding human behavior has opened up neuroscience to consideration of what are, from an evolutionary perspective, more fundamental behavioral capacities – and, in so doing, has thrown into high relief the crucial role of social experience – the ability to navigate social relationships – in a species whose social competence is critical to survival. No coherent biologically based model of human development can ignore this dimension of our behavioral repertoire.

This type of model de-emphasizes the role of the executive system, focusing instead on the species-specific and adaptively critical role of social functioning – and the length of time it takes to acquire proficiency. Recognition of this crucial component of human development – and of adolescence as the crucial period for consolidating the learning – has led Blakemore and her colleagues [61] to develop a model for which the driving force is social learning. The model aims to specify relationships between the neuroanatomic, cognitive, and functional processes available through the adolescent years in order to understand the developmental trajectories of this developmental epoch. Neuroimaging and anatomical investigations of changes in the neural substrate post-puberty and beyond inform and are informed by the work of developmental psychologists mapping the progress of functional competence in this life stage.

Modeling by disorder

The strategy of exploring the impact of neurological disorders on behavior that has served adult neuropsychology well is equally potent in the developmental arena, and has been productively utilized in the context of such disorders as the myelodysplasias, traumatic brain injury, pediatric cancers, and genetic and metabolic disorders. The strategy is framed very differently when developmental disorders are considered, however, with the interaction of *timing-of-insult* × *developmental-status* being central. Disorder undermines already established neural organization in the adult; in the child, disorder undermines the actual process of organization.

Maureen Dennis and her colleagues have elucidated many of the challenges to be tackled in their work with individuals with spina bifida [62]. Most recently, in her 2009 Birch lecture to the International Neuropsychological Society, Dennis offered a comprehensive view of the impact of the biological disruption in development associated with spina bifida and the disturbance in structural development that ensues. Specifically, very early embryonic defects

lead to perturbations of normal processes of organization. Exploring the logic of the developmental disturbances as they influence the laying down of structural elements, Dennis has described a full range of anatomical outcomes: elements are absent, attenuated, enhanced, delayed, dysmorphic, or designed differently. These outcomes underlie anomalous neural activation, atypical automatization, under- and over-recruitment of networks, developmental delay and time-lagged deficits, and atypical cognitive profiles. The radical reorganization that can take place leads to "inelegant and strange solutions" (Dennis, Birch lecture, INS, 2009).

Dennis's work indicates that the neural substrate for behavior in spina bifida is markedly reconfigured, changing the otherwise expectable brain–behavior relationships. This reconfiguration notwithstanding, clinical observations indicate quite clearly that individuals with spina bifida can achieve a high degree of adaptive success. The ability of even a reconfigured nervous system, in this and other developmental conditions, to respond plastically, take advantage of environmental input, and succeed adaptively is remarkable. How it does so remains to be elucidated.

Modeling by lesion

Neurodevelopmental disorders bring with them a high degree of complexity. However, at times, the type of injury may appear to reflect a uniform insult, which in an adult patient would be anticipated to cause limited impact. Not so with the developing organism. As an example, the research program of Elizabeth Bates and her colleagues has studied the impact of a specific lesion, unilateral stroke, to a brain that is presumably appropriately developed prior to the lesion forming. They have investigated the effects of the early lesion on later skill development in a variety of areas. Their data on language development [63] support the relationship of left-hemisphere mechanisms underlying language functions, even in young children. This suggests that at this point in our evolutionary history, left-hemisphere specialization for language is now part of our biological preparedness. Bates notes, however, that this does not entail that language is organized as it is in the adult brain. Language capacities considered to be mediated by posterior brain systems in the adult were disrupted by frontal lesions in the young child. Why? The answer could be "biological" or "behavioral", or both. Is it that temporal systems are not available to the young child? Hardly. The children studied behaved normally with respect to other functions associated with the temporal lobes. Or do they lack the capacity to support this skill in particular? If so, it is not clear why. Or is it that the fact that the skill is *being learned* – rather than having been automatized (as, arguably, in the adult) – and that active learning recruits different brain systems than routinized maintenance? Given that effort engages frontal brain networks, the impact of disrupted frontal systems in a young child may well undermine the learning of language and its use, rather than the skill itself.

Modeling the brain–experience interface

Rerouting and reorganization of neural systems does not only occur under the aberrant biological conditions associated with different neurodevelopmental disorders. Atypical neural architectures and behavioral profiles can result from atypical experience as brain systems are being assembled. Models derived from the experience of individuals born prematurely are informative [64]. The brain systems being assembled in the third trimester should be able to count on the more or less highly controlled sensory conditions of the womb: regular and consistent auditory background (with the rhythmic organizing experience of the maternal heartbeat) and no visual input. Instead, the immature preterm brain is subjected to the complex auditory stimulation and the visual shock of the outer world. Models can focus on the nature of brain development when the environment is aberrant or on the impact of the expectable environment when the brain cannot "receive" its inputs. Such models will require a close analysis of those systems that are in active development later in intrauterine life, the behaviors they subserve, and the impact of having them engage in transactions with the environment in an undeveloped state. Therapeutic interventions will need to focus on promoting developmental processes by modifying the child's immediate experience and shaping its later interactions in the world. The potential of manipulations of the extrauterine environment for supporting expected developmental outcomes in such individuals remains to be thoroughly explored (See. Als [65] for a neonatal care intervention strategy based on the synactive model of the premature child).

Even with a presumably adequately developed full-term brain, the developmental consequences of atypical experience in the guise of adverse early child care are well documented in studies of children whose early life was spent in the orphanages of totalitarian states. "Adversity" can be also be indexed by exposure of a previously appropriately developing brain to toxic agents in the intrauterine environment, in the outer environment or in the course of (necessary) medical treatments. A central element of the organizing model in all of these types of studies is behavioral outcome as a function of the chronological-age-×-time/duration-of-the-adverse-exposure interaction.

The specificity of action of the plastic processes that drive such changes in response to the environment does not need seriously adverse conditions for its demonstration. One can simply lack opportunities in life. The neural bases of perhaps the most powerful of our cultural products, reading, have been well studied to date; largely in "horizontal" paradigms that seek to explicate the components of the skill. A more clearly developmental analysis can be applied, however. Reading is a complex cultural product that modern societies expect their members to acquire: literacy makes for greater adaptive success in such a society (but see Grigorenko and O'Keefe [66]), increasing the likelihood that an individual will have the economic basis for effective mating, reproduction, and raising of young. The plasticity of the nervous system in response to experience predicts that acquiring reading will change the brain; and so it does. In a series of studies of individuals from the fishing community of southern Portugal in which some individuals do not achieve literacy for social and not biological reasons, Petersson and colleagues [67] have demonstrated different patterns of neural activity as a function of having a reading brain rather than a nonreading brain. While their data only pertain to exposure to reading decoding, and their reading subjects were not highly educated (raising the question of the functional reorganization that might be expected to take place as more sophisticated reading skills are elaborated over the course of formal education throughout childhood and adolescence), Petersson et al. note that the acquisition of literacy "appears to influence the auditory-verbal system in a non-trivial way" [67], and also selectively influences the functional architecture of non-language systems. That is, change in brain architecture is not limited to simply committing some neural networks to the reading skill, but also results in a reorganization of neural structures that influence the way in which other skills develop. Failing to acquire reading does not simply mean one is non-literate; it may commit one to a different developmental course with respect to the acquisition of behavioral capacities and, potentially, result in an altered pattern of adaptive success.

Reasoning backwards from data of this type, we can assume that the acquisition of each new addition to the behavioral repertoire is likely to entail reorganization of brain systems. This is true not only of a major behavioral system such as language, the acquisition of which, at least at this point in our behavioral history, is supported by innate proclivities, but also of the application of language in written form, a more recently invented cultural product. Neuropsychological performance varies as a function of literacy or lack of literacy in the presence of brain damage [68] and in the context of different sociocultural experience [69]. The brain is also shaped to meet the specific culturally determined requirements of different language groups: reading Italian activates different networks than reading English [70], for example. Culture plays an important role in shaping brain – and one that clinicians ignore at their peril. In the clinical setting the practitioner must take seriously the individual's experience with cultural products in interpreting observations. This goes beyond the awareness of and sensitivity to cultural variables as more traditionally conceived that is expected in culturally competent care.

Modeling from typical to atypical and back

Understanding typical development from a neuroscientific perspective raises ethical challenges. Children cannot be subjected to brain lesions, nor can their access to the expectable environments of growth and development be deliberately limited. One way around these limitations is the investigation of the "natural experiment" of disease and disorder, as exemplified by the work of Dennis and her colleagues above. Another adds the comparative method to the investigative armamentarium. Diamond's research program has mined a wide range of neuroscientific models, tools and techniques that can be mobilized. Working initially in the developmental psychology tradition, Diamond revealed the trajectory of the very young child's ability to recall and to inhibit more primitive responding and to tolerate delay in a hiding-retrieval task – an executive capacity [71]. She then turned to comparative psychology for insights into brain–behavior relationships for executive capacities and used with typically developing young children tasks

whose neuropsychological properties had been closely mapped in studies of monkeys with targeted brain lesions [72]. The neural substrate for the executive capacities in question was thus outlined – and the importance of the dopamine pathways serving the critical brain regions highlighted [73]. Diamond then turned to the traditional disorder-based strategy and investigated the executive capacities of children with a disorder of dopamine metabolism [74]. This allowed for analysis of the genetics of dopamine production and action [75]. Using these additional techniques, Diamond has come full circle and explored the cognitive performance in typically developing children [76].

Modeling by time

In learning about brain–behavioral relationships as defined in lesion studies, neuropsychologists are taught to pay attention to and differentiate between age at time of lesion and age at time of testing. In the adult context the distinction is important in understanding the role of the lesion in and the role of recovery that may have occurred. Specifying these two time points is equally necessary when working with children. However, it appears from the work of Karmiloff-Smith and her colleagues that two time points are not enough for a comprehensive developmental analysis. A third time point indexing the endstate of the child's developmental trajectory – his or her adaptive success as an independent member of society – is critical. Few studies have explicitly targeted adaptive success and explored the developmental trajectories by which it is attained; the longitudinal studies needed are difficult to mount.

The work of Bellugi and her colleagues has yielded important insights in the differences between two genetic syndromes – Williams (WS) and Down (DS) – and contributed to an improved characterization of the behavioral profiles of both disorders, yielding in particular details of the WS behavioral phenotype [77]. Subject to a developmental analysis, the data from WS and DS provide a more provocative picture. For example, the start-state for vocabulary acquisition is equivalent for WS and DS toddlers; however, the end-state is quite different. Language is much better in WS adolescents and adults [78] in comparison to those with DS. In contrast, for number, the start-state differs: young WS children do better; but so does the end-state: DS individuals do better [79].

A horizontal analysis at a given time will suggest a deficit in one group relative to the other. The developmental (vertical) analysis not only implies different routes to the achieved end-state in the two groups, but also calls into question the meaning and predictive value of the earlier "deficit". Cross-sectional investigative designs and horizontal analyses of behavior apparently fail to help us to predict how well an individual will succeed in achieving the adult end-state that is the goal of the developmental process – and of the clinical assessment.

Modeling by domain

Neuropsychological investigation has a long history of focusing on executive and linguistic capacities in the here-and-now. An individual's ability to achieve adaptive success – the desired developmental outcome – is, however, more realistically indexed by social functioning and adjustment. Accordingly, Yeates and his colleagues [80] have proposed a model with this outcome as its driving force. The emphasis on outcome, rather than disease or disorder, makes it applicable to a range of disorders that derail development. As noted by Yeates and colleagues, age/developmental stage at time of injury and neural substrates involved are expected to be salient in predicting outcomes, rather than the nature of the derailing process. The model brings findings from developmental psychology together with those of social neuroscience with the goal of "specifying the relationships between social adjustment, peer interactions and relationships, social problem solving and communication, social-affective and cognitive-executive processes, and their brain substrates" [80]. In formulating the model, the authors pay attention to the necessarily contextualized nature of social functioning (involving both self and others) and recognize the multiple competencies that must be acquired and the need to characterize the developmental trajectories of the components of these competencies.

Modeling brain–behavior relationships

Neuropsychology developed originally in response to "where?" questions, in the context of lesions to the adult brain secondary to disease and trauma: i.e., given observations of specific "broken behavior", where in the brain is the damage? The goal was to determine the brain–behavior relationships for different dimensions of behavior – to determine the neural substrate(s) for language, for visual processing, for motor output and control, and to outline their localization. The

organizing question in the adult setting was and still regularly is: *what is the neural substrate for domain X?* Similarly, within the historic downward extension of adult neuropsychology to the pediatric context, this question has subsequently guided investigations into brain–behavior relationships in children. But as is now well known, children are not small adults – and downwards-extension thinking is not appropriate to the task as it is understood. In the developmental context, the guiding question cannot be *what is the neural substrate for domain X?* but instead must be formulated as *what is(are) the neural substrate(s) for the development of domain X?*

In exploring brain–behavior relationships over development, one line of questioning includes the following: *which components of which neural system(s) will need to recruited – and when – for this or that component of behavioral domain X?* An important corollary question is: *which components of which neural systems are available for recruitment at specific times?* Different cognitive capacities and their associated neural networks come "on line" in response to the expression of the relevant developmental genes at different times. One must also hold as a possibility that building a brain is somewhat like building a new road: during the building (developmental) process, if the traffic has to keep flowing, then some structures will need to be built (available) that will later be dismantled (no longer used to support the specific operation in question). In addition, the expression of information from the genome requires exposure to and experience with the expectable environment of the organism to activate the processes of epigenesis. This entails not only that the environment be "good enough" but also that the organism be able to take advantage of it at any given time. This latter has implications for modeling atypical development: *what constraints are imposed by a given disease process?* and *how do they influence the acquisition of reserve capacities?*

It also has implications for modeling in typical development. In modeling the capacities of the "symbolic species", Deacon [81] explores the interaction between the child's available capacities and the information available in the environment, arguing that the former determines what can be selected from (or by) the latter. The linguistic elements that the infant responds to (and learns from) are those that are with the range of its overall neural and cognitive capacities at a given point in time. Thus, early on the infant is sensitive to larger features of the communicative environment (that express relationships between and intentions towards objects in the environment) and learns initially from features that are not parsed into computational units (phonology, syntactics, semantics). At the same time, the child appears to be sensitive to patterns among features that will support analysis of computational elements in due course. Saffran [82] has demonstrated, for example, that infants are sensitive to the statistical regularities in the sound stream, regularities that will eventually cue the sound features of the child's mother tongue.

The interaction with environmental information can be strikingly specific. A provocative investigation by Neville, Mills, and Lawson [83] highlighted the complexity that ensues. In an evoked potential paradigm in infants, they showed that, initially, activity in response to word recognition is widely dispersed through the brain. Then, at the point when the child has acquired a 200-word vocabulary, activity focuses on the left temporal lobe – irrespective of maturational age. But a child's vocabulary is determined by the number of words spoken to it. Hart and Risley [19] demonstrated the impact of environmental variables (in their case, in the form of discrepancies in SES) on vocabulary growth in the 0 to 3-year period. The vocabulary of economically advantaged 3-year-olds was more than 3-times greater than that of the most disadvantaged children, with the vocabulary of a less disadvantaged group lying in between. Not only the number of words but also the kind of words were related to SES: higher SES parents used more encouraging and fewer prohibiting utterances than low SES – and the number of encouraging versus prohibiting utterances was related to later psychometric IQ: more encouragement, higher IQ scores; more prohibitions, lower IQ scores. The neural substrate for language is directly shaped by experience, in this case the child's language environment. The brain–environment interaction is clear.

The modularity of the brain–behavior relationships of language in the adult is well established; in adults, language as a behavioral domain may, in some sense, stand alone. The trajectory to that modular architecture is, however, not yet well established and, in the child, language cannot easily be disembedded from its context of use. The goal of the most important models is not delineation of *brain–behavior relationships of language in the child*, but the characterization of the *brain–behavior relationships of language development*; these must be explored in developmental terms; they will be non-linear; they will be dependent on expectable experience [84]. Breakdown in the trajectory of language development can be expected to occur in response to changes in brain and changes in expectable experience, both interacting with ongoing developmental experience and expectations. We can expect that a similar analysis will be needed for attention [85], for prosocial behavior of all types [86], for executive skills [87], and the like.

Heterogeneity of outcomes

One lesson to be drawn from the above discussion is the level of complexity that is entailed by studying anything in a developmental framework. One consequence of this is the sheer range of outcomes that must be accounted for in developmental analyses. In such analyses heterogeneity is to be expected – and to be explicated.

In developmental models the core expectation of nonlinearity entails heterogeneity of outcomes, both typical and atypical, secondary to the interactions of nonlinearity and individual differences – in the development of systems, in behavioral characteristics, and in disease processes. Developmental trajectories of typically developing children include variability related to inherited individual characteristics (gender, temperament, IQ), family characteristics (education, resources, parenting styles, disciplinary beliefs) and cultural and societal values and opportunities. Derailment of developmental trajectories subsequent to disease, disorder, injury, experiential restriction, or adverse conditions takes place in the context of the above and is compounded by variability secondary to differences in the nature of the derailing condition, the brain systems affected, the time at onset, the timing with respect to the development of other systems, the treatments available, and their impact on the developing nervous system and person. Modeling in development must account for heterogeneity.

Heterogeneity of outcomes is part and parcel of typical development as manifest in normal human variation and diversity. In spite of their differences, however, most individuals are recognizable as members of one species and achieve acceptable adaptive success as adults. Adaptive competence can be achieved by different routes. Rampant heterogeneity is evidently constrained. The information in the genome is one source of major constraint. Evolution has provided the body maps and the biological proclivities for behaviors that are species-specific. The species-specific environment constrains the unfurling of these throughout development, not just via the physical properties that "afford" [88] the behavioral repertoire of any organism, but also by means of the social and psychological expectations that nudge the human individual specifically towards the central tendency for "good enough" communication and social interaction with conspecifics that is at the core of human nature. Clinicians are very familiar with this concept given their experience with the range of difference in neuropsychological profiles that is elicited in the course of assessments and the ability of young individuals to achieve a high level of functional independence and adaptive success nonetheless [89]. The adaptation model of learning disorders described by Holmes-Bernstein and Waber [90] and the harmful dysfunction concept of mental disorder articulated by Wakefield [91] highlight the necessary interaction of constitution and context in both creating – and avoiding or compensating for – learning deficits.

In the face of adversity there are other constraints on derailment: reserve is built over time; resilience is deployed from the beginning. The concept of "reserve" was derived from adult literature to account for the fact that, as individuals age, functional competence and disease burden are not well correlated. Satz [92] characterized the concept of "brain reserve". Stern [93] extended the concept to include "cognitive reserve" as indexed by education and/or by psychometric IQ. Both brain and cognitive reserve must get their start in inherited potentialities but must also be the product of developmental processes. Cognitive reserve surely reflects an end-state – outcome-to-date – of a learning process. An individual's cognitive reserve at any stage will depend on the inherited capacity for learning, the quality of both the nurturing and learning environments she/he has participated in, and the presence or otherwise of disease processes of different types.

Reserve is an equally important concept in the developmental context. It plays a role in the understanding of both risk and recovery and must be evaluated in the investigation of disease/disorder outcomes [94]. For the child en route to adulthood, the age (the index of how long the child has been in the world having developmentally necessary learning experiences) and the quality of those experiences are important factors.

Resilience is also associated with the ability to buffer adversity. It appears not to reflect an end-state (the reserve capacity of the outcome-to-date) but rather to be shaped by a start-state and reflected in temperament variables such as reactivity, exploratory drive, etc. [95]. Although the manifestations of early temperamental characteristics can be modulated by contextual variables (such as parenting style), temperament variables are typically seen as the bedrock of the personality and the style in which one will engage socially with the world. Is resilience then the start-state and what might be called "socio-emotional reserve" the endpoint of the trajectory of resilience? The ability to maintain effective functioning in adulthood has been demonstrated to reflect social-emotional competencies such as curiosity about the world, interest in other people, and the ability to participate in and sustain social networks [96]. The role of these capacities in the preservation of behavioral function as disease burden accumulates is beginning to be explored [97].

Methodological issues

This discussion does not cover the many methodological issues raised by the study of behavior in the developmental frame. The issue of measurement of behavior merits comment, however. The most widely used outcome measures are the various forms of IQ test. In the neuroscience context, strong genetic control of both different neural substrates and the heritability of psychometric IQ is claimed [98], with an argument for generalized, rather than modularized, g [35]. Psychometric IQ tests, however, are typically taken to index knowledge. Anderson and Nelson [99] have argued that knowledge is acquired via two processing routes (central processes of thought and dedicated processing modules [25]) that have different acquisition trajectories and that must therefore be examined closely in models of behavioral development. The distinction has implications for the nature of psychometric IQ as an outcome measure in developmental studies and for the selection of control and comparison groups when working with neurodevelopmental disorders that derail developmental trajectories in different ways and at different times.

In measuring behavioral competencies, the psychometric IQ measures are not sufficient; an understanding of the full range of component processes that underlie actual behavioral output is required. This requires careful analysis of the nature of tasks to be used. The lesson from both comparative and developmental psychology is that the animal has to be "met" in its own ecological setting and at the level at which it is currently functioning: specific tasks have to be within the repertoire of the organism and motivationally salient for the animal at a given developmental stage. (Applying this principle can reveal, for example, advanced memory capacities – previously thought to be unique to humans – in species as "far" from humans as scrub jays [100].) In pursuit of the principle, developmentally referenced neuropsychological models that specify brain–behavior relationships of underlying processes can be very useful in constructing measures that target a particular behavioral domain and are user-friendly for the desired age/stage.

What lessons can one take from these examples? One is the importance of considering adaptive success as a time point in the analysis. A second is the added value of a comparative strategy in explicating developmental trajectories – of individuals with disorders that have different anatomical outcomes, of individuals who experience similar perturbing events that are sustained at different times. These lessons have the potential for clarifying the nature of targeted interventions. The focus on differentiating levels is also important for intervention planning.

Implications

What are the implications of the foregoing discussion for clinical and research practice, and more specifically, how can these considerations contribute to clinical work and research occurring within a developmental framework? First and foremost is the importance of modeling itself. The clinician-scientist's job is to map the theory of THIS child – developed on the basis of the information obtained from evaluation – to the theory of THE child – the product of the clinician's training and experience. Continuing education over time in the field will update the latter. The former takes place, however, in the 'micro' timeframe of the clinical evaluation. As data are collected, the theory of THIS child is constructed on a dynamic, moment-to-moment basis via models that generate hypotheses to be tested; the working model is refined and shaped on an ongoing basis. Thus, clinicians and clinical researchers must not only keep abreast of new knowledge in the relevant neurosciences, but must also consider carefully how new knowledge and new paradigms inform the way in which questions about behavioral function are asked and interpretations are made – and refine the way in which they view (model)

the organism as needed. Different models have different implications for the design and methodology of the clinical assessment as a whole.

In light of the above, multiple principles must be operative to guide a clinical assessment model and inform the clinician's behavior. Some principles guide all assessments that are clinical; others are particular to the neuropsychological assessment of behavior.

Clinical assumptions

The primary goal of any assessment is to make a difference to the child and family who come to you seeking guidance and direction. A diagnosis or an explanation is not sufficient. The clinician must formulate a plan to promote the client's welfare

- The model that guides the assessment will guide both the evaluation component and the management component – and will specify the relation between them. The evaluation generates a portrait of the child and a diagnostic formulation that guides the management plan. The latter can include a specific goal such as the identification of a targeted remedial approach, or suggest a broader intervention program, or focus on strategies to promote the child's ongoing developmental progress – or all of these.

- The outcome of the assessment must be ecologically valid, that is, providing a management plan and recommendations that respond to the risks that the child can be expected to face, are relevant to the individual child's and family's experience, that are realistic and respect the capacities, resources and feelings of the child and the members of his/her 'treatment team' (family, educators, other professionals).

Clinical neuropsychological assumptions

- The "unit of analysis" is a child (the owner of the brain in question) and his/her experience in the world, not a behavioral domain and not a test performance.

- The clinical analysis of the developing child that is neuropsychological must have the *brain-context-development* matrix at its core. The observed behavior that the brain supports cannot be understood with reference to its experience; the brain–context interaction must be explored over the course of development.

35

- The brain-context-development matrix shapes the diagnostic stance, influencing the data collection strategy, the types of data collected, the range of tools and techniques employed. To meet the brain requirement, the evaluation must sample (at least) the full range of behavior that brain supports, that is, be comprehensive of "thinking", "feeling", social and regulatory capacities; it must account for both typical and disrupted behavior. It must integrate qualitative and quantitative observations. The body of data to be collected is large; the selection and implementation of data reduction heuristics is not a trivial issue. To meet the context requirement: it must collect and integrate into the diagnostic formulation data on relationships and experience – past and current – in evaluation, family, peer, community, and social settings; it must relate in a systemic fashion the behavior collected in the structured evaluation setting to the behavior of the child in the real world of his/her everyday experiences. This will, in the clinical setting, necessarily include models of the potential disorders that could be operating (the members of the differential diagnosis) or a model of the specific disorder where this is known. To meet the development requirement, both the theory of THE child and the theory of THIS child will be developmentally framed. The behavioral profile generated at the time of evaluation is an outcome of the developmental course to date; the clinician cannot simply provide a description of the child that fits some nosological scheme and accesses resources now, but must act to promote optimal future outcomes and longer-term adaptive success.

Perhaps more than anything else, the centrality of context to developmental modeling makes these models clinically relevant. Clinical work always deals with the individual whose behavior is uniquely shaped by the particularities of his or her day-to-day experiences. Attempting to specify a given individual's interaction with all of the contextual variables in his or her life is thus integral to the clinician's practice. A better understanding of how contextual variables shape, perturb, or derail developmental processes, their trajectories and outcomes is important for clinical analyses of behavior; more nuanced analyses inform intervention strategies that are more closely specified and produce improved outcomes for children and their families.

Intervening

The implications of the rapidly expanding neuroscience knowledge base for intervening are exciting. The contributions to be made to the developmental neurosciences by neuropsychologists at both the group/conceptual – research – level and the individual/intervention – clinical – level are significant. In the clinical arena, change is central to intervention; developmentally, changed outcomes are the goal. The plastic change that is the foundation of all learning is dependent not only on the inherent physiological properties of the nervous system but also on experience, functional significance and meaning. These entail behavior-in-the-world and, as such, are the particular purview of neuropsychological clinicians. Modifying, mitigating, and maximizing behavioral outcomes at a variety of levels will be a crucial element in intervention planning to optimize development – normally proceeding or subsequent to insult – on the one hand and to minimize non-optimal fashioning of the brain by experience subsequent to injury or developmental perturbation.

There are two major contributions from the developmental perspective with respect to intervention. One, the centrality of context to developmental thinking entails that the application of knowledge gained from the group-level analysis of the research investigation to the individual-level analysis of the clinical interaction must be tailored to specific circumstances and capabilities. One size is unlikely to fit all. This is the job of the clinician. An understanding of contextual variables in characterizing the experience of the individual child is a *sine qua non* for the creation and implementation of an effective intervention plan (see the explanatory role of family variables on outcomes in TBI: TBI section this volume). The second is one that is only just beginning to be thought through in a systemic fashion. Both the timing and nature of an intervention need to be individualized. Interventions cannot simply be targeted towards individual behavioral skills; they must be applied in the context of an understanding of the developmental status of an individual. Karmiloff-Smith et al.'s [101] work provides the rationale for questions of the following type: What do you intervene on? When? Should the manifest symptom be the target of intervention? Or underlying processes? In either case, how?

Intervention strategies explicitly building on the neuroscientific evidence base pertaining to the nature of CNS plasticity are in their infancy but show considerable promise. The work of Posner and Rothbart and their colleagues [85] exemplifies important thinking in this regard. They have demonstrated that systematic instruction and practice in attentional behaviors facilitates attentional performance in children – and is most effective for those children whose attentional skills are weakest at the outset. An important element in their research is the role of developmental theory in their intervention strategy. The tripartite network of focus–awareness–control identified in their research program leads to specification of behavioral tasks as targets of intervention. This allows intervention outcomes to be evaluated in terms of both behavioral improvement and changed neural processing. Findings related to acquisition and stabilization of different behavioral components of the attentional network allow the intervention to be targeted in time also. Applying the tenets of developmental sensitive periods leads to interventions that match the expected developmental acquisition trajectory.

Conclusions

Construction of models to guide thinking is an ongoing process. As more and more knowledge is gained, our model of the world and of the nature of knowledge (the "zeitgeist") shifts, opening the way for new and different questions about how the natural world "works" and how its denizens play out their lives. New modes of thought in science generally lead to new ways of asking questions and to answers not previously conceived. In neuropsychology, these new modes of thought lead to advances in our appreciation of the organism, how it works, the nature of its capacities, which in turn leads to shifts in the models that shape our knowledge of psychological functions and then of the relationship of such functional capacities to brain. For the clinician, this knowledge then shapes the assessment strategy; the contribution of different types of data is reconsidered, new psychological techniques are developed, new tests are constructed, and interpretation of the observations is framed within the new understanding of the organism and its capacities. With a better model of the neurobehavioral capacities of the individuals we work with and their ecological significance, our management planning becomes increasingly tailored to the needs of individuals, our interventions more effectively targeted, and the outcomes more positive. It all starts to sound impossibly complex and overwhelming but, in fact, it is wondrously exciting and the reason why so many neuropsychological clinicians love their work!

References

1. Kirp DL. *The Sandbox Investment. The Preschool Movement and Kids-First Politics.* Cambridge, MA: Harvard University Press; 2007.

2. Richerson PJ, Boyd R. *Not by Genes Alone. How Culture Transformed Human Evolution.* Chicago, IL: University of Chicago Press; 2004.

3. Kenrick DT. Evolutionary psychology, cognitive science and dynamical systems. Building an integrative paradigm. *Curr Dir Psychol Sci.* 2001;**10**:13–17.

4. Preuss TM, Caceres M, Oldham MC, Geschwind DH. Human brain evolution: insights from microarrays. *Nat Rev* 2004;**5**(11):850–60.

5. Dayan P, Abbott IF. *Theoretical Neuroscience: Computational and Mathematical Modeling of Neural Systems.* Cambridge, MA: MIT Press; 2005.

6. Karmiloff-Smith A. *Beyond Modularity. A Developmental Perspective on Cognitive Science.* Cambridge, MA: MIT Press; 1992.

7. Mayr E. *Animal Species and Evolution.* Cambridge, MA: Harvard University Press; 1963.

8. Dumont L. The modern conception of the individual: notes on its genesis and that of concomitant institutions. *Contrib Indian Sociol* 1965;**8**:13–61.

9. Wertsch JV, Sammarco JG. Social precursors to individual cognitive functioning: the problem of units of analysis. In Wertsch JV, ed. *Vygotsky and the Social Formation of Mind.* Cambridge, MA: Harvard University Press; 1985.

10. Institute of Medicine (U.S.). Committee on Quality of Health Care in America. *Crossing the Quality Chasm: A New Health System for the 21st Century.* Washington DC: National Academy Press; 2001.

11. Tversky A, Kahneman D. Judgment under uncertainty: heuristics and biases. *Science* 1974;**185**(4157):1124–31.

12. Ahn W, Kim NS. Causal theories of mental disorder concepts. *Psychol Sci Agenda* 2008;**22**(6).

13. Bernstein JH. Developmental neuropsychological assessment. In Yeates KO, Ris DM, Taylor HG, eds. *Pediatric Neuropsychology; Research, Theory, and Practice.* New York: Guilford Press; 2000: 405–38.

14. Ash J, Gallup GG. Paleoclimatic variation and brain expansion during human evolution. *Human Nat* 2007;**18**(2):109–24.

15. Calvin WH. *A Brain for All Seasons: Human Evolution and Abrupt Climate Change.* Chicago, IL: University of Chicago Press; 2002.

16. Gunnar MR. Quality of early care and the buffering of neuroendocrine stress reactions: potential effects on the developing human brain. *Prev Med* 1998;**27**:208–11.

17. Fries AB, Ziegler TE, Kurian JR, Jacoris S, Pollak SD. Early experience in humans is associated with changes in neuropeptides critical for regulating social behavior. *Proc Nat Acad Sci USA* 2005;**102**(47):17237–40.

18. Nelson CA, ed. *The Effects of Early Adversity on Neurobehavioral Development*. Mahwah, NJ: Lawrence Erlbaum Associates; 2000.

19. Hart B, Risley T. *Meaningful Differences in the Everyday Experiences of Young American Children*. Baltimore, MD: Brookes; 2005.

20. Taylor HG, Yeates KO, Wade SL, Drotar D, Stancin T, Burant C. Bidirectional child-family influences on outcomes of traumatic brain injury in children. *J Int Neuropsychol Soc* 2001;**7**(6):755–67.

21. Richardson K. *Models of Cognitive Development*. Hove, UK: Psychology Press; 1998.

22. Karmiloff-Smith A, Scerif G, Ansari D. Double dissociations in developmental disorders? Theoretically misconceived, empirically dubious. *Cortex*. 2003 Feb;**39**(1):161–3.

23. Llinas RR. *I of the Vortex. From Neurons to Self*. Cambridge, MA: MIT Press; 2001.

24. Gibbs RW. *Embodiment and Cognitive Science*. New York: Cambridge University Press; 2006.

25. Fodor J. *The Modularity of Mind*. Cambridge, MA: MIT Press; 1983.

26. Tooby J, Cosmides L. The psychological foundations of culture. In Barkow JB, Cosmides L, Tooby J, eds. *The Adapted Mind: Evolutionary Psychology and the Generation of Culture*. New York: Oxford University Press; 1992: 19–36.

27. Buller DJ, Hardcastle VG. Evolutionary psychology, meet developmental neurobiology: against promiscuous modularity. *Brain Mind* 2000;**1**:307–25.

28. O'Leary DD. Development of connectional diversity and specificity in the mammalian brain by the pruning of collateral projections. *Curr Op Neurobiol* 1992;**2**(1):70–7.

29. Bishop DVM. Cognitive neuropsychology and developmental disorders: uncomfortable bedfellows. *Q J Exp Psychol* 1997;**50a**(4):899–923.

30. Johnson MH, Grossmann T, Cohen Kadosh K. Mapping functional brain development: building a social brain through interactive specialization. *Dev Psychol* 2009;**45**(1):151–9.

31. Elman JL, Bates EA, Johnson MH, Karmiloff-Smith A, Parisi D, Plunkett K. *Rethinking innateness. A Connectionist Perspective on Development*. Cambridge, MA: MIT Press; 1996.

32. Anderson M. The concept and development of general intellectual ability. In Reed J, Warner-Rogers J, eds. *Child Neuropsychology, Concepts, Theory and Practice*. Malden, MA: Wiley–Blackwell; 2008.

33. Laughlin SB, Sejnowski TJ. Communication in neuronal networks. *Science* 2003;**301**(5641):1870–4.

34. Petronis A, Gottesman II, Crow TJ, DeLisi LE, Klar AJ, Macciardi F, et al. Psychiatric epigenetics: a new focus for the new century. *Mol Psychiatry* 2000;**5**(4):342–6.

35. Plomin R, Spinath FM. Genetics and general cognitive ability (g). *Trends Cogn Sci* 2002;**6**(4):169–76.

36. Kovas Y, Plomin R. Generalist genes: implications for the cognitive sciences. *Trends Cogn Sci* 2006;**10**(5):198–203.

37. Caspi A, Sugden K, Moffitt TE, Taylor A, Craig IW, Harrington H, et al. Influence of life stress on depression: moderation by a polymorphism in the 5-HTT gene. *Science* 2003;**301**(5631):386–9.

38. Pascual-Leone A, Amedi A, Fregni F, Merabet LB. The plastic human brain cortex. *Annu Rev Neurosci* 2005;**28**:377–401.

39. Buonomano DV, Merzenich MM. Cortical plasticity: from synapses to maps. *Annu Rev Neurosci* 1998;**21**:149–86.

40. Merabet LB, Rizzo JF, Amedi A, Somers DC, Pascual-Leone A. What blindness can tell us about seeing again: merging neuroplasticity and neuroprostheses. *Nat Rev Neurosci* 2005;**6**(1):71–7.

41. Ramachandran VS. Plasticity and functional recovery in neurology. *Clin Med* 2005;**5**(4):368–73.

42. Flor H. Phantom limb pain: characteristics, causes and treatment. *Lancet* 2002;**1**:182–9.

43. Kopp B, Kunkel A, Muhlnickel W, Villringer K, Taub E, Flor H. Plasticity in the motor system related to therapy-induced improvement of movement after stroke. *Neuroreport* 1999;**10**(4):807–10.

44. Gaser C, Schlaug G. Gray matter differences between musicians and nonmusicians. *Ann N Y Acad Sci* 2003;**999**:514–7.

45. Atherton M, Zhuang J, Bart WM, Hu XP, He S. A functional MRI study of high-level cognition. I. The game of chess. *Cogn Brain Res* 2003;**16**:26–31.

46. Baumeister J, Reinecke K, Liesen H, Weiss M. Cortical activity of skilled performance in a complex sports related motor task. *Eur J Appl Physiol* 2008;**104**(4):625–31.

47. Burton H. Visual cortex activity in early and late blind people. *J Neurosci* 2003;**23**(10):4005–11.

48. Stiles J. The fundamentals of brain development. *Integrating Nature and Nurture*. Cambridge, MA: Harvard University Press; 2008.

49. Silverstein FS, Jensen FE. Neonatal seizures. *Ann Neurol* 2007;**62**(2):112–20.

50. Newport EL. Contrasting concepts of the critical period for language. In Carey S, Gelman R, eds. *The Epigenesis of Mind: Essays on Biology and Cognition*. Hillsdale, NJ: Lawrence Erlbaum Associates; 1991: 111–31.

51. Filley CM. *The Behavioral Neurology of White Matter*. New York: Oxford University Press; 2001.

52. Yakovlev PI, Lecours AR. *The Myelogenetic Cycles of Regional Maturation of the Brain*. Oxford: Blackwell; 1967.

53. Paus T, Zijdenbos A, Worsley K, Collins DL, Blumenthal J, Giedd JN, et al. Structural maturation of neural pathways in children and adolescents: in vivo study. *Science* 1999;**283**(5409):1908–11.

54. Sowell ER, Peterson BS, Thompson PM, Welcome SE, Henkenius AL, Toga AW. Mapping cortical change across the human life span. *Nat Neurosci* 2003;**6**(3):309–15.

55. Hasan KM, Kamali A, Iftikhar A, Kramer LA, Papanicolaou AC, Fletcher JM, et al. Diffusion tensor tractography quantification of the human corpus callosum fiber pathways across the lifespan. *Brain Res* 2009;**1249**:91–100.

56. Bernstein JH, Waber DP. Executive capacities from a developmental perspective. In Meltzer L, *Understanding Executive Function: Implications and Opportunities for the Classroom*. New York: Guilford Publications; 2007.

57. Jerison HJ. Evolution of prefrontal cortex. In Krasnegor NA, Lyon GR, Goldman-Rakic P, eds. *Development of the Prefrontal Cortex*. Baltimore, MD: Brookes; 1997: 9–26.

58. Pennington BF. Dimensions of executive functions in normal and abnormal development. In Krasnegor NA, Lyon GR, Goldman-Rakic P, eds. *Development of the Prefrontal Cortex*. Baltimore, MD: Brookes; 1997: 265–81.

59. Roth G, Dicke U. Evolution of the brain and intelligence. *Trends Cogn Sci* 2005;**9**(5):250–7.

60. Mesulam M-M. *Principles of Behavioral and Cognitive Neurology*. New York: Oxford University Press; 2000.

61. Blakemore S-J, Choudhury S. Brain development during puberty: state of the science. *Dev Sci* 2006;**9**(1):11–14.

62. Dennis M, Landry SH, Barnes M, Fletcher JM. A model of neurocognitive function in spina bifida over the life span. *J Int Neuropsychol Soc* 2006;**12**(2):285–96.

63. Bates E, Reilly J, Wulfeck B, Dronkers N, Opie M, Fenson J, et al. Differential effects of unilateral lesions on language production in children and adults. *Brain Lang* 2001;**79**:223–65.

64. Luciana M. Cognitive development in children born preterm: implications for theories of brain plasticity following early injury. *Dev Psychopathol* 2003;**15**(4):1017–47.

65. Als H. *Program Guide – Newborn Individualized Developmental Care and Assessment Program (NIDCAP): An Education and Training Program for Health Care Professionals*. Boston: NIDCAP Federation International 2008.

66. Grigorenko EL, O'Keefe PA. What do children do when they cannot go to school? In Sternberg RJ, Grigorenko EL, eds. *Culture and Competence: Contexts of Life Success*. Washington DC: American Psychological Association; 2004: 23–53.

67. Petersson KM, Reis A, Ingvar M. Cognitive processing in literate and illiterate subjects: a review of some recent behavioral and functional neuroimaging data. *Scand J Psychol* 2001;**42**(3):251–67.

68. Lecours AR, Mehler J, Parente MA, Caldeira A, Cary L, Castro MJ, et al. Illiteracy and brain damage–1. Aphasia testing in culturally contrasted populations (control subjects). *Neuropsychologia* 1987;**25**(1B):231–45.

69. Manly JJ, Jacobs DM, Sano M, Bell K, Merchant CA, Small SA, et al. Effect of literacy on neuropsychological test performance in nondemented, education-matched elders. *J Int Neuropsychol Soc* 1999;**5**(3):191–202.

70. Paulesu E, McCrory E, Fazio F, Menoncello L, Brunswick N, Cappa SF, et al. A cultural effect on brain function. *Nat Neurosci* 2000;**3**(1):91–6.

71. Diamond A. Development of the ability to use recall to guide action, as indicated by infants' performance on AB. *Child Dev* 1985;**56**(4):868–83.

72. Diamond A. The development and neural bases of memory functions as indexed by the AB and delayed response tasks in human infants and infant monkeys. *Ann N Y Acad Sci* 1990;**608**:267–309; discussion 309–17.

73. Diamond A. Evidence for the importance of dopamine for prefrontal cortex functions early in life. *Phil Trans R Soc Lond* 1996;**351**(1346):1483–93; discussion 94.

74. Diamond A, Prevor MB, Callender G, Druin DP. Prefrontal cortex cognitive deficits in children treated early and continuously for PKU. *Monogr Soc Res Child Dev* 1997;**62**(4):i–v, 1–208.

75. Diamond A. Consequences of variations in genes that affect dopamine in prefrontal cortex. *Cerebral Cortex* 2007;17 Suppl **1**:i161–70.

76. Diamond A, Briand L, Fossella J, Gehlbach L. Genetic and neurochemical modulation of prefrontal cognitive functions in children. *Am J Psychiatry* 2004;**161**(1):125–32.

77. Bellugi U, Lichtenberger L, Jones W, Lai Z, St George M. The neurocognitive profile of Williams Syndrome: a complex pattern of strengths and weaknesses. *J Cogn Neurosci* 2000;**12** Suppl 1:7–29.

78. Paterson SJ, Brown JH, Gsodl MK, Johnson MH, Karmiloff-Smith A. Cognitive modularity and genetic disorders. *Science* 1999;**286**(5448):2355–8.

79. Paterson SJ, Girelli L, Butterworth B, Karmiloff-Smith A. Are numerical impairments syndrome specific? Evidence from Williams syndrome and Down's syndrome. *J Child Psychol Psychiatry* 2006;**47**(2):190–204.

80. Yeates KO, Bigler ED, Dennis M, Gerhardt CA, Rubin KH, Stancin T, et al. Social outcomes in childhood brain disorder: a heuristic integration of social neuroscience and developmental psychology. *Psychol Bull* 2007;**133**(3):535–56.

81. Deacon TW. The symbolic species. *The Co-evolution of Language and the Brain*. New York: Norton; 1997.

82. Saffran JR. Words in a sea of sounds: the output of infant statistical learning. *Cognition* 2001;**81**(2):149–69.

83. Neville HJ, Mills DL, Lawson DS. Fractionating language: different neural subsystems with different sensitive periods. *Cerebral Cortex* 1992;**2**(3):244–58.

84. Locke JL. A theory of neurolinguistic development. *Brain Language* 1997;**58**(2):265–326.

85. Posner MI, Rothbart MK. *Educating the Human Brain*. Washington DC: American Psychological Association; 2007.

86. Tomasello M, Carpenter M. Shared intentionality. *Dev Sci* 2007;**10**(1):121–5.

87. Zelazo PD, Müller U, Frye D, Marcovitch S, Argitis G, Boseovski J, et al. The development of executive function in early childhood. *Monogr Soc Res Child Dev* 2003;**68**:vii–137.

88. Gibson. *The Ecological Approach to Visual Perception*. New York: Houghton Mifflin; 1979.

89. Rey-Casserly C, Bernstein JH. Making the transition to adulthood for individuals with learning disorders. In Wolf LE, Schreiber HE, Wasserstein J, eds. *Adult Learning Disorders: Contemporary Issues*. New York: Psychology Press; 2008: 363–88.

90. Holmes-Bernstein JM, Waber DP. Developmental neuropsychological assessment. The systemic approach. In Boulton AA, Baker GB, Hiscock M, eds. *Neuromethods, vol. 17: Neuropsychology*. Clifton, NJ: Humana Press; 1990: 311–71.

91. Wakefield JC. Evolutionary versus prototype analyses of the concept of disorder. *J Abnorm Psychol* 1999;**108**:374–99.

92. Satz P. Brain reserve capacity on symptom onset after brain injury: a formulation and review of evidence for threshold theory. *Neuropsychology* 1993;**7**:273–95.

93. Stern Y. What is cognitive reserve? Theory and research application of the reserve concept. *J Int Neuropsychol Soc* 2002;**8**(3):448–60.

94. Dennis M, Yeates KO, Taylor HG, Fletcher JM. Brain reserve capacity, cognitive reserve capacity, and age-based functional plasticity after congenital and acquired brain injury in children. In Stern Y, ed. *Cognitive Reserve. Theory and Applications*. New York: Taylor and Francis; 2007: 53–83.

95. Masten AS. Resilience in developing systems: progress and promise as the fourth wave rises. *Dev Psychopathol* 2007;**19**:921–30.

96. Everson-Rose SA, Lewis TL. Psychosocial factors and cardiovascular diseases. *Annu Rev Public Health* 2005;**26**:469–500.

97. Zunzunegui M, Alvarado BE, Del Ser T, Otero A. Social networks, social integration, and social engagement determine cognitive decline in community-dwelling Spanish older adults. *J Gerontol B Psychol Sci Soc Sci* 2003;**58**:S93–S100.

98. Toga AW, Thompson PM. Genetics of brain structure and intelligence. *Annu Rev Neurosci* 2005;**28**:1–23.

99. Anderson M, Nelson J. Individual differences and cognitive models of the mind: using the differentiation hypothesis to distinguish general and specific cognitive processes. In Duncan J, McLeod P, Phillips L, eds. *Measuring the Mind: Speed, Control and Age*. New York: Oxford University Press; 2005: 89–113.

100. Dally JM, Emery NJ, Clayton NS. Food-caching western scrub-jays keep track of who was watching when. *Science* 2006;**312**(5780):1662–5.

101. Karmiloff-Smith A, Thomas M, Annaz D, Humphreys K, Ewing S, Brace N, et al. Exploring the Williams syndrome face-processing debate: the importance of building developmental trajectories. *J Child Psychol Psychiatry* 2004;**45**(7):1258–74.

Models of developmental neuropsychology: adult and geriatric

Tyler J. Story and Deborah K. Attix

Neuropsychologists often assess cognitive function to distinguish normal aging from pathological conditions. For elders, interpretation hinges on accurate conceptualization of cognitive performances associated with normal neurological aging versus deficits indicative of central nervous system injury or illness, such as those found in neurodegenerative dementias. Early research indicated that aging in the absence of disease is not associated with standard focal deficits that are typical of an *injured* central nervous system [1, 2]. Rather, age-related declines were characterized as a more diffuse, gradual loss of efficiency and flexibility. Cross-sectional observations provided an important foundation for estimating abilities across various age groups, and these normative studies have traditionally informed models of normal aging.

More recently, neuropsychologists and neuroscientists have expanded our understanding of the longitudinal course of neurological function in older adults by including intraindividual observations of anatomical and functional changes over time. And yet, the relationship between aging and cognitive function is actually quite complex and difficult to characterize for several reasons. For instance, there are considerable methodological challenges to conducting well-controlled longitudinal studies that span beyond 5–7 years, such that aging models typically rely on relative snapshots of neurodevelopment when considered within the context of a 70–80-year lifespan. Also, influences on how humans age continue to evolve in a manner that probably parallels societal and technological progress. It appears that environmental, nutritional, and technological factors that can influence aging are changing with increasing speed. The relative impact of these factors may also be mediated by regional differences, further complicating the concept of normal aging across socioeconomic, racial, and cultural groups. Some of these factors may explain why the variability of neuropsychological function in adults increases with age, and how descriptive studies and resulting models can over-simplify patterns of age-related versus pathological decline in performance. Therefore, a clear neurodevelopmental model explaining how the brain ages in the absence of significant disease or injury remains somewhat elusive.

In the following chapter, we review recent research and theory describing models of aging within adult and geriatric neuropsychology. The chapter is organized into two primary sections. The first section provides a review of concepts related to adult neuropsychology and *normal* aging, with a particular focus on the challenges to establishing a universal neurodevelopmental model. The second section of this chapter presents recent research that characterizes neuroanatomical and functional changes associated with aging. Finally, we close with a discussion of future directions for understanding the neuropsychology of normal aging, with a particular emphasis on the dynamic nature of this field as medical advances and technology interact with the aging process.

Normal neurobiological aging: conceptual issues

Defining normal, healthy, and optimal aging

The aging process involves the accrual of molecular damage through oxidative stress, DNA mutations, and the interactions between free radicals, glucose, and related metabolites [3]. Over time, interactions between genetic predisposition and environment produce physiological stress with accumulating cellular remnants that are akin to an inflammatory process [4]. Thus, by definition, aging is a biological process that involves progressive cellular damage and dysfunction. Beyond broad generalizations, the terms "normal" and "healthy" aging become difficult to clearly define in this context since degradation of function represents a normal course for biological systems over time.

One might consider defining normal or healthy as the absence of disease, or the absence of disability and dysfunction in daily living [5]. These definitions, however, may over-simplify the relationships between aging, health, and disease when applied to specific individuals and conditions. For example, forms of sensory loss, such as blindness and deafness, often represent a disability, although these conditions do not universally equate to illness or poor health (for further discussion, see chapters by Noll and Harder, and Kammerer et al., this volume). In older patients, some degree of sensory loss may be consistent with *normal* aging. Additionally, if aging is a natural process of maturation that increases susceptibility to illnesses and loss of function, then the terms *healthy* and *normal* may describe different constructs at different ages. Poor vascular health, poor vision, and osteoporosis may be considered *normal* age-related changes in patients who are 80 years and older because of population base rates. In contrast, the presence of these conditions in younger groups may not be age-appropriate, and thus more clearly indicative of illness.

As an illustration, some conditions affecting neurocognitive function, such as mild small-vessel ischemic disease, are more common in older adult groups than the absence of such conditions. De Leeuw and colleagues [6] randomly sampled 1077 adult patients from the general population and found that 92% of their sample of volunteers ranging in age from 60 to 90 years showed some presence of subcortical white matter lesions. Only 13% of the youngest group (60–70 years) were completely free of subcortical lesions, while 0% of the oldest group (80–90 years) could be classified as lesion-free. If 100% of a randomly selected sample of older adults over the age of 80 showed some degree of subcortical ischemic change, one is left to wonder whether this is truly a disease process, or simply a reflection of how the human brain ages in the eighth and ninth decades of life. More importantly, if we continue to identify such conditions as "diseases", then it appears that normal aging and disease cannot be considered mutually exclusive in older age groups.

Evolving healthcare practices, medical interventions, and technology also complicate our ability to study and define healthy neurobiological aging. Many individuals now survive illnesses (e.g. various cancers) and acute medical events (e.g. cerebrovascular accidents) that would have been fatal several decades ago. How treatments for diseases interact with *normal* or pathological aging is largely unknown. The trajectory for neurobiological aging after such illnesses and treatments is also unknown; it is uncertain whether the aging process is advanced in certain biological systems by these treatments and conditions. Many patients who are now in their 80s and 90s may have at one time undergone treatment for a life-threatening medical condition, such as cancer, but now remain cognitively intact. These individuals could still fall within a *normal* trajectory of neuropsychological function in old age. Should individuals with a history of any serious medical illnesses be excluded from epidemiological studies of aging? This is a question still unanswered.

Given the prevalence of some conditions in older adults, we consider "healthy aging" to be somewhat of a misnomer within the context of the maturing central nervous system. Thus, we will discuss neurodevelopment in older adults using three descriptions: (1) abnormal aging, which reflects early onset of a disease and/or premature shortening of the lifespan; (2) normal aging, which describes age-appropriate disease onset with corresponding functional declines; (3) optimal aging, in which individuals demonstrate uncommon physical and cognitive resilience to age-associated diseases and decline that are typical of the ninth decade of life and beyond. These variants of aging probably fall on a continuum, with most adults fitting somewhere between categories based on current functioning and history (see Fig. 2b.1). In addition, the application of models of this nature should vary across patient groups, as cultural, regional, genetic, and technological factors influence base rates of various conditions and produce somewhat unique *normal* aging profiles. Finally, as addressed above, this model characterizes a process that is likely to keep evolving along with societal and scientific progress. Therefore, within the next several years, the patient examples presented in Figure 2b.1 may no longer be consistent with optimal, normal, and abnormal aging due to advances that continue to expand the human lifespan.

Attributes of normal and optimal aging

Several large, longitudinal studies have identified physical and mental variables that predict resistance to age-associated decline. For example, the MacArthur Foundation studies [7] identified several factors that were associated with physical and cognitive longevity over a period of 7 years. Researchers followed 1189 people between ages 70 and 79. Physical functioning was determined by measures of balance, gait, and

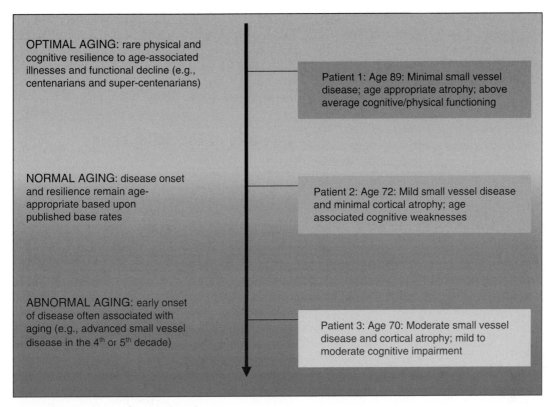

Figure 2b.1. Continuum of neurobiological aging.

upper body strength; memory, language, abstraction, and praxis comprised the primary cognitive variables that were considered. Factors most associated with minimal physical decline were optimal lung functioning, regular physical activity, and participation in social activities, including both work and volunteer activities. Patients with chronic medical conditions also showed benefits from these lifestyle factors. High-functioning groups tended to report higher incomes and higher education, and they showed higher levels of sulfated dehydroepiandrosterone (DHEA-S) and peak exhalation of carbon dioxide, which are positive indicators of immune and respiratory function. Participants with higher functioning over the course of the study also showed fewer psychiatric symptoms than individuals who declined over time [8].

The Victoria Longitudinal Study represents another longitudinal, community-based study that used fewer exclusion criteria for participants than most studies of its nature [9]. Hultsch and colleagues obtained cognitive data on three occasions over 6 years for 250 community-dwelling adults ranging in age from 55 to 86 years. Patients were tested on recall of general world facts, immediate word recall, immediate story recall,

vocabulary recognition, verbal fluency for synonyms, antonyms, and figures of speech, reading comprehension and speed, semantic speed (lexical decision-making), working memory, and personality. Overall, participants showed decreasing participation in more intellectually engaging activities (e.g. novel information processing) as they aged. While greater reported participation in intellectually engaging activities was associated with cognitive resilience over the course of the study, self-reported health, personality variables, and physical activity were not strong predictors of cognitive decline. Unfortunately, there was no way to differentiate cause and effect in this study; intellectually engaging activities may serve to slow cognitive decline, or individuals with greater baseline cognitive reserve and less susceptibility to early decline may seek out intellectually engaging activities. Indeed, the associative rather than causal nature of these relationships should be considered in all studies of aging.

In addition to the pro-health factors described above, the MacArthur Foundation Studies also highlighted potential risk factors for age-associated decline. Interleukin-6 is a cytokine with pro-inflammatory and anti-inflammatory roles, with links to several progressive neurological disorders; this particular cytokine was associated with cognitive decline over time [10]. At baseline, plasma interleukin levels were only modestly related to cognitive functioning. At 2.5- and 7-year follow-up assessments, individuals falling within the top third of the sample in interleukin-6 plasma concentration showed the greatest risk of decline in total cognitive performance. Total cognitive performance was composed of measures assessing verbal memory, spatial recognition, abstraction, spatial ability, and naming. Although it is unclear why the authors chose to dichotomize outcome (decline versus no decline) and categorize interleukin concentration into tertiles, this study provided evidence of a link between CNS inflammatory responses and cognitive decline with aging. In the same sample, low vitamin B was associated with the greatest cognitive decline over 7 years after controlling for elevated plasma homocysteine concentration [11].

Whereas the studies above identify variables that differentiate normal from abnormal cognitive aging, research with centenarians may provide some insight into *optimal* aging. Centenarians represent a very specific subset of the population, who have demonstrated remarkable resistance to disease, physical disability, and cognitive decline. Interestingly, while individuals in this group tend to show less history of disease, they do demonstrate increases in inflammatory responses with age, similar to those observed in diseases such as Alzheimer's disease, cancer, and diabetes [4]. The risk, however, of constructing a neurodevelopmental model for *normal* aging based on this group is that it probably represents a unique subset of the population in terms of genetic make-up, environmental exposure, and life experience. As of 2004 in the USA, actuarial formulas using life expectancy data predicted that roughly 6 in 1000 men and 21 in 1000 women will reach the age of 100 [12]. Considering these statistics, centenarians may provide interesting data regarding disease resistance, but they are hardly representative of a *normal* aging process.

Finally, our understanding of abnormal, normal, and optimal aging is limited by the variables that we select. Variables are often chosen from prior studies that used different designs (cross-sectional versus longitudinal comparisons), cohorts, and outcome measurements than subsequent investigations. Societal and scientific advances may not only influence how we *age*, but also how we *study* aging. For example, advances in neuroimaging over the last several decades have provided us with an array of variables that could not be considered in early aging research. As we will see in the following section, these technologies provide helpful pictures of aging, but these pictures are not always consistent because the tools and techniques often vary between studies.

Integrity of the aging brain

Structural changes

Advances in neuroimaging have allowed us to visualize the brain at various stages of aging. Clearly identifying structural changes that are typical of *normal* versus abnormal aging remains difficult. As we review in the following section, there is consistent evidence that the human brain physically declines with age, although the regions and characteristics of this decline vary somewhat by study methodology and sample.

Several studies have shown an inverse relationship between age and brain volume. For example, Coffey and colleagues [13] found lower frontal and temporal lobe volumes in older versus younger volunteers, as well as age-related ventricular enlargement. Based on their cross-sectional comparison, they extrapolated estimates of percent decline by year by region, with frontal lobes showing 0.55% per year, hippocampus and amygdala declining 0.30% per year, and the temporal lobes losing 0.28% per year. An individual's odds of cortical atrophy and ventricular enlargement increased 8.9% per year and 7.7% year respectively. Jack and colleagues [14] found a similar association between age and decreased volume in the hippocampus and anterior temporal lobe.

Consistent with other areas of research (e.g. anoxic brain injury), the hippocampus appears to be particularly vulnerable to age-related degradation. While the key pathways between the entorhinal cortex, hippocampus, and association cortices are most susceptible to neuronal death in Alzheimer's disease, these areas also exhibit age-associated structural decline in the absence of disease. For example, it appears that most individuals have a small number of neurofibrillary tangles in the entorhinal cortex by age 55 [15]. In addition, healthy patients also exhibit greater age-associated degradation in some regions of the hippocampus. Whereas patients with Alzheimer's disease show the greatest structural changes in CA1 of the hippocampus, normal aging is associated with changes in the subiculum [16], suggesting that Alzheimer's disease does not simply reflect a process of rapid neurological aging.

As just described, neuroimaging studies have revealed age-associated volume loss in temporal and frontal regions of interest; however, there has been some indication that volume loss due to aging may differ by sex. For example, using a sample of healthy controls ranging in age from 18 to 80 years, Cowell and colleagues [17] found general volume loss in frontal and temporal lobes. More specifically, men showed greater volume loss than women despite controlling for neurological/medical, psychiatric, and cognitive conditions that might confound results. Similarly, Raz and colleagues [18] compared volumes of 13 regions of interest in 200 adults ranging in age from 20 to 80 years. They found significant age-related volume differences, with lateral prefrontal cortex volume showing the greatest negative association with age. Men differed from women by showing larger volumes in all regions of interest after controlling for height, and increased rates of decline in the hippocampus and fusiform gyrus [18]. Post-mortem cerebral volume comparisons by Witelson et al., [19] showed sex-specific relationships between regional volume loss and intellectual abilities, with men showing a greater relationship between cerebral volume loss and declining visual-spatial abilities. In another investigation, Shan and colleagues [20] found greater left hemisphere volume loss in elderly men (mean age = 70) than in elderly women (mean age = 69), particularly in the left frontal lobe.

Thus, region-of-interest studies highlight the frontal and temporal lobes in the aging process, and suggest that men may be vulnerable to greater loss than women. Evidence, however, for age-related white versus gray matter pathology is inconsistent. White matter hyperintensities (WMH) are common in healthy older adults, with a distribution pattern that is similar to disease processes such as angiopathies and Alzheimer's disease [21]. In Holland and colleagues' [21] study, WMH were most prevalent in the deep periventricular white matter for healthy controls, patients with amyloid angiopathy, and patients with Alzheimer's disease. The density of lesions was greater in the patient populations. A recent study using diffusion tensor imaging showed a reduction in association fibers based on age [22]. Similarly, as we previously described, De Leeuw and colleagues [6] found WMH in 92% of their total sample of healthy adults, and in 100% of those participants aged 80 to 90 years.

Using volumetric analyses, Guttmann and colleagues [23] compared magnetic resonance images of healthy participants ranging in age from 18 to 81 years. They found that older adults showed a greater percent of CSF and lower percent of white matter than younger adults, even after covarying white matter hyperintensities. Relative percent of gray matter volume, however, remained comparable at approximately 48% between the oldest and youngest age groups. Interestingly, the middle-aged group (50–59 years) showed less relative (percentage) gray matter volume than the youngest and oldest groups, which may suggest some variance associated with cohort effects.

Consistent with other region-of-interest studies, Jernigan and colleagues [24] showed specific age-associated changes in hippocampal volume, as well as disproportionate declines in frontal lobe volume and supporting white matter in older volunteers. Gray matter loss typically preceded white matter volume loss, though white matter volume decline was more severe than gray matter change in the oldest participants. The authors estimated average losses of 35% in the hippocampus, 14% in the cerebral cortex, and 26% in white matter between the ages of 30 and 90. While older participants were living independently and free of cognitive impairment or serious medical conditions, they were not excluded if they suffered from "common medical conditions of the elderly, such as hypertension and cardiac conditions", if their conditions were medically stable [24].

While these studies suggest progressive, age-associated declines in both gray and white matter regions, they all share a common methodological weakness – cross-sectional design. Many also utilized self-reported health screenings, in which participants were excluded for known, reported serious medical conditions. Therefore, many participants may have suffered from the early stages of undiagnosed medical conditions that could have been identified with physical exams and blood tests prior to enrollment. Determining the degree to which volumetric differences are due to aging versus commonly discussed cohort effects (e.g. nutrition, exposure to pollutants, educational history, life stressors) and sampling strategies is nearly impossible in such studies. Each generation is exposed to new variations in pollutants, education, technology, medical intervention, cultural shifts, and various other external factors that continue to evolve with unknown positive and negative implications for long-term health. As an illustration, the current cohort comprising many *older age* groups lived through two of the greatest stressors of the twentieth century, the Great Depression and World War II. Several studies link small hippocampal volumes with depression and traumatic stress [25], and it is impossible to know to what degree these structural differences are due to aging in this particular cohort.

Multi-year neuroimaging studies are rare, due primarily to costs and the challenges of following the same individual over long periods. Despite the practical limitations of longitudinal neuroimaging studies, the Baltimore Longitudinal Study of Aging (BLSA) collected repeated neuroimaging on a sample of older adults over a 4-year period. Participants were aged 59 to 85 years and were free of epilepsy, stroke, bipolar disorder, dementia, severe cardiovascular disease, severe pulmonary disease, and metastatic cancer. In addition, no patients developed dementia by year-5 follow-up. A small subsample of participants ($N = 24$) was labeled "very healthy" due to the absence of any medical condition or cognitive impairment throughout the 4-year study [26].

BLSA participants showed significant loss of both gray and white matter across age groups, including in the "very healthy" subsample. Although tissue loss was significant for all four major cerebral lobes, frontal and parietal regions were most susceptible to tissue loss regardless of age and sex [26]. The average yearly brain volume loss for the entire sample amounted to 5.3 cm^3, although the very healthy group's yearly decline was also notable, at roughly 3 cm^3/year. There were no significant differences in rate of change for gray versus white matter. Mild lateralized patterns were also observed, with greater right than left inferior frontal and anterior temporal gray matter volume changes. White matter loss was also greater on the left than the right in temporal lobe. Finally, the rate of increasing central brain atrophy, as indicated by ventricular volume, was greater in older than in young adults [26].

The studies described above represent a small sample of the rapidly expanding neuroimaging literature. Although there is variation by study in the degree of white versus gray matter volume loss, and to some extent variation in region as well, there is convincing evidence that tissue loss in the brain occurs with normal aging. We have some concern, however, that the concept of a *shrinking brain* is overrepresented in neuroimaging studies addressing normal aging, with far less attention directed to the potential for dendritic growth and neurogenesis, and how these positive

potentials change over time. In the absence of neurological disease, new learning continues to occur across the lifespan. This process of continued expansion of associative networks presumably has a direct physiological correlate.

Neurogenesis and its clinical implications in the adult brain remain controversial and require some extrapolation from primate research and in vitro studies. Primate models have shown patterns of neurogenesis in prefrontal, inferior temporal, and posterior parietal cortex in adult macaques [27]. In this particular study, new neurons originated in the subventricular region and migrated via white matter tracts to the neocortex. Research has suggested that the adult human hippocampus is capable of neurogenesis when examined in vitro (e.g. [28]). In addition, Jin and colleagues [29] have found evidence of the early stages of neurogenesis in the dentate gyrus of patients with Alzheimer's disease. This study, however, showed only immature marker proteins for neurogenesis, with no indication of actual neuronal growth. This burgeoning area of research has exciting implications for both disease-modifying interventions and our understanding of neural plasticity in the aging brain. Interventions that modify disease progress or actually initiate successful neurogenesis in adults would represent a technological/medical intervention that would revolutionize models of aging and the structural integrity of the brain.

Functional changes

General functioning

Our understanding of age-associated functional changes differs depending on the cognitive domain, and, to some extent, the associated developmental theory and imaging literature being considered. To a large extent, normative samples form the basis for estimations of cognitive decline in neuropsychology. These norms provide us with descriptive data that we often use as an atheoretical neurodevelopmental model; i.e. we decide whether or not an individual fits within a normative range of strengths and weaknesses, with the understanding that this range varies by age, and sometimes by education, sex, and race. These norms, however, were often not developed with a priori hypotheses regarding the trajectory of cognitive functions over time. Instead, they represent samplings of groups without serious medical and psychiatric illnesses that show a somewhat steady decline in specific abilities when compared across age groups.

For example, Digit Symbol-Coding raw scores at the 50th percentile on the Wechsler Adult Intelligence Scale-III [30] decline from a peak of 83 points to 37 points between ages 16 and 85. Thus, a raw Digit Symbol-Coding score of 37 is consistent with impairment at age 25, but within expectation at 85 years. In contrast, average performance on the Vocabulary subtest remains relatively stable across age groups. When examining an older individual, neuropsychologists typically consider a certain degree of decline in coding speed (relative to estimated ability at a younger age) to be unremarkable or consistent with aging. Therefore, we are essentially using cross-sectional norms to estimate which cognitive changes are associated with *normal* aging and which might be associated with impairment. These cross-sectional data form one perspective in converging lines of research that contribute to an evolving neurodevelopmental model of aging. Figure 2b.2 illustrates the relative changes in average-level performance across age groups for the Vocabulary, Digit Symbol-Coding, and Block Design subtests. To graph performance changes on the same scale for all three subtests, we used the scaled score equivalents for a young reference group (age 20–24 years) generated by the average subtest raw score (50th percentile) for each age group. For example, an average Digit Symbol-Coding raw score for a 65-year-old is 54, which equals a scaled score of 6 for the 20–24-year-old reference group (see Fig. 2b.2).

A large, early body of work in the area of general cognitive decline has focused on two descriptive categories for cognitive function: crystallized intelligence and fluid intelligence [31]. Crystallized intelligence is broadly defined as education-dependent skill, consisting of vocabulary, verbal reasoning, and general knowledge base. In contrast, fluid intelligence represents the ability to solve novel problems, apply skills in a novel context, and more generally process new information. On the WAIS-III [30], the verbal subtests are thought to capture crystallized intelligence, while the nonverbal subtests capture fluid intelligence.

As adults age, crystallized intelligence is thought to remain stable or gradually increase [32]. Fluid intelligence has been considered more sensitive to aging and composed of functions that enable one to learn from, adapt to, and respond to one's environment (e.g. information processing and cognitive flexibility). Figure 2b.2 illustrates the stability of vocabulary relative to specific nonverbal subtests when compared *across* age groups. Studies testing age-associated changes in crystallized and fluid intelligence have yielded a variety of findings both between studies and within study samples across time [33].

Initially, age-related changes were expected to be lateralized because crystallized skills were associated with verbal functioning (left-hemisphere for most right-hand dominant individuals), while fluid abilities were associated with nonverbal processes (more right-hemisphere-dependent in most individuals). While many tests associated with fluid intelligence and

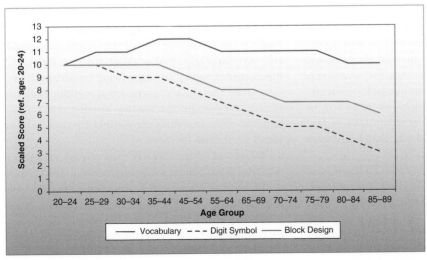

Figure 2b.2. WAIS-III average performance for each age group when plotted as scaled scores for 20–24-age reference group: Vocabulary, Digit Symbol-Coding, Block Design.

speed of information processing are sensitive to right-hemisphere damage, several studies addressed this lateralized model by presenting information to visual half fields [34] and controlling for speed and familiarity [35]. Each failed to show a hemispheric difference in normal aging. Therefore, previous evidence (WAIS-III normative samples) of potentially lateralized effects of aging may instead reflect changes in processing speed, which tend to emerge more on tests assessing fluid abilities.

Using structural equation modeling, McArdle and colleagues [33] examined these broad categories as they changed in a sample of 1193 individuals over an average of 2.7 years, finding that crystallized and fluid abilities both followed nonlinear growth curves. These nonlinear growth curves resembled those of other specific functional domains, such as memory, processing speed, and auditory and visual information processing. While each curve illustrated a different acceleration rate relative to age, they all predicted a similar pattern of decline. The different rates of decline were largely consistent with previous distinctions between crystallized and fluid ability over time, but also suggested that the use of broad factors oversimplifies the trajectories of age-associated functional decline. For example, processing speed exhibited a different rate of decline than fluid reasoning skills, although traditional definitions of fluid abilities would typically lump these skills together.

McArdle et al.'s [33] study produced interesting and complex models of age-associated cognitive decline that clearly contribute to adult neurodevelopmental theory. Unfortunately, the study employed a short retest interval and relied on mathematical predictions of change, both of which limit ecological validity. The authors also acknowledge an assumption in this study, one that is found in most norming and longitudinal studies, that the cognitive constructs being considered remain invariant in factor structure and expression (how they might be observed or assessed) across the lifespan. Whether that is true remains an open question, and one that is complex and rarely addressed longitudinally.

Sensory loss is another poorly controlled confound in many of these studies that can affect measurement and validity. Changes in sensory functioning in older adults may alter how memory, verbal processing, and visual processing are expressed, and these changes may limit the validity of current instruments for older populations. While declines in sensory functioning

may parallel changes in cognitive processes due to a common underlying cause (e.g. aging, injury, or neurodegeneration), thorough vision and hearing exams are not often included to rule out this confound in neuropsychological assessments. Lindenberger and Baltes [36] proposed that vision and hearing loss accounted for more age-associated cognitive variance than processing speed. In their study of participants ranging in age from 70 to 103, sensory acuity (visual and auditory) accounted for over 90% of age-associated variance and nearly 50% of total variance in cognitive performance. The process of assessing sensory functioning and using these variables to explain age-associated variance in cognitive performance carries its own potential reliability and validity concerns, and we caution against generalizing findings of this nature to individual cognitive profiles. Nevertheless, such studies highlight the significance of sensory changes in understanding the neuropsychology of aging.

Specific cognitive functions

Cross-sectional studies have repeatedly shown declines in executive functions, processing speed, verbal memory, and even vocabulary, excluding an initial increase in verbal skills between the third and sixth decades [37]. Salthouse [38] proposed that processing speed represented the fundamental function that accounted for age-related differences in other cognitive functions, including memory and problem-solving. More recently, Park and colleagues [39] studied a cross-sectional sample of community-dwelling adults. The resulting latent variable model of cognitive functioning supported processing speed as a general factor influencing working memory, verbal recall, and visual recall. In addition, the model implicated the unique role of visual and verbal working memory systems in memory functioning and age-associated decline in performance. This study suggested that working memory systems are domain-specific (e.g. visual versus verbal), and that these functions are distinct from verbal and visual short-term memory.

Based on this research, age-related functional declines could follow domain-specific paths, similar to the varying rates of change presented by McArdle and colleagues [33]. This argues against a diffuse, *dedifferentiated* (i.e. single process and trajectory) decline in cognitive ability. Nevertheless, processing speed remained the strongest construct in the latent model, and cross-sectional performance declines (between age groups) followed the same trajectory for all domains. Therefore, processing speed was again highlighted as a functional marker for aging [39].

There have been some recent longitudinal data to support a model of general functional decline, with a higher rate of loss of processing speed. Growth-curve analyses were conducted on changes in cognitive performance for individuals aged 44 to 88 years in the Swedish Adoption/Twin Study of Aging [32]. Participants were followed for 6 years and assessed on three occasions. While memory and other cognitive domains maintained a relatively linear decline over time, skills associated with information processing and response speed showed accelerated rates of decline after age 65.

In another cross-sectional comparison, Schretlen and colleagues [40] found that differences between older and younger adults in processing speed, executive ability, and frontal lobe volume each made independent contributions to the total explained variance for cognitive performance. In other words, differences in processing speed alone did not account for the general pattern of poorer fluid/executive functioning in older than younger adults. Their sample, however, included participants with "minor … and moderate health problems", which included hypertension, diabetes, major depression, emphysema, congestive heart failure, prior myocardial infarction, and substance abuse. While they argue that this is more representative of *normal* aging than *optimal* aging, a majority of their sample (roughly 60%) suffered from Type II diabetes, hypertension, or depression in remission, all conditions that can influence cognition to some degree.

Alternatively, Hasher and colleagues [41] have argued that age-related changes in cognitive functioning result from changes in the ability to effectively filter or inhibit processing of extraneous information. This susceptibility to distracting data results in slower performance and less processing of target information under timed conditions. Hasher and colleagues, however, propose that this increased distractibility also leads to a larger quantity of processed information. While in many instances the extraneous information that is not filtered remains irrelevant, in some contexts this additional information may prove useful or relevant [42]. A series of studies [42] demonstrated that older adults responded more accurately than younger adults to questions about nontarget (i.e. presumed irrelevant) information, providing some support for this alternative theory of information processing in older adults.

Finally, the confounds that we have discussed that plague cross-sectional aging research are particularly critical to neuropsychological research attempting to characterize individual changes in function over time. Some of the most commonly considered confounds to cross-sectional studies of function include quality of education, cultural factors, and the Flynn effect. Although not likely to be independent of educational and cultural factors, how the Flynn effect uniquely impacts age-group differences is not well understood. More generally, cohort effects may especially influence performance on formal assessments because cultural and educational factors can impact how an individual *expresses* ability, even if the underlying function is only marginally affected by these factors. The relative cohort differences in average ability may vary by region and culture, and this pattern may vary by specific abilities. For example, with the relatively recent explosion of the computer/video gaming industry, younger generations may develop and hone visual-spatial abilities to a far greater extent than any previous cohort. Additionally, as we have previously mentioned, humans are surviving illnesses that were fatal to previous generations, and the long-term impact of these illnesses and medical interventions on cognitive function as we age is unclear. These examples again highlight the variability of cognitive functioning across age groups and specific populations, as well as the likelihood that the functional expression of *normal aging* will continue to evolve with societal and technological progress.

Age and variability

Older adults represent a physically and functionally diverse group [43]. While variability between individuals is often the focus of research and clinical work, *intraindividual* variability has emerged as an important construct in aging research as well – i.e. performance changes from trial to trial, and testing session to testing session over short intervals of time [44]. Hultsch and MacDonald [44] have hypothesized that such intraindividual variability tends to be largest during developmental periods of the greatest relative growth or decline, such as during childhood/adolescence and older age. In general, older adults tend to show greater intraindividual variability than younger adults [45, 46], suggesting that intraindividual variability may represent a marker for neuropsychological decline associated with age. While Hultsch and colleagues [47] have suggested that an individual's degree of performance variability remains stable over short periods (four testing sessions over 5 weeks), there is currently little longitudinal evidence confirming that intraindividual variability actually changes over time in the same individuals and in a manner that parallels a disease or aging process.

Assuming, however, that intraindividual variability does increase as a result of aging, then the simplest and most general interpretation relates to the integrity of the central nervous system. As age-associated CNS changes occur (e.g. white matter lesions, gray matter atrophy), an individual becomes potentially more susceptible to various endogenous (e.g. hormone changes, medication side-effects) and exogenous (e.g. environmental distractions, stress) factors that transiently impact function. This pattern would suggest that memory performance is particularly susceptible to encoding and organizational weaknesses as we age, which has been substantiated to some degree. For example, older adults show greater intraindividual variability across learning trials on memory testing than younger adults [45], and the degree of variability independently predicts performance on episodic and working memory tasks [48].

Providing a functional explanation of intraindividual variability in older adults has been challenging, as decreased processing speed does not fully explain this phenomenon [49]. Hultsch and colleagues' [47] study uniquely demonstrated that variability between testing sessions was not restricted to reaction time and processing speed, as older adults exhibited variability on memory function as well. Similarly, Li et al. [50] showed substantial variability on basic concentration, spatial memory, and verbal memory tasks in older adults. In addition, increased intraindividual variability in older adults is not necessarily observed on all cognitive tasks, and it may reflect abnormal aging (illness) in some individuals. For example, intraindividual variability is higher among patients with neurological conditions than it is for healthy older adults. Specifically, healthy older adults differ from patients with dementia in reaction time variability across testing sessions [51]. Similarly, patients with Alzheimer's disease show greater intraindividual variability in memory and reaction time than patients with Parkinson's disease, while healthy controls show less variability than either clinical group [52].

Differentiating the effects of intraindividual variability versus legitimate longitudinal change on neuropsychological performance will require sophisticated approaches that consider the roles of alternate forms, practice effects, sensory loss, and measurement error. Salthouse et al. [37] attempted to circumvent some of these challenges by administering alternate forms at each of three testing sessions, while a companion group received the forms in counterbalanced order. Participants were tested on three occasions over short intervals (within 2–10 weeks). Intraindividual variability was nearly one-half the magnitude of interindividual variability, suggesting that a single assessment may have limited validity for evaluating an older adult's level of functioning.

In general, this remains a relatively nascent area of neuropsychological science and additional, larger studies are needed. As previously mentioned, intraindividual variability research has involved short intervals (i.e. several assessments within 4–5 weeks), with no longitudinal follow-up that tracks this phenomenon over time for the same individuals. We currently do not understand whether or not variability actually increases with age, or whether observed differences have simply reflected cohort effects. In addition to test interval concerns, most studies in this area have included small sample sizes that need replication in larger samples to increase external validity and application to large developmental models.

Despite these limitations, intraindividual variability appears to be relevant to both age-associated changes in cognitive performance and pathological aging [37]. More importantly, current neuropsychological science indicates that this construct remains a potential confound in the assessment of cognitive function in older adults. This body of literature strongly suggests that cognitive functions in older adults are unlikely to be fixed, even across short intervals. Therefore, neuropsychologists must consider the ramifications of interpreting a *moving target* when differentiating profiles associated with normal versus abnormal aging.

Summary and future directions

Our understanding of the neuroscience of aging continues to evolve, but the progress to date has been truly inspiring. Early observational and cross-sectional studies built a critical foundation by distinguishing neurological aging from brain injury and neurodegenerative disease. While recognizing these accomplishments, this chapter outlined many of the persisting challenges to establishing a clear neurodevelopmental model of *normal aging*, particularly if the intention is to apply such a model to individual patients from various age groups and backgrounds. On a general level, there is convincing evidence that aging involves a gradual decline in the structure and function of the brain. White and gray matter densities decline with age, and there are parallel functional declines, with the most consistent and rapid changes occurring in cognitive efficiency. The degree to which these losses are independent of disease is difficult to quantify, as age-specific base rates would suggest that some *diseases* reflect a normal aging process (e.g. small-vessel ischemia).

As a field, we continue to work towards greater consistency across studies in terms of variables of interest, experimental controls, and patient samples. Only recently have researchers attended to the potential value of assessing intraindividual variability when differentiating normal from abnormal aging. Evidence now suggests that this is an important factor to the accuracy of clinical assessments in older adults, and potentially our ability to identify susceptibility to cognitive decline.

Perhaps the single greatest challenge to these endeavors is determining whether or not neurodevelopment is a fixed process that can be accurately captured across age groups, cultures, and societies. As we have discussed throughout this chapter, societal and medical advances directly impact our physical and mental lives in ways that probably change how we age. These technologies and social norms rapidly evolve, and their shifting interaction with aging is not well understood.

How we choose to study the construct of aging is critical for neuropsychologists and neuroscientists, and these choices will guide our understanding of this process. For example, we must reach some consensus regarding age-appropriate diseases and related recruitment and exclusion criteria for normal aging studies. We would benefit from studies that help establish clearer standards for "healthy" research subjects at specific ages that are rooted in epidemiological research with published base rates for various physical diseases. In addition, further movement towards longitudinal designs that track samples through adult developmental transitions (e.g. from the fifth to seventh decades of life) would provide important data regarding intraindividual change. Finally, new statistical modeling and imaging techniques provide a level of unprecedented sophistication to neuropsychological studies of aging, building on the progress provided by longitudinal research design. Integrating these techniques in ways that complement versus replace longitudinal studies is critical to maximizing the implications of such research. Given these challenges and choices, we eagerly anticipate the thoughtful collaboration across disciplines that will yield the next generation of aging models.

References

1. Reitan R. Psychologic changes associated with aging and with cerebral damage. *Mayo Clin Proc* 1967;**42**:653–73.

2. Kaszniak AW, Newman MC. Toward a neuropsychology of cognitive aging. In Qualls SH, Abeles N, eds. *Psychology and the Aging Revolution: How we adapt to longer Life*. Washington DC: American Psychological Association; 2000: 43–67.

3. Rattan SIS. Increased molecular damage and heterogeneity as the basis of aging. *Biol Chem* 2008;**389**:267–72.

4. Franceschi C, Bonafe M. Centenarians as a model for healthy aging. *Biochem Soc Trans* 2003;**31**:457–61.

5. Matthews KA. A behavioral medicine perspective on aging and health. In Qualls SH, Abeles N, eds. *Psychology and the Aging Revolution: How we adapt to longer life*. Washington DC: American Psychological Association; 2000: 197–205.

6. de Leeuw FE, de Groot JC, Achten E, et al. Prevalence of cerebral white matter lesions in elderly people: a population based magnetic resonance imaging study. The Rotterdam Scan Study. *J Neurol Neurosurg Psychiatry* 2001;**70**:9–14.

7. Rowe JW, Kahn RL. *Successful Aging*. New York: Pantheon; 1998.

8. Berkman LF, Seeman TE, Albert M, et al. High, usual and impaired functioning in community-dwelling older men and women: findings from the MacArthur Foundation Research network on successful aging. *J Clin Epidemiol* 1993;**10**:1129–40.

9. Hultsch DF, Hertzog C, Small BJ, et al. Use it or lose it: engaged lifestyle as a buffer of cognitive decline in aging? *Psychol Aging* 1999;**14**:245–63.

10. Weaver JD, Huang MH, Albert M, et al. Interleukin-6 and risk of cognitive decline: MacArthur studies of successful aging. *Neurology* 2002;**59**:371–8.

11. Kado DM, Karlamangla AS, Huang MH, et al. Homocysteine versus the vitamins folate, B6, and B12

as predictors of cognitive function and decline in older high-functioning adults: MacArthur studies of successful aging. *Am J Med* 2005;**118**:161–7.

12. Social Security Administration. Actuarial Publications: Period Life Table, 2004. http://www.ssa.gov/OACT/ STATS/table4c6.html (Accessed June 4, 2008).

13. Coffey C, Wilkinson W, Parashos I, et al. Quantitative cerebral anatomy of the aging human brain: a cross-sectional study using magnetic resonance imaging. *Neurology* 1992;**42**:527–36.

14. Jack C, Petersen R, O'Brien P, et al. MR-based hippocampal volumetry in the diagnosis of Alzheimer's disease. *Neurology* 1992;**42**:183–8.

15. Bouras C, Hof PR, Giannakopoulos P, et al. Regional distribution of neurofibrillary tangles and senile plaques in the cerebral cortex of elderly patients: a quantitative evaluation of a one-year autopsy population from a geriatric hospital. *Cereb Cortex* 1994;**4**:138–50.

16. Chételat G, Fouquet M, Kalpouzos G, et al. Three-dimensional surface mapping of hippocampal atrophy progression from MCI to AD and over normal aging as assessed using voxel-based morphometry. *Neuropsychologia* 2008;**46**:1721–31.

17. Cowell PE, Turetsky BI, Gur RC, et al. Sex differences in aging of the human frontal and temporal lobes. *J Neurosci* 1994;**14**:4748–55.

18. Raz N, Gunning-Dixon F, Head D, et al. Aging, sexual dimorphism, and hemispheric asymmetry of the cerebral cortex: replicability of regional differences in volume. *Neurobiol Aging* 2004;**25**:377–96.

19. Witelson SF, Beresh H, Kigar DL. Intelligence and brain size in 100 postmortem brains: sex, lateralization, and age factors. *Brain* 2006;**129**:386–98.

20. Shan ZY, Liu JZ, Sahgal V, et al. Selective atrophy of left hemisphere and frontal lobe of the brain in old men. *J Gerontol A Biol Sci Med Sci* 2005;**60**:165–74.

21. Holland CM, Smith EE, Csapo I, et al. Spatial distribution of white matter hyperintensities in Alzheimer's disease, cerebral amyloid angiopathy, and healthy aging. *Stroke* 2008;**39**:1127–33.

22. Stadlbauer A, Salomonowitz E, Strunk G, et al. Age-related degradation in the central nervous system: assessment with Diffusion-Tensor Imaging and Quantitative Fiber Tracking. *Radiology* 2008;**247**:179–88.

23. Guttmann CRG, Jolesz FA, Kikinis R, et al. White matter changes with normal aging. *Neurology* 1998;**50**:972–8.

24. Jernigan TL, Achibald SL, Fennema-Notestine C, et al. Effects of age on tissues and regions of the cerebrum and cerebellum. *Neurobiol Aging* 2001;**22**:581–94.

25. Hickie I, Naismith S, Ward PB, et al. Reduced hippocampal volumes and memory loss in patients with early- and late-onset depression. *Br J Psychiatry* 2005;**186**:197–202.

26. Resnick SM, Pham DL, Kraut MA et al. Longitudinal magnetic resonance imaging studies of older adults: A shrinking brain. *J Neurosci* 2003;**23**:3295–301.

27. Gould E, Reeves AJ, Graziano MSA, et al. Neurogenesis in the neocortex of adult primates. *Science* 1999;**286**:548–52.

28. Roy NS, Wang S, Jiang L, et al. *In vitro* neurogenesis by progenitor cells isolated from the adult human hippocampus. *Nat Med* 2000;**6**:271–7.

29. Jin K, Peel AL, Mao XO, et al. Increased hippocampal neurogenesis in Alzheimer's disease. *Proc Natl Acad Sci USA* 2004;**101**:343–7.

30. Wechsler D. *WAIS-III Administration and scoring manual.* San Antonio: The Psychological Corporation; 1997.

31. Horn JL, Cattell RB. Age differences in fluid and crystallized intelligence. *Acta Psychol (Amst)* 1963;**26**:107–29.

32. Finkel D, Reynolds CA, McArdle JJ, et al. Latent growth curve analyses of accelerating decline in cognitive abilities in late adulthood. *Dev Psychol* 2003;**39**:535–50.

33. McArdle JJ, Ferrer-Caja E, Hamagami F, et al. Comparative structural analyses of the growth and decline of multiple intellectual abilities over the life span. *Dev Psychol* 2002;**38**:115–42.

34. Cherry BJ, Hellige JB, McDowd JM. Age differences and similarities in patterns of cerebral asymmetry. *Psychol Aging* 1995;**10**:191–203.

35. Mittenberg W, Seidenberg M, O'Leary DS, et al. Changes in cerebral functioning associated with normal aging. *J Clin Exp Neuropsychol* 1989;**11**:918–32.

36. Lindenberger U, Baltes PB. Sensory functioning and intelligence in old age: a strong connection. *Psychol Aging* 1994;**9**:339–55.

37. Salthouse TA, Nesselroade JR, Berish DE. Short-term variability in cognitive performance and the calibration of longitudinal change. *J Gerontol B Psychol Sci Soc Sci* 2006;**61**:P144–51.

38. Salthouse TA. The processing-speed theory of adult age differences in cognition. *Psychol Rev* 1996;**103**:403–28.

39. Park DC, Lautenschlager G, Hadden T, et al. Models of visuospatial and verbal memory across the adult life span. *Psychol Aging* 2002;**17**:299–320.

40. Schretlen D, Pearlson GD, Anthony JC, et al. Elucidating the contributions of processing speed, executive ability, and frontal lobe volume to normal age-related

differences in fluid intelligence. *J Int Neuropsychol Soc* 2000;**6**:52–61.

41. Hasher L, Lustig C, Zacks RT. Inhibitory mechanisms and the control of attention. In Conway A, Jarrold C, Kane M, Miyake A, Towse J, eds. *Variation in Working Memory*. New York: Oxford University Press; 2007: 227–49.

42. Healy MK, Campbell KL, Hasher L. Cognitive aging and increased distractibility: costs and potential benefits. *Prog Brain Res* 2008;**169**:353–63.

43. Nelson EA, Dannefer D. Aged heterogeneity: fact or fiction? The fate of diversity in gerontological research. *Gerontologist* 1992;**32**:17–23.

44. Hultsch DF, MacDonald SWS. Intraindividual variability in performance as a theoretical window into cognitive aging. In Dixon RA, Backman L, Nilsson L-G, eds. *New Frontiers in Cognitive Aging*. Oxford: Oxford University Press; 2004: 65–88.

45. Miller SB, Odell KH. Age-related intraindividual performance variability with practice. *Int J Aging Hum Dev* 2007;**65**:97–120.

46. Robertson S, Myerson J, Hale S. Are there age differences in intraindividual variability in working memory performance? *J Gerontol B Psychol Sci Soc Sci* 2006;**61B**:P18–24.

47. Hultsch DF, MacDonald SWS, Hunter MA, et al. Intraindividual variability in cognitive performance in older adults: comparison of adults with mild dementia, adults with arthritis, and healthy adults. *Neuropsychology* 2000;**14**:588–98.

48. Hultsch DF, MacDonald SWS, Dixon RA. Variability in reaction time performance of younger and older adults. *J Gerontol B Psychol Sci Soc Sci* 2002;**57**:P101–15.

49. Allaire JC, Marsiske M. Intraindividual variability may not always indicate vulnerability in elders' cognitive performance. *Psychol Aging* 2005;**20**:390–401.

50. Li SC, Aggen SH, Nesselroade JR, et al. Short-term fluctuations in elderly people's sensorimotor functioning predict text and spatial memory performance: the MacArthur Successful Aging Studies. *Gerontology* 2001;**47**:100–16.

51. Strauss E, MacDonald SWS, Hunter M, et al. Intraindividual variability in three groups of older adults: cross-domain links to physical status and self-perceived affect and beliefs. *J Int Neuropsychol Soc* 2002;**8**:893–906.

52. Burton CL, Strauss E, Hultsch DF, et al. Intraindividual variability as a marker of neurological dysfunction: a comparison of Alzheimer's disease and Parkinson's disease. *J Clin Exp Neuropsychol* 2006;**28**:67–83.

Multicultural considerations in lifespan neuropsychological assessment

Thomas Farmer and Clemente Vega

Introduction

Neuropsychological assessment has the ability to detect a variety of brain-based pathologies and their impact on cognitive and behavioral functioning across the lifespan. Yet, despite this capability, it has become increasingly clear that neuropsychological assessments are not a pure measure of an individual's abilities, nor do they directly or specifically demonstrate brain–behavior interactions. Rather, research has indicated that many facets of an individual's cultural background impact the assessment procedure and its interpretation. In response, it has become increasingly important to understand the effects cultural and environmental factors have on the practice of neuropsychological assessment and diagnosis. Without an understanding of the unique contribution of culture and environment to a patient's performance on tests, neuropsychologists may risk misdiagnosis as well as fail to notice important opportunities to engage the patient and family in the eventual rehabilitative or treatment process.

The importance of understanding the role of culture in assessment and treatment of neurological issues has been very well highlighted in the last decade. As one example, Anne Fadiman, in her book *The Spirit Catches You and You Fall Down*, writes about a young girl born into a family of Hmong refugees from Laos living in Merced, California [1]. The author discusses the treatment of and eventual tragedy that results when this young Hmong girl, Lia, is diagnosed with epilepsy, by emphasizing the interweaving role that culture plays in the diagnostic and treatment process. Lia's story showcases how, despite the greatest efforts of physicians and her family to try to help her survive, varying cultural approaches to understanding the disease process and its impact and treatment contributed to a rift between the Hmong culture and modern Western biomedical culture, which led each to misunderstand one another's efforts. This rift eventually resulted in a series of choices being made by the family that left Lia experiencing a very poor outcome. When attempting to make sense of

the perceived medical failure, one doctor involved in the girl's care shared his interpretation of the situation, stating that "[t]he language barrier was the most obvious problem, but not the most important. The biggest problem was the cultural barrier. There is a tremendous difference between dealing with the Hmong and dealing with anyone else. An infinite difference" (p. 91) [1]. His statement highlights, for the reader, the immense role cultural practice and interpretation can have in the understanding of and acceptance of recommendations regarding development and disease. Essentially, what Lia's story demonstrates is that significant differences in language and ideology can contribute to a family's working from a very different perspective than that desired by the clinicians who are attempting to treat their patient.

As illustrated above, when a patient arrives for a neuropsychological assessment, language barriers can be a clear impediment from the moment of contact. Yet, too often, culture is not viewed by the clinician to be an important consideration until language differences present themselves. In response, the focus of this chapter will be to examine and clarify the cultural factors that affect neuropsychological assessment, whether explicitly or implicitly. These include, but are not limited to, ethnicity, race, gender, age, and poverty. As culturally competent neuropsychological assessments and interventions are crucial to best practice, this chapter attempts to look beyond just the cultural variables of language that are most frequently considered, and offers an examination of the multiple components of culture that exist as important factors in the neuropsychological assessment and interpretation process.

Theoretical considerations

Historically, multicultural considerations in neuropsychological assessment were often, as with many domains of psychology, largely dismissed or even ignored. This was mainly due to the belief that the field of neuropsychology was immune from cultural biases. Evidence of this fact has been well represented by the fundamentally Eurocentric approach taken in the field of assessment. Kamphaus has reminded us that the tradition of modern intelligence testing arose in Western countries, including France, Germany, Britain, and North America [2]. However, a predominantly Western viewpoint has not been monolithic; for example, culture and its impact on assessment findings became an important consideration for Luria during his travels in the Republic of Uzbekistan. It was during these travels that he began to hypothesize that culture is one of the principal determinants underlying cognitive processes. Over the past decades, many psychologists have come to share this belief. For example, modern standardization of tests (e.g. WISC-IV-Spanish) have begun to oversample ethnic minorities in order to capture specific ethnic group demographics [3].

Neuropsychological functioning is not distinct from cultural variables; yet the field of neuropsychology still struggles with understanding how to incorporate cultural considerations into practice and assessment. Ardila has suggested that, even now, some practitioners lack training and understanding of how to achieve an appropriate, culturally sensitive neuropsychological assessment [4]. He argues that considerable biases concerning assessment and its interpretations about brain–behavior relations can exist within the practitioner; similarly, biases exist with regard to the development and application of neuropsychological instruments that are available. Consequentially, Ardila has strongly supported approaches towards research and policy that address disparity in multicultural assessment. These views are shared by others in the field who believe that a goal of cross-cultural psychology should be the systematic study of the association between cultural contexts and the specific behaviors that develop out of that context [5, 6]. More specifically, multicultural research should address the generalizability of current theories regarding neuropsychological assessment and diagnosis, considering culturally specific behaviors, and integrating findings that contain an understanding of a universal approach to assessment applicable across a wide range of cultures. While the impact of such variables as ethnicity, race, gender, age, and acculturation will be directly addressed, given the limited scope of this chapter it is also recommended that the practitioner be aware that culture can encompass myriad variables such as sexuality, educational experience, and immigration status, as well.

Defining cultural variables

Culture

Over the past several years, the American Psychological Association (APA) has made multicultural education, training, research, and practice a high priority within the field of psychology [7]. However, in concert with this positive effort, there has remained some confusion and even controversy about the precise definitions of race, culture, and ethnicity, and how they are best emphasized in practice, training, and research. These three constructs are often used interchangeably, which contributes to the confusion. Still, several definitions exist for each specific construct, which can provide guidance.

Culture has been defined in a variety of ways, yet many psychologists agree that it can be difficult to effectively classify. Gardiner and Kosmitzki have defined culture as "the cluster of learned and shared beliefs, values (achievement, individualism, collectivism), practices (rituals and ceremonies), behaviors (roles, customs, traditions), symbols (institutions, language, ideas, objects, and artifacts), and attitudes (moral, political, religious), that are characteristic of a particular group of people and that are communicated from one generation to another" (p. 4) [8]. The APA has defined culture as "the embodiment of a worldview, through … learned and transmitted beliefs, values, and practices, including religious and spiritual traditions. It also encompasses a way of living informed by the historical, economic, ecological, and political forces on a group" [9]. As one can see by following these definitions, culture encompasses a great deal of one's existence, and it strongly influences the ways in which individuals and groups come to understand experience. Importantly, culture is passed along with language. This transmittal of both deliberate and unintentional information that accompanies both overt and unconscious behavior occurs not only through the semantic meanings of a specific language, but also through the underlying values and attitudes individuals share and show. Oftentimes, it is the influence these cultural variables have on behavior, emotion, and cognitive functioning that can be particularly difficult to understand without (some) knowledge of the language a patient uses. This impacts how experience and knowledge are able to be shared and understood during the assessment process.

Ethnicity

Ethnicity refers to the "acceptance of the group mores and practices of one's culture of origin and the concomitant sense of belonging" those beliefs and practices offer [9]. As such, ethnicity refers to how identity is commonly tied to a group, based on sets of behavioral characteristics and norms, common historical roots, and self-identified group characteristics and experiences. In the USA, the most commonly cited ethnic breakdown includes Whites, African Americans, Hispanics, Native Americans, and Asian Americans. However, it is important to recognize that ethnicity is different from culture. Whereas culture refers to the basic characteristics of behaviors and values that apply to a particular group, ethnicity refers more specifically to the group of people who share those cultural features. Given this definition, it is observed that many different ethnic groups may share a common culture. Moreover, one particular ethnic group may have several subcultures. Hence, while culture is a more abstract term that refers to multiple attributes and is often variable in its meaning, ethnicity is more frequently used to characterize specific groups of people, and as such is more readily identifiable, based on the group characteristics that have been assigned or accepted as definitional.

Race

Based on the definitions considered above, both culture and ethnicity imply that learned behaviors are passed down from generation to generation, leading to a means of categorizing a group of individuals based on shared characteristics and behavior. In contrast, race is often perceived as something that is not learned; instead, it has an implied biological basis. This understanding of race as being biologically determined has created significant debate among psychologists and other social scientists, as well as within medicine. Thus, while no general consensus exists to the exact definition of race, the APA has expressed the view that race is socially constructed, defined as the "category to which others assign … individuals on the basis of physical characteristics, such as skin color or hair type, and the generalizations and stereotypes made as a result" [9].

Culture, ethnicity, and race: influences on assessment

While many factors may account for weak performance on neuropsychological testing, such as brain impairment

or variable effort, culture is also an influential factor with regard to performance ability [5]. In fact, culture appears to be a potent variable, even when demographic factors such as age, years of formal education, gender, and income are controlled. In the past, these discrepancies have often been attributed to biological differences due to ethnicity [10]. However, current studies offer support to the idea that the differences based on ethnic classifications are not likely to be the result of underlying biological mechanisms, but rather a result of a dynamic relationship between neurobiological and sociocultural systems [11]. Kennepohl suggests that at a young age the brain has significant plasticity, probably enabling the environment (culture included) to have a profound impact on brain development. More than just a moderating effect, culture may have a direct impact on brain development. For example, debate exists about the relationship between culture and handedness, as well as culture and hemispheric specialization [12, 13]. Debate continues as to whether culture is a direct variable impacting brain development, with research continuing to investigate this issue.

Studies have identified several moderating factors that play a role in differences of racial group performance on assessment measures, which include the quality of education, literacy rates, understanding of the testing process, stereotype threat, and level of acculturation [4, 14–17]. When these factors are not clearly delineated, the possibility of significant differential treatment of minorities increases [18]. Research that blindly discusses racial differences in terms of only race, and not other important cultural variables, may actually create disparity and contribute to barriers. Gasquoine has argued that measured cognitive differences between groups of people have led to the belief in racially based intellectual superiority, without accounting for underlying factors contributing to the observed differences [19].

In addition, racism and discrimination have also been shown to have a detrimental impact on physical and psychological well-being, including performance on test measures [20]. Stress-based theories of poor health and mental health outcomes suggest that there is a higher level of risk in ethnic and racial minority populations [21]. Furthermore, while society has changed drastically over the past several decades with regard to overt racism, contemporary forms of racism continue to persist in more subtle, often unintentional or unconscious modes. For example, it has been observed that some White European Americans inadvertently present with negative body language when encountering individuals perceived to be from another race or culture [22]. Becoming aware of these influences on aspects of the social and professional interactions is extremely important for neuropsychologists, particularly when engaged in such practices as assessment and feedback of diagnostic information, given the natural position of privilege and power that is present in their professional and personal roles. Prevaricating around the possibility of unconscious biases may increase the risk of conveying power dynamics in cross-cultural interactions. As a result, the actual testing situation may be ruptured in a manner that decreases the ability to create and maintain alliances, and increase the stress level of the patient, thus impacting their ability to perform. Therefore, it is essential to understand how the stress of racism may impact the alliance-building process.

Furthermore, ethnic differences in neuropsychological assessment may be more characteristic of expectations about the process and its findings, rather than the patient's actual neuropsychological functioning itself [23]. Research has shown that when race or gender is cued, women and many racial minorities perform worse on tests [16]. Steele has termed this phenomenon "stereotyped threat". Essentially, when minority stereotypes are associated with a lower test performance, stereotype threat has been shown to trigger underperformance. These stereotypes persist in many testing situations for a variety of minority populations. Based on this model, Steele has proposed that ethnic minorities may be extremely sensitive to experiencing negative judgment about their capacities and capabilities, particularly on standardized measures such as those used during neuropsychological assessment (e.g. the Wechsler Scales), because of a history of oppression and past experiences of rejection. As a result, any subtle bias from the examiner may activate this response to stereotype threat. Steele accentuates the importance of practitioners being aware of subtle interactions during assessment, such as negative facial expressions and voice tone, which may convey to the examinee a critical and underlying biased stance. Steele further attests that practitioners must focus on proper exploration, reflection, and interpretation, as well as facilitating the expression of affect and attending to patients' experiences in order to fully understand their cultural background. Subsequently, the practitioner will be positively contributing to the alliance by alleviating the stress of the assessment procedure, thus decreasing the possibility of misinterpreting past or current behavior, overpathologizing, developing poor rapport, or over- or underestimating symptom presentation.

Assessment expectations and covert prejudices are not the only factors that can affect the testing process. A variety of other possible cultural influences exist that may present as well. For example, differences in the general approach to responding to questions may vary by culture. Horn and Cattell have suggested that older populations have fluid intelligence that declines with age, whereas crystallized aspects of intelligence tend to improve [24]. While age may be a significant variable with regard to being able to adequately respond to fluid problems, Gardiner and Kosmitzki have presented data suggesting that intellectual speed associated with fluid intelligence appears to be much more valued in Western societies as well [8]. The suggestion is that populations of individuals raised in Western societies will differ from those from non-Western societies. Collectivist cultures may be slower to respond to specific stimuli as they often consider others in the group before responding. Essentially, they may value reflective responses more so than rapid responses. The suggestion is that while overall age may impact fluid intelligence, culture may also impact the underlying response patterns on measures of fluid intelligence.

Acculturation

When considering culture as a moderating factor in assessment, practitioners must be capable of assessing the extent to which retained traditions and practices from a patient's native culture may potentially contribute to findings, as well as understand the level to which an individual's acquisition of mainstream values and norms will also impact performance (e.g. responses to verbal measures found on the Wechsler Scales). Level of acculturation, often measured by the length of time one has lived in the USA (or other country of relevance), is a particularly important variable to consider when completing neuropsychological assessments [25]. Acculturation varies significantly between newly arrived individuals and natural-born citizens; however, length of time in a country, in and of itself, does not define acculturation. Acculturation is clearly associated with language proficiency, and individuals from non-English-speaking countries who are less acculturated to US norms will often present with a substantial disadvantage on English-only measures. Yet language should not be the only consideration when discussing acculturation, since immigrants who are English-speaking may have substantially different experiences and views about health care, mental health, and treatment, which can impact performance.

While level of acculturation is related to the number of years an individual has resided in a country, there is not a perfect correlation between the two. In addition to residency length, unique patterns of migration can often account for variations in experience and understanding of concepts being addressed through a particular test. This can lead to differential (i.e. low) scores in assessment that are unrelated to actual brain dysfunction [26]. While length of time is certainly a factor, when and where the migration occurred may impact one group of individuals very differently from other members of the same ethnic group [5]. Furthermore, acculturation may be a transparent issue when working with immigrants; however, the need to assess acculturation is probably applicable in any non-majority population. For example, Landrine and Klonoff have developed the African American Acculturation Scale (AAAS) in order to measure this variable [27]. They reported that the level of acculturation seen even within a native group of individuals can have a significant impact on performance on a variety of neuropsychological tests. As a result, having a general idea of the degree to which a patient has adopted the mainstream culture is of significant importance for the practitioner, when taking into account variables that can influence test findings.

To add another level in the understanding of acculturation, one must move away from thinking of acculturation in a linear manner. The theory of acculturation assumes that people move along a spectrum from their traditional culture to adapting to the mainstream culture. This adaptation toward their new environment is seen as essential to promote optimal functioning. However, the term transnationalism may better encompass the dynamic process that occurs through immigration. Immigrants undergo cultural deliberations in a bidirectional flow between their country of origin and the country of immigration. While immigrants may assimilate many mainstream practices, this is combined with maintaining a transnational connection. As clinicians, we try to predict the level of acculturation by examining the length of residency. However, as stated previously, specific migration patterns may vary the acculturation level significantly. Furthermore, specific experiences associated with race, social class, gender, unique stories of strength, and unique stories of discrimination and oppression have a dynamic interaction with transnational identities of immigrants. This

dynamic process can simply not be marginalized and simplified by examining only the number of years since immigration.

Age

Age is an important factor taken into account with regard to the development, standardization, and use of most neuropsychological tests [28]. Research has begun to attend to the specific needs of older, culturally diverse adults. In 2030, approximately one in five US residents are projected to be 65 and older, with the numbers of this age group expecting to double from 2008 to 2050 [29]. As the population of older people is ever growing, several issues need to be addressed in order to conduct culturally competent assessments with adults. Neuropsychologists need to consider the etiology of communication difficulties resulting from brain trauma associated with age (e.g. stroke, Parkinson's disease) and how they may impact performance differently, or the effects of declining visual or auditory acuity on test performance when considering performance on measures [30]. Of additional importance is the need to understand the client's identity and how this impacts their understanding of aging, from his or her perspective. For instance, a clinician will conduct a thorough background interview to gain an understanding of how the client views him/herself in relation to such variables as age, physical status, or cognitive functioning; additional concerns to be considered are such variables as religious faith and practice, and ethnicity, and how aging is viewed by the client's ethnic group. On the other hand, we must consider that gathering such information can be difficult, as older clients might be hesitant to discuss such issues as faith or ethnicity, given their experience of the myriad political and social periods they have lived through during their lives.

Importantly, age should not be seen as an isolated moderating variable, but rather taken in conjunction with other factors such as socioeconomic status, race, acculturation level, and education. Given the broad range of educational experiences that persons who are older may have experienced, it is important to take education into specific consideration, as literacy has been shown to have a significant impact across verbal and nonverbal measures [31]. Of note, research by Manly and her colleagues has suggested that literacy is a protective factor in memory decline for older adults; hence, literacy is a factor that is of significant importance in adult assessment. In tandem with literacy, it is important to recognize that older adults, especially those from ethnically diverse populations, may have had significantly different educational exposure from the cultural norm in the USA. As a result, an older patient's reading and mathematical understanding level may have a more significant moderating impact than just knowing their years of education alone.

Gender

Gender is also an important issue taken into account with neuropsychological assessment, particularly during the neurobehavioral maturation periods. Boys and girls have been shown to have different rates of development, and as a result differing patterns of cognitive progression. Girls have been shown to often outperform boys on some neuropsychological instruments, particularly ones requiring language and aspects of early executive control [28]. Additionally, Levy and Heller have suggested that lateral asymmetry may be less noticeable in women [32]. Furthermore, differential patterns of aging have been noted; women still typically outlive men, and this has an impact on considerations regarding neurological disease process, and its impact on cognition and behavior. Neuropsychological and psychopathological disorders have also been shown to occur differentially with regard to gender. During early development, males are more likely to display and be referred for assessment for externalizing disorders such as attention deficit hyperactivity disorder [33]. During the adult years, while males are more commonly diagnosed with psychotic disorders in the early adult period, there are data to suggest an increased vulnerability and distinct disadvantage to later life diagnosis for women [28, 34].

The disparity in neurological development and diagnostic vulnerabilities between males and females must be further considered when examining individuals from immigrant populations. Because educational opportunities often vary among men and women who are members of immigrant groups, this variability in educational exposure and associated behavioral and cognitive fluency serves as a potential source of neurocognitive variance. For instance, women may not have been offered the educational opportunities of their male counterparts, and as a result show indications of decreased effectiveness and efficiency on neuropsychological measures.

Socioeconomic status

Socioeconomic status (SES) appears to be one of the most significant moderating factors when considering culture and test performance. Lezak et al. observed

that SES is the defining factor underlying racial differences [28]. For example, they suggest that the vast majority of between-group differences seen on neuropsychological tests when examining performances by Whites and African Americans disappear when controlling for SES. This is not a uniformly accepted interpretation, however, nor does it appear to fully reflect the range of research available [16, 27]. Notably, differences in performance believed to be accounted for by SES may be marginal when one considers a contextual viewpoint of culture and SES [35]. This view suggests that differences in performance are less likely to be based on factors associated with SES, but rather on the environmental context of the developing individual. Nevertheless, one of the clearest and most intuitive impacts that SES may have on neuropsychological development is the lack of adequate resources such as health care and nutritional meals for those living in poverty. Poor health care and nutrition have a significant impact on brain development, and neural maturation can be significantly disrupted. For example, research has shown that children from lower SES backgrounds who are exposed to lead experience a significantly greater negative impact on their cognitive functioning than do children from more affluent backgrounds. SES has been shown to have a moderating effect on neuropsychological functioning given the limited access to good-quality medical care for many adults as well [36]. In addition, differences in SES and consequent exposure to educational and enrichment opportunities play a significant role in development and vulnerability to neurocognitive difficulties. Hart and Risley reported on the relationship between the number and complexity of words used in the home and SES [37]. The lack of exposure to more complex language and its subsequent impact on vocabulary can have a greater impact on individuals living in poverty; in particular, such individuals may not be exposed to the range of language that is more typically used by affluent cultures. This may significantly impact the range of performances that are possible when an individual who is impoverished is presented with neuropsychological measures that have been developed for use with middle- to upper-class SES groups, and in turn contribute to misdiagnosis of cognitive dysfunction. Furthermore, variability in language development has been shown to have a greater effect on individuals of lower SES, leading to diminished performance on knowledge-based tasks such as the oral language scales on the Woodcock Johnson Psychoeducational Battery [38].

While language exposure may be a significant moderating factor for individuals of lower SES, exposure to other factors that serve as stressors may serve as an underlying variable for a variety of augmenting and diminishing experiences for such children in their environments. While all families experience stress in some form, poorer families tend to experience a great deal of stress, and this contributes to variability across a number of performance domains. Exposure to long-term stress has been shown to have a number of adverse effects on the brain. The significance and length of such stressful experiences can limit available cognitive resources required for more effective learning and problem-solving. Noble et al. have suggested that the stress poverty can induce can potentially be the reason for lower scores across a variety of domains including language, memory, and attention [39]. Individuals living at a low SES often do not have positive exposure to education, health care, and other environmentally stimulating activities that promote cognitive and behavioral success. They may also have an increased vulnerability to exposure to harmful environmental stimuli such as toxic agents or violence that hamper neuronal patterning and organization [40]. Children and families living in older housing continue to live under the threat of serious exposures to common toxic hazards, such as mercury and lead-based paint. Many of these older homes continue to persist in poor, urban areas.

It should not be automatically assumed that minorities and individuals presenting in the clinic who are living in poverty always experience significant stressors that negatively impact their psychological and neuropsychological functioning. More importantly, some research has pointed to culture as a protective factor. Palloni and Morenoff describe a Hispanic Paradox, in which there exists a unique resilience to negative health outcomes of poverty and other psychosocial challenges [41]. While this phenomenon is rare, practitioners need to be aware of not only the barriers such as race, poverty, and experiences of oppression of color, but also of the strengths and resilience that exist within these populations.

Ethical considerations for the culturally competent neuropsychologist

Nearly all diverse populations experience some degree of disenfranchisement based on the simple fact of *difference*. Neuropsychologists have an ethical duty to respect the dignity and worth of individuals in the context of their culture. These duties are becoming increasingly important given that over the past several decades the demographic make-up of the USA has shifted dramatically with regard to racial and ethnic diversity. Minority populations have grown disproportionately faster than Whites in the US population [42]. From 1980 to 2000, the Asian and Pacific Islander populations doubled in size, whereas the Hispanic population increased by one and a half times. These rates are predicted to continue to rise through the next half century. As a result, it is important not to underestimate the value of having culturally competent practitioners within the field of neuropsychology available to address the needs of these growing communities.

Psychologists can certainly agree that formal education, recruitment of qualified cross-cultural neuropsychologists, and the life-long process of examination are essential to best practice. However, several debates exist in terms of the ethical practice of cross-cultural neuropsychology. This issue becomes even more pronounced when considering some of the high-stake assessments that neuropsychologists may conduct with minority populations. Findings from neuropsychological assessment may impact applications and consideration for such privileges as citizenship and government assistance, and these results are frequently components of consideration in forensic matters and school placement. The potential for misinterpretations by less-successfully trained neuropsychologists with regard to cross-cultural factors is substantially increased, given the higher representation of multicultural individuals referred for assessment under these circumstances. The assessment may thereby be counterproductive, leaving individuals vulnerable to misclassification and misdiagnosis. In these cases, the results of the assessment may produce more harm than actual good.

Many APA programs and internships have adopted a core multicultural foundation of training within their curricula, as outlined by the Guidelines and Principles for Accreditation of Programs in Professional Psychology [43]. Actions to incorporate multicultural training include long-term efforts to attract diverse faculty and a coherent plan to provide relevant multicultural knowledge and experiences. The Houston Conference on Specialty Education in Clinical Neuropsychology noted the need to recruit professionals from a variety of backgrounds specifically into neuropsychology programs at all levels [44]. These efforts remain important given that the ethnic and racial make-up of students enrolled in such programs currently tends to be relatively homogeneous. On the other hand, guidelines have yet to be outlined to address specific training requirements in internship and residency education and training with respect to neuropsychology specialization; although practitioners have been encouraged to recognize multicultural issues in assessment and treatment, no formal outlines for training have been officially presented. Neuropsychologists need to closely examine their own beliefs through continued professional development and ongoing study of research concerning multicultural considerations within neuropsychology, in order to minimize variables which can contribute to needless negative interactions with patients and have the potential for biases in administration, interpretation, and diagnosis.

Similar to the Houston Conference, Brickman et al. have highlighted four specific ethical issues that should be considered when assessing a client from a diverse background [45]. First, race alone should not be considered as the reason for discrepant findings in neuropsychological assessments. Hence, practitioners need to consider additional factors that ride in tandem with or influence findings separate from race when conducting an assessment. The culturally sensitive neuropsychologist should approach assessment with an understanding of the cultural background of the examinee, including paying attention to such possible moderating factors as the quality of education, or the level of acculturation the individual presents with, and how these may impact performance.

Secondly, it is important that the examiner understands the normative information that underlies the use of their assessment instruments. Practitioners should be able to reflect on the degree to which their client's education and other background experiences align with the normative group for the measures being utilized; this is relevant even when the normative group has included race as a factor. One caveat expressed by Manly and Echemendia to the requirement that assessments be used that have been race-normed is that some processes used in developing specific racial norms may be harmful [46]. While more sensitive norms may assist in detecting cognitive impairment, they may also have the unintended impact of denying ethnic minorities needed services. Test developers need to be cautious not to use race as a proxy for underlying cultural and educational factors.

Thirdly, practitioners should strive to refer clients to an appropriate neuropsychologist who has an understanding of the examinee's language and culture whenever possible. If an appropriate referral is not accessible, practitioners are recommended to seek consultation when available. A translator should only

be used as a last resort, with a well-considered understanding of the caveats that apply when using a translator. Specifically, the fluency of interpreters can be quite variable, and the translator's knowledge of the language may be specific to a particular dialect that differs from the one used by the patient (e.g. Castilian Spanish versus Mexican Spanish). Additionally, for the nonfluent neuropsychologist using a translator, there may be no way to determine the accuracy of the translation that is utilized; this can significantly hamper efforts at obtaining verbally based information during the testing. It is strongly suggested that the use of a translator for assessment be preceded by a formal interview with the translator prior to the day of the assessment, which includes a thorough description of the assessment procedures and tools that will be used. A clear understanding must be reached of the intention and purpose of the evaluation, as well as possible outcomes that may influence the patient's future.

Finally, the practitioner should maintain competence when completing neuropsychological testing by gaining continued education in the area of multicultural issues [7]. As is evident from each of the presented explanations, these ethical considerations are extremely complex. Future research regarding the best means of addressing these issues within the professional assessment and diagnosis context is strongly needed.

There are other ethical considerations that should be addressed beyond those mentioned above. Clinicians must understand and maintain awareness of the power differential between the neuropsychologist and the patient by being aware of their own values, assumptions, and behaviors, as well as work to appreciate the unique cultural background of each examinee. Culturally competent assessment requires a persistent effort on the part of the practitioner to be cognizant of their own biases and the biases embedded in the tests that are being administered. We must be mindful at all times of the culture of the individual being assessed and how to best appreciate this difference, while simultaneously considering culture variability in interpreting and understanding the data obtained. Ardila has suggested that because many clinicians are still unaware of cultural variables, the degree to which such variables impact a neuropsychological assessment remains quite significant [4]. While psychologists are frequently required to assess patients who have different cultural backgrounds and beliefs from themselves, often they may not have the basic knowledge or self-awareness to bridge these cultural differences [47]. Furthermore, clinicians may quickly judge an aspect of behavior without the appropriate cultural context, which increases the risk of misinterpreting behavior and cognitive profiles, thus leading to a potential misdiagnosis. In sum, one of the most important steps a practitioner can take to minimize the power differential and cultural gap is to be aware of their own biases and their lack of information.

Approaches to culturally competent neuropsychology

Preassessment procedures

A key component to conducting accurate cross-cultural evaluations begins with effective communication, regardless of language continuity between the examiner and the patient. Neuropsychologists need to be conscious that decisions made following evaluations can ultimately guide the direction of a patient's neurorehabilitative treatment and affect their functionality in the future. Patients may experience anxiety as a result of this knowledge, which may potentially affect their performance prior to even entering the testing room [48]. As such, when faced with a referral to evaluate an individual from another culture, there are several key preparation points a clinician must consider. First, gathering background information begins during the process of setting up the initial appointment. At this point, preliminary data should be gathered about culture; mainly the clinician has the opportunity to inquire about family caregivers and/or informants, and ensure that the patient will be accompanied by others who can provide detailed historical information. This is also an opportunity to establish the native or preferred language spoken, as well as request additional informative materials such as medical and academic records.

Following the initial contact and prior to the appointment date, the clinician is encouraged to gather information about the customs and beliefs of the patient's culture, views of psychology/mental illness within the culture, as well as neuropsychological measures available that are norm-specific for this population. This period is also an opportunity for the clinician to reach out to colleagues who may have had direct personal or professional experiences with the patient's culture. The practitioner should strive to understand how culture may affect symptom formation and expression of distress, gain knowledge of any culture-bound syndromes, as well as appreciate culture's impact on assessment expectations, therapeutic alliance, family involvement, and interpretation of

assessment results. Overall, during the initial intake process, relevant cultural factors that should be considered through the course of the assessment include generational history, citizenship or residency status, language, family support systems or history of dissolution in the family structure, community resources, level of education, factors associated with immigration such as change of social status, work history, and the level of stress linked to acculturation or oppression [9].

Multiculturally sensitive practitioners should always be aware of the limitations of their instruments and personal assessment practices [6]. Specifically, psychologists are encouraged to consider the validity of specific instruments, understand the reference population for standardization, and test biases. A debate exists regarding the appropriateness of conducting a neuropsychological evaluation with a patient who has a limited knowledge of the language of the assessment. This issue is discussed by Artiola i Fortuny and Mullaney, who question testing outside a patient's native language by asking "Can the absurd be ethical?" [49]. Appropriately, they argue that a practitioner who does not have fluency in a patient's language is unlikely to detect language-related issues such as difficulties with prosody, or the impact and presentation of unusual syntax. Furthermore, behavioral observations are limited because of the inability to perceive incongruent affect. Neuropsychologists should always strive to place patients with culturally matched practitioners. However, it is also understood that neuropsychologists receiving a referral may not be fluent in the patient's native language *and* not have available to them another practitioner to whom the patient can be referred. Traditional examples include rural areas with a limited number of clinicians with the required expertise; patients who lack transportation resources; and acute care setting practices. It is suggested that practitioners schedule a pre-evaluation meeting with the translator in order to discuss the main points of the evaluation and determine the most direct translation and/or explanations for psychological language. Furthermore, practitioners are encouraged to obtain translation of questionnaires normally used in their practice to gather biographical and historical data. This provides structure and organization for record-keeping that is consistent with the evaluation process to which the clinician is accustomed; however, when translating we must keep in mind that the *gold standard* is to use translation with back-translation as additional processes to ensure the best possible conversion. One final but important note with regard to the use of translation services, clinicians must keep in mind that the use of translators may have an impact on rapport-building and are encouraged to themselves remain active in the discussion.

Measuring pre-morbid estimates of function

Arguably the biggest challenge faced by neuropsychologists during the evaluation process is determining accurately a patient's pre-morbid level of function. Dementia studies have generally utilized adapted variations of the National Adult Reading Test as a measure of pre-morbid intellectual ability, including versions from various Western European countries, South America, and Hispanics living in the USA [50, 51]. The use of this measure as an estimate of pre-morbid function across cultures is further supported by literature suggesting that years of education alone overlook the more important factor of quality of education [31]. Nevertheless, it is important to keep in mind there is variability across cultures, especially the emphasis placed on formal education and literacy; thus findings of one measure (e.g. NART) as a strong predictor of pre-morbid function may not always be applicable. Furthermore, total years of education as a variable to predict cognitive function can be ambiguous when considering the likelihood of systemic differences between the USA and other, less-developed countries. Quality of education as a factor in neuropsychological test performance has been identified within minority populations educated in the USA and outside the USA [52, 53].

Certainly, an objective measure of reading ability can provide a good estimate of intellect; however, a clinician should not be encouraged to limit gathering additional information about the person's history related to intellect and academic performance to just one measure. What other materials may be useful tools in formulating an estimate of function prior to neurological insult? Ideally, every piece of informative material available should be explored. These include any collateral reports or data from school performance such as grades and/or teacher reports. In addition, a detailed educational history should be gathered beyond the last grade completed, including subject-matter strengths and weaknesses, average grades, familial attitudes towards formal education, etc. Furthermore, the educational history of immediate family should be explored, if possible. What is the level of education of the patient's parents and grandparents? How does the patient's academic performance compare to siblings? This is particularly important as some authors have argued that early environmental factors such as learning opportunities in the home, including the availability of educationally oriented material and parental attitude, are important predictors of cognition [54]. For adults, an extensive occupational history should also be included, looking specifically at upward movement or promotion within employment ranks. Work colleagues and supervisors may provide valuable information as well. Again, not all countries/cultures place a great emphasis on formal education and literacy, and lacking these does not necessarily indicate level of function or competence. For these patients in particular, a thorough occupational history may provide a more accurate estimate of functional capacity prior to neurological disease.

Neuropsychological measures

According to the literature, the quest to develop a "culture-free" measure of cognitive function in the USA dates back to Raymond Cattell and his theory of intelligence, a feat that has been described as "mythical" following numerous studies [55, 56]. Despite his best efforts, Cattell's unsuccessful history of developing a culture-free measure of cognition has left neuropsychologists to ultimately focus on *minimizing* the cultural biases of our instruments rather than attempting to eliminate them. Assessment instruments can be culturally biased in several ways, including culturally insensitive content or construction of test items, formatting, mode of administration, or the inappropriate application of the assessment [57]. Stimulus material may only incorporate terms and situations relevant to mainstream culture. Additionally, specific questionnaires may not account for the expression of symptoms [58]. Specifically, Smith et al. cited a history of misdiagnosing African Americans as cognitively impaired based on the WAIS-R [59]. Findings of this magnitude highlighted the importance of cultural and demographic-specific normative data. Awareness of the disparity in neuropsychological test performance across cultures has encouraged researchers to propose normative data that account for these differences.

Practitioners need to be aware of limitations in the assessment practices, from intakes to the use of standardized assessment instruments. When the validity or reliability has not been adequately established, neuropsychologists must describe the strengths and limitations of test results and the overall interpretation.

Furthermore, when these issues arise, it becomes imperative to comprehensively assess the cultural and socio-political relevant factors that may be producing possible deficits across myriad domains of functioning. Reynolds reported that several issues need to be considered with regard to cultural biases in neuropsychological tests [60]. These include (1) inappropriate content-exposure, (2) inappropriate standardization samples, (3) examiners' and language bias, (4) inequitable social consequences, (5) measurement of different constructs, (6) differential predictive validity, and (7) qualitatively distinct aptitude and personality that may vary by culture.

Professional manuals published by Heaton and colleagues have helped lessen the occurrence of misclassification of individuals as impaired with normative data that are more specific to gender, age, and education for a number of neuropsychological instruments [14, 61]. In terms of cultural variations, norms are available for African Americans (and Whites) through an expanded Halstead-Reitan Battery that includes executive functioning, attention/working memory, processing speed, spatial skills, verbal skills, academic achievement, as well as sensorimotor and psychomotor skills. Furthermore, additional normative data for the WAIS-III and WMS-III are available, corrected for ethnicity, age, gender, and education to include Hispanics in the USA, as well as African Americans and Whites.

Publication of normative data specific to African Americans has extended beyond the aforementioned neuropsychological batteries, with large-scale studies providing corrected normative data for the Rey Auditory Verbal Learning Test, Hopkins Verbal Learning Test, and the Stroop, among others [62–64]. Other studies have provided an alternate version for the Mini Mental Status Examination [65]. In addition to normative data, Lautenschlager and colleagues suggest an alternative scoring method (latent semantic analysis), so as to reduce cultural biases [66].

More recently, there has been significant cross-cultural research over the past decade within the USA that has focused largely on Hispanic populations [66]. For this reason, as well as language differences, and the forecast that Hispanics will become the largest minority in the USA by the middle of this century, this population is largely represented within the norm-specific neuropsychological instruments available when compared to other minority groups [40]. There have been a number of large-scale research studies conducted within the USA and Latin America that have collected normative data for Hispanics. For example, Spanish norms have been developed for the WISC-IV, which enables comparisons with English-speaking children [3]. The standardization procedure included Latinos from several countries of origin such as Mexico, Cuba, Puerto Rico, Dominican Republic, as well as Central and South America. The norms have also been adjusted demographically to enable comparisons with children with similar US educational experience and parental education level.

In addition to collecting specific cross-cultural normative data and creating neuropsychological batteries that are culture-specific, researchers have focused on comparing existing measures of neuropsychological function across cultures in an attempt to identify various factors with minimal cultural biases. Tests for executive functioning, attention, memory, visuoperceptual processing, and language have all been considered. A full discussion of the findings regarding these measures is, however, beyond the scope of this chapter.

In summary, practitioners should work to assess their patients in the most culturally competent and ethical manner. They should be able to recognize multicultural differences and be sensitive to their patients and aware of their own biases. Neuropsychologists should continue to seek out continued education on the topic of cross-cultural assessment. Understanding cultural influences on behavior is essential to conceptualizing the patient's symptoms and diagnosis. One of the most important aspects of the assessment is a thorough interview. As previously stated, one should strive to corroborate information from other pertinent sources related to the patient. While referring out is not always a possibility, practitioners should be aware of their limitations (e.g. language, understanding of the culture). Practitioners should avoid translators and translated tests, as well; however, they should follow best practices if there is a need to do so. When available, they should seek out cross-culturally validated tests. Lastly, practitioners should also report on limitations and possible cultural barriers that may have impacted the assessment.

Summary and conclusions

- By understanding an individual's culture, neuropsychologists maximize accuracy in diagnosis as well as the effectiveness of treatment/rehabilitative services.

- Culture, ethnicity, and race are defined individually. These factors interact actively, and affect/influence a person's cognitive development at different levels.

- Covert racism and/or discrimination continue to exist; either in the form of the examiner's biased interpretations or the examinee's reservations about their expected performance.

- Other cultural variables such as age, gender, socioeconomic status, acculturation, and education need consideration, not independently, but collectively as part of an individual's culture and as influencing neuropsychological performance.

- Ethical standards in our field highlight the importance of cultural diversity training, both at the graduate and post-graduate level in order to ensure best clinical practices.

- Preparation for an assessment with individuals from different cultures begins prior to the appointment, and it includes gathering information specific to the patient as well as researching cultural background.

- Estimating pre-morbid level of function extends beyond total years of education, especially in cultures where literacy and education are not readily available. Other factors may include the quality of the education and performance, previous employment, familial details about education and employment, home environment, etc.

- Language introduces many challenges for assessments. There has been a recent trend in neuropsychology to conduct projects that create measures and norms to be used with Spanish-speaking individuals. Bilinguals create even greater challenges in testing, but should generally be tested in their preferred language.

- Culturally appropriate norms should be used when available, with few exceptions. Currently, educational and racial norms are available for many neuropsychological measures published by Heaton and colleagues.

- Research on the use of "language-free" measures developed in the USA with other cultures is beginning to show no significant differences across cultures. Nevertheless, this issue is controversial and clinical judgment should determine the use of these measures as well as the quality of an individual's performance.

- Incorporating culture into neuropsychological assessments will decrease the risk of misdiagnosis, increase the participation of the patient and the patient's family, and also promote social justice by treating people with dignity and humanity. Appreciating a patient's culture allows practitioners to more acceptably recognize cognitive deficits, but also increases the ability to more fully appreciate the person.

- The field of neuropsychology needs to continue to focus on developing and training multiculturally diverse clinicians. The field should work to set general guidelines to address multicultural issues in postdoctoral training. Standardization methods of assessment instruments should continue to be expanded in order to best embrace myriad cultural groups.

References

1. Fadiman A. *The Spirit Catches You and You Fall Down*. New York: Farrar, Strauss, & Giroux; 1997.

2. Kamphaus RW. *Clinical Assessment of Children's Intelligence*. Boston: Allyn & Bacon; 1993.

3. Wechsler D. *Wechsler Intelligence Scale for Children-Fourth Edition, Spanish*. San Antonio, TX: Harcourt Assessments; 2004.

4. Ardila A. Directions of research in cross-cultural neuropsychology. *J Exp Psychol* 1995;**17**:143–50.

5. Manly JJ, Jacobs DM, Touradji P, Small SA, Stern Y. Reading level attenuates differences in neuropsychological test performance between African American and white elders. *J Int Neuropsychol Soc* 2002;**8**:341–8.

6. Ries JK, Potter BS, Llorente AM. Multicultural aspects of pediatric neuropsychological intervention and rehabilitation. In Hunter S, Donders J, eds. *Pediatric Neuropsychological Interventions*. New York: Cambridge University Press, 2007: 47–67.

7. American Psychological Association. Ethical principles of psychologists and code of conduct. *Am Psychol* 2002;**57**:1060–73.

8. Gardiner HW, Kosmitzki C. *Lives Across Cultures: Cross-cultural Human Development*. New York: Pearson Education; 2005.

9. American Psychological Association. Guidelines on multicultural education, training, research, practice, and organizational change for psychologists. *Am Psychol* 2003;**58**:377–402.

10. Neisser U, Boodoo G, Bouchard TJJ, Boykin AW, Brody N, Ceci SJ, et al. Intelligence: knowns and unknowns. *Am Psychol* 1996;**51**:77–101.

11. Kennepohl S. Toward a cultural neuropsychology: an alternative view and a preliminary model. *Brain Cogn* 1999;**41**:365–80.

12. De Agostini M, Khamis AH, Ahui AM, Dellatolas G. Environmental influences in hand preference: an African point of view. *Brain Cogn* 1997;**35**(2):151–67.

13. Hatta T, Kawakami A. Image generation and handedness: is the hemi-imagery method valid for studying the hemisphere imagery generation process? *Neuropsychologia* 1997;**35**:1499–502.

14. Heaton RK, Taylor M, Manly J. Demographic effects and demographically corrected norms with the WAIS-III and WMS-III. In Tulsky D, et al., eds. *Clinical interpretations of the WAIS-II and WMS-III*. San Diego: Academic Press; 2003: 183–210.

15. Manly JJ, Touradji P, Tang MX, Stern Y. Literacy and memory decline among ethically diverse elders. *J Clin Exp Neuropsychol* 2003;**25**:680–90.

16. Steele CM. Stereotyping and its threat are real. *Am Psychol* 1998; **53**: 680–81.

17. Manly JJ, Byrd DA, Touradji P, Stern Y. Acculturation, reading level, and neuropsychological test performance among African American elders. *Appl Neuropsychol* 2004;**11**:37–46.

18. Mensh E, Mensh H. *The IQ Mythology: Class, Race, Gender, and Inequality*. Carbondale, IL: Southern University Press; 1991.

19. Gasquoine PG. Variables moderating cultural and ethnic differences in neuropsychological assessment: the case of Hispanic Americans. *Clin Neuropsychol* 1999;**13**(3):376–83.

20. Clark VR, Williams DR. Racism as a stressor for African Americans: a biopsychosocial model. *Am Psychol* 1999;**54**:1070–77.

21. Mendelson T, Kubzansky LD, Datta GD, Buka SL. Relation of female gender and low socioeconomic status to internalizing symptoms among adolescents: a case of double jeopardy? *Soc Sci Med* 2008;**66**(6):1284–96.

22. Dovidio JF, Kawakami K, Gaertner SL. Implicit and explicit prejudices and interracial interaction. *J Pers Soc Psychol* 2002;**82**:62–8.

23. Shepherd I, Leathem J. Factors affecting performance in cross-cultural neuropsychology: from a New Zealand bicultural perspective. *J Int Neuropsychol Soc* 1999;**5**:83–4.

24. Horn JL, Cattell RB. Age differences in fluid and crystallized intelligence. *Acta Psychol* 1967;**26**:107–29.

25. Sue S. Measurement, testing, and ethnic bias: Can solutions be found? In: Sodowsky GR, Impara JC, eds. *Multicultural Assessment in Counseling and Clinical Psychology*. Lincoln, NB: Buros Institute of Mental Measurement; 1998: 7–36.

26. Rey GJ, Feldman E, Rivas-Vazquez R, Levin BE, Benton A. Neuropsychological test development for Hispanics. *Arch Clin Neuropsychol* 1998;**14**:593–601.

27. Landrine H, Klonoff EA. The African American Acculturation Scale: development, reliability and validity. *J Black Psychol* 1994;**20**:102–27.

28. Lezak MD, Howleson DB, Loring DW. *Neuropsychological Assessment*, 4th edn. New York: Oxford University Press; 2004.

29. US Census Bureau. 2008 National Population Projections [document on the internet]. Washington DC: USCB; 2008 August [cited 2008 October 30]. Available from http://www.census.gov/ipc/www/usinterimproj.

30. Hays PA. Culturally responsive assessment with diverse older clients. *Prof Psychol Res Pr* 1996;**27**(2):188–93.

31. Manly JJ, Byrd DA, Touradji P, Sanchez D, Stern Y. Literacy and cognitive change among ethnically diverse elders. *Int J Psychol* 2004;**39**(1):47–60.

32. Levy J, Heller W. Gender differences in human neuropsychological function. In Gerall AA, Moltz H, Ward IL, eds. *Handbook of Behavioral Neurobiology*, Vol. 11. New York: Plenum; 1992.

33. Cuffe SP, Moore CG, McKeanan RE. Prevalence and correlates of ADHD symptoms in the National Health Interview Survey. *J Atten Disord* 2005;**9**:392–401.

34. Seeman MN. Gender differences in schizophrenia across the life span. In: Cohen CI, ed. *Schizophrenia Into Later Life*. Washington DC: American Psychiatric Publishing; 2003.

35. Valencia RR, Suzuki LA. *Intelligence Testing and Minority Students: Foundations, Performance Factors, and Assessment Issues*. Thousand Oaks, CA: Sage; 2001.

36. Centers for Disease Control and Prevention. *Use of race and ethnicity in public health surveillance summary of the CDC/ATSDR workshop*. Washington DC: MMWR Wkly 1993; **10**.

37. Hart B, Risley TR. *Meaningful Differences in the Everyday Experiences of Young American Children*. Baltimore: Brookes; 1995.

38. Campbell T, Dollaghan C, Needleman H, Janosky J. Reducing bias in language assessment: processing-dependent measures. *J Speech Hear Res* 1997;**40**:519–25.

39. Noble KG, McCandliss BD, Farah MJ. Socioeconomic gradient predict individual differences in neurocognitive abilities. *Dev Sci* 2007;**10**(4):464–80.

40. Van Gorp WG, Myers HF, Drake EB. Neuropsychology training: ethnocultural considerations in the context of general competency training. In Fletcher-Janzen E, Strickland TL, Reynolds CR, eds. *Handbook of Cross-cultural Neuropsychology*. New York: Kluwer Academic/Plenum; 2000: 19–27.

41. Palloni A, Morenoff JD. Interpreting the paradoxical in the Hispanic paradox: demographic and epidemiologic approaches. *Ann N Y Acad Sci* 2001;**954**:140–74.

42. US Census Bureau. *Census 2000 brief*. Washington DC: USCB; 2001. USCB publication.

43. American Psychological Association. Guidelines and principles for accreditation of programs in professional psychology [document on the Internet]. Washington DC: APA; 2008 [cited 2009 Feb 25]. Available from: http://www.apa.org/ed/accreditation/G&P0522.pdf.

44. Hannay HJ, Bieliauskas LA, Crosson BA, Hammeke TA, Hamsher K, Koffler SP. Proceedings of the Houston Conference on Specialty Education and Training in Clinical Neuropsychology. *Arch Clin Neuropsychol* 1998;**13**:157–250.

45. Brickman AM, Cabo R, Manly J. Ethical issues in cross-cultural neuropsychology. *Appl Neuropsychol* 2006;**13** (2):91–100.

46. Manly J, Echemendia RJ. Race-specific norms: using the model of hypertension to understand issues of race, culture, and education in neuropsychology. *Arch Clin Neuropsychol* 2007;**22**(3):319–25.

47. Wong TM, Strickland TL, Fletcher-Janzen E, Ardila A, Reynolds CR. Theoretical and practical issues in the neuropsychological assessment and treatment of culturally dissimilar patients. In Fletcher-Janzen E, Strickland TL, Reynolds CR, eds. *Handbook of Cross-cultural Neuropsychology*. New York: Kluwer Academic/ Plenum; 2000: 3–18.

48. Nell V. *Cross-cultural Neuropsychological Assessment: Theory and Practice*. Mahwah, NJ: Lawrence Erlbaum Associates; 2000.

49. Artiola i Fortuny L, Mullaney H. Assessing patients whose language you do not know: can the absurd be ethical? *Clin Neuopsychol* 1998;**12**:113–26.

50. Nelson HE. *The National Adult Reading Test (NART): Test Manual*. Bury St. Edmunds, UK: Thames Valley Test Company; 1982.

51. Schrauf RW, Weintraub S, Navarro E. Is adaptation of the word accentuation test of premorbid intelligence necessary for use among older, Spanish-speaking immigrants in the United States? *J Int Neuropsychol Soc* 2006;**12**(3):391–99.

52. Manly JJ, Jacobs DM. Future directions in neuropsychological assessment with African Americans. In Ferraro FR, ed. *Minority and Cross-cultural Aspects of Neuropsychological Assessment*. Leiden, The Netherlands: Swets & Zeitlinger; 2001.

53. Shuttleworth-Edwards AB, Kemp RD, Rust AL, Muirhead J, Hartman NP, Radloff SE. Cross-cultural effects on IQ test performance: a review and preliminary normative indications on WAIS-III test performance. *J Clin Exp Neuropsychol* 2004;**26**(7):903–20.

54. Byrd DA, Miller SW, Reilly J, Weber S, Wall TL, Heaton RK. Early environmental factors, ethnicity, and adult cognitive test performance. *Clin Neuropsychol* 2006;**20**:243–60.

55. Cattell R. A culture-free intelligence test. *J Educ Psychol* 1940;**31**:161–79.

56. Levav M, Mirsky AF, French LM, Bartko JJ. Multinational neuropsychological testing: performance of children and adults. *J Clin Exp Neuropsychol* 1998;**20**(5):658–72.

57. Padilla AM. Issues in culturally appropriate assessment. In Suzuki L, Ponterotto JG, Meller PJ, eds. *Handbook of Multicultural Assessment*, 2nd edn. San Francisco: Jossey-Bass; 2001

58. Sue D, Sue S. Cultural factors in the clinical assessment of Asian Americans. *J Consult Clin Psychol* 1987;**55**:479–87.

59. Smith GE, Ivnik RJ, Lucas JA. Assessment techniques: tests, test batteries, norms, and methodological approaches. In Morgan J, Ricker J, eds. *Textbook of Clinical Psychology*. New York: Taylor & Francis; 2008.

60. Reynolds CR. Methods for detecting and evaluating cultural bias in neuropsychological tests. In Fletcher-Janzen E, Strickland TL, Reynolds CR, eds. *Handbook of Cross-cultural Neuropsychology*. New York: Kluwer Academic/Plenum; 2000: 249–86.

61. Heaton RK, Miller SM, Taylor MJ, Graft I. *Revised comprehensive norms for an expanded Halstead-Reitan Battery: demographically adjusted neuropsychological norms for African Americans and Caucasian Adults*. Lutz, FL: Psychological Assessment Resources; 2004.

62. Ferman TJ, Lucas JA, Ivnik RJ, Smith GE, Willis FB, Petersen RC, et al. Mayo's older African American normative studies: Auditory Verbal Learning Test norms for African American elders. *Clin Neuropsychol* 2005;**19**(2):214–28.

63. Friedman MA, Schinka JA, Mortimer JA, Graves AB. Hopkins Verbal Learning Test – Revised: norms for elderly African Americans. *Clin Neuropsychol* 2002;**16**(3):356–72.

64. Moering RG, Schinka JA, Mortimer JA, Graves AB. Normative data for elderly African Americans for the Stroop Color Word Test. *Arch Clin Neuropsychol* 2004;**19**(1):61–71.

65. Brown LM, Schinka JA, Mortimer JA, Graves AB. 3MS normative data for elderly African Americans. *J Clin Exp Neuropsychol* 2003;**25**(2):234–41.

66. Lautenschlager NT, Dunn JC, Bonney K, Flicker L, Almeida OP. Latent semantic analysis: an improved method to measure cognitive performance in subjects of non-English-speaking-background. *J Clin Exp Neuropsychol* 2006;**28**:1381–87.

Structural and functional neuroimaging throughout the lifespan

Brenna C. McDonald and Andrew J. Saykin

Introduction

From a neuroimaging perspective, the changes that occur over the lifespan in brain structure and functional capacity, both developmental and degenerative, must be considered in combination with the cognitive, behavioral, and psychosocial status of an individual when utilizing neuroimaging for either clinical or research purposes. In this chapter we selectively review some common conventional neuroimaging techniques and their application, followed by discussion of advanced structural and functional neuroimaging methods and likely future directions.

Conventional neuroimaging methodologies

Historically speaking, older structural and functional neuroimaging techniques are often referred to as "conventional" imaging methodologies, though the categorization of what techniques are considered cutting-edge versus those which are labeled conventional continues to evolve over time as ever-newer imaging technologies are developed. Structural imaging techniques such as computed axial tomography (CAT or CT) and magnetic resonance imaging (MRI) have become routine neuroimaging methodologies, with wide availability in terms of both scanning technology and technical capacity for their implementation and interpretation. CT scanning was the earliest method of structural brain imaging to come into common clinical and research use, and utilizes computerized integration of multiple X-ray images to generate cross-sectional views of the brain. While CT remains the optimal method for some neuroimaging purposes (e.g. visualization of bone or acute hemorrhage), the exposure to radiation involved in the technique and its relatively low contrast between classes of brain tissue have led CT largely to be supplanted by structural MRI in research and for many clinical applications.

Structural MRI capitalizes on variations in the inherent magnetic properties (resonance and water content) of different body tissues to provide visualization of normal and abnormal neuroanatomy with increasingly high levels of resolution, typically of the order of 1 mm^2 in plane. Different MR pulse sequences are optimized to image normal neuroanatomic details and atrophy (e.g. T1-weighting) versus visible pathology such as hyperintense microvascular and inflammatory lesions (e.g. T2-weighting, fluid-attenuated inversion recovery (FLAIR)). In addition to visual inspection for clinical abnormalities, semi-automated or manual analysis methods can be used to segment or classify structural MR images into the main brain tissue compartments (grey and white matter (GM and WM) and cerebrospinal fluid (CSF)), or to demarcate brain structures, regions of interest (ROI), or particular abnormalities (e.g. WM lesions). Volume and other tissue characteristics can then be quantitated and compared using imaging analysis and statistical software. For example, manual or semi-automated delineation of WM hyperintensities, which can reflect microvascular changes or areas of demyelination, is often conducted in studies of multiple sclerosis or other WM disorders [1–3]. Similarly, tracing of brain tumors can be utilized in treatment planning or to compare efficacy of treatment strategies [4, 5]. In other clinical populations, ROI analysis of various structures is commonly used to compare patient and control groups or examine disease progression over time. Medial temporal lobe (MTL) abnormalities have been documented in older adults with mild cognitive impairment (MCI) and Alzheimer's disease (AD), where MTL atrophy has been demonstrated to worsen with disease progression [6, 7]. Other brain regions have also been investigated in MCI, AD, and healthy older adults with cognitive complaints, with findings suggesting that diminished volume of the corpus callosum is sensitive to very early stages of cognitive decline, while volume loss is not seen in the fornix and mammillary bodies until the point of conversion to AD [8, 9]. In psychiatric conditions such as schizophrenia and autism-spectrum disorders, studies using

ROI analyses have pointed to multiple brain regions which may underlie aspects of the cognitive and behavioral symptom profiles [10–14].

Molecular functional neuroimaging methods such as positron emission tomography (PET) are able to demonstrate changes in brain activity over time or differences between study groups through the use of short-lived radiotracers. In early work, O^{15}-labeled water or ^{18}F-fluorodeoxyglucose (FDG) were utilized to measure blood flow and glucose metabolism, respectively, either at rest or during task performance. While O^{15}-water PET has largely been supplanted by MR imaging methodologies such as functional MRI (fMRI) and MR perfusion sequences which are capable of noninvasive blood flow measurements (e.g. arterial spin labeling, discussed below), FDG PET has come into regular clinical use in some neurocognitive populations due to approval for payment for the service by the Centers for Medicare and Medicaid Services (CMS), the US federal agency that administers Medicare, Medicaid, and the State Children's Health Insurance Program. CMS approval for FDG PET to aid in localization of seizure focus in refractory epilepsy was granted in 2000. A clinical indication for FDG PET in aiding the differential diagnosis of Alzheimer's disease versus frontotemporal dementia was approved in 2004, for the first time broadening the routine clinical use of PET to include assisting in diagnostic clarification of a disorder whose primary symptoms are cognitive and behavioral. Most recently (2005), CMS announced approval for payment for FDG PET for patients with brain tumors provided that data are submitted to the National Oncologic PET Registry (implemented in 2006) to provide empirical data to assist in future determinations of appropriate indications for this service. Novel research using FDG PET has also demonstrated the potential utility of neuroimaging techniques as biomarkers for treatment response, for both medication and psychotherapy. In a longstanding program of research, Mayberg and colleagues have demonstrated characteristic patterns of hypermetabolism in the subgenual cingulate (BA25) in treatment-resistant depression, and have shown that deep brain stimulation to this region can lead to symptom remission and normalization of brain metabolic activity [15]. In later work, this group demonstrated that patterns of alterations in brain metabolism on PET are also associated with clinical improvement in response to antidepressants or cognitive behavioral therapy, and that these alterations in neural activity vary with treatment type [16–18].

Single photon emission computed tomography (SPECT) is used for similar clinical applications as FDG PET (e.g. in epilepsy and brain tumor, as well as in cerebrovascular disease and neurodegenerative disorders; for review, see [19]). SPECT utilizes injected radiotracers to visualize brain perfusion (blood flow) or receptor density, and has the advantage of being less expensive and more readily accessible than PET. However, its limited spatial resolution (about 6–8 mm) and restricted range of uses for functional imaging have led to less widespread utilization of SPECT in clinical research than other neuroimaging techniques.

Advanced neuroimaging research methods

Recent advances in neuroimaging have been centered less on the development of entirely new imaging technologies than on innovations within a given modality, such as MRI or PET, which improve the capabilities of the method. In MRI, wider availability of high-field magnets (3.0 tesla field strength and above) has greatly improved image spatial resolution for structural series, signal-to-noise ratios for fMRI, and ability to detect neurochemical peaks in MR spectroscopy. Hardware improvements such as advanced head coil designs with greater numbers of channels have facilitated the development of parallel imaging approaches which can dramatically decrease scan acquisition time and improve MR image quality. In addition to technological advances in hardware, development in MR pulse sequences and image analysis techniques has improved clinical care while also enabling neuroimaging to be incorporated into a broader array of research programs.

Advanced MRI techniques

Voxel-based morphometry (VBM) approaches allow the quantification of GM and WM density (or concentration) and volume on a voxel-by-voxel basis throughout the entire brain through computational analysis of conventional T1-weighted anatomic images (e.g. SPGR, MP-RAGE, or TFE series) [20–22]. Through statistical parametric mapping techniques routinely used to analyze functional neuroimaging data, VBM can evaluate a particular tissue compartment across every voxel in the brain relative to a user-defined a priori statistical threshold. VBM therefore provides a fully automated method for assessing tissue characteristics, overcoming some limitations of morphological methods which rely on manual segmentation of brain regions or structures and offering an unbiased, comprehensive, and reliable technique sensitive to local changes in tissue volume or density. In temporal lobe epilepsy VBM has confirmed findings of brain abnormalities noted in previous manual segmentation studies, and has also elucidated a pattern of more widespread extratemporal differences, which may help to explain the patterns of cognitive deficit found in this disorder [23]. VBM has likewise confirmed previous ROI analyses demonstrating MTL volume loss in MCI, and recent data suggest that similar abnormalities are present in individuals with cognitive complaints who do not meet clinical criteria for the diagnosis of MCI, suggesting the possibility of an even earlier "pre-MCI" stage [24]. While VBM has more commonly been used to examine GM changes, brain WM can also be studied using this technique. In a recent paper investigating structural brain changes following chemotherapy for acute lymphoblastic leukemia (ALL), Carey et al. found decreased regional WM volume in two areas in the superior and middle frontal gyri which correlated with cognitive performance [25]. These findings confirmed prior studies showing WM abnormalities following chemotherapy for ALL, but provided greater specificity of localized ROIs for future investigation.

Another MR-based technique, diffusion tensor imaging (DTI), capitalizes on variation in diffusion of water molecules in different brain tissue types to map pathways and assess tissue integrity (Fig. 4.1). Diffusion of water molecules in GM and CSF is largely random (isotropic), but is directionally restricted (anisotropic) in WM by axonal membranes and myelin. WM fiber tracts are therefore highly non-random in diffusion characteristics in healthy brain tissue. The integrity of WM pathways can be quantitatively indicated by the degree of anisotropy, while the degree and orientation of anisotropy can demonstrate the directionality of fiber tracts [26] and the neuroanatomical connectivity of fiber pathways between brain regions involved in a particular network [27, 28]. Pathological changes in GM can also be detected by examining differences in mean diffusivity of tissue, though to date DTI has primarily been used to investigate WM changes, documenting abnormalities in clinical populations where WM disease is a hallmark on neuroimaging. In multiple sclerosis, DTI has demonstrated decreased WM and GM integrity in regions which appear normal on conventional MR sequences [29]. In specific disorders, use of structural MR techniques optimized for detection of particular pathology in GM or WM can also build upon prior neuroimaging findings (e.g. see [30] for discussion of detection of iron deposition and myelin loss via T2 hypointensities and relaxometry and T1 mapping in multiple sclerosis). In AD, abnormalities in mean diffusivity have been found in GM of the MTL, as well as regions in the frontal and parietal lobes, using a fully automated DTI approach [31].

Magnetic resonance spectroscopy (MRS) allows graphic representation and quantification of metabolite concentration, synthesis rates, and relative volumes in brain tissue based on the varying magnetic characteristics of biochemical compounds. The most recent advances in spectroscopic methods allow

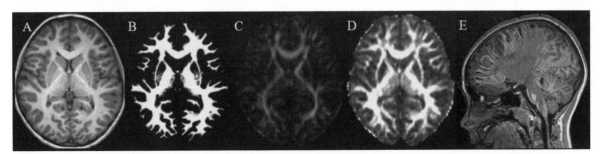

Figure 4.1. See color plate section. Sample DTI image acquired in a healthy 8-year-old girl. The FA map (C and D) is registered to the participant's T1-weighted MP-RAGE volume (A) and shown with the segmented white matter map from the MP-RAGE (B). Higher signal intensity in the raw FA image (D) reflects the highly directional intra-axonal diffusion of water molecules indicating major fiber pathways and white matter integrity. In (C) fiber tracts are color-coded to denote directionality of orientation of white matter pathways (red = lateral/medial, green = anterior/posterior, blue = superior/inferior, other colors indicate crossing fibers). In (E) the use of fiber tractography to follow the course of white matter pathways is demonstrated, with color coding indicating seed regions used to generate tracts (beige = corpus callosum, pink = internal capsule, blue = external capsule).

increasingly specific measurements of brain neurotransmitters (e.g. glutamate, glycine, and GABA) and metabolite markers of neuronal status and integrity (e.g. NAA, creatine, choline, and myoinositol). Such findings have offered new insights into neurochemical abnormalities in frontal and temporal lobe regions in first-episode schizophrenia [32], and have further characterized the nature of abnormal tissue in epileptiform cortical malformations [33]. These results can have important treatment implications as well. For example, MRS-derived biomarkers have been found to predict survival in children with CNS tumor better than standard histopathology [34], and to demonstrate evidence of compromised neural functioning in children during diabetic ketoacidosis, which can be improved with treatment [35].

While no longer a "new" imaging technique, fMRI continues to require a high level of specialized expertise for stimulus task design and interpretation of results. As a result, while clinical applications have increased, bringing fMRI into more routine use, it is not yet a standard technique in the manner of those methods discussed under conventional imaging above. Rather, fMRI is most commonly used in clinical research with the goal of detecting alterations in brain function which improve understanding of abnormalities in clinical populations in aggregate or measuring changes in neuronal activity in response to pharmacological or behavioral treatment at the group level. These observations may in the future translate into biomarkers to predict individual likelihood of treatment response, allowing increased "personalization" of medical care. fMRI demonstrates activation of brain regions during the performance of cognitive or sensorimotor tasks via detection of increases in local signal intensity attributable to changes in local blood flow and oxygenation and detectable due to the differing magnetic susceptibility of oxyhemoglobin and deoxyhemoglobin. This use of deoxyhemoglobin as an endogenous contrast agent eliminates the need for a radioactive contrast agent to measure changes in brain activity, and has become known as blood oxygen level dependent (BOLD) contrast.

For both clinical and research applications, fMRI has the advantage of being a repeatable, noninvasive procedure, with no significant known health risks for most individuals. Stimulus paradigms can also be developed to assess a virtually limitless range of sensorimotor, cognitive, behavioral, or emotional questions, making fMRI a highly versatile tool (Fig. 4.2).

In 2007, a current procedural terminology (CPT) code was implemented to allow payment for clinical fMRI as part of preoperative neurosurgical planning, paving the way for reimbursement for this service by federal and private insurers. Most commonly fMRI is used to localize sensorimotor or language cortex as part of comprehensive presurgical assessment in patients with a brain tumor, epileptic focus, or arteriovenous malformation (AVM) thought likely to affect these functions. In brain tumor and AVM populations clinical fMRI referrals commonly request mapping of hand or foot motor functioning in preparation for resection of a lesion in the vicinity of the motor strip. Motor mapping may also be useful in patients with focal frontal lobe epilepsy if the presumed seizure focus is a lesion (e.g. cortical dysplasia) in motor cortex. Another major indication for fMRI mapping in patients with a tumor or AVM is language lateralization and localization, if the lesion or planned resection approach is likely to affect frontal or temporal brain regions that may be critical for language functioning in the presumed dominant hemisphere. A recent validation study comparing fMRI mapping of language and hand motor functioning with intraoperative electrocortical mapping (ECM) demonstrated good sensitivity and specificity of fMRI compared to ECM results and noted good functional outcomes, confirming the utility of fMRI for presurgical mapping [36]. Furthermore, there are data to suggest that the additional functional data provided by presurgical language or motor maps can allow modification of treatment plans and facilitate a more aggressive resection, shorter surgical time, or less extensive craniotomy [37]. Another important direction is the incorporation of fMRI brain mapping information into surgical navigation systems, permitting use during surgery. Recent work also suggests the feasibility of obtaining updated fMRI data during surgery itself. Future directions in presurgical planning may include the use of "real-time" fMRI data. While most clinical fMRI exams are conducted as far in advance of surgery as possible due to the time needed for image processing and analysis, recent studies of sensorimotor, visual, and language mapping suggest that use of real-time fMRI t-maps for preoperative planning and/or intraoperative motor cortex localization may be feasible in some cases, eliminating the need for image postprocessing and potentially saving considerable time and effort for both the patient and the treatment team [38, 39]. Increasingly scanner vendors are marketing prepackaged fMRI

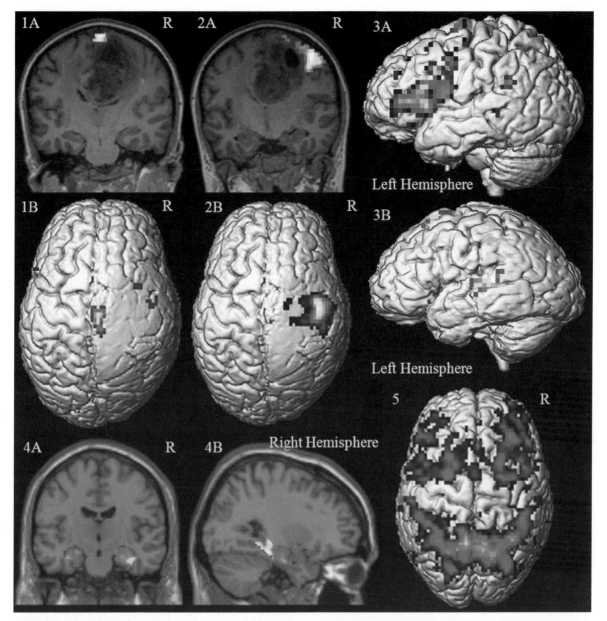

Figure 4.2. See color plate section. fMRI brain activation patterns elicited by different task paradigms displayed over the participants' high-resolution T1-weighted MP-RAGE volume and rendered anatomy. Motor mapping in a patient with a right frontal anaplastic astrocytoma demonstrates contralateral motor strip activation in medial regions for left foot movement (1A and B) and lateral regions for left hand movement (2A and B). In (3) representative activation patterns are shown for individuals with typical left-hemisphere dominance for expressive language (3A, using a verb generation paradigm in an adult) and receptive language (3B, during processing of novel and familiar words in a child). In (4) bilateral medial temporal lobe activation during episodic memory processing is shown in an 11-year-old boy with right temporal lobe epilepsy while encoding novel scenes. In (5) the typical pattern of bilateral frontal and parietal activation observed during working memory processing is demonstrated in an adult using a visual-verbal n-back task.

mapping protocols capable of producing preoperative activation maps for some functions. Effective use of such protocols requires appropriate professional training and experience, however, given the importance of the clinical decisions involved [40].

Another major clinical use of fMRI is in comprehensive evaluation for epilepsy surgery, where functional mapping can be of great relevance (for reviews, see [41, 42]). Language lateralization and localization is particularly important in temporal lobe epilepsy, the epilepsy subtype most amenable to surgical treatment, as the most utilized surgical approaches, standard anterior temporal lobectomy or selective amygdalo-hippocampectomy, may pose a risk to language functioning if the seizure focus is in the language dominant hemisphere. Language mapping may also be beneficial for patients with frontal lobe epilepsy whose seizure focus is thought to lie in anterior regions important for expressive language. There is evidence that individuals with epilepsy have a higher incidence of atypical language dominance than is found in the general population, making careful assessment of language functioning of even greater importance [43–47]. While historically presurgical assessment of language and memory has been conducted using an invasive angiographic procedure, the intracarotid amobarbital test (IAT or Wada test), multiple studies have demonstrated the capacity of fMRI to assess hemispheric dominance for language as effectively as the IAT. As fMRI also affords localization of frontal and temporal language-related regions in a way not possible with the IAT, many epilepsy surgery centers are moving toward utilization of fMRI rather than IAT when possible (for review of language mapping, see [48]). In this population in particular, it would be of great benefit to be able also to assess hemispheric capability of supporting memory using fMRI, providing a non-invasive method for obtaining data currently gathered via the IAT. This is an active area of clinical research, and a few studies have presented data which are highly promising in this regard, with preliminary evidence that fMRI activation patterns correlate with postsurgical memory outcome [49–53]. At present, however, fMRI has not been demonstrated to evaluate hemispheric support of memory functions reliably at the level of the individual patient.

As noted above, the scope of fMRI research includes a broad range of studies examining cognitive, emotional, motor, and sensory processing. One advantage of fMRI as compared to functional neuroimaging techniques which require use of a radioactive tracer is the safety and relative ease of conducting repeat studies in the same participants. fMRI can therefore be used more readily to study brain function in healthy individuals and children, and as part of longitudinal studies. Through such work, there have been significant insights into the underlying neural processes critical to effective cognition, confirming and extending theories previously derived from studies of individuals with a particular type or location of brain lesion or clinical disorder with a known brain correlate. fMRI has also been used to examine alterations in brain function following emotional or physical trauma, or in response to behavioral or pharmacological treatment. For example, abnormalities in working memory-related brain activation have been observed in adults after even very mild traumatic brain injury (TBI) [54], while, in PTSD, fMRI activation patterns have been identified during processing of fearful faces that may predict response to cognitive behavioral therapy [55]. In a study examining patients with MCI before and after treatment with donepezil, a cholinesterase inhibitor, Saykin et al. found reduced working memory-related frontoparietal fMRI activation in the MCI group relative to controls at baseline, which increased with treatment in conjunction with improved task performance [56].

Perfusion MRI techniques can also be utilized to examine features of both brain structure and function, with some overlapping capability with BOLD fMRI. Arterial spin labeling (ASL) utilizes arterial blood water which has been magnetically "labeled" using radiofrequency pulses to measure brain perfusion, avoiding the exposure to radioactivity necessary for O^{15}-water PET or gadolinium as required for other MRI perfusion approaches such as dynamic susceptibility contrast (DSC) imaging. The two major approaches, continuous and pulsed arterial spin labeling (CASL and PASL), have varying strengths and weaknesses, but both provide the ability to generate absolute quantification of blood flow. As a result, ASL allows statistical calculations which are not possible using the arbitrary units generated by BOLD fMRI. ASL has been shown to be of use in clinical research in cerebrovascular disease, brain tumor, epilepsy, and neurodegenerative and neuropsychiatric disorders, as well as in the study of development and aging. For example, ASL imaging is capable of distinguishing between high- and low-grade gliomas, and of demonstrating brain changes related to AD and frontotemporal dementia which correlate with functional status. ASL perfusion fMRI has great potential utility in examining outcomes following pharmacological or physiological interventions which affect resting cerebral blood flow (CBF), to distinguish effects of interest. ASL images of resting CBF (Fig. 4.3A) also provide a map of brain function analogous to that provided by FDG PET metabolic studies (Fig. 4.3B), allowing examination of the relationship between resting CBF and cognitive performance on out-of-scanner tasks (for recent review of these and other uses of ASL, see

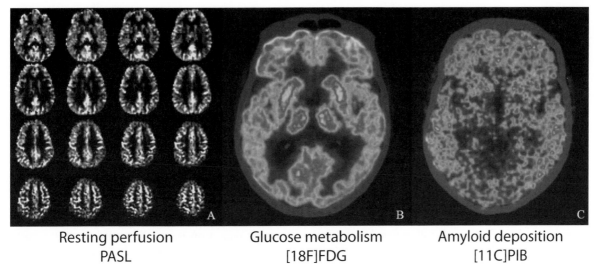

| Resting perfusion | Glucose metabolism | Amyloid deposition |
| PASL | [18F]FDG | [11C]PIB |

Figure 4.3. See color plate section. Functional imaging using PASL and PET. In (A) the resting grey matter perfusion CBF map of a healthy adult is shown using a PASL Q2TIPS sequence with parallel imaging at 3T. In (B) normal resting glucose metabolism is demonstrated using the [18F]FDG tracer in a 75-year-old patient with MCI (CDR 0.5, MMSE 29), while in (C) amyloid deposition is demonstrated in the same individual using [11C]PIB.

[57]). ASL can also be conducted during cognitive processing, similar to BOLD fMRI, with the two techniques appearing to provide complementary information [58]. Although ASL has less sensitivity to detect activation than BOLD fMRI, the advantages of having a stable baseline and being able to quantify change in physiological units (mL/100 g/min) are significant.

Like fMRI, functional near-infrared spectroscopy (fNIRS) also utilizes measurement of hemoglobin oxygenation to detect tissue changes reflective of brain activity (for reviews, see [59, 60]). While fMRI uses the magnetic characteristics of hemoglobin, fNIRS is an optical imaging technique that measures relative oxygen concentration by capitalizing on the differential absorption of light in tissues with varying degrees of oxygenation. Advantages of fNIRS include its capacity to tolerate a greater degree of subject motion, as well as the fact that it can be conducted in everyday environments using portable, wearable technology such that an extensive (and expensive) imaging suite is not needed. fNIRS also has fewer restrictions in terms of patient-specific factors or risks (i.e. no magnetic fields, RF pulses or radioactivity are required), and can be used in otherwise difficult to study populations (e.g. fetuses and neonates [61–63]). These factors give fNIRS the ability to help answer questions not easily addressed using other functional imaging techniques. However, fNIRS has relatively low spatial resolution (~30 mm), and is not capable of imaging deep brain structures, limiting its utility in assessment of regions below the cortical surface.

Advanced PET techniques

Advances in PET tracer development now allow targeted examination of specific neurotransmitter systems, including the dopaminergic, cholinergic, and serotonergic systems. Tracers have also been developed to study receptor binding for opioids and benzodiazepines (for review, see [64]). Utilization of these techniques permits research to move well beyond basic imaging of blood flow or glucose metabolism, to visualize more directly the neural pathology and pathophysiology underlying brain disorders. As for fMRI, particularly active areas of PET research include its use to predict risk of disease development, assist in differential diagnosis, monitor treatment response, or detect biomarkers that may predict likelihood of response to one treatment versus another. In dementia, development of PET tracers for amyloid protein deposition is a major milestone, in that the senile plaques described by Alzheimer a century ago are composed of beta amyloid. PET amyloid imaging using ^{11}C-PIB has been shown to differentiate between healthy elderly individuals and those with MCI or AD, as well as to correlate with memory performance [65–68]

(Fig. 4.3C). Several other PET tracers have been developed for AD pathology as well, including ^{18}F-FDDNP and ^{18}F-AV-45. Various tracers have also been used to demonstrate changes in brain metabolic patterns following drug treatment that correlate with clinical status in AD [69–75]. In healthy participants, PET data suggest that dopamine D2 receptor activity in the hippocampus shows a relationship to cognitive performance in memory and other domains, suggesting a potential target for pharmacological agents to treat memory disorders [76]. Similarly, in chronic TBI Kraus et al. found improvements in executive functions following amantadine treatment that correlated with increased left prefrontal glucose metabolism [77]. Forssberg and colleagues have noted regional abnormalities in dopaminergic function in adolescents with ADHD which correlated with attentional and hyperactivity symptoms, offering a potential method for monitoring treatment response or targeted pharmacotherapeutics [78, 79]. The understanding of the neural basis for efficacy of antipsychotic medications has also been greatly advanced by PET studies demonstrating a relationship between symptomatic improvement and receptor occupancy, which have also pointed toward novel target receptors for drug development to maximize treatment response while minimizing neuroleptic side effects (for review, see [80]). In substance abuse, PET research has furthered the understanding of the neural basis of addiction, again pointing toward possible treatment mechanisms [81, 82].

Integration of structural and functional imaging techniques such as those described above can be a particularly powerful tool for increasing understanding of the neural substrate of brain disorders and potentially identifying biomarkers for disease risk, course, or response to treatment. For example, DTI can be combined with fMRI to relate anatomic connectivity to functional brain activation patterns during cognitive or motor processing and to recovery from brain injury or insult [83, 84]. Image-guided neurorehabilitation is likely to become a major area of research, and ultimately clinical practice, over the next decade. The integration of advanced neuroimaging techniques with genetic information, which has come to be known as neuroimaging genomics, is likely to be particularly fruitful in this regard, given the potential to elucidate molecular mechanisms underlying individual differences in cognition, brain injury, and recovery trajectory [85, 86].

Limitations and considerations

Each neuroimaging technique discussed above has advantages and disadvantages with regard to answering a specific research question or appropriateness of use in a particular clinical population or context. Due to the strength of the magnetic field, MRI techniques are not usually appropriate for individuals with ferrous metal or electronic devices in their bodies (e.g. shrapnel, infusion pumps, neurostimulators, pacemakers) due to safety risks. Other common concerns for MRI are factors such as braces or surgical hardware, which may not pose a health risk to the individual but can cause imaging artifacts that result in substandard or unusable imaging data. Concerns with regard to device safety and artifact are increased as the standard moves to higher-field magnets. Medical devices which have been tested and found to be safe on a 1.5 tesla system may have been found to be unsafe or may not have been tested at 3.0 tesla or higher. Particular MR pulse sequences are also more likely to cause heating (increasing potential risk) or be more vulnerable to artifact than others. Unfortunately, pulse sequences such as echoplanar imaging (used for fMRI and DTI) are among those most likely to be affected, limiting the potential use of some advanced MRI techniques in certain individuals. The problem of signal dropout and other susceptibility artifacts in particular brain regions is also a concern for some advanced neuroimaging techniques. In addition, the potential effect of various structural brain abnormalities and participant-related factors (e.g. vascular lesions and related blood flow disruption, tumor mass effect, neurochemical effects of medications or drugs of abuse) on brain anatomy, function, and activation patterns is of critical importance in evaluation of functional neuroimaging data.

In addition to limitations of the technology involved, patient factors are a critical consideration in neuroimaging. Individuals prone to claustrophobia or panic attacks may not be able to tolerate the MRI scanner environment. While for clinical purposes this difficulty can be overcome to some degree by "open" magnets, such scanner designs are generally inadequate at present for producing high-quality images of the brain for preoperative mapping or clinical research. Similarly, while sedative agents can be used to help patients tolerate the scanner for structural series, such medications can affect CBF and BOLD activity, and are likely to hamper the ability of the participant to complete fMRI tasks or diminish the

Table 4.1. Selected resources for neuroimaging clinical practice guidelines.

Professional organization	Guideline description	Weblink (as of September 24, 2009)
American Academy of Child and Adolescent Psychiatry	Practice parameters	http://www.aacap.org/cs/root/member_information/practice_information/practice_parameters/practice_parameters
American Academy of Family Physicians	Clinical recommendations	http://www.aafp.org/online/en/home/clinical/clinicalrecs.html Search for neuroimaging
	Practice guidelines	http://www.aafp.org/online/en/home/publications/journals/afp.html Search for practice guidelines neuroimaging
American Academy of Neurology	Practice guidelines	http://www.aan.com/go/practice/guidelines
	Practice parameters	http://www.aan.com/go/home Search for practice parameter
American Academy of Pediatrics	Policy statements/Clinical practice guidelines	http://aappolicy.aappublications.org/ Search for neuroimaging
American College of Radiology	Appropriateness criteria for imaging modalities by medical condition	http://www.acr.org/SecondaryMainMenuCategories/quality_safety/app_criteria/pdf/TableofContents.aspx
	Practice guidelines	http://www.acr.org/secondarymainmenucategories/quality_safety/guidelines.aspx
American Psychiatric Association	Practice guidelines	http://www.psych.org/MainMenu/PsychiatricPractice/PracticeGuidelines_1.aspx
American Psychological Association, Division 40 (Clinical Neuropsychology)	Position statement on the role of neuropsychologists in clinical fMRI	http://www.div40.org/Committee_Activities_Pages/Advisory_Committee/Practice/TCN18_3_349_351.pdf
National Guideline Clearinghouse	Department of Health and Human Services resource for evidence-based clinical practice guidelines	http://www.guideline.gov/

activation detected. Individuals who cannot tolerate an MRI scan without these agents are therefore generally not included in research studies, though in some circumstances clinical scans may be attempted with use of anxiolytic medication. While PET does not share the same limitations as MRI in terms of ferromagnetic metal or device restrictions, for some individuals claustrophobia may preclude scanning, though this is typically far less of a problem than for MRI. The exposure to radiation involved in PET can limit its use in nonclinical settings, however. For example, while children and adolescents with cancer or epilepsy may undergo FDG PET as part of their standard clinical care, the potential concerns with regard to unnecessary exposure of the healthy developing body or brain to radiation and attendant assent/consent issues limit the degree to which imaging tools which utilize radiation (CT) or radioactive tracers (PET and SPECT) are used in minors or other vulnerable populations for purely research purposes.

Given these concerns, as well as the likelihood of any specific imaging modality yielding meaningful data relevant to a particular clinical condition, many professional organizations have issued practice recommendations or position papers discussing the appropriateness of particular imaging modalities in specific patient populations, or reviewing recommended professional qualifications for administration and interpretation of neuroimaging techniques (Table 4.1). In addition, insurance companies likewise typically issue policy statements regarding conditions for which particular neuroimaging modalities will and will not be reimbursed (i.e. for which a specific neuroimaging study is deemed "medically necessary").

In addition to general safety and feasibility issues for neuroimaging in any given individual, there are further considerations to be addressed when utilizing advanced neuroimaging techniques with children and adolescents, which tend to be most pronounced at younger ages [87–89]. While vigilance regarding increased motion is important both in clinical populations and in younger participants in general, many groups have found that scanning can be successful with minimal in-scanner head restraints (i.e. only foam padding and/or tape across the forehead) when preceded by adequate preparation, including practicing the fMRI tasks out of the scanner and instruction and discussion of the importance of remaining as still as possible. Use of a mock scanner can also be beneficial, particularly when behavioral training is being implemented to improve the participant's ability to restrict motion [90].

Careful planning is essential for fMRI task design, to create a paradigm which appropriately probes the function(s) of interest while controlling for potential confounds or nuisance factors. The level of developmental functioning and cognitive ability of the patient or target population must be carefully considered, to avoid demonstrating effects due only to task failure rather than true differences in the cognitive process of interest. At times task paradigms must be modified or replaced entirely to examine similar cognitive constructs at different ages or cognitive/functional ability levels. For example, studies of reading and learning disabilities may employ tasks based on an individual's level of reading proficiency. Similarly, an increasing body of research has demonstrated that aspects of executive functioning can be demonstrated even in very young children, yet the behavioral probes required to assess such higher-order abilities differ greatly for children and adults. Studies addressing language-related functions may choose to use auditory tasks in younger children, who may not have adequate reading skills to allow examining the cognitive process of interest using a visual/verbal format. However, for individuals with diminished hearing (e.g. the elderly), scanner noise may interfere with auditory perception of task paradigms, making visual presentation preferable.

Consideration also needs to be given to the choice of statistical thresholds when analyzing functional neuroimaging data across the lifespan, or between clinical populations and healthy comparison samples. Research has suggested that the relative level of brain activation (i.e. of signal to be detected) can differ between children and adults, or between patients and controls, requiring careful consideration of statistical thresholds to be used, depending on the question of interest. For example, much more stringent thresholds may be used in research studies examining between-group differences in larger samples versus smaller case series or when processing individual case data for presurgical mapping. The savvy reader of functional neuroimaging research should also be mindful of other aspects of image acquisition and analysis that have a critical impact on results. For example, studies may report analyses of activation differences only within discrete ROIs, while others assess alterations in activation patterns throughout the brain. Such differences in analytic approach have a pivotal effect on statistical power and the results and conclusions which can be drawn regarding the nature and extent of the neural circuits subserving various cognitive functions.

Finally, as noted above, many neuroimaging studies focus on reporting positive or negative correlations between imaging variables of interest (e.g. regional brain activation or tissue volume) and level of clinical symptomatology, behavioral ratings, cognitive performance, or treatment outcome, particularly as these differ between clinical populations and healthy comparison samples. Much published work, however, does not attempt to explicitly address the degree of shared variance between structural or functional brain changes and these other factors. In addition, particularly for functional neuroimaging studies, sample sizes are often too small to allow meaningful statements about the predictive validity of imaging biomarkers (or vice versa, the degree to which clinical or behavioral variables predict brain differences), though recent trends towards larger-scale and multicenter studies may diminish this concern in the future. It is often the case that neuroimaging data provide complementary rather than redundant information, highlighting the need for studies which evaluate both brain structure and function through multiple modalities (e.g. neuroimaging, emotional/behavioral measures, cognitive testing, genetic assays, physiological monitoring, etc.). At times, neuroimaging results may appear to contradict other data, which may be attributable to the limitations of the particular imaging modality being utilized (e.g. relative temporal or spatial resolution, signal to noise characteristics, etc.), or in some cases the greater sensitivity of imaging to particular types of pathology, especially early in the course of a disorder. Neuroimaging findings will be most clinically meaningful when they can be put to practical use at the individual level; for example, by facilitating accurate diagnosis or predicting response to different treatment options, allowing clinical care to be "personalized".

Integrative and future directions

In addition to examination of specific research questions regarding brain dysfunction in particular clinical populations, the neuroimaging tools discussed above can be used to investigate broader questions of interest with relation to both normal and pathological development and degeneration over the lifespan. For example, functional neuroimaging can be used to illustrate age-related differences in capacity for functional reorganization of the brain in response to injury or disease that have important implications for understanding neural development and plasticity. This can be investigated in developmental animal models (e.g. [91]) as well as human studies. Structural imaging tools can likewise be used to model longitudinal growth and degeneration in different brain regions over time, to further understanding of normal and abnormal brain development, and facilitate understanding of the interaction between brain and cognitive maturation. This has additional importance in the context of the potential influence of developmental and experiential risk factors over the course of the lifespan. For example, the presence of early risk factors for epilepsy can have important implications for seizure and cognitive outcome. Similarly, several medical and lifestyle factors have been shown to affect lifetime risk of the development of AD. Examination of the interaction of these factors with differences in brain structure and function may help us understand the mechanisms of these changes. As research continues to integrate findings related to clinical status, cognitive function, and genetic variability with structural, functional, and molecular neuroimaging data, we will be able to further develop a unified framework for understanding functional brain changes related to development and aging over the course of the lifespan.

Acknowledgements

This work was supported in part by members of the Partnership for Pediatric Epilepsy Research, which includes the American Epilepsy Society, the Epilepsy Foundation, the Epilepsy Project, Fight Against Childhood Epilepsy and Seizures (FACES), and Parents Against Childhood Epilepsy (PACE), as well as by the Indiana Economic Development Corporation (grant #87884), and grants from the National Institute on Aging (P30AG010133 and R01AG019771) and National Cancer Institute (R01CA101318).

References

1. Anbeek P, Vincken KL, van Osch MJP, et al. Automatic segmentation of different-sized white matter lesions by voxel probability estimation. *Med Image Anal* 2004; **8**:205–15.

2. Ashton EA, Takahashi C, Berg MJ, et al. Accuracy and reproducibility of manual and semiautomated quantification of MS lesions by MRI. *J Magn Reson Imaging* 2003;**17**:300–8.

3. Sastre-Garriga J, Ingle GT, Chard DT, et al. Grey and white matter atrophy in early clinical stages of primary progressive multiple sclerosis. *Neuroimage* 2004;**22**: 353–9.

4. Beyer GP, Velthuizen RP, Murtagh FR, et al. Technical aspects and evaluation methodology for the application of two automated brain MRI tumor segmentation methods in radiation therapy planning. *Magn Reson Imaging* 2006;**24**:1167–78.

5. Xie K, Yang J, Zhang ZG, et al. Semi-automated brain tumor and edema segmentation using MRI. *Eur J Radiol* 2005;**56**:12–19.

6. Du AT, Schuff N, Amend D, et al. Magnetic resonance imaging of the entorhinal cortex and hippocampus in mild cognitive impairment and Alzheimer's disease. *J Neurol Neurosurg Psychiatry* 2001;**71**:441–7.

7. Jack CR Jr, Shiung MM, Weigand SD, et al. Brain atrophy rates predict subsequent clinical conversion in normal elderly and amnestic MCI. *Neurology* 2005; **65**:1227–31.

8. Copenhaver BR, Rabin LA, Saykin AJ, et al. The fornix and mammillary bodies in older adults with Alzheimer's disease, mild cognitive impairment, and cognitive complaints: a volumetric MRI study. *Psychiatry Res* 2006;**147**:93–103.

9. Wang PJ, Saykin AJ, Flashman LA, et al. Regionally specific atrophy of the corpus callosum in AD, MCI and cognitive complaints. *Neurobiol Aging* 2006;**27**:1613–17.

10. Baiano M, David A, Versace A, et al. Anterior cingulate volumes in schizophrenia: a systematic review and a meta-analysis of MRI studies. *Schizophr Res* 2007;**93**: 1–12.

11. Bigler ED, Mortensen S, Neeley ES, et al. Superior temporal gyrus, language function, and autism. *Dev Neuropsychol* 2007;**31**:217–38.

12. Cleavinger HB, Bigler ED, Johnson JL, et al. Quantitative magnetic resonance image analysis of the cerebellum in macrocephalic and normocephalic children and adults with autism. *J Int Neuropsychol Soc* 2008;**14**:401–13.

13. Nestor PG, Kubicki M, Kuroki N, et al. Episodic memory and neuroimaging of hippocampus and fornix in chronic schizophrenia. *Psychiatry Res* 2007;**155**:21–8.

14. Shenton ME, Dickey CC, Frumin M, et al. A review of MRI findings in schizophrenia. *Schizophr Res* 2001; **49**:1–52.

15. Mayberg HS, Lozano AM, Voon V, et al. Deep brain stimulation for treatment-resistant depression. *Neuron* 2005;**45**:651–60.

16. Goldapple K, Segal Z, Garson C, et al. Modulation of cortical-limbic pathways in major depression: treatment-specific effects of cognitive behavior therapy. *Arch Gen Psychiatry* 2004;**61**:34–41.

17. Kennedy SH, Evans KR, Kruger S, et al. Changes in regional brain glucose metabolism measured with positron emission tomography after paroxetine treatment of major depression. *Am J Psychiatry* 2001; **158**:899–905.

18. Kennedy SH, Konarski JZ, Segal ZV, et al. Differences in brain glucose metabolism between responders to CBT and venlafaxine in a 16-week randomized controlled trial. *Am J Psychiatry* 2007;**164**:778–88.

19. Masdeu JC, Arbizu J. Brain single photon emission computed tomography: technological aspects and clinical applications. *Semin Neurol* 2008;**28**:423–34.

20. Ashburner J, Friston KJ. Voxel-based morphometry – the methods. *Neuroimage* 2000;**11**:805–21.

21. Ashburner J, Friston KJ. Why voxel-based morphometry should be used. *Neuroimage* 2001;**14**:1238–43.

22. Good CD, Johnsrude IS, Ashburner J, et al. A voxel-based morphometric study of ageing in 465 normal adult human brains. *Neuroimage* 2001;**14**:21–36.

23. Keller SS, Roberts N. Voxel-based morphometry of temporal lobe epilepsy: an introduction and review of the literature. *Epilepsia* 2008;**49**:741–57.

24. Saykin AJ, Wishart HA, Rabin LA, et al. Older adults with cognitive complaints show brain atrophy similar to that of amnestic MCI. *Neurology* 2006;**67**:834–42.

25. Carey ME, Haut MW, Reminger SL, et al. Reduced frontal white matter volume in long-term childhood leukemia survivors: a voxel-based morphometry study. *AJNR Am J Neuroradiol* 2008;**29**:792–7.

26. Le Bihan D, Mangin JF, Poupon C, et al. Diffusion tensor imaging: concepts and applications. *J Magn Reson Imaging* 2001;**13**:534–46.

27. Basser PJ, Mattiello J, Le Bihan D. MR diffusion tensor spectroscopy and imaging. *Biophys J* 1994;**66**: 259–67.

28. Pierpaoli C, Jezzard P, Basser PJ, et al. Diffusion tensor MR imaging of the human brain. *Radiology* 1996;**201**:637–48.

29. Zivadinov R, Cox JL. Neuroimaging in multiple sclerosis. *Int Rev Neurobiol* 2007;**79**:449–74.

30. Neema M, Stankiewicz J, Arora A, et al. T1- and T2-based MRI measures of diffuse gray matter and white matter damage in patients with multiple sclerosis. *J Neuroimaging* 2007;**17**: 16S–21S.

31. Rose SE, Janke AL, Chalk JB. Gray and white matter changes in Alzheimer's disease: A diffusion tensor imaging study. *J Magn Reson Imaging* 2008;**27**:20–6.

32. Olbrich HM, Valerius G, Rusch N, et al. Frontolimbic glutamate alterations in first episode schizophrenia: evidence from a magnetic resonance spectroscopy study. *World J Biol Psychiatry* 2008;**9**:59–63.

33. Simister RJ, McLean MA, Barker GJ, et al. Proton magnetic resonance spectroscopy of malformations of cortical development causing epilepsy. *Epilepsy Res* 2007;**74**:107–15.

34. Marcus KJ, Astrakas LG, Zurakowski D, et al. Predicting survival of children with CNS tumors using proton magnetic resonance spectroscopic imaging biomarkers. *Int J Oncol* 2007;**30**:651–7.

35. Wootton-Gorges SL, Buonocore MH, Kuppermann N, et al. Cerebral proton magnetic resonance spectroscopy in children with diabetic ketoacidosis. *AJNR Am J Neuroradiol* 2007;**28**:895–9.

36. Bizzi A, Blasi V, Falini A, et al. Presurgical functional MR imaging of language and motor functions: validation with intraoperative electrocortical mapping. *Radiology* 2008;**248**:579–89.

37. Petrella JR, Shah LM, Harris KM, et al. Preoperative functional MR imaging localization of language and motor areas: effect on therapeutic decision making in patients with potentially resectable brain tumors. *Radiology* 2006;**240**:793–802.

38. Feigl GC, Safavi-Abbasi S, Gharabaghi A, et al. Real-time 3T fMRI data of brain tumour patients for intra-operative localization of primary motor areas. *Eur J Surg Oncol* 2008;**34**:708–15.

39. Kesavadas C, Thomas B, Sujesh S, et al. Real-time functional MR imaging (fMRI) for presurgical evaluation of paediatric epilepsy. *Pediatr Radiol* 2007;**37**:964–74.

40. Bobholz JA, Rao SM, Saykin AJ, et al. Clinical use of functional magnetic resonance imaging: reflections on the new CPT codes. *Neuropsychol Rev* 2007;**17**:189–91.

41. McDonald BC, Saykin AJ, Williams JM, et al. fMRI Wada test: prospects for presurgical mapping of language and memory. In Faro SH, Mohamed FB, eds. *Functional MRI: Basic Principles and Clinical Applications*. New York: Springer; 2006: 278–314.

42. McDonald BC, Saykin AJ. Functional magnetic resonance imaging in neurosurgical planning for temporal lobe epilepsy: language, memory, and seizure outcome. In Hillary FG, DeLuca J, eds. *Functional*

Neuroimaging in Clinical Populations. New York: Guilford Press; 2007: 185–218.

43. Devinsky O, Perrine K, Llinas R, et al. Anterior temporal language areas in patients with early onset of temporal lobe epilepsy. *Ann Neurol* 1993;**34**:727–32.

44. Gaillard WD, Berl MM, Moore EN, et al. Atypical language in lesional and nonlesional complex partial epilepsy. *Neurology* 2007;**69**:1761–71.

45. Springer JA, Binder JR, Hammeke TA, et al. Language dominance in neurologically normal and epilepsy subjects: a functional MRI study. *Brain* 1999;**122**: 2033–46.

46. Weber B, Wellmer J, Reuber M, et al. Left hippocampal pathology is associated with atypical language lateralization in patients with focal epilepsy. *Brain* 2006;**129**:346–51.

47. Woermann FG, Jokeit H, Luerding R, et al. Language lateralization by Wada test and fMRI in 100 patients with epilepsy. *Neurology* 2003;**61**:699–701.

48. Bookheimer S. Pre-surgical language mapping with functional magnetic resonance imaging. *Neuropsychol Rev* 2007;**17**:145–55.

49. Frings L, Wagner K, Halsband U, et al. Lateralization of hippocampal activation differs between left and right temporal lobe epilepsy patients and correlates with postsurgical verbal learning decrement. *Epilepsy Res* 2008;**78**:161–70.

50. Janszky J, Jokeit H, Kontopoulou K, et al. Functional MRI predicts memory performance after right mesiotemporal epilepsy surgery. *Epilepsia* 2005;**46**: 244–50.

51. Rabin ML, Narayan VM, Kimberg DY, et al. Functional MRI predicts post-surgical memory following temporal lobectomy. *Brain* 2004;**127**:2286–98.

52. Richardson MP, Strange BA, Thompson PJ, et al. Pre-operative verbal memory fMRI predicts post-operative memory decline after left temporal lobe resection. *Brain* 2004;**127**:2419–26.

53. Richardson MP, Strange BA, Duncan JS, et al. Memory fMRI in left hippocampal sclerosis: optimizing the approach to predicting postsurgical memory. *Neurology* 2006;**66**:699–705.

54. McAllister TW, Flashman LA, McDonald BC, et al. Mechanisms of working memory dysfunction after mild and moderate TBI: evidence from functional MRI and neurogenetics. *J Neurotrauma* 2006;**23**:1450–67.

55. Bryant RA, Felmingham K, Kemp A, et al. Amygdala and ventral anterior cingulate activation predicts treatment response to cognitive behaviour therapy for post-traumatic stress disorder. *Psychol Med* 2008;**38**:555–61.

56. Saykin AJ, Wishart HA, Rabin LA, et al. Cholinergic enhancement of frontal lobe activity in mild cognitive impairment. *Brain* 2004;**127**:1574–83.

57. Wolf RL, Detre JA. Clinical neuroimaging using arterial spin-labeled perfusion magnetic resonance imaging. *Neurotherapeutics* 2007;**4**:346–59.

58. Fernandez-Seara MA, Wang J, Wang Z, et al. Imaging mesial temporal lobe activation during scene encoding: comparison of fMRI using BOLD and arterial spin labeling. *Hum Brain Mapp* 2007;**28**:1391–400.

59. Chakravarti S, Srivastava S, Mittnacht AJC. Near infrared spectroscopy (NIRS) in children. *Semin Cardiothorac Vasc Anesth* 2008;**12**:70–9.

60. Hoshi Y. Functional near-infrared spectroscopy: potential and limitations in neuroimaging studies. *Int Rev Neurobiol* 2005;**66**:237–66.

61. Minagawa-Kawai Y, Mori K, Hebden JC, et al. Optical imaging of infants' neurocognitive development: recent advances and perspectives. *Dev Neurobiol* 2008;**68**:712–28.

62. Hebden JC, Austin T. Optical tomography of the neonatal brain. *Eur Radiol* 2007;**17**:2926–33.

63. Wolfberg AJ, du Plessis AJ. Near-infrared spectroscopy in the fetus and neonate. *Clin Perinatol* 2006;**33**: 707–28.

64. Heiss W-D, Herholz K. Brain receptor imaging. *J Nucl Med* 2006;**47**:302–12.

65. Forsberg A, Engler H, Almkvist O, et al. PET imaging of amyloid deposition in patients with mild cognitive impairment. *Neurobiol Aging* 2008;**29**:1456–65.

66. Jack CR Jr, Lowe VJ, Senjem ML, et al. 11C PiB and structural MRI provide complementary information in imaging of Alzheimer's disease and amnestic mild cognitive impairment. *Brain* 2008;**131**:665–80.

67. Kemppainen NM, Aalto S, Wilson IA, et al. PET amyloid ligand [11C] PIB uptake is increased in mild cognitive impairment. *Neurology* 2007;**68**:1603–6.

68. Pike KE, Savage G, Villemagne VL, et al. Beta-amyloid imaging and memory in non-demented individuals: evidence for preclinical Alzheimer's disease. *Brain* 2007;**130**:2837–44.

69. Kadir A, Andreasen N, Almkvist O, et al. Effect of phenserine treatment on brain functional activity and amyloid in Alzheimer's disease. *Ann Neurol* 2008;**63**:621–31.

70. Kadir A, Darreh-Shori T, Almkvist O, et al. PET imaging of the in vivo brain acetylcholinesterase activity and nicotine binding in galantamine-treated patients with AD. *Neurobiol Aging* 2008;**29**:1204–17.

71. Mega MS, Dinov ID, Porter V, et al. Metabolic patterns associated with the clinical response to galantamine

therapy: a fludeoxyglucose f 18 positron emission tomographic study. *Arch Neurol* 2005;**62**:721–8.

72. Potkin SG, Anand R, Fleming K, et al. Brain metabolic and clinical effects of rivastigmine in Alzheimer's disease. *Int J Neuropsychopharmacol* 2001;**4**:223–30.

73. Stefanova E, Wall A, Almkvist O, et al. Longitudinal PET evaluation of cerebral glucose metabolism in rivastigmine treated patients with mild Alzheimer's disease. *J Neural Transm* 2006;**113**:205–18.

74. Tune L, Tiseo PJ, Ieni J, et al. Donepezil HCl (E2020) maintains functional brain activity in patients with Alzheimer disease: results of a 24-week, double-blind, placebo-controlled study. *Am J Geriatric Psychiatry* 2003;**11**:169–77.

75. Volkow ND, Ding YS, Fowler JS, et al. Imaging brain cholinergic activity with positron emission tomography: its role in the evaluation of cholinergic treatments in Alzheimer's dementia. *Biol Psychiatry* 2001;**49**:211–20.

76. Takahashi H, Kato M, Hayashi M, et al. Memory and frontal lobe functions; possible relations with dopamine D2 receptors in the hippocampus. *Neuroimage* 2007;**34**:1643–9.

77. Kraus MF, Smith GS, Butters M, et al. Effects of the dopaminergic agent and NMDA receptor antagonist amantadine on cognitive function, cerebral glucose metabolism and D2 receptor availability in chronic traumatic brain injury: a study using positron emission tomography (PET). *Brain Inj* 2005;**19**:471–9.

78. Forssberg H, Fernell E, Waters S, et al. Altered pattern of brain dopamine synthesis in male adolescents with attention deficit hyperactivity disorder. *Behav Brain Funct* 2006;**2**:40.

79. Jucaite A, Fernell E, Halldin C, et al. Reduced midbrain dopamine transporter binding in male adolescents with attention-deficit/hyperactivity disorder: association between striatal dopamine markers and motor hyperactivity. *Biol Psychiatry* 2005;**57**:229–38.

80. McGuire P, Howes OD, Stone J, et al. Functional neuroimaging in schizophrenia: diagnosis and drug discovery. *Trends Pharmacol Sci* 2008;**29**:91–8.

81. Fowler JS, Volkow ND, Kassed CA, et al. Imaging the addicted human brain. *Sci Pract Perspect* 2007;**3**:4–16.

82. Volkow ND, Fowler JS, Wang G-J, et al. Dopamine in drug abuse and addiction: results of imaging studies and treatment implications. *Arch Neurol* 2007;**64**:1575–9.

83. Werring DJ, Clark CA, Barker GJ, et al. The structural and functional mechanisms of motor recovery: complementary use of diffusion tensor and functional magnetic resonance imaging in a traumatic injury of the internal capsule. *J Neurol Neurosurg Psychiatry* 1998;**65**:863–9.

84. Werring DJ, Clark CA, Parker GJ, et al. A direct demonstration of both structure and function in the visual system: combining diffusion tensor imaging with functional magnetic resonance imaging. *Neuroimage* 1999;**9**:352–61.

85. Hariri AR, Weinberger DR. Imaging genomics. *Br Med Bull* 2003;**65**:259–70.

86. Viding E, Williamson DE, Hariri AR. Developmental imaging genetics: challenges and promises for translational research. *Dev Psychopathol* 2006;**18**:877–92.

87. Bookheimer SY, Dapretto M, Karmarkar U. Functional MRI in children with epilepsy. *Dev Neurosci* 1999;**21**:191–9.

88. Gaillard WD, Grandin CB, Xu B. Developmental aspects of pediatric fMRI: Considerations for image acquisition, analysis, and interpretation. *Neuroimage* 2001;**13**:239–49.

89. Hertz-Pannier L, Chiron C, Vera P, et al. Functional imaging in the work-up of childhood epilepsy. *Childs Nerv Syst* 2001;**17**:223–8.

90. Slifer KJ, Koontz KL, Cataldo MF. Operant-contingency-based preparation of children for functional magnetic resonance imaging. *J Appl Behav Anal* 2002;**35**:191–4.

91. Duhaime A-C, Saykin AJ, McDonald BC, et al. Functional magnetic resonance imaging of the primary somatosensory cortex in piglets. *J Neurosurg* 2006;**104**:259–64.

Disorders
Attention deficit hyperactivity disorder in children and adolescents

David Marks, Joey Trampush and Anil Chacko

ADHD Phenomenology

Attention deficit hyperactivity disorder (ADHD) is a complex psychiatric syndrome characterized by developmentally excessive manifestations of inattention, hyperactivity, and impulsivity which have their onset prior to age 7 and are associated with impairments in at least two domains of psychosocial functioning (e.g. scholastic achievement, family interactions, peer relations) [1]. Widely considered to be the most common psychiatric disorder of childhood, ADHD affects approximately 5% of school-aged children worldwide [2], with diagnostic rates in males exceeding those of females by 4:1 in non-referred investigations and 9:1 in clinically referred samples [3].

Comorbidity profiles in children with ADHD

Upwards of two-thirds of children and adolescents with the disorder meet criteria for one or more comorbid psychiatric conditions. In particular, approximately 50–60% meet criteria for oppositional defiant disorder (ODD), 30–50% meet criteria for conduct disorder (CD), 25% meet criteria for one or more anxiety disorders, and 15–25% have a comorbid mood disorder [4]. Relative to same-aged peers, children with ADHD are also at heightened risk for tic disorders, learning disabilities, and substance use disorders [4]. The high prevalence of psychiatric comorbidity among youth with ADHD may reflect common etiological mechanisms and/or temperamental features (e.g. impulsivity), as well as associated psychosocial consequences of the disorder (e.g. demoralization stemming from impaired social functioning). ADHD is also considered a significant risk factor for adverse outcomes during adolescence and adulthood [5]; however, the relative contributions of ADHD vs. psychiatric comorbidity to subsequent outcomes have been difficult to isolate.

Chapter premise and objectives

Since its inception as a diagnostic entity, efforts have been undertaken to identify the underlying etiological mechanisms associated with ADHD, based on the assumption that deficient neuropsychological processes underlie the heterogeneous array of behavioral difficulties associated with the disorder. Although technological and methodological advances have ushered in a flurry of scientific exploration and helped to resolve numerous ambiguities, such investigations have also raised additional questions, and, with a few exceptions, have neglected to approach the search for constituent deficiencies from a developmental perspective.

In the current chapter, specific emphasis has been placed on reviewing: (i) neuropsychological profiles of ADHD in children and adolescents; (ii) the stability of neuropsychological functioning across the aforementioned developmental periods in youth with ADHD (including relationships between the stability of neuropsychological functioning and the continuity/persistence of ADHD symptoms); (iii) potential moderators of neuropsychological functioning; (iv) patterns of structural and functional neuroimaging; and (v) pharmacological, psychosocial, and neurocognitive remediation strategies for children with ADHD.

Neuropsychology of pediatric ADHD across development

Initially conceptualized as a condition largely confined to boys who were hyperactive or hyperkinetic, the role of attentional dysfunction in ADHD was introduced by Douglas in 1972 [6], who examined vigilance deficits in these children. Research characterizing the precise nature of attentional dysfunction, as well as cognitive correlates of hyperactivity and impulsivity, has since increased. Neuropsychological research of ADHD has informed modern clinical practice and contemporary models of underlying pathophysiology, and guided neuroimaging approaches. However, only recently have investigators begun to appreciate the limitations of time-locked snapshots of neuropsychological functioning in ADHD and the importance of developmental factors (e.g. age, symptom stability, environmental changes) that have the potential to confound concurrent estimates of neurocognitive dysfunction in youth with ADHD. As such, current knowledge about the developmental trajectory of neurocognitive dysfunction in ADHD largely comes from *cross-sectional* interpretations of a vast literature, which are highlighted in the forthcoming sections.

Neuropsychological characterization of ADHD

Neuropsychological research studies of pediatric ADHD frequently dichotomize cognitive performance into "higher-order executive functions" and "lower-order non-executive functions". Other terms used to describe this dichotomy include "top-down" vs. "bottom-up", and "effortful" vs. "automatic". Higher-order executive functions broadly encompass attentional control, working memory, response inhibition, cognitive flexibility, planning, organization, and set-shifting. In contrast, lower-order functions include state regulation, activation/arousal, processing speed, and basic language processing, as well as long-term memory and basic sensory and motor functions. As detailed below, recent findings have cast doubt on whether ADHD constitutes a pure disorder of executive function given that many children with ADHD perform poorly on both higher-order and lower-order measures [7].

Neuropsychological profiles of preschool children with ADHD

Despite the fact that the symptoms of ADHD frequently have their onset during the preschool period [8], the preponderance of studies examining neuropsychological correlates of ADHD have been conducted using school-age children. The limited literature examining preschoolers with ADHD has yielded inconsistent results regarding the presence of neurocognitive impairments. Sonuga-Barke et al. examined planning, working memory, and inhibition in preschoolers with and without high ADHD symptom counts and found that only inhibition was associated with ADHD symptoms [9]. In a later study, these investigators observed that, while both executive dysfunction (working memory, set shifting, planning) and delay aversion (reward sensitivity) factors made significant and independent contributions to predictions of ADHD symptoms, only the executive dysfunction factor correlated significantly with age, suggesting that, while executive dysfunction may emerge

during early childhood, delay aversion may be more developmentally independent [10]. Others have found preschoolers with ADHD to perform more poorly than controls on tests of vigilance, motor control, and working memory [11], as well as measures of early academic skills [12].

More recently, investigators have suggested that lower-order regulatory deficits are most prominent during the preschool period. For example, Marks et al. demonstrated that, despite overall weaker performance of preschoolers at risk for ADHD on measures of working memory and inhibitory control, such weaknesses could not be attributed to executive function impairments after accounting for groupwise disparities in lower-level processes [13]. Similarly, Berwid and colleagues showed that at-risk preschoolers do not exhibit specific deficits in either inhibitory control or sustained attention; rather, the most consistent effect related to risk status across tasks was the greater number of errors, and longer, more variable reaction times of at-risk preschoolers [14]. These findings suggest that ADHD-associated decrements in performance on executive function tasks in preschool children are probably related to state regulatory impairments rather than insufficiently developed executive function systems.

Neuropsychological profiles of school-age children with ADHD

Relative to their typically developing counterparts, school-age ADHD cohorts have been shown to exhibit weaknesses on higher-order executive measures as well as lower-order, nonexecutive indices, with effect sizes generally falling within the moderate range [15]. In a recent meta-analysis of 123 studies, ADHD probands scored significantly lower than controls on measures of general intellectual functioning and academic achievement, as well as on an array of executive and non-executive indices [16]. Among youth with ADHD, effect sizes for FSIQ were larger than those for several executive function measures, while effect sizes for measures of academic achievement and computerized indices of vigilance were significantly larger than those for FSIQ.

A number of other meta-analyses have examined specific neuropsychological domains and measures relevant to pediatric ADHD. For example, a meta-analysis of working memory performance revealed strong effects for *spatial* storage and central executive domains and relatively weaker effects for *verbal* storage and central executive measures [17]. Recently, several meta-analyses have reviewed the literature on interference control in ADHD, as assessed via the Stroop Color-Word Test [e.g. 16, 18–20]. Some have reported minimal interference effects across different developmental periods [18, 20] while others have shown more pronounced interference deficits in ADHD [16, 19]. In addition, two recent meta-analyses applied to the Stop-Signal Task as an index of response inhibition found that children with ADHD exhibited slower and more variable reaction times to primary task stimuli (i.e. go-stimuli), as well as slower Stop-Signal reaction times; effects sizes of moderate strength were observed across analyses [21, 22]. Finally, in a review of 18 studies of Continuous Performance Tests (CPTs) in both children and adults with ADHD, 16 found significantly greater RT variability (RTSD) in patients with ADHD compared to controls [23], a pattern that was not attributable to overall slower or faster responding. Across virtually all of the above studies, measures of RTSD yielded among the strongest effect sizes [23].

Neuropsychological profiles of adolescents with ADHD

Relative to the plethora of neuropsychological research in school-age children with ADHD, comparatively little research has examined neuropsychological profiles of adolescents with the disorder. Small to moderate executive function weaknesses have been reported in this age group and have been linked to symptoms of inattention but not hyperactivity-impulsivity [24]. Recent findings from a large Finnish cohort indicated that adolescents with ADHD performed more poorly on measures of reading fluency, working memory, inhibition, response variability, and set-shifting relative to those with subthreshold ADHD and typically developing controls [25]. Approximately half of the ADHD cohort was classified as having a categorically derived executive function deficit relative to 29% of the subthreshold ADHD group and 10% of the control group [25].

Potential moderators of group differences in neuropsychological functioning

Attempting to reconcile disparities across studies, several investigators have looked to potential moderators of group differences in studies completed to date. Beyond differences in age, inclusion/exclusion criteria, comorbidity, treatment status, etc., one such factor has involved the practice of statistical covariance for overall IQ. This issue has been somewhat controversial, with some investigators arguing that removing the

effect of IQ is necessary to isolate groupwise EF discrepancies [26] and others [27] suggesting that doing so may obfuscate any detectable EF disparities. Ultimately, reconciliation of such issues (e.g. reporting findings with and without IQ covariation) will be critical for leveling the interpretive playing field across investigations.

Stability of neuropsychological functions across development

Although some symptoms of ADHD typically diminish with age [28], limited data exist regarding the stability of neuropsychological functioning over development and the extent to which neuropsychological functions covary with or predict symptom stability over time. In light of the fact that such issues are addressed in Chapter 5b by Semrud-Clikeman and Fine, we provide only a cursory discussion below.

Neuropsychological stability relative to symptom stability

To date, few studies have investigated the extent to which neuropsychological functioning has paralleled ADHD symptom stability or remission over development. Such analyses are critical to understanding the centrality (or lack thereof) of neuropsychological dysfunction to ADHD. Kalff et al. examined the neurocognitive profiles of 5- and 6-year-old children who were diagnosed as either having ADHD or subthreshold ADHD 18 months later, as well as typically developing children without ADHD symptoms [29]. Poorer performance on measures of visuomotor integration, verbal working memory, and visual attention at baseline were predictive of ADHD 18 months later. Further, the performance of subthreshold ADHD children 18 months prior generally fell between that of ADHD children and controls [29].

Recently, our group found that executive and nonexecutive skills correlated with the presence or absence of childhood ADHD at early adult follow-up [30]. Specifically, when divided into subgroups of ADHD persisters and remitters, performance on putative measures of executive or effortful processes closely paralleled adolescent/young adult clinical status, with remitters performing more similarly to controls than persisters. In contrast, measures of less effortful, bottom-up, processes generally differentiated those with childhood ADHD from controls irrespective of adolescent/young adult clinical status. Overall, elements of the neurocognitive profile of ADHD (e.g. lower-order processes) appear to reflect stable traits that heighten diagnostic liability, while others (e.g. higher-order executive processes) may constitute state-like and/or compensatory epiphenomena.

Diagnostic utility of neuropsychological measures

Although clearly beneficial for elucidating neurocognitive substrates, approximately 50% of pediatric ADHD cohorts perform in the "normal" range on any given neurocognitive measure, suggesting poor sensitivity [31]. Further, the absence of an "impaired" score on neuropsychological tasks seldom rules out the presence of ADHD, contributing to reduced specificity [31]. Despite these limitations, neuropsychological assessment in pediatric ADHD remains important, particularly with respect to issues of differential diagnosis and/or psychiatric comorbidity (e.g. learning disabilities, language and/or pervasive developmental disorders), identification of individual learning styles (e.g. reconciliation of speed vs. accuracy), and establishment of home- and/or school-based interventions

Etiological mechanisms in ADHD

Data from numerous studies indicate that both genetic and environmental factors interact to produce the diverse constellation of behavioral characteristics that define ADHD. However, results from family, twin, and adoption studies have shown that ADHD tends to cluster in families and that genetic factors alone reportedly explain up to 80% of the variance in the ADHD phenotype [32]. Beyond general heritability, molecular genetic studies have focused primarily on genetic alterations that may interfere with proper functioning of brain catecholamines dopamine and norepinephrine. Dopamine and norepinephrine neurons are functionally expressed in many interconnected brain pathways involved in top-down (e.g. prefrontal cortex) and bottom-up (e.g. locus coeruleus) cognitive control, respectively. Further, the majority of effective pharmacological treatments for ADHD (e.g. stimulants and nonstimulants) interact with dopamine and norepinephrine systems to dramatically improve the core symptoms of inattention and hyperactivity/impulsivity. Indeed, association (i.e. case-control analysis) and linkage (i.e. family pedigree analysis) approaches have shown that polymorphisms in a variety of dopaminergic and noradrenergic genes are preferentially associated with ADHD. For example, a recent meta-analysis of molecular genetic studies of ADHD identified four dopamine genes as being significantly associated with ADHD [32]. A more recent large-scale study examining children with ADHD Combined Type and their affected siblings confirmed the association of several dopamine-related genes to ADHD [33].

An emerging line of research involves the study of molecular genetic influences on neuropsychological functioning in ADHD. For instance, Swanson and colleagues demonstrated that, contrary to expectations, the absence of the 7-repeat allele of the dopamine D4 receptor (DRD4–7R) in ADHD children was associated with impaired performance on measures of attention and inhibitory control; those with the DRD4–7R allele performed similarly to controls [34]. Thus, genetic factors, particularly those associated with both normal cognitive functions and ADHD (e.g. dopaminergic and noradrenergic system genes), may help identify subgroups of ADHD children with a partial syndrome characterized by behavioral excesses without neurocognitive deficits.

Neuroimaging in pediatric ADHD

Prior to the availability of modern imaging data, frontal lobe dysfunction was presumed to be the neural substrate for ADHD based on the resemblance between patients with frontal lobe lesions and the ADHD phenotype (e.g. poor impulse control and inattention). While neuroimaging research has supported frontal lobe pathology in ADHD, support has also been provided for diffuse and dynamic neurologic dysfunction.

Structural magnetic resonance imaging

Cerebral cortex

Studies conducted to date have demonstrated overall reductions in total cortical volume in children with ADHD relative to age- and sex-matched controls through age 19 by approximately 3% overall and 3–5% in the right hemisphere [35]. Abnormal morphology (bilateral volumetric *reduction*) has been documented in virtually all areas of the frontal cortex. In contrast, prominent *increases* in grey matter have been reported in the posterior temporal and inferior parietal cortices bilaterally in ADHD [36]. In limbic regions, larger bilateral hippocampus as well as reduced bilateral amygdala over the area of the basolateral complex have been reported in ADHD [37].

Basal Ganglia

The basal ganglia have been implicated in the pathophysiology of ADHD due to their input-output role as a mediator of frontal-subcortical communication and catecholamine modulation of motor and cognitive functions. Subtle caudate nucleus volume and symmetry differences have been reported in ADHD in childhood; however, caudate normalization in ADHD typically occurs by adolescence [38].

Corpus callosum

The corpus callosum is the largest interhemispheric commissure connecting the right and left cerebral hemispheres, and reductions in size may lead to a decrease in the amount of fibers that normally traverse the hemispheres. Reduced area of the corpus callosum in ADHD has been reported in the anterior (rostrum, genu, rostral body) and posterior (splenium) portions (see [35] for review). In contrast, a comparison of the corpus callosum of children diagnosed with ADHD to that of their non-affected siblings demonstrated no differences in corpus callosum morphometry between the two groups, either in local anatomy or total structure, suggesting corpus callosum abnormalities may be more environmentally sensitive than genetically mediated in ADHD [39].

Cerebellum

Differentiation in cerebellar morphometry between children with ADHD and typically developing controls is arguably among the most consistent structural imaging finding to date [35]. An early quantitative examination of the cerebellum in general and the cerebellar vermis in particular reported that overall volumes were significantly reduced in boys with ADHD [40]. The decrease was localized to the posterior-inferior lobule, but not to the posterior-superior lobule, and remained significant after adjusting for total cerebral volume and IQ.

Functional magnetic resonance imaging

Functional MRI studies have consistently implicated connectivity among the prefrontal cortex, basal ganglia, thalamus, and cerebellum in the pathophysiology of pediatric ADHD. Yet specific neural substrates have not been identified, as both hypoactivation and hyperactivation within this connectivity have been observed.

Prefrontal-subcortical connectivity

A series of studies have examined response inhibition in ADHD with mixed results. Schulz et al. prospectively examined response inhibition in adolescents diagnosed with ADHD during childhood compared to adolescents with no history of ADHD [41]. Adolescents with childhood ADHD exhibited markedly greater activation of frontal regions, while controls activated a distinct neural network including temporal, cerebellar, and hippocampal regions. Activation of the anterior cingulate gyrus was inversely related to performance, with greater activation in individuals who had more difficulty inhibiting the prepotent response [41]. Rubia et al. examined inhibition and error-processing in adolescents with ADHD and controls [42]. In controls, successful inhibition was characterized by increased neural activation in a fronto-cerebellar network, while adolescents with ADHD showed no significant activations within this network. Activation patterns during error-processing were similar in ADHD and control adolescents overall; however, controls showed significantly increased activation of the posterior cingulate and precuneus relative to ADHD participants [42]. Finally, recent work by Durston and colleagues [43] has suggested that inhibitory deficits in ADHD appear to be genetically mediated and may involve compromised activation of the inferior frontal gyrus and anterior cingulate gyrus.

To help better determine whether hypo- or hyperactivation is more indicative of ADHD, Dickstein et al. employed the recently developed activation likelihood estimation (ALE) technique to carry out a quantitative meta-analysis of published fMRI studies of ADHD [44]. When the individual ALE maps for the two groups (ADHD and controls) were compared statistically, controls demonstrated significantly greater probability of activation in a variety of regions relative to individuals with ADHD, including the left ventral and dorsolateral prefrontal cortex, anterior cingulate cortex, bilateral parietal lobe, right thalamus, left middle occipital gyrus, and an area centered at the right claustrum extending from insula to the striatum. In contrast, greater probability of activation in ADHD vs. controls included the left frontal lobe, insular cortex and portions of middle frontal gyrus, left thalamus and the right paracentral lobule.

Developing vs. mature neural systems

Recent longitudinal MRI studies have demonstrated substantial neuroanatomic differences in pediatric ADHD that fluctuate dynamically. The first study to examine neural changes over time followed a large sample of individuals with ADHD and age-matched healthy controls (age range 4.5–19 years) using a mixture of longitudinal and cross-sectional MRI analytical methods [38].

At baseline, healthy controls had significantly greater total cerebral volume than ADHD patients, as well as larger frontal grey and white matter. However, after adjustment for total cerebral volume, no significant difference in frontal volume remained between the two groups. Further, analysis of a subset of follow-up scans 2–3 years later demonstrated no disparity in frontal morphometry in ADHD; rather, the frontal lobes had the smallest effect sizes of any anatomical region. Baseline differences in cerebellar volume persisted, with a non-significant tendency for this difference to increase over time [38]. Longitudinal cerebellar growth has been linked recently to different clinical outcomes in ADHD: the growth trajectory of total cerebellar volume in children with ADHD with better clinical outcomes parallels that of normally developing controls, whereas cerebellar growth in those with poorer outcomes is characterized by a progressive decrease in total cerebellar volume that falls further away from the normal trajectory over time [45].

Automated measures of cortical thickness across the entire cortex have recently demonstrated an association between rates of cortical thinning and symptom improvement in ADHD [46]. As a group, children with ADHD had significantly reduced cortical thickness; however, such observations were most prominent in prefrontal and anterior temporal regions. On baseline scans examined retrospectively, ADHD probands with poor clinical outcomes displayed relative thinning in medial and superior prefrontal regions and cingulate cortex bilaterally relative to those with better clinical outcomes, even after adjustment for IQ and overall cortical thickness. Probands with favorable outcomes differed minimally in cortical thickness from controls except for a small region of thinning in the left dorsolateral PFC, and showed normalization of right parietal cortical thickness over time.

Most recently, work by Shaw and colleagues has suggested that ADHD is characterized by a delay rather than deficiency in regional cortical maturation [47]. Cortical maturation progressed in a similar manner regionally in both children with and those without ADHD, with primary sensory areas attaining peak cortical thickness before higher-order association areas. However, there was a marked delay in attaining peak thickness throughout most of the cortex in ADHD: the median age by which 50% of the cortical points attained peak thickness for this group was 10.5 years, which was significantly later than the median age of 7.5 years for typically developing controls. The delay was most prominent in the lateral prefrontal cortex and in the posterior portions of the middle/superior temporal gyrus bilaterally [47].

Evidence-based interventions

The following section is devoted to a discussion of what is considered to be the two most empirically well-supported interventions to date: behavioral interventions and psychopharmacological treatment. In addition, we will also briefly review two large-scale intervention studies for ADHD – the Multimodal Treatment of ADHD (MTA) Study as well as the Preschool ADHD Treatment Study (PATS) – that have been instrumental in developing practice guidelines for the treatment of ADHD in youth.

Behavioral interventions

Behavioral parent training

Behavioral parent training (BPT) has been a well-studied intervention for various childhood mental health disorders including ADHD [48]. BPT is a treatment approach wherein parents are taught how to manipulate antecedents (e.g. rules, commands) and consequences (e.g. rewards, time out) of their child's behavior (e.g. aggression, noncompliance) in order to improve behavior. Although effects of BPT on core ADHD symptoms have been reported [49], it appears that the primary evidence for BPT as an intervention for ADHD is founded on the effects of BPT on co-occurring oppositional problems and impairment in children versus improvements in the core symptoms of ADHD per se [50]. Given that children with ADHD often present with comorbid ODD, the effect of BPT on ODD is noteworthy. Lastly, BPT for families of children with ADHD has also demonstrated improvements in parental functioning [49]. Thus, the evidence for BPT for ADHD suggests that BPT improves co-occurring oppositional/defiant behavior, impairment, parental functioning, and, to a lesser extent, core ADHD symptoms. Collectively, the evidence is substantial that BPT improves the functioning of children with ADHD and their families; however, further empirical investigation is necessary to determine for whom BPT works best as well as how best to maximize BPT for traditionally difficult-to-engage and difficult-to-treat ADHD populations [48].

Classroom behavior management

Given the notable difficulties that children with ADHD have within the school setting, it is not surprising that a primary emphasis for treatment is to target classroom behavior and academic productivity. In fact, interventions implemented in the classroom, primarily in the form of behavioral interventions, have been studied to a greater extent relative to other psychosocial interventions for ADHD, including BPT [51]. Classroom behavior management often takes the form of psychoeducation and direct consultation with the teacher to better understand and manage the child's difficulties across academic, peer, and teacher–child contexts. This often requires educating/instructing the teacher on the appropriate application of praise, planned ignoring, effective commands, classroom rules, use of contingent rewards/reinforcers, time-out from positive reinforcement, and the use of a daily report card. Studies on classroom behavioral interventions for ADHD demonstrate that this form of intervention is highly effective, with significant effects on direct observation and teacher ratings of child behavior in the classroom [3]. Effect size data from one meta-analysis of classroom behavior management for ADHD reported a mean effect size of 0.60 for between-subject designs, approximately 1.00 for within-subject designs, and approximately 1.40 for single-case designs [52]. Clearly, classroom behavior management procedures result in substantial improvements in the behavior of children with ADHD. Although meta-analyses indicate the benefits of academically focused interventions for ADHD [52], these are relatively few compared to studies focusing on behavior management in the classroom. Next-generation studies should further explore the specific effects of academic interventions on academic outcomes in children with ADHD and how best to combine behavior management and academic interventions in the classroom for youth with ADHD.

Summer Treatment Program

The Summer Treatment Program (STP) for children with ADHD is an intensive psychosocial program that seamlessly integrates multiple evidence-based treatment components for school-age children, including BPT, praise, effective commands, point systems, time-out, daily report cards, social skills training, and problem-solving training (see ref. 53 for details). Children are grouped according to developmental level and spend the entire day together with highly trained and supervised counselors and an experienced lead counselor. This offers children the opportunity to learn how to develop appropriate social skills, problem-solving skills, and peer relationships under the support and encouragement of their counselors. Over the past decade, the effectiveness of the STP has been evaluated in large between-group [54], large crossover [55] and several single-subject designs [56], indicating the acute benefits of the STP

for youth with ADHD. It is clear that intensive interventions, such as the STP, are an important aspect of comprehensive care for youth with ADHD; however, data are sorely needed regarding the longer-term benefits of this intensive intervention when children return to school. How best to maximize and sustain the often dramatic treatment gains found in the STP to post-STP settings remains an essential empirical question.

Pharmacological interventions

Stimulant medications are the first-line pharmacological intervention for ADHD [57] and include short- and long-acting preparations of methylphenidate and amphetamine salts. The literature on stimulant medication for ADHD has demonstrated acute benefits on multiple behavioral outcomes (see ref. 58 for reviews), including improvements in core symptoms of ADHD, compliance, aggression, and academic productivity. Although a dose-dependent response to stimulant medication has been cited in the literature [59], such increases may also be accompanied by the emergence and/or exacerbation of adverse events. In addition, several studies have noted that the dose of stimulant medication can be reduced substantially if a combined approach is taken whereby both stimulant medication and behavioral interventions are in place [60]. The opposite is also true; that is, the intensity of behavioral interventions can be substantially reduced if concurrent stimulant medication is provided. Given the noted side effects associated with stimulant medication and that many parents prefer nonpharmacological approaches to treating ADHD [61], the use of behavioral interventions alone or at least in combination with stimulant medication may be a more palatable treatment regimen for most families. Within the past several years, nonstimulant alternatives (e.g. atomoxetine) have come to market and may constitute a viable option for individuals for whom stimulants are either ineffective or poorly tolerated. Given that as many as 30% of youth do not respond to or have an adverse response to stimulant medication [62], the development of alternative pharmacological interventions is clearly necessary.

Key clinical trials

Multimodal Treatment Study of Children with ADHD (MTA)

The MTA Study constitutes the largest clinical trial of a childhood mental health disorder funded by the NIMH to date and included 579 children between the ages of 7 and 9 who were diagnosed with ADHD, Combined type [63]. The study was developed to compare the most evidence-based interventions for ADHD on multiple outcomes over a 14-month period and to gauge the extent to which the intensive interventions provided through the study fared better than treatments received in the community. Children were randomized to one of four treatment conditions: (1) behavioral treatment (BPT, STP, classroom behavior management); (2) medication management (primarily stimulant medication); (3) combined behavioral and medication management; or (4) a community comparison condition. The immediate 14-month post-treatment data indicated that medication management alone was as effective as the combined treatment condition in reducing ADHD symptoms, suggesting that there was no incremental benefit of behavioral interventions [64]. However, compared to the medication management condition, the combined treatment condition resulted in greater improvement in key domains of functioning, including children's social skills and parent–child relationships [65]. Moreover, normalization of functioning was more likely to occur from participation in the combined treatment condition [66]. Although many accolades have been showered upon the MTA study, and practice guidelines have been guided by its outcomes, data regarding normalization of functioning in key domains over the long term have been sobering. Swanson and colleagues found that between 32 and 64% of children continued to exhibit clinically significant levels of ADHD despite the intensive MTA stimulant medication and behavioral treatment regimens [67]. Moreover, children continued to have significant difficulties in peer relationships – a key domain of functioning related to children's long-term positive outcomes [68]. It therefore appears that while stimulant medication and/or behavioral interventions appear to help to reduce the breadth and severity of ADHD symptoms, many remain deviant relative to their peers in key areas of functioning.

Preschool ADHD Treatment Study (PATS)

Despite the fact that symptoms of ADHD typically have their onset during the preschool period [8] there has been a relative dearth of studies examining the efficacy and safety of stimulant medication in young children. Although several investigations have highlighted the potential benefits of stimulant treatment for young children with ADHD (e.g. ref. 60), it was clear that a large, representative stimulant medication trial of preschool children with ADHD using well-validated and broad-based measures assessing multiple outcomes, including

safety and tolerability, was needed. The Preschool ADHD Treatment Study (PATS; see ref. 69) was conducted as a 6-site, 8-phase, 70-week clinical trial of stimulant medication for preschool-aged children with ADHD. An initial, intense screening phase followed by a 10-week BPT program was conducted to exclude children who responded well to the psychosocial intervention from the subsequent pharmacological trial, thereby retaining more severe ADHD cases. Following this, an open-label safety lead-in was conducted to determine whether children could tolerate the doses of stimulant medication that were to be used in the study (i.e. 1.25 mg TID, 2.5 mg TID, 5 mg TID, and 7.5 mg TID). This was followed by a 5-week, double-blind, placebo-controlled, crossover titration to determine optimal dosing and then a 4-week, double-blind, placebo-controlled parallel study of best-dose or placebo. The last two phases of the study involved an open-label maintenance phase and a discontinuation phase to determine safety and relative long-term effectiveness of stimulant medication. Results indicated that all but the smallest dose was effective in reducing ADHD symptoms [70]; however, even the lowest dose was effective in improving functioning in some settings (i.e. classroom). Similar to other studies, there were notable increases in side effects (e.g. emotional lability), particularly at higher dosages. Compared to school-age children enrolled in the MTA Study, effect size data were smaller for preschool-age children enrolled in the PATS study, indicating that stimulant medication may be less effective for younger children. Moreover, the fact that stimulant medication did not normalize ADHD symptoms in a majority of children suggests that alternative and adjunctive interventions may be necessary to maximize outcomes for preschoolers with more severe manifestations of ADHD.

Cognitive remediation strategies for children with ADHD

Although both pharmacological and psychosocial interventions provide acute benefits with respect to symptom reduction and impairment (e.g. parent–child relationships), these interventions seldom result in sustained benefits once the intervention has been discontinued [48] nor do they yield long-term improvements in psychosocial functioning [71]. Limitations of these "evidence-based" interventions have consequently spurred the development of alternative interventions for ADHD, particularly those that target either attention [72, 73] or working memory [74, 75].

Remediation of attentional functioning

Two studies have been conducted that focus on improving attention in children with ADHD through intensive, targeted attention-focused training programs. Kerns et al. [72] evaluated the program, Pay Attention!, which includes materials designed to enhance sustained, selective, alternating, and divided attention through both visual and auditory activities. Results indicated that, compared to those who were engaged in computer-based activities (e.g. games and puzzles), ADHD probands who participated in Pay Attention! improved their performance on several neurocognitive tests as well as measures of academic achievement. Parent reports of ADHD symptoms did not improve as a function of treatment; however, a trend toward improvement in teacher-reported inattention and impulsivity was reported for children in the Pay Attention! condition.

Recently, a computerized progressive attentional training (CPAT) program was evaluated in a sample of children with ADHD; it includes four training tasks designed to activate sustained attention, selective attention, orienting of attention, and executive attention [73]. Relative to children with ADHD who took part in computer games and paper-and-pencil activities, participation in the 8-week CPAT program resulted in improved performance on non-standardized academic tests as well as a reduction in parent-reported ADHD symptoms.

Collectively, programs that have focused on improving attention have resulted in improvements on several neurocognitive tests, academic achievement, and reports of children's behavior. Clearly, attention-focused interventions hold promise as a therapeutic modality for children with ADHD; however, there are notable limitations that will necessitate further empirical investigation (e.g. lack of comparison with empirically supported interventions). Further, the extent to which these programs can be implemented under "real-world" conditions is critical. Consequently, such interventions, while promising, warrant additional studies of both efficacy and generalizability.

Remediation of working memory

In addition to interventions that have focused on directly targeting attention, the Cogmed Working Memory Training Program (Cogmed) has demonstrated evidence for enhancing working memory and reducing behavioral symptoms of inattention and hyperactivity/impulsivity in children with ADHD [74, 75]. This software-based training program was developed to improve working memory abilities, particularly in children with ADHD or severe attention problems. The training is implemented with a software product (RoboMemo© from Cogmed Cognitive Medical Systems AB, Stockholm, Sweden) and includes a set of computerized visual-spatial and auditory-verbal working memory tasks. All tasks involve: (a) maintenance of simultaneous mental representations of multiple stimuli; (b) unique sequencing of stimulus order in each trial; and (c) progressive adaptation of difficulty level as a function of individual performance. Training plans are individualized and are modified according to performance; however, the typical plan includes 13 tasks, with 15 trials of eight tasks each day.

In two clinical trials, the Cogmed intervention was compared to an identical computer program using low working memory load tasks that were not adjusted based on child performance. In the initial, double-blind, controlled study, the Cogmed intervention, relative to the low working memory load condition, yielded significantly greater improvements on measures of working memory, nonverbal complex reasoning, response inhibition, and motor activity [74]. In a larger, multi-site clinical trial similar beneficial effects of Cogmed were reported, with significant intervention effects observed for measures of verbal and nonverbal working memory, nonverbal complex reasoning, and response inhibition relative to participants in the low memory load condition [75]. However, contrary to the initial investigation, no treatment effects were observed for measures of motor activity. Importantly, the above gains in neurocognitive functioning were maintained at 3-month follow-up for those receiving the Cogmed intervention [58]. Although behavioral ratings obtained at post-intervention did not reveal changes in teacher reports of ADHD severity, significant treatment effects were observed using standardized and nonstandardized parent ratings of ADHD severity, many of which were maintained at follow-up.

Although promising, the results of the above working memory interventions must be considered in the context of high rates of treatment noncompliance (approximately one-third) and restrictive inclusion and exclusion (e.g. required computer access, exclusion of ODD participants) The lack of significant improvement in teacher-rated ADHD behaviors is also a significant concern, as one would expect improvements in working memory to translate into improvements within settings in which these abilities are most taxed and/or impaired (i.e. at school). The absence of teacher-identified behavioral changes may reflect an expectancy bias on the part of parents who may have not been as blind to the nature of the interventions in question. Ultimately, closer examination of treatment effects across multiple outcomes coupled with prospective investigations of long-term efficacy will be key steps in future studies of this intervention.

Enhancement of executive function development

As we close this section on cognitive interventions, one recent study is worth noting. Although it is not directly aimed at children with ADHD, Diamond and colleagues [76] evaluated "Tools of the Mind", a comprehensive preschool curriculum designed to enhance executive function development, which is particularly relevant to ADHD given reported impairments in time management and organizational skills in children with ADHD [15]. Tools of the Mind is grounded in established developmental theory and was developed based on Luria's [77] and Vygotsky's [78] theory of development and includes 40 activities interwoven into classroom activities that promote executive functioning throughout the preschool day, including the use of self-regulatory (internalized) speech, dramatic play, and aids to support memory and attention. In a sample of children from low-income, urban preschools, Tools of the Mind was compared to the school district's existing literacy program, which focused on similar academic content but did not address executive functioning development. Results indicated that children randomized to Tools of the Mind classrooms demonstrated significant improvements in inhibitory control, working memory, and cognitive flexibility relative to those assigned to the conventional literacy program.

Importantly, the Tools of the Mind program includes several design elements that may inform interventions in general, and cognitive interventions in particular. First, the intervention emphasizes early childhood, a time when executive functioning skills are coming on line developmentally. Efforts to target executive functioning when skills are emerging may be preferable to remediation that occurs past the point of typical skill acquisition/development [79]. Second, rather than solely relying on the involvement of professionals, familiar and potentially transformative adult figures (i.e. teachers) implement the intervention within a setting in which these children live and learn (i.e. school), thereby intensifying the potency and

palatability of the intervention. Moreover, the fact that the intervention is seamlessly woven into the existing curriculum and relies on activities that children find to be enjoyable and that teachers can readily support bolsters the sustainability of the intervention and resulting improvement(s).

Thus, while the aforementioned studies have notable limitations, considerable progress has been made on how to ameliorate patterns of neurocognitive dysfunction of children with ADHD. Contrary to existing methods, such techniques may improve both the acute difficulties children with ADHD experience as well as the long-term outcomes for these children. Although many questions remain, several clear directions exist for future work in this area (e.g. comparison and/or augmentation with well-validated treatments) that may ultimately help to reduce the severity of ADHD symptoms and breadth of psychosocial impairment.

Summary and future directions

ADHD is a heterogeneous psychiatric disorder characterized by clinically significant manifestations of inattention, hyperactivity, and impulsivity, which persist in a significant subset of affected individuals and portend risk for a number of adverse psychosocial outcomes. Within the past several decades, a variety of models have been proposed identifying various "core" cognitive deficits in children with ADHD, based on the suspicion that deficient neuropsychological functioning underlies the diverse array of behavioral difficulties associated with the disorder. Although numerous theoretical models have emphasized frontally-mediated executive functions with regard to the underlying pathophysiology and resulting symptomatic expression [80], recent reviews and meta-analyses [15] have suggested that executive function deficiencies do not account for most of the variance in ADHD symptoms, discounting the clinical utility of such measures in diagnostic assessment. Yet the apparent schism between executive function development on the one hand, and the presence of ADHD symptoms on the other, suggests that alternative models may be required to account for the emergence of early externalizing behaviors. One recent model [28] has proposed that distinct mechanisms underlie the etiology of, and recovery from, ADHD, with the former posited to result from noncortical dysfunction that remains static through development, and the latter a byproduct of cortically mediated, effortful control. Consequently, targeted efforts to augment top-down processes, which have already demonstrated acute benefits with respect to both neurocognitive and behavioral functioning [78], may hold promise in altering the long-term trajectories of children with ADHD. In addition to emphasizing ecologically sensitive measures, remedial strategies would be well-served to examine the role of psychiatric comorbidity in remediation techniques and whether developmental status impacts responsivity to such methods.

ADHD phenomonology

- ADHD is a highly prevalent, often chronic psychiatric disorder that, by definition, is associated with impairment in multiple spheres of psychosocial functioning.

- Co-occurrence with other psychiatric disorders, particularly other disruptive behavior disorders, is clearly the rule rather than the exception; however, the contributions of ADHD vs. psychiatric comorbidity to later outcomes have been difficult to isolate.

Neuropsychological profiles

- During both childhood and adolescence, many individuals with ADHD display impairment(s) in one or more domains of neuropsychological functioning; however, such deficits are neither necessary nor sufficient to make the diagnosis and may vary as a function of several moderating factors (e.g. inclusion criteria, IQ covariation, etc.)

- Although distinctions between lower-order and higher-order functions may not have discriminative utility during childhood, this dichotomy may hold promise for distinguishing between persisters and remitters.

Etiological mechanisms

- Catecholaminergic systems (i.e. dopamine and norepinepherine) have been most consistently implicated in the pathophysiology of ADHD and are targeted neurochemical systems for treatment

- ADHD is considered among the most heritable psychiatric disorders and has been linked to allelic variations in the dopamine D4 receptor (DRD4) and transporter (DAT).

Structural and functional neuroimaging

- Findings from structural and functional neuro-imaging studies have consistently implicated perturbations in fronto-thalamo-striatal regions; however, support has also been provided for diffuse and dynamic neurological dysfunction.

- Recent investigations have suggested that ADHD is characterized by a delay rather than deficiency in regional cortical maturation (i.e. attainment of peak cortical thickness).

Psychosocial and psychopharmacological intervention

- First-line pharmacological interventions for ADHD include both psychostimulants (e.g. methylphenidate and amphetamine salts) as well as non-stimulants (e.g. atomoxetine; bupropion); however, the jury is out as to which preparation works most effectively for which children or symptom cluster.

- Evidence-based psychosocial treatments include parent management training; teacher consultations; summer treatment programs; social skills interventions; and paraprofessional programs; and have been shown to produce reductions in ADHD symptoms and associated patterns of psychiatric comorbidity.

- Recently developed methods of cognitive remediation have targeted attention and/or working memory and may hold promise vis-à-vis acute manifestations of ADHD as well as the long-term outcomes for affected individuals.

References

1. American Psychiatric Association. *Diagnostic and Statistical Manual of Mental Disorders*, 4th edn, text revision. Washington DC: 2000.

2. Faraone SV, Sergeant J, Gillberg C, et al. The worldwide prevalence of ADHD: is it an American Condition? *World Psychiatry* 2003;**2**(2):104–13.

3. Barkley, RA. *Attention Deficit Hyperactivity Disorder: A Handbook for Diagnosis and Treatment*, 3rd edn. New York: Guilford Press; 2005.

4. Biederman, J, Newcorn, J, Sprich, S. Comorbidity of attention deficit hyperactivity disorder with conduct, depressive, anxiety, and other disorders. *Am J Psychiatry* 1991;**148**(5):564–577.

5. Mannuzza S, Klein RG, Bessler AG, et al. Adult status of hyperactive boys grown up. *Am J Psychiatry* 1998;**155**(4):493–8.

6. Douglas VI. Stop, look and listen: the problem of sustained attention and poor impulse control in hyperactive and normal children. *Canad J Behav Sci* 1972;**4**:259–82.

7. Rommelse NN, Altink ME, de Sonneville LM, et al. Are motor inhibition and cognitive flexibility dead ends in ADHD? *J Abnorm Child Psychol* 2007;**35**(6):957–67.

8. Ross DM, Ross SA. *Hyperactivity: Current Issues, Research, and Theory.* New York: John Wiley and Sons; 1982.

9. Sonuga-Barke EJ, Dalen L, Daley D, et al. Are planning, working memory, and inhibition associated with individual differences in preschool ADHD symptoms? *Dev Neuropsychol* 2002;**21**(3):255–72.

10. Sonuga-Barke EJ, Dalen L, Remington B. Do executive deficits and delay aversion make independent contributions to preschool attention-deficit/hyperactivity disorder symptoms? *J Am Acad Child Adolesc Psychiatry* 2003;**42**(11):1335–42.

11. Mariani MA, Barkley RA. Neuropsychological and academic functioning in pre-school boys with attention deficit hyperactivity. *Dev Neuropsychol* 1997;**13**:111–29.

12. DuPaul GJ, McGoey KE, Eckert TL, et al. Preschool children with attention-deficit/hyperactivity disorder: impairments in behavioral, social, and school functioning. *J Am Acad Child Adolesc Psychiatry* 2001;**40**(5):508–15.

13. Marks DJ, Berwid OG, Santra A, et al. Neuropsychological correlates of ADHD symptoms in preschoolers. *Neuropsychology* 2005;**19**(4):446–55.

14. Berwid OG, Curko Kera EA, Marks DJ, et al. Sustained attention and response inhibition in young children at risk for Attention Deficit/Hyperactivity Disorder. *J Child Psychol Psychiatry* 2005;**46**(11):1219–29.

15. Willcutt EG, Doyle AE, Nigg JT, et al. Validity of the executive function theory of attention-deficit/hyperactivity disorder: a meta-analytic review. *Biol Psychiatry* 2005;**57**(11):1336–46.

16. Frazier TW, Demaree HA, Youngstrom EA. Meta-analysis of intellectual and neuropsychological test performance in attention-deficit/hyperactivity disorder. *Neuropsychology* 2004;**18**(3):543–55.

17. Martinussen R, Hayden J, Hogg-Johnson S, et al. A meta-analysis of working memory impairments in children with attention-deficit/hyperactivity disorder. *J Am Acad Child Adolesc Psychiatry* 2005;**44**(4):377–84.

18. van Mourik R, Oosterlaan J, Sergeant JA. The Stroop revisited: a meta-analysis of interference control in AD/HD. *J Child Psychol Psychiatry* 2005;**46**(2):150–65.

19. Lansbergen MM, Kenemans JL, van Engeland H. Stroop interference and attention-deficit/hyperactivity disorder: a review and meta-analysis. *Neuropsychology* 2007;**21**(2):251–62.

20. Schwartz K, Verhaeghen P. ADHD and Stroop interference from age 9 to age 41 years: a meta-analysis of developmental effects. *Psychol Med* 2008;**38**:1607–16.

21. Lijffijt M, Kenemans JL, Verbaten MN, et al. A meta-analytic review of stopping performance in attention-deficit/hyperactivity disorder: deficient inhibitory motor control? *J Abnorm Psychol* 2005;**114**(2):216–22.

22. Alderson RM, Rapport MD, Kofler MJ. Attention-deficit/hyperactivity disorder and behavioral inhibition: a meta-analytic review of the stop-signal paradigm. *J Abnorm Child Psychol* 2007;**35**(5):745–58.

23. Klein C, Wendling K, Huettner P, et al. Intra-subject variability in attention-deficit hyperactivity disorder. *Biol Psychiatry* 2006;**60**(10):1088–97.

24. Martel M, Nikolas M, Nigg JT. Executive function in adolescents with ADHD. *J Am Acad Child Adolesc Psychiatry* 2007;**46**(11):1437–44.

25. Loo SK, Humphrey LA, Tapio T, et al. Executive functioning among Finnish adolescents with attention-deficit/hyperactivity disorder. *J Am Acad Child Adolesc Psychiatry* 2007;**46**(12):1594–604.

26. Werry JS, Elkind GS, Reeves JC. Attention deficit, conduct, oppositional, and anxiety disorders in children: III. Laboratory differences. *J Abnorm Child Psychol* 2002;**15**(3):409–28.

27. Nigg JT. Is ADHD a disinhibitory disorder? *Psychol Bull* 2001;**127**:571–98.

28. Halperin JM, Schulz KP. Revisiting the role of the prefrontal cortex in the pathophysiology of attention-deficit/hyperactivity disorder. *Psychol Bull* 2006;**132**(4):560–81.

29. Kalff AC, Hendriksen JGM, Kroes M, et al. Neurocognitive performance of 5- and 6-year-old children who met criteria for attention deficit/hyperactivity disorder at 18 months follow-up: results from a prospective population study. *J Abnorm Child Psychol* 2002;**30**(6):589–98.

30. Halperin JM, Trampush JW, Miller CJ, et al. Neuropsychological outcomes of ADHD in adolescence/young adulthood: profiles of persisters, remitters and controls. *J Child Psychol Psychiatry.* 2008;**49**:958–66.

31. Nigg JT, Willcutt EG, Doyle AE, et al. Causal heterogeneity in attention-deficit/hyperactivity disorder: do we need neuropsychologically impaired subtypes? *Biol Psychiatry* 2005;**57**(11):1224–30.

32. Faraone SV, Perlis RH, Doyle AE, et al., Molecular genetics of attention-deficit/hyperactivity disorder. *Biol Psychiatry* 2005;**57**(11):1313–23.

33. Brookes K, Xu X, Chen W, et al. The analysis of 51 genes in DSM-IV combined type attention deficit hyperactivity disorder: association signals in DRD4, DAT1 and 16 other genes. *Mol Psychiatry* 2006;**11**(10): 934–53.

34. Swanson J, Oosterlaan J, Murias M, et al. Attention deficit/hyperactivity disorder children with a 7-repeat allele of the dopamine receptor D4 gene have extreme behavior but normal performance on critical neuropsychological tests of attention. *Proc Natl Acad Sci USA* 2000;**97**(9):4754–9.

35. Valera EM, Faraone SV, Murray KE, et al. Meta-analysis of structural imaging findings in attention-deficit/hyperactivity disorder. *Biol Psychiatry* 2007;**61**(12):1361–9.

36. Sowell ER, Thompson PM, Welcome SE, et al. Cortical abnormalities in children and adolescents with attention-deficit hyperactivity disorder. *Lancet* 2003;**362**(9397):1699–707.

37. Plessen KJ, Bansal R, Zhu H, et al. Hippocampus and amygdala morphology in attention-deficit/hyperactivity disorder. *Arch Gen Psychiatry* 2006;**63**(7):795–807.

38. Castellanos FX, Lee PP, Sharp W, et al. Developmental trajectories of brain volume abnormalities in children and adolescents with attention-deficit/hyperactivity disorder. *JAMA* 2002;**288**(14):1740–8.

39. Overmeyer S, Simmons A, Santosh J, et al. Corpus callosum may be similar in children with ADHD and siblings of children with ADHD. *Dev Med Child Neurol* 2000;**42**(1):8–13.

40. Berquin PC, Giedd JN, Jacobsen LK, et al. Cerebellum in attention-deficit hyperactivity disorder: a morphometric MRI study. *Neurology* 1998;**50**(4):1087–93.

41. Schulz KP, Fan J, Tang CY, et al. Response inhibition in adolescents diagnosed with attention deficit hyperactivity disorder during childhood: an event-related FMRI study. *Am Journal Psychiatry* 2004;**161**(9):1650–7.

42. Rubia K, Smith AB, Brammer MJ, et al. Abnormal brain activation during inhibition and error detection in medication-naive adolescents with ADHD. *Am Journal Psychiatry* 2005;**162**(6):1067–75.

43. Durston S, Mulder M, Casey BJ, et al. Activation in ventral prefrontal cortex is sensitive to genetic vulnerability for attention-deficit hyperactivity disorder. *Biol Psychiatry* 2006;**60**(10):1062–70.

44. Dickstein SG, Bannon K, Castellanos FX, et al. The neural correlates of attention deficit hyperactivity disorder: an ALE meta-analysis. *J Child Psychol Psychiatry* 2006;**47**(10):1051–62.

45. Mackie S, Shaw P, Lenroot R, et al. Cerebellar development and clinical outcome in attention deficit hyperactivity disorder. *Am J Psychiatry* 2007;**164**(4):647–55.

46. Shaw P, Lerch J, Greenstein D, et al. Longitudinal mapping of cortical thickness and clinical outcome in children and adolescents with attention-deficit/hyperactivity disorder. *Arch Gen Psychiatry* 2006;**63**(5):540–9.

47. Shaw P, Eckstrand K, Sharp W, et al. Attention-deficit/hyperactivity disorder is characterized by a delay in cortical maturation. *Proc Natl Acad Sci USA* 2007;**104**(49):19649–54.

48. Chronis AM, Chacko A, Fabiano GA, et al. Enhancements to the behavioral parent training paradigm for families of children with ADHD: review and future directions. *Clin Child Fam Psychol Rev* 2004;**7**(1):1–27.

49. Anastopoulos AD, Shelton TL, DuPaul GJ, et al. Parent training for attention-deficit hyperactivity disorder: its impact on parent functioning. *J Abnorm Child Psychol* 1993;**21**(5):581–96.

50. Horn WF, Ialongo N, Popovich S, et al. Behavioral parent training and cognitive-behavioral self-control therapy with ADD-H children: comparative and combined effects. *J Clin Child Psychol* 1987;**15**(1):57–68.

51. Pelham WE Jr, Fabiano GA. Evidence-based psychosocial treatments for attention-deficit/hyperactivity disorder. *J Clin Child Adolesc Psychol* 2008;**37**(1):184–214.

52. DuPaul GJ, Eckert T. The effects of school-based interventions for attention deficit hyperactivity disorder: a meta-analysis. *School Psychol Rev* 1997;**26**:5–27.

53. Pelham WE Jr, Fabiano GA, Gnagy E. et al. The role of Summer Treatment Program in the context of comprehensive treatment for Attention-Deficit/Hyperactivity Disorder. In E. Hibbs, P Jensen, eds *Psychosocial Treatments for Child and Adolescent Disorders: Empirically Based Strategies for Clinical Practice*, 2nd edn. APA; 2007: 455–89.

54. Pelham WE Jr, Gnagy EM, Greiner AR, et al. Behavioral vs. behavioral and pharmacological treatment in ADHD children attending a summer treatment program. *J Abnorm Child Psychol* 2000;**28**(6):507–26.

55. Chronis AM, Fabiano GA, Gnagy EM, et al. An evaluation of the Summer Treatment Program for children with attention-deficit/hyperactivity disorder using a treatment withdrawal design. *Behav Ther* 2004;**35**:561–85.

56. Coles EK, Pelham WE Jr, Gnagy EM, et al. A controlled evaluation of behavioral treatment with children with ADHD attending a summer treatment program. *J Emot Behav Disord* 2005;**13**:99–112.

57. American Academy of Child and Adolescent Psychiatry. Practice parameters for the assessment and treatment of children and adolescents with attention-deficit/hyperactivity disorder. *J Am Acad Child Adolesc Psychiatry* 2007;**46**(7): 894–921.

58. Swanson JS, McBurnett K, Wigal T. Stimulant medications and the treatment of children with ADHD. *Adv Clin Child Psychol* 1995;**17**:265–322.

59. Pelham WE, Bender ME, Caddell J, et al. Methylphenidate and children with attention deficit disorder. Dose effects on classroom academic and social behavior. *Arch Gen Psychiatry* 1985;**42**(10):948–52.

60. Chacko A, Pelham WE Jr, Gnagy EM, et al. Stimulant medication effects in a summer treatment program among young children with attention-deficit/hyperactivity disorder. *J Am Acad Child Adolesc Psychiatry* 2005;**44**(3):249–57.

61. Power TJ, Hess LE, Bennett DS. The acceptability of interventions for attention-deficit hyperactivity disorder among elementary and middle school teachers. *J Dev Behav Pediatr* 1995;**16**(4):238–43.

62. Biederman J, Spencer T. Psychopharmacological Interventions. *Child Adolesc Psychiatric Clin N Am* 2008;**17**:439–58.

63. Arnold LE, Abikoff HB, Cantwell DP, et al. National Institute of Mental Health Collaborative Multimodal Treatment Study of Children with ADHD (the MTA). Design challenges and choices. *Arch Gen Psychiatry* 1997;**54**(9):865–70.

64. MTA Cooperative Group. A 14-month randomized clinical trial of treatment strategies for attention-deficit/hyperactivity disorder. Multimodal Treatment Study of Children with ADHD. *Arch Gen Psychiatry* 1999;**56**(12):1073–86.

65. Hinshaw SP, Owens EB, Wells KC, et al. Family processes and treatment outcome in the MTA: negative/ineffective parenting practices in relation to multimodal treatment. *J Abnorm Child Psychol* 2000;**28**(6):555–68.

66. Conners CK, Epstein JN, March JS, et al. Multimodal treatment of ADHD in the MTA: an alternative outcome analysis. *J Am Acad Child Adolesc Psychiatry* 2001;**40**(2):159–67.

67. Swanson JS, Kraemer HC, Hinshaw SP, et al. Clinical relevance of the primary findings of the MTA: success rates based on severity of ADHD and ODD symptoms at the end of treatment. *J Am Acad Child Adolesc Psychiatry* 2001;**40**(2):168–79.

68. Hoza B, Gerdes AC, Mrug S, et al. Peer-assessed outcomes in the multimodal treatment study of children with attention deficit hyperactivity disorder. *J Clin Child Adolesc Psychol* 2005;**34**(1):74–86.

69. Kollins S, Greenhill L, Swanson J, et al. Rationale, design, and methods of the Preschool ADHD Treatment Study (PATS). *J Am Acad Child Adolesc Psychiatry* 2006;**45**(11):1275–83.

70. Greenhill L, Kollins S, Abikoff H, et al. Efficacy and safety of immediate-release methylphenidate treatment for preschoolers with ADHD. *J Am Acad Child Adolesc Psychiatry* 2006;**45**(11):1284–93.

71. Molina BS, Flory K, Hinshaw SP, et al. Delinquent behavior and emerging substance use in the MTA at 36 months: prevalence, course, and treatment effects. *J Am Acad Child Adolesc Psychiatry* 2007;**46**(8):1028–40.

72. Kerns KA, Eso K, Thomson J. Investigation of a direct intervention for improving attention in young children with ADHD. *Dev Neuropsychol* 1999;**16**(2):273–95.

73. Shalev L, Tsal Y, Mevorach C. Computerized progressive attentional training (CPAT) program: effective direct intervention for children with ADHD. *Child Neuropsychol* 2007;**13**(4):382–8.

74. Klingberg T, Forssberg H, Westerberg H. Training of working memory in children with ADHD. *J Clin Exp Neuropsychol* 2002;**24**(6):781–91.

75. Klingberg T, Fernell E, Olesen PJ, et al. Computerized training of working memory in children with ADHD – a randomized, controlled trial. *J Am Acad Child Adolesc Psychiatry* 2005;**44**(2):177–86.

76. Diamond A, Barnett WS, Thomas J, et al. Preschool program improves cognitive control. *Science* 2007;**318**(5855):1387–8.

77. Luria AR. *The Higher Cortical Functions in Man*. New York: Basic Books; 1966.

78. Vygotsky LS. *Mind in Society: The Development of Higher Psychological Processes*. Cambridge, MA: Harvard University Press; 1978.

79. Tremblay RE. Prevention of youth violence: why not start at the beginning? *J Abnorm Child Psychol* 2006;**34**(4):481–7.

80. Barkley RA. Behavioral inhibition, sustained attention, and executive functions: constructing a unifying theory of ADHD. *Psychol Bull* 1997;**121**(1):65–94.

Attention deficit hyperactivity disorder in adults

Margaret Semrud-Clikeman and Jodene Goldenring Fine

Introduction

Attention deficit hyperactivity disorder (ADHD) is a disorder that involves difficulty with attention, impulse control, and hyperactivity. There has been controversy regarding whether ADHD remits by adulthood or continues into adolescence and adulthood with similar symptom patterns [1]. Many now suggest that the symptoms change over time and development, from high activity levels to problems primarily with attention.

For children and early adolescents, significant difficulty is often seen with hyperactivity. Difficulties with academic subjects and behavior in school are prevalent for children with ADHD, due to problems with attention and impulse control/hyperactivity [2]. The main challenge for adults with ADHD is generally impulse control and attention. Problems with attention and impulse control can impact the work environment in areas such as difficulty with meeting deadlines and paying attention to details. In addition, adults with ADHD tend to attain lower socioeconomic status and rates of professional employment, and have higher rates of separation and divorce [3].

Therefore, emerging data indicate that ADHD probably continues for many individuals throughout the life span. Thus, it is important to explore how ADHD in adults is diagnosed, assessed, and treated. The aim of this chapter is to critically review the literature on adult ADHD, including findings on neuropsychological functioning, neuroimaging, neuropsychological assessment, and interventions currently available that have ecological and strong empirical validity. It is not our intent to duplicate what is written on pediatric ADHD, which is discussed in the previous chapter, but to rather complement this information and apply it appropriately to adults.

Epidemiology of ADHD in adults

The incidence of ADHD is approximately 3% to 9% for children and around 4% to 5% for adults [4]. Familial studies have found that parents of children with ADHD have a significantly increased risk of being diagnosed with ADHD [5]. Fathers of children with ADHD show a 24% incidence of also having ADHD, while the incidence is 7% for control families. Furthermore, mothers of children with ADHD show a prevalence rate of 15%, while mothers of control children have an incidence of 3%. In addition, relatives of adults with ADHD were found to show prevalence rates of 49% compared to 2.5% of adults without ADHD [6].

It has been estimated that approximately 60% of childhood diagnosed ADHD cases continue to show a sufficient number of symptoms into late adolescence and adulthood that are considered to be clinically significant [7, 8]. These symptoms have been also found to be a risk factor for lower levels of employment and academic attainment, marital problems, substance abuse, higher levels of automobile accidents and infractions, and more financial difficulties [3, 9]. It is not clear why some children, as they age, show remission of symptoms of ADHD while others continue to struggle and show significant clinical difficulty with ADHD. While most studies have focused on the continuity of ADHD into adolescence, there have been factors that seem to predict persistence of ADHD into adulthood. These include severity of ADHD in childhood, existence of other comorbid disorders, and social, emotional, and environmental difficulties [10].

Diagnostic issues in adult ADHD

The Diagnostic and Statistical Manual of Mental Disorders, Fourth Edition, Text Revision (DSM-IV-TR) [11] identifies three subtypes of ADHD – predominately inattentive, hyperactive-impulsive, and combined. DSM-IV-TR does not address diagnosis of ADHD in adults except to state that hyperactivity may decrease over time, and become internal restlessness in older adolescents and adults. Thus, diagnosis of ADHD in adulthood generally presumes a previous diagnosis of ADHD in childhood. Several studies have supported the occurrence of ADHD in adults as well as the concordance between childhood and adult ADHD symptomatology [12]. Notably as well, newly diagnosed adults tend to be those diagnosed with ADHD predominately inattentive subtype, rather than the combined subtype [13].

Age-of-onset controversy

While clinicians and researchers generally accept the presence of ADHD in adults, there is controversy about the timing of diagnosis. An initial diagnosis of ADHD that occurs in adulthood requires the report of symptoms that occurred in childhood. This requirement of retrospective reporting of symptoms in previously undiagnosed adults has led some to question the validity of the diagnosis [14], while others have provided evidence for neuropsychological and neurological bases for adult ADHD [15] that confirms the validity of the diagnosis.

Faraone et al. [16] suggest that there are two particularly troublesome diagnostic questions regarding adult ADHD. The first is whether the age of onset set by DSM-IV-TR, symptoms occurring prior to age 7, should be applied to adults. The second issue is how should the diagnostic criteria and symptom list be modified for adults, particularly when retrospective diagnoses are being made. Some researchers suggest that this age of onset is arbitrary, and believe it may not be a useful heuristic for diagnosis, particularly since it has not been empirically validated [17]. In line with this criticism, Schaughency et al. [18] studied adolescents before the age of 13 and those older than 13 with regard to the relationship between age of onset, severity of symptoms, problems with adjustment, and persistence of ADHD. They found no difference in these variables for children with onset either before or after 13 years of age.

Similarly, Rohde et al. [19] compared two groups of adolescents diagnosed with ADHD. Both groups met criteria for the diagnosis of ADHD, but with only one group meeting the age-of-onset criteria. No difference was found between these groups in clinical presentation. The authors concluded that age of onset may not be an appropriate criterion for diagnosis and suggested it should be revised. Finally, field trials during the development of DSM-IV found that when an age of onset of 7 years was applied, cases that were being evaluated were not as likely to be identified with ADHD. Moreover, clinician agreement decreased when a strict adherence was given to age of onset compared to when age of onset was not applied [20].

Some suggest that the threshold for age of onset needs to be changed, particularly for adults [16]. However, it is likely that changing these criteria may result in higher levels of false positive diagnoses. Still, it has been suggested that this risk is required in order to identify adults with ADHD who need services and who may not have been identified as children [6].

Faraone et al. [21] sought to more fully explore age of onset and number of symptoms required for a diagnosis of ADHD in adults by comparing four groups of adults with ADHD. The first group met all DSM-IV criteria including age of onset; the second group met all ADHD criteria but not age of onset; the third group had three or more inattentive symptoms and three or more hyperactive/impulsive symptoms but did not meet full criteria (subthreshold group); and the fourth group did not meet ADHD criteria. The group who met full criteria and the group who met all criteria except for age of onset did not differ significantly on clinical symptomatology. There were roughly equal proportions of participants in each of the two ADHD groups who showed lifetime presentation of ADHD (70% for the full ADHD group and 68% for the group without age of onset).

Conclusions from these studies suggest that the age-of-onset criteria may be too strict, limiting diagnosis of patients, specifically adult-age patients, who require intervention and support. It has been suggested that, based on the empirical data, the age-of-onset cut-off should be later than 7, possibly to symptoms occurring before or at age 12 [21]. It has also been suggested that when adults present with age of onset after age 12, the diagnosis should be made with extreme care after ruling out other possibilities [22].

Comorbidity issues

Children with ADHD frequently show additional disorders including higher incidences of learning disabilities, antisocial behaviors, and mood and anxiety disorders. Several studies have found similar rates of psychiatric comorbidity in adults, with elevations in antisocial and substance abuse behaviors [23]. In a follow-up of hyperactive children into adulthood, Fischer et al. [24] studied young adults with ADHD: combined-subtype diagnoses, who had a history of ADHD as children, and control young adults without any ADHD symptoms. The ADHD group showed a higher risk for at least one psychiatric disorder compared to the control group. Twenty-six percent of the ADHD group vs. 12 percent of the control group were found to show a significantly higher incidence of major depression, while no statistically significant difference was found for incidence of anxiety disorders or oppositional or conduct disorders.

Additional studies have found increased incidence of bipolar disorder, oppositional defiant disorder, and substance abuse in adults with ADHD combined-subtype diagnoses compared to adults with ADHD predominately inattentive type [25]. Others have found a higher incidence of dysthymia, alcohol and drug dependence/abuse, and learning disabilities in adults with ADHD predominately inattentive type [26]. In this same study, adults with a diagnosis of ADHD combined type were found to show more oppositional behavior, higher levels of suicidality, a greater number of arrests, and an increased reporting of interpersonal problems compared to those with ADHD predominately inattentive type.

Most of the above disorders are considered Axis I (mood and behavioral) disorders. Less research has explored the incidence of Axis II (personality) disorders in adults with ADHD. Some researchers have suggested that Cluster B personality disorders are related to ADHD due to their externalizing characteristics [27]. These disorders include borderline personality disorder, histrionic personality disorder, narcissistic personality disorder, and obsessive-compulsive personality disorder. An overlap between ADHD and borderline personality disorder (BPD) has been found in investigations looking at childhood ADHD and later development of BPD in adulthood [28].

A study of adults with ADHD combined type found that, compared to controls, there was a significantly higher incidence of the following personality disorders: passive-aggressive, histrionic, borderline (BPD), and antisocial [24]. Another study evaluated whether personality disorders differed depending on ADHD subtype as well as investigating whether ADHD and the attendant symptoms influenced the degree of impairment beyond the Axis II diagnosis [27]. The only cluster that showed highly significant results was Cluster B, with a higher incidence of BPD (20.3% vs. 3.9%) compared to controls. For CLuster C (avoidant, dependent, obsessive-compulsive), ADHD was significantly associated with an increased incidence of all three personality disorders. To determine whether ADHD symptoms were related to more significant forms of personality disorder, the authors used hierarchical multiple regression and found that ADHD did account for greater levels of impairment,

particularly symptoms consistent with antisocial personality disorder and BPD, as well as generalized anxiety disorder and major depression. This study underscores the need to evaluate possible co-occurring Axis I and Axis II diagnoses in adults. It also highlights the importance of recognizing that ADHD symptoms in conjunction with one of these diagnoses increase the likelihood of greater impairment and the need for more intensive intervention.

Gender differences in adult ADHD

In children the ratio of males to females diagnosed with ADHD ranges from 2:1 to 9:1 [29]. Studies with adults have found a more balanced ratio and some have pointed to this difference between adults and children as evidence that many adults are inaccurately identified with ADHD [30]. Others have suggested that this imbalance is due to females showing fewer disruptive behaviors and not being referred for assistance until entering college or work positions that require sustained attention [31].

Biederman et al. [32] sought to evaluate whether the clinical presentation of ADHD in women differs from that in men and whether this difference in expression of symptoms accounts for the later referral of women for evaluation. A previous study by this group found that women with ADHD have higher rates of mood disorders, conduct problems, learning problems, and neuropsychological deficits compared to normally functioning women [31]. Others studies have found similar rates of higher levels of depression, anxiety, and sensitivity to stress [33]. In addition, it has been hypothesized that the finding of a higher likelihood for a later diagnosis in women results in these emotional problems partly due to the lack of support provided to these women at a younger age.

The Biederman et al. [32] study utilized a new sample of women with ADHD from previous work, while also supplementing the study with additional neuropsychological measures and statistical analyses. For this study, there were 82 women and 137 men with a diagnosis of ADHD, and 81 women and 134 men in the control group. When ADHD symptoms were evaluated, *talking excessively* was the only symptom that discriminated between women and men with ADHD, with women talking more frequently. No statistically significant differences were found on the lifetime number of total, inattentive, or hyperactive-impulsive symptoms. Women with ADHD were found to show

99

more inattentive symptoms compared to men with ADHD and to have, proportionately, a higher incidence of ADHD predominately inattentive subtype diagnoses.

When looking at comorbidity of Axis I and Axis II diagnoses in this sample, it was found that men with ADHD had a higher frequency of substance abuse disorder and/or antisocial personality disorder compared to women with ADHD. A further analysis found that while ADHD was associated with bipolar disorder, social phobia, and the anxiety disorders, no gender effects were present except for substance abuse. In addition, 34% of women participants with ADHD and 7% of control women were found to have one comorbid diagnosis while men with ADHD showed rates of 50% and 15% of men in the control group. Further analysis found that men were more likely than women to have a psychiatric disorder, with any participant diagnosed with ADHD more likely to have a psychiatric disorder compared to those without ADHD.

Conclusion

Given this brief review of the literature, it appears that there is sufficient evidence that ADHD continues into adulthood. Moreover, there are emerging data indicating that ADHD may be diagnosed in adulthood, with late identification of ADHD occurring particularly for females and possibly for males with ADHD predominately inattentive subtype presentation. For many clinicians working with late adolescents or adults, the problem of establishing an age of onset may make diagnosis problematic. Evolving findings from research on age of onset are, for the most part, not supportive of the cut-off of 7 years of age for meeting criteria; rather, researchers suggest that a more appropriate cut-off may be 12 years of age for the identification of symptoms that are disruptive to the child's functioning.

For issues of comorbidity it was found that adults with ADHD tend to show a higher risk for the development of substance abuse disorder, mood disorders, anxiety disorders, and some Axis II disorders, particularly BPD and antisocial personality disorder. Men with ADHD were found to be much more likely to develop substance abuse disorder and antisocial personality disorder compared to women with ADHD. Finally, one issue that was raised in the research was the finding that women were commonly diagnosed much later than men, and were more likely to be diagnosed as adults than men. These findings also

have been related to somewhat higher rates of depression and anxiety in these women, possibly because treatment was delayed and stress levels increased as women with ADHD attempted to cope.

Another issue that arises in the literature is that the subtypes may differ not only in age of diagnosis but also in relation to other comorbid diagnoses. Many of the studies reviewed did not report subtype differences, but those that did found that the ADHD combined subtype was more commonly related to conduct and substance abuse problems. ADHD predominately inattentive type has been linked to difficulties in school, retention in a grade, and mood disorders. Further study is needed to differentiate between these subtypes as well as to describe possible gender differences within adult populations.

Neuropsychological functioning

This section reviews recent neuropsychological research on adult ADHD. Consistent with child research to date, the domains covered include cognitive functioning, attention, impulse regulation, executive functioning and adaptive functioning. Table 5b.1 lists the tests commonly used in research and clinical evaluation.

Cognitive functioning

Cognitive functioning in adults with ADHD has generated controversy in the literature. Some findings suggest that cognitive functioning is similar across groups with ADHD and control comparisons (e.g. ref. 34), while others indicate no substantial differences between the populations (e.g. ref. 35). A meta-analysis that included methodological variables indicated that the differences in research findings were related to how the groups were diagnosed, the use of DSM-based criteria, and the presence of comorbid disorders, all of which affected the level of ability seen across samples.

The type of IQ estimate used also influences research outcomes on cognitive functioning. Differences between ADHD and non-ADHD groups are likely to be wider when IQ tests include tasks for short-term memory and processing speed. Another factor that may influence studies of adult ADHD is that children with ADHD who become adults with ADHD may have a more severe form of the disorder. Variability in research outcomes may also be influenced by time of onset. Those with later onset are more likely to have the inattentive form of ADHD rather than the combined form and may have greater

Table 5b.1. Selected neuropsychological tests for the evaluation of adults with ADHD.

Domain/test	Task(s) / scores / usage	Publisher
Cognition		
Wechsler Adult Intelligence Scale, Third Edition (WAIS-III)	Multi-subtest battery yielding Full Scale IQ and index scores of Verbal Comprehension, Perceptual Organization, Working Memory and Processing Speed. Considered the gold standard for intellectual assessment.	Psychological Corporation
Stanford-Binet, Fifth Edition (SB-5)	Multi-subtest battery with five domains: Fluid Reasoning, Knowledge, Quantitative Reasoning, Visual-Spatial Processing and Working Memory. Full scale IQ is a summary of ability. Subtests at different levels measure different skills/abilities. Good overall measure with low floor and high ceiling.	Riverside Publishing
Woodcock-Johnson Cognitive, Third Edition (WJ COG III)	Three cognitive categories: Verbal Ability, Thinking Ability, and Cognitive Efficiency as well as Full Scale IQ. Broad factors and clusters based on the Cattell-Horn-Carroll concept of intelligence. Computer scoring required.	Riverside Publishing
Attention / inhibition		
Conners Continuous Performance Test (Conners CPT)	Computerized visual continuous performance test yielding multiple indexes of attention, response rate, and vigilance. Considered to be sensitive to problems with attention and inhibition. Includes an algorithm for likelihood of ADHD.	Multi-Health Systems
Test of Variable Attention (TOVA)	Similar to the Conners CPT but also includes an auditory condition.	Universal Attention Disorders
Stroop Test	Test of inhibition of automatic reading response. See Executive Functions, below under the Delis-Kaplan Executive Function System (D-KEFS)	
Paced Auditory Serial Addition Test (PASAT)	Auditory attention and working memory task. Serial addition of numbers with increasing pace. Considerable age and practice effects. Sensitive to expressive language problems.	
Memory		
Wechsler Memory Scale (WMS)	Multi-test battery including auditory, visual, and visuo-spatial tests of short-term memory and longer-term (30 minutes) recall. Measures include both contextual and more abstract information. Good for observing organization of simple versus complex information (e.g. memory for sentences vs. memory for stories).	Psychological Corporation
California Verbal Learning Test, Second Edition (CVLT-II)	Task of verbal list learning, with an interference trial. Multiple analyses including semantic/serial organization strategies, learning curve, perseverations.	Psychological Corporation
Rey Complex Figure Test and Recognition Trial (RCFT)	This Rey Complex Figure test is favored because of the recognition trial, which can help differentiate among those who can recall the information, but not organize a motor response to reproduce it.	
Digit Span	Short-term storage and working memory. A subtest of the WAIS, described above.	Psychological Corporation
Other executive functions		
Delis-Kaplan Executive Function System (D-KEFS)	An update on time-honored executive function tests such as Trails AB, Stroop, and Tower. Added conditions help tease out motor, sequencing, and set-switching problems. Verbal and design fluency are included, along with a sorting test, a 20-questions test, and a proverb test.	Psychological Corporation
ADHD rating scales		
Brown ADD Scale for Adults	ADHD symptoms and executive functioning, including memory, emotional regulation and self-monitoring.	
Conners' Adult ADHD Rating Scale	Inattention, impulsivity, hyperactivity, self-concept. Self-report and observer scales. Long and short versions.	

protective factors offsetting early diagnosis. Finally, adults with ADHD who have a comorbid diagnosis may experience more significant deficits in cognition and other important areas of functioning.

Core symptoms: attention and impulsivity

In adults, the two core symptoms of ADHD are attention and impulsivity. While often present in children, hyperactivity is clinically uncommon in adults, although restlessness is often reported. When inattention is the primary symptom, the diagnosis is ADHD predominantly inattentive (ADHD:PI). This subtype of ADHD is characterized by problems with attention regulation, without significant symptoms of impulsivity or hyperactivity. Even when adults *do* have symptoms of hyperactivity, it is still the problems related to inattention and disorganization that have the greatest effect on daily life, according to recent research on the relative contributions of specific executive functions to adaptive functioning [36].

Inattention

Among the most common direct measures of sustained attention are the computerized continuous performance tests (CPTs). Two of the most widely used are the Conners' CPT and the Test of Variables of Attention (TOVA). For these measures, the patient is asked to distinguish specific visual targets (Conners' CPT; TOVA) and/or auditory stimuli (TOVA) while refraining from responding to non-targets. The number of omissions, or not responding to the target stimuli, is considered to be a robust indicator of inattention that consistently distinguishes adults who have ADHD from those who do not [37]. Persons with ADHD have also been found to have more variable responses than normal controls on the CPT. CPT exams also identify individuals with learning problems and also those with subclinical symptoms of ADHD. Thus, caution is advised in these cases.

The Paced Auditory Serial Addition Task (PASAT) is a non-computerized auditory test that requires the participant to add numbers in serial fashion with increasingly shorter inter-stimulus intervals. It is a very challenging test requiring rapid organization of auditory material that has been shown to be effective in discriminating adults with ADHD from non-affected adults [37].

Response inhibition

Although most adults with ADHD experience a reduction in symptoms of hyperactivity as they mature, signs of motoric disinhibition have been observed in commission errors on CPTs [37] and stop-signal tests [38]. Commission errors occur when the person responds with an action when they are expected to inhibit a response.

The Stroop Color-Word Interference task is also considered a measure of inhibitory ability because a learned response (reading words) must be suppressed while a novel response (reading print color) is enacted. Data on the interference condition of the Stroop, however, have not been consistent in adult ADHD research and it has generally proven to be a relatively poor measure of between-group differences [37, 39]. Given the high comorbidity of reading problems and ADHD, it may be that reading words is not as automatic in many people with ADHD as it is for typically developing persons. If the reading rate is slower to begin with, the interference effect of having to inhibit reading will not be as large [37].

Although inattention and impulsivity form the core symptoms of ADHD, adults with ADHD demonstrate a variety of other neuropsychological differences that can significantly impair day-to-day functioning. Many of these are collected under the umbrella term of executive functions, referring to the abilities required to effectively assimilate and organize, plan, and execute tasks. Working memory, planning/organization and mental flexibility are among the executive functions that have been studied in adults with ADHD.

Memory

Deficits in memory are considered a hallmark of ADHD for both children and adults, as is suggested by the DSM-IV criteria of forgetfulness and difficulty following through with tasks. Research has suggested that there are problems in both visual and verbal working and long-term memory in persons with ADHD.

Verbal memory

Agreement has largely been found with regard to deficits in verbal memory for adults with ADHD. Tests with more complex demands such as the Wechsler Memory Scales-III Logical Memory subtest (WMS-III) appear to be more sensitive than shorter tests such as the Digit Span subtest of the WAIS III. The Logical Memory subtest requires the patient to recall an entire story, while Digit Span requires immediate recall of number sequences. The numbers of story elements recalled immediately and after 30 minutes for Logical Memory have both been found to be lower for adults with ADHD. In children, the digits backwards condition of the Digit Span subtest has been shown to be more sensitive than digits forward to symptoms of ADHD [40].

Word-list learning tasks such as the California Verbal Learning Test (CVLT) and Rey Auditory Verbal Learning Test (RAVLT) have also been used to examine deficits in verbal memory, with strong results [37, 41]. The CVLT is a rich test that includes five trials for learning a list of words, an interference trial, short delay, long delay, recognition and measures for strategic approach to learning the list. Persons with ADHD have been shown to do more poorly than controls on nearly all of the CVLT measures. Adults with ADHD have been found to use serial rather than semantic clustering of the words (repeating in the order heard rather than grouping by category, e.g. *furniture, animals*) [35]. Anxiety has also been found to be an important factor in CVLT performance [42].

Visual memory

The strong findings for deficits in verbal memory have not been found in the visual domain. More complex tasks, such as the Rey–Osterrieth Complex Figure Test, appear to better differentiate control and ADHD groups than do simpler tasks such as the WMS Visual Reproduction test, which presents one relatively simple figure at a time [43]. Anxiety and depression may also affect performance on visual memory tasks. The WMS Spatial Span has not been useful in distinguishing ADHD from control groups [44]. In Hervey's meta-analysis, adults with ADHD did not appear to have a specific difficulty with visual-spatial memory; rather a general problem with encoding, retrieval, and organization of material was evident [37].

Additional executive functions

The term "executive functions" refers to the set of higher-level cognitive processes that control and regulate the behaviors needed for purposeful, goal-directed activity. They typically include working memory, and inhibition, discussed above, as well as planning, organization, and cognitive flexibility as well as the ability to self-monitor behaviors.

Planning

Tower tasks (i.e. Tower of London, Tower of Hanoi, Delis-Kaplan Executive Function System Tower Task) are typically used to assess planning. In this task, colored beads or disks are stacked in specific configurations on three pegs. Following specific rules, the patient must move the pegs to make a target configuration. In a study of young adults with average or better cognitive ability, The Tower of London–Drexel Edition was not found to distinguish between ADHD and control groups, or to strongly correlate with other

executive functioning variables except processing speed [45]. Although planning and organization has been widely recognized clinically as an area of difficulty for those with ADHD, tests that measure it do not seem to be effective in discriminating symptoms of ADHD.

Mental flexibility, fluency, and speed

Previous work with children has suggested that mental flexibility, or the ability to shift easily and effectively from one task to another, is compromised in persons who have ADHD. Unprompted word retrieval, such as is required on the Controlled Oral Word Association Task (COWAT), has been demonstrated to distinguish between ADHD and control groups [39]. Trails B has also been effective in differentiating adults with ADHD from those without ADHD [37]. Because fluency and flexibility tasks are generally performed under timed conditions, it is important to consider whether deficits in overall speed of processing are present.

Daily functioning

In reviewing the literature on group differences in performance on executive functioning measures, it seems clear that difficulties seen in daily life may not always map onto neuropsychological measures. For example, adults with ADHD are known to have a greater number of automobile accidents [46], poorer graduation rates and more problems at work [47], yet neuropsychological measures meant to assess planning, organization, strategy formation, and response to feedback do not seem to be effective discriminatory measures. Research indicates that children and adults with and without problems in executive functioning can have similar levels of primary ADHD symptoms [48], indicating a lack of specificity of executive functioning deficits for the disorder of ADHD. Moreover, differences observed in neuropsychological functioning with regard to executive functions reveal group differences in ADHD that are generally too small to be clinically significant at the individual level [49].

Clinically, it makes sense when working with adults to assess the domains of functioning most applicable to life success, such as social and work functioning. Research suggests that the high comorbidity of mood and anxiety disorders found in children extends to adults [50]. Adults with ADHD have been found to have had fewer years of education, lower rates of employment, and more multiple marriages than their unaffected peers [51]. Although adults with ADHD have been found to have higher rates of substance abuse, longitudinal studies suggest that people who received pharmacological treatment were less likely or at least not more likely to have drug abuse problems [52] than untreated peers after 10 years.

Neuropsychological measurement of adult ADHD

Measures of inhibition and sustained attention appear to be most universally reliable in the research literature on adult ADHD, mirroring findings in child research. Other neuropsychological measures of purported symptoms of ADHD are less reliable, suggesting broad heterogeneity and imperfect mapping of neuropsychological tasks onto real-world symptoms. Moreover, while group differences between people with and without ADHD may be seen on some measures, often the differences are too small to be clinically useful. Many research papers with significant findings reveal differences that may nonetheless be within the average range of functioning. Table 5b.1 shows the areas of functioning usually assessed, along with some current tests used for clinical evaluation.

Recently, more attention has been given to the possibility that executive functions may be divided into "hot" and "cool" processes, a concept first suggested by Zelazo and colleagues [53]. Cool executive functions are those of executive control, thought to be aspects of Barkley's [1] executive function pathway. Hot processes are suggested as the motivational and behavioral dysregulation seen in children with ADHD, and are distinct neurologically from cool processes. It may be that real-world functioning is ultimately based on the latter (hot) functions, meaning that on a day-to-day basis the motivation for performing a task, as well as executing the appropriate level of alertness and behavioral self-monitoring, affects success. In contrast, the cooler, purely cognitive aspects of functioning are more likely to be measured in the neuropsychological testing environment. This literature review suggests that there is more work to be done in better aligning clinical evaluation with ADHD symptoms.

Conclusion

Studies of neuropsychological functioning in adults with ADHD confirm that the core deficits in this disorder are attention and inhibition. These problems can be identified though assessment. The impact on executive functions, while theoretically persuasive, is not well documented empirically, specifically with the measurement tools that are available for assessment. It appears to be of primary importance to assess the daily functioning of adults with ADHD, and to consider the many other difficulties that this population brings to the clinical environment, such as problems with mood, conduct, and substance use/abuse, when considering factors contributing to distress. When reviewing the research literature, it is important to be aware of which specific ADHD populations the findings may apply to and whether the differences seen between groups are large enough to be clinically meaningful. There is much work to be done in the adult ADHD population to better understand how this childhood disorder manifests across development and impacts maturity.

The following section will review the findings from neuroimaging with adults with ADHD and how they relate to neuropsychological functioning and tests. These studies are just emerging and this overview will be fairly brief in nature. Both functional magnetic resonance imaging (fMRI) and structural imaging will be reviewed as well as their relation to neuropsychological functioning. In addition the relation between medications and brain activation will be discussed.

Neuroimaging in ADHD

Recently there has been an increase in studies that evaluate ADHD in adults using MRI. The research generally involves either structural analysis of anatomical structures in ADHD or functional magnetic resonance imaging which evaluates the activation of the brain as the participant completes a task. There are a few studies that also use positron emission tomography (PET) to study the effects of medication on brain activation. Table 5b.2 summarizes the findings from these studies.

MRI findings

Smaller volumes in cortical gray matter, the prefrontal cortex and anterior cingulate volumes in adults with larger volumes in white matter overall and in the gray matter of the nucleus accumbens have been found [54]. Other areas that have been found to be thinner in adults with ADHD include the dorsolateral prefrontal cortex and the anterior cingulate; areas associated with attention and executive functioning [55].

Table 5b.2. Findings from neuroimaging in adults with ADHD.

Author	Participants	Findings
Volumetric studies		
Hesslinger et al. [54]	8 ADHD:C[a]	C = ADHD for total brain volume
	17 Controls	C > ADHD in left orbitofrontal cortex volume
Seidman et al. [69]	24 ADHD	C > ADHD cortical gray matter
	18 Controls	C > ADHD prefrontal volume
		C > ADHD ACC[b] volume
		C < ADHD overall white matter volume
Nakris et al. [55]	24 ADHD	C > ADHD R[c] inferior parietal volume
(extension of Seidman et al. 2006 study)	18 Controls	C > ADHD R dorsolateral prefrontal volume
		C > ADHD R ACC
Functional MRI		
Bush et al. [56]	8 ADHD	Counting Stroop Task
	8 Controls	C > ADHD ACC
Schweitzer et al. [58]	6 ADHD	C > ADHD frontal and temporal regions
rCBF study[d]	6 Controls	C < ADHD widespread activation
		C < ADHD occipital lobe
Valera et al. [57]	20 ADHD	Working Memory Task
	20 Controls	C > ADHD cerebellar and occipital activation
		C = ADHD when participants with LD[e] removed
Hale et al. [70]	12 ADHD	Forward digit span
	12 Controls	C < ADHD left linguistic regions
		C < ADHD right dorsolateral and inferior frontal lobe
		C < ADHD right superior parietal lobe
		Backward digit span
		C < ADHD left linguistic regions
		C > ADHD bilateral parietal lobes
Castellanos et al. [71]	20 ADHD	Inhibition and working memory
	20 Controls	C > ADHD ACC
		C > ADHD precuneus and PCC[f] activation
Diffusion Tensor Imaging		
Ashtari et al. [72]	18 ADHD	More white matter in the following areas for C > ADHD
	15 Controls	Right premotor
		Right striatal
		Left cerebellum
		Left parieto-occipital
		Bilateral cerebral peduncles
Nakris et al. [55]	12 ADHD	More white matter in the following areas for C > ADHD
	17 Controls	Right superior longitudinal fasciculus
		Right cingulum bundle

[a] Attention deficit hyperactivity disorder: combined type.
[b] Anterior cingulate cortex.
[c] Right.
[d] Regional cerebral blood flow.
[e] Learning disability.
[f] Posterior cingulate cortex.

Functional magnetic resonance imaging (fMRI) studies have assisted in linking attention and executive functioning directly to brain activation. For volumetric studies this link is generally correlational in nature while for fMRI the relationship is more direct. Given the importance of the anterior regions for attention and executive control, many fMRI studies in adults have sought to evaluate the integrity of these systems in participants with ADHD. Table 5b.2 summarizes the findings from the fMRI studies. One of the earliest studies using fMRI in adults with ADHD found that patients showed less activation in the anterior cingulate while completing a task that requires response selection and inhibition [56]. There was greater activation in the brains of the participants with ADHD, suggesting less efficient processing.

Frontal lobe activation in adults with ADHD

With the advent of fMRI the frontal lobes remain an area of interest. Studies with adult participants have found that right frontal regions show less activation in adults with ADHD compared to controls on tasks that evaluate inhibition and working memory; this difference is evident even when no difference is found behaviorally [57]. It may well be that the areas that are involved in higher-order reasoning do not coordinate well with executive functioning, organization, and planning capacities of the frontal lobes, thus resulting in poorer performance in participants with ADHD. Moreover, widespread activity may result in inefficient processing of information. A regional cerebral blood flow (rCBF) study supports this conclusion. Findings from this study indicated that blood flow changes in women and men with ADHD differed from typical adults in that activation was more widespread and generally in the occipital regions. In contrast, the participants without ADHD showed higher levels of activation in the frontal and temporal regions [58].

Diffusion tensor imaging (DTI)

Diffusion tensor imaging (DTI) allows for the visualization of white matter tracts. DTI is used to evaluate the integrity of these tracts as well as the connectivity to various brain areas. Studies utilizing DTI have found less white matter in the right premotor, right striatal regions, and left cerebellar and parieto-occipital regions as well as in connections between the anterior and posterior regions of the brain [55]. This difference in white matter tracts may be related to the difficulties described above where there appeared

to less efficient processing of information. Thus, these differences also serve to support the idea that fewer connections across (front to back) the brains of people with ADHD contribute to a disconnect between reasoning skills and those involved in association and previous learning. Both of these difficulties are present in ADHD and appear to be active throughout adolescence and adulthood.

Medication and imaging

A new area of investigation is the use of fMRI to evaluate the effects of medication on performance. Current research has suggested that catecholamine dysregulation, particularly with dopamine, is associated with the frontostriatal deficits seen in ADHD. These deficits include problems with activity level as well as difficulties in reward-seeking behaviors. Studies using PET imaging to compare adults with ADHD with those without ADHD have found a relation between the structures associated with the regulation of dopamine and brain differences in participants with ADHD, particularly in the right caudate. In addition, the caudate reacts differentially in people with ADHD when methylphenidate is administered [59].

Conclusion

Neuroimaging studies have shown promise for understanding brain structure and activation differences in adults with ADHD. Initial studies have found results similar to those of children with activation differences present in the dorsolateral prefrontal regions as well as in the basal ganglia. The brain activation found in neuroimaging appears to be sensitive to medication with a lessening of differences in activation between adults with and without ADHD when there is a history of stimulant medication use. White matter tracts have also been found to differ in adults with ADHD from those without, with fewer tracts found in the right hemisphere. These white matter differences probably interfere with efficient processing of information, particularly attentional abilities, through the tracts that are important in determining what and where aspects of a task. Further study of the effects of medication as well as activation differences in subtypes of ADHD in adults is important. As there is emerging evidence of gender differences in activation in adults with ADHD, additional study as to gender variations would also be helpful. Moreover, given the initial discussion of the age-of-onset controversy, it may be interesting to study late onset versus early onset to determine whether there are activation differences and/or white matter tract variations.

Treatment for adults with ADHD

For children with ADHD, pharmacotherapy and psychotherapy are treatment options that are used frequently. There is also a rich literature on how best to adjust the environment for children with ADHD, as well as guidance for parents and teachers on behavioral management (refer to the previous chapter for an extended discussion of this literature). In general, the treatment focus for children tends to be on the child's surrounding adult system. For adults with ADHD, environmental modification options are often more limited. Few job supervisors are willing to provide interventions that are frequently used for children, for example, color-coded folders, timers, frequent breaks, or tangible immediate rewards and post-task check-ups multiple times per day. While the research on adult therapies is less substantive than for children, some studies on pharmacological management and psychotherapies have been conducted. Overall, the treatment options for adults fall into three categories: pharmacotherapy, psychotherapy/psychoeducation and coping strategies/environmental modification.

Pharmacological treatments

Following the substantial literature on child ADHD medication treatment, stimulant treatment for adults with ADHD has been the primary model of care. In early studies of adult response to stimulants, an unexplained difference in response rate between adults and children to stimulants was found. Controlled studies on children reported a 70% response rate, while the adult response was lower, at about 50% [60]. More recent studies, however, have demonstrated outcomes consistent with the child research. Spencer et al. [60] suggest that earlier studies were characterized by doses that were too low, around 0.6 mg/kg per day. In a study of methylphenidate (MPH) including a double-blind placebo-controlled design, Spencer et al. used a target dose of 1 mg/kg per day and found a 78% response rate.

Of the stimulant medications, methylphenidate (MPH) has been identified as the preferred treatment for most adults with ADHD. One of the biggest risks of medication· for ADHD is appetite suppression/loss. Longer-acting stimulants are associated with greater appetite loss than are shorter-acting stimulants. A meta-analysis of 22 placebo-controlled studies concluded that immediate-release MPH had the most

"favorable balance of benefits and harms" [61]. Non-stimulant medications such as atomoxetine (Strattera) are also being used to treat symptoms of ADHD. Atomoxetine has been shown to reduce ADHD symptoms by 25–30% in roughly half to about 70% of the participants in a recent study, depending on previous medication history [62].

The use of antidepressants has been extended to treat symptoms of ADHD. The tricyclics imipramine, desipramine, and buproprion have been studied in children, adolescents and adults, with positive effects reported [62]. Monoamine oxidase inhibitors (MAOIs) have not been studied to the same extent as the other antidepressants. A few small studies have been done on fluoxetine and venlafaxine, with reports of up to a 77% response rate, but the dropout rate due to adverse effects ranged from 21% to 25% [62].

In general, pharmacological treatment of ADHD symptoms in adults has mirrored the success of treatment with children. However, the measures used to evaluate success have solely relied on reduction of behavioral symptoms, typically in the range 25%–30%. No studies were found that evaluated psychosocial variables such as academic or occupational performance, risky behavior, or social interaction so important to adult functioning. Moreover, the studies reported above have usually included heterogeneous ADHD groups, thus little is known about the relative efficacy of medication for specific subgroups of ADHD.

Psychotherapy and psychoeducation

While medication can alleviate symptoms of ADHD, it does not provide guidance on the coping skills and strategies needed for adults with ADHD to be successful in daily functioning. Adults with ADHD experience much higher rates of failure in relationships, work, and academic environments, which suggests that such strategies are needed to improve their long-term outcomes. Moreover, the high rates of comorbidity with mood and anxiety disorders, conduct problems, and substance abuse call for treatment that addresses highly complex clinical presentations.

Although psychoeducation may play an important role in treating ADHD, particularly for clinic-referred adults who were not treated or identified in childhood, Barkley et al. [63] caution that ADHD leads primarily to deficits in *performance*, not knowledge. A person with ADHD may not behave appropriately even though they clearly understand, for example, that they should not drink and drive, blow up at the boss, or defer an important task for the sake of immediate pleasure. Thus, a combination of psychoeducation and cognitive-behavioral therapy (CBT) has been suggested as the best way to provide non-medication support for adults with ADHD [64].

Outcome studies of CBT for adults with ADHD are limited and have been generally of poor quality. Most are chart-reviews, include small clinical samples, and typically have been conducted without control groups. All of these studies looked at short-term reduction of ADHD symptoms based on DSM-IV-related self-rating scales. Only one study reviewed clearly identified the sample with a report on socio-economic status, employment, and education [65], indicating a well-educated, high-functioning group. Each of the studies reviewed reported a reduction in ADHD core symptoms in the short term, but none followed real-world outcomes in the long term. No study formally evaluated their treatment against the efficacy of medication alone. In a study of combined medication and CBT treatment, participants improved, but it was not possible to determine the effect of CBT above that of medication [66]. The authors suggest that therapy might have helped participants cope with depression and anxiety, and increase their persistence when faced with challenges.

At this time, no strong support regarding the efficacy of psychotherapy alone or in combination with medication is evident for adults with ADHD. In children, the effects of cognitive-behavioral therapy have not demonstrated strong benefits beyond that of parent training and medication [67]. Children appear to benefit more from behavioral interventions such as contingency systems that are less applicable to the adult population. Barkley et al. [63] suggest that behavioral training that is disassociated from the moment of actual performance of the task will be less effective than treatment that occurs in the moment, because people with ADHD often do not perform according to their own best knowledge, and associating actions with choices in the past is more difficult. Moreover, insight into why things go awry may be more limited. Thus, treatment in the form of environmental modification and *in situ* coaching may be more effective forms of support for adults with ADHD.

Coping strategies/environmental modification

There is no research documenting whether individual coaching or workplace accommodations are effective for adults with ADHD. Barkley et al. [63] have outlined theoretical principles for supporting adults through these approaches, based on both child evidence of effective behavioral treatments and areas of failure to which clinicians should pay attention. They recommend, first, that identification of and attention to comorbid disorders such as substance abuse and depression occur; such difficulties should be identified and treated. Educational and occupational impairments are likely to be present, requiring knowledge of the applicability of the Americans with Disabilities Act in order to design accommodations for problematic environments. Financial management assistance is another area in which adults with ADHD are often suggested to need assistance; similarly, health management may be an area of focus, as well.

Taking a hint from child studies, Barkley et al. [63] recommend that tangible reinforcement systems may be needed for adults to accomplish tasks. This system places a burden on family and workplace cohorts to provide the motivational structure that cannot be generated internally by an adult with ADHD. Similar to the methods used for children, "chunking" of work tasks into manageable units, with immediate feedback and rewards for appropriate performance, may assist in work completion. Making the internal timeline public, for example providing visual cues of the work stream, may also assist with task completion and on-time behavior. Barkley et al. [63] conclude that although these interventions may work at least partially, there is no empirical evidence supporting them at this time.

Conclusion

The current state of treatment research strongly indicates that medication therapy is the best frontline approach for adults with ADHD. Successful application of pharmacotherapy can positively affect the core symptoms that cascade into problems in daily functioning. Still, research into the long-term outcomes of the various medication types utilized is needed. Comorbidity continues to pose special problems. Stimulant medications have been shown to mitigate symptoms specific to ADHD, but most adults presenting with ADHD have complex profiles.

Cognitive behavioral psychotherapy appears to be largely ineffective above the effects of medication, although rigorous studies like those conducted in children have not been pursued. Modest gains may be related to improvement in mood; specifically, there is evidence that ADHD symptom self-report scales, often used to assess symptom reduction, are also sensitive to Axis I mood and anxiety disorders [68]. Thus, with therapy, adults with ADHD may feel better in the short term, which is reflected in changes in scores on the rating scales used for ADHD assessment. Barkley et al.'s [63] conceptualization of adult ADHD suggests that any treatment that is temporally removed from the moment, particularly when an action is needed or taken, will not be successful. Adjustment of the environment, externalization of motivation and temporal cues, and tangible rewards are suggested. Although no research has investigated the efficacy of these ideas, they are derived from the substantial research in child ADHD.

Treatment for ADHD in adults has lagged far behind that of child research. Specific areas that need further investigation include differential response to medications based on subtypes and comorbidities, long-term outcomes for daily functioning, and efficacy of *in situ* behavioral treatments. Improvements in the lives of adults with ADHD most likely require a multisystemic approach including medication, treatment of comorbid disorders, and family/workplace support.

Final thoughts

As research progresses, a link between the neuropsychological deficits seen in adults with ADHD, neuroimaging results, and response to medication is beginning to be forged. Diagnostic issues as well as the existence of comorbid disorders continue to be areas that require further study and clarification. It is also not clear from the research how we may be able to predict which adolescents will be able to sufficiently compensate for their attentional difficulties and no longer require medication.

There are few studies that evaluate brain structure and function while controlling for medication response and/or treatment history. Studies with children with ADHD with and without a treatment history have found differences both neuropsychologically as well as structurally/functionally [45]. These issues need further study and evaluation.

Similar to research with children and adolescents with ADHD, there are few studies that evaluate possible differences between subtypes. Most studies use adults with a broad array of ADHD symptoms and do not control for number of hyperactive/impulse symptoms. Adults with ADHD who evidence higher levels of impulsivity may well differ from those with a sole deficit in attention. These differences require

further study, as do the developmental issues that are present in individuals with ADHD. Given the finding that white matter differences are present from young to older children, it would be interesting to analyze whether there are developmental changes that mirror that of typically developing individuals. It would be very exciting if we become able to predict which individuals will improve on neuropsychological tests and are able to respond to particular interventions, and whether these interventions are related to brain structure and function.

Further study as to alternative interventions with or without medication is another avenue of research that may assist in our understanding of ADHD in adults. There are few studies that evaluate the efficacy of therapy with adults with ADHD; this is quite problematic and of concern. One of the most commonly prescribed therapies is CBT – yet there were only four studies that were found in our review of the literature and they did not provide evidence for the efficacy of such therapy. Thus, an area that has been sorely neglected in work with adults with ADHD is what the most appropriate behavioral treatment is, in addition to medication. This issue is particularly important given the finding that many adults do not achieve their potential, are under-employed, and have a higher risk for accidents as well as substance abuse. These deficits in our understanding of adults with ADHD are an area of particular importance similar to the importance of interventions with children. Empirically supported interventions are key not only to understanding the disorder but also in treatment of ADHD.

Key chapter points

1. ADHD in adults presents differently from ADHD in children. The primary difficulty is found in attention and executive functioning in adults, while for children overactivity is the prime area of concern, as well as inattention.

2. Age of onset for an ADHD diagnosis is an area of controversy and has not been resolved. Some suggest a cut-off of 12 for symptoms to appear while others adhere to a cut-off of 7. This cut-off appears to differentially affect women compared to men.

3. Neuropsychological testing needs to be comprehensive when evaluating the presence or absence of ADHD. There is currently not a particular profile that definitively diagnoses ADHD, but rather a group of strengths and weaknesses that

may be individual in their impact, but have in common a difficulty in functioning when attentional resources are limited.

4. Neuroimaging is uncovering differences in areas of the brain that are associated with ADHD. These include the caudate, frontal white matter, and anterior cingulate regions. Further study is needed that links these anatomic areas with functional differences in performance and behavior.

5. Interventions include psychopharmacology and cognitive behavioral treatment. These treatments when used in conjunction have been found to be the most efficacious.

References

1. Barkley RA, Behavioral inhibition, sustained attention, and executive functions: Constructing a unifying theory of ADHD. *Psychol Bull* 1997;**121**:65–94.

2. Semrud-Clikeman M, et al. Rapid naming deficits in children and adolescents with reading disabilities and attention deficit hyperactivity disorder. *Brain Lang*, 2000; **74**:70–83.

3. Biederman J, Faraone SV, Spencer T. Patterns of psychiatric comorbidity, cognition, and psychosocial functioning in adults with attention deficit hyperactivity disorder. *Am J Psychiatry*, 1993;**150**:1792–8.

4. Wilens T, Faraone SV, Biederman, J. Attention-deficit/hyperactivity disorder in adults. *JAMA*, 2004;**292**:619–23.

5. Faraone SV, et al. Attention-deficit/hyperactivity disorder in adults: an overview. *Biol Psychiatry* 2000;**48**:9–20.

6. Faraone SV. Attention deficit hyperactivity disorder in adults: implications for theories of diagnosis. *Curr Dir Psychol Sci* 2000;**9**:33–6.

7. Rasmussen P, Gillberg C. Natural outcome of ADHD with developmental coordination disorder at age 22 years: a controlled, longitudinal, community-based study. *J Am Acad Child Adolesc Psychiatry* 2000;**39**:1424–31.

8. Biederman J, Mick E, Faraone SV. Age-dependent decline of ADHD symptoms revisited: impact of remission, definition, and symptom subtype. *Am J Psychiatry* 2000;**157**:9–20.

9. Barkley RA, et al. Driving in young adults with attention deficit hyperactivity disorder: knowledge, performance, adverse outcomes, and the role of executive functioning. *J Int Neuropsychol Soc* 2002;**8**:656–72.

10. Kessler RC, Merikangas KR. The National Comorbidity Survey Replication (NCS-R): background and aims. *I J Methods Psychiatric Res* 2004;**13**:60–8.

11. American Psychiatric Association. *Diagnostic and Statistical Manual of Mental Disorders*, 4th text revision edn. American Psychiatric Association; 2000.

12. Murphy K, Barkley RA. Attention deficit hyperactivity disorder adults: Comorbidities and adaptive impairments. *Compr Psychiatry* 1996;**37**:393–401.

13. Downey K, et al. Adult attention deficit hyperactivity disorder: Psychological test profiles in a clinical population. *J Nerv Mental Disord* 1997;**185**:32–8.

14. Manuzza S, et al. Accuracy of adult recall of childhood attention deficit hyperactivity disorder. *Am J Psychiatry* 2002;**159**:1882–8.

15. Faraone SV. Genetics of adult attention-deficit/hyperactivity disorder. *Psychiatr Clin North Am*, 2004;**27**:303–21.

16. Faraone SV, et al. Neuropsychological studies of late onset and subthreshold diagnosis of adult Attention-Deficit/Hyperactivity Disorder. *Biol Psychiatry* 2006; **60**:1081–7.

17. Barkley RA, Biederman J. Toward a broader definition of the age-of-onset criterion for attention-deficit hyperactivity disorder. *J Am Acad Child Adolesc Psychiatry* 1997;**36**:1204–10.

18. Schaughency EA, et al. Self reported inattention, impulsivity, and hyperactivity at ages 15 and 18 in the general population. *J Am Acad Child Adolesc Psychiatry* 1994;**33**:173–84.

19. Rohde LA, et al. Exploring ADHD age-of-onset criterion in Brazilian adolescents. *Eur Child Adolesc Psychiatry* 2000;**9**:212–18.

20. Applegate B, et al. Validity of the age of onset criterion for Attention-Deficit/Hyperactivity Disorder: a report from the DSM IV field trials. *J Am Acad Child Adolesc Psychiatry* 1997;**36**:1211–21.

21. Faraone SV, et al. Diagnosing adult Attention Deficit Hyperactivity Disorder: are late onset and subthreshold diagnoses valid? *Am J Psychiatry* 2006;**163**:1720–9.

22. McGough JJ, Barkley RA. Diagnostic controversies in adult attention deficit hyperactivity disorder. *Am J Psychiatry* 2004;**161**:1948–56.

23. Faraone SV, et al. Substance use among ADHD adults: implications of late onset and subthreshold diagnoses. *Am J Addict* 2007;**16**:24–34.

24. Fischer M, et al. Young adult follow-up of hyperactive children: self-reported psychiatric disorders, comorbidity, and the role of childhood conduct problems and teen CD. *J Abnorm Child Psychol* 2002;**30**:463–72.

25. Millstein R, et al. Presenting ADHD symptoms and subtypes of clinically referred adults with ADHD. *J Attent Disord* 1997;**2**:159–66.

26. Murphy K, Barkley RA, Bush T. Young adults with attention deficit hyperactivity disorder: subtype differences in comorbidity, educational and clinical history. *J Nerv Ment Dis* 2002;**190**:147–57.

27. Miller TW, Nigg JT, Faraone SV. Axis I and II comorbidity in adults with ADHD. *J Abnorm Psychol*, 2007;**116**:519–28.

28. Fossati A, et al. History of childhood attention deficit/hyperactivity disorder symptoms and borderline personality disorder: a controlled study. *Compr Psychiatry* 2002; **43**:369–77.

29. Biederman J, et al. Family-genetic and psychosocial risk factors in DSM III attention deficit disorder. *J Am Acad Child Adolesc Psychiatry* 1990;**29**:526–33.

30. Hill J, Schoener E. Age-dependent decline of attention deficit hyperactivity disorder. *Am J Psychiatry* 1996;**153**:1143–6.

31. Biederman J, et al. Influence of gender on attention deficit hyperactivity disorder in children referred to a psychiatric clinic. *Am J Psychiatry* 2002;**159**:36–42.

32. Biederman J, et al. Gender effects on Attention-Deficit/Hyperactivity Disorder in adults, revisited. *Biol Psychiatry* 2004;**55**:692–700.

33. Rucklidge JJ, Kaplan BJ. Psychological functioning of women identified in adulthood with Attention-Deficit/Hyperactivity Disorder. *J Atten Disord* 1997;**2**:167–76.

34. Rashid FL, Morris MK, Morris R. Naming and verbal memory skills in adults with Attention Deficit Hyperactivity Disorder and Reading Disability. *J Clin Psychol* 2001;**57**(6):829–38.

35. Seidman LJ, et al. Neuropsychological function in adults with attention-deficit hyperactivity disorder. *Biol Psychiatry* 1998;**44**(4):260–8.

36. Stavro GM, Ettenhofer ML, Nigg JT. Executive functions and adaptive functioning in young adult attention-deficit/hyperactivity disorder. *J Int Neuropsychol Soc* 2007;**13**(2):324–34.

37. Hervey AS, Epstein JN, Curry JF. Neuropsychology of adults with Attention-Deficit/Hyperactivity disorder: a meta-analytic review. *Neuropsychology* 2004;**18**(3):485–503.

38. Logan GD. On the ability to inhibit thought and action. A user's guide to the Stop Signal Paradigm. In Dagenbach D, Carr T, eds. *Inhibitory Processes in Attention, Memory, and Language*, San Diego, CA: Academic Press; 1994:189–239.

39. Boonstra AM, et al. Executive functioning in adult ADHD: a meta-analytic review. *Psychol Med* 2005; **35**:1097–108.

40. Rosenthal EN, et al. Digit Span components as predictors of attention problems and executive functioning in children. *Arch Clin Neuropsychol* 2006;**21**(2):131–9.

41. Dige N, Wik G. Adult attention deficit hyperactivity disorder identified by neuropsychological testing. *Int J Neurosci* 2005;**115**(2):169–83.

42. Roth RM, et al. Contribution of organizational strategy to verbal learning and memory in adults with attention-deficit/hyperactivity disorder. *Neuropsychology* 2004;**18**(1):78–84.

43. Johnson DE, et al. Neuropsychological performance deficits in adults with attention deficit/hyperactivity disorder. *Arch Clin Neuropsychol* 2001;**16**(6):587–604.

44. Schweitzer JB, Hanford RB, Medoff DR. Working memory deficits in adults with ADHD: is there evidence for subtype differences *Behav Brain Funct* 2006;**2**:43.

45. Semrud-Clikeman M, Pliszka SR, Liotti M. Executive functioning in children with ADHD:Combined Type with and without a stimulant medication history. *Neuropsychology* 2008;**22**:329–40.

46. Barkley RA. Driving impairments in teens and adults with attention-deficit/hyperactivity disorder. *Psychiatr Clin North Am* 2004;**27**:233–60.

47. Biederman J, Faraone SV. The effects of attention-deficit/hyperactivity disorder on employment and household income. *Med Gen Med* 2006;**8**(3).

48. Biederman J, et al. Impact of executive function deficits and attention-deficit/hyperactivity disorder (ADHD) on academic outcomes in children. *J Consul Clin Psychol* 2004;**72**(5):757–66.

49. Sonuga-Barke EJS, et al. Executive dysfunction and delay aversion in Attention Deficit/Hyperactivity Disorder: nosologic and diagnostic implications. *Child Adolesc Psychiatr Clin* 2008;**17**:367–84.

50. Tannock R. Attention-Deficit/Hyperactivity Disorder with anxiety disorders. In Brown TE, ed. *Attention-Deficit Disorders and Comorbidities in Children, Adolescents, and Adults*. Washington DC: American Psychiatric Press; 2000: 125–70.

51. Faraone SV, et al. Attention-deficit/hyperactivity disorder in adults: an overview. *Biolog Psychiatry* 2000;**48**(1):9–20.

52. Biederman J, Petty CR, Wilens TE, Fraire MG, Purcell CA, Mick E, Monuteaux MC, & Faraone SV (2008). Familial risk analyses of attention deficit hyperactivity disorder and substance abuse disorders. *American Journal of Psychiatry*, **165**, 107–15.

53. Zelazo PD, et al. Abstract. *Monogr Soc Res Child Dev* 2003;**68**(3):vii–viii.

54. Hesslinger B, et al. Frontoorbital volume reductions in adult patients with attention deficit hyperactivity disorder. *Neurosci Lett* 2002;**328**:319–21.

55. Nakris N, et al. Cortical thinning of the attention and executive function networks in adults with Attention-Deficit/Hyperactivity Disorder. *Cereb Cortex* 2007;**17**:1364–75.

56. Bush G, et al. Anterior cingulate cortex dysfunction in Attention-Deficit/Hyperactivity Disorder revealed by fMRI and the counting Stroop. *Biol Psychiatry* 1999;**45**:1542–52.

57. Valera EM, et al. Functional neuroanatomy of working memory in adults with Attention-Deficit/Hyperactivity Disorder. *Biol Psychiatry* 2005;**57**:439–47.

58. Schweitzer JB, et al. Alterations in the functional anatomy of working memory in adult Attention Deficit Hyperactivity Disorder. *Am J Psychiatry* 2000;**157**:278–80.

59. Bush G, et al. Functional magnetic resonance imaging of methylphenidate and placebo in Attention-Deficit/Hyperactivity Disorder during the multi-source interference task. *Arch Gen Psychiatry* 2008;**65**:102–14.

60. Spencer TJ, Biederman J, Wilens T. Stimulant treatment of adult attention-deficit/hyperactivity disorder. *Psychiatr Clin North Am* 2004;**27**(2):361–72.

61. Peterson K, McDonagh MS, Fu R. Comparative benefits and harms of competing medications for adults with attention-deficit hyperactivity disorder: a systematic review and indirect comparison meta-analysis. *Psychopharmacology (Berl)* 2008;**197**(1):1–11.

62. Spencer TJ, Biederman J, Wilens T. Nonstimulant treatment of adult attention-deficit/hyperactivity disorder. *Psychiatr Clin North Am* 2004;**27**(2):373–83.

63. Barkley RA, Murphy K, Fischer M. *ADHD in Adults: What the Science Says.* New York, NY: The Guildford Press; 2008.

64. McDermott SP. Cognitive therapy for adults with Attention-Deficit/Hyperactivity Disorder. In Brown TE, ed. *Attention-Deficit Disorders and Comorbidities in Children, Adolescents, and Adults.* Washington DC: American Psychiatric Press; 2000; 569–606.

65. Solanto MV, et al. Development of a new psychosocial treatment for adult ADHD. *J Atten Disord* 2008;**11**(6):728–36.

66. Rostain AL, Ramsay JR. A combined treatment approach for adults with ADHD – results of an open study of 43 patients. *J Atten Disord* 2006;**10**(2):150–9.

67. Semrud-Clikeman M, et al. An intervention approach for children with teacher- and parent-identified attentional difficulties. *J Learn Disabil* 1999;**32**(6):581–90.

68. Solanto MV, Etefia K, Marks DJ. The utility of self-report measures and the continuous performance test in the diagnosis of ADHD in adults. *CNS Spectr* 2004;**9**(9):649–59.

69. Seidman L, Valera E, Markris N, Monuteaux MC, Boriel D, Kelkar K. Dorsolateral prefrontal and anterior cingulate cortex volumetric abnormalities in adults with attention deficit/hyperactivity disorder identified by magnetic resonance imaging. *Biol Psychiatry* 2006;**60**: 1071–80.

70. Hale TS, Bookheimer S, McGough JJ, Phillips JM, McCracken JT. Atypical brain activation during simple and complex levels of processing adult ADHD. *J Attent Disord* 2007;**11**:125–40.

71. Castellanos FX, Margulies DS, Kelly C, Uddin LQ, Ghaffari M, Krisch A, Shaw D, Shehzad Z, Di Martino A, Biswal B, Sonuga-Barke EJS, Rotrosen J, Adler LA, Milham MP. Cingulate-precuneus interactions: a new locus of dysfunction in adult attention-deficit/hyperactivity disorder. *Biol Psychiatry* 2008;**63**: 332–7.

72. Ashtari M, Kumra S, Bhaskar SL, Clarke T, Thaden E, Cerbellione KL. Attention-deficit/hyperactivity disorder: a preliminary diffusion tensor imaging study. *Biol Psychiatry* 2005;**57**:448–55.

Attention deficit hyperactivity disorder: a lifespan synthesis

Jeffrey M. Halperin, Anne-Claude V. Bedard and Olga G. Berwid

Introduction

Taken together, the data presented in the previous two chapters paint a clear picture of attention deficit hyperactivity disorder (ADHD) as a highly prevalent, heterogeneous, and oftentimes lifelong neurobehavioral disorder that results in considerable functional impairment for afflicted individuals. Further, while efficacious treatments are available, most provide limited long-term benefits. As discussed in the prior chapters, ADHD is quite prevalent in childhood, making it more the rule than the exception that classrooms will have at least one child with the disorder. Prevalence rates are generally estimated to be lower among adults, but it is this group that is beginning to be clinically referred and identified at much higher rates in recent years, and this primarily accounts for the substantial increase in medication prescriptions written to treat ADHD. Yet knowledge regarding continuity between the childhood, adolescent, and adult conditions in ADHD remains quite limited.

That ADHD is a heterogeneous disorder is generally well accepted throughout the scientific literature, and these multiple sources of variability are problematic for the diagnosis, study, and treatment of ADHD. This heterogeneity is perhaps most apparent phenomenologically with regard to the core defining symptom domains, as evidenced by the three distinct subtypes (predominantly inattentive [ADHD-I], predominantly hyperactive/impulsive [ADHD-HI], and combined [ADHD-C]), as well as with regard to associated features and comorbidities. As described in the previous chapters, it is the exception rather than the rule when an individual with ADHD does not meet criteria for at least one other psychiatric disorder and/or a learning disability. Further, individuals diagnosed with ADHD are neuropsychologically heterogeneous with regard to the nature of their neurocognitive impairments and abilities, and most likely their underlying neural pathophysiology. Finally, when taking a developmental or lifespan perspective, ADHD appears to be highly variable in its clinical manifestations during differing phases of life. Thus, during the preschool years, those with ADHD are most clearly characterized by extreme hyperactivity, often accompanied by low frustration tolerance and marked inhibitory control deficits. Throughout the school-age years, hyperactivity tends to diminish, while emerging impairments in attention, goal-directed effort, and impulsivity are observed, with each of these later difficulties associated with high levels of functional impairment. Finally, by later adolescence and in adulthood, severe difficulties associated with hyperactivity are relatively uncommon; instead, impairments resulting from disorganization, forgetfulness, and failure to sustain effort are observed, often with impulsiveness and risk-taking behaviors also occurring.

It is unclear the extent to which these distinct "faces" of ADHD at different phases of life are associated with or due to similar or distinct underlying neural substrates. Some data suggest that, early on, ADHD is characterized by a rather heterogeneous set of nonspecific neuropsychological deficits that become more specific to executive functioning later in life [1], and several brain regions that appear deviant in children with ADHD normalize over development [2, 3]. However, far more data from longitudinal samples are required to fully elucidate these developmental variations and to begin to determine the degree to which differences in the clinical manifestations of ADHD are due to developmentally sensitive neural mechanisms inherent to the disorder, or an epiphenomenon related to ever-changing environmental (e.g. social, educational, vocational) demands placed on the individual.

While it is becoming increasingly well accepted that ADHD is a lifelong disorder for many if not most afflicted individuals, this observation too deserves further scrutiny. Historically, ADHD has been conceptualized as a disorder of early onset, most typically beginning during the preschool years, but with clear signs before the age of 7 years. However, as described by Semrud-Clikeman and Fine (Chapter 5b), several investigators have suggested that evidence of early childhood onset should not be required, and that those whose symptoms and impairments emerge later in life are phenotypically and perhaps genetically similar to those with early onset. Similarly, for many children, ADHD may not be an enduring lifelong disorder. While there is considerable evidence from longitudinal studies that ADHD frequently persists into adulthood, this does not appear to be the case for all children with the disorder [4, 5]. Thus, further conceptual exploration and empirical research into the neural and environmental factors that account for this developmental variation in emergence and persistence are warranted.

With regard to treatment, the greatest empirical support for efficacy is for psychostimulant medication, with accumulating evidence supporting the utility of some non stimulant medications as well. Several psychosocial interventions, primarily in the form of behavior modification procedures taught to parents and teachers, have also shown considerable, albeit less consistent, promise, particularly with children. As described by Semrud-Clikeman and Fine, these latter interventions have more limited utility with adults, since there are typically fewer individuals in their environments who can help to apply these procedures. While active medication and behavior-modification treatments have a substantial impact on symptom severity and impairment for many afflicted individuals, these effects do not heal the underlying pathophysiology or determinants of the disorder. Further, the impact of these treatment modalities on neuropsychological functioning is moderate in strength at best. Thus, to the extent that ADHD can be considered a neuropsychological disorder, some goals of treatment may be only partially achieved. Finally, due to the side effects of many medications, and the challenges in continuing psychosocial interventions for longer periods, it is the rule, rather than the exception, that these treatments are implemented for relatively short durations. As such, there is usually a disconnect between the generally accepted chronicity of ADHD and the typical short-term duration of most interventions. Not only do most symptoms and impairment return shortly after treatment is terminated, but there are few data that support the highly desired goal of treatment improving long-term outcomes of individuals with ADHD. Thus, new directions for treatment development, with an eye towards long-term benefits across the lifespan, are sorely needed.

Below, we will explore in greater depth the above-outlined issues with a focus on the developmental/lifespan perspective. Specifically, we will examine (a) the continuities/discontinuities between the preschool, middle childhood, adolescent and adult manifestations of ADHD, both behaviorally and neuropsychologically; (b) the impact of phenotypic and potentially underlying heterogeneity on our ability to diagnose and elucidate the underlying biological substrates of ADHD; and (c) possible directions for novel approaches to treatment that will have greater potential for changing the overall developmental trajectory for this lifelong disorder. While resisting constraint by a particular perspective or theoretical conceptualization of ADHD, much of our discussion will be framed by the developmental perspective outlined by Halperin and Schulz [6], which posits distinct neural mechanisms for the etiology and subsequent developmental trajectories of ADHD across the lifespan.

Theoretical conceptualizations of ADHD

Theoretical characterizations of what we now call ADHD have evolved considerably throughout the past century, from what was originally conceptualized as a "moral defect" [7], to a disorder that was primarily behavioral in nature and related to hyperkinesis and/or impulse control deficits, to more of a cognitive disorder of attention, to one of higher-order executive functions [8]. Yet it is notable that, unlike many psychiatric disorders, throughout most of its history ADHD has been conceptualized as a disorder of neurological dysfunction rather than a condition of primarily psychogenic origin. Scientific consensus has clearly and consistently rallied around the point that ADHD is not caused by bad parents or teachers. This is not to say that the symptom expression and behavioral functioning of individuals with ADHD are not influenced substantially by environmental factors and that an array of environmental factors clearly affect neural development and behavior. However, a core understanding of ADHD requires a brain-based perspective.

To date, data derived from an array of neurocognitive and neuroimaging studies have generated a number of compelling conceptualizations regarding the "core deficit" underlying ADHD. Among the most clearly articulated are what are generally referred to as (1) the "state regulation" model [9], (2) the "delay aversion model" [10], and (3) the "inhibitory control" model [8]. The state-regulation model [9] posits core deficits in underlying "arousal" and "activation" systems that most likely emanate from the brainstem, are highly influenced by noradrenergic and serotonergic neurotransmission, and terminate in cognitive control regions of the dorsolateral prefrontal cortex. The delay aversion model [10], which is more motivationally based, posits an inability to delay rewards and a characterization of behavior that seeks smaller immediate rewards over larger rewards for which the individual must wait. This model is most closely linked with dopaminergic pathways originating in the ventral striatum that ascend primarily via pathways in the medial prefrontal cortex. The inhibitory control model [8] posits that a core inability to delay actions results in secondary deficits in four aspects of executive control: nonverbal working memory, internalization of speech, self-regulation of affect/motivation/effort, and reconstitution. These executive deficits, in turn, produce the phenotypic deficits and impairments that characterize ADHD. Barkley [8] posits that these deficits are caused by anomalies in primarily right lateralized circuits connecting the basal ganglia and prefrontal cortex.

Borrowing heavily from these models, Halperin and Schulz [6] have attempted to conceptualize ADHD from a developmental lifespan perspective. At the core of this model is the notion that distinct mechanisms underlie the etiology and the course/trajectory of ADHD severity throughout the lifespan. Specifically, it was posited that ADHD is due to subcortical neural dysfunction that is present early in ontogeny and remains present and relatively static throughout the lifetime. This subcortical dysfunction could be analogous to brainstem-related state-regulation deficits posited by Sergeant, reward-related deficits in the ventral striatum posited by Sonuga-Barke, and/or cerebellar-related impairments associated with timing and motor control, as suggested by more recent neuroimaging studies [11]. In contrast to the notions of others [8, 12], according to this conceptualization, ADHD is not *caused* by higher cortical or executive impairments. Rather, these more rostral brain regions and their associated neuropsychological processes are posited to be highly influential in the developmental course and trajectory of ADHD across the lifespan. Specifically, it is hypothesized that the development of these higher cortical (perhaps executive)

functions throughout childhood and adolescence is involved in the diminution of symptoms often seen with age and the degree to which individuals with ADHD adapt or can compensate for their subcortically driven deficits through "top-down" regulatory control [6]. Thus, from this perspective, ADHD is a life-long disorder that emerges very early in development. The degree to which symptoms persist and cause impairment throughout the lifespan is largely dependent upon the degree to which later-developing brain regions can compensate for these early-emerging deficits.

Sources of phenotypic variability across the lifespan

That preschoolers, school-age children, adolescents and adults with ADHD appear different is well described in the scientific and clinical literature. In general, these developmental changes occur gradually, in a dimensional fashion, rather than as abrupt "all-or-none" phenomena. Patterns of extreme hyperactivity, which are characteristic of the preschool years, generally diminish over time, while symptoms falling more within the realm of the inattention domain become more prominent and impairing with increasing age [13]. The degree to which impulsiveness has large developmental variation is less clear, as it is a source of considerable impairment associated with both younger and older manifestations of the disorder.

Not surprisingly, developmental variations in clinical presentation result in age-related differences in diagnosis, particularly as related to DSM-IV-based ADHD subtypes. ADHD-HI is most commonly diagnosed in early childhood, ADHD-C is most commonly diagnosed in clinical samples during the school-age years (although ADHD-I may be more common in epidemiological samples), and ADHD-I is most prevalent by adolescence and adulthood. Thus, many, if not most, individuals with ADHD change subtype within their lifetime [14].

Further, even within childhood, data suggest considerable instability of ADHD subtypes [15]. Undoubtedly, some of the subtype instability is related to the imposition of a categorical system (DSM-IV) on dimensional measurement (e.g. six inattentive and six hyperactive/impulsive items = ADHD-C, but six inattentive and five hyperactive/impulsive items = ADHD-I). As such, variations related to measurement error, small behavioral changes or environmental adjustments can appear to exaggerate these minimal differences. Further, many individuals with ADHD-I or ADHD-HI may have a less severe presentation of ADHD-C (i.e. short a symptom or two) rather than a truly distinct subtype. While there are data suggesting the existence of a "purer" form of ADHD-I, characterized by few if any hyperactive/impulsive symptoms, and perhaps a "sluggish cognitive tempo" [16], most [17], but not all [18], studies have failed to find differences between this group and individuals with ADHD-C on key neuropsychological measures. Further research is needed to determine the extent to which this group represents a truly distinct subtype of ADHD and whether such a group should be considered to fall within the same category as ADHD-C.

Distinct from these small, potentially measurement-error-related shifts in symptoms and severity over short periods, more substantive changes in behavior over longer periods of development are also frequently observed. These latter changes are more important to understand from a lifespan perspective. Some systematic variations, such as the shift from ADHD-HI during the preschool years to ADHD-C following school entry [15], are likely to be related, at least in part, to the lack of attentional demand placed on preschoolers, thus limiting the ability to detect impairments in attention. However, other apparent shifts become somewhat more problematic to understand and result in several unanswered questions. For example, as hyperactivity diminishes with increasing age, there is a frequently observed developmental shift from ADHD-C during childhood to ADHD-I during adolescence/young adulthood. This begs the question, "should adolescents and adults who meet diagnostic criteria for ADHD-I, but who met criteria for ADHD-C in childhood, be considered to have ADHD-I or ADHD-C in partial remission?" From a clinical/treatment perspective this question may be more academic than substantive because the answer is unlikely to impact treatment decisions, which are largely determined by currently presenting symptoms. However, this is a critical question for scientists trying to understand the neurobiological substrates of the disorder. Are inattentive individuals who were hyperactive in childhood biologically similar to those who have always had ADHD-I since childhood? We know of no available data that directly answer this key question. However, solid-state actigraph recordings from the ankle of an adolescent group diagnosed with ADHD-C in childhood indicated that these individuals continued to be more active than never-ADHD-diagnosed controls at 10-year follow-up, irrespective of whether they met criteria for ADHD-C or ADHD-I or no longer met criteria for the disorder [5]. However, this study did not include individuals with ADHD-I in childhood, so a direct comparison could not be made. Based upon the model of Halperin and Schulz [6], we would suggest that these elevated actigraph counts reflect a persisting underlying or core deficit that causes ADHD, but through the development of top-down cognitive control many individuals can adequately compensate for this underlying deficit, resulting in minimal, if any, functional impairment.

Considering the substantial developmental variation in the clinical presentation of ADHD, it has been suggested that diagnostic criteria should reflect these age-related differences [14]. Lowering the diagnostic symptom threshold for adults from the six-item cut-off to four or five items has been proposed, implicitly acknowledging the diminished symptom severity (or at least diversity of symptoms) that often presents in adults with the disorder [19]. However, this approach does not address other *qualitative* differences in ADHD across the lifespan. In particular, many of the hyperactive/impulsive items in DSM-IV are inappropriate for application to adolescents and adults (e.g. "runs and climbs excessively"). Similarly, it has been questioned whether a distinct set of criteria, perhaps focusing more on hyperactivity and less on inattention, should be applied to preschool children [15]. Placing the diagnostic criteria for ADHD into a developmental framework is clearly a challenge for future iterations of the DSM.

From a scientific perspective, one also needs to question why the behavioral manifestations of what appears to be a single disorder vary so much across distinct phases of life. Clearly, a piece of the answer lies in context and the ever-changing life demands placed upon individuals as they develop. During early childhood, adults tend to structure, organize, and plan the environment for children. However, as they age, children begin to take on more of these responsibilities for themselves, and by adulthood individuals are primarily accountable for guiding their own lives. Within this contextual framework, it becomes readily apparent why attention-related symptoms would become more prominent across development and into adulthood. However, environmental context and demands, while important, do not fully account for developmentally related variations in ADHD, and in particular, the individual variability in ADHD trajectories seen across development. Here we must look to the brain and view ADHD within a neuro-developmental context.

Human brain development proceeds in a systematic manner that begins before conception and continues at least into early adulthood. The human brain develops largely in utero and is approximately 80% of adult size by the age of 2 years (ref. 20; also see Williamson, Chapter 1 of this volume). Myelination begins in utero and proceeds rapidly up to age 2 years [21]. This is also a period of rapid synapse formation that varies in rate and timing in different brain regions, reaching maximum density at age 3 months in the auditory cortex and at age 15 months in the prefrontal cortex, with an overproduction of synapses [22]. Synaptogenesis is followed by a period during which neurons begin to form complex dendritic trees [23]. Although no doubt controversial (for example, see Marks et al., Chapter 5a of this volume), we would argue that the neural determinants of ADHD are probably in place and already impacting behavior by this early stage in development.

Beginning at about the age of 5 years, neural development is marked by increased cortical organization and refinement, as well as by neuronal growth. Cortical gray matter continues to thicken during the school-age years, with about half of the cortical regions attaining peak thickness by the median age of 7.5 years [2], and cortical thickness peaking at around 10.2 to 12.8 years in the parietal cortex and around 11.0 to 12.1 years in the frontal lobe [24]. Although following the same general trajectories across brain regions, cortical thickness peaks later in children with ADHD as compared to controls [2]. Experience-dependent pruning of inefficient synapses in the cortex in a regionally specific manner is also taking place during this time [20, 22, 24]; although it is mostly after puberty and into early adulthood that the developmental process of cortical thinning occurs. In addition, the process of myelination, which facilitates rapid neurotransmission, continues well into adulthood in many cortical regions. We hypothesize that it is the top-down control that is associated with these later neurodevelopmental processes that underlies the diminution of hyperactivity over development, and that individual variability in these experience-dependent processes accounts for the diversity of outcomes associated with ADHD.

Developmental heterogeneity of ADHD and psychiatric comorbidities

From a treatment perspective, ADHD is still often viewed as a relatively homogeneous disorder, with only minimal evidence of tailoring treatments to individuals. Nevertheless, from a phenomenological, neuropsychological, genetic and developmental perspective, variation abounds and is well described in the extant literature. Heterogeneity with regard to psychiatric comorbidity has been extensively studied. Unfortunately, comorbid disorders are often conceptualized as independent conditions that co-occur with ADHD (e.g. like a sore throat and a broken leg). This may make sense from a medical or treatment perspective (e.g. treat the ADHD and treat the depression), but is extremely unlikely to be true from an etiological perspective; rates of overlap are far too high for this to be possible. Several thoughtful reviews [25] have proposed potential explanations for the high comorbidity rates, which include similar risk factors for multiple disorders, one disorder increasing risk for another, and problems with definitional criteria. There is likely to be some truth to all of these possible explanations. However, it will become increasingly important that studies of ADHD abandon largely fruitless attempts to "control" for comorbidity and begin to incorporate the co-occurring clinical phenomena into their conceptualization of the disorder as part and parcel of the syndrome.

One approach to unraveling these overlapping conditions might be to examine the interrelations of patterns of comorbidity over development. As stated previously, among individuals with ADHD of all ages, the presence of comorbid disorders is the rule rather than the exception. Nevertheless, there is variability across developmental phases of life: children with ADHD most commonly present with comorbid oppositional-defiant disorder (ODD), conduct disorder (CD) and anxiety disorders; a smaller, yet not insignificant, percentage also present with comorbid depression or other mood difficulties [26]. Data regarding comorbidity in adolescents and adults with ADHD have been less consistent, with some of the variability associated with whether the sample had been prospectively followed since childhood, or whether the participants were recruited as adults [27]. Most longitudinal data derived from samples diagnosed in childhood indicate outcomes characterized by high rates of antisocial personality disorder and substance use disorders [28], although some report elevated rates of depressive and anxiety disorders [29], and other personality disorders [30] as well. Studies of newly recruited adults with ADHD generally report higher rates of comorbid internalizing and personality disorders. These differences are probably due to substantive differences seen in samples diagnosed in childhood and prospectively followed versus samples of individuals with ADHD recruited as adults. First, and perhaps most importantly, samples recruited as adults represent individuals experiencing significant impairment related to ADHD. In contrast, samples of adults who had been followed from childhood include many individuals who no longer meet criteria for or experience impairment related to ADHD. Thus, while newly recruited adult samples inform us about ADHD as manifested in adulthood, they tell us little about the natural history or outcome of childhood ADHD. Longitudinal follow-up samples tell us about outcomes of childhood ADHD, but unless the sample is examined relative to adult ADHD status (i.e. "persistence" vs. "partial remission" vs. "full remission"), the data may be less informative about the patterns of psychiatric comorbidity associated with adult ADHD, and perhaps, more importantly, the role comorbidity plays in longitudinal outcome of the disorder. Examinations of adult manifestations of ADHD and related comorbidities are most accurately reviewed with an eye towards a given individual's prospectively acquired history, and must include those who are no longer diagnosable in adulthood.

Beyond the certainty of childhood onset, there are probably other important differences between samples followed from childhood in comparison to those recruited as adults. For example, it would seem that individuals with childhood ADHD who have the poorest outcomes (e.g. criminality, antisocial behavior, unemployment) are less likely to self-refer for treatment as compared to those with relatively positive outcomes, yet are struggling with the impact of their symptoms on their academic or vocational success. Particularly in samples of adults with ADHD recruited from outpatient clinical and/or private practice settings, the range of severity may be skewed toward the better or higher functioning outcomes, and probably toward higher socio-economic status.

Very few longitudinal studies have systematically examined the continuity of childhood comorbidity into adulthood. As such, relatively little is known about the role this source of heterogeneity in development may play in longitudinal presentation. Some studies suggest considerable homotypic continuity, such that childhood CD, anxiety and mood disorders predict later antisocial personality disorder (ASPD), anxiety, and mood disorders, respectively [31]. Yet Mannuzza et al. [28] found that a substantial proportion of children with ADHD went on to develop ASPD and substance use disorders in adolescence despite the fact that they excluded aggressive individuals and those with CD from their childhood cohort. Insights into the developmental trajectories of comorbid disorders are also likely to be limited by the fact that most children with ADHD have multiple comorbid disorders (e.g. ADHD+CD+anxiety disorder). The ability to carefully parse children into more homogeneous subgroups without overlapping comorbidities that can be followed over development requires an extremely large sample size and is thus problematic to achieve.

Neuropsychological heterogeneity

ADHD is also characterized by considerable neuropsychological heterogeneity. Several meta-analyses provide clear documentation that, on the group level, children [32–34] and adults [35, 36] with ADHD differ significantly from non-ADHD comparison groups on a wide array of neuropsychological measures. However, in general, effect sizes have been modest and too small to suggest that any single type of neuropsychological deficit could account for or be accounted for by ADHD alone. As such, the practice of using neuropsychological tests to make the diagnosis of ADHD is quite problematic and such data should be used cautiously and always interpreted within the context of a more complete psychological or psychiatric evaluation. For example, among a small battery of executive function tests, Nigg et al. [37] found that the Stop-Signal Task had the greatest sensitivity to ADHD, yet only 51% of diagnosed individuals performed poorly on that measure. Identification of individuals with ADHD increased to 79% when the criterion was shifted to poor performance on any of their executive measures. However, this criterion erroneously identified 47% of non-ADHD controls. It is unlikely that any single neuropsychological test, set of tests, or construct can adequately characterize all individuals with ADHD.

Some investigators have been exploring the scientific and clinical utility of exploiting this neuropsychological heterogeneity to identify more homogeneous subgroups of individuals with ADHD. Nearly 20 years ago, Halperin et al. [38] attempted to parse children with ADHD based upon whether or not they performed poorly on a continuous performance test (CPT) measure of attention. They found that "inattentive" children with ADHD had more learning and cognitive problems relative to their "non-inattentive" ADHD peers. In contrast, those who were not inattentive by this measure presented with higher levels of conduct problems. A more recent, theoretically driven attempt by Solanto et al. [39] found that different individuals with ADHD were identified using the Stop-Signal and Delay tasks. This finding supports what has been referred to as the Dual Pathway Theory of ADHD [40], which posits that ADHD is composed of individuals from two distinct subgroups; those with primary deficits in inhibitory control and those with impairments more closely linked to reward-related delay processes. Similar approaches could be used to identify specific subgroups with apparent state-regulation or executive function deficits.

From an empirical perspective, the identification of more homogeneous subgroups based on neuropsychological performance can be advantageous. Assuming that neurocognitive deficiencies are more rooted in the neurobiological substrates of the disorder than are the behavioral symptoms, subgroups based on narrowly defined neuropsychological profiles may represent potential "endophenotypes" that could lead to increasingly valid subgroups for the ADHD taxonomy and pave the way for the identification of genetic determinants of this complex disorder [41]. In addition, reduced variability would provide greater power for the study of differences in longitudinal course.

There is also some evidence to suggest that the nature of the neuropsychological deficits associated with ADHD change over development. During the preschool years, ADHD appears to be characterized by a diverse set of neuropsychological impairments. While poor performance on measures of executive functions has been frequently reported [42, 43], preschoolers with ADHD also perform poorly on a wide array of non executive neuropsychological tests. Studies that have employed experimental manipulations to isolate specific domains of impairment such as perceptual or motor conflict, set shifting, and visual working memory have generally failed to identify such specific impairments [44, 45]. Rather, they tend to find that preschoolers with ADHD perform more poorly across both experimental and control conditions, with little evidence of specificity in any cognitive domain.

Nonetheless, preschoolers with ADHD were reported to have greater reaction time variability across multiple measures [45], which is often cited as a marker of state regulation deficiencies or attentional lapses.

Most research examining neuropsychological functioning in ADHD has focused on school-age children. Three meta-analyses [46–48] examined interference control, as measured using the Stroop Test, and provided minimal evidence for specific impairments in this domain. Similarly, a meta-analysis [49] examining studies of visuospatial orienting found little or no evidence for any visuospatial attention deficits in ADHD, including functions typically attributed to the anterior or executive attention system.

As already discussed, two additional meta-analyses examined a broader array of executive functions. The first [12] found that those with ADHD performed more poorly than controls on about two-thirds of executive function measures. More recently, Willcutt et al. [32] conducted a meta-analysis of 83 studies (total $N = 6703$) focusing on 13 executive function tasks. The data indicated that groups of children with ADHD perform more poorly than controls on many executive function measures, but effect sizes were consistently in the medium range (0.46–0.69) and significant group differences were again found for only 65% of comparisons. In view of the relatively modest effect sizes and variability of findings, these investigators concluded that executive function weaknesses are "neither necessary nor sufficient to cause all cases of ADHD".

Further, executive function deficits are not selective; children with ADHD differ from controls on several measures of non executive abilities, such as motor coordination, language, visuomotor integration, and learning and memory (as reviewed by Halperin and Schulz [6]). A meta-analysis [50] that compared groups with ADHD to controls and included several non-executive function measures reported an effect size of 0.61 for Full Scale IQ and even larger effect sizes for measures of academic achievement as assessed by the Wide Range Achievement Test. Thus, at least in school-age children, there do not appear to be larger effect sizes for executive function deficits in ADHD relative to impairments in other cognitive domains. Finally, a recent study [51] reported that after controlling for "lower order" cognitive processes, there was little evidence for primary executive function deficits in children with ADHD.

Fewer studies have examined neuropsychological deficits in adolescents and adults with ADHD, although findings generally suggest impairments similar to those in children. Adolescents with ADHD typically exhibit impaired performance compared with a non-ADHD group across an array of executive function measures [52, 53]. One meta-analysis [35] reported that adults with ADHD performed worse than controls across multiple neuropsychological domains, whereas another reported that executive functions were not generally reduced in adult ADHD patients [36]. Consistent impairments on several CPT paradigms were reported, whereas more traditional executive function tests such as the Stroop, Wisconsin Card Sorting Test, and Trail-Making Tests only differentiated the groups moderately well, when at all [35, 37].

While it is difficult to ascertain through the use of cross-sectional data the degree to which neuropsychological impairments, as they relate to ADHD, change over development, a recent meta-analysis of studies using the Stop-Signal Task to differentiate individuals with ADHD from controls reported evidence for substantially larger inhibitory control deficits for adults as compared to children [1]. This would suggest that executive function deficits, at least as gauged by a measure of inhibition, become more prominent in adults with ADHD.

Longitudinal studies of children with ADHD followed into adolescence and beyond have generally found that neuropsychological dysfunction persists throughout development. Fischer et al. [54] examined neuropsychological outcomes of childhood ADHD relative to the persistence of ADHD in early adulthood. Those with persistent ADHD made significantly more errors on a CPT than controls, while those with ADHD in childhood, but not adulthood, did not differ from either group on these measures. Persisters, remitters, and controls earned similar amounts on a card task designed to measure inhibitory control, although the ADHD groups performed the task slower than controls. Hinshaw et al. [55] prospectively followed girls with ADHD, along with a matched comparison sample, 5 years after childhood assessment. The childhood-diagnosed ADHD group displayed moderate to large deficits in executive/attentional performance relative to the comparison group at follow-up. Control of childhood IQ reduced executive function differences yet when the subset of girls meeting diagnostic criteria for ADHD in adolescence was compared with the remainder of the participants, neuropsychological deficits emerged even with full statistical control.

Reasoning that core deficits of ADHD should persist in adults no longer meeting diagnostic criteria, but more epiphenomenal characteristics should parallel symptom recovery, Carr et al. [56] compared adults with ADHD, adults with retrospectively assessed childhood histories of ADHD but partial recovery, and controls on an anti-saccade task. They found that directional errors on the task behaved like epiphenomenal symptoms in that the ADHD group, but not the partially remitted group, differed from controls. In contrast, anticipatory errors seemed more like a core deficit; those with childhood ADHD differed from controls irrespective of adult status. This approach provides insight into the developmental trajectory of neurocognitive functioning in ADHD and the dissociation of potentially causal versus secondary deficits.

Finally, our group [5] examined neuropsychological functioning in a longitudinal sample of adolescents/young adults who were diagnosed with ADHD during childhood as compared to a well-matched never-ADHD comparison group. Despite similar Full Scale IQ scores, relative to controls, those with childhood ADHD performed significantly worse across a wide array of measures. Notably, persisters, but not remitters, performed poorly relative to the never-ADHD comparison group on a wide array of measures believed to assess executive or conscious control functions. In contrast, measures posited to be more automatic or under less conscious control distinguished both persisters and remitters from the comparison group. These findings, in line with the reasoning of Carr et al. [56], were interpreted to suggest that these latter impairments, which were evident in both persisters and remitters, were likely to reflect core deficits of the disorder. According to the reasoning of Carr et al. [56], the neuropsychological deficits that were only evident in persisters could be considered epiphenomenal. However, they could also be interpreted as supportive of our hypothesis that the development of top-down control resulted in a diminution of ADHD severity over development. These data cannot shed light on which of these two interpretations is likely to be correct.

Current treatments and new directions

The chapters on childhood (Marks et al.) and adult (Semrud-Clikeman and Fine) ADHD provide excellent reviews regarding the benefits of empirically

question about how those with and without ADHD are different, one can use a within-subjects longitudinal design to elucidate individual trajectories of the disorder. This, in turn, can lead to the discovery of unique factors associated with improving and deteriorating trajectories over development. Early childhood differences that might serve as prognostic indicators of course and outcome could be elucidated and potentially serve as markers for the identification of individuals for early intervention. Moderating factors during childhood that impact these varying trajectories can be identified and built into treatment programs. Therefore, at this stage, it is arguable that the most reasonable approach to studying this complicated disorder is to take the long-term approach to understanding the lifelong course of ADHD rather than focusing on short-term and oftentimes transient differences. There is no doubt that ADHD is a developmental disorder that changes in substantive ways on both the group and individual level throughout life. Conceptualizing, investigating, and treating it through the lens of a developmental perspective may provide one pathway to elucidating ADHD's still hidden complexities.

References

1. Lijffijt M, et al. A meta-analytic review of stopping performance in attention-deficit/hyperactivity disorder: deficient inhibitory motor control? *J Abnorm Psychology* 2005;**114**(2):216–22.

2. Shaw P, et al. Attention-deficit/hyperactivity disorder is characterized by a delay in cortical maturation. *Proc Natl Acad Sci USA* 2007;**104**(49):19649–54.

3. Castellanos FX, et al. Developmental trajectories of brain volume abnormalities in children and adolescents with attention-deficit/hyperactivity disorder. *JAMA* 2002; **288**(14):1740–8.

4. Polanczyk G, Rohde LA. Epidemiology of attention-deficit/hyperactivity disorder across the lifespan. *Curr Opi Psychiatry* 2007;**20**(4):386–92.

5. Halperin JM, et al. Neuropsychological outcome in adolescents/young adults with childhood ADHD: profiles of persisters, remitters and controls. *J Child Psychol Psychiatry* 2008;**49**(9):958–66.

6. Halperin JM, Schulz KP. Revisiting the role of the prefrontal cortex in the pathophysiology of attention-deficit/hyperactivity disorder. *Psycholog Bull* 2006;**132**(4):560–81.

7. Still GF. Some abnormal psychical conditions in children: excerpts from three lectures. *J Atten Disord* 2006;**10** (2):126–36.

8. Barkley RA. Behavioral inhibition, sustained attention, and executive functions: constructing a unifying theory of ADHD. *Psycholog Bull* 1997;**121**(1):65–94.

9. Sergeant J. The cognitive-energetic model: an empirical approach to attention-deficit hyperactivity disorder. *Neurosci Biobehav Rev* 2000;**24**(1):7–12.

10. Sonuga-Barke EJ, et al. Hyperactivity and delay aversion – I. The effect of delay on choice. *J Child Psychol Psychiatry* 1992;**33**(2):387–98.

11. Dickstein SG, et al. The neural correlates of attention deficit hyperactivity disorder: an ALE meta-analysis. *J Child Psychol Psychiatry* 2006;**47**(10):1051–62.

12. Pennington BF, Ozonoff S. Executive functions and developmental psychopathology. *J Child Psychol Psychiatry* 1996;**37**(1):51–87.

13. Biederman J, Mick E, Faraone SV. Age-dependent decline of symptoms of attention deficit hyperactivity disorder: impact of remission definition and symptom type. *Am J Psychiatry* 2000;**157**(5):816–8.

14. Todd RD, Huang H, Henderson CA. Poor utility of the age of onset criterion for DSM-IV attention deficit/hyperactivity disorder: recommendations for DSM-V and ICD-11. *J Child Psychol Psychiatry* 2008;**49**(9):942–9.

15. Lahey BB, et al. Instability of the DSM-IV Subtypes of ADHD from preschool through elementary school. *Arch Gen Psychiatry* 2005;**62**(8):896–902.

16. McBurnett K, Pfiffner LJ, Frick PJ. Symptom properties as a function of ADHD type: an argument for continued study of sluggish cognitive tempo. *J Abnorm Child Psychol* 2001;**29**(3):207–13.

17. Solanto MV, et al. Neurocognitive functioning in AD/HD, predominantly inattentive and combined subtypes. *J Abnorm Child Psychol* 2007;**35**(5):729–44.

18. Huang-Pollock CL, Nigg JT, Halperin JM. Single dissociation findings of ADHD deficits in vigilance but not anterior or posterior attention systems. *Neuropsychology* 2006;**20**(4):420–9.

19. Kooij JJ, et al. Internal and external validity of attention-deficit hyperactivity disorder in a population-based sample of adults. *Psychol Med* 2005;**35**(6):817–27.

20. Giedd JN, et al. Brain development during childhood and adolescence: a longitudinal MRI study. *Nat Neurosci* 1999;**2**(10):861–3.

21. Brody BA, et al. Sequence of central nervous system myelination in human infancy. I. An autopsy study of myelination. *J Neuropathol Exp Neurol* 1987; **46**(3):283–301.

22. Huttenlocher PR, de Courten C. The development of synapses in striate cortex of man. *Hum Neurobiol* 1987; **6**(1):1–9.

23. Mrzljak L, et al. Neuronal development in human prefrontal cortex in prenatal and postnatal stages. *Prog Brain Res* 1990;**85**:185–222.

24. Giedd JN, et al. Quantitative magnetic resonance imaging of human brain development: ages 4–18. *Cereb Cortex* 1996;**6**(4):551–60.

25. Rhee SH, et al. Testing hypotheses regarding the causes of comorbidity: examining the underlying deficits of comorbid disorders. *J Abnorm Psychol* 2005;**114**(3):346–62.

26. Spencer TJ. ADHD and comorbidity in childhood. *J Clin Psychiatry* 2006;**67** Suppl 8:27–31.

27. Marks DJ, Newcorn JH, Halperin JM. Comorbidity in adults with attention-deficit/hyperactivity disorder. *Ann N Y Acad Sci* 2001;**931**:216–38.

28. Mannuzza S, et al. Significance of childhood conduct problems to later development of conduct disorder among children with ADHD: a prospective follow-up study. *J Abnorm Child Psychol* 2004;**32**(5):565–73.

29. Biederman J, et al. New insights into the comorbidity between ADHD and major depression in adolescent and young adult females. *J Am Acad Child Adolesc Psychiatry* 2008;**47**(4):426–34.

30. Miller CJ, et al. Childhood attention-deficit/hyperactivity disorder and the emergence of personality disorders in adolescence: a prospective follow-up study. *J Clin Psychiatry* 2008;**69**(9):1477–84.

31. Biederman J. Impact of comorbidity in adults with attention-deficit/hyperactivity disorder. *J Clin Psychiatry* 2004;**65** Suppl 3:3–7.

32. Willcutt EG, et al. Validity of the executive function theory of attention-deficit/hyperactivity disorder: a meta-analytic review. *Biol Psychiatry* 2005;**57**(11):1336–46.

33. Alderson RM, Rapport MD, Kofler MJ. Attention-deficit/hyperactivity disorder and behavioral inhibition: a meta-analytic review of the stop-signal paradigm. *J Abnorm Child Psychol* 2007;**35**(5):745–58.

34. Martinussen R, et al. A meta-analysis of working memory impairments in children with attention-deficit/hyperactivity disorder. *J Am Acad Child Adolescent Psychiatry*, 2005;**44**(4):377–84.

35. Hervey AS, Epstein JN, Curry JF. Neuropsychology of adults with attention-deficit/hyperactivity disorder: a meta-analytic review. *Neuropsychology* 2004;**18**(3):485–503.

36. Schoechlin C, Engel RR. Neuropsychological performance in adult attention-deficit hyperactivity disorder: meta-analysis of empirical data. *Arch Clin Neuropsychology* 2005;**20**(6):727–44.

37. Nigg JT, et al. Causal heterogeneity in attention-deficit/hyperactivity disorder: do we need neuropsychologically impaired subtypes? *Biol Psychiatry* 2005;**57**(11):1224–30.

38. Halperin JM, et al. Specificity of inattention, impulsivity, and hyperactivity to the diagnosis of attention-deficit hyperactivity disorder. *J Am Acad Child Adolesc Psychiatry* 1992;**31**(2):190–6.

39. Solanto MV, et al. The ecological validity of delay aversion and response inhibition as measures of impulsivity in AD/HD: a supplement to the NIMH multimodal treatment study of AD/HD. *J Abnorm Child Psychol* 2001;**29**(3):215–28.

40. Sonuga-Barke EJ. The dual pathway model of AD/HD: an elaboration of neuro-developmental characteristics. *Neurosci Biobehav Rev* 2003;**27**(7):593–604.

41. Crosbie J, et al. Validating psychiatric endophenotypes: inhibitory control and attention deficit hyperactivity disorder. *Neurosci Biobehav Rev* 2008;**32**(1):40–55.

42. Winsler A, et al. Verbal self-regulation over time in preschool children at risk for attention and behavior problems. *J Child Psychol Psychiatry* 2000;**41**(7):875–86.

43. Mariani MA, Barkley RA. Neuropsychological and academic functioning in preschool boys with attention deficit hyperactivity disorder. *Dev Neuropsychol* 1997;**13**:111–29.

44. Marks DJ, et al. Neuropsychological correlates of ADHD symptoms in preschoolers. *Neuropsychology* 2005;**19**(4):446–55.

45. Berwid OG, et al. Sustained attention and response inhibition in young children at risk for Attention Deficit/Hyperactivity Disorder. *J Child Psychol Psychiatry* 2005;**46**(11):1219–29.

46. Lansbergen MM, Kenemans JL, van Engeland H. Stroop interference and attention-deficit/hyperactivity disorder: a review and meta-analysis. *Neuropsychology* 2007;**21**(2):251–62.

47. Schwartz K, Verhaeghen P. ADHD and Stroop interference from age 9 to age 41 years: a meta-analysis of developmental effects. *Psychol Med* 2008;**38**(11):1607–16.

48. van Mourik R, Oosterlaan J, Sergeant JA. The Stroop revisited: a meta-analysis of interference control in AD/HD. *J Child Psychol Psychiatry* 2005;**46**(2):150–65.

49. Huang-Pollock CL, Nigg JT. Searching for the attention deficit in attention deficit hyperactivity disorder: the case of visuospatial orienting. *Clin Psychol Rev* 2003;**23**(6):801–30.

50. Frazier TW, Demaree HA, Youngstrom EA. Meta-analysis of intellectual and neuropsychological

test performance in attention-deficit/hyperactivity disorder. *Neuropsychology* 2004;18(3):543–55.

51. Rommelse NN, et al. Are motor inhibition and cognitive flexibility dead ends in ADHD? *J Abnorm Child Psychol* 2007;35(6):957–67.

52. Martel M, Nikolas M, Nigg JT. Executive function in adolescents with ADHD. *J Am Acad Child Adolesc Psychiatry* 2007;46(11):1437–44.

53. Loo SK, et al. Executive functioning among Finnish adolescents with attention-deficit/hyperactivity disorder. *J Am Acad Child Adolesc Psychiatry* 2007;46(12):1594–604.

54. Fischer M, et al. Executive functioning in hyperactive children as young adults: attention, inhibition, response perseveration, and the impact of comorbidity. *Dev Neuropsychol* 2005;27(1):107–33.

55. Hinshaw SP, et al. Neuropsychological functioning of girls with attention-deficit/hyperactivity disorder followed prospectively into adolescence: evidence for continuing deficits? *Neuropsychology* 2007;21(2):263–73.

56. Carr LA, Nigg JT, Henderson JM. Attentional versus motor inhibition in adults with attention-deficit/hyperactivity disorder. *Neuropsychology* 2006;20(4):430–41.

57. Sonuga-Barke EJ, et al. Parent-based therapies for preschool attention-deficit/hyperactivity disorder: a randomized, controlled trial with a community sample. *J Am Acad Child Adolesc Psychiatry* 2001;40(4):402–8.

58. Greenhill L, et al. Efficacy and safety of immediate-release methylphenidate treatment for preschoolers with ADHD. *J Am Acad Child Adolesc Psychiatry* 2006;45(11):1284–93.

59. American Academy of Pediatrics/American Heart Association clarification of statement on cardiovascular evaluation and monitoring of children and adolescents with heart disease receiving medications for ADHD: May 16, 2008. *J Dev Behav Pediatr* 2008;29(4):335.

60. A 14-month randomized clinical trial of treatment strategies for attention-deficit/hyperactivity disorder. The MTA Cooperative Group. Multimodal Treatment Study of Children with ADHD. *Arch Gen Psychiatry* 1999;56(12):1073–86.

61. Pietrzak RH, et al. Cognitive effects of immediate-release methylphenidate in children with attention-deficit/hyperactivity disorder. *Neurosci Biobehav Rev* 2006;30(8):1225–45.

62. Rapport MD, Kelly KL. Psychostimulant effects on learning and cognitive function: Findings and implications for children with Attention Deficit Hyperactivity Disorder. *Clin Psychol Rev* 1991;11(1):61–92.

63. Chamberlain SR, et al. Atomoxetine improved response inhibition in adults with attention deficit/hyperactivity disorder. *Biol Psychiatry* 2007;62(9):977–84.

64. Faraone SV, et al. Atomoxetine and Stroop task performance in adult attention-deficit/hyperactivity disorder. *J Child Adolesc Psychopharmacol* 2005;15(4):664–70.

65. Spencer T, et al. Effectiveness and tolerability of Atomoxetine in adults with attention deficit hyperactivity disorder. *Am J Psychiatry* 1998;155(5):693–5.

66. Gualtieri CT, Johnson LG. Medications do not necessarily normalize cognition in ADHD patients. *J Atten Disord* 2008;11(4):459–69.

67. Bedard AC, Tannock R. Anxiety, methylphenidate response, and working memory in children with ADHD. *J Atten Disord* 2008;11(5):546–57.

68. Scheres A, et al. The effect of methylphenidate on three forms of response inhibition in boys with AD/HD. *J Abnorm Child Psychol* 2003;31(1):105–20.

69. Bedard AC, et al. Effects of methylphenidate on working memory components: influence of measurement. *J Child Psychol Psychiatry* 2007;48(9):872–80.

70. Rhodes SM, Coghill DR, Matthews K. Methylphenidate restores visual memory, but not working memory function in attention deficit-hyperkinetic disorder. *Psychopharmacology (Berl)* 2004;175(3):319–30.

71. Mannuzza S, Klein RG, Moulton JL. Persistence of Attention-Deficit/Hyperactivity Disorder into adulthood: what have we learned from the prospective follow-up studies? *J Atten Disord* 2003;7(2):93–100.

72. Fischer M, et al. The adolescent outcome of hyperactive children diagnosed by research criteria: II. Academic, attentional, and neuropsychological status. *J Consult Clin Psychol* 1990;58(5):580–8.

73. Toplak ME, et al. Review of cognitive, cognitive-behavioral, and neural-based interventions for Attention-Deficit/Hyperactivity Disorder (ADHD). *Clin Psychol Rev* 2008;28(5):801–23.

74. Shalev L, Tsal Y, Mevorach C. Computerized progressive attentional training (CPAT) program: effective direct intervention for children with ADHD. *Child Neuropsychol* 2007;13(4):382–8.

75. O'Connell RG, et al. Cognitive remediation in ADHD: effects of periodic non-contingent alerts on sustained attention to response. *Neuropsychol Rehabil* 2006;16(6):653–65.

76. Rapport MD, et al. Methylphenidate and attentional training. Comparative effects on behavior and neurocognitive performance in twin girls with attention-deficit/hyperactivity disorder. *Behav Mod* 1996;20(4):428–30.

77. Kerns K, Eso K, Thomson J. Investigation of a direct intervention for improving attention in children with ADHD. *Dev Neuropsychol* 1999;**16**:273–95.

78. Thorell LB, et al. Training and transfer effects of executive functions in preschool children. *Dev Sci* 2009;**12**(1):106–13.

79. Klingberg T, et al. Computerized training of working memory in children with ADHD – a randomized, controlled trial. *J Am Acad Child Adolesc Psychiatry* 2005;**44**(2):177–86.

80. Klingberg T, Forssberg H, Westerberg H. Training of working memory in children with ADHD. *J Clin Exp Neuropsychol* 2002;**24**(6):781–91.

81. Olesen PJ, Westerberg H, Klingberg, T. Increased prefrontal and parietal activity after training of working memory. *Nat Neurosci* 2004;**7**(1):75–9.

Learning disorders in children and adolescents

Gregory M. Stasi and Lori G. Tall

Introduction

Academic concerns and problems are quite common in children and adolescents. While it has been estimated that approximately 20% of the general population in the USA experience difficulties with some form of academic performance [1], current prevalence rates suggest that approximately 6% of the general population meet the necessary diagnostic criteria for a specific learning disorder [2]. There is significant discussion both in the literature and among clinicians and researchers regarding how to appropriately classify and subsequently diagnose a specific learning disorder (LD). Traditionally, it was assumed that a specific learning disorder exists when there is a significant discrepancy between a child's cognitive ability and achievement in reading, mathematics, or written expression. However, within the USA, changes have occurred over the past decade regarding the criteria used for determining a specific learning disorder. These changes have taken place mainly in response to the demonstrated limitations of the ability–achievement model of LD [3]. Currently, categorization of a child's LD is based on a multi-tiered process involving, ideally, early identification and intervention, and review of response to intervention (RTI).

Three primary specific learning disorders are classified in the DSM-IV-TR: Reading Disorder, Mathematics Disorder, and Disorder of Written Expression. A fourth, Learning Disorder, Not Otherwise Specified (LD-NOS), serves as a grouping for patterns of learning difficulty that are not academic subject specific (i.e. nonverbal learning disorder is characterized as LD-NOS). Many children have been found to exhibit multiple learning disorders; for example, it is quite common for a child to meet criteria for both a reading disorder and a comorbid disorder of written expression. In addition, children with specific learning disorders often have co-occurring psychological conditions, such as attention deficit hyperactivity disorder, anxiety and mood disorders, and Tourette syndrome. As such, it is important to recognize that the utilization of DSM-IV-TR-based criteria solely when considering learning difficulties may prove inexact. This will be discussed more fully in the relevant sections below.

Children with documented learning disorders are at risk for social and emotional concerns. Prior studies have indicated that up to 75% of children with learning disorders demonstrate significant social skills deficits, expressed by peer rejection and social isolation [4]. Therefore, it is believed to be of importance that a child's social and emotional functioning be carefully assessed whenever a child is being evaluated for a learning disorder.

Neuropsychologists strongly emphasize that, in order to most effectively address a child's specific learning disorder, it is important that the child undergo a comprehensive evaluation in order to effectively classify and make sense of the patterns of difficulty the child presents, to rule out additional comorbid factors of concern, and to better determine what specific interventions are warranted. There exists an extensive literature detailing an array of interventions for children with learning disorders. Typically, recommended interventions are specific based on the area of weakness a child displays, both across testing measures and within the learning environment. Interventions can be administered either in a one-on-one manner or within the regular education classroom, in order to support the child with mastering academic demands.

Children with learning disabilities tend to exhibit deficits in their achievement on academic-based tasks throughout their lives; adult impact of learning disorder will be addressed in the following chapter by Sparrow. There has been considerable research focusing on the characterization of children and adolescents with specific learning disabilities, and this research has posited five academic characteristics of children and adolescents with LD [5]. Specifically, children with LD may (1) lack the basic skills necessary to meet academic demands; (2) possess knowledge of a variety of basic skills but fail to use them systematically in problem-solving situations; (3) fail to use effective or efficient learning strategies; (4) fail to have sufficient knowledge in order to learn to the level of new content presented at an advancing level; and (5) often fail to take advantage of learning enhancers within the environment. In line with these characteristics, there is ongoing discussion within the literature regarding how to use current research on LD to more effectively identify and define the impact of various learning disorders and their effects at varying points during the learning process.

At present, three main models exist regarding the identification and placement of children with LD in special education services: the discrepancy model; the intraindividual differences model; and the "problem-solving" or response to intervention (RTI) model. Each of these models is directly considered within the current legal criteria applicable to learning disorders, as specified in the Individuals with Disabilities Education Act (IDEA) that was reauthorized in 2004. IDEA provides specific federal guidelines for the diagnosis of a specific learning disability, as well as articulating criteria for establishing eligibility for special educational programming. The guidelines set by IDEA have traditionally emphasized that a diagnosis of a specific learning disability be based on a significant discrepancy between scores that measure cognitive ability and scores that measure achievement in one or more of the following academic areas: oral expression, listening comprehension, written expression, basic reading skills, reading fluency skills, reading comprehension, mathematics calculation, and mathematics problem-solving [6]. Additionally, children who do not necessarily meet criteria for services based upon IDEA may be eligible for special accommodations under federal law through Section 504 of the Rehabilitation Act of 1973 [6]. As the above authors pointed out, "the definition of a disability under Section 504 and ADA is a 'mental or physical impairment that substantially limits one or more major life activities'".

Two recent additional models have been posited with regard to identifying LD: the intraindividual differences model and the problem-solving model [3]; and aspects of both of these models have been considered in the reauthorization of IDEA [3, 6, 64]. The intraindividual differences model emphasizes the importance of neuropsychological assessment in the identification of learning disabilities. Specifically, as articulated in a paper presented by the National

Center for Learning Disabilities (NCLD) in 2002, "while IQ tests do not measure or predict a student's response to instruction, measures of neuropsychological functioning and information processing could be included in evaluation protocols in ways that document the areas of strengths and vulnerabilities needed to make informed decisions about eligibility for services, or more importantly, what services are needed". As the name of the model indicates, the focus is on internal differences within individuals rather than differences between children. This model also focuses on the limitations of an IQ and achievement discrepancy model, specifically because of a lack of relationship with intervention outcomes.

The problem-solving model highlights that the important consideration with regard to any learning disorder is how to intervene and improve functioning [3, 64]. The focus of this model is on functional ipsative assessment of behavior and learning, as opposed to utilizing a normative model. Identification of a child with a learning disorder under the problem-solving model is based on failure to respond to intervention. The main feature of this failure to respond to intervention is the implementation of ongoing academic and behavioral screening with a valid assessment measure, and continued monitoring if substantial progress has not been demonstrated [7]. Proponents of the problem-solving (RTI) model often argue that a combination of interviewing and behavioral observation is sufficient for identification of problems as well as to determine appropriate interventions [8]. This approach is most beneficial for children who have emotional or behavioral disorders that are secondary to defined environmental factors such as inappropriate or inconsistent reinforcement or punishment. However, this response to intervention definition leaves many unanswered questions in that the screening measures to be used are not defined or explained. Another critique of the response to intervention or problem-solving model of learning disabilities is that identification of actual learning disabilities may not occur for some children until they have failed and a strict following of the model may lead to denial of services for some children who are at risk for learning disorders [7]. Debate concerning the most appropriate model for classification and intervention is ongoing at this time and is influential with regard to how diagnosis and intervention will continue to evolve [64].

Specific learning disorders in childhood

Learning disorders are not homogeneous. The DSM-IV-TR delineates learning disabilities as falling into four main categories: Reading Disorder, Mathematics Disorder, Disorder of Written Expression, and Learning Disorder Not Otherwise Specified [9]. Diagnostic criteria listed in the DSM-IV-TR indicate that a learning disorder exists when there is a discrepancy of more than two standard deviations between academic achievement and cognitive capability [9]. This definition continues to be applied within the broad field of medicine and psychiatry specifically, but is no longer considered educationally applicable following changes in classification under IDEA. Each of the learning disorders will be considered separately.

Reading disorder

Reading is the process of extracting and constructing meaning from written text for a specific purpose [10]. Research indicates that a child's reading achievement develops in a two-tier hierarchical manner [1]. The earliest stage of reading is represented by mastery of the visual-orthographic properties of letters, memorization of a limited repertoire of sight words, and the use of visual associative skills to foster word recognition from pictures that accompany text (word identification). Going along with this stage is the child's ability to decode and process phonemes.

The second stage is associated with the child's ability to decompose speech into component structures and also readily identify graphemes with phonemes (language comprehension). Skilled readers are able to primarily rely on automatized orthographic skills. Reading deficits can occur at either stage of the hierarchy; affected children can struggle either with the phonological aspects of decoding and sight word reading or in their ability to imply meaning from the visual component of language.

Prevalence

Reading disorders are the most common form of learning problems in the USA, with an estimated prevalence rate ranging from 5 to 15% of the general population [8]. Although reading disorders account for the greatest number of children with diagnosed learning disorders, the actual prevalence rate may still be higher than indicated. Research has suggested that the stated prevalence rates for children with learning disorders are probably inaccurate, and in fact may be an under-representation of actual rates of reading disorder among the general population, because many children are not accurately identified due to problems associated with the discrepancy model of diagnosis [11], or as a result of underdiagnosis. Similarly, there is suggestion that reading disorder rates may be inflated for some populations, particularly children from lower socioeconomic communities, given poorer reading instruction and remediation at early ages of schooling. Fletcher and his colleagues have shown that early intervention for many readers who present with environmentally based deficiencies in decoding and comprehension often successfully remediates the need for more extensive identification as reading disordered and for placement in more intensive programming [3, 64].

Epidemiology of reading disorder

There is strong evidence that reading disorders are substantially more common in boys than in girls [8]. The specific neurodevelopmental causes of reading disorders in children are unknown [1]. However, there is considerable evidence that genetic factors contribute to the development of reading disorders; specifically with deficits in phonological decoding and awareness [12]. There is some evidence that there are differences between children who have a primarily genetic versus acquired reading disorder [8]; this suggests that some reading disorders are probably attributable to organic biological causes while others are secondary to environmental factors. Recent research has indicated that as much as 70% of individual differences in 7-year-old children's reading achievement is attributable to genetic effects [13]. However, a genetic predisposition is, obviously, not the only factor that accounts for reading disabilities. The current speculation is that children who have severe reading disabilities most likely have a biological precursor which interacts with characteristics from the environment, which ultimately results in the display of the reading disorder phenotype [8]. For example, a child's socioeconomic status (SES) has been implied as a reliable predictor of outcome for both oral language and literacy skills [14]. Prior research has revealed that children who are classified as being good readers spend a greater extent of time outside school reading for pleasure than do poor readers. Specifically, Cunningham and Stanovich [14] documented that good readers read more materials outside school in two days than poor readers do in an entire year.

Differential diagnosis

The DSM-IV-TR indicates that prior to making a formal diagnosis of a reading disorder, a clinician must differentiate learning concerns from normal variation in academic attainment, and from scholastic difficulties due to a lack of opportunity, poor teaching, or cultural factors [9]. It is fairly common for children with a reading disorder to have a comorbid learning disorder affecting mathematics and written expression [15]. There also exists a high comorbidity between Reading Disorder and Attention Deficit Hyperactivity Disorder (ADHD) [16]. Additionally, it is fairly common for children with a reading disorder to demonstrate deficits with their social and emotional functioning and often exhibit symptoms of depression and anxiety [7].

Although children who are identified as having a reading disorder at an early age may have the advantage of early intervention, they are more likely to demonstrate continued deficits with reading throughout their lifespan. Research has indicated that kindergarteners who have language disabilities are at an increased risk for later reading deficits in their grade-school years [17]. Young children who demonstrate reading deficits often have an accompanying deficit in decoding and manipulating basic phonemes.

As stated above, the first stage of reading is associated with the visual-orthographic representation and phonological decoding of sounds and letters. Thus, children with language disorders are likely to demonstrate deficits with their ability to accurately phonetically decode letters and words. Extensive research has documented that early language impairment is associated with significant reading difficulties [17].

Specific deficits with reading disorders

The analysis of reading disorders requires careful assessment of reading skill at four levels: phonemic analysis, word identification, reading fluency, and reading comprehension [1]. Children with reading disorders often have associated language deficits including deficiencies in phonemic discrimination, sound blending and sound segmentation, receptive vocabulary, naming, oral word fluency, semantic knowledge, and grammatical and syntactical analysis. These children often have associated deficits with perception, rapid auditory processing, rapid visual processing, and/or auditory discrimination, attention, auditory sequencing and/or sentence recall, and verbal memory.

Children with deficits with their phonemic awareness can have problems with auditory processing and receptive language. These children have a poor sound–symbol awareness, which is represented by a poor metalinguistic understanding that words can be broken down into their basic phonemic elements [8]. Oftentimes, children with primary deficits with phonological awareness rely on compensatory approaches when reading, including using a sight word approach and/or guessing at words based on their general configuration. Children with phonological processing and decoding deficits often use a sight word approach to reading which results in errors in reading because they frequently mistake words based on their general configuration [8]. These children often make sight word decoding errors and very often present with expressive and/or receptive language deficits. As a result, they are likely to be recognized by parents and teachers as having a learning disorder.

Children with primary word identification problems, also known as orthographic dyslexia due to deficits with visual processing of written text, demonstrate little difficulty with their ability to decipher words that make "phonemic sense". In contrast, these children have extensive deficits with sight word decoding of text. For example, they would probably be able to accurately decipher and state the word "grand" quite well, but have difficulty decoding the word "right", most likely stating "rig-hut" [8].

There has been little research on reading fluency, timing, and retrieval speed. Research has indicated that fluent reading is rapid, smooth, and automatic, without attention paid to reading mechanics such as decoding. Children with reading disorders who have adequate phonological processing and decoding but have poor rapid automatized naming skills are likely to demonstrate average sight word decoding skills, but tend to read slowly and make a vast amount of spelling errors on measures of orthographic accuracy [8]. Prior research has indicated five primary factors that affect a child's reading fluency. These factors include:

1. the proportion of words recognized as morphemes or orthographic units

2. speed variations in sight word processing

3. processing speed during novel word identification

4. use of context clues to facilitate word identification

5. speed of semantic access of word meaning [8, 19].

A child with a reading fluency deficit can show weakness with all or just one or two of the above factors. Interventions are specifically aimed at addressing the area of reading fluency in which a child demonstrates weakness. Therefore, when conducting an evaluation for a reading disorder, the neuropsychologist must take into consideration the various factors that compose a child's ability to read accurately and rapidly, and to then demonstrate which areas show a particular strength or weakness. There has been little evidence to suggest that a child's phonemic awareness is related to reading fluency; however, when a child is unable to read a word it is often evident that rapidly reading written text will be affected. Overall, children with deficits with reading fluency are more often identified as being learning-disabled later in life, as opposed to during the early reading years, since they typically demonstrate adequate pre reading skills.

The final potential area of reading weakness for children is with the ability to comprehend text that one has read [1]. Reading comprehension requires accuracy and proficiency at lower-level processes such as phonemic awareness, word identification, and reading fluency, and with integration of prior knowledge. Adequate comprehension of text also requires working memory and numerous executive skills in order for the child to interpret text meaning and draw conclusions about the passages [8]. Two main aspects associated with a child's reading comprehension have been identified: semantics and pragmatics. A child's semantic knowledge includes an understanding of morpheme root words, prefixes, and suffixes. Additionally, a child's knowledge and understanding of semantics applies to both the underlying meaning of individual words as well as sentence structure. Hale and Fiorello [8] suggest that a child's word knowledge and use is deeply connected to syntax (i.e. system of rules for word order) and grammar. They postulate that well-developed semantic and syntactic knowledge is likely to lead to increased comprehension competency. The other aspect of reading comprehension, pragmatics, is the function of the message conveyed. Pragmatic knowledge is based on personal experience and individual values.

Research has indicated that children with deficits in both phonological processing and awareness and naming speed have a much greater risk of developing a severe reading disorder [19]. Thus, it is clearly

Table 6a.1.

Neurobehavioral characteristics	Neuroanatomical correlates
Phonological processing and awareness deficits	Greater occipital-temporal lobe activity Larger right planum temporale, perisylvian temporal regions Middle temporal gyrus Wernicke's area, Angular and supramarginal parietal gyri Striate and Extrastriate cortex Left hemisphere of the frontal lobe
Reading speed and fluency	Thalamus and M pathway Cerebellum Broca's area Dorsolateral prefrontal cortex
Reading comprehension	Bilateral activation in occipital lobe fusiform and lingual cortices Superior temporal lobe activity More widespread frontal lobe activity

pertinent that an evaluation for reading disabilities assess not only a child's phonological awareness and decoding but also the child's automaticity and rapid naming.

Neuroanatomical features of reading disabilities

Research has indicated that various neuroanatomical structures have specific impact on a child's ability to read. The cognitive correlates are broken down in Table 6a.1 by their influence on specific reading characteristics: phonological processing and awareness, reading speed and fluency, and reading comprehension.

There has been substantial research examining the neurological correlates associated with various aspects of reading disabilities. Research has indicated that the neuroanatomical locations associated with primary phonological processing and awareness deficits include greater occipital-temporal lobe activity because of the inherent use of memory-based strategies for word recognition and enlarged right planum temporale [20–22]. In addition, several studies have indicated relatively specific cortical areas that have an involvement in phonological decoding and awareness, including perisylvian temporal regions which act as the primary and association auditory cortex, the middle temporal gyrus, Wernicke's area, angular and supramarginal parietal gyri, striate and extrastriate cortex, and the left hemisphere of the frontal lobe [8].

131

Prior neuroanatomical research suggests that the specific brain regions associated with reading speed and fluency include the thalamus and M pathway, the cerebellum, Broca's area, and the dorsolateral prefrontal cortex [8]. As well, research has documented that approximately 80% of children with a diagnosed reading disorder associated with fluency concerns have cerebellar impairment [23]. The cerebellum has a direct impact on the automatization of motor skills and implicit learning, which are two obvious critical skills utilized in reading fluency [24].

Functional MRI (fMRI) studies have indicated that, when a child engages in reading comprehension, the neuroanatomical structures identified as active include strong bilateral activation of the occipital fusiform and lingual cortices for both word recognition and semantic processing [25]. Additionally, superior temporal lobe activity when a child is engaged in comprehension tasks has been noted, specifically within the posterior Wernicke's area and the middle temporal gyrus [8]. Although frontal lobe activity has been shown for all aspects of reading, there is increasing evidence that frontal activity tends to be more widespread and bilateral during reading comprehension in comparison to word reading [26].

Interventions for reading disorders

The IDEA-2004 states that children who struggle with reading comprehension should participate in an empirically validated remedial teaching approach [16]. Until recently, there has been a paucity of comprehensive research evaluations that assess the benefits of interventions for reading disorders [18, 64]; however several recent studies have been published highlighting the likely impact of selective approaches available. For example, a series of recent fMRI studies indicate that effective reading intervention actually changes the pattern of brain activation among readers. Specifically, as children with phonological processing and awareness deficits develop more effective decoding strategies and improve their reading, their pattern of brain activation shifts towards the pattern that is consistently observed in strong readers [8, 16]. This research has added greater impetus to the utilization of phonologically based reading interventions for students with RD.

There are a small number of commercially available interventions that have shown consistent, positive gains in children's phonetic awareness and decoding. These include the Orton-Gillingham approaches,

Lindamood Phoneme Sequencing Program, Earobics, and the Wilson Method. Fast ForWord has also shown some limited impact, although negative findings are well documented as well [8, 27, 28]. An intervention study examining the efficacy of various phonological decoding and awareness interventions indicated that both Earobics and the Lindamood Phoneme Sequencing Program demonstrate significant improvements with phonological awareness, with gains maintained at 6 weeks after intervention [27]. Regardless of the method of intervention approach, research has consistently indicated that the most efficacious phonological intervention includes early identification of "at risk" and struggling readers, who are provided with specific strategies to better phonetically decode [16, 64].

Interventions established to improve a child's reading comprehension have focused on developing text-analysis skills, such as vocabulary-building, fact-finding, and identifying major themes, as well as improving the child's metacognitive awareness of reading including his or her ability to predict, justify, and confirm meaning between text and prior knowledge [16]. Specific reading interventions aimed at improving a child's comprehension of text include Reading Recovery [28] and the Accelerated Reader/Reading Renaissance Program [29]. The Reading Recovery program is designed as a short-term comprehension intervention, which supplements classroom instruction with one-on-one tutoring in an out of classroom environment. The Accelerated Reader/Reading Renaissance Program is a two-part intervention. The first part is a set of recommended principles on guided reading with a focus on the teacher's direct instruction. The second component of the program is the utilization of a computer program that facilitates reading practice by providing students and teachers with immediate feedback regarding the student's performance on a set of comprehension questions. Across studies, effective reading comprehension programs focus on instruction that is explicit, well supported and guided, adjusted to the individual, and generalizable across multiple texts [3, 16].

Mathematics disorder

Mathematics disorder has been previously called developmental arithmetic disorder, developmental acalculia, or dyscalculia. It is estimated to affect from 3% to as high as 14% of school-age children, depending on how the disorder is defined and operationalized

[30]. While these prevalence rates suggest that mathematics disorder is as common as reading disorder, less research regarding mathematics disorder has occurred, and there is significant disagreement in the literature regarding the underlying deficits associated with this diagnosis [2]. Several factors impact prevalence rates for mathematics disorder, including a paucity of studies, inconsistent or narrow understanding of mathematics difficulties, and the changing methods utilized for identifying a student with a learning disorder, e.g. response to intervention versus the discrepancy model [31].

In order to understand how to define a mathematics disorder, it is necessary to recognize how math skills develop in children [8]. Mathematic ability develops in a hierarchical manner, including the gaining of an understanding of one-to-one correspondence, classification, seriation, and conservation. After these foundation skills develop, children are next able to learn addition, subtraction, multiplication, and division, with skills applicable to higher mathematics being acquired based on mastery of these lower-level capabilities. Advanced topics such as algebra and geometry are taught as children enter adolescence, when mastery of higher-order reasoning capacities has occurred.

When a child is identified as having a mathematics disorder, one or more of the following skill areas may underlie the difficulties observed: visual spatial skills, linguistic abilities, and working memory. Visual spatial skills are necessary for aligning numerals in columns for calculation problems, understanding the base ten system, interpreting maps, and understanding geometry. Linguistic abilities are needed when performing word problems, following procedures of how to carry out operations, understanding math syntax [32], knowledge of math facts and relationships between numbers [33]. Working memory capabilities underlie the online manipulation of numbers and their operations.

Epidemiology of mathematics disorder

Several studies have provided strong evidence for a genetic predisposition for a mathematics disorder. A familial predisposition was observed in half of all children diagnosed with a deficit in mathematics. Research has also implicated chromosomes 6 and 15 as playing an important role in the development of a mathematics disorder [34]. There is also evidence to support different mathematics disorder profiles, corresponding to different phenotypes of mathematics

deficiency [35]. For example, studies have shown that girls with Turner syndrome exhibit difficulties in recalling visual details, which impact mathematical skill development, whereas girls with Fragile-X syndrome demonstrate difficulty in comprehending and recalling the "big picture", particularly with regard to visual information, and therefore hampering aspects of mathematical problem-solving. Of note, the specific deficits in visual spatial processing seen in the Fragile-X group were more strongly correlated with poor math performance, while the deficits in Turner syndrome were not. Studies examining the various patterns of information-processing difficulty may provide stronger evidence of specific subtypes of mathematics disorder, as well as indicating possible genetic contributions that are not as obvious when studying children with a general mathematics disorder [35].

Mathematics disorder is often comorbid with ADHD, with a prevalence ranging from 15% to 44% [36]. Researchers have examined comorbidity prevalence rates between LDs and other genetically based psychopathology, such as bipolar disorder, ADHD combined type, autism, and spina bifida; they found that 60 to 79% of children with these primary disorders also had a co-occurring learning disorder, whether mathematics, reading, or written language specific [37]. The presence of a math disorder ranged from 21% to 33% in the various groups.

A number of environmental factors have been posited to contribute to the development of a mathematics disorder. These include poor teaching, unreliable mathematics teaching programs, overcrowded classrooms, lack of available appropriate interventions for learning difficulties, and familial deprivation. Additionally, cognitive factors such as low intellectual skill and mood difficulties, including anxiety over math performance, have been identified as potential contributors to math underachievement [38].

Subtypes of mathematics disorder

Levine and associates [39] have posited a 16-subcomponent model that classifies the skills necessary for performing mathematics. Subcomponents of the model include the following:

Learning facts: all mathematical procedures involve underlying facts (i.e. multiplication tables and simple addition and subtraction)

Understanding details: all math procedures involve attention to and understanding of detail

Mastering procedures: the processes involved in multiplication, division, reducing fractions, and regrouping)

Using manipulations: the ability to manipulate facts, details, and procedures to solve more complex mathematical problems

Recognizing patterns: recognition of recurring patterns that give hints about the procedures required

Relating to words: knowledge of math vocabulary

Analyzing: drawing inferences from word problems

Processing images: interpretation of differences of size, shape and measurement

Performing logical processes: using reasoning and logic to problem-solve

Estimating solutions: estimating answers to problems

Conceptualizing and linking: understanding that two sides of an equation are equal

Approaching the problem systematically: using a strategic approach when problem-solving

Accumulating abilities: a hierarchy of knowledge and skills must be constructed over time

Applying knowledge: using math in everyday life

Fearing the subject

Having an affinity for the subject.

Following their model, which proposes that many skills are necessary for the successful completion of math problems, it is unlikely that there is one cause that leads to a diagnosis of a mathematics disorder. Instead, research has demonstrated that children with mathematics disorder are heterogeneous as a group. Nonetheless, it has been shown that children with mathematics disorder exhibit distinct impairment in three areas: deficits in semantic memory, deficits in sequencing multiple steps (i.e. procedural difficulties), and visuospatial deficits (i.e. difficulties representing numerical information spatially) [40]. In line with this, evidence has been provided supporting several mathematic disorder subtypes, including a semantic/long-term memory subtype, a procedural/working memory subtype, and a visual spatial motor subtype [35].

Neuroanatomical features of mathematics disorders

While mathematics disorder has not received the attention given to reading disorders, research has suggested that lesions in both hemispheres and select

Table 6a.2.

Neurobehavioral characteristics	Neuroanatomical correlates
Numerical magnitude Semantic understanding of math concepts and procedures	Bilateral inferior parietal lobes
Constructional apraxia Visual spatial sketchpad – holds visual spatial information in temporary storage Mental math Magnitude comparisons Geometric proofs	Right parietal lobe
Calculation deficits	Left parietal lobe
Allocation of attention Inhibition of distracters when problem-solving Attention to math operational signs Retrieval of learned facts	Anterior cingulate cortex
Organization of a response to solve complex problems Determining plausibility of results Deciphering word problems Retrieval of learned facts	Dorsolateral prefrontal cortex
Modulates affective problem-solving and judgment Consistent recall of learned facts	Orbitofrontal cortex
Numbers are encoded as sequences of words (eighteen versus 18) Retrieval of math facts Addition facts Multiplication facts	Left perisylvian region
Math computation	Prefrontal and inferior parietal lobe
Phonological loop – holds and manipulates acoustic information Knowledge of base-10 system Writing dictated numbers	Left temporal lobe
Procedural Code – numbers are symbols representing quantity in a sequenced order Regrouping skills Long division	Bilateral occipital-temporal lobes

subcortical difficulties probably contribute to a disorder in mathematics [41]. Mathematical computation and problem-solving has been linked to both hemispheres, depending on aspects of the problem being attended to and managed. The various neurobehavioral characteristics of mathematics disorders and the corresponding neuroanatomical correlates are described in Table 6a.2.

The temporal lobes have been implicated in children with a mathematics disorder, as early math skills tend to be verbally encoded [42]. The left perisylvan region of the temporal lobe has been implicated in the understanding that numbers can be encoded as a sequence of words [43]. The English language, which uses a base-10 numbering system, also probably contributes to language-related issues in the development of math skill [44]. Word problems present a unique challenge combining language and mathematics. In word problems the use and understanding of terms that include such concepts as *all*, *neither*, and *some* may complicate a child's ability to demonstrate math knowledge [45]. Bilateral areas within the occipital and temporal lobes are involved in number-identification skills, including knowledge that numbers are encoded as fixed symbols representing quantity in a specific order [46].

Working memory skills involved in mathematic ability include the phonological loop, which holds and manipulates acoustic information and is housed in the left temporal lobe [47]. The visual spatial sketch-pad theorized to hold visual, spatial, and kinesthetic information in temporary storage is housed along inferior portions of the right parietal lobes. The ability to allocate attentional resources to perform tasks that required dual attention resides in the anterior cingulate and in the frontal lobes. The frontal lobes are also involved in inhibiting any distracters interfering with problem-solving necessary for completing complex math equations [48].

The understanding that numbers are encoded as analog quantities (magnitude code) allows a child to judge that "7" is larger than "2" [49]. The encoding of analog quantities involves the bilateral inferior parietal lobes. The parietal lobes are also involved in the semantic understanding of math concepts and procedures and the evaluation of the plausibility of a response.

The frontal lobes, which principally manage executive functioning skills, have been implicated in mathematics disorder in several studies [50]. Skills such as planning, organizing and allocating attention to execute a goal-directed task and following an algorithm when problem-solving require adequate executive functioning skills for success.

Interventions for mathematics disorder

Classroom-wide interventions, such as Houghton Mifflin Mathematics [51] and Everyday Mathematics, have reported significant improvements with children's mathematics abilities. Research has suggested that, on an individual level, interventions should be established based on the specific mathematics deficit a child displays. For example, children with a predominant procedural, visuospatial, or conceptual problem-solving deficiency would be likely to benefit from an approach that models effective problem-solving techniques, followed by backward chaining after the student has gained mastery [16]. Still, mathematics intervention remains an open area for the development of additional approaches, and a child's specific neuropsychological profile may guide our understanding of applicability.

Disorder of written expression

It is often thought that gaining proficiency in written expression is the culmination of a child's education. However, the ability to express oneself in written form is required for academic progress across a wide swath of schooling. Despite the fact that written expression is the most difficult academic skill to master, it is the least researched of all the learning disorders [52]. Several reasons for the lack of research have been cited, including the belief that written language is an extension of oral language [8]. As our understanding of what is involved in written expression expands, there is increased evidence that multiple cognitive processes are involved in written expression, and that a disorder can appear in this academic domain if one or more of these cognitive processes are impaired.

Written language involves multiple cognitive processes, including the ability to spell and then write words, formulate and then express ideas, organize one's ideas into a combination of sentences and paragraphs, evaluate and edit the finished product, and use one's words as a means to communicate meaning and connect ideas. A written language disorder can manifest as a result of impairments in the development of any of the above-mentioned skills [8].

The exact percentage of children in the population with disorders of written expression has been difficult to calculate [53]. Factors contributing to the varying estimates of incidence include the lack of agreement on definitions of learning disorders, as well as variation in the procedures that lead to school determinations among states and individual school districts. Most information available about the prevalence of the disorder of written expression is based on studies of reading disorders or learning disorders in general. As such, a disorder of written expression is assumed to occur with a similar frequency to other learning disorders. Estimates are that about 6% of the school-aged population has a disorder of written expression [8]. In neuropsychological research with adults with acquired deficits, reading and writing appear to be independent skills areas, with dysgraphia occurring without dyslexia. This has not been well studied in children. A disorder of written expression, without pre-occurring or concurrent learning disorders of reading and/or mathematics, is considered rare.

Development of written language

Models that attempt to outline the development of written language abilities include those proposed by Abbott and Berninger [54], Ellis [55], Hayes and Flower [56] and Roeltgen [57]. Hayes and Flower [56] stated that written language encompasses a complex set of neurocognitive interactions. They proposed a continuous interaction between the formal task of writing, executive functions (e.g. language organization, self-monitoring, implementing grammatical structure), and the accessing of key memory-based information. They also suggested that knowledge communication in written form is strongly influenced by one's relative strengths or weaknesses in verbal expression, such that expressive language deficits interfere with the development of written language.

Whereas Hayes and Flower focus on multiple cognitive steps involved in writing, Ellis [55] has emphasized the steps involved when retrieving information from memory, such that inefficiencies in written language can be traced to failures of memory access or implementation. Ellis makes a strong case for the importance of memory in written language, but does not consider the impact of other cognitive variables (e.g. fine motor skills).

Similar to Hayes and Flower, Roeltgen [57] conceptualized the process of writing as complex and multifaceted. Additionally, he recognized that specific brain regions were likely to be responsible for the varied processes which synergistically combined to create the end result of written language. This has evolved into the current belief that written language disorders can be broken down into subtypes, and that the processes underlying written communication have specific localization within the human brain.

In their studies of written language skill, Abbot and Berninger [54] have focused on developmental changes in capacity, utilizing sophisticated neuropsychological batteries. They identified that at earlier stages of development, written language deficits are largely influenced by reading skill. However, as a child ages, writing skill is based on an interactive relationship between reading, oral language, and verbal cognitive capability (reflected by Verbal IQ). The utilization of neuropsychological tests calibrated to assess nuances of cognitive development and their effect on written language makes this model particularly relevant to the current mode of testing and treatment.

Written language disorder subtypes

A disorder of written language can occur at many different levels, including spelling, handwriting, semantic knowledge, executive functions, memory processes, and metacognitive processes. The age of the child is another important factor when determining what part of the writing process is potentially impacted, and how it affects written language competency [58].

Spelling

Spelling is an important part of written language even if the development of computer programs, such as spell check, have made the importance of accurate spelling less relevant than in the past. Children develop spelling skills in stages, beginning with their initial efforts at creating letter-like forms, transitioning to spelling words phonetically, and ending with spelling words according to orthographic rules and checking for their accuracy against memory. The most common error patterns in spelling include letter additions and omissions, letter reversals, sequencing errors, consonant substitutions, and vowel substitutions [8].

Phonological awareness is also necessary for spelling. If a child cannot decode language in order to read, then it is highly likely that the same child will struggle when decoding the sound–symbol relationship required to spell [59]. Reduced graphomotor skill can also interfere with formulating letters, spelling, and the amount of output produced when writing. Accurate spelling also requires retrieval from memory, specifically the unique way letters are ordered to produce a correctly spelled word.

Handwriting

Handwriting and poor visual motor integration skills can also contribute to a written language disorder and impact a child's motivation for producing written work. Assessing a child's ability to shape letters,

Table 6a.3.

Neurobehavioral characteristics	Neuroanatomical correlates
Attention, memory, and executive functions	Frontal lobe
Long-term semantic memory retrieval	Right prefrontal cortex
Verbs/Nouns	Frontal and temporal areas
Grammar and syntax	Inferior frontal: Broca's area

correctly space letters and words, align words correctly and the overall quality of penmanship is important when determining the quality of handwriting skills [8].

Written language processes

Spelling words accurately and writing legibly are involved in written language, with impairments in expressive language skills and executive functioning abilities constituting the remainder of skills involved in written language disorders. However, the skills required for expressive language and executive functioning are multi-layered and complex, including long-term and working memory, self-planning, monitoring, evaluation, and modification [8].

Neuroanatomical features of written language disorders

There is a paucity of research examining the neuroanatomical features associated with disorders of written expression. Prior research has pointed out that written language is without a doubt the most difficult academic subject because it requires virtually every part of the brain to work concertedly toward a final product [8]. A brief summary of the important neuroanatomical correlates associated with specific writing characteristics is presented in Table 6a.3.

A child's ability to write text incorporates most cerebral regions. The frontal lobes are taxed in that a child has to be able to attend to tasks at hand, organize his or her work, and recall prior information [8]. Long-term memory plays a vital role in a child's ability to write comprehensive text. The child has to be able to recall the important details and aspects associated with the information he or she is writing. Thus, the right prefrontal cortex has a direct impact on the child's written expression [60]. Research has shown that a child's knowledge of nouns is situated in the frontal

areas. Thus, as Hale and Fiorello [8] point out, noun–verb agreement is probably related to the interaction between the frontal and temporal lobes. Finally, prior research has suggested that the frontal region, in association with Broca's area, is involved with a child's knowledge of syntax and grammar [8].

Interventions for written expression

Research is limited regarding assessment and intervention of written expression. Unlike reading and mathematics (which have definite input and output characteristics), written expression is predominantly an output task. As a result, approaches taken with intervention are often focused on how a child reaches the final product. For example, the ability to accurately spell words is an integral component of written expression. Research indicates that children who have spelling deficits often present with predominant deficits in phonological awareness and difficulties with executive functioning [8]. As a result, interventions for children who demonstrate a primary deficit with spelling focus not only on developing the phoneme (sound) – grapheme (symbol) relationship but also on improving the child's visual memory retrieval [8]. Although supportive technology devices such as keyboarding, voice dictation, and word prediction software are quite often prescribed to children with writing disorders, there has been little empirical evidence suggesting the long-term efficacy in improving a child's written expression [16]. It has been documented that effective interventions for writing include use of explicit coaching in discourse structure as well as executive training with a focus on organizational strategies [16].

Role of neuropsychological assessment in learning disorders

A comprehensive neuropsychological assessment is not always necessary or required for many children who have specific learning disabilities [64]. Traditional school-based evaluations, which utilize an RTI approach coupled with the examination of ability and achievement development, may be sufficient to effectively identify and then remediate a specific learning disorder. However, there remain a significant number of children for whom this approach may be insufficient; this is particularly the case when a child is provided with a series of supportive services, but continues to show slow or non-existent gains. In such situations, or when likely comorbidities are present, a more detailed neuropsychological assessment is warranted. A multidimensional, quantitative and qualitative analysis of neuropsychological functioning can offer informative data regarding a child's specific problems, in addition to their pattern of strengths, which can aid and guide the development of an effective, empirically based intervention plan [61]. Prior research has indicated that a careful examination of the various interplays between and relationships among neurological, cognitive, and behavioral characteristics of children with psychological and learning disorders can provide practitioners with the information necessary to confirm initial diagnostic impressions, rule out confounding or conflicting data, and monitor intervention efficacy [61].

One important aspect of a comprehensive neuropsychological evaluation is the ability to obtain information regarding potential underlying etiological causes of observed phenomena and concerns [8]. Therefore, an effective neuropsychological evaluation should focus on processes driving observed low performances on academic-based measures. Additionally, it has been suggested that screening children on predictor variables including working memory, attention, and executive functioning may be helpful for monitoring the child's response to specific interventions and also identifying children who are at increased risk for a learning disorder [61]. This is a consultative resource the neuropsychologist can provide to the school setting. Important to note as well, there are limitations regarding the incremental validity of adding additional assessment measures when determining whether a child has a learning disorder. Specifically, as the number of measures increases, the likelihood of finding discrepant results also increases, thus an increase in Type I error [8]. This must be taken into consideration by the neuropsychologist consultant when working with families and school.

Psychosocial correlates of learning disorders

Children who have LD are at increased risk for difficulties with social and emotional functioning [62]. Studies have suggested that up to 75% of children with LD manifest significant deficits in social skills, and experience peer rejection and social isolation as a result. Yet there is debate regarding what impact a specific type of learning disorder may have on a child's social and emotional functioning. Many earlier studies examining psychosocial correlates of learning disorders were inconclusive because children with a learning disorder were categorized as one homogeneous group [63]. Still, there remains evidence that indicates children with LD are at increased risk for social and emotional problems that further impact learning and adaptation.

One specific concern is with self-esteem and self-efficacy. Children who struggle with reading, writing, or mathematics are often more likely to exhibit lower levels of self-esteem. Failure experiences with learning contribute to the belief that one is less capable. Similarly, peers are more rejecting of classmates who require support academically. As a result, children with LD are at greater risk for experiencing social isolation, peer rejection, and loneliness [62]. This in turn contributes to attributions of poor efficacy and lowered self-regard. Additionally, children with LD demonstrate not only lowered academic self-concept but also lowered self-concept within the social domain. Similarly, some research has indicated that children with a specific learning disorder exhibit significantly poorer social skills and are less socially competent than their non-learning-disabled peers [8]. This may stem, in part, from difficulties with rapidly processing social information and missing subtle social nuances.

Research has also demonstrated that children who have multiple learning disabilities have greater deficits with their social and emotional functioning than children with learning deficits in one domain [62]. The authors speculated that the reason children with multiple learning disabilities are at a greater disadvantage is that students with learning problems in one area are often able to compensate for their academic difficulties and therefore experience fewer academic failures. As a result, they are better adjusted than students with problems in multiple areas.

Conclusions and future directions

Learning disorders are fairly common in childhood, and, as Sparrow in the next chapter indicates, they are typically life-long in some aspects of their impact. It has been estimated that up to 20% of school-age children demonstrate significant deficits with their achievement in some academic domain [1]. Current diagnostic standards provided by the DSM-IV-TR delineate three major types of learning disorders: reading disorder, mathematics disorder, and a disorder of written expression [9]. These disorders are not homogeneous and thus children will often demonstrate deficits with multiple domains (e.g. reading and mathematics). Additionally, it is quite common for children with documented learning disorders to exhibit comorbid psychological and emotional disorders. Children with learning disorders often exhibit deficits with their daily social functioning [31, 32]. There is a definite need for extensive research to discern the impact that social functioning has on a child's academic achievement. There has also been a paucity of research regarding appropriate accommodations and interventions for children with co-existing social and learning disorders. Existing programs appear to offer some children a greater opportunity for success, but not all programs are appropriate or suitable for the individual needs of the child with LD. As a result, continued investigation of optimal, effective, and cost-neutral options for classroom as well as individual intervention is required. Making sense of the role comorbidities play in the development and maintenance of learning disorders also remains an important area of study; this will be likely to guide efforts at better identifying and then intervening with children with LDs, and preparing them for the move towards advanced adult-level learning.

References

1. Slomka G. In Snyder PJ, Nussbaum PD, eds. *Clinical Neuropsychology: A Pocket Handbook for Assessment.* Washington DC: APA Press; 2003: 141–69.

2. Hale J, Fiorello C, Bertin M, Sherman R. Predicting math achievement through neuropsychological interpretation of WISC-III variance components. *J Psychoeduc Assess* 2003;**21**:358–80.

3. Fletcher J, Morris R, Lyon G. In Swanson HL, Harris KR, Graham S, eds. *Handbook of Learning Disabilities*. New York: Guilford Press; 2003: 158–81.

4. Margalit M, Tur-Kaspa H, Most T. Reciprocal nominations, reciprocal rejections, and loneliness among students with learning disorders. *Educ Psychol* 1999;**19**:79–90.

5. Larkin M, Ellis E. In Wong BYL, ed. *Learning About Learning Disabilities*. New York: Academic Press; 1998: 557–77.

6. Maedgen J, Semrud-Clikeman M. In Hunter SJ, Donders J. eds. *Pediatric Neuropsychological Intervention.* Cambridge: Cambridge University Press; 2007: 68–87.

7. Semrud-Clikeman M. Neuropsychological aspects for evaluating learning disabilities. *J Learn Disabil*, 2005; **38**: 563–8.

8. Hale J, Fiorello C. *School Neuropsychology: A Practitioner's Handbook*. New York: Guilford Press.

9. American Psychiatric Association. *Diagnostic and Statistical Manual of Mental Disorders, Fourth Edition, Text Revision*. Washington DC: American Psychiatric Association; 2000.

10. Vellutino F, Fletcher J, Snowling M, Scanlon D. Specific reading disability (dyslexia): What have we learned in the fast four decades? *J Child Psychol Psychiatry* 2004;**45**:2–40.

11. Shaywitz S, Escobar M, Shaywitz B, Fletcher J, Makuch R. Evidence that dyslexia may represent the lower tail of a normal distribution of reading ability. *N Engl J Med*, 1992;**326**:145–50.

12. Thomson J, Raskind W. In Swanson HL, Harris KR, Graham S, eds. *Handbook of Learning Disabilities*. New York: Guilford Press; 2003: 256–70.

13. Harlaar N, Spinath F, Dale P, Plomin R. Genetic influences on word recognition abilities and disabilities: A study of 7 year old twins. *J Child Psychol Psychiatry* 2005;**46**:373–84.

14. Cunningham A, Stanovich K. Assessing print exposure and orthographic processing skill in children: a quick measure of reading experience. *J Educ Psychol* 1998;**82**:733–40.

15. Fletcher J. Predicting math outcomes: reading predictors and comorbidity. *J Learn Disabil* 2005;**38**:308–12.

16. Wills K. In Hunter SJ, Donders J, eds. *Pediatric Neuropsychological Intervention*. Cambridge: Cambridge University Press; 2007.

17. Catts H, Fey M, Tomblin J, Zhang X. A longitudinal investigation of reading outcomes in children with language impairments. *J Speech Lang Hear Res* 2002;**45**:3–18.

18. Bowers P. In Wolf M, ed. *Dyslexia, Fluency, and the Brain*. Timonium, MD: York Press; 2001: 41–64.

19. Lovett M, Steinbach K, Frijeters J. Remediating the core deficits of developmental reading disability: A double-deficit perspective. *J Learn Disabil* 2000;**33**:334–58.

20. Shaywitz S, Shaywitz B, Fulbright R, Constable R, Mencl W. Neural systems for compensation and persistence: Young adult overcome of childhood reading disability. *Biol Psychiatry* 2003;**54**:25–33.

21. Hynd G, Semrud-Clikeman M, Lorys A, Novey E, Eliopulos D. Brain morphology in developmental dyslexia and attention deficit hyperactivity disorder. *Arch Neurol* 1990;**47**:919–26.

22. Nicholson R, Fawcett A, Dean P. Developmental dyslexia: the cerebellar deficit hypothesis. *Trends Neurosci* 2001;**24**:508–11.

23. Miller C, Sanchez J, Hynd G. In Swanson HL, Harris KR, Graham, S, eds. *Handbook of Learning Disabilities*. New York: Guilford Press; 2003: 158–81.

24. Vicari S, Marotta L, Menghini D, Molinari M, Petrosini D. Implicit learning deficit in children with developmental dyslexia. *Neuropsychologia* 2003;**41**:108–14.

25. Booheimer S, Zeffiro T, Blaxton T, Gaillard W, Theodore W. Regional cerebral blood flow during object naming and word reading. *Hum Brain Mapp* 1995;**3**:93–106.

26. Silver C, Blackburn L, Arffa S, Barth J, Bush S, Koffler S, Pliskin N, Reynolds C, Ruff M, Troster A, Moser R, Elliot R. The importance of neuropsychological assessment for the evaluation of childhood learning disorders NAN policy and planning committee. *Arch Clin Neuropsychol* 2006;**21**:741–4.

27. Barbaresi W, Kautsic S, Colligan R, Weaver A, Jacobsen S. The incidence of autism in Olmstead County, Minnesota. *Arch Pediatr Adolesc Med* 2005;**159**:37–44.

28. Baenen N, Bernhole A, Dulane C, Banks K. Reading recovery: long-term progress after three cohorts. *J Educ Students Placed at Risk* 1997;**2**:161.

29. Ross S, Nunnery J, Goldfeder E. *A Randomized Experiment on the Effects of Accelerated Reader/Reading Renaissance in an Urban School District: Preliminary Evaluation Report.* Memphis, TN: The University of Memphis Center for Research in Educational Policy; 2004.

30. Desoete A, Roeyers H, De Clercq A. Children with mathematics learning disabilities in Belgium. *J Learn Disabil* 2004;**37**:50–61.

31. Fuchs L. Prevention research in mathematics: improving outcomes, building identification models, and understanding disability. *J Learn Disabil* 2005;**38**:293–304.

32. Hiebert J, LeFevre P. In Hiebert J, ed., *Conceptual and Procedural Knowledge in Mathematics.* Hillsdale, NJ: Erlbaum Press; 1987: 1–27.

33. Hallahan D. Some thoughts on why the prevalence of learning disabilities has increased. *J Learn Disabil* 1992;**8**:523–8.

34. Shalev R, Manor O, Kerem B, Ayali M, Badichi N, Friedlander Y, Gross-Tsur V. Developmental Dyscalculia is a familial learning disability. *J Learn Disabil*, 2001; **34**:59–65.

35. Mazzocco M. Challenges in identifying target skills: math disability screening and intervention. *J Learn Disabil* 2005;**38**:318–23.

36. Rapport M. Bridging theory and practice: conceptual understanding of treatments for children with attention deficit hyperactivity disorder (ADHD), obsessive-compulsive disorder (OCD), autism, and depression. *J Clin Child Psychol* 2001;**30**:3–7.

37. Mayes S, Calhoun S Frequency of reading, math, and writing disabilities in children with clinical disorders. *Learn Individ Differ* 2006;**16**:145–57.

38. Ginsburg, H. Mathematics learning disabilities: a view from developmental psychology, *J Learn Disabil* 1997;**30**:20–33.

39. Levine M. *A Mind at a Time.* New York: Simon & Schuster; 2002.

40. Geary D. In Geary, DC, ed. *Children's Mathematical Development.* Washington DC: American Psychological Association Press; 1995: 261–88.

41. Branch W, Cohen M, Hynd G. Academic achievement and attention-deficit/hyperactivity disorder in children with left-or right-hemisphere dysfunction. *J Learn Disabil* 1995;**28**:35–43.

42. Shalev R, Auerback J, Manor O, Gross-Tsur V. Developmental Dyscalculia: prevalence and prognosis. *Eur Child Adolesc Psychiatry* 2000;**9**:58–64.

43. Dehaene S, Cohen L. Cerebral pathways for calculation: double dissociation between rote verbal and quantitative knowledge of arithmetic. *Cortex* 1997;**33**:219–50.

44. Campbell JI, Xue Q. Cognitive arithmetic across cultures. *J Exp Psychol Gen* 2001;**130**:299–315.

45. Levine M. *Developmental Variation and Learning Disabilities.* Cambridge, MA: Educators Pub Service; 1987.

46. Von Aster M. Developmental cognitive neuropsychology of number processing and calculation: varieties of developmental dyscalculia. *Eur Child Adolesc Psychiatry* 2000;**9**:41–57.

47. Baddeley A. Recent developments in working memory. *Curr Op Neurobiol* 1998;**8**:234–8.

48. Hopko D, Ashcraft M, Gute J, Ruggiero K, Lewis C. Mathematics anxiety and working memory support for the existence of a deficient inhibition mechanism. *J Anxiety Disord* 1998;**12**:343–55.

49. Chocon F, Cohen L, van de Moortele P, Dehaene S. Differential contributions of the left and right inferior parietal lobules to number processing. *J Cogn Neurosci* 1999;**11**:617–30.

50. Menon V, Rivera S, White C, Eliez S, Glover G, Reiss A. Dissociating prefrontal and parietal cortex activation during arithmetic processing. *Nuroimage* 2000;**12**:357–65.

51. EDSTAR Inc. *Large-scale Evaluation of Student Achievement in Districts Using Houghton Mifflin.* Raleigh-Durham, NC: EDSTAR, 2004.

52. Lerner J. *Learning Disabilities: Theories, Diagnosis, and Teaching Strategies*, 8th edn. Boston: Houghton-Mifflin; 2000.

53. Swanson H, Ashbaker M. Working memory, short-term memory, speech rate, word recognition, and reading comprehension in learning disabled readers: does the executive system have a role? *Intelligence* 2000;**28**:1–30.

54. Abbot R, Berninger V. Structural equation modeling of relationships among developmental skills and writing skills in primary and intermediate grade writers. *J Educ Psychol* 1993;**85**:478–508.

55. Ellis A. *Reading, Writing, and Dyslexia: A Cognitive Analysis.* New York: Psychology Press; 1982.

56. Hayes J, Flower L. *Cognitive Processes in Writing.* New York: Erlbaum; 1980.

57. Roeltgen D. In Heilman KM, Valenstein E, eds. *Clinical Neuropsychology.* New York: Oxford University Press; 1985: 75–96.

58. Berninger V, Mizokawa D, Bragg D. Theory-based diagnosis and remediation of writing disabilities. *J School Psychol*, 1991;**29**:57–79.

59. Torgesen J. In Lyon GR, Krasnegor NA, eds. *Attention, Memory, and Executive Functioning.* Baltimore: Brookes; 1996: 157–84.

60. Cardebat D, Demonet J, Villard G, Faure S, Puel M, Celsis P. Brain functional profiles in formal and semantic fluency tasks: a SPECT study in normals. *Brain Lang*, 1996;**52**:305–13.

61. Keefe R. The contribution of neuropsychology to psychiatry. *Am J Psychiatry* 1995;**152**:6–15.

62. Margalit M, Al-Yagon M. In Wong BYL, Donahue M, eds. *The Social Dimensions of Learning Disabilities.* Mahwah, New Jersey: Erlbaum; 2002: 53–75.

63. Rourke B. In Lyon GR, ed. *Frames of Reference for the Assessment of Learning Disabilities.* Baltimore, MD: Brookes; 1994: 475–509.

64. Fletcher JM, Lyon GR, Fuchs LS, Barnes MA. *Learning Disabilities: From Identification to Intervention.* New York: Guilford Press; 2007.

Learning disorders in adults

Elizabeth P. Sparrow

Overview

Learning disorders (LD) are not limited to school-aged youth, and their impact extends beyond the academic realm. An LD is a life-long condition that affects individuals in the social, emotional, behavioral, and cognitive domains. Many adults do not know why they have always struggled more than peers as LDs were not as widely recognized or diagnosed in the past. Given increased awareness of LDs in adults, neuropsychologists and other allied health professionals must be prepared to identify LDs and plan interventions to help the adults we see clinically.

Diagnosis

Many terms are used to describe difficulties in learning, including "learning disorder" and "learning disability." In US publications, these terms are used interchangeably other than when exact diagnostic terms are required. Note that the term "learning disability" has a broader application in the UK, where it includes all developmental disabilities such as mental retardation and autism; this is an important consideration when reviewing results of research conducted outside the USA. Differences in diagnostic terms and models determine the number of people classified as having LD, and thus impact access to services [1]. Decisions about selecting a diagnostic model have significant financial implications (e.g. funding services), emotional implications (e.g. families feeling their needs are being met), and legal implications (e.g. employee retention, support requirements). As a result, political agendas are often involved in selecting diagnostic models. Three primary models for identification of LD are presented here, followed by an overview of relevant diagnostic systems and laws as they pertain to diagnosis of adult LD.

Diagnostic models

Many diagnosticians were trained to use a score discrepancy model, requiring a numerical discrepancy[1] between ability (i.e. IQ scores) and academic achievement (i.e. achievement testing scores). The discrepancy model has been criticized for excluding people who develop compensatory strategies to cope with an LD, as test scores do not reflect the amount of effort exerted on the test. Another argument against the discrepancy model is that test scores are not always predictive of functional performance, thus a reliance on test scores may misclassify individuals who are not functioning at expected levels. Finally, although the discrepancy model may identify a deficit in academic achievement, it fails to identify the cognitive processes that are involved in the deficit and thus limits treatment efficacy.

In contrast, the clinical performance model focuses on performance-based measures that are compared with peer-referenced expectations. This model is based on level of functioning relative to expectations, rather than test scores. Within the performance model, there are differences of opinion about which peers should be referenced in establishing expectations (e.g. age-matched versus ability-matched). The choice of comparison has important implications regarding who is provided with accommodations. The performance model has been criticized for reducing expectations for individuals to the general population average when age-based comparisons are used (e.g. a person with superior-range IQ but low average reading scores would not meet LD criteria using age-based standards).

A third model, "response to intervention" (RTI), is based on identifying an individual's weaknesses, providing a scientific, research-based intervention, and determining whether the individual shows improvement with that intervention. Although RTI has been used for decades, it gained popularity when RTI was included in the Individuals with Disabilities Education Improvement Act (IDEA) [2], which described RTI as a way to identify students with LD. Proponents of RTI focus on providing necessary services rather than "labeling a problem". RTI has been criticized as an overly inclusive method that may result in a

Table 6b.1. Summary of diagnostic models.

Model	Diagnosis	Strengths	Weaknesses
Score discrepancy	Discrepancy between IQ and achievement scores	• Simple to apply, requires little interpretation • Linked to statistical guidelines for significance	• Excludes those who are compensating for deficits • Excludes those whose IQ score is lowered by symptoms of LD • Does not identify cognitive processes to remediate
Clinical performance	Performance-based measures (e.g., school assignments, work tasks) are compared with peer-referenced expectations	• Based on actual functioning rather than results from individualized, structured tests • When ability-matched peers are used, allows for diagnosis of LD across range of intellectual functioning	• Lack of consensus about which peers should be the reference • When age-matched peers are used, does not allow for diagnosis of LD in people with non-average intellectual abilities
Response to intervention (RTI)	Not the primary focus of this model	• Focus is on the individual making progress with interventions	• Does not produce a diagnosis • May increase the number of people who qualify for services

significant increase in the number of people who qualify for services. Thus far, RTI has been applied to school-aged youth, but RTI concepts have potential for adults with LD [3].

See Table 6b.1 for a summary of diagnostic models.

Diagnostic terms and criteria

Two major classification systems are used for diagnosis of LD: the Diagnostic and Statistical Manual of Mental Disorders, Fourth Edition, Text Revision (DSM-IV-TR) [4] and the International Statistical Classification of Diseases and Health Related Problems (ICD)[5]. The DSM-IV-TR uses the broad category "Learning Disorders" to describe learning problems that significantly interfere with academic achievement or everyday functioning that requires reading, writing, or math. Diagnostic criteria for LD in the DSM-IV-TR require a discrepancy between individual achievement test scores and individual expectations, based on chronological age, age-appropriate education, and intellectual ability. The deficit in achievement must interfere with academic achievement or activities of daily living. Specific LD diagnoses in the DSM-IV-TR include:

• Reading Disorder (RD)[2]: based on deficient reading accuracy, speed, or comprehension; qualitatively, people with RD read slowly, have difficulty with reading comprehension, and make reading

errors (omissions, substitutions, and/or distortions);

• Disorder of Written Expression: based on standardized test or functional assessment of writing skills; difficulties can include grammar/punctuation, organization, spelling, and handwriting, although spelling and handwriting difficulties alone are not sufficient to establish this diagnosis;

• Mathematics Disorder: based on deficient mathematical calculation or reasoning; this disorder is not limited to numbers, and can involve:

  • language (e.g. "word problems," math terms, operations, concepts)

  • perception (e.g. clustering objects into groups, identifying operations/signs)

  • attention (e.g. copying problems correctly, remembering borrowed/carried figures, noting correct operation)

  • memory (e.g. learning basic math facts)

  • sequencing (e.g. steps involved in long division problems);

• Learning Disorder Not Otherwise Specified (LD-NOS): based on other problems in learning that do not meet specific criteria for the other three LD diagnoses; the DSM-IV-TR offers the example of a combination of reading, writing, and math difficulties that interfere with academic achievement even if individually administered standardized test results are not substantially below expectations.

Another classification system, the ICD, handles LD in a slightly different way (ICD-10) [5].[3] Within the ICD-10, "Mental and Behavioral Disorders: Disorders of Psychological Development" includes "specific developmental disorders of scholastic skills". Diagnostic requirements state that skill acquisition must be impaired beginning with early development, and that the impairment cannot be solely attributed to lack of opportunity to learn, mental retardation, acquired brain trauma, or disease. Disorders in this subcategory of the ICD-10 include:

- specific reading disorder, including reading comprehension, word recognition, oral reading, and all tasks involving reading; alternate terms include backward reading, developmental dyslexia, and specific reading retardation;

- specific spelling disorder,[4] which is impaired spelling skills (oral and written) in the absence of a specific reading disorder; an alternate term is specific spelling retardation (without reading disorder);

- specific disorder of arithmetical skills,[5] specifically mastery of the basic computational skills (addition, subtraction, multiplication, division); this set of diagnostic criteria is not based on abstract reasoning skills used in advanced math courses (e.g. algebra, geometry); other acceptable terms include: developmental acalculia, developmental arithmetical disorder, and developmental Gerstmann's syndrome; math difficulties that are secondary to reading or spelling disorders are excluded;

- mixed disorder of scholastic skills, which requires a specific disorder of arithmetical skills in the presence of either specific reading disorder or specific spelling disorder;

- other developmental disorders of scholastic skills, which references only a "developmental expressive writing disorder;"[6]

- developmental disorder of scholastic skills, unspecified, which includes "knowledge acquisition disability NOS" and LD-NOS.

Note that the DSM-IV-TR and ICD-9-CM do not exclude acquired conditions from the LD criteria, while the ICD-10 limits the use of these LD diagnoses to developmental conditions only. This has implications for prevalence rates.

Legal definitions

The language of US federal law also defines LD, particularly in IDEA 2004. LD is also referenced in key places including the Americans with Disabilities Act [6], Section 504 [7], and Section 508 [8]. IDEA 2004 applies to young adults (up through 21 years old) who are still in high school, and has continued relevance for adults with LD given political implications of changes enacted in IDEA 2004. IDEA 2004 includes "specific learning disability" (SLD) within the definition of child with a disability, including impaired listening, thinking, reading, writing, spelling, and math calculating. The federal definition of SLD includes perceptual disabilities, brain injury, minimal brain dysfunction, dyslexia, and developmental aphasia. IDEA 2004 excludes from the definition of SLD any learning problems that are secondary to visual/hearing/motor disabilities, mental retardation, emotional disturbance, environmental/cultural/economic disadvantage, limited English proficiency, or lack of appropriate instruction.

New terminology was introduced in IDEA 2004 regarding identifying SLDs in students. The final IDEA 2004 rules and regulations clearly indicate that a state must not require a severe discrepancy between achievement and intellectual ability in identifying an SLD. (This ultimate decision softened the language of an earlier draft that *prohibited* use of the discrepancy model.) The concept of RTI was introduced into federal law in IDEA 2004, as well as permission to use other research-based methods to identify an SLD. Furthermore, IDEA 2004 allows determination of an SLD in the following circumstances:

- the student does not achieve adequately for his age;

- the student does not meet state grade-level standards in one of the following areas (contingent on appropriate learning experiences and instruction):
  - oral expression
  - listening comprehension
  - written expression
  - basic reading skill
  - reading fluency skills
  - reading comprehension
  - mathematics calculation
  - mathematics problem-solving;

- the student does not make sufficient progress to meet age- or grade-level standards when RTI is being employed, or

- the student shows a pattern of strengths and weaknesses in performance and/or achievement when compared with expectations for age, grade, or intellectual ability.

IDEA 2004 establishes precedence for use of diagnostic models that are not discrepancy-based by considering functional performance and failure to make progress as equally important factors. Like the DSM-IV-TR, IDEA 2004 allows acquired conditions to be included under the term SLD.

The Americans with Disabilities Act (ADA) [6] provides protection from discrimination on the basis of disability, including discrimination against people with LD, in five categories:

- employment setting
- federal and local government and any entity receiving federal funding
- private sector providers of public goods and services
- telecommunication services for the deaf and hearing-impaired
- Federal Department of Transportation, as well as state and local public transit systems.

Within the ADA, SLDs are listed as an example of a mental impairment under the definition of individuals with disabilities. The ADA specifies that in order for an SLD to be considered a disability, it must substantially limit a major life activity (e.g. self-care, speaking, learning, or working). If an impairment restricts the conditions, manner, or duration under which a major life activity can be performed (relative to most people), then it is considered a substantial limitation. Assessment of disability is based on untreated impairments, even if available treatments mitigate the impact of those impairments.

Once an individual is determined to have an SLD under ADA definitions, he still may not be considered qualified for protection under the ADA unless he or she meets basic eligibility requirements for the school or workplace. For example, a woman seeking to practice as a lawyer must complete law school and pass the bar exam,[7] regardless of an SLD. The presence of the SLD may qualify her for modified courses or examinations, but does not allow her to bypass the law degree or examination. The finding that an individual is qualified does not guarantee the implementation of specific accommodations; employers are not required to provide accommodations that would impose undue hardship on the operation of the business.

The ADA specifies three ways that the needs of a qualified individual with a disability can be met:

- reasonable modifications of policies, practices, or procedures; for example, providing extended time for a person who has slow information-processing;
- auxiliary aids and services (required only for people with limited ability to communicate); for example, providing a qualified reader;
- removal of barriers, including architectural and communication barriers that are structural in nature; for example, revising conventional signage.

Section 504 of the Rehabilitation Act [7] made it illegal for any federally funded program or activity to discriminate against a person on the basis of disability (extending Title VI of the Civil Rights Act of 1964, which addressed discrimination on the basis of race, color, or national origin). Although Section 504 provided the foundation for the ADA, it was not entirely replaced by the ADA. Key differences include:

- section 504 indicates that agencies that discriminate against people with disabilities may lose federal funding; the ADA does not include this condition;
- section 504 includes entities that are not addressed under the ADA (e.g. housing that is built or operated by any entity that receives federal funds, as opposed to state/local government housing) [9].

Finally, Section 508 of the 1973 Rehabilitation Act was amended in 1998 to address accessibility of electronic and information technology to people with disabilities. For adults with LD, this might include access to books on tape/CD, computer or word processor, calculator, and voice recognition/dictation software.

In summary, while IDEA 2004 does not directly apply to most adults with LD, it establishes several models for diagnosis of LD that could be extended to the adult population. The ADA, Section 504, and Section 508 protect the rights of people with disabilities, including LD, from discrimination. A history of qualifying for special education and related services under IDEA 2004 does not guarantee qualification under federal laws pertaining to adults. Adult laws strive to ensure equal *access*, rather than equal outcome for people with LD.

Characteristics and features

This section describes research about the etiology of LD, including genetic and acquired forms. Typical course and prognosis, prevalence, demographics, and comorbidity of LD are summarized. Finally, other associated features are presented, including cognitive profiles, medical issues, life success, and relative strengths.

Etiology

Most research on the genetics of LD has focused on reading disorders (RD). RD and spelling disorders appear to aggregate familially; 50 to 60% of the variance in RD can be explained by genetics [10, 11]. Some 25 to 50% of people with RD show heritable, familial factors [12]. There is increased prevalence of LD in first-degree biological relatives of people with RD [4]. Research has indicated the involvement of chromosomes 6 and 15 in some families with strong histories of RD [13]; these chromosomes may also be involved with spelling difficulties [10]. Different genotypes may be linked to very specific phenotypes (e.g. chromosome 6 and deficits in phonological awareness; chromosome 15 and deficits in single-word reading [13]). Regions of chromosome 1 have been linked with RD and spelling disorder in some studies, particularly when there is a strong history of expressive speech disorder; chromosome 2 has been weakly implicated [10].

At times, there is no strong evidence of genetic transmission. An increased rate of LDs has been identified in children of mothers who used certain substances during pregnancy [14, 15], including alcohol [16], barbiturates [17], cigarettes [18], and cocaine [19]. LDs have also been identified as a common outcome for prenatal exposure to environmental toxins, such as lead and air pollution [20, 21]. Children who are born preterm show increased rates of LD [22]. Other birth risk factors associated with later diagnosis of LD include very low birthweight, low APGAR score, low maternal education, and substandard prenatal care [23]. Several studies suggest that maternal auto-immune disease during pregnancy is associated with higher rates of LD in offspring [24].

Course and prognosis

Symptoms of an LD are usually first recognized when formal instruction involves that particular academic skill (i.e., 1st grade for reading, 1st to 3rd grade for math, and 1st or 2nd grade for written expression [4]). In people with above average intelligence, symptoms may not become apparent until later years due to compensation. Although referral for diagnosis may not occur in early childhood, retrospective review of records often reveals early warning signs of LD. Diagnostic symptoms of an LD are most impairing when the deficient academic skill is required; associated features of LD are usually pervasive across settings. An LD is lifelong[8] and cannot be cured, although many adults show improved functioning as the consequence of compensatory strategies and choosing settings that maximize their strengths while minimizing weaknesses.

A study of successful[9] adults with LD identified the following shared characteristics: persistence, adaptive coping mechanisms, good match between abilities and job placement, support network, expectations and desire for success, goal-orientation, and positive reframe of LD [25]. The authors summarized these characteristics as representing the adult's conscious decision to take control over his/her life, accepting the LD, and adapting to move forward (rather than just survive). Factors that predict employment for adults with LD include: completing high-school degree, male gender (although employed females had higher rates of skilled as opposed to unskilled labor positions), higher socioeconomic status (which was in turn associated with specialized instruction in childhood), higher IQ scores, intact practical math skills, history of high-school job experience, and parents who are actively involved prior to high-school graduation [26, 27]. Family and social networks play a role in post-high-school employment; the majority of young adults with LD who are employed found their jobs through personal connections [28]. Young adults with LD who receive appropriate support in college are more likely to continue using compensatory strategies, and are more likely to graduate rather than withdraw [28].

Prevalence

The DSM-IV-TR [4] indicates that LD occurs in 2 to 10% of the general population. Other sources estimate higher prevalence in the adult population, up to 15% [29]. In a 2004 survey, 2.8% of college freshmen reported having an LD [30]. One federal agency estimates that 40–50% of adults receiving social services or related programs have an LD [31]. Federal data indicate that in 2003, 2.9 million children and adolescents in the USA were classified as having a primary disability of SLD (4.3% of school-aged youth); the SLD category accounts for almost 50% of students receiving services under IDEIA 2004 Part B [32]. An estimated 4% of school-aged youth have a reading disorder and 1% have a math disorder; prevalence of written language disorder was not estimated because this occurs in isolation so rarely [4]. Among people with LD, 80% are estimated to have a form of RD [33].

Demographics

Age is not a clear predictive factor for LD. The impact of an LD may be lessened over time with appropriate interventions and compensation. Severe cases of LD are more likely to be identified at younger ages, and milder cases more likely to be missed at younger ages [28]. Thus, early age of diagnosis can be associated with worse prognosis (i.e. because the symptoms are more severe), although this is not absolute in that late diagnosis of LD can result in worse prognosis due to the development of secondary issues.

Some studies have indicated that gender is a key demographic factor in prevalence of LD; for example, studies of RD have reported gender ratios up to 3:1 (male:female) [34]. Other researchers believe uneven gender ratios are due to sampling issues. Shaywitz and colleagues [35] demonstrated that when a large number of children are tested (i.e. the sample is not based on clinic referrals or school-based identification), RD occurs at similar rates in boys and girls (no statistically significant difference); in contrast, school-identified samples showed significantly more boys than girls classified with an RD. Another study reported that in their sample of adults who had reading or arithmetic deficiencies, the men were more likely to have a history of special education services than the women [36]. Given common comorbidities such as the disruptive behavior disorders that occur more frequently in males, this may represent a referral bias in that disruptive students are more likely to be referred for evaluation and treatment. These findings suggest that referral bias, sampling bias, and comorbidity may impact gender ratios more than the actual diagnosis of an LD when comparing people with LD to people in the general population.

When considering gender within LDs, some researchers have reported higher percentages of women than men with arithmetic deficiencies [36, 37]. There appears to be an interaction between gender, LD status, and employment. Results from several studies indicate that women with LD have higher rates of unemployment than men with LD or women in the general population [28].

Limited data are available about race/ethnicity and LD. Although a higher percentage of minority schoolchildren were categorized as having SLD in 2003 (relative to the general population) [32], this trend was apparent across all disability categories and does not appear to be specific to SLD. Socioeconomic status (SES; which covaries with race in some areas of the USA) and referral bias based on race may be partially responsible for these findings [38]. Studies have documented the positive impact of higher SES on outcome for people with LD [28]. Possible mechanisms include financial resources for private intervention, increased parent availability/involvement, and a broader network of job placement resources. Lower SES is associated with higher rates of risk factors, including environmental toxins.

Historically, many research studies reported increased rates of sinistrality in people with dyslexia. Studies utilizing broad samples (rather than clinic-referred samples) do not consistently support this finding. One study showed a strong association between deficits in phonological processing and sinistrality, but no statistically significant relationship between handedness and a diagnosis of dyslexia [39].

Research about intellectual ability and LD are confounded by the impact that LD can have on IQ scores. People with RD often have lower Verbal IQ scores than predicted based on other indicators of intellectual ability [40]. One study suggested that the heritability of RD varies with IQ level, with greater environmental influences involved when IQ is lower (i.e., heritability was 0.72 in the sample with FSIQ ≥ 100, and 0.43 for FSIQ < 100) [11]. It is possible that this represents an interaction with other variables, including socioeconomic status, education, and literacy exposure.

Comorbidity

LDs have high rates of comorbidity with each other, as well as with other psychiatric and medical conditions. Among LDs, Reading Disorder is often comorbid with Disorder of Written Expression and/or Mathematics Disorder. Disorder of Written Expression and Mathematics Disorder are rarely found in isolation. There are also high rates of co-occurrence between LD and other psychiatric disorders, including Attention-Deficit/Hyperactivity Disorder (ADHD) and disruptive behavior disorders, mood disorders, anxiety disorders, and substance use disorders [26, 41–43].

Associated features

Neuropsychological findings show that impaired functioning is not limited to the specific academic skill named by an LD diagnosis. Brain structure and function are atypical in people with LD. Other associated issues include legal difficulties, substance use, underachievement, and underemployment. Despite these problems, many adults with LD have succeeded in life.

Studies of *neuropsychological performance* in adults with LD show that people with math difficulties often have impaired visuospatial skills (including RCFT Copy and WJ-R Spatial Relations) and slower motor performance (including hand tapping and Grooved Pegboard), while people with reading difficulties often have impaired linguistic skills including spelling, word retrieval, rapid automatic naming, word recognition, decoding, and phonologic awareness/processing [26, 29, 36, 40, 44–46]. Caution must be used in generalizing these findings as most of these studies based group membership solely on achievement test scores (primarily the WRAT-R). Although many studies matched their groups by IQ score, Greiffenstein and Baker's [36] findings suggest that this may be misleading. Their sample of adults with low WRAT-R arithmetic scores also had statistically lower FSIQ scores than their group with low reading/spelling scores. These lower FSIQ scores were associated with lower perceptual organization index scores and lower PIQ scores. Their sample of adults with low WRAT-R reading recognition or spelling scores had statistically lower VIQ scores than their group with low arithmetic scores. These findings of non-independent variation of achievement test scores and IQ test scores provide some support for arguments against an achievement–ability discrepancy model for diagnosing LD.

Attention and executive functioning have been described as problematic for people with LD (e.g. lower TMT-B scores for young adults with LD; see [46]). Given that studies of neuropsychological functioning in adults with LD have focused on achievement test scores for group classification without examining comorbidity, it is possible that these attention and executive deficits are a function of high rates of comorbidity with disorders such as ADHD (cf. [29]). Memory deficits in LD have been described by some, including reports of short-term and working memory deficits [47]. Again, samples limit use of these findings; for example, Isaki and Plante's [47] clinical sample combined adults with a history of LD with adults who had a history of general language deficits. It is probable that problems with remembering are secondary to primary input processes for adults with LD [29, 40].

Most of the neuroimaging and post-mortem brain studies involving LD have focused on RD. Studies of people with dyslexia describe *structural brain abnormalities* in language/language association areas and frontal regions. Specific structural atypicalities identified in the brains of people with dyslexia include the planum temporale, portions of the thalamus (including bilateral medial geniculate nucleus and posterior nuclei), corpus callosum, and portions of the anterior cortex (including orbitofrontal and dorsolateral cortexes) [39, 40, 48–50]. Although early studies identified high numbers of polymicrogyria and other cortical abnormalities in the brains of people with dyslexia, this does not appear to be strongly associated with this particular diagnostic group (cf. [49]). One study identified perisylvian gyral/sulcal differences in children with atypical performance on neurolinguistic tests, but found these structural differences were not reliably associated with diagnostic group (i.e. dyslexia, ADHD, or no diagnosis) [51]. This finding shows that structural differences between a clinical group and a nonclinical group do not necessarily indicate that the structural differences are diagnostic. Studies of *functional brain abnormalities* in people with LD have also focused on RD. During phonological analysis tasks, adults with dyslexia showed atypical brain activation levels relative to non-impaired readers; this included anterior overactivation (including inferior frontal gyrus) and posterior underactivation (including Wernicke's area, angular gyrus, and striate cortex) [52].

Other medical findings have been reported anecdotally, but not validated. These include increased prevalence of childhood ear infections and family history of autoimmune disorders (cf. [49]). Given that certain facial structures (e.g. ear canals) develop concurrently with key cortical structures, it is reasonable to hypothesize that people with cortical variations such as those described in LD might have a greater proclivity toward ear infections. If a person had vulnerabilities in the immune system, he or she would be more susceptible to prenatal or early childhood exposures that could impact brain development and result in an LD.

Another common pattern among adults with LD is *"life underachievement"*, meaning that the symptoms of LD have limited them from reaching potential. This can be apparent through academic underachievement, underemployment, legal difficulties, and substance use. In the USA, 26% of public-school students with LD (over 750 000 students with at least average intelligence) dropped out of high school before completing the 12th grade in 2003 [53]. It is interesting that one study found higher education levels in a group of adults with "arithmetic deficiency" when compared with adults who had "reading deficiency" or combined

Table 6b.2. Average annual earnings in 1992 [54].

Education	Literacy	
	Low	High
High school degree	$14,570	$19,300
Post-secondary education	$17,120	$23,020

reading and arithmetic deficiencies [36]. For students with LD who completed high school, only 35% pursued post-secondary education, and the majority of these youth attended 2-year colleges rather than 4-year colleges [53].

Given findings that annual earnings increase with increased education and increased literacy, this has significant implications for the earning potential of adults with an LD that impacts literacy (see Table 6b.2).[10] Underemployment has been reported for adults with LD. The exception is found in studies of adults with LD who completed college and were employed appropriately; job success for adults with LD has been linked to the goodness-of-fit between strengths and job choice [28].

Self-report data from surveys of state and federal inmates show a high incidence of learning problems [55], suggesting that people with LD may be at risk for legal difficulties. In the USA, 50% of young adults who received special education under the classification of LD had been involved with the criminal justice system when interviewed in their early 20s [56]. Two-thirds of state prison inmates with a self-reported LD had not completed high school or a GED [57]. Studies of recidivism show lower rates of re-arrest, re-conviction, and re-incarceration for inmates who participated in educational programming, and higher employment success for parolees who participated in educational programming [58]. While the study did not draw connections between these findings and LD status of the inmates and parolees, it is reasonable to think that a person with an LD would be less likely to participate in or benefit from educational programming without appropriate supports and interventions.

There are increased rates of LD among people who have substance use disorders, with estimates ranging from 40 to 70% of chemically dependent adolescents; this comorbidity is associated with decreased effectiveness of substance use treatment programs [59]. The relationship between LD and substance use is probably multifactorial, including variables such as LD characteristics that are also risk factors for substance use (e.g. low self-esteem, academic difficulty, depression) and shared etiological pathways (e.g. prenatal substance exposure associated with increased rates of LD, parental substance use associated with increased rates of offspring substance use).

Unfortunately, statistics are typically collected about problems and deficits. Although there are no statistics about relative strengths and skills in adults with LD, clinical experience, anecdotal information, and generalization of neuropsychological findings suggest that many people with LD show a number of strengths. These include curiosity, imagination, and intuition. Successful adults with LD are often resourceful and persistent, with good compensatory strategies and intact support systems. People with LD tend to be outgoing and sociable, with good empathy.

Assessment

Those who evaluate adults for possible LD must have a solid foundation in differential diagnosis of childhood disorders. Without this knowledge base, it is difficult to identify the early manifestations of an LD and to determine the best diagnosis to account for these early symptoms. Many adults have developed compensatory mechanisms for coping with an LD, making it difficult to evaluate the disorder based solely on current performance. Adults with LD may have made education and employment decisions based on fear of failure rather than actual ability and interest; in these cases, the lack of challenge relative to ability may result in the appearance of no functional impairment. At times, a bright adult may have no history of an LD diagnosis, but may be experiencing increased difficulty as demands become more complex and there is not sufficient time to compensate. This is often the case for adults in educational settings such as college, graduate school, or other higher education. This can also occur for adults who are promoted to a career level that requires more efficient and integrative work. It is important for the clinician to have experience with assessing early development so that he or she will recognize evidence of vulnerabilities even when there is no history of an LD diagnosis. If the adult is (or plans to be) enrolled in academic coursework, a clinician with a background in working with school-aged youth will be well suited to provide specific recommendations for appropriate academic accommodations as well as study strategies.

Clinicians evaluating adults for LD must also have experience working with adults. Critical differential diagnosis issues such as the personality disorders are less familiar to clinicians who work primarily with children. Professionals who work with adults tend to be more aware of possible secondary gain as a motivating factor for diagnosis and/or performance. Many treatment issues are unique to adults, such as marriage, financial management, and gainful employment. The most effective clinician for an adult LD evaluation is one who has this unique combination of child and adult experience.

This section provides general guidelines for important topics to address in an assessment, including key topics to explore in obtaining the background history, determining differential diagnostic decisions, and compiling the test battery. The reader is referred to Mapou [45] for detailed guidelines for evaluation of LD in adults.

Background history

An adult LD evaluation should include a thorough background history, with particular focus on early development, academic performance, and diagnostic criteria of LD. Past history of special education and related services for learning difficulties can support a diagnosis of LD. In the absence of official school services, an adult may have survived school because of extracurricular instruction or extensive support. School records and report cards should be reviewed when possible, with attention to comments that suggest early warning signs of LD.

Red flags for possible LD

- Late talker
- Jumbled word pronunciation and mispronunciation in reading and speech
- Difficulty learning basic pre-academic skills, including rhyming, alphabet letters/sounds, numbers, colors, names of objects
- Difficulty segmenting words into syllables and syllables into phonemes
- Poor use of phonics to "sound out" words
- Nonfluent speech and reading, including circumlocution, word substitution, filler words, nonspecific words, and blocking
- Slow response to questions
- Slow and effortful academic work; easily fatigued by academic work; avoids academic work
- Difficulty remembering names of people and places
- Prefers pictures, diagrams, or demonstration over written text or numbers; prefers telling rather than writing answers

Adults with an LD often describe a pattern of learning best in hands-on settings rather than lecture rooms. They may choose to attend trade/vocational schools rather than pursue higher education in a college/university setting. Underachievement is common for adults with LD, and should be suspected when an adult with adequate cognitive skills repeated a grade, was placed in remedial or basic courses, or earned low grades. As mentioned previously, some adults with LD barely survive high school or withdraw. Some adults with LD who withdraw from high school are able to earn a GED as they complete focused coursework in smaller classes with fewer simultaneous demands.

Family history can also support consideration of an LD. When evaluating for adult LD, it is important to inquire not only about family of origin, but also about academic functioning in the adult's offspring. Many adults present for an evaluation after a son or daughter is diagnosed, commenting that they experienced similar difficulties in childhood.

Premorbid LD should be considered when there is a history of brain injury. Although the sequelae of neurological damage may mask the symptoms of an LD, a careful background history may reveal pre-existing symptoms. Remember that the presence of an LD may actually increase an individual's risk for brain injury, as slow processing or perceptual difficulties may result in greater probability of being injured. In cases where the symptoms of LD were not evident prior to the injury, some definitions consider acquired symptoms as fitting within a diagnosis of LD.

Patterns of substance use are also important to inquire about in the background history. If the adult was using substances during the school years, this could impact learning in the absence of an LD; however, it is important to consider whether the substance use could be secondary to the LD. People with LD often experience social and emotional difficulties, as well as increased stress academically and vocationally. This places them at risk for using substances as a coping mechanism. Therefore, it is important to carefully inquire about academic functioning prior to onset of substance use.

Differential diagnosis

Given the high rates of comorbidity, the differential diagnosis of LD is usually a selection of which combination of diagnoses best explain the symptoms. Psychiatric considerations include:

- Attention-Deficit/Hyperactivity Disorder (ADHD). Establish whether the attentional problems occur in certain subjects or are pervasive across settings. For example, people with RD often appear inattentive and fidgety in language-based settings, but show intact attention and self-control in other settings.

- Communication disorders, including expressive or receptive language disorders. People with LD can have difficulties with spoken language, such as word-finding errors and comprehension. People with communication disorders can have difficulty with reading and written expression. When language is impaired and academic achievement is significantly below expectations based on nonverbal intellectual functioning, it is reasonable to consider comorbid diagnoses of communication disorder and LD.

- Intellectual disability (ID). The presence of deficient cognitive functioning does not exclude a diagnosis of LD. These diagnoses can be comorbid if achievement is significantly below expectations given the adult's education and severity of ID. It is important to consider the possibility of severe LD in some cases where an adult has previously been diagnosed with ID. If the previous diagnosis of ID was assigned based on low IQ scores from traditional assessment of intelligence (which relies heavily on language and symbols), it is important to consider other ways to assess ability.

- Pervasive Developmental Disorders (PDD), including autistic disorder and Asperger's disorder. People with PDD diagnoses often have difficulty with learning. It is important to consider whether learning difficulties exceed those expected for the individual's education and intellectual functioning, which would warrant an additional diagnosis. The DSM-IV-TR indicates that it is possible to have comorbid LD and PDD.

- Personality disorder. In adults, the possibility of an Axis II diagnosis must be considered. Certain patterns, particularly those observed in people with Histrionic or Borderline Personality Disorder, could be associated with academic struggles. The background history can help determine whether a personality disorder causes attributions that mask an LD. For example, an adult with LD and Narcissistic Personality Disorder might describe incompetent instructors rather than admitting academic struggles.

- Anxiety disorders and mood disorders. Symptoms of depression and anxiety can interfere with learning. A key in identifying comorbid LD is persistence of the symptoms. If the learning difficulties are secondary to depression/anxiety, they should recur and remit in conjunction with these symptoms; if there is a comorbid LD learning problems will persist regardless of emotional stability.

Differential diagnosis of LD is not limited to psychiatric considerations, and should include sensory factors (e.g. vision, hearing, motor functioning). Most diagnostic guides indicate that the presence of sensory deficits does not rule out an LD; the evaluator must establish that the academic difficulties are in excess of those usually associated with sensory impairment. Medical factors should also be considered, particularly when a medical syndrome may include symptoms of LD.

It is important to think about other factors that can be associated with academic difficulties. Lack of appropriate instruction must be ruled out before an LD can be diagnosed. This includes opportunity to receive instruction, quality of instruction, and attendance at school. If an adult was not present for instruction (e.g. chronic illness, frequent relocation, tardiness, truancy) or was not offered appropriate instruction, it is difficult to determine the presence of an LD. Similarly, if English was not the adult's primary language during childhood or adolescence and this was not addressed, it is unreasonable to expect that he or she gained adequate instruction.

Cultural factors may play a role. Some cultures emphasize physical appearance or social connections over academic success for females. Some families need their children to contribute financially, spending more hours at a job than at homework. It is important to obtain information about these factors and consider them as possible explanations for academic struggles, either in addition to or in place of an LD.

Normal variations in academic achievement should be considered. It is typical for a student to do better in some content areas than others; this pattern does not necessarily indicate an LD. Finally, there are situations in which an adult may have a secondary motivation to do poorly academically or on tests.

Keys to assessing LD in adults

- Do not rule out an LD diagnosis solely on the basis of average individual achievement test scores.

- Fluency is a critical issue for all content areas. Does the adult read, write, and do math fluently?

Consider the amount of time and effort required to earn each test score.

- Test the limits. Complete a test with standardized administration, then modify the test to evaluate your hypotheses (e.g. allow additional time, read text aloud, provide fill-in-the-blank response formats). Compare performance from the standardized administration with the modified administration to determine appropriate accommodation recommendations.

- Analyze the format of the test that produced a given score.

- Discuss relevant issues in the recommendations (e.g. fatigues quickly when mental arithmetic is required, reading comprehension is more accurate when a word is presented in context).

Areas to assess

A psychoeducational evaluation (i.e. IQ and achievement testing) can document an ability–achievement discrepancy, but provides little information about which cognitive processes are contributing to the academic deficit. A psychoeducational evaluation does not produce sufficient data to consider alternative diagnoses. A full evaluation battery should be used when evaluating possible LD for an adult [60], including the following areas:

- Intelligence (IQ)
- Academic achievement: prioritize the primary area of concern, but be sure to include screens of other content areas given the high rates of comorbidity among LDs
- Reading, including phonological awareness, vocabulary development, comprehension, and decoding. Single-word recognition and decoding scores may not show the deficit, as time and effort are not taken into account. Note qualitative errors and effort as the adult reads a passage aloud
- Spelling
- Written language
- Math, including calculation and applied math
- Speed of information-processing and responding
- Timed academic tests, including reading, math, and writing fluency. Consider tests that offer standardized ways to test the limits (e.g. Nelson-Denny Reading Test has normative data for extended time)

- Compare timed academic tasks with other timed tests. Remember that subtests such as Coding and Symbol Search involve symbols, and thus are not a fair measure of processing speed for people with LD
- Attention: prerequisite of learning, differential diagnosis of ADHD
- Executive functioning, even when ADHD is not comorbid with the LD
- Memory and learning, including:
  - Pairs of tests that contrast area of academic difficulty and relatively intact skills, e.g.
    - Linguistic versus spatial
    - Auditory versus visual
    - Rote (e.g. word list) versus meaningful (e.g. story memory)
  - Tests that inform specific study/learning strategy recommendations
- Language, including tests of receptive/expressive, visual/auditory, and academic/conversational language
- Visuospatial, including perception and generation of information
- Sensory and motor functioning: to identify possible sensory/motor disorder as comorbid/competing diagnosis
- Personality and emotional functioning:
  - Consider personality disorders and patterns that impact functioning. Remember that LD can impact perceptual processing and verbal complexity, and can affect results from standard projective tests
  - Emotional evaluation to identify comorbid/secondary diagnoses and factors that may be limiting functional learning
- Vocational skills and interests
- Validity indicators

Specific evaluation needs

If the adult is seeking the evaluation in order to obtain accommodations in a specific setting, review relevant criteria prior to beginning the evaluation. Settings with very specific requirements include entrance examinations (e.g. LSAT, MCAT, GMAT, GRE) and college/university accommodations offices. Most review boards require the following:[11]

- evaluation conducted by a qualified professional within the past 5 years (older evaluations are accepted in some cases)

- history of symptoms and difficulties (particularly when there is no history of prior diagnosis)

- evidence of functional impairment (past and current)

- psychological/neuropsychological test scores to document deficits in academic functioning

- differential diagnosis discussion, including alternative explanations and why they were rejected

- statement of impairment, and how the LD substantially limits functioning

- specific DSM or ICD diagnosis, with support from evaluation

- specific accommodation and treatment recommendations with rationale and link to evaluation findings (including a history of past accommodations).

Some review boards specify which tests are "approved" and what qualifications must be held by the examiner. Although a qualified professional is certainly in a position to educate the review board about the suitability of an alternate test or method, this may delay the adult's access to needed accommodations. The examiner must weigh potential costs and benefits of modifying the recommended protocol when seeking accommodations in one of these specific settings.

Inclusion of strengths

Report of an LD evaluation should discuss the adult's relative strengths. A statement of deficit can be contrasted with intact skills. Even when the research literature (or clinical experience) suggests that a domain is likely to be intact, it is important to directly assess these skills as not every individual follows the group pattern. Many settings require documentation of individual data to support accommodations/modifications; it is not sufficient to say, "Most people with LD benefit from hands-on learning". Consideration of strengths is another good reason to assess all domains of functioning rather than just the areas of concern. Without knowledge of intact skills, it is difficult to develop an effective treatment plan that maximizes strengths while compensating for weaknesses.

Treatment

An assessment that stops with the diagnosis of LD is inadequate. Simply obtaining a label does not address the issues that led the adult to seek an evaluation, although it is a starting place for understanding the history of struggles. Professionals who see adults with LD must be knowledgeable about types of treatment and settings in which the adult requires interventions. Self-advocacy is a critical skill that should be addressed when providing services to adults with LD.

Types of treatment and treatment issues

The primary treatment modality for children with LD is direct intervention, which includes specialized instructional techniques to remediate the specific deficits. The introduction of RTI into federal legislation has led to increased awareness of scientifically validated treatment programs for use with children (see What Works Clearinghouse [61]). If an adult had the time and financial resources to devote to relearning a specific skill, these techniques would probably also work (although the materials might seem juvenile). Some adult literacy programs use placement testing to help identify which reading skills should be targeted in instruction. Although adult education programs are available for all content areas, instructors may not have training in LD-specific instruction issues.

Keys to instruction and accommodation for LD [62]

- Be structured and systematic

- Teach manageable chunks of information

- Explicitly connect new information to past knowledge ("scaffolding") and course goals

- Give feedback about expectations and how the adult can improve

- Use direct instruction; monitor progress

- Teach in short and frequent increments until skill is mastered; use periodic review to reinforce/maintain concepts

- Teach to the adult's strengths, accommodate cognitive deficits

- Help apply and generalize knowledge and skills

- Use techniques supported by research (when possible)

- Meet individual needs

- Use qualified teachers with specialized training in LD instruction

- Use relevant assistive technology (e.g. text-to-speech software, digital recordings, word processing, dictation software, calculators, spreadsheets)

Most effective treatment plans for adults focus on coping with the LD and related issues through a combination of accommodations/modifications, support groups, and psychotherapy, and medication content, includes a combination of compensatory strategies, niche identification, and adjunct treatment of associated issues. Remember the shared characteristics of successful adults with LD; many of these can be taught or supported in therapy sessions.

Accommodations and modifications are terms that have legal meaning under federal laws. Generally speaking, these terms refer to ways of changing the environment or altering expectations for a person with an LD. Examples of accommodations and modifications that may be helpful for an adult with LD include extended time, reduced workload, individual workspace (e.g. reduced distractions), and use of assistive technology (cf. [63, 64]). Two research papers have documented the specific efficacy of extended time for students with LD, including reading comprehension [65], algebra [66], and the Scholastic Aptitude Test (SAT) [67].

There are many benefits to an adult with LD who participates in a support group, whether in person or online. Support groups normalize the experience of having an LD and reduce feelings of isolation. These groups provide education about the diagnosis, associated features, effective interventions, and survival strategies. People in the group can offer insight to newly diagnosed adults and young adults with childhood diagnoses of LD. Support group members may have suggestions about which local resources are helpful for diagnosis or treatment.

Therapy sessions can help an adult with LD, particularly when the therapist is familiar with LD and associated features. The therapist should adjust treatment modalities to match the adult's cognitive strengths and weaknesses (e.g. avoid bibliotherapy for an adult with RD). Education about LD can be integrated into the sessions. The primary focus of individual therapy sessions is often secondary or comorbid emotional symptoms. Some therapists are equipped to offer "coaching" services to an adult with LD, including help with organization and planning. A referral to the local vocational rehabilitation office may be appropriate. Couples therapy or family therapy may be indicated in some instances, as LD-related issues can impact everyone in the adult's family. Proactive intervention may help reduce the chance of secondary emotional distress or substance abuse/dependence.

Support groups and therapy sessions can help educate and support adults with LD about social issues. Socially, some adults with LD have difficulty with interpersonal relationships, including romantic partnerships, family relations, social support networks, and professional contacts (cf. [68]). The issue is usually with application and interpretation, rather than absence of social skills or knowledge. For adults with language-related LD, social difficulties may be related to limited comprehension skills that reduce social inferencing. Adults with perceptual difficulties may have difficulty reading body language and facial expression. Timing may be off in social interactions, resulting in awkward conversations. People with LD may have been teased or bullied as children. These issues may lead to feelings of isolation, rejection, and loneliness, resulting in emotional sequelae. Social difficulties can prevent an adult with LD from developing a social support network, and thus limit prognosis. Remember that not all people with LD struggle socially. Some people with LD have exceptional social skills, and are well-known and liked, particularly the subset of people with LD who have extraordinary athletic abilities and excel in that arena.

Emotional issues are important to address in support groups and therapy sessions. People with LD describe feeling overwhelmed, inadequate, and incompetent. This pattern can lead to learned helplessness and dependency, particularly when childhood interventions did not encourage self-sufficiency and age-appropriate independence. Adults with LD, especially those with social struggles, often have low self-confidence and self-concept. These features increase the risk for anxiety and depression, even in the absence of genetic risk. Parents with LD may feel guilty when their children struggle academically; emotional reactions can impede assistance for the children. It is important to inquire about emotional issues if the adult does not describe them in the initial referral. If the adult with LD seems at risk for emotional sequelae, teach and practice coping skills before he or she reaches crisis.

Research has not revealed a medication or nutritional supplement to cure or remediate LD. When comorbid diagnoses such as anxiety, depression, or ADHD are present, it is appropriate to consider a medication trial to address these symptoms.

Primary treatment settings

Adults with LD may be enrolled in classes, including community college, university, or continuing adult education classes. They may be studying for a GED or entrance examination such as LSAT, GRE, MCAT, or GMAT. Job requirements may include certain certifications, such as Microsoft certification in information technology or Qualified Elevator Inspector certification. It is important to discuss these possibilities with the adult to determine whether he or she is currently in an academic setting or whether this may be a future goal. Keep in mind that adults may have avoided academic commitments in the past given their deficits, but that a good evaluation and treatment plan will support them in considering future possibilities. Results from the evaluation should help the adult with LD know how to compensate for deficits. Skills addressed might include note-taking, listening, studying, writing, and test-taking. If the adult meets criteria established by the ADA or other legislation, accommodations/modifications such as reduced courseload or extended deadlines may be appropriate to recommend.

Whether employed or seeking employment, adults with LD should be given strategies for maximizing performance in the workplace. For example, an adult with a Disorder of Written Expression might benefit from using dictation software for written work. An adult with a Reading Disorder might indicate a preference for meetings rather than written briefs. In some instances, it is appropriate to recommend vocational counseling, particularly if the individual is in a job that is a poor match for his or her strengths and weaknesses (e.g. an adult with dyslexia who works as a proofreader).

In the home, an adult with LD needs to perform activities of daily living and maintain good relationships with family members or housemates. Working with the adult to create a list of domestic problems (e.g. misplacing keys/wallet, neglecting to wash clothes for work, losing bills/paperwork, failing to manage finances, and forgetting appointments/deadlines) can guide strategy development. Domestic harmony can be improved by addressing such issues, but these practical areas do not solve all relationship issues in the home. Some adults with LD will need pointers about reasonable expectations and common courtesy, while others will benefit from couples therapy.

Community issues may include relationships, legal compliance, housing, transportation, health, and leisure activities. Adults with LD may benefit from support with appropriate social skills. Strategies to increase compliance with legal regulations may improve the adult's functioning (e.g. adults with RD might need to review common parking signs so that they do not continue to be towed for parking inappropriately). Adults may require assistance to comprehend and complete legal forms (e.g. leases, contracts). It may be helpful to address transportation tasks (e.g. bus/train schedules, driving directions). An adult with LD may benefit from entering recurring calendar reminders for health-related appointments (e.g. annual examination, monthly allergy shots). Leisure activities should also be planned and scheduled.

Self-advocacy

This may be the most important skill for an adult with LD.[12] Learning to effectively communicate about personal strengths/and deficits increases the chance of success in all settings. Common questions that relate to self-advocacy include:

- *Who should I tell?* Think about this on a "need to know" basis. If the symptoms of LD impact functioning in the workplace, share appropriate amounts of information with supervisors and perhaps coworkers. In academic situations, disclosure of the disability opens the door to services. When the adult is in a committed relationship, it is usually a good idea to inform the partner. Therapists and physicians will be more effective if they are aware of an LD diagnosis.

- *What information should I share?* Share the amount of information that is necessary for the adult's success. In some cases, it may be appropriate to give another person the full neuropsychological assessment report to read. At times, an excerpt or summary letter from the neuropsychologist is sufficient. It may be adequate to simply describe needs (e.g. "I have difficulty understanding what I read. Can we discuss information by telephone rather than by e-mail?").

- *When should I tell?* This can be a difficult decision. Legally, an applicant cannot be rejected (from school or a job) purely on the basis of his disability, as long as he or she meets minimum requirements for acceptance when provided with appropriate accommodations and modifications. In situations where an adult with LD discloses the diagnosis during the application process, this information may lead to special consideration of the hurdles he or she has surmounted in the process of reaching adulthood (e.g. providing a context for understanding grades or past performance reviews). It is helpful to obtain information from knowledgeable resources (e.g. career or college counselor) about the climate in a university or company. If adults with LD choose not to disclose disability status during the application process, they may face difficulty finding appropriate supports once admitted or hired. If they are the first adult with LD in an organization, they may spend time and energy trail-blazing rather than working or studying. Once admitted or hired, adults with LD should disclose disability status if they will require any accommodations or modifications to function successfully.

- *How do I obtain accommodations/ modifications?* In the workplace, contact the human resources (HR) office. Academic settings have a student services (SS) office or ADA compliance office. By law, these offices must support a qualified person with disabilities (including LD) in obtaining necessary supports as specified by the ADA, Section 504, and Section 508.[13] These offices are responsible for ensuring that the company/university is legally compliant, not for obtaining what is best for the adult with LD. Adults with LD may benefit from working with an advocate or lawyer who specializes in these issues. Regardless of the people involved, the best results are usually obtained through teamwork. It is difficult for an adult with LD to survive in an environment that is hostile. Once the HR or SS office is in agreement that the adult qualifies as a person with a disability, they will facilitate the dispersion of information to appropriate supervisors or professors. When an evaluation is completed prior to application, it is important for the evaluator to review services typically offered in that setting, ensure documentation is consistent with requirements, and discuss these options with the adult client. Many evaluators who see college students help the young adult establish a connection with the appropriate university office after obtaining a signed release of information form.

- *What accommodations/modifications can I get?* It is important to remind adults with LD that they are not guaranteed the same services that were provided under IDEIA 2004, as this federal law does not apply after high school. The range of accommodations/modifications required of employers and universities tends to be narrower than those required of primary and secondary public school systems. Most settings require documentation of a recent evaluation by a qualified examiner that supports each accommodation/modification request with individual data. There is no comprehensive list of provisions that must be made for adults with LD, as each adult has unique needs. After providing the appropriate person with the evaluation report, it is important for the adult with LD to discuss the results and recommendations with them to develop strategies that will be mutually beneficial. Some professionals are available to participate in this conversation after completing an evaluation; however, it is important that the adult with LD is a participant as he or she will be the one interacting with the company/university on a daily basis. Within the academic setting, the SS office tends to be familiar with the needs of students with LD, and may have additional recommendations about services that may be helpful.

Resources

There are many resources for people with LD, including support groups, educational materials, assistive technologies, and treatment programs. The majority of direct intervention programs target school-aged youth, but can be altered to address the needs of adults with LD (particularly adults in educational settings). Primary organizations that serve people with LD include:

- International Dyslexia Association, http://www.interdys.org
- LD Association of America, http://www.ldaamerica.org
- National Center for LD, http://www.ld.org

Summary and future directions

In sum, LDs are lifelong and impact many aspects of adult functioning. While there is some debate about the best operational definition of an LD, diagnosis in adults is largely guided by the DSM-IV-TR. Comorbidity and associated features of LD remind the evaluator to consider all domains of functioning when conducting an evaluation and planning interventions. There is no cure for LD, but many adults learn effective ways to compensate for their weaknesses by maximizing areas of strength. Neuropsychologists and other allied health professionals can help adults with LD by evaluating all areas of functioning, completing a detailed background interview, assessing all areas of current need, and providing specific treatment recommendations that are relevant to individual needs.

Research in this field has focused primarily on school-aged youth with LD; it is important to expand research efforts to consider the needs of adults with LD. The most critical issue that remains is developing direct interventions for use with adults, and establishing the efficacy of these research-based interventions. Otherwise, adults with LD will continue to struggle as professionals apply upward extensions of child-based research. Given the prevalence of LD in adults, it is important for funds and effort to be directed toward this research and practice topic to address a nationwide problem that directly impacts the financial, vocational, social, and emotional success of these many adults.

Future studies of LD in adults should take into account the variables that have been considered in child-based research, including large population samples, gender, IQ, SES, educational attainment, etiology, family background, and support network. Samples must be well-defined, including how LD was determined and recruitment methods. Clinical comparison groups are recommended, in addition to general population control groups.

Notes

1. One to two standard deviations is the range typically used.
2. Although not a DSM-IV-TR diagnosis, the term "dyslexia" is used in the research literature and popular press to describe RD. According to prominent researchers, "Developmental dyslexia is characterized by an unexpected difficulty in reading in children and adults who otherwise possess the intelligence and motivation considered necessary for accurate and fluent reading" (ref. 33, p. 147). Although early studies suggested visual deficits, recent work supports a linguistic basis for dyslexia (i.e. letter reversals are due to misnaming the letter rather than misperceiving the symbol).
3. In 2008, the USA still used the ICD-9-Clinical Modification (ICD-9-CM) [69] rather than the ICD-10 for insurance coding purposes. The ICD-9-CM includes alexia and dyscalculia within LD; ICD-10 categorizes these elsewhere.
4. A subcategory of "Specific Reading Disorder" in the ICD-9-CM.
5. "Mathematics disorder" in the ICD-9-CM.
6. "Other specific learning difficulties: Disorder of written expression" in the ICD-9-CM.

7. The ADA Title III Technical Assistance Manual [70] provides specific guidance regarding instructional courses, admission examinations, and licensing examinations (sections 4.6100 and 4.6200).
8. For example, see Bruck's findings that adults with a history of childhood dyslexia continue to show slow and inaccurate decoding [71], poor phoneme awareness [72], and spelling errors [73].
9. Success ratings were based on a combination of five variables: income level, job classification, education level, prominence in job field, and job satisfaction.
10. The National Adult Literacy Survey of 1992 [74] found the average prose literacy level for adults with LD was Level 1, the lowest category assigned.
11. For example, see guidelines published by the Association on Higher Education and Disability [75] and the Educational Testing Service [76].
12. Interestingly, one survey found that although 73% of young adults with LD reported that LD symptoms impact their job performance, only 55% of the sample self-disclosed LD status to employers [77].
13. If an institution is receiving any federal funding in grants, loans, or special projects, then that institution is required to accommodate a person with a disability.

References

1. Hoy C, Gregg N, Wisenbaker J, Bonham SS, King M, Moreland C. Clinical model versus discrepancy model in determining eligibility for learning disabilities services at a rehabilitation setting. In Gregg N, Hoy C, Gay AF, eds. *Adults with Learning Disabilities: Theoretical and Practical Perspectives.* New York: The Guilford Press; 1996: 55–67.
2. Individuals with Disabilities Education Improvement Act (IDEA 2004). Public Law 2004; 108–446.
3. Gregg N, Coleman C, Davis M, Lindstrom W, Hartwig J. Critical issues for the diagnosis of learning disabilities in the adult population. *Psychol Schools* 2006;**43**(8): 889–99.
4. American Psychiatric Association (APA). *Diagnostic and Statistical Manual of Mental Disorders*, 4th edn. text revision; DSM-IV-TR. Washington DC: American Psychiatric Association; 2000.
5. World Health Organization. *ICD-10: The International Statistical Classification of Diseases and Related Health Problems*, vol. 1–3, 10th revision, 2nd edn. Geneva: World Health Organization; 2004.
6. Americans with Disabilities Act (ADA). Public Law 1990; 101–336.
7. Section 504 of the 1973 Rehabilitation Act, Public Law 93–112.
8. Section 508 of the Rehabilitation Act (29 U.S.C. 794d), as amended by the Workforce Investment Act of 1998, Public Law 105–220.

9. The National Council on Disability (NCD, 2003). *Rehabilitating Section 504.* Accessed 22 Apr 2008 from http://www.ncd.gov/newsroom/publications/2003/section504.htm.

10. Schulte-Körne G. Genetics of reading and spelling disorder. *J Child Psychol Psychiatry* 2001;**42**(8):985–97.

11. Wadsworth SJ, Olson RK, Pennington BF, DeFries JC. Differential genetic etiology of RD as a function of IQ. *J Learn Disabil* 2000;**33**:192–9.

12. DeFries JC, Fulker DW. Multiple regression analysis of twin data: Etiology of deviant scores versus individual differences. *Acta Genet Med Gemollol* 1988;**37**:205–16.

13. Grigorenko EL, Wood FB, Meyer MS, Hart LA, Speed WC, Shuster A, Pauls DL. Susceptibility loci for distinct components of developmental dyslexia on chromosomes 6 and 15. *Am J Hum Genet* 1997;**60**:27–39.

14. Pulsifer MB, Butz AM, O'Reilly FM, Belcher HM. Prenatal drug exposure: effects on cognitive functioning at 5 years of age. *Clin Pediatr (Phila)* 2008;**47**(1):58–65.

15. Vorhees CV. Developmental neurotoxicity induced by therapeutic and illicit drugs. *Environ Health Perspect* 1994;**102**(Suppl 2):145–53.

16. Howell KK, Lynch ME, Platzman KA, Smith GH, Coles CD. Prenatal alcohol exposure and ability, academic achievement, and school functioning in adolescence: a longitudinal follow-up. *J Pediatr Psychol* 2006;**31**(1):116–26.

17. Reinisch JM, Sanders SA. Early barbiturate exposure: the brain, sexually dimorphic behavior and learning. *Neurosci Biobehav Rev* 1982;**6**(3):311–19.

18. Batstra L, Hadders-Algra M, Neeleman J. Effect of antenatal exposure to maternal smoking on behavioural problems and academic achievement in childhood: prospective evidence from a Dutch birth cohort. *Early Hum Dev* 2003;**75**(1–2):21–33.

19. Morrow CE, Culbertson JL, Accornero VH, Xue L, Anthony JC, Bandstra ES. Learning disabilities and intellectual functioning in school-aged children with prenatal cocaine exposure. *Dev Neuropsychol* 2006;**30**(3):905–31.

20. Fergusson DM, Horwood LJ, Lynskey MT. Early dentine lead levels and educational outcomes at 18 years. *J Child Psychol Psychiatry* 1997;**38**(4):471–8.

21. Margai F, Henry N. A community-based assessment of learning disabilities using environmental and contextual risk factors. *Soc Sci Med* 2003;**56**(5):1073–85.

22. Allen MC. Neurodevelopmental outcomes of preterm infants. *Curr Opin Neurol* 2008;**21**(2):123–8.

23. Stanton-Chapman TL, Chapman DA, Scott KG. Identification of early risk factors for learning disabilities. *J Early Intervent* 2001;**24**(3):193–206.

24. Ross G, Sammaritano L, Nass R, Lockshin M. Effects of mothers' autoimmune disease during pregnancy on learning disabilities and hand preference in their children. *Arch Pediatr Adolesc Med* 2003;**157**:397–402.

25. Gerber PJ, Ginsberg R, Reiff HB. Ientifying alterable patterns in employment success for highly successful adults with LD. *J Learn Disabil* 1992;**25**:475–87.

26. Feldman E, Levin BE, Lubs H, Rabin M, Lubs ML, Jallad B, Kusch A. Adult familial dyslexia: A retrospective developmental and psychosocial profile. *J Neuropsychiatry Clin Neurosci* 1993;**5**:195–9.

27. Fourqurean JM, Meisgeier C, Swank PR, Williams RE. Correlates of postsecondary employment outcomes for young adults with LD. *J Learn Disabil* 1991;**24**:400–5.

28. Adelman PB, Vogel SA. Issues in the employment of adults with LD. *Learn Disable Q* 1993;**16**:219–32.

29. Goldstein S, Kennemer K. Learning disabilities. In Goldstein S, Reynolds CR, eds. *Handbook of Neurodevelopmental and Genetic Disorders in Adults.* New York: The Guilford Press; 2005: 91–114.

30. Ward MJ, Merves ES. *Full-time freshmen with disabilities enrolled in 4-year colleges: a statistical profile.* Information from HEATH: a quarterly newsletter (Summer 2006). Accessed 10 Jul 2008 from http://www.heath.gwu.edu/archived/newsletter/issue18/new_freshman_data.htm.

31. The National Institute for Literacy. *Bridges to practice.* Accessed 21 Apr 2008 from http://www.nifl.gov/nifl/ld/bridges/bridges.html.

32. United States Department of Education (U.S. DOE), Office of Special Education and Rehabilitative Services, Office of Special Education Programs. *27th Annual (2005) Report to Congress on the Implementation of the Individuals with Disabilities Education Act,* vol. 1. Washington DC: 2007.

33. Shaywitz SE, Shaywitz BA. Dyslexia (specific reading disability). *Pediatrics Rev* 2003;**24**:147–53.

34. Rutter M, Caspi A, Fergusson D, Horwood LJ, Goodman R, Maughan B, Moffitt TE, Meltzer H, Carroll J. Sex differences in developmental reading disability: new findings from 4 epidemiological studies. *JAMA* 2004;**291**:2007–12.

35. Shaywitz SE, Shaywitz BA, Fletcher JM, Escobar MD. Prevalence of reading disability in boys and girls. Results of the Connecticut Longitudinal Study. *JAMA* 1990;**264**(8):998–1002.

36. Greiffenstein MF, Baker WJ. Neuropsychological and psychosocial correlation of adult arithmetic deficiency. *Neuropsychology* 2002;**16**(4):1332–3.

37. Shafrir U, Siegel LS. Subtypes of learning disabilities in adolescents and adults. *J Learn Disabil* 1994;**27**:123–34.

38. Artiles AJ, Aguirre-Munoz Z, Abedi J. Predicting placement in learning disabilities programs: do predictors vary by ethnic group? *Except Child* 1998;**64**(4):543–59.

39. Beaton AA. The relation of planum temporale asymmetry and morphology of the corpus callosum to handedness, gender, and dyslexia: a review of the evidence. *Brain Lang* 1997;**60**:255–322.

40. Bigler ED. The neurobiology and neuropsychology of adult learning disorders. *J Learn Disabil* 1992;**25**:488–506.

41. Carroll JM, Iles JE. An assessment of anxiety levels in dyslexic students in higher education. *Br J Educ Psychol* 2006;**76**(Pt 3):651–62.

42. Huntington DD, Bender WN. Adolescents with learning disabilities at risk? Emotional well-being, depression, suicide. *J Learn Disabil* 1993;**26**(3):159–66.

43. The National Center on Addiction and Substance Abuse at Columbia University (2000). *Substance abuse and learning disabilities: peas in a pod or apples and oranges?* Accessed 11 Jul 2008 from http://www.casacolumbia.org/absolutenm/articlefiles/379-Substance%20Abuse%20and%20Learning%20Disabilities.pdf.

44. McCue M, Shelly C, Goldstein G, Katz-Garris L. Neuropsychological aspects of LD in young adults. *Clin Neuropsychol* 1984;**6**:229–33.

45. Mapou RL. Assessment of learning disabilties. In Ricker, JH, ed. *Differential Diagnosis in Adult Neuropsychological Assessment.* New York: Springer; 2004: 370–420.

46. Spreen O, Strauss E. *A Compendium of Neuropsychological Tests: Administration, Norms, and Commentary*, 2nd ed. Oxford: Oxford University Press; 1998.

47. Isaki E, Plante E. Short-term and working memory differences in language/LD and normal adults. *J Commun Disord* 1997;**30**:427–37.

48. Bigler ED, Lajiness-O-Neill R, Howes N. Technology in the assessment of learning disability. *J Learn Disabil* 1998;**31**:67–82.

49. Hynd GW, Semrud-Clikeman M. Dyslexia and brain morphology. *Psychol Bull* 1989;**106**:447–82.

50. Morgan AE, Hynd GW. Dyslexia, neurolinguistic ability, and anatomical variation of the planum temporale. *Neuropsychol Rev* 1998;**8**:79–93.

51. Heimenz JR, Hynd GW. Sulcal/gyral pattern morphology of the perisylvian language region in developmental dyslexia. *Brain Lang* 2000;**74**:113–33.

52. Shaywitz SE, Shaywitz BA, Pugh KR, Fulbright RK, Constable RT, Mencl WE, Shankweiler DP, Liberman AM, Skudlarski P, Fletcher JM, Katz L, Marchione KE, Lacadie C, Gatenby C, Gore JC. Functional disruption in the organization of the brain for reading in dyslexia. *Proc Nat Acad Sci USA* 1998;**95**:2636–41.

53. Wagner M, Newman L, Cameto R, Levine P. *Changes over time in the early postschool outcomes of youth with disabilities: a report of findings from the National Longitudinal Transition Study (NLTS) and the National Longitudinal Transition Study-2 (NLTS2).* Menlo Park, CA: SRI International; 2005.

54. The National Institute for Literacy. *Workforce education.* Accessed 21 Apr 2008 from www.nifl.gov/nifl/facts/workforce.html.

55. Maruschak LM, Beck AJ. Medical problems of inmates, 1997. Bureau of Justice Statistics: Special Report, NCJ 181644, 2001. Accessed 21 Apr 2008 from http://www.ojp.usdoj.gov/bjs/pub/pdf/mpi97.pdf.

56. Wagner M, Newman L, Cameto R, Levine P, Garza N. *An Overview of Findings from Wave 2 of the National Longitudinal Transition Study-2 (NLTS2).* Menlo Park, CA: SRI International; 2006.

57. Harlow CW. *Education and correctional populations.* Bureau of Justice Statistics: Special Report, NCJ 195670, 2003. Accessed 21 Apr 2008 from http://www.ojp.usdoj.gov/bjs/pub/pdf/ecp.pdf.

58. The National Institute for Literacy. *Correctional education facts.* Accessed 21 Apr 2008 from www.nifl.gov/nifl/facts/correctional.html.

59. Yu JW, Buka SL, Fitzmaurice GM, McCormick MC. Treatment outcomes for substance abuse among adolescents with learning disorders. *J Behav Health Serv Res* 2006;**33**(3):275–86.

60. Hawks R. Assessing adults with learning disabilities. In Gregg N, Hoy C, Gay AF, eds. *Adults with Learning Disabilities: Theoretical and Practical Perspectives.* New York: The Guilford Press; 1996: 144–61.

61. United States Department of Education (U.S. DOE), Institute of Education Sciences (undated). *What works clearinghouse.* Accessed 11 Jul 2008 from http://ies.ed.gov/ncee/wwc/reports/.

62. Fantine JA (undated). *ProLiteracy America: learning disabilities trainer's guide* (based on *Bridges to practice: a research-based guide for literacy practitioners serving adults with learning disabilities*). Accessed 21 Apr 2008 from http://www.nifl.gov/nifl/ld/bridges/training/docs/GuidebookFinal.doc.

63. Lindstrom JH. Determining appropriate accommodations for postsecondary students with reading and written expression disorders. *Learn Disabil Res Pract* 2007;**22**(4):229–36.

64. Ofiesh NS. Math, science, and foreign language: evidence-based accommodation decision making at the postsecondary level. *Learn Disabil Res Pract* 2007;**22**(4):237–45.

65. Runyan MK. The effect of extra time on reading comprehension scores for university students with and without learning disabilities. *J Learn Disabil* 1991;**24**:104–8.

66. Alster EH. The effects of extended time on algebra test scores for college students with and without learning difficulties. *J Learn Disabil* 1997;**30**:222–7.

67. Lindstrom JH, Gregg N. The role of extended time on the SAT* for students with learning disabilities and/or attention-deficit/hyperactivity disorder. *Learn Disabil Res Pract* 2007;**22**(2):85–95.

68. Gajar A. Adults with learning difficulties: current and future research priorities. *J Learn Disabil* 1992;**25**:507–19.

69. Centers for Disease Control and Prevention (CDC). *The International Statistical Classification of Diseases and Related Health Problems*, 9th revision, Clinical Modification (ICD-9-CM) 2007. Accessed 22 Jan 2008 from http://www.cdc.gov/nchs/icd9.htm.

70. Americans with Disabilities Act (ADA). Title III Technical Assistance Manual: Covering Public Accommodations and Commercial Facilities (undated). Accessed 22 Apr 2008 from http://www.ada.gov/taman3.html.

71. Bruck M. Word recognition skills of adults with childhood diagnoses of dyslexia. *Dev Psychol* 1990;**26**:439–54.

72. Bruck M. Persistence of dyslexics' phonological awareness deficits. *Dev Psychol* 1992;**28**:874–86.

73. Bruck M. Component spelling skills of college students with childhood diagnoses of dyslexia. *Learn Disabil Q* 1993;**16**:171–84.

74. United States Department of Education (U.S. DOE), Office of Special Education and Rehabilitative Services, Office of Special Education Programs (2000). 1992 National Adult Literacy Survey. Washington DC.

75. Association on Higher Education and Disability (AHEAD, undated). *AHEAD Best Practices Disability Documentation in Higher Education*. Accessed 10 Jul 2008 from http://www.ahead.org/resources/bestpracticesdoc.htm.

76. Educational Testing Service (ETS), Office of Disability Policy. ETS Revised Policy Statement for Documentation of a Learning Disability in Adolescents and Adults (*Documenting Learning Disabilities*, 2nd edn). Princeton, NJ: 2007. Accessed 10 Jul 2008 from http://www.ets.org/Media/Resources_For/Test_Takers_with_Disabilities/pdf/documenting_learning_disabilities.pdf.

77. Madaus JW. Employment self-disclosure rates and rationales of university graduates with learning disabilities. *J Learn Disabil* 2008;**41**(4):291–9.

Synthesis of chapters on learning disabilities: overview and additional perspectives

H. Lee Swanson

This chapter reviews key concepts identified and discussed in the preceding chapters on learning disabilities (i.e. learning disorders) by Stasi and Tall, and Sparrow. Although both provide an extensive review of assessment models, policy, legal definitions, and treatments for individuals with learning disabilities (LD), the chapter by Stasi and Tall focuses on children and adolescents, and the chapter by Sparrow focuses on adults. In my synthesis of key concepts, I will complement their thorough review with further information related to large-scale syntheses of findings on adults and children with LD as they relate to controversies in the field.

Common themes

Both chapters share common themes, and they highlight the current emphasis placed on these issues within the field of neuropsychology. For example, both review diagnostic models, incidence and etiology, neurological correlates, key psychological processes, treatment, and current practices for individuals with LD. Each chapter reviews the primary diagnostic models regarding LD: IQ and achievement discrepancy, response to intervention, and clinical performance. Each reviews major classification systems used in the diagnosis of LD, with particular attention given to the criteria established in the Diagnostic and Statistical Manual of Mental Disorders (DSM-IV-TR [1]), as well as legal definitions (e.g. Individuals with Disabilities Education Improvement Act of 2004 [2]) currently in place in the USA. Sparrow further analyzes federal definitions related to adults (e.g. Americans with Disabilities Act of 1990 [3] and related changes in interpretation authored by the US Supreme Court). Both chapters provide information on the characteristics and features related to the etiology of LD, with the majority of research-based findings focusing primarily on reading disorders. Both note that sampling biases may lead to more boys being identified with LD than girls, and consider the high rate of co-occurrence of LD and inattention/hyperactivity. Notably, both chapters

suggest that different genotypes may be linked to very specific phenotypes of LD, and stress that corresponding symptoms of LD become apparent in the early elementary grades.

Children and adolescents

Each chapter, however, provides critical information related to the age group under study. The chapter by Stasi and Tall reviews research on academic concerns and problems in children and adolescents with LD, albeit selectively, given the breadth of studies available. They review four primary aspects of learning disorders that are commonly considered in the literature, based on DSM-IV-TR: reading disorder, math disorder, disorder of written expression, and nonverbal learning disabilities. The authors briefly review several MRI studies that have suggested a correspondence between brain activation and psychological deficits, and that currently underlie ongoing physiological investigations within the field.

Stasi and Tall clearly indicate that the majority of published research focuses on reading disorders (RD, also referred to as reading disabilities). Although research on the specific neural developmental causes of RD is emerging, there is some growing consensus that a core problem of RD is related to phonological awareness (also see Shaywitz et al. [4]). In contrast to RD, the core problems of math disabilities (MD) appear related to processes that include numerosity and working memory (e.g. see Berch et al. [5] for review). Their associated neuropsychological underpinnings are still being elucidated, however. Importantly, the relationships between disorders of written expression and nonverbal learning disabilities and underlying alterations in brain activation are less clearly understood. Yet, despite this dearth of clear findings, hypotheses regarding neuroanatomical and behavioral manifestations of the four primary aspects of LD are discussed by Stasi and Tall, with a goal of stimulating continued theory development.

A thorough review is provided of the role of neurological assessment. The chapter concludes with interventions related to LD and future directions for the field.

Adults

Sparrow cites studies suggesting that the success of adults with LD (e.g. such as in the area of employment) is related to such factors as persistence of the learning disorder, as well as family and social networks, and their ability to provide effective support, engagement, and accommodation. Some research suggests that adults with LD experience limits in reaching their potential, such as difficulties related to employment, post-secondary education, and legal matters (e.g. vulnerability to substance abuse). As with children, Sparrow notes that the majority of research available for review focuses on RD. She highlights that cognitive variables considered important in differentiating adults with RD from average readers were linked to areas of phonological awareness and executive functioning, with some suggestive evidence that these psychological correlates are linked to atypical brain activation levels. In terms of assessment, special attention is given to the importance of background history, including underachievement; appropriate instruction and accommodation; and cultural factors and language. Sparrow notes that, in the clinical assessment of adult LD, this background information needs to be integrated with measures of intelligence, academic achievement, psychological processes (e.g. attention, memory), vocational skills and emotional functioning. Importantly, Sparrow observes that few treatment plans for adults with LD have a strong research base. The primary treatment settings for adults with LD include the community college and/or continuing adult classes. The chapter concludes with the observation that adults with LD can have lifelong difficulties, and that these concerns benefit from appropriate attention and support.

Three questions plaguing the field

Both chapters provide an excellent foundation for understanding and thinking about the assessment and treatment of LD. However, I would like to conclude by answering three questions that continue to exist within the field. Answers to these questions can vary among researchers, but my response to these questions is an attempt to bring some consensus related to identification and treatment (see Swanson [6], for further discussion). These questions are: *what is a learning disability?*; *what role does IQ play?*; and *what treatment programs yield the best outcomes?*

Before answering these questions, I would like to concur with the authors that the majority of experimental research on LD focuses on children and adults with RD. While another subtype of learning disabilities which has received more recent experimental work is math disabilities (e.g. see Berch et al. [5] for review), the number of data-based articles that have been published are few compared to RD. Within these studies, however, children and adults with LD are usually operationally defined among researchers as having average IQ scores (e.g. standard score at or above 85) and standardized reading and/or math scores below the 25th percentile (standard score at or below 90). The incidence of children with LD is conservatively estimated to be 2% of the public school population and reflects the largest category of children served in special education. For adults the incidence of reading disabilities (RD) or math disabilities (MD) is unclear. For example, there has been no major epidemiological study focusing on RD among adults [7], although RD has been conservatively estimated at approximately 3–5% of the general population [8]. Nonetheless, RD is considered a persistent chronic condition across adulthood. For example, in the Connecticut longitudinal project approximately 70% of children identified with RD in grade 3 had RD as adults [9, 10].

What is a learning disability?

Currently, children (as well as adults) classified with LD are typically individuals of normal intelligence who experience mental information-processing difficulties that underlie poor academic achievement. Several definitions across the last four decades have referred to children with LD as reflecting a heterogeneous group of individuals with "intrinsic" disorders that are manifested by specific difficulties in the acquisition and use of listening, speaking, reading, writing, reasoning, or mathematical abilities. These definitions assume that the learning difficulties of such individuals are:

1. *not* due to inadequate opportunity to learn, general intelligence, or to significant physical or emotional disorders, but to *basic* disorders in specific psychological processes (such as remembering the association between sounds and letters);

2. *not* due to poor instruction, but to specific psychological processing problems; these problems have a neurological, constitutional, and/or biological base;

3. *not* manifested in all aspects of learning; such individual's psychological processing deficits depress only a limited aspect of academic behavior. For example, such individuals may suffer problems in reading, but not arithmetic.

To assess LD at the cognitive and behavioral level, systematic efforts are made to detect: (a) normal psychometric intelligence, (b) below-normal achievement on standardized measures of achievement (e.g. word recognition below the 25th percentile), (c) below normal performance on measures of specific cognitive processes (e.g. phonological awareness, working memory), (d) that evidence-based instruction has been presented under optimal conditions, and (e) that academic and/or cognitive processing deficits are not directly caused by environmental factors or contingencies (e.g. SES). In essence, the predominant model for identification of children with LD requires the documentation of normal intelligence (i.e. individuals do not suffer from mental retardation) and deficient academic performance that persists after best instructional practices have been systematically provided.

What role does IQ play in the diagnosis?

Perhaps one of the most contentious aspects concerning the definition of LD relates to establishing a discrepancy between IQ and reading. Since the inception of the field of learning disabilities, the classification of LD has been partly based on the presence of an aptitude (IQ)–reading discrepancy. That is, the diagnosis and assessment of RD has been based on uncovering a significant discrepancy between achievement in reading and general psychometric intellectual ability (see Hoskyn and Swanson [11] for a review of this literature). This discrepancy criterion was included in the federal definition of LD since the development of the US Department of Education's guidance and regulations in 1977 [12] for P.L. 94–142 (1975) and has remained unchanged until recent passage of the Individuals with Disabilities Education Improvement Act of 2004 (IDEA). The concept of unexpected underachievement in students with LD has been translated into a discrepancy between ability as demonstrated by intelligence testing and achievement measures. However, the recent reauthorization of IDEA [2] has raised validity concerns related to the usability of IQ discrepancy scores in the identification of individuals with RD. These policy decisions were partly based on research showing that children with low reading scores and low IQ scores were behaviorally similar to children with high IQ and low reading

scores, thus calling into question the discriminant validity of discrepancy scores for identification. Several studies have suggested that variations in IQ tell us little about differences in processing when groups are defined at low levels of reading (e.g. Francis et al. [13]).

A comprehensive review of the literature suggests, however, that variations between IQ and reading are important in the diagnostic process. Three meta-analyses were done before the passage of IDEA [2, 11, 14, 15] that addressed the relevance of IQ. The contradictions in the three meta-analyses are reviewed in Stuebing et al. [15]. Stuebing et al. considered the Hoskyn and Swanson [11] selection process of studies more conservative of the three, and therefore some of these findings will be highlighted. Hoskyn and Swanson [11] analyzed published literature comparing children who are poor readers, but who either had higher IQ scores than their reading scores or had IQ scores commensurate with their reading scores. The findings of the synthesis were consistent with previous studies outside the domain of reading that report on the weak discriminative power of discrepancy scores. Although the outcomes of Hoskyn and Swanson's synthesis generally supported current notions about comparable outcomes on various measures among the discrepancy and non discrepancy groups, verbal IQ significantly *moderated* effect sizes (the magnitude of difference) between the two groups. That is, although the degree of discrepancy between IQ and reading was irrelevant in predicting effect sizes, the magnitude of differences in performance (effect sizes) between the two groups was significantly related to verbal IQ. They found that when verbal IQ for the discrepancy group was in the high-average range, the chances their overall performance on cognitive measures would differ from the low achiever (nondiscrepancy group) were increased. In short, although the Hoskyn and Swanson [11] synthesis supports the notion that "differences in IQ and achievement" are unimportant in predictions of effect size differences on various cognitive variables, the magnitude of differences in verbal IQ between these two ability groups did significantly moderate general cognitive outcomes.

Alternatives to the discrepancy model

One popular alternative to defining LD based on the IQ–Achievement discrepancy model as mentioned in the chapters is referred to as "response to instruction" (RTI). The goal of RTI is to monitor the intensity of instruction and make systematic changes in the instructional context as a function of a student's overt performance. This is done by considering various tiers of instructional intensity. This approach is compatible with those that attempt to identify the cognitive and neuropsychological (i.e. psychometric) aspects of LD. RTI focuses on a systematic manipulation of the environmental context (i.e. instruction, classroom, school) to determine procedures that maximize learning, whereas cognitive and neurological approaches focus on mapping the internal dynamics of learning. The unique application of cognitive and neurological approaches to the field of LD is (1) to explain "why" and predict "how" individual differences emerge in children at risk for LD after intense exposure to valid instructional procedures and (2) to document whether functional brain anatomy changes emerge as a function of intervention (see Swanson [6], for a review).

Historically, the concept of RTI as a means to further refine the definition of LD has been discussed since the inception of the field. Unfortunately RTI as an assessment approach to define LD has a weak experimental base. At the time of this writing, there have been no controlled studies randomly assigning children seriously at risk for LD to assessment and/or delivery models (e.g. tiered instruction vs. special education (resource room placement)) that have measured outcomes on key variables (e.g. over-identification, stability of classification, academic and cognitive growth in response to treatment). The few studies that compare RTI with other assessment models (e.g. discrepancy-based or low-achievement-based models) involve post hoc assessments of children divided at post-test within the same sample. In addition, different states and school districts have variations in their interpretations of how RTI should be implemented, thereby weakening any uniformity linking the science of instruction to assessing children at risk for LD.

Although there is enthusiasm for RTI as a means to provide a contextual (or more ecologically valid) assessment of children at risk for LD when compared to other models (e.g. models based on inferences from behavioral data about internal processing), the use of RTI as a scientific means to identify children at risk for LD has several obstacles to overcome. The first obstacle is that in contrast to standardized formats of testing and assessment, there are no standardized applications of evidence-based instruction.

A second obstacle is that teacher effects cannot always be controlled. The teacher variable plays a key role in mediating treatment outcomes for children.

Further, this variance cannot be accounted for by merely increasing treatment fidelity. Procedures that control for treatment fidelity in applying evidence-based treatments account for a very small amount of variance in student outcomes. Although the role of teacher effects can be controlled to some degree, there is no "expert teaching model" that has been operationalized and implemented for instructional delivery in evidence-based practices.

Another obstacle is that even under the best instructional conditions, individual differences in achievement in some cases will increase. There will be some instructional conditions that vastly improve achievement in both average achievers and children at risk for LD, but these robust instructional procedures will increase the performance gap between some children. Thus, significant performance differences will remain for some children with LD when compared to their counterparts even under the most intensive treatment conditions. Perhaps even more fundamental than these three major obstacles is the lack of consensus about what "non responsiveness" entails and how it should be uniformly measured.

What treatments work?

A meta-analysis, funded by the US Department of Education, synthesized experimental intervention research conducted on children with LD over a 35-year period. Swanson and several colleagues [16–20] synthesized articles, technical reports, and doctoral dissertations that reported on group design and single design studies published between the years of 1963 and 2000. Condensing over 3000 effect sizes, they found a mean effect size (ES) of 0.79 for LD treatment versus LD control conditions for group design studies [19] and 1.03 for single subject design studies [20]. According to Cohen's [21] classification system, the magnitude of the ES is small when the absolute value is at 0.20 or below, moderate when the ES is 0.50 and large when the ES is 0.80 or above. Thus, on the surface, the results are consistent with the notion that children with LD are highly responsive to intense instruction. However, when children with LD were compared to nondisabled children of the same grade or age who also were receiving the same best-evidence intervention procedure, effect sizes (ES M = 0.97, SD = 0.52) were substantially in favor of nondisabled children (see Swanson et al. [22], pp. 162–169). More importantly, the mean effect size difference increased in favor of children without LD (ES = 1.44; see [22], p. 168) when psychometric scores related to IQ and reading were not included as part of sample reporting. Thus, the magnitude of the treatment outcomes could not be adequately interpreted without recourse to psychometric measures.

In terms of general treatment models, methodologically sound studies (those studies with well-defined control groups and clearly identified samples) found that positive outcomes in remediation were directly related to a *combination* of direct and strategy instructional models. Components of direct instruction emphasize fast-paced, well-sequenced, highly focused lessons. The lessons are delivered in small groups to students who are given several opportunities to respond and receive feedback about accuracy and responses. Components related to effective strategy include advanced organizers (provide students with a type of mental scaffolding on which to build new understanding, i.e. consist of information already in the students' minds and the new concepts that can organize this information), organization (information or questions directed to students, stopping from time to time to assess their understanding), elaboration (thinking about the material to be learned in a way that connects the material to information or ideas already in their mind), generative learning (learners must work to make sense out of what they are learning by summarizing the information), and general study strategies (e.g. underlining, note-taking, summarizing, having students generate questions, outlining, and working in pairs to summarize sections of materials), thinking about and controling one's thinking process (metacognition), and attributions (evaluating the effectiveness of a strategy). They also found that only a few instructional components from a broad array of activities were found to enhance treatment outcomes. Regardless of the instructional focus (reading, math, writing), two instructional components emerged in the analysis of treatments for children with LD. One component was explicit practice, which included activities related to distributed review and practice, repeated practice, sequenced reviews, daily feedback, and/or weekly reviews. The other component was advanced organizers, which included: (a) directing children to focus on specific material or information prior to instruction, (b) directing children about task concepts or events before beginning, and/or (c) the teacher stating objectives of the instruction.

Summary

In conclusion, the aforementioned chapters provided an extensive overview of the field of LD related to assessment, etiology, and treatment. I have merely highlighted some of the key points made in the chapters. The scientific research shows that children and adults with LD can be assessed, and significant gains can be made in academic performance as a function of treatment. However, there is considerable evidence that some children (less information is available on adults) with normal intelligence when exposed to the best instructional conditions fail to efficiently master skills in such areas as reading, mathematics, and/or writing. Some literature suggests that individuals with LD are less responsive to intervention than individuals with similar primary academic levels but without LD, and that these academic problems persist into adulthood. Finally, these difficulties in academic mastery reflect fundamental cognitive deficits (e.g. phonological process, working memory). Further research is required to continue to help us understand these issues, both behaviorally and neuropsychologically, and to more effectively determine when and how intervention, as well as accommodation, can support affected individuals, and promote better outcomes academically and functionally.

References

1. American Psychiatric Association. *Diagnostic and statistical manual of mental disorders, Fourth Edition, Text Revision*. Washington DC: American Psychiatric Association; 2000.

2. Individuals with Disabilities Education Improvement Act of 2004 (IDEA), Pub. L. No. 108–446,118 Stat. 2647 (2004). [Amending 20 U.s.c. §§ 1400 et. Seq.).

3. Americans with Disabilities Act (ADA; 1990). Public Law 101–336; 2004 Reauthorization.

4. Shaywitz SE, Mody M, Shaywitz BA. Neural mechanisms in dyslexia. *Curr Dir Psychol Sci* 2006;15:278–81.

5. Berch DB, Mazzocco MMM. *Why is Math so Hard for Some Children?* Baltimore, MD: Brookes; 2007.

6. Swanson HL. Neuroscience and response to instruction (RTI): a complementary role. In Reynolds C, Fletcher-Janzen E, eds. *Neuropsychology Perspectives on Learning Disabilities in the era of RTI: Recommendation for Diagnosis and Intervention*. New York: John Wiley & Sons; 2008: 28–53.

7. Corley M, Taymans J. Adults with learning disabilities: a review of the literature. In Comings J, Garner B, Smith C,

eds. *Annual Review of Adult Learning and Literacy*, Vol. 3 San Francisco, CA: Wiley & Sons; 2002: 44–83.

8. National Adult Literacy Survey U.S. Department of Education, National Center for Education: 1992.

9. Shaywitz SE, Fletcher JM, Holahan JM, Schneider AE, Marchione KE, Stuebing KK, Francis DJ, Shaywitz BA. Persistence of dyslexia: The Connecticut longitudinal study at adolescence. *Pediatrics* 1999;**104**:1351–9.

10. Shaywitz BA, Shaywitz SE, Blachman BA, Pugh KR, Fulbright RK, Skudlarski P, et al. Development of left occipitotemporal systems for skilled reading in children after a phonologically-based intervention. *Biol Psychiatry* 2004;**55**:926–33.

11. Hoskyn M, Swanson HL. Cognitive processing of low achievers and children with reading disabilities: a selective meta-analytic review of the published literature. *School Psychol Rev* 2000;**29**:102–19.

12. U.S. Office of Education. Assistance to states for education for handicapped children: Procedures for evaluating specific learning disabilities. Federal Register, 42, GI082-G1085, 1977.

13. Francis DJ, Fletcher JM, Stuebing KK, Lyon GR, Shaywitz BA, Shaywitz SE. Psychometric approaches to the identification of LD: IQ and achievement scores are not sufficient. *J Learn Disabil* 2005;**38**(2):98–108.

14. Fuchs D, Fuchs L, Mathes PG, Lipsey M. Reading differences between low achieving students with and without learning disabilities. In Gersten R, Schiller EP, Vaughn S, eds. *Contemporary Special Education*

Research: Synthesis of Knowledge Base of Critical Issues. Mahwah, NJ: Erlbaum; 2000.

15. Stuebing KK, Fletcher JM, LeDoux JM, Lyon GR, Shaywitz SE, Shaywitz BA. Validity of IQ-discrepancy classifications of reading disabilities: a meta-analysis. *Am Educ Res J* 2002;**39**:469–518.

16. Swanson HL. Reading research for students with LD: A meta-analysis in intervention outcomes. *J Learn Disabil* 1999;**32**:504–32.

17. Swanson HL. Searching for the best cognitive model for instructing students with learning disabilities: A component and composite analysis. *Educ Child Psychol* 2000;**17**:101–21.

18. Swanson HL, Deshler D. Instructing adolescents with learning disabilities: Converting a meta-analysis to practice. *J Learn Disabil* 2003;**36**:124–35.

19. Swanson HL, Hoskyn M. Experimental intervention research on students with learning disabilities: a meta-analysis of treatment outcomes. *Rev Educ Res* 1998;**68**:277–321.

20. Swanson HL, Sachse-Lee C. A meta-analysis of single-subject-design intervention research for students with LD. *J Learn Disabil* 2000;**33**:114–36.

21. Cohen J. *Statistical Power Analysis for the Behavioral Sciences*, 2nd edn. Hillsdale, NJ: Erlbaum, 1988.

22. Swanson HL, Hoskyn M, Lee CM. *Interventions for Students with Learning Disabilities: A Meta-analysis of Treatment Outcomes*. New York: Guilford, 1999.

Chapter 7a

Infants and children with spina bifida

Heather B. Taylor, Susan H. Landry, Lianne English and Marcia Barnes

Introduction

Spina bifida myelomeningocele (SB) is the most common severely disabling birth defect in North America. However, knowledge of this condition is limited, especially regarding the impact of SB in infancy and early childhood. This chapter discusses the neuropsychological profile present in infants and children with SB, including findings from the first longitudinal study to our knowledge with a cohort of children with SB who were recruited in infancy and followed to their present age of 8½ years. Research conducted as part of a larger multidisciplinary research program, directed toward characterizing SB and the biological and environmental factors that account for variability in outcomes, will also be reviewed.

In this chapter, we identify the nature of SB relevant to development and cognitive functioning, followed by a summary of the neurobehavioral profile including the core deficits and the subsequent cognitive and functional difficulties. We then discuss the potential psychosocial and behavioral difficulties present in this population. The important role of the environment, especially parenting, as a potential moderator is also highlighted. Finally developmental assessment and intervention with this population are discussed with suggestions for future research.

Spina bifida myelomeningocele

SB is a neural tube defect that is associated with significant spine and brain malformations. The current prevalence level in North America is 0.3–0.5 per 1000 births (post dietary fortification data, Williams et al. [1]). The primary CNS insult in SB affects both ends of the neural tube. The defining spinal lesion, myelomeningocele, is a fluid-filled sac that herniates and protrudes through the spinal cord and meninges. This can occur at any level of the spine and is evident from the first weeks of gestation, before many women have confirmed their pregnancy, and it requires neurosurgical repair shortly after birth. SB is often associated with major orthopedic and urological impairments, including paraplegia of the lower limbs and neurogenic bladder and bowel functioning [2].

SB is the product of a complex pattern of gene/environment interactions that is associated at birth with distinctive physical, neural, and behavioral phenotypes [3]. The spinal lesion level is a visible source of phenotypic diversity that can be explained in part by genetic factors [4]. In addition to variations in the level of spinal lesion, there is variation in the neural phenotype which involves varying degrees of anomalies of the brain, including the midbrain and tectum, dysgenesis and/or hypoplasia of the corpus callosum, and selective thinning of posterior cerebral cortex [5, 6]. The Chiari II malformation, present in most children with myelomeningocele, is a pattern of hindbrain/cerebellar deformation of varying severity. This malformation includes a small posterior fossa, which results in distortion of the posterior fossa contents and their herniation through the tentorial incisures and foramen magnum. This in turn blocks the flow of cerebro spinal fluid (CSF), resulting in hydrocephalus. Hydrocephalus occurs in 60–95% of children with myelomeningocele [7], often resulting in the stretching and damage of periventricular brain structures, particularly the corpus callosum [8, 9]. Depending upon the severity of hydrocephalus, shunting is usually required and this complication is also associated with more severe impairment [2, 10, 11]. Difficulties regulating CSF due to shunt malfunctions and infections may produce further secondary brain injury.

Model of neurocognitive function in spina bifida

Although as a group children with SB have modal core deficits and assets in particular aspects of cognitive functioning, it is important to keep in mind that SB is also a disorder that is associated with significant variability in motor, cognitive, academic, and social functioning. For example, some children with SB may have minor motor functioning difficulties whereas others may have major motor disabilities. One of the purposes of the programmatic work on SB [3] is to explain the sources and nature of this variability for both scientific and practical/clinical purposes. Dennis et al. [12] propose a model of neurocognitive functioning in SB over the lifespan that identifies sources of variability in neurocognitive functioning as well as accounting for typical or modal neurocognitive profile. Specifically, Dennis et al. [12] suggest that the primary CNS insult varies with regard to impact at the neural level (neural phenotype; i.e. spinal cord, cerebellum, brainstem, and callosal dysgenesis). This in turn may result in a secondary CNS insult as discussed above (e.g. including potential for hydrocephalus, callosal hypoplasia, thinning of the posterior cortex, and further insult potential if a shunt malfunction occurs). The model stipulates that the primary CNS insults lead directly to a set of core deficits, present in infancy, that interfere with cognitive and motor development and are strongly correlated with specific congenital brain dysmorphologies. These deficits include difficulty with motor functioning (including motor learning/control and timing) and attention orienting. Together, these impact the infant's ability to learn from the environment and impact functional skills in the cognitive phenotype. The model also identifies the environment as a potential moderator (e.g. parenting and poverty).

The review below emphasizes core deficits and functional strengths and weaknesses specific to infants and young children with SB. A more comprehensive review of core deficits and assets across the lifespan for individuals with SB can be found in Dennis et al. [12].

Cognitive functioning in infants and children with SB

Core deficits: factors that impact learning

Infants with SB may demonstrate core deficits in motor functioning (motor control/learning and timing) and attention orienting. Combined performance in these critical areas is believed to become part of a foundation that guides learning in children at-risk for developmental difficulties as well as typical developing children [13].

Motor functioning: control/movement and timing

Infants' successful motoric organization and exploration of the environment is thought to be essential in development of skills necessary for appropriate cognitive development [14, 15]. For example, a key motor milestone is the onset of self-generated locomotion (creeping, crawling, walking), the timing of which affects the development of perceptual-cognitive skills [16]. In addition, visually guided reaching is a key motor milestone that is integral to the development of skills in other domains. The infant's ability to obtain objects serves to expand his or her experiences in a similar fashion to self-generated locomotion. Motor impairment restricts the infant's ability to explore the environment, thereby restricting sensory experiences [14].

Children with SB have impaired upper and lower limb control [17, 18] and eye movement [19, 20]. The higher the level of the meningomyelocele, the more motor functioning (e.g. ambulation) will be impaired [21], with lesion level being directly related to lower limb gross motor deficits. Nonetheless, motor functioning variability in this area is related to the integrity of brain regions such as the cerebellum that control truncal and axial movement [22, 23], and the cerebellum and midbrain that control eye movements [24]. Deficits in the upper extremities involve control, organization, and quality of gross and fine motor movements, mediated by the cerebellum and dependent on visual cortex and parietal areas for guidance. Some of the fine motor deficits of children with SB represent timing rather than movement impairments. Functions mediated by the cerebellum, such as speech articulation, precise motor movements, and rhythm perception, are impaired regardless of the degree to which a motor response is required [25] and are related to cerebellum volume.

Early motor skills were evaluated in our longitudinal study in 165 children, 91 with SB and 74 developing typically. Assessments were given at five time points (6, 12, 18, 24, and 36 months of age). Having SB was associated with lower levels of motor performance. Furthermore, having a shunt or a higher lesion level also predicted significantly lower scores than having SB without a shunt or having lower lesion levels, respectively [26]. This finding is consistent with those identified in school-age children and adults with SB [17, 27] with relation to higher lesion and more severe motor deficit.

Attention

Infants' ability to attend to their environment fosters learning from their surroundings. At a very young age, typically developing infants are able to modulate arousal states and activate early attention behaviors. These attention modulation and activation skills improve with the support of mediators such as neurophysiological maturation and parent interactions [28–31]. Two important aspects of attention include *attention orienting* (i.e. turning toward a stimulus), and *attention holding* (i.e. sustained fixation on the stimulus after turning). Adequate development in these attentional processes allows infants to move on to, and learn about, other environmental stimuli [32].

Attention orienting is a core deficit in children with SB arising from a specific set of brain abnormalities in the midbrain, and including the superior colliculus [33]. In our research conducted on infants with SB (SB = 47; control = 40), 18-month-old infants with SB took significantly longer to shift their attention from a blinking light to a face stimulus projected on a screen (i.e. attention orienting) than typically developing infants [34]. This same study reported no difference in infants' ability to habituate, or show a decremental response, to a familiar stimulus when compared to typically developing infants, suggesting that while infants with SB have difficulty in attention orienting, once they attend to a stimulus they learn about (habituate to) that stimulus at a rate comparable to their typically developing peers.

Functional strengths and weaknesses

Many children with SB have significant functional difficulties, despite average intelligence and proficiency with certain aspects of language and academic skills. The impact of deficits in core areas in combination with environment/experiences and intervention appears to produce a pattern of strengths and weaknesses by the time these children reach school age.

Motor learning/adaptation

Dennis et al. [25] conducted a study and found that children with SB performed comparably to controls in a motor learning task, demonstrating intact motor adaptation despite lower limb dysfunction and upper limb motor deficits. These findings suggest a distinction between motor performance/control and motor adaption/learning as it relates to functioning in this population. Dennis et al. [25] further posit that motor learning may be subserved by a neural system that includes the basal ganglia as well as the cerebellum.

Visual perception

An important correlate of regulation of attention is visual perception. Children with SB often have ocular-motor difficulties such as nystagmus or strabismus that result in difficulties in visual fixation, gaze-shifting, tracking, and scanning abilities. These children often have relative strengths on visual perception tasks involving categorical relations (e.g. face perception) and relative deficits on visual perception tasks of figure-ground delineation and relational coordinates [27]. Perceptual difficulties have been related to posterior cortex thinning [35, 36]. Early visual processing problems have important implications for infants' early spatial learning and rule-based learning. Scanning and tracking abilities assist in the development of spatial and contingency learning skills such as object permanence and object constancy, as they assist in helping infants perceive and attend to salient stimuli [27].

Goal-directed behavior: rule-based problem-solving

Goal-directed behavior is an important component of motivation, playing an essential role in successful learning [37]. This can also be described as executive functioning or, in other cases, rule-based problem-solving. It is a complex, multifaceted construct that involves more than one psychological process. Some important components necessary for goal-directed behavior to occur include (1) identifying a particular interest, (2) planning the actions necessary to carry out the activity, (3) initiating and persisting in these actions in order to achieve an identified goal, as well as (4) self-monitoring and self-regulating, or adjusting behavior, to achieve a goal. A critical component of these goal-directed behaviors is that the child self-initiates purposeful action rather than being dependent on the structure provided by others.

Research suggests that older children with SB tend to have difficulty in regulating their behavior toward the achievement of particular goals. In one study, children with SB and normal cognitive development had below-average adaptive behavior skills, lack of initiative, and inadequate follow-through skills, compared to typically developing children [38]. Findings regarding the performance of school-aged children with SB working on independent problem-solving tasks showed that these children had more difficulty maintaining goal-directed activities during play than did age- and IQ-matched typically developing children [11]. More specifically, children with SB had difficulty sequencing their own behavior in order to reach a goal.

In one study, a group of school-age children with and without SB were evaluated in the number of task-oriented play activities performed and the time spent on independent task-oriented activities. The children with SB showed less task-oriented behavior and more time in simple manipulation of the play materials. They also appeared to have more difficulty with demonstrating a level of exploration that involved functional use of play materials, suggesting difficulty establishing a goal (e.g. forming shapes with Playdoh, finding small red buttons), and self-monitoring to move successfully toward that goal on their own [39]. The development of persistent goal-directed behavior is an important step that may be linked to the development of adaptive behaviors and goal achievement as children mature. In addition, children's ability to self-monitor their activities and then self-correct or self-regulate to adjust their behavior accordingly is critical for adaptive problem-solving and successful goal attainment.

While these kinds of problems have been characterized by some as "frontal" deficits, Denckla [40] noted that these problems are commonly found in individuals with nonfrontal anomalies. Fletcher et al. [41] and Snow [42] found that school-age children with SB have difficulties on a number of executive function tasks. However, Fletcher et al. [41] noted that patterns of performance reflected motor demands and difficulties with arousal and regulation of attention that lead to slower speed of processing as opposed to classic "frontal" patterns.

Language

Despite often strong development of vocabulary and syntax, difficulties with the flexible use of language in a social context is a well-documented problem for children with SB [12, 43, 44]. Children with SB were found to be less efficient in their ability to relay information in a concise manner, produce fewer clauses that communicate the content of a story and require more time to reproduce the story than typically developing children. In another study, children with SB were less likely to generate a well-sequenced progression of events in their narratives or to provide fully elaborated meaning [44]. In conversation, individuals with SB generally have been described as tangential and appear to have difficulty assembling verbal information to provide appropriate responses in a quickly changing social interaction. These kinds of difficulties seem to reflect not only problems with contextual language, but also a lack of efficiency in integration of information [43, 45] and inferencing [46, 47]. During early childhood (6 months to 36 months), children with SB have been found to show slower rates of growth in language compared to typically developing children [26].

Impact on academic skills in school-age children with SB

In a population-based sample of school-age children and youth with SB [3, 5, 48], 58% of children had learning difficulties defined as academic achievement below the 25th percentile. Only 3% of children had specific reading difficulties; in contrast, 29% had specific math difficulties, and 26% had problems in both reading and math. These academic deficits are interesting when considered in relation to lesion level and ethnicity, the latter being a proxy for socio-economic status (SES) in our studies. Although upper level lesions are associated with greater brain dysmorphology and worse neurocognitive outcomes such as IQ, academic outcomes are particularly affected in Hispanic children with upper-level lesions. For example, the average word reading abilities of Hispanic children with upper-level lesions is in the borderline range, while the average word-reading abilities of non-Hispanic children with upper level lesions are within the average range. For math, Hispanic ethnicity and higher-level lesions produced the worst outcomes (severely deficient range), but lower-level lesions and less social economic disadvantage still resulted in math outcomes that were below average [5]. These findings suggest that: (1) spina bifida affects academic achievement in reading and math, though math is more affected than reading; (2) children who have upper-level lesions and are socially and economically disadvantaged are at greatest risk for severe academic difficulties; and (3) as is the case for neurologically intact children, social economic disadvantage is a source of considerable influence with respect to academic achievement in children with SB.

In studies of school-age children with SB who are not socially and economically disadvantaged there is a modal academic profile that includes better developed reading than math and good word-decoding accompanied by less skilled comprehension [48–58]. These patterns are evident from the preschool years [56] and persist across the lifespan into adulthood [55, 57, 58].

Many children with spina bifida develop adequate to above-average word-reading abilities and vocabulary knowledge and grammar commensurate with age peers [49, 53]. In contrast, reading and discourse comprehension is less well developed, particularly when comprehension requires considerable integration of ideas such as including the making of inferences within text and between the text and general knowledge, and the suppressing of previously activated information that is no longer relevant to ongoing comprehension as text or discourse unfolds across time [43, 47]. The difficulties that children with spina bifida have in text and discourse comprehension should not be categorized as problems with "complex language"; for example, these children are quite capable of making inferences [47], but they are less efficient at doing so particularly when the information-processing load increases (e.g. when information has to be integrated across longer chunks of text [43]).

Math is a particular area of difficulty in spina bifida. As early as 36 months of age, the ability of preschoolers with spina bifida to count and their conceptual counting knowledge (e.g. knowing that objects can be counted only once) are not as well developed as for their typically developing peers [56]. By school age many children with spina bifida look similar to neurologically normal children with math disabilities in that they are slow at single-digit arithmetic and they have difficulty with the procedures involved in multi-digit arithmetic such as borrowing across zero [48]. In contrast to what was hypothesized about the origins of mathematical difficulties in spina bifida in earlier studies (e.g. Wills [52]), these difficulties in arithmetic at school age are not related to visual-spatial skills. However, children with spina bifida also have difficulty with aspects of mathematics such as geometry, estimation, and word problem-solving, all of which are related to visual-spatial skill [54]. Although the modal academic difficulties in SB are generally consistent with those proposed as markers of nonverbal learning disabilities (NLD) [59], our population-based studies of SB have provided a more nuanced picture of the cognitive and academic strengths and weaknesses in this condition. For example, we have found that: greater verbal than performance IQ does not characterize the subgroup of Hispanic children with SB; although the rate of math disabilities is high in SB, about half of the children with math disability also have reading disability; and the cognitive characteristics of difficulties in arithmetic for those children with specific math disabilities are remarkably similar to those of children with both reading and math disabilities.

Spina bifida, because it is diagnosed during gestation or at birth, provides an opportunity to study the developmental precursors of later emerging academic abilities and disabilities, including those in mathematics. In our longitudinal study, English [60] found that level and growth in working memory and inhibitory control (using a delayed response task) from 12 months to 26 months of age predicted a broad range of skills at 60 months that are related to later reading acquisition, including phonological awareness, rapid automatized naming and identification of letters of the alphabet and simple words. By age 7 and a half, however, working memory/inhibitory control was only related to reading fluency and not to word-reading accuracy or reading comprehension. In contrast, level and growth in working memory/inhibitory control were a robust predictor of informal math skills at 60 months of age (rote verbal counting, adding to and taking away from visual displays involving small set sizes) as well as fluency in single-digit arithmetic and accuracy in single- and multi-digit arithmetic at age 7. Studies of this nature have the potential to provide information relevant for early identification and intervention for neurodevelopmental disorders such as spina bifida as well as providing knowledge about the early developmental precursors of academic skills more generally.

Although recent studies have begun to elucidate relations between the neural phenotype in SB and particular neurocognitive outcomes [12], not a great deal is known about the connection between the neural phenotype in SB and academic outcomes. However, researchers [12, 61] have suggested that there is considerable cortical plasticity in SB that may support the acquisition of skills in some domains to a level commensurate with neurologically intact peers. For example, using magnetic source imaging they demonstrated bilateral activation of only the frontal part of the typical network for reading in a child with good word-recognition skills [61].

Psychosocial adaptation and behavior adjustment

We have highlighted the variability that is present in cognitive functioning of children with SB. There is equal if not greater variability in the psychosocial and adaptive functioning among these young children.

This is probably due to multiple factors, including the child's developmental stage, potential biological basis for learning difficulties and psychological problems, as well as the child's individual strengths and weaknesses (emotionally and physically) and family environment (e.g. SES, support). These factors and small sample size in many studies complicate research efforts. As a result, findings of current research in this area are varied for young children with SB. Nonetheless, the available research to date suggests that children with SB are at increased risk for symptoms that characterize psychosocial adaptation (e.g. depression, anxiety, somatic concerns) and behavioral adjustment (e.g. behavior and conduct problems).

Psychosocial adaptation

Infancy through the preschool years is a time when children appear to be less aware or unconcerned about differences among themselves. Usually, cognitive growth in early elementary school allows children to develop their self-concept and begin to see differences between themselves and others. This becomes even more evident as children transition into adolescence. As a result, low self-concept is believed to be a significant predictor of psychological problems in young children and adolescents with disabilities [62]. In a longitudinal study on predictors of psychosocial adaptation, 68 children with SB were followed and evaluated at three time points from 8 years of age to 13 years of age [63]. Results suggested that intrinsic motivation, verbal IQ, behavioral conduct, copying style, and physical appearance were the best predictors for both children with SB and their age-matched typically developing peers. Moreover, the single best predictor of psychosocial adaptation was intrinsic classroom motivation (i.e. autonomy-seeking behaviors in the classroom), followed by verbal IQ.

It is important to note that medical problems, including adverse reactions to medication, problems with ventricular shunt, and infections, can cause depressive symptoms and must be ruled out [18]. Nonetheless, youth with SB have been found to be at greater risk of depressive mood, low self-worth, and suicidal ideation compared to their typically developing peers [64, 65], with girls with SB having an increased risk for depression and higher levels of suicidal ideation [65]. In one study, self-worth and perceived parental support mediated the effect of physical appearance self-concept on depressed mood among young people with SB [64]. Preliminary findings from our study of 8½-year-old children with and without SB (control = 30; SB = 36) found children with SB to be significantly higher in self-reported symptoms of anxiety. High responses indicate a high number of anxious feelings (e.g. being nervous, worrying). There was no significant difference between groups on depression or self-esteem. Somatic concerns and anxiety have also been reported in children and adolescents with SB [66]. Another study found continence to be related to self-concept in children with SB, with incontinent girls at a high risk for poor self-esteem [67].

A review of the literature of social competence among children with chronic conditions, including SB, identified children with SB as being less competent socially and in school. Children with SB were found to have fewer interactions with peers and to be more frequently alone than their typically developing peers. However, children with SB initiated interactions with peers equally, but were neglected by peers compared to typically developing children. The level of social skills demonstrated by children and adolescents with SB did not differ from typically developing children; however, multiple studies identified that children with more severe presentations (IQ < 85, obesity, walking problems) were less socially competent compared to those with less severe presentations [68].

Behavior adjustment

Behavioral adjustment is an important issue for children with SB. Fletcher et al. [69] found that hydrocephalus was related to the presence of behavior adjustment problems in children with SB (5 to 7 years of age). Another study demonstrated that 33% of children with SB met criteria for attention deficit hyperactivity disorder (ADHD) and 13% met the criteria for oppositional defiant disorder [66].

Research is beginning to evaluate factors that may attenuate the risk for psychosocial and behavioral maladjustment. An active coping style and behavioral autonomy are thought to be two ways that children with SB may have more successful adaptation [63, 70]. Overall, psychosocial and behavior problems cannot be attributed solely to the effects of physical disability, cognitive functioning, and the environment and need to take into account a broader range of biological, family, and individual child characteristics.

Environmental influences

Brain development in the early years (birth to 5 years) is influenced by experiences that affect learning, behavior, and physical and mental health throughout life [71–74]. These findings may be especially true for children with SB who have to manage various physical, environmental, and cognitive challenges that impact their development.

The impact of environmental factors such as socioeconomic status and the quality of parental interaction experienced by children with SB is likely to influence the developmental areas discussed above, particularly in terms of enhancing strengths and ameliorating the impacts of weaknesses in cognitive development. Although it is thought that core deficits persist and cut across outcome domains, their influence on at least some aspects of the cognitive phenotype (such as attention regulation, some academic skills, etc.) may be moderated by the influence of environmental variables, which has obvious implications for intervention.

Socioeconomic status

A higher risk of having a child with SB has been found in populations with lower SES [75]. Low SES can have multiple implications for a family of a child with SB both on the family and on the child. Holmbeck et al. [76] conducted a study comparing families of children with SB (8–9 years of age) to typical developing children. They found that families from lower SES backgrounds demonstrated higher levels of observed mother–child conflict, less family cohesion, and more reported life events impacting the family system. Their findings further suggested that low SES families who also have a child with SB are particularly at-risk for low levels of cohesion.

At the child level, SES has been found to impact cognition and education. Typically developing children from lower SES backgrounds show lower average levels of academic achievement than do those from middle and higher SES backgrounds [77]. Furthermore, SES has been found to relate to lower score outcomes in studies on children with SB, especially in language and reading [5].

In our longitudinal study on children with SB, evaluated from 6 months of age to 36 months of age, SES was found to impact growth in language and cognition. Children from lower SES backgrounds, regardless of etiology, demonstrated slower growth

than those from higher SES backgrounds. Children with SB demonstrated slower growth in these areas compared to typically developing children; however, the presence of SB impacted development in these areas above and beyond SES [26]. This suggests that although SES indeed impacts development in children, the presence of SB has an additional impact regardless of SES. Therefore, children with SB who are socially and economically disadvantaged may be at a heightened risk for developmental difficulties. Without intervention, these children could also be at a greater risk for learning impairments when they reach school age.

Parenting

Parenting a child with SB is a complex topic. Readers are referred to the following chapter for details regarding functioning in families of children and adolescents with spina bifida for more details (i.e. stress, adjustment, development of autonomy). This section focuses on parenting as it relates to cognition and learning outcomes in children with SB. Parenting style has been related to learning outcomes among children at-risk for developmental difficulties, including children with SB [13, 78–82]. Studies suggest that when a young child has special needs, the influence of the parenting environment may be even greater than what is seen in typically developing children [13, 83–85]. In light of the core deficits of children with SB one aspect of parenting thought to be important is a responsive parenting style. This style includes the use of behaviors that involve accurate perception of children's needs and responses that are contingent to those needs. For the child with SB, who has difficulty gaining a sense of autonomy over learning due to motor, visual, and attention problems, this style of parenting may be particularly important because it strikes a balance between supporting learning and still providing the child with some control over the process [13].

The literature supports at least four types of responsive behaviors: contingent responding, emotional/affective support, language input that supports developmental needs, and support for infant foci of attention. Two components of a responsive parenting style include behaviors related to an affective-emotional style and those that are cognitively supportive. This style of parenting may help to buffer developmental difficulties that could compromise learning. For example, assisting a child in maintaining attentional focus is thought to be an important supportive behavior because it does not require the child to inhibit a response to something of interest and redirect their attention to another topic. In this way, young children do not tax their limited attentional and cognitive capacity trying to reorient and organize a response but can use this capacity to process information about the original object of interest [13].

In our longitudinal study of children with SB, the impact of parenting and motor skills on the development of cognitive, language, and daily living skills was examined in 165 children (91 with SB), from 6 to 36 months of age. Children with SB were found to show higher levels and faster growth trajectories in cognitive skills through 3 years of age when their mothers used higher levels of maintaining behaviors, even after controlling for family SES and child's motor development [78]. Similar results were found for language development, and the influence of maternal maintaining on these outcomes was comparable for those with SB and typically developing children. Bi-directionality was evaluated demonstrating that both the 12-month child language and responsive parenting constructs were significantly related to the 18-month child language construct, with both the maternal and child 12-month parenting relating to the 18-month parenting. Nonetheless, at later ages, only the 18-month parenting predicted the 24-month parenting construct. This was consistent with the "back and forth" influence noted by others [86, 87] in that at the earlier age bidirectional influence was seen, while at later ages the relation became one of mother's effects on the child.

As the child's learning occurs through direct interactions with the parent, it is important to recognize that the parent's ability to be responsive may be hindered and/or buffered by factors such as characteristics of the child, family economic status, and social and personal attributes of the caregiver. For example, characteristics of a child at risk for developmental delays can disrupt positive mother–child interactions [88, 89], particularly when the mother is already burdened with the problems associated with low SES [90]. Since mothers with low SES, regardless of the medical status of their infants, have often been described as believing that their actions have little effect on their children, and as having lower expectations for their development [91], these infants are likely to be in double jeopardy for poor mother–child interactions. Furthermore, having a child with SB may present a considerable challenge to parents. However, a review of research on adjustment in families of children with SB suggested that the extent to which SB affects parents depends on the quality of parents' partner relationship, family climate, and support from informal social networks [92]. In a recent intervention study on children born preterm, social support was found to be a unique predictor of mothers' ability to move from an unresponsive style to a responsive style of parenting [93]. This is an encouraging finding as interventions can provide greater degrees of social support for mothers with high-risk characteristics or from high-risk backgrounds [94].

Clinical implications

The first 3 years of a child's life are an important time for brain growth and offer a window of opportunity to optimize children's development in many ways. Neuropsychology is in an ideal role to provide consultation and evaluation regarding a child with SB's cognitive level of function and to make appropriate interventions, including ways to ameliorate the impact of brain impairment on cognitive, social, academic, and emotional functioning. Because of the variability among children with SB, it is important to evaluate and monitor each skill area to ensure a comprehensive personalized intervention program that is relevant to the individual. Serial neuropsychological assessments can be an important tool in monitoring children with SB, as cognitive changes can indicate problems including shunt malfunction and hydrocephalus [95], and to make appropriate referrals to help guide development.

Assessment

The rates of academic difficulties such as math disabilities have been well established from population-based studies of SB [3, 48], and difficulties in informal aspects of mathematical functioning such as counting procedures and counting knowledge such as one-to-one correspondence emerge in this group as early as 3 years of age [56]. Consequently, the ability exists to assess risk in SB at an early age and to provide prevention or early intervention in areas of greatest risk. Although we have found that deficits in early aspects of executive functions (e.g. working memory and inhibitory control) measured in infancy and toddlerhood are related to a range of academic outcomes, particularly math [60], assessment and prevention in infants with SB awaits further advances in both early assessment technology and early targeted interventions.

The role of childhood intervention

Referrals to early intervention services may help children with SB get a good start during their first three years. In the USA, most states provide early intervention services to infants and toddlers who have a diagnosed physical or mental condition which may affect their development or impede their education. Rowley [96] identifies the role of early child intervention services as including an individualized family service plan designed to meet the child's needs in multiple developmental areas: physical development, cognitive development, communication, social or emotional development, and adaptive development. When children turn 3 years of age, they are eligible for special education services through their parents' local school system and may be eligible to continue receiving services including physical therapy, occupational therapy, speech therapy and early childhood special education.

Equally important may be intervention services for parents. Landry et al. [13] highlight the importance of the parenting environment for children at risk for developmental difficulties; including children with SB. Responsive parenting has been related to better developmental outcomes in preterm and full-term children [85, 97–99]. Furthermore, a responsive parenting intervention has demonstrated changes in parenting style, and positive impacts on developmental outcomes for preterm children [100]. Interventions specifically designed for parents of children with SB may have the potential to provide a buffering effect on the developmental problems often seen in children with SB.

Medical procedures: preparing and supporting families

Children who have spina bifida may spend a great deal of time in clinics and hospitals when they are very young. They often receive numerous medical tests, surgeries, and hospitalizations. Spina bifida is a condition that can be very medically complicated and at times children may experience periods of medical fragility. The importance of preparing children for medical procedures has been long understood and it can be critical when a child will require multiple procedures [101]. The developmental age of the child is an important consideration when preparing children. For example, children under 2 years of age benefit from parent involvement. Separation should be minimized when possible. Children from 2 to 7 years of age

benefit from medical play right before the procedure to prepare them. This can include toys and/or books about the condition/procedure. Most hospitals have child-life specialists who can be instrumental in helping children prepare for and get through painful or frightening medical procedures. As children get developmentally older they can often benefit from verbal explanations in appropriate terms. To our knowledge there are no studies that evaluate appropriate preparation for children with SB regarding medical procedures. Nonetheless, recommendations for preparing children with chronic conditions for medical procedures may help guide future research and intervention (e.g. Hallowell et al. [102]; LeRoy et al. [103]).

Concluding comments: future research

In this chapter we have provided an overview of the neurobehavioral profile of infants and children with SB. We reviewed evidence that infants and children with SB show early developmental vulnerability which may impact their ability to grow and learn. These areas include motor control and attention orientation, as well as later cognitive strengths and weaknesses in motor adaptation, visual perception, and language. We then highlighted academic skills in school-age children with SB, which have implications for intervention. When core and functional difficulties hamper children's abilities in these areas, they are at increased risk for continuing learning problems.

Young children with SB may also be more vulnerable and reliant than typically developing children on the support they receive through sensitive, responsive parenting. Our study has identified responsive parenting as related to greater growth in cognitive skills (language and cognition) among young children with SB. Additional longitudinal research needs to be conducted using larger samples to continue to evaluate this finding. Moreover, the potential for parents to be empowered to use skills that may impact children's later cognitive functioning lends itself to intervention research. Recent findings that a responsive parenting style can be taught to parents of preterm infants and toddlers, and that these skills have a positive impact on the child, are promising for parents of children with SB.

This chapter also highlights the importance of using longitudinal data to correlate core deficits and early functioning with later development. There are numerous advantages of longitudinal studies which can evaluate these relations over time using growth curve analyses. We are continuing to follow our cohort of children with and without SB through 9½ years of age. This will allow us to correlate the core deficits identified in infancy with later learning difficulties and brain structures present through MRI analyses (conducted when children are assessed at 9½ years of age). Findings from this research should begin to bridge some of the gaps currently in the literature along with further longitudinal research in this area taking into account potential interactions of biological and environmental risk and protective factors.

Acknowledgement

This research was supported, in part, by Grant PO1HD35946 funded by the National Institute for Child Health and Development and the National Institute of Neurological Disease and Stroke.

References

1. Williams LJ, Rasmussen SA, Flores A, et al. Decline in the prevalence of spina bifida and anencephaly by race/ethnicity: 1995–2002. *Pediatrics* 2005;**116**(3):580–6.

2. Charney EB. Neural tube defects: spina bifida and myelomeningocele. In Batshaw ML, Perret YM, eds. *Children with Disabilities: A Medical Primer*. Baltimore: Brookes, 1992: 471–88.

3. Fletcher JM, Northrup H, Landry SH, et al. Spina bifida: genes, brain, and development. *Int Rev Res Ment Retard* 2004;**29**:63–117.

4. Volick KA, Blanton SH, Tyerman GH, et al. Methylenetetrahydrofolate reductase and spina bifida: evaluation of level of defect and maternal genotypic risk in Hispanics. *Am J Med Genet* 2000;**95**:21–7.

5. Fletcher JM, Copeland K, Frederick JA, et al. Spinal lesion level in spina bifida: A source of neural and cognitive heterogeneity. *J Neurosurg* 2005;**102**(Suppl. 3):268–79.

6. Juranek J, Fletcher JM, Hasan KM, et al. Neocortical reorganization in spina bifida. *NeuroImage* 2008;**40**(4):1516–22.

7. Griebel ML, Oakes WJ, Worley G. The Chiari malformation associated with meningomyelocele. In Rekate HL, ed. *Comprehensive Management of Spina Bifida*. Boca Raton, FL: CRC Press, 1991: 67–92.

8. Del Bigio MR. Neuropathological changes caused by hydrocephalus. *Acta Neuropathol (Berl)* 1993;**85**:573–85.

9. Del Bigio MR. Cellular damage and prevention in childhood hydrocephalus. *Brain Pathol* 2004;**14**:317–24.

10. Dennis M. Acquired disorders of language in children. In Feinberg TE, Farah MJ, eds. *Behavioral neurology and neuropsychology*. New York: McGraw-Hill, 1996: 737–54.

11. Landry SH, Robinson SS, Copeland D, et al. Goal-directed behavior and perception of self-competence in children with spina bifida. *J Pediatr Psychol* 1993;**18**(3):389–96.

12. Dennis M, Landry SH, Barnes M, et al. A model of neurocognitive function in spina bifida over the lifespan. *J Int Neuropsychol Soc* 2006;**12**(2):285–96.

13. Landry SH, Taylor HB, Guttentag C, et al. Responsive parenting: closing the learning gap for at-risk children. In Glidden L, ed. *International Review of Research in Mental Retardation*, vol. 36. New York: Academic Press; 2008.

14. Thelen E, Smith LB. *A Dynamic Systems Approach to the Development of Cognition and Action*. Cambridge, MA: MIT Press; 1995.

15. Landry SH, Lomax-Bream L, Barnes M. The importance of early motor and visual functioning for later cognitive skills in preschoolers with and without spina bifida. *J Int Neuropsychol Soc* 2003;**9**:176.

16. Bertenthal BI, Campos JJ, Barreto KC. Self-produced locomotion: An organizer of emotional, cognitive, and social development in infancy. In Emde R, Harmon R, eds. *Continuities and Discontinuities in Development*. New York: Plenum; 1984: 175–210.

17. Hetherington R, Dennis M. Motor function profile in children with early onset hydrocephalus. *Dev Neuropsychol* 1999;**15**:25–51.

18. Liptak GS. Neural tube defects. In Batshaw ML, ed. *Children with Disabilities*, 5th edn. Washington DC: Brookes; 2002: 467–92.

19. Salman MS, Sharpe JA, Lillakas L, et al. Smooth ocular pursuit in Chiari Type II malformation. *Dev Med Child Neurol* 2007;**49**:289–93.

20. Salman MS, Sharpe JA, Eizenman M, et al. Saccades in children with spina bifida and Chiari Type II malformation. *Neurology* 2005;**64**:2098–101.

21. McDonald CM. Rehabilitation of children with spina dysraphism. *Neurosurg Clin N Am* 1995;**6**:393.

22. Miall RC, Reckess GZ, Imamizu H. The cerebellum coordinates eye and hand tracking movements. *Nat Neurosci* 2001;**4**:638–44.

23. Miall RC, Christensen LOD, Cain O, et al. Disruption of state estimation in the human lateral cerebellum. *PLoS Biol* 2007;**5**(11):e316.

24. Leigh RJ, Zee DS. The saccadic system. *The Neurology of Eye Movements*, 3rd edn. New York: Oxford University Press; 1999: 90–134.

25. Dennis M, Jewell D, Edelstein K, et al. Motor learning in children with spina bifida: Intact learning and performance on a ballistic task. *J Int Neuropsychol Soc* 2006;**12**:598–608.

26. Lomax-Bream L, Barnes M, Copeland K, et al. The impact of spina bifida on development across the first three years. *Dev Neuropsychol* 2007;**31**(1):1–20.

27. Dennis M, Fletcher JM, Rogers T, et al. Object-based and action-based visual perception in children with spina bifida and hydrocephalus. *J Int Neuropsychol Soc* 2002;**8**(1):95–106.

28. Block JH, Block J. The role of ego-control and ego-resiliency in the organization of behavior. In Collins WA, ed. *Minnesota Symposia on Child Psychology*. Hillsdale, NJ: Lawrence Erlbaum; 1979.

29. Mischel W, Patterson CJ. Effective plans for self-control in children. In Collins WA, ed. *Minnesota Symposia on Child Psychology*. Hillsdale, NJ: Lawrence Erlbaum; 1979: 199–230.

30. Wertsch JV. From social interaction to higher psychological processes. *Hum Dev* 1979;**22**:1–22.

31. Kopp CB. Antecedents of self-regulation: A developmental perspective. *Dev Psychol* 1982;**18**:199–214.

32. Ruff HA, Lawson KR. Assessment of infants attention during play with objects. In Schaefer CE, Critlin K, Sandgrund A, eds. *Play Diagnosis and Assessment*. New York: Wiley; 1991: 115–29.

33. Rafal R, Henik A. The neurology of inhibition: Integrating controlled and automatic processes. In Dagenback D, Carr T, eds. *Inhibitory Process in Attention, Memory, and Language*. San Diego, CA: Academic Press; 1994: 1–51.

34. Taylor HB, Landry SH, Cohen L, et al. *Early information processing among infants with spina bifida*. Presented at the 34th annual meeting of International Neuropsychological Society in Boston, MA, 2006.

35. Dennis M, Fitz CR, Netley CT, et al. The intelligence of hydrocephalic children. *Arch Neurol* 1981;**38**:607–15.

36. Fletcher JM, Bohan TP, Brandt ME, et al. Morphometric evaluation of the hydrocephalic brain: relationships with cognitive abilities. *Childs Nerv Syst* 1996;**12**:192–9.

37. White RW. Motivation reconsidered: the concept of competence. *Psychol Rev* 1959;**66**:297–333.

38. Tew JB. Spina bifida in ordinary schools: handicap, attainment and behavior. *Z Kinderchir* 1988;**43**(suppl 11):46–8.

39. Landry SH, Copeland D, Lee A, et al. Goal-directed behavior in children with spina bifida. *Dev Behav Pediatr* 1990;**11**(6):306–11.

40. Denckla MB. A theory and model of executive function: a neuropsychological perspective. In Lyons GR, Krasnegor NA, eds. *Attention, Memory, and Executive Functioning*. Baltimore, MD: Brookes; 1996: 263–77.

41. Fletcher JM, Brookshire BL, Landry SH, et al. Attentional skills and executive functions in children with early hydrocephalus. *Dev Neuropsychol* 1996;**12**(1):53–76.

42. Snow JH. Executive processes for children with spina bifida. *Child Health Care* 1999;**28**(3):241–53.

43. Barnes MA, Huber J, Johnston A, et al. A model of comprehension in spina bifida meningomyelocele: Meaning activation, integration, and revision. *J Int Neuropsychol Soc* 2007;**13**:854–64.

44. Dennis M, Jacennik B, Barnes MA. The content of narrative discourse in children and adolescents after early-onset hydrocephalus and in normally developing age peers. *Brain Lang* 1994;**46**(1):129–65.

45. Badell-Ribera A, Shulman K, Paddock N. The relationship of nonprogressive hydocephalus to intellectual functioning in children with spina bifida cystica. *Pediatrics* 1966;**37**(5):787–93.

46. Barnes MA, Dennis MF. Reading comprehension deficits arise from diverse sources: evidence from readers with and without developmental brain pathology. In Cornoldi C, Oakhill J, eds. *Reading Comprehension Difficulties: Processes and Interventions*. New Jersey: Lawrence Erlbaum; 1996: 251–78.

47. Barnes MA, Faulkner H, Wilkinson M, et al. Meaning construction and integration in children with hydrocephalus. *Brain Lang* 2004;**89**(1):47–56.

48. Barnes MA, Wilkinson M, Boudousquie A, et al. Arithmetic processing in children with spina bifida: calculation accuracy, strategy use, and fact retrieval fluency. *J Learn Disabil* 2006;**39**:174–87.

49. Barnes MA, Dennis M. Discourse after early-onset hydrocephalus: core deficits in children of average intelligence. *Brain Lang* 1998;**61**(3):309–34.

50. Barnes MA. The decoding-comprehension dissociation in the reading of children with hydrocephalus: a reply to Yamada. *Brain Lang* 2002;**80**:260–3.

51. Barnes MA, Johnston AM, Dennis M. Comprehension in a neurodevelopmental disorder, spina bifida myelomeningocele. In Cain K, Oakhill J, eds. *Children's Comprehension Problems in Oral and Written Langauge: A Cognitive Perspective*. New York: Guilford Press; 2007: 193–217.

52. Wills KE. Neuropsychological functioning in children with spina bifida and/or hydrocephalus. *J Clin Child Psychol* 1993;**22**(2):247–65.

53. Barnes MA, Dennis M. Reading in children and adolescents after early-onset hydrocephalus and in their normallly-developing age peers: phonological analysis, word recognition, word comprehension and passage comprehension skill. *J Pediatr Psychol* 1992;**17**(4):445–65.

54. Barnes MA, Pengelly S, Dennis M, et al. Mathematics skills in good readers with hydrocephalus. *J Int Neuropsychol Soc* 2002;**8**:72–82.

55. Barnes MA, Dennis M, Hetherington R. Reading and writing skills in young adults with spina bifida and hydrocephalus. *J Int Neuropsychol Soc* 2004;**10**:680–88.

56. Barnes MA, Smith-Chant B, Landry SH. Number processing in neurodevelopmental disorders: Spina bifida myelomeningocele. In Campbell JID, ed. *Handbook of mathematical cognition*. New York: Psychology Press; 2005: 299–314.

57. Dennis M, Barnes MA. Numeracy skills in adults with spina bifida. *Dev Neuropsychol* 2002;**21**:141–56.

58. Hetherington R, Dennis M, Barnes MA, et al. Functional outcome in young adults with spina bifida and hydrocephalus. *Childs Nerv Syst* 2006;**22**:117–24.

59. Ris MD, Ammerman RT, Waller N, et al. Taxonicity of nonverbal learning disabilities. *J Int Neuropsychol Soc* 2007;**13**:50–8.

60. English L. *The impact of infant executive functions on reading and math outcomes in children with spina bifida.* Unpublished masters thesis, 2008.

61. Papanicolaou AC, Simos PG, Fletcher JM, et al. Early development and plasticity of neurophysiological processes involved in reading. In Foorman B, ed. *Preventing and Remediating Reading Difficulties. Bringing Science to Scale.* Timonium, MD: York Press; 2003: 3–21.

62. King GA, Shultz IZ, Steel K, et al. Self-evaluation and self-concept of adolescents with physical disabilities. *Am J Occup Ther* 1993;**47**:132.

63. Coakley RM, Holmbeck GN, Bryant FB. Constructing a prospective model of psychosocial adaptation in young adolescents with spina bifida: an application of optimal data analysis. *J Pediatr Psychol* 2006;**31**(10):1084–99.

64. Appleton PL, Ellis NC, Minchom PE, et al. Depressive symptoms and self-concept in young people with spina bifida. *J Pediatr Psychol* 1996;**22**(5):707–22.

65. Wallander JL, Feldman WS, Varni JW. Physical status and psychosocial adjustment in children with spina bifida. *J Pediatr Psychol* 1989;**14**(1):89–102.

66. Ammerman RT, Kane VR, Slomka GT, et al. Psychiatric symptomology and family functioning in children and adolescents with spina bifida. *J Clin Psychol Med Settings* 1998;**5**:449–65.

67. Moore C, Kogan BA, Parekh A. Impact of urinary incontinence on self-concept in children with spina bifida. *J Urol* 2004;**171**:1659–62.

68. Nassau JH, Drotar D. Social competence among children with central nervous system-related chronic health conditions: a review. *J Pediatr Psychol* 1997;**22**(6):771–93.

69. Fletcher JM, Brookshire BL, Landry SH, et al. Behavioral adjustment of children with hydrocephalus: relationships with etiology, neurological, and family status. *J Pediatr Psychol* 1995;**20**(1):109–25.

70. Holmbeck GN, Westhoven VC, Shapera WE, et al. A multi-method, multi-informant, and multi-dimensional perspective on psychosocial adjustment in pre-adolescents with spina bifida. *J Consult Clin Psychol* 2003;**71**(4):782–96.

71. DiPietro JA. Baby and the brain: advances in child development. *Annu Rev Public Health* 2000;**21**:455–71.

72. Dawson G, Klinger LF, Panagiotides H, et al. Frontal lobe activity and affective behavior of infants of mothers with depressive symptoms. *Child Dev* 1992;**63**:725–37.

73. Neville HJ, Bavelier D, Corina D, et al. Cerebral organization for language in deaf and hearing subjects: biological constraints and effects of experience. *Proc Natl Acad Sci USA* 1998;**95**:922–9.

74. Elman JL, Bates EA, Johnson MH, et al. *Rethinking Innateness.* Boston: MIT Press; 1996.

75. Yang J, Carmichael SL, Canfield M, et al. Socioeconomic status in relation to selected birth defects in a large multicentered US case-control study. *Am J Epidemiol* 2008;**167**:145–54.

76. Holmbeck GN, Coakley RM, Hommeyer JS, et al. Observed and perceived dyadic and systemic functioning in families of preadolescents with spina bifida. *J Pediatr Psychol* 2002;**27**(2):177–89.

77. Natriello G, McDill EL, Pallas AM. *Schooling Disadvantaged Children: Racing Against Catastrophe.* New York: Teachers College Press; 1990.

78. Lomax-Bream L, Taylor HB, Landry SH, et al. Role of early parenting and motor skills on development in children with spina bifida. *J Appl Dev Psychol* 2007;**28**(3):250–63.

79. Landry SH, Smith KE, Swank PR. Responsive parenting: establishing early foundations for social, communication, and independent problem-solving skills. *Dev Psychol* 2006;**42**(4):627–42.

80. Landry SH, Chapieski ML. Visual attention during toy exploration in preterm infants: effects of medical risk and maternal interactions. *Infant Behav Dev* 1988;**11**:187–204.

81. Landry SH, Chapieski ML. Joint attention of six-month-old Down syndrome and preterm infants: I. Attention to toys and mother. *Am J Ment Retard* 1990;**94**(5):488–98.

82. Taylor HB, Anthony J, Aghara R, et al. The interaction of early maternal responsiveness and children's cognitive abilities on later decoding and reading comprehension skills. *Early Educ Dev* 2008;**19**(1):188–207.

83. Bornstein MH. How infant and mother jointly contribute to developing cognitive competence in the child. *Proc Natl Acad Sci USA* 1985;**82**(21):7470–3.

84. Landry SH, Denson SE, Swank PR. Effects of medical risk and socioeconomic status on the rate of change in cognitive and social development for low birth weight children. *J Clin Exp Neuropsychol* 1997;**19**(2):261–74.

85. Landry SH, Smith KE, Miller-Loncar CL, et al. Predicting cognitive-linguistic and social growth curves from early maternal behaviors in children at varying degrees of biological risk. *Dev Psychol* 1997;**33**(6):1–14.

86. Bell RC. Contributions of human infants to caregiving and social interaction. In Handel G, ed. *Childhood Socialization*. Hawthorne, NY: Aldine de Gruyter; 1988: 103–22.

87. Braungart-Rieker J, Garwood MM, Stifter CA. Compliance and noncompliance: The roles of maternal control and child temperament. *J Appl Dev Psychol* 1997;**18**:411–28.

88. Goldberg S. Prematurity: Effects on parent-infant interaction. *J Pediatr Psychol* 1978;**3**:137–44.

89. Kogan KL. Interaction systems between preschool handicapped or developmentally delayed children and their parents. In Field T, Goldberg S, Stern D *et al.*, eds. *High-risk Infants and Children: Adult and Peer Interactions*. New York: Academic Press; 1980: 227–47.

90. Drillien CM. *The Growth and Development of the Prematurely Born Infant*. Edinburgh, Scotland: E. & S. Livingstone; 1964.

91. Hess RD, Shipman VC. Early experience and the socialization of cognitive modes in children. *Child Dev* 1965;**36**(4):869–86.

92. Vermaes I, Gerris J, Janssen J. Parents' social adjustment in families of children with spina bifida: a theory-driven review. *J Pediatr Psychol* 2007;**32**(10):1214–26.

93. Guttentag C, Pedrosa-Josic C, Landry SH, et al. Individual variability in parenting profiles and predictors of change: effects of an intervention with disadvantaged mothers. *J Appl Dev Psychol* 2006;**27**(4):349–69.

94. Dieterich SE, Landry SH, Smith KE, et al. Impact of community mentors on maternal behaviors and child outcomes. *J Early Intervention* 2006;**28**(2):111–24.

95. Matson MA, Mahone EM, Zabel TA. Serial neuropsychological assessment and evidence of shunt malfunction in spina bifida: a longitudinal case study. *Child Neuropsychol* 2005;**11**(4):315–32.

96. Rowley L. Welcoming babies with spina bifida: a message of hope and support from new and expectant parents. 2007. Available at: http://www.waisman.wisc.edu/nrowley/sb-kids/wbwsb.html.

97. Landry SH, Smith KE, Miller-Loncar CL, et al. Responsiveness and initiative: Two aspects of social competence. *Infant Behav Dev* 1997;**20**(2):259–62.

98. Landry SH, Smith KE, Miller-Loncar CL, et al. The relation of change in maternal interactive styles to the developing social competence of full-term and preterm children. *Child Dev* 1998;**69**(1):105–23.

99. Landry SH, Smith KE, Swank PR, et al. Early maternal and child influences on children's later independent cognitive and social functioning. *Child Dev* 2000;**71**(2):358–75.

100. Landry SH, Smith KE, Swank PR, et al. Responsive parenting: the optimal timing of an intervention across early childhood. *Dev Psychol* 2008;**45**(5):1335–53..

101. Salmon K. Commentary. Preparing children for medical procedures: taking account of memory. *J Pediatr Psychol* 2006;**31**:859–61.

102. Hallowell L, Stewart S, Silva CA, et al. Reviewing the process of preparing children for MRI. *Pediatr Radiol* 2008;**38**(3):271–9.

103. LeRoy S, Elixson EM, O'Brien P, et al. Recommendations for preparing children and adolescents for invasive cardiac procedures: a statement from the American Heart Association Pediatric Nursing Subcommittee of the Council on Cardiovascular Nursing in collaboration with the Council on Cardiovascular Diseases of the Young. *Circulation* 2003;**108**:2550–64.

Adolescence and emerging adulthood in individuals with spina bifida: a developmental neuropsychological perspective

Kathy Zebracki, Michael Zaccariello, Frank Zelko and Grayson N. Holmbeck

Introduction

Adolescence and early adulthood are transitional periods characterized by numerous biological, psychological, cognitive, and social changes [1, 2]. More changes are seen in adolescence than in any other period of development except infancy. The late teens through twenties are marked by profound change, exploration of possible life directions, and decision-making that has enduring implications [1]. "Change" is the defining construct for these developmental periods and is particularly salient in individuals with chronic health conditions (CHC).

Spina bifida myelomeningocele (SBM) is a prototypical example of a CHC with core neurological features (Table 7b.1) and diverse complications (Table 7b.2) impacting development and outcome. Readers are referred to the previous chapter for details regarding the etiology, features, and clinical course of SBM. Individuals with SBM experience not only typical ongoing challenges of adolescence and adult development, but also unique changes owing to their health condition. Both normative and illness-specific changes occur within a larger environmental context that itself undergoes transformation over time. Individuals with SBM also face health system discontinuities such as the transition from pediatric medical care to adult care, and the transition from parent-controlled health care to self-management.

We begin this chapter with conceptual frameworks for considering the critical developmental milestones of adolescence and emerging adulthood, and a discussion of the interplay between the developmental issues of these periods and the experience of a CHC. Second, we consider major empirical findings relevant to SBM in adolescence and adulthood. Third, we examine the clinical implications of these findings for the care of adolescents and young adults with SBM. Fourth, we consider the role of the neuropsychologist and neuropsychological assessment in SBM. We conclude with comments and recommendations for assessment, intervention, and research pertaining to adolescents and young adults with SBM.

Models of adolescent and adult development

Biopsychosocial-contextual model of normative adolescent development (ages 10–18)

Holmbeck and Shapera [3] proposed a contextual framework for understanding adolescent development and adjustment (Fig. 7b.1), emphasizing biological, psychological, and social changes of adolescence. In this model, the relationship between primary developmental changes of adolescence (e.g. biological/puberty, psychological/cognitive, social roles) and developmental outcomes (e.g. achievement, autonomy, and identity) is mediated by the interpersonal contexts in which adolescents develop (e.g. family, peer, and school). Developmental changes impact relationships and environmental factors which, in turn, influence the individual's ability to master critical milestones of adolescence. Causal and mediational effects in this model may be moderated by demographic, intrapersonal, and interpersonal factors. In applying this model to CHCs, primary changes could also include features of an illness such as its visibility, neuropsychological compromise, and motor and sensory limitations. Three areas of change – biological/pubertal, social roles, and psychological/cognitive – are described below.

Biological/pubertal changes

Substantial physical growth and change are characteristic of adolescence, varying considerably between individuals with regard to time of onset, duration, and termination of the pubertal cycle [4]. Both pubertal status and pubertal timing impact quality of family relationships and indicators of psychosocial adaptation and psychopathology [5]. Early maturing girls are at risk for a variety of adaptational difficulties, including depression, substance use, early sexual risk behaviors, eating problems and disorders, and family conflicts. Precocious puberty, which occurs more frequently in females with SBM than females without a CHC, thus places adolescents at risk for such disruptions of adaptation [6]. Early pubertal onset may also incorrectly suggest advanced cognitive sophistication, resulting in premature transfer of responsibility for medical care management from parent to adolescent.

Table 7b.1. Primary neurological features of spina bifida myelomeningocele.

Myelodysplasia (spinal cord malformation)
Hydrocephalus
Agenesis/dysgenesis of the corpus callosum
Chiari II cerebellar anomaly
Cortical dysplasia
Neurogenic bladder and bowel

Changes in social roles

Although change from childhood to adolescent social status is universal, specific changes are culturally dependent. In Western industrialized societies, social role redefinition is associated with greater social responsibility, accountability, and rights in political, economic, and legal arenas. Adolescence also brings increased status in interpersonal relationships. CHCs such as SBM affect the nature and timing of these

Table 7b.2. Secondary features/complications of spina bifida myelomeningocele.

Ventricular shunt malfunction
Scoliosis
Orthopedic impairment
Urologic difficulties (e.g. urinary tract infections)
Renal dysfunction/failure
Spinal cord tethering
Sensory/motor impairment
Skin breakdown (i.e. pressure sores)
Reduced mobility
Epilepsy
Obesity
Allergies (e.g. latex)
Fractures
Cardiovascular disease
Metabolic syndrome

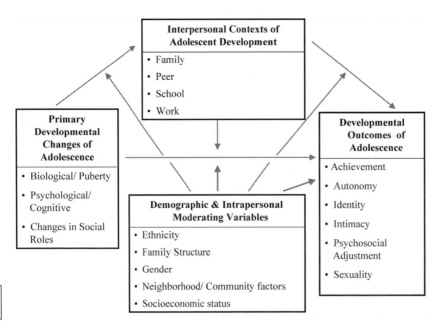

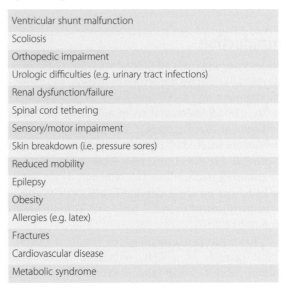

Figure 7b.1. A framework for understanding adolescent development and adjustment. From Holmbeck GN, Shapera WE. Research methods with adolescents. In Kendall PC, Butcher JN, Holmbeck GN, eds. *Handbook of Research Methods in Clinical Psychology*, 2nd edn. New York: Wiley; 1999: 634–61.

changes. For example, adolescents with motor disabilities may not be able to obtain a driver's license, a coveted privilege of adolescence. Alternative modes of transportation for those adolescents may leave them feeling socially isolated and limited in their level of independence.

Cognitive/psychological changes

Adolescence has long been described as a critical period of cognitive development, with particular growth of the capacity for complex and abstract reasoning, and increases in processing capacity, knowledge base, cognitive self-regulation, and socially relevant cognitions (e.g. empathy). The presence of a CHC may affect the emergence of these cognitive and psychological changes during adolescence. For example, CHCs involving the central nervous system may limit adolescents' growth towards autonomy in both medical self-care and normative activities of daily living. Cognitive limitations may diminish their ability to establish age-appropriate peer relationships, thus increasing risk for social isolation and psychological maladjustment, particularly in the form of internalizing problems (e.g. depression, anxiety).

Emerging adulthood as a distinct developmental period (ages 18–25)

While adolescence is traditionally viewed as the primary transitional period between childhood and adulthood, Arnett [1] posits an additional developmental period, distinct from adolescence and young adulthood, that occurs between the ages of 18 and 25, namely, *emerging adulthood*. The primary developmental challenges of emerging adulthood include: taking responsibility for one's self, making independent decisions, becoming financially independent, and exploring one's identity [1]. Risk behaviors (e.g. unprotected sex, substance abuse) also peak in the early 20s, in part due to experimentation with new and different identities and a significant decrease in parental monitoring. The processes of emerging adulthood are no different and no less complex in those with CHCs than in other individuals. Adults with CHCs, however, are often faced with unique barriers to normative milestones in the areas of education, employment, marital status, parental status, and residential and economic independence [7].

Social support during emerging adulthood is a crucial factor for positive development. Peer relationships among young adults with CHCs not only serve as a key source of emotional support, they also facilitate adjustment to living with a CHC and medical adherence [8]. As in adolescence, factors such as visibility, neuropsychological compromise, and motor and sensory limitations increase risk for social isolation and maladaptive social skills in individuals with CHCs, and affect the rate at which they gain independence. Attainment of higher education and steady employment may also be hampered due to sequelae of a CHC (e.g. cognitive impairment) or its treatment (e.g. increased school absences), further decreasing social interaction.

Families also play an important role in facilitating positive development. Adolescents entering emerging adulthood are expected to take on more responsibility in the areas of self-advocacy, self-care, and management of their health condition. HIPAA and privacy laws, in fact, can limit parental influence in these areas. Consequently, parents and families play a crucial role in promoting the development of these skills in youth with CHCs.

Empirical findings in adolescents and emerging adults with SBM

Medical factors

Neurodevelopmental anomalies are at the core of the medical challenges faced by individuals with SBM. Features such as agenesis of the corpus callosum, the Chiari II malformation involving the cerebellum, and hydrocephalus are common [9], and other subcortical anomalies have been reported as well [10]. These and other medical factors affect the cognitive and psychosocial functioning of individuals with SBM, which together make the medical management of SBM a complex affair, influencing the developmental processes of adolescence and adulthood. For example, bladder and bowel management are major challenges of individuals with SBM. Without careful adherence to routines such as clean intermittent self-catheterization, the risk of serious medical complications such as renal hypertension increases, contributing to an 8-fold increase in renal failure relative to the general population [11]. The common problems of orthopedic disability, reduced mobility, activity limitations, and obesity also confer risk for further disabling conditions such as metabolic syndrome, fractures, and skin breakdown/pressure sores.

185

Cognition

Executive functions

Individuals with SBM experience a wide range of cognitive difficulties. A common theme underlying their concerns is the impaired ability to monitor, integrate, and assemble information from a variety of sources and within a specific cognitive domain [12]. Significant difficulties with planning/organization, metacognition, and self-monitoring have also been documented in adolescents with SBM [13]. This impairment closely resembles the multidimensional construct of executive functions (EF), a series of higher-order cognitive skills employed in problem-solving. The demonstration of such deficits is particularly noteworthy in light of the presumed neural substrate of executive processes, and the overlap between this substrate and anatomical findings in individuals with SBM. A neural network of frontal, thalamic and striatal systems, densely loaded with white matter tracks, is commonly associated with executive functions [14]. One plausible explanation for EF deficits, therefore, is dysmyelination [15]. The varied cerebral anomalies associated with SBM, however, also allow for the possibility that other neural mechanisms may underlie deficits of EF in this population.

Attention

Youth with SBM experience generally perform well on tasks requiring anterior attention system functions (e.g. detecting interesting events, suppressing irrelevant information); however, they often experience difficulty on items requiring posterior attention functions (e.g. disengaging, shifting) [12]. Specific deficits in the attentional processes of encoding, sustaining, focus/execute and shifting have also been noted [16]. Attentional difficulties in SBM are thought to be mediated by posterior white matter regions [15]. Midbrain structures such as the pulvinar, reticular nuclei, and locus ceruleus have been identified as part of an orienting and altering attention system. Dysgenesis or damage to these regions may account for the corresponding attentional weaknesses.

Language

Despite intact basic structure and fund of knowledge, individuals with SBM are known to demonstrate difficulties in various aspects of language, such as pragmatics, inferential skills, and fluency [17]. The "cocktail party syndrome" involving expressive language marked by superficial content (i.e. "empty" conversation) has long been reported [18]. Adolescents with SBM have also been shown to experience difficulty with stringing words together to explain themselves [19]. These deficits seem to become more apparent with age and increased linguistic demands in social and academic settings.

Visual-spatial abilities

Despite early descriptions of visuospatial deficits, the current literature does not support the presence of global visual perceptual impairment in individuals with SBM. Simple tasks (e.g. face and object perception) are often intact [12], though tasks requiring the integration of a visual gestalt are more problematic [20]. Moreover, static visual properties such as size and length are readily perceived, but multifaceted dimensions requiring ongoing flexibility are more difficult [21]. As noted for EF, the neural underpinnings of visual perceptual skills appear to overlap with brain structures often found to be anomalous in SBM, such as the splenium of the corpus callosum, dorsal parietal-occipital pathways, and other white matter structures.

Memory

Data concerning the impact of SBM on memory in adolescence and young adults are limited [12, 22]. Deficits in immediate and delayed episodic memory and prospective memory for goals have been noted. Working memory is impaired on tasks requiring high information maintenance, as is rate of verbal learning. Memory deficits intensify with an increased number of lifetime shunt revisions. Bilateral hippocampal atrophy due to hydrocephalus and poor subcortical white matter myelination may be two features of SBM that are related to these impairments in memory [23].

Academic achievement

Individuals with SBM exhibit a relatively stable pattern of reading strengths and weaknesses. Most studies conducted with children suggest intact single-word reading but poor comprehension (e.g. Barnes et al. [24]). Poor visual-spatial ability and slowed processing speed may contribute to the effortful process of reading. Impairment is seen in multiple domains of math including speed, computation accuracy, and applied mathematical problem-solving [25]. Data concerning academic achievement in late adolescents and young adults are limited. Neural substrates of academic achievement have not been directly studied in individuals with SBM. Rather, it is surmised that the substrates of specific deficits of visuospatial abilities, attention/executive function and memory contribute to functional deficits in achievement.

Motor functions

A wide variety of motor deficits are seen in individuals with SBM affecting functions such as coordinated fine and gross motor control, strength, balance and dexterity, and oculomotor and oral-motor skills. Many of these deficits are related to lesion level, degree of spinal cord involvement, and the Chiari II cerebellar malformation [26]. Dyspraxia has been associated with frequency of shunt revisions and symptoms of hydrocephalus that may continue into adulthood [27].

Psychosocial adaptation

Emotional adjustment

The numerous medical features of SBM necessitate adherence to complex treatment regimens which place substantial physical, psychological, and social demands on affected individuals and their families. Rates of internalizing symptoms (e.g. depression and anxiety) are higher in adolescents with CHC than in youth without a CHC [28]. Levels of guilt, suicidal ideation, and somatic concerns are elevated within this population, and reported self-worth is lower [29, 30]. Although some individuals with SBM experience difficulties in emotional adjustment, others demonstrate resiliency and similar psychosocial adjustment to the general population.

Family functioning

Adolescence is often marked by increased friction with parents and emotional distance [5]. Families play a critical role in fostering adolescents' autonomy and psychological adjustment, enhancing outcomes when the family environment is high in support and cohesiveness and low in conflict [31]. Several parenting factors have been shown to affect adolescent well-being in SBM: (1) responsiveness to adolescents' needs for increasing responsibility and decision-making, (2) appropriate monitoring of and clear expectations for their child's behavior, and (3) parental psychological health, stress, and coping [31]. Families

of adolescents with SBM experience higher stress and lower cohesion than other families [32]. Moderating variables such as other stressors (e.g. economic strain) and lower adolescent cognitive functioning may partly explain these findings. Many families of individuals with SBM, however, demonstrate considerable resilience as well.

Patterns of parental oversight in medical care activities can influence adolescents' development of autonomy [33]. With transition to adolescence, a gradual shift is seen in responsibility for medical care away from parents. The manner in which these changes occur has important implications for adolescents' short- and long-term health. If the transfer occurs before adolescents are cognitively and psychologically ready, a decline in medical adherence is often observed [34]. On the other hand, parents who maintain control over medical tasks long after adolescents have developed necessary skills for self-care management may foster a sense of dependency and low self-efficacy [35]. A gradual transfer of responsibility in synchrony with adolescents' levels of maturity and cognitive development may best serve the goals of promoting autonomy and appropriate health-related behaviors.

Peer social functioning

Peer relationships are critical during adolescence, exerting positive effects on cognitive, social-cognitive, linguistic, sex role, and moral development. Concerns about conformity to peer norms reach a peak during this developmental period, producing stress and preoccupation about belonging to a particular peer group. Indeed, one of the most robust predictors of difficulties during adulthood is poor peer relationships during childhood and adolescence [36]. Multiple factors may contribute to social isolation in individuals with SBM, including its symptoms and consequences (e.g. limited mobility), psychological adjustment (e.g. depression), and reduced expectations for participation (e.g. by family and friends). Youth with CHCs spend less time than their peers socializing and participating in extracurricular activities and sports, and more time in self-care and passive activities [37]. Adolescents with chronic illnesses requiring prolonged school absences may be perceived by classmates as socially withdrawn, affecting opportunities for meaningful peer relationships. Physical appearance is also associated with social acceptance in individual with CHCs [38].

To date, most of the work on social functioning in SBM has been with children and pre-adolescents; less is known about adolescents and adults. Children with SBM tend to be socially immature and passive, have fewer friends, less peer support and limited social contacts outside of school, and date less during adolescence than their peers [28]. Cognitive limitations associated with SBM such as impaired social cue recognition may also contribute to restriction of social networks and social competence.

Sexuality

While most individuals with SBM receive instruction in sex education at school, relatively few are provided instruction specific to SBM [39, 40]. Women appear more likely to receive SBM-related information about sexuality and reproduction than men [40]. In an Australian sample, 95% of adolescents and adults reported inadequate knowledge about sexual and reproductive health pertaining to their SBM, suggesting that education in sexuality and reproduction specific to SBM is an unmet need in many individuals with this condition [41].

Predictably, the desire for intimate relationships and sexual contact is high among adolescents and adults with SBM, but their sexual activity appears to be delayed [39]. Only 60% of the Australian sample had dated, though nearly all expressed an interest in having a boyfriend/girlfriend [41]. Sexual activity decreases with SBM severity, being significantly more common in individuals with lumbar and sacral lesions, and much less likely among those with hydrocephalus [39, 40]. Urinary incontinence and latex sensitivity are examples of specific factors that may complicate sexual activity in SBM [40, 41]. Furthermore, individuals with spina bifida and hydrocephalus report being more dissatisfied with their sexuality and partnerships than those without hydrocephalus, and their satisfaction is lower than that of individuals without SBM [42]. In the same study, satisfaction with sexuality appeared to be particularly low among men with SBM. Nevertheless, aspirations of SBM individuals with respect to relationships and reproduction appear to be high [41].

Functional adaptation

General independence skills

Due to advances in medical and surgical care, survival to adulthood is becoming the norm in SBM. Many young adults attain independence in specific activities of daily living (e.g. bathing, dressing, and toileting),

important prerequisites to independent living [43]. However, rates of independent residence and community participation are lower than expected [44]. Though adolescents with SBM are hopeful about their future, with generally positive beliefs and expectations about independent functioning, their actual participation in adolescent activities such as decision-making, household responsibilities, and friendship activities is often limited [45]. Independent functioning in SBM has been shown to correlate with spinal lesion level and the presence of hydrocephalus [43], with lesions above the lumbar level strongly associated with dependence on others. The generally disappointing rate of functional independence in adults with SBM is a source of great concern among families and caretakers of individuals with this condition.

Driving

The task of driving a motor vehicle is a rite of passage for most adolescents but a major obstacle to those with SBM. Only 45% of individuals of driving age with SBM in a US sample had obtained a drivers license [46]. In a British study of long-term outcome, 54% of an adult sample had passed a driver's test, but only 19% were actually driving [47], others having stopped for medical or financial reasons. The outlook for independent driving is, therefore, limited, compelling individuals with SBM to rely heavily on others for essential transportation.

Employment

Employment prospects for adults with SBM are commonly reduced by health, psychosocial, and educational factors. Only 38% of a sample of Swedish adults with SBM were employed [48]. In a British long-term follow up sample, only 26% were engaged in open employment, with an additional 18% in sheltered work situations [47]. Little other research has considered the challenge of employment in individuals with SBM.

Clinical implications

Academic functioning

Children with SBM are more likely to experience success in the early elementary years, when learning is highly structured and focuses on foundation skills. In contrast, adolescents and adults with SBM often struggle to meet demands for efficiency and speed in high school and post-secondary academic settings. They have particular difficulty with tasks that require long-term planning, organization, problem-solving, self-monitoring during task engagement, and focused attention. Comprehension of complex and unfamiliar instructional materials is often a challenge and youth with SBM struggle as they are required to use such materials independently. The aforementioned neuro-psychological difficulties (e.g. executive function, attention, memory) may contribute to incomplete assignments and homework as well as poor perform-ance on tests.

Academic supports are often necessary to max-imize academic achievement and minimize potential frustration as well as effects on self-esteem due to struggles in school. As previously mentioned, rates of mental health issues are elevated in teenagers with CHC [29–30] and can be further exacerbated by aca-demic struggles. The use of adaptive curriculum and accommodations serve two inter-related functions: to enhance the learning environment and to mitigate the emergence of depressive or anxiety symptomology when a youth with SBM is unable to maintain adequate progress at school. Examples of appropriate support consist of work accommodations, instruction in organizational techniques, and educational efforts designed to increase the efficiency of the student's academic pursuits.

Executive function

With entry into adolescence and subsequent adult-hood, it is expected that individuals increasingly mon-itor themselves and their environment, and engage more effectively in novel problem-solving activities. Increased organizational competence is expected in the face of more complex demands by society and one's environment. In essence, there is a dynamic interchange between stage of development, stage of cognitive skill, and environmental demands [49]. The association between SBM and executive dysfunction predicts that this interchange will be suboptimal, and that adolescents and adults with SBM will have diffi-culty mastering the necessary skills and compensatory strategies to function on an independent basis. Executive function (EF) deficits may thus affect the ability to secure and maintain employment, live inde-pendently, and have meaningful social relationships.

Data are accumulating to support the view that EF is a key area of vulnerability in SBM, necessitating interventions targeting EF in this population. EF skills

should ideally be taught, implemented, and practiced in the situations where they will be needed (e.g. job, school) as opposed to a sterile environment devoid of contextual factors. Multistep tasks should be broken down into independent parts and additional steps should not be introduced until prior steps have been adequately rehearsed and mastered. In conjunction, creating an environment that is structured and routi-nized will ameliorate EF weaknesses. Specific interven-tions and strategies to manage executive dysfunction in individuals with CHC are outlined in other reports [50]. The overarching goal is to have EF skills become more automatic for the adolescent and young adult with SBM.

Vocational training

Vocational training has been cited as a critical need by individuals with SBM and their families. Adolescents with CHCs who participate in vocational training are more likely to seek out, secure, and maintain paid employment following high school [51]. Transitions to post-secondary education work and educational activities are, by law, part of the special education process, and deserve consideration as early as the junior high years. Early transition planning should focus on mastery of general life skills (e.g. shopping and money handling, transportation training) useful to adolescents regardless of career preference. During middle to late adolescence, the focus of transition planning should include skills relevant to the student's specific employment and education goals.

Transition to adult care

Children with SBM and their families ultimately face a transition from familiar, multidisciplinary pediatric health care settings to adult settings that are likely to vary in structure and the level of psychosocial support they provide [47]. This transition is often experienced as difficult and frustrating [52]. The transition from pediatric to adult care should be carefully planned, to help individuals with SBM and their families become accustomed to a more independent and active role as consumers in the health care setting. A well-planned transition that decreases the dependency between the pediatrician and young person, by facilitating the notion of personal responsibility for decision-making by the young adult, will promote well-being for the youth and strengthen their relationship with an adult provider [53]. Special support should be provided during the initial period of transition, to facilitate adjustment to the new care environment. Transition strategies should be flexible and implemented gradually to accommodate the unique circumstances of each individual with SBM and his/her family. An appropriate transition plan will attend not only to medical needs, but also to the spectrum of care required in SBM, addressing emotional, developmental, and social issues [54]. Unfortunately, despite the importance of providing a transition program, few transition programs exist for young people with a CHC [55].

Assistive technology

Though assistive technologies are commonly used to enhance mobility in SBM, the application of technology to cognitive and other functional handicaps is in its infancy [56]. Great potential exists for the development of assistive software applications on personal computers, personal digital assistants, and emerging hardware platforms. Some examples of applications relevant to SBM would include temporal reminders for medications and treatments, information storage and retrieval systems, organizational/management systems, and productivity tools for writing, speech recognition, written text-to-speech conversion, and math. Another application of technology, the use of the internet as an information source about SBM, has recently been surveyed [57]. Results revealed numerous sources of information and indicate that it is relatively accessible online, though it requires a high reading level (10.9 grade) and varies considerably in quality.

Protective factors

An over-arching goal through adolescence and adulthood is to become an independent and productive contributor to one's environment and society. A series of studies have considered the factors that facilitate positive life outcomes in individuals with SBM and other CHCs. Perceived family encouragement appears to be positively related to whether or not an adult with SBM is employed, socially active, and able to travel independently in the community [58]. Level of hope in adolescents with SBM, and active coping via social support, are related to higher quality of life [59]. Being treated by parents in an age-appropriate fashion and being allowed to participate in various social activities are related to positive self-esteem [30]. Furthermore, Coakley and colleagues [60]

found that late childhood and preadolescence motivation in an educational setting, verbal ability, and positive behaviors predict positive psychosocial adaptation. Together, these data suggest several factors that should be a focus of monitoring and intervention efforts in individuals with SBM and their families.

The role of the neuropsychologist and neuropsychological assessment

The neuropsychologist can play several important roles in the care of adolescents and adults with SBM. The neuropsychologist is uniquely suited to consider neurological, cognitive, emotional/behavioral, and environmental factors impacting individuals with SBM, and to provide consultation, assessment, and therapeutic expertise. Some examples of common activities of the neuropsychologist working with individuals with SBM are provided below.

1. Consultative/educational:
   help families and individuals with SBM understand developmental processes that underlie academic and social functioning, and how they may be affected by SBM;

   provide education about difficulties that individuals with SBM often face in social, academic, and other performance contexts;

   help families and individuals with SBM to understand the educational system and the special education process;

   advocate for appropriate support services for individuals with SBM in academic and vocational settings;

   assist families and individuals with SBM in planning transition to post-secondary employment and education.

2. Assessment:
   conduct evaluations of individuals with SBM in an effort to characterize their neuropsychological, educational, and emotional functioning;

   help parents and individuals with SBM understand evaluation results and their ramifications for functioning (e.g. academic, vocational) and intervention;

   consult with individuals, families, and medical caretakers about the relationship between NP evaluation results and medical issues in SBM;

   based on evaluation results, assist in intervention planning for the educational setting, mental health services, rehabilitation services, and vocational activities.

3. Therapeutic:

provide psychotherapeutic services to the individual with SBM;

provide support and therapeutic services to families of individuals with SBM;

assist others working with the individual with SBM to facilitate adaptation in emotional, behavioral, and social domains.

Neuropsychological evaluations of individuals with SBM serve several important purposes. With a cornucopia of tools to assess both basic (e.g. language, motor) and higher-order functions (e.g. executive functions), neuropsychological evaluations can be instrumental in characterizing profiles of ability that identify the presence of depressed cognitive functioning, learning disabilities and disorders of attention. These profiles often have direct relevance to educational and vocational programming. Neuropsychological assessment techniques, as contrasted with other approaches (e.g. psychoeducational), are especially well suited to examining aspects of functioning such as processing speed, memory, and attention, which are particularly sensitive indicators of neurological dysfunction.

Neurosurgeons may request neuropsychological evaluations to help judge the need for placement or revision of a ventricular shunt to treat hydrocephalus. Serial evaluations can also be used to track an individual's cognitive functioning over time as an indication of neurologically based changes in mental status. Neuropsychological evaluations can also serve as a rough "report card" of interventions, providing information on the efficacy of various services and treatments an individual with SBM is receiving. Furthermore, results of neuropsychological assessment can offer input into the process of vocational planning, by identifying strengths and weaknesses that help an adolescent or adult with SBM to define a vocational path.

Concluding comments

In this chapter we have provided an overview of empirical findings and clinical implications related to SBM in adolescence and adulthood, in the context of models of development that have been recently proposed and applied to CHCs. It is useful to consider the transitions of individuals with SBM from childhood to adolescence to adulthood within these frameworks to better understand how primary and secondary features of their condition influence processes of normative development. Not only is the negotiation of developmental milestones more difficult for this population [61] but

individuals with SBM confront transitions that are not faced by their peers, such as the transition to self-care from parent-managed health care. Moreover, transitions to education, employment, marriage, living on one's own, and parenthood are more complicated, and the degree to which these goals are attainable varies across young adults. As noted above, there is considerable variability across individuals in the ease with which they are able to manage the demands of the complex transition to adulthood. Depending on a variety of individual and environmental conditions, individuals with SBM may have very different outcomes (i.e. multifinality) [62]. Our challenge is to better understand the diverse individual and environmental factors that contribute to positive outcomes in SBM, with the ultimate goal of optimizing them.

There is tremendous need for research addressing basic processes of cognition, psychosocial adaptation, and functional adaptation in relation to both primary and secondary features of SBM. Rapid advances in structural and functional imaging technologies should fuel further progress in understanding the neuropathological features of SBM, and how they are related to cognitive and functional handicaps associated with this condition. Developmentally oriented longitudinal research should consider the multidimensional processes of transition to adulthood in individuals with SBM, with the goal of enhancing them. Randomized clinical trials are necessary to determine the intervention methods – cognitive, psychosocial, health-related, and environmental – that promote positive vocational and functional outcomes. Future research addressing the questions *why* and *for whom* specific interventions and prevention programs work is crucial to facilitating a seamless transition from childhood to adolescence and into adulthood for youth affected by SBM.

Acknowledgements

Completion of this chapter was supported by research grants from the National Institute of Child Health and Human Development (R01-HD048629) and the March of Dimes Birth Defects Foundation (12-FY04–47).

References

1. Arnett JJ. Emerging adulthood: a theory of development from the late teens through the twenties. *Am Psychol* 2000;**55**:469–80.

2. Williams PG, Holmbeck GN, Greenley RN. Adolescent health psychology. *J Consult Clin Psychol* 2002;**70**:828–42.

191

3. Holmbeck GN, Shapera WE. Research methods with adolescents. In Kendall PC, Butcher JN, Holmbeck GN, eds. *Handbook of Research Methods in Clinical Psychology*, 2nd edn. New York: Wiley; 1999: 634–61.

4. Brooks-Gunn J, Reiter EO. The role of pubertal processes. In Feldman SS, Elliott GR, eds. *At the Threshold: The Developing Adolescent*. Cambridge: Harvard University Press; 1990: 16–53.

5. Paikoff RL, Brooks-Gunn J. Do parent-child relationships change during puberty? *Psychol Bull* 1991;**110**:47–66.

6. Blum R. Chronic illness and disability in adolescence. *J Adolesc Health* 1992;**13**:364–8.

7. Wells T, Sandefur GD, Hogan DP. What happens after the high school years among young persons with disabilities? *Soc Forces* 2003;**82**:803–32.

8. La Greca AM, Bearman KJ, Moore H. Peer relations of youth with pediatric conditions and health risks: promoting social support and healthy lifestyles. *Dev Behav Pediatr* 2002;**23**:271–80.

9. Menkes JH, Sarnet HB, Flores-Sarnet L. Malformations of the nervous system. In Menkes JH, Sarnet HB, Bernard ML, eds. *Child Neurology*, 7th edn. Philadelphia: Lippincott Williams & Wilkins; 2006: 287–302.

10. Del Bigio MR. Neuropathological changes caused by hydrocephalus. *Acta Neuropathologica* 1993;**85**:573–85.

11. Lawrenson R, Wyndaele JJ, Vlachonikolis I, et al. Renal failure in patients with neurogenic lower urinary tract dysfunction. *Neuroepidemiology* 2001;**20**:138–43.

12. Dennis M, Landry SH, Barnes M, et al. A model of neurocognitive function in spina bifida over the life span. *J Int Neuropsychol Soc* 2006;**12**:285–96.

13. Mahone EM, Zabel TA, Levey E, et al. Parent and self-report ratings of executive function with myelomeningocele and hydrocephalus. *Child Neuropsychol* 2002;**8**:258–70.

14. Royall DR, Lauterbach EC, Cummings JL, et al. Executive control function: a review of its promise and research. *J Neuropsychiatry Clinl Neurosci* 2002;**14**:377–405.

15. Fletcher JM, Bohan TP, Brandt ME, et al. Morphometric evaluation of the hydrocephalic brain: relationship with cognitive development. *Childs Nerv Syst* 1996;**12**:192–99.

16. Loss N, Yeates KO, Enrile BG. Attention in children with myelomeningocele. *Child Neuropsychol* 1998;**4**:7–20.

17. Dennis M, Hendrick EB, Hoffman HJ, et al. The language of hydrocephalic children. *J Clin Exp Neuropsychol* 1987;**9**:593–621.

18. Tew, B. The "cocktail party syndrome" in children with hydrocephalus and spina bifida. *Br J Dis Comm* 1979;**14**:89–101.

19. Brookshire BL, Fletcher JM., Bohan TP, et al. Specific language deficiencies in children with early onset hydrocephalus. *Child Neuropsychol* 1995;**1**:106–17.

20. Fletcher JM, Brookshire BL, Bohan TP, et al. Early hydrocephalus. In Rourke BP, ed. *Syndrome of Nonverbal Learning Disabilities: Neurodevelopmental Manifestations*. New York: Guilford Press; 1995: 206–36.

21. Dennis M, Rogers T, Barnes, MA. Children with spina bifida perceive visual illusions but not multistable figures. *Brain Cogn* 2002;**46**:108–13.

22. Dennis M, Jewell D, Drake J, et al. Prospective, declarative, and nondeclarative memory in young adults with spina bifida. *J Int Neuropsychol Soc* 2007;**13**:312–23.

23. Zola-Morgan S, Squire LR. Neuroanatomy of memory. *Annu Rev Sci* 1993;**16**:547–63.

24. Barnes M, Dennis M, Hetherington R. Reading and writing skills in young adults with spina bifida and hydrocephalus. *J Int Neuropsychol Soc* 2004;**10**:655–63.

25. Dennis M, Barnes, M. Math and numeracy in young adults with spina bifida and hydrocephalus. *Dev Neuropsychol* 2002;**21**:141–55.

26. Fletcher JM, Copeland K, Frederick JA, et al. Spinal lesion level in spina bifida: a source of neural and cognitive heterogeneity. *J Neurosurg* 2005;**102**:268–79.

27. Hetherington R, Dennis M, Barnes M, et al. Functional outcome in young adults with spina bifida and hydrocephalus. *Childs Nerv Syst* 2006;**22**:117–24.

28. Holmbeck GN, Westhoven VC, Shapera W, et al. A multi-method, multi-informant, and multi-dimensional perspective on psychosocial adjustment in pre-adolescents with spina bifida. *J Consult Clin Psychol* 2003;**71**:782–96

29. Borjeson MC, Lagergren J. Life conditions of adolescents with myelomeningocele. *Dev Med Child Neurol* 1990;**32**:698–706.

30. Wolman C, Basco DE. Factors influencing self-esteem and self-consciousness in adolescents with spina bifida. *J Adolesc Health* 1994;**15**:543–48.

31. Friedman D, Holmbeck GN, Jandasek B, et al. Parent functioning in families of preadolescents with spina bifida: longitudinal implications for child adjustment. *J Fam Psychol* 2004;**18**:609–19.

32. Holmbeck GN, Greenley RN, Coakley RM. Family functioning in children and adolescents with spina bifida: an evidence-based review of research and interventions.*J Dev Behav Pediatr* 2006;**27**:249–77.

33. Anderson BJ, Brackett J, Ho J, et al. An intervention to promote family teamwork in diabetes management tasks: relationships among parental involvement, adherence to blood glucose monitoring, and glycemic control in young adolescents with type 1 diabetes. In: Drotar D, ed. *Promoting Adherence to Medical*

Treatment in Chronic Childhood Illness: Concepts, Methods, and Interventions. Mahwah, NJ: Lawrence Erlbaum; 2000: 347–65.

34. Wysocki T, Taylor A, Hough BS, et al. Deviation from developmentally appropriate self-care autonomy. *Diabetes Care* 1996;**19**:119–25.

35. Coyne JC, Anderson BJ. The "psychosomatic family" reconsidered: diabetes in context. *J Marital Fam Ther* 1988;**14**:113–23.

36. Parker JG, Asher SR. Peer relations and later personal adjustment: are low-accepted children at risk? *Psychol Bull* 1987;**102**:357–89.

37. Fuggle P, Shand PA, Gill LJ, et al. Pain, quality of life, and coping in sickle cell disease. *Arch Dis Child* 1996;**75**:199–203.

38. LaGreca AM. Social consequences of pediatric conditions: fertile area for future investigation and intervention. *J Pediatr Psychol* 1990;**15**:285–307.

39. Verhoef M, Barf HA, Vroege JA et al. Sex education, relationships, and sexuality in young adults with spina bifida. *Arch Phys Med Rehabil* 2005;**86**:979–87.

40. Cardenas DD, Topolski TD, White CJ, et al. Sexual functioning in adolescents and young adults with spina bifida. *Arch Phys Med Rehabil* 2008;**89**:31–35.

41. Sawyer SM, Roberts KV. Sexual and reproductive health in young people with spina bifida. *Dev Med Child Neurol* 1999;**41**:671–5.

42. Barf HA, Post MW, Verhoef M, et al. Life satisfaction of young adults with spina bifida. *Dev Med Child Neurol* 2007;**49**:458–63.

43. Verhoef M, Barf HA, Post MW, et al. Functional independence among young adults with spina bifida, in relation to hydrocephalus and level of lesion. *Dev Med Child Neurol* 2006;**48**:114–19.

44. Mukherjee S. Transition to adulthood in spina bifida: changing roles and expectations. *Sci World J* 2007;**7**:1890–5.

45. Buran CF, Sawin KJ, Brei T, et al. Adolescents with myelomeningocele: activities, beliefs, expectations, and perceptions. *Dev Med Child Neurol* 2004;**46**:244–52.

46. Leger RR. Severity of illness, functional status, and HRQOL in youth with spina bifida. *Rehabil Nurs* 2005;**30**:180–7.

47. Oakeshott P, Hunt GM. Long-term outcome in open spina bifida. *Br J Gen Pract* 2003;**53**:632–6.

48. Valtonen K, Karlsson AK, Alaranta H, et al. Work participation among persons with traumatic spinal cord injury and meningomyelocele. *J Rehabil Med* 2006;**38**:192–200.

49. Bernstein JH. Developmental neuropsychological assessment. In Yeates KO, Ris MD, Taylor HG, eds. *Pediatric Neuropsychology: Research, Theory and Practice.* New York: Guilford; 2000: 405–38.

50. Mahone EM, Slomine BS. Managing dysexecutive disorders. In Hunter SJ, Donders J, eds. *Pediatric Neuropsychological Intervention.* New York: Cambridge University Press; 2007: 287–313.

51. Wagner MM, Blackorby J. Transition from high school to work or college: how special education students fare. *Future Child* 1996;**6**:103–20.

52. Buran CF, McDaniel AM, Brei TJ. Needs assessment in a spina bifida program: a comparison of the perceptions by adolescents with spina bifida and their parents. *Clin Nurse Spec* 2002;**16**:256–62.

53. Bailey S, O'Connell B, Pearce J. The transition from paediatric to adult health care services for children with acquired or congenital disorders. *Aust Health Rev* 2003;**26**:64–9.

54. Soanes C, Timmons S. Improving transition: a qualitative study examining the attitudes of young people with chronic illness transferring to adult care. *J Child Health Care* 2004;**8**:102–12.

55. LoCasale-Crouch L, Johnson B. Transition from pediatric to adult medical care. *Adv Chronic Kidney Dis* 2005;**12**:412–17.

56. Johnson KL, Dudgeon B, Kuehn C, et al. Assistive technology use among adolescents and young adults with spina bifida. *Am J Public Health* 2007;**97**:330–6.

57. Bergman J, Konijeti, R, Lerman SE. Myelomeningocele information on the internet is accessible and of variable quality, and requires a high reading level. *J Urol* 2007;**177**:1138–42.

58. Loomis JW, Javornisky JG, Monahan JJ, et al. Relations between family environment and adjustment outcomes in young adults with spina bifida. *Dev Med Child Neurol* 1997;**39**:620–7.

59. Sawin KJ, Brei TJ, Buran CF. Factors associated with quality of life in adolescents with spina bifida. *J Holist Nurs* 2002;**20**:279–304.

60. Coakley RM, Holmbeck GN, Bryant FB. Constructing a prospective model of psychosocial adaptation in young adolescents with spina bifida: an application of optimal data analysis. *J Pediatr Psychol* 2006;**31**:1084–99.

61. Schultz AW, Liptak GS. Helping adolescents who have disabilities negotiate transitions to adulthood. *Issues Compr Pediatr Nurs* 1998;**21**:187–201.

62. Holmbeck GN, Friedman D, Abad M, et al. (2006). Development and psychopathology in adolescence. In Wolfe DA, Mash EJ, eds. *Behavioral and Emotional Disorders in Adolescence: Nature, Assessment, and Treatment.* New York: Guilford Press; 2006: 21–55.

Spina bifida/myelomeningocele and hydrocephalus across the lifespan: a developmental synthesis

Ilana Gonik, Scott J. Hunter and Jamila Cunningham

Introduction

As has been well outlined in the two chapters regarding spina bifida/myelomeningocele (SB), SB is a still quite common and often severely disabling birth defect that is typically associated with bowel and bladder complications, complete paralysis, and other congenital defects [1], as well as varying degrees of anomalies in the brain. SB affects many aspects of early and later development, impacting opportunities for academic achievement and vocational success, as well as ongoing independence. It is often associated with neurodevelopmental changes, such as Chiari II malformation or acqueductal stenosis, that can result in hydrocephalus [2–5], leading to the need for shunting. Medical management of the conditions associated with SB (e.g. shunting, catheterization) influence the developmental process of cognitive and psychological functioning into adolescence and adulthood.

As both chapters discussed, SB is associated with significant variability in medical, motor, cognitive, psychosocial, academic, and functional adaptation throughout the lifespan. Complications of SB can range from minor physical problems to severe physical and mental disabilities. Generally, the degree and severity of the primary central nervous system (CNS) insult and its potential secondary CNS insults (e.g. hydrocephalus) lead directly to the set of deficits, such as motor functioning and attention orienting [6], that can be seen as early as infancy. This chapter aims to synthesize information shared in the previous two chapters, by reviewing the core deficits and strengths across the lifespan for individuals with SB, and to highlight issues pertinent to assessment, diagnosis, and intervention.

Cognitive funtioning

Attention

Infants and children

Typically developing infants are able to modulate their attention in order to learn about environmental stimuli. Children with SB show deficits in their ability to properly orient and shift their attention towards environmental stimuli due to abnormalities in the midbrain. Additionally, children with shunted hydrocephalus perform more slowly on simple tests of attention and processing speed [7]. In contrast, infants with SB show a normal ability to sustain their fixation and habituate to a stimulus in a manner that is comparable to developmentally normal infants [8].

Adolescents and adults

Adolescents with SB show deficits on tasks of sustained attention, orienting, focusing, and attention shifting [9]. These deficits have been associated with sustained damage to posterior white matter regions, midbrain structures, tectum, and superior colliculus [10]. In addition, hydrocephalus has been associated with hypoplasia, a thinning of components of the posterior attention system such as the parietal cortex and corpus callosum [11]. In contrast, adolescents appear to have normal abilities in orienting their attention towards unexpected events and disengaging from old information in order to eliminate extraneous input. These functions have been associated with the anterior attention system, which includes areas of the midprefrontal cortex [9].

Executive functions

Infants and children

Children with SB show deficits in several areas of executive functioning. Research has shown that executive function deficits identified in children with SB may be related to frontal cortex disruption, but also to likely alterations in subcortical controls [12]. They are also linked to difficulties with motor functioning and attention regulation [7]. Overall, the greatest deficits on neuropsychological tests with regard to executive dysfunction are shown in children with shunted hydrocephalus, whether there is a history of SB or not [12].

Adolescents and adults

Many adolescents with SB show development of significant executive dysfunction [6]. In general, the range of dysfunction becomes more evident in adolescence as individuals with SB fail to meet age-appropriate expectations in areas such as independent initiation of goal-directed activity and flexibility [13]. Executive functioning deficits that characterize individuals with SB lead to difficulty engaging in the complex demands of adulthood (i.e. employment, social relationships, independent living); difficulties with progressing to independence in college and with establishing a vocational path are observed. Adults with SB may need additional attention and instruction in developing and implementing executive function skills in order for them to become more automatic [14].

Language

Infants and children

Children with hydrocephalus typically have normal phonological, semantic, and syntactic language abilities [15]. However, the use of complex language in social contexts has been characterized as lacking in content, and it can be tangential, redundant, and contain irrelevant stereotypical phrases. Children with SB can also have difficulty sequencing events in a logical and meaningful order, to produce a cohesive and meaningful story. In general, they require more time than children of the same age to develop and produce a narrative, and are less efficient at providing information [15]. This may relate to executive weaknesses discussed above.

Adolescents and adults

Language deficits can become more apparent during adolescence and adulthood due to the increased linguistic demands of social and academic settings. Problems with language pragmatics, elaboration, clarity, fluency, and making inferences regarding narrative content become more pronounced [16]. This can hamper acceptance in social contexts and limit interactions.

Motor functioning

Infants and children

Children with higher-level meningomyelocele typically show greater lower limb motor impairments [17]. Motor functioning variability depends upon the integrity of the cerebellum [18]; cerebellar and subcortical involvement can impact coordination and sequencing of motor responses. As discussed in Taylor et al., having a shunt, due to excess CSF, has been associated with lower levels of motor performance, with impaired motor planning and sequencing observed [19].

Adolescents and adults

Physical phenotype (level of the spinal cord lesion), cerebellar impairment, and spinal cord involvement continue to impact motor functioning into adolescence and adulthood. Adults continue to show deficits in fine and gross motor control, stability, motor coordination, and oral–motor regulation. Depending on the level of the lesion, some adults with SB are able to gain independence in specific activities of daily living (e.g. personal hygiene and toileting); however, a decreased level of motor ability generally relates to a lower level of functional ability (e.g. household responsibilities) [20], and a need for physical supports and accommodations. This can significantly impact opportunities for independent living and vocational choices.

Visual–spatial abilities

Infants and children

As a result of the primary brain dysmorphologies and secondary CNS insults, children with SB show deficits in the development of visual perceptual abilities. Perceptual problems are associated with disordered development of the midbrain and tectum, and widening of the third ventricle, which limits the development of binocular vision, stereopsis, and depth perception [21]. Children with shunted hydrocephalus typically have a thin posterior cortex which impacts movement in relation to visual input. Hypoplasia of the corpus callosum also impacts visual motor integration [10]. On tasks of visual perception, children with SB generally exhibit normal abilities in face recognition, visual closure, line orientation, and tasks of dorsal stream visual processing. They have weaker abilities on tasks of dorsal visual input such as stereoscopic depth perception, visual figure-ground, and mental rotation [22].

Adolescents and adults

In terms of visuospatial cognition, previous studies have shown that young adults with SB show a lower Performance IQ and demonstrate difficulties reflecting a central impairment in visuospatial processing and right-hemisphere dysfunction [23, 24]. Generally, visual spatial functions that were intact in childhood remain well-developed into adolescence and young adulthood (e.g. facial recognition); however, tasks that require complex dimensions of visual properties and a plasticity of skills are more effortful [25]. Integrative and sequential processing are often affected, hampering efforts at fluid visuoperceptual problem-solving.

Memory

Infants and children

Children with SB and shunted hydrocephalus perform more poorly than both typically developing children and those without hydrocephalus. While implicit memory and motor learning are preserved, deficits in working memory span and information maintenance are observed [26]. Children with SB and shunted hydrocephalus have been found to acquire verbal information more slowly over the course of learning trials; to display a pronounced recency effect; to demonstrate deficits in long-delay free-recall of information; and show encoding and retrieval deficits on both verbal and nonverbal memory tasks. Overall, pervasive disturbances in memory processes have been noted. In addition, children with SB and shunted hydrocephalus demonstrate deficits in the metacognitive process involved in their learning and memory. This again highlights the impact of executive dysfunction on aspects of learning and recall [27, 28].

Adolescents and adults

Adolescents and adults with SB and hydrocephalus have poorer memory overall than both normal individuals and those with occult spina bifida. Nondeclarative memory, semantic memory, and working memory processes requiring response inhibition are generally intact. Episodic declarative memory and working memory processes involving high information retention and flexibility are significantly weaker [29].

Young adults with SB can have difficulty learning and recalling word lists, and often have poor spatial memory [30]. This impacts such opportunities as developing independence in travel. Overall, while memory processes are developmentally stable in many individuals with SB from childhood to young adulthood, problems with prospective memory, working memory, and components of episodic memory have been reported.

Academic achievement

Infants and children

Research has shown that children with SB often show deficits with both reading, specifically comprehension, and math; however, math ability is more typically impaired. Additionally, upper-level lesions, which are associated with poorer cognitive outcomes, are linked with demonstration of greater academic difficulties. Furthermore, children with upper-level lesion SB who come from disadvantaged socioeconomic backgrounds are found to be at the greatest risk for poor academic outcomes [2].

In children with SB, specific deficits have been demonstrated in math accuracy, speed, and strategy-use. These deficits have been related to poorer procedural knowledge, inattentive slips, a slower retrieval of math facts, and less mature strategies to solve problems. Children with SB also show increased vulnerability to interference when completing sets of math problems, suggesting difficulties with perception and self-organization that inhibit retrieval and lead to inaccuracy [31].

Adolescents and adults

Deficits in reading decoding and writing fluency seen in childhood continue to impact the academic performance of young adults [32]. In addition, deficits specific to executive function, memory, attention, motor functioning, and visual spatial ability contribute to an often increased pattern of academic impairment that is commonly seen in adolescence. The demands of high school require greater speed, autonomy, and organization, which is difficult to maintain without academic and parental supports and accommodations. Academic strategies should focus on strengthening organizational techniques, providing resource support in their areas of weakness, and providing psychological supports to minimize depressive and anxious symptoms that may accompany their frustrations with school [32].

Psychosocial adaptation

Psychosocial adjustment

Infants and children

Higher incidences of both internalizing and externalizing behavior problems have been reported by parents of children with SB as compared to typically developing children [33]. Children with higher verbal aptitude, autonomy in the classroom, behavioral regulation, physical appearance, parental support, and coping mechanisms showed better psychological outcomes over time [34]. In addition, medical problems associated with SB including issues with medication, shunt revisions, and continence, among others, place children at risk for psychological problems [35].

Children with SB have also shown increased psychosocial and behavioral comorbidities, including attention deficit hyperactivity disorder (ADHD) and oppositional defiant disorder (ODD) [36]. Better coping mechanisms are associated with improved behavioral outcomes in children and positive family psychosocial characteristics [34, 37].

Adolescents and adults

Holmbeck and Shapera's [38] contextual model regarding adolescent development and psychological adjustment posits that interpersonal relationships, such as family and friends, mediate the relationship between the changes of adolescence and their eventual developmental outcomes. Early puberty in girls with SB has been associated with higher risk for depression, substance abuse, eating disorders, family arguments, and sexual promiscuity [39]. Circumstances such as the inability to obtain a driver's license and the impact of having weaker social skills contribute to poor peer relations and social isolation, which place adolescents with SB at risk for developing internalizing symptoms.

Greater levels of social activities and inclusion are associated with higher levels of self-esteem. In general, the medical, psychological, and social demands on individuals with SB are associated with a greater risk for developing internalizing symptoms including depression, anxiety, feelings of guilt, suicidal thoughts, and somatic complaints [37, 40].

Social adjustment

Infants and children

Children with SB are at significant risk for peer difficulties. They tend to be socially immature and have fewer friends. They are also involved in fewer extracurricular and social activities, which can then hamper the development of better social skills. Children with SB may show highly dependent behavior and require adult guidance for decision-making and interpersonal direction; this serves to diminish opportunities for age-cohort interactions and opportunities for making independent choices. In social and school settings, these children often exhibit less intrinsic motivation, increased passivity, a lack of assertiveness, less involvement in social discussions and conversations, and less confidence in their abilities [37]. Children's social passivity may be linked with their nonverbal deficits (i.e. nonverbal cues) which limit their understanding of social exchanges and intentions [36]; it may also reflect weaknesses in executive skill development. In general, children with more cognitive, physical, and medical problems have poorer social competence and greater levels of social isolation [41].

Adolescents and adults

Differences with regard to behavioral autonomy and physical appearance between adolescents with SB and their peers cause anxiety about peer conformity [42]. Poor peer relationships, cognitive difficulties, reduced motor abilities, and other medical complications are associated with reduced independence and poorer social skills in adulthood. Individuals who are intermittently employed and not involved in advanced educational programs have fewer opportunities to socialize. Adults with greater levels of autonomy and social support and intimacy have higher levels of emotional adjustment, and a better quality of life. Interestingly, they have also been shown to have more persistent adherence to medical treatment [43], which may mediate their opportunities for independence.

Family functioning

Infants and children

The clinical symptoms associated with SB put intensive physical, psychological, and social demands on the children and families involved, placing them at risk for increased levels of psychosocial problems and family distress [37]. As a result, parents of children with SB have elevated psychosocial concerns [44]. Research has shown that the parenting environment is crucial to the developmental outcomes of children [45], particularly children with medical and neurodevelopmental concerns. Responsive parenting is directly associated with better development of cognitive and language skills in young children with SB [46]. However, low family socioeconomic status, risk of child developmental delays, and poor social skill and support of the parent impact the caregiver's ability to appropriately parent and respond to the child [47].

Adolescents and adults

Family conflict and parenting stress in families of adolescents with SB are significant predictors of less adaptive parenting behaviors and poor adolescent outcomes longitudinally [48]. Positive parenting practices are important predictors of adolescent adjustment and resilience [49]. Additionally, regarding the adolescent with SB in an age-appropriate manner and providing the appropriate level of care and supervision to medical activities, including increased independence in medical decision-making, can also influence adolescents' self-esteem and autonomy. Overall, familial support and encouragement is associated with better opportunities for adult employment, positive social skills, and community independence [50].

Environmental issues

Infants and children

As noted in several domains above, socioeconomic status (SES) has been directly linked with poor developmental outcomes in infants and children with SB. Children with SB from lower SES backgrounds show reduced academic achievement and greater risk for developmental problems [51]. Families from low SES environments often have more conflict and less unity and solidity [52], which impacts opportunities for developing independence and increasing autonomy.

Adolescents and adults

Making the transition from pediatric health care to an appropriate adult medical care can be stressful on both the young adult and their family [53]. A gradual transition in services that is premeditated and well planned can result in a more positive health care management experience [54]. Similarly, educational transitions benefit from careful discussion and review, with communication regarding accommodations and physical support needs being crucial. Additionally, participation in vocational training can be beneficial to the development of education and employment goals [55]. Increased independence in the activities of daily living is associated with a higher likelihood of independent living opportunities and success [20]. Assistive technology to improve mobility, cognitive dysfunction, and other disabilities may also prove beneficial to enhancing independence [56]. Consideration of family resources, based on SES, is not to be shied away from by the transition team and the individual with SB. The need for potential support services and explorations of how to best provide and pay for these services must be openly considered.

The role of neuropsychology

Assessment

Infants and children

The neuropsychological assessment can provide crucial information regarding the cognitive, academic, and psychological delays of the child with SB. Cognitive changes can signal problems with shunt insertions and help guide medical treatment. Additionally, early assessment can identify delays and guide intervention efforts early in the child's life [57].

Adolescents and adults

The neuropsychologist can continue to be beneficial throughout the adolescent and adult years. The neuropsychologist can provide evaluations of cognitive, academic, and psychological functioning to understand the individual's strengths and weaknesses. This can guide academic interventions, employment decisions, rehabilitation choices, medical interventions, and therapeutic options. Additionally, the neuropsychologist can provide education regarding barriers to individual functioning and act as an advocate with regard to accommodations in school and employment settings, as well as supporting financial planning through the identification of ongoing life skill needs.

Therapy

Infants and children

Identification of significant developmental delays through neuropsychological testing can help guide children towards early intervention (EI) services. Additionally, parenting training programs which promote responsive parenting practices can help promote better developmental and psychological outcomes in children with SB [58].

Adolescents and adults

Identification of depressed or anxious psychological profiles as a result of neuropsychological testing can help guide individuals with SB towards supportive therapeutic services. Neuropsychologists can assist therapy providers in facilitating an appropriate method of intervention to meet the cognitive, psychological, behavioral, and social needs of the young adult. Family interventions and therapy may also be beneficial to help promote familial support and encouragement.

Future directions

This chapter has reviewed and highlighted the core deficits and strengths across the lifespan for individuals with SB, as identified in the previous two chapters. Although research concerning aspects of development and intervention for individuals with SB and hydrocephalus has become increasingly comprehensive, there remain several areas which have not been fully examined that require ongoing additional research. Research examining the importance of preparing children and adults with SB for the multitude of medical procedures that they may encounter is essentially absent from the literature. While interventions such as medical play, having a parent involved in the process, and verbal explanations of medical procedures in child-friendly terms have all been thought to be beneficial in reducing anxiety and stress, there have surprisingly been few formal studies conducted examining these types of intervention for children with SB [59].

Longitudinal research involving responsive versus less involved parenting and their long-term effects on development in children with SB should also be conducted. Studies to date have suggested that responsive parenting is highly influential with regard to the development of greater success and independence; however, it is uncertain how titrations in responsivity over time actually contribute to increased self-control and effectiveness. This remains an important area of research with regard to understanding how to best promote self-efficacy and success with independence in persons with SB.

Additionally, longitudinal studies examining early cognitive, social, and emotional deficits and later functioning (i.e. through adulthood) remain necessary, particularly given the variabilities in development that are observed. Understanding brain development through the use of functional imaging technologies, and how they may elucidate structure–function relationships across the life span, could lead to greater understanding of the patterns of cognitive deficit observed, given differing types of SB, as well as the influence of associated neurological insults, and their long-term effects on capability. For example, research differentiating between individuals with hydrocephalus secondary to SB and those with congenital hydrocephalus has suggested that there are significant variabilities in outcome [60]. By examining the differing trajectories in neural development, better predictions may be possible regarding potential patterns of neuropsychological development and achievement. Similarly, research examining the treatment procedures utilized beginning in childhood, which can lead to optimal functioning and appropriate transitions into adulthood, remains needed.

Future research should focus on the numerous differential outcomes that exist between individuals with SB. Having a better understanding of the direct associations between early cognitive, psychological, social, and environmental influences and later outcomes could help guide interventions. Furthermore, an examination of intervention methods available at the adult level that promote employment and adaptive skills should be conducted to determine which interventions are appropriate for the level of independence, cognition, and psychological health of the individual.

References

1. Charney EB. Neural tube defects: Spina bifida and myelomeningocele. In Batshaw ML, Perret YM, eds. *Children with Disabilities: A Medical Primer.* Baltimore: Brookes; 1992: 471–88.

2. Fletcher JM, Copeland K, Frederick JA, et al. Spinal lesion level in spina bifida: A source of neural and cognitive heterogeneity. *J Neurosurg* 2005;**102**:268–79.

3. Juranek J, Fletcher JM, Hasan KM, et al. Neocortical reorganization in spina bifida. *Neuroimage* 2008;**40**:1516–22.

4. Del Bigio MR. Neuropathological changes caused by hydrocephalus. *Acta Neuropathol (Berl)* 1993;**85**:573–85.

5. Del Bigio MR. Cellular damage and prevention in childhood hydrocephalus. *Brain Pathol* 2004;**14**:317–24.

6. Mahone EM, Zabel TA, Levey E, et al. Parent and self-report ratings of executive function in adolescents with myelomeningocele and hydrocephalus. *Child Neuropsychol* 2002;**8**:258–70.

7. Fletcher JM, Brookshire BL, Landry SH, et al. Attentional skills and executive functions in children with early hydrocephalus. *Dev Neuropsychol* 1996;**12**:53–76.

8. Taylor HB, Landry SH, Cohen L, et al. *Early information processing among infants with spina bifida*. Presented at the 34th annual meeting of International Neuropsychological Society in Boston, MA, 2006.

9. Dennis M, Landry SH, Barnes M, et al. A model of neurocognitive function in spina bifida over the life span. *J Int Neuropsychol Soc* 2006;**12**:285–96.

10. Fletcher JM, Bohan TP, Brandt ME, et al. Morphometric evaluation of the hydrocephalic brain: relationship with cognitive development. *Childs Nerv Syst* 1996;**12**:192–99.

11. Dennis M, Edelstein K, Frederik J, et al. Peripersonal spatial attention in children with spina bifida: Associations between horizontal and vertical line bisection and congenital malformations of the corpus callosum, midbrain, and posterior cortex. *Neuropsychologia* 2005;**43**:2000–10.

12. Snow JH. Executive processes for children with spina bifida. *Child Health Care* 1999;**28**:241–53.

13. Tarazi R, Mahone EM, Zabel TA. Self-care independence in children with neurological disorders: An interactional model of adaptive demands and executive dysfunction. *Rehabilitation Psychology* 2007;**52**:196–205.

14. Mahone EM, Slomine BS. Managing dysexecutive disorders. In Hunter SJ, Donders J, eds. *Pediatric Neuropsychological Intervention*. New York: Cambridge University Press; 2007: 287–313.

15. Dennis M, Jacennik B, Barnes MA. The content of narrative discourse in children and adolescents after early-onset hydrocephalus and in normally developing age peers. *Brain Lang* 1994;**46**:129–65.

16. Dennis M, Hendrick EB, Hoffman HJ, et al. The language of hydrocephalic children. *J Clin Exp Neuropsychol* 1987;**9**:593–621.

17. McDonald CM. Rehabilitation of children with spina dysraphism. *Neurosurg Clin N Am* 1995;**6**:393.

18. Miall RC, Reckess GZ, Imamizu H. The cerebellum coordinates eye and hand tracking movements. *Nat Neurosci* 2001;**4**:638–44.

19. Landry SH, Lomax-Bream L, Barnes M. The importance of early motor and visual functioning for later cognitive skills in preschoolers with and without spina bifida. *J Int Neuropsychol Soc* 2003;**9**:176.

20. Verhoef M, Barf HA, Post MW, et al. Functional independence among young adults with spina bifida, in relation to hydrocephalus and level of lesion. *Dev Med Child Neurol* 2006;**48**:114–19.

21. Lennerstrand G, Gallo JE, Samuelsson L. Neuro-ophthalmological findings in relation to CNS lesion in patients with myelomeningocele. *Dev Med Child Neurol* 1990;**32**:423–31.

22. Dennis M, Fletcher JM, Rogers T, et al. Object-based and action-based visual perception in children with spina bifida and hydrocephalus. *J Int Neuropsychol Soc* 2002;**8**:95–106.

23. Rourke BP. The syndrome of nonverbal learning disabilities: developmental manifestations in neurological disease, disorder, and dysfunction. *Clinical Neuropsychol* 1988;**2**:293–330.

24. Hommet C, Billard C, Gillet P, et al. Neuropsychologic and adaptive functioning in adolescents and young adults shunted for congenital hydrocephalus. *J Child Neurol* 1999;**14**:144–50.

25. Dennis M, Rogers T, Barnes, MA. Children with spina bifida perceive visual illusions but not multistable figures. *Brain Cogn* 2002;**46**:108–13.

26. Yeates KO, Enrile BG. Implicit and explicit memory in children with congenital and acquired brain disorder. *Neuropsychology* 2005;**19**:618–28.

27. Scott MA, Fletcher JM, Brookshire BL, et al. Memory functions in children with early hydrocephalus. *Neuropsychology* 1998;**12**:578–89.

28. Yeates KO, Enrile BG, Loss N, et al. Verbal learning and memory in children with myelomeningocele. *J Pediatric Psychol* 1995;**20**:801–15.

29. Dennis M, Jewell D, Drake J, et al. Prospective, declarative, and nondeclarative memory in young adults with spina bifida. *J Int Neuropsychol Soc* 2007;**13**:312–23.

30. Barf HA, Verhoef M, Jennekens-Schinkel A, et al. Cognitive status of young adults with spina bifida. *Dev Med Child Neurol* 2003;**45**:813–20.

31. Barnes MA, Wilkinson M, Boudousquie A, et al. Arithmetic processing in children with spina bifida: calculation accuracy, strategy use, and fact retrieval fluency. *J Learn Disabil* 2006;**39**:174–87.

32. Barnes MA, Dennis M, Hetherington R. Reading and writing skills in young adults with spina bifida and hydrocephalus. *J Int Neuropsychol Soc* 2004;**10**:680–8.

33. Lemanek KL, Jones ML, Lieberman B. Mothers of children with spina bifida: adaptational and stress processing. *Children's Health Care* 2000;**29**:19–35.

34. Coakley RM, Holmbeck GN, Bryant FB. Constructing a prospective model of psychosocial adaptation in young adolescents with spina bifida: an application of optimal data analysis. *J Pediatr Psychol* 2006;**31**:1084–99.

35. Moore C, Kogan BA, Parekh A. Impact of urinary incontinence on self-concept in children with spina bifida. *J Urol* 2004;**171**:1659–62.

36. Fletcher JM, Brookshire BL, Landry SH, et al. Behavioral adjustment of children with hydrocephalus: relationships with etiology, neurological, and family status. *J Pediatr Psychol* 1995;**20**:109–25.

37. Holmbeck GN, Westhoven VC, Shapera WE, et al. A multi-method, multi-informant, and multi-dimensional perspective on psychosocial adjustment in pre-adolescents with spina bifida. *J Consult Clin Psychol* 2003;**71**:782–96.

38. Holmbeck GN, Shapera WE. Research methods with adolescents. In Kendall PC, Butcher JN, Holmbeck GN, eds. *Handbook of Research Methods in Clinical Psychology, 2nd Edn*. New York: Wiley; 1999: 634–61.

39. Blum R. Chronic illness and disability in adolescence. *J Adolesc Health* 1992;**13**:364–8.

40. Wolman C, Basco DE. Factors influencing self-esteem and self-consciousness in adolescents with spina bifida. *J Adolesc Health* 1994;**15**:543–8.

41. Nassau JH, Drotar D. Social competence among children with central nervous system-related chronic health conditions: a review. *J Pediatr Psychol* 1997;**22**:771–93.

42. Friedman D, Holmbeck GN, DeLucia C, et al. Trajectories of autonomy development across the adolescent transition in children with spina bifida. *Rehabil Psychol* 2009;**54**:16–27.

43. Sawin KJ, Brei TJ, Buran CF. Factors associated with quality of life in adolescents with spina bifida. *J Holist Nurs* 2002;**20**:279–304.

44. Holmbeck GN, Gorey-Ferguson L, Hudson T, et al. Maternal, paternal, and marital functioning in families of preadolescents with spina bifida. *J Pediatr Psychol* 1997;**22**:167–81.

45. Landry SH, Smith KE, Miller-Loncar CL, et al. Predicting cognitive-linguistic and social growth curves from early maternal behaviors in children at varying degrees of biological risk. *Dev Psychol* 1997;**33**:1–14.

46. Lomax-Bream L, Taylor HB, Landry SH, et al. Role of early parenting and motor skills on development in children with spina bifida. *J Appl Dev Psychol* 2007;**28**(3):250–63.

47. Vermaes I, Gerris J, Jansses J. Parents' social adjustment in families of children with spina bifida: A theory-driven review. *J Pediatr Psychol* 2007;**32**:1214–26.

48. Greenley RN, Holmbeck GN, Rose BM. Predictors of parenting behavior trajectories among families of young adolescents with and without spina bifida. *J Pediatric Psychol* 2006;**31**:1057–71.

49. Friedman D, Holmbeck GN, Jandasek B, et al. Parent functioning in families of preadolescents with spina bifida: longitudinal implications for child adjustment. *J Fam Psychol* 2004;**18**:609–19.

50. Loomis JW, Javornisky JG, Monahan JJ, et al. Relations between family environment and adjustment outcomes in young adults with spina bifida. *Dev Med Child Neurol* 1997;**39**:620–7.

51. Natriello G, McDill EL, Pallas AM. *Schooling Disadvantaged Children: Racing Against Catastrophe*. New York: Teachers College Press; 1990.

52. Holmbeck GN, Coakley RM, Hommeyer JS, et al. Observed and perceived dyadic and systemic functioning in families of preadolescents with spina bifida. *J Pediatr Psychol* 2002;**27**:177–89.

53. Buran CF, McDaniel AM, Brei TJ. Needs assessment in a spina bifida program: a comparison of the perceptions by adolescents with spina bifida and their parents. *Clin Nurse Spec* 2002;**16**:256–62.

54. Bailey S, O'Connell B, Pearce J. The transition from paediatric to adult health care services for children with acquired or congenital disorders. *Aust Health Rev* 2003;**26**:64–9.

55. Wagner MM, Blackorby J. Transition from high school to work or college: how special education students fare. *Future Child* 1996;**6**:103–20.

56. Johnson KL, Dudgeon B, Kuehn C, et al. Assistive technology use among adolescents and young adults with spina bifida. *Am J Public Health* 2007;**97**:330–6.

57. Barnes MA, Smith-Chant B, Landry SH. Number processing in neurodevelopmental disorders: spina bifida myelomeningocele. In Campbell JID, ed. *Handbook of Mathematical Cognition*. New York: Psychology Press; 2005: 299–314.

58. Landry SH, Smith KE, Swank PR, et al. Responsive parenting: the optimal timing of an intervention across early childhood. *Dev Psychol* in press.

59. Salmon K. Commentary. Preparing children for medical procedures: taking account of memory. *J Pediatr Psychol* 2006;**31**:859–61.

60. Lacy M, Pyykkonen BA, Hunter SJ, et al. Intellectual functioning in children with early-shunted post-hemorrhagic hydrocephalus. *Pediatric Neurosurg* 2008;**44**:376–81.

Cerebral palsy across the lifespan

Seth Warschausky, Desiree White and Marie Van Tubbergen

Introduction

Definition

In one of the earlier definitions of cerebral palsy (CP), Bax described CP as "A disorder of movement and posture due to a defect or lesion of the immature brain" [1]. Over the decades, it became apparent that greater precision in the definition was needed to improve the accuracy and consistency of diagnosis and to enhance communication among researchers and health care providers. In 2004, the workgroup of the International Workshop on Definition and Classification of Cerebral Palsy undertook this challenge [2]. Motor impairment continued to be recognized as the central feature of CP, but the workgroup also appreciated the limitations of defining the disorder exclusively on this basis. It was recommended that a multidimensional and multidisciplinary approach be used to redefine CP, resulting in the following definition:

> Cerebral palsy (CP) describes a group of permanent disorders of the development of movement and posture, causing activity limitation, that are attributed to non-progressive disturbances that occurred in the developing fetal or infant brain. The motor disorders of cerebral palsy are often accompanied by disturbances of sensation, perception, cognition, communication, and behaviour, by epilepsy, and by secondary musculoskeletal problems.

The workgroup provided a detailed rationale for each of the terms composing its definition, several of which are of interest to the neuropsychologist [2]. For example, "permanent" reflects the persistence of CP throughout the lifespan, although the clinical presentation may evolve as individuals with CP age. Limits were not placed on "development", but it was noted that motor impairments usually appear before 18 months of age. Of particular relevance to neuropsychology, "accompanied by" was included in the definition to acknowledge the frequent occurrence of concomitant disorders and impairments in nonmotor domains (e.g., cognition and behavior). Depending on the subtype of CP, accompanying impairments are present in 25 to 80% of cases [3].

Classification

As the definition of CP evolved over time, so did the classification of subtypes of CP. For many years, classification was based on a system developed in Sweden [4]. An understanding of this system is important because all but the most recent studies used it as the basis for classification. In this system, CP is divided into spastic, dyskinetic, ataxic, and mixed subtypes, each reflecting the presence of specific abnormalities in muscle tone and/or movement. In spastic CP, an abnormal increase in muscle tone (hypertonicity) results in rigidity. Spastic CP is further subdivided based on variations in the distribution of hypertonicity across the affected limbs. Specifically, diplegia primarily affects the legs, quadriplegia affects all limbs (although the legs tend to be more involved), and hemiplegia primarily affects the arm and leg on one side of the body. Dyskinetic CP affects all limbs and the trunk of the body. This subtype is further divided on the basis of movement and postural abnormalities (e.g. choreoform, dystonic). Ataxic CP is characterized by an abnormal decrease in muscle tone (hypotonicity), as well as impairments in balance, coordination, and gait. Finally, mixed CP is self-explanatory, reflecting the presence of more than one subtype of CP.

More recently, the working group of the International Workshop on Definition and Classification of Cerebral Palsy provided guidance regarding the classification of CP [2]. This system is largely consistent with that of the collaborative group for the Surveillance of Cerebral Palsy in Europe [5]. In the new classification system, four key dimensions were considered [2]. In the first dimension, "motor abnormality" was recognized as the central feature of CP. It was recommended that classification be based on the predominant type of tone or movement abnormality, with less-prominent abnormalities listed secondarily. Thus, use of the term "mixed" was discarded. It was also suggested that the severity of motor abnormalities be graded using scales specifically designed for this purpose. For example, the Gross Motor Function Classification System [6] and the Bimanual Fine Motor Function Scale [7] may be used to grade the severity of restrictions in ambulation and upper extremity function, respectively. The second dimension of importance in classifying CP was "accompanying impairment", which includes epilepsy, cognitive deficits, behavioral or emotional difficulties, and impairments in vision or audition. It was suggested that the presence or absence, as well as the severity, of such limitations be recorded. The third dimension considered was "anatomical and neuroimaging findings". The workgroup recommended that the terms "unilateral" and "bilateral" be paired with a description of the type of motor impairment observed. As such, spastic diplegia and spastic quadriplegia were replaced with bilateral spastic CP, and spastic hemiplegia was replaced with unilateral spastic CP. In addition, it was recommended that neuroimaging be conducted and findings reported when possible. Finally, "cause and timing" were considered, with the recommendation that probable causative events and the timeframe of such events be reported, with the understanding that it is frequently impossible to identify the causative antecedents of CP.

Epidemiology and etiology

Recent reviews indicate that the worldwide prevalence of CP is over 2/1000 live births [3, 8]. The reported prevalence of subtypes of CP varies, but findings from most epidemiological studies are relatively consistent with those of a large-scale survey conducted by the collaborative group for the Surveillance of Cerebral Palsy in Europe [9]. Data were examined from approximately 5000 children with CP born between 1976 and 1990 in eight European countries. Among these children, 55% had bilateral spastic CP, 29% had unilateral spastic CP, 7% had dyskinetic CP, 4% had ataxic CP, and 4% had CP of unknown subtype. In addition, 31% of children in the sample had severe intellectual impairment (i.e. IQ < 50), 21% had epilepsy, 11% had severe visual impairment, and there were more males than females (ratio of 1.33:1).

The etiology of CP is varied and, as noted earlier, in many instances it is not possible to determine the cause of CP. That said, several predominant antecedents of CP have been identified. In industrialized nations, prematurity and low birthweight are often associated with CP. Children born between 32 and 42 weeks gestation and below the 10th percentile in birthweight are 4 to 6 times more likely to be diagnosed with CP than are children of similar gestational age and average birthweight [3]. Birth plurality is another significant factor, as the prevalence of CP is approximately 2/1000 in singletons, 13/1000 in twins, and 45/1000 in triplets [3].

In developing nations, the etiology of CP is dominated by different factors [8]. Due to less sophisticated medical care, survival is limited among children born prematurely or of low birthweight, and CP is more often related to perinatal asphyxia and maternal complications. There is also a higher prevalence of postnatally acquired CP due to factors such as infection and head injury.

Neuropathology

Four types of brain abnormality are typically associated with CP: white matter damage, cortical and subcortical lesions, brain malformations, and postnatal injuries [3]. In a review of MRI and CT studies, it was estimated that brain abnormalities are detectable in 80–90% of children across all subtypes of CP [10]. Abnormal white matter, typically periventricular leukomalacia (PVL), is the most common finding and occurs in 38% of cases. Disrupted development of the corpus callosum has been associated with PVL. Among individuals with bilateral spastic, dyskinetic, or ataxic CP, 65% have abnormalities confined to the white matter. Combined abnormalities in the white and gray matter are most often found in individuals with unilateral spasticity, occurring in 31% of these cases. Brain malformations, usually resulting from disruption of the migration of neurons, and damage confined to the gray matter are less common, occurring in 10% and 6% of CP cases, respectively. Additional features include ventriculomegaly (enlarged ventricles), abnormalities in cerebrospinal space, and cerebral atrophy. It is important to note that no brain abnormalities are identified using MRI or CT in almost 20% of individuals with CP, and further research is needed to understand the neuropathology underlying CP in these cases. Neuroimaging findings suggest that approximately one-third of CP is associated with pre-natal insult, 40% with perinatal insult, and the remainder occurring post-natally [10].

Impairments

Apart from gross motor impairments, individuals with CP are at significant risk for impairments in multiple aspects of body structure and function that affect development, participation and adult outcomes. Complex neuropsychological risks are described in a separate section. Neurological impairments include epilepsy, with the highest risk associated with hemiplegic CP [11].

Sensory impairments are prevalent in this population. Visual impairments are present in a majority of persons with CP, with differing risk by subtype [12, 13]. Vision is abnormal in about 80% of children with quadriplegia, strabismus is common among children with diplegia, and visual field defects are noted in approximately 25% of children with hemiplegia. Hearing impairments, although not as common, occur in a significant percentage of children with CP and are quite common in children with quadriplegia. There is also increasing evidence of impaired proprioception in children with CP, and findings suggest complex age and laterality effects [14].

Additional areas of impairment have been noted as well. Oromotor function is frequently impaired, adversely affecting the development of speech and feeding, placing individuals with CP at risk for aspiration. Evidence suggests that almost 50% of children with quadriplegia have feeding difficulties [12]. Comorbid impairments are noted in other domains, including gastrointestinal and genitourinary functions, as well as growth [13]. Clearly, there is a complex set of needs associated with CP comorbidities that require a multidisciplinary approach to assessment and intervention.

Neuropsychology

CP is a highly heterogeneous disorder in terms of clinical presentation, etiology, neuropathology, and comorbid impairments. Most research has focused on cognition in children with bilateral spastic CP or groups of children in which subtypes of CP are combined. Studies focusing solely on dyskinetic or ataxic CP are rare. Thus, as Fennell and Dikel noted in their discussion of cognition across various subtypes of CP, the complexity of the disorder makes it "… difficult, if not impossible, to make satisfactory generalizations

about the relationship of cerebral palsy and cognitive functioning" [15]. In addition to the difficulty in making generalizations about CP, our knowledge of function in specific cognitive domains is quite limited. Although intelligence (IQ) has been examined in a considerable number of studies, there is a great need for additional research examining specific aspects of cognition such as memory, language, and executive abilities.

The following discussion focuses on both general and specific aspects of cognition. Rather than providing an exhaustive review, findings from a sampling of studies have been selected to demonstrate issues of importance in understanding the neuropsychology of CP.

Intelligence

The distribution of IQ among individuals with CP spans the full range. At the group level, however, older versions of the Wechsler scales showed that Full Scale IQ (FSIQ), Verbal Scale IQ (VSIQ), and Performance Scale IQ (PSIQ) were reduced in comparison with typically developing children, with PSIQ particularly affected. This pattern is demonstrated by findings from a study in which the Wechsler Preschool and Primary Scale of Intelligence was administered to 127 Icelandic children with all subtypes of CP (82% bilateral spastic) [16]. The median FSIQ, VSIQ, and PSIQ were 84, 92, and 77, respectively, with 40% of children having FSIQs below 70. More severe motor impairment was associated with lower IQ. That said, the combination of degree of motor impairment and history of epilepsy accounted for 22% of the variance in IQ, indicating that motor impairment is not a perfect predictor of intellect. Further, as will be discussed in detail later in the chapter, there is concern regarding the accuracy to which the cognitive abilities of individuals with significant motoric impairments can be measured.

A few studies have been conducted to examine possible neuroimaging and medical correlates of IQ. Ultrasound is often used to determine the extent and location of brain damage in neonates, but the severity of ultrasound findings does not predict IQs that are obtained later in childhood in individuals with CP [17]. On the other hand, MRI findings of ventricular enlargement, reduced periventricular white matter, and thinning of the corpus callosum have been significantly correlated with FSIQ and PSIQ (but not VSIQ) [18]. Medical variables may be of greater importance in terms of predicting IQ. In a study of children with unilateral spastic CP, lesion laterality failed to correlate significantly with any IQ; in contrast, the FSIQ, VSIQ, and PSIQ of children with seizures were significantly lower than those of children without seizures [19]. IQs also tend to be decrease to a greater degree as the severity of CP increases [3].

Psychomotor speed

Given the clinical presentation of CP, it is not surprising that impairments in psychomotor speed are extremely common. It is important to note that impairments have been identified using not only tests requiring speeded manual responses [20], but also using those requiring oral [21] and ocular [20] responses. As such, it is crucial that the contribution of psychomotor speed be considered when interpreting the results of either timed tests or untimed tests that place significant demands of motor output, regardless of the specific cognitive domain being assessed.

Attention

Impairments in selective visual attention have been identified in children with CP [22, 23]. Attention deficit hyperactivity disorder (ADHD) is also more common than in the general population, and it has been estimated that 19% of children with CP carry this diagnosis [24]. Few studies have examined the utility of pharmacological treatment in individuals with a dual diagnosis of ADHD and CP. In one such study, however, teacher ratings on the Abbreviated Conners' Rating Scale indicated that 4 weeks of treatment with methylphenidate significantly improved ADHD symptomatology in children with CP and ADHD [25]. Thus, although further research is needed to thoroughly examine the issue, drug therapies hold promise for alleviating at least some of the impairments in attention that are associated with CP.

Executive abilities

Executive abilities represent an assemblage of cognitive processes (e.g. strategic processing, working memory, and inhibitory control) that facilitate higher-order thought and action. Little research has been conducted in which executive abilities were the primary focus of investigation in individuals with CP. Results from studies using large test batteries or assessing other domains of cognition, however, provide evidence of impairments in children with CP.

For example, on the Tower test of the NEPSY, the strategic planning of children with CP was found to be poorer than that of controls [17]. Similarly, in examining learning and memory using the California Verbal Learning Test – Children's Version, it was found that children with CP strategically clustered semantically related words less often than controls [26]. Thus, these limited findings indicate that strategic processing is an area of concern.

Findings regarding working memory are mixed. Jenks and colleagues found that children with CP had lower scores than controls on forward digit span, backward digit span, and one-syllable word span [27]. In contrast, White and colleagues [21] found that memory span for one-, two-, and three-syllable words was comparable for children with bilateral spastic CP and controls. Further research is needed to determine the reason for the discrepancy in these findings, as is research assessing working memory for different types of materials (e.g. verbal versus nonverbal) that are presented in different modalities (e. g. visual versus auditory).

In terms of inhibitory control, a study focusing on this facet of executive ability provided converging evidence from three tasks that pointed to impairment in children with bilateral spastic CP [20]. Using a Stroop paradigm, it was shown that children with CP were slower than typically developing controls when required to inhibit a prepotent reading response and instead name the color in which words were printed. In another task, children viewed lateralized stimuli and were asked to respond manually by pressing a key either on the same side as the stimuli or on the opposite side. On this task, children with CP made more errors than controls when the prepotent same-sided response had to be suppressed in favor of the opposite-sided response. Finally, using an antisaccade task it was shown that children with CP were both slower and made more errors than controls when asked to move their eyes in the direction opposite to that of a lateralized stimulus. Thus, the impairment in inhibitory control was apparent regardless of response modality (oral, manual, or ocular).

Learning and memory

To thoroughly characterize learning and memory in individuals with CP, it is important to appreciate the intricacies involved in acquiring, retaining, and retrieving information, as is demonstrated by findings from the following studies. For example, in a study in which the California Verbal Learning Test – Children's Version was administered, the performance of children with bilateral spastic CP was comparable to that of typically developing controls in terms of learning a list of words following a single presentation (i.e. Trial 1 recall) and retaining previously learned words over delay intervals (i.e. short- and long-delay recall) [26]. That said, children with CP exhibited poorer learning across repeated trials, such that fewer words were recalled following the fifth presentation of the list (i.e. Trial 5 recall) [26]. Children with CP also exhibited more false positive errors, particularly at younger ages when delayed recall was assessed using a recognition format. These results suggest that some aspects of learning and memory may be relatively well preserved, whereas others are significantly compromised in children with CP.

It is also important to consider the effects that presentation and response modality may have on learning and memory. To examine this issue, children with bilateral spastic CP were administered four paired associate tasks [28]. Stimuli and responses were either visual/nonverbal (designs) or auditory/verbal (words), with each possible combination of stimulus-response pairing represented in separate tasks (i.e. word-word, design-design, word-design, and design-word). Memory for the pairings was assessed using a multiple-choice recognition format, thereby minimizing motor demands. Results showed that children with CP recalled fewer pairings than controls only on the two tasks requiring visual/nonverbal responses, indicating a disproportionate compromise in learning and memory for visual/nonverbal material.

Learning and memory have also been examined in individuals with unilateral spastic CP, in this instance using subtests from the Wechsler Memory Scale to assess prose recall, verbal paired-associate learning, and memory for nonverbal designs [19]. Although the performance of individuals with CP was compromised compared with that of controls, the more interesting findings of this study arose when performance within the CP group was considered within the context of lesion laterality, lesion severity, and the presence or absence of seizures. A particularly interesting result was that neither lesion laterality nor lesion severity was related to performance on any of the memory subtests. This is surprising given that all of the individuals with CP had unilateral brain abnormalities that might be expected to differentially affect memory for

verbal versus nonverbal information. It also would have been reasonable to expect that more severe lesions would result in poorer performance, but this was not the case. The presence or absence of seizures, however, was a significant factor, in that individuals with CP and seizures performed more poorly than either controls or individuals with CP and no seizures. Thus, care must be taken in generalizing findings even within a group of individuals with a given subtype of CP.

Visual spatial and perceptual abilities

A substantial reduction in PSIQ has been one of the most ubiquitous findings in the CP literature. The majority of tests that assessed PSIQ placed considerable demands on visual spatial and perceptual abilities, and one might assume that poorer PSIQ reflected impairment in these abilities. It is important to remember, however, that many tests used to assess PSIQ also place considerable demands on psychomotor speed. As such, caution must be used in interpreting findings. When assessing visual spatial and perceptual abilities outside the context of determining IQ, it is preferable to administer untimed tests that minimize motor demands.

A study examining performance on the Developmental Test of Visual Perception in children with bilateral CP born preterm and full-term demonstrates the importance of independently evaluating visual motor and nonmotor visual perceptual abilities [29]. For children born preterm, overall performance was below average (median score of 79). When performance on subtests assessing visual motor versus nonmotor visual perceptual abilities was examined, an interesting pattern emerged. Median Visual-Motor Integration and Motor-Reduced Visual-Perceptual Quotients were 75 and 85, respectively. Thus, although both visual motor and nonmotor visual perceptual abilities were reduced in children born preterm, the impairment in visual motor ability was more pronounced.

An additional issue addressed in this study was gestational age [29]. In contrast with findings of impairment in children born preterm, the overall performance of children born full-term was average (median score of 103). In addition, there was no discrepancy between the Visual-Motor Integration and Motor-Reduced Visual-Perceptual Quotients (medians of 98 and 100, respectively). Because general cognitive and MRI findings were similar in the

209

preterm and full-term groups, these findings suggest that the effects of gestational age and CP may be independent and that the effects of each should be contrasted in studies of children with CP.

Language

A number of studies have shown that VSIQ is generally reduced in children with CP, but, as is the case for other domains of cognition, little research has been conducted to examine specific aspects of language. There is, however, some evidence of impairments in both expressive and receptive language abilities beyond those that are attributable to difficulties in speech [30]. For example, naming abilities, vocabulary knowledge, grammatical skills, and conceptual understanding of language have been identified as areas of deficit. In addition, problems in expressive and receptive language are more frequent in children with more severe CP or having IQs below 70.

Phonological awareness, the ability to consciously represent and reflect on phonological properties [31], is the most robust predictor of reading in the general population [32, 33]. It has generally been found that the performance of children with CP is comparable to that of typically developing controls on most tasks assessing phonological awareness [37, 38]. Larsson and Sandberg [34], however, showed that children with CP performed more poorly than controls on a visual rhyming task that required identification of rhyming words presented as pictures. In addition, in comparing the performance of typically developing children and children with anarthria, Card and Dodd found that children with CP and anarthria were poorer in detecting rhyme in written words, segmenting syllables, and manipulating phonemes [35]. Findings from these studies indicate that articulation may not be necessary for the development of many aspects of phonological awareness, but impaired or absent speech is associated with increased difficulty on some phonological tasks.

Academic abilities

Academic abilities are of crucial importance in terms of later vocational outcomes and, in turn, quality of life. It has been estimated that over 50% of children with spastic CP have either a learning disability or a specific learning impairment (e.g. dyslexia, dyscalculia) [24]. In spite of a clear need, there is a paucity of research in which predictors of academic outcomes have been examined in individuals with CP. For example, although reading is of fundamental importance to learning and participation in society, little research has been conducted to examine this ability in individuals with CP.

As noted earlier, phonological awareness is essential to the development of reading. In children with anarthria and CP, better phonological awareness is related to better reading [36]. Adequate development of phonological awareness early in childhood in children with CP, however, does not necessarily predict intact reading later in childhood. Thus, the relationship between phonological awareness and long-term reading outcomes among children with CP differs from that of typically developing children. More generally, these findings point to the need for ongoing assessment as individuals with CP age, as cognitive abilities and the interactions among cognitive abilities may change over time.

Few other aspects of academic ability have been examined in individuals with CP. In one of the few studies of this nature, predictors of mathematical ability (assessed by addition and subtraction accuracy) were examined in children with CP in both mainstream and special education classrooms [27]. Performance was compared with that of controls. Structural equation modeling revealed that mathematical ability was mediated by intelligence, working memory (memory span), early numeracy (counting and number concepts), and instruction time. Between-group comparisons indicated that mathematical ability was comparable for children with CP in mainstream classrooms and controls, whereas children with CP in special education classrooms performed more poorly. As such, a finding of particular concern was that children with CP in special education classrooms received less instruction in mathematics. These findings have clear implications for the education of children with CP, particularly those receiving special education services. Additional research is needed to guide the development of remediation programs to improve academic outcomes in individuals with CP.

Table 8.1 summarizes the key neurobehavioral characteristics of CP described in the preceding discussion.

Universal assessment issues

There is long-standing concern that motor and communicative impairments render traditional cognitive assessment instruments inaccessible and inaccurate. Losch and Dammann [37] examined a variety of

Table 8.1. Summary of neurobehavioral characteristics.

Intelligence
Generally reduced, with Performance Scale IQ particularly compromised. Greater risk of reduced IQs in presence of white matter abnormalities, ventricular enlargement, seizures, and increased severity of CP

Psychomotor speed
Impairments during speeded tasks requiring manual, oral, and ocular responses

Attention and executive abilities
Impairments in selective visual attention, planning, strategic processing, and inhibitory control. Mixed evidence regarding working memory

Learning and memory
Impairments in learning slope and increased interference by irrelevant information. Memory for nonverbal material particularly compromised. Likelihood of impairment increases in presence of seizures

Visual spatial and perceptual abilities
Impairments particularly evident if born preterm

Language
Impairments in both expressive and receptive abilities. Risk increases with greater severity of CP and IQ below 70

Academic abilities
Anarthria increases likelihood of impairment in phonological awareness and reading. Impairment in mathematical ability more pronounced if in special education

Behavior
Higher incidence of ADHD than in general population; pharmacological treatment may be beneficial. Risk for depression comparable to that of general population, with decreased risk in individuals with lower intellect. Social risks across the lifespan include less-frequent social contact and lower-quality friendships

cognitive tests and found that motor abilities accounted for 16% of the variance in scores obtained by children with CP, whereas a language/cognition factor accounted for 49% of the variance. The language/cognition factor included elements of articulation and speech, overlapping with and undifferentiated from general cognitive abilities. Thus, impairments in articulation and hand movement may negatively affect performance on measures purported to describe specific cognitive domains.

Techniques used to address the accessibility needs of individuals with CP have ranged from forced-choice formats [38] to the measurement of event-related brain potentials [39]. Although event-related potentials yield clinically relevant findings, their application requires expensive equipment and significant expertise. Forced-choice formats are effective for constraining response options, particularly in a clinical population that is experienced at this form of communication [38]. For example, Sabbadini and colleagues provided individuals with speech and motor impairments with three response option methods including multiple-choice, dichotomous yes/no responses, and sensor pointer techniques [40]. These methods allowed participation in neuropsychological assessment to a degree that limited cognitive profiles could be produced.

Developments in technology also provide opportunities for accommodated assessments. For example,

Raven's Coloured Progressive Matrices [41] is a standardized assessment tool that utilizes a multiple-choice response format presented in a booklet form. The examinee may either point to or state the number of their chosen answer. There are a number of strategies to accommodate speech and motor impairments with this task. Items may be presented on a computer screen using software that provides multiple-choice options, and examinees can utlize an AT device to indicate their choice (e.g. HeadMouse, pressure switch) [42]. However, adaptations may affect psychometric properties; further research is needed to identify reliable, valid, and accessible cognitive measures and assessment techniques.

Assessing choice-making capabilities

Children with significant speech and motor impairments may lack experience participating in an assessment milieu. In the previous example of Raven's Coloured Progressive Matrices [41], a child may have the sensory and motor skills necessary to participate but have little experience in systematically responding to questions that are unrelated to any aspect of the immediate environment. Children are expected to have an internal drive to demonstrate their knowledge and respond to the requests of the examiner. The child must be able to repeat this process many times to fully participate in the assessment. For children with significant speech and motor impairments, the expectations inherent in assessment may be unique in their daily experiences, as even accessible testing procedures rely upon consistent and reliable choice-making abilities.

Choice-making is often defined and assessed as the expression of personal preference, and constitutes a core concept of self-determination. For children diagnosed with CP who have a combination of motor, speech, and possible cognitive impairments, communicating basic knowledge also involves making a choice from predetermined options. Individuals may have only specified signals or gestures that are understood by others, and even someone highly proficient with augmentative and alternative communication will need to choose words or pictures from an array that displays a finite number of choices at any one time. Even invested communication partners may have difficulty distinguishing between the speech and motor impairments that preclude typical means of response (i.e. talking or gesturing) and the underlying cognitive abilities involved in making choices. It is therefore critical to accurately assess choice-making abilities across the spectrum of domains, including choice-making to express knowledge and skills, prior to formal cognitive assessment.

Case illustration

P, an 8-year-old female diagnosed with quadriplegic CP, was placed in a designated classroom for students with cognitive and physical impairments (multiple impairments). She was anarthric. Her cognitive abilities were estimated to be more than three standard deviations below the mean, although standardized assessments were perceived to be inaccessible. Parents and teachers consistently reported that P was "in there", as evidenced by her emotional reactions, which were often consistent with the content of higher-level conversations going on around her and her age-appropriate tastes in games and movies. P used specific eye movements to indicate yes and no, but questions posed to P were usually related to her activities and preferences. P used the eye movements to communicate with less familiar partners, but when asked to use eye movements to answer factual questions in an assessment context, P's responses were often inconsistent and/or ambiguous.

If P had access to an adapted version of Raven's Coloured Progressive Matrices and was competent in the use of a HeadMouse, the assessment may result in

conclusions that underestimate or otherwise misrepresent her actual abilities. It would be difficult to discern whether her errors resulted from deficits in intelligence, visuospatial skills, choice-making skills, or unidentified factors. If P chose her answers randomly when taking the test, or out of preference for her favorite design on the page, her score on the test is not solely an estimation of the targeted cognitive domains, but, at least in part, a measure of difficulty in using the presented format to make choices. Therefore, imprecise conceptualization and assessment of choice-making skills may weaken even the most thorough cognitive assessments or, worse yet, promote an assumption that speech and motor impairments preclude meaningful assessment or even the existence of complex cognitive abilities.

To date, there are few objective, systematic approaches toward conceptualization and assessment of choice-making abilities. Van Tubbergen and colleagues [43] propose a model showing a progression of skills involved in choice-making, and a framework for understanding the abilities that constitute the foundation for these skills and behaviors (Table 8.2). The model describes a hierarchy of behaviors beginning with the ability to focus attention on a stimulus, moving from general to specific signals to express preferences, and finally using specific signals to express concrete and abstract knowledge.

A conceptual hierarchy of choice-making abilities, independent of speech and motor abilities, will provide individuals and their families with significant benefits. Accurate identification of abilities would allow stakeholders to set concrete, realistic goals toward the next level of communicating choice and inform coordinated interventions to develop more advanced skills

Psychosocial development and quality of life

Population-based studies indicate that children with CP are at risk for psychosocial difficulties, although the majority exhibit adjustment similar to that of typically developing peers [44–46]. In a recent European study, approximately 26% of children with CP had significant psychosocial concerns [46]. Key predictors of psychosocial risk included better gross motor function, poorer intellect, greater pain, a sibling with disabilities and residence in a rural or smaller urban setting. Pain, experienced by most children with CP [47], has been shown to predict depression and lower health-related

Table 8.2. Model for the progression of choice-making skills [43].

Skill level	Skill description	Multiple choice	Yes / no
Orienting responsive	Will notice and attend, at least briefly, to novel stimulus		
Preference	Will communicate a general, affective response regarding personal preference	"Which picture do you like best?"	"Do you like this dog?"
Preference – advanced	Will communicate a specific response signal regarding personal preference	"Which picture do you like best?"	"Do you like this dog?"
Directed	Will communicate a specific response signal to questions unrelated to personal desires	"Which one is a fish?" "Which one is a dog?"	"Does this dog have a nose?" "Is this dog black?"
Prediction	Will communicate a specific response signal to questions requiring indirect application of knowledge	"Which one does not show an animal?" "Which one barks?"	"Is this an animal?" "Can he fly?"

quality of life. Regarding children's reports of psychosocial status, approximately 50% of children with CP can self-report information in multiple domains; importantly, there is relatively low parent–child concordance in perceptions of the child's emotional functioning, highlighting the importance of including the child perspective in clinical assessments [48].

Healthy social development is associated with academic success, positive psychological childhood adjustment and adult outcomes [49]. There is significant evidence that children with neurodevelopmental conditions are at increased risk for social developmental difficulties [50, 51]. Children with CP are at risk for impairments in prosocial behavior, as well as specific social problem-solving deficits [52, 53]. Regarding peer relations and friendships, recent findings indicate significant social risks in the regular classroom setting, with evidence of gender-specific risks associated with CP [54]. Girls with CP had weaker prosocial behavior, fewer reciprocated friendships, and were more isolated and victimized. Other findings have shown that children with congenital neurodevelopmental conditions (CP and spina bifida) have fewer friends, a higher percentage of adult friends, less contact with friends and self-reports of less validation and caring in their peer relationships; however, a recent community-based study did not find a significant interaction between gender and disability [55].

There is a paucity of research that examines social problem-solving skills in children with CP. In a preliminary study that compared the social problem-solving profiles of children with CP or spina bifida and children who sustained a head injury, similar difficulties were noted, including poorer ability to generate prosocial solutions to social problems [56]. Findings suggested that group differences in the neuropsychological correlates of social problem-solving skills included associations with executive functions in the congenital, but not the acquired neurodevelopmental condition group. There is evidence to suggest that level of intellect, in particular, mediates aspects of social development in children with congenital neurodevelopmental conditions. For example, Holmbeck and colleagues [57] found that lower intellect was associated with greater passivity in family interactions.

Family influences on social development

Parenting style differs in families of children with congenital neurodevelopmental conditions and cognitive impairments, including self-reports of less restrictive but also less nurturant attitudes in parenting [58, 59]. There is also evidence of less parental responsiveness in parents of children with cognitive impairments [60]. Parenting has an effect on children's development, with evidence from typically developing populations of both direct and indirect effects on social development [61]. Direct effects are noted in parents' efforts to facilitate social interactions with peers, whereas indirect effects stem from parenting characteristics and attitudes. There are few studies of these influences on the social development of children with CP; however, recent evidence suggests that there are important dissociations between parenting and the social development of children with CP. Thomas and colleagues [62] found no significant associations between parents' direct social facilitation efforts, such as setting up playdates, and children's social development. Similarly, Cunningham and colleagues [63] found that, controlling for intellect, there were no significant associations between indirect parenting factors and the social functioning of children with CP and spina bifida, although such associations were found in a typically developing sample. These findings may in part be related to the finding that greater parental overprotectiveness in families of children with spina bifida was associated with child intellect [57]. In families of children with congenital neurodevelopmental conditions, parenting style and attitude may be strongly influenced by specific child characteristics, perhaps more so than in the typically developing population. Findings suggest the need to modify current models of parenting influences on social development for children with such conditions, including CP. Other socioenvironmental factors typically not included in the study of social development, such as access to social activities and the negative effects of stigmatization, also may be key predictors of trajectory and outcomes.

Regarding disability stigmatization, the literature has largely focused on the reaction of typically developing children to children with disabilities, with very few studies focusing on the lives of individuals with CP [64]. The insidious effects of social stigmatization can affect child development through indirect paths. For example, perceived stigmatization of children with disabilities can have adverse effects on parents, including increased maternal distress. Furthermore, there is evidence that parents' reactions to perceived stigmatization can adversely affect the peer contact of their children with disabilities [65].

Quality of life

Recently, there has been a significant research focus on the quality of life (QoL) of children with CP, with some inconsistencies in findings in part due to heterogeneity in samples and instrumentation. There are distinctions between QoL as subjective well-being, and the multidimensional understandings of health-related QoL. Rosenbaum and colleagues [66] provide evidence to suggest that QoL and health-related QoL are distinct sets of weakly associated constructs. At this point, there is some agreement regarding relevant domains of QoL but no universal definition. In a European population-based study of children with CP between 8 and 12 years of age, child perceptions of quality of life were generally similar to those of typically developing peers [46]. In general, motor impairment was not associated with QoL, similar to recent US findings in adolescents with CP [66]. A high percentage (54%) of the children with CP had experienced pain the previous week and, similar to findings in other studies, pain was associated with QoL. Overall, a small percentage of the variance in QoL was explained by impairments (3%) and more so by pain (7%).

Issues specific to adulthood and aging

In recent years there has been increasing awareness that the lifespan needs of individuals with congenital neurodevelopmental conditions are not being met. At the fundamental level, these needs include standard as well as specialized medical care [67, 68]. Pediatricians often have difficulty identifying colleagues who can provide care for adult patients with CP who were supposed to "graduate" from pediatrician care. Adults with CP report the need for more sensitive and informed medical care. There are compelling reasons why access to appropriate medical services is particularly important for this population, including high risk for comorbid conditions and evidence of loss of function including ambulatory status, over time [69, 70]. In addition to loss of mobility, eating can be affected [71]. There is evidence that the mortality rates during childhood are elevated [72], and in general CP of greater severity is associated with higher mortality rates; but of those who survive to adulthood, the subsequent 85% survival rate at age 50 is close to that of the general population (96%) [73]. At this point, there is no empirical evidence of decline in cognition associated with aging with CP.

To date, psychosocial research with the adult population with CP has largely focused on social and employment domains. Regarding psychological health, there is limited evidence suggesting that the severity of depression among individuals with CP but no mental retardation does not differ significantly from that of the general population. In contrast, the severity of depression among individuals with CP and low intellect appears *lower* than that of the general population [74].

Social participation

Adults with CP are at significant risk for low social participation in the community. The social risks associated with CP are clearly noted early in development but there is evidence that, in the transition from adolescence to young adulthood, people with CP become even less socially active [75]. In a population-based study in Denmark, 55% of adults with CP had no competitive employment, cohabiting partner or biological children, compared with 4% of the general population [76]. Only 28% cohabited with another person, and of those cohabiting only 15% were married. These rates are much lower than those noted in the general population, in which 69% are cohabiting and 42% are married. Key predictors of cohabitation included higher intellect, less motor impairment and no epilepsy. Although the majority of adults with CP (67%) in this study lived independently, the level was lower than that of the general population (92%). In light of these findings, it is not surprising that there is preliminary evidence that middle-age and older adults with CP experience relatively high levels of loneliness; however, these findings are from a sample in which a majority of individuals reside in group or nursing home settings [77]. Interestingly, there were no significant differences in the loneliness levels of those with CP who did or did not use augmentative and alternative communication. It is important to note that while level of intellect predicts aspects of community integration among adults with disabilities, intellect is not a strong predictor of self-determination. Rather, self-determination is associated with self-perceptions of opportunities to make personal choices [78]. This finding highlights the importance of promoting choice opportunities for persons with disabilities.

Employment

There is increasing awareness of the poor employment prospects for persons with CP, although data regarding employment outcomes remain quite limited. There may be differences in employment between countries. In Denmark, the estimated competitive employment rate is 29% [68, 79]. There is evidence of differences in the employment rates associated with subtypes of CP, with the lowest rate (12%) noted in individuals with quadriplegia. Those with hemiplegia are at lower risk than those with diplegia. Other key predictors of employment among ambulatory persons with CP and IQs greater than 50 are less severe cognitive impairment and absence of epilepsy, with only a minor influence of motor impairment.

Research directions

There are a number of critical research issues inherent in the study of a condition associated with significant heterogeneity in etiology, neuropathology, clinical presentation, and associated comorbidities. The significant refinement in classification of CP and the recent development of instruments to assess aspects of motor functioning have led to a greater understanding of risks and needs associated with varying dimensions of functioning. In the USA, however, there is a paucity of multisite research that focuses on CP. Given the complexity of the disorder, it is only through such collaborative endeavors that key research questions may be addressed. The lack of accessible cognitive measures, including specific measures of language and information-processing speed, has hindered progress in neuropsychological research. Clearly, further psychometric work is needed to set the stage for studies that can include children with CP and significant sensory, speech, and motor impairments. The risks for impairments in specific domains, such as aspects of visual perception and/or visual motor functions, are not well understood. At this point, studies are needed that utilize more precise measurement. Very little of the neuropsychological work to date has included neuroimaging data, and much remains to be learned about the developmental trajectories associated with underlying neuropathology.

In the psychosocial spheres, there are significant risks for less-frequent social contact, poorer-quality friendships and perhaps increasing isolation in adult-hood. At this point, there is the need for greater emphasis on intervention outcome research including prospective studies of interventions to address social isolation and passivity. Children with disabilities are at great risk for passivity, yet the most commonly used behavioral rating instruments do not assess this aspect of functioning. There is increasing awareness of the prevalence of comorbid ADHD in children with CP, but little is known about the efficacy of pharmacological and behavioral interventions in this population. In addition, current ADHD rating scales were not designed for use in a population with significant motor impairments.

Researchers and society have only recently begun to understand that children with CP become adults with CP. There is tremendous need to develop research and service programs that serve the needs of these adults. The significant medical care concerns, as well as very low marriage and employment rates, present clear opportunities for research, public policy, and increased community awareness that will lead to concrete and meaningful improvements in the lives of individual with CP.

Acknowledgements

Preparation of this chapter was supported by funds from the National Institutes of Health, HD052592–01A, HD057344–01, and US Department of Education, National Institute on Disability and Rehabilitation Research, H133G070044.

References

1. Bax MC. Terminology and classification of cerebral palsy. *Dev Med Child Neurol* 1964;**11**:295–7.

2. Rosenbaum P, Paneth N, Leviton A, Goldstein M, Bax M, Damiano D, et al. A report: the definition and classification of cerebral palsy. *Dev Med Child Neurol Suppl* 2007;**109**:8–14.

3. Odding E, Roebroeck ME, Stam H J. The epidemiology of cerebral palsy: Incidence, impairments and risk factors. *Disabil Rehabil* 2006;**28**:183–91.

4. Hagberg B, Sanner G, Steen M. Disequilibrium syndrome in cerebral-palsy – clinical aspects and treatment. *Acta Paediatr Scand* 1972;**226**:1–63.

5. Cans C, Dolk H, Platt MJ, Colver A, Prasauskiene A, Krageloh-Mann I, et al. Recommendations from the SCPE collaborative group for defining and classifying cerebral palsy. *Dev Med Child Neurol* 2007;**49**:35–8.

6. Palisano R, Rosenbaum P, Walter S, Russell D, Wood E, Galuppi B. Development and reliability of a system to classify gross motor function in children with cerebral palsy. *Dev Med Child Neurol* 1997;**39**:214–23.

7. Beckung E, Hagberg G. Neuroimpairments, activity limitations, and participation restrictions in children with cerebral palsy. *Dev Med Child Neurol* 2002;**44**:309–16.

8. Blair E, Watson L. Epidemiology of cerebral palsy. *Semin Neonatal Med* 2006;**11**:117–25.

9. Johnson A. Prevalence and characteristics of children with cerebral palsy in Europe. *Dev Med Child Neurol* 2002;**44**:633–40.

10. Korzeniewski SJ, Birbeck G, DeLano MC, Potchen MJ, Paneth N. A systematic review of neuroimaging for cerebral palsy. *J Child Neurol* 2008;**23**:216–27.

11. Krageloh-Mann I, Hagberg G, Meisner C, Schelp B, Haas G, Eeg-Olofsson KE, et al. Bilateral spastic cerebral palsy–a comparative study between south-west Germany and western Sweden. I: Clinical patterns and disabilities. *Dev Med Child Neurol* 1993;**35**:1037–47.

12. Venkateswaran S, Shevell MI. Comorbidities and clinical determinants of outcome in children with spastic quadriplegic cerebral palsy. *Dev Med Child Neurol* 2008;**50**:216–22.

13. Green LB, Hurvitz E. Cerebral palsy. *Phys Med Rehabil Clin N Am.* 2007;**18**:859–82.

14. Goble DJ, Lewis CA, Hurvitz EA, Brown SH. Development of upper limb proprioceptive accuracy in children and adolescents. *Hum Movement Sci* 2005;**24**:155–70.

15. Fennell EB, Dikel TN. Cognitive and neuropsychological functioning in children with cerebral palsy. *J Child Neurol* 2001;**16**:58–63.

16. Sigurdardottir S, Eiriksdottir A, Gunnarsdottir E, Meintema M, Arnadottir U, Vik T. Cognitive profile in young Icelandic children with cerebral palsy. *Dev Med Child Neurol* 2008;**50**:357–62.

17. Pirila S, van der Meere J, Korhonen P, Ruusu-Niemi P, Kyntaja M, Nieminen P, et al. A retrospective neurocognitive study in children with spastic diplegia. *Dev Neuropsychol* 2004;**26**:679–90.

18. Fedrizzi E, Inverno M, Bruzzone MG, Botteon G, Saletti V, Farinotti M. MRI features of cerebral lesions and cognitive functions in preterm spastic diplegic children. *Pediatr Neurol* 1996;**15**:207–12.

19. Vargha-Khadem F, Isaacs E, van der Werf S, Robb S, Wilson J. Development of intelligence and memory in children with hemiplegic cerebral palsy. The deleterious consequences of early seizures. *Brain* 1992;**115** Pt 1:315–29.

20. Christ SE, White DA, Brunstrom JE, Abrams RA. Inhibitory control following perinatal brain injury. *Neuropsychology* 2003;**17**:171–8.

21. White DA, Craft S, Hale S, Park TS. Working memory and articulation rate in children with spastic diplegic cerebral palsy. *Neuropsychology* 1994;**8**:180.

22. Schatz J, Craft S, White D, Park TS, Figiel GS. Inhibition of return in children with perinatal brain injury. *J Int Neuropsychol Soc* 2001;**7**:275–84.

23. Craft S, White DA, Park TS, Figiel G. Visual attention in children with perinatal brain injury: asymmetric effects of bilateral lesions. *J Cognitive Neurosci* 1994;**6**:165.

24. Schenker R, Coster WJ, Parush S. Neuroimpairments, activity performance, and participation in children with cerebral palsy mainstreamed in elementary schools. *Dev Med Child Neurol* 2005;**47**:808–14.

25. Gross-Tsur V, Shalev RS, Badihi N, Manor O. Efficacy of methylphenidate in patients with cerebral palsy and attention-deficit hyperactivity disorder (ADHD). *J Child Neurol* 2002;**17**:863–6.

26. White DA, Christ SE. Executive control of learning and memory in children with bilateral spastic cerebral palsy. *J Int Neuropsychol Soc* 2005;**11**:920–4.

27. Jenks KM, de Moor J, van Lieshout EC, Maathuis KG, Keus I, Gorter JW. The effect of cerebral palsy on arithmetic accuracy is mediated by working memory, intelligence, early numeracy, and instruction time. *Dev Neuropsychol* 2007;**32**:861–79.

28. Schatz J, Craft S, Koby M, Park TS. Associative learning in children with perinatal brain injury. *J Int Neuropsychol Soc* 1997;**3**:521–7.

29. Pagliano E, Fedrizzi E, Erbetta A, Bulgheroni S, Solari A, Bono R, et al. Cognitive profiles and visuoperceptual abilities in preterm and term spastic diplegic children with periventricular leukomalacia. *J Child Neurol* 2007;**22**:282–8.

30. Pirila S, van der Meere J, Pentikainen T, Ruusu-Niemi P, Korpela R, Kilpinen J, et al. Language and motor speech skills in children with cerebral palsy. *J Commun Disord* 2007;**40**:116.

31. Smith M. *Literacy and Augmentative and Alternative Communication*. Burlington, MA: Elsevier Academic Press; 2005.

32. Stanovich KE, Seigel LS. Phenotypic performance profile of children with reading disabilities: a regression-based test of the phonological-core variable-difference model. *J Educ Psychol* 1994;**86**:24–53.

33. Vellutino FR, Fletcher JM, Snowling MJ, Scanlon DR. Specific reading disability (dyslexia) what have we learned in the past four decades? *J Child Psychol Psyc* 2004;**45**:2–40.

34. Larsson M, Dahlgren Sandberg A. Phonological awareness in Swedish-speaking children with complex communication needs. *J Intellect Dev Dis* 2008;**33**:22–35.

35. Card R, Dodd B. The phonological awareness abilities of children with cerebral palsy who do not speak. *Augment Altern Comm* 2006;**22**:149–59.

36. Sandberg AD, Hjelmquist E. Language and literacy in nonvocal children with cerebral palsy. *Read Writ* 1997;**9**:107–33.

37. Losch HH, Dammann OO. Impact of motor skills on cognitive test results in very-low-birthweight children. *J Child Neurol* 2004;**19**:318–22.

38. Berninger VW, Gans BM, St James P, Connors T. Modified WAIS-R for patients with speech and/or hand dysfunction. *Arch Phys Med Rehabil* 1988;**69**:250–5.

39. Byrne JM, Dywan CA, Connolly JF. An innovative method to assess the receptive vocabulary of children with cerebral palsy using event-related brain potentials. *J Clin Exp Neuropsychol* 1995;**17**:9–19.

40. Sabbadini M, Bombardi P, Carlesimo GA, Rosato V, Pierro MM. Evaluation of communicative and functional abilities in Wolf-Hirshhorn syndrome. *J Intellect Disabil Res* 2002;**46**:575–82.

41. Raven J, Raven JC, Court JH. *Manual for Raven's Progressive Matrices and Vocabulary Scales. Section 2: Coloured Progressive Matrices*. Oxford, England: Oxford Psychologists Press; 1998.

42. ACAL. Adapted Cognitive Assessment Laboratory. 2008 [July 23, 2008]; Available from: http://www.med.umich.edu/pmr/acal/index.htm.

43. Van Tubbergen M, Warschausky S, Birnholz J, Baker S. Choice beyond preference: conceptualization and assessment of choice-making skills in children with significant impairments. *Rehabil Psychol* 2008;**53**:93–100.

44. Lavigne JV, Faier-Routman J. Psychological adjustment to pediatric physical disorders: a meta-analytic review. *J Pediatr Psychol* 1992;**17**:133–57.

45. McDermott S, Coker A, Mani S, Krishnaswami S, Nagle R, Barnett-Queen L, et al. A population-based analysis of behavior problems in children with cerebral palsy. *J Pediatr Psychol* 1996;**21**:447–63.

46. Parkes J, White-Koning M, Dickinson HO, Thyen U, Arnaud C, Beckung E, et al. Psychological problems in children with cerebral palsy: a cross-sectional European study. *J Child Psychol Psyc* 2008;**49**:405–13.

47. Tervo RC, Symons F, Stout J, Novacheck T. Parental report of pain and associated limitations in ambulatory children with cerebral palsy. *Arch Phys Med Rehab*. 2006;**87**:928–34.

48. Varni JW, Burwinkle TM, Sherman SA, Hanna K, Berrin SJ, Malcarne V L, et al. Health-related quality of life of children and adolescents with cerebral palsy: hearing the voices of the children. *Dev Med Child Neurol* 2005;**47**:592–7.

49. Parker JG, Asher SR. Peer Relations And Later Personal Adjustment – Are Low-Accepted Children At Risk. *Psychol Bull* 1987;**102**:357–89.

50. Thomas PJ, Warschausky S, Farmer JE, Donders J, Warschausky S. Social Integration of Children with Physical Disabilities. *Treating neurodevelopmental disabilities: Clinical research and practice*. New York: Guilford Press; 2006: 234.

51. Yeates KO, Bigler ED, Dennis M, Gerhardt CA, Rubin KH, Stancin T, et al. Social outcomes in childhood brain disorder: A heuristic integration of social neuroscience and developmental psychology. *Psychol Bull* 2007;**133**:535.

52. Dallas E, Stevenson J, McGurk H. Cerebral-palsied children's interactions with siblings: II. Interactional structure. *J Child Psychol Psyc* 1993;**34**:649.

53. Warschausky S, Argento AG, Hurvitz E, Berg M. Neuropsychological status and social problem-solving in children with congenital or acquired brain dysfunction. *Rehabil Psychol* 2003;**48**:250–4.

54. Nadeau L, Tessier R. Social adjustment of children with cerebral palsy in mainstream classes: peer perception. *Dev Med Child Neurol* 2006;**48**:331–6.

55. Cunningham SD, Thomas PD, Warschausky S. Gender differences in peer relations of children with neurodevelopmental conditions. *Rehabil Psychol* 2007;**52**:331.

56. Warschausky S, Argento AG, Hurvitz E, Berg M. Neuropsychological status and social problem solving in children with congenital or acquired brain dysfunction. *Rehabil Psychol* 2003;**48**:250.

57. Holmbeck GN, Coakley RM, Hommeyer JS, Shapera WE, Westhoven VC. Observed and perceived dyadic and systemic functioning in families of preadolescents with spina bifida. *J Pediatr Psychol* 2002;**27**:177–89.

58. Beck A, Daley D, Hastings R P, Stevenson J. Mothers' expressed emotion towards children with and without intellectual disabilities. *J Intellect Disabil Res* 2004;**48**:628.

59. Woolfson L, Grant E. Authoritative parenting and parental stress in parents of pre-school and older children with developmental disabilities. *Child Care Hlth Dev* 2006;**32**:177.

60. Kim J-M, Mahoney G. The effects of mother's style of interaction on children's engagement: Implications for using responsive interventions with parents. *Topics Early Child Spec* 2004;**24**:31.

61. Ladd GW, Profilet SM, Hart CH. Parents' management of children's peer relations: facilitating and supervising children's activities in the peer culture. In Parke RD, Ladd GW, eds. *Family-peer Relationships: Modes of Linkage*. Hillsdale, NJ: Lawrence Erlbaum; 1992: 215.

62. Thomas PD, Warschausky S, Golin R, Meiners K. Direct parenting methods to facilitate the social functioning of children with cerebral palsy. *J Dev Phys Disabil* 2008;**20**:167–74.

63. Cunningham SD, Warschausky S, Thomas PD. Parenting and social functioning of children with and without congenital neurodevelopmental conditions. *Rehabil Psychol* 2009;**54**:109–15.

64. McLaughlin ME, Bell MP, Stringer DY. Stigma and acceptance of persons with disabilities understudied aspects of workforce diversity. *Group Organ Manage* 2004;**29**:302.

65. Green SE. "What do you mean 'what's wrong with her?'": stigma and the lives of families of children with disabilities. *Soc Sci Med* 2003;**57**:1361–74.

66. Rosenbaum PL, Livingston MH, Palisano RJ, Galuppi BE, Russell DJ. Quality of life and health-related quality of life of adolescents with cerebral palsy. *Dev Med Child Neurol* 2007;**49**:516–21.

67. Green LB, Hurvitz EA. Cerebral palsy. *Phys Med Rehabil Clin N Am* 2007;**18**:859–82, vii.

68. Liptak GS, O'Donnell M, Conaway M, Chumlea WC, Wolrey G, Henderson RC, et al. Health status of children with moderate to severe cerebral palsy. *Dev Med Child Neurol* 2001;**43**:364–70.

69. Day SM, Wu YW, Strauss DJ, Shavelle RM, Reynolds RJ. Change in ambulatory ability of adolescents and young adults with cerebral palsy. *Dev Med Child Neurol* 2007;**49**:647–53.

70. Strauss D, Ojdana K, Shavelle R, Rosenbloom L. Decline in function and life expectancy of older persons with cerebral palsy. *NeuroRehabilitation* 2004;**19**:69–78.

71. Krakovsky G, Huth MM, Lin L, Levin RS. Functional changes in children, adolescents, and young adults with cerebral palsy. *Res Dev Disabil* 2007;**28**:331–40.

72. Blair E, Watson L, Badawi N, Stanley FJ. Life expectancy among people with cerebral palsy in Western Australia. *Dev Med Child Neurol* 2001;**43**:508–15.

73. Hemming K, Hutton JL, Pharoah PO. Long-term survival for a cohort of adults with cerebral palsy. *Dev Med Child Neurol* 2006;**48**:90–5.

74. McDermott S, Moran R, Platt T, Issac T, Wood H, Dasari S. Depression in adults with disabilities, in primary care. *Disabil Rehabil* 2005;**27**:117.

75. Stevenson C, Pharoah P, Stevenson R. Cerebral palsy-the transition from youth to adulthood. *Dev Med Child Neurol* 1997;**39**:336–42.

76. Michelsen SI, Uldall P, Hansen T, Madsen M. Social integration of adults with cerebral palsy. *Dev Med Child Neurol* 2006;**48**:643–9.

77. Balandin S, Berg N, Waller A. Assessing the loneliness of older people with cerebral palsy. *Disabil Rehabil* 2006;**28**:469.

78. Wehmeyer ML, Garner NW. The impact of personal characteristics of people with intellectual and developmental disability on self-determination and autonomous functioning. *J Appl Res Intellect* 2003;**16**:255–65.

79. Michelsen SI, Uldall P, Kejs AMT, Madsen M. Education and employment prospects in cerebral palsy. *Dev Med Child Neurol* 2005;**47**:511–7.

Intellectual disability cross the lifespan

Bonnie Klein-Tasman and Kelly Janke

Introduction

Intellectual disability, which until recently was referred to as "mental retardation", is characterized by intellectual functioning falling well below population norms, in tandem with difficulties with everyday functioning. Historically, both the label and the definition of this disability have undergone changes. The first body to attempt to clearly define the characteristics of this disorder was the American Association on Mental Deficiency, in 1908. This most recent reworking of the definition, described in the 10th edition of Mental Retardation: Definition, Classification, and Systems of Supports [1], is as follows: "Mental retardation is a disability characterized by significant limitations both in intellectual functioning and in adaptive behavior as expressed in conceptual, social, and practical adaptive skills. This disability originates before the age of 18." Relevant to this discussion, in 2007 the American Association on Mental Retardation (AAMR) spearheaded a change in the diagnostic label for mental retardation, due largely to concerns about the stigma this term holds [2]. The membership approved adoption of the term "intellectual disability", and an accompanying change to the organization name, to the American Association on Intellectual and Developmental Disabilities (AAIDD). As a result, the common term now is "intellectual disability", which will be used throughout this chapter, even though DSM-IV-TR [3] has not yet updated its terminology.

In this chapter, the history of definitions of intellectual disability will first be briefly reviewed, with an emphasis on current controversies regarding diagnostic conceptualization and criteria. Next, various etiologies of intellectual disability will be described. This will be followed by discussion of common areas of difficulty and relevant treatment approaches used for individuals with intellectual disabilities, with emphasis on the status of empirical support for these approaches. Finally, junctures of developmental challenge, and the nature of these challenges at each juncture, will be discussed; accompanying this will be a consideration of the role of neuropsychology in the study of intellectual disability and in it its assessment, in relation to these issues.

Definitions of intellectual disability: history, components, and contemporary controversies

As mentioned, the first definition of mental retardation put forth by the AAMD was introduced in 1908. To take into account changes in clinical practice and scientific advances, this definition has been updated ten times (as has the name of the organization, to reflect the changes in definition and terminology; i.e. AAMD became the AAMR, and now the AAIDD). Traditionally, diagnosis of mental retardation (now intellectual disability, or ID) has included both the notion that intellectual functioning is at least two standard deviations below the mean, and that there are difficulties present in everyday functioning, typically referred to as adaptive behavior. While there are numerous diagnostic systems containing definitions of ID, the most widely accepted and influential body in the field is the AAIDD. This body has taken primary responsibility for honing the definition of disability. Other definitions of ID are typically based in some part on the AAIDD definition. In particular, there are two other commonly used diagnostic systems: DSM-IV-TR [3] and International Classification of Functioning, Disability, and Health (ICF [4]). This latter classification system is distributed by the World Health Organization and is generally not used in North America. In terms of the operationalization of diagnostic criteria, the AAIDD and the DSM-IV diagnostic criteria specify that a diagnosis of ID is based on performance on a measure of intellectual abilities (such as the Wechsler Scales) that yields a Full Scale IQ score below 70, together with deficits in adaptive behavior. In addition, the concept of "levels of support" to reflect the severity of the intellectual disability is endorsed; this component addresses the varying needs an individual with ID may have in regard to meeting adaptive demands.

Diagnostic criteria for intellectual disability

- Significant limitation in intellectual functioning
- Significant limitations in at least two areas of adaptive functioning
- Onset before age 18
- Determination of level of severity

The AAIDD and other bodies have emphasized several considerations when making a diagnosis of ID. These include taking into account the context of the individual, in particular the age, peer group, and culture. The AAIDD reminds clinicians to "take into account the individual's cultural and linguistic differences as well as communication, sensory, motor, and behavioral factors" [5] although the guidelines regarding precisely how to accomplish this are lacking. Most importantly, there is emphasis placed on considering each person as an individual, within his or her own context, who presents with a unique pattern of relative strengths and weakness.

Components of the current AAIDD definition and current controversies

There are several areas of controversy regarding definitions of intellectual disability. First, there is controversy about the precise cut point in intellectual functioning warranting consideration of a diagnosis of ID. Second, there is controversy regarding the place of adaptive behavior in the definition, with some placing more emphasis on this construct than others. Relatedly, there are systems for determining "levels" of intellectual disability based on both intellectual functioning and adaptive behavior levels.

Areas of controversy

- *Intellectual functioning*:
  - monolithic approach to consideration of intellectual functioning
  - cut point for determination of significant limitation in intellectual functioning

- *Adaptive functioning*:
  - operationalization of adaptive functioning
  - centrality of adaptive functioning to diagnostic decision
- *Level of severity of intellectual disability*: Two approaches:
  - Level of intellectual functioning (mild, moderate, severe, profound)
  - Level of support required (intermittent, limited, extensive, or pervasive)

Intelligence

Intelligence is the most clearly operationalized component of the intellectual disability diagnosis. Determination of intellectual abilities is typically made based on performance on a standardized measure of intellectual functioning with well-demonstrated psychometric properties (including internal consistency, test-retest reliability, and demonstrated validity). This construct forms the bedrock of the diagnosis. Without intellectual functioning deficits, the diagnosis of intellectual disability is not considered. However, it is a necessary but not sufficient criterion for diagnosis.

While assessment of intelligence may appear straightforward in comparison to other components forming the diagnostic criteria for ID, it is not without its murkiness. There are a broad array of measures of intellectual functioning, each with its historical and contemporary features and "quirks", and patterns of strengths and weaknesses. In addition to these measurement issues, neuropsychologists are likely to be particularly perplexed by the lack of a process-based conceptualization of intellectual disability. There is no consensus on variability in the ability of particular aspects of intellectual functioning to reflect intellectual disability. In fact, there appears to be a preference to consider Full Scale IQ primarily in the determination of intellectual functioning. In other words, equal weight is given to processing speed, verbal reasoning abilities, and nonverbal reasoning abilities in intellectual measures. This monolithic approach ignores the patterns of functioning of children, which can include areas of relative strength and weakness that are not clearly reflected by an overall IQ score. For example, an individual might have a Verbal IQ of 82 and a Nonverbal IQ of 57, with an overall Full Scale IQ of 65. While the omnibus IQ may fall in the range of intellectual disability, verbal abilities fall in the low-average range. As a result, the person under consideration may not truly show ID, but instead may have a specific learning disability profile that hampers nonverbal problem-solving. The procedures for considering components of IQ test performance are not clearly delineated or agreed upon.

Second, there has long been concern that measures of intellectual functioning are not culturally neutral (also see Farmer and Vega, Chapter 3 of this volume). While differences between individuals are more substantial than differences between ethnic groups, individuals of Hispanic, Native American, or African descent score lower on IQ tests as a whole. These differences may reflect a bias in intelligence tests, as these measures assume knowledge of the English language, are often administered by White examiners, and emphasize completion time. However, discrepancies are not due to testing biases alone, and research supports the role of environmental factors, including socioeconomic status and differences in expectations or cultural values. A study that used gross matches on SES to compare young children from different ethnic backgrounds to White children found much smaller IQ differences than studies that assessed adolescents or adults [6]. The authors suggested that consideration of additional variables such as medical and nutritional history, household income, and the quality and amount of parent–child interaction may reduce or even eliminate the differences between children of different ethnicities.

Finally, there is considerable debate regarding how and whether to take into account confidence intervals and measurement unreliability in estimates of intellectual functioning. In the 1992 AAMR definition [7], the cut point was essentially changed to 75, which resulted in a doubling of the number of people eligible for a diagnosis of intellectual disability [8]. However, without allowing for some variability in this cut point, we are ignoring the psychometric properties of our measures, which all have some degree of unreliability.

Adaptive behavior

As mentioned, a decrement in intellectual functioning is a necessary but not sufficient criterion for the diagnosis of intellectual disability. The second important component is the presence of impairments in "adaptive behavior". In the current AAIDD conceptualization, such adaptive behavior impairment is "expressed in conceptual, social, and practical adaptive skills", with difficulties in one of these areas required for diagnosis. The importance and conceptualization of

the adaptive behavior construct has been revisited frequently in the AAIDD literature. This criterion was originally included to avoid "false positive" diagnoses of individuals who don't do well on IQ measures but nevertheless function effectively in their daily lives. In the most recent set of criteria, there is an attempt to increase the role of adaptive behavior in the conceptualization of intellectual disability.

There is controversy regarding how central adaptive behavior should be to our conceptualization of intellectual disability. Some would like this construct to be front and center in the ID construct, arguing that it is the deficits in adaptive function that are at the core of the challenges of people with ID, rather than their IQ decrements. However, there are several challenges to this contention. First, current measures of adaptive behavior do not have the same track record of containing strong psychometric properties (e.g. test-retest reliability, validity), when compared with intellectual measures. Second, this construct is not usually operationalized to rely on information culled from just one measure (as is IQ), but rather is often explored through a collection of measures (e.g. parent and teacher reports of adaptive behavior, performance on academic testing). Complicating this, different measures of adaptive behavior can yield quite different findings. Third, decrements in adaptive behavior are not monolithic within the population with ID. Difficulties across all areas of the adaptive behavior construct (conceptual, social, and practical adaptive skills) are not required, presumably because use of such a criterion would exclude too many individuals. Finally, the incremental validity of the adaptive behavior construct has not been clearly demonstrated. Notably, performance on measures of adaptive behavior is usually highly correlated with performance on IQ measures [9]; this does suggest that more often than not, much of the information utilized for forming a diagnosis of ID comes from the assessment of intellectual functioning.

Level of functioning

Researchers, clinicians, and educators are often concerned about the level of functioning of individuals with ID. The AAIDD approach to defining ID emphasizes level of functioning, by focusing on the "level of support" needed by each individual in order to meet daily goals and expectations (i.e. intermittent, limited, extensive, or pervasive support required). Classification of support as intermittent reflects the

223

observation that the individual requires support on an "as-needed" basis, while limited support reflects the fact that a person with ID requires time-limited, but consistent support over time. Extensive classification reflects support being required daily in at least some environments, and pervasive classification reflects a need for support at all times. Other systems (e.g. DSM-IV-TR) emphasize the range of intellectual functioning as the source of conclusions regarding level of functioning (i.e. DSM-IV-TR classifies ID as being mild, moderate, severe, or profound). However, there have been few investigations of the level of correspondence between these different approaches. Researchers generally adhere to the *level of functioning* approach, as the operationalization of this approach is more straightforward and therefore is likely to have greater reliability. In contrast, practitioners and ID support personnel favor a *level of support* approach as, conceptually, this approach better reflects the reasons for, and process of determination of, the nature of services an individual with ID requires. The lack of agreement between these systems of classification contributes to the ongoing bifurcation within the field, and makes integration of basic and applied research more challenging.

Additionally, there has been virtually no attention paid to whether, either for scientific or practice purposes, different approaches may be appropriate at different points in development, or at different levels of functioning. During early and middle childhood, parents play a very strong role in children's adaptive behavior – by scaffolding development to support optimal functioning, failing to do so, or by compensating for areas of difficulty. During this period, parents and teachers of children with mild ID may also focus primarily on academic functioning and progress in developing cognitive competencies. Hence, definitions of adaptive functioning at this developmental time point are predicated on the individual child as well as the environment and its differing sets of requirements. In contrast, when a child enters adolescence and adulthood, the definition of adaptive functioning alters, in response to increased expectations for the development of general independence and work-related skills.

It is possible that in a child with very limited cognitive abilities, attention might be better placed on characterizing and targeting adaptive functioning in particular, across development, whereas for a child with only mild to moderate delays, characterization of

intellectual functioning may need to be prioritized to establish reasonable expectations for performance at school. With advancement towards adulthood, the same individual might better be characterized according to adaptive functioning needs, in tandem with consideration of intellectual skill level, in order to more effectively outline needed supports as well as areas where independence can be expected. Research is needed to determine whether the utility of different approaches to level of functioning characterization varies based on the age and developmental stage of the child.

Etiologies of intellectual disability

As mentioned, the diagnosis of intellectual disability typically gives little consideration to individual patterns of strength and weakness in functioning, and the diagnostic process is often blind to etiology. However, the majority of research concerning the neuropsychology of intellectual disability examines patterns characteristic of particular etiologies, and practitioners in the field increasingly incorporate etiology into their conceptualizations of the form of ID being evaluated, and the supports needed for individual children presenting with ID. When considering the context of the individual and his or her patterns of strength and weakness, neuropsychologists are particularly likely to be interested in incorporating information about the etiology of the intellectual disability into their diagnosis, given that research has indeed revealed that in many cases there are characteristic patterns of functioning representative of a specific neurodevelopmental disorder. Dykens and colleagues [10, 11] in particular have written extensively about the value of an etiologically based approach to understanding intellectual disability, when the etiology is known. As well, while Pennington [8] cautions that even though individuals with intellectual disability of known etiology differ in levels of functioning, such an approach to classification, incorporating both level of functioning and etiology, is needed. Nevertheless, there is very little research available to date that addresses phenotypes of individuals of different levels of cognitive and adaptive functioning and their differing treatment needs; there is more research regarding patterns seen for particular etiologies. This section of the chapter will attempt to provide guidance and direction regarding the role etiology may play in helping

Table 9a.1. Etiologies associated with developmental stages.

Stage	Manifestations
Preconceptual	Genetics, unknown etiology
Intrauterine	Infections, substance exposure, metals and chemicals, nutrition
Perinatal or postnatal	Birth complications
Childhood	Environmental exposures, injury, deprivation

define and understand specific patterns of ID and their presentation.

The prevalence of intellectual disability is between 1 and 3%, with the majority presenting with mild ID [12]. McDermott et al. [13] reviewed recent research regarding epidemiology and etiology of ID, dividing the spectrum based on the developmental stage at which the disorder presents. We will borrow from this approach as we provide examples of the common etiologies of ID below (see Table 9a.1). In particular, preconceptual-stage etiology includes genetic etiologies of ID (i.e. chromosomal, sex-linked single gene, autosomal dominant, metabolic, segmental autosomal, and genetic and nutritional contributors to the development of ID). Intrauterine etiology includes infections, substance exposure, metals and chemicals, and nutritional contributors. Perinatal or postnatal etiologies include birth complications. Childhood etiologies include environmental exposures, injury, and deprivation.

It is notable that McDermott and colleagues [13] indicate in their review that approximately 50% of cases of intellectual disability are of unknown etiology, with 75–90% of cases classified as mild or moderate, and 10–25% as severe to profound. Severe to profound intellectual disabilities are disproportionally genetic in origin, while environmental etiologies are more common for mild to moderate intellectual disability [8]. Within the intellectual disability literature there is reference to the existence of a "bimodal tail" of the normal distribution, with part of the tail of the distribution simply being part of the normal curve (representing the majority of cases of mild intellectual disability) together with the presence of a bump at the bottom of the distributions (representing more significant perturbations of the developing system) [8]. Evidence from investigations of siblings of affected individuals has demonstrated that siblings of

individuals with mild ID tend to have similar levels of intellectual functioning, whereas siblings of individuals with more severe presentations of ID tend to show average-range intellectual functioning [14]. This suggests that mild ID is more likely to be "familial" and less likely to result from a specific genetic or environmental etiology unique to the affected individual, in comparison to moderate to profound intellectual disability.

Also important to consider, regarding both genetic and environmental etiologies, is the range of effect of the etiology. For some etiologies, association with intellectual disability is strong, in that the presence of the etiological risk factor almost always results in intellectual disability (e.g. Down syndrome). However, for other etiologies of ID, the effects are often milder and more probabilistic; in such cases, the likelihood of developing intellectual disability may be a more common outcome for that specific etiological population, when compared with the general population, but ID is not always a characteristic outcome of the etiology (e.g. Neurofibromatosis Type 1). Most genetic and environmental etiologies are indeed probabilistic to some extent, in that other environmental factors contribute to variability in effect and ultimate outcomes.

Manifestations associated with preconceptual stage

With the exception of the "unknown etiology" category, ID secondary to a defined genetic disorder represents the most common etiology of ID. With advances in the field of molecular genetics and the successful sequencing of the genome, genetic etiologies are increasingly implicated in intellectual disabilities, and new genetic etiologies are identified on a regular basis. Typically, genetic abnormalities that contribute to ID come about at conception. These genetic abnormalities emerge due to a variety of developmental perturbations that impact gene expression. While a comprehensive review of the phenotypes of all genetic disorders is beyond the scope of this chapter, we will review the main kinds of genetic abnormalities and provide some examples of characteristic phenotype. For this discussion, we will borrow our typology from Dykens et al. [11], who divide the categories of genetic disorders as follows: numerical chromosomal abnormalities, structural chromosomal abnormalities (deletions, duplications, translocations, and mosaicism), parental imprinting, and single-gene disorders, with some overlaps between these categories. In addition, there are a few etiologies of intellectual disability that are genetic and affected by nutrition. Genetic disorders also differ in their mode of transmission; these can be autosomal dominant, autosomal recessive, or X-chromosome-linked ("X-linked").

Numerical chromosomal

Chromosomal abnormalities generally involve extra copies of large segments of a given chromosome. The most common chromosomal abnormality affecting intellectual functioning is Down syndrome, with an incidence of approximately 1 in 800 live births. In the majority of cases, Down syndrome results from an extra copy of chromosome 21, but mosaicism (in which some cells are affected and others are not) is also apparent. Physical features of Down syndrome include characteristic facial dysmorphologies and congenital heart abnormalities. Notably, there is an increased risk of early-onset Alzheimer's disease in Down syndrome [15].

Intellectual functioning is typically in the range of moderate mental retardation [16, 17]. Some individuals with Down syndrome, typically those with a mosaic genetic presentation, have intellectual abilities in the broadly average range [18, 19]. A particular weakness with the grammatical aspects of language and a relative strength on spatial tasks is often reported [16, 19], and verbal short-term memory is typically more impaired than is visual [20]. Memory deficits have also been reported [17]. Individuals with Down syndrome typically show a relative strength in their social skills and a relative weakness in daily living skills [21]. A number of studies have indicated that parents report lower levels of behavior problems in children with Down syndrome than are reported for children with other developmental disabilities [22, 23], and that children with Down syndrome generally have an "upbeat" personality [24]. Dykens and Kasari [23] also found an increase in internalizing symptoms with age, including anxiety, depression, and withdrawal.

Sex-linked single gene

Fragile-X syndrome is a single gene disorder in which the fragile mental retardation 1 gene (FMR1) becomes inactivated because it contains a large number of repeats, and therefore does not effectively produce a critical FMR1 protein [25, 26]. As the X chromosome is affected, males are more strongly impacted than females and show poorer abilities. The physical features associated with Fragile-X include distinctive facial features, including long faces and prominent ears [27], and connective tissue abnormalities [28]. The median range of intellectual abilities for males is in the moderate impairment range, with median intellectual abilities in the low average range for females [29]. Articulation difficulties [30] and pragmatic difficulties (e.g. echolalia, stereotyped language) are often reported and sequential processing and spatial reasoning are also areas of weakness. Relative strengths in expressive and receptive vocabulary have been observed [31, 32]. While a relative strength in early reading and spelling skills has been reported [31, 33], academic difficulties include poor math and abstract reasoning skills, and difficulty with planning. Across the lifespan, there tends to be a decline in IQ scores with chronological age [34] that is most characteristic of males with the disorder [35]. Socialization is typically an area of relative weakness for people with Fragile-X, and social anxiety and gaze aversion are commonly reported [36]. Daily living skills are an area of relative strength [21]. Boys with Fragile-X syndrome show a very high prevalence rate of comorbid attention-deficit/hyperactivity disorder (ADHD), with estimates of occurrence falling between 72% [37] and 90% [38]. Girls with Fragile-X often show emotional and social difficulties such as social anxiety, loneliness, and proneness to depression [39].

Structural abnormality

There are a number of structural abnormalities involving a segment of a chromosome that are associated with intellectual disability. A segmental autosomal disorder is one in which a segment of a chromosome from one parent is missing or altered. Examples of such disorders include 22q11 syndrome (also referred to as Velocardiofacial syndrome) and Williams syndrome, both of which involve hemizygous microdeletions and usually result in mild to moderate intellectual disability. Inverted duplication 15 (also called Autism15 or Idic 15) is another segmental autosomal disorder, in this case involving extra copies of material on chromosome 15, either interstitially or as a marker chromosome.

Metabolic

There are a small number of etiologies of intellectual disability that are genetic and also involve nutritional input. The most commonly known disorder is phenylketonuria (PKU) in which the gene directing metabolism of phenylalanine to tyrosine is affected, and there is a build-up of phenylalanine in the body [40]. As tyrosine is a precursor to dopamine, this has the effect of altering production of dopamine. If the intake of phenylalanine is not restricted by diet, severe neurodevelopmental consequences can occur. This genetic disorder has received considerable attention because it provides an example of how the environment contributes to the expression of genetic disorders, and is also an example of a potentially debilitating disorder that can be identified early and managed nutritionally.

Manifestations associated with intrauterine exposures

Intrauterine exposures to substances and chemicals increase the risk of intellectual disability. Alcohol exposure in utero is the best-documented intrauterine exposure that frequently results in intellectual disability [41, 42]. In a recent review [43], the author concluded that the pattern seen in children affected by alcohol exposure is generalized and includes intellectual disability for many, including slowed processing, language deficits, and memory difficulties. Additionally, behavior problems and attention problems (especially inattention) are also common.

Intrauterine exposures to high levels of methylmercury and lead have also been linked to intellectual disability, while exposure at lower levels typically results in only subtle effects [44, 45]. Cocaine and cigarette exposure, as well as nutritional deficits in utero, have all been associated with increased rates of learning, attention, and behavioral regulation problems, with decrements in intellectual functioning common, sometimes (thought not usually) resulting in intellectual disability [46].

Each of these potential teratogens continues to be studied in detail, with accumulating data regarding developmental impact emerging at a strong pace. Nonetheless, variable methods used for the study of these concerns, coupled with their association with SES and class factors, have contributed to inconsistent findings regarding potential and actual effects. Sophisticated research protocols utilizing multimethod approaches for ascertaining risk, exposure, and impact are required to tease apart the impact teratogens have on prenatal developmental processes.

Manifestations associated with perinatal complications

Perinatal complications include prematurity and obstetrical or delivery complications. Definitional difficulties make a discussion of the impact of perinatal complications on intellectual functioning complex. In particular, there are indications that perinatal complications may themselves reflect a vulnerable neural system and increase the likelihood of premature birth rather than prematurity causing subsequent deficits [13]. Regardless of the direction of this relationship, there appears to be a connection between restricted growth or low birth weight and ID. Lee and colleagues [47] assessed 49 extreme-low-birth-weight infants with the Griffiths Mental Development Scale and the Reynell Developmental Language Scale as part of the High Risk Follow-up program. Twenty-four percent of infants who weighed 750 g or less and 13% of infants who weighed between 751 and 999 g had intellectual impairment. A lower percentage of physical and cognitive disabilities was associated with delivery by cesarean section, whereas greater risk was associated with postnatal steroid use, which may impair cerebral cortical growth [48].

A more useful variable may be intrauterine growth, which accounts for gestational age and the infant's gender. Leonard and colleagues [49] assessed this growth with percentage of optimal growth and analyses were adjusted for sociodemographic variables. Suboptimal intrauterine growth, regardless of gestational age, and poor head growth was associated with ID. Yaqoob and colleagues [50] also found small head circumference to be an independent predictor of ID.

Neurological problems are often not a result of birth injuries, but may be a consequence of prematurity or asphyxia [13, 51]. Constable and colleagues [51] found that the neural connectivity of individuals born prematurely was significantly different from controls when the groups were assessed at the age of 12. Their findings suggest that the decrease in white matter tract organization is related to the significantly poorer cognitive performance of the preterm group. Similarly, significant variabilities in availability of oxygen during the birth process have been associated with increased risk for cognitive impairment. Interference with regulatory and processing capacities within the brain, particularly those skills coordinated through the subcortical tracts, which occurs secondary to the impact of hypoxia and anoxia, may contribute to disruptions in sensory, motor, and cognitive development [13].

Manifestations associated with childhood etiologies

There are several etiologies of intellectual disability that emerge as important after the prenatal and perinatal periods. These include environmental exposures, deprivation, and head injury. All of these etiologies have been shown to have some impact on intellectual functioning. The extent of the effect is often variable, with some individuals showing decrements in intellectual functioning significant enough to result in functioning in the range of intellectual disability.

In addition to the environmental exposures in utero discussed above, there is also evidence of neuropsychological effects of exposures during early childhood and beyond. In particular, lead exposure has been associated with learning problems, attention problems, and, in some cases, intellectual disability [52, 53]. Baghurst and colleagues [54] found an inverse relationship between lead exposure and IQ even after controlling for gender, birth weight, birth order, feeding method (breast, bottle, or both), duration of breast-feeding, parental education, maternal IQ and age at delivery, exposure to cigarette smoke, quality of the home environment (including whether the child's biological parents were living together), and socioeconomic status.

Needleman and colleagues have also observed the negative impact of childhood lead exposure on both early development and long-term neurobehavioral functioning [55–57]. Their meta-analysis examining the relationship between childhood lead exposure and IQ found substantial evidence for the impairing effect of lead on intellectual functioning [57]. In an 11-year follow-up of children assessed in first and second grade, Needleman and colleagues [56] found that higher lead levels in childhood were significantly related to high-school absenteeism and dropout rates, a diagnosis of a reading disability, slower reaction times and finger-tapping, and poorer eye–hand coordination. Needleman and Bellinger [55] discussed the complexity of identifying the true effects of lead exposure given the numerous factors that can influence a child's development; however, they conclude that consistent evidence remains for the negative

effects of low-level lead exposure on intellectual and behavioral functioning.

Another substance that can affect intellectual functioning postnatally is mercury. Though a majority of the literature concerning the effects of mercury has examined the relationship between prenatal exposure and neuropsychological deficits, significant medical effects have also been reported from exposure to mercury in over-the-counter medicines in the first half of the century, house paint, thermometers, and fungicide [58, 59]. More recently, there have been investigations of developmental effects of mercury exposure by studying populations who consume large amounts of fish, which can be a significant source of mercury [60]. High doses of methylmercury may cause intellectual impairment; however, findings regarding the association between fish consumption and neuropsychological functioning have been inconsistent [60–62].

There is a more sparse literature about the role of early environmental deprivation and malnutrition. However, these have been identified as a source of intellectual disability [50]. Yaqoob and colleagues [50] examined the etiology of mild ID for 40 children followed longitudinally. Social deprivation and malnutrition were the primary sources of ID for 28% of the sample. Ornoy and colleagues [63] compared children of average socioeconomic status to children with environmental deprivation and to children born to a mother or father with a heroin dependency. The children born to a heroin-dependent parent and children who experienced environmental deprivation showed significantly higher rates of attention problems and scored significantly lower on measures of intelligence, visuospatial abilities, reading, and arithmetic.

Finally, research into head injury suggests that some kinds of injuries may be associated with intellectual disability. Parker and Rosenblum [64] observed a 14-point decrease in IQ scores when comparing the participants' post-injury scores to estimated pre-injury scores based on population norms. Ewing-Cobbs and colleagues [65] examined the intellectual and academic functioning of 23 children who suffered a brain injury before the age of 6. Nearly half of the children had IQ scores below the 10th percentile and were having significant difficulties in school. Additionally, brain injuries appear to be related to deficits in executive function, attention, memory, and linguistic abilities [66, 67]. However, clinicians must be cautious when interpreting post-injury assessment results because the individual could have had

Table 9a.2. Psychosocial and pharmacological interventions.

Area of challenge	Psychosocial interventions	Pharmacological interventions
Mood disorders	Social reinforcement, modeling, role playing, token economies, cognitive therapy	SSRIs, lithium, anticonvulsants (e.g. carbamazepine, valproic acid)
Anxiety	Social skills training, relaxation training, systematic desensitization, exposure	Medications used for general population
Psychotic disorders	Social skills training and psychoeducation	Antipsychotics (e.g. clozapine)
Stereotyped behaviors	Reinforcement-based treatments (e.g. extinction, differential reinforcement)	SSRIs and antipsychotics (e.g. risperidone, olanzapine)
Aggression	Anger management, stress reduction, relaxation exercises, learning appropriate coping methods, improving communication skills, social skills training	Antipsychotics (e.g. risperidone)
ADHD	Travel cards	Methylphenidate, risperidone, amphetamine
Language difficulties	Speech-language therapy, sign language when appropriate	
Other difficulties	Physical and occupation therapy for motor development and activities of daily living, use of assistive technology	

preexisting cognitive impairment, as ID is a risk factor for trauma [68].

Description and interventions for common difficulties

Neuropsychologists play a critical role in assessing individuals' strengths and weaknesses and suggesting appropriate, empirically supported interventions. See Table 9a.2 for a listing of areas of challenge and representative interventions. Because intelligence is considered a largely stable trait, tertiary prevention methods should capitalize on these strengths and minimize the weaknesses or negative effects of ID across the lifespan. While improvements in intellectual functioning may occur with educational support and therapies for individuals with very mild intellectual impairments or borderline intelligence, it is generally agreed that it is unlikely that intellectual abilities of more severely affected individuals can be substantially improved [69]. However, intervention programs can target the maladaptive behaviors and conditions that often accompany intellectual impairment [69]. There is very little etiology-specific research about interventions (see Klein-Tasman et al. [70] for a review of interventions for children with intellectual disabilities of genetic origin). This section will concentrate on research regarding people with intellectual disabilities more generally. Characteristics often associated with ID include high rates of co-occurring psychopathology,

self-injurious and repetitive behaviors, and adaptive behavior deficits. In addition, speech and occupational therapy needs and assistive technology needs are often present. Research about interventions in these domains is discussed.

Psychopathology and problem behavior

Mood disorders

It is difficult to draw conclusions regarding the prevalence of mood disorders in individuals with ID and the efficacy of treatments because the studies examining these variables are limited by a lack of appropriate controls and other methodological flaws. Matson and Laud [71] noted that prevalence rates of depression range from 0.9 to 3.2%, while the prevalence of bipolar disorder remains unclear. Estimations of the rates of these disorders may not be an accurate representation of how many individuals with ID experience symptoms of depression and mania because of diagnostic overshadowing [72]. Clinicians may falsely attribute symptomatology to the intellectual disability, rather than make a co-morbid mood or behavior diagnosis. It is important to adapt DSM criteria to accurately capture the signs and symptoms that may be present for those with ID. Rush and colleagues [73] discuss the importance of also modifying and evaluating assessment measures because diagnosis with the DSM relies

229

heavily on self-report and may underestimate the prevalence of psychopathology in this population.

A depressed mood and decrease in interest and pleasure may manifest as withdrawal, decreased emotional reactivity, and apathetic facial expressions in individuals with ID. Additionally, psychomotor agitation may sometimes underlie the self-injurious behavior and increased aggression observed in this population; however, clinicians should not assume that challenging behaviors are depressive equivalents [74, 75]. Self-injury may also be a result of the irritability associated with a manic state. Other manic symptoms may be present as inaccurate beliefs of having mastered daily living skills, disorganized speech, decreased sleep, or increased maladaptive behavior [71].

Once practitioners recognize mood disorders in individuals with ID, developmentally appropriate interventions must then be implemented. There appears to be a relationship between depressive symptoms and social skills deficits [76], so behavior modification that incorporates social reinforcement, modeling, and role playing may be effective [76]. Token economies can also be used to reinforce behaviors incompatible with depressed responses [77]. Behavior programs aimed at reducing aggression and self-injury can be used to decrease manic symptoms [78]. Additionally, research has shown that individuals with ID can benefit from cognitive therapy, but may require additional education and training to understand the concepts of this modality [79, 80]. Studies [81] have shown selective serotonin reuptake inhibitors (SSRIs) to be effective for individuals with ID; however, additional studies using adequate controls are needed [71]. King and colleagues [82] found that symptoms of bipolar disorder can be successfully reduced with a combination of lithium and anticonvulsants such as carbamazepine (CMZ) and valproic acid (VPA).

Anxiety disorders

Research has shown that the intellectually disabled population may experience higher levels of anxiety following stress, which may be due in part to poor coping skills and low self-esteem [83]. Given that social interactions are often stressful for individuals with intellectual disability, interventions should focus on developing social skills and a positive self-image [80]. There is also evidence that behavioral relaxation training can be used to reduce anxiety as well as improve general functioning [84]. In a review of psychosocial interventions, Hatton [85] found that cognitive-behavior methods such as systematic desensitization and exposure may be appropriate treatments, though outcomes have mostly been examined on a case-by-case basis. Pharmacotherapy can also be used to reduce anxiety symptoms [86], but studies that compare the efficacy of these medications for the general population to the intellectually disabled population are warranted [87].

Psychotic disorders

There is controversy regarding the dual diagnosis of schizophrenia and ID, as some of the behavioral symptoms thought to be associated with psychotic disorders may instead result from a neurological abnormality related to the ID [71]. However, the prevalence rates of schizophrenia appear to be higher for the ID population compared to the general population. Antipsychotics such as clozapine have been shown to effectively reduce the number of psychotic symptoms experienced by those with dual diagnosis [88]. Though pharmacotherapy is typically the primary intervention, it may be helpful to combine the medications will social skills training and psychoeducation [71].

Stereotyped and self-injurious behavior

Repetitive and stereotyped behaviors are present in many neurodevelopmental disorders. Stereotyped behaviors such as hand-flapping, spinning, and body-rocking occur in up to 60% of individuals with intellectual disability, and self-injurious behaviors including head-banging, skin-picking and biting have been observed in up to 46% of these individuals [89]. A meta-analysis conducted by McClintock and colleagues [90] indicated that these behaviors are significantly more likely in individuals with severe or profound intellectual disability compared to a more mild form. Reinforcement-based treatments such as extinction and differential reinforcement can be effective for decreasing self-injurious behavior and lower-order sensory and repetitive behaviors such as thumb-sucking and hand-flapping [91]. Noncontingent attention can be used for behavior maintained by attention and noncontingent sensory stimulation may be useful for behavior maintained by automatic reinforcement. Alternatively, attention can be withheld to extinguish self-injurious behavior maintained by attention. Only in severe cases does it appear to be necessary to use restrictive procedures to prevent serious injury [91]. There is also evidence that SSRIs and antipsychotics such as risperidone and olanzapine are effective treatments for stereotyped and self-injurious behaviors [91].

Aggression

A meta-analysis that examined the challenging behavior of individuals with ID did not find a significant relationship between aggression and the degree of ID [90]. Aggressive acts appear to be learned behaviors that are maintained by psychological, medical, and social factors; therefore, treatment must be appropriately modified to address the antecedents of each individual's behavior [92]. Research examining pharmacological interventions is limited, but there is some evidence that antipsychotics (e.g. risperidone) may reduce aggression in children and adults [93]. Effective psychosocial strategies include anger management, stress reduction, relaxation exercises, learning appropriate coping methods, and improving communication skills [94]. Poor emotional control and social incompetence also appear to be risk factors for acts of sexual aggression [95]. Nezu and colleagues [96] designed *Project STOP*, an outpatient treatment for men at risk for sex-offending behavior. The program employs CBT techniques aimed at improving social skills and self-control, including interpersonal skills training and sexual education.

ADHD

Research generally indicates that attention deficit hyperactivity disorder (ADHD) is a valid diagnosis for both children and adults with ID [97, 98] and that rates are higher among those with ID compared to siblings and the general population [99]. Some are reluctant to diagnose ADHD, and rather attribute the attention problems and impulsivity seen to the intellectual disability [97]. Pearson and colleagues [100] compared 48 children with intellectual disability and comorbid ADHD to 47 children with intellectual disability alone. Parents of the children with ADHD reported significantly more internalizing symptoms, academic problems, family conflict, and social skills deficits on the Personality Inventory for Children–Revised. A comorbid diagnosis of ADHD therefore puts individuals with ID at risk for additional social, academic, and vocational difficulties.

To date, intervention research has focused largely on the use of psychostimulants. Filho and colleagues [101] compared the efficacy of risperidone and methylphenidate (MPH) in reducing ADHD symptomatology in 45 children and adolescents with moderate ID. Risperidone and MPH were found to be effective for reducing both hyperactive and inattentive symptoms. This reduction was significantly greater for the risperidone group, a result that is consistent with previous findings. The results of this study also indicate that the side effects associated with MPH and risperidone are the same in the ID and the general population. Filho et al. [101] noted that risperidone may be especially useful for children with ID who exhibit ADHD and other disruptive behaviors. Research with adults is very limited; however, a recent retrospective study [102] found that methylphenidate ($N = 3$) and amphetamine ($N = 7$) significantly reduced hyperactivity and irritability with minimal side effects.

While behavioral strategies such as assistance with organization, breaking tasks into smaller components, and frequent reinforcement are certainly used with individuals with ID, there has been little research about their effectiveness with this population. Access to the general education curriculum can be increased for individuals with ID and attention difficulties with the use of Travel Cards [103]. The Travel Card is a behavior management strategy that provides immediate feedback, prompts from instructors, and reinforcement. It allows students to earn points or tokens for following class rules and completing their assignments, which can be traded in for rewards. The results of Carpenter's [104] study indicate that this strategy effectively increases student productivity, collaboration between special education teachers and general education teachers, and communication between parents and teachers.

Language difficulties

Language delay is common for individuals with ID, and adaptive functioning deficits related to communication are often seen. Therefore, improving the language and communication skills of these individuals is a critical component of treatment and education. Before beginning speech-language therapy, it is important to consider comorbid problems such as hearing impairments and motor disorders as well as the level and etiology of ID. These variables greatly influence the nature and severity of the individual's language deficits and therefore influence the focus of treatment. Individuals with Fragile X Syndrome, for instance, often have articulation and pragmatic difficulties, with relative strengths in expressive and receptive vocabulary. Individuals with Down syndrome generally show a particular weakness with grammatical aspects of language such as syntax and morphology [19]. Fluid linguistic abilities are usually present in individuals with Williams syndrome, although delays in early language acquisition are the norm rather than the exception [105]. Interventions must not only be tailored for specific syndromes, but must consider the general phenotype of these conditions. For example, it has been suggested that the use of sign language may be appropriate for those with language delays. However, this may not be effective for individuals with Fragile X syndrome, a syndrome associated with fine motor deficits, or for Williams syndrome, where gestural development and visuospatial construction are typically delayed.

Occupational and physical therapy needs

Individuals with ID often show impairment in self-care, home living, health, and safety [3]. Research has indicated that there is a relationship between the level of ID and an individual's ability to perform activities of daily living (ADLs). When individuals with ID struggle to care for themselves or carry out daily routines, occupational therapy can be used to increase their sense of autonomy. When designing an intervention program, an occupational therapist should consider what clients can do and what they would like to be capable of doing at the end of therapy. The Assessment of Motor and Process Skills [106, 107] can be used to evaluate an individual's performance of ADLs. ADL motor skills include the movements that are necessary to complete a task, such as the manipulation of any required objects. ADL process skills include the individual's sequential reasoning and problem-solving abilities. When a client's strengths and weaknesses have been assessed, interventions can be designed to reach the individual's goals. Jenkins and Sells [108] found that the gross and fine motor skills can be significantly improved with just one therapy session per week. However, controlled research about the efficacy of occupational therapy is sparse.

Use of assistive technology

Assistive technology devices are "any item, piece of equipment, or product system whether acquired, commercially off the shelf, modified, or customized, that is used to increase, maintain, or improve functional capabilities of a child with a disability" and assistive technology services are any services that assist individuals with ID "in the selection, acquisition, or use of an assistive technology device" [109]. The goal of these devices is to compensate for the individual's disability to improve his or her functioning in the home and community.

In a review of 40 studies that examined the use of assistive technology (AT), Mechling [110] found that manual antecedent prompts and computer-aided systems were helpful for persons with ID. Several studies have shown picture cues to be effective for prompting participation in activities and completing multi-step tasks to improve vocational and daily living skills. Pairing these pictures with auditory prompts that provide additional reminders and information may be particularly beneficial. Additional research is needed to examine the usefulness of tactile prompts such as vibrating pagers. One aid that can integrate these various prompts is the palmtop personal computer. For example, a light or beep can be used to draw the individual's attention to the device, where reminders and other messages or images are displayed on the screen. These devices have been efficacious in decreasing the need for supervision and increasing performance accuracy. However, these aids are currently underutilized; commonly reported barriers include a lack of instruction and knowledge regarding availability as well as the cost of the devices.

Developmental junctures of importance and the role of neuropsychology

Developmental junctures of importance

Developmental junctures may be times when families are more likely to seek out a neuropsychological evaluation, as planning for the next step becomes important. In this section, we will briefly review some of the central issues at play at different developmental periods for individuals with intellectual disability, with a focus on those areas most central to neuropsychologists.

Infancy and preschool years

Individuals with intellectual disabilities are typically identified as showing developmental delays beginning in the preschool years. Delays in language acquisition, motor development, and self-care skills are often early indicators of difficulty that bring families to the attention of early childhood educators and professionals. Because of the lack of stability of measures of intellectual abilities, together with the considerable normal variability in rates of development in early childhood, a definitive diagnosis of intellectual disability is generally not made until the child reaches approximately the age of 6. Before that time, the difficulties shown by the child are most often characterized as "developmental delays" rather than as "intellectual disability". It is important to keep in mind that while preschool measures of cognitive functioning may indeed lack reliability within the middle of the distribution, their reliability at the extremes is considerably stronger, such that young children identified as showing extreme delays relative to their peers (performance more than 2 standard deviations below the mean) are highly likely to continue to have some degree of difficulty over time.

Common services during the infancy and preschool years include speech, occupational, physical, and developmental therapies concentrating on helping children move through important early developmental milestones (reviewed below). Within this infancy and preschool timeframe, one common transition point is from Birth to Three services to Early Childhood services, which takes place around the child's third birthday. The most pronounced difference at this point is that support services for the child are likely to shift from taking place in the family's home to taking place in a school environment, as the school system takes over case management. In this transition, goals of socialization are also typically added to the cognitive, language, and motor goals previously identified for the child.

Grade-school and middle-school years

In the grade-school years, families and school personnel are faced with decisions regarding how much of the regular education curriculum can be accessed effectively by each individual child. Because of the range of intellectual and adaptive functioning that exists within the category of intellectual disability, such decision-making is by necessity individualized. Certainly, the requirement of placement in the "least restrictive environment" often means that inclusion approaches are central in the grade-school years. However, the extent to which a child is included in the regular education classroom, and the nature of that inclusion, varies widely from one area of the country to another and from one school district to another. Nevertheless, inclusion approaches are very common in the grade-school years, with children receiving pull-out speech, physical, and occupational therapy, and also commonly participating in social skills groups or friendship circles to support social development.

High-school years: transition to independence

Beginning in the high-school years, there is typically a gradual incorporation of preparation for independent functioning and vocational aspirations within the school setting and in the community. This typically begins at approximately age 14, and active involvement of the adolescent in the planning is encouraged. Development of friendships and networks of social support continues to be important, and during this period differences between the individual with ID and same-aged typically developing peers may be more evident. As we have mentioned previously [70], the area of transition to independence is one with a sparse empirical literature, although several recent initiatives promoting self-determination in adolescents with ID have shown some success [111].

Adulthood and independence

Most individuals with ID show continued support needs as adults, with an increased focus on independence from parents and other primary caregivers. While many continue to live with their parents into adulthood [112], independent and semi-independent living opportunities are also sought. Parents of adults with ID become increasingly concerned with planning for a time when they will no longer be able to play an active support role [113]. Vocational opportunities and establishments of outlets for social interaction and social support are important areas for intervention, and risk of social isolation is heightened. Appropriate residential supports and meaningful life activities combined with friendship and support from others is associated with increased happiness for these adults [114]. In adulthood, many individuals are vulnerable to experiencing mental and physical health problems which may not be well recognized [115]. It is important to continue to keep in mind the individual's level of functioning and specific strengths and challenges.

Role of neuropsychologists

There has been a general paucity of writing about the neuropsychology of intellectual disability per se (see Bregman et al. [39] for a discussion). There is a tension in the study of the neuropsychology of intellectual disabilities between the etiological approach and the level-of-functioning approach, as discussed for the field more generally by Dykens and Hodapp as the "two cultures" of intellectual disabilities research. Pennington [8] terms these two approaches the "developmental" and the "specific deficit" approach. In the developmental approach, there is a desire to uncover deficits that are common across etiologies of intellectual disability. In the specific deficit approach, there is greater emphasis on patterns of strength and weakness that may be specific to particular etiologies. For the most part, there is an emphasis on the etiological approach among neuropsychologists, which is not surprising given the promise of identification of gene-brain-behavior research. While there is certainly less focus on the level-of-functioning or developmental approach, consideration of more general characteristics of intellectual disability is necessary given that etiology is known in fewer than half of the cases. Additionally, the etiology-based focus may place more weight than is appropriate on a modular approach to the understanding of intelligence, neglecting evidence that intellectual functions are often tied closely to one another in individuals with intellectual disability. In fact, interrelations among intellectual functioning domains may be stronger in individuals with ID than in those without [116]. Intellectual disability has been broadly related to slower processing speed and cognitive efficiency, and working memory deficits [40].

As we have argued elsewhere, a central role of neuropsychologists, and developmental neuropsychologists in particular, is to apply an understanding of neurocognitive disorders to the assessment of a child's pattern of strengths and weaknesses, and to point families in the direction of appropriate interventions. Advances in molecular and clinical genetics and perinatal medicine in general have resulted in a growth in research examining the phenotypes associated with a broad range of identified etiologies of neurodevelopmental disorders. For neuropsychologists in particular, knowledge of etiology can play an important role in the assessment and intervention process, as certain etiologies appear to be associated with particular patterns of cognitive functioning and behavior. Given the focus of neuropsychologists on information-processing styles and patterns of individual strength and weakness, consideration of etiology when it is known is consistent with a neuropsychological approach to assessment and intervention. Knowledge of the etiology of mental retardation can add greater nuance to the portrait of the child with a cognitive disability by providing initial hypotheses about the patterns of strengths and weaknesses that are likely to be present. There is also research pointing to particular aspects of cognitive functioning that are most likely to be affected for individuals with intellectual disabilities more generally. Expectations about the nature of strengths and weaknesses can assist neuropsychologists in choosing appropriate assessment tools to sample the areas of functioning most likely to be relevant to the child at hand. Moreover, neuropsychologists have much to contribute to the study of effective interventions. Their careful characterization of patterns of ability may suggest that particular interventions are likely to be most beneficial. There is a particular role of neuropsychologists in designing and conducting treatment research to examine the fit between profiles of abilities and difficulties and particular interventions (see Klein-Tasman et al. [70] for further discussion).

References

1. Luckasson R, et al. *Mental Retardation: Definition, Classification, and Systems of Supports* 10th edn. Washington DC: American Association on Mental Retardation; 2002.

2. Schalock RL, et al. The renaming of mental retardation: understanding the change to the term intellectual disability. *Intellect Dev Disabil* 2007;**45**(2):116–24.

3. APA. *Diagnostic and Statistical Manual of Mental Disorders*, 4th edn, *text revision [DSM-IV-TR]*. Washington DC: American Psychiatric Association; 2000.

4. World Health Organization. *International Classification of Functioning, Disability, and Health (ICF)*. Geneva: 2001.

5. AAIDD. *Frequently asked questions on intellectual disability and the AAIDD definition (updated January 2008)*. [cited 03/15/2009]; Available from: http://www.aamr.org/content_185.cfm.

6. Prifitera A, Weiss LG, Saklofske DH. The WISC-III in context. In Saklofske A, ed. *WISC-III Clinical use and Interpretation: Scientist-practitioner Perspectives*. San Diego: Academic Press; 1998:1–38.

7. Luckasson R, et al. *Mental Retardation: Definition, Classification, and Systems of Support*, 9th edn.

Washington DC: American Association on Mental Retardation; 1992.

8. Pennington BF. *The Development of Psychopathology: Nature and Nurture*. New York: Guilford; 2002.

9. Clausen JA. Mental deficiency: Development of a concept. *Am J Ment Defic* 1967; **71**: 727–45.

10. Dykens EM, Hodapp RM. Research in mental retardation: toward an etiologic approach. *J Child Psychol Psychiatry* 2001;**42**(1):49–71.

11. Dykens EM, Hodapp RM, Finucane B. *Genetics and Mental Retardation Syndromes: A New Look at Behavior and Interventions*. Baltimore, MD: Brookes; 2000.

12. Hodapp RM, Dykens EM. Mental retardation. In Mash R, Barkley R, eds. *Child Psychopathology*, New York: Guilford; 1996:326–89.

13. McDermott S, et al. Epidemiology and etiology of mental retardation. In Mulick J, Rojahn J, Jacobson J, eds. *Handbook of Intellectual and Developmental Disabilities*. Springer; 2007:3.

14. Nichols PL. Familial mental retardation. *Behav Genet* 1984;**14**(3):161–70.

15. Zigman WB, et al. Alzheimer's disease in Down syndrome: neurobiology and risk. *Ment Retard Dev Disabil Res Rev* 2007;**13**(3):237–46.

16. Klein BPM, Mervis CB. Contrasting patterns of cognitive abilities of 9- and 10-year-olds with Williams Syndrome or Down Syndrome. *Dev Neuropsych* 1999;**16**:177–96.

17. Pennington BF, et al. The neuropsychology of Down syndrome: evidence of hippocampal dysfunction. *Child Dev* 2003;**74**:75–93.

18. Fishler KK, et al. Mental development in Down syndrome mosaicism. *Am J Ment Retard* 1991;**96**(3):345–51.

19. Abbeduto L, et al. The linguistic and cognitive profile of Down syndrome: Evidence from a comparison with fragile X syndrome. *Down Syndr Res Pract* 2001;**7**:9–15.

20. Wang PP. A neuropsychological profile of Down syndrome: cognitive skills and brain morphology. *Ment Retard Dev Disabil Res Rev* 1996;**2**:102–8.

21. Zigler EHR. Behavioral functioning in individuals with mental retardation. *Annu Rev Psychol* 1991;**42**:29–50.

22. Myers BA, Pueschel SM. Psychiatric disorders in persons with Down syndrome. *J Nerv Ment Dis* 1991;**179**:609–13.

23. Dykens EMK, Casari C. Maladaptive behavior in children with Prader-Willi syndrome, Down syndrome, and nonspecific mental retardation. *Am J Ment Retard* 1997;**102**:228–37.

24. Hodapp R, Desjardin J. Genetic etiologies of mental retardation; issues for intervention and interventionists. *J Dev Phys Disabil* 2002;**14**:323–38.

25. DeBoulle K, Verkerk AJMH, Reyniers E, Vits L, Hendrikx J, Van Roy B, Ven Den Bos F, et al. A point mutation in the FMR-1 gene associated with Fragile X mental retardation. *Nat Genet* 1993;**3**:31–5.

26. Tassone F, Hagerman RJ, et al. FMRP expression as a potential prognostic indicator in Fragile X syndrome. *Am J Med Genet* 1999;**84**:250–61.

27. Butler MG, Allen GA, et al. Anthropometric comparison of mentally retarded males with and without the Fragile X syndrome. *Am J Med Genet* 1991;**38**:260–8.

28. Hagerman RJ, Van Housen K, et al. Consideration of connective tissue dysfunction in the Fragile X syndrome. *Am J Med Genet* 1984;**17**:111–21.

29. Bennetto, L, Pennington BF, Porter DT, Taylor AK, Hagerman RJ. Profile of cognitive functioning in women with the Fragile X mutation. *Neuropsychology* 2001;**15**:290–9.

30. Abbeduto, L, Hagerman RJ. Language and communication in fragile X syndrome. *Ment Retard Dev Disabil Res Rev* 1997;**3**:313–22.

31. Kemper MB, Hagerman RJ, Altshul-Stark D. Cognitive profiles of boys with Fragile X syndrome. *Am J Med Genet* 1988;**30**:191–200.

32. Powell L, Houghton S, Douglas G. Comparison of etiology-specific cognitive functioning profiles for individuals with Fragile X and individuals with Down Syndrome. *J Spec Educ* 1997;**31**:362–76.

33. Hagerman RJ, Kemper M, Hudson M. Learning disabilities and attentional problems in boys with Fragile X syndrome. *Am J Dis Child* 1985;**139**:674–8.

34. Fisch GS, Simensen, R, Tarleton J, Chalifoux M, Holden JJA, Carpenter, N, et al. Longitudinal study of cognitive abilities and adaptive behavior in Fragile X males: A prospective multicenter analysis. *Am J Med Genet* 1996;**64**:356–61.

35. Fisch GS, Carpenter N, Holden JJA, Howard-Peoples PN, Maddalena A, Borghgraef, M, et al. Longitudinal changes of cognitive and adaptive behavior in Fragile X females: a prospective multicenter analysis. *Am J Med Genet* 1999;**83**:308–12.

36. Einfeld SL, Tonge BJ, Florio T. Behavioral and emotional disturbance in Fragile X syndrome. *Am J Med Genet* 1994;**51**:386–91.

37. Backes M, Genc B, Schreck J, Doerfler W, Lehmkuhl G, von Gontard A. Cognitive and behavioral profile of fragile X boys: correlations to molecular data. *Am J Med Genet* 2000;**95**:150–6.

38. Bregman JD, Leckman JF, Ort SI. Fragile X syndrome: genetic predisposition to psychopathology. *J Autism Dev Disabil* 1988;**18**:343–54.

39. Hagerman J, Sobesky WE. Psychopathology in fragile X Syndrome. *Am J Orthopsychiat* 1989;**59**(1):142–52.

40. Pennington BF, Bennetto L. Toward a neuropsychology of mental retardation. In Burack J, Hodapp R, Zigler E, eds. *Handbook of Mental Retardation and Development.* Cambridge: Cambridge University Press; 1998: 80–114.

41. Kaemingk K, Paquette A. Effects of prenatal alcohol exposure on neuropsychological functioning. *Dev Neuropsychol* 1999;**15**(1):111–140.

42. Wass TS, Mattson SN, Riley EP. Neuroanatomical and neurobehavioral effects of heavy prenatal alcohol exposure. In Brick J, ed. *Handbook of the Medical Consequences of Alcohol and Drug Abuse.* New York: Haworth Press; 2004: 139–69.

43. Kodituwakku PW. Defining the behavioral phenotype in children with fetal alcohol spectrum disorders: a review. *Neurosci Biobehav Rev* 2007;**31**(2):192–201.

44. Dietrich KN. Environmental neurotoxicants and psychological development. In Yeates KO, Ris MD, Taylor HG, eds. *Pediatric Neuropsychology: Research, Theory, and Practice.* New York: Guilford 2000: 206–34.

45. Mendola P, et al. Environmental factors associated with a spectrum of neurodevelopmental deficits. *Ment Retard Dev Disabil Res Rev* 2002;**8**(3):188–97.

46. Sampson PD, et al. Incidence of fetal alcohol syndrome and prevalence of alcohol-related neurodevelopmental disorder. *Teratology* 1997;**56**(5):317–26.

47. Lee BH, Stoll BJ, McDonald SA. Neurodevelopmental outcomes of extreme-low-birth-weight infants born between 2001 and 2002. *Hong Kong Med J* 2008;**14**(1):21–8.

48. Barrington KJ. Postnatal steroids and neurodevelopmental outcomes: a problem in the making. *Pediatrics* 2001;**107**(6):1425–6.

49. Leonard H, et al. Relation between intrauterine growth and subsequent intellectual disability in a ten-year population cohort of children in Western Australia. *Am J Epidemiol* 2008;**167**(1):103–11.

50. Yaqoob M, et al. Mild intellectual disability in children in Lahore, Pakistan: aetiology and risk factors. *J Intellect Disabil Res* 2004;**48**(Pt 7):663–71.

51. Constable RT, et al. Prematurely born children demonstrate white matter microstructural differences at 12 years of age, relative to term control subjects: an investigation of group and gender effects. *Pediatrics* 2008;**121**:306–16.

52. Lanphear BP, et al. Low-level environmental lead exposure and children's intellectual function: an international pooled analysis. *Environ Health Perspect* 2005;**113**(7):894–9.

53. Tong S, et al. Lifetime exposure to environmental lead and children's intelligence at 11–13 years: the Port Pirie cohort study. *Br Med J* 1996. **312**(7046):1569–75.

54. Baghurst PA, et al. Environmental exposure to lead and children's intelligence at the age of seven years: the Port Pirie cohort study. *N Engl J Med* 1992;**327**(18):1279–84.

55. Needleman HL, Bellinger D. Studies of lead exposure and the developing central nervous system: a reply to Kaufman. *Arch Clin Neuropsychol*, 2001; **16**(4):359–74.

56. Needleman HL, Schell A, Bellinger D, Leviton A, Allred EN. The long-term effects of exposure to low doses of lead in childhood. An 11-year follow-up report. *N Engl J Med* 1990;**322**(2):83–8.

57. Needleman HLGCA. Low-level lead exposure and the IQ of children. A meta-analysis of modern studies. *J Am Med Assoc* 1990;**263**(5):673–8.

58. Goldman LR, Shannon MW. Technical report: mercury in the environment: Implications for pediatricians. *Pediatrics* 2001;**108**(1):197–205.

59. Graff JC, et al. In-home toxic chemical exposures and children with intellectual and developmental disabilities. *Pediatr Nurs* 2006;**32**(6):596–603.

60. Koger SM, Schettler T, Weiss B., Environmental toxicants and developmental disabilities: A challenge for psychologists. *Am Psychol* 2005;**60**(3):243–55.

61. Axtell CD, et al. Association between methylmercury exposure from fish consumption and child development at five and a half years of age in the Seychelles child development study: An evaluation of nonlinear relationships. *Environ Res Sect* 2000;**84**:71–80.

62. Myers GJ, Davidson, PW. Does methylmercury have a role in causing developmental disabilities in children? *Environ Health Perspect* 2000;**108 Suppl** 3:413–20.

63. Ornoy A, et al. Developmental outcome of school-age children born to mothers with heroin dependency: importance of environmental factors. *Dev Med Child Neurol* 2001;**43**(10):668–75.

64. Parker RS, Rosenblum A. IQ loss and emotional dysfunctions after mild head injury incurred in a motor vehicle accident. *J Clin Psychol* 1996;**52**(1):32–43.

65. Ewing-Cobbs L, et al. Late intellectual and academic outcomes following traumatic brain injury sustained during early childhood. *J Neurosurg* 2006;**105**(4):287–96.

66. Anderson V, et al. Attentional skills following traumatic brain injury in childhood: A componential analysis. *Brain Injury* 1998;**12**(11):937–49.

67. Ewing-Cobbs L, et al., Longitudinal neuropsychological outcome in infants and preschoolers with traumatic brain injury. *J Int Neuropsychol Soc* 1997;**3**(6):581–91.

68. Sherrard J, Tonge BJ, and Ozanne-Smith J. Injury risk in young people with intellectual disability. *J Intellect Disabil Res* 2002;**46**(1):6.

69. Hartley SL, Horrell SV, Maclean WE. Jr. Science to practice in Intellectual Disability: the role of empirically supported treatments. In Jacobson J, Mulick J, Rojahn J, eds. *Handbook of Intellectual and Developmental Disabilities*. New York: Springer; 2007: 425–43.

70. Klein-Tasman BP, Phillips KD, Kelderman J. Interventions for children with genetic syndromes associated with intellectual disability. In Hunter S, Donders J, eds. *Pediatric Neuropsychology Interventions*. London: Cambridge University Press; 2007: 193–223.

71. Matson JL, Laud RB. Assessment and treatment: psychopathology among people with developmental delays. In Jacobson J, Mulick J, Rojahn J, eds. *Handbook of Intellectual and Developmental Disabilities*. New York: Springer; 2007: 507–39.

72. Reiss S, Levitan GW, Szyszko J. Emotional disturbance and mental retardation: Diagnostic overshadowing. *Am J Ment Defic* 1982;**86**:567–74.

73. Rush KS, et al., Assessing psychopathology in individuals with developmental disabilities. *Behav Modif* 2004;**28**(5):621–37.

74. Tsiouris JA, et al. Challenging behaviours should not be considered as depressive equivalents in individuals with intellectual disability. *J Intellect Disabil Res* 2003;**47** (Pt 1):14–21.

75. McBrien JA. Assessment and diagnosis of depression in people with intellectual disability. *J Intellect Disabil Res* 2003;**47**(1):1.

76. Matson JL, et al. Depression and social skills among individuals with severe and profound mental retardation. *J Dev Phys Disabil* 2006;**18**(4):393–400.

77. Matson JL. The treatment of behavioral characteristics of depression in the mentally retarded. *Behav Ther*, 1982;**13**:209–18.

78. Reudrich SL. Treatment of bipolar mood disorder in persons with mental retardation. In Fletcher RJ, Dosen A, ed. *Mental Health Aspects of Mental Retardation*. Lexington, MA: Lexington Books; 1993: 268–80.

79. Dagnan D, Chadwick P. Cognitive-behaviour therapy for people with learning disabilities. In Kroese B, Dagnan D, Loumidis K, eds. *Cognitive-behaviour Therapy for People with Learning Disability*. London: Routledge; 1997: 110–23.

80. Dagnan D, Jahoda A. Cognitive-behavioral intervention for people with intellectual disability and anxiety disorders. *J Appl Res Intellect Disabil* 2006;**19**:91–7.

81. Racusin R, Kovner-Kline K, King BH. Selective serotonin reuptake inhibitors in intellectual disability. *Ment Retard Dev Disabil Res Rev* 1999;**5**(4):264–9.

82. King R, Fay G, Croghan P. Rapid cycling bipolar disorder in individuals with developmental disability. *Ment Health Aspects Dev Disabil* 2000;**2**:50–8.

83. Feinstein C, Reiss AL Psychiatric disorder in mentally retarded children and adolescents: the challenges of meaningful diagnosis. *Child Adolesc Psychiatric Clin N Am*, 1996;**5**:827–52.

84. Lindsay WR, Morrison FM., The effects of behavioural relaxation on cognitive performance in adults with severe intellectual disabilities. *J Intellect Disabil Res* 1996;**40**(4):285.

85. Hatton C. Psychosocial interventions for adults with intellectual disabilities and mental health problems: a review. *J Ment Health* 2002;**11**(4):357–73.

86. Crabbe H.F. Treatment of anxiety disorders in persons with mental retardation. In Dosen A, Days K, eds. *Treating Mental Illness and Behavior Disorders in Children and Adults with Mental Retardation*. Washington DC: American Psychiatric Press; 2001: 227–41.

87. Khreim I, Mikklesen E. Anxiety disorders in adults with mental retardation. *Psychiatric Ann*, 1997;**27**:175–81.

88. Thalayasingam S, Alexander RT, Singh I. The use of clozapine in adults with intellectual disability. *J Intellect Disabil Res* 2004;**48**(6):572–9.

89. Bodfish JW, et al. Compulsions in adults with mental retardation: prevalence, phenomenology, and co-morbidity with stereotypy and self-injury. *Am J Ment Retard* 1995;**100**:183–92.

90. McClintock K, Hall S, Oliver C. Risk markers associated with challenging behaviors in people with intellectual disabilities: A meta-analytic study. *J Intellect Disabil Res* 2003;**47**(6):405–16.

91. Bodfish, JW. Stereotypy, self-injury, and related abnormal repetitive behaviors. In Jacobson J, Mulick J, Rojahn J, eds. *Handbook of Intellectual and Developmental Disabilities*. New York: Springer; 2007; 481–505.

92. Gardner WI. *Aggression and Other Disruptive Behavioral Challenges: Biomedical and Psychosocial Assessment and Treatments*. Kingston, NY: NADD; 2002.

93. Aman MGR. Pharmacotherapy. In Jacobson J, Mulick J, Rojahn J, eds. *Handbook of Intellectual and Developmental Disabilities*. New York: Springer; 2007; 657–71.

94. Gardner WI. Aggression in persons with intellectual disabilities and mental disorders. In Jacobson J, Mulick J, Rojahn J, eds. *Handbook of Intellectual and Developmental Disabilities*. New York: Springer; 2007; 541–62.

95. Nezu CM, et al. Sex offending behavior. In Jacobson J, Mulick J, Rojahn J, eds. *Handbook of Intellectual and Developmental Disabilities*. New York: Springer; 2007; 635–55.

96. Nezu CM, Greenberg J, Nezu AM. Project STOP: cognitive behavioral assessment and treatment for sex offenders with intellectual disability. *J Forensic Psychol Pract* 2006;**6**(3):87.

97. Antshel KM, et al. Is ADHD a valid disorder in children with intellectual delays? *Clin Psychol Rev* 2006;**26**:555–72.

98. LaMalfa G, Lassi S, Bertelli M, et al. Detecting attention-deficit/hyperactivity disorder (ADHD) in adults with intellectual disability. *Res Rev Disabil* 2008;**29**(2):158–64.

99. Hastings RP, et al. Symptoms of ADHD and their correlates in children with intellectual disabilities. *Res Dev Disabil* 2005;**26**:456–68.

100. Pearson DA, et al. Patterns of behavioral adjustment and maladjustment in mental retardation: comparison of children with and without ADHD. *Am J Ment Retard* 2000;**105**(4):236–51.

101. Filho AGC, et al. Comparison of risperidone and methylphenidate for reducing ADHD symptoms in children and adolescents with moderate mental retardation. *J Am Acad Child Adolesc Psychiatry* 2005;**44**(8):748–55.

102. Jou R, Handen B, Hardan A, Psychostimulant treatment of adults with mental retardation and attention deficit/hyperactivity disorder. *Austral Psychiat* 2004;**12**(4):376–9.

103. Jones VF, Jones LS. *Comprehensive Classroom Management: Creating Positive Learning Environments for All Students* 4th edn. Boston: Allyn and Bacon; 1995.

104. Carpenter LB. Utilizing travel cards to increase productive student behavior, teacher collaboration, and parent-school communication. *Education and Training in Mental Retardation and Developmental Disabilities*, 2001. **36**(3):318–22.

105. Mervis CB, Robinson BF. Expressive vocabulary ability of toddlers with Williams syndrome or Down syndrome: a comparison. *Dev Neuropsychol* 2000;**17**(1):111–26.

106. Fisher AG. *Assessment of Motor and Process Skills: Development, Standardization, and Administration Manual*, vol. 1, 4th edn. Fort Collins: Three Star Press; 2001.

107. Fisher AG. *Assessment of Motor and Process Skills: User Manual*, vol. 2, 4th edn. Fort Collins: Three Star Press; 2001.

108. Jenkins JR, Sells CJ. Physical and occupational therapy: Effects related to treatment, frequency, and motor delay. *J Learn Disabil* 1984;**17**(2):89–95.

109. *Individuals with Disabilities Education Act*. 1990.

110. Mechling LC. Assistive technology as a self-management tool for prompting students with intellectual disabilities to initiate and complete daily tasks: a literature review. *Educ Train Dev Disabil* 2007;**42**(3):252–69.

111. Wehmeyer ML, et al. *Promoting Self Determination in Students with Developmental Disabilities*. New York: Guilford Press; 2007.

112. Lakin KC, Prouty R, Coucouvanis K. HCBS recipients are increasingly likely to live with parents or other relatives. *Intellect Dev Disabil* 2007;**45**(5):359–61.

113. Heller T, Caldwell J, Factor A. Aging family caregivers: policies and practices. *Ment Retard Dev Disabil Res Rev*, 2007;**13**(2):136–42.

114. Emerson E, Hatton C. Self-reported well-being of women and men with intellectual disabilities in England. *Am J Ment Retard* 2008;**113**:143–55.

115. The Surgeon General, *Closing the gap: a national blueprint to improve the health of persons with mental retardation*. Washington DC: Department of Health and Human Services, Office of the Surgeon General; 2002.

116. Detterman DK, Daniel MH. Correlations of mental tests with each other and with cognitive variables are highest for low IQ groups. *Intelligence* 1989;**13**(4):349.

Lifespan aspects of PDD/autism spectrum disorders (ASD)

Julie M. Wolf and Sarah J. Paterson

Introduction

Autism is a neurodevelopmental disorder that involves impairment in three broad areas as identified by the Diagnostic and Statistical Manual of Mental Disorders, 4th edition [1]: socialization, communication, and repetitive or restricted behaviors and interests. With regard to socialization, individuals with autism may show limited use of nonverbal behaviors, such as eye contact or facial expressions directed to others. They may demonstrate limited social and emotional reciprocity, may not seek to share their enjoyment of activities and interests with others, and often fail to develop appropriate peer relationships. In the area of communication, individuals with autism may have a significant language delay and have difficulties with symbolic play. Those individuals with strong verbal skills still tend to have communication impairments, including difficulty with reciprocal conversation, and use of unusual or repetitive language. Finally, in the area of restricted and repetitive behaviors, individuals with autism may show a preoccupation with parts of objects (e.g. repeatedly spinning the wheel of a toy car), or an intense preoccupation with an unusual topic of interest (e.g. radiators, train schedules). In some individuals, these areas of interest become almost all-consuming, such that it is difficult for them to relate to others without bringing up their preoccupation. Individuals with autism often show a need for routine and predictability, and may exhibit ritualistic behavior or become upset by disruptions in their usual routine. Finally, some individuals with autism exhibit repetitive movements, such as hand-flapping or body-rocking. The DSM-IV-TR specifies that in order to meet criteria for a diagnosis of autism, an individual must have six of these symptoms in total, including at least two in the social domain, and at least one in each of the other two domains. Thus, an individual does not need to display all of the characteristics of autism, and in fact the presentation of autism is highly heterogeneous, with two individuals rarely showing the identical pattern of symptoms.

Autism is one of several of the pervasive developmental disorders (also referred to as autism spectrum disorders, or ASD) identified in the DSM-IV-TR. Also included in this category are Asperger's disorder, Rett's disorder, childhood disintegrative disorder, and pervasive developmental disorder, not otherwise specified (PDD-NOS). Rett's disorder and childhood disintegrative disorder are very rare, and are not discussed in this chapter. Asperger's disorder involves impairments in socialization and repetitive/restricted behaviors, with normal to above-average cognitive and communication ability. Individuals with Asperger's disorder are often highly verbal, and may have intense interests about which they collect vast amounts of information [2]. PDD-NOS is the diagnosis assigned to individuals who show significant symptoms of an autism spectrum disorder, but in a pattern that does not meet criteria for any of the other ASDs.

Recent estimates of the prevalence of ASD is 1 in 150 individuals in the USA [3], with a male:female ratio of approximately 4:1. There have been recent reports that the incidence of autism is increasing [4], although it is not clear whether this represents a true rise in incidence or whether other factors such as greater awareness of the disorder or changes in application of the diagnostic criteria may contribute to this increase. Autism is known to be highly heritable, with current thinking that it is a polygenic disorder, with multiple interacting genetic factors [5]. This is consistent with the significant heterogeneity in phenotype across the autism spectrum.

Pathophysiology of autism spectrum disorders

Head and brain growth in autism

One of the most salient biomarkers for ASD appears to be increased head size. Numerous head circumference (HC) studies have confirmed the association between autism and macrocephaly [6–8]. Along with this indirect measure of brain size, MRI studies have found increased brain volume in ASD [9–12]. Schultz [13] analyzed high-resolution structural MRI data from 117 males compared to 108 healthy male controls. The volume of the whole brain and of the frontal, temporal, and parietal lobes was significantly increased between 3.4% and 9.0% in the autism group compared to controls. No significant differences were found in the brain stem, cerebellum, subcortical complex, and the occipital lobes. Overall, brain size was 5% greater in all subtypes of ASD than controls. There were no significant differences within ASD subtypes.

Studies have shown that brain volume may be enlarged by as much as 10% in toddlers with autism [10, 12, 14], which is a larger increase than is seen in older children and adults. These cross-sectional data suggest that the abnormality is one of early overgrowth followed by relatively slower growth during which time healthy controls "catch up" to some degree; however, caution is warranted until true longitudinal studies are conducted. The current literature is not entirely clear about whether increased brain size is present at birth or emerges over development. Courchesne and colleagues [15] found that HC was slightly smaller at birth in their sample and Gillberg and de Souza [16] reported a mean HC that is enlarged at birth. Another study reports normal HC at birth [6]. The majority of the data at present point to differences in the developmental trajectory and this fits with an emerging hypothesis that tissue growth and elaboration of neural architecture and connectivity may occur prematurely in autism, with less guidance and shaping by functional experiences and adaptive learning, thus contributing directly to the expression of autistic behaviors [10]. This evidence from brain development coincides with recent results, which have pointed to the emergence of early behavioral signs of ASD at around 12 months [17].

It appears that this aberrant brain growth is primarily driven by differences in white matter development. A study of 2–3-year-olds with autism showed they had 18% more cerebral white matter and 12% more cerebral gray matter than age-matched controls, but in 12–16-year-olds these comparisons favored controls. Evidence of decreased cerebral white matter in adolescents and adults with autism [10] is also consistent with other studies showing size reductions in the cross-sectional area of the splenium [18] and the genu [11] of the corpus callosum measured at midline. However, other data suggest that white matter remains overgrown into adulthood. In a large sample [13], there was a 7% enlargement of white matter compared to a 3.2% enlargement of cortical gray matter. Regionally, the white matter enlargement was greatest in the temporal lobes (10–11% enlargement). Increased white matter has been found in other studies and has been used to argue for a fundamental problem with cortical connectivity [19, 20]. The corpus collosum, which consists of long-range fiber tracts, is reduced in volume in individuals with ASD and it had been demonstrated that white matter consists of an abundance of short-range fibers [19]. These studies are consistent with neuropathological evidence of decreased neuronal cell size in ASDs, suggesting a paucity of long-range fibers since longer fibers require larger cell bodies to support their metabolic needs [21]. DTI is an MRI modality that enables the assessment of fiber pathway orientation, estimation of structural connectivity, and an estimate of the "integrity" of the cerebral white matter. Using DTI in a small sample of children and adolescents with ASD, Barnea-Goraly et al. [20] found reduced fractional anisotropy (a measure of axonal coherence using the diffusion properties of water) in the anterior cingulate, body and genu of the corpus callosum, ventromedial prefrontal areas, subgenual prefrontal regions, superior temporal sulcus, fusiform gyrus, and amygdala.

Abnormalities in social brain circuitry

Given that social impairments are at the core of ASD, it is not surprising that impairments in a number of brain areas underlying social ability have been documented in ASD. Involvement of the amygdala is supported by animal models in which lesions to the amygdala and other temporal lobe structures result in reduced social behaviors in prairie voles [22], rats [23], and primates [24]. Structural abnormalities of the amygdala in individuals with autism have been reported by a number of studies, although the nature of these findings has been inconsistent, with some studies suggesting smaller amygdala volumes [25–28], and others suggesting increased amygdala volumes [12, 29]. Abnormal functional activity in the amygdala has also been demonstrated [28, 30].

The fusiform gyrus, known for its involvement in face processing, has also been implicated in autism. Schultz et al. [31] were the first to report hypoactivation of the fusiform gyrus in individuals with ASD when viewing faces, and this finding has since been replicated numerous times [28, 32, 33]. Fewer studies have investigated structural abnormalities in the fusiform gyrus, although one MRI study found abnormal asymmetry in the posterior temporal fusiform gyrus in

Table 9b.1.

Neurobehavioral characteristics of ASD	Neuroanatomical correlates
Social/emotional processing impairments	Structural abnormalities and hypoactivation within limbic system (including amygdala, fusiform gyrus, superior temporal sulcus)
Deficits in some areas of attention, including shifting, orienting, disengaging; possible strengths in other areas, e.g. divided attention	Mixed findings showing either normal activation or hypoactivation of frontal, parietal, and occipital regions
Deficits in verbal and source memory; accounts of exceptional episodic and rote memory	Research is limited, but some reports of enlarged or abnormally shaped hippocampus
Language impairments	Reduced Broca's area activity; increased Wernicke's area activity; engagement of visual cortex and parietal areas
Strong visual-spatial skills (in some individuals); local perceptual bias; possible global processing deficit	Reduced activation of premotor, parietal, occipital, and ventral temporal regions; recruitment of right primary visual cortex and bilateral extrastriate areas
Mixed reports of normal and impaired executive functioning; performance may be task-specific	Mixed findings involving frontal lobes, parietal lobs, cerebellum, insula, and anterior cingulate; recruited areas likely also task-specific

individuals with autism [19], and another MRI study found slightly, but not significantly, smaller fusiform volumes in individuals with autism as compared to controls [28].

The superior temporal sulcus (STS) also appears to be involved in the pathophysiology of autism. The STS plays a role in social cognition, and appears to contribute to some of the social impairments observed in ASD, including voice perception, theory of mind/understanding the intentions of others, and eye gaze (see Zilbovicius et al. [34] for a review of the role of the STS in ASD).

Thus, it is clear that a network of limbic and other social brain structures is involved in ASD. Recent research attention has moved toward examining interconnectivities between these and other brain areas [35, 36], consistent with the notion of autism as a disorder of connectivity.

Cognitive manifestations of autism spectrum disorders

The heterogeneity seen in the behavioral phenotype of ASD extends to its cognitive manifestations, with no clear pattern emerging as to a cognitive profile that characterizes the disorder. Individuals with ASD often display a cognitive profile characterized by a high degree of variability (i.e. with more pronounced strengths and weaknesses than typically developing individuals [37]), although the particular pattern of strengths and weaknesses is not uniform across individuals. In this regard, the cognitive profiles of individuals with autism are akin to the cognitive profiles of typically developing individuals, who also show individual differences with regard to areas of strength and weakness. With this caveat, what follows is a review of the patterns of strengths and weaknesses that may be most often observed in individuals with ASD, with a summary provided in Table 9b.1.

Attention

Individuals with autism have demonstrated difficulties with shifting, orienting, and disengaging attention [38, 39], although these impairments may be task-specific [40]. Such difficulties are already present in infancy [17]. Impairment in the ability to disengage attention from one stimulus to shift it to another in 12-month-old infants at risk for ASD is predictive of ADOS scores at 24 months. This impairment is likely to contribute to difficulty with joint attention, which has implications for social and language development [41]. However, there are aspects of attention in which some individuals with ASD excel. For example, some evidence suggests that adults with autism are better able to divide attention than are typically developing individuals [42]. Consistent with these strengths, Kennedy and Courchesne [43] found normal organization of the dorsal attention network (including pre-supplementary motor area, intraparietal sulcus, and superior precentral sulcus). Behavioral deficits in spatial attention in individuals with ASD have been found to be associated with hypoactivation in frontal, parietal, and occipital regions, and particularly in the inferior parietal lobule [44].

Memory

The findings with regard to memory skills of individuals with autism are mixed. Some studies suggest impairments in verbal memory [45] and source memory [46]. Deficits in episodic memory are also reported [47], although there are many clinical accounts of individuals with ASD who have exceptional episodic memory, as well as exceptional memory in general for topics that interest them. Very few studies have directly examined the brain mechanisms involved in memory ability in ASD, although there are reports of structural abnormalities of the hippocampus [48, 49], an area known to be involved in memory function.

Language

Several studies are now focusing on the early language skills of infants at risk for autism, and those who are newly diagnosed. Wetherby and colleagues [50] found that 18-month-olds who were later diagnosed with ASD engaged in fewer communicative acts than their typically developing counterparts, with particular impairments in communication to establish joint attention and the use of deictic gestures, for example showing and pointing. In addition, videos taken around the first birthday suggest that infants with ASD babble less than typically developing infants and use fewer gestures [51]. Using the Macarthur Communicative Development Inventory, a parent report questionnaire, Mitchell et al. [52] also found that 12-month-olds who developed ASD exhibited fewer gestures, and were delayed in language comprehension at 18 months.

The language skills of children and adults with ASD are quite variable. Children with classic autism tend to show a deficit in verbal ability relative to their performance on nonverbal or visuospatial tasks, whereas children with Asperger's disorder often show the opposite pattern, with verbal skills emerging as a significant strength. Some individuals with autism are completely nonverbal, while others (particularly those with Asperger's disorder) are highly verbal with advanced knowledge of vocabulary. The grammar skills of children with ASD are mixed, and many children with ASD demonstrate lower receptive than expressive language abilities. Even individuals with Aperger's disorder, despite their relative verbal strength, demonstrate impairments in their functional use of language. They may demonstrate unusual word choice, or repetitive, perseverative, or overly formal language. They also tend to have impairments in pragmatic skills (i.e. in appropriately using their language in a social context).

Children with ASD also demonstrate atypical perception and production of voice prosody. For example, Paul et al. [53] found that individuals with ASD are impaired in their ability to perceive stress patterns in speech when used either for grammatical functions or for pragmatic or affective functions. Children with ASD often speak with an atypical voice inflection, which may be overly sing-song, nasal, mechanical, or monotone. See Tager-Flusberg and Caronna [54] for a comprehensive review of language abilities in ASD.

During language-processing tasks, studies have demonstrated reduced activity in Broca's area, and increased activity in Wernicke's area [55, 56] among individuals with ASD. There is also evidence to suggest that individuals with ASD employ perceptual processing areas when processing language, including visual cortex and parietal areas [57, 58], suggesting that individuals with autism utilize mental imagery when processing language.

Visual-spatial/perceptual skills

Visual-spatial skill is an area of relative strength for some individuals with autism [59], as evidenced by strong performance on the Block Design task of the Wechsler intelligence scales [60] and on embedded figures tasks [61]. Some studies suggest that individuals with ASD are detail-focused and demonstrate a local bias in perceptual processing [62, 63]. However, there is disagreement as to whether this local bias is accompanied by a deficit in global processing [63] or whether global processing is intact [62]. Consistent with the visuospatial strengths of some individuals with ASD, Lee et al. [64] found reduced cortical involvement of left dorsolateral and medial premotor, parietal, occipital, and ventral temporal regions in individuals with ASD when performing an embedded-figures task. With regard to local processing, Manjaly et al. [65] report that individuals with ASD recruit right primary visual cortex and bilateral extrastriate areas, whereas control participants recruited left parietal and premotor areas. The authors suggest that this recruitment of early visual areas is consistent with the notion of enhanced local processing in ASD.

Although visual processing is sometimes an area of strength, deficits emerge when the visual information is social in nature. For example, young children with ASD fail to show a differential electrophysiological response to familiar versus unfamiliar faces, but do so for objects [66] and 2-year-olds with ASD have difficulty with face recognition assessed using a visual paired comparison paradigm [67]. An extensive literature suggests that these impairments in face processing continue into childhood and adulthood (see Sasson [68] for a recent review).

Executive functioning

Executive functioning (EF) deficits have been documented in autism in the areas of mental flexibility, planning, cognitive switching, strategy use, visual working memory, and verbal fluency [69–71]. However, other studies have failed to find EF deficits in individuals with autism [72]. It may be that EF performance is task-specific, as was suggested by Gilbert et al. [73], who found differential brain activation for different EF tasks. A random response-generation task yielded abnormal activity in cerebellar but not frontal areas, while a task involving selection between stimulus-oriented and stimulus-independent thought yielded abnormal functional organization of prefrontal cortex. In another study, individuals with ASD showed increased activation of the left inferior and orbital frontal gyrus during a motor inhibition task; of the left insula during an interference-inhibition task; and of the parietal lobes during a set-shifting/cognitive flexibility task [74]. Finally, Kana et al. [75] found hypoactivation of anterior cingulate among individuals with ASD on a response inhibition task, and greater activation of premotor areas on a task with a high working memory load. Individuals with ASD also showed reduced synchrony between neural circuitries involved in inhibition (including anterior cingulate, middle cingulate, and insula) and frontal and parietal regions.

Psychosocial and behavioral manifestations of ASD

Infancy

Studies of behavior conducted with infant siblings who are at risk for ASD and who are later diagnosed with ASD point to several behavioral markers, which appear to be common in most infants. Infants who later develop ASD are often reported to be irritable and find transitions difficult and are either under- or over-reactive to their environment [17]. In addition, these infants are often gaze-avoidant, fail to orient to their name, exhibit fewer social smiles than their peers, show decreased social interest, and have difficulty with imitation [17, 76]. It is also important to note that repetitive movements of either the body or with

objects can be seen in infants. In fact, in one prospective study the amount of repetitive behavior seen at 12 months was highly predictive of later ASD diagnosis [17, 77]. Studies are also pointing to impairment of motor skills in at-risk infants [17].

Childhood

In addition to the core symptoms of ASD, children with ASD often show any of a number of associated symptoms. These include sensory impairments (either over-sensitivity or undersensitivity to sensory information or a tendency to seek out sensory stimulation [78]), sleep and eating disturbances (often refusing foods of particular textures [79]), mental retardation, which occurs in as many as 50% of children with autism [5], anxiety [80] and disruptive behaviors, including tantrums, oppositionality, and aggression [81].

Adolescence

In adolescence, the difficulties of childhood may persist, while mood-related problems increase in concern, particularly among higher-functioning individuals who may be acutely aware of their impairments. Adolescence is a time of increased social demands, during which peer acceptance is of utmost importance. Adolescents with Asperger's disorder or high-functioning autism may yearn to fit in with their peers, but not have the social skills to do so. They may also be more prone to peer victimization than lower-functioning individuals, because their impairments are less noticed, making teachers less likely to intervene [82].

Adulthood

In adulthood, some individuals show an abatement of symptoms in the area of communication, although significant socialization impairments and restricted/repetitive behaviors persist [83]. Early language ability and IQ are the best predictors of outcome, although they only account for a small percentage of the variance [83]. Co-morbidities are common among adults with ASD, including mood disorders, anxiety, and behavior problems [80, 83]. Seltzer et al. [83] note that some behavior problems may appear to become more severe in adulthood, not because the behavior itself has changed, but because the social context and expectations surrounding those behaviors have changed. For example, while behaviors such as hitting and kicking are problematic in childhood, if these behaviors persist into adulthood they are viewed as quite dangerous and violent. Sexuality also often becomes an issue in adolescence and adulthood. The majority of individuals with ASD demonstrate an interest in sexuality, but may lack the social skills to act appropriately upon those interests, and may in turn engage in deviant or inappropriate sexual behaviors [84].

Although individuals with ASD continue to make progress throughout their lives, adult outcomes are often still poor. A minority of adults go to college, attain employment, have true friendships, or achieve true independent living status [85–87]. The best predictor of quality of life for adults with ASD appears to be the amount of support that is available to the individual [85], with the adult's *perception* of the support they receive perhaps being more important than the actual support received [86].

Very little research has been conducted concerning geriatric issues in ASD, which may be a result of the relatively recent awareness and recognition of the disorder. Older adults with ASD probably grew up during a time when their diagnosis was not identified, and when the common approach to treatment was institutionalization. Identifying the needs of older adults with ASD is an important area for future research, as the many children and young adults now being identified will need appropriate and empirically validated services throughout their lives.

The role of assessment in diagnosing ASD

The "gold standards" in autism diagnosis are the Autism Diagnostic Observation Schedule (ADOS) [88] and the Autism Diagnostic Interview – Revised (ADI-R) [89]. The ADI-R is a semi-structured parent interview that assesses symptoms in the areas of social interaction, communication, and repetitive and stereotyped patterns of interest and behavior, consistent with the DSM-IV criteria for autism. The ADI-R has demonstrated good reliability and validity [90]. Some have criticized it for its lengthy administration time (2 to 3 hours), which limits its utility in clinical settings. The ADOS is a semi-structured assessment of social interaction, communication, play and imagination, and repetitive behaviors and interests, and provides a standardized context in which to observe behaviors. The ADOS has demonstrated good inter-rater reliability, test–retest reliability, and diagnostic validity [91]. The ADOS is intended to be administered in conjunction with the ADI-R, so that both parent-report and direction observation data inform

diagnosis. Both the ADOS and ADI-R include algorithms that provide cut-off scores suggestive of an autism spectrum diagnosis, although these scores are not meant to be conclusive, but rather are intended to be considered along with other data to determine whether DSM-IV-TR criteria for ASD are met.

Although the ADOS and ADI-R are considered the gold standards in ASD diagnosis, a number of other diagnostic measures are available. Among these is the Diagnostic Interview of Social and Communication Disorders (DISCO) [92], which is a semi-structured interview that covers a wider range of behaviors than the ADI-R, with high inter-rater reliability [92]. Another interview which allows for a dimensional (rather than categorical) assessment of ASD as well as other co-morbid disorders is the Developmental, Dimensional, and Diagnostic Interview (3di) [93]. This interview also demonstrates strong inter-rater and test–retest reliability, strong concurrent and criterion validity, and good sensitivity and specificity in differentiating ASD from non-ASD conditions.

With regard to direct observation measures, a widely used alternative to the ADOS is the Childhood Autism Rating Scale (CARS) [94]. While the CARS has good sensitivity, specificity, reliability, and validity, it does not provide a standardized set of activities during which to observe the child, and a critique is that it may simply serve to confirm pre-existing clinician impressions. Thus, Tidmarsh and Volkmar [95] have suggested that the CARS may be best suited as a measure of overall impression, rather than a descriptive measure, and thus may be best used as a screening tool.

There have been recent efforts to develop observation measures suitable for use with children under 2, in order to document early signs of ASD, or important risk markers for these children. The Autism Observational Scale for Infants (AOSI) [96] consists of a semi-structured play session with systematic presses for 18 specific risk markers for autism. The presses target behaviors such as early social interaction, visual tracking and attentional disengagement, imitation, affective responses, reactivity, and sensory-motor development. The presence of seven or more of these markers at 12 months identified 85% of those children later diagnosed at 2 years [17]. Inter-rater agreement on the AOSI total score is excellent at 6, 12, and 18 months, and test–retest reliability (at 12 months) is also good [96]. The ADOS-T is also currently under development and is intended for use with infants between 12 and 30 months who are able to walk. There are currently two algorithms for use with these infants, one for those with no words and one for those with some words [97]. In a study of 272 children between 12 and 30 months, the ADOS-T could distinguish between ASD, developmental disability, and typical development with a sensitivity of 93% and specificity of 93%. Both these instruments hold a great deal of promise for early detection of the first signs of ASD, but it is important for further longitudinal prospective studies to be conducted to investigate the relationship of early signs to later diagnoses. It appears that between 24 and 36 months diagnosis remains quite stable, but we need more data comparing findings in infancy to those in toddlerhood [67].

Autism diagnosis also typically includes an evaluation of adaptive behavior. The Vineland Adaptive Behavior Scales [98] is the most commonly used measure of adaptive functioning in the assessment of autism spectrum disorders, and assesses functioning in the areas of communication, daily living, and socialization. Individuals with autism typically display a highly variable profile on the Vineland, with the most pronounced deficits in socialization [99].

Interventions for individuals with ASD

Of the many treatments available for ASD, behavioral interventions have received the greatest empirical support. Applied Behavioral Analysis (ABA) involves intensive discrete trial instruction in a one-on-one context, with emphasis on generalizing learned skills to other settings. Discrete trials involve providing the child with a prompt or instruction (e.g. "touch cup"), awaiting the child's response, providing a prompt if needed (e.g. guiding the child's hand toward the cup), and feedback (e.g. reinforcement for a correct response). Behavioral interventions are most effective when begun early (prior to age 4), when treatment is intensive (up to 40 hours per week) and long-term, and when generalization to the natural environment is emphasized [100]. Support for the effectiveness of ABA comes from Lovaas's work [101], suggesting significant long-term improvement in children who had received the intervention, as well as from numerous follow-up studies. Despite its extensive empirical support, ABA has been criticized for producing "robotic" behaviors, and because it is expensive and time-intensive, making it infeasible for many families.

Another intervention model for children with ASD is the Treatment and Education of Autism and Related Communication-Handicapped Children (TEACCH) model [102]. TEACCH is a structured teaching program which places emphasis on providing visual and other supports to foster independence. Although the TEACCH method has not undergone extensive empirical investigation, there are some studies supporting its effectiveness [103, 104].

Children with ASD may benefit from a number of assistive devices and technologies to aid in communication. These include the Picture Exchange Communication System (PECS) [105], sign language, and keyboards. Typically, consultation with a specialist in assistive technologies is helpful in determining which augmentative communication system may be warranted for a particular child or adult.

Although no medications are available to treat the core symptoms of ASD, pharmacotherapy can be beneficial in alleviating some of the symptoms that are associated with ASD. SSRIs, mood stabilizers, psychostimulants, and atypical antipsychotics may be effective in treating disruptive behaviors, self-injury, mood and anxiety [81]. Owley [106] provided a summary of approaches for addressing co-morbid emotional and behavioral regulation concerns with pharmacotherapies, and discussed the collaborative role neuropsychologists can play in monitoring and elaborating on the success of medication-based interventions.

Given the social impairments in ASD, there is a clear need for interventions targeting social skill development, and a number of models have been developed and empirically validated. Many of these models involve teaching social skills in an explicit manner, given that children with ASD do not seem to pick up these rules implicitly. These models have demonstrated effectiveness in improving social skills such as greeting and play skills [107]; social initiation, eye contact, experience-sharing, interest in peers, problem-solving skills, and emotional knowledge [108]; conversational skills, topic selection, and self-perception [109]; and increased social interaction time with peers [110]. Gray [111] has developed "social stories" and "comic strip conversations", which are social skills lessons presented in story or cartoon format that are individualized around a specific event or situation that is causing the child difficulty. Outcome studies have demonstrated improved socialization skills and increased duration of social engagement with peers as a result of interventions using social stories; however, only limited generalization and maintenance of these improvements was found [112–114].

Although early interventions show great promise in improving the outcomes of individuals with ASD, some degree of impairment continues into adulthood for most individuals. Unfortunately, services for adults are often lacking. Some recent work has begun to focus on interventions for adults. For example, Howlin et al. [115] report that a supportive employment scheme for adults with ASD (involving work preparation, job finding, and support in the workplace) effectively increased success in finding and maintaining employment. The authors note that investing in appropriate support services such as these could reduce the long-term costs associated with autism. Thus, broadening the array of services and empirically validated interventions for adults is a critical area of future research and policy.

Future research directions

Given the complexity of this heterogeneous disorder, researchers have a long way to go in understanding the etiology of autism and in developing effective interventions appropriate for individuals across the broad autism spectrum. With regard to diagnostic practices, further research is necessary to evaluate whether the current DSM-IV classification system appropriately captures the heterogeneous presentations of ASD. Continued development of assessment measures is also important to ensure that our measures are sensitive to the milder end of the spectrum, while maintaining specificity and not contributing to over-diagnosis. It is also extremely important to continue prospective studies of infant siblings at risk for autism because such studies should shed light on the timing of the emergence of first signs of ASD. Knowing this could help us provide interventions as early as possible in development.

Research into the genetics of autism has come a long way, but continued research is needed to understand the multiple genetic pathways that may lead to ASD, as well as to understand how genetic/environmental interactions may contribute to the disorder. With regard to the physiology of ASD, recent research has begun to suggest abnormalities in white matter tracts combined with atypical functional connectivity. Continued work exploring ASD as a disorder of brain connectivity is needed.

Research is also needed to develop new empirically validated interventions for ASD, and to provide empirical support for the many interventions already in use. As noted, only behavioral approaches have received extensive empirical support. Thus, research is needed to assess the validity of other intervention approaches, so that a wider array of treatment options is available to families.

Finally, it is important that researchers attend to issues throughout the lifespan. Much recent attention

has been on early development, with the recognition that early intervention is essential to optimal outcome. However, adolescents and adults with ASD continue to have functional impairments, and it is essential that research and services attend to this population as well. Furthermore, research on geriatric issues in ASD is notably absent. This is another vital area of work, given that the large numbers of children now being diagnosed with ASD will someday reach adulthood and old age.

References

1. American Psychiatric Association. *Diagnostic and Statistical Manual of Mental Disorders*, 4th edn, text revision. Washington DC: APA; 2000.
2. Klin A, Volkmar FR. Asperger syndrome: diagnosis and external validity. *Child Adolesc Psychiatric Clin N Am* 2003;**12**(1):1–13.
3. CDC. Prevalence of autism spectrum disorders – Autism and Developmental Disabilities Monitoring Network, 14 sites, United States, 2002. *MMWR Surveil Summ* 2007;**56**(SS-1):12–28.
4. Newschaffer CJ, Falb MD, Gurney JG. National autism prevalence trends from United States special education data. *Pediatrics* 2005;**115**(3):e277–82.
5. Muhle R, Trentacoste SV, Rapin I. The genetics of autism. *Pediatrics* 2004;**113**(5):e472–86.
6. Lainhart JE, Piven J, Wzorek M, Landa R, Santangelo SL, Coon H, Folstein SE. Macrocephaly in children and adults with autism. *J Am Acad Child Adoles Psychiatry* 1997;**36**:282–90.
7. Miles JH, Hadden LL, Takahashi TN, Hillman RE. Head circumference is an independent clinical finding associated with autism. *Am J Med Genet* 2000;**95**:339–50.
8. Aylward EH, Minshew NJ, Goldstein G, Honeycutt NA, Augustine AM, Yates KO, Barta PE, Pearlson GD. Effects of age on brain volume and head circumference in autism. *Neurology* 2002;**59**:175–83.
9. Piven J, Arndt S, Bailey J, Havercamp S, Andreasen NC, Palmer P. An MRI study of brain size in autism. *Am J Psychiatry* 1995;**152**:1145–9.
10. Courchesne E, Karns CM, Davis HR, Ziccardi R, Carper RA, Tigue ZD, Chisum HJ, Moses P, Pierce K, Lord C, Lincoln AJ, Pizzo S, Schreibman L, Haas RH, Akshoomoff NA, Courchesne RY. Unusual brain growth patterns in early life in patients with autistic disorder: an MRI study. *Neurology* 2001;**57**:245–54.
11. Hardan A, Minshew N, Keshavan M. Corpus collosum size in autism. *Neurology* 2000;**55**:1033–6.
12. Sparks BF, Friedman SD, Shaw DW, Aylward EH, Echelard D, Artru AA, Maravilla KR, Giedd JN, Munson J, Dawson G, Dager SR. Brain structural

abnormalities in young children with autism spectrum disorder. *Neurology* 2002;**59**:184–92.

13. Schultz RT. Developmental deficits in social perception in autism: the role of the amygdala and fusiform face area. *Int J Dev Neurosci* 2005;**23**:125–41.

14. Hazlett HC, Poe M, Gerig G, Smith RG, Provenzale J, Ross A, Gilmore J, Piven J. An MRI and head circumference study of brain size in autism: birth through age two years. *Arch Gen Psychiatry* 2005;**62**:1366–76.

15. Courchesne E, Carper R, Akshoomoff N. Evidence of brain overgrowth in the first year of life in autism. *J Am Med Assoc* 2003;**290**:337–44.

16. Gillberg C, de Souza L. Head circumference in autism, Asperger syndrome, and ADHD: a comparative study. *Dev Med Child Neurol* 2002;**44**(5):296–300.

17. Zwaigenbaum L, Bryson S, Rogers T, Roberts W, Brian J, Szatmari P. Behavioral manifestations of autism in the first year of life. *Int J Dev Neurosci* 2005;**23**:143–52.

18. Manes F, Piven J, Vrancic D, Nanclares V, Plebst C, Starkstein SE. An MRI study of the corpus callosum and cerebellum in mentally retarded autistic individuals. *J Neuropsychiatry Clin Neurosci* 1999;**11**(4):470–4.

19. Herbert MR, Harris GJ, Adrien KT, Ziegler DA, Makris N, Kennedy DN, Lange NT, Chabris CF, Bakardjiev A, Hodgson J, Takeoka M, Tager-Flusberg H, Caviness VSJ. Abnormal asymmetry in language association cortex in autism. *Ann Neurol* 2002;**52**:588–96.

20. Barnea-Goraly N, Kwon H, Menon V, Eliez S, Lotspeich L, Reiss AL. White matter structure in autism: preliminary evidence from diffusion tensor imaging. *Biol Psychiatry* 2004;**55**:323–6.

21. Casanova MF, Buxhoeveden DP, Switala AE, Roy E. Minicolumnar pathology in autism. *Neurology* 2002;**58**(3):428–32.

22. Kirkpatrick B, Carter CS, Newman SW, Insel TR. Axon-sparing lesions of the medial nucleus of the amygdala decrease affiliative behaviors in the prairie vole (microtus ochrogaster): Behavioral and anatomical specificity. *Behav Neurosci* 1994;**108**:501–13.

23. Daenen EWPM, Wolterink G, Gerrits MAFM, Van Ree JM. The effects of neonatal lesions in the amygdala or ventral hippocampus on social behaviour later in life. *Behav Brain Res* 2002;**136**:571–82.

24. Bachevalier J. Medial temporal lobe structures and autism: a review of clinical and experimental findings. *Neuropsychologia* 1994;**32**:627–48.

25. Bauman M, Kemper TL. Histoanatomic observations of the brain in early infantile autism. *Neurology* 1985;**35**:866–74.

26. Kemper TL, Bauman ML. The contribution of neuropathologic studies to the understanding of autism. *Neurol Clin* 1993;**11**:175–87.

27. Aylward EH, Minshew NJ, Goldstein G, Honeycutt NA, Augustine AM, Yates KO, Barta PE, Pearlson GD. MRI volumes of amygdala and hippocampus in non-mentally retarded autistic adolescents and adults. *Neurology* 1999;**53**:2145–50.

28. Pierce K, Muller R, Ambrose J, Allen G, Courchesne E. Face processing occurs outside the fusiform 'face area' in autism: evidence from functional MRI. *Brain* 2001;**124**(10):2059–73.

29. Howard MA, Cowell PE, Boucher J, Broks P, Mayes A, Farrant A, Roberts N. Convergent neuroanatomical and behavioural evidence of an amygdala hypothesis of autism. *Neuroreport* 2000;**1**:2931–5.

30. Baron-Cohen S, Ring HA, Bullmore ET, Wheelwright S, Ashwin C, Williams SCR. The amygdala theory of autism. *Neuroscience and Biobehav Rev* 2000;**24**:355–64.

31. Schultz RT, Gauthier I, Klin A, Fulbright RK, Anderson AW, Volkmar F, Skudlarski P, Lacadie C, Cohen DJ, Gore JC. Abnormal ventral temporal cortical activity during face discrimination among individuals with autism and asperger syndrome. *Arch Gen Psychiatry* 2000;**57**(4):331–40.

32. Wang AT, Dapretto M, Hariri AR, Sigman M, Bookheimer SY. Neural correlates of facial affect processing in children and adolescents with autism spectrum disorder. *J Am Acad Child Adolesc Psychiatry* 2004;**43**(4):481–90.

33. Deeley Q, Daly EM, Surguladze S, Page L, Toal F, Robertson D, Curran S, Giampietro M, Seal M, Brammer M. An event related functional magnetic resonance imaging study of facial emotion processing in asperger syndrome. *Biol Psychiatry* 2007;**62**(3):207–17.

34. Zilbovicius M, Meresse I, Chabane N, Brunelle F, Samson Y, Boddaert N. Autism, the superior temporal sulcus and social perception. *Trends Neurosci* 2006;**29**(7):359–66.

35. Kleinhans NM, Richards T, Sterling L, Stegbauer KC, Mahurin R, Johnson LC, Greenson J, Dawson G, Aylward E. Abnormal functional connectivity in autism spectrum disorders during face processing. *Brain* 2008;**131**(4):1000–12.

36. Wicker B, Fonlupt BH, Tardif C, Gepner B, Deruelle C. Abnormal cerebral effective connectivity during explicit emotional processing in adults with autism spectrum disorder. *Soc Cogn Affect Neurosc* 2008;**3**:135–43.

37. Joseph RM, Tager-Flusberg H, Lord C. Cognitive profiles and social-communicative functioning in children with autism spectrum disorder. *J Child Psychol Psychiatry* 2002;**43**(6):807–21.

38. Townsend J, Courchesne E, Egaas B. Slowed orienting of covert visual-spatial attention in autism: Specific deficits associated with cerebellar and parietal abnormality. *Dev Psychopathol* 1996;**8**:563–84.

39. Courchesne E, Townsend J, Akshoomoff NA, Saitoh O, Yeung-Courchesne R, Lincoln AJ, James HE, Haas RH, Schreibman L, Lau L. Impairment in shifting attention in autistic and cerebellar patients. *Behav Neurosci* 1994;**108**(5):848–65.

40. Pascualvaca DM, Fantie BD, Papageorgiou M, Mirsky AF. Attentional capacities in children with autism: Is there a general deficit in shifting focus? *J Autism Dev Disord* 1998;**28**(6):467–78.

41. Mundy P, Neal R. Neural plasticity, joint attention and a transactional social-orienting model of autism. *Int Rev Men Retard* 2001;**23**:139–68.

42. Rutherford MD, Richards ED, Moldes V, Sekuler AB. Evidence of a divided-attention advantage in autism. *Cogn Neuropsychol* 2007;**24**(5):505–15.

43. Kennedy DP, Courchesne E. The intrinsic functional organization of the brain is altered in autism. *Neuroimage* 2008;**39**(4):1877–85.

44. Haist F, Adamo M, Westerfield M, Courchesne E, Townsend J. The functional neuroanatomy of spatial attention in autism spectrum disorder. *Dev Neuropsychol* 2005;**27**(3):425–58.

45. Toichi M, Kamio Y. Verbal memory in autistic adolescents. *Jpn J Child Adolesc Psychiatry* 1998;**39**:364–73.

46. O'Shea AG, Fein DA, Cillessen AH, Klin A, Schultz RT. Source memory in children with autism spectrum disorders. *Dev Neuropsychol* 2005;**27**(3):337–60.

47. Millward C, Powell S, Messer D, Jordan R. Recall for self and other in autism: children's memory for events experienced by themselves and their peers. *J Autism Dev Disord* 2000;**30**(1):15–28.

48. Schumann CM, Hamstra J, Goodlin-Jones BL, Lotspeich LJ, Kwon H, Buonocore MH, et al. The amygdala is enlarged in children but not adolescents with autism; the hippocampus is enlarged at all ages. *J Neurosci* 2004;**24**(28):6392–401.

49. Dager SR, Wang L, Friedman SD, Shaw DW, Constantino JN, Artru AA, Dawson G, Csernansky JG. Shape mapping of the hippocampus in young children with autism spectrum disorder. *Am J Neuroradiol* 2007;**28**(4):672–7.

50. Wetherby A, Watt N, Morgan L, Shumway S. Social communication profiles of children with autism spectrum disorders late in the second year of life. *J Autism Dev Disord* 2007;**37**(5):960–75.

51. Werner E, Dawson G. Validation of the phenomenon of autistic regression using home videotapes. *Arch Gen Psychiatry* 2005;**62**(8):889–95.

52. Mitchell S, Brian J, Zwaigenbaum L, Roberts W, Szatmari P, Smith I, Bryson S. Early language and communication development of infants later diagnosed with Autism Spectrum Disorder. *J Dev Behav Pediatr* 2006;**27**:69–78.

53. Paul R, Augustyn A, Klin A, Volkmar FR. Perception and production of prosody by speakers with autism spectrum disorders. *J Autism Dev Disord* 2005;**35**(2):205–20.

54. Tager-Flusberg H, Caronna E. Language disorders: autism and other pervasive developmental disorders. *Pediatr Clin N Am* 2007;**54**(3):469–81.

55. Harris GJ, Chabris CF, Clark J, Urban T, Aharon I, Steele S, McGrath L, Condouris K, Tager-Flusberg H. Brain activation during semantic processing in autism spectrum disorders via functional magnetic resonance imaging. *Brain Cogn* 2006;**61**(1):54–68.

56. Just MA, Cherkassky VL, Keller TA, Minshew NJ. Cortical activation and synchronization during sentence comprehension in high-functioning autism: Evidence of underconnectivity. *Brain* 2004;**127**(8):1811–21.

57. Gaffrey MS, Kleinhans NM, Haist F, Akshoomoff N, Campbell A, Courchesne E, Muller R. A typical participation of visual cortex during word processing in autism: an fMRI study of semantic decision. *Neuropsychologia* 2007;**45**(8):1672–84.

58. Kana RK, Keller TA, Cherkassky VL, Minshew NJ, Just MA. Sentence comprehension in autism: thinking in pictures with decreased functional connectivity. *Brain* 2006;**129**(9):2484–93.

59. Caron MJ, Mottron L, Berthiaume C, Dawson M. Cognitive mechanisms, specificity and neural underpinnings of visuospatial peaks in autism. *Brain: J Neurol* 2006;**129**(7):1789–802.

60. Shah A, Frith U. Why do autistic individuals show superior performance on the block design task? *J Child Psychol Psychiatry* 1993;**34**(8):1351–64.

61. Jolliffe T, Baron-Cohen S. Are people with autism and Asperger syndrome faster than normal on the embedded figures task? *J Child Psychol Psychiatry* 1997;**38**:527–34.

62. Mottron L, Burack JA, Iarocci G, Belleville S, Enns JT. Locally oriented perception with intact global processing among adolescents with high-functioning autism: Evidence from multiple paradigms. *J Child Psychol Psychiatry* 2003;**44**(6):904–13.

63. Schlooz WAJM, Hulstijn W, van den Broek PJA, van der Pijll ACAM, Gabreels F, van der Gaag RJ, Rotteveel JJ. Fragmented visuospatial processing in children with pervasive developmental disorder. *J Autism Dev Disord* 2006;**36**(8):1025–37.

64. Lee PS, Foss-Feig J, Henderson JG, Kenworthy LE, Gilotty L, Gaillard WD, Vaidya CJ. Atypical neural substrates of embedded figures task performance in children with autism spectrum disorder. *Neuroimage* 2007;**38**(1):184–93.

65. Manjaly ZM, Bruning N, Neufang S, Stephan KE, Brieber S, Marshall JC, et al. Neurophysiological

correlates of relatively enhanced local visual search in autistic adolescents. *Neuroimage* 2007;**35**(1):283–91.

66. Dawson G, Carver L, Meltzo AN, Pagagiotides H, McPartland J, Webb SJ. Neural correlates of face and object recognition in young children with autism spectrum disorder, developmental delay and typical development. *Child Dev* 2002;**73**:700–17.

67. Chawarska K, Volkmar F. Impairments in monkey and human face recognition in 2-year-old toddlers with Autism Spectrum Disorder and Developmental Delay. *Dev Sci* 2007;**10**(2):266–79.

68. Sasson NJ. The development of face processing in autism. *J Autism Dev Disord* 2006;**36**(3):381–94.

69. Ozonoff S, Jensen J. Brief report: Specific executive function profiles in three neurodevelopmental disorders. *J Autism Dev Disord* 1999;**29**(2):171–7.

70. Kleinhans N, Akshoomoff N, Delis DC. Executive functions in autism and Asperger's disorder: flexibility, fluency, and inhibition. *Dev Neuropsychol* 2005;**27**(3):379–401.

71. Verte S, Geurts HM, Roeyers H, Oosterlaan J, Sergeant JA. Executive functioning in children with autism and Tourette syndrome. *Dev Psychopathol* 2005;**17**(2):415–45.

72. Liss M, Fein D, Allen D, Dunn M, Feinstein C, Morris R, Waterhouse L, Rapin I. Executive functioning in high-functioning children with autism. *J Child Psychol Psychiatry* 2001;**42**(2):261–70.

73. Gilbert SJ, Bird G, Brindley R, Frith CD, Burgess PW. Atypical recruitment of medial prefrontal cortex in autism spectrum disorders: an fMRI study of two executive function tasks. *Neuropsychologia* 2008;**46**(9):2281–91.

74. Schmitz N, Rubia K, Daly E, Smith A, Williams S, Murphy DGM. Neural correlates of executive function in autistic spectrum disorders. *Biol Psychiatry* 2006;**59**(1):7–16.

75. Kana RK, Keller TA, Minshew NJ, Just MA. Inhibitory control in high-functioning autism: decreased activation and underconnectivity in inhibition networks. *Biol Psychiatry* 2007;**62**(3):198–206.

76. Chawarska K, Klin A, Paul R, Volkmar F. Autism spectrum disorder in the second year: stability and change in syndrome expression. *J Child Psychol Psychiatry* 2007;**48**(2):128–38.

77. Wetherby AM, Woods J, Allen L, Cleary J, Dickenson H, Lord C. Early indicators of autism spectrum disorders in the second year of life. *J Autism Dev Disord* 2004;**34**:473–93.

78. Liss M, Saulnier C, Fein D, Kinsbourne M. Sensory and attention abnormalities in autistic spectrum disorders. *Autism Int J Res Pract* 2006;**10**(2):155–72.

79. Ahearn WH, Castine T, Nault K, Green G. An assessment of food acceptance in children with autism

or Pervasive Developmental Disorder-Not Otherwise Specified. *J Autism Dev Disord* 2001;**31**(5):505–11.

80. Gillott A, Standen PJ. Levels of anxiety and sources of stress in adults with autism. *J Intellect Disabil* 2007;**11**(4):359–70.

81. Aman MG. Management of hyperactivity and other acting-out problems in patients with autism spectrum disorder. *Semi Pediatr Neurol* 2004;**11**(3):225–8.

82. Shtayermman O. Peer victimization in adolescents and young adults diagnosed with Asperger's syndrome: a link to depressive symptomatology, anxiety symptomatology and suicidal ideation. *Issues Compr Pediatr Nurs* 2007;**30**(3):87–107.

83. Seltzer MM, Shattuck P, Abbeduto L, Greenberg JS. Trajectory of development in adolescents and adults with autism. *Ment Retard Dev Disabil Res Rev* 2004;**10**(4):234–47.

84. Hellemans H, Colson K, Verbraeken C, Vermeiren R, Deboutte D. Sexual behavior in high-functioning male adolescents and young adults with autism spectrum disorder. *J Autism Dev Disord* 2007;**37**(2):260–9.

85. Howlin P, Goode S, Hutton J, Rutter M. Adult outcome for children with autism. *J Child Psychol Psychiatry* 2004;**45**(2):212–29.

86. Renty JO, Roeyers H. Quality of life in high-functioning adults with autism spectrum disorder: The predictive value of disability and support characteristics. *Autism Int J Res Pract* 2006;**10**(5):511–24.

87. Orsmond GI, Krauss MW, Seltzer MM. Peer relationships and social and recreational activities among adolescents and adults with autism. *J Autism Dev Disord* 2004;**34**(3):245–56.

88. Lord C, Rutter M, DiLavore PC, Risi S. *Autism Diagnostic Observation Schedule*. Los Angeles, CA: Western Psychological Services; 2002.

89. Rutter M, LeCouteur A, Lord C. *The Autism Diagnostic Interview – Revised*. Los Angeles, CA: Western Psychological Services; 2003.

90. Lord C, Pickles A, McLennan J, Rutter M, Bregman J, Folstein S, Fombonne E, Leboyer M, Minshew N. Diagnosing autism: analyses of data from the Autism Diagnostic Interview. *J Autism Dev Disord* 1997;**27**(5):501–17.

91. Lord C, Risi S, Lambrecht L, Cook EH Jr, Leventhal BL, DiLavore PC, Pickles A, Rutter M. The Autism Diagnostic Observation Schedule-Generic: a standard measure of social and communication deficits associated with the spectrum of autism. *J Autism Dev Disord* 2000;**30**(3):205–23.

92. Wing L, Leekam SR, Libby SJ, Gould J, Larcombe M. The diagnostic interview for social and communication

disorders: Background, inter-rater reliability and clinical use. *J Child Psychol Psychiatry* 2002;**43**(3):307–25.

93. Skuse D, Warrington R, Bishop D, Chowdhury U, Lau J, Mandy W, Place M. The Developmental, Dimensional and Diagnostic Interview (3di): a novel computerized assessment for autism spectrum disorders. *J Am Acad Child Adolesc Psychiatry* 2004;**43**(5):548–58.

94. Schopler E, Reichler RJ, Renner BR. *Childhood Autism Rating Scale*. Circle Pines, MN: AGS Publishing; 1986.

95. Tidmarsh L, Volkmar FR. Diagnosis and epidemiology of autism spectrum disorders. *Canad J Psychiatry* 2003;**48**(8):517–25.

96. Bryson SE, McDermott C, Rombough V, Zwaigenbaum L. The Autism Observational Scale for Infants: scale development and assessment of reliability. *J Autism Dev Disabil* 2008;**38**(4):731–8.

97. Luyster R, Guthrie W, Gotham K, Risi S, DiLavore P, Lord C. *The Autism Diagnostic Observation Schedule – Toddler module: preliminary findings using a modified version of the ADOS*. Paper presented at the 7th Annual International Meeting for Autism Research, London, England; 2008.

98. Sparrow SS, Cicchetti D, Balla DA. *Vineland Adaptive Behavior Scales*, 2nd edn. Circle Pines, MN: AGS Publishing; 2005.

99. Carter AS, Volkmar FR, Sparrow SS, Wang JJ, Lord C, Dawson G, Fombonne E, Loveland K, Mesibov G, Schopler E. The Vineland Adaptive Behavior Scales: supplementary norms for individuals with autism. *J Autism Dev Disord* 1998;**28**(4):287–302.

100. Lovaas OI. *Teaching Individuals with Developmental Delays: Basic Intervention Techniques*. Austin, TX: Pro-Ed; 2003.

101. McEachin JJ, Smith T, Lovaas OI. Long-term outcome for children with autism who received early intensive behavioral treatment. *Am J Men Retard* 1993;**97**(4):359–91.

102. Mesibov GB, Shea V, Schopler E. *The TEACCH approach to autism spectrum disorders*. New York: Springer; 2004.

103. Van Bourgondien ME, Reichle NC, Schopler E. Effects of a model treatment approach on adults with autism. *J Autism Dev Disord* 2003;**33**(2):131–40.

104. Panerai S, Ferrante L, Zingale M. Benefits of the treatment and education of autistic and

communication handicapped children (TEACCH) programme as compared with a non-specific approach. *J Intellect Disabil Res* 2002;**46**(4):318–27.

105. Bondy A, Frost L. The Picture Exchange Communication System. *Behav Modif* 2001;**25**(5):725–44.

106. Owley T. Pharmacological interventions for neurodevelopmental disorders. In Hunter SJ, Donders J, eds. *Pediatric Neuropsychological Intervention: A Critical Review of Science and Practice*. Cambridge University Press; 2007.

107. Barry TD, Klinger LG, Lee JM, Palardy N, Gilmore T, Bodin SD. Examining the effectiveness of an outpatient clinic-based social skills group for high-functioning children with autism. *J Autism Dev Disord* 2003;**33**(6):685–701.

108. Bauminger N. The facilitation of social-emotional understanding and social interaction in high-functioning children with autism: intervention outcomes. *J Autism Dev Disord* 2002;**32**(4):283–98.

109. Mesibov GB. Social skills training with verbal autistic adolescents and adults: A program model. *J Autism Dev Disord* 1984;**14**(4):395–404.

110. Morrison L, Kamps D, Garcia J, Parker D. Peer mediation and monitoring strategies to improve initiations and social skills for students with autism. *J Positive Behav Intervent* 2001;**3**(4):237–50.

111. Gray CA. Social stories and comic strip conversations with students with Asperger Syndrome and high-functioning autism. In Schopler E, Mesibov GB, Kunce LJ, eds. *Asperger Syndrome or High-Functioning Autism?* New York: Plenum Press; 1998: 167–98.

112. Greenway C. Autism and Asperger syndrome: strategies to promote prosocial behaviours. *Educ Psychol Pract* 2000;**16**(4):469–86.

113. Thiemann KS, Goldstein H. Social stories, written text cues, and video feedback: effects on social communication of children with autism. *J Appl Behav Anal* 2001;**34**(4):425–46.

114. Delano M, Snell ME. The effects of social stories on the social engagement of children with autism. *J Positive Behav Intervent* 2006;**8**(1):29–42.

115. Howlin P, Alcock J, Burkin C. An 8 year follow-up of a specialist supported employment service for high-ability adults with autism or Asperger syndrome. *Autism Int J Res Pract* 2005;**9**(5):533–49.

Chapter 9c

Autism spectrum disorders and intellectual disability: common themes and points of divergence

Marianne Barton, Colby Chlebowski and Deborah Fein

The preceding chapters by Wolf and Paterson and Klein-Tasman and Janke reveal similarities as well as differences between the related fields of intellectual disabilities and autistic spectrum disorders, and suggest distinct as well as overlapping areas for continued study. Both sets of authors note difficulties inherent in the fact that the disorders are defined by behavioral characteristics that have been subject to change over time. In the field of intellectual disability, confusion has been most marked in the debate over the statistical cut-off for the ID diagnosis, and over the role of adaptive skills in the conceptualization of the disability. In 1992, the American Association for Mental Retardation recommended changing the IQ cut-off from 70 to 75, a decision that would have doubled the number of individuals diagnosed with ID [1]. After a period of considerable debate, clinicians and researchers retained the cut-off score of 70 for both cognitive measures and adaptive skills. Klein-Tasman and Janke describe several caveats to this decision, including recognition of the psychometric limitations of IQ tests, and the danger of excessive reliance on overall scores and attendant disregard for evidence of variability in cognitive function. Similarly, despite dissenting opinions, deficits in adaptive functioning are now regarded as central to the diagnosis. Klein-Tasman and Janke note that this decision, while useful, introduces a variety of concerns, including questions about the validity of adaptive measures and the extent to which they reflect variance unique to adaptive functioning and distinct from cognitive ability.

In the autism spectrum disorder (ASD) field, the behavioral basis of diagnosis is believed to have contributed to the recent reported increase in the incidence of the disorder [2]. DSM-IV [3] promoted broader and more inclusive diagnostic criteria, which have probably contributed to the more frequent diagnosis of individuals with the disorder at both ends of the spectrum of impairment. That is, individuals with significant cognitive impairments who might once have been labeled with ID may now be more likely to be diagnosed with ASD because their deficits in social functioning are more readily recognized. Individuals who are higher functioning, and would previously be diagnosed with a personality disorder or with no diagnosis, may also be diagnosed with an ASD on the basis of a broader definition of social impairments and restricted interests. While it is impossible to rule out changes in the incidence of the disorder which might be associated with environmental events (e.g. exposure to toxins), the available data suggest that changes in the behaviorally driven diagnostic system probably contribute to increases in the prevalence rate for autism spectrum disorders, and associated decreases in the prevalence rate of intellectual disability [4]. Changes in the behavioral descriptors of both ASD and ID have been informed by research and have clearly enriched our understanding of both disorders. Nonetheless, they underscore the vulnerability of behavioral diagnostic categories and the danger of assuming that any such category "carves nature at its joints".

Comparison of the data presented in the two chapters suggests that the two fields of ID and ASD research are at different stages of conceptual and empirical development. As Wolf and Paterson note, despite the clear recognition that ASD is heavily genetically determined, little is known about specific genetic abnormalities that underlie the disorder, beyond the assertion that these are likely to involve multiple interacting factors [5]. Indeed, there are few specific hypotheses about etiological sub-groups which might underlie differing presentations of ASD.

Equally important, while there is widespread recognition that ASD includes individuals with enormous phenotypic variability, efforts to establish valid subcategories within ASD have been largely unsuccessful. Studies comparing clinical characteristics of ASD subtypes have found significant variation within both intellectual functioning and autistic symptomatology, which may vary somewhat independently of each other, making accurate classification of individuals along the autism spectrum very difficult [6]. Partially as a result of phenotypic heterogeneity, descriptive as well as prospective studies of individuals with ASD have produced inconsistent findings and frequent failures to replicate results.

In the absence of clear etiological data or reliable sub-classification schemes, the ASD research community has built on its rich clinical literature to develop a model of the disorder based upon behavioral patterns and emerging brain studies. Data in support of the view that ASD may be conceptualized as a disorder of inter-connectivity between the limbic system and other areas of the brain are carefully reviewed by Wolf and Paterson. This hypothesis offers a thoughtful integration of much of the behavioral and the neuropsychological data, but it remains largely theoretical and awaits further explication and empirical support. The fact that individuals with some genetic conditions, such as Fragile X syndrome and tuberous sclerosis, are at greater risk for ASDs [7, 8], suggests that there may be multiple etiological conditions which contribute to the development of ASD in a probabilistic model. Among the more challenging questions confronting ASD researchers is explication of the manner in which different etiological conditions may result in common neurological and behavioral pathways and overlapping sets of functional deficits.

The field of ID has made greater progress toward the delineation of sub-types of the disorder based on etiology, although Klein-Tasman and Janke note that only about 50% of cases of ID have a known etiology. Research in the neuropsychology of ID has focused heavily on identifying characteristics specific to disorders of known etiology. In the clinical literature as well, an etiological approach to intellectual disability is strongly advocated, particularly when an etiological approach can be paired with a functional analysis in an individual case [9]. Klein-Tasman and Janke report that identification of etiological sub-categories has resulted in improved treatment design and clearer prognostic estimates, and they review the extensive database regarding the characteristic patterns associated with multiple etiological categories. Undoubtedly, the relatively simpler genetic models known to underlie some forms of ID (e.g. Down syndrome) as compared to the more complex polygenic models believed

to underlie ASDs have contributed to advances in this research, as has the much longer history of investigation into the causes of ID. Nonetheless, the progress made in the ID literature underscores the need for continued research into carefully specified diagnostic sub-categories and etiological models as well as further explication of genetic models for both ID and ASD.

Among the more compelling differences between these two bodies of research is the expected trajectory of individuals diagnosed, in particular the potential for marked progress, sometimes called "optimal outcome", in some children diagnosed with an ASD. Research suggests that a minority of children diagnosed with an ASD can lose the diagnosis and score in the normal range on measures of cognitive, adaptive, and social skills. Factors that appear to predict "optimal outcome" in ASD are higher intelligence, receptive language skills, imitation ability, motor development, and early age of diagnosis and intervention (see Helt et al. [10] for a complete review). It is unclear what proportion of children diagnosed with an ASD can be expected to make such marked progress, whether their gains can be attributed to remediation of deficits or the development of compensatory skills, and what functional changes may be identified in their brains. These and other questions remain the focus of ongoing research efforts. Given the possibility of such change over time, and the recognition that interventions for children with ASD may show diminishing returns as the child gets older [11], early intervention services for individuals diagnosed with an ASD are targeted, intensive, and extensive (e.g. 20 hours per week).

In contrast, ID is thought to be a disorder that is relatively stable through the lifespan. Unlike infants with ASD, infants with ID show relative stability in cognitive functioning from early scores on developmental measures. While intervention in ID is not designed to reverse the effects of the disability, proponents argue that early, targeted intervention has the potential to alter developmental trajectories and prevent associated deficits. For example, Guralnick [12] argues that although the intellectual deficits in children with Down syndrome (DS) are significant and apparent at an early age, the continued decline in intellectual development that often occurs in the first 5 years of life of a child with DS may result from the absence of early intensive intervention. Other interventions for ID focus on targeting accompanying conditions (e.g. self-injurious behavior) rather than directly addressing the cognitive deficits.

Additionally, animal models of Rett syndrome and Fragile X syndrome have introduced the idea that some forms of mental retardation can be reversed either through silencing then reactivating a gene that causes a disorder or by exposing animals to enriched environments [13]. These models suggest that, for these syndromes, neuronal plasticity may remain and opportunities to study potential mechanisms for intervention and treatment are possible.

Any discussion of clinical challenges facing the fields of ID and ASD reveals clear similarities between the two. Researchers in both fields have made marked progress toward the development of assessment tools that permit early, valid diagnosis. Researchers and clinicians now have reliable measures of cognitive functioning at every developmental stage as well as increasingly valid indices of adaptive function, and highly reliable assessments of autistic symptoms. Interestingly, the diagnostic tools also appear to work with individuals with co-morbid ASD and ID. Since low mental ages may account for less developed social behavior and delayed communication skills [14], differentiating the impairments associated with low IQ from primary social impairments can be challenging. Additionally, the presence of stereotyped behaviors (e.g. hand-flapping and body-rocking) in both individuals with ASD and low functioning individuals with ID complicates the differentiation between the disorders. However, research suggests that reliable ASD diagnostic instruments (i.e. the ADI-R and ADOS) can accurately classify ASD in a sample of children with ID [15]. Concerns remain with clinicians' ability to diagnose milder presentations of both disorders, but especially ASD, and with the need to balance sensitivity of diagnosis with the potential for over-identification.

Despite increased confidence in diagnostic tools, the impact of cultural and socio-economic variables on the expression of symptoms, likelihood of diagnosis, and age at diagnosis remains a significant concern [16]. Early identification of children suspected of intellectual disability has long been prominent in pediatric practice, but progress toward the early detection of autistic spectrum disorders has been more recent (e.g. Robins et al. [17]). In ASD screening, studies indicate that ethnic minority children are screened with autism-specific screeners and evaluated and diagnosed later than White children [18]. These differences do not appear to be influenced by the socio-economic status (SES) of the families, but may reflect other variables such as cultural differences with regard to identifying symptoms or seeking services, or differences in pediatrician practice with families of different ethnicities. While fewer studies have addressed the cultural influence on the screening and diagnosis of ID, one study indicated that referral rates for mild cases of ID (as compared to more severe cases) were influenced by SES, with fewer referrals of mild ID in low-SES areas [19].

Socio-economic factors may also be related to the availability of intervention services for both the ID and the ASD population [20]. Most states in the USA have Early Intervention programs in place to serve children under the age of 3 with ID and ASD, and all public schools are mandated to provide appropriate services to diagnosed children aged 3 and above. There are well-documented intervention models which have been associated with positive outcomes in the ASD population, and there is a considerable body of data regarding effective tertiary prevention programs for the ID population. The nature of services available and their intensity is widely divergent across communities, however, with availability often determined by socio-economic variables and ideological commitments rather than by empirical data.

While some treatment modalities have significant empirical support (e.g. Applied Behavior Analysis), others, despite being widely used, have been much less studied (e.g. Sensory Integration Therapy). As the number of individuals identified with ASD increases, the need for carefully controlled, well-designed outcome studies grows ever more acute. These studies will be refined, of course, by researchers' ability to describe the characteristics of homogeneous subgroups of participants, which might eventually permit the matching of individuals with effective intervention tools.

Both Wolf and Paterson and Klein-Tasman and Janke note that transitional periods in the lives of children with ID and ASD appear to be points of particular vulnerability as children and their families move between systems of care with differing intervention models and environmental supports. This occurs initially as families negotiate the transition from home-based, family-centered early intervention programs, to school-based, child-centered education programs in the public schools. The progression from typically smaller elementary school communities to the larger, more complex communities of the middle school or high school involves another transition, this one often complicated by the vagaries of puberty, hormonal challenges, and increased social demands. Finally the transition from the relatively sheltered school setting to the workplace or supported community can be especially difficult. At each transition point, there is a need for careful planning, informed by identification of individual strengths and unique vulnerabilities, and leading to specification of the supports likely to be needed in the new setting. Klein-Tasman and Janke make a strong case for the delineation of fit between an individual and his/her environment, and the thorough assessment of functional skills and requirements for support in the natural environment. That view has gained wide acceptance in the ID literature, and is increasingly explicit in intervention models for individuals with ASD (e.g. Social Communication, Emotion Regulation and Transactional Supports (SCERTS) and Treatment, and Education of Autism and Related Communication-Handicapped Children (TEACCH), which specify the provision of visual and transactional supports in the natural environment.

In both the ID and the ASD community, but especially in the latter group, there is a paucity of supports available to young adults as they move out of the educational system and there is a sparse literature about how best to tailor those supports. Due to the relatively limited implementation of targeted adaptive behavior interventions for individuals with ASD in childhood, the difficult transition to adulthood is perhaps not surprising. Wolf and Paterson note that the majority of adults with ASD are unable to obtain employment, develop relationships or live independently, and that adult independence is best predicted by the perceived availability of support. The nature of needed support services for adults, the mechanisms for providing them within existing communities and the training of service providers remain areas about which research has been largely silent. Finally, the support of adults with ID and ASD as they age represents an area of even greater and potentially more complex need, and even more limited knowledge base.

Among individuals diagnosed with both ID and ASD there is a high co-morbidity of psychiatric disorders that may further limit an individual's ability to function. Furthermore, the assessment of those conditions, which include anxiety disorders, depression and behavior problems, is complicated by the underlying developmental disability. Clearly neuropsychologists in clinical settings have a significant role to play

in the assessment of individuals with complex presentations and co-morbid conditions, and in the design and monitoring of multifaceted intervention strategies.

Individuals with intellectual disability and autistic spectrum disorders present challenges to the field of neuropsychology, as well as opportunities to advance our understanding of brain–behavior relationships. Klein-Tasman and Janke point out the tension in the study of intellectual disability between the etiological (or developmental) approach and the functional (or specific deficit) approach, a tension that exists to some degree in the field of ASD as well. They argue that both research and clinical practice require an integration of the two models in support of the goal of providing assessments of an individual's unique pattern of strengths and weaknesses informed by a growing understanding of neurocognitive disorders. That integration will be supported by ongoing efforts to delineate etiological models and sub-groups, to refine diagnostic tools, to evaluate treatment options carefully, and to continue prospective studies which might reveal the earliest presentation and the progression of these disorders.

References

1. McDermott S, Durkin MS, Schupt N, Stein, Z. Epidemiology and etiology of mental retardation. In Mulick J, Rojahn J, Jacobson J, eds. *Handbook of Intellectual and Developmental Disabilities.* New York: Springer; 2007.

2. Newschaffer C, Croen L, Daniels J, Giarelli E, Grether J, Levy S, et al. (2007) The epidemiology of autism spectrum disorder. *Annu Rev Publ Health*, 2007;**28**:235–58.

3. American Psychiatric Association *Diagnostic and Statistical Manual of Mental Disorders*, 4th edn. Washington DC: American Psychiatric Association; 1994.

4. Coo H, Ouellette-Kuntz H, Lloyd J, Kasmara L, Holden J, Lewis M. Trends in autism prevalence: Diagnostic substitution revisited. *J Autism Dev Disord* 2008;**38**:1036–46.

5. Muhle R, Trentacoste S, Rapin I. The genetics of autism. *Pediatrics* 2004;**113**:472–86.

6. Walker D, Thompson A, Zwaigenbaum L, Goldberg J, Bryson S, Mahoney W, Strawbridge C, Szatmari P. Specifying PDD-NOS: a comparison of PDD-NOS, Asperger Syndrome, and autism. *J Am Acad Child Adolesc Psychiatry* 2004;**43**:172–80.

7. Baker P, Piven, J, Sato Y. Autism and tuberous sclerosis complex: prevalence and clinical features. *J Autism Dev Disord* 1998;**28**:279–85.

8. Rogers S, Wehner E, Hagerman R. The behavioral phenotype in Fragile X: symptoms of autism in very young children with Fragile X Syndrome, idiopathic Autism, and other developmental disorders. *J Dev Behav Pediatr* 2001;**22**:409–17.

9. Pennington B. *The Development of Psychopathology: Nature and Nurture*. New York: Guilford.

10. Helt M, Kelley E, Kinsbourne M, Pandey J, Boorstein H, Herbert M, Fein D. Can children with autism recover? If so, how? *Neuropsychol Rev* 2008;**18**:339–66.

11. Mars A, Mauk J, Dowrick P. Symptoms of pervasive developmental disorders as observed in prediagnostic home videos of infants and toddlers. *J Pediatr* 1998;**132**:500–4.

12. Guralnick M. Effectiveness of early intervention for vulnerable children: a developmental perspective. *Early Intervention: The Essential Readings*. Malden, MA US: Blackwell; 2004.

13. Restivo L, Ferrari F, Passino E, Sgobio C, Bock J, Oostra B, et al. Enriched environment promotes behavioral and morphological recovery in a mouse model for the fragile X syndrome. *PNAS Proc Nat Acad Sci USA* 2005;**102**:11557–62.

14. Wing L. The history of ideas on autism. *Autism* 1997;**1**:13–23.

15. de Bildt, A, Sytema S, Ketelaars C, Kraijer D, Mulder E, Volkmar F, Minderaa R. Interrelationship between Autism Diagnostic Observation Scheduled Generic (ADOS-G), Autism Diagnostic Interview-Revised, (ADI-R), and the diagnostic and statistical manual of mental disorders (DSM-IV-TR) classification in children and adolescents with mental retardation. *J Autism Dev Disord* 2004;**34**:129–37.

16. Bhasin T, Schendel D. Sociodemographic risk factors for autism in a US metropolitan area. *J Autism Dev Disord* 2007;**37**:667–77.

17. Robins D, Fein D, Barton M, Green J. The modified checklist for autism in toddlers: An initial study investigating the early detection of autism and pervasive developmental disorders. *J Autism Dev Disord* 2001;**31**:131–44.

18. Troyb E, Maltempo A, Boorstein H. *The influence of ethnicity and SES on age at diagnosis of autism.* Poster presented at the International Meeting for Autism Research, London.

19. Slone M, Durrheim K, Lachman P, Kaminer D. Association between the diagnosis of mental retardation and socioeconomic factors. *Am J Ment Retard* 1998;**102**:535–46.

20. Brown J, Rogers S. Cultural issues in autism. In Ozonoff S, Rogers S, Hendren R, eds. *Autism Spectrum Disorders: A Research Review for Practitioners*. Arlington, VA: American Psychiatric Publishing; 2003: 209–26.

Hearing loss across the lifespan: neuropsychological perspectives

Betsy Kammerer, Amy Szarkowski and Peter Isquith

Introduction

Unlike many conditions described in this volume, having a hearing loss or being deaf does not necessarily result in specific deficits in functioning. Functional outcomes depend on a complex interplay of physiological, developmental and environmental factors. We start with the premise that hearing loss by itself will often have an impact on cognitive organization but not necessarily or consistently on intellectual, neuropsychological, emotional, social or behavioral functioning. Disruption of these functions depends heavily on other factors that may be associated with etiology of the hearing loss or the interaction between individuals and their environment, including communication, family, educational, emotional and sociolinguistic environments. At the same time, effects related to a hearing loss can have significant negative impact in each of these areas, particularly without comprehensive and appropriate supports.

Hearing loss cannot be viewed as a single disorder or characteristic. A child with a congenital hearing loss secondary to prenatal infection is quite different from an older adult with hearing loss associated with the cumulative effects of aging, even if the mechanical aspects are similar. The child is likely to have had limited early access to language, potentially altering the child's educational, social and familial environments, whereas the adult has probably had typical developmental experiences. Even two children born with the same etiology and mechanics of hearing loss can develop along quite different trajectories depending on environmental variables. This chapter will discuss the parameters involved in defining and understanding the impact of hearing loss on neuropsychological and psychosocial outcomes across the lifespan. We avoid the broad term "hearing impaired", which can be perceived as an oversimplification that collapses the broad spectrum of hearing loss and its associated facets into a single, nonspecific view. Further, it connotes that hearing loss constitutes an

"impairment" or disability in and of itself, a premise with which many individuals with hearing loss disagree. We refer to individuals with hearing loss as hard of hearing (HH), deaf (D), or Deaf. In this discussion, *hearing loss* refers to the mechanical aspects of hearing, *deaf or deafness* refers to hearing loss sufficient to prevent auditory access to verbal language even with aids, *hard of hearing* refers to a more modest hearing loss that allows for some functional auditory input, and *Deaf* refers to a cultural identification of oneself with the Deaf Community, a recognized cultural and linguistic minority.

Hearing-loss characteristics

The physiological characteristics of hearing loss directly impact the individual's life and types of available intervention. Information on the degree, frequency range, site, clarity, and benefit derived from assistive devices such as hearing aids (HAs) is contained in an audiogram generated after an audiological evaluation. This information is essential to the neuropsychological evaluation.

Degree

The degree of hearing loss is typically first described by thresholds at which sound is detected across the frequency spectrum and measured by amplitude in decibels hearing level (dBHL). Broad categories of hearing loss are defined as: normal = 0–20 dB; mild = 21–40 dB; moderate = 41–55 dB; moderately severe = 56–70 dB; severe = 71–90 dB, and; profound > 90 dB. Hearing loss in the milder ranges has not been associated with significant language or academic outcomes in children with normal intelligence [1] but the impact of even a mild loss can complicate attention, communication, and learning for children with other developmental challenges. More severe hearing losses have educational and often communication significance, typically requiring support with language development (sign language or spoken language), personal assistive devices such as hearing aids (HA) or cochlear implants (CI), and educational supports.

Frequency

The pattern of hearing loss across the frequency spectrum affects the degree to which an individual can access spoken language via auditory channels. Impact on speech reception is greater if the hearing loss is in the primary speech frequencies, ranging from 500 to 4000 Hz, than losses outside of that range.

Site

Hearing loss is further defined by the general site of disruption in the transmission of sound and categorized as conductive, sensorineural, mixed (both conductive and sensorineural components) or auditory neuropathy/dys-synchrony.

Conductive hearing loss stems from disruption in the external or, more likely, middle ear components that conduct sound from the ear canal to the tympanic membrane, through the small bones of the middle ear to the inner ear [2]. Conductive hearing loss is a common effect of otitis media (ear infections) in children, but can also be caused by anything that blocks the transmission of sound (e.g. ear wax). Common treatments include antibiotics or removal of the obstruction. This type of hearing loss is most often of limited duration. Additionally, conductive hearing loss results in hearing loss no greater than moderately severe, as sound levels greater than 55–60 dB vibrate in the skull and translate sound energy to the fluid in the inner ear, effectively bypassing the middle ear.

Sensorineural hearing loss (SNHL) stems from deficits in the inner ear, most commonly damaged cochlear hair cells or auditory (VIII) nerve. Since sound is received through nerves that may be damaged or absent, increasing the loudness of sound does not necessarily equate with an increase in ability to discriminate sounds. Sensorineural losses are permanent, and can progress. The majority of children and adults with educationally or communicatively significant hearing loss have sensorineural losses.

Mixed hearing loss is a combination of both conductive and sensorineural factors.

Auditory neuropathy/auditory dys-synchrony (AN/AD) stems from disordered transmission from inner hair cells to the auditory nerve or disordered auditory brainstem transmission with normal cochlear function. AN/AD is often associated with medical risk factors

such as anoxia or hyperbilirubinemia [3]. Hearing loss in AN/AD can cause significant inconsistencies in hearing levels, with periods of near normal hearing and periods of significant loss, can remain severe, or can become normal hearing in the first years of life.

Time of onset

Timing of onset can be categorized as congenital, prelingually acquired, or postlingually acquired. Congenital and acquired prelingual hearing losses are more likely to interfere with acquisition of spoken language, while postlingual occurs after the child has already developed spoken language. While over 50% of individuals with hearing loss experience onset after the age of 65 (estimated 314 per 1000) [4], the much smaller number of children with prelingual onset (< 1 per 1000) experience the greatest developmental risks. Postlingually deafened individuals typically have sufficient experience with spoken language to enable continued speech and language development.

Identification and management

Identification of hearing loss before 6 months of age results in significantly better cognitive and language outcomes regardless of degree of hearing loss, socioeconomic status, or presence of other disabilities [5]. Historically, many children, even those with profound hearing loss, were not identified until 2 years of age or later. Fortunately, newborn hearing screening is now required in most of the USA and in many other countries, facilitating identification and intervention at a time when auditory input is crucial for language development, and communication can be initiated with knowledge of the child's hearing status.

Access to language, whether spoken or visual (e.g. sign language), is of primary concern for people with all manner of hearing loss across the age spectrum, but more so with young children, for whom language development is essential to their cognitive, social, and emotional development and to outcomes including mastery of academic skills and later vocational success. The impact of a hearing loss depends largely on the degree of loss experienced and the timing of onset. Many children with mild to moderate losses have good access to spoken language through hearing aids (HA), external devices that amplify sound and increase awareness of the acoustic features of speech. Others with more severe to profound losses may access spoken language through HA (if they receive exceptional benefit from them) or cochlear implants (CI), surgically implanted devices that transduce sound to electrical impulses and directly stimulate the auditory nerve. CIs have significantly changed the potential for developing spoken language in deaf children, with a majority of the children implanted early showing age-appropriate language skills [6]. While neither type of device replaces hearing or is a panacea for hearing loss, both may be viable options depending on hearing-loss characteristics and available environmental supports.

For those without reasonable and timely access to spoken language, however, access to visual language is essential. Visual languages include those that sign each word in the order of written language (e.g. Signing Exact English) or use manual cues to aid speech reading (e.g. Cued Speech). The most common form of visual language is sign language, a full linguistic system with all the properties of other natural languages [7]. Sign languages convey the same range of meanings and have complex phonology, morphology and syntax akin to spoken languages. Children exposed to natural models of sign language demonstrate language development patterns that parallel those of their hearing peers [8].

Epidemiology of hearing loss

Approximately 1 in 1000 children is born annually with severe to profound deafness, but that number increases to 3 per 1000 when hard-of-hearing children are included [9]. Some 17 per 1000 individuals have hearing loss onset by the age of 18 years, and over 300 per 1000 adults over the age of 65, or 1/3rd of the older population, have hearing loss sufficient to affect communication. The prevalence of hearing loss increases substantially with age, with 40–65% of adults over 75 years and more than 80% of those 85 years and older having communicatively significant hearing loss.

Epidemiological data collected by the Gallaudet Research Institute [10] describe the characteristics of D/HH children from 0 to 18 years who are identified as having special education needs in the USA. Of children in the sample, 41% had congenital hearing loss, 16% had hearing loss prior to their second birthday, and 7% after age 2 years, but onset was unknown for 36%. Twenty-three percent of hearing loss was attributed to genetic causes, 10% to prenatal infection, 12% to postnatal disease, and the majority (57%) of hearing loss was due to unknown causes. The percentage of those with hearing loss in each category was described

as 13% mild, 14% moderate, 12% moderate to severe, 14% severe, and 28% profound.

Anatomy of the hearing system

The human peripheral (versus central) hearing system is divided into three distinct components that linearly transduce sounds to nerve impulses: the external, middle and inner ear [2]. The external ear transmits sound from the environment to the tympanic membrane/ear drum (the entry point to the middle ear), which transduces sound vibrations into mechanical energy which is then transmitted through the three ossicles (malleus, incus and stapes) to the oval window (the entry point to the inner ear), where the sound is transduced again into fluid vibrations in the cochlea and the vestibule. These vibrations stimulate receptors (stereocilia or hair cells) that synapse with the auditory nerve (VIII) and encode amplitude and frequency tonotopically.

The translation of sound energy to neural signals becomes increasingly complicated but more organized upon entering the central auditory system via the auditory nerve at the brainstem auditory nuclei, where information bifurcates into separate monaural and binaural pathways. Monaural pathways carry amplitude and pitch signals from each cochlea separately to the contralateral auditory cortex. Binaural pathways follow a more complex course, transmitting signals from each cochlea both ipsilaterally and contralaterally, allowing for comparison of signals based on timing and loudness differences from each ear and facilitating sound localization and discrimination. This feature is important in unilateral hearing loss. Because pitch and volume data from each ear are carried separately to the auditory cortex, information from one ear is preserved. Without comparison of timing and amplitude data from both cochlea, unilateral hearing loss prevents localization and sound separation. Individuals with unilateral hearing loss thus have difficulty listening in background noise and identifying the location of sounds. Both monaural and binaural pathways are reunited at the inferior colliculus and are transmitted through the thalamus to the primary auditory cortex. Tonotopic organization is maintained within the auditory cortex, with low frequencies processed rostrally and high frequencies processed caudally [2].

Etiology of hearing loss

Knowing the etiology of a hearing loss is essential to understanding its potential impact on development (Table 10a.1). While hearing loss itself does not cause

Table 10a.1. Etiology of hearing loss.

Type	Etiology	Hearing-loss characteristics	Neurological/neuropsychological correlates
Hereditary			
Syndromic			
	Waardenburg syndrome	Range of sensorineural hearing loss from unilateral to bilateral, characteristically a low frequency hearing loss	No known cognitive, psychiatric or neurological implications
	Usher syndrome	Sensorineural hearing loss coupled with vision loss (retinitis pigmentosa), variable age of onset depending on type (Types I, II, III)	No known cognitive or psychiatric implications; progressive vision loss; vestibular and gross motor deficits may be involved
	Pendred syndrome	Congenital, non-progressive, severe to profound sensorineural hearing loss	No known cognitive, psychiatric or neurological implications
	Mitochondrial DNA mutations	Sensorineural, variable range	Cognitive and neurological implications
Non-syndromic			
	Otosclerosis	Conductive hearing loss, progressive in nature	Can lead to social isolation
	GJB2 gene mutation (Connexin 26)	Accounts for up to 50% of all non-syndromic sensorineural deafness	No known cognitive, psychiatric or neurological implications
Non-hereditary			
Congenital infections			
	Cytomegalovirus (CMV)	Most common cause of non-hereditary deafness. 40% of neonates with CMV develop sensorineural hearing loss	Significant neurological implications: mircocephaly, chorioretinitis, seizures, hypo/hypertonia, cerebral palsy, mental retardation, behavioral disorders
	Rubella	Exposure to rubella virus in utero can cause sensorineural hearing loss of varying severity	Can present with mental retardation and autistic features; significant physical implications: retinopathy, micro-ophthalmia, microencephaly, cardiac defects
	Toxoplasmosis, syphilis, herpes simplex virus	Sensorineural hearing loss of varying severity	Neurological symptoms may include mental retardation, visual impairment, seizures
Other etiologies			
	Auditory nerve tumors	Often complete sensorineural loss resulting from noncancerous tumor often arising from vestibular nerve	Associated with balance problems; surgery may lead to hemi-facial paralysis; difficult emotional adjustment to sudden loss and possible facial paralysis
	Bacterial meningitis	Sensorineural hearing loss	Cognitive, language, behavioral and academic problems often manifest; neurological sequelae may include: mental retardation, spasticity or paresis, seizure disorders; specific language deficits are common
	Measles, mumps, varicella zoster	Rarely causes sensorineural hearing loss	Usually no disease sequelae
	Hypoxia	Variable sensorineural hearing loss, often associated with prematurity	Outcomes depend on effects of hypoxia; associated sequelae are reduced secondary to current treatment
	Noise-induced hearing loss	Sensorineural, variable in range, often progressive	No cognitive, psychiatric or neurological implications

Table 10a.1. (cont.)

Type	Etiology	Hearing-loss characteristics	Neurological/neuropsychological correlates
	Ototoxic drugs	Sensorineural, variable in range, can appear long after drug exposure	Hearing loss can be a reminder of the illness, making adaptation difficult
	Presbycusis	Progressive hearing loss mainly in older adults, bilateral, impacts higher frequencies initially	Associated with depression, anxiety, paranoia and decrease in social activity
	Otitis media	Conductive, mild to moderate degree of loss	Mild deficits in working memory and language processing, associated with later language and learning disabilities

neuropsychological deficits, certain etiologies carry additional risk factors for neural disruption. Although the cause of hearing loss was previously unknown for the majority of affected children, the ability to identify genetic causes has significantly increased in this decade; the majority of them not associated with other neurodevelopmental risk factors. In addition, use of ototoxic drugs for medical treatments has led to a recent increase in the incidence of known causes of hearing loss in children (e.g. some chemotherapy agents used to treat cancers). In adults, hearing loss can be caused by trauma or auditory nerve tumors, although the vast majority of hearing loss is associated with the cumulative effects of aging, namely noise-induced hearing loss and presbycusis.

Hereditary deafness

As many as 1000 genes are involved in the hearing system. Over 350 genetic conditions associated with hearing loss are described in the literature, accounting for over 50% of SNHL and some conductive hearing loss in children [11]. Of genetic causes, 70–80% of are autosomal recessive, 15–20% are autosomal dominant, and 1–3% are sex-linked or mitochondrial. Approximately 30% of the causative genes have been identified. Genes primarily associated with hearing loss are indicated by DFNA for dominant and DFNB for recessive, with a following number indicating order of discovery (e.g. DFNA 1).

Non-syndromic hereditary deafness

Non-syndromic genetic causes of deafness are typically autosomal recessive and result in congenital, bilateral severe to profound hearing loss without other neurological concerns. The best-known association, accounting for over 50% of non-syndromic hearing loss, is a mutation in the GJB2 gene responsible for production of connexin 26, an inner-ear protein gene.

While most forms of genetic hearing loss occur early in life, otosclerosis typically presents in adolescence and is a progressive hearing loss. This non-syndromic conductive hearing loss results from hardening around the stapes at the oval window, restricting movement and reducing sound transduction.

Syndromic hereditary deafness

The majority of syndromes associated with sensorineural hearing loss are hereditary. The most common dominant syndrome is Waardenburg and the most common non-dominant syndromes are Usher and Pendred syndromes.

Waardenburg syndrome is an autosomal dominant genetic syndrome with four known subtypes [12], each with varying mutations of the PAX-3 gene. Hearing loss in Waardenburg syndrome may be unilateral or bilateral and varies from mild to profound with a characteristic low-frequency loss. There are no documented cognitive or neurological sequelae associated with Waardenburg syndrome.

Usher syndrome is an autosomal recessive disorder with three subtypes, the first two with congenital, bilateral SNHL and onset of visual impairment with retinitis pigmentosa later in life. Type I is characterized by profound loss and onset of retinitis pigmentosa by 10 years, while Type II includes mild to severe bilateral hearing loss and onset of retinitis pigmentosa between 10 and 20 years. Type III is characterized by progressive SNHL typically with post-lingual onset, some involvement of the vestibular system, and variable onset of retinitis pigmentosa. There are no other known neurological conditions common to Usher syndrome.

Pendred syndrome is also a recessive syndrome with congenital, non-progressive severe to profound bilateral hearing loss along with bilateral dilatation of the vestibular aqueducts. It is not associated with other neuropsychological deficits.

Sex-linked disorders involving hearing loss are far less common, explaining only 1 to 3% of hearing loss in children. Syndromes include Norrie disease, Alport syndrome, and Nance deafness.

There are also many syndromic disorders attributed to inherited mitochondrial DNA mutations that involve hearing loss, including MELAS (mitochondrial myopathy, encephalopathy, lactic acidosis, and stroke), MIDD (maternally inherited diabetes and deafness, a rare form of Type-2 diabetes), MERRF (myoclonic epilepsy associated with ragged-red fibers) and Kearns-Sayre syndromes. These disorders are typically accompanied by systemic and/or neurological problems, often severe.

Several fairly rare genetic syndromes include conductive hearing loss, typically resulting from bone growth deformities. These are often quite recognizable from the facial features and include Treacher Collins, Klippel-Feil, Crouzon syndromes, and osteogenesis imperfecta.

Non-hereditary causes

Non-hereditary causes of hearing loss in children are becoming less common secondary to available prevention and treatment. Varying degrees of hearing loss are often associated with specific congenital and acquired infections. While on the decline, these causes remain important as they are often associated with other, sometimes severe, neurological sequelae that affect multiple domains of functioning in children.

Congenital infections

Hearing loss is frequently associated with prenatal TORCH (toxoplasmosis, others, rubella, cytomegalovirus and herpes) infections that can infect the placenta and disrupt the developing fetal central nervous system. Cytomegalovirus (CMV) is probably the most common cause of nonhereditary sensorineural hearing loss and is associated with jaundice, hepatomegaly, splenomegaly, rash, intrauterine growth retardation and respiratory distress. Over 90% of infants with these symptoms have additional neurological consequences including microcephaly, periventricular leukomalacia, polymicrogyria, pachygyria or lissencephaly along with chorioretinitis, seizures, hypo/hypertonia, cerebral palsy, mental retardation, and behavioral disorders [13].

Rubella resulted in thousands of cases of congenital rubella syndrome (CRS), the most common cause of hearing loss in children born in the early 1960s during a rubella epidemic in the USA. CRS is rarely seen in many countries since the introduction of the rubella vaccine, but remains a significant problem in countries where use of the vaccine is not consistent. Infants born with CRS exhibit a broad spectrum of symptoms including SNHL, cataracts, retinopathy, micro-ophthalmia, microcephaly, and cardiac defects (myocarditis, patent ductus arteriosus, valvular stenosis, and septal defects). Neurological symptoms can include autistic features and mental retardation.

Other infections, including toxoplasmosis, syphilis, and herpes simplex virus, are less frequent but can be associated with SNHL and significant neurodevelopmental disorders including mental retardation, visual impairment, and seizures [14].

Acquired infections

Both viral and bacterial infections, particularly in the first few years of life, can be associated with SNHL. As with prenatal infections, timing and severity are important considerations in evaluating the likelihood of neurological impairments other than hearing loss. The increasing availability of effective vaccinations or treatments has decreased the incidence of postnatal infectious causes of hearing loss. Bacterial meningitis, specifically *Haemophilus influenzae* type b (Hib), accounted for the majority of hearing loss in infants and children but is now rare due to vaccination programs [15]. Pneumococcal meningitis, meningococcal meningitis and group B streptococcal infections remain the most common forms of early meningitis. Of children who survive bacterial meningitis, some 40% exhibit acute neurological complications, with severe to profound hearing loss the most common residual sequelae. Some 6% are also left with mental retardation, 4% with spasticity or paresis, and 4% with seizures. Neurological symptoms during the acute infection phase increase the likelihood of residual, long-term cognitive, language, behavioral and academic difficulties. Language disorders may be a secondary result of the hearing loss, but are also often neurologically based and a direct result of the infection.

More rarely, viral infections can be associated with hearing loss. These include measles, mumps, and varicella zoster. Again, vaccinations have made these causes quite rare.

Hypoxia

The incidence of sensorineural hearing loss associated with perinatal or neonatal complications has varied substantially over the past 30 years. In the 1960s, hypoxia accounted for less than 2% of hearing loss in children. With increased survival of high-risk infants in the 1990s along with ventilation, oxygen, and acidosis, however, that incidence increased to between 25 and 30%. Newer treatments, however, have again reduced the incidence of hearing loss associated with prematurity [16].

Ototoxic drugs

Several classes of medications are associated with SNHL. Some are associated with hearing loss in a developing fetus, including salicylates (aspirin), nonsteroidal anti-inflammatory drugs, diuretics, and quinine. Others cause hearing loss in individuals across the age spectrum such as certain classes of antibiotics (e.g. erythromycin) and chemotherapeutic agents (e.g. cisplatin). Hearing loss which occurs as a side effect of treatment for cancer, for example, can be particularly difficult for patients since it can be a lifelong reminder of the cancer diagnosis and treatment.

Noise-induced hearing loss

Noise-induced hearing loss typically occurs in adults and is the cumulative effective of damage to the hair cells from repeated, prolonged exposure to loud sounds, though can also result from a single exposure such as a blast explosion. Noise-induced losses have a characteristic audiogram with a precipitous drop in hearing level between 3000 and 6000 Hz, affecting ability to discriminate consonant sounds. Current frequency of use of music players at higher volumes is of concern related to potential noise-induced hearing loss [17].

Presbycusis

SNHL associated with aging is known as presbycusis, a term encompassing general deterioration of the hair cells in the cochlea. It is progressive and bilateral with greater impact at higher frequencies. Presbycusis might be more correctly thought of as the cumulative effects of a lifetime of exposure to noise, caffeine, ototoxic medications, and other factors [18]. It is the most common type of hearing loss but affects primarily older adults. Hearing loss of this type can be associated with depression, anxiety, paranoia, and decrease in social activity.

Otitis media

Childhood ear infections are quite common and can be associated with conductive hearing loss. Fluid can block Eustachian tubes, preventing normal air and fluid flow in the middle ear, interfering with tympanic membrane movement and inhibiting sound conduction to the cochlea. Associated hearing loss is often mild but can be moderate and is usually temporary. Most children by the age of 3 years have had at least one such ear infection, and about half have had two or more. If untreated, otitis media can lead to permanent damage and permanent hearing loss. There has long been debate in the literature and medical community as to whether temporary, periodic hearing loss associated with otitis media is associated with any other developmental problems [19]. Recent research, however, demonstrates mild deficits in working memory and language processing that are associated with later language and learning disabilities in children with histories of severe, prolonged and/or frequent otitis media [20].

Neuropsychological correlates of hearing loss

There has been long-term interest in potential differences in brain functioning in D/HH individuals secondary to decreased or absent auditory stimulation. Early studies were often confounded by including diverse groups of individuals with differing levels of hearing loss. Recent studies have more rigorously defined coherent participant groups and/or separated groups into those with hereditary deafness and those who are neurologically at risk, often demonstrating that deficits found in previous studies were related to neurological issues and not to hearing loss per se [21]. Similarly, some earlier studies of children with cochlear implants did not consistently attend to etiology or have adequate sample sizes to address critical issues including age of implantation and duration of implant use. Recent controlled studies have increased understanding of brain plasticity by tracking function in congenitally deaf children who had auditory stimulation from a CI at differing stages of brain development.

The advent of modern imaging techniques has contributed to an explosion of research into cognitive functioning in deaf individuals. Event-related potential (ERP), functional magnetic resonance imaging (fMRI), and cognitive behavioral studies have consistently demonstrated different organization of brain function in deaf individuals [22]. Deafness from birth results in less myelination and fewer fibers projecting to and from the auditory cortex [8]. Even with conductive hearing loss, which should cause only mild decreases in auditory stimulation, animal models suggest altered temporal processes in the auditory cortex [23]. Recent studies of brain utilization in those who are deaf, however, have found greater multimodal connectivity in the auditory cortex area relative to the brains of those who are hard of hearing or who develop progressive hearing loss, suggesting that the brain might not simply reorganize and use the auditory cortex for another purpose, but that it may use other sensory information to accommodate for the lack of access to sound [24].

Studies of unilateral cochlear implantation at different ages provide insights into the functioning of the primary auditory cortex. In congenitally or early deafened individuals, non-auditory processing (i.e. perceiving and understanding sign language) involves the area of the cortex believed selective for human voice. The first 2 years of life may be the sensitive period for establishing a preference for processing human voice or visual communication [25]. In deaf children, when the auditory cortex is primed for listening via early introduction of sound through a cochlear implant, that area of the brain can be activated. Using measures of P1 cortical auditory evoked potentials, Sharma and colleagues identified a sensitive period of increased plasticity from birth to approximately 3.5 years for central auditory system development [26]. Beyond that window, plasticity is greatly reduced, though some children still receive significant benefit from an implant. Cortical stimulation studies in children born deaf suggest that this sensitive period seems to close at around 7 years, by which time the auditory system has been recruited for other functions.

Although research on bilateral implantation is in its infancy, early work reveals ipsilateral, but not necessarily contralateral, auditory cortex activation [26]. The second, later implanted, device may be attempting to access cortex that no longer has typical connections to higher-order auditory and language areas. Near-simultaneous bilateral implantation may facilitate more rapid development of central auditory pathways [27].

In this brief discussion of current findings, we focus primarily on examples of recent studies of neuropsychological function in deaf signers, with attention to the developing body of information on children with cochlear implants.

General cognitive functioning

Historically, deaf individuals were viewed as intellectually inferior; then decades ago as not inferior but as concrete; and eventually as intellectually normal, with much of the distinction in viewpoints determined by measures used. With appropriate measures, the distribution of intellectual functioning among D/HH individuals is similar to that of hearing individuals, although differences can be found in specific skill areas [28]. The heterogeneity of the hearing loss group, combined with differing access to early language and educational opportunities, are factors that contribute significantly to varied outcomes. When hearing loss is addressed early in life and the appropriate interventions are provided to D/HH individuals without other neurological issues, the cognitive reorganization of some functions does not seem to have an impact on general cognitive or intellectual functioning, at least at the level of index scores.

Attention and executive functioning

Attention and executive control processes are particularly critical for D/HH individuals. They must monitor multiple visual cues (e.g. people's reactions) since they cannot rely solely on auditory cues (e.g. car horns), and signers must integrate written language with native language in learning situations. For those who rely on HAs or CIs, continuous sustained attention to the speaker is required to process language, and concentrated effort is required in groups; often all speakers cannot be understood. D/HH students are often misread as having attentional issues due to their normal need to frequently look around to find who is speaking, to understand instructions they could not easily process, or to alleviate the strain on sustained attention.

Early studies typically found greater inattention and impulsivity in deaf than hearing children, probably related to etiologies of deafness that also involved frontal brain systems or to executive functioning deficits which in turn impair language processing. In comparing children with CIs and deaf children without CIs, Pisoni and colleagues proposed that auditory deprivation impacts both the auditory cortex and frontal cortex [29].

Current studies offer mixed results, in part based on the nature of the task. D/HH children perform equally as well as hearing children on tests of planning, impulse control, and cognitive flexibility when tasks are appropriate and accessible for both groups [30]. Deaf students exhibited greater inattention and impulsivity on continuous performance tests, though their performance style appeared to reflect adaptations appropriate in their environments more than pathology [31]. No differences were noted between hearing children, HH children and children with CIs on a similar task. Behavioral inventories of executive function suggest that, while deaf children overall are described as more impulsive and inattentive than hearing children, these problems are more often seen in deaf children with other neurological risk factors and not children with hereditary deafness [32]. Hereditarily deaf children were described as having similar everyday executive abilities compared to age-matched peers in their ability to inhibit, shift, modulate emotions, initiate, plan, organize, and self-monitor. Hauser and colleagues found similar patterns with deaf adults' self-reported executive functions [33].

Language

Communication development is a primary concern for those with all degrees of hearing loss, as language substantially impacts cognitive, academic and social–emotional outcomes. For D/HH individuals, language does not develop in isolation and is not related entirely to specific hearing loss factors, but results from the complex interplay of biological and environmental factors. Understanding how to support development of language and language-related learning skills has been a longstanding priority for families and educators of D/HH children.

Given the importance of language acquisition in deaf children, many studies have focused on understanding how sign language users may differ from hearing individuals. Although early studies suggested that spatial characteristics of sign language might lead it to be processed in the right hemisphere, later studies confirmed that it is indeed processed in the left hemisphere using much the same brain regions as spoken languages [34]. Left-hemisphere lesions cause aphasia for sign language in deaf adults. Injury to Wernicke's area can result in fluent sign jargon and injury to Broca's area can result in agrammatic and dysfluent signing while non-linguistic gestures remain intact. Sign language skills remain largely intact after right-hemisphere injury, with the exception of some pragmatic elements, subtle use of space errors, and facial processing errors [34]. Thus, while the right hemisphere may play a larger role in language processing for deaf signers, language is typically lateralized to the left hemisphere.

Functional imaging studies shed light on brain organization for language in deaf signers. Increased activity is seen in the left superior temporal region during comprehension of ASL for both deaf and hearing signers [35], with increased activity in the auditory association cortex but not primary auditory cortex in deaf signers [36]. After activation of a CI, however, the primary auditory cortex was activated by spoken words while there was no effect in the auditory association cortex. Plasticity appeared limited to auditory association cortex and not primary auditory areas that are more dedicated to fundamental processing of auditory input. Re-assignment of the auditory comprehension areas to sign language comprehension is probably age-dependent, with greater plasticity occurring in deaf individuals with early or congenital hearing loss than in those with later-onset hearing loss [25].

The availability of CIs has increased the potential for developing spoken language in profoundly deaf children. Although some children with CIs use sign language, spoken language is typically the goal. Language outcomes after receiving a CI are variable, with more than half showing age-appropriate language skills when implanted early [6]. There is also a small group of children who show little development of spoken language with a CI, although they may well benefit from access to sound. Early age of implantation and auditory experience pre-implant have consistently been associated with positive language outcomes [37]. Explaining the remaining variability in outcomes is currently an important area of research. One theory is that differences relate in part to the verbal rehearsal process in working memory causing limitations in information-processing capacity, associated with early lack of auditory stimulation [29].

Although children with mild hearing loss or unilateral hearing loss readily gain spoken-language skills, their language levels are also below their hearing peers [38].

Visuospatial cognition

Visual processing skills have often been used as a measure of intellectual functioning in D/HH persons, under the assumption that only language skills will be impacted by deafness. The common belief that loss of one sense leads to enhancement of other senses (e.g. visual processing) is not, however, a straightforward trade-off in deaf individuals. Recent studies of visual cortex size and responsivity found no differences between hearing and deaf adults, although visual responses were stronger in the auditory cortex for deaf versus hearing subjects [39]. There may be effects of hearing loss and sign language use at more complex, higher levels of visual information processing. For example, deaf individuals attend to the peripheral visual fields more than their hearing peers when those aspects are attentionally demanding, though not in general [40].

Differences seen in controlled research tasks are not likely to be observable in a typical neuropsychological evaluation. Hauser and colleagues [41] found no differences between congenitally, genetically deaf native ASL users and hearing subjects on a battery of typical clinical visuospatial tasks, suggesting that deviations on such standard measures can be interpreted to imply neuropsychological deficits and not attributed to hearing loss or sign language use. Similarly, in assessment of those who are HH or use CIs, performance on visual processing tasks is not affected by hearing loss, although performance is vulnerable to neurological sequelae associated with some etiologies [29].

Memory

Memory and working memory vary in D/HH individuals depending on the nature of the stimuli. Deaf signers show an advantage on visual span/working memory tasks [42] but a disadvantage for the same tasks with linguistic information [43]. Kowalska and Szelag [44] suggest that deaf individuals may distribute attentional resources between visual and temporal processing differently than hearing individuals, creating a limitation in working memory.

Children with CIs have also shown inconsistent memory functioning, particularly for sequential and working memory tasks [29]. When given a battery of neuropsychological tests, a group of early implanted children with CIs performed comparably to their hearing peers with the exception of digit span, and auditory and visual sequential memory tasks that contained verbal stimuli [6].

Even adults with mild to moderate hearing loss show decreased auditory working memory [45]. McCoy and colleagues proposed the *effortfulness hypothesis*, which states that an HH person must expend effort to perceive the environment that might otherwise have been available for encoding information into memory.

Motor development

Although deaf children and adolescents have similar motor skill acquisition patterns compared to hearing peers [46], early studies noted motor deficits in this population. Horn and colleagues suggest that these deficits were related to etiologies of deafness with associated neurological impairment and balance issues connected with vestibular problems. Deaf children with no additional neurological issues demonstrate motor skills similar to their hearing peers [47, 48], and signing deaf adults show visual-motor skills comparable to hearing adults [30]. In fact, deaf children who are fluent signers may develop enhanced finger dexterity compared to non-signers. Studies of children with CIs are of interest since the surgery could potentially impact balance and therefore motor skills. Studies of deaf children with and without CIs, however, reveal delays in broad motor development [49] and in complex motor sequencing and balance [50], suggesting no specific effect of the CI. In children with CIs, however, higher ratings of general motor function by parents [51] and better fine motor skills [47] were both associated with better language outcomes post-implantation, suggesting a link between motor and language development in deaf children [29].

Social–emotional development

As might be expected given the multitude of hearing-loss and linguistic characteristics, there is no singular course of social–emotional development amongst individuals with hearing loss. The course of emotional development is altered in many ways at all ages and ranges of hearing loss [52]. An essential tenet is that attitudes about hearing loss and congruence between the person's communication mode and that of their environment are related to life satisfaction [53], identify formation, and social–emotional functioning [54].

Persons with progressive hearing loss

Individuals with progressive hearing loss experience unique emotional challenges. The grief process lasts longer and is experienced more deeply, as the person gradually feels significant losses in what they hear. Later hearing loss is not identity-forming; it is perceived as a deficit. Hearing loss in older people can result in restricted communication with others and can limit social interactions. This may be a significant contributing factor to the social withdrawal seen in many older individuals [55]. As a result, feelings of frustration, shame, stigmatization and depression can occur.

Individuals who are hard of hearing

Relative to members of the Deaf Community and to typically hearing persons, HH individuals are often more socially isolated [56]. Deaf signers and hearing participants rated their quality of life and general and behavioral health similarly, while the HH group reported significantly worse relationships then either of the other groups. HH individuals are at greater risk for problems with identity formation and with social relationships.

Cochlear implant users

With the increased number of children receiving implants, understanding the factors which promote healthy emotional development and positive self-esteem in this group is essential. Thus far, research has focused primarily on parent-reported quality of life, despite the absence of validated hearing-loss-related quality-of-life instruments [57] and poor correlations between child and parent reports regarding social–emotional status. Studies suggest that less stress in the family system correlates with better communication outcomes and increased social relationships in young children with CIs [58].

Late-deafened adults have been particularly open to pursuing a CI, since their life experience has been so changed by loss of hearing [55]. While some experience difficulty adjusting to the implant, the majority of adult CI users report improved self-worth and higher levels of life satisfaction 2 years post-surgery.

Deaf sign language users

Prevalence rates of psychiatric disorders in deaf signers mirror those in the general public. The presentation of mental illness in this population, however, can be markedly different [59]. Deaf individuals tend to have greater gaps in their social networks and often present with feelings of loneliness or isolation, as well as frustration with feeling marginalized. Additionally, because facial expressions are of greater importance in Deaf culture, deaf individuals are more likely to attend to and describe types and degrees of emotions of the characters they discuss, but are less likely to mention causal factors [56]. As with any cultural group, clinicians should consider the impact of the patient's culture on his/her presentation and avoid incorrectly attributing their actions or feelings to their hearing loss or membership in the Deaf Community [59]. Alternatively, behaviors that are in line with Deaf cultural norms may appear to be clinically important when they are in fact cultural.

Assessment

Neuropsychological assessment, including psychosocial evaluation, is frequently a critical component of planning appropriate interventions for D/HH children and adults, in part because the etiology of the hearing loss may be associated with neurological vulnerabilities in functioning across neuropsychological domains. Hearing loss with no other neurological risks can also create challenges, particularly to communication, language skills, and psychosocial adaptation, that require definition and monitoring via thorough assessment. As evident from the above discussion, historical variables are of particular importance when assessing individuals with hearing loss, including age of onset and characteristics of hearing loss, age, type and continuity of interventions (e.g. CI, HA, exposure to sign), educational and therapeutic history, and presence of additional disabilities. Added to these are factors with specific impact on D/HH children; opportunities for socialization with others, exposure to specific content, and access to communication [60]. Careful integration of biological, experiential, and psychosocial factors is essential to comprehensive evaluation and to ensuring appropriate interventions.

Appropriate evaluation of people with hearing loss, however, raises multiple concerns, which are detailed in chapters on this topic [60, 61]. For assessment of deaf signers, direct communication and in-depth knowledge of deafness are essential skills for the evaluator, as use of an interpreter can lead to unreliable results. Referral to a professional with competence in deaf-related issues is a preferable option [62], yet limited availability of neuropsychologists fluent in sign language necessitates flexibility in approach to assessment. Neuropsychologists who are not familiar with working with the deaf often collaborate with school or clinical psychologists who work directly with deaf students, providing better psychometric quality and enabling the understanding of important cultural components of a person's presentation. People who are strong verbal communicators such as those with milder hearing losses, children who benefit well from HAs or CIs and are in mainstream educational settings, and later-deafened individuals will make up the majority of individuals referred to neuropsychologists not specializing in working with D/HH individuals. Even in these more common situations when professionals may feel comfortable with communication and testing procedures, consultation with an evaluator experienced in working with D/HH persons is advisable. The professional should understand the following: the person's assistive listening devices (HA, FM systems, CI), appropriate modifications to maximize hearing in the testing room, how to relate ability to hear in a quiet test room with listening in a classroom, cognitive and social–emotional issues related to hearing loss, and differentiation of effects of hearing loss or neuropsychological vulnerabilities in specific areas such as attention and language (see Table 10a.2).

Table 10a.2.* There are variations in the overarching organization of various neuropsychological constructs, administrative demands of assessment tasks, and scoring procedures which may impact recommendations as to the use of any given task with D/HH individuals. The following chart is provided as an aide for individual assessment, research, and test battery development. The chart describes general cautions and suggestions that will be appropriate for some, but not all D/HH, examinees.

Domain Assessment task	Caveats	Complexity of administration Language demands		Additional comments and potential confounds
		Receptive	Expressive	
Executive/attention				
Verbal fluency	S, I, L	MED	LOW	Adequate understanding of the category is essential. Speech production demands may decrease speed and increase anxiety, stress or fatigue.
Visual fluency	V, C	MED	LOW	
Inhibition (Stroop) tasks	S, V	HIGH	LOW	Examinee must be secure in color naming and word reading. Speech production demands may decrease speed.
Trail-making	M	LOW	LOW	Examinee must be secure in alphabet and number series sequences.
Tower	M, C	HIGH	LOW	
Card-sorting	M, C	HIGH	LOW	Repeated task interruptions by examiner may interfere with performance.
Continuous performance	M	HIGH	LOW	CPTs utilizing words or numbers may add an additional variable.
Auditory span	H, R, C	HIGH	LOW	Stress of hearing without context may decrease memory. Signed versions are not equivalent.
Visual span	M,C	HIGH	LOW	
Language				
Articulation	H, S	LOW	LOW–MED	Speech production demands may increase anxiety or stress. Audiogram should be checked to understand which errors are related to hearing loss.
Naming	S, I, L	MED–HIGH	LOW	Semantic cuing is often more appropriate then phonemic cuing.
Receptive vocabulary	H, R, I, L	MED–HIGH	LOW	
Expressive vocabulary	S, I, L	LOW–HIGH	LOW	
Language formulation	H, S, L	LOW–HIGH	LOW–HIGH	Examinees with a history of sign language use may display mixed grammatical features of sign and English.
Language comprehension	H, R, I, L	MED–HIGH	MED–HIGH	Reading skills may be negatively impacted in many examinees.
Phonological awareness	H, R, S	MED–HIGH	LOW	Pressure to hear correctly may increase anxiety, stress, or fatigue.
Automaticity	S	MED–HIGH	LOW	Speech production demands may increase anxiety or stress.
Visual/nonverbal				
Complex figure copying	M	MED–HIGH	LOW	Organizational style may differ without being pathological. Part-oriented approaches are common.

Table 10a.2.* (cont.)

Domain Assessment task	Caveats	Complexity of administration Language demands		Additional comments and potential confounds
		Receptive	**Expressive**	
Visual-spatial (mental rotation, patterns)	M	MED–HIGH	LOW	These tasks may be performed in an advanced fashion by many deaf people.
Visual-constructive	M	HIGH	LOW	Process analysis is particularly relevant, with attention to visual detail or spatial errors.
Memory				
Semantic memory (story, sentence)	H, R, S, I, L	LOW–HIGH	LOW–HIGH	Translations may significantly alter the structure and grammar of the targeted English language items. Communication via speech-reading will increase attentional demands.
Visual memory (facial, design, picture, spatial location)	M	LOW–MED	LOW	D/HH examinees may be at a disadvantage when verbal labels are useful.
Word list learning	H, R, I, S	LOW	LOW	Categorization strategies may differ; semantic categories are more common.
Object list learning	I, M	LOW	LOW	D/HH examinees may be at a disadvantage when verbal labels are useful.
Motor				
Visual-motor	M	LOW	LOW	Organizational style may differ without being pathological. Part-oriented approaches are common.
Pegboard; fingertapping; praxis	M	LOW–MED	LOW	Deaf signers may have an advantage in finger speed.
Motor sequencing	M	LOW	LOW	Tasks which are demonstrated or signed frequently elicit only motoric imitation.
Vestibular/balance	M	LOW	LOW	Enhanced visual compensation strategies may offset vestibular/balance deficits. Caution must be used for balance tasks involving closed eyes. Sensorineural hearing loss may be associated with balance or vestibular difficulties.
Cognition				
Verbal measures	H,R,S,I,V, C,L	LOW–HIGH	LOW–HIGH	Verbal test performance as a measure of cognitive potential is used only with great caution. Use of verbal tests to understand skills in learning environments may be appropriate.
Nonverbal measures	M,V,C	LOW–HIGH	LOW	Nonverbal test performance is often a better indicator of cognitive potential, but caution should be used when motor or visual problems are present.

*Review of measures and table contributed to this work by Steven Hardy-Braz.
Caveats Key: H: Hearing: For D/HH examinees using oral/aural communication, particular attention must be paid to adequacy of listening environment on these tasks, including lighting, carpets, functioning of HA/CI, and clarity of examiner's speech. R: residual hearing may alter administration complexity; increased tendency to mishear information. M: motor impairment may be present related to etiology of hearing loss (e.g. cytomegalovirus, meningitis). S: speech production demands may hinder performance. I: inconsistent information access due to hearing loss may influence ability and results. V: visual loss may be present related to etiology of hearing loss (e.g. Usher syndrome, toxoplasmosis). C: with complex instructions, examiner demonstrations and practice items are often required to ensure task comprehension. l: language: limited English fluency, vocabulary, or phonological awareness may limit production or performance.

In all assessments, there is an ethical obligation to evaluate with tools that are appropriate and fair. Few psychological tests have been normed with deaf people, and those identified as "deaf" on the few so normed tests, or those with a D/HH sample, may in fact be a heterogeneous group of persons who happen to have a hearing loss. Although language portions of intelligence tests should not be used to estimate cognitive potential in any person with a hearing loss, exclusion of language testing to bypass communication issues can also bias test results. Language may be a relative strength in the profile despite hearing loss, and strengths and weaknesses in specific language areas may well be important diagnostic information. Careful task analysis is particularly essential to understanding implications of test results in this population. Essential information on defining appropriate test procedures can be found in the recent test manuals of the Wechsler Intelligence Scale for Children–Fourth Edition [63], for example, which offers detailed cautions in testing and applicability of specific subtests for individuals with hearing loss. Common modifications and accommodations in test procedures to increase fairness, however, have not been validated or standardized [64], and it is essential for professionals to document all nonstandard aspects of test administration. Given multiple threats to test validity with D/HH individuals, non-test procedures, such as review of records, observations, and collateral interviews, take on greater importance for people with hearing loss [62].

Intervention

The focus of intervention planning for D/HH children, as for all children, should be to optimize cognitive, academic, and adaptive outcomes and to enhance quality of life through appropriate management of social and emotional needs. For D/HH children, research has consistently demonstrated positive language and academic outcomes from early identification of hearing loss and from the efficacy of early intervention [65, 66]. Universal newborn screening is now viewed as the standard of care by the American Academy of Pediatrics [67], with specific recommendations for comprehensive follow-up support services. These services need to include all medical/audiological management required, but also intervention for any identified language, motor, cognitive, or emotional needs. Early intervention services need to address the significantly lower health-related quality of life reported in families with a child with hearing loss [37]. Also of primary importance to both cognitive progress and positive emotional adjustment is early access to communication through the modality (spoken or visual language) most appropriate for the child. Without early and appropriate communication, delays in both cognitive and emotional areas are noted [68, 69]. Access to language specifically increases emotional maturity and understanding, as well as development of perspective and social reciprocity.

Family-focused early intervention programs have been particularly successful, as they can begin to address the family's adjustment to having a child with a permanent condition that can affect natural parent/child communication [38, 70]. Restoring a parent's comfort and natural intuitions with parenting is primary. Parental attitudes toward deafness strongly influence how the parents will perceive their child with hearing loss. Parents can benefit significantly from creating or entering an environment that is supportive of them and understanding of the needs of their child. Participation in parent support groups, parent-focused chat rooms on the topic, and other outlets are important for many parents as they navigate new territory in learning how to parent a D/HH child (see Table 10a.3).

For D/HH children, many interventions to address the potential neuropsychological vulnerabilities associated with the hearing loss or the etiology of the hearing loss occur in the school setting. Neuropsychological assessments are often useful in specifically defining the comprehensive needs of the D/HH student. Although 25% of students are in residential schools specifically designed for deaf students, most D/HH students are in regular education settings with an additional 12% having some resource-room time and 20% attending a self-contained classroom within a comprehensive school setting [10]. An educational placement that matches the communication mode of deaf students increases life satisfaction. For children who are mainstreamed, it is essential to ensure that all professionals working with the child understand the impact of the hearing loss in both the educational demands and the potential social isolation. Since the primary causes of hearing loss are also primary causes of neurological dysfunction, a child with a hearing loss is more likely to have a learning disability, yet teachers have often been trained in either deaf education or special education, and may not be trained to deal with the deaf student with learning disabilities [71]. Deaf students often require specialized instruction as research shows different learning styles for both reading [72] and mathematics [73]. Intervention programs in school are also needed to address the needs of children with unilateral and mild/moderate hearing loss, whose needs are often underappreciated and not adequately managed [74].

Interventions should include the psychosocial domain, as D/HH youths experience greater levels of psychological stress than hearing peers [52]. Hearing-loss-specific concerns include psychological stress,

Table 10a.3. Related websites.

Organization	Website address	Description
Alexander Graham Bell	www.agbell.org	Information and resources for all ages emphasizing spoken language development
Experience Journal: Children's Hospital, Boston	www.experiencejournal.com	Children and adults with hearing loss, their parents and siblings, and the professionals who work with them share experiences and feelings
Hands & Voices	www.handsandvoices.org	Parent-driven, parent/professional collaborative group supporting all communication modalities
Hearing Exchange Kids	www.HearingExchangeKids.com	Place for elementary and middle school-age children with hearing loss to learn games and tips, and communicate with each other; particularly for mainstreamed children who do not have peers with hearing loss
Healthy Hearing	www.healthyhearing.com	Current patient-focused consumer information on hearing aids, cochlear implants, and hearing health
Laurent Clerc National Deaf Education	http://clerccenter.gallaudet.edu	Resources for deaf and hard-of-hearing children and adults, including research and websites
Listen-Up	www.listen-up.org	Information related to D/HH children, with optional listserve group limited to parents and caretakers
National Institute on Deafness and Communication Disorders	www.nidcd.nih.gov/	NIH website covering research, funding, and health information related to hearing loss
CI-Circle	www.cicircle.org	For parents whose children use or are considering cochlear implants
My Baby's Hearing (Boys Town National Research Hospital)	www.babyhearing.org	Comprehensive information on hearing loss in young children, for parents and professionals

identity formation and peer relationships. Research suggests intervention should be geared to enhancement of the D/HH adolescent's identity, which leads to better social–emotional outcomes, and higher level of satisfaction with life [54]. Assisting youths with identity formation can take many forms, such as counseling with a professional in this field or all means of building associations with similar peers, including therapy or activity groups with peers, attending events for D/HH youth, having a D/HH mentor, or, for those who do not have peers nearby, having a D/HH "penpal". Social integration in inclusive settings has been found to significantly enhance life satisfaction and decrease isolation in those with hearing loss [75].

Psychotherapy is often an appropriate intervention. For all levels of hearing loss, the therapist should be able to communicate directly with the person and should be familiar with working with the D/HH population [76]. Culturally affirmative therapy ensures that the person's identity and perspectives are respected and not marginalized by the therapeutic experience [77]. Concerns have been raised about the lack of adequate numbers of professionals to deal with the psychosocial and emotional needs of the D/HH population [78], and expansion of current mental health services is essential.

Future research directions

Future hearing-loss-related research should continue to work toward prevention of medically based hearing loss, early identification, and better management. Acquired SNHL rates have significantly decreased in countries with advanced neonatal care and comprehensive vaccine programs [11]. The same benefits have yet to be realized in many countries where such treatments are unavailable, yet are important given the potentially severe social and medical consequences associated with acquired hearing loss. Newborn screening in recent years has also dramatically changed the developmental course of D/HH individuals. Continued enhancement of newborn screening where available remains important, as increased access to early hearing evaluation and intervention programs for D/HH children would offer substantial benefits in developing countries where such essential services are limited.

Our understanding of critical periods in brain development and brain reorganization capacity has widened through cognitive neuroscience research on children with cochlear implants and those raised in signing environments. It will be important to translate this wealth of knowledge into practical implications to enhance the lives of D/HH individuals. How these exciting neuroscience developments might influence academic and language-learning programs for D/HH children remains to be seen. In particular, the new body of knowledge regarding information-processing needs of D/HH individuals of varying backgrounds might translate to programs tailored to their specific learning styles that are distinct from hearing individuals. Also, there remains much to understand about neurological substrates and neuropsychological factors associated with the wide variability in outcomes with cochlear implants [29]. Research on this question is of paramount importance in helping parents and professionals to make the best decisions for deaf children contemplating implants. Given the relative low incidence of hearing loss, however, it is difficult for any one program to find well-defined, cohesive, research populations. Thus, multisite research programs should be established to enable comprehensive, longitudinal studies [79], with emphasis on translational research that cuts across neurobiology, neuroscience, neuropsychology and education.

Despite the importance of comprehensive neuropsychological evaluations for D/HH individuals, researchers and clinicians are restricted by the paucity of adequate assessment tools in most neuropsychological domains. There continues to be a need for assessment instruments that are informed by cognitive neuroscience research to address the complex and varying cognitive processing patterns of D/HH people with different etiologies, degrees of hearing loss, auditory experiences, modes of communication and educational and emotional environments. Only recently have test publishers begun attending to the needs of D/HH individuals and the appropriateness of their measures [63].

While neuroscience research continues to move forward, scant research addresses the quality of life for D/HH individuals across the lifespan in a comprehensive fashion. Although there are known stressors potentially connected with neurological and/or environmental factors associated with hearing loss, we do not yet understand the risk and resilience factors that arise from the deaf experience, nor do we know what factors might enhance quality of life for D/HH individuals with differing degrees of hearing loss and various modes of communication. With more carefully defined participant groups that consider a host of biological, social and environmental variables, cognitive neuroscience and neuropsychological research have demonstrated that presumed general knowledge about deaf and hard-of-hearing individuals is suspect. Until substantial strides are made that can better inform clinical practice, neuropsychological assessment with deaf and hard-of-hearing individuals remains an art.

Acknowledgement

The authors wish to express their gratitude to Steven Hardy-Braz for reviewing the full range of tests and contributing a table on their appropriateness with deaf/hard of hearing individuals.

References

1. Wake M, Tobin S, Cone-Wesson B, Dahl HH, Gillam L, McCormick L, et al. Slight/mild sensorineural hearing loss in children. *Pediatrics* 2006;**118**:1842–51.

2. Møller A R. *Hearing: Anatomy, Physiology, and Disorders of the Auditory System*, 2nd edn. Amsterdam: Academic Press; 2006.

3. Rance G. Auditory neuropathy/dys-synchrony and its perceptual consequences. *Trends Amplif* 2005;**9**:1–43.

4. American Speech-Language-Hearing Association. The prevalence and incidence of hearing loss in adults. 2008 [November 20, 2008]; Available from: http://www.asha.org/public/hearing/disorders/prevalence_adults.htm.

5. Yoshinga-Itano C. Early identification, communication modality and the development of speech and spoken language skills. Patterns and considerations. In Spencer P E, Marschark M, eds. *Advances in the Spoken Language Development of Deaf and Hard-of-hearing Children*. Oxford: Oxford University Press; 2006: 298–327.

6. Fagan MK, Pisoni DB, Horn DL, Dillon CM. Neuropsychological correlates of vocabulary, reading, and working memory in deaf children with cochlear implants. *J Deaf Stud Deaf Educ* 2007;**12**:461–71.

7. Fischer SD, van der Hulst H. Sign language structures. In Marschark M, Hauser PC, eds. *Deaf Cognition: Foundations and Outcomes*. Oxford: Oxford University Press; 2003:319–31.

8. Emmorey K, Allen JS, Bruss J, Schenker N, Damasio H. A morphometric analysis of auditory brain regions in congenitally deaf adults. *Proc Natl Acad Sci USA* 2003;**100**:10049–54.

9. National Institute on Deafness and Other Communication Disorders. Fact sheets. 2007; Available from: http://www.nidcd.nih.gov/health/statistics/hearing.asp.

10. Gallaudet Research Institute. *Regional and national summary report of data from the 2006–2007 annual survey of deaf and hard of hearing children and youth.* Washington DC: GRI, Gallaudet University; 2006; Available from: http://gri.gallaudet.edu/Demographics/.

11. Smith RJ, Bale JF Jr, White KR. Sensorineural hearing loss in children. *Lancet* 2005;**365**:879–90.

12. Nadol JB Jr, Merchant SN. Histopathology and molecular genetics of hearing loss in the human. *Int J Pediatr Otorhinolaryngol* 2001;**61**:1–15.

13. Noyola DE, Demmler GJ, Nelson CT, Griesser C, Williamson WD, Atkins JT, et al. Early predictors of neurodevelopmental outcome in symptomatic congenital cytomegalovirus infection. *J Pediatr* 2001;**138**:325–31.

14. Roizen NJ. Nongenetic causes of hearing loss. *Ment Retard Dev Disabil Res Rev* 2003;**9**:120–7.

15. Anderson VA, Taylor HG. Meningitis. In Yeates KO, Ris MD, Taylor HG, eds. *Pediatric Neuropsychology: Research, Theory, and Practice.* New York: Guilford Press; 2000:117–48.

16. Cristobal R, Oghalai JS. Hearing loss in children with very low birth weight: current review of epidemiology and pathophysiology. *Arch Dis Child Fetal Neonatal Ed* 2008;**93**:F462–8.

17. Fligor BJ. Do headphones cause hearing loss? Risk of music induced hearing loss for the music consumer. In Churin M, ed. *Hearing Loss in Musicians.* San Diego: Plural Publishing; 2009: in press.

18. Gates GA, Mills JH. Presbycusis. *Lancet* 2005;**366**:1111–20.

19. Sonnenschein E, Cascella PW. Pediatricians' opinions about otitis media and speech-language-hearing development. *J Commun Disord* 2004;**37**:313–23.

20. Nittrouer S, Burton LT. The role of early language experience in the development of speech perception and phonological processing abilities: evidence from 5-year-olds with histories of otitis media with effusion and low socioeconomic status. *J Commun Disord* 2005;**38**:29–63.

21. Remine MD, Brown PM, Care E, Rickards F. The relationship between spoken language ability and intelligence test performance of deaf children and adolescents. *Deaf Educ Intl* 2007;**9**:147–64.

22. MacSweeney M, Woll B, Campbell R, McGuire PK, David AS, Williams SC, et al. Neural systems underlying British Sign Language and audio-visual English processing in native users. *Brain* 2002;**125**:1583–93.

23. Xu H, Kotak VC, Sanes DH. Conductive hearing loss disrupts synaptic and spike adaptation in developing auditory cortex. *J Neurosci* 2007;**27**:9417–26.

24. Lee H-J, Truy E, Mamou G, Sappey-Marinier D, Giraud A-L. Visual speech circuits in profound acquired deafness: a possible role for latent multimodal connectivity. *Brain* 2007;**130**:2929–41.

25. Sadato N, Yamada H, Okada T, Yoshida M, Hasegawa T, Matsuki K, et al. Age-dependent plasticity in the superior temporal sulcus in deaf humans: a functional MRI study. *BMC Neurosci* 2004;**5**:56.

26. Sharma A, Dorman MF, Kral A. The influence of a sensitive period on central auditory development in children with unilateral and bilateral cochlear implants. *Hearing Res* 2005;**203**:134–43.

27. Bauer PW, Sharma A, Martin K, Dorman M. Central auditory development in children with bilateral cochlear implants. *Arch Otolaryngol Head Neck Surg* 2006;**132**:1133–6.

28. Marschark M, Hauser PC. Cognitive underpinnings of learning by deaf and hard-of-hearing students. In Marschark M, Hauser, PC, eds. *Deaf cognition: Foundations and Outcomes.* Oxford: Oxford University Press; 2008:3–24.

29. Pisoni DB, Conway CM, Kronenberger WG, Horn DL, Karpicke J, Henning SC. Efficacy and effectiveness of cochlear implants in deaf children. In Marschark M, Hauser PC, eds. *Deaf Cognition: Foundations and Outcomes.* Oxford: Oxford University Press; 2008:52–101.

30. Dye MW, Hauser PC, Bavelier D. Deaf cognition: foundations and outcomes. In Marschark M, Hauser PC, eds. *Perspectives on Deafness.* Oxford: Oxford University Press; 2008:250–64.

31. Parasnis I, Samar VJ, Berent GP. Deaf adults without attention deficit hyperactivity disorder display reduced perceptual sensitivity and elevated impulsivity on the Test of Variables of Attention (T.O.V.A.). *J Deaf Stud Deaf Educ* 2003;**46**:1166–83.

32. Rhine, S. *Assessment of executive function.* Unpublished doctoral dissertation. Washington DC: Gallaudet University; 2002.

33. Hauser PC, Lukomski J, Hillman T. Development of deaf and hard-of-hearing students' executive function. In Marschark M, Hauser PC, eds. *Deaf Cognition: Foundations and Outcomes.* Oxford: Oxford University Press; 2008:286–308.

34. Campbell R, MacSweeney M, Waters D. Sign language and the brain: a review. *J Deaf Stud Deaf Educ* 2008;**13**:3–20.

35. Petitto LA, Zatorre RJ, Gauna K, Nikelski EJ, Dostie D, Evans AC. Speech-like cerebral activity in profoundly deaf people processing signed languages: implications for the neural basis of human language. *Proc Natl Acad Sci USA* 2000;**97**:13961–6.

36. Bavelier D, Brozinsky C, Tomann A, Mitchell T, Neville H, Liu G. Impact of early deafness and early exposure to sign language on the cerebral organization for motion processing. *J Neurosci* 2001;**21**:8931–42.

37. Yoshinaga-Itano C. From screening to early identification and intervention: discovering predictors to successful outcomes for children with significant hearing loss. *J Deaf Stud Deaf Educ* 2003;**8**:11–30.

38. Stredler-Brown A. Minimal hearing loss: impact and treatment. *Plenary Panel Discussion National Early Hearing Detection and Intervention Conference*, Atlanta, Georgia; 2005.

39. Fine I, Finney EM, Boynton GM, Dobkins KR. Comparing the effects of auditory deprivation and sign language within the auditory and visual cortex. *J Cogn Neurosci* 2005;**17**:1621–37.

40. Bavelier D, Dye MW, Hauser PC. Do deaf individuals see better? *Trends Cogn Sci* 2006;**10**:512–8.

41. Hauser PC, Dye MW, Boutla M, Green CS, Bavelier D. Deafness and visual enumeration: not all aspects of attention are modified by deafness. *Brain Res* 2007;**1153**:178–87.

42. Geraci C, Gozzi M, Papagno C, Cecchetto C. How grammar can cope with limited short-term memory: simultaneity and seriality in sign languages. *Cognition* 2008;**106**:780–804.

43. Boutla M, Supalla T, Newport EL, Bavelier D. Short-term memory span: insights from sign language. *Nat Neurosci* 2004;**7**:997–1002.

44. Kowalska J, Szelag E. The effect of congenital deafness on duration judgment. *J Child Psychol Psychiatry* 2006;**47**:946–53.

45. McCoy SL, Tun PA, Cox LC, Colangelo M, Stewart RA, Wingfield A. Hearing loss and perceptual effort: downstream effects on older adults' memory for speech. *Q J Exp Psychol* 2005;**58**:22–33.

46. Dummer GM, Haubenstricker JL, Stewart DA. Motor skill performances of children who are deaf. *Adapt Phys Activ Q* 1996;**13**:400–14.

47. Horn DL, Pisoni DB, Miyamoto RT. Divergence of fine and gross motor skills in prelingually deaf children: implications for cochlear implantation. *Laryngoscope* 2006;**116**:1500–6.

48. Kutz W, Wright C, Krull KR, Manolidis S. Neuropsychological testing in the screening for cochlear implant candidacy. *Laryngoscope* 2003;**113**:763–6.

49. Gheysen F, Loots G, Van Waelvelde H. Motor development of deaf children with and without cochlear implants. *J Deaf Stud Deaf Educ* 2008;**13**:215–24.

50. Schlumberger E, Narbona J, Manrique M. Non-verbal development of children with deafness with and without cochlear implants. *Dev Med Child Neurol* 2004;**46**:599–606.

51. Horn DL, Davis RAO, Pisoni DB, Miyamoto RT. Visumotor integration ability of pre-lingually deaf children predicts audiological outcome with a cochlear implant: a first report. *Int Cong Ser* 2004;**1273**:356–9.

52. Hauser PC, Wills K, Isquith PK. Hard of hearing, deafness, and being deaf. In Farmer JE, Donders J, Warschausky SA, eds. *Treating neurodevelopmental disabilities: clinical research and practice*. New York: Guilford Press; 2006.

53. Gilman R, Easterbrooks SR, Frey M. A preliminary study of multidimensional life satisfaction among deaf/hard of hearing youth across environmental settings. *Soc Indicators Res* 2004;**66**:143–64.

54. Calderon R, Greenberg M. Social and emotional develoment of deaf children. In Marschark M, Spencer PE, eds. *Oxford Handbook of Deaf Studies, Language, and Education*. Oxford: Oxford University Press; 2003:177–89.

55. Mitchell RLC. Age-related decline in the ability to decode emotional prosody: Primary or secondary phenomenon? *Cogn Emot* 2007;**21**:1435–54.

56. Fellinger J, Holzinger D, Dobner U, Gerich J, Lehner R, Lenz G, et al. Mental distress and quality of life in a deaf population. *Soc Psychiatry Psychiatr Epidemiol* 2005;**40**:737–42.

57. Lin FR, Niparko JK. Measuring health-related quality of life after pediatric cochlear implantation: a systematic review. *Int J Pediatr Otorhinolaryngol* 2006;**70**:1695–706.

58. Bat-Chava Y, Martin D, Kosciw JG. Longitudinal improvements in communication and socialization of deaf children with cochlear implants and hearing aids: evidence from parental reports. *J Child Psychol Psychiatry* 2005;**46**:1287–96.

59. Schonauer K, Achtergarde D, Suslow T, Michael N. Comorbidity of schizophrenia and prelingual deafness: its impact on social network structures. *Soc Psychiatry Psychiatr Epidemiol* 1999;**34**:526–32.

60. Maller SJ. Intellectual assessment of deaf people: a critical review of core concepts and issues. In Marschark M, Spencer PE, eds. *Oxford Handbook of Deaf Studies, Language, and Education*. Oxford: Oxford University Press; 2003:451–63.

61. Sattler JM, Hardy-Braz ST, Willis J. Hearing impairments. In Sattler JM, Hoge RD, eds. *Assessment of*

Children: Behavioral, Social, and Clinical Foundations 5th edn. San Diego: J.M. Sattler; 2006.

62. Brice PJ. Ethical issues in working with deaf children, adolescents and their families. In Gutman V, ed. *Ethics in Mental Health and Deafness*. Washington DC: Gallaudet University Press; 2002:52–67.

63. Hardy-Braz S. In Wechsler D, ed. *Wechsler Intelligence Scale for Children (WISC-IV) Administration and Scoring Manual*, 4th edn. San Antonio: Harcourt Assessment; 2004:12–18.

64. Hill-Briggs F, Dial JG, Morere DA, Joyce A. Neuropsychological assessment of persons with physical disability, visual impairment or blindness, and hearing impairment or deafness. *Arch Clin Neuropsychol* 2007;**22**:389–404.

65. Vohr B, Jodoin-Krauzyk J, Tucker R, Johnson MJ, Topol D, Ahlgren M. Early language outcomes of early-identified infants with permanent hearing loss at 12 to 16 months of age. *Pediatrics* 2008;**122**:535–44.

66. Yoshinaga-Itano C. Levels of evidence: universal newborn hearing screening (UNHS) and early hearing detection and intervention systems (EHDI). *J Commun Disord* 2004;**37**:451–65.

67. Nelson HD, Bougatsos C, Nygren P. Universal newborn hearing screening: systematic review to update the 2001 US Preventive Services Task Force Recommendation. *Pediatrics* 2008;**122**:e266–76.

68. Meadow-Orleans RP, Sass-Lehrer M, Mertens DM. *Parents and their Deaf Children: The Early Years*. Washington DC: Gallandet University Press; 2003.

69. Moeller MP. Early intervention and language development in children who are deaf and hard of hearing. *Pediatrics* 2000;**106**:E43.

70. Kushalnagar P, Krull K, Hannay J, Mehta P, Caudle S, Oghalai J. Intelligence, parental depression, and behavior adaptability in deaf children being considered for cochlear implantation. *J Deaf Stud Deaf Educ* 2007;**12**:335–49.

71. Soukup M, Feinstein S. Identification, assessment, and intervention strategies for deaf and hard of hearing students with learning disabilities. *Am Ann Deaf* 2007;**152**:56–62.

72. Harris M, Moreno C. Deaf children's use of phonological coding: evidence from reading, spelling, and working memory. *J Deaf Stud Deaf Educ* 2004;**9**:253–68.

73. Blatto-Vallee G, Kelly RR, Gaustad MG, Porter J, Fonzi J. Visual spatial representation in mathematical problem solving by deaf and hearing students. *J Deaf Stud Deaf Educ* 2007;**12**:432–48.

74. Holstrum WJ, Gaffney M, Gravel JS, Oyler RF, Ross DS. Early intervention for children with unilateral and mild bilateral degrees of hearing loss. *Trends Amplif* 2008;**12**:35–41.

75. Israelite N, Ower J, Goldstein G. Hard-of-hearing adolescents and identity construction: influences of school experiences, peers, and teachers. *J Deaf Stud Deaf Educ* 2002;**7**:134–48.

76. Harvey MA. *Psychotherapy with Deaf and Hard of Hearing Persons: A Systemic Model*, 2nd edn. Mahwah, NJ: Lawrence Erlbaum; 2003.

77. Glickman NS, Gulati S. *Mental Health Care of Deaf People: A Culturally Affirmative Approach*. Mahwah, NJ: Lawrence Erlbaum; 2003.

78. Roush J, Bes FH, Gravel JS, Harrison M, Lenihan S, Marvelli A. Preparation of personnel to serve children with hearing loss and their families: current status and future needs. *Summit on Deafness Proceedings: Spoken Language in the 21st Century – Predicting Future Trends in Deafness*, Washington DC: 2004.

79. Fink NE, Wang NY, Visaya J, Niparko JK, Quittner A, Eisenberg LS, et al. Childhood Development after Cochlear Implantation (CDaCI) study: design and baseline characteristics. *Cochlear Implants Int* 2007;**8**:92–116.

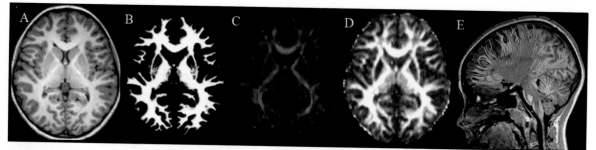

Figure 4.1. Sample DTI image acquired in a healthy 8-year-old girl. The FA map (C and D) is registered to the participant's T1-weighted MP-RAGE volume (A) and shown with the segmented white matter map from the MP-RAGE (B). Higher signal intensity in the raw FA image (D) reflects the highly directional intra-axonal diffusion of water molecules indicating major fiber pathways and white matter integrity. In (C) fiber tracts are color-coded to denote directionality of orientation of white matter pathways (red = lateral/medial, green = anterior/posterior, blue = superior/inferior, other colors indicate crossing fibers). In (E) the use of fiber tractography to follow the course of white matter pathways is demonstrated, with color coding indicating seed regions used to generate tracts (beige = corpus callosum, pink = internal capsule, blue = external capsule).

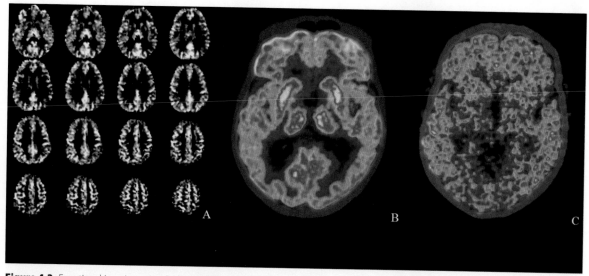

Figure 4.3. Functional imaging using PASL and PET. In (A) the resting grey matter perfusion CBF map of a healthy adult is shown using a PASL Q2TIPS sequence with parallel imaging at 3T. In (B) normal resting glucose metabolism is demonstrated using the [18F]FDG tracer in a 75-year-old patient with MCI (CDR 0.5, MMSE 29), while in (C) amyloid deposition is demonstrated in the same individual using [11C]PIB.

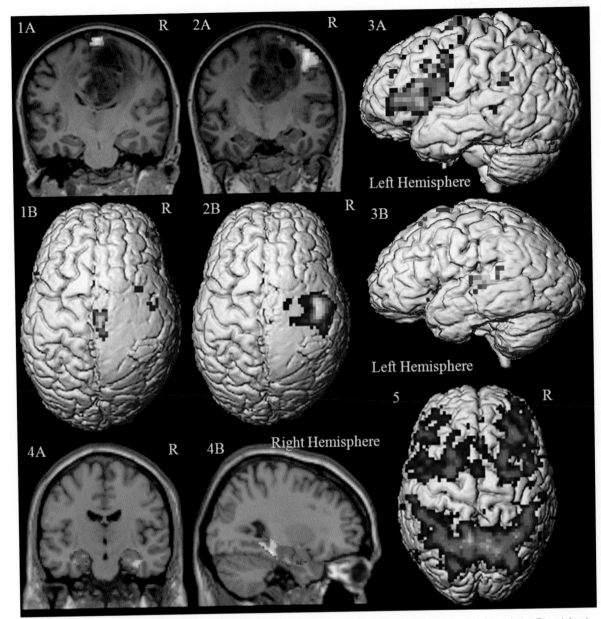

Figure 4.2. fMRI brain activation patterns elicited by different task paradigms displayed over the participants' high-resolution T1-weighted MP-RAGE volume and rendered anatomy. Motor mapping in a patient with a right frontal anaplastic astrocytoma demonstrates contralateral motor strip activation in medial regions for left foot movement (1A and B) and lateral regions for left hand movement (2A and B). In (3) representative activation patterns are shown for individuals with typical left-hemisphere dominance for expressive language (3A, using a verb generation paradigm in an adult) and receptive language (3B, during processing of novel and familiar words in a child). In (4) bilateral medial temporal lobe activation during episodic memory processing is shown in an 11-year-old boy with right temporal lobe epilepsy while encoding novel scenes. In (5) the typical pattern of bilateral frontal and parietal activation observed during working memory processing is demonstrated in an adult using a visual-verbal n-back task.

Chapter

10b

Visual impairment across the lifespan: neuropsychological perspectives

Lisa M. Noll and Lana L. Harder

Introduction

Vision is often an essential capacity for the interaction between individuals and their environment. Yet, for some individuals, an impaired visual system alters that opportunity. Visual loss can be lifelong, present from birth; for others, it can be progressive or abrupt. For some individuals, particularly those who lose vision later in life, the loss of vision is associated with a corresponding loss of independence, and impact on their emotional status. A lifespan perspective regarding visual impairment (VI) holds that the experience of VI since birth or early childhood is qualitatively different from the experience of individuals who acquire VI later in life. For example, in early childhood, VI impacts psychomotor and cognitive development that relies upon visual information processing and places challenges on the educational system, which must provide appropriate supports. In contrast, when acquired later in life, VI may place challenges on the ability to complete tasks of daily living, be independent, and engage in leisure activities, but not affect learning status or how knowledge is shared.

While VI may impact the trajectory of lifespan development, it also taps an individual's (and their family's) ability to cope effectively with the challenges VI elicits. Professionals working with individuals with VI must take into consideration the developmental trajectory and cognitive, behavioral and psychological sequelae of VI when assessing neurocognitive functioning, to determine the most appropriate educational, vocational, and/or rehabilitative setting to optimize quality of life.

Epidemiology and pathophysiology

Risk factors for VI are associated with increasing rates of premature infant survival and increasing life expectancy among the elderly. Moreover, the complexity and breadth of the visual system increase the chances of dysfunction, from the eye to caudal portions of the brain. Insult or disruption at any point in this system

may lead to VI. Variability of VI and the resulting functional impact, as well as individual differences across levels of impairment, make it difficult to describe this population in a one-size-fits-all manner.

VI, according to the United States Department of Health and Human Services, may refer to "any chronic visual deficit that impairs everyday function and is not correctable by ordinary eyeglasses or contact lenses" [1]. According to the World Health Organization (WHO), VI includes low vision and blindness [2]. Low vision refers to visual acuity of less than 6/18 (values expressed in meters) but greater than or equal to 3/60, or visual field loss at less than 20 degrees, in the better eye with correction. Blindness is defined by the WHO as visual acuity of less than 3/60, or visual field loss at less than 10 degrees, in the better eye with correction.

VI may be due to reduction in visual acuity or the ability to see objects clearly, or to visual field loss. Underlying causes for VI include damage to or abnormality of the eye itself, through either structural abnormalities or refractive errors, or dysfunction in areas of the brain responsible for processing visual information (e.g. cortical VI) [3]. This chapter will describe conditions and underlying mechanisms that lead to VI as well as their cognitive and behavioral manifestations across the lifespan. Additionally, the role of neuropsychological assessment and associated challenges will be discussed. Finally, prevention and intervention for persons with VI and future directions will be considered.

Prevalence

According to the WHO [2], recent global estimates indicate a reduction in VI related to disease processes, accompanied by an increase in impairment related to increased lifespan. More than 161 million people were visually impaired worldwide; of those, 124 million people had low vision and 37 million were blind. Greater than 82% of people who are blind are

50 years of age and older and 1.4 million are under age 15. In terms of gender, females are at significantly higher risk for VI compared to males. The vast majority (i.e. 90%) of persons with VI reside in developing countries.

Rates in the USA are considerably lower than worldwide estimates. Approximately 1 in 1000 children in the USA are visually impaired [3]. Based on estimates from the 2000 US Census, approximately 0.78% of Americans 40 years or older were blind, while 1.98% had low vision [4]. Congdon and colleagues noted that underlying causes of VI varied according to race/ethnicity. For Whites, age-related macular degeneration (AMD) was the leading cause (54.4%) of blindness. Cataract and glaucoma were responsible for greater than 60% of blindness in African-Americans. For Whites, African-Americans, and Hispanics, cataracts are the primary cause (50%) of low vision.

Infancy and childhood

While advancements in medical technology over the last several decades have increased the survival rates of premature infants, placing them at increased risk for sensory impairment [5], there has been a decrease in the rate of neurosensory deficits among infants, including blindness [6]. Nevertheless, the risk of such deficits is significantly greater for premature infants, particularly those of very or extremely low birth weight (< 1500 g) [7]. For children under the age of 5 years, the most prevalent visual conditions are cortical VI, retinopathy of prematurity, and optic nerve hypoplasia [8]. However, children with VI are a heterogeneous group, with approximately 50 to 60% of children with VI also presenting with other disabilities such as hearing impairment, epilepsy, cerebral palsy, or developmental delay [3, 7]. A discussion of conditions which lead to VI, organized by underlying causes, follows. Please see Table 10b.1 for a summary of conditions and corresponding mechanisms and impairment.

Structural abnormality

VI can be caused by structural abnormality or damage to the eye itself. Cataracts are seen in both pediatric and adult populations, and are one of the most common causes of VI across the lifespan. Due to the resulting opaque lens, light cannot pass through to reach the retina and thus vision is obscured.

Cataracts vary according to size and location and affect visual acuity differently across patients [9]. Cataracts may be inherited or the result of maternal illness (e.g. rubella) during the prenatal period. Additionally, cataracts may be present in the context of other syndromes (e.g. Marfan syndrome, Turner syndrome, Down syndrome) [3].

Glaucoma exists when there is increased pressure from fluid within the anterior chamber of the eye, which can lead to permanent damage of the optic nerve [3]. Such damage may cause loss of peripheral vision and, eventually, the loss of central vision. The level of impairment associated with glaucoma is highly dependent on factors such as the age of onset and the timeliness of diagnosis and intervention [3]. Glaucoma may be associated with conditions including Sturge-Weber syndrome, neurofibromatosis, and retinopathy of prematurity [3].

Strabismus is a common condition among children and occurs when eyes are not aligned properly [3]. For example, one or both eyes may turn inward or outward. Inward turning of the eye is known as "esotropia" while the outward turning of the eye is known as "exotropia". Functional VI may include decreased binocular vision.

Amblyopia is present when the brain suppresses the image received through one eye and the other eye is utilized. This often happens when one eye has superior acuity, or when one eye is affected by strabismus. The degree of vision loss ranges from mild to severe.

Nystagmus is involuntary movement of the eyes alternating in smooth pursuit in one direction and saccadic fashion in the other direction. This movement may occur in horizontal or vertical directions and typically involves both eyes. Nystagmus results in reduced visual acuity [3].

Retinopathy of prematurity (ROP) is caused by damage to the retina, which may lead to vision impairment or blindness in premature infants [3]. There is an inverse relationship between birth weight and risk for ROP. Infants born at or before 28 weeks gestation and weighing 1500 grams or less are at greatest risk. Associated vision problems include strabismus, glaucoma, amblyopia, refractive errors, and even total blindness.

Optic nerve hypoplasia (ONH) is the leading cause of infant blindness and prevalence estimates indicate that 7 in 100 000 are affected [10]. Those with ONH are at significant risk for poor developmental outcomes. ONH is a congenital anomaly characterized by a

Table 10b.1. Eye conditions, localization of dysfunction, and nature of impairment.

Condition	Site or mechanism of dysfunction	Nature of visual impairment
Cataract	Cloudiness of the lens of the eye	Obscured vision; mild to complete blindness; myopia
Glaucoma	Increased pressure in the anterior chamber of the eye; places optic nerve at risk	Mild to complete blindness; loss of peripheral vision and then central vision; nearsightedness and astigmatism
Strabismus	Poor alignment of the eyes (e.g. esotropia, exotropia)	Decreased binocular vision
Amblyopia	Use of one eye is suppressed	Degree of vision loss ranges from mild to severe
Nystagmus	Involuntary movement of the eyes, alternating in smooth pursuit and saccadic fashion, horizontally or vertically	Reduced visual acuity
Retinopathy of prematurity (ROP)	Damage to the retina	Vision impairment to complete blindness
Optic nerve hypoplasia (ONH)	Reduced number of optic nerve axons; affects development of visual pathways	Mild to severe impairment in the form of decreased visual acuity and reduced visual fields
Myopia	Cornea and lens	Distant objects appear blurry
Hyperopia	Cornea and lens	Difficulty focusing on nearby objects
Anisometropia	Notable difference between refractive power of each eye	Amblyopia; poor stereoacuity
Astigmatism	Irregularity of the cornea; eye's ability to focus is compromised	Distorted or blurry vision for objects near and far
Presbyopia	Loss in elasticity of lens	Difficulty focusing sharply on nearby objects
Cortical visual impairment (CVI)	Results from neurological insult; absence of sufficient ocular or pupillary abnormality to explain level of visual impairment	Mild to severe visual impairment; some preservation of visual acuity, color perception, and visual field; complete blindness is rare
Age-related macular degeneration (AMD)	Degeneration of the macula	Loss of central vision; blurring and distortion of vision; "dry" AMD shows slow progression and "wet" AMD is associated with rapid progression
Diabetic retinopathy (DRP)	Retinal neurodegeneration and microvascular complications	Mild visual impairment to complete blindness
Traumatic brain injury (TBI)	[a]Acquired neurological damage	[a]Difficulty with binocular function; occulomotor skills; convergence/divergence of eyes; accommodation; visual fields; visual perceptual skills; and/or visual attention
Cerebrovascular accident (CVA)	[a]Acquired neurological damage	[a]Optic apraxia; optic ataxia; simultagnosia; achromotopsia; palinopsia; prosopagnosia; hemianopia; hemispatial neglect

[a] Nature of impairment is dependent upon location of neurological insult.

below-normal number of optic nerve axons, affecting the development of the visual pathways [11]. VI associated with ONH varies considerably and ranges from mild to severe, in the form of decreased visual acuity and reduced visual fields.

Refractive errors

Disproportion of the various parts of the eye can lead to refractive error, or problems with visual acuity [3]. Such errors may be inherited or part of a specific condition such as retinopathy of prematurity or glaucoma. These errors can worsen during childhood and are most often treated with corrective lenses. Specific refractive errors include myopia or nearsightedness, hyperopia or farsightedness (also known as hypermetropia), anisometropia, and astigmatism.

In the case of myopia, the eye is too big and is not compensated for by a reduction in the curvature of the cornea or of the lens surface, causing objects to appear blurry from a distance [9]. Hyperopia occurs when the cornea is fairly flat, the eye is not as long, or the eye's ability to focus is weak, resulting in difficulty focusing on objects which are nearby [3]. Anisometropia occurs when there is a notable difference between the refractive power of each eye, which can result in amblyopia and below-average stereoacuity, or depth perception [12]. Astigmatism refers to a refractive error resulting from an abnormal shape of the cornea and the eye's ability to focus is compromised [3, 9]. Objects far and near may appear blurry, depending on the severity of the astigmatism. Finally, presbyopia is a visual condition which tends to emerge in middle age [13]. Due to loss in elasticity of the lens, the patient has reduced ability to focus sharply on objects which are nearby.

Cortical vision impairment (CVI)

The most common cause of VI in children in developed countries is CVI [8, 14–16], and it is believed to be related to increased survival rates of premature infants [17]. CVI is diagnosed when neurological insult and associated visual dysfunction occur, in the absence of sufficient ocular or pupillary abnormality [18]. Patients may have an abnormality at the level of the eye itself, but the degree of VI in patients observed is greater than would be expected based on the abnormalities alone [16].

Adult CVI typically results from trauma or vascular insult, while in children CVI is most commonly the result of perinatal hypoxia [14, 16]. Other etiologies include prematurity, hydrocephalus, trauma, encephalitis, meningitis, structural central nervous system abnormalities, and seizures [14, 16]. Ophthalmic abnormalities associated with CVI include esotropia, exotropia, nystagmus, optic atrophy, and significant refractive error [16]. Neurological conditions associated with CVI include cerebral palsy, global developmental delay, periventricular leukomalacia, hemiparesis, and hearing loss [16, 17].

The severity of vision impairment in children with CVI ranges from mild to severe [17]. Complete blindness is rare in children with CVI. Patients often show variability in preserved visual acuity, visual field, or color perception. Some affected individuals show improvement across time. Longitudinal follow-up studies of patients with CVI indicate improvement in visual function in 46 to 57% of patients [15–17]. Greater neurological damage reduces the chances for recovery of vision [17].

Adulthood

The prevalence and risk for VI increases significantly with age [19]. Additionally, the prevalence of VI increases with reduced cognitive functioning [20] and it is known to interfere with the successful completion of activities of daily living. VI is also related to an increase in psychological problems (e.g. depression) and reduced quality of life [20–22]. Four major causes of adult VI include cataracts, glaucoma, macular degeneration, and diabetic retinopathy [19]. Additionally, acquired brain injury (e.g. traumatic brain injury and cerebrovascular accident) is commonly associated with VI [23]. With the exception of developed countries, cataract is the leading cause of blindness globally, followed by glaucoma [2].

Age-related macular degeneration (AMD)

Within developed countries, AMD is the leading cause of blindness and ranks third globally [2]. In the USA, approximately 8 million individuals, aged 55 or older, have AMD [24]. AMD is considered to be a complex disease and multiple genes and environmental factors are believed to play a role [25]. AMD is a progressive, chronic, degenerative disease of the macula, which typically leads to central vision loss [21] and is also characterized by blurry and distorted vision [24]. Whereas the most common form, termed "dry" AMD, shows a slow progression, "wet" AMD, in contrast, is characterized by newly formed blood vessels beneath the retina and affects approximately 10% of those with AMD, and often has a rapid progression [24]. Associated risk factors include aging, smoking, sunlight exposure, diet, cardiovascular disease, and light iris pigmentation [24, 25].

Diabetic retinopathy (DRP)

DRP is one of the leading causes of vision loss in the USA [19]. VI resulting from diabetes mellitus (DM) is characterized by retinal neurodegeneration and microvascular complications [26, 27] and may develop years after the initial diagnosis of DM [28]. Close monitoring through annual ophthalmological screenings is recommended for patients with DM.

Acquired injury

Acquired brain injury is the leading cause of neurological dysfunction within the USA [29]. Of those who survive a cerebrovascular accident (CVA) or traumatic brain injury (TBI), many will have visual disturbance [29] as a complication. Individuals recovering from TBI may show specific difficulties with binocular function, oculomotor skills, convergence and divergence of the eyes, accommodation, and visual field changes [29]. Other impairments resulting from TBI frequently include visual perceptual dysfunction and deficits in visual attention [30].

CVA often results in multiple impairments including cognition, vision, language, and motor functions [31]. The second most common impairment in patients with posterior cerebral artery (PCA) CVA, which accounts for 5 to 10% of all strokes, is visual field defects [31]. Specific visual cognitive impairments include optic apraxia, optic ataxia, simultagnosia, achromatopsia, palinopsia, and prosopagnosia. Strokes of the middle cerebral artery (MCA) may cause hemisensory loss, hemianopia, and hemispatial neglect. Left visuo-spatial neglect is often observed in patients following right-hemisphere stroke and is considered a predictor of poor functional outcome [23].

Cognitive and psychosocial sequelae in visual impairment

Traditionally, research with blind and visually impaired children and adults has compared their behaviors with that of sighted controls, hypothesizing differences given variation in sensory function. However, a more recent perspective suggests that behavior may play a similar function for both groups [32, 33]. This perspective draws from the observation that identical behaviors may serve a different purpose, and may result from unique underlying processes, while differing behaviors may have the same utility. Thus, applied to visual impairment, individuals with VI may show unique patterns of development that contrast with traditional developmental trajectories seen in sighted individuals; still, this is not a uniform expectation. This model holds relevance when considering assessment of developmental outcome, specifically for purposes of intervention. The developmental implications of VI impact individuals differently, based on their particular stage of development, and co-occurring developmental challenges. For example, adults with early-onset blindness during childhood typically display cognitive and psychosocial sequelae that influence the way professionals assess and support their needs, in contrast with adults who acquire VI later in life. The following section addresses the developmental trajectories seen in persons with VI.

Childhood

Developmental issues

The presence of VI impacts development of early functional behaviors in infancy, including perceptual problem-solving, hand–mouth coordination, independent exploration, and formation of adaptive and play skills. The way VI impacts early development is complicated by the degree to which the CNS has been altered, and whether other sensory deficits are present [34]. The development of the visual system begins during the first months of gestation and continues past birth. Underlying this development is the need to respond to increasing elements of visual processing. Infants utilize their vision to enhance their understanding of the world before they can demonstrate understanding. Visual experience also allows infants to identify important caregivers; learn associations between sounds, objects, and language; and respond to and initiate social interactions and communication [35]. Much of development occurs as a result of incidental learning, much of which initially relies on vision. Furthermore, visual imitation, such as when the parent engages the child in social games, is deeply connected to cognitive development, reflecting the association between imitation and language [35, 36]. The manner in which children with VI come to develop associations and expectations about the environment and how this translates to differences in their development given VI continues to be an area of debate [36].

Developmental acquisition

Research examining differences in cognitive development between children with VI and sighted children indicates that sensorimotor schemas are delayed in children with VI (e.g. object permanence, cause–effect relationships) [37, 38]. Children with profound VI are at significant risk for displaying a plateau or even regression in the development of cognitive and language skills, and a consequent slower rate of learning [32, 37]. However, a caveat to these findings is that many of the standardized instruments used to assess early cognitive competence in children rely on vision for such tasks as sorting, matching and block-building.

For example, Dale and Sonksen [38] found that children with profound versus severe VI, secondary to congenital disorders of the peripheral visual system, were at an increased risk for displaying uneven patterns of development across measures of early learning. Furthermore, children with profound VI presented with global learning delays across tasks assessing sensorimotor understanding and verbal comprehension, between 27 and 54 months of age [38], when compared with children with severe VI.

Cognitive impairment and VI often co-occur, reflecting the presence of multiple disabilities [39]. For example, toddlers with bilateral optic nerve dysplasia (ONH), assessed with the Battelle Developmental Inventory between 36 and 60 months of age, achieved scores within the delayed range, while children with unilateral ONH were less delayed [10]. Similarly, children with ONH and CNS involvement (hypoplastic corpus callosum) showed significantly greater delays in skill development in the areas of adaptive functioning, personal–social interactions, communication and overall cognition. Thus, children with ONH are at greater risk for neurodevelopmental delays in the presence of CNS involvement and medical concerns.

Normal visual acuity is not always associated with normal visual function [15]. As a result, improvements in visual acuity such as can be seen in children with cortical visual impairment (CVI) may or may not be associated with more favorable cognitive outcome. Similarly, children with improved visual acuity may not display commensurate improvements in motor or cognition [15]. This highlights the heterogeneity among children with CVI, such that the underlying neurological process and/or event contributing to visual impairment may be related to neurodevelopmental impairments outside the visual pathway that further impact learning.

Motor development

Research supports the observation that blindness negatively impacts motor development. Children's ability to explore their environment with their hands, a source of early learning, and their ability to explore their environment through active movement are both influenced by vision. However, individual differences across children and their environments complicate the delineation of specific time frames for motor skill development [32].

Reaching and grasping

In comparison to sighted infants, blind infants are not observed to visually explore their hands [40]. Fraiberg [41] observed that blind infants at 5 months of age typically did not grasp their own hands, play with their fingers, hold a cube in each hand, or transfer objects, in comparison to sighted peers. Blind children also used a palmar grasp at 9 months of age, rather than a pincer grasp.

Haptic or tactile exploration is limited, often because the posturing of the blind infant does not

facilitate such exploration. The absence of midline exploration of objects limits the development of such skills as transferring and reaching of objects, and hinders the infant's understanding of how actions impact upon objects [40]. Reaching and grasping is a function of smooth motor control and is seen in response to the infant's perceptual processing of information originating from objects in the environment [32]. While sighted infants are able to reach for objects visually perceived between 4 and 5 months of age, reaching in response to auditory information develops later in VI infants (i.e. 10 months) [42]; this is further supported by Fraiberg [41], who describes ear–hand coordination as developing later than eye–hand coordination. Landau [43] has suggested that sound may not be a sufficient cue early on for infants with VI, as sound does not provide the same level of information about shape, texture, and movement as vision. As a result, a blind infant is unable to discern an object's qualities by sound and is often unable to associate the object with what is being grasped [43]. Furthermore, sound is an inconsistent source of information, as it changes based on the actions of the object, acoustical interference, and the child's position in space in relation to the object.

Children have been found to reach earlier (i.e. 6–8 months of age) when the object emitting auditory information was removed or fell from their grasp [44]. This correlates with Piaget's third substage of sensorimotor development, when coordination develops between vision and prehension (i.e. hand–eye coordination) [45]. Thus, previous experience with an object drives the accommodation of motor movements to reach for the object that was just in their grasp. In contrast to blind infants, the presence of any visual capacity is believed to serve a useful function. Infants with any degree of response to light perception are more likely to wave their hands across the visual field, assume a prone position, and to display similar developmental sequences to those of sighted infants [46].

Gross motor skills and locomotion

As the sighted infant begins to sit, crawl, and walk, she learns such concepts as space, distance, and orientation [40]. The input of visual information allows the infant to move toward objects of interest, thus expanding her experience and understanding of the world. Motor skills are influenced by visual imitation as well as motivation to move towards an object of interest.

Whether towards a toy or caregiver, locomotion is both self-initiated and motivated by engagement with the external reward.

Motorically, infants with VI seem to develop similarly to sighted infants in terms of stability patterns such as sitting and standing; but they reveal delays in self-initiated mobility, including reaching, crawling, and walking [47]. Adelson and Fraiberg [47] found a greater time difference (i.e. 8 months) between blind and sighted children advancing from leaning on hands and knees to crawling, and then walking with support to walking independently (i.e. 15.3 months). Locomotion benefits from the drive that comes from seeing an object and moving towards it, while auditory cues do not motivate movement towards objects until object permanence is achieved [41, 43].

Visual impairments also impact the way children learn to use their muscles, since they are unable to watch and imitate others, and then practice these skills in response. In the absence of vision, children may form a mental representation of motor sequences based on alternate sensory input, including touch, language, or other sensory models. However, this representation will differ from the representation generated by visual perception [40].

The diversity across motor development emphasizes the notion of differences across individual experiences and sensory input. Warren [32] has suggested that "opportunity" in the form of access to engage in motor activities is important for the motor development of blind children. An additional consideration is the relationship between specific maternal behaviors and their positive influence on blind children's development [48].

Cognitive development in children

Vision is involved in approximately 80% of what children learn during childhood and thus plays an important role in a child's ability to discern relationships and establish perceptual experiences essential to support development [49]. In the absence of vision, children rely on their other senses such as hearing, smell, touch, and taste for information-processing; however, intersensory coordination is more challenging because sensory information for the blind child is experienced as parts-of-the-whole. The task is thus to learn how to integrate this information. Webster and Roe discuss the notion of conceptual bridging, in which parents play an important role in making "bridges" between the child's inner or sensory pictures and that of the real

world [9]. While all children display conceptual confusion, children with VI cannot rely on direct observation to clarify their understanding, requiring more systematic and structured explanations from adults, with language as the medium [9]. An enduring belief is that children with VI display heightened acuity across other modalities to compensate for visual loss; however, research has not substantiated this idea [32].

Most children with VI have average intellectual functioning. However, while VI is not equated with cognitive limitations, some children with VI have cognitive limitations and/or other disabilities that impact development (e.g. hearing, motor impairments) [50].

Object permanence

Object permanence reflects a child's understanding that an object continues to exist in the absence of ongoing direct sensory information. This reflects the beginning of conceptual memory. Given the absence of vision to guide exploration, blind children develop object permanence later than sighted children [32, 33, 40]. Bigelow [44] found that blind children initially use tactile information to assist with object location, and later use auditory information. However, when presented with contradictory cues, blind children used more simplistic means of tactile exploration, even though they had learned to search by sound, a more sophisticated searching tool. Thus, blind children attain object permanence through the same cognitive sequence as sighted children but organize the information differently.

While studies support the delays in object permanence in blind children [41, 44, 51], individual variation also is observed. Rogers and Puchalski [51] found that while both blind and visually impaired children achieved object permanence within similar age ranges, but later than sighted children, vision alone did not solely account for the delay [48]. Rather, the provision of opportunities for learning and presence of positive parental interactions were thought to play a supportive and influential role in the development of object permanence [47].

Conservation

Conservation emerges between 7 and 11 months of age and reflects an infants' understanding that objects have physical properties [45]. Conservation is typically assessed visually; however, because blind children explore physical properties through haptic exploration

[40], assessment of conservation requires an alternate approach. Studies comparing the development of conservation in blind and sighted children reveal that the order of skills between the two groups follows a similar sequence [52], but blind children are delayed in their acquisition [53]. Furthermore, the presence of some functional vision in the child with VI assists the child in understanding the physical properties of conservation [32]. Conservation knowledge is best interpreted through both verbal and gestural information, as Iverson and Goldin-Meadow [54] found that both blind and sighted children verbalized similar subject matter across explanations of conservation, conveying information through gestures that was not relayed in speech.

Additional research has explored the manner in which blind children process properties of physical states. Blind children have been observed to engage in more sophisticated hand movements than sighted subjects, and utilize strategies that consider multiple properties (e.g. decentration), suggesting a similar form of decentration used by sighted children in visual conservation tasks [53]. Children with VI and additional disabilities encounter multiple challenges, which also must be reviewed when considering the provision of opportunities for both learning and social–emotional growth [55]. For example, children with VI and multiple disabilities have difficulty generalizing information and are limited by the extent that other sensory input can be incorporated into learning.

In summary, research looking across early cognitive development, which relies closely on experience, suggests that while children with VI tend to be delayed in the attainment of developmental tasks, skills are attained in the expected sequence. However, the timing of these skills is variable and depends on the degree of visual function, the quality of the interactive relationships with caregivers (e.g. level of scaffolding), and the opportunity to experience the environment.

Executive function in children and adolescents

Executive functioning describes a set of brain processes that guide one's thoughts and behaviors and thus relate to such abilities as attention, memory, adaptation, and organization and planning. A paucity of research exists concerning the development of executive functioning in persons with VI, although recent research has highlighted important considerations. Children with VI have been found to display delays

in the shift to more logical thinking and abstract reasoning that may impact higher-order reasoning required in secondary school [9].

Attention and memory

Selective attention is intertwined with the notion of concept formation, in which the individual comes to focus on some features over others. Davidson and colleagues [53] found that with increasing age, children developed improved ability to attend to and distinguish among tactile features across conservation tasks. Children with cortical visual impairment (CVI) held a longer gaze, as measured by increased visual attention, when presented with color and motion, in comparison to gray and static displays [18]. Children with CVI do not appear to display a preference for specific color, but the presence of any colors is reportedly sufficient to capture gaze. In summary, these results suggest differences in the way in which attention impacts concept formation across tactile information among differing forms of VI. Across measures of intellectual ability, blind children tend to perform best on measures assessing verbal memory span in comparison to other subtests [32].

Language and communication development

Early language development

Blind children have been found to babble less than their sighted peers, which may reflect increased listening [41]. Furthermore, studies across speech production suggest that children with VI may have difficulty producing some speech sounds, specifically those that have visible lip patterns (e.g. 'm,' 'b' or 'f'), whereas other sounds that are invisible to the lips are produced at the same rate as sighted children [56]. This delay in speech sounds is said to resolve by 5 years of age. Across areas of communication, children with VI vocalize and imitate words at the same rate as sighted children, but demonstrate fewer skills to make wants known or speak in two-word phrases, suggesting that VI may cause a delay in concept formation at the rate of sighted peers [32, 33].

Linguistics

While cognitive skills among blind versus sighted school age children are not seen as broadly different, blind children do not perform as well as their sighted peers on tasks assessing abstract concepts [32, 55], and are often delayed in the acquisition of positional concepts such as *between* and *behind*, and in conservation concepts [33]. Studies in linguistics with children with VI reveal that they misuse pronouns (e.g. substitute "you" for "I"), display less generalization about the properties of objects, identify with one property of an object, ask fewer questions, and focus more on self as a topic in conversations [57]. This misuse of pronouns may be related to the child's difficulties understanding cognitive representations of self [58], or may reflect problems in differentiating spatially between self and others [59].

Classification

Children construct word meaning and conceptual categories based on their own unique experiences. Research indicates that most children organize their thinking based on properties such as shape, movement, and size [9, 57, 60]. Categorization is important because it allows the child to move from using a word learned in one context to denote a particular situation to using the word more widely to refer to other symbols that share similar perceptual features [57]. While children with VI do not differ in their rate of word acquisition, their first 50 words tend to reflect their own actions [60]; they tend to reflect the here and now of daily life, and relate to social events and familiar routines. Children with VI also appear to have fewer general names for classes of objects such as cat, and more specific names for toys, pets, and people. They also tend to use fewer modifiers, such as qualities of objects like cold or hard, or function words (e.g. "What's that?"), but use more words common to social interaction, such as "Thank you".

Social communication

Among peers, children with VI display use of more restrictive types of sentences that reflect either the different or reduced social cues they perceive or receive. A delay in self-awareness and pretend play may impact the child's communication with others [3]. For example, 3-year-olds with profound VI demonstrate less-developed social communication skills in relation to peers with severe VI, and perform lower across measures of referential communication (e.g. sharing of interests and attention to objects with an adult) in comparison to peers with intact vision [38]. Children with VI also have greater difficulty with reciprocal communication. This probably relates to

the absence of eye contact to confirm attention to a speaker, the absence of visual cues to indicate change in a communication partner, and differences in nonverbal gestures [32, 61, 62]. Furthermore, parents' conversations with their infants tend to focus on labeling and on topics that are related to the infant, as opposed to other environment-related topics. As a result, conversations parents have with infants with VI may focus more directly on topics related to the child, limiting opportunities for broadened representation.

Perspective-taking and theory of mind

The ability to understand another person's perspective and thoughts in relation to one's self is thought to be related to nonverbal communication, perspective-taking, and joint attention. These skills play a role in the development of *theory of mind*, which signals an individual's understanding that mental states, rather than physical events, can account for differences in behavior [63]. Discussions related to the development of theory of mind in blind children include the development of shared reference, which is most often achieved through verbal interactions, but can also reflect shared visual communicaton. Because blind children are typically delayed in the use of, or even fail to engage in, protodeclarative pointing, which can reflect social referencing, they are often hampered in their ability to show joint attention. Nonetheless, blind children do use hearing and touch as a means of sharing attention (e.g. place parent's hand on an object or cry for an object to be returned) [33]; the difficulty with this is that it may place the blind child at a disadvantage in social communication.

In a study of social cognition, visually impaired subjects generated fewer correct justifications for the intentions of characters in a series of stories in comparison to sighted peers [64]. This may reflect differences in the VI individual's understanding of the uses of language that call for insight into the beliefs and intentions of others. It may be that social cognition in visually impaired children is affected by their difficulty with processing visual information such as social cues, rather than an absence of visual experience that facilitates understanding of the mental states of others. Children's understanding of perceptual cues in language may reflect differences in making inferences about whether a person can see versus not see an object, as well as the semantic value that they place on such words as "see" and "perceive" [65, 66].

Autism-like behaviors and VI

The presence of delays across social and early communicative development and play behaviors in visually impaired children has raised questions regarding a link between VI and autism. For example, within social interactions, echolalia observed during social exchanges has been suggested to reflect an individual's lack of understanding about to how to respond to others [9]. However, Pérez-Pereira and Conti-Ramsden [33] suggest that "autistic-like" behaviors reported in blind children may not reflect the same underlying mechanisms as those observed in children with autism; instead, stereotyped and echolalic behaviors in children with blindness may have adaptive functions. For example, repeated head-turning and rocking back and forth may provide blind children with proprioceptive feedback that provides information regarding their body position in space [33]. However, it is also the case that blind children can present with other impairments such as deafness, cerebral palsy, or mental retardation that share a vulnerability to stereotyped behaviors seen in children with a neurodevelopmental disorder such as autism. Thus, when discussing behaviors in children with VI, it is important for researchers to identify the characteristics of the children in their studies, and to consider the range of reasons behind select behavioral presentations.

Academic functioning

Literature is limited regarding the impact of impaired visual acuity on academic functioning. Several studies have found a relationship between visual difficulties and reading [67] and visual difficulties and attention [68]. The presence of a learning disability in children with strabismus was observed in approximately 20% of subjects, compared to 4–6% of the general population [69]. However, perceptual problems that often present with strabismus can impact reading and other academic performance; these include difficulty with contrast and crowding [70].

Young children with VI learn to read in a similar way to a sighted child. Both blind and sighted children learn the meaning of symbolic representations (print and/or Braille characters) and how those representations form words, sentences, and paragraphs, which when put together communicate a unique message. Research suggests that when children with VI read Braille, both tactual and phonological encoding occurs, with both operating interdependently [32]. Children with VI are able to draw inferences when reading at a similar level to that of sighted peers, while children with VI are more skilled at comprehending literal questions presented auditorially than sighted peers [64]. Children with VI may have an auditory advantage when processing literal information, which has a low semantic content and is thus stored verbatim in the absence of additional semantic encoding.

Behavioral characteristics of visual impairment

Various emotional and behavioral difficulties have been related to VI. Opir-Cohen and colleagues [71] identified that the presence of an emotional or behavioral deficit was significantly related to level of gross motor and visual motor integration, language, and social development. Gross motor development may contribute to a child's sense of safety within the environment, their interest in social interactions, and their desire for exploration.

Additional studies across specific etiologies of visual impairment also reveal behavioral sequelae. Children with CVI who exhibit specific color preferences and responses to movement [72] may attend to unusual objects such as a light or a ceiling fan, or they may have difficulty viewing objects under certain environmental conditions, giving the impression that their vision is variable. Vision behaviors characteristic of CVI are often related to the severity of CVI and may change over time and/or improve; however, few children develop normal vision [15]. Children with optic nerve hypoplasia (ONH) also present with distinct behavioral characteristics. Specifically, children with ONH may demonstrate a wide spectrum of visual abilities ranging from a loss of detailed vision in both central and peripheral fields to subtle peripheral field loss. In addition, there may be a deficient depth perception; mild photophobia (i.e. squinting, lowering their head, or avoiding light by turning away); as well as feeding issues and restricted food preferences (e.g. diminished taste and smell related to associated hormonal problems) [10, 11]. Children with ONH may also present with inattentiveness and irritability, secondary to hypoglycemia.

Social and emotional development in childhood and adolescence

Social–emotional development in early childhood

One of the first developmental issues that parents and infants face is the regulation of biological processes such as sleeping, eating, and modulation of states of alertness. Parents and babies typically rely on a visual vocabulary; however, a visually impaired baby is unable to see the parent, thereby lacking that shared visual vocabulary. The infant may not reach for the parent until she is able to reach toward sound. As a result, the relationship may be impacted, as the parent may interpret the baby as unaffectionate or uninterested [41].

Vision plays an important role in the development of play skills including determining the boundaries of the play area, engaging in group activities (e.g. hide and seek), and learning through modeling, imitation, and role-playing. Vision also plays an important role in the emergence of symbolic thinking where children can relate to the world through different symbols (e.g. Lego bricks can represent a specific object). Research suggests that children with VI engage in less symbolic play, and sighted children engage in more complex play earlier in development than those with VI [73]. However, Bishop and colleagues [74] found that socially able blind children did not display difficulties across symbolic representation and play, with the exception of anchoring individual roles to play objects. Differences in symbolic play may relate more to difficulty in role-taking and social engagement that are present in some congenitally blind children [33, 66], as opposed to reflecting the impact of visual impairment per se. Similarly, it has been proposed that the lack of exploration seen in play behaviors among children with VI relates to a lack of appropriately organized and designed play areas, as opposed to an inherent predisposition to engage in self-directed play. This means that toys need to be accessible and tap more than the visual sensory system [73].

Social interaction

All children differ in their innate ability to interact with others; however, children with VI may have more difficulty initiating social interactions, engaging in cooperative play with peers, and choosing play activities. Observation of preschoolers with VI reveals that their strategies to initiate peer interactions are not as successful as those employed by sighted peers. This is in part related to challenges with interpreting non-verbal communication [75]. School-age children with VI do not automatically repair communication exchanges with sighted peers, due to their reliance on physical contact, rather than eye contact [76]. Children with VI may also face issues of acceptance by peers in

light of facial differences (e.g. appearance of the eyes), or engagement in stereotypical behaviors such as rocking [55].

Children with VI may also display greater self-consciousness than their sighted peers, given their reliance on adaptive devices, which can set them apart from others. Social isolation may accompany VI. Children may retreat from social interactions, particularly those that rely on visual cues [77]. The reliance on others also places youth with VI at risk for becoming more passive and dependent. Children learn socially appropriate behaviors by modeling the behaviors of others. This can leave children with VI without a range of appropriate role models who can provide information on social behaviors [75, 76], challenging their development of social maturity.

Parent–child interaction

Achieving state regulation for the baby with VI requires more conscious efforts on the part of the parent [41]. The role of parent–child interaction is well documented and these interactions are most often mediated by eye-contact. Early studies of interactions between mothers and infants with VI revealed that mothers had greater difficulty distinguishing and assigning meaning to their infants' behaviors [41]. Studies examining the negative risks associated with parent–infant interactions in VI children [41, 78] suggest that mothers of VI infants have difficulty reading their infants' cues and subsequently are more directive and intrusive, while their infants are more passive and reactive. However, other studies have found no differences in the quality and appropriateness of the interaction [35, 79]. Warren [32] cites situational factors which may contribute to parents' ability to fully interact with their blind infant, including increased medical care and hospitalization, financial strain, level of adaptation needed to meet infants' needs, and alterations in family life.

An infant's developing capacity for language plays an important role in creating social interaction. Hughes and colleagues [48] found that maternal behaviors across play sequences, such as quality of maternal control and appropriateness of directiveness, were positively related to a child's language development, while the frequency of these behaviors was negatively related to language development. Overall, findings suggest that it is the quality and amount of maternal goal-directed behaviors and the quality of responsiveness that promotes language skills, environmental exploration, and sensorimotor development [35, 48, 79].

Adolescence

Adolescents with VI face different issues than their sighted peers, in part related to variability in adolescent identity development. Most teens look forward to the milestone of obtaining their driver's license, but for teens with VI this is a symbol of independence they cannot share. In a study looking at the perceptions of teens with VI and their best friends, Rosenbaum found that regardless of the age of onset of the VI, almost all of the teens expressed negative feelings about their own VI [80]. Coping skills among teens varied widely, from attempting to hide their VI from others to describing it as a positive experience, suggestive of greater acceptance. Additional themes included negative impact on self-esteem secondary to exclusion from families, feelings of isolation at school, difficulties fitting in with peers, and struggles in establishing best friends.

The role of peers has been found to play an important role for teens with VI. Kef and Dekovic [81] found a positive linear relationship between peer support and well-being among adolescents with VI, while well-being was not influenced by peer support for sighted adolescents. Furthermore, parental support appears to play a bigger role in the feelings of well-being among sighted adolescents, in comparison to adolescents with VI; reflecting the visually impaired teens' need for independence from their parents and their desire to fit in with their nonimpaired peers [81].

Adulthood

Cognitive development in adulthood

The link between cognition and sensory functioning in adults has been documented in several studies; findings from a longitudinal study examining individuals age 70 years plus demonstrated a parallel decline in visual function and memory, and a parallel decline in hearing and cognitive function over an 8-year period [82]. Research has suggested common pathophysiology between Alzheimer's disease and macular degeneration, while VI alone places individuals at risk for cognitive decline [83]. The coexistence of VI and cognitive impairment placed older adults at greater risk for disabilities across tasks related to instrumental activities (e.g. shopping, finances), mobility, and activities of daily living (e.g. self-care), more than VI or cognitive impairment alone.

The global impact of cognitive dysfunction can hide the presence of visual impairment [23]. The prevalence of VI increases with age, and individuals with cognitive limitations have a higher prevalence of VI. Additionally, the presence of VI appears to place older individuals at greater risk. Cognitive impairment may impact an older individual's ability to both perceive and understand the functional impact of their visual loss, thus resulting in less endorsement across questions assessing visual function [84]. Furthermore, it may be that individuals with cognitive impairment are not able to understand the questions posed, thus resulting in less endorsement of visual problems.

Executive functioning in adults

Attention and memory

The presence of residual functional vision hampers the attentional strategies needed for haptic exploration, which interferes with focused attention to solely tactile information [85]. Joyce and colleagues [85] revealed that adults who sustained blindness early in life displayed better attention to shape and structure across discrimination tasks in comparison to adults who became blind later in life. This suggests that adults with residual vision may have more difficulty learning to attend to tactile information. Furthermore, adults with late-life blindness may not benefit from learning to read Braille, given their difficulty with attentional skill needed for haptic exploration.

Research regarding sensory impairment has emphasized the notion of neuronal plasticity and possible reorganization that occurs in response to these sensory differences [86, 87]. Hugdahl and colleagues [87] performed a dichotomous listening task with congenitally blind and sighted individuals. Results revealed hemispheric reorganization for speech production and enhanced modification of attention to facilitate processing of speech, and thus improved auditory attention originating from the prefrontal cortex. It remains unclear whether spatial modification in the sensory system for auditory information is related to the loss of vision, or is a result of repeated exposure and attention to speech sounds. Research in adult memory functioning in the blind has shown that individuals who experienced blindness early on in life performed better on average across various verbal memory tasks, in comparison to sighted controls, suggesting compensatory mnemonic performance [88].

Psychological and social functioning in visually impaired adults

Emotional functioning

Loss of vision is described as one of the more fear-provoking conditions in aging adults, characterized by feelings of incompetence, helplessness, anxiety, and depression. Loss of vision also potentially undermines activities of daily living, professional life and leisure, contributing to feelings of vulnerability [89]. The onset of visual loss can coincide with transitions such as moving from work to retirement, subsequently further impacting a change in identity and life plans. It may also coincide with health concerns, contributing to the increased distress that the condition fosters. Feelings of insecurity can result as the adult with VI struggles to cope with feelings of incompetence, dependence, and a lack of productivity [89].

Research has suggested a strong association between depression and low vision in older adults [22, 90]. Lower subjective well-being and loneliness also are reported. Vision quality of life has been negatively associated with difficulties reading medication labels, maneuvering around homes and neighborhoods, and losing access to driving [20]. Endorsements of dependency and associated emotional concerns highlight the isolating effect of bilateral moderate to severe VI. Thus, there appears to be a strong bidirectional relationship between functional impairment and low mood/depression [22]. Older adults with VI often experience co-morbid medical conditions, further impacting physical, adaptive and social functioning. Among adults over age 65, greater than 50% of those with VI may be at risk for depression [91].

Social issues among visually impaired adults

Social support plays an important role in the lives of adults with VI. Less-optimal feelings of well-being appear related to an absence of support as well as negative support [92], which can include insensitivity, criticism, or overprotection. Quality of life research in patients with AMD revealed that depression is more strongly associated with the loss of vision in one eye as opposed to both eyes [21]. Bilateral visual loss may be associated with greater acceptance of the condition while visual loss in one eye may give rise to uncertainty of future visual loss of the other eye.

Neuropsychological assessment

Most standardized tests of intellectual functioning rely on vision for completion. This impacts the extent to which comparisons can be made between individuals with VI and those who are sighted. The number of assessment measures specifically designed for individuals with VI is limited and the manner in which more traditional assessment measures can and should be modified and/or adapted remains an area of debate [93]. Furthermore, an important area of assessment is adaptive functioning. Yet, most tests available to assess environmental adaptation are based on sight and their items heavily rely on vision for navigating the environment. The need for measures that capture the variables essential to individuals with VI remains strong, in order to effectively assess the abilities of children and adults with VI [94].

Overarching issues

A thoughtful assessment of the neuropsychological status of an individual with VI calls for consideration of what is affected in terms of the individual's particular presenting disability(ies), allowing for an effective assessment of what is impacted, developing, and in need of more and less support [55]. Several factors are cited in the literature when considering the absence of tests for assessing individuals with VI across the lifespan. In the case of children with VI, research cites variability across the acquisition of developmental milestones, which affects the development of normative standards that are both valid and reliable [34, 36, 41, 50]. The VI population is heterogeneous, impacting the selection of an appropriate and consistent normative sample. Visual acuity, functional vision, CNS involvement, and additional disabilities (e.g. motor, hearing) are factors to be considered when selecting an appropriate population for a normative sample that reflects the variability found in the VI population [32, 36, 37, 41, 43, 50].

Because there are a limited set of assessment measures for individuals with VI, tests standardized on sighted children and adults are frequently used. This leads to a cautious interpretation of the resulting data. Specifically, when assessing children and adults with childhood VI, it is important to take into consideration differences in experience, development, and the environment, all of which may differ from the visually intact normative sample used for the test under consideration. The notion of "blind-versus-sighted comparison" suggests that visually impaired individuals perform similarly to sighted individuals; however, Warren [95] has shown that this comparison is often not meaningful. Rather, results are best interpreted as revealing a *different*, rather than slower, course of development for visually impaired individuals in comparison with sighted peers. Additionally, it is important to recognize that the manner in which tests are often modified for use with visually impaired individuals, including changes in the pattern of responses deemed acceptable, delivery of instructions, and test format (i.e. Braille or enlarged print), typically violates the standardization practices of the test, and impacts interpretation of results. Therefore, test results may be questionable at best, and often inadequate depending on the degree of modification [32, 37, 96].

The individual's response to stimuli in the environment drives the manner in which tests and the environment may need to be manipulated and/or adapted to facilitate assessment. Visual performance should be considered during any assessment of visually impaired persons [37, 94, 95]. Factors to consider include brightness and contrast (e.g. black writing on buff to reduce glare and pictures or objects displayed on yellow on black, blue, green or purple); adaptation of time, viewing distance of stimuli, and size of the images (e.g. large font for low-vision children); testing milieu and adaptation of materials (e.g. increasing item size, intensifying contrast); and special aids such as magnifying lenses and large font. Interpretation of test results must account for any adaptations and/or modifications of the environment and stimuli [96, 97].

Visual status plays an important role in the assessment process. It is important to ascertain whether the observed pattern of responding is related to visual loss and/or limited cognitive abilities. Considerations include visual acuity, visual field defects, eye movement disorders, balance, and cortical processing of visual information. The presence of multiple issues can impact test administration and interpretation of results. Clarification of these concerns will allow for modifications such as magnification and enlarged visual stimuli, positioning of stimuli (e.g. to address visual field defects), lighting and color, seating, and administration of standardized measures if the individual has usable vision [37].

Establishing rapport

In addition to the standard practices that psychologists and neuropsychologists employ to establish rapport with individuals, additional procedures should be adopted when working with the visually impaired population. Children with VI may require additional time when separating from an adult in comparison to sighted children, given that the introduction to a new environment requires adaptation to the sounds, smells, temperatures, and unfamiliar persons [98]. The environment should include few physical obstacles to facilitate the individual's mobility and limit such distractions from auditory and vibrotactile stimuli. Additional time should be allotted for reading Braille given that it takes approximately 2.5-times longer to read Braille in comparison to normal print [98]. Additional time also should be provided before a standardized response is required, given that individuals may need time to explore and manipulate the objects and stimuli [97]. Interactions with the individual should rely on verbal directions and associated tactile cues (e.g. telling the child that the block will be placed in their hand and then touching the block to the hand), thus minimizing nonverbal gestures [98].

Family context

A comprehensive assessment of a child and adult includes gathering pertinent information beyond demographic and developmental history to include the nature of the visual loss, current visual acuity, timetable of developmental milestones, adaptive functioning, as well as the individual's acceptance of the visual loss [20–22, 96]. Furthermore, it is important to take into account family members' perceptions of the person with VI's abilities and limitations, their fears regarding development and independence, and their expectations or overprotectiveness [77, 92]. Consideration of family needs and resources plays an important role in the assessment of individuals with VI [37] and can be assessed through administration of specific measures tapping social support, need for financial assistance, family functioning, and family needs.

Ethical considerations

Conducting neuropsychological assessments on visually impaired children and adults requires appropriate selection of assessment instruments, based on the visual characteristics of the individual and knowledge of the impact of VI on the developmental trajectory across learning and adaptive functioning. This allows for appropriate interpretation of the data and conclusions [96]. Descriptive language to guide testing plays an important role in how the individual responds and how data are both collected and interpreted. Observation of both typical and dysfunctional behaviors should be noted and interpreted cautiously given the discussions of behavioral characteristics in VI persons [97, 98]. Thus, delineating significance of cognitive impairment and/or developmental delays in a VI population based on low test scores from a test battery standardized on a sighted population could result in inappropriate labeling and remediation [32].

Neuropsychological assessment in specific visually impaired populations

The research is limited with regard to the development of assessment batteries for individuals with VI. While several specific measures have been developed, many standardized measures have been modified, making it difficult to evaluate persons with VI, particularly when considering the heterogeneity of the visually impaired population. Recent research has explored testing measures and practices specific for VI populations [37, 97, 99, 100]. Additional information is available from local and state agencies for the visually impaired detailing test administration and adapted test materials (e.g. American Foundation for the Blind and American Printing House for the Blind).

Assessing developmental acquisition in early childhood

Given the innate difficulties in assessing children with VI, the inclusion of information across various sources, including standardized tests, criterion-referenced tests, behavioral observations, curriculum-based tests, and assessment of adaptive functioning, allows for greater confidence when making recommendations based on test results [96]. The assessment process of infants and children with VI is further complicated by the correlation between vision, sensory, motor, cognitive, and psychological characteristics that call into question the validity and reliability of test measures based on skills acquisition in sighted young children. Such measures as the Bayley Scales of Infant and Toddler Development, Third Edition (Bayley-3), and the Battelle Developmental Inventory, Second Edition (BDI-2), do not account for how either omission (Bayley-3) or adaptation of items (BDI-2) impacts obtained test scores, based on the absence of infants and toddlers with VI included in the standardization process [97].

An additional concern with regard to adaptation of test stimuli for infants and toddlers relates to the substitution of tactual for visual stimuli. Warren and Hatton [40] discuss the notion that it is unclear whether the tactual items tap the same cognitive process assessed by visual stimuli, calling into question any comparison regarding information-processing and learning that is made between VI and sighted young children. Similarly, factors associated with the physical and environmental circumstances may impact the child's performance and may not reflect the child's true skills and abilities [97]. Thus, in review of the limitations across reliable and valid assessments for VI infants and toddlers, test data are best expressed *as a range* as opposed to reporting a single score [37].

Assessing intelligence and learning

The Wechsler Verbal subtests are typically administered to individuals with VI, as these subtests do not require significant adaptation from standardized procedure [93, 97]. However, assessment of intellectual functioning solely based on verbal processing does not capture the range of abilities that may be unique to the VI population, and information tapped in verbal subtests may have developmental roots in visual learning and processing [101]. Furthermore, the Wechsler Scales have not included visually impaired or multiply disabled youngsters or adults in their normative sample, so the applicability of norms is unclear and a cautious interpretation of performance is advised.

The Blind Learning Aptitude Test (BLAT) [102] is an untimed nonverbal, culture-free measure that assesses the ability to discern differences in information through tactile perception of a pattern of dots. However, the absence of clear information regarding exactly what processes the BLAT is tapping, and whether these processes occur equally in children and teens with varying levels of visual acuity, weakens the reliability of this test. Another assessment tool, The Cognitive Test for the Blind and Visually Impaired (CTB) [103], is a component of the Comprehensive Vocational Evaluation System (CVES), designed to assess the vocational and educational potential of individuals who are visually impaired or blind [104]. While the CTB is considered a valid measure of cognitive functioning for individuals with varying levels of visual impairment [101], questions concerning the impact of individual differences on test interpretation weaken its reliability and validity.

291

Assessing older adults

A question concerning the presence of dementia in the VI population is based on their shared demographics and symptomatology, which include depression, social withdrawal and isolation, and diminished ability to use nonverbal cues [100]. Most standardized neuropsychological assessment measures used in the clinical diagnosis of dementia include processing of visual images and therefore do not account for potential differences across visual impairment, including visual acuity. While removal of all visual items may be viewed as an effective adaptation, it may compromise the integrity of testing [99, 100].

For example, assessment of older adults with VI such as AMD involves the adequate assessment of cognitive functioning in light of the accommodations that must be made across measures for low vision. Bertone and colleagues [100] proposed a test battery that includes administration of verbal measures, select nonverbal measures appropriate for the visual acuity of the individual, a depression inventory, and a "blind" adapted version of the Mini-Mental Status Evaluation to assess for depression and dementia. By administering measures appropriate for the level of visual loss and adapting the environment appropriately to capture individual visual characteristics, the proposed battery distinguishes visual information-processing from cognition, thus allowing for a "more accurate" measure of current cognitive functioning.

Testing older adults must also consider the comorbid neurological and medical issues that may impact sensory and motor functioning [100]. These issues should be considered across test selection, administration, and interpretation. Based on the discussion of assessment practices, evaluations with VI should be guided by an understanding of the characteristics across learning and functioning of a person with VI, along with consideration of individual differences across life experiences and visual functioning, so as to generate a specific profile of the individual, which subsequently drives intervention.

Prevention and intervention

The WHO estimates that up to 75% of all blindness globally is actually avoidable [14]. According to these estimates, approximately half of the cases of childhood blindness are avoidable. In 1999, VISION 2020, the Global Initiative for the Elimination of Avoidable Blindness, was launched and aims to eliminate avoidable blindness by 2020.

Early intervention in infancy and childhood

For visual disturbance detected in infancy and early childhood, treatment and intervention are often recommended as early as is feasible in order to promote the child's development. Both early intervention and multidisciplinary models for the treatment of young children with VI are recommended to allow them to reach their potential.

Given that young children spend a great deal of time within schools, it is important to acknowledge intervention provided within this system, as well as laws which have been put in place to support and protect individuals with disabilities. Early Childhood Intervention (ECI), funded at state and national levels through the Individuals with Disabilities Education Improvement Act (IDEIA), provides assessment and intervention (e.g. occupational therapy) for infants and toddlers, 0 to 3 years of age. Similar services are provided through the Preschool Program for Children with Disabilities (PPCD) beginning at age 3 years through the preschool years. Both IDEIA and Section 504 of the Rehabilitation Act of 1973 (42 U.S. C. Sec. 12102 [2]) provide support for persons with disabilities and mandate free and appropriate public education (FAPE). The Americans with Disabilities Act (ADA) extends coverage of Section 504 to employment settings and higher education institutions. Under ADA, students with disabilities, including VI, are eligible for services (e.g. academic accommodations) during the college years.

In conclusion, as emphasized by the WHO, prevention is achieved for many at-risk populations (e.g. diabetic patients) through regular ophthalmological care as well as early detection and intervention. Prevention and early intervention are also highlighted given the implications for the developmental sequelae associated with VI. Intervention is guided by the underlying cause of impairment, and often surgical or pharmacological interventions are indicated and effective for improving VI. Additionally, rehabilitation efforts, which focus on diminishing the functional impact of VI, are viable options for many VI populations (e.g. TBI and CVA patients). Continued efforts toward improving and developing prevention methods as well as technological and rehabilitation interventions are warranted given the significant impact of VI on developmental, cognitive, adaptive, social, and emotional functioning in these patients across the lifespan.

Future directions

The research reflects the growing need and importance of considering the development of visually impaired children and adults given the rise in prematurity and accompanying CNS involvement, as well as the increase in the aging population. Research will be called on to provide improved means of assessing and intervening given the demands placed on schools, medical and mental health care professionals, local and federal agencies, as well as families to care for a family member with VI. With regard to assessment, psychometrically sound instruments are needed across the life span. The heterogeneity of the VI population calls for normative samples to reflect the VI population, composed of both individuals with an isolated VI and those with multiple disabilities. In addition, research investigating the utility of adapted measures, as well as those measures specifically developed for the visually impaired, is necessary to ascertain whether we are truly assessing the underlying cognitive process that the measure was originally designed to assess. Consideration of cultural diversity also is limited in the VI literature, but is needed to both adequately understand the impact of individual differences on opportunity and family functioning, and also to provide culturally sensitive assessment and intervention practices.

Future efforts also should be directed towards empirically validated intervention programs. With respect to children, increased focus in education programs is called for, dedicated to preparing teachers to work with youth with VI, in the presence or absence of additional disabilities. Intervention practices should be comprehensive, thus addressing the learning/educational, social–emotional, and adaptive needs of VI children and adolescents in the classroom and the school environment as a whole. Greater inclusion calls for improved diversity training and tolerance in schools and availability of adaptive technology. Professionals who interface with older adults require ongoing training and education regarding the impact of VI on global functioning and ways in which to delineate decreased functioning due to the presence of VI versus dementia. Empirically validated intervention programs, which consider emotional and social functioning (e.g. engagement in leisure activities), are needed given the comorbidity of VI and depression, and the subsequent impact on global functioning. Furthermore, further research is called for to develop adaptive technology and resources to facilitate quality of life across the life span.

Throughout the discussion of VI, the notion of individual differences was emphasized. An important aspect of this is the family context in which the individual with VI lives. Research involving the parents and caregivers of the visually impaired will allow for a greater understanding of what families within a particular stage of development require. Intervention programs looking at the way in which interactions foster or hinder development also are noteworthy, so as to provide intervention programs to both parents of young children and caregivers of older adults in the hope of fostering beneficial outcomes.

References

1. US Department of Health and Human Services. *Vision research – a national plan 1999–2003: a report of the National Eye Advisory Council.* Bethesda: National Eye Institute; 1998. NIH Publication No. 98–4120.

2. The World Health Organization. Magnitude and causes of visual impairment. Fact sheet 282. 2004. http://www.who.int/mediacentre/factsheets/fs282/en/ [accessed February 19, 2008].

3. Holbrook MC. *Children with Visual Impairments: A Parents' Guide,* 2nd edn. Bethesda: Woodbine House; 2006.

4. Congdon N, O'Colmain B, et al. Causes and prevalence of visual impairment among adults in the United States. *Arch Ophthalmol* 2004;**122**:477–85.

5. Alexander GR, Slay M. Prematurity at birth: trends, racial disparities, and epidemiology. *Ment Retard Dev Disabil Res Rev* 2002;**8**:215–20.

6. O'Connor AR, Fielder AR. Visual outcomes and perinatal adversity. *Semin Fetal Neonat Med* 2007;**12**:408–14.

7. Rudanko SL, Fellman V, Laatikainen L. Visual impairment in children born prematurely from 1972 through 1989. *Ophthalmology* 2003;**110**:1639–45.

8. Hatton DD, Schwietz E, Boyer B, Rychwalski P. Babies count: the national registry for children with visual impairments, birth to 3 years. *JAAPOS* 2007;**11**:351–5.

9. Webster A, Roe J. *Children with Visual Impairments: Social Interaction, Language and Learning.* New York: Routledge; 1998.

10. Borchert MS, Garcia-Filion PC, et al. Developmental outcomes in young children with optic nerve hypoplasia: a prospective study. *JAAPOS* 2006;**10**:83.

11. Hellström A, Wiklund LM, Svensson E. The clinical and morphologic spectrum of Optic Nerve Hypoplasia. *JAAPOS* 1999;**3**:212–20.

12. Richardson SR, Wright CM, et al. Stereoacuity in unilateral visual impairment detected at preschool screening: outcomes from a randomized controlled trial. *Invest Ophthalmol Vis Sci* 2005;**46**:150–4.

13. Sakimoto M, Rosenblatt MI, Azar DT. Laser eye surgery for refractive errors. *Lancet* 2006;**367**:1432–47.

14. Huo R, Burden SK, Hoyt CS, Good WV. Chronic cortical visual impairment in children: Aetiology, prognosis, and associated neurological deficits. *Br J Ophthalmol* 1999;**83**:670–5.

15. Matsuba CA, Jan JE. Long-term outcome of children with cortical visual impairment. *Dev Med Child Neurol* 2006;**48**:508–12.

16. Khetpal V, Donahue SP. Cortical visual impairment: etiology, associated findings, and prognosis in a tertiary care setting. *JAAPOS* 2007;**11**:235–9.

17. Watson T, Orel-Bixler D, Haegerstrom-Portnoy G. Longitudinal quantitative assessment of vision function in children with cortical visual impairment. *Optom Vis Sci* 2007;**84**:471–80.

18. Cohen-Maitre SA, Haerich P. Visual attention to movement and color in children with cortical visual impairment. *J Vis Impair Blind* 2005:389–402.

19. Morse AR, Rosenthal BP. Vision and vision assessment. *J Ment Health Aging* 1996;**2**:197–212.

20. Varma R, Wu J, et al. Impact of severity and bilaterality of visual impairment on health-related quality of life. *Ophthalmology* 2006;**113**:1846–53.

21. Slakter J, Stur M. Quality of life in patients with age-related macular degeneration: Impact of the condition and benefits of treatment. *Surv Ophthalmol* 2005;**50**:263–73.

22. Evans JR, Fletcher AE, Wormald RPL. Depression and anxiety in visually impaired older people. *Ophthalmology* 2007;**114**:283–8.

23. Luauté J, Halligan P, et al. Visuo-spatial neglect: A systematic review of current interventions and their effectiveness. *Neurosci Biobehav Rev* 2006;**30**:961–82.

24. Schmier JK, Halpern MT, Covert D, Delgado J, Sharma S. Impact of visual impairment on use of caregiving by individuals with age-related macular degeneration. *Retina J Retinal Vitreous Dis* 2006;**26**:1056–2.

25. Chamerlain M, Baird P, et al. Unraveling a complex genetic disease: Age-related macular degeneration. *Surv Ophthalmol* 2006;**51**:576–86.

26. Zhang X, Norris SL, et al. Effectiveness of interventions to promote screening for diabetic retinopathy. *Am J Prevent Med* 2007;**33**:318–35.

27. Gardner TW, Antonetti DA, et al. Diabetic retinopathy: more than meets the eye. *Surv Ophthalmol* 2002;**47**: S253–62.

28. Polak BCP, Crijns H, et al. Cost-effectiveness of glycemic control and ophthalmological care in diabetic retinopathy. *Health Policy* 2003;**64**:89–97.

29. Park WL, Mayer S, et al. Rehabilitation of hospital inpatients with visual impairments and disabilities from systemic illness. *Arch Phys Med Med Rehabil* 2005;**86**:79–81.

30. Sarno S, Erasmus LP, et al. Electrophysiological correlates of visual impairments after traumatic brain injury. *Vis Res* 2000;**40**:3029–38.

31. Ng YS, Stein J, et al. Clinical characteristics and rehabilitation outcomes of patients with posterior cerebral artery stroke. *Arch Phys Med Med Rehabili* 2005;**86**:2138–43.

32. Warren DH. *Blindness and Children: An Individual Differences Approach.* Cambridge: Cambridge University Press; 1994.

33. Pérez-Pereira M, Conti-Ramsden G. *Language Development and Social Interaction in Blind Children.* East Sussex: Psychology Press; 1999.

34. Sonksen PM, Dale N. Visual impairment in infancy: impact on neurodevelopmental and neurobiological processes. *Dev Med Child Neurol*, 2002;**44**:782–91.

35. Preisler G. Social and emotional development of blind children: a longitudinal study. In Lewis V, Collins GM, eds. *Blindness and Psychological Development in Young Children.* Leicester: BPS Books; 1997: 69–85.

36. Bigelow AE. The effect of blindness on the early development of the self. In Rochat P, ed. *The Self in Infancy: Theory and Research.* Amsterdam: Elsevier Science; 1995: 327–47.

37. Bradley-Johnson S. *Psychoeducational Assessment of Students who are Visually Impaired or Blind: Infancy Through High School.* Austin: Pro-Ed; 1994.

38. Dale N, Sonksen PM. Towards an assessment schedule for social communicative development for young visually impaired children. *Dev Med Child Neurol* 1998;**40**(Suppl.79):30–1.

39. Kwok SK, Chan AKH, Gandhi SR, et al. Ocular defects in children and adolescents with severe mental deficiency. *J Intellect Disabil Res* 1996;**40**:330–5.

40. Warren DH, Hatton, DD. Cognitive development in children with visual impairment. In Boller F, Grafman J, eds. *Handbook of Neuropsychology*, 2nd edn. Vol. 8, Pt. II. Amsterdam: Elsevier Science; 2003:439–58.

41. Fraiberg S. *Insights from the Blind: Comparative Studies of the Blind and Sighted Infants.* New York: Basic Books; 1977.

42. Freedman DA, Fox-Kolenda BJ, Margileth DA, et al. The development of the use of sound as a guide to affective

and cognitive behavior: A two-phase process. *Child Dev* 1969;**49**:1099–105.

43. Landau B. Knowledge and its expression in the blind child. In Keating D, Rosen H, eds. *Constructive Perspectives on Developmental Psychopathology and Atypical Development*. Hillsdale: Erlbaum; 1991:173–92.

44. Bigelow AE. The development of reaching in blind children. *Br J Dev Psychol* 1986;**4**:355–66.

45. Piaget J. *The Construction of Reality in the Child*. New York: Basic Books; 1954.

46. Freedman DA. On hearing, oral language, and psychic structure. In Holt RR, Peterfreund E, eds. *Psychoanalysis and Contemporary Science*. New York: Macmillan; 1972: 57–69.

47. Adelson E, Fraiberg S. Gross motor development in infants blind from birth. *Child Dev* 1974;**45**:114–26.

48. Hughes M, Dote-Kwan J, Dolendo J. Characteristics of maternal directiveness and responsiveness with young children with visual impairments. *Child Care Health Dev* 1999;**25**:285–98.

49. Padula WV. Vision and its influence on development of the visually impaired child. In Mulholland ME, Wurster MV, eds. *Help Me Become Everything I Can Be*. New York: American Foundation for the Blind; 1983.

50. Dale N, Sonksen P. Developmental outcome, including setback, in young children with severe visual impairment. *Dev Med Child Neurol* 2002;**44**:613–22.

51. Rogers SJ, Puchalski CB. Development of object permanence in visually impaired infants. *J Vis Impair Blind* 1988;**82**:137–42.

52. Lister C, Leach C, Ballinger S, et al. Extent of similarity in concept development for visually impaired and sighted children. *Early Child Dev Care* 1996;**117**:21–8.

53. Davidson PW, Dunn G, Wiles-Kettenmann M, et al. Haptic conservation of amount in blind and sighted children: Exploratory movement effects. *J Pediatr Psychol* 1981;**6**:191–200.

54. Iverson JM, Goldin-Meadow S. What's communication got to do with it? Gesture in congenitally blind children. *Dev Psychol* 1997;**33**:453–67.

55. Hunter SJ, Griffin-Shirley N, Noll L. Visual impairments. In Farmer JE, Donders J, Warschausky S, eds. *Treating Neurodevelopmental Disabilities: Clinical Research and Practice*. New York: The Guilford Press; 2006: 132–46.

56. Mills AE. Acquisition of speech sounds in the visually-handicapped child. In Mills AE, ed. *Language Acquisition in the Blind Child: Normal and Deficient*. London: Croom Helm; 1983:45–56.

57. Dunlea A. *Vision and the Emergence of Meaning: Blind and Sighted Children's Early Language*. Cambridge: Cambridge University Press; 1989.

58. Fraiberg S, Adelson E. Self-representation in language and play: observations of blind children. *Psychoanal Q* 1973;**42**:539–62.

59. Brambring M. Divergent development of verbal skills in children who are blind or sighted. *J Vis Impair Blind* 2007;**101**:749–62.

60. Bigelow AE. Early words of blind children. *J Child Lang* 1987;**14**:47–56.

61. Bigelow AE. The development of joint attention in blind infants. *Dev Psychopathol* 2003;**15**:259–75.

62. Ferrel KA. Your child's development. In Holbrook MC, ed. *Children with Visual Impairments: A Parent's Guide*, 2nd edn. Bethesda: Woodbine House; 2006: 85–108.

63. Pring L, Dewart H, Brockbank, M. Social cognition in children with visual impairments. *J Vis Impair Blind* 1998;**92**:754–68.

64. Edmonds CJ, Pring L. Generating inferences from written and spoken language: a comparison of children with visual impairment and children with sight. *Br J Dev Psychol* 2006;**24**:337–51.

65. Landau B, Gleitman LR. *Language and Experience: Evidence from the Blind Child*. Cambridge: Harvard University Press; 1985.

66. Pérez-Pereira M, Castro J. Language acquisition and the compensation of visual deficit: New comparative data on a controversial topic. *Br J Dev Psychol* 1997;**15**:439–59.

67. Romani A, Conte S, Callieco R, et al. Visual evoked potential abnormalities in dyslexic children. *Funct Neurol* 2001;**16**;219–29.

68. Tonge BJ, Lipton GL, Crawford C. Psychological and educational correlates of strabismus in school age children. *Aust N Z J Psychiatry* 1984;**18**:71–7.

69. Reed MJ, Stevens JKE, Steinbach MJ, et al. Contrast letter thresholds in the non-affected eye of early-onset strabismic subjects and unilateral eye enucleated subjects. *Vis Res* 1996;**36**:3011–18.

70. Reed MJ, Kraft SP, Bunic R. Parents' observations of the academic and nonacademic performance of children with strabismus. *J Vis Impair Blind* 2004;**98**:276–89.

71. Opir-Cohen M, Ashkenazy E, Cohen A, et al. Emotional status and development in children who are visually impaired. *J Vis Impair Blind* 2005;**99**:478–5.

72. Jan JE, Groenveld M, Sykanda AM, Hoyt CS. Behavioral characteristics of children with permanent cortical visual impairment. *Dev Med Child Neurol* 1987;**29**:571–6.

73. Tröster H, Brambring M. The play behavior and play materials of blind and sighted infants and preschoolers. *J Vis Impair Blind* 1994;**88**:421–32.

74. Bishop M, Hobson, R, Lee A. Symbolic play in congenitally blind children. *Dev Psychopathol* 2005;**17**:447–65.

75. Erwin EJ. Social participation of young children with visual impairments in integrated and specialized settings. *J Vis Impair Blind* 1993;**5**:138–42.

76. Keklis LS, Sacks SZ. The effects of visual impairment on children's social interactions in regular education programs. In Sacks SZ, Kekelis LS, Gaylord-Ross RJ, eds. *The Development of Social Skills by Blind and Visually Impaired Students*. New York: American Foundation for the Blind; 1992.

77. Tuttle DW, Tuttle NR. Psychosocial needs of children and youths. In Holbrook MC, Koenig AJ, eds. *Foundations of Education, 2nd edn, Vol. 1. History and Theory of Teaching Children and Youths with Visual Impairments*. American Foundation for the Blind; 2005.

78. Baird SM, Mayfield P, Baker P. Mothers' interpretations of the behavior of their infants with visual and other impairments during interactions. *J Vis Impair Blind* 1997;**91**:467–83.

79. Dote-Kwan J. Impact of mothers' interactions on the development of their young visually impaired children. *J Vis Impair Blind*, 1995;**89**:47–58.

80. Rosenbaum LP. Perceptions of the impact of visual impairment on the lives of adolescents. *J Vis Impair Blind* 2000;**94**:434–45.

81. Kef S, Dekovic M. The role of parental and peer support in adolescents well-being: A comparison of adolescents with and without visual impairment. *J Adolesc* 2004;**27**:453–66.

82. Anstey KJ, Hofer SM, Luczcz MA. A latent growth curve analysis of late-life sensory and cognitive function over 8 years: evidence for specific and common factors underlying change. *Psychol Aging* 2003;**18**:714–26.

83. Uhlmann RF, Larson EB, Koepsell TD, et al. Visual impairment and cognitive dysfunction in Alzheimer's disease. *J Gen Intern Med* 1991;**6**:126–32.

84. Holmen K, Anderson L, Ericsson K, et al. Visual impairment related to cognition and loneliness in old age. *Scand J Caring Sci* 1994;**8**:99–105.

85. Joyce A, Isom R, Dial JG et al. Implications of perceptual-motor differences within blind populations. *J Appl Rehabil Counsel* 2004;**35**:3–7.

86. Amedi A, Merabet LB, Bermpohl F, et al. The occipital cortex in the blind: lessons about plasticity and vision. *Curr Dir Psychol Sci* 2005;**14**:306–11.

87. Hugdahl K, Ek M, Takio F, et al. Blind individuals show enhanced perceptual and attentional sensitivity for identification of speech sounds. *Cogn Brain Res* 2004;**19**:28–32.

88. Roder B, Rosler F. Memory for environmental sounds in sighted, congenitally blind and late blind adults: evidence for cross-modal compensation. *Int J Psychophysiol* 2003;**50**:27–39.

89. Wahl HW. Visual impairment: psychological implications. *Encyclopedia Psychol* 2000;**8**:204–7.

90. Hayman KJ, Kerse NM, LaGrow SJ, et al. Depression in older people: visual impairment and subjective ratings of health. *Optom Vis Sci* 2007;**84**:1024–30.

91. Crews JE, Jones GC, Kim JH. Double jeopardy: the effects of comorbid conditions among older people with vision loss. *J Vis Impair Blind* 2006; Special Supplement: 824–48.

92. Cimarolli VR, Boerner K. Social support and well-being in adults who are visually impaired. *J Vis Impair Blind* 2005;**99**:521–34.

93. Chaudry NM, Davidson PW. Assessment of children with visual impairment and blindness. In Simeonsson RJ, Rosenthal SL, eds. *Psychological and Developmental Assessment: Children with Disabilities and Chronic Conditions*. New York: Guilford Press; 2001: 225–47.

94. Fewell RR. Assessment of visual functioning. In Bracken BA, ed. *The Psychoeducational Assessment of Preschool Children*, 3rd edn. Boston: Allyn and Bacon; 2000: 234–48.

95. Warren DH. Visual impairment. In Kaufman JM, Hallahan DP, eds. *Handbook of Special Education*. Eaglewood Cliffs: Prentice-Hall; 1981.

96. Van Hasselt VB, Sisson LA. Visual impairment. In Frame C, Matson J, eds. *Handbook of Assessment in Child Psychopathology: Applied Issues in Diagnosis and Treatment Evaluation*. New York: Plenum Press; 1987: 593–618.

97. Aiken LR. *Assessment of Intellectual Functioning: Perspectives on Individual Differences*, 2nd edn. New York: Springer; 1996.

98. Semrud-Clikeman M, Hynd GW. Assessment of learning and cognitive dysfunction in young children. In Culbertson JL, Willis DJ, eds. *Testing Young Children: A Reference Guide for Developmental, Psychoeducational, and Psychosocial Assessments*. Austin: ProEd; 1993: 167–261.

99. Hill-Briggs F, Dial JG, Morere DA, et al. Neuropsychological assessment of persons with physical disability, visual impairment or blindness, and hearing impairment or deafness. *Arch Clin Neuropsychol* 2007;**22**;389–404.

100. Bertone A, Wittich W, Watanabe D, et al. The effect of age-related macular degeneration on non-verbal neuropsychological test performance. *Int Congr Ser* 2005;**1282**;26–30.

101. Nelson PA, Dial JG, Joyce A. Validation of the Cognitive Test for the Blind as an assessment of intellectual functioning. *Rehabil Psychol* 2002;**47**:184–93.

102. Newland TE. The Blind Learning Aptitude Test. *J Vis Impair Blind* 1971;**73**:134–9.

103. Dial J, Mezger C, Gray S, et al. *Manual: Comprehensive Vocational Evaluation System*. Dallas: McCarron-Dial Systems; 1990.

104. Dial J, Chan F, Mezger C, et al. Comprehensive vocational evaluation system for visually impaired and blind persons. *J Impair Blind* 1991;**85**:153–7.

Traumatic brain injury in childhood

Michael W. Kirkwood, Keith Owen Yeates and Jane Holmes Bernstein

Introduction

Traumatic brain injury (TBI) is one of the leading causes of morbidity and mortality in youth worldwide. Though much remains to be learned, research focused on pediatric TBI has flourished in the last two decades. The current chapter will emphasize recent scientific literature relevant to understanding the consequences of moderate to severe TBI and the role of neuropsychological assessment in particular in characterizing and managing these difficulties. Epidemiological, pathophysiological, and intervention data will be highlighted as well. Outcomes and clinical care after uncomplicated mild TBI in children can be expected to differ from more severe injury; comprehensive reviews of this literature are available elsewhere [1, 2].

Epidemiology

In the USA, more than one million children and adolescents sustain TBI each year. Among children aged 0 to 14 years, TBI accounts for approximately 2700 annual deaths, 37 000 hospitalizations, and 435 000 emergency department visits [3]. Not surprisingly given such frequency, the associated financial costs are considerable. Annual hospitalization charges alone exceed $1 billion [4]. Rates and costs of all childhood TBI are undoubtedly much larger, as many milder injuries go unreported entirely or are treated in outpatient settings and remain unaccounted for in hospital-based estimates.

The incidence of TBI varies by severity, with mild TBI comprising 80 to 90% of all treated cases. Throughout childhood, boys are at considerably greater risk for TBI than girls. Children aged 0 to 4 years have the highest rate of TBI-related emergency department visits, although TBI in adolescents aged 15 to 19 years results in many more inpatient hospitalizations and deaths [3]. Age at injury is also associated with different causal mechanisms, which helps to account for varying pathology and outcomes across development. Inflicted trauma is the leading cause of

serious injury during infancy; falls are heavily represented throughout childhood, especially in the toddler and preschool years; sport- and motor-vehicle-related TBI increases in middle childhood; and TBI from motor-vehicle-related trauma and assaults peaks during older adolescence [5]. The frequency and outcome of TBI may also vary by race and socioeconomic status, with some data suggesting higher rates and worse outcomes in nonwhites and families of lower income [6, 7].

Pathophysiology

The pathological effects of TBI are typically classified as either primary or secondary. Primary injury occurs at the time of trauma as a direct result of the impact or acceleration-deceleration forces applied to the head. Common primary effects include skull fractures, contusion, and hematoma, as well as more widely distributed lesions such as diffuse axonal shearing and diffuse vascular injury. Though therapeutic options to address primary injury could emerge in the future (e.g. stem cell technologies), prevention efforts are the only current means by which these injuries can be minimized. Secondary effects include additional insults (e.g. brain swelling and edema, hypoxia, hypotension, hydrocephalus, seizures) that follow primary injury and serve to compound the initial effects. These can be particularly deleterious after more severe TBI. The primary injury also leads to a secondary pathophysiological cascade that can include impaired blood flow, increased intracranial pressure, excitotoxicity, energy failure, inflammation, and cell death.

Although there are pathophysiological commonalities among all types of TBI, the response of an immature brain differs from that of the more mature brain of the adult [8, 9]. For example, children are more likely to display post-traumatic brain swelling, hypoxic-ischemic insult, and diffuse, rather than focal, injuries. The biomechanical properties of the young brain probably explain at least some of these differences: compared to adults, children have a greater head-to-body ratio, less myelination, and more water content and cerebral blood volume. Once children reach adolescence, TBI-related pathology begins to more closely resemble that seen in adults.

Non-accidental trauma has unique biomechanical and pathological properties compared with other mechanisms of injury, which contributes to the particularly poor outcomes seen in many of these cases. In addition to the specific psychosocial complexities often present, these injuries are not uncommonly complicated by very young age at time of injury, repeated trauma, delay in treatment (resulting in hypoxic-ischemic injury), seizures, and concomitant injury to the cervical spine [9].

Neurobehavioral and familial consequences of pediatric TBI

Numerous international research groups have contributed substantially to characterizing the childhood outcomes of pediatric TBI. Less work has focused on outcomes into adulthood, though an increasing amount of data are available in this regard (see Beauchamp, Dooley, and Anderson, Chapter 11b, this volume). TBI-related consequences can be classified within several broad-based domains including cognitive, psychosocial, functional, educational, and familial. Table 11a.1 outlines the common childhood consequences of severe TBI and provides empirically grounded estimates of the magnitude for effects within each area.

Cognitive

Childhood TBI results in a multitude of well-documented cognitive effects, which are strongly related to injury severity. Partial cognitive recovery is often seen within the first months of injury, although longitudinal work demonstrates a plateau after 6 months to a year and persistent cognitive deficits thereafter, especially following more severe injury [10]. Across cognitive areas, effects become more prominent as effortful processing increases. Thus, overlearned knowledge and automatized skills can be relatively unaffected by TBI, whereas tasks dependent upon integrative, novel, or speeded processing usually reveal more problems.

On measures of IQ, injuries occurring in infancy or the preschool years are associated with a broad-based diminution in scores and/or less rapid growth over time [11]. As children become older, IQ effects

Table 11a.1. Common consequences of severe pediatric TBI in school-aged children and empirical evidence for effects

Domain	Specific area	Evidence for effects
Cognitive	Basic linguistic skills	−
	Pragmatic communication skills	++
	Nonverbal abilities	+
	Learning and memory	++
	Processing speed	++
	Attentional processes	+
	Test-based executive functioning	+
	Everyday executive functioning	+
Psychosocial	Social problem-solving and competence	++
	Personality change	++
	ADHD	++
	Other novel psychiatric disorders	+
Functional	Adaptive functioning	++
	Health-related quality of life	+
	Somatic, cognitive, and behavior complaints	+
Educational	Performance on math achievement tests	+
	Performance on reading/spelling achievement tests	−
	Classroom performance	++
	Special education need	++
Familial	Family distress, burden, negativity	++

++ indicates evidence of a strong or well-established relationship;
+ indicates evidence of a modestly established relationship;
− indicates minimal or equivocal evidence.

become more heterogeneous but are greatest on speeded tasks. Research with the Wechsler Intelligence Scale for Children–Third Edition, for instance, has documented clear effects on the Processing Speed Index [12]. A recent study with the Wechsler Intelligence Scale for Children–Fourth Edition suggests that the Processing Speed factor is apt to once again have the best criterion validity after TBI [13].

In terms of language functioning, TBI has been found to result in persistent problems with discourse, pragmatics, and other higher-level communication skills. In contrast, vocabulary, syntax, and other basic linguistic skills are relatively spared, especially after the early stages of recovery and in children injured later in development [14]. TBI also undermines a range of nonverbal capacities including spatial orientation and perceptual-motor functioning [15, 16]. Negative effects on learning and memory, especially involving more demanding tasks such as list-learning recall [17] and prospective memory [18], have been documented. Speeded and/or sustained attention and more complex attentional control processes are also compromised [19]. Post-injury deficits on tasks tapping executive functioning include problems with working memory [20], self-regulation and inhibition [21, 22], planning [23], and concept formation and verbal fluency [21]. These performance-based executive functioning difficulties correspond to executive problems observed in everyday settings [24].

Psychosocial

Pediatric TBI increases the risk for a variety of psychosocial and functional problems as well, which are not necessarily related strongly to the cognitive consequences. Compared with the cognitive effects, psychosocial outcomes are more multifactorially determined, depending in part on injury severity but also heavily on non-injury-related factors such as family stress, coping, and socioeconomic status. Moreover, in contrast to many cognitive difficulties that tend to show recovery in the initial months after injury, psychosocial difficulties are more likely to show a stable or even worsening pattern over time [10, 25].

In general, social outcomes have received relatively little attention after pediatric TBI, though the conceptual groundwork for future work exists [26]. Extant studies have documented poorer social problem-solving and less social competence in children with TBI compared with non-injured peers [27]. Numerous studies have also documented that moderate to severe TBI increases the risk for a wide range of behavioral problems. In a recent prospective controlled study, Schwartz et al. [28] found that 36% of the severe TBI group displayed significant behavioral problems at 4 years post-injury, compared with 22% of the moderate TBI group, and 10% of the orthopedic control children.

Pediatric TBI is also associated with a variety of psychiatric symptoms and disorders. Generally speaking, novel disorders occur much less frequently after moderate injuries when traits of the disorder are not present premorbidly. Personality change is a frequent psychiatric consequence of more severe TBI. Changes involving lability, aggression, and disinhibition are most common, whereas apathy and paranoia occur less frequently [29]. "Secondary" attention-deficit/hyperactivity disorder (S-ADHD) has been found to develop in approximately 15–20% of children with TBI who did not display premorbid ADHD [30, 31]. TBI also increases the risk for other disruptive

behavioral disorders such as oppositional defiant disorder [32]. Depressive and anxiety symptomatology and disorders are also observed more frequently in children with TBI than controls [33, 34]. In contrast, manic and psychotic symptoms are documented much less frequently after childhood injury.

Functional

Moderate or severe TBI is also associated with persistent adaptive behavior deficits (e.g. poorer communication and daily living skills) and functional limitations [25, 35]. In addition, declines in children's health-related quality of life are often apparent – more frequently reported by the parent than by the child [36].

Following milder TBI, a variety of somatic, cognitive, and behavioral complaints are often reported, which are commonly referred to as "post-concussive symptoms". After severe TBI, the onset or exacerbation of similar symptomatology is seen, typically with more persistence than after milder injury. Yeates et al. [37] found that in comparison to children with orthopedic injury or moderate TBI, children with severe TBI reported more frequent cognitive/somatic symptoms (e.g. headache, fatigue, attention and memory problems) and emotional/behavioral symptoms (e.g. moodiness, impulsivity, aggressiveness) through 12 months post-injury.

Educational

Children injured during infancy or the preschool years are at risk for difficulties in the acquisition of a broad range of academic skills [11]. In contrast, TBI in later childhood or adolescence is generally associated with age-appropriate basic academic achievement [38]. Despite adequate performance on most standardized academic tests, however, children injured at any age often display remarkably poor everyday classroom functioning. Across development, pediatric TBI significantly increases the risk for failing grades, need for special education services, and parental and teacher concerns about academic competence [11, 38]. Although the entire range of factors contributing to these classroom difficulties remains to be elucidated, post-injury compromise of neurobehavioral capacities (e.g. attention, self-regulation, speeded responding, memory) that are necessary for effective everyday school performance can be expected to play a major role, as can the student's emotional and behavioral adjustment [39].

Familial

Research examining the effects of moderate to severe pediatric TBI on families has been accumulating quickly in recent years. TBI increases the risk for psychological symptoms in parents and siblings and contributes significantly to family distress, burden, and negativity [40, 41]. Family-related problems can persist for years post-injury and may become especially apparent during developmental transition periods [42]. Families with increased stress, fewer resources, and poorer coping appear to be most likely to develop post-injury problems [43].

Influences on outcome

The outcomes of pediatric TBI have now been adequately described in many neurobehavioral domains. Nonetheless, across studies, the amount of unaccounted variance remains substantial, and the specific consequences for a given individual are difficult to predict. Variables that influence pediatric outcomes can be classified into three broad categories: injury-related, contextual, and developmental.

Injury-related

The relationship between injury severity and outcome has been investigated in many studies, resulting in the identification of a clear dose–response relationship. Uncomplicated mild TBI (i.e. mild TBI without clear intracranial pathology) has typically been found to produce transient neuropsychological effects. Although subjectively reported post-concussive complaints may linger in a minority of children, problems on cognitive/psychoeducational tests are generally not apparent, particularly after the initial days or weeks [1, 44]. As the severity of TBI increases, however, so do the risks for a host of neurobehavioral problems, with severe injuries responsible for the greatest morbidity.

A number of injury severity markers have been linked consistently to pediatric outcomes following TBI, including depth of coma, length of coma, duration of post-traumatic amnesia (PTA), and neuroimaging abnormalities. Across most studies, results support statements that a particular severity marker is associated with a poorer neurobehavioral outcome. However, generally speaking, the data do not allow more precise predictions about the likelihood of a specific neuropsychological or functional outcome given a particular marker. In adult populations, enough data have accumulated to produce several empirically-based "threshold values", above or below which a certain outcome is especially likely or unlikely [45]. For example, if PTA lasts more than 3 months, an adult is very unlikely to achieve a "good" recovery on the Glasgow Outcome Scale. For childhood populations, there are limited data in this regard, at least when predicting long-term morbidity.

The Glasgow Coma Scale (GCS), or a modified version for infants and toddlers, has probably been investigated more than any other severity measure in pediatric studies, with lower scores associated with worse early and long-term outcomes. In contrast to static measurements such as a one-time GCS score, however, markers that are presumed to index neurobiological recovery, such as duration of coma, length of impaired consciousness, or duration of PTA, may serve as even better predictors of neurobehavioral outcome [46].

Data from neuroimaging studies indicate that the more prevalent the structural abnormalities, the greater the morbidity. Studies have also documented an anterior–posterior gradient in the focal lesions associated with pediatric TBI, with larger and more numerous lesions found in the frontal and anterior temporal regions [47]. This frontotemporal susceptibility to injury relates to how these regions are positioned in the skull and has long been assumed to be the basis of the core neurobehavioral problems seen after TBI. In pediatric populations, multiple studies have found expected brain–behavior associations supporting this assumption. Levin and Hanten [48] review much of this literature as it pertains to executive functioning, highlighting relationships between frontal lobe pathology and neuropsychological deficits in children that match well with expectations based on classic models of brain–behavior relationships.

Several studies have also made it clear, however, that brain–behavior relationships based on adult models cannot be assumed after childhood TBI. For example, in a population of school-aged children with TBI, Slomine et al. [49] found that frontal lesion volume failed to predict performance on any measure of executive function. Power et al. [50] failed to find a relationship between frontal lesion severity and performance on measures of attentional control. Salorio et al. [51] found that performance on a list-learning memory measure was more strongly related to lesions outside the frontotemporal regions than lesions within those regions. Taken together, these studies support the position that pediatric brain–behavior relationships differ from those of adults, reflecting the differences in maturation of cortical regions in individuals at different stages of development.

Given the multi-layered nature of TBI pathology, a diverse set of techniques and technologies will undoubtedly prove useful in more fully explaining brain–behavior relationships in children. Depth-of-lesion models will be important to elucidate the impact of injury on subcortical regions, which may index injury severity more effectively and relate more strongly to long-term neurobehavioral outcomes than cortical lesions [52]. Newer MRI technologies that show increased sensitivity to the effects of diffuse brain injury are also being developed and utilized after pediatric TBI, including susceptibility-weighted MR imaging [53], diffusion tensor imaging [54], and magnetic resonance spectroscopy [55]. At present, the contribution of neurochemical indices (e.g., S100B neuron-specific enolase) and genetic markers (e.g. APOE status) in pediatric populations is less clear, although this may change with the rapid technological advances in these areas.

Contextual

The need to consider variables beyond injury severity in predicting post-injury outcomes is now well appreciated, including the importance of a number of contextual factors. In general, such variables have been found to have a greater effect on psychosocial and academic outcomes than physical and cognitive outcomes. Socioeconomic status, family resources, and both pre-injury and post-injury family functioning have all been shown to be important moderators of long-term outcome [10, 25]. The mechanisms by which the environment exerts its effect have not yet been clarified. It could be that families from disadvantaged environments lack the resources or availability to enhance the child's recovery or to optimally manage post-injury neurobehavioral problems; family adversity could also differentially affect neurologically compromised children, as these children may be more dependent on the environments because of their limitations [25]. In any case, the relationships between child and environment are likely to prove bidirectional in at least some situations. Taylor and colleagues [56] found that higher family distress at 6 months post-injury predicted worse child behavior at 12 months and also that increased child behavior problems at

6 months predicted poorer family outcomes at 12 months.

Developmental

A number of developmental variables have been shown to influence outcomes as well. At a general level, developmental skills and functional status of the child prior to the injury can strongly impact post-injury adaptive and behavioral functioning [28, 30, 57]. Post-injury psychiatric problems are also predicted by a number of pre-injury child variables including intellectual status, adaptive skills, and psychiatric condition [10, 58].

Several time-specific developmental variables have also been studied as moderators. Age at injury, time since injury, and age at testing have all received scientific attention, although age at injury has clearly been investigated the most thoroughly. Historically, earlier age at injury was thought to produce better outcomes because of the young brain's "plasticity". Better outcomes can indeed be seen in immature nonhuman animals under certain well-defined conditions [59] and in humans after early focal or discrete injuries such as perinatal stroke [60]. Nonetheless, more recent investigations have demonstrated that the immature child brain is more vulnerable, not more accommodating, to diffuse, evolving injuries such as TBI. Multiple studies have now shown that TBI during the infancy and preschool years is associated with worse outcomes than injury occurring in later childhood or adolescence [11, 61]. Skills that have not yet developed or are currently in development at the time of injury may be particularly susceptible to injury effects and may show an altered course of post-injury development [19, 62]. Explanations to account for this increased vulnerability in young children include potential restrictions on functional recovery imposed by the injured child's smaller repertoire of skills, the damaging impact of diffuse injury on systems responsible for later skill acquisition and maintenance (e.g. self-regulation, learning and memory), and the potentially limiting effects of prolonged hospitalization and treatment on learning.

Neuropsychological assessment

With increasingly sophisticated acute medical care and technology, neuropsychologists are rarely asked to assist in making an initial diagnosis of TBI, except perhaps in certain cases of milder TBI, when the medical or neuroimaging evidence for injury may be less clear. Of course, neuropsychological assessment has value above and beyond simply diagnosing TBI. Neuropsychological assessment can be used to delineate the neurobehavioral consequences of injury, disentangle injury effects from other factors that may be contributing to or moderating post-injury behavior, assist with post-injury diagnostic decision-making, and develop rehabilitation and educational management plans appropriate to the child's needs and circumstances.

Empirical investigation of the contributions of neuropsychological assessment after pediatric TBI is still in its infancy, and thus few interventions or recommendations are as yet evidence-based. However, the general "neurological" validity of psychometric testing has been demonstrated throughout the extensive outcome literature – that is, numerous tests and certain rating scales have been shown to discriminate youth with moderate to severe TBI from other children. This discriminatory power clearly provides support for the utility of neuropsychological testing in characterizing the impact of TBI. The ability of tests to predict or change specific functional outcomes – the "ecological" validity of the tests – has received far less study. As discussed below, clinical neuropsychological assessment involves more than simply "testing"; the benefits of the neuropsychological assessment process beyond the sensitivity of the actual test scores remain to be investigated in detail.

Whether explicitly stated or not, all clinical neuropsychological assessments are based on a theoretical framework, which drives data collection, interpretation, and management. We approach our clinical neuropsychological assessments from the perspective of the Neurodevelopmental Systems Model, first detailed by Holmes-Bernstein and Waber [63] and elaborated further on a number of occasions. The model is founded on several conceptual assumptions about childhood behavior and specifies a particular methodology by which neuropsychological assessments are conducted. We believe these assumptions and methods have relevance for clinically framing the TBI outcome literature and guiding clinical assessments after pediatric TBI.

The model's first assumption is that clinical assessments should be conducted with the goal of improving the real-world **adaptation** of the child. The days are long past when the value of a neuropsychological assessment was to document a cognitive or behavioral

profile in order to determine the presence or location of "organic brain damage". Neuropsychological assessment as a clinical endeavor has evolved to find its fundamental utility in systematically describing the functional consequences of brain perturbation and using these data to facilitate the adaptation of the child within a given environmental and developmental context.

The model's next assumption is that the **brain** is the necessary substrate for all behavior. Thus, understanding injury-related neuropathology is crucial to documenting post-injury behavior. The past reliance of pediatric neuropsychology on adult models of brain–behavior relationships is rapidly giving way to more nuanced and developmentally framed models to guide both research and practice. Newer imaging technologies, in particular, hold promise for relating the behavior of children of different ages to more specific neural substrates in typically developing and injured youngsters alike.

Understanding the role of the brain in behavior is never sufficient in isolation, however, as behavior is always the product of a dynamic interplay between both brain and **contextual** variables. Thus, in order to fully appreciate the impact of TBI on a child, the clinician must examine both the pre-injury environment in which the child developed and the post-injury environment in which the child will be expected to function.

Finally, when assessing the child specifically, neuropsychologists need to have a solid grasp of the principles of **development**. As typically developing youngsters negotiate their way through childhood and adolescence, the contexts in which they are expected to function change in tandem with expected neurobiological maturation – typically becoming more demanding as youngsters gain in skill and capacity. For the child with TBI, the developmental trajectory may well be derailed as a function of behavioral deficits secondary to brain insult. Such a child is then at significant risk for failing to meet the contextual expectations of the wider environment – and for further limitations on optimal development. An important contribution of the neuropsychologist is the careful evaluation of the match between the child's capacities and the expectations to be met – with the goal of designing interventions that will promote optimal developmental progress.

In addition to these core assumptions, the Neurodevelopmental Systems Model specifies that clinical neuropsychological assessment encompasses two primary tasks: evaluation and management. Evaluation is focused on collecting and interpreting data relevant to understanding the *brain-context-development* matrix for any given child, and management is focused on using these data to facilitate the real-world adaptation of the particular child.

Neuropsychological evaluation

Within the framework of the developmental systems model, data for the neuropsychological evaluation are derived from three, equally weighted sources: historical information, systematic observations, and test data. Research focused on the impact of pediatric TBI has clearly highlighted the necessity of considering each of these sources when conducting neuropsychological assessments.

Historical data

To fully appreciate the consequences of TBI, the importance of collecting thorough pre-injury historical information cannot be overstated. Brain injuries in children are not randomly distributed in the general population: different patterns of pre-injury functioning are associated with increased risk for injury. Inattentive or impulsive children engage in more risky behavior that increases their likelihood of injuries, including head injuries. As discussed previously, the rate of pre-injury ADHD in children who go on to suffer TBI is probably at least twice as high as that seen in the general population. Rates of premorbid cognitive and academic difficulties and familial stressors may also be higher in children who sustain TBI [64]. For the clinician, this means that behaviors attributed to the injury must be scrutinized carefully to determine precisely what is new, changed, or unexpected in the child's post-injury functioning.

Not only are pre-injury characteristics likely to dispose certain children to sustain injuries, but as previously explored, pre-injury child and family variables have also been found to independently contribute to or moderate post-injury child outcomes, over and above injury-related and developmental factors. Thus, a comprehensive understanding of pre-injury status is important not only for evaluating the accuracy of post-injury attributions, but also for making predictions about which children are likely to be at most risk for post-injury problems.

The clinical history after TBI also needs to include detailed injury-related information, with particular attention to the severity of injury. Length of hospital stay and the type and intensity of inpatient and outpatient treatment may provide indirect information about injury status. GCS scores can be used to document severity level more specifically, though clinicians should be mindful of the interpretive challenges of the GCS, especially in very young children [65]. As mentioned, markers of neurobiological recovery such as PTA may relate better to certain neurobehavioral outcomes than GCS scores; however, in practice, PTA is documented inconsistently in medical records and retrospective ratings can be unreliable. When examining neuroimaging data, clinicians should consider that the technology and timing of the study will influence results. Computed tomography (CT) scans have been used for decades to rapidly detect surgically significant lesions in the acute care setting, a task that they still perform impressively well. However, in comparison to MRI, CT scans are less effective in detecting subtle neuropathology and can be expected to correlate less well with neurobehavioral outcome. Moreover, any type of neuroimaging conducted on the day of injury or in the sub-acute period may not adequately characterize the extent of injury-related pathology, as it may take several weeks to months before the full extent of trauma-induced neural degeneration and other pathology become manifest.

From a clinical perspective, relevant historical data need to include, at a minimum, information about the injury mechanism, severity, and circumstances; recovery and treatment course; family factors such as pre- and post-injury coping styles/functioning, socioeconomic status, educational background, and familial-genetic history; and the child's pre-injury development including information about pregnancy, labor, and delivery, attainment of developmental milestones, medical status, educational experience, and psychosocial functioning. The means by which these developmental data can be collected include pre-injury parental ratings using behavioral checklists, although clinicians should bear in mind that such ratings may underestimate premorbid psychiatric problems [66]. A thorough clinical interview is always indicated, to allow for in-depth coverage of pre-injury child development and functioning, as well as family and school environmental factors. Given the subjective nature of parental and patient report, corroborative data such as educational and medical records are likely to be particularly useful in ensuring the accuracy of the historical information.

Observational data

Observational data after TBI can provide information beyond that which can be gathered by history or tests alone. In general, pediatric behavioral observations can be subsumed heuristically under five categories: (1) observations reported or elicited either in interviews with individuals familiar with the child's behavior in non-clinical (natural) contexts or from structured questionnaires; (2) direct examination of the child (e.g. size, body habitus, facial features, personal hygiene, dress); (3) direct observation of the child–parent interaction during the clinical contacts; (4) analysis of the child's behavior in the examiner–child dyad; and (5) observation of the child under specific performance demands [67].

Clinician observations of child–adult and child–peer interactions and child behavior in general can be direct, as in observations of parent–child interactions in the clinical interview or in the course of evaluation, or indirect, as obtained from careful interviewing by a skilled clinician either in person or by telephone. After TBI specifically, observations of parent–child interactions can serve as a useful window into the often disrupted post-injury family dynamics. Analysis of the child's behavior can also offer information about neurobehavioral domains that are commonly affected by TBI but may be difficult to capture through tests alone (e.g. self-regulation), as well as data about how a child qualitatively responds to conditions likely to be encountered in everyday settings (e.g. time demands, possible distractions, expectation for initiation). Observation of the child during the completion of formal tests also provides a critical check on the validity of the test data. Both interview data and behavioral observations during evaluation are also the source of specific anecdotes that can be used to help facilitate parent or teacher understanding of the results. As yet, no identified studies have demonstrated the incremental value of examiner-based observations after pediatric TBI, although data do suggest standardized and norm-referenced measures of test session behavior have utility in pediatric assessment more generally [68].

The value of parent-based observational data after pediatric TBI has been demonstrated in a number of studies using the Behavior Rating Inventory of Executive Function (BRIEF [69]). The BRIEF is a rating scale developed to evaluate executive functioning of individuals in everyday settings. Normative data and psychometric properties are well established. The parent-completed version has been found to be sensitive to the severity of TBI [24, 70]. The BRIEF provides data about executive functions distinct from performance-based measures, which have been criticized as lacking ecological validity after pediatric TBI. Relationships between the BRIEF and real-world outcomes have also been established, with parental ratings showing associations with child behavioral adjustment and adaptive functioning, as well as parental psychological distress, family burden, and general family functioning [24].

Psychological test data

In addition to a thorough history and systematic observation, well-standardized, performance-based psychological and psychoeducational tests are indispensable to understanding a child's unique post-injury neuropsychological profile. The worth of testing is unlikely to derive exclusively from a specific test or test battery, which will change as psychometric technology evolves. Rather, the primary value of testing stems from the fact that TBI is known to impact a variety of neurobehavioral domains, and psychometric testing is the best-demonstrated methodology to evaluate neurobehavioral performance relative to age expectations.

After pediatric TBI, no particular battery of tests has been shown to be more or less sensitive or valid. However, the literature on the outcomes of TBI does indicate that clinicians should avoid an over-reliance on tests of automatized information or functioning (e.g. many academic tests) and ensure sufficient coverage of more dynamic processes such as speeded processing, learning and memory, and attention/executive control. Given the differences in outcome expected at different ages, clinicians should consider targeting different skills depending on the age at injury. For example, in terms of language skills, clinicians may want to conduct a more thorough evaluation of basic linguistic skills (e.g. phonological awareness and lexical skills) when evaluating a child injured in infancy or the preschool years, while focusing on higher-level communication skills for older children. Numerous resources are available to assist in the development of a comprehensive, pediatric-focused test battery. Baron [71] and Strauss et al. [72] may be especially worthwhile, as they include coverage of both the general and TBI-related psychometric properties of many commonly used pediatric tests.

Of the many available tests, the California Verbal Learning Test–Children's Version (CVLT-C [73]) stands out as an example of a particularly well-investigated instrument after pediatric TBI. The CVLT-C measures verbal learning and memory in children from age 5 through 16 using a five-trial list-learning paradigm. Internal consistency has been well documented; test–retest reliabilities are less robust. Relevant validity data for the CVLT-C after TBI have been reported in a number of studies. Mottram and Donders [74] demonstrated that a four-factor model (Attention Span, Learning Efficiency, Delayed Recall, and Inaccurate Recall) underlies performance of children with TBI, similar to that seen in healthy children. Criterion-related evidence has also been provided, as performance has been shown to be sensitive to injury severity [75]. Speed of information-processing may in part mediate the effect of injury on CVLT-C performance [76], and males may be at increased risk for retrieval problems following TBI [77]. A study by Miller and Donders [78] found that children who obtained a composite T score of less than 45 on the total list-learning trials soon after a moderate-severe TBI were 8–13-times more likely to be placed in special education 1–2 years later. This was above and beyond both injury severity indicators and demographic characteristics, nicely illustrating the potential predictive validity of post-TBI test data in accounting for real-world outcomes.

Neuropsychological management

Evidence-based practice depends not only on research evidence but also on the clinician's expertise – the ability to select and apply relevant evidence in the service of the child and family (see Bernstein, Chapter 2a, this volume). The clinician's expertise is nowhere more important than during clinical management. Within the Neurodevelopmental Systems Model, management consists of two components: (1) education of the child, family, educators, and/or allied health professionals; and (2) delineation of a set of specific recommendations that can optimally promote the child's success. Each component is shaped by the *brain-context-development* framework of the guiding assessment model [79].

Education of the child, family, and wider community takes place during both the feedback or interpretative session(s) held with the child and parents, and the written neuropsychological report. No identified studies have examined the specific contribution of the neuropsychologist in providing education about moderate to severe TBI or its consequences. Parents do, however, consistently report a general desire for more information and education after pediatric TBI [80]. Given the extensive data collected during a neuropsychological assessment and neuropsychologists' background and training in both neurological and psychological principles, they are uniquely positioned to play an important role in meeting this educational need.

When developing child-specific recommendations, the neuropsychologist must make the link between the evaluation data and those interventions that are most likely to optimize the child's progress [79]. In doing so, the clinician draws from a considerable knowledge base about child development, psychological adjustment, behavioral management, educational techniques and accommodations, family systems, medical interventions, and brain injury rehabilitation. However, as yet, the direct evidence for interventions that respond specifically to the outcomes of pediatric TBI remains relatively sparse, with a particular dearth of randomized controlled trials. Empirical work that can be expected to have most application to neuropsychological management can be grouped into several areas: rehabilitation, pharmacological, psychosocial, and educational.

Rehabilitation

In adult populations, considerable evidence supports the efficacy of rehabilitation in addressing cognitive deficits, at least in certain domains. In children, only a few Class I or Class II rehabilitation studies exist. A recent review by Laatsch et al. [81] resulted in two practice guidelines: (1) service providers should consider providing attention remediation to assist recovery after acquired brain injury, and (2) comprehensive pediatric rehabilitation programs should consider involving the family members as active treatment providers in the rehabilitation treatment team. These guidelines were based largely on the noteworthy work of van't Hooft and colleagues in Sweden and Braga and colleagues from Brazil (as well as Butler and Copeland's work focused on pediatric cancer).

van't Hooft et al. [82] randomized 38 children aged 9 to 16 years with TBI and other types of acquired brain injures into treatment and control groups. The treatment group trained for 30 minutes per day for

17 weeks with the Amsterdam Memory and Attention Training program for children (AMAT-C). The primary training was provided by the child's parent or teacher, with weekly professional consultation. At the end of training, significant treatment effects were seen on lab-based tests of attention and memory, with minimal effect on speeded performance. These beneficial effects were maintained at 6-month follow-up [83]. The results of these studies are quite promising, though further research will be needed to investigate whether the effects generalize to children's everyday functioning and whether the results would be maintained in groups of TBI children exclusively.

Braga and colleagues [84] randomized 87 children aged 5 to 12 years with TBI to receive cognitive and physical rehabilitation services from hospital-based clinicians or by family members with clinician training and supervision. All children received 12 months of intensive individualized services. The study demonstrated that parents, many of whom were not well educated, were able to learn the skills needed to deliver interventions within the everyday routines of the child. Both groups demonstrated improvements, although only the children in the family-supported group demonstrated statistically significant improvement on the Wechsler Intelligence Scale for Children–Third Edition and measures of physical functioning.

Pharmacological intervention

In recent years attention has been given to developing evidence-based guidelines for the use of psychopharmacological agents in managing the neurobehavioral consequences of TBI in adults. In children, the treatment of TBI-related problems with psychotropic medication is not at all well studied, despite common use in practice. Psychostimulants are the most researched agent, probably because of the frequency of attention/regulatory problems after TBI and the success of stimulants in treating developmentally based ADHD. However, even with stimulants, results of TBI-focused studies have been mixed. Existing studies suggest that treatment effects on behavior (hyperactivity, impulsivity) may be greater than on cognition, but that effects overall may be less apparent than those seen in developmental ADHD populations [85].

Psychosocial intervention

Few randomized, controlled studies have investigated psychosocial interventions after pediatric TBI, though

management ideas can be garnered from the child psychology literature generally and a number of TBI-specific models and case studies. The limited pediatric TBI-specific research does suggest that interventions derived from traditional applied behavioral analysis methodologies, as well as those grounded in the provision of proactive, antecedent-focused support, may reduce behavioral problems after TBI [86].

Though not focused on child psychosocial functioning exclusively, the randomized controlled studies of Wade and colleagues aimed at improving family functioning deserve particular mention, given their quality and the contribution of familial-related variables to child psychosocial outcomes. Wade et al. [87] developed a family problem-solving program to provide information to families about TBI, as well as training in problem-solving skills, family communication, and antecedent behavior management. The intervention was provided originally in face-to-face sessions that included parents, children with TBI, and siblings over a 6-month period. This intervention resulted in improvements in childhood internalizing symptoms, depression/anxiety, and withdrawal. The intervention was then adapted to be provided in an on-line format, which was found in a small non-randomized study to reduce childhood behavioral problems and improve parent–child conflict [88]. These researchers also reported on a randomized clinical trial involving 40 families assigned to receive the online intervention or general internet resource support [89]. The intervention group displayed reduced parental levels of global distress, depressive symptoms, and anxiety. These findings were consistent with a small study by Singer and colleagues [90], which also found that a stress-management group was more effective in reducing parental anxiety and depression than simply providing information during a parent-based support group.

Educational support

In the USA, the average length of a hospital stay after pediatric TBI has been decreasing in recent years, and comprehensive outpatient rehabilitation programs have become less available. Thus, much post-injury rehabilitation and support is now expected to occur within the educational system. Unfortunately, quality research examining specific educational interventions after pediatric TBI is strikingly absent, perhaps in part because of the significant variability in the needs and settings of each child. Given the lack of direct empirical support, at this point, empirically backed school intervention following TBI must rely on indirect studies conducted with populations who may display similar manifest problems (e.g. ADHD). Ylvisaker et al. [91] have summarized much of this research.

Prevention

The frequency and consequences of pediatric TBI and the few proven interventions make clear the importance of prevention efforts. Approaches to prevention have traditionally been classified as primary, secondary, or tertiary. Primary TBI prevention aims to prevent the trauma entirely, which can be expected to be most effective when grounded in an understanding of the common causes of injury across development. In children, a number of such programs have demonstrated success, including home visitation by trained professionals focused on preventing child abuse [92], mandatory youth bicycle-helmet legislation [93], and graduated driver licensing programs for teens [94]. Because primary prevention will never be entirely successful in eliminating TBI, minimizing adverse outcomes and disability once injury occurs will have value as well. Secondary TBI prevention is geared toward limiting the evolving and delayed neurobiological effects of injury and is the major goal of all pre-hospital and acute health care. The recent attempts to establish evidence-based guidelines for the acute medical management of severe pediatric TBI is an example of a comprehensive secondary prevention effort [95]. Tertiary prevention aims to maximize the child's functioning once the effects of injury become manifest and includes the various approaches to pediatric rehabilitation and symptom management highlighted above.

Future research directions

Neuropsychologically focused research has contributed substantially to the rapidly growing scientific knowledge base of pediatric TBI. Practicing neuropsychologists now have sufficient data to anticipate and evaluate the common consequences of injury, examine plausible factors affecting individual outcomes, and assist in developing scientifically informed management plans. Despite this solid research foundation, considerable future work remains.

Neuropsychological outcome studies have recently moved away from the historical emphasis on neurocognition to consider the broader impact of TBI.

Nonetheless, ongoing investigation will be necessary to more fully capture the socioemotional effects of injury, as well as the everyday functional consequences for children with TBI, families, and the educational and healthcare systems. Further delineation of the mechanisms by which neural, contextual, and developmental variables influence outcomes will also be necessary, which should be especially valuable in allowing early identification and intervention for those youth and families at greatest risk. Preliminary data suggest that certain areas of neurobehavioral deficit may be "primary" (e.g. slowed processing, poor working memory), which may in turn account for downstream problems in other cognitive and functional areas (e.g. memory deficits, school failure). Initial data also suggest that brain–behavior relationships will differ at least to some extent in children compared with adults following TBI. Increasingly sophisticated models will be needed to clarify these relationships, with an eye toward developmentally minded evaluation and treatment prioritization. Given the limited amount of sound longitudinal research available currently, following children over lengthier post-injury periods should continue to be a high priority. Such research will be necessary to appreciate the evolving consequences of pediatric TBI and how child and family needs change over different developmental periods.

Clinically, newer imaging methods and biological markers will undoubtedly gain prominence in the years ahead in documenting the pathological effects of TBI. A key question will be whether or not these technologies add to outcome prediction and the understanding of brain–behavior relationships beyond currently available data. In order to substantiate the value of neuropsychological evaluation, ongoing research will be required to establish that psychometric instruments have sufficient reliability and validity in TBI populations specifically. A pressing long-term goal for the field will also be to move past the examination of specific tests to demonstrate the incremental validity of the neuropsychological assessment process (and neuropsychologist) more broadly – in predicting outcomes, in developing principled and effective intervention strategies, and as a change agent in and of itself. In other words, research is needed to show that neuropsychological evaluations, recommendations, feedback meetings, reports, etc. make a difference in the real-world lives of children and families. Once established, an even more significant challenge awaits: specifying exactly which aspects of the assessment process benefit whom under what circumstances. Finally, one of the most glaring areas of need continues to be TBI-specific intervention, where few randomized, controlled trials exist. Particularly worthwhile for neuropsychologists will be emphasizing how neuropsychological data can help to drive efficacious intervention by, for example, classifying children and/or families into groups using evaluation results and then demonstrating group by treatment interactions.

References

1. Carroll LJ, Cassidy JD, Peloso PM, Borg J, von Holst H, Holm L, et al. Prognosis for mild traumatic brain injury: results of the WHO collaborating centre task force on mild traumatic brain injury. *J Rehabil Med* 2004;**43** (Suppl):84–105.

2. Kirkwood MW, Yeates KO, Taylor HG, Randolph C, McCrea M, Anderson V. Management of pediatric mild traumatic brain injury: a neuropsychological review from injury through recovery. *Clin Neuropsychol* 2007;**22**:769–800.

3. Langlois JA, Rutland-Brown W, Thomas KE. *Traumatic brain injury in the United States: Emergency department visits, hospitalizations, and deaths.* Atlanta: Centers for Disease Control and Prevention, National Center for Injury Prevention and Control; 2006.

4. Schneier AJ, Shields BJ, Hostetler SG, Xiang H, Smith G. Incidence of pediatric traumatic brain injury and associated hospital resource utilization in the United States. *Pediatrics* 2006;**118**(2):483–92.

5. Keenan HT, Bratton SL. Epidemiology and outcomes of pediatric traumatic brain injury. *Dev Neurosci* 2006;**28**(4–5):256–63.

6. Langlois JA, Rutland-Brown W, Thomas KE. The incidence of traumatic brain injury among children in the United States: differences by race. *J Head Trauma Rehabil* 2005;**20**(3):229–38.

7. Kraus JF. Epidemiological features of brain injury in children: occurrence, children at risk, causes, and manner of injury, severity, and outcomes. In: Broman SH, Michel ME, eds. *Traumatic Head Injury in Children.* New York: Oxford University Press; 1995: 22–39.

8. Giza CC, Mink RB, Madikians A. Pediatric traumatic brain injury: not just little adults. *Curr Opin Crit Care* 2007;**13**(2):143–52.

9. Kochanek PM. Pediatric traumatic brain injury: quo vadis? *Dev Neurosci* 2006;**28**(4–5):244–55.

10. Anderson VA, Catroppa C, Haritou F, Morse S, Rosenfeld JV. Identifying factors contributing to child and family outcome 30 months after traumatic brain injury in children. *J Neurol Neurosurg Psychiatry* 2005;**76**(3):401–8.

11. Ewing-Cobbs L, Prasad MR, Kramer L, Cox CS Jr., Baumgartner J, Fletcher S, et al. Late intellectual and academic outcomes following traumatic brain injury sustained during early childhood. *J Neurosurg* 2006;**105**(4 Suppl):287–96.

12. Tremont G, Mittenberg W, Miller L. Acute intellectual effects of pediatric head trauma. *Child Neuropsychol* 1999;**5**:104–14.

13. Donders J, Janke K. Criterion validity of the Wechsler Intelligence Scale for Children-Fourth Edition after pediatric traumatic brain injury. *J Int Neuropsychol Soc* 2008;**14**(4):651–5.

14. Ewing-Cobbs L, Barnes M. Linguistic outcomes following traumatic brain injury in children. *Semin Pediatr Neurol* 2002;**9**(3):209–17.

15. Lehnung M, Leplow B, Herzog A, Benz B, Ritz A, Stolze H, et al. Children's spatial behavior is differentially affected after traumatic brain injury. *Child Neuropsychol* 2001;**7**(2):59–71.

16. Yeates KO, Taylor HG, Wade SL, Drotar D, Stancin T, Minich N. A prospective study of short- and long-term neuropsychological outcomes after traumatic brain injury in children. *Neuropsychology* 2002;**16**(4):514–23.

17. Catroppa C, Anderson V. Recovery in memory function, and its relationship to academic success, at 24 months following pediatric TBI. *Child Neuropsychol* 2007;**13**(3):240–61.

18. Ward H, Shum D, McKinlay L, Baker S, Wallace G. Prospective memory and pediatric traumatic brain injury: effects of cognitive demand. *Child Neuropsychol* 2007;**13**(3):219–39.

19. Catroppa C, Anderson VA, Morse SA, Haritou F, Rosenfeld JV. Children's attentional skills 5 years post-TBI. *J Pediatr Psychol* 2007;**32**(3):354–69.

20. Mandalis A, Kinsella G, Ong B, Anderson V. Working memory and new learning following pediatric traumatic brain injury. *Dev Neuropsychol* 2007;**32**(2):683–701.

21. Anderson V, Catroppa C, Morse S, Haritou F, Rosenfeld J. Attentional and processing skills following traumatic brain injury in early childhood. *Brain Inj* 2005;**19**(9):699–710.

22. Ganesalingam K, Sanson A, Anderson V, Yeates KO. Self-regulation and social and behavioral functioning following childhood traumatic brain injury. *J Int Neuropsychol Soc* 2006;**12**(5):609–21.

23. Levin HS, Song J, Ewing-Cobbs L, Roberson G. Porteus Maze performance following traumatic brain injury in children. *Neuropsychology* 2001;**15**(4):557–67.

24. Mangeot S, Armstrong K, Colvin A, Yeates K, Taylor H. Long-term executive function deficits in children with

traumatic brain injuries: assessment using the Behavior Rating Inventory of Executive Function (BRIEF). *Child Neuropsychol* 2002;**8**(4):271–84.

25. Taylor HG, Yeates KO, Wade SL, Drotar D, Stancin T, Minich N. A prospective study of short- and long-term outcomes after traumatic brain injury in children: behavior and achievement. *Neuropsychology* 2002;**16**(1):15–27.

26. Yeates KO, Bigler ED, Dennis M, Gerhardt C, Rubin K, Stancin T, et al. Social outcomes in childhood brain disorder: a heuristic integration of social neuroscience and developmental psychology. *Psychol Bull* 2007;**133**(3):535–56.

27. Yeates KO, Swift E, Taylor HG, Wade SL, Drotar D, Stancin T, et al. Short- and long-term social outcomes following pediatric traumatic brain injury. *J Int Neuropsychol Soc* 2004;**10**(3):412–26.

28. Schwartz L, Taylor HG, Drotar D, Yeates KO, Wade SL, Stancin T. Long-term behavior problems following pediatric traumatic brain injury: prevalence, predictors, and correlates. *J Pediatr Psychol* 2003;**28**(4):251–63.

29. Max JE, Koele SL, Castillo CC, Lindgren SD, Arndt S, Bokura H, et al. Personality change disorder in children and adolescents following traumatic brain injury. *J Int Neuropsychol Soc* 2000;**6**(3):279–89.

30. Yeates KO, Armstrong K, Janusz J, Taylor HG, Wade S, Stancin T, et al. Long-term attention problems in children with traumatic brain injury. *J Am Acad Child Adolesc Psychiatry* 2005;**44**(6):574–84.

31. Levin H, Hanten G, Max J, Li X, Swank P, Ewing-Cobbs L, et al. Symptoms of attention-deficit/hyperactivity disorder following traumatic brain injury in children. *J Dev Behav Pediatr* 2007;**28**(2):108–18.

32. Max JE, Castillo CS, Bokura H, Robin DA, Lindgren SD, Smith WL, Jr., et al. Oppositional defiant disorder symptomatology after traumatic brain injury: a prospective study. *J Nerv Ment Dis* 1998;**186**(6):325–32.

33. Luis CA, Mittenberg W. Mood and anxiety disorders following pediatric traumatic brain injury: a prospective study. *J Clin Exp Neuropsychol* 2002;**24**(3):270–9.

34. Vasa RA, Gerring JP, Grados M, Slomine B, Christensen JR, Rising W, et al. Anxiety after severe pediatric closed head injury. *J Am Acad Child Adolesc Psychiatry* 2002;**41**(2):148–56.

35. Max JE, Koele SL, Lindgren SD, Robin DA, Smith WL, Jr., Sato Y, et al. Adaptive functioning following traumatic brain injury and orthopedic injury: a controlled study. *Arch Phys Med Rehabil* 1998;**79**(8):893–9.

36. McCarthy ML, MacKenzie EJ, Durbin DR, Aitken ME, Jaffe KM, Paidas CN, et al. Health-related quality of life during the first year after traumatic brain injury. *Arch Pediatr Adolesc Med* 2006;**160**(3):252–60.

37. Yeates K, Taylor H, Barry C, Drotar D, Wade S, Stancin T. Neurobehavioral symptoms in childhood closed-head injuries: changes in prevalence and correlates during the first year postinjury. *J Pediatr Psychol* 2001;**26**(2):79–91.

38. Ewing-Cobbs L, Barnes M, Fletcher JM, Levin HS, Swank PR, Song J. Modeling of longitudinal academic achievement scores after pediatric traumatic brain injury. *Dev Neuropsychol* 2004;**25**(1–2):107–33.

39. Yeates KO, Taylor HG. Behavior problems in school and their educational correlates among children with traumatic brain injury. *Exceptionality* 2006;**14**(3):141–54.

40. Wade SL, Taylor HG, Drotar D, Stancin T, Yeates K, Minich N. A prospective study of long-term caregiver and family adaptation following brain injury in children. *J Head Trauma Rehabil* 2002;**17**(2):96–111.

41. Sambuco M, Brookes N, Lah S. Paediatric traumatic brain injury: a review of siblings' outcome. *Brain Inj* 2008;**22**(1):7–17.

42. Wade SL, Taylor HG, Yeates KO, Drotar D, Stancin T, Minich NM, et al. Long-term parental and family adaptation following pediatric brain injury. *J Pediatr Psychol* 2006;**31**(10):1072–83.

43. Wade SL, Stancin T, Taylor H, Drotar D, Yeates KO, Minich NM. Interpersonal stressors and resources as predictors of parental adaptation following pediatric traumatic injury. *J Consult Clin Psychol* 2004;**72**(5):776–84.

44. Yeates KO, Taylor HG, Rusin J, Bangert B, Dietrich A, Nuss K, et al. Longitudinal trajectories of post-concussive symptoms in children with mild traumatic brain injuries and their relationship to acute clinical status. *Pediatrics* 2009;**123**:735–43.

45. Kothari S. Prognosis after severe TBI: a practical, evidence-based approach. In Zasler ND, Katz DI, Zafonte RD, eds. *Brain Injury Medicine: Principles and Practice.* New York: Demos Medical Publishing; 2007: 169–200.

46. Yeates KO. Closed-head injury. In Yeates KO, Ris MD, Taylor HG, eds. *Pediatric Neuropsychology: Research, Theory, and Practice.* New York: The Guilford Press; 2000.

47. Wilde EA, Hunter JV, Newsome MR, Scheibel RS, Bigler ED, Johnson JL, et al. Frontal and temporal morphometric findings on MRI in children after moderate to severe traumatic brain injury. *J Neurotrauma* 2005;**22**(3):333–44.

48. Levin HS, Hanten G. Executive functions after traumatic brain injury in children. *Pediatr Neurol* 2005;**33**(2):79–93.

49. Slomine BS, Gerring JP, Grados MA, Vasa R, Brady K, Christensen J, et al. Performance on measures of executive function following pediatric traumatic brain injury. *Brain Inj* 2002;**16**(9):759–72.

50. Power T, Catroppa C, Coleman L, Ditchfield M, Anderson V. Do lesion site and severity predict deficits in attentional control after preschool traumatic brain injury (TBI)? *Brain Inj* 2007;**21**(3):279–92.

51. Salorio CF, Slomine BS, Grados MA, Vasa RA, Christensen JR, Gerring JP. Neuroanatomic correlates of CVLT-C performance following pediatric traumatic brain injury. *J Int Neuropsychol Soc* 2005;**11**(6):686–96.

52. Bonnier C, Marique P, Van Hout A, Potelle D. Neurodevelopmental outcome after severe traumatic brain injury in very young children: role for subcortical lesions. *J Child Neurol* 2007;**22**(5):519–29.

53. Babikian T, Freier MC, Tong KA, Nickerson JP, Wall CJ, Holshouser BA, et al. Susceptibility weighted imaging: neuropsychologic outcome and pediatric head injury. *Pediatr Neurol* 2005;**33**(3):184–94.

54. Wilde EA, Chu Z, Bigler E, Hunter J, Fearing M, Hanten G, et al. Diffusion tensor imaging in the corpus callosum in children after moderate to severe traumatic brain injury. *J Neurotrauma* 2006;**23**(10):1412–26.

55. Babikian T, Freier MC, Ashwal S, Riggs ML, Burley T, Holshouser BA. MR spectroscopy: predicting long-term neuropsychological outcome following pediatric TBI. *J Magn Reson Imaging* 2006;**24**(4):801–11.

56. Taylor HG, Yeates KO, Wade SL, Drotar D, Stancin T, Burant C. Bidirectional child-family influences on outcomes of traumatic brain injury in children. *J Int Neuropsychol Soc* 2001;**7**(6):755–67.

57. Catroppa C, Anderson VA, Morse SA, Haritou F, Rosenfeld J. Outcome and predictors of functional recovery 5 years following pediatric traumatic brain injury (TBI). *J Pediatr Psychol* 2008;**33**(7):707–18.

58. Max JE, Levin HS, Schachar RJ, Landis J, Saunders A, Ewing-Cobbs L, et al. Predictors of personality change due to traumatic brain injury in children and adolescents six to twenty-four months after injury. *J Neuropsychiatry Clin Neurosci* 2006;**18**(1):21–32.

59. Kolb B, Gibb R. Brain plasticity and recovery from early cortical injury. *Dev Psychobiol* 2007;**49**(2):107–18.

60. Bates E, Reilly J, Wulfeck B, Dronkers N, Opie M, Fenson J, et al. Differential effects of unilateral lesions on language production in children and adults. *Brain Lang* 2001;**79**(2):223–65.

61. Anderson V, Catroppa C, Morse S, Haritou F, Rosenfeld J. Functional plasticity or vulnerability after early brain injury? *Pediatrics* 2005;**116**(6):1374–82.

62. Ewing-Cobbs L, Prasad MR, Landry SH, Kramer L, DeLeon R. Executive functions following traumatic brain injury in young children: a preliminary analysis. *Dev Neuropsychol* 2004;**26**(1):487–512.

63. Holmes-Bernstein J, Waber DP. Developmental neuropsychological assessment: The systematic approach. In Boulton AA, Baker GB, Hiscock M, eds. *Neuromethods:* Vol. 17, *Neuropsychology*. Clifton, NJ: Humana Press; 1990: 311–71.

64. Goldstrohm SL, Arffa S. Preschool children with mild to moderate traumatic brain injury: an exploration of immediate and post-acute morbidity. *Arch Clin Neuropsychol* 2005;**20**(6):675–95.

65. Simpson DA, Cockington RA, Hanieh A, Raftos J, Reilly P. Head injuries in infants and young children: the value of the Paediatric Coma Scale. Review of literature and report on a study. *Childs Nerv Syst* 1991;**7**(4):183–90.

66. Bloom DR, Levin HS, Ewing-Cobbs L, Saunders AE, Song J, Fletcher JM, et al. Lifetime and novel psychiatric disorders after pediatric traumatic brain injury. *J Am Acad Child Adolesc Psychiatry* 2001;**40**(5):572–9.

67. Holmes JM. History and observations. In Rudel RG, Holmes JM, Pardes JR, eds. *Assessment of Developmental Learning Disorders: A Neuropsychological Approach*. New York: Basic Books; 1988: 144–65.

68. Glutting JJ, Youngstrom EA, Oakland T, Watkins M. Situational specificity and generality of test behaviors for samples of normal and referred children. *School Psychology Review* 1996;**25**:94–107.

69. Gioia GA, Isquith PK, Guy SC, Kenworthy L. *Behavior Rating Inventory of Executive Function Professional Manual*. Odessa, FL: Psychological Assessment Resources; 2000.

70. Nadebaum C, Anderson V, Catroppa C. Executive function outcomes following traumatic brain injury in young children: a five year follow-up. *Dev Neuropsychol* 2007;**32**(2):703–28.

71. Baron IS. *Neuropsychological Evaluation of the Child*. Oxford: Oxford University Press; 2004.

72. Strauss E, Sherman EMS, Spreen O. *A Compendium of Neuropsychological Tests: Administration, Norms, and Commentary*, 3rd edn. Oxford: Oxford University Press; 2006.

73. Delis DC, Kramer JH, Kaplan E, Ober BA. *California Verbal Learning Test–Children's Version*. Austin, TX: The Psychological Corporation; 1994.

74. Mottram L, Donders J. Construct validity of the California Verbal Learning Test – Children's Version (CVLT-C) after pediatric traumatic brain injury. *Psychol Assess* 2005;**17**(2):212–7.

75. Mottram L, Donders J. Cluster subtypes on the California verbal learning test-children's version after pediatric traumatic brain injury. *Dev Neuropsychol* 2006;**30**(3):865–83.

76. Donders J, Minnema MT. Performance discrepancies on the California Verbal Learning Test-Children's Version (CVLT-C) in children with traumatic brain injury. *J Int Neuropsychol Soc* 2004;**10**(4):482–8.

77. Donders J, Hoffman NM. Gender differences in learning and memory after pediatric traumatic brain injury. *Neuropsychology* 2002;**16**(4):491–9.

78. Miller LJ, Donders J. Prediction of educational outcome after pediatric traumatic brain injury. *Rehabilitation Psychology* 2003;**48**:237–41.

79. Bernstein JH. Developmental neuropsychological assessment. In Yeates KO, Ris MD, Taylor HG, eds. *Pediatric Neuropsychology: Research, Theory, and Practice*. New York: The Guilford Press; 2000.

80. Aitken ME, Mele N, Barrett K. Recovery of injured children: parent perspectives on family needs. *Arch Phys Med Rehabil* 2004;**85**(4):567–73.

81. Laatsch L, Harrington D, Hotz G, Marcantuono J, Mozzoni M, Walsh V, et al. An evidence-based review of cognitive and behavioral rehabilitation treatment studies in children with acquired brain injury. *J Head Trauma Rehabil* 2007;**22**(4):248–56.

82. van't Hooft I, Andersson K, Bergman B, Sejersen T, Von Wendt L, Bartfai A. Beneficial effect from a cognitive training programme on children with acquired brain injuries demonstrated in a controlled study. *Brain Inj* 2005;**19**(7):511–8.

83. van't Hooft I, Andersson K, Bergman B, Sejersen T, von Wendt L, Bartfai A. Sustained favorable effects of cognitive training in children with acquired brain injuries. *Neurorehabilitation* 2007;**22**(2):109–16.

84. Braga LW, Da Paz AC, Ylvisaker M. Direct clinician-delivered versus indirect family-supported rehabilitation of children with traumatic brain injury: a randomized controlled trial. *Brain Inj* 2005;**19**(10):819–31.

85. Jin C, Schachar R. Methylphenidate treatment of attention-deficit/hyperactivity disorder secondary to traumatic brain injury: a critical appraisal of treatment studies. *CNS Spectr* 2004;**9**(3):217–26.

86. Ylvisaker M, Turkstra L, Coehlo C, Yorkston K, Kennedy M, Sohlberg M, et al. Behavioural interventions for children and adults with behaviour disorders after TBI: a systematic review of the evidence. *Brain Inj* 2007;**21**(8):769–805.

87. Wade SL, Michaud L, Brown T. Putting the pieces together: preliminary efficacy of a family problem-solving intervention for children with traumatic brain injury. *J Head Trauma Rehabil* 2006;**21**(1):57–67.

88. Wade SL, Wolfe C, Brown T, Pestian J. Putting the pieces together: preliminary efficacy of a web-based family intervention for children with traumatic brain injury. *J Pediatr Psychol* 2005;**30**(5):437–42.

89. Wade SL, Carey J, Wolfe CR. An online family intervention to reduce parental distress following pediatric brain injury. *J Consult Clin Psychol* 2006;**74**(3):445–54.

90. Singer GHS, Glang A, Nixon C, Cooley E, Kerns KA, Williams D, et al. A comparison of two psychosocial interventions for parents of children with acquired brain injury: An exploratory study. *J Head Trauma Rehabil* 1994;**9**:38–49.

91. Ylvisaker M, Todis B, Glang A, Urbanczyk B, Franklin C, DePompei R, et al. Educating students with TBI: themes and recommendations. *J Head Trauma Rehabil* 2001;**16**(1):76–93.

92. Bilukha O, Hahn RA, Crosby A, Fullilove M, Liberman A, Moscicki E, et al. The effectiveness of early childhood home visitation in preventing violence: a systematic review. *Am J Prev Med* 2005;**28**(2 Suppl 1):11–39.

93. Macpherson A, Spinks A. Bicycle helmet legislation for the uptake of helmet use and prevention of head injuries. *Cochrane Database Syst Rev* 2007;(2):CD005401.

94. Chen LH, Baker SP, Li G. Graduated driver licensing programs and fatal crashes of 16-year-old drivers: a national evaluation. *Pediatrics* 2006;**118**(1):56–62.

95. Adelson PD, Bratton SL, Carney NA, Chesnut RM, du Coudray HE, Goldstein B, et al. Guidelines for the acute medical management of severe traumatic brain injury in infants, children, and adolescents. Chapter 1: Introduction. *Pediatr Crit Care Med* 2003;**4**(3 Suppl):S2–4.

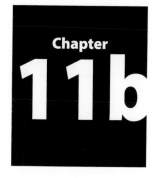

Chapter 11b

Adult outcomes of pediatric traumatic brain injury

Miriam Beauchamp, Julian Dooley and Vicki Anderson

Introduction

Traumatic brain injury (TBI) is one of the most common causes of acquired disability during childhood. While the majority of such injuries are mild, and result in few, if any, functional sequelae, children sustaining more significant insults may experience permanent cognitive and behavioral deficits. Clinical reports indicate residual impairments in a range of skills, particularly information-processing, attention, memory, learning, social function and behavior. These deficits impact on a child's capacity to interact with the environment effectively, resulting in lags in skill acquisition, and increasing gaps between injured children and their age peers, as they move through childhood and into adulthood. Secondary deficits may also emerge, relating to family stress and adjustment difficulties. Treatment and management of the child with TBI and family requires long-term involvement, where the role of the neuropsychologist is to understand the child's difficulties, to inform parents and the wider community of their cognitive and behavioral implications, to liaise with teachers and rehabilitation workers, to design academic and vocational interventions and behavior-management programs, and to provide counseling with respect to adjustment issues for the child and family.

Epidemiology

Population-based studies have recently reported that 750:100 000 children will suffer TBI each year. Of these, fewer than half will seek medical care, 10% will be hospitalized and only 7% will sustain significant head injury [1]. Between 5 and 10% will experience temporary and/or permanent neuropsychological impairment, and 5 to 10% will sustain fatal injuries [2]. When considering adult outcome from such insults, it is frequently assumed that only children with more severe injuries will continue to experience significant sequelae long-term after insult. Examination of data specific to this severe injury group shows that

the mortality rate is approximately one-third, with another third of children making a good recovery, and the last third exhibiting residual disability, at least in the first few years post-injury [3]. To date, very few studies have followed injured children into adulthood to document the frequency and nature of any ongoing deficits.

When considering the long-term impact of TBI in childhood, there are several factors that must be considered, some of which are specific to this particular stage of the life cycle. First, and as for adults, more severe insult is consistently associated with poorer prognosis [4]. In addition, children sustaining TBI are not representative of the population. Boys are more than twice as likely to suffer a TBI [1]. Further, TBI is more common in socially disadvantaged children [5, 6] and in children with pre-existing learning and behavioral deficits [7]. These pre-existing characteristics may increase the young person's risk of experiencing post-injury problems and limit their capacity to access necessary rehabilitation and educational resources, resulting in slower than expected recovery and development and likelihood of residual impairments through childhood and into adulthood. Finally, age is also a key predictor [4], with the nature of pediatric TBI varying with age. Infants are more likely to sustain injury due to falls or child abuse. In fact, infancy is the only developmental stage with a high rate of non-accidental injury, which commonly results in more severe injury and higher mortality and morbidity than accidental injuries [8]. Older children and adolescents are more commonly victims of sporting, cycling, and pedestrian accidents, and assaults.

Pathophysiology

TBI is usually due to a blow or wound to the head, sufficient to cause altered consciousness, and may be classified as penetrating (or open) head injury or closed head injury. The mechanics and underlying pathophysiology of these injuries will differ, depending on the cause of injury, and the degree of the force involved, and may result in a range of possible outcomes. Pathophysiology may be classified according to characteristics of the insult: (i) *primary impact injuries* occur as a direct result of force to the brain, and include fractures, diffuse axonal damage, contusions, and lacerations. Such injuries are generally permanent, and show little response to early treatment; and (ii) *secondary injuries*, such as extradural, subdural, and intracerebral hemorrhage, may result from the primary injury, and are predictive of poor outcome in children [9]. Raised intra-cranial pressure, brain swelling, hypoxia, infection, and metabolic changes, including hypothermia, electrolyte imbalance, and respiratory difficulties may also occur [10]. If not treated quickly, usually via surgical intervention, these secondary complications may cause cerebral herniation and ultimately death. Recent investigations have found that secondary damage may also result from neurochemical processes. Elevated levels of excitatory amino acids, such as glutamate and aspartate, have been detected in cerebrospinal fluid immediately post TBI, and found to persist for several days, causing disruption to cell function, and eventual cell death [11].

Penetrating injuries account for approximately 10% of all childhood TBI, and refer to injuries which involve penetration of the skull by some form of "missile". Injury tends to be localized around the path of the missile, with additional damage resulting from skull fragments or shattered fragments from the missile itself. Secondary damage may occur due to cerebral infection (from the alien object entering the brain), swelling, bleeding, and raised intra-cranial pressure. Loss of consciousness is relatively uncommon, but neurological deficits and post-traumatic epilepsy are frequently observed. Neurobehavioral sequelae tend to reflect the focal nature of the insult, and children often exhibit specific deficits consistent with the localization of the lesion, with other skills intact.

Closed head injury is more common and refers to an insult where the skull is not penetrated, but rather the brain is shaken within the skull cavity, resulting in multiple injury sites, as well as diffuse axonal damage. Damage results from compression and deformation of the skull at the point of impact. The primary pathology includes contusion, or bruising, at point of impact of the blow and at other cerebral sites. Specific areas of the brain are particularly vulnerable to such damage, including the temporal lobes and basal frontal regions.

The characteristic pattern of neurobehavioral consequences reflects involvement of these regions, and includes impaired attention, processing speed and executive abilities.

Functional manifestations

Consequences of adult TBI are well established, with findings indicating significant problems (physical, cognitive dysfunction, educational, vocational opportunity, psychological) persisting even several decades post-injury, and including social and psychiatric disturbance [12, 13]. In comparison, the long-term consequences of childhood TBI remain poorly understood. One of the major difficulties faced by professionals working with children with TBI is predicting outcome and determining priorities for intervention and follow-up. Some researchers argue for the presence of serious and persisting sequelae, even after the mildest of insults; however, opportunities to follow these children into adulthood are limited, and it is likely that clinical perceptions of long-term outcome may be negatively skewed, with only those children with severe ongoing problems presenting for services in the long term post-injury.

To date, only a handful of studies have followed survivors of childhood TBI into adulthood, with somewhat conflicting results, possibly due to inherent methodological problems of longitudinal research, including sample attrition and bias and changes in diagnostic and treatment approaches over time. While only a few studies have reported on adult outcome after mild TBI in childhood, results are consistent, and suggest very few long-term neurobehavioral consequences [14, 15], although psychological problems are more common [16, 17].

In contrast, there is a growing body of research addressing adult outcome from more severe TBI in childhood. Even in these studies reports of gross neurobehavioral impairment are rare, and most survivors tend to manage adequately through their school years [18, 19]. Where cognitive problems are detected, they tend to be in the more dynamic domains of attention, memory, and processing speed [20–22]. Persisting medical and physical problems are more common [17, 23], as are vocational and educational difficulties [13, 17, 18, 22]. Social and psychiatric problems are, however, the most highly represented and include social maladjustment and isolation, poor quality of life, depression, attention deficits, and family problems

Table 11b.1. Functional characteristics of adults with childhood TBI.

Cognitive difficulties	Attention Processing speed Executive deficits
Psychiatric disorders	ADHD Depression Adjustment disorder
Adaptive disorders	Academic failure Unemployment
Social problems	Isolation Low rates of participation

[13, 17, 21], with an association between both pre-injury factors and injury severity and presence of disabilities. See Table 11b.1 for a list of the common functional characteristics of adults with childhood TBI.

Outcome from child TBI is highly variable, and a number of factors have been established as contributing to recovery, at least up to 5 years post-insult: injury severity and injury age, pre-morbid characteristics of the child and psychosocial factors [4, 14, 23]. Other factors of potential importance include access to rehabilitation and other resources, child and family adjustment and degree of residual disability [4, 24]. The limited body of research addressing long-term effects of childhood TBI suggests that similar factors may be relevant for long-term outcome [22, 25], although the research emphasis has been almost entirely on injury-based predictors to date.

Assessment of neurobehavioral outcomes and functional abilities

Neuropsychological assessment plays an important part in diagnostic, recovery and rehabilitation processes post-TBI, and the characteristics of such childhood assessments at the acute stage are described in Chapter 11a.

Assessment is more frequent and long-term for severely injured individuals who suffer serious deficits that impact significantly on their ability to function in daily life. Ongoing assessment of function is necessary to track the development of cognition post-injury and to identify changing needs as the brain recovers and environmental demands change (e.g. re-integration to school or work). This is true for the post-acute phase, but is equally important in the very long term. Though cognitive deficits usually improve during

the 2 years post-injury in children, recovery plateaus after this time and remaining deficits will continue to impact on functioning into adulthood [26, 27]. Survivors of pediatric TBI may even appear to make a full recovery in the initial stages post-injury, with "latent" TBI symptoms emerging only months or even years after injury as later developmental milestones fail to be attained [28].

Neuropsychological assessment is of benefit throughout the lifespan. By the time individuals injured during childhood reach early adulthood, they are generally well aware of the lasting effects of their injury on various spheres of their lives. As they move through the transitions to adulthood, it may be necessary to re-evaluate their capacity to cope, both cognitively and emotionally, with new demands and responsibilities. For example, a change in employment may cause new challenges by tapping previously unused skills or by increasing cognitive demands. Difficulties in dealing with such changes may require an assessment to identify areas of dysfunction and how these may be compensated so the individual can better manage their new environment.

Neuropsychological outcomes after childhood TBI are partially a function of brain plasticity. Long-term evaluation therefore requires an understanding of neural reorganization, maturation and degeneration, as well as their interaction with developmental growth and experience. Contrary to traditional views, findings now indicate that infants and children who sustain severe injuries are particularly vulnerable to residual cognitive impairments [4]. Long-term follow-up, monitoring and management is of particular importance for these at-risk individuals. Although some restoration of function may occur, the late appearance of cognitive and behavioral problems may be associated with a failure of particular brain regions (and their associated cognitive skills) to develop, either as a direct result of TBI or due to progressive atrophy or loss of neural activity [28, 29]. These processes may lead to atypical patterns of cognitive function due to structural and functional re-assignment in the injured brain. Accordingly, individuals who demonstrate similar performance levels on a particular test may in fact be relying on different neural substrates. This suggests that assessments in the long term should rely on refined methods capable of detecting subtle cognitive variations and compensation strategies.

The unique characteristics of adult outcomes of childhood TBI have consequences for the goal and structure of remote neuropsychological assessment, which must be considered as distinct from the early, post-acute and developmental evaluations following injury and different to the acute assessment of mature adults who sustain injuries. Some of the objectives of these 'late' assessments may include: (a) developing an up-to-date cognitive profile in keeping with the patient's environment; (b) identifying "chronic" neuropsychological impairments; (c) re-assessing cognitive, behavioral and social functions in light of adult milestones and evolving roles and responsibilities; (d) tailoring assessment to pinpoint subtle areas of dysfunction; (e) generating cognitive strategies to assist with daily life; and (f) investigating the potential effects of brain plasticity and the role of reorganization/recruitment on cognitive and behavioral function.

In keeping with a shift in goals, there is also a shift in focus when conducting neuropsychological assessments in adults with childhood injuries. As in the acute phase, testing in the long term remains an individualized undertaking, tailored to the needs and characteristics of the client; however, these types of evaluations have their own qualities. First, long-term follow-up assessments need to be specific and sensitive, as the major areas of difficulty for the patient will have been previously identified. Second, the clinician needs to be aware that subjective complaints and self-reports of daily functioning may be greatly influenced by compensatory strategies established over the years post-injury, as well as habituation to existing deficits. In this sense, a lack of subjective complaints may not accurately reflect absence of cognitive dysfunction (nor lack of insight), as adults may have developed adaptations and compensatory mechanisms which mask the nature and extent of existing problems. Third, age at injury is an important consideration, as it will affect the extent and nature of the neurocognitive skills likely to have been affected by brain injury. Donders and Warschauwsky [30] demonstrated that early-onset childhood TBI results in worse outcomes in higher-level cognitive skills and social integration than later "transition age" (17–21 years) injuries. The relative impact of TBI on cognitive and social skills is a function of the stage of development at injury; skills that are emerging and not yet solidified may be particularly vulnerable to trauma. Fourth, the ongoing review of the impact of childhood TBI into adulthood may need to rely increasingly on measures that reflect real-life skills and behavior in order to address the daily impact of chronic TBI sequelae. There is increasing interest in the ecological validity of the neuropsychological assessment, though adequate measures are still scarce [31, 32]. Results obtained within the confines of a standard assessment need to be interpreted with a consideration of real-world environments which can be chaotic and noisy and hence more difficult for individuals with brain injuries to negotiate. Obtaining an adequate history and information from third parties can help in achieving an accurate picture of an individual's functioning in the real world [33].

Cognitive assessment

The evaluation of cognitive function remains the cornerstone of neuropsychological assessment at any stage post-injury and at any age. Identifying mental strengths and weaknesses is of fundamental importance to providing individuals with brain injury and their families with an accurate depiction of their current abilities. Neuropsychological assessment in the long term following childhood TBI should continue to be based on individualized systemic evaluation of cognitive skills. Measurement of IQ is useful to obtain an up-to-date representation of global intellectual functioning. In order to minimize overuse of full IQ scales abbreviated IQ tools can be helpful (e.g. Wechsler Abbreviated Scale of Intelligence) [34]. Using standardized measures of cognitive function, particularly those that are applicable to wide age brackets, procures the advantage of providing scores that can be compared across the lifespan from one assessment to another, enabling the neuropsychologist to track change over time. However, practice effects should be considered when interpreting results from individuals exposed to multiple assessments over the years, particularly when these are conducted in relatively short time spans, even when efforts are made to use alternate forms of tests.

Specific cognitive domains of interest include attention, memory and learning, processing speed, executive function, visuospatial and visuomotor skills, language, reading, and mathematics. Though standardized assessments exist for most of these areas, the need for a more specific and subtle evaluation in the long term suggests that it will be useful for the clinician to carefully choose particular tests which are valid and reliable and that span child and adult age bands such as the Test of Everyday Attention [35], Delis-Kaplan Executive Function System [36], the Wechsler Memory Scale-III [37], and the Wechsler Individual Achievement

Test-II [38]. Measures that focus on specific cognitive domains may also be included: memory (California Verbal Learning Test-II [39]; Rey Auditory Verbal Learning Test [40]); attention (Continuous Performance Test-II [41]; Paced Auditory Serial Addition Test [42]), executive function (Rey-Osterreith Complex Figure [43]; Wisconsin Card Sorting Test [44]; Stroop Test [45]; Verbal Fluency Test [46]).

Vocational assessment

Research findings demonstrate that injuries sustained during childhood affect vocational outcome. Ewing-Cobbs and colleagues [47] found that almost 50% of patients with TBI failed a school grade or required placement in special education classrooms and the odds of unfavorable academic performance were 18-times higher for patients versus controls. Such poor academic success has significant implications for later vocational outcomes. Koskiniemi and colleagues [48] further showed that, following preschool TBI, normal school performance or intelligence does not necessarily translate to good vocational outcome, suggesting that almost any child with brain injury may be at risk for professional problems or unemployment later in life. In light of these findings, assessment of vocational status is an important element of neuropsychological assessment in adulthood.

TBI survivors in full-time employment demonstrate better intellectual capacities, fewer executive deficits [19, 49], as well as largely intact perceptual, complex visual processing, attention and memory capacities [50, 51], suggesting that assessment of these skills is an important aspect of the neuropsychological evaluation of vocational outcomes. While such cognitive factors are of a fundamental importance in determining an individual's ability to undertake and maintain full-time work, research also shows that they cannot alone predict vocational outcome. Environmental demands and social and emotional factors are also critical when determining the need for vocational rehabilitation and support [52–54]. Self-awareness, in particular, has been identified as an important factor in successful return to work and should therefore be considered as related to vocational success [55].

Emotional, social and behavioral assessment

There is increasing evidence that, after childhood TBI, social and emotional deficits increase and persist into adulthood, having unfavorable effects on daily living, ability to engage in work and social activities and coping with adult responsibilities. These difficulties may be exacerbated by accumulated failures and frustrations throughout development, which may cause survivors to withdraw from regular work and leisure activities and to accumulate significant emotional problems. As noted previously, available research has identified social and psychological problems as the major complaint of adult survivors. Yeates and colleagues [56] suggest that these difficulties are related to executive abilities, pragmatic language and social problem-solving skills, and are important in determining social functioning throughout the lifespan post-TBI. Measures of social functioning are often limited to general, parent-based reports, which are not useful with adults. Few of the existing measures are standardized and no appropriate tools exist for evaluating the long-term social implications of TBI into adulthood. Some measures that may be of use for evaluating adaptive, functional and psychosocial outcomes in adults are the Community Integration Questionnaire [57] and Sydney Psychosocial Reintegration Scale [58]. Also, the Dysexecutive Questionnaire, part of the Behavioural Assessment of the Dysexecutive Syndrome [59], can be useful for identifying everyday signs of executive problems which may impact on social and behavioral function.

TBI is also associated with a high rate of emotional and behavioral problems in adulthood including increased anxiety, depression and poor coping skills [60–62]. Maladaptive behaviors are related to the psychiatric sequelae of pediatric TBI, which have become an important focus of the evaluation of TBI outcomes in the long term. Although some patients suffer from lifetime psychiatric disorders, there is also evidence for the emergence of novel disorders, particularly following severe injury during childhood. Bloom and colleagues [63] reported that attention deficit hyperactivity disorder and depression are the most common novel diagnoses, though a variety of psychiatric diagnoses may be present, with 74% of disorders persisting in 48% of injured children. Post-injury personality disorders have also been identified in a high proportion of TBI survivors (66%), though there does not appear to be a TBI-specific personality syndrome given that common post-TBI disorders range between borderline, avoidant, paranoid, obsessive-compulsive and narcissistic personality types [64]. Given the prevalence of both Axis I and II psychiatric diagnoses following childhood TBI, an initial screening of such disorders and of more general emotional and behavioral problems (e.g. Minnesota Multiple Personality Inventory-2) [65] can be useful when frank psychiatric problems are suspected and to evaluate the need for further referral for full psychiatric evaluation using structured clinical interview techniques to complement the neuropsychological profile of cognitive, social, and emotional abilities.

In summary, neuropsychological assessment is important for the life-long management of childhood TBI-related dysfunction and ongoing monitoring of recovery, adaptation and compensation as a function of fluctuating environmental demands and responsibilities. Assessment of childhood TBI in adulthood is distinct from evaluations performed acutely and brings with it a number of challenges and particular considerations. Evaluations must make allowances for ongoing development and aging, reorganization of structure and function, compensatory mechanisms and habituation, practice effects, real-world functioning, changing life situations and the demands of the current environment. Thorough assessments remain important, though there may be a shift in focus from cognitive domains to the evaluation of social, emotional and behavioral problems, as well as vocational outcomes and adaptive capabilities. Continued collaboration with other health professionals remains essential as well as ongoing referral to rehabilitation and intervention programs when needed.

Interventions

Recently, significant advances have been made in evidence-based, acute medical care and diagnostic technology used to assess the extent and severity of TBI, but the status of knowledge with respect to behavioral interventions is much less developed, and there have been relatively few studies which have addressed child-based post-acute rehabilitation and long-term intervention specifically. A wide variety of strategies have been used to treat post-TBI impairments in adults, with similar techniques generally reported within child populations. Within clinical contexts, rehabilitation models are traditionally multidisciplinary, taking a holistic view of the patient, and employing an eclectic range of treatments. Commonly, these interventions are not confined to evidence-based methods. Within such contexts, the neuropsychologist's role is often focused on specific evidence-based models, which are frequently domain-specific (e.g. attention).

There is little empirical evidence detailing the treatment of post-TBI impairments in children and adolescents that can be of use to clinicians. Navigating the comparatively sparse intervention literature is made difficult due to a number of factors that influence a clinician's ability to effectively evaluate studies: the heterogeneity of patients and their differing pre-injury characteristics, length and type of intervention used, degree of injury severity, sites of brain damage, timing of assessments, methods of data collection, and the outcome measures used. The majority of intervention studies include only adults, although it is clear that outcome after TBI is different for children than for adults. Further, much intervention research is based on single-case or small group designs, limiting the generalizability of results. Consistent with this, Teasell and colleagues [66] reported that across all ages, less than 30% of studies used randomized controlled trial (RCT) designs.

Cognitive interventions

A number of approaches have demonstrated success in treating cognitive impairments in children with TBI. In one such study, involving both adult and child survivors of TBI, Wilson and colleagues [67] used a pager system to treat post-TBI memory and planning impairments. Their randomized control cross-over study was structured so that patients were allocated to a pager or wait list group before choosing what they wanted to be reminded about. After 5 weeks with the pager, participants achieved over 70% of their tasks compared with less than 50% for the wait list group. A follow-up assessment 7 weeks later demonstrated that the pager group still achieved significantly more tasks than they did at baseline, indicating that the pager system performed well even after completion of the training program.

Similarly, Suzman et al. [68] used an intervention consisting of several training "modules" focusing on metacognitive, self-instructional, self-regulation training, attribution and reinforcement, and administered using a computerized problem-solving program. The authors reported substantial gains on trained tasks, as well as improvements on some of the post-intervention standardized tests of problem-solving. Clearly, the multi-focused approach to the treatment of post-injury cognitive impairments resulted in improved functioning in specific skills with a consequent run-on effect to other related skills. However, in this study, training consisted of three 40-minute sessions per week which lasted for over 3 weeks. Unfortunately, this level of time and commitment is not going to be suitable for many families. Other, more hands-off, approaches have been developed and appear promising. For example, preliminary evidence from a telephone-based cognitive training intervention study suggests that, in addition to improved neuropsychological performance, this approach also resulted in improved self-esteem ratings in children, having the additional benefit of enhanced feelings of task-mastery and motivation to face new challenges [69].

To date, most approaches to intervention have focused on more severe TBI, and have usually involved a considerable patient burden, in terms of time commitment. In contrast, in their intervention with mildly injured children and adults, Ponsford et al. [70], utilized a simple, efficient method, providing patients and their families with an information booklet, documenting the likely symptoms following minor injuries. They reported that behavioral symptoms and cognitive difficulties were reduced in children with mild TBI who participated in the intervention, compared to those in a control group. The authors reported that providing this information early in the treatment phase successfully reduced parent and child stress. Similarly, Kirkwood et al. [71] have presented preliminary evidence that for patients with mild TBI, provision of a comprehensive information booklet at acute presentation was as effective as a follow-up meeting with a clinician. Thus, there may be significant cost-effective benefits in educating parents on the commonly reported symptom presentation and resolution, at least with injuries at the mild end of the severity spectrum.

Emotional, social and behavioral interventions

Impairments in behavior and social functioning have been associated with parental stress, family turmoil, problems in school and impaired peer relations and, collectively, constitute the number one reason that families seek intervention and rehabilitation services [72]. In a recent review, Ylvisaker et al. [73] reported that the majority of studies since 2000 were based on a positive behavior intervention and support system using proactive, antecedent-focused strategies, and that, to date, only two such studies used RCT designs. For example, Wade et al. [74] successfully reduced problem behaviors in children with TBI, using a 6-month family-centered intervention, consisting of seven bi-weekly core sessions and up to four individualized sessions each lasting approximately 1.5 hours, and based on a proactive problem-solving approach. Medd and Tate [75] have also demonstrated successful outcomes for post-TBI anger problems using a variety of antecedent control procedures (e.g. self-awareness training) in individual therapy sessions with a clinical psychologist for 5 to 8 weeks. In this treatment, participants were required to keep a daily log of their aggressive outbursts, a task that is difficult for patients in general and especially those with prospective memory impairment.

Intervention strategies from the field of applied behavior analysis have proven somewhat successful in the treatment of post-TBI behavior problems. For example, Feeney and Ylvisaker [76] used photographic and written cues for desired behaviors, verbal rehearsal of plans, and a performance review with three adolescent patients with severe TBI. The strategy effectively reduced the frequency of aggressive and challenging behaviors but these improvements were not maintained once the cues were withdrawn. Other strategies have included the use of token economies [77], verbal contracts [78], reinforcement and informational feedback [79], initial reduction of task demands [80], caregiver education [81], stress inoculation training [82], extinction [83], and home-based mentoring [84]. All these intervention strategies have demonstrated success in treating post-TBI behavior problems.

In the first published study to describe an intervention targeting post-TBI emotion perception deficits, Bornhofen and McDonald [85] reported that participants significantly improved both in their ability to judge basic emotional stimuli and in the more complex task of making social inferences based on the demeanor of a speaker. These results are promising as it has been suggested that impairments in certain skills related to emotion perception, such as facial expression, vocal prosody and body posture [86–89], underlie the lack of improvement frequently observed in many patients with TBI.

Educational, vocational interventions

Educational and vocational difficulties are frequent post-TBI and have been reported to persist through childhood and into adulthood. Survivors of serious TBI often find it difficult to meet educational demands, and are at risk of leaving school early. As a result, further education opportunities are limited, and the range of potential employment contexts restricted. Many young people will need support in choosing appropriate careers and entering the workforce. Commonly, such support is provided based on the results of neuropsychological evaluation, which describes the young person's cognitive strengths and weaknesses, and assists in identifying employment contexts that meet these profiles. In some instances, survivors are able to utilize such information independently, and require no additional input. Where more serious difficulties are present, the neuropsychologist may become involved in consultations with employers or vocational counselors, and may even play a role in task analysis of job demands, in order to develop strategies to compensate for the individual's difficulties.

Hux and colleagues [90] found that nearly 29% of students with reported TBIs had received special education services. In addition to the post-TBI academic challenges, the biggest challenge reported by adolescents with TBI was reintegrating back into the classroom and school environment [91]. It is well established that impairments in cognitive or behavioral functioning are related to, and possibly underlie, the poor academic performance often seen after TBI. For example, Catroppa and Anderson [92] reported that children with TBI demonstrated impairments in memory functioning 2 years post-injury and their academic success was dependent on both the demands of the tasks they completed and the severity of their injury. These results suggest that, when minimal demands are placed on students with TBI, their impairments may not be apparent. However, when students are working within a busy classroom, full of noise and distraction, their capacity to complete tasks which tax higher-order cognitive skills (e.g. solving math problems in your head) may be reduced, and any TBI-related impairments are likely to be much more apparent. The nature and extent of impairment in social function may also impact on the young person's academic capabilities. Along these lines, Yeates and Taylor [93] noted that poorer behavioral adjustment predicted both poorer classroom performance and an increased likelihood of educational intervention, suggesting that successful intervention in certain areas is likely to positively impact on academic functioning.

In a large-scale follow-up of survivors of severe TBI, Asikainen and colleagues [94] found that coma scores, duration of unconsciousness and traumatic amnesia, all traditional markers of injury severity, significantly predicted occupational outcome up to 20 years post-injury. This group [95] also noted that those who sustained their injuries earlier in life, coupled with poor educational attainment, were the least likely to be gainfully employed as adults. Although no neuropsychological test data were provided, it is likely that cognitive and behavioral impairments had a detrimental effect on academic achievement, followed by a knock-on effect to occupational success. This evidence suggests that leaving post-TBI impairments untreated or not treating them successfully using appropriate intervention strategies can have wide-reaching and long-term implications.

Novel, innovative intervention approaches

Recently a number of novel and innovative techniques have been utilized in the treatment of TBI-related impairments. For example, virtual reality (VR) environments have been developed to assist clinicians when treating impairments in general executive functions [96], memory [97], and social cognition [98]. VR environments have the advantage of permitting the presentation of numerous and varied problems or tasks which can be repeated until improvement or mastery is achieved. VR environments are often more ecologically valid and accessible than traditional rehabilitation methods. For example, using an image of the patient rather than an avatar reduces cybersickness by not requiring the use of head-mounted display units, and not isolating the patient from the real world, enabling the clinician to readily and easily intervene and provide feedback during the session. One of the promising areas of VR-based rehabilitation is prospective memory impairment. Preliminary studies demonstrate that VR-based prospective memory tasks consistently discriminate between patients with frontal lobe injury and controls, and provide evidence of their potential utility to improve these impairments [99]. Although there are clear benefits to using VR-based interventions, the costs associated with this technology make it unavailable to the vast majority of clinicians.

Another example of a successful approach to intervention is the SARAH program. The program, which began in the 1970s, is run across eight hospitals in Brazil and is based on the philosophy that children with TBI should be treated as a whole rather than a collection of parts. In addition, as TBI often results in impairments in various areas of functioning, the SARAH program actively includes parents, family members and teachers in the recovery process. To date, this approach has proven successful in treating broad-spectrum cognitive impairments [100] and holds promise for the treatment of emotional and behavioral difficulties commonly observed after TBI. Although there is little that is inherently novel about the SARAH approach, the active involvement of both the patient and their support network (both immediate and extended) ensures that the skills acquired during the intervention will not be context-dependent and will provide the patient with the confidence and the skill set with which to competently navigate their environment.

Finally, web-based technology has, of late, been utilized in the treatment of social skills impairments post-TBI. Wade and colleagues [101, 102] used the internet to deliver a series of therapeutic training sessions, based on cognitive-behavioral principles, with improved post-injury adjustment and self-management skills as well as self-reported parental distress. Families involved in the intervention were provided with a home computer, and completed sessions from home. The training module was structured as a 14-session package consisting of eight core sessions, each addressing specific topics (e.g. Steps of problem solving, Communication) and six sessions focusing on stressors experienced by some but not all families. The modules were designed to encourage family members to be actively involved and include tips, video clips demonstrating specific skills, as well as exercises that provide opportunities to practice the skills learned in that session.

In sum, a variety of intervention options are available for the treatment of post-TBI impairments. As described above, intervention strategies administered directly by clinicians (including rehabilitation nurses, physical therapists, and neuropsychologists among others), administered indirectly to families and teachers, using face-to-face problem-solving strategies or advanced computer-based technologies have all proven useful to treat cognitive, emotional, social, and behavioral impairments in children, adolescents and adults with TBI. There are a number of factors that a clinician should consider prior to engaging a patient with TBI in intervention, including: the capabilities of the patient, the fit between patient and intervention requirements, the practical demands of the intervention, the empirical

evidence supporting the intervention, the competence of the clinician in delivering the intervention according to its principles, and the likelihood of successful completion. While RCTs have the potential to greatly inform about the efficacy of the intervention, the lessons learned from single-case studies provide valuable information on appropriate and available strategies especially in terms of the patients' and their families' response and level of engagement in the intervention.

Future directions

Despite significant advances in the study of childhood TBI, the consequences of brain injuries sustained early in development remain less clear than those of similar injuries in adults. Nonetheless, there now exists good evidence demonstrating that a child's brain is vulnerable to early trauma and that skills that have not developed or are emerging at the time of injury may be permanently impaired, suggesting that childhood TBI can impact on an individual's cognitive, behavioral, emotional and social functioning well into adulthood and, indeed, throughout the lifespan. As a result of the previously widespread and erroneous notion that children's brains were "plastic" and could recover well from injury through transfer of function to undamaged areas, the chronicity of childhood TBI deficits is often underappreciated. The distinct outcomes of childhood versus adult TBI further highlight the importance of considering these types of injuries separately and avoiding inferring knowledge from the adult domain when considering children's brain injuries.

Notwithstanding the increasing evidence base that children are particularly vulnerable to brain injuries and that the consequences of these have long-lasting impacts on survivors' functioning and quality of life, further studies are needed to specifically describe the extent and severity of such life-long deficits. Although there are significant methodological difficulties and time requirements related to longitudinal studies, more "very long-term" follow-up studies on the outcome of childhood TBI are required to improve our knowledge of the lasting implications of such injuries, not just into adulthood, but throughout the entire lifespan. In particular, little is known of the interaction between early brain injuries and the normal degenerative processes related to the aging brain.

Much of the intervention research conducted to date has focused on the cognitive domain. As a result, specific outcomes in the areas of attention, memory, language and executive function are clearly described. More recently, however, the focus of scientific attention has shifted to emotional and social domains and preliminary reports suggest that social dysfunction following childhood TBI is common, persistent, and represents the most debilitating of all sequelae. Nevertheless, evidence for this is still limited and more research is needed before we have a clear picture of the social outcomes of TBI. Progress in this area is currently limited by the paucity of adequate measures for assessing social function, suggesting there is a pressing need to develop specific, validated, reliable and standardized measures of social skills, which can be used in both research and clinical contexts.

Similarly, rehabilitation of social and emotional problems following childhood TBI is constrained by the lack of data evaluating the efficacy of behavioral interventions. While randomized controlled trials have become the gold standard in appraising the worth of such treatments, consideration of case studies and efficacy studies can provide valuable information in this regard. There are currently some useful resources available to clinicians which can provide additional information and assist when making a decision about intervention options. For example, *PsychBite* (http://www.psychbite.com) is a website which presents independent reviews (conducted by trained volunteer reviewers) of published intervention studies which are focused specifically on TBI-related impairments. Although the scores awarded to a study do not necessarily reflect the overall utility of the intervention, the review process nonetheless provides some useful information about the study and its methodological strengths. With the increase in calls for more methodologically rigorous studies, large multi-center trials may be necessary and it is important that the structure and focus of these studies take into account important developmental issues.

It is also recommended that clinicians and therapists investigate interventions that have been developed to address areas of impairment in other clinical populations (e.g. cognitive functioning in patients with Alzheimer's disease or aggression in adolescents with conduct disorder) as these strategies may have direct applications in the treatment of post-TBI impairments. Finally, following on from the suggestion by Catroppa and Anderson [103] that future intervention studies targeting executive functions should use appropriate and valid measures, it is also recommended that technological advances be utilized to engage and motivate patients and their families to participate in interventions that provide them with realistic and age-appropriate challenges to best prepare them for the transition back to the home, school, or workplace.

References

1. Mitra B, Cameron P, Butt W. Population based study of pediatric head injury. *J Ped Child Health* 2007;**43**(3):154–9.

2. Goldstein, FC, Levin, HS. Epidemiology of pediatric closed head injury: incidence, clinical characteristics and risk factors. *J Learn Disabil* 1987;**20**(9):518–25.

3. Michaud LJ, Rivara FP, Grady MS, Reay DT. Predictors of survival and severe disability after severe brain injury in children. *Neurosurgery* 1992;**31**(2):254–64.

4. Anderson V, Catroppa C, Morse S, Haritou F, Rosenfeld J. Functional plasticity or vulnerability after early brain injury? *Pediatrics* 2005;**116**(6):1374–82.

5. Rivara JB, Jaffe KM, Fay GC, Polissar NL, Martin KM, Shurtleff HA, et al. Family functioning and injury severity as predictors of child functioning one year following traumatic brain injury. *Arch Phys Med Rehabil* 1993;**74**(10):1047–55.

6. Taylor HG, Drotar D, Wade S, Yeates K, Stancin T, Klein S. Recovery from traumatic brain injury in children: the importance of the family. In Broman SH, Michel ME, eds. *Traumatic Head Injury in Children.* New York: Oxford University Press; 1995: 188–218.

7. Asarnow RF, Satz P, Light R, Lewis R, Neumann E. Behavior problems and adaptive functioning in children with mild and severe closed head injury. *J Pediatr Psychol* 1991;**16**(5):543–55.

8. Holloway M, Bye A, Moran K. Non-accidental head injury in children. *Med J Aust* 1994;**160**(12):786–9.

9. Quattrocchi KB, Prasad, P, Willits, NH, Wagner FC. Quantification of midline shift as a predictor of poor outcome following head injury. *Surg Neurol* 1991;**35**(3):183–8.

10. Pang D. Pathophysiologic correlates of neurobehavioral syndromes following closed head injury. In Ylvisaker M, ed. *Head Injury Rehabilitation: Children and Adolescents.* London: Taylor & Francis; 1985: 3–70.

11. Yeates KO. Closed-head injury. In Yeates KO, Ris MD, Taylor HG, eds. *Pediatric Neuropsychology: Research, Theory, and Practice.* New York: Guilford Press; 2000: 92–116

12. Engberg A, Teesdale G. Psychosocial outcome following traumatic brain injury in adults: A long-term

population-based follow-up. *Brain Inj* 2004;**18**(6):533–45.

13. Hoofien D, Gilboa A, Vakil E, Donovick P. Traumatic brain injury (TBI) 10–20 years later: a comprehensive outcome study of psychiatric symptomatology, cognitive abilities and psychosocial functioning. *Brain Inj* 2001;**15**(3):189–209.

14. Hessen E, Anderson V, Nestvold K. Neuropsychological function 23 years after mild traumatic brain injury: a comparison of outcome after pediatric and adult head injuries. *Brain Inj* 2007;**21**(9):963–79.

15. McKinlay A, Dalrymple-Alford JC, Horwood LJ, Fergusson DM. Long term psychosocial outcomes after mild head injury in early childhood. *J Neurol Neurosurg Psychiatry* 2002;**73**(3):281–88.

16. Hessen E, Anderson V, Nestvold K. MMPI-2 profiles 23 years after paediatric mild traumatic brain injury. *Brain Inj* 2008;**22**(1):39–50.

17. Klonoff H, Clark C, Klonoff, PS. Long-term outcome of head injuries: a 23 year follow up study of children with head injuries. *J Neurol Neurosurg Psychiatry* 1993;**56**(4):410–15.

18. Jonsson CA, Horneman G, Emanuelson I. Neuropsychological progress during 14 years after severe traumatic brain injury in childhood and adolescence. *Brain Inj* 2004;**18**(9):921–34.

19. Nybo T, Sainio M, Muller K. Stability of vocational outcome in adulthood after moderate to severe preschool brain injury. *J Int Neuropsychol Soc* 2004;**10**(5):719–23.

20. Asikainen I, Nybo T, Müller K, Sarna S, Kaste M. Speed performance and long-term functional and vocational outcome in a group of young patients with moderate or severe traumatic brain injury. *Eur J Neurol* 1999;**6**(2):179–85.

21. Cattelani R, Lombardi F, Brianti R, Mazzucchi A. Traumatic brain injury in childhood: intellectual, behavioural and social outcome into adulthood. *Brain Inj* 1998;**12**(4):283–96.

22. Nybo T, Koskiniemi M. Cognitive indicators of vocational outcome after severe traumatic brain injury (TBI) in childhood. *Brain Inj* 1999;**13**(10):759–66.

23. Koskiniemi M, Kyykka T, Nybo T, Jarho L. Long-term outcome after severe brain injury in preschoolers is worse than expected. *Arch Pediatr Adolesc Med* 1995;**149**(3):249–54.

24. Yeates KO, Taylor HG, Drotar D, Wade SL, Klein S, Stancin T, et al. Pre-injury family environment as a determinant of recovery from traumatic brain injuries in school-age children. *J Int Neuropsychol Soc* 1997;**3**(6):617–30.

25. Hoofien D, Vakil E, Gilboa A, Donovick PJ, Barak O. Comparison of the predictive power of socio-economic variables, severity of injury and age on long-term outcome of traumatic brain injury: sample specific variables versus factors as predictors. *Brain Inj* 2002;**16**(1):9–27.

26. Yeates KO, Taylor HG, Wade SL, Drotar D, Stancin T, Minich N. A prospective study of short- and long-term neuropsychological outcomes after traumatic brain injury in children. *Neuropsychology* 2002;**16**(4):514–23.

27. van Heugten CM, Hendriksen J, Rasquin S, Dijcks B, Jaeken D, Vles JH. Long-term neuropsychological performance in a cohort of children and adolescents after severe paediatric traumatic brain injury. *Brain Inj* 2006;**20**(9):895–903.

28. Giza CC, Prins ML. Is being plastic fantastic? Mechanisms of altered plasticity after developmental traumatic brain injury. *Dev Neurosci* 2006;**28**(4–5):364–79.

29. Giza CC, Mink RB, Madikians A. Pediatric traumatic brain injury: not just little adults. *Curr Opin Crit Care* 2007;**13**(2):143–52.

30. Donders J, Warschausky S. Neurobehavioral outcomes after early versus late childhood traumatic brain injury. *J Head Trauma Rehabil* 2007;**22**(5):296–302.

31. Silver CH. Ecological validity of neuropsychological assessment in childhood traumatic brain injury. *J Head Trauma Rehabil* 2000;**15**(4):973–88.

32. Chaytor N, Temkin N, Machamer J, Dikmen S. The ecological validity of neuropsychological assessment and the role of depressive symptoms in moderate to severe traumatic brain injury. *J Int Neuropsychol Soc* 2007;**13**(3):377–85.

33. Sbordone RJ. Limitations of neuropsychological testing to predict the cognitive and behavioral functioning of persons with brain injury in real-world settings. *NeuroRehabilitation* 2001;**16**(4):199–201.

34. Wechsler, D. *The Wechsler Abbreviated Scale of Intelligence.* San Antonio, TX: The Psychological Corporation; 1999.

35. Robertson IH, Ward T, Ridgeway V, Nimmo-Smith I. *The Test of Everyday Attention.* Bury St. Edmunds: Thames Valley Test Company; 1994.

36. Delis DC, Kaplan E, Kramer JH. *Delis Kaplan Executive Function System (D-KEFS).* San Antonio, TX: The Psychological Corporation; 2001.

37. Wechsler, D. *Wechsler Memory Scale-Third Edition: Administration and scoring manual.* San Antonio, TX: The Psychological Corporation; 1997.

38. Wechsler, D. *Wechsler Individual Achievement Test – Second Edition (WIAT-II).* San Antonio, TX: The Psychological Corporation; 2002.

39. Delis D, Kramer J, Kaplan E, Ober B. *California Verbal Learning Test-Second Edition.* San Antonio, TX: The Psychological Corporation; 2000.

40. Rey A. *L'examen clinique en psychologie (Clinical tests in psychology).* Paris, France: Presses Universitaires de France; 1964.

41. Conners CK, MHS Staff, eds. *Conners' Continuous Performance Test II: Computer Program for Windows Technical Guide and Software Manual.* North Tonwanda, NY: Mutli-Health Systems; 2000.

42. Gronwall D, Sampson H. *The Psychological Effects of Concussion.* Auckland, New Zealand: University Press/ Oxford University Press; 1974.

43. Rey A. L'examen psychologique dans les cas d'encéphalopathie traumatique. *Arch Psychol* 1941;**28**:286–340.

44. Berg EA. A simple objective technique for measuring flexibility in thinking. *J Gen Psychol* 1948;**39**:15–22.

45. Stroop JR. Studies of interference in serial verbal reactions *J Exp Psychol* 1935;**18**:643–62.

46. Strauss E, Sherman E, Spreen O. *A Compendium of Neuropsychological Tests: Administration, Norms and Commentary*, 3rd edn. Oxford: Oxford University Press; 2006.

47. Ewing-Cobbs L, Prasad MR, Kramer L, Cox CS Jr, Baumgartner J, Fletcher S, et al. Late intellectual and academic outcomes following traumatic brain injury sustained during early childhood. *J Neurosurg* 2006;**105**(4 Suppl):287–96.

48. Koskiniemi M, Kyykka T, Nybo T, Jarho L. Long-term outcome after severe brain injury in preschoolers is worse than expected. *Arch Pediatr Adolesc Med* 1995;**149**(3):249–54.

49. Nybo T, Sainio M, Muller K. Middle age cognition and vocational outcome of childhood brain injury. *Acta Neurol Scand* 2005;**112**(5):338–42.

50. Lachapelle J, Bolduc-Teasdale J, Ptito A, McKerral M. Deficits in complex visual information processing after mild TBI: electrophysiological markers and vocational outcome prognosis. *Brain Inj* 2008;**22**(3):265–74.

51. Ownsworth T, McKenna K. Investigation of factors related to employment outcome following traumatic brain injury: a critical review and conceptual model. *Disabil Rehabil* 2004;**26**(13):765–83.

52. Johnstone B, Hexum CL, Ashkanazi G. Extent of cognitive decline in traumatic brain injury based on estimates of premorbid intelligence. *Brain Inj* 1995;**9**(4):377–84.

53. Guerin F, Kennepohl S, Leveille G, Dominique A, McKerral M. Vocational outcome indicators in atypically recovering mild TBI: a post-intervention study. *NeuroRehabilitation* 2006;**21**(4):295–303.

54. Mateer CA, Sira CS. Cognitive and emotional consequences of TBI: intervention strategies for vocational rehabilitation. *NeuroRehabilitation* 2006;**21**(4):315–26.

55. Shames J, Treger I, Ring H, Giaquinto S. Return to work following traumatic brain injury: trends and challenges. *Disabil Rehabil* 2007;**29**(17):1387–95.

56. Yeates KO, Swift E, Taylor HG, Wade SL, Drotar D, Stancin T, et al. Short- and long-term social outcomes following pediatric traumatic brain injury. *J Int Neuropsychol Soc* 2004;**10**(3):412–26.

57. Willer, BS, Ottenbacher, KJ, Coad ML. The Community Integration Questionnaire: a comparative examination. *Am J Phys Med Rehabil* 1994;**73**(2):103–11.

58. Tate R, Hodgkinson A, Veerabangsa A, Maggiotto S. Measuring psychosocial recovery after traumatic brain injury: Psychometric properties of a new scale. *J Head Trauma Rehabil* 1999;**14**(6):543–57.

59. Wilson BA, Alderman N, Burgess PW, Emslie H, Evans JJ. BADS: Behavioural Assessment of the Dysexecutive Syndrome. London, UK: Thames Valley Test Company; 1996.

60. Anson K, Ponsford J. Who benefits? Outcome following a coping skills group intervention for traumatically brain injured individuals. *Brain Inj* 2006;**20**(1):1–13.

61. Draper K, Ponsford J, Schonberger M. Psychosocial and emotional outcomes 10 years following traumatic brain injury. *J Head Trauma Rehabil* 2007;**22**(5):278–87.

62. Ponsford J, Draper K, Schonberger M. Functional outcome 10 years after traumatic brain injury: Its relationship with demographic, injury severity, and cognitive and emotional status. *J Int Neuropsychol Soc* 2008;**14**(2):233–42.

63. Bloom DR, Levin HS, Ewing-Cobbs L, Saunders AE, Song J, Fletcher JM, et al. Lifetime and novel psychiatric disorders after pediatric traumatic brain injury. *J Am Acad Child Adolesc Psychiatry* 2001;**40**(5):572–9.

64. Hibbard MR, Bogdany J, Uysal S, Kepler K, Silver JM, Gordon WA, et al. Axis II psychopathology in individuals with traumatic brain injury. *Brain Inj* 2000;**14**(1):45–61.

65. Hathaway S, McKinley J. *MMPI-2 Manual for Administration and Scoring.* Minneapolis, MN: University of Minnesota Press; 1989.

66. Teasell R, Bayona N, Marshall S, Cullen N, Bayley M, Chundamala J, et al. A systematic review of the

rehabilitation of moderate to severe acquired brain injuries. *Brain Inj* 2007;**21**(2):107–12.

67. Wilson BA, Emslie H, Quirk K, Evans J, Watson P. A randomized control trial to evaluate a paging system for people with traumatic brain injury. *Brain Inj* 2005;**19**(11):891–4.

68. Suzman KB, Morris RD, Morris MK, Milan MA. Cognitive-behavioral remediation of problem solving deficits in children with acquired brain injury. *J Behav Ther Exp Psychiatry* 1997;**28**(3):203–12.

69. Madsen Sjö N, Weidner S, Spellerberg S, Kihlgren M. Cognitive training in local settings: two methodological versions. *New Frontiers in Pediatric Traumatic Brain Injury*; 2007 Nov 8–10; San Diego, USA.

70. Ponsford J, Willmott C, Rothwell A, Cameron P, Ayton G, Nelms R, et al. Impact of early intervention on outcome after mild traumatic brain injury in children. *Pediatrics* 2001;**108**(6):1297–303.

71. Kirkwood M, Dise-Lewis J, Wathen J, Brent A, Wilson P. Comparison of three early educational interventions following pediatric mild TBI. *New Frontiers in Pediatric Traumatic Brain Injury*; 2007 Nov 8–10; San Diego, USA.

72. Max JE, Roberts MA, Koele SL, Lindgren SD, Robin DA, Arndt S, et al. Cognitive outcome in children and adolescents following severe traumatic brain injury: influence of psychosocial, psychiatric, and injury-related variables. *J Int Neuropsychol Soc* 1999;**5**(1):58–68.

73. Ylvisaker M, Turkstra L, Coehlo C, Yorkston K, Kennedy M, Sohlberg MM, et al. Behavioral interventions for children and adults with behaviour diorders after TBI: a systematic review of the evidence. *Brain Inj* 2007;**21**(8):769–805.

74. Wade SL, Michaud L, Maines-Brown T. Putting the pieces together: preliminary efficacy of a family problem-solving intervention for children with traumatic brain injury. *J Head Trauma Rehabil* 2006;**21**(1):57–67.

75. Medd J, Tate RL. Evaluation of an anger management therapy program following acquired brain injury: a preliminary study. *Neuropsych Rehabil* 2000;**10**(2):185–201.

76. Feeney T, Ylvisaker M. Choice and routine: antecedent behavioral interventions for adolescents with severe traumatic brain injury. *J Head Trauma Rehabil* 1995;**10**(3):67–86.

77. Burke W, Weslowski M. Applied behavior analysis in head injury rehabilitation. *Rehabil Nurs* 1988;**13**(4):186–8.

78. Zencius A, Weslowski M, Burke W, McQuade D. Antecedent control in the treatment of brain injured clients. *Brain Inj* 1989;**3**(2):199–205.

79. O'Reilly MF, Green G, Braunling-McMorrow D. Self-administered written prompts to teach home accident prevention skills with brain injuries. *J Appl Behav Anal* 1990;**23**(4):431–46.

80. Kennedy CH. Manipulating antecedent conditions to alter the stimulus control of problem behavior. *J Appl Behav Anal* 1993;**27**(1):161–70.

81. Carnevale GJ. Natural-setting behaviour management for the individuals with traumatic brain injury: Results of a three year caregiver training program. *J Head Trauma Rehabil* 1996;**11**(1):27–38.

82. Aescheman SR, Imes C. Stress inoculation training for impulsive behaviors in adults with traumatic brain injury. *J Rational-Emotive Cogn Behav Ther* 1999;**17**(1):51–65.

83. Treadwell K, Page T. Functional analysis: identifying the environmental determinants of severe behavior disorders. *J Head Trauma Rehabil* 1996;**11**(1):62–74

84. Willis T, LaVigna G. The safe management of physical aggression using multi-element positive practices in community settings. *J Head Trauma Rehabil* 2003;**18**(1):75–87.

85. Bornhofen C, McDonald S. Treating deficits in emotion perception following traumatic brain injury. *Neuropsychol Rehabil* 2008;**18**(1):22–44.

86. Hornak J, Rolls ET, Wade D. Face and voice expression identification in patients with emotional and behavioural changes following ventral frontal lobe damage. *Neuropsychologia* 1996;**34**(4):247–61.

87. McDonald S. Putting communication disorders in context after traumatic brain injury. *Aphasiology* 2000;**14**(4):339–47.

88. McDonald S. Traumatic brain injury and social function: let's get social. *Brain Impair* 2003;**4**(1):36–47.

89. Trower P. Situational analysis of the components and processes of behaviour of socially skilled and unskilled patients. *J Consult Clin Psychol* 1980;**48**(3):327–39.

90. Hux K, Marquardt J, Skinner S, Bond V. Special education services provided to students with and without parental reports of traumatic brain injury. *Brain Inj* 1999;**13**(6):447–55.

91. Sharp NL, Bye RA, Llewellyn GM, Cusick A. Fitting back in: adolescents returning to school after severe acquired brain injury. *Disabil Rehabil* 2006;**28**(12):767–78.

92. Catroppa C, Anderson V. Recovery in memory function, and its relationship to academic success at 24 months following pediatric TBI. *Child Neuropsychol* 2007;**13**(3):240–61.

93. Yeates KO, Taylor HG. Behavior problems in school and their educational correlates among children with

traumatic brain injury. *Exceptionality* 2006;**14**(3):141–54.

94. Asikainen I, Kaste M, Sarna S. Predicting late outcome for patients with traumatic brain injury referred to a rehabilitation programme: a study of 508 Finnish patients 5 years or more after injury. *Brain Inj* 1998;**12**(2):95–107.

95. Asikainen I, Kaste M, Sarna S. Patients with traumatic brain injury referred to a rehabilitation and re-employment programme: social and professional outcome for 508 Finnish patients 5 or more years after injury. *Brain Inj* 1996;**10**(12):883–99.

96. Elkind JS, Rubin E, Rosenthal S, Skoff B, Prather P. A simulated reality scenario compared with the computerized Wisconsin Card Sorting test: an analysis of preliminary results. *Cyberpsychol Behav* 2001;**4**(4):489–96.

97. Matheis RJ, Schultheis MT, Rizzo AA. Learning and memory in a virtual office environment. In Burdea G, Thalmann D, Lewis JA, eds. *Proceedings of the 2nd International Workshop in Virtual Rehabilitation*; 2003 Sep 21–22; Piscataway, NJ, USA.

98. Osborne K, Preston AM. Brain training: social cognition in a virtual reality setting. *New Frontiers in Pediatric Traumatic Brain Injury*; 2007 Nov 8–10; San Diego, USA.

99. Morris RG, Kotitsa M, Bramham J, Brooks B, Rose FD. Virtual reality investigation of strategy formation, rule breaking and prospective memory in patients with focal prefrontal neurosurgical lesions. In Sharkey P, Lányi CS, Standen P, eds. *Proceedings of the 4th International Conference on Disability, Virtual Reality & Associated Technologies*; 2002 Sep 18–21; Veszprém, Hungary.

100. Braga LW, Da Paz AC, Ylvisaker M. Direct clinician-delivered versus indirect family-supported rehabilitation of children with traumatic brain injury: a randomized controlled trial. *Brain Inj* 2005;**19**(10):819–31.

101. Wade SL, Carey J, Wolfe CR. The efficacy of an online cognitive-behavioral family intervention in improving child behaviour and social competence following pediatric brain injury. *Rehabil Psychol* 2006;**51**(3):179–89.

102. Wade SL, Carey J, Wolfe CR. An online family intervention to reduce parental distress following pediatric brain injury. *J Consult Clin Psychol* 2006;**74**(3):445–54.

103. Catroppa C, Anderson V. Planning, problem-solving and organizational abilities in children following traumatic brain injury: Intervention techniques. *Pediatr Rehabil* 2006;**9**(2):89–97.

Neurobehavioral aspects of traumatic brain injury sustained in adulthood

Tresa Roebuck-Spencer, James Baños, Mark Sherer and Thomas Novack

Introduction

Traumatic brain injury (TBI) is an important public health issue in the USA, with estimates of over 1.5 million new cases a year, most commonly due to motor vehicle accidents and falls [1]. TBI ranges in severity from mild to severe and results in some disturbance in cognitive, behavioral, emotional, or physical functioning. Often the effects of TBI are not physically observable to others, and thus are not well understood or appreciated by the general public. For persons with mild injuries, these effects may be first recognized, diagnosed, and treated by neuropsychologists. Thus, it is imperative that neuropsychologists have a good understanding of the short- and long-term cognitive, neurobehavioral, and psychosocial effects of TBI and how these effects change over the course of TBI recovery.

Although no particular demographic group is biologically predisposed to brain injury, certain groups are at higher risk. In adults, rates for TBI peak between the ages of 15 and 24 years and for persons older than 64 [2]. Other than for the very young or the very old, TBI rates are universally higher for men than women [3]. Other risk factors for brain injury include alcohol consumption [4], prior brain injury [5], and low socioeconomic status [6]. TBIs related to sports and recreation activities are receiving more attention, with an estimated 300 000 sports-related injuries with loss of consciousness each year [7]. Estimates rise to between 1.6 and 3.8 million per year when milder injuries without loss of consciousness and non-medically treated injuries are considered [3]. This chapter will focus on the most common forms of civilian TBI, as caused by motor vehicle accidents, falls, and recreational activities. The current scientific controversy regarding the physiological effects of military blast injuries and the overlap of their consequences with possible post-traumatic stress disorder is complex and beyond the scope of this chapter.

Classification of injury severity

The most commonly used index of injury severity is the Glasgow Coma Scale (GCS) [8], which is determined by eye-opening, motor movement, and verbal communication. Severe, moderate, and mild injuries are typically designated by scores of 3 to 8, 9 to 12, and 13 to 15, respectively [9]. On the mild end of the spectrum, individuals without abnormalities on neuroimaging are often described as having uncomplicated mild TBI. Individuals with mild TBI and abnormal findings on initial neuroimaging are often referred to as having sustained a complicated mild TBI and have been shown to have outcomes more similar to individuals with moderate TBI [10].

Injury severity can also be determined by the length of coma or the time it takes an individual to return to a conscious or responsive state, often defined as the time from injury until a person is able to follow commands. Another common indicator of injury severity is the duration of post-traumatic amnesia (PTA), which refers to the phase of recovery following TBI during which the patient is responsive, but acutely confused, disoriented, and unable to retain new memories. Duration of PTA can be assessed retrospectively through patient interview or, preferably, it can be assessed prospectively by serial assessment of orientation. While some have questioned the validity of retrospective assessment of PTA duration, studies have shown that PTA estimates are similar across these two assessment methods with high correlations between the two and similar ability to predict late outcome [11]. The commonly used criteria developed by Russell and Smith [12] classify PTA as slight (< 1 hour), moderate (1 to 24 hours), severe (1 to 7 days) or very severe concussion (beyond 7 days). Although these classification systems are not typically used clinically and have less empirical support than GCS, it is nonetheless important to be aware of them because they are frequently used in the research literature and GCS scores are not available for every patient.

Effects of TBI on the brain

TBI can occur in a variety of ways, resulting in a diverse pattern of brain insult. Closed head injury refers to blunt trauma where an object strikes the head or the head strikes an object. It also describes acceleration/deceleration injuries where brain tissue experiences shear, tensile, and compressive strain due to unrestricted movement of the head [13]. Open or penetrating head injury occurs when an object penetrates the dura and causes direct damage to the brain (e.g. stab wounds, gun-shot wounds, penetrating or comminuted skull fracture).

Resulting pathology to the brain is individual to the person and largely determined by mechanism of injury. The pathology resulting from a penetrating brain injury may be focal in nature and may include injury to the scalp, skull fracture, and associated intracerebral hematomas or contusions. Pathology resulting from acceleration/deceleration injuries often includes tearing of bridging veins (with resulting subarachnoid hemorrhage and/or subdural hematomas) and diffuse axonal injury [13]. Secondary or delayed complications can also occur, including swelling/edema, hypoxia/ischemia, raised intracranial pressure, associated vascular changes, and less commonly meningitis, and abscess [13].

Contusions to the brain following TBI are common and often occur in a characteristic distribution involving the frontal and temporal poles, the lateral and inferior aspects of the frontal and temporal lobes, and less commonly the inferior aspects of the cerebellum [14]. This pattern of findings is most probably due to abrasion of the brain against the bony ridges on the surface of the skull in these areas. These parenchymal contusions can result in focal signs and symptoms and have been blamed in some studies for the frontal executive and behavioral deficits following TBI [15].

Intracranial hematomas, which include subarachnoid, epidural, and subdural hematomas, are commonly seen following TBI and are the most common cause of clinical deterioration in patients who initially present well [16]. Hematomas may also be related to early focal cognitive signs and symptoms. Diffuse axonal injury (DAI) is commonly seen following acceleration/deceleration injuries and refers to a number of pathologies including hemorrhages and tissue tears seen throughout the brain. The cerebral commissures and other white matter tracts of the brainstem are particularly vulnerable to stretching and shearing as a result of mechanical forces. The extent of DAI may be the principal pathological substrate responsible for

decreased arousal levels and the range of neurological deficits from mild to severe brain injury [13].

By its nature TBI results in diffuse effects on the brain. When present, focal cognitive and behavioral symptoms, such as aphasia or apraxia, tend to be observed early in the course of recovery. While there is some evidence that location and size of lesion is related to type and extent of cognitive impairment [15, 17], other studies have not supported the presence

Table 11c.1. Major neurobehavioral characteristics of TBI.

Cognitive impairments	Neuroanatomical correlates
Impaired alertness/ arousal	Diffuse axonal injury and/or brainstem injuries with greater severity associated with depth of coma
Slowed cognitive processing	Diffuse axonal injury/white matter disruption
Poor attention	Diffuse cerebral contusions and/or diffuse axonal injury
Impaired learning and memory	Frontal and/or temporal lobe contusions
Working memory impairment	Diffuse axonal injury; white matter lesions; frontal lobe dysfunction
Impaired executive functioning	Contusions to the frontal and temporal poles, the lateral and inferior aspects of the frontal and temporal lobes, and less commonly to the inferior aspects of the cerebellum; damage to frontal/subcortical loops
Aphasia	Focal injury to left hemisphere or left subcortical structures through hematomas or cerebral contusions
Limb apraxia	Focal injury to left hemisphere from hematoma or cerebral contusion

Neurobehavioral syndromes	Neuroanatomical correlates
Disinhibition syndromes	Loss of tonic inhibition by the orbitofrontal system, often through damage to the orbital frontal cortex and its associative connections
Impairments in initiation	Lack of integration between drive-related behaviors and cognitive mediators of behavioral expression, often through damage to the medial frontal cortex and its associative connections
Impairments in self-awareness	Poorly understood, but frequently associated with damage to the prefrontal cortex and temporal poles
Neuropsychiatric disorders	Disruption of distributed neurotransmitter systems (particularly early in recovery); psychosocial factors may play an increasing role in later recovery

of a specific pattern of neurobehavioral impairment based on lesion location [14, 18]. See Table 11c.1 for a description of the most common neurobehavioral characteristics of TBI.

Cognitive effects of TBI

The effect of TBI on cognition and subsequent recovery varies as a function of injury severity. Shortly following injury, individuals sustaining a mild TBI typically experience transient symptoms of mild confusion, difficulty maintaining attention, and forgetfulness. Over several weeks, these individuals may complain of difficulty paying attention in the face of distraction, difficulty multitasking, and cognitive fatigue. The majority of available research shows that individuals with mild TBI and no associated findings on structural neuroimaging (i.e. uncomplicated mild TBI) typically recover to baseline levels of cognitive functioning within 1 to 3 months post-injury and are expected to have a favorable long-term outcome [10, 19, 20]. However, a subset of individuals do not recover within this timeline, with prolonged symptoms often described as post-concussion syndrome. There is controversy about the cause of these prolonged symptoms, with many believing that they are driven by emotional/personality factors and secondary gain issues, as opposed to underlying neurological impairment [20].

Individuals with moderate to severe TBI typically pass through a series of predictable stages during the initial recovery period. While order of progression through these stages is constant, some stages may be absent and duration varies considerably. Impaired consciousness is typically seen immediately following injury, with coma representing the most extreme end of the spectrum. Coma is a temporary non-responsive state in which the patient has closed eyes, follows no instructions, gives no communication, and shows no purposeful movements [8]. Following resolution of coma, a small percentage of surviving patients remain in a nonresponsive vegetative state [21], characterized by eye-opening, recovery of some brainstem functioning and return of sleep/wake cycles but without behavioral evidence for self or environmental awareness. Surviving, non-vegetative patients who go on to recover a limited degree of responsiveness to the environment may be classified in a minimally conscious state, with inconsistent, minimal evidence of awareness of self or the environment [22].

In most cases, resolution of coma is followed by a responsive, but markedly confused state, commonly referred to as Post-Traumatic Amnesia (PTA) [23]. Hallmarks of this stage include deficits in arousal, orientation, attention, and memory encoding [24]. Based on recent research it may be more accurate to characterize this phase of recovery in terms of delirium or as a post-traumatic confusional state (PTCS) rather than a purely amnestic state [25].

Following resolution of PTA, the majority of individuals with moderate to severe TBI demonstrate continued cognitive and neurobehavioral impairments. Cognitive deficits are variable and dependent on many factors, including premorbid functioning, comorbid neurological and psychiatric status, nature and severity of the injury, and timing of assessment relative to injury. Multiple studies document greater levels of cognitive impairment as severity of injury worsens (e.g. Schretlen and Shapiro [19], Dikmen and Machamer [26]). The magnitude and pattern of cognitive impairment depend on the timing of the assessment relative to onset of injury. Almost all patients with moderate or severe TBI have detectable cognitive impairments at 1 month post-injury [27]. Cognitive functioning typically improves with time, with the most recovery occurring during the first 6 months post-injury and continuing for 18 months or longer [19, 28]. Improvement is typically seen across most areas of cognitive functioning, with improvement seen in basic cognitive skills, such as immediate attention, preceding improvement in more complex cognitive skills, such as problem-solving and complex attention [28, 29]. At 1 year post-injury, almost all patients with very severe injuries continue to have cognitive impairment and more than half of patients with moderate to severe impairment have residual deficits [30]. While the expected course is recovery of function until a plateau is reached usually around 18–24 months, a subgroup of patients will improve beyond this point while another subgroup may show late decline [28, 31]. Greater age at time of injury and increased levels of depression may be associated with increased risk of late decline [28, 31].

Consistent with the heterogeneous nature of injury, the pattern of impairment varies across individuals. Although circumscribed cognitive deficits may be seen in patients with focal injuries, they are generally superimposed on global cognitive dysfunction resulting from diffuse injury. Intellectual functioning may be relatively spared [32]. Commonly seen impairments include some combination of slowed fine-motor speed, impaired attention, slowed cognitive processing speed, learning and memory impairment, impaired complex language and discourse, and impaired executive functions (e.g. Levin [23], Millis et al. [28]).

Severe TBI has been accepted as a risk factor for degenerative neurological diseases such as Alzheimer's [33] and Parkinson's [34]. It has been convincingly demonstrated that multiple proteins associated with these neurodegenerative disorders accumulate as a result of TBI [35]. There could also be a genetic component increasing the association between TBI and Alzheimer's disease [36], although the relationship has not been established beyond doubt [37]. These disorders do not arise in the early stages of recovery, although the accumulation of proteins begins with the trauma onset. One interpretation is that the TBI accelerates development of a condition that the person might have experienced even without the traumatic event.

Neurobehavioral effects of TBI

A range of neurobehavioral changes are frequently seen following brain injury. Emotional and behavioral changes following mild TBI, when present, are typically transient in nature and less intense in magnitude. In contrast, for individuals with moderate to severe TBI, such changes can be severe and often pose the greatest challenge to return to previous levels of functioning. Neurobehavioral deficits tend to be united by a common theme of impaired regulatory control, often accompanied by poor awareness of the dysregulation. In this sense, they share features with some of the cognitive deficits associated with TBI and are often considered to fall within the larger category of executive dysfunction. However, the neurobehavioral manifestations of TBI are often enduring and introduce a unique element of impairment that can often place greater burden on caregivers than cognitive or physical deficits [38], and can prove to be a formidable barrier to community integration and vocational rehabilitation [39]. Although the range of neurobehavioral problems after TBI is broad, they can be considered under the categories of disinhibition syndromes, impairments in initiation, impairments of self-awareness, and neuropsychiatric disorders.

Disinhibition syndromes

Damage to the orbitofrontal cortex has long been associated with cognitive, behavioral, and neuropsychiatric

disinhibition. The orbitofrontal cortex has a unique vulnerability to injury with the sudden acceleration and deceleration associated with a traumatic blow to the head. Behavioral changes after TBI are best conceptualized as a loss of tonic balance in a regulatory system that includes the orbitofrontal cortex, other areas of the brain, and corresponding associative pathways. In this system, the more ventrally located cortical areas (primarily the orbitofrontal cortex) selectively inhibit and release behavioral programs initiated by the more dorsally located cortex [40]. Damage to these areas or their associated pathways can disrupt this balance between initiation and inhibition across motor, cognitive, and behavioral domains. The orbitofrontal cortex is, however, unique in that it has direct efferent connectivity with limbic/diencephalic structures as well as brainstem biogenic amine nuclei, all of which are significant determinants of behavior [41]. The net result can be a failure to inhibit emotionally guided behaviors, or a failure to incorporate cues as to reinforcement value and behavioral relevance into the behavioral repertoire. As such, common behavioral features of TBI include aggression/agitation, social disinhibition, impulsivity, risk-taking behavior, and affective lability [42, 43].

Aggression and agitation are among the most common (and problematic) manifestations of behavioral disinhibition following moderate to severe TBI. These behaviors are often poorly directed and not always related to environmental triggers in a predictable fashion. They are consistently rated as being one of the most distressing behavioral sequelae of TBI by family and caregivers, and interfere with rehabilitation efforts [44]. Aggression and agitation are associated with poor community and vocational re-integration. They predict domestic violence and relationship failure, which is of particular concern given that loss of social support may in turn exacerbate aggressive behavior [45]. In more severe cases, aggressive behavior is a leading factor in long-term institutional placement [46].

Agitated behavior is quite common during the acute period of recovery, occurring in 35–96% of patients [42]. Agitation that occurs in this period of recovery is best conceptualized as non-purposeful behavior occurring in the context of generalized confusion. Risk factors include frontotemporal injury, disorientation, comorbid medical complications, and use of anticonvulsant medications. During post-acute rehabilitation, aggression and agitation are associated with younger age, environmental cues, and mood disorder [47, 48]. The more enduring patterns of aggression and agitation seen in post-acute recovery and in the chronic phase of TBI tend to be more complex manifestations of behavioral dyscontrol that are complicated by environmental factors and premorbid personality and behavioral characteristics. The behavior tends to be more frequently verbal than physical, except in extreme cases. Risk factors for long-term aggressive behavior include neurocognitive impairments [49], problems with family support or family structure [45], and unemployment [50].

Impairments in initiation

Although perhaps not as dramatic and unsettling as the disinhibition syndromes, impairments in initiation can be equally disabling. The behavioral presentation of initiation syndromes can range from extreme apathy and avolition, to more subtle impairments in initiating and persisting with goal-directed activities. Severe apathy and avolition can greatly hinder participation in even basic activities of daily living and place a substantial burden on caregivers, who must frequently cue and guide behavior. The more subtle impairments may not interfere as much with basic self-care, but may be more problematic in the context of independent living, vocational rehabilitation, and educational pursuits [51]. Neuroanatomically, impairments in initiation can be associated with lesions of the medial aspects of the frontal lobes, particularly those affecting the cingulate gyrus or its subcortical connections [52, 53]. Among many other functions, the cingulate gyrus serves as an integration point between behavioral influences of limbic origin and higher-level cognitive regulation of behavior. A failure of this system results in limbic and drive-related behaviors that are not incorporated into behavioral expression.

Impairments of self-awareness

The types of awareness deficits encountered after TBI are not often as dramatic as the frank anosognosia syndromes seen in stroke. However, these deficits can be complex and pose a significant barrier across many domains of functioning. Diminished awareness of a basic physical deficit (e.g. weakness of an extremity) may sometimes be encountered during the acute/post-acute period of recovery in the context of more global cognitive deficits, but does not often persist into the chronic stages of recovery. Impaired awareness of

cognitive and behavioral deficits is more likely to persist past the post-acute period, although awareness often improves with time [54]. In the more chronic phase of recovery, deficits in awareness are more likely to involve awareness of functional implications of deficits or ability to make generalizations about one's abilities when new situations are encountered. In this sense, such deficits can be viewed as an extension of cognitive impairments in judgment, self-monitoring, and ability to process corrective cues from the environment. The neuroanatomic substrate of self-awareness is not well understood. Clinical and empirical evidence implicates damage to the prefrontal cortex and temporal poles, possibly by disrupting the integration of intrapersonal information and extrapersonal performance feedback. Specific studies have documented that the number of brain lesions, but not volumes of lesions within specific areas, is associated with more severely impaired self-awareness, suggesting that impaired self-awareness may be related to disruptions in broadly distributed networks [55].

Neuropsychiatric disorders

Depression and anxiety are the most common neuropsychiatric sequelae of TBI. Prevalence estimates for depression range from 15% to 60% [56, 57]. This variability is due in part to the challenge posed by symptom overlap with TBI (e.g. apathy, fatigue, sleep disturbance, memory problems, etc.). Disruption of distributed neurotransmitter systems (e.g. the serotonin system) is one hypothesized cause of depression after TBI, particularly earlier in recovery. Depression later in recovery may be more strongly related to psychosocial stressors and emerging awareness of deficits. Not surprisingly, depression after TBI is associated with poorer psychosocial outcome [58]. Risk factors include pre-injury depression, psychosocial stress, and social isolation. Recent research has increasingly implicated coping style as a factor influencing the development and maintenance of depression in the chronic phase of TBI recovery as well [59]. Anxiety after TBI is often generalized in nature, with rates ranging from 2% to 44% [56]. Anxiety in the form of post-traumatic stress disorder (PTSD) remains a point of controversy in the field because memory for the traumatic event itself is often lacking. PTSD symptoms are more common in milder injuries where there is more likely to be at least partial recall of the event [60], although there is evidence that PTSD symptoms in more severe injuries may develop secondary to the trauma of hospitalization, medical procedures, and pain [61, 62]. Incidence and prevalence of psychotic disorders after TBI is difficult to ascertain due to lack of clear operational definitions and inconsistent methodology, but these disorders are generally not considered to be common following TBI [57].

Psychosocial effects of TBI

The upheaval caused by moderate to severe TBI in adults is understandably associated with changes in personal and family roles as well as community activities such as employment, education, driving, and engagement in leisure activities. The cognitive, behavioral, and emotional impairments following TBI often pose a substantial and enduring barrier to resuming these roles and activities. The impact is particularly acute for the high proportion of young adult TBI survivors, who are in an important developmental epoch when social, vocational, and family roles have not already been established and refined.

Except in more severe cases, basic living skills tend to have a favorable long-term outcome after TBI [58]. Personal and family roles are more likely to be strained by personality and behavioral changes after TBI. Aggression and other manifestations of disinhibition can obviously be problematic in close relationships. However, impaired social skills and social problem-solving (particularly in conjunction with poor awareness) also negatively affect relationships [63]. For TBI survivors, attrition of friendships often accompanies such changes, further narrowing social support. Even subtle social and behavioral impairments can lead to more distant familial relationships and attrition of social relationships. Unfortunately, this can exacerbate the problem, as familial and social support are in turn predictors of more favorable psychosocial outcome [45].

In addition to changes in interpersonal roles, TBI survivors often experience substantial changes in their participation in the community at large, including independent living, community mobility, vocational pursuits, and participation in leisure activities. Return to work and maintenance of employment are particularly important, not only as key components of independence, but as an opportunity for development of social support and leisure opportunities, and enhancement of community integration in the larger sense. Unfortunately, employment is consistently identified

as among the poorest areas of psychosocial outcome [58], with post-injury unemployment estimates ranging from 10% to 70% [64–66]. This extreme range in estimates relates to the definition of employment. While some studies refer to return to a previous job, lower rates of unemployment may be seen in studies that refer to any type of employment or return to productive activity, which, in addition to employment, includes return to school, homemaking, and sometimes volunteer activity. It should be noted that many of those able to return to work report problems on the job and the stability of work is uncertain [67]. Vocational stability after a return to work is also an important issue, as many TBI survivors may have the basic skills to perform a job but may be unable to manage the social and behavioral constraints imposed in vocational settings.

Injury severity has the biggest impact on return to employment [68], but other factors also contribute, including pre-injury unstable work histories, lower education, minority status, being unmarried, driving limitations, and working at unskilled positions [65, 69–71]. Mood, fatigue, and behavioral problems can also interfere with return to work following TBI [72]. Despite the prevalence of the problem, substance use prior to injury has not been explored extensively as a predictor of outcome after injury. Most attention focuses on substance abuse after injury [73], which has a deleterious effect on participation in vocational training and employment [74].

Return to driving is a key outcome after TBI in that driving affords greater opportunity for social and community integration, including employment. TBI survivors frequently cite inability to drive as among the most functionally limiting problems they face [75]. The problem is made more complex by the fact that driving poses an issue of safety, yet procedures for assessing this risk lack standardization. Many TBI survivors return to driving without any formal evaluation. On-the-road driving evaluations are the preferred means of assessing readiness to return to driving, although such evaluations are costly and not available to all TBI survivors. In-office screening measures are available [76], but need further development and standardization. Although assessment of neurocognitive factors such as attention and executive functioning may be helpful, the impact of factors such as poor judgment, behavioral impulsivity, and self-awareness of limitations is more difficult to assess. In addition to injury severity, premorbid personality factors (e.g. risk-taking behavior) and indices of premorbid driving safety (e.g. traffic violations and accidents) may be useful in predicting driving risk. A return to driving with restrictions (e.g. light traffic, familiar routes, no driving at night or in bad weather) can be a means of mitigating risk, although the burden of enforcing such restrictions frequently falls upon the primary caregiver.

Neuropsychological assessment following adult TBI

The focus of neuropsychological assessment is determined by the goals of the assessment, the severity of the injury, and the individual's stage of recovery. Information from neuropsychological evaluations is invaluable and can be used to provide feedback to the patient, caregivers, and treatment staff regarding treatment and discharge planning, assessment of effectiveness of drug trials and other interventions, supervision needs, decision-making capacity, driving capacity, and readiness to return to work, school, or other independent activities [77].

Assessment following mild TBI

Traditionally patients with mild TBI are seen for comprehensive neuropsychological testing to assess cognitive abilities and make recommendations regarding return to functional activities and treatment needs. In such evaluations, it is essential to consider the expected duration of TBI-related symptoms, given research showing that symptoms are expected to resolve within 1–3 months following injury [19, 20]. Consideration of potential etiological factors other than TBI should be considered for individuals reporting symptoms outside this time window or excessive complaints, given that evidence of prolonged or excessive symptoms may be associated with psychiatric/emotional factors, secondary gain issues, substance abuse, or other comorbid factors [20]. Individuals with complicated mild TBI may perform somewhat worse on cognitive testing than those with uncomplicated mild TBI when assessed several days following injury and a year after injury deficits may still be evident in some cases [78]. Other evidence suggests that long-term outcome for the majority of individuals with complicated mild TBI is still very good overall [79].

In some settings, particularly those treating sports-related concussions, initial neuropsychological testing following mild TBI or concussion can occur within hours or days after injury. This testing can take the form of serial assessments using sensitive measures of attention, processing speed, and symptom report with the goal of tracking recovery from injury. This procedure is gaining momentum from the sports concussion literature where paper and pencil tests [80] or computerized testing batteries [81, 82] are used to measure attention and processing speed, areas of cognition known to be sensitive to mild TBI. Although there is controversy regarding incremental validity, sensitivity, and reliability of computerized testing following concussion [83], these testing procedures have been shown to document recovery of cognitive functioning over 1–2 weeks following concussion [81, 82] and to have incremental validity over and above symptom report and other measures tracking concussion recovery [84].

Assessment following moderate to severe TBI

For individuals with moderate to severe TBI, early neuropsychological assessment may focus on determining level of responsiveness and tracking cognitive status and recovery. Measures such as the Coma Recovery Scale–Revised [85] can be used to assess arousal, attention, and other key behavioral elements for individuals in coma or minimally conscious state. With responsive but confused patients, measures of orientation [86, 87] are well suited to assist with determination of when a patient has recovered basic cognitive skills.

Disagreement exists regarding when to first perform neuropsychological assessment. Traditionally, administration of neuropsychological tests has been contingent on PTA resolution, as it is assumed that significant disorientation, confusion, and poor attention would compromise validity of testing. However, research suggests that administration of selected neuropsychological measures to patients still in PTA can result in useful prognostic data [9, 88]. In a survey of neuropsychologists with extensive clinical and research experience in TBI [77], guidelines for timing of assessments were contingent on injury severity and time since injury. In general, preliminary testing at resolution of PTA was recommended for all levels of TBI severity. For individuals with mild TBI, initial testing was recommended between 1 week and 1 month post-injury with repeat assessment at 1 year. For individuals with moderate to severe TBI, initial follow-up testing intervals were recommended at 3 months, 6 months, 1 year, and 2 years post-injury. These guidelines provide general suggestions only. While there is no published research specifically addressing appropriate post-injury testing intervals, it is essential to be aware of severity of injury and time since injury when interpreting research using TBI samples.

There are no objective guidelines regarding the selection of specific neuropsychological tests to evaluate the effects of TBI. While the Halstead-Reitan Neuropsychological Battery has been used successfully in the area of TBI (e.g. Dikmen et al. [30]), concerns regarding this battery of tests include a potential "floor" effect for very severely injured individuals and limited ecological validity [77]. Most neuropsychologists today use an eclectic battery of tests with a focus on adequate normative values and criterion validity. Regardless of specific battery or specific tests, key domains to target when evaluating an individual with TBI should include orientation, fine motor skills, attention, cognitive speed, learning and memory, language skills, visual-perceptual skills, and executive functions [9]. Despite compelling evidence of a TBI, some individuals may either consciously or unconsciously exaggerate symptoms when seen for follow-up evaluations, particularly those engaged in litigation or with other secondary gain issues. Thus, symptom validity measures should be included in assessment batteries when appropriate. It also is essential to include assessment of neurobehavioral status, particularly areas of functioning described earlier in this chapter, given that such behavioral changes can exist even when cognitive functioning is within normal limits. Further, evaluation of emotional and psychiatric status is imperative given high rates of psychopathology, and in particular high rates of depression, after TBI, and the association of poor outcome with emotional distress.

Neuropsychological test results, in aggregate, have the capacity to predict community functioning. Sherer and colleagues [89] found that early cognitive status made independent contributions to the prediction of productivity at 1 year post-injury, while other studies [90, 91] have documented strong concurrent relationships between cognitive functioning and functional status at 1 to 10 years post-injury. In studies reviewed by Sherer and Novack [77], it was found that results from neuropsychological evaluations are generally predictive of personal safety, independent living, driving safety, and return to work.

It is also important to note that neuropsychological testing is predictive of later productivity even when controlling for demographic and injury severity variables [89]. A recent prospective study found that a brief battery of neuropsychological tests administered early in the recovery course was predictive of handicap, functional outcome, supervision needs, and employability at 1 year [92]. This battery was also found to predict functional outcome at 1 year above and beyond functional and injury severity variables, providing strong support for the incremental validity of neuropsychological testing in moderate to severe TBI.

Interventions for TBI

While the effects of mild TBI are expected to be transient, they can limit an individual's return to work and, in some individuals, persist past the window of expected recovery. There is good empirical evidence that early single-session treatment providing education about the effects and recovery of mild TBI in conjunction with reassurance and appropriate attribution of symptoms can improve outcome following mild TBI [93]. Single-session treatments have been shown to be as effective as more extensive assessment and treatment, with effects lasting up to 1 year post-injury [94].

Individuals with moderate to severe TBI often have persisting impairments that impact their ability to return to their previous level of functioning. These patients are much more likely than patients with mild injuries to require inpatient rehabilitation. Upon discharge from inpatient rehabilitation, most individuals with moderate to severe TBI still require supervision within the home and are not ready to return to work, school, or other previous levels of independent functioning. Comprehensive-integrated post-acute rehabilitation programs are specialized in treating persons with TBI with cognitive and behavioral difficulties that may render them unable to benefit from traditional rehabilitation programs. Such programs provide all aspects of rehabilitation treatment in an integrated format with disciplines creating collaborative goals related to the client's individual needs, such as work re-entry, school re-entry, or independence. Improved functional outcome has been demonstrated for individuals participating in such programs, including improvements in independent living, participation in household activities, productive activity, and vocational reentry [95, 96], with gains in functioning maintained for most participants up to 4 years post-injury [97]. Further, there is evidence that these programs result in improved outcome even for individuals with chronic TBI and for whom improvement due to spontaneous neurological recovery can be ruled out [98].

Treatments for cognitive impairments following TBI are often classified as "restitution training", defined as the direct attempt to restore underlying impaired function, or "strategy training", defined as development of strategies to compensate for residual cognitive deficits. The former has limited empirical support and generalization outside specific tasks. Studies and reviews addressing cognitive rehabilitation techniques often come under fire for the limited number of Class I studies or randomized controlled trials (RCTs) and lack of data regarding duration of treatment effects and generalization of effects to everyday functioning or real-world tasks.

In the most recent extensive review of the effectiveness of cognitive rehabilitation, Cicerone and colleagues [99] surveyed the literature from 1998 to 2002 with a concentration on class I studies. Cognitive linguistic therapies were found to be effective for language-based impairments. Group communication treatment was found to improve language functioning, communication, and pragmatics. With regard to visual spatial impairments, compensatory visual scanning strategies were helpful for unilateral neglect, and there was promising support for computer-based restitution training to reduce the extent of visual disorder. Self-management strategies to improve attention were found to be effective in post-acute but not acute periods of recovery. Remediation of memory impairments focused on compensatory strategies and use of assistive technology. For those with relatively mild memory impairments and intact self-management abilities, internal compensatory strategies (such as visual imagery) and external strategies (such as memory logs or diaries) have been found to be effective. For those with more moderate to severe memory problems, external memory aids, such as paging devices, are effective in improving independent functioning. Effective remediation of executive functioning deficits included training in formal problem-solving strategies and their application to everyday situations and functional activities. Maintenance of gains achieved by these treatments needs further study given evidence that initial improvements seen for some forms of cognitive rehabilitation, specifically memory training, are not seen at 6 months post-treatment [100].

Neurobehavioral and emotional changes following TBI are often the most challenging to treat and the most distressing to families and caregivers. For instance, by its very nature, poor self-awareness is resistant to treatment, given that individuals do not consistently acknowledge their own difficulties and do not realize when behavioral or compensatory strategies need to be employed. Interventions including feedback regarding performance, education about impairments, and implementation of self-performed prediction and goal-setting exercises have been explored in the literature. A recent study, using a randomized controlled trial, demonstrated improvements in functional tasks and self-regulation following participation in an awareness training intervention, in which individuals were asked to rate performance levels prior to and following a task [101]. A similar study compared an awareness training intervention, consisting of education, prediction, performance, and evaluation, to conventional therapy and found improved self-awareness but no differences between groups on the functional task [102]. Studies of social communication skills training showed improved communication and improved overall life satisfaction for individuals with TBI [103]. Group-based supportive therapy has been found to be successful for improving coping skills and adjustment following TBI [104]. With regard to psychosocial consequences of TBI, vocational rehabilitation, and more specifically supported employment, has been shown to increase return to work rates and job stability in survivors of TBI (e.g. Wehman et al. [105]).

Medications are a common treatment for the cognitive and neurobehavioral impairments following TBI across all severity levels. In a recent review of pharmacological interventions following TBI [106] three major areas were included as potential treatment targets including cognition, aggression, and affective disorders/anxiety/psychosis. Treatment "standards" by definition would be concluded from good evidence of effectiveness of a treatment based on at least one well-designed class I study or overwhelming class II evidence. Although there were an adequate number of studies to review, due to recurrent methodological problems the quality of the evidence did not support any treatment standards. "Guidelines" for treatment are based on well-designed class II studies that provide fair evidence of treatment effectiveness. Treatment "options" are based on class II or class III studies whose results support a recommendation for treatment for a specific group. With respect to cognition, treatment guidelines included the use of stimulants (specifically methylphenidate) for treatment of attention

Table 11c.2. Empirically supported treatments for TBI.

Target problems	Treatment(s)
Mild TBI	
Neuropsychological effects of mild TBI	Single-session educational treatment
Cognition	
Language/communication impairments	Cognitive linguistic therapies; group communication treatment
Visual spatial; unilateral neglect	Training of compensatory visual scanning strategies
Apraxia	Gestural or strategy training
Attentional impairment	Self-management attention-processing strategies (for post-acute periods only)
	Medication (e.g. methylphenidate)
Learning and memory	Internal compensatory strategies (e.g. visual imagery; memory logs/diaries) (mild impairment)
	External memory aids such as pagers or phone alarms (moderate–severe impairment)
	Medication (e.g. donepezil)
Executive dysfunction	Formal problem-solving training and training of self-regulation strategies
	Medication (e.g. bromocriptine)
Neurobehavioral deficits	
Impairment in language pragmatics	Group communication treatment
Poor self-awareness	Awareness training interventions
Aggression	Medication (e.g. beta-blockers)
Depression/anxiety	Psychotherapy (individual and group)
	Medication (tricyclic antidepressants and serotonin reuptake inhibitors)
Psychosis	Medication (e.g. olanzapine)
Coping skills	Group-based supportive therapy
Community reintegration	Comprehensive-integrated post-acute rehabilitation programs
Return to work	Supported employment
	Comprehensive-integrated post-acute rehabilitation programs

and speed of processing deficits, the use of cholinesterase inhibitors (specifically donepezil) for treatment of attention and memory function, and the use of dopamine agonists (specifically bromocriptine) for treatment of executive dysfunction. Guidelines for treatment of aggression included the use of beta-blockers (e.g. propranolol and pindolol). Evidence was insufficient to support the development of guidelines and standards for the treatment of TBI-related depression, mania, anxiety and psychosis. However, provided options included the use of tricyclic antidepressants and serotonin reuptake inhibitors (specifically sertraline) for treatment of depression and the use of atypical antipsychotics (specifically olanzapine) for treatment of psychosis. See Table 11c.2 for list of common treatments following TBI.

There is no cure for TBI; thus, the best treatment is prevention. In conjunction with the Centers for Disease Control, one of the largest prevention programs is the Think First National Injury Prevention Foundation. This, and other similar programs, seeks to prevent brain injuries by providing public education, implementing specific public health programs, and affecting public policy. Resulting public health education programs frequently focus on vehicular safety (e.g. wearing seatbelts, wearing approved helmets, obeying traffic laws, etc.) and firearms safety [107]. There is good evidence that bicycle and motorcycle helmets, seatbelts, and airbags reduce severity of brain injury following accidents [108–110]. More recently, researchers are examining specific types of sports helmets designed to lessen impact of injuries during contact sports [111].

Future directions

Traditional, in-office services are not sufficient to address the post-hospital cognitive, behavioral, and emotional needs following TBI [112]. Alternative means of assessment and intervention may help address this service gap. In particular, telemedicine is showing promise for patients whose participation in follow-up care is complicated by disability, transportation, or distance. In a recent study, telephone-based counseling and education at intervals after TBI led to improved functional status at 1 year follow-up [113]. A mail survey specifically addressing telerehabilitation needs revealed that individuals with TBI are interested in receiving services through telemedicine and are particularly interested in services to assist with memory, attention, problem-solving, and activities of daily living [114].

Computer administration of tests offers the advantage of consistency of presentation, including timing of the presentation of materials and responses, in addition to rapid scoring, which has been essential to assessment in athletic venues where brief evaluations are performed to provide before and after assessments in cases of concussion. Computers have been playing a role in test scoring for a number of years and individual tests can now be administered by computer. Entire neuropsychological batteries have been developed for the computer [115]. This also presents challenges: if tests can be administered, scored, and interpreted by computer, what is the role of the neuropsychologist? Test security also needs to be considered, as does the loss of flexibility in administration that can be essential in assessing some patients.

Neuropsychologists can anticipate playing a strong role in research on brain physiology and structure in relation to behavior as documented by increasingly sophisticated neuroimaging techniques. To date, fMRI studies have shown altered patterns of brain activation during working memory tasks in individuals with moderate to severe TBI [116] and in individuals with mild TBI [117]. These results suggest that individuals with TBI may utilize different strategies or solve problems in less efficient ways than non-injured controls. fMRI also has great promise for improving our current understanding of neuroplasticity during recovery from TBI and may assist with understanding the neural mechanisms underlying recovery during various rehabilitation therapies.

Diffusion tensor imaging (DTI) is a noninvasive imaging technique that measures the structural integrity of white matter tracts, including detecting abnormalities not seen on traditional structural imaging and changes in white matter integrity following mild TBI [118]. DTI findings also correlate with injury severity, suggesting a potential future role in early diagnosis and prognosis of TBI [119]. Neuropsychologists are in a position to lead such studies as well as assisting others in developing methodologies that highlight cognitive performance.

The promise of virtual reality has been touted [120] but applications are still scarce, perhaps due to the expense of the technology. However, technologies incorporating virtual reality are beginning to surface, such as driving-simulation devices and programs [121]. Recent versions of video games that respond to body movements of the players approximate virtual reality and may provide physical and cognitive stimulation for rehabilitation purposes. It appears likely that virtual reality in some guise will play a role in interventions to address rehabilitation following brain injury, if not in the assessment of problems.

Acknowledgements

Completion of this chapter was partially supported by the National Institute on Disability and Rehabilitation Research Grant # H133A070039 and the Texas TBI Model System of TIRR (Grant # H133A070043).

References

1. Rutland-Brown W, Langlois JA, Thomas KE, et al. Incidence of traumatic brain injury in the United States, 2003. *J Head Trauma Rehabil* 2006;**21**:544–8.

2. Kraus JF, Chu LD. Epidemiology. In Silver JM, McAllister TW, Yudofsky SC, eds. *Textbook of Traumatic Brain Injury*. Washington DC: American Psychiatric Publishing; 2005: 3–26.

3. Langlois JA, Rutland-Brown W, Wald MM. The epidemiology and impact of traumatic brain injury: a brief overview. *J Head Trauma Rehabil* 2006;**21**:375–8.

4. Smith GS, Kraus JF. Alcohol and residential, recreational, and occupational injuries: a review of the epidemiologic evidence. *Annu Rev Public Health* 1988;**9**:99–121.

5. Salcido R, Costich JF. Recurrent traumatic brain injury. *Brain Inj* 1992;**6**:293–8.

6. Kraus JF, Fife D, Ramstein K, et al. The relationship of family income to the incidence, external causes, and outcomes of serious brain injury, San Diego County, California. *Am J Public Health* 1986;**76**:1345–7.

7. Thurman DJ, Branche CM, Sniezek JE. The epidemiology of sports-related traumatic brain injuries in the United States: recent developments. *J Head Trauma Rehabil* 1998;**13**:1–8.

8. Teasdale G, Jennett B. Assessment of coma and impaired consciousness. A practical scale. *Lancet* 1974;**2**:81–4.

9. Hannay HJ, Sherer M. Assessment of outcome from head injury. In Narayan RK, Wilberger JE, Povlishock JT, eds. *Neurotrauma*. New York: McGraw-Hill; 1996: 723–47.

10. Williams DH, Levin HS, Eisenberg HM. Mild head injury classification. *Neurosurgery* 1990;**27**:422–8.

11. McMillan TM, Jongen EL, Greenwood RJ. Assessment of post-traumatic amnesia after severe closed head injury: retrospective or prospective? *J Neurol Neurosurg Psychiatry* 1996;**60**:422–7.

12. Russell WR, Smith A. Post-traumatic amnesia in closed head injury. *Arch Neurol* 1961;**5**:4–17.

13. Gennarelli TA, Graham DI. Neuropathology. In Silver JM, McAllister TW, Yudofsky SC, eds. *Textbook of Traumatic Brain Injury*. Washington DC: American Psychiatric Publishing; 2005: 27–50.

14. Levin HS, Williams DH, Eisenberg HM, et al. Serial MRI and neurobehavioural findings after mild to moderate closed head injury. *J Neurol Neurosurg Psychiatry* 1992;**55**:255–62.

15. Levin HS, Amparo E, Eisenberg HM, et al. Magnetic resonance imaging and computerized tomography in relation to the neurobehavioral sequelae of mild and moderate head injuries. *J Neurosurg* 1987;**66**:706–13.

16. Rockswold GL, Leonard PR, Nagib MG. Analysis of management in thirty-three closed head injury patients who "talked and deteriorated". *Neurosurgery* 1987;**21**:51–5.

17. Levin HS, Culhane KA, Mendelsohn D, et al. Cognition in relation to magnetic resonance imaging in head-injured children and adolescents. *Arch Neurol* 1993;**50**:897–905.

18. Anderson CV, Bigler ED, Blatter DD. Frontal lobe lesions, diffuse damage, and neuropsychological functioning in traumatic brain-injured patients. *J Clin Exp Neuropsychol* 1995;**17**:900–8.

19. Schretlen DJ, Shapiro AM. A quantitative review of the effects of traumatic brain injury on cognitive functioning. *Int Rev Psychiatry* 2003;**15**:341–9.

20. Iverson GL. Outcome from mild traumatic brain injury. *Curr Opin Psychiatry* 2005;**18**:301–17.

21. Lippert-Gruner M, Wedekind C, Klug N. Outcome of prolonged coma following severe traumatic brain injury. *Brain Inj* 2003;**17**:49–54.

22. Giacino JT, Ashwal S, Childs N, et al. The minimally conscious state: definition and diagnostic criteria. *Neurology* 2002;**58**:349–53.

23. Levin HS. Neurobehavioral sequelae of closed head injury. In Cooper PR, ed. *Head Injury*. Baltimore: Williams & Wilkins; 1993: 525–51.

24. Stuss DT, Binns MA, Carruth FG, et al. The acute period of recovery from traumatic brain injury: posttraumatic amnesia or posttraumatic confusional state? *J Neurosurg* 1999;**90**:635–43.

25. Sherer M, Nakase-Thompson R, Yablon SA, et al. Multidimensional assessment of acute confusion after traumatic brain injury. *Arch Phys Med Rehabil* 2005;**86**:896–904.

26. Dikmen S, Machamer J. Neurobehavioral outcomes and their determinants. *J Head Trauma Rehabil* 1995;**10**:74–86.

27. Kalmar K, Novack T, Nakase-Richardson R, et al. Feasibility of a brief neuropsychological test battery during acute inpatient rehabilitation after TBI. *Arch Phys Med Rehabil* 2008;**89**:942–9.

28. Millis SR, Rosenthal M, Novack TA, et al. Long-term neuropsychological outcome after traumatic brain injury. *J Head Trauma Rehabil* 2001;**16**:343–55.

29. Dikmen S, Reitan RM, Temkin NR. Neuropsychological recovery in head injury. *Arch Neurol* 1983;**40**:333–8.

30. Dikmen S, Machamer J, Winn R, et al. Neuropsychological outcome at 1-year post head injury. *Neuropsychology* 1995;**9**:80–90.

31. Ruff RM, Young D, Gautille T, et al. Verbal learning deficits following severe head injury: heterogeneity in recovery over 1 year. *J Neurosurg* 1991;**75**:S50–8.

32. Johnstone B, Hexum CL, Ashkanazi G. Extent of cognitive decline in traumatic brain injury based on estimates of premorbid intelligence. *Brain Inj* 1995;**9**:377–84.

33. Plassman BL, Havlik RJ, Steffens DC, et al. Documented head injury in early adulthood and risk of Alzheimer's disease and other dementias. *Neurology* 2000;**55**: 1158–66.

34. Goldman SM, Tanner CM, Oakes D, et al. Head injury and Parkinson's disease risk in twins. *Ann Neurol* 2006;**60**:65–72.

35. Uryu K, Chen XH, Martinez D, et al. Multiple proteins implicated in neurodegenerative diseases accumulate in axons after brain trauma in humans. *Exp Neurol* 2007;**208**:185–92.

36. Mayeux R, Ottman R, Maestre G, et al. Synergistic effects of traumatic head injury and apolipoprotein-epsilon 4 in patients with Alzheimer's disease. *Neurology* 1995;**45**:555–7.

37. Millar K, Nicoll JA, Thornhill S, et al. Long term neuropsychological outcome after head injury: relation to APOE genotype. *J Neurol Neurosurg Psychiatry* 2003;**74**:1047–52.

38. Riley GA. Stress and depression in family carers following traumatic brain injury: the influence of beliefs about difficult behaviours. *Clin Rehabil* 2007;**21**:82–8.

39. Winkler D, Unsworth C, Sloan S. Factors that lead to successful community integration following severe traumatic brain injury. *J Head Trauma Rehabil* 2006;**21**:8–21.

40. Starkstein SE, Robinson RG. Mechanism of disinhibition after brain lesions. *J Nerv Ment Dis* 1997;**185**:108–14.

41. Cummings JL, Coffey CE. Neurobiological basis of behavior. In Coffey CE, Cummings JL, eds. *Textbook of Geriatric Neuropsychiatry*, 2nd edn. Washington DC: American Psychiatric Press; 2000: 81–108.

42. Kim E. Agitation, aggression, and disinhibition syndromes after traumatic brain injury. *NeuroRehabilitation* 2002;**17**:297–310.

43. Grafman J, Schwab K, Warden D, et al. Frontal lobe injuries, violence, and aggression: a report of the Vietnam Head Injury Study. *Neurology* 1996;**46**:1231–8.

44. Lequerica AH, Rapport LJ, Loeher K, et al. Agitation in acquired brain injury: impact on acute rehabilitation therapies. *J Head Trauma Rehabil* 2007;**22**:177–83.

45. Leach LR, Frank RG, Bouman DE, et al. Family functioning, social support and depression after traumatic brain injury. *Brain Inj* 1994;**8**:599–606.

46. Elsinger P, Grattan L, L G. Impact of frontal lobe lesions on rehabilitation and recovery from acute brain injury. *NeuroRehabilitation* 1995;**5**:161–85.

47. Baguley IJ, Cooper J, Felmingham K. Aggressive behavior following traumatic brain injury: how common is common? *J Head Trauma Rehabil* 2006;**21**:45–56.

48. Klonoff PS, Lamb DG, Henderson SW, et al. Outcome assessment after milieu-oriented rehabilitation: new considerations. *Arch Phys Med Rehabil* 1998;**79**:684–90.

49. Wood R, Liossi C. Neuropsychological and neurobehavioral correlates of aggression following traumatic brain injury. *J Neuropsychiatry Clin Neurosci* 2006;**18**:333–41.

50. Sander AM, Kreutzer JS, Fernandez CC. Neurobehavioral functioning, substance abuse, and employment after brain injury: implications for vocational rehabilitation. *J Head Trauma Rehabil* 1997;**12**:28–41.

51. Reid-Arndt SA, Nehl C, Hinkebein J. The Frontal Systems Behaviour Scale (FrSBe) as a predictor of community integration following a traumatic brain injury. *Brain Inj* 2007;**21**:1361–9.

52. Middleton FA, Strick PL. Basal ganglia and cerebellar loops: motor and cognitive circuits. *Brain Res Brain Res Rev* 2000;**31**:236–50.

53. Cohen RA, Kaplan RF, Zuffante P, et al. Alteration of intention and self-initiated action associated with bilateral anterior cingulotomy. *J Neuropsychiatry Clin Neurosci* 1999;**11**:444–53.

54. Hart T, Sherer M, Whyte J, et al. Awareness of behavioral, cognitive, and physical deficits in acute traumatic brain injury. *Arch Phys Med Rehabil* 2004;**85**:1450–6.

55. Sherer M, Hart T, Whyte J, et al. Neuroanatomic basis of impaired self-awareness after traumatic brain injury: findings from early computed tomography. *J Head Trauma Rehabil* 2005;**20**:287–300.

56. Rogers JM, Read CA. Psychiatric comorbidity following traumatic brain injury. *Brain Inj* 2007;**21**:1321–33.

57. Kim E, Lauterbach EC, Reeve A, et al. Neuropsychiatric complications of traumatic brain injury: a critical review of the literature (a report by the ANPA Committee on Research). *J Neuropsychiatry Clin Neurosci* 2007;**19**:106–27.

58. Draper K, Ponsford J, Schonberger M. Psychosocial and emotional outcomes 10 years following traumatic brain injury. *J Head Trauma Rehabil* 2007;**22**:278–87.

59. Anson K, Ponsford J. Coping and emotional adjustment following traumatic brain injury. *J Head Trauma Rehabil* 2006;**21**:248–59.

60. Mayou RA, Black J, Bryant B. Unconsciousness, amnesia and psychiatric symptoms following road traffic accident injury. *Br J Psychiatry* 2000;**177**:540–5.

61. Bryant RA Posttraumatic stress disorder and mild brain injury: controversies, causes and consequences. *J Clin Exp Neuropsychol* 2001;**23**:718–28.

62. Bryant RA, Marosszeky JE, Crooks J, et al. Posttraumatic stress disorder and psychosocial functioning after severe traumatic brain injury. *J Nerv Ment Dis* 2001;**189**:109–13.

63. Burridge AC, Huw Williams W, Yates PJ, et al. Spousal relationship satisfaction following acquired brain injury: the role of insight and socio-emotional skill. *Neuropsychol Rehabil* 2007;**17**:95–105.

64. Ezrachi O, Ben-Yishay Y, Kay T, et al. Predicting employment in traumatic brain injury following neuropsychological rehabilitation. *J Head Trauma Rehabil* 1991;**6**:71–84.

65. Gollaher K, High W, Sherer M, et al. Prediction of employment outcome one to three years following traumatic brain injury (TBI). *Brain Inj* 1998;**12**:255–63.

66. Engberg AW, Teasdale TW. Psychosocial outcome following traumatic brain injury in adults: a long-term population-based follow-up. *Brain Inj* 2004;**18**:533–45.

67. Sander AM, Kreutzer J, Rosenthal M, et al. A multicenter longitudinal investigation of return to work and community integration following traumatic brain injury. *J Head Trauma Rehabil* 1996;**11**:70–84.

68. Doctor JN, Castro J, Temkin NR, et al. Workers' risk of unemployment after traumatic brain injury: a normed comparison. *J Int Neuropsychol Soc* 2005;**11**:747–52.

69. Kreutzer JS, Marwitz JH, Walker W, et al. Moderating factors in return to work and job stability after traumatic brain injury. *J Head Trauma Rehabil* 2003;**18**:128–38.

70. Dikmen SS, Temkin NR, Machamer JE, et al. Employment following traumatic head injuries. *Arch Neurol* 1994;**51**:177–86.

71. Vanderploeg RD, Curtiss G, Duchnick JJ, et al. Demographic, medical, and psychiatric factors in work and marital status after mild head injury. *J Head Trauma Rehabil* 2003;**18**:148–63.

72. McCrimmon S, Oddy M. Return to work following moderate-to-severe traumatic brain injury. *Brain Inj* 2006;**20**:1037–46.

73. Corrigan JD, Rust E, Lamb-Hart GL. The nature and extent of substance abuse problems in persons with traumatic brain injury. *J Head Trauma Rehabil* 1995;**10**:29–46.

74. Corrigan JD. Substance abuse as a mediating factor in outcome from traumatic brain injury. *Arch Phys Med Rehabil* 1995;**76**:302–9.

75. Hopewell CA. Driving assessment issues for practicing clinicians. *J Head Trauma Rehabil* 2002;**17**:48–61.

76. Novack TA, Banos JH, Alderson AL, et al. UFOV performance and driving ability following traumatic brain injury. *Brain Inj* 2006;**20**:455–61.

77. Sherer M, Novack T. Neuropsychological assessment after traumatic brain injury in adults. In Prigatano GP, Pliskin NH, eds. *Clinical Neuropsychology and Cost Outcome Research*. New York: Psychology Press; 2003: 39–60.

78. Kashluba S, Hanks RA, Casey JE, et al. Neuropsychologic and functional outcome after complicated mild traumatic brain injury. *Arch Phys Med Rehabil* 2008;**89**:904–11.

79. Iverson GL. Complicated vs uncomplicated mild traumatic brain injury: acute neuropsychological outcome. *Brain Inj* 2006;**20**:1335–44.

80. McCrea M, Guskiewicz KM, Marshall SW, et al. Acute effects and recovery time following concussion in collegiate football players: the NCAA Concussion Study. *J Am Med Assoc* 2003;**290**:2556–63.

81. Iverson GL, Brooks BL, Collins MW, et al. Tracking neuropsychological recovery following concussion in sport. *Brain Inj* 2006;**20**:245–52.

82. Bleiberg J, Cernich AN, Cameron K, et al. Duration of cognitive impairment after sports concussion. 2004;**54**:1073–8.

83. Randolph C, McCrea M, Barr WB. Is neuropsychological testing useful in the management of sport-related concussion? *J Athl Train* 2005;**40**:139–52.

84. McCrea M, Barr WB, Guskiewicz K, et al. Standard regression-based methods for measuring recovery after sport-related concussion. *J Int Neuropsychol Soc* 2005;**11**:58–69.

85. Giacino JT, Kalmar K, Whyte J. The JFK Coma Recovery Scale-Revised: measurement characteristics and diagnostic utility. *Arch Phys Med Rehabil* 2004;**85**:2020–9.

86. Levin HS, O'Donnell VM, Grossman RG. The Galveston Orientation and Amnesia Test: a practical scale to assess cognition after head injury. *J Nerv Ment Dis* 1979;**167**:675–84.

87. Jackson WT, Novack TA, Dowler RN. Effective serial measurement of cognitive orientation in rehabilitation: the Orientation Log. *Arch Phys Med Rehabil* 1998;**79**:718–20.

88. Pastorek NJ, Hannay HJ, Contant CS. Prediction of global outcome with acute neuropsychological testing following closed-head injury. *J Int Neuropsychol Soc* 2004;**10**:807–17.

89. Sherer M, Sander AM, Nick TG, et al. Early cognitive status and productivity outcome after traumatic brain injury: findings from the TBI model systems. *Arch Phys Med Rehabil* 2002;**83**:183–92.

90. Atchison TB, Sander AM, Struchen MA, et al. Relationship between neuropsychological test performance and productivity at 1-year following traumatic brain injury. *Clin Neuropsychol* 2004;**18**:249–65.

91. Ponsford J, Draper K, Schonberger M. Functional outcome 10 years after traumatic brain injury: its relationship with demographic, injury severity, and cognitive and emotional status. *J Int Neuropsychol Soc* 2008;**14**:233–42.

92. Hanks RA, Millis SR, Ricker JH, et al. The predictive validity of a brief inpatient neuropsychologic battery for persons with traumatic brain injury. *Arch Phys Med Rehabil* 2008;**89**:950–7.

93. Mittenberg W, Canyock EM, Condit D, et al. Treatment of post-concussion syndrome following mild head injury. *J Clin Exp Neuropsychol* 2001;**23**:829–36.

94. Paniak C, Toller-Lobe G, Reynolds S, et al. A randomized trial of two treatments for mild traumatic brain injury: 1 year follow-up. *Brain Inj* 2000;**14**:219–26.

95. Cope DN. The effectiveness of traumatic brain injury rehabilitation: A review. *Brain Inj* 1995;**9**:649–70.

96. Malec JF, Basford JS. Postacute brain injury rehabilitation. *Arch Phys Med Rehabil* 1996;**77**:198–207.

97. Sander AM, Roebuck TM, Struchen MA, et al. Long-term maintenance of gains obtained in postacute rehabilitation by persons with traumatic brain injury. *J Head Trauma Rehabil* 2001;**16**:1–19.

98. High WM, Jr., Roebuck-Spencer T, Sander AM, et al. Early versus later admission to postacute rehabilitation: impact on functional outcome after traumatic brain injury. *Arch Phys Med Rehabil* 2006;**87**:334–42.

99. Cicerone KD, Dahlberg C, Malec JF, et al. Evidence-based cognitive rehabilitation: updated review of the literature from 1998 through 2002. *Arch Phys Med Rehabil* 2005;**86**:1681–92.

100. Milders M, Deelman B, Berg I. Rehabilitation of memory for people's names. *Memory* 1998;**6**:21–36.

101. Goverover Y, Johnston MV, Toglia J, et al. Treatment to improve self-awareness in persons with acquired brain injury. *Brain Inj* 2007;**21**:913–23.

102. Cheng SK, Man DW. Management of impaired self-awareness in persons with traumatic brain injury. *Brain Inj* 2006;**20**:621–8.

103. Dahlberg CA, Cusick CP, Hawley LA, et al. Treatment efficacy of social communication skills training after traumatic brain injury: a randomized treatment and deferred treatment controlled trial. *Arch Phys Med Rehabil* 2007;**88**:1561–73.

104. Anson K, Ponsford J. Evaluation of a coping skills group following traumatic brain injury. *Brain Inj* 2006;**20**:167–78.

105. Wehman PH, Revell WG, Kregel J, et al. Supported employment: an alternative model for vocational rehabilitation of persons with severe neurologic, psychiatric, or physical disability. *Arch Phys Med Rehabil* 1991;**72**:101–5.

106. Warden DL, Gordon B, McAllister TW, et al. Guidelines for the pharmacologic treatment of neurobehavioral sequelae of traumatic brain injury. *J Neurotrauma* 2006;**23**:1468–501.

107. Think First National Brain Injury Prevention Foundation (Online). Fast Facts: Traumatic Brain Injury. 2008. http://www.thinkfirst.org/Documents/FastFacts/TFbrain368.pdf. (Accessed July 1, 2008.)

108. Attewell RG, Glase K, McFadden M. Bicycle helmet efficacy: a meta-analysis. *Accid Anal Prev* 2001;**33**:345–52.

109. Pintar FA, Yoganandan N, Gennarelli TA. Airbag effectiveness on brain trauma in frontal crashes. *Annu Proc Assoc Adv Automot Med* 2000;**44**:149–69.

110. Hillary FG, Schatz P, Moelter ST, et al. Motor vehicle collision factors influence severity and type of TBI. *Brain Inj* 2002;**16**:729–41.

111. Collins M, Lovell MR, Iverson GL, et al. Examining concussion rates and return to play in high school football players wearing newer helmet technology: a three-year prospective cohort study. *Neurosurgery* 2006;**58**:275–86.

112. Corrigan JD, Whiteneck G, Mellick D. Perceived needs following traumatic brain injury. *J Head Trauma Rehabil* 2004;**19**:205–16.

113. Bell KR, Temkin NR, Esselman PC, et al. The effect of a scheduled telephone intervention on outcome after moderate to severe traumatic brain injury: a randomized trial. *Arch Phys Med Rehabil* 2005;**86**:851–6.

114. Ricker JH, Rosenthal M, Garay E, et al. Telerehabilitation needs: a survey of persons with acquired brain injury. *J Head Trauma Rehabil* 2002;**17**:242–50.

115. Levinson DM, Reeves DL. Monitoring recovery from traumatic brain injury using automated neuropsychological assessment metrics (ANAM V1.0). *Arch Clin Neuropsychol* 1997;**12**:155–66.

116. Perlstein WM, Cole MA, Demery JA, et al. Parametric manipulation of working memory load in traumatic brain injury: behavioral and neural correlates. *J Int Neuropsychol Soc* 2004;**10**:724–41.

117. McAllister TW, Sparling MB, Flashman LA, et al. Differential working memory load effects after mild traumatic brain injury. *Neuroimage* 2001;**14**:1004–12.

118. Rutgers DR, Toulgoat F, Cazejust J, et al. White matter abnormalities in mild traumatic brain injury: a diffusion tensor imaging study. *AJNR Am J Neuroradiol* 2008;**29**:514–9.

119. Benson RR, Meda SA, Vasudevan S, et al. Global white matter analysis of diffusion tensor images is predictive of injury severity in traumatic brain injury. *J Neurotrauma* 2007;**24**:446–59.

120. Rizzo AA, Buckwalter JG, Neumann U. Virtual reality and cognitive rehabilitation: a brief review of the future. *J Head Trauma Rehabil* 1997;**12**:1–15.

121. Lengenfelder J, Schultheis MT, Al-Shihabi T, et al. Divided attention and driving: a pilot study using virtual reality technology. *J Head Trauma Rehabil* 2002;**17**:26–37.

Traumatic brain injury in older adults

Felicia C. Goldstein and Harvey S. Levin

Introduction

Traumatic brain injury (TBI) in older adults poses a critical health problem, a statement which is supported by epidemiological studies indicating that persons aged 65 years and older are especially vulnerable. In the USA, the rate of TBI-related emergency room visits, hospitalizations, and deaths for the period 1995–2001 was 267.4/100 000 in persons aged 65–74 years. The figure for those 75 years and older dramatically increased to 659.1/100 000, and this group was found to have the highest rate of TBI-related hospitalizations and deaths compared to any other ages [1]. Analysis of data from a Centers for Disease Control and Prevention 15-state TBI surveillance system indicated that persons 85 years and older were twice as likely to be hospitalized as those 75–84 years, and more than 4-times as likely as those 65–74 years [2]. The above statistics are coupled with shifts in the percentage of older persons in the USA. Thirty-five million people were 65 years and older in the year 2000, representing a 12% increase over the past decade. This figure is projected to rise to 53 million in the year 2020, with the elderly comprising over 20% of the US population by the year 2030 [3].

In this chapter, we present research findings concerning the functional, cognitive, and emotional outcomes from TBI sustained in older adults. Our review focuses on adults who were injured in late life as opposed to at a young age, in order to understand the ability of the aging brain to withstand the acute effects of TBI. We first begin with an appreciation of risk factors that affect the clinical presentation and recovery from TBI, followed by a review of the neurobehavioral consequences. We conclude with continued gaps in knowledge and suggestions for future research.

Risk factors affecting outcome of TBI in older adults

Age

Numerous studies demonstrate that advanced age is a risk factor for greater morbidity and mortality from TBI [4–15]. Older age may also affect the response to clinical interventions. For example, the first hypothermia trial [16] found that this intervention resulted in higher mortality of treated than untreated patients with severe TBI who were over 45 years old. Investigations reveal that older patients, when matched to young adults on Glasgow Coma Scale (GCS) [17] scores, have worse functional outcomes and a higher death rate (Table 11d.1). Mosenthal and colleagues [9] found that the mortality rate for persons 65 years and older was twice as high as for younger persons. Of the patients who survived, those 65 years and older were more likely to remain in a persistent vegetative state or to be left with severe disability as determined by the Glasgow Outcome Scale (GOS) [18]. Based on data from the New York State Trauma Registry, Susman et al. [14] found that a greater percentage of patients 65 years and older had poorer outcomes on the Functional Independence Measure (FIM) [19] than those 18–64 years. In addition, 54% of the older patients were discharged to extended care facilities. Ulvik and colleagues [20] found a linear rise in the 30-day mortality rate from TBI beginning at age 50 years, with an increase of 32% for each subsequent decade. In contrast, a relationship between age and mortality was not found in patients who were less than 50 years old. These findings prompted the investigators to suggest that "elderly" as applied to patients with TBI needs to be re-conceptualized as younger than the traditional definition of 65 years.

Severity of injury

Although age is an important predictor of outcome, there is evidence that it interacts with TBI severity such that a better prognosis occurs with milder injuries (see Table 11d.1). In general, studies in older adults who sustain severe TBI (GCS scores of 3–8) have reported mortality rates of $\geq 70\%$, whereas good outcomes occur in $< 10\%$ [4, 6, 7, 11, 12, 15, 21]. In contrast, good outcomes have been observed in up to 28% of patients with moderate TBI (GCS scores of 9–12) and

Table 11d.1. Glasgow Outcome Scale as a function of age in representative studies of traumatic brain injury.

Investigators	n	Sample characteristics	Findings[a]
Alberico et al., 1987 [4]	330	Patients 0–80 years old; prospective series of hospitalized patients with GCS scores 7 or less for at least 6 hours; outcome at 1 year	GR: 0–20 yrs=45%, 21–40 yrs=35%, 41–60 yrs=15%, 61–80 yrs=5% Dead: 0–20 yrs=25%, 21–40 yrs=32%, 41–60 yrs=50%, 61–80 yrs=70%
Dikmen et al., 1995 [5]	466	Patients < 20 – ≥ 70 years old; prospective series of hospitalized patients with GCS scores 3–15; time to follow commands <1 hr – ≥29 days; outcome at 1 year	GR: < 20–29 yrs=>75%, 30–39 yrs=70%, 40–49 yrs=60%, 50–59 yrs=30%, 60–69 yrs=25%, ≥ 70 yrs=20%
Gomez et al., 2000 [6]	810	Patients > 14 years old; admitted to hospital; GCS scores 8 or less; outcome at 6 months	GR/MD: 15–25 yrs=47%; 26–35 yrs=40%; 36–45 yrs=30%; 46–55 yrs=32%; 56–65 yrs=15%; > 65 yrs=8% Dead: 15–25 yrs=41%; 26–35 yrs=47%; 36–45 yrs=56%; 46–55 yrs=38%; 56–65 yrs=65%; > 65 yrs=87%
Jennett et al., 1976 [7]	600	Patients 0 – ≥ 60 years old; prospective series of patients in coma for ≥ 6 hours	GR/MD: 0–19 yrs=56%, 20–59 yrs=39%, ≥ 60 yrs=5% Dead: 0–19 yrs=37%, 20–59 yrs=53%, ≥ 60=88%
Katz and Alexander, 1994 [8]	243	Patients 8–89 years old; admitted to rehabilitation; coma >1 hr (n=97); outcome at 1 year	GR: < 20 yrs=55%, 20–39 yrs=40%, 40–59 yrs=10%, ≥ 60 yrs=43% MD: < 20 yrs=38%, 20–39 yrs=50%, 40–59 yrs=78%, ≥ 60 yrs=10% SD: < 20 yrs=8%, 20–39 yrs=10%, 40–59 yrs=10%, ≥ 60 yrs=43%
Mosenthal et al., 2002 [9]	694	Patients 0–≥ 80 years old; retrospective analysis of patients admitted to level I trauma centers; GCS scores 3–15; outcome at discharge	SD/Veg: 0–< 64 yrs=5%; ≥ 65 yrs=13% Dead: 0–< 65 yrs=14%; ≥ 65 yrs=30%
Mosenthal et al., 2004 [10]	128	Patients 18–64 and ≥ 65; prospective, multicenter investigation of patients admitted to trauma centers; outcome at 6 months examined in those with GCS scores 13–15	GR: 18–64 years=80%, >65=62% MD: 18–64 years=15%, >65=10%
Pennings et al., 1993 [11]	92	Patients 20–40 and ≥ 60 years old; admitted to hospital and alive 6 hours after admission; GCS scores 5 or less; outcome at discharge	GR/MD: 20–40 yrs=38%, ≥ 60 yrs=2% SD: 20–40 yrs=18%, ≥ 60 yrs=5% Veg/Dead: 20–40 yrs=44%, ≥ 60 yrs=93%
Pentland et al., 1986 [12]	2019	Patients < and > 65 years old; Prospective series of hospitalized patients; GCS scores 3–14; outcome at discharge or 1 month	GR/MD: GCS 3–7: < 65 yrs=22%, > 65 yrs=4%, GCS 8–12: < 65 yrs=86%, > 65=46%, GCS 13–14: < 65 yrs=99%, > 65 yrs=96%; SD/Veg/Dead: GCS 3–7: < 65 yrs=78%, > 65 yrs=96%, GCS 8–12: < 65 yrs=14%, > 65=55%, GCS 13–14: < 65 yrs=1%, > 65 yrs=4%;
Rothweiler et al., 1998 [13]	411	Patients 18–89 years old; prospective series of hospitalized patients; GCS scores 3–15; outcome at 1 year	GR: time to follow commands (TFC) ≥ 14 days: 18–29 yrs=18%, 30–39 yrs=30%, 40–49 yrs=0%, 50–59 yrs=15%, ≥ 60 yrs=8% TFC 25 hrs–13 days: 18–29 yrs=80%, 30–39 yrs=70%, 40–49 yrs=100%, 50–59 yrs=18%, ≥ 60 yrs=0% TFC 24 hrs or less: 18–29 yrs=95%, 30–39 yrs=80%, 40–49 yrs=81%, 50–59 yrs=75%, ≥ 60 yrs=40%
Vollmer et al., 1991 [15]	661	Patients ≥ 15 years old; prospective sample of hospitalized patients with traumatic coma; outcome at 6 months	GR/MD: 16–25 yrs=49%, 26–35 yrs=48%, 36–45 yrs=33%, 46–55 yrs=22%, ≥ 56 yrs=9% SD/Veg/Dead: 16–25 yrs=50%, 26–35 yrs=52%, 36–45 yrs=66%, 46–55 yrs=77%, ≥ 56 yrs=91%

Figures cited in the table are estimates when data were presented in graph form.
[a] GR = good recovery (resumption of normal activities with some possible minor deficits); MD = moderate disability (disabled but independent in daily activities); SD = severe disability (dependent on others for daily support); Veg = vegetative.

in up to 80% of patients with mild TBI (GCS scores of 13–15) [10, 22, 23]. A particularly encouraging recovery pattern was reported by Mosenthal et al. [10], who examined the 6-month GOS and modified FIM scores of patients with mild TBI. While the FIM score was lower, indicative of less independence in the older (≥ 65 years) versus younger patients, and they were less likely to achieve a "good outcome", almost one-third demonstrated continued improvements compared to their hospital discharge status, and over 80% were performing at an independent level. Their results highlight, as the investigators point out, that a large percentage of older patients can achieve a clinically satisfactory outcome even though the data are "statistically" worse when compared to young patients.

Pathophysiological considerations

In addition to age and severity of injury, unique pathophysiological responses must be considered in any model of outcome. Older persons are at an increased risk for intracranial bleeds, especially subdural hematoma (SDH), due to brain atrophy, which causes stretching of the bridging veins and thus greater vulnerability to shearing effects from the trauma [24, 25]. The risk for SDH rises to almost 25% in patients 50–74 years, and to > 25% at 75 years and older [26]. SDH is diagnostically challenging in the older patient because it is common in the setting of mild TBI (GCS scores of 13–15), low-velocity falls, and no visible external head trauma. Thus, trauma may escape suspicion by the patient and significant other, and remain undetected until there is a deteriorating mental status. Guidelines formulated by investigators in the USA (New Orleans Criteria) [27] and Canada (Canadian CT Head Rule) [28] both recommend that persons who are in their 60s and present to the emergency room within 1–2 hours of sustaining a mild TBI should undergo a head computerized tomography scan (CT).

Unlike the young patient in whom the clinical signs of SDH typically manifest within 72 hours of injury, the scenario of the older adult frequently involves a chronic development phase due to enlargement of the subdural space which allows a large amount of blood to accumulate before cerebral compression and resultant neurological sequelae become apparent [25]. Another major risk factor for SDH includes treatment with anticoagulant and antiplatelet medications [29–31]. In a retrospective analysis of almost 400 patients with TBI who were 55 years or older, Lavoie and colleagues [30] found that the pre-injury use of warfarin, an anticoagulant, was associated with a significantly greater risk of a more severe head injury and higher mortality, even though the patients taking warfarin were more likely to sustain their injuries from low-velocity falls.

Physical and cognitive status

Advanced age often carries an increased risk of developing associated medical conditions which, in turn, can produce frailty and cognitive deficits. A 2007 CDC report, The State of Aging and Health in America, noted that approximately 80% of older adults had at least one chronic medical condition, and 50% had at least two conditions. Collapsed across ethnicity and race, the most prevalent conditions in persons ≥ 65 years were hypertension (54%), arthritis (48%), diabetes (20%), coronary heart disease (18%), cancer (14%), and stroke (9%) [32]. Extrapolating to the elderly TBI population, these statistics suggest that medical comorbidities and resulting sequelae of these diseases are common at the time of injury. Falls, a frequent mechanism of TBI in persons who are ≥ 65 years old [2, 14], are themselves associated with numerous risk factors including disorders of gait, balance, weakness, decreased vision, peripheral neuropathy, and cognitive disorders [33, 34]. Motor-vehicle accidents, the second most common mechanism of TBI in the elderly, are associated with medical conditions including stroke, heart disease, and arthritis as well as certain medications such as benzodiazepines, nonsteroidal anti-inflammatory drugs, and angiotensin converting enzyme (ACE) inhibitors [35]. Coronado and colleagues [2] found that hypertension, diabetes mellitus, cardiac arrhythmias, and electrolyte disturbances were prevalent conditions for both mechanisms of injury. In addition, Alzheimer's disease and other dementias were present in up to 10% of the elderly fallers. This figure is likely to be an underestimate since neuropsychological evaluations, if performed, may have detected cases of undiagnosed dementia and mild cognitive impairment.

Cognitive outcome

Table 11d.2 summarizes the findings to date concerning the cognitive outcome of older patients with TBI including the commonly affected areas, recovery over time, the relationship to severity of injury, and distinguishing features from Alzheimer's disease.

Table 11d.2. Cognitive outcome following TBI sustained in older adults.

Investigators	Sample characteristics	Findings
Aharon-Peretz et al., 1997 [45]	18 patients > 60 years old with mild and moderate TBI; 10 orthopedic and 10 healthy controls	At 6 weeks post-injury, patients with TBI performed significantly worse than healthy, but not orthopedic, controls in semantic fluency, visual and verbal memory, and abstract reasoning.
Goldstein et al., 1994 [36]	22 patients ≥ 50 years old with mild and moderate TBI; 16 healthy controls	Up to 7 months post-injury, patients performed significantly worse than controls in confrontation naming, phonemic fluency, visual and verbal memory, and verbal reasoning.
Goldstein et al., 1996 [54]	Patients > 50 years old with mild and moderate TBI; 14 patients with Alzheimer's disease (AD) and 14 healthy controls	Although both patient groups showed impaired recall relative to controls, the patients with TBI also displayed significantly better recall than those with AD and were more likely, similar to controls, to recall words equally from the primacy, middle, and recency positions of a word list. Unlike the patients with AD, the patients with TBI showed a normal facilitation in generating words belonging to categories compared with words beginning with specific letters.
Goldstein et al., 2001 [51]	Patients ≥ 50 years old with mild ($n = 18$) and moderate ($n = 17$) TBI; 14 healthy controls	Up to 2 months post-injury, patients with mild TBI differed significantly from controls on only one cognitive measure (phonemic fluency). In contrast, patients with moderate TBI performed significantly worse than both mild patients and controls in visuomotor processing speed and set-shifting, verbal memory, confrontation naming, reasoning, and hypothesis generation.
Luukinen at al., 1999 [46]	Population-based sample of 588 adults ≥ 70 years old who were assessed at baseline and 2 years later with the MMSE	Persons who sustained major head injuries from falls (e.g. requiring hospitalization) exhibited a greater decline in the MMSE score compared to non-fallers; In contrast, minor head injuries were not associated with decline in the MMSE.
Mazzucchi et al., 1992 [50]	70 patients ≥ 50 years old with mild, moderate, and severe TBI	A high incidence of generalized deterioration and dementia was observed at 6 months to 3 years post-injury. There were no significant differences in outcome as a function of increasing severity.
Rapoport et al., 2006 [48]	49 patients ≥ 50 years old with mild and moderate injuries; 49 healthy controls	At 1 year post-injury, patients with moderate, but not mild, TBI performed significantly worse than healthy controls on measures of overall cognitive status, processing speed, language, and executive functioning.
Rapoport et al., 2008 [49]	30 patients ≥ 50 years old with mild and moderate injuries; 46 healthy controls	At 2 years post-injury, patients did not perform significantly worse than healthy controls on any cognitive measures. The presence of the apolipoprotein E-ε4 allele was not associated with conversion to mild cognitive impairment or dementia.

Early cognitive manifestations

Goldstein et al. [36] evaluated the cognitive outcome within 2 months of injury of 22 older adults (mean age = 67.8 years, SD = 12.0) with mild (GCS scores of 13–15, normal CT scan) or moderate (GCS scores of 9–12, or 13–15 with an abnormal CT scan) TBI who were prospectively recruited from acute care hospitals. In addition to reviewing medical records to exclude patients with pre-injury conditions such as strokes which could affect their cognitive performance, significant others were interviewed close in time to the injury using the Blessed Dementia Rating Scale [37] to screen for pre-existing dementia. Patients

and non-head-injured controls received measures that examined automatic attention (alphabet recitation, sequencing numbers with a pencil), effortful attention (counting by 3s, alternating between numbers and letters with a pencil) [38, 39], memory (recalling words, recognizing pictures) [40, 41], language (generating words, naming pictures) [42], and executive functioning (inferring similarities, generating hypotheses, and shifting responses) [43, 44]. Compared to demographically comparable control subjects, the patients exhibited significantly poorer word-list learning and visual recognition memory, naming of pictured items, generation of words under timed conditions, inferences of similarities, and generation of hypotheses/shifting response sets. Effortful attention such as serial 3s was also more compromised in the patients.

In a follow-up study, Aharon-Peretz et al. [45] observed a similar pattern of cognitive deficits up to 6 weeks post-injury in 18 patients > 60 years old with mild, moderate, and severe TBI. The investigators excluded patients with subdural and intracerebral hematomas in order to examine the effects of diffuse as opposed to focal brain injury. Compared to a healthy control group, the patients exhibited impairments in verbal and visual memory, word fluency, and verbal similarities. However, there were no significant differences in cognitive functioning between the patients with TBI and an orthopedic control group. The authors attributed this latter result to the possibility that the orthopedic controls had pre-existing cognitive impairments that predisposed them to having accidents.

Cognitive recovery

Only a few studies have examined cognitive recovery following TBI sustained in late life. In a population-based study conducted in Finland, Luukinen et al. [46] followed 588 individuals 70 years and older who received a baseline shortened Mini-Mental State Examination [47] and who then underwent a repeat MMSE approximately 2.5 years later. Of these individuals, 31 had sustained fall-related head injuries in the interim. It was found that major head injury (e.g. seeking medical attention, requiring inpatient care) was associated with an increased risk of a decline in the MMSE score, even after controlling for potential confounders such as level of education and medical comorbidities. In contrast, minor head injury was not an independent predictor of change in the MMSE score. A limitation of the study in understanding the effects of brain injury, per se, on cognitive outcome, as the investigators noted, is that the definition of severity of the fall-related head injury was based on qualitative rather than neurological indices such as the GCS score.

Rapoport and colleagues [48] prospectively recruited patients ≥ 50 years old who sustained mild (GCS score 13–15, PTA < 24 hours, loss of consciousness/confusion ≥ 20 minutes) or moderate (GCS 9–12, PTA < 1 week, or GCS 13–15 with intracranial complication) TBI. The investigators screened and excluded patients with pre-injury dementia and major neurological, medical, or psychiatric conditions. Patients received a comprehensive battery of cognitive measures within 2 months of

injury and were then re-evaluated at 1 year. After controlling for demographic factors and severity of medical comorbidities, it was found that the patients with TBI performed significantly worse than community controls at the 1 year assessment on measures of overall cognitive status, verbal memory, timed letter fluency, visuomotor speed, and expressive language (naming).

In a follow-up study, Rapoport et al. [49] investigated the 2-year cognitive outcome of the same cohort of older TBI adults. In addition, they examined whether the apolipoprotein E-ε4 allele, a risk factor for Alzheimer's disease (AD), was associated with the development of dementia or mild cognitive impairment (MCI). Strengths of the study included the administration of the same neuropsychological measures to a demographically matched uninjured group at all occasions (baseline, 1 year, 2 years) in order to control for practice effects. Moreover, ratings of dementia or MCI were conducted by clinicians who were unaware of the participants' status (TBI vs. control). Rapoport and colleagues did not find any significant differences in cognitive performance between the two groups, nor was there an effect of APOE-ε4 on cognitive outcome. At the 2-year follow-up, 3 of 30 (10%) patients with TBI were classified as having MCI or dementia compared to 2 of 46 controls (4.3%), a statistically nonsignificant difference.

Cognitive outcome according to injury severity

Up to 80% of older adults who sustain mild TBI achieve a good functional outcome on the GOS, raising the possibility that cognitive potential is also better after mild TBI. However, an early investigation by Mazzucchi and colleagues [50] did not fulfill this expectation. The investigators administered tests of intellectual functioning, memory, language, and visuomotor performance to patients 50–75 years old at injury who sustained mild, moderate, or severe TBI. There was a high incidence of generalized deterioration and dementia in half their sample of 70 patients at 6 months to 3 years post-injury, whereas only one-fourth had a mild decline or normal findings. Patients with mild TBI (no loss of consciousness, GCS scores of 13–15, post-traumatic amnesia less than 1 day, and normal CT head scans) did not have a better outcome than those with severe injuries. Limitations of the study included the investigators' use of a global definition of impairment based on poor performance on any measure as opposed to examining specific domains, and the possibility that some patients had pre-existing dementia. In addition, patients were referred for evaluations, which could have biased the results since cognitive deficits may have prompted their referrals.

Subsequent studies [51, 52] have observed a dose–response relationship between injury severity and magnitude of cognitive deficits based on using prospective methodologies and screening of premorbid conditions. Goldstein and colleagues [51] prospectively recruited 18 patients (mean age = 62.3 years, SD = 9.7) with mild head injuries (GCS scores of 13–15, loss of consciousness < 20 minutes, and normal neurological and neuroradiological findings) who had been hospitalized on neurosurgery units. Minimum study entry criteria included evidence of a head injury of sufficient intensity to produce a TBI (e.g. striking the head during a fall) as well as a period of confusion and retrograde/post-traumatic amnesia substantiated by ambulance reports, emergency room records, and interviews using the Galveston Orientation and Amnesia Test [53]. Seventeen patients (mean age = 65.2 years, SD = 10.2) with moderate TBI (GCS scores 9–12, or 13–15 with intracranial complications) were selected from a larger pool of study participants based on demographic features and injury–test intervals similar to those of the mild patients. Patients underwent cognitive testing an average of 1 month post-injury to assess attention, language, memory, and executive functioning. There were no significant differences between the patients with mild TBI versus community-residing controls on any cognitive measure except for a timed letter fluency task where the patients generated fewer words. In contrast, the mild patients and controls both performed significantly better than the moderate patients in visuomotor processing speed and set-shifting, verbal memory, confrontation naming, reasoning and hypothesis generation. Consistent with these results, Rapoport et al. [48] noted that there were cognitive differences at 1 year post-injury between the moderate patients and normal controls, whereas patients with mild TBI did not significantly differ from the control group.

Goldstein and colleagues subsequently examined whether there is a difference in outcome between patients with and without intracranial complications but comparable GCS scores of 13–15 [52]. Patients were classified as having either uncomplicated mild TBI (GCS scores of 13–15, normal neuroradiological findings), complicated mild TBI (GCS scores of 13–15, abnormal neuroradiological findings), or moderate TBI (GCS scores of 9–12 with or without abnormal neuroradiological findings). The uncomplicated patients with mild TBI performed significantly better on language (naming, fluency) and executive functioning (number of categories) measures than patients with complicated mild TBI. This latter group, in turn, performed comparably to patients with moderate TBI with the exception of faster set-shifting ability.

Cognitive performance associated with TBI versus Alzheimer's disease

The differential diagnosis of cognitive impairments due to TBI versus AD is clinically challenging. As previously discussed, cognitive impairment is a risk factor for falls, raising the possibility that some patients may have a pre-injury neurodegenerative disorder such as AD. Moreover, the initial neurobehavioral sequelae of older adults with mild and moderate TBI, including difficulties in storing and retrieving new material, reduced verbal fluency, and naming impairments, are the same cognitive manifestations of AD. In a study to identify possible distinguishing features, Goldstein and colleagues [54] compared the neuropsychological profiles of older adults who sustained mild and moderate TBI or were diagnosed with probable AD. The groups were similar in demographics and overall cognitive status on the MMSE. Patients with TBI were carefully screened for pre-existing dementia and were recruited during their initial hospitalization or shortly after discharge while in an early stage of recovery. Although both patient groups showed impaired recall of a word list relative to normal controls, the patients with AD also displayed poorer recall than those with TBI. Moreover, whereas the patients with TBI and normal controls exhibited a nearly equal distribution of recall from the primacy, middle, and recency positions of the word list, the patients with AD recalled a significantly higher proportion of words from the end of the list. This latter finding was interpreted as demonstrating the inability of the patients with AD to retrieve earlier items, possibly due to a storage deficit. Letter and category fluency tasks also differentiated the patient groups. Unlike the patients with TBI, those with AD did not show a normal facilitation in generating words belonging to categories compared with words beginning with specific letters. Moreover, relative to normal control performance, patients with AD, in contrast to those with TBI, exhibited a disproportionate impairment on the category versus the letter fluency task.

More recently, Breed and colleagues [55] examined cognitive profiles in patients with TBI and AD. Their patients with TBI were older than 55 years at the time of the study, they had been injured an average of 15.8 years previously, and determination of severity of injury was based on self-report information concerning length of loss of consciousness and post-traumatic amnesia. Despite differences in methodology compared with the Goldstein et al. [54] study, however, the investigators replicated findings of poorer timed letter fluency and memory functioning in the AD group. In addition, the patients with AD exhibited significantly lower percent retention scores for both verbal and visual material relative to TBI and normal controls, whereas the latter groups did not significantly differ from each other. This suggests that rapid forgetting is more characteristic of AD versus TBI.

Affective functioning

Depression is common in older patients with TBI, consistent with the high frequency of mood disturbance documented in young survivors. Self-reported depression is found at 1 month post-injury in 30% of mild and moderate patients ≥ 50 years old, with continued or new-onset depression in 25% at 7 months, and 12% at 13 months [56]. We observed that almost 20% of mild and moderate patients who were not initially depressed at 1 month post-injury endorsed symptoms of new-onset depression at 7 months. In addition, patients with greater depression were rated by their significant others as showing a post-injury decline in social functioning and activities of daily functioning. The presence and worsening over time of mood disturbance was also confirmed in a study [57] that asked informants of 17 mild and moderate patients to complete the Geriatric Evaluation of Relative's Rating Instrument [58], a questionnaire inquiring about the patient's cognition, affect, interpersonal relations, and daily activities. The significant others provided retrospective ratings of pre-injury functioning and then completed the same ratings an average of 4 and 13 months post-injury. Compared to their pre-injury status, patients at the initial follow-up were noted to exhibit mood changes (happy one day, sad the next day) and hypersensitivity to sudden noises and sights. By 1 year, however, relatives observed a worsening in the patients' mood, including reports of hopelessness, worthlessness, and pessimism concerning the future.

In their longitudinal investigation of mild and moderate patients with TBI, Rapoport and colleagues [48] used the Structured Clinical Interview [59] to diagnose the presence of major depression. At baseline, 11/69 (15.9%) patients exhibited one episode, whereas at 1 year 6/49 patients (12.2%) met criteria. In contrast, none of the 68 community-residing older adult control participants had major depression at baseline, and only one (1.5%) met criteria at 1 year. Minor depression was present in 15/69 (21.7%) patients at baseline and 9/49 (18.8%) at 1 year, versus 3.8% and 2.9% of the controls, respectively. The figures for major depression in patients with TBI are higher than those reported in epidemiological studies of community-residing elderly persons (prevalence of 1–5%) but are similar to figures for medically ill persons (11.5%) and for those requiring home health care (13.5%). In contrast, the figures reported by Rapoport and colleagues for minor depression in their patients, but not the controls, are similar to prevalence findings of up to 26% of community-based samples and 23% of hospitalized patients [60]. Although direct comparisons are difficult due to diverse sampling and measurement techniques, it is clear that older patients with TBI are at risk for depression, probably due to functional disability and chronic illness, which in themselves are associated factors in epidemiological studies [60].

Conclusions

A review of risk factors for recovery from TBI sustained in older adults underscores the fact that a direct comparison with younger patients is complicated by numerous mediators apart from age that affect their course. Although age emerges as an independent predictor when these other factors are "statistically controlled", it is conceptually difficult to think of age alone as influencing outcome since these other features are so intimately linked to recovery. The influence of these additional risk factors has led investigators to suggest that modified severity indices and outcome measures need to be constructed to capture the uniqueness of the older TBI population [10, 12]. It has been proposed that the GCS score may underestimate severity of injury in older persons since it does not take into account the presence of intracranial complications such as SDH which are common in this patient population. As a result, the "matching" of a younger versus older sample on the basis of GCS scores alone may give the impression of a poorer outcome in older persons. Non-injury-related factors including social support, living arrangement, and employment status are important to consider as well in models of outcome. For example, Lawes [61] examined the reasons for hospital admission for patients with TBI who were 75 years and older. Approximately half of the patients sustaining mild TBI were admitted because they lived alone or needed further assistance at home, rather than due to complications related to their head injuries. Thus, gauges of recovery in the older patient such as the ability to return home may need to be reformulated.

A review of neuropsychological functioning in older patients with TBI indicates that the same cognitive domains as young adults are affected, involving attention, memory, language, and executive functioning. The available studies indicate that a good cognitive outcome is possible after mild-moderate TBI. Consistent with investigations in young adults [62–65], uncomplicated mild head injury in adults ≥ 50 years old does not produce clinically significant, persistent cognitive deficits. While these findings are limited to premorbidly healthy and independently functioning individuals, and thus cannot be generalized to the population at large, they indicate the potential for a positive outcome. The finding of depression in up to one-third of older adults with mild and moderate TBI and the fact that this may become noticeable only after several months have passed indicates that it is an important secondary condition that requires diagnosis and follow-up. Moreover, its presence can interfere with cognitive and functional recovery. Rapoport et al. [66], for example, found that patients with major depression were rated by their informants as being less independent in performing instrumental activities of daily living at 1 year post-injury.

Finally, qualitative aspects of neuropsychological performance such as an exaggerated recency effect in recalling a word list, a disproportionate loss of learned material after a delay, or reduced semantic versus phonemic fluency may be able to clinically distinguish cognitive deficits due to TBI versus AD, and they could potentially provide a yardstick to track the possible development of AD. However, further research is needed in order to test the sensitivity, specificity, and predictive power of these and other abilities as diagnostic markers. Positron emission tomography using compounds for imaging beta amyloid could be a powerful tool as well for differential diagnosis. The identification of cognitive markers could assist with patient/family planning and early pharmacological treatment interventions. In addition, research on the effects of TBI in persons already exhibiting symptoms of mild cognitive impairment or AD has not been conducted to our knowledge. Given the reduced cerebral reserve caused by a pre-existing cognitive disorder, one might predict that a new TBI, even one that is relatively mild, might disproportionately magnify the symptoms and accelerate the disease course.

Unlike the extensive literature on children and young adults, little is known about the rehabilitation needs of older persons with TBI. Despite a slower rate of functional recovery compared to young patients, older adults with TBI who are in rehabilitation settings are able to demonstrate significant improvements from admission to discharge [67, 68]. Additional research is needed to examine the risk factors, apart from age, that influence rehabilitation potential, as well as whether the timing and intensity of treatment services need to be altered to fit this unique patient population.

References

1. Langlois JA, Rutland-Brown W, Thomas KE. *Traumatic brain injury in the United States: Emergency department visits, hospitalizations, and deaths.* Atlanta, Georgia: Centers for Disease Control and Prevention, National Center for Injury Control and Prevention; 2006.

2. Coronado VG, Thomas KE, Sattin RW, Johnson RL. The CDC Traumatic Brain Injury Surveillance System: Characteristics of persons aged 65 years and older hospitalized with a TBI. *J Head Trauma Rehabil* 2005; **20**:215–28.

3. United States Census Bureau, *The 65 Years and Over Population.* U.S. Department of Commerce, Economics, and Statistics Administration; 2000.

4. Alberico AM, Ward JD, Choi S, Marmarou A, Young HF. Outcome after severe head injury: relationship to mass lesions, diffuse injury, and ICP course in pediatric and adult patients. *J Neurosurg* 1987;**67**:648–56.

5. Dikmen SS, Ross BL, Machamer JE, Temkin NR. One year psychosocial outcome in head injury. *J Int Neuropsych Soc* 1995;**1**:67–77.

6. Gomez PA, Lobato RD, Boto GR, De la Lama A, Gonzalez PJ, de la Cruz J. Age and outcome after severe head injury. *Acta Neurochir* 2000;**142**:373–80.

7. Jennett B, Teasdale G, Braakman R, Minderhoud J, Knill-Jones R. Predicting outcome in individual patients after severe head injury. *Lancet* 1976;**1**:1031–4.

8. Katz DI, Alexander MP. Traumatic brain injury: predicting course of recovery and outcome for patients admitted to rehabilitation. *Arch Neurol* 1994;**51**:661–70.

9. Mosenthal AC, Lavery RF, Addis M, Kaul S, Ross S, Marburger R, et al. Isolated traumatic brain injury: age is an independent predictor of mortality and early outcome. *J Trauma* 2002;**52**:907–11.

10. Mosenthal AC, Livingston DH, Lavery RF, Knudson MM, Lee S, Morabito D, et al. The effect of age on functional outcome in mild traumatic brain injury: 6-month report of a prospective multicenter trial. *J Trauma* 2004;**56**:1042–8.

11. Pennings JL, Bachulis BL, Simons CT, Slazinski T. Survival after severe brain injury in the aged. *Arch Surg* 1993;**128**:787–93.

12. Pentland B, Jones PA, Roy CW, Miller JD. Head injury in the elderly. *Age Ageing* 1986;**15**:193–202.

13. Rothweiler BR, Temkin NR, Dikmen SS. Aging effect on psychosocial outcome in traumatic brain injury. *Arch Phys Med Rehabil* 1998;**79**:881–7.

14. Susman M, DiRusso SM, Sullivan T, Risucci D, Nealon P, Cuff S, et al. Traumatic brain injury in the elderly: Increased mortality and worse functional outcome at discharge despite lower injury severity. *J Trauma* 2002;**53**:219–24.

15. Vollmer DG, Torner JC, Jane JA, Sadornic B, Charles-Bois D, Eisenberg HM. Age and outcome following traumatic coma: why do older patients fare worse? *J Neurosurg* 1991;**75**:S37–49.

16. Clifton GL, Miller ER, Choi SC, Levin HL, McCauley S, Smith KR, et al. Hypothermia on admission in patients with severe brain injury. *J Neurotrauma* 2002;**19**:293–301.

17. Teasdale G, Jennett B. Assessment of coma and impaired consciousness: a practical scale. *Lancet* 1974;**2**:281–4.

18. Jennett B, Bond MR. Assessment of outcome after severe brain damage. *Lancet* 1975;**1**:480–4.

19. Granger CV, Hamilton BB. UDS report. The uniform data system for medical rehabilitation report of first admissions for 1992. *Am J Phys Med Rehab* 1992;**71**:108.

20. Ulvik A, Wentzel-Larsen T, Flaatten H. Trauma patients in the intensive care unit: short- and long-term survival and predictors of 30-day mortality. *Acta Anaesthesiol Scand* 2007;**51**:171–7.

21. Ushewokunze S, Nannapaneni R, Gregson BA, Stobbart L, Chambers IR, Mendelow AD. Elderly patients with severe head injury in coma from the outset – has anything changed? *Brit J Neurosurg* 2004;**18**:604–7.

22. Kotwica Z, Jakubowski JK. Acute head injuries in the elderly. An analysis of 136 consecutive patients. *Acta Neurochir* 1992;**118**:98–102.

23. Ross AM, Pitts LH, Kobayashi S. Prognosticators of outcome after major head injury in the elderly. *J Neurosci Nursing* 1992;**24**:88–93.

24. Adhiyaman V, Asghar M, Ganeshram KN, Bhowmick BK. Chronic subdural haematoma in the elderly. *Postgrad Med J* 2002;**78**:71–5.

25. Flanagan SR, Hibbard MR, Riordan B, et al. Traumatic brain injury in the elderly: diagnostic and treatment challenges. *Clin Geriatr Med* 2006;**22**:449–68.

26. Luerrsen TG, Klauber MR, Marshall LF. Outcome from head injury related to patient's age: a longitudinal prospective study of adult and pediatric head injury. *J Neurosurg* 1988;**68**:409–16.

27. Haydel MJ, Preston CA, Mills TJ, Luber S, Blaudeau E, DeBlieux PM. Indications for computed tomography in patients with minor head injury. *N Engl J Med* 2000;**343**:100–5.

28. Stiell IG, Wells GA, Vandemheen K, Clement C, Lesiuk H, Laupacis A, et al. The Canadian CT Head Rule for patients with minor head injury. *Lancet* 2001;**357**:1391–6.

29. Karni A, Holtzman R, Bass T, Zorman G, Carter L, Rodriguez L, et al. Traumatic head injury in the anticoagulated elderly patient: a lethal combination. *Am Surg* 2001;**67**:1098–100.

30. Lavoie A, Ratte S, Clas D, Demers J, Moore L, Martin M, et al. Preinjury warfarin use among elderly patients with closed head injuries in a trauma center. *J Trauma* 2004;**56**:802–7.

31. Reynolds FD, Dietz PA, Higgins D, Whitaker TS. Time to deterioration of the elderly, anticoagulated, minor head injury patient who presents without evidence of neurologic abnormality. *J Trauma* 2003;**54**:492–6.

32. *The State of Aging and Health in America* 2007. Atlanta, Georgia: Centers for Disease Control and Prevention, National Center for Injury Control and Prevention; 2007.

33. Rubenstein LZ. Falls in older people: epidemiology, risk factors and strategies for prevention. *Age Ageing* 2006;**35**-S2:ii37–ii41.

34. Thurman DJ, Stevens JA, Rao JK. Practice parameter: assessing patients in a neurology practice for risk of falls (an evidence-based review). *Neurology* 2008;**70**:473–9.

35. McGwin G, Sims RV, Pulley L, Roseman JM. Relations among chronic medical conditions, medications, and automobile crashes in the elderly: A population-based case-control study. *Am J Epidemiol* 2000;**152**:424–31.

36. Goldstein FC, Levin HS, Presley RM, Searcy J, Colohan ART, Eisenberg HM, et al. Neurobehavioural consequences of closed head injury in older adults. *J Neurol Neurosurg Psychiatry* 1994;**57**:961–6.

37. Blessed G, Tomlinson BE, Roth M. The association between quantitative measures of dementia and of senile change in the cerebral grey matter of elderly subjects. *Br J Psychiatry* 1968;**114**:797–811.

38. Army Individual Test Battery. *Manual of Directions and Scoring*. Washington DC: War Department, Adjutant General's Office; 1944.

39. Wechsler D. *Wechsler Memory Scale-Revised*. New York: Psychological Corporation; 1987.

40. Hannay HJ, Levin HS. *The Continuous Recognition Memory Test*. Houston: Neuropsychological Resources; 1988.

41. Libon DJ, Mattson RE, Glosser G, Kaplan E, Malamut BL, Sands LP, et al. A nine-word dementia version of the California Verbal Learning Test. *Clin Neuropsychol* 1996;**10**:237–44.

42. Benton AL, Hamsher KdeS. *Multilingual Aphasia Examination*. Iowa City: University of Iowa; 1976.

43. Nelson HE. A modified card sorting test sensitive to frontal lobe deficits. *Cortex* 1976;**12**:313–24.

44. Wechsler D. *Wechsler Adult Intelligence Scale-Revised*. New York: Psychological Corporation; 1981.

45. Aharon-Peretz J, Kliot D, Amyel-Zvi E, Tomer R, Rakier A, Feinsod M. Neurobehavioural consequences of closed head injury in the elderly. *Br Inj* 1997;**11**:871–5.

46. Luukinen H, Viramo P, Koski K, Laippala P, Kivela S-L. Head injuries and cognitive decline among older adults: a population-based study. *Neurology* 1999;**52**:557–62.

47. Folstein MF, Folstein SE, McHugh PR. Mini-mental state: A practical method for grading the cognitive state of patients for the physician. *J Psychiatric Res* 1975;**12**:189–98.

48. Rapoport MJ, Herrmann N, Shammi P, Kiss A, Phillips A, Feinstein A. Outcome after traumatic brain injury sustained in older adulthood: a one-year longitudinal study. *Am J Geriatr Psychiatry* 2006;**14**:456–65.

49. Rapoport M, Wolf U, Hermann N, Kiss A, Shammi P, Reis M, et al. Traumatic brain injury, apolipoprotein E-e4, and cognition in older adults: a two-year longitudinal study. *J Neuropsychiatry Clin Neurosci* 2008;**20**:68–73.

50. Mazzucchi A, Cattelani R, Missale G, Gugliotta M, Brianti R, Parma M. Head-injured subjects aged over 50 years: correlations between variables of trauma and neuropsychological follow-up. *J Neurol* 1992;**239**:256–60.

51. Goldstein FC, Levin HS, Goldman WP, Clark AN, Kenehan-Altonen T. Cognitive and neurobehavioral functioning after mild and moderate traumatic brain injury. *J Int Neuropsych Soc* 2001;**7**:373–83.

52. Goldstein FC, Levin HS. Cognitive outcome after mild and moderate traumatic brain injury in older adults. *J Clin Exp Neuropsychol* 2001;**23**:739–53.

53. Levin HS, O'Donnell VM, Grossman RG. The Galveston Orientation and Amnesia Test: a practical scale to assess cognition after head injury. *J Nerv Mental Dis* 1979;**167**:675–84.

54. Goldstein FC, Levin HS, Roberts VJ, Goldman WP, Kalechstein AS, Winslow M, Goldstein SJ. Neuropsychological effects of closed head injury in older adults: a comparison with Alzheimer's Disease. *Neuropsychology* 1996;**10**:147–54.

55. Breed S, Sacks A, Ashman TA, Gordon WA, Dahlman K, Spielman L. Cognitive functioning among individuals with traumatic brain injury, Alzheimer's disease, and no cognitive impairments. *J Head Trauma Rehabil* 2008;**23**:149–57.

56. Levin HS, Goldstein FC, MacKenzie EJ. Depression as a secondary condition following mild and moderate traumatic brain injury. *Sem Clin Neuropsychiatry* 1997;**2**:207–15.

57. Goldstein FC, Levin HS, Goldman WP, Kalechstein AD, Clark AN, Kenehan-Altonen T. Cognitive and behavioral sequelae of closed head injury in older adults according to their significant others. *J Neuropsychiatry Clin Neurosci* 1999;**11**:38–44.

58. Schwartz GE. Development and validation of the Geriatric Evaluation by Relative's Rating Instrument (GERRI). *Psychol Rep* 1983;**53**:479–88.

59. First MB, Gibbon M, Spitzer RL, Williams JBW, Benjamin LS. *User's Guide for the Structured Clinical Interview for DSM-IV Axis II Personality Disorders (SCID-II)*. Washington, DC: Am Psychiatric Press; 1997.

60. Hybels CF, Blazer DG. Epidemiology of late-life mental disorders. *Clin Geriatr Med* 2003;**19**:663–96.

61. Lawes D. A retrospective review of emergency admission for head injury in the over 75s. *Injury* 2002;**33**:349–51.

62. Dikmen S, Machamer J, Temkin N. Mild head injury: facts and artifacts. *J Clin Exp Neuropsychol* 2001;**23**:729–38.

63. Levin HS, Mattis S, Ruff RM, Eisenberg HM, Marshall LF, Tabaddor K, et al. Neurobehavioral outcome following minor head injury: a three center study. *J Neurosurg* 1987;**66**:234–43.

64. Ponsford J, Willmott C, Rothwell A, Cameron P, Kelly AM, Nelms R. Factors influencing outcome following mild traumatic brain injury in adults. *J Int Neuropsych Soc* 2000;**6**:568–79.

65. Williams DH, Levin HS, Eisenberg HM. Mild head injury classification. *Neurosurgery* 1990;**27**:422–8.

66. Rapoport MJ, Kiss A, Feinstein A. The impact of major depression on outcome following mild-to-moderate traumatic brain injury in older adults. *J Affect Disord* 2006;**92**:273–6.

67. Cifu DX, Kreutzer JS, Marwitz JH, Rosenthal M, Englander J, High W. Functional outcomes of older adults with traumatic brain injury: a prospective, multicenter analysis. *Arch Phys Med Rehabil* 1996;**77**: 883–8.

68. Frankel JE, Marwitz JH, Cifu DX, Kreutzer JS, Englander J, Rosenthal M. A follow-up study of older adults with traumatic brain injury: taking into account decreasing length of stay. *Arch Phys Med Rehabil* 2006; **87**:57–62.

Chapter

11e

Traumatic brain injury across the lifespan: a long-term developmental perspective

Jacobus Donders

The four exciting chapters in this section show clearly that traumatic brain injury (TBI) is common across the lifespan, and that a number of general principles apply. For example, regardless of age of onset, uncomplicated mild TBI is typically associated with only transient sequelae but as injury severity increases, there are more significant and persistent morbidities in the survivors. In addition, behavioral and psychosocial sequelae tend to be relatively most concerning in the long run, even when cognitive impairments are not trivial. These chapters also illustrate that variation in age of onset of TBI is associated with important differences in pathophysiology as well as predictors of outcome. Those at the extremes of the age spectrum appear to be relatively most vulnerable to the effects of TBI, whereas the specific detrimental impact of prefrontal involvement has been established much more clearly in adult than in pediatric samples. Different age levels are also associated with distinct necessities to consider comorbid complicating factors, ranging from learning disability in children, to alcohol abuse in young adults, to hypertension and diabetes mellitus in the elderly.

It is evident from the preceding four chapters that a long-term developmental perspective is needed when considering the impact of TBI. When severe TBI affects children, some sequelae may not become fully manifest until many years post-injury, and there also is concern about the possible acceleration of onset of degenerative diseases in older adults who sustained severe TBI decades earlier. In this context, it is important to consider various moderating variables, such as socioeconomic adversity, family dynamics and possibly genetics. Unfortunately, the level of precision with which neuropsychologists can currently predict outcomes becomes increasingly modest, the more years pass since injury. Relatively few studies have evaluated sufficiently large and representative samples in a prospective manner for more than a handful of years [1, 2].

This is clearly an avenue for future research, with a need for application of more sophisticated statistical techniques such as general linear modeling and path analysis [3, 4], as well as inclusion of more advanced neuroimaging procedures such as diffusion tensor and magnetic resonance spectroscopy applications [5, 6].

In today's healthcare climate, where there are increasing demands for empirical data to support the necessity of specific services, the onus is on neuropsychologists to present evidence for the value-added nature of their assessment and intervention procedures. There have been a few recent investigations that have provided support for the incremental merit of neuropsychological assessment in the prediction of outcome after TBI [7, 8], but studies are still lacking with regard to the application of such findings to specific therapeutic or preventative interventions. Furthermore, although there have been a number of successful applications of randomized clinical trials with regard to brief psychotherapy and cognitive rehabilitation in samples with TBI [9, 10], there is a need for more Class I evidence for the lasting effectiveness of specific interventions, all the way from acute care to long-term follow-up. Further application of such designs with innovative technologies such as web-based family intervention [11] and virtual reality [12] is also desirable.

Beyond direct practical applications, the field is in need of more integrated biopsychosocial models to provided sound theoretical guidance for future research. A few such models have recently appeared in the literature but they have typically focused on a restricted age range [13, 14] and expansion of such models to offer a true life-span developmental neuropsychological perspective is a primary challenge for the next decade. This will need to include utilization of the full range of resources, from animal models [15] to psychological intervention methods [16] to incorporation of cultural issues [17]. In addition, it needs to be appreciated that "outcome" is a multidimensional construct and that different predictors, moderators, and mediators are likely to be found for various dimensions [18]. The four chapters in this section provide excellent groundwork from which to begin the next generation of interdisciplinary research into the prevention, treatment, and follow-up of TBI across the lifespan.

References

1. Ponsford J, Draper K, Schönberger M. Functional outcome 10 years after traumatic brain injury: its relationship with demographic variables, injury severity, cognitive and emotional status. *J Int Neuropsychol Soc* 2008;**14**:233–42.

2. Catroppa C, Anderson VA, Morse SA, et al. Outcome and prediction of functional recovery 5 years following pediatric traumatic brain injury (TBI). *J Ped Psychol* 2008;**33**:707–18.

3. Ewing-Cobbs L, Barnes M, Fletcher JM, et al. Modeling of longitudinal academic achievement scores after pediatric traumatic brain injury. *Dev Neuropsychol* 2004;**25**:107–33.

4. Yeates KO, Swift E, Taylor HG, et al. Short- and long-term social outcomes following pediatric traumatic brain injury. *J Int Neuropsychol Soc* 2004;**10**:412–26.

5. Sidaros A, Engberg AW, Sidaros K, et al. Diffusion tensor imaging during recovery from severe traumatic brain injury and relation to clinical outcome: a longitudinal study. *Brain* 2008;**131**:559–72.

6. Shutter L, Tong KA, Lee A, et al. Prognostic role of proton magnetic resonance spectroscopy in acute traumatic brain injury. *J Head Trauma Rehabil* 2006;**21**:334–49.

7. Miller LJ, Donders J. Prediction of educational outcome after pediatric traumatic brain injury. *Rehab Psychol* 2003;**48**:237–41.

8. Hanks RA, Millis SR, Ricker JH, et al. The predictive validity of a brief inpatient neuropsychologic battery for persons with traumatic brain injury. *Arch Phys Med Rehabil* 2008;**89**:950–7.

9. Paniak C, Toller-Lobe G, Reynolds S, et al. A randomized trial of two treatments for mild traumatic brain injury: 1 year follow-up. *Brain Inj* 2000;**14**:219–26.

10. Van't Hooft I, Andersson K, Bergman B, et al. Beneficial effect from a cognitive training programme on children with acquired brain injuries demonstrated in a controlled study. *Brain Inj* 2005;**19**:511–18.

11. Wade SL, Carey J, Wolfe CR. The efficacy of an online cognitive-behavioral family intervention in improving child behavior and social competence following pediatric traumatic brain injury. *Rehabil Psychol* 2006;**51**:179–89.

12. Matheis RJ, Schultheis MT, Tiersky LA, et al. Is learning and memory different in a virtual environment? *Clin Neuropsychol* 2007;**21**:146–61.

13. Yeates KO, Bigler ED, Dennis M et al. Social outcomes in childhood brain disorder: A heuristic integration of social neuroscience and developmental psychology. *Psychol Bull* 2007;**133**:535–66.

14. Kieffaber PD, Marcoulider GA, White MH, et al. Modeling the ecological validity of neurocognitive assessment in adults with acquired brain injury. *J Clin Psychol Med Set* 2007;**14**:206–18.

15. Duhaime A. Large animal models of traumatic injury to the immature brain. *Dev Neurosci* 2006;**28**:380–7.

16. Coetzer R. Psychotherapy following traumatic brain injury: integrating theory and practice. *J Head Trauma Rehabil* 2007;**22**:39–47.

17. Kennepohl S, Shore D, Nabors N, Hanks R. African-American acculturation and neuropsychological test performance following traumatic brain injury. *J Internat Neuropsychol Soc* 2004;**10**:566–77.

18. Wood RL, Rutherford NA. Demographic and cognitive predictors of long-term psychosocial outcome following traumatic brain injury. *J Int Neuropsychol Soc* 2006;**12**:350–8.

Pediatric aspects of epilepsy

Lindsey Felix and Scott J. Hunter

Introduction

Epilepsy is the most common neurological condition in childhood and patients frequently present to neuropsychological clinics due to a number of factors related to their seizures, including difficulties with attention, learning, and behavior. Specific cognitive impairments often accompany epileptic syndromes, and these translate to academic underachievement. Patients also present with psychiatric symptoms including inattention, depression, and anxiety. Treatment, including antiepileptic drugs (AEDs) and surgery, can be related to alterations in cognition. As such, continual monitoring for changes in neurocognitive functioning is recommended.

Classification of seizures

Etiology

A seizure is defined as the discharge of abnormal electrical activity in the brain; a diagnosis of epilepsy is made when an individual has recurrent seizures with electroencephalographic (EEG) confirmation [1, 2]. While EEG affirmatively diagnoses up to 70% of individuals with epilepsy, clinical, subjective, and objective observations typically corroborate EEG findings in order to support a diagnosis.

Three mechanisms that occur at the cellular level have been implicated in the development of epilepsy [1]. Defects involving ion channels may result in the prolonged opening of sodium or calcium channels, excessively depolarizing the presynaptic membrane, and resulting in epileptiform activity [3]. The presence of excessive excitatory (glutamate and aspartate) or deficient inhibitory (GABA and glycine) neurochemicals may also increase brain activity, leading to seizures [2]. Third, cellular changes, such as the development of excitatory pathways or synaptic reorganization, can lead to epilepsy, also known as the "kindling" effect [3].

Generalized and localization-related seizures

Classification of seizure type involves localization of electrical discharge [1, 2]. Seizures can be classified as generalized, localized, or undetermined [4]. Primary generalized seizures have an abrupt onset of synchronized bilateral discharges accompanied by a sudden loss of consciousness [2, 4]. Primary generalized seizures include tonic-clonic seizures, atonic seizures, and absence seizures. Tonic-clonic seizures are the most common type of primary generalized seizures. Lasting less than 5 minutes, they involve the tonic stiffening of the trunk and extremities, followed by clonic rhythmic jerking. Tonic-clonic seizures are followed by postictal unresponsiveness.

Atonic seizures are identified by a sudden loss of muscle tone that results in an abrupt fall [2]. Myoclonic seizures consist of brief, single symmetrical jerks of the head and upper extremities which typically occur upon awakening and may occur in a cluster. Absence seizures account for approximately 2 to 11% of all seizure diagnoses, with the highest rates before the age of 10 [5]. Absence seizures are nonconvulsive, last a few seconds, and consist of brief staring episodes with a sudden cessation of activity [2]. A classification of atypical absence seizures is applied when seizures begin early in childhood and are accompanied by other generalized seizures.

Localization-related, or focal, seizures occur when groups of neurons simultaneously release electrical discharges. Secondary generalized seizures occur when seizures of focal onset spread to the surrounding neurons, or the contralateral hemisphere. Partial seizures are seizures of focal onset that account for 40 to 60% of those seen in children with epilepsy, with complex partial seizures being more common than simple partial seizures [4]. They begin within a localized area of the brain and involve an aura or warning, such as a feeling of fear, nausea, foul odor or taste, dizziness, or sense of déjà vu [2]. Simple partial seizures involve no alteration of consciousness, whereas complex partial seizures, also known as psychomotor seizures, involve a loss of consciousness. Complex partial seizures last a few minutes and are followed by postictal confusion and fatigue.

A patient with pseudoseizures presents similarly to patients with other epilepsy syndromes [6]. In contrast with other seizures, there is no clinical support for epileptiform activity. Pseudoseizures are often seen in patients with epilepsy, and patients with comorbid psychiatric conditions [2].

At the second level of classification, causation-related variables are implicated. Symptomatic epilepsy involves an identified origin or cause of the seizure activity, including brain anomalies, metabolic derangements, birth anoxia, cerebrovascular insults, central nervous system infections, central nervous system neoplasm, and head trauma [5]. Symptomatic epilepsy can be contrasted with idiopathic epilepsy, in which there is no identified cause of seizures. Cryptogenic epilepsy indicates that there is probably a structural brain abnormality that has not yet been identified [4, 5].

Epilepsy syndromes

Several identified epileptic syndromes occur in childhood and each follows a typical course [5].

Generalized idiopathic epilepsies

Childhood absence seizures, juvenile absence seizures, and juvenile myoclonic epilepsy comprise the majority of generalized idiopathic epilepsies [4]. In childhood absence epilepsy, brief periods of a lack of awareness, seen as staring incidents, occur several times per day and typically occur in clusters [5]. Girls are more frequently affected than boys. This disorder is responsive to treatment and usually spontaneously resolves [2]. Juvenile absence epilepsy has a peak onset during puberty, distinguishing it from childhood absence epilepsy [2, 4, 5]. Patients with juvenile absence epilepsy have a poorer prognosis than patients with childhood absence epilepsy, as generalized convulsive seizures and persistence of epilepsy into adulthood usually follow [2]. Males and females are equally affected.

Onset of juvenile myoclonic epilepsy, also termed impulsive petit mal epilepsy, occurs in late childhood to early adolescence, usually between the ages of 12 and 18 [5]. It is characterized by myoclonic jerks of the upper extremities, following awakening [4]. Resolution of seizures is infrequent. Juvenile myoclonic

epilepsy is genetically inherited; specifically, chromosome 6p21.3 has been implicated [5].

Focal idiopathic epilepsies of childhood

Focal idiopathic epilepsies of childhood, also referred to as benign focal epilepsies, are among the most common seizure disorders in children between the ages of 3 and 12 [4]. With benign focal epilepsy of childhood, seizures occur rarely, and usually resolve by mid-adolescence [5]. Males are more frequently affected than females. The most common type is known as benign rolandic epilepsy, in which seizures occur nocturnally and include unilateral clonic activity of the head and upper extremities [5]. Genetic links have been identified by twin studies; chromosome 15q14 has been implicated [4].

Occipital lobe epilepsy accounts for 6 to 8% of all epilepsies, and children are more affected than adults [4]. Benign childhood occipital epilepsy involves visual symptoms, including seeing stars, illusions, and hallucinations [2]. Temporal lobe epilepsy is one of the most common types of epilepsy in adults and children, although childhood onset has a poorer prognosis [7]. Auras often precede temporal lobe seizures and involve somatosensory symptoms: epigastric rising sensation, olfactory symptoms, and emotional symptoms [7].

Frontal lobe epilepsy accounts for 30% of partial epilepsies, and is the largest subgroup of extra-temporal-lobe epilepsies [4]. Frontal lobe seizures have a difficult presentation, making diagnosis complicated. They rarely present with clear interictal or even ictal EEG abnormalities, and are often misidentified as pseudoseizures.

Epileptic encephalopathies

Epileptic encephalopathies consist of a group of syndromes characterized by deterioration in sensory and/or motor functioning as a result of epileptiform activity [4]. Prognosis is typically poor. Regression or failure to meet developmental milestones is common.

Dravet's Syndrome is estimated to occur in 1/40 000 children under the age of 7 [4]. Onset is within the first year of life in typically developing children [5]. Dravet's syndrome is characterized by frequent prolonged seizures that lead to recurrent status epilepticus. Seizure focus switches hemispheres and seizures are typically unresponsive to AED therapy. Developmental delay has ranged from 26 to 42% and hyperactivity is frequently observed [4].

West syndrome (infantile spasms) has an onset in infancy, and prevalence rates have been estimated at 2 to 4.5/10 000 live births annually [2, 4]. A typical presentation involves myoclonic seizures. Characterization of West syndrome includes infantile spasms, psychomotor deterioration, and hypsarrhythmia [5]. Other types of seizures occur in 50 to 75% of cases. Lennox-Gastaut syndrome comprises 20 to 50% of cases.

Patients with Lennox-Gastaut syndrome have mixed seizures, including atypical absence, atonic, and myoclonic seizures [2]. This syndrome is very rare, and prevalence has been estimated between 1.3 and 2.6/10 000 children [4]. Between 20 to 60% of children have a history of infantile spasms. Comorbid status epilepticus is common [5]. Prognosis is poor as 91% exhibit mental retardation [4].

Myoclonic astatic epilepsy begins between the ages of 2 and 5 in typically developing children [5]. Seizures begin as generalized tonic-clonic, but are followed by myoclonic astatic seizures of increasing frequency. Patients who have comorbid developmental delay are often misdiagnosed with idiopathic Lennox Gastaut syndrome. There appear to be two distinct prognostic categories: seizure remission and mild cognitive impact versus deterioration in cognitive function due to persisting seizures [4].

Continuous spike-wave discharges during sleep (electrical status epilepticus during sleep) involves continuous spike and wave activity during more than 85% of non-rapid-eye-movement sleep [2]. Age of onset is typically between 4 and 14, and it usually occurs between 5 and 7 years. Boys are affected more frequently than girls. Pre-existing neurological abnormalities are reported in approximately one-third of patients and premorbid developmental delay is commonly reported [4]. The majority of patients experience neuropsychological regression as a direct consequence of the continuous spike and waves during sleep. Seizures are often present and partial motor seizures typically occur prior to identification of the syndrome. Seizures often remit spontaneously during adolescence.

Landau-Kleffner syndrome (LKS; acquired aphasia with convulsive disorder) is the most commonly known disorder associated with continuous spike and waves during slow sleep [4, 5]. It has a typical onset between the ages of 2 and 11 [2]. LKS is characterized by a sudden or gradual onset of auditory agnosia, preceded by typical development [5]. Language impairment varies, but it generally impacts comprehension first, followed by productive language. Other cognitive functions are left unimpaired [4]. Seizures occur in approximately 70 to 80% of affected children; however, seizures are responsive to anticonvulsant medication. Epileptiform activity is prominent in the temporal lobe, often occurring bilaterally. Behavioral changes are often present, and are typically related to alterations in neural function or linguistic frustration.

Epidemiology

Epidemiological studies indicate that epilepsy affects 1 to 2% of school-aged children, which translates to 150 250 to 325 000 active cases in children aged 5 to 14 in the USA [8]. Worldwide, approximately 4 to 9 out of every 1000 pediatric patients have epilepsy, equaling the most common pediatric neurological conditions [2]. Onset typically occurs during childhood and adolescence; 75% of individuals with epilepsy have their first seizures before the age of 20. About 25% of those who experience one convulsive episode will ultimately meet formal criteria for epilepsy. In fact, half of childhood epilepsy occurs during the first 5 years of life. For reasons unknown, epilepsy affects boys slightly more than girls [6].

Neuropsychological findings in pediatric patients with epilepsy

Overall cognitive functioning

Most forms of cognitive impairment seen in epilepsy patients are captured by the DSM-IV-TR category of Mild Neurocognitive Disorder [9]. Most studies using the Wechsler scales to assess cognitive functioning have documented low average range [10, 11, 12] to average range capability [13–17]. Several studies have identified no significant differences in intellectual functioning according to hemispheric lateralization of epileptiform discharges [11, 12, 16, 18] or seizure frequency [1, 16]; however, Caplan et al. [18] and Buelow et al., [19] both indicated that increased seizure frequency was associated with decreased cognitive capability. Patients with frequent EEG discharges during testing perform worse than patients with infrequent seizures [12].

Patients with more severe neuropathology, including comorbid hippocampal sclerosis and cortical dysplasia, hippocampal sclerosis and tumor [20], the presence of febrile or prolonged seizures [18], and comorbid attention deficit hyperactivity disorder (ADHD) [21], perform significantly worse on cognitive measures than patients with less severe neuropathology. Several studies have indicated that patients with earlier age of onset perform worse than patients with later age of onset [19, 20, 22]; whereas other studies have yielded no relationship between age of onset and cognitive functioning [14, 16]. Gender is not related to cognitive functioning [14, 19].

Academic achievement

In patients with well-controlled or benign epilepsies, performance on achievement tests is typically within the average range, whereas in patients with less successfully controlled epilepsy, academic deficits are frequently observed, relative to age-based norms [15, 20, 23–26]. Similarly, parent-rated academic performance of patients with epilepsy is lower than that of typically developing peers [18, 27]. As well, pediatric patients with epilepsy are more likely to be placed in specialized medical and educational institutions [28] and provided with special education supports [3] than typically developing peers. Epilepsy variables, including seizure frequency [23], age of onset and duration of disease [22, 23, 28], are correlated with academic test performance [23] and placement in specialized or adapted schools [22, 28]. Cognitive variables, such as decreased overall cognitive functioning [22], verbal comprehension [18, 24], nonverbal processing and executive functioning, [27], and attention and memory [24], are correlated with academic achievement test performance [18, 24], placement in specialized classrooms [22], and parent-rated academic performance [27]. In pediatric patients with comorbid epilepsy and learning disability, academic achievement is approximately one half year behind that of nonaffected, learning disabled peers [20].

Psychosocial variables including externalizing behaviors are related to decreased academic skill development [23], placement in specialized schools [28], and parent-rated academic problems [13]. Internalizing behaviors in adolescents are related to academic skill development [23], but are not related to academic skill development in younger patients [24] or placement in specialized schools [28]. Overall, children with epilepsy, particularly uncontrolled epilepsy, are at risk for academic underachievement, and this is confounded by type of epilepsy, cognitive functioning, and psychosocial variables.

Linguistic processing

Low average [11, 13] to average range [14–17, 24] verbal comprehension has been identified in several studies using the Wechsler intelligence scales. Receptive language skills are typically within the low average range [15, 29]. Expressive language capabilities have been observed to be more severely impaired [13, 15]. Complex neuropathology, including epilepsy pathophysiology and the presence of congenital hemiparesis, is related to decreased linguistic processing [20]. In contrast, seizure frequency [14, 16], hemispheric lateralization [16, 29], and duration of disease [14, 16] do not correlate with linguistic deficits.

A discussion of linguistic processing would not be complete without addressing cortical language reorganization. Language reorganization in pediatric and adult patients with left-onset complex partial epilepsy has been observed [25, 30]. For example, in patients with identified reading and/or spelling deficits, greater activation and earlier onset of late, language-specific magnetoencephalographic activity in posterior temporal and inferior parietal areas of the right hemisphere, relative to the left, have been observed.

Visuospatial processing

On the perceptual organizational subtests of the Wechsler intelligence scales, pediatric patients with epilepsy generally exhibit low average [11, 13, 14] to average range skill [16, 17]. More specifically, patients with generalized and benign epilepsies [15, 30, 31] have typically exhibited average visuospatial analysis and synthesis skills. However, Høie and colleagues [32] found "severe nonverbal problems", indicated by performance below the 10th percentile on the Raven Matrices, in 79 (43%) epilepsy patients, compared to four controls (3%). Similarly, children with frontal lobe epilepsy [31] exhibited significant impairment on the copy trial of the Rey Complex Figure Test; however, patients with temporal epilepsies [20, 31] have not consistently exhibited impairment in this domain.

The literature regarding the impact of etiological and seizure variables in relation to perceptual and organizational skill is inconsistent. Increased seizure frequency and younger age of onset have been associated with "severe nonverbal problems" by Høie et al. [32]; however, Riva et al. [16] and Kramer et al. [14] have both documented no relationship between seizure frequency and nonverbal processing. Aldenkamp et al. [20] indicated that duration of disease was correlated with performance on perceptual tasks, while

Kramer et al. [14] and Riva et al. [16] did not. Demographic evaluations revealed no relationship between parental income, occupation, and education level and the presence of "severe nonverbal problems" in pediatric patients with epilepsy [32].

Processing speed

Processing-speed tasks require speeded reaction time and motor control. Pediatric patients with mixed epilepsy presentations [10] and those with frontal lobe epilepsy [31] have both shown impairment on Wechsler scale processing-speed tasks. In contrast, children with generalized absence epilepsy and temporal lobe epilepsy perform within the average range [31]. Reaction times to computer-presented stimuli were delayed in two studies [12, 30]; however, Boelen et al. [10] demonstrated average range reaction times. Reaction time was related to etiology, such that patients with generalized epilepsies had more impaired reaction times than patients with partial [12] and absence epilepsies [30]. Lower seizure frequency was associated with faster reaction times than higher seizure frequency [12].

Pediatric patients with epilepsy exhibit average simple motor control and finger dexterity [10, 16, 17]. Motor control is related to type of epilepsy, such that patients with frontal lobe and absence epilepsy performed significantly worse than patients with temporal lobe and generalized epilepsies [33]. Patients with younger age of onset performed worse than those with an older age of onset [16]. Motor control was not associated with hemispheric lateralization, seizure frequency, or duration of having epilepsy [16].

Everyday memory

Parent- and child-rated everyday memory performance was evaluated by Kadis et al. [34]. Parent ratings of decreased everyday memory performance were related to parent-rated indices of attention, overall cognitive abilities, auditory working memory, and vigilance. Child ratings of everyday decreased memory performance were related to parent-rated attention, auditory working memory, and vigilance. Mood and emotional state were not related to changes in everyday memory, a distinction from studies evaluating everyday memory in adults.

Verbal learning and memory

Most studies have documented average range list-learning and recall [14, 16, 17, 24, 26, 31, 35] and story recall [14, 21, 24] in children with epilepsy. In contrast, Billingsley et al. [36] reported deficits in recall and recognition. Patients with absence epilepsy [30] and frontal lobe epilepsy [31] appear to perform worse on verbal memory tasks than patients with temporal lobe epilepsy. Patients with stronger cognitive abilities perform better on verbal memory tasks [37] than those whose cognitive profile is hampered.

Hemispheric lateralization [17, 21, 31, 36, 38] and seizure frequency [14, 16] variables are not observed to be associated with performance on list-learning and story recall tasks. Age of onset and duration of disease have been correlated with performance on verbal list-learning and recall [16, 36] and story recall [37] in some studies, such that those with an earlier age of onset and longer duration of disease performed worse than their counterparts. However, this finding is not consistent [14, 35, 37, 38].

Nonverbal learning and memory

Pediatric patients with epilepsy exhibit low average range [15] to average range [14, 37, 39] simple nonverbal recall. Patients with higher intellectual functioning exhibited better visual memory performance [37]. Across patients with temporal lobe epilepsy, right-sided focus was associated with significantly decreased visual retention [20, 37]. On the other hand, patients with frontal lobe [37] and partial epilepsy [29] do not exhibit the same effect of lateralization. Complex etiological variables (e.g. congenital hemiparesis) were negatively correlated with visual retention [29]. Age of onset was not associated with nonverbal learning [14, 37]. Parental adaptation to diagnosis correlated positively and long-standing behavioral problems correlated negatively with nonverbal recall [39].

Several studies have employed the Rey Complex Figure Test to assess learning and recall of complex visual information. Pediatric patients with epilepsy exhibit low average [15, 37] to average range [30, 37] recall of the Rey figure. Cognitive functioning was positively correlated with performance on recall trials [37]. However, research has demonstrated inconsistencies with regard to localization. Nolan et al. [37] found that children with temporal lobe epilepsy performed worse than children with frontal lobe epilepsy, whereas Hernandez et al. [31] demonstrated that children with frontal lobe epilepsy performed worse than those with temporal lobe epilepsy. No relationships between hemispheric lateralization [21, 31], seizure frequency, and duration of disease [14, 37] and recall of the Rey figure have been documented.

Attention

Impairments in verbal attention and auditory working memory [9, 15, 24, 29, 30, 34, 39], visual attention and visual working memory [30, 31, 33], and sustained concentration [29, 31] have been documented in studies. Patients with uncontrolled epilepsy have impaired attention relative to patients with successful seizure control [26, 39]. Children and adults with absence epilepsy performed worse than children and adults with temporal lobe and juvenile myoclonic epilepsy on visual sustained attention tasks [35]. Hemispheric lateralization effects [29, 30, 31] and gender differences [33] in attentional regulation and working memory have not been identified as impacting attention.

Executive functioning

Parent-rated executive dysfunction, as ascertained with the Behavior Rating Inventory of Executive Function (BRIEF), contributes to poor quality of life in pediatric patients with epilepsy [40]. In general, children with epilepsy fall in the average range on the BRIEF [40]. Still, 42% of one sample showed clinical-level impairments in developing executive skill.

Høie et al. [27] developed a broad executive-functioning factor composed of visual-motor functioning, verbal learning, word fluency, set-shifting, and visual working memory. Patients with lower intellectual abilities, active epilepsy, earlier age of onset, and parent-rated depressive symptoms performed significantly worse on the executive-functioning composite than their counterparts.

Shifting cognitive set, as assessed by the Wisconsin Card Sorting Test (WCST), is impaired, both in overall categories achieved [17], as well as in perseveration [17, 33, 35] in pediatric patients with epilepsy. Performance on the WCST was related to epilepsy variables including hemispheric lateralization [16, 33], age of onset [17], seizure frequency, and duration of disease [16]. Planning skill, assessed by performance on the Tower of London, was impaired in children with frontal lobe epilepsy, but preserved in children with temporal lobe and generalized epilepsies [33]. Pediatric patients with epilepsy exhibited significantly impaired design fluency production in both free and fixed forms, and significantly more perseverative errors than age-based norms [16, 17]. Average range phonemic [17] and semantic [16, 17] word fluency has

been observed; however, patients with absence epilepsy [30] and frontal lobe epilepsy [33] exhibited significant impairment relative to patients with generalized tonic-clonic epilepsy and temporal lobe absence epilepsy.

Psychological functioning and comorbidities

Prevalence rates of ADHD have been documented at 31% for inattention and 31% for hyperactivity-impulsivity [41, 42]. The prevalence rate of behavioral problems has not been directly studied; however, in pediatric patients with comorbid epilepsy and ADHD, 31% of the sample also had comorbid oppositional defiant disorder (ODD) [24]. Rates for depressive disorders range from 5 to 33% in children and adolescents with epilepsy [13, 43]. Rates of anxiety disorders range between 16 and 48% [43, 44].

Differential diagnosis between seizures and inattention

Similarities between absence seizures and ADHD-inattentive type symptoms confound proper diagnosis [41]. Parents of children with epilepsy or ADHD-I frequently endorse "staring behavior" [42]. However, two behaviors occur nearly exclusively in ADHD-I patients: off-task behavior and starting but not completing homework. These findings are particularly useful in clinical interviews where clinical and EEG findings are inconclusive.

Depression and anxiety symptoms

Depressive symptom presentation is likely to be reflected in increased somatic complaints [41], irritability, and social withdrawal [26]. Of utmost importance, significantly more patients with epilepsy (20%) endorsed suicidal ideation when compared to a healthy control group (9%) [13]. Oguz et al. [45] identified age-related distinctions in anxiety symptoms among children with epilepsy, utilizing the State Trait Anxiety Inventory (STAI). Younger patients (between the ages of 9 and 11) exhibited elevated trait anxiety, whereas older patients had both elevated state and trait anxiety; puberty onset could exacerbate the number and degree of anxious symptoms exhibited.

Social functioning

Children and adolescents with normal intelligence and epilepsy exhibit impairments in parent-rated activity in clubs and sociability with children outside school, compared to healthy children and adolescents [13, 46]. Patients with lower cognitive abilities exhibit a greater number of social deficits than those with higher cognitive abilities [19, 47]. Gender and ethnic differences are evident, such that girls with epilepsy participate in social activities less frequently than boys [46], and children with epilepsy who are of ethnic minority status exhibit lower social competence and participation in activities [47], when assessed by parent report [46].

Treatment

Antiepileptic drugs (AEDs)

Seizures can be controlled in approximately 70 to 80% of children with epilepsy, through the administration of AEDs [2]. Most children who have been seizure-free for at least 2 years can be withdrawn from AEDs successfully [2, 4]. The use of one AED (i.e. monotherapy) is recommended, as polytherapy is associated with a greater number of side effects [8]. Dosage is individual-specific; some children require subtherapeutic serum levels of AEDs, whereas other children's seizures remain intractable even at presumably toxic levels.

AED side effects

A large body of literature has developed regarding the side-effect profiles of AEDs [48]. Older-line medications have been shown to impact aspects of cognitive development. Many newer (i.e. second and third generation) AEDs are believed to have a lessened impact on cognition, but findings are limited by sparse long-term data. Ultimately, studies evaluating the side effects of AEDs have often proved both inconclusive and contradictory [48]. As such, Bourgeois [48] has suggested continual monitoring for the development of cognitive impairment and the corresponding need for subsequent adjustments with anti-epilepsy medications.

Studies evaluating the side effects of monotherapy have indicated little to no neuropsychological impairments [48]. However, studies evaluating side effects of AEDs often utilize parent report, rather than performance on neurocognitive measures [48]. Parent-rated AED side effects were more commonly impacted by seizure frequency and severity, and not AED load [49]. Commonly reported cognitive side effects of AED polytherapy include impairments in overall cognitive abilities [18, 22, 37], receptive and expressive language [15], nonverbal processing [32], parent-rated attention [49], processing speed [15, 49], and learning and memory [15]. Academically, administration of polytherapy is associated with decreased parent-rated school performance [49] and placement in specialized or adaptive educational programming [22, 28]. Psychiatrically, polytherapy is associated with increases in parent-rated behavior problems, hyperactivity, and temper tantrums [49], depression and anxiety [43, 44, 45], and a decrease in self-rated quality of life [40, 43, 50]. Physical side effects include loss of appetite, headache, and fatigue [2, 49]. These side effects are believed to be caused by one or more of four mechanisms, including an alteration in metabolizing cerebral monoamines (serotonin), an alteration in endocrine functioning, drug-induced folate deficiency, or neuronal damage [3].

Surgical management

Because 20 to 30% of pediatric patients with epilepsy are unresponsive to AEDs, surgical management has become more prevalent [2]. Early surgery is strongly recommended, in order to prevent the cognitive and psychosocial ramifications of ongoing seizures and need for polydrug therapy. Surgery in childhood is associated with increased seizure control and improved developmental outcome [51].

Wada testing

Intracarotid sodium amobarbital testing (Wada) was originally developed to confirm hemispheric lateralization of speech for epilepsy surgery candidates [52]. The Wada test is utilized to predict postoperative speech function, verbal learning, and memory. The process involves paralyzing the epileptogenic hemisphere, by injecting amobarbital (or a similar compound) into the carotid artery. Next, neuropsychological testing is conducted in order to evaluate the contralateral hemisphere's ability to sustain linguistic and memory functions [52]. This procedure is controversial in children, as accurate language cortex identification is difficult in children younger than 10 [53]. However, Lee et al. [54] found that hemisphere of seizure onset prediction using Wada memory testing was significantly more accurate for children with temporal and extra-temporal seizures; however, onset laterality in children with left temporal lobe seizures was less reliable.

Cortical language mapping

Prior to dominant hemisphere epilepsy surgery, electrical stimulation mapping of language allows for identification of essential language cortex [55]. By doing so, sufficient epileptogenic tissue can be removed while preserving language functions. In children, a mental age of 5 years is the general rule for participation in intra-operative mapping. Tasks include object-naming, counting, reading, and following simple commands. Electrical stimulation mapping has been documented as safe in young children. Its utility is controversial, as some studies have reported no difference in the amount of cortex devoted to language in adults and children, whereas others noted increases with advancing age.

Surgical interventions

Three primary types of surgery are utilized to elicit seizure freedom. Focal resection involves the removal of a localized seizure focus. This type of surgical management is used with structural lesions and complex partial seizures occurring in the temporal lobe. Approximately 80% of patients become seizure-free, and outcome studies have shown little evidence of cognitive decline post-surgery [56]. A corpus callosotomy involves partial or complete division of the corpus callosum. This type of surgical management is typically used with intractable generalized seizures, thereby limiting the bilateral spread of seizures. Seizure freedom has occurred in 25 to 75% of individuals following this type of procedure [56]. A functional hemispherectomy is utilized with medically intractable partial seizures in children who are usually already hemiplegic. The procedure involves partial resection of the involved hemisphere. Complex partial seizures are typically controlled in 80 to 90% of cases using functional hemispherectomy [2].

Postoperative results

In a study evaluating cognitive changes pre- and post-surgery in preschool children, 66% were seizure-free, 26% had substantial seizure reduction, and 8% were unchanged [52]. At 6 to 12 months post-resection, 41 children showed stability of development, three children showed cognitive gains of equal to or greater than 15 points, three had developmental decline (transient in two children), and three moved from not assessable to assessable. These numbers increased at second follow-up; 11 children showed cognitive gains of 15 points or more. However, these gains were only made in children who were seizure-free and stable, over time.

Pediatric and adult patients with temporal lobe epilepsy who underwent surgery at least 6 months prior to testing performed significantly worse than preoperative and control children and adults on the recognition trial of a verbal learning task [36]. On the other hand, there were no differences according to surgical status on the delayed recall trial, word identification, and verbal fluency.

In total, current studies indicate that the post-surgical prognosis in children is good, indicating that cognitive abilities remain intact. Improvement in cognitive functioning following surgery remains variable, given multiple factors affecting development and support. These findings are especially true for patients who achieve and maintain seizure freedom. Specific cognitive functions (e.g. recognition) may be decreased following surgery in children and adults; however, overall verbal abilities appear to remain intact.

Long-term outcomes

The impact of childhood-onset epilepsy on later quality of life was evaluated in 91 participants with active epilepsy from 1961 to 1964 at a hospital in Finland [50]. At follow-up in 1997, 61 of the patients were in remission off medication, 13 were in remission on medication, and 17 were not in remission. In Japan, the long-term medical, educational, and social outcomes of childhood-onset epilepsy were evaluated in 155 participants with active epilepsy between 1961 and 1992 [57]. At follow-up in 1998, 93 patients had achieved remission off medication and 12 were in remission on medication. Patients with normal intelligence ($n = 106$) had significantly higher remission rates than patients with mental retardation ($n = 49$).

The results indicated that long-term prognosis is favorable in terms of seizure remission, emotional well-being, and physical health [50, 57]. Outcome was unfavorable in terms of mortality, education, employment, marriage, having one's own children, and licensed driving. The worst prognoses were in those patients with mental retardation and active epilepsy [57].

Summary

Overall, it appears that cognitive abilities are relatively preserved for pediatric patients with epilepsy, such that they exhibit low average to average range capability. Pediatric patients with epilepsy are at an increased risk for academic underachievement, as assessed by psychometric measures, school placement, and teacher- and parent-reported academic skills. Expressive language appears to be more frequently impaired than receptive language. In terms of visuo-spatial processing, patients with frontal lobe epilepsy are more commonly, and significantly, impaired than patients with other localizations. Processing-speed task performance is more likely to be impaired than general cognitive abilities, specifically in patients with increased seizure frequency. Impairment in these domains is related to increased seizure frequency and complex neuropathology.

Surprisingly, memory has been documented as relatively intact in pediatric patients with epilepsy, although this can vary according to hemispheric lateralization and the type of memory task (e.g. verbal versus visual) being utilized and examined. Attentional and executive dysregulation have been consistently reported within the literature. Patients with epilepsy exhibit decreased cognitive flexibility and perseveration. This is particularly true on fluency tasks. Planning is most impaired in patients with frontal lobe epilepsy.

With regard to psychological functioning, children with epilepsy often exhibit ADHD symptoms and behavioral problems. Differential diagnosis between absence seizures and inattention is important, as children with these diagnoses can present similarly. Additionally, anxiety and depression have been documented at higher rates than in the general population.

Treatment through the administration of AEDs has proven successful, although monotherapy is recommended as polytherapy is associated with impairment in several neurocognitive domains. Surgical management is being utilized at increasing rates, as it is associated with increased neurocognitive functioning and seizure remission. Surgical procedures must be preceded by cortical language-mapping or Wada testing to avoid removal of necessary language cortex. Long-term outcome studies have demonstrated that patients with epilepsy have relatively similar lives to people in the normal population, specifically those who obtain seizure freedom.

Future directions

At specific issue is the need to better understand the cognitive and behavioral effects of newer AEDs, as they are developed and then introduced. Because the goal is to more effectively treat seizures and their potential impact on development, it is important that potential neurocognitive side-effect profiles are identified and, ideally, addressed prior to drug implementation. This is an important role to be played by neuropsychology, and in particular developmental neuropsychology, given the need to address differing levels of impact and effect of these medications across the lifespan. With regard to pediatric patients with epilepsy, the ability to utilize monotherapeutic approaches with minimal cognitive and behavioral impact is likely to have a significant impact on a child's developmental outcome.

Similarly, ongoing investigation of surgical approaches and their targeted success at both diminishing to stopping seizures, and on promoting effective developmental growth, is strongly needed. Given the continued prevalence of seizures, an emphasis on understanding the impact of interventions, and on developing accompanying psychologically based approaches that enhance cognitive and behavioral development and functioning, remains an important domain for neuropsychology.

Key points to remember

1. Patients with more severe neuropathology perform worse across cognitive domains.

2. Patients with epilepsy are at risk for academic underachievement, particularly patients with poorly controlled epilepsy, lower cognitive abilities, and psychosocial stressors.

3. Processing speed, attention, and executive functioning are particularly vulnerable to disruption.

4. A good clinical interview is mandatory in distinguishing between seizures, particularly absence seizures, and ADHD-I.

5. Long-term outcomes are good, specifically in patients with seizure control.

References

1. Kolb B, Whishaw IQ. Neurological disorders. In Atkinson RC, Lindzey G, Thompson R, eds. *Fundamentals of Human Neuropsychology*. New York: Worth Publishers; 2003: 697–722.

2. Williams J, Sharp G. Epilepsy. In Yeates K, Ris M, Taylor H, eds. *Pediatric Neuropsychology: Research, Theory, and Practice*. New York: The Guilford Press; 2000: 47–73.

3. Julien RM. *A Primer of Drug Action: A Comprehensive Guide to the Actions, Uses and Side Effects of Psychoactive Drugs*. New York: Worth Publishers; 2004.

4. MacAllister WS, Schaffer SG. Neuropsychological deficits in childhood epilepsy syndromes. *Neuropsychol Rev* 2007;**17**:427–44.

5. Nordli DR. In Pellock JM, Bourgeous BF, Dodson WE, Nordli WE, Sankar R, eds. *Pediatric Epilepsy: Diagnosis and Therapy*, 3rd edn. New York; Demos Medical Publishing; 2008: 137–46.

6. Hauser WA, Banerjee PN. Epidemiology of epilepsy in children. In Pellock JM, Bourgeous BF, Dodson WE, Nordli WE, Sankar R, eds. *Pediatric Epilepsy: Diagnosis and Therapy*, 3rd edn. New York: Demos Medical Publishing; 2008: 147–64.

7. Houser CR, Vinters HV. Neuropathological substrates of epilepsy. In Pellock JM, Bourgeous BF, Dodson WE, Nordli WE, Sankar R, eds. *Pediatric Epilepsy: Diagnosis and Therapy*, 3rd edn. New York: Demos Medical Publishing; 2008: 75–100.

8. Dreisbach M, Ballard M, Russo DC, et al. Educational intervention for children with epilepsy: a challenge for collaborative service delivery. *J Spec Educ* 2001;**16**:111–21.

9. Aldenkamp AP, Baker GA, Meador KJ. The neuropsychology of epilepsy: what are the factors involved? *Epilepsy Behav* 2004;**5**:S1–2.

10. Boelen S, Niuwenhuis S, Steenbeek L, et al. Effect of epilepsy on psychomotor function in children with uncomplicated epilepsy. *Dev Med Child Neurol* 2005;**47**:546–50.

11. Caplan R, Guthrie D, Komo S, et al. Social communication in children with epilepsy. *J Child Psychol Psychiatry* 2002;**43**:245–53.

12. Tromp SC, Weber JW, Aldenkamp AP, et al. Relative influence of epileptic seizures and of epilepsy syndrome on cognitive function. *J Child Neurol* 2003;**18**:407–12.

13. Caplan R, Siddarth P, Gurbani S, et al. Depression and anxiety disorders in pediatric epilepsy. *Epilepsia* 2005;**46**:720–30.

14. Kramer U, Kipervasser S, Neufield MY, et al. Is there any correlation between severity of epilepsy and cognitive abilities in patients with temporal lobe epilepsy? *Eur J Neurol* 2006;**13**:130–4.

15. Northcott E, Connolly AM, Berroya A, et al. The neuropsychological and language profile of children with benign rolandic epilepsy. *Epilepsia* 2005;**46**:924–30.

16. Riva D, Avanzini G, Franceschetti S, et al. Unilateral frontal lobe epilepsy affects executive functions in children. *Neurol Sci* 2005;**26**:263–70.

17. Riva D, Saletti V, Nichelli F, et al. Neuropsychologic effects of frontal lobe epilepsy in children. *J Child Neurol* 2002;**17**:661–7.

18. Caplan R, Sagun J, Siddarth P, et al. Social competence in pediatric epilepsy: insights into underlying mechanisms. *Epilepsy Behav* 2005;**6**:218–28.

19. Buelow JM, Austin JK, Perkins SM, et al. Behavior and mental problems in children with epilepsy and low IQ. *Dev Med Child Neurol* 2003;**45**:683–92.

20. Aldenkamp AP, Overweg-Plandsoen W, Diepman LA. Factors involved in learning problems and educational delay in children with epilepsy. *Child Neuropsychol* 1999;**5**:130–6.

21. Bigel MG, Smith ML. Single and dual pathologies of the temporal lobe: effects on cognitive function in children with epilepsy. *Epilepsy Behav* 2001;**2**:37–45.

22. Bulteau C, Jambaque I, Viguier D, et al. Epileptic syndromes, cognitive assessment, and school placement: a study of 251 children. *Dev Med Child Neurol* 2000;**42**:319–27.

23. Adewuya AO, Oseni SB, Okeniyi JA. School performance of Nigerian adolescents with epilepsy. *Epilepsia* 2006;**47**:415–20.

24. Gonzalez-Heydrich J, Dodds A, Whitney J, et al. Psychiatric disorders and behavioral characteristics of pediatric patients with both epilepsy and attention-deficit hyperactivity disorder. *Epilepsy Behav* 2007;**10**:384–8.

25. Williams J, Phillips T, Griebel ML, et al. Factors associated with academic achievement in children with controlled epilepsy. *Epilepsy Behav* 2001;**2**:217–23.

26. Williams J, Sharp G. Academic achievement and behavioral ratings in children with absence and complex partial epilepsy. *Educa Treat Child* 1996;**19**:143–53.

27. Høie B, Mykletun A, Waaler PE, et al. Executive functions and seizure-related factors in children with epilepsy in western Norway. *Dev Med Child Neurol* 2006;**48**:519–25.

28. Sabbagh SE, Soria C, Escolano S, et al. Impact of epilepsy characteristics and behavioral problems on school placement in children. *Epilepsy Behav* 2006;**9**:573–8.

29. Kolk A, Beilmann A, Tomberg T, et al. Neurocognitive development of children with congenital unilateral brain lesion and epilepsy. *Brain Dev* 2001;**23**:88–96.

30. Henkin Y, Sadeh M, Kivity S, et al. Cognitive function in idiopathic generalized epilepsy of childhood. *Child Neurol* 2005;**47**:126–32.

31. Hernandez M, Sauerwein HC, Jambaqué I, et al. Attention, memory, and behavioral adjustment in children with frontal lobe epilepsy. *Epilepsy Behav* 2003;**4**:522–36.

32. Høie B, Mykletun A, Sommerfelt K, et al. Seizure-related factors and non-verbal intelligence in children with

epilepsy: a population-based study from western Norway. *Seizure* 2005;**14**:223–31.

33. Hernandez M, Sauerwein HC, Jambaqué I, et al. Deficits in executive functions and motor coordination in children with frontal lobe epilepsy. *Neuropsychologia* 2002;**40**:384–400.

34. Kadis DS, Stollstorff M, Elliot I, et al. Cognitive and psychological predictors of everyday memory in children with intractable epilepsy. *Epilepsy Behav* 2004;**5**:37–43.

35. Levav M, Mirsky AF, Herault J, et al. Familial association of neuropsychological traits in patients with generalized and partial seizure disorders. *J Clin Exp Neuropsychol* 2002;**24**:311–26.

36. Billingsley RL, McAndrews MP, Smith ML. Intact perceptual and conceptual priming in temporal lobe epilepsy: neuroanatomical and methodological implications. *Neuropsychology* 2002;**16**:92–101.

37. Nolan MA, Redoblado MA, Lah S, et al. Memory function in childhood epilepsy syndromes. *J Paediatr Child Health* 2004;**40**:20–7.

38. Williams J, Phillips T, Griebel M, et al. Patterns of memory performance in children with controlled epilepsy on the CVLT-C. *Child Neuropsychol* 2001;**7**:15–20.

39. Schouten A, Oostrom KJ, Pestman WR, et al. Learning and memory of school children with epilepsy: A prospective controlled longitudinal study. *Dev Med Child Neurol* 2002;**44**:803–11.

40. Sherman EM, Slick DJ, Eyrl KL. Executive dysfunction is a significant predictor of poor quality of life in children with epilepsy. *Epilepsia* 2006;**47**:1936–42.

41. Høie B, Sommerfelt K, Waaler PE, et al. Psychosocial problems and seizure-related factors in children with epilepsy. *Dev Med Child Neurol* 2006;**48**:213–19.

42. Williams J, Sharp GB, DelosReyes E, et al. Symptom differences in children with absence seizures versus inattention. *Epilepsy Behav* 2002;**3**:245–8.

43. Adewuya AO, Ola BA. Prevalence of and risk factors for anxiety and depressive disorders in Nigerian adolescents with epilepsy. *Epilepsy Behav* 2005;**6**:342–7.

44. Williams J, Steel C, Sharp GB, et al. Anxiety in children with epilepsy. *Epilepsy Behav* 2003;**4**:729–32.

45. Oguz A, Kurul S, Dirik E. Relationship of epilepsy-related factors to anxiety and depression scores in epileptic children. *J Child Neurol* 2002;**17**:37–40.

46. Jakovljević V, Martinović Ž. Social competence of children and adolescents with epilepsy. *Seizure* 2006;**15**:528–32.

47. Caplan R, Guthrie D, Komo S, et al. Social communication in children with epilepsy. *J Child Psychol Psychiatry* 2002;**43**:245–53.

48. Bourgeois BF. Differential cognitive effects of antiepileptic drugs. *J Child Neurol* 2002;**17**:2S28–33.

49. Carpay JA, Vermeulen J, Stroink H, et al. Parent-reported subjective complaints in children using antiepileptic drugs: What do they mean? *Epilepsy Behav* 2002;**3**:322–9.

50. Sillanpää M, Haataja L, Shinnar S. Perceived impact of childhood-onset epilepsy on quality of life as an adult. *Epilepsia* 2004;**45**:971–7.

51. Freitag H, Tuxhorn I. Cognitive function in preschool children after epilepsy surgery: rationale for early intervention. *Epilepsia* 2005;**46**:561–7.

52. Tripathi M, Jain S. In Schachter SC, Holmes GL, Trenité DG, eds. *Behavioral Aspects of Epilepsy: Princples & Practice*. New York: Demos Medical Publishing; 2008: 297–306.

53. Schevon CA, Carlson C, Zaroff CM, et al. Pediatric language mapping: sensitivity of neurostimulation and Wada testing in epilepsy surgery. *Epilepsia* 2007;**48**:539–45.

54. Lee GP, Park YD, Hempel A, et al. Prediction of seizure-onset laterality by using Wada memory asymmetries in pediatric epilepsy surgery candidates. *Epilepsia* 2002;**43**:1049–55.

55. Hamberger MJ. Cortical language mapping in epilepsy: a critical review. *Neuropsychol Rev* 2007;**17**:477–89.

56. Patil S, Cross H, Harkness W. Outcome of epilepsy surgery in childhood. In Pellock JM, Bourgeous BF, Dodson WE, Nordli WE, Sankar R, eds. *Pediatric Epilepsy: Diagnosis and Therapy*, 3rd edn. New York: Demos Medical Publishing; 2008: 801–810.

57. Wakamoto H, Nagao H, Hayashi M, et al. Long-term medical, educational, and social prognoses of childhood-onset epilepsy: a population-based study in a rural district of Japan. *Brain Dev* 2000;**22**:246–55.

Chapter 12b

A lifespan perspective of cognition in epilepsy

Michael Seidenberg and Bruce Hermann

Introduction

Epilepsy is a chronic neurological disorder, affecting approximately 1% of the population, or over 2 million Americans, with an incidence of 30% of cases younger than age 18 years at diagnosis (see Hauser and Hesdorffer [1]; also see Felix and Hunter, Chapter 12a of this volume). Epilepsy is an umbrella term for various syndromes with distinct profiles of clinical semiology, etiology, age of onset, EEG, and other neurophysiological underpinnings. For many individuals, antiepileptic drug (AED) treatment provides a successful route to seizure control. However, a significant number of people continue onto an intractable and chronic course which can last for many years, and in some for the better part of their life.

Viewed from a lifespan perspective, childhood-onset chronic epilepsy potentially impacts the early years of brain and cognitive development and also leaves the underlying neurobiological substrate vulnerable to the effects of subsequent insults (i.e. seizures) including the additional impact associated with aging. To date, there have been few attempts to consider the lifespan natural course of epilepsy and its implications for neurobehavioral status. This is the primary objective of this chapter.

Cognitive reserve

The concepts of brain reserve capacity and cognitive reserve were initially proposed as a potential mediator of the cognitive course in older individuals. According to this proposal, individuals have different thresholds for exhibiting neuropsychological and behavioral symptoms in the face of seemingly similar cerebral insults [2]. Persons with greater cognitive reserve are hypothesized to be able to sustain more neurobiological insults before manifesting cognitive symptoms than someone with less cognitive reserve. Both genetic and environmental factors are believed to contribute to cognitive reserve. Evidence in favor of the cognitive reserve hypothesis has been reported in a number of clinical conditions, including Alzheimer's disease, multiple sclerosis, and HIV encephalopathy.

Dennis et al. proposed that the concept of cerebral reserve may have important implications for understanding the cognitive trajectory in people who have suffered an early brain insult [3]. Specifically, they hypothesized that an early brain insult confers an increased risk for disrupted cognitive development and accelerated aging effects due to reduced cerebral reserve. Since a substantial number of people with epilepsy have their onset in childhood, the concept of cerebral reserve may be a useful construct in conceptualizing the lifespan course of cognitive and brain development in epilepsy.

Early onset and cognitive status

The effect on cognition of an early childhood brain insult in people with epilepsy has been studied in two ways. One approach has examined children with epilepsy directly while the other approach has examined adults with epilepsy characterized by their developmental stage at onset of epilepsy (i.e. early versus late onset). Both lines of research confirm that age of epilepsy onset is a robust correlate of cognitive status; early age of epilepsy onset is associated with more pronounced cognitive impairment than later onset. This relationship has been observed across various seizure types and impacts several basic cognitive domains including memory, intelligence, and language [4]. This is also discussed in detail in the preceding chapter by Felix and Hunter in this volume.

Many of these studies have been conducted with people with active epilepsy; however, a recent study of 158 adult patients on AED and without epileptic seizures for at least 2 years also reported that age of seizure onset less than 18 years was a powerful predictor of neuropsychological status [5]. There is also a marked increased risk for mental retardation in children with an age of seizure onset in the first 2 years of life [6]. In a study of 79 children with temporal lobe epilepsy with onset ranging from the first year of life till 18 years of age, Cormack et al. [7] found that age of onset was the best predictor of presurgical neuropsychological status and that children with onset in the first year of life were significantly more likely to show intellectual impairment. Furthermore, those with an age of onset after 5 years of age showed a reduced risk of intellectual dysfunction.

Of interest, cognitive and behavioral impairments have also been demonstrated close to the time of recurrent seizure onset. Children with newly diagnosed epilepsy examined prior to the administration of antiseizure medications showed significantly poorer performance in the areas of attention, reaction time, academic achievement, and visual memory [8]. Comparable results were reported in children with new-onset localization-related and idiopathic generalized epilepsy when compared to controls [9]. In both studies, a pattern of mild generalized cognitive impairment was evident across measures of intelligence, language, attention, executive function, and psychomotor speed.

Why might these neuropsychological deficits appear so early in the course of the disorder? In contrast to adults with epilepsy, where a developed and reasonably stable cognitive substrate is the target of potentially adverse epilepsy factors, children present with a dynamic pattern of cognitive and brain development. Cortez et al. [10] pointed out that the onset of recurrent spontaneous seizures is the end result of the complex process of epileptogenesis involving a cascade of transcriptional changes in brain triggered by an interaction of genetic and environmental factors. The neurobiological results of these transcriptional changes include plasticity, apoptosis and further neurogenesis, all of which could conceivably affect

cognitive and brain development. Subsequently, ictal and interictal activities may further impact brain development during a period of major dendritic and synaptic growth. Thus, the epileptic process may interfere with normal cerebral development.

Early onset and brain status

The cognitive findings in adults with childhood-onset epilepsy are consistent with the notion that an early brain insult which occurs during the course of brain maturation can negatively influence cerebral development. Indeed, recent studies have confirmed the presence of structural and functional brain abnormalities in children with epilepsy across a variety of syndromes [11]. Hermann et al. [12] compared 37 temporal lobe epilepsy adults with early-onset temporal lobe epilepsy to 16 TLE subjects with a late onset of epilepsy using high-resolution quantitative volumetrics. Most subjects in both groups had been diagnosed with epilepsy for over 20 years. The childhood-onset group showed significant volume abnormalities compared to normals in both temporal and extratemporal regions, especially affecting cerebral white matter and increased CSF. Furthermore, the white matter reduction was seen on a bilateral basis. In contrast, subjects with late onset of recurrent temporal lobe seizures did not exhibit significant volumetric differences compared to controls. This is quite extraordinary considering that this group had been diagnosed with epilepsy for nearly 20 years. See Figure 12b.1.

The corpus callosum (CC) is the largest neural pathway connecting the two cerebral hemispheres and plays an important role in the interhemispheric transfer of information. Brain connectivity reduction in the corpus callosum as measured by quantitative

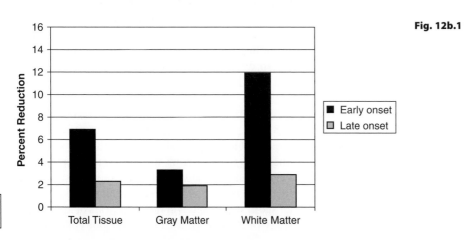

Fig. 12b.1

MR volumes is also greater in childhood-onset epilepsy as compared to adult-onset epilepsy. Hermann and colleagues matched an early- and late-onset TLE epilepsy group on duration of epilepsy and found that the early-onset TLE group showed significantly smaller corpus callosum volume (compared to healthy controls) than a later-onset age TLE group [13]. Furthermore, corpus callosum volume was significantly correlated with performance on measures of information-processing speed and efficiency. More recently, Weber et al. also observed that epilepsy was associated with a decreased thickness in the posterior callosal regions, particularly among those with an early age of seizure onset [14]. Thus, white matter vulnerability appears to be a critical feature of childhood-onset epilepsy.

There is additional evidence from animal research attesting to the increased vulnerability of white matter development with early onset seizures. Dwyer and Wasterlain [15] examined the effects of electroconvulsive (EC)-induced seizures (two per day for 10 days) in rats at different developmental stages (2–11 days, 9–18 days, 19–28 days). Animals were later sacrificed, and results showed that seizures in early development selectively impaired myelin accumulation out of proportion to their overall effect on brain growth. These effects varied regionally in that they were reversible in the cerebellum but not in the forebrain. Further, examination of cerebroside (CER) and proteolipid protein (PLP), relatively specific myelin lipids, showed they were reduced 13% and 11% in rats who seized between days 2 through 11 and 9 through 18, but were not reduced in mature rats subjected to a comparable number of seizures. Examination of the ratio of lipid to DNA showed that CER and PLP were reduced to a greater degree than would be explained on the basis of cell loss alone, suggesting that early seizures affected myelin accumulation. In addition, Wasterlain et al. more broadly demonstrated that in addition to the curtailment of myelin and selectively and permanently affected myelin-specific lipids, repeated EC-induced seizures in the immature rat reduced brain growth and resulted in a reduction of synaptic markers in the absence of markers of neuronal cell body loss [16]. These effects on brain growth and development were dependent on the developmental stage of the animal when seizures were induced, again more severe when seizures occurred at younger ages, and these brain changes were evident in the absence of histological lesions.

The link between age of epilepsy onset and white matter brain tissue is particularly intriguing given that the normal developmental trajectory of white matter development extends over a very substantial period. Courchesne and colleagues found that white matter volume increased 74% from early childhood (19–33 months) to adolescence (12–15 years) with an ongoing but slower rate of growth until the fourth decade [17]. Of interest, Nagy and colleagues showed that maturation of white matter regions was correlated with the development of cognitive functions during childhood [18]. In childhood-onset epilepsy, both overall cerebral white matter volume and corpus callosum volume have been shown to significantly correlate with cognition [13].

MR volumetric studies in children with epilepsy have primarily involved children with *chronic* epilepsy and the findings reveal abnormalities in cerebrum, cerebellum and hippocampus [19]. A recent voxel-based morphometric investigation of children with chronic temporal lobe epilepsy reported a distributed pattern of abnormality in temporal and extratemporal lobe gray matter [20], similar to that reported in the adults with temporal lobe epilepsy [21]. Byars et al recently investigated 249 children within 3 months of the first recognized seizure and reported a relationship between cognition and clinically significant magnetic resonance abnormalities. In addition, among recently diagnosed children with epilepsy, there is a high rate (about 30%) of diagnosable attention deficit hyperactivity disorder (ADHD) [22]. These children with comorbid ADHD symptoms also show quantitative MRI abnormalities in a neural network consisting of the frontal lobe, thalamus, and brain stem [23].

Cognitive progression in epilepsy

When considering the lifespan implications of epilepsy on cognition, an important issue concerns the changes that occur over time. This issue is commonly referred to as "progression", and has been the focus of investigation at the molecular, physiological, and cellular level [24]. From a neuropsychological perspective, the issue of progression entails the possibility that continued cognitive decline is evident among people with epilepsy over the course of the disorder.

To date, research relevant to the issue of progression has relied primarily on cross-sectional designs, which have obvious limitations for inferring change or progression. The most direct method is through longitudinal designs that specifically retest the same subject cohort over a specified interval of time. Despite the importance of the progression issue, there have been a decidedly limited number of studies using a longitudinal design in the investigation of cognitive change in epilepsy.

Dodrill surveyed the published literature of cognitive longitudinal studies in both children and adults with epilepsy [25]. He listed 13 studies of adults dating back to 1942 and nine studies with children dating back to 1924. Based on this review, Dodrill concluded that there was evidence for "losses in mental abilities over time" that was more evident among children than adults. Nevertheless, he cautioned that additional investigation was necessary and stressed the need for including a control group to account for potential developmental and aging changes.

Earlier longitudinal studies which did not include a control group concluded that the epilepsy group did not show evidence of a progressive decline in cognition [26] because their scores remained stable or improved over the test–retest interval (within-group comparison). When control groups are used, one finds consistent evidence for a significant difference in cognitive course between epilepsy groups and controls [27]. However, the degree of cognitive change observed for the epilepsy group is frequently characterized by a lack of or less improvement compared to the controls, rather than an absolute level of decline. Improvement over the test–retest interval is often referred to as a practice effect. Baseline testing can be viewed as an initial exposure and potential learning experience (episodic memory) for both groups and follow-up performance reflects the degree of learning as a function of the prior exposure. Viewed in this context, the "lack of a practice effect" similar to the control group indicates that the epilepsy group did not benefit to the same degree from the previous exposure to the testing protocol. Thus, test–retest memory performance can be stable or even show an improvement, but it still may not be "normal".

It is important to note that actual levels of decline, not simply a lack of practice effect, have also been noted, particularly in memory performance [28]. It appears that specific subgroups exist with different cognitive course within the "overall" epilepsy group that may show distinct patterns of cognitive vulnerability. Hermann et al. identified three subgroups of TLE patients based on a cluster analysis of baseline cognitive functioning; mildly impaired, memory impaired, and memory plus executive impaired [29]. Following a 4-year interval, the latter group showed the most adverse cognitive course. This group was characterized by a significantly longer duration of epilepsy, lower baseline level of cognition, and increased baseline volumetric abnormalities compared to the other two groups. Cognitive decline was not limited to a single cognitive domain, but encompassed a wide range of abilities. This may be secondary to the more widespread structural, EEG, and metabolic disturbances that are often observed in partial complex epilepsy [30]. See Figure 12b.2.

The relationship between "cognitive reserve" and risk for cognitive decline in epilepsy has been suggested. Several investigations have shown that educational level, a proxy for cognitive reserve, moderated the effect of duration of epilepsy on cognition. For example, when epilepsy patients were divided into two groups based on education level (high or low), differential relationships with duration have been

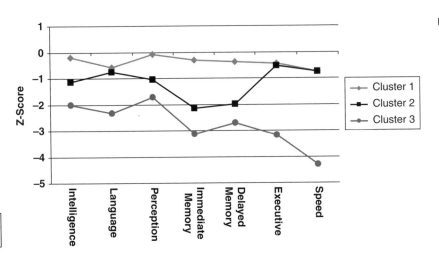

Fig. 12b.2

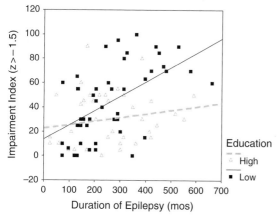

Fig. 12b.3

observed. There was a significant association of cognition and duration only in the low-education group, but not the high-education group [31]. It appears that people with more years of education (i.e. cognitive reserve) have greater capacity to withstand the neurobiological insults associated with epilepsy (e.g. duration) and its treatment secondary to the favorable biological and environmental effects of increasing education (Fig 12b.3).

In addition, more direct measures of cognitive reserve, based on MRI volumes, also provide support for the reserve model. Baseline measures of whole brain white matter volume, increased CSF, and generalized cerebral atrophy have been significantly associated with an adverse cognitive outcome. Baseline hippocampal volume is also associated with change in memory performance over a 4-year interval. People with less baseline hippocampus volume showed the greatest test–retest decline in memory performance [28].

Aging and cognitive status

People with chronic epilepsy are exposed to several factors which place them at increased risk for abnormal cognitive and brain aging, including decades of seizures and the potential iatrogenic effects of treatment with medications. For those whose seizures begin in childhood, the consequences of the aging process will be superimposed on an already compromised substrate of cognition and brain health. Compared to healthy controls, community-dwelling elders with chronic partial epilepsy exhibited significantly poorer performance across all scales of the Mattis Dementia Rating Scale [32]. A related investigation compared

matched groups of community-dwelling elders with chronic partial epilepsy, healthy control elders and healthy elders with amnestic mild cognitive impairment, a known precursor to AD [33]. Compared to patients with amnestic MCI, community-dwelling elders with epilepsy exhibited a comparable degree of memory impairment and even greater impairment in executive function. Furthermore, cognitive impairment in early-onset TLE is more pronounced with increasing years of duration and exceeds the normal age-related change observed in healthy controls.

Aging with epilepsy is fraught with a set of detrimental medical complications which can impact cognitive course. Population-based investigations of medical comorbidities demonstrate a significantly higher rate of dementia and AD in persons with epilepsy compared to controls [34]. It is widely appreciated that seizures are part of the natural history of AD. Population-based studies demonstrate that unprovoked seizures occur with increased incidence in persons with AD compared to nondemented elderly controls. However, less appreciated is evidence suggesting that dementia may develop with greater frequency in elders with chronic and established epilepsy compared to controls. Breteler et al. [35], in the EURODEM project, re-analyzed eight case control studies and reported that the risk for AD was significantly elevated in persons with established epilepsy (duration $\geq$ 10 years). In a later study, Breteler et al. [36] demonstrated an age-accelerated risk of dementia in 4505 persons with epilepsy, aged 50–75, compared to age-matched persons with other medical disorders over an 8-year observation period.

In the general aging literature, prospective studies have confirmed the association of various risk factors with abnormal cognitive and brain aging and even the risk of dementia. Hermann et al. considered three classes of risk variables (vascular disease, inflammatory markers, and lifestyle factors) for dementia and describe the evidence which suggests that they are overrepresented in epilepsy [37].

Persons with chronic epilepsy may be at increased risk of abnormal cognitive and brain aging and dementia because of an increased prevalence of vascular risk factors that may result at least in part from treatment with antiepilepsy drugs (AEDs). Valproic acid (VPA) treatment has been associated with several metabolic disorders including hyperinsulinemia and insulin resistance and substantial weight gain/increased body mass index (BMI) [38]. In addition to alterations in insulin sensitivity and body mass, commonly prescribed enzyme-inducing medications (e.g. phenytoin [PHT], carbamazepine [CBZ]) disturb folate metabolism, leading to significantly increased levels of homocysteine [39]. Especially troubling are reports of elevated insulin resistance and hyperhomocysteinemia in children with epilepsy caused by AEDs since early exposure to vascular risk factors predicts cerebrovascular disease in adults in the general population [40]. Adults with chronic epilepsy have significantly increased carotid artery intima-media thickness (IMT) and early death from ischemic heart disease. Population-based surveys of medical comorbidities also document higher rates of hypertension, ischemic heart disease, heart failure, diabetes, and cerebrovascular disease in persons with epilepsy [41].

Mounting evidence points to the role of inflammation in the pathogenesis of cognitive decline and dementing disorders including AD. Overall, prospective studies suggest that inflammatory markers (hs-CRP, IL-6, fibrinogen) are important predictors of adverse cognitive outcomes, and recent reports link inflammatory biomarkers to age-accelerated cerebral atrophy as well [42]. Chronic epilepsy is associated with an increased risk of exposure to inflammatory risk factors associated with abnormal cognitive aging and dementia. Evidence that persons with epilepsy may be particularly vulnerable to inflammation comes from both human and animal studies. For example, experimentally induced seizures trigger a prominent inflammatory response in neural areas involved in the onset and propagation of seizures. Increased inflammatory markers have been detected in serum, CSF and brain in persons with epilepsy. Pertinent are findings of increased IL-6 following recent tonic-clonic seizures. IL-6 has also been reported to be elevated secondary to CBZ but not VPA treatment with elevated fibrinogen in chronic epilepsy [43].

Lifestyle factors are associated with the risk of cognitive decline and dementia in the general population. Fratiglioni et al. reviewed 28 community-based *prospective* studies examining relationships between extent of social networks, physical activity, and leisure-time mental stimulation with the risk of cognitive decline, dementia and AD [44]. The evidence is persuasive. With regard to the risk of prospective cognitive decline, 18 of 22 studies reported positive relationships. Chronic epilepsy is associated with an increased prevalence of lifestyle factors associated with abnormal cognitive aging and dementia. Compared to healthy controls, epilepsy patients are less likely to participate in regular physical exercise/activity and demonstrate poorer aerobic capacity and diminished muscle strength and endurance [45, 46]. These lifestyle differences probably contribute to reports of elevated BMI in both adults and children. Persons with epilepsy also have decreased contacts with available social networks, consistent with the known psychosocial consequences and felt stigma associated with epilepsy [47].

Summary and conclusion

We have presented a viewpoint of childhood and adult epilepsy from a lifespan perspective. It appears that the onset of childhood/adolescent epilepsy may be associated with disruption in the development of the early cognitive and neural substrate. Consistent with the notion of cognitive reserve, we hypothesize that this in turn places these individuals at risk for effective utilization of the typical educational and social opportunities which augment development. This in turn places them at increased risk for cognitive decline in the face of added lifetime insults, either epilepsy-related (e.g. status epilepticus) or non-epilepsy-related (e.g. vascular risk factors), including potentially increased vulnerability to the neurobiological effects of aging. Long-term prospective investigations of individuals with childhood-onset epilepsy have reported considerably poorer psychosocial outcomes in adulthood, outcomes that involve salient areas of life performance and quality of life including employment, marriage and family characteristics, psychiatric status, income and socioeconomic status [48]. An important clinical implication of these findings is that efforts are needed to identify and remediate these early neurobehavioral problems, especially in light of the known poor long-term psychosocial prognosis of persons with childhood epilepsy, as well as the potential impact of early-onset epilepsy on progressive adult development and aging.

Acknowledgements

This chapter was written with support of NIH RO1 44351 and MO1 RR 03186 (GCRC).

References

1. Hauser WA, Hesdorffer DC. *Epilepsy, Frequency, Causes, Consequences.* New York: Demos Publications; 1990.

2. Satz P. Brain reserve capacity on symptom onset after brain injury: a formulation and review of evidence for threshold theory. *Neuropsychology* 1993;7:273–95.

3. Dennis M, Spiegler BJ, Hetherington R. New survivors for the new millennium. Cognitive risk and reserve in adults with childhood brain insults. *Brain Cogn* 2000;42:102–5.

4. O'Leary DS, Seidenberg M, Berent S, et al. Effect of age of onset of tonic-clonic seizures on neuropsychological performance in children. *Epilepsia* 1983;22:197–204.

5. Hessen E, Lossius MI, Reinvag I, et al. Predictors of neuropsychological impairment in seizure-free epilepsy patients. *Epilepsia* 2006;47:1870–8.

6. Vasconcellos E, Wyllie E, Sullivan S, Stanford L, Bulacio J, Kotagal P, Bingaman W. Mental retardation in pediatric candidates for epilepsy surgery: the role of early seizure onset. *Epilepsia* 2001;42(2):268–74.

7. Cormack F, Cross JH, Harkness W, et al. The development of intellectual abilites in pediatric temporal lobe epilepsy. *Epilepsia* 2007;48:201–4.

8. Oostrom KJ, Smeets-Schouten A, Kruitwagen CL, et al. Not only a matter of epilepsy: early problems of cognition, and behavior in children with epilepsy "only" – a prospective controlled study starting at diagnosis. *Pediatrics* 2003;112:1338–44.

9. Hermann B, Jones J, Sheth R, et al. Children with new onset epilepsy: Neuropsychological status and brain structure. *Brain* 2006;129:2609–19.

10. Cortez MA, Perez Velazquez JL, et al. Animal models of epilepsy and progressive effects of seizures. *Adv Neurol* 2006;97:293–304.

11. Lawson JA, Vogrin S, Bleasel AF, et al. Predictors of hippocampal, cerebral, and cerebellar volume reduction in childhood epilepsy. *Epilepsia* 2000;41:1540–5.

12. Hermann BP, Seidenberg M, Bell B, et al. The neurodevelopmental impact of childhood onset temporal lobe epilepsy on brain structure and function. *Epilepsia* 2002;43:1062–71.

13. Hermann B, Hansen R, Seidenberg M, et al. Neurodevelopmental vulnerability of the corpus callosum to childhood onset localization-related epilepsy. *NeuroImage* 2003;18:284–92.

14. Weber B, Ludrs E, Faber J, et al. Distinct regional atrophy in the corpus callosum of patients with temporal lobe epilepsy. *Brain* 2007;130:3149–54.

15. Dwyer BE, Wasterlain CG. Electroconvulsive seizures in the immature rat adversely affects myelin accumulation. *Exp Neurol* 1982;78:616–28.

16. Wasterlain CG, Thompson KW, Kornblum H, et al, Long-term effects of recurrent seizures on the developing brain. In Nehlig A, Motte J, Moshe SL, et al, eds. *Childhood Epilepsies and Brain Development*. London: John Libbey; 1999.

17. Courchense E, Chisum HJ, Townsend J, et al. Normal brain development and aging: quantitative analysis of in-vivo MR imaging in healthy volunteers. *Radiology* 2000;216:672–82.

18. Nagy Z, Westerberg H, Klingberg T. Maturation of white matter is associated with the development of cognitive functions during childhood. *J Cogn Neurosci* 2004;16:1227–33.

19. Lawson JA, Volgrin S, Bleasel AF, et al. Cerebral and cerebellar reduction in children with intractable epilepsy. *Epilepsia* 2000;41:1456–62.

20. Cormack F, Gadian DG, Vargha-Khadem F, et al. Extra-hippocampal grey matter density abnormalities in paediatric mesial temporal lobe sclerosis. *Neuroimage* 2005;27:635–43.

21. Marsh L, Morrell M, Shear P, et al. Cortical and hippocampal volume deficits in temporal lobe epilepsy. *Epilepsia* 1997;38:576–87.

22. Byars AW, deGrauw TJ, Johnson CS, et al. The association of MRI findings and neuropsychological functioning after the first recognized seizure. *Epilepsia* 2007;48:1067–74.

23. Hermann B, Jones J, Dabbs K, et al. The frequency, complications, and aetiology of ADHD in new onset paediatric epilepsy. *Brain* 2007;130:3135–48.

24. Pitkanen A, Sutula T. Is epilepsy a progressive disorder? Prospects for new therapeutic approaches in temporal lobe epilepsy. *Lancet Neurol* 2002;1:103–8.

25. Dodrill C. Neuropsychological effects of seizures. *Epilepsy Behav* 2004;5:S21–4.

26. Selwa L, Berent S, Giordani B, et al. Serial cognitive testing in temporal lobe epilepsy: longitudinal changes in medical and surgical therapies. *Epilepsia* 1994;35:743–9.

27. Seidenberg M, Pulsipher D, Hermann B. Cognitive progression in epilepsy. *Neuropsychol Rev* 2007;17:444–54.

28. Hermann B, Seidenberg M, Dow C, et al. Cognitive prognosis in chronic temporal lobe epilepsy. *Ann Neurol* 2006;60:70–7.

29. Hermann B, Seidenberg M, Lee EJ, et al. Cognitive phenotypes in temporal lobe epilepsy. *J Int Neuropsychol* 2007;13:12–20.

30. Keller SS, MacKay CE, Barrick TR, et al. Voxel-based morphometric comparison of hippocampal and extrahippocampal abnormalities in patients with left and right hippocampal atrophy. *Neuroimage* 2002;16:23–31.

31. Oyegbile T, Hermann BP, Seidenberg M. The nature and course of neuropsychological morbidity in chronic temporal lobe epilepsy. *Neurology* 2004;**62**:1736–42.

32. Martin R, Griffith R, Faught E. Cognitive functioning in community dwelling older aduts with chronic partial epilepsy. *Epilepsia* 2005;**46**:298–303.

33. Griffith HR, Martin RC, Bambara JK, et al. Older adults with epilepsy demonstrate cognitive impairments compared with patients with amnestic mild cognitive disorder. *Epilepsy Behav* 2006;**8**:161–8.

34. Gaiatzis A, Caroll K, Majeed A, et al. The epidemiology of the comorbidity of epilepsy in the general population. *Epilepsia* 2004;**45**:1613–22.

35. Breteler MM, de Groot RR, van Romunde LK, et al. Risk of dementia in patients with Parkinson's disease, epilepsy, and severe head trauma: a register based follow up study. *Am J Epidemiol* 1995;**142**:1300–5.

36. Breteler MM, van Dujin CM, Chandra V, et al. Medical history and the risk of Alzheimer's disease: a collaborative re-analysis of case control studies. EURODEM Risk Factors Research Group. *Int J Epidemiol* 1991;**20**:S36–42.

37. Hermann B, Seidenberg M, Jones J. Neurobehavioral comorbidites of epilepsy: can a natural history be developed? *Lancet Neurol* 2008;**7**:151–60.

38. Luef GJ, Waldmann M, Sturm W, Naser A, et al. Valproate therapy and nonalcoholic fatty liver disease. *Ann Neurol* 2004;**55**:729–32.

39. Sheth RD. Metabolic concerns associated with antiepileptic medications. *Neurology* 2004;**63**:S24–9.

40. Attilakos A, Papakonstantinou E, Schulpis K, et al. Early effect of sodium valproate and carbamazepine monotherapy on homocysteine metabolism in children with epilepsy. *Epilepsy Res* 2006;**71**:229–32.

41. Tellez-Zenteno JF, Matijevic S, Wiebe S. Somatic comorbidity of epilepsy in the general population in Canada. *Epilepsia* 2005;**46**:1955–62.

42. Hamed SA, Nabeshima T. The high atherosclerotic risk among epileptics: the atheroprotective role of multivitamins. *J Pharmacol Sci* 2005;**98**:340–53.

43. Verotti A, Pascarella R, Trotta D, et al. Hyperhomocysteinemia in children treated with sodium valproate and carbamazepine. *Epilepsy Res* 2000;**41**:253–7.

44. Fratiglioni L, Paillard-Borg S, Winblad B. An active and socially integrated lifestyle in late life might protect against dementia. *Lancet Neurol* 2004;**3**:343–53.

45. Wong J, Wirrell E. Physical activity in children/teens with epilepsy compared with that in their siblings without epilepsy. *Epilepsia* 2006;**47**:631–9.

46. Jalava M, Sillanpää M. Physical activity, health-related fitness, and health experience in adults with childhood-onset epilepsy: a controlled study. *Epilepsia* 1997;**38**:424–9.

47. Jacoby A, Snape D, Baker GA. Epilepsy and social identity: the stigma of a chronic neurological disorder. *Lancet Neurol* 2005;**4**:171–8.

Chapter 13a

Leukemia and lymphoma across the lifespan

Kevin R. Krull and Neelam Jain

Introduction

Leukemia is the most common form of pediatric cancer, accounting for 25% of all cancers occurring before 20 years of age [1]. Acute lymphoblastic leukemia (ALL) accounts for roughly 75% of all leukemia diagnoses, with roughly 3000 new cases diagnosed annually [1]. Lymphomas are the third most common form of childhood cancer, occurring in roughly 1700 new cases annually [1]. Improvements in the treatment of leukemia and lymphoma have led to a remarkable increase in the survival rate, which currently exceeds 80% [2]. At these incidence and survival rates, it is estimated that 1 out of every 640 young adults will be a pediatric cancer survivor [3]. As many as two-thirds of all pediatric cancer survivors experience one or more permanent side effects of their treatment, often referred to as "late effects" (i.e. persisting or developing 5 or more years following cancer diagnosis) [4]. The late effects that commonly occur in patients with leukemia include neurocognitive impairment, obesity, short stature, osteoporosis, osteonecrosis, and cardiac dysfunction [5]. Neurocognitive late effects are often associated with treatment for leukemia, given that central nervous system (CNS) prophylaxis is a standard of care. As pediatric cancer survivors constitute a significant proportion of young adults, and as neurocognitive late effects appear relatively common, the public health consequences are substantial. This chapter will provide a review of the basic pathophysiology of acute lymphoblastic leukemia (ALL), acute myelogenous leukemia (AML), Hodgkin lymphoma (HL), and non-Hodgkin lymphoma (NHL) as well as a review of treatment factors, mediators and moderators that may influence neurocognitive and psychosocial outcomes, and evaluation, management, and prevention of these outcomes.

Pathophysiology of leukemia

Acute lymphoblastic leukemia (ALL) is a malignant disorder of lymphoid cells produced in the bone marrow that can migrate via the circulatory system to almost every organ system, including the central nervous system (CNS) [6]. The peak age of onset of ALL is roughly 4 years, with higher rates in Whites and males [1]. Survival rates, which are now estimated to exceed 80%, are, in part, related to more effective CNS prophylaxis therapies [2].

Acute myelogenous leukemia (AML), a malignant disorder of myeloid cells produced in the bone marrow, represents approximately 15–20% of childhood leukemia cases and accounts for greater than 30% of deaths from leukemia [7]. In 2004, AML accounted for 17% of newly diagnosed leukemia cases in children and adolescents younger than 20 [8]. Children of Hispanic background have higher rates of AML than African American children, who have higher rates than White children. Current cure rates for AML are between 50 and 60% with long-term survival of 40–50% [7].

Pathophysiology of lymphoma

Hodgkin lymphoma (HL) is a malignant disorder of the lymph nodes characterized by the presence of abnormal cells that arise from white blood cells. The most common symptom of HL is the presence of a painless enlargement of one or more lymph nodes in the region of the neck [9]. The occurrence of HL is rare in children younger than 4 years of age; there were fewer than 16 cases reported in infants and in children between the ages of 1 and 4 in 2004 [8]. HL has a male predominance in early onset and an even sex distribution for adolescent onset. The 5-year survival rate for children under 20 years of age with HL is greater than 90% [1].

Non-Hodgkin lymphoma (NHL) is a malignant disorder of the lymph nodes typically classified into one of four categories including Burkitt's and Burkitt-like lymphomas, lymphoblastic lymphomas, diffuse large B-cell lymphomas, and anaplastic large cell lymphomas. Each of these types of lymphoma involves different chromosomal translocations and can present in clinically distinct locations [10]. Burkitt's and Burkitt-like lymphoma are most often found in the intra-abdominal area and lymphoblastic lymphomas are often present as mediastinal masses. Burkitt's and Burkitt-like lymphoma are the predominant type to occur in children between the ages of 5 and 14, while diffuse large-cell lymphomas are the most common type in 15–19-year-olds. Roughly 50% of newly diagnosed NHL cases involve children between the ages of 5 and 14, while an additional 37% occur in the 15–19-year-old age group [8]. NHL occurs more often in males and more frequently in Whites compared to African Americans [1]. The 5-year survival rate for children and adolescents under 20 is approximately 72% [1].

Treatment factors

Table 13a.1 presents a summary of the various treatment agents associated with pediatric cancer diagnoses.

Cranial radiation therapy (CRT) was the standard of care for CNS prophylaxis of leukemia in the 1960s and 70s [6]. Since that time, standards have shifted to CNS prophylaxis with chemotherapy. Despite this change in the standard of care, approximately 10–15% of ALL patients in the highest risk categories still receive prophylactic or therapeutic CRT. CRT is associated with physiological late effects including growth suppression, obesity, and endocrine dysfunction [11]. Steno-occlusive disease of large and small cerebral vessels, abnormal vascular collateralization, aneurysms, and vascular malformations are a particularly morbid complication of CRT because of the increased risk for ischemic stroke and intraparenchymal hemorrhage [12, 13]. Children and adolescents diagnosed with AML, HL, or NHL do not typically receive cranial radiation therapy as part of their treatment regimens.

Low-dose, involved-field radiation therapy (IFRT) to lymph nodes is part of the standard of care for children and adolescents with HL [9]. Radiation therapy for HL has been associated with systemic complications such as bone and soft-tissue hypoplasia, increased risk of cardiac morbidity including atherosclerotic heart disease, valvular dysfunction, and pericardial disease, and pulmonary and endocrine sequelae [9, 14].

Antimetabolite chemotherapeutic agents including methotrexate (MTX), 6-mercaptopurine (6-MP), and cytarabine (Ara-C) are commonly used for the treatment of pediatric leukemia and lymphoma. These agents function by interfering with DNA production,

Table 13a.1. Cancer type and common treatments.

Cancer type	Common treatments
Acute lymphoblastic leukemia (ALL)	Antimetabolites Anthracyclines Bacterial enzymes Cranial radiation Glucocorticoids Vinca alkaloids
Acute myelogenous leukemia (AML)	Antimetabolites Anthracyclines Glucocorticoids
Hodgkin lymphoma (HL)	Antimetabolites Anthracyclines Glucocorticoids Involved-field radiation therapy Vinca alkaloids
Non Hodgkin lymphoma (NHL)	Antimetabolites Anthracyclines Glucocorticoids Vinca alkaloids
Relapsed leukemia and lymphoma	High-dose chemotherapy Total body irradiation Bone marrow transplantation

thereby affecting cell growth and division, resulting in a very efficient way to treat many hematological and oncological malignancies. MTX is typically used in the treatment of ALL and NHL while 6-MP is typically used for the treatment of ALL, and Ara-C for ALL, AML, and NHL [7, 10, 15]. MTX is administered intrathecally (IT; i.e. directly into the cerebrospinal fluid through the spinal canal) at doses based upon the age of the child, a strategy that was derived from CNS volume considerations in order to reduce neurotoxicity associated with IT MTX treatment [16]. Children younger than 12 months of age are typically given 6 mg per dose, children who are between 12 and 23 months of age are typically given 8 mg per dose, children who are between 24 and 35 months of age are typically given 10 mg per dose, and children who are age 3 or older are typically given 12 mg per dose. This administration route bypasses the blood–brain barrier (BBB) and leads to direct CNS exposure. MTX is also administered through high-dose intravenous (IV) administration at doses typically ranging from 1 gm to 30 gm/m^2 administered via prolonged IV infusion [15]. MTX administered through IV readily crosses the BBB and also leads to direct CNS exposure.

The primary mechanism of action of MTX is inhibition of dihydrofolate reductase (DHFR), the enzyme primarily responsible for the conversion of dihydrofolates to their active form of folate [17]. Folate acts to convert homocysteine to methionine;

homocysteine in turn may lead to neuronal injury through excessive excitation in amino acid pathways [18]. Another key enzyme in folate metabolism is methylenetetrahydrofolate reductase (MTHFR), which catalyzes the primary form of circulating folate, and is a co-substrate for homocysteine remethylation to methionine [19]. Deficiency in MTHFR activity results in hyperhomocysteinemia. Alterations in the function of folate pathway enzymes impact CNS folate levels, thereby increasing toxic levels of homocysteine. This is one of the primary reasons that high-dose IV MTX is typically followed by a course of the rescue agent leucovorin, the active form of folate that serves to rescue cells from folate depletion [20].

White matter abnormalities have been reported in the frontal lobes, particularly the right frontal lobe, during active therapy with MTX, though the duration of changes and their relationship to long-term pathology are unclear [21, 22]. Brain MRI studies reveal rates of leukoencephalopathy as high as 86% after seven courses of high-dose IV MTX, with a reduction to roughly 40% prevalence by the end of therapy [21]. Transient changes in white matter may be the result of demyelination, which could lead to decreased axonal density and brain atrophy.

Glucocorticoids (i.e. prednisone, prednisolone, dexamethasone) are also used for the treatment of leukemia and lymphoma. These agents affect metabolism and have anti-inflammatory and immunosuppressive effects. Their inhibition of glucose utilization by neurons and glia increases concentration of glutamate, particularly in the hippocampus, which causes excitotoxic neuronal death as a result of overstimulation [23]. Glucocorticoid treatment has been shown to cause damage to the hippocampus in rodents and primates [24]. Dexamethasone has been shown to be a potent cytotoxic agent, with higher rates of CNS penetrance than prednisone and prednisolone [25].

There are many other chemotherapeutic agents that are used in the treatment of leukemias and lymphomas. Common agents that are potentially associated with cognitive or behavioral dysfunction include anthracyclines (e.g. adriamycin, daunomycin, doxorubicin), vinca alkaloids (e.g. vincristine and vinblastine), and bacterial enzymes (e.g. asparaginase). Anthracyclines operate by structurally distorting base pairs of a DNA/RNA strand in order to inhibit DNA and RNA synthesis and stop the replication of cancer cells [26]. Anthracyclines are associated with cardiovascular toxicity, though direct cerebrovascular impact has not

yet been demonstrated [27]. Vinca alkaloids act as mitotic inhibitors which prevent cell growth [20]. These agents have been associated with acute peripheral neuropathy [28]. Bacterial enzymes such as asparaginase reduce levels of circulating asparagine, which leukemic cells require in quantities higher than non-leukemic cells [20]. Asparaginase is associated with cerebrovascular complications including venous thrombosis and cerebral hemorrhage [29]. There are many other chemotherapeutic agents used in the treatment of leukemia and lymphoma although few have been studied well or tied to adverse neurocognitive outcomes.

Children and adolescents with bone marrow relapse of ALL or a diagnosis of AML, HL, or NHL are candidates for bone marrow transplant (BMT), which is also known as hematopoietic stem cell transplantation (HSCT). BMT is the transplantation of the blood stem cells which are derived in the bone marrow [30]. For children and adolescents with ALL or AML the process of BMT involves both high-dose chemotherapy and total body irradiation followed by IV infusion of bone marrow or purified peripheral blood stem cells from a compatible donor [30]. For children and adolescents with HL or NHL the process of BMT involves high-dose chemotherapy with or without the addition of total body irradiation [31].

Mediators and moderators

Sex is a risk factor in pediatric malignancies that impacts treatment outcomes. Although boys develop ALL more often than girls, girls typically have a better prognosis since boys often experience extramedullary testicular relapse, have a higher incidence of T-cell disease, and have a lower incidence of favorable DNA index [1, 6]. As such, boys are often given chemotherapy for longer durations than girls, with a typical 36-month course for boys and a 30-month course for girls [2]. Sex has also been examined as a moderator of neurocognitive outcomes; this will be discussed later in this chapter.

Age at diagnosis is an important prognostic factor which influences treatment selection and outcome for leukemia and lymphoma. ALL is most often diagnosed between the ages of 2 and 5, with a peak incidence of 4 years of age [15]. Treatments for children diagnosed with ALL between the ages of 1 and 9 are different than those for infants and children who are diagnosed at 10 years of age and older. Infants and children older

381

than 10 at diagnosis are at higher risk for disease severity and treatment adjustments are made accordingly [15]. In the case of HL there are two distinct disease types with different typical age at onset and treatment varies accordingly. NHL treatment is dependent upon the particular type of lymphoma although age at diagnosis does not appear to affect choice of treatment.

Risk allocation refers to whether a patient is considered low, standard, or high risk upon initial diagnosis. Staging refers to the extent the disease has spread. Staging of HL or NHL has an influence on risk allocation, while ALL and AML are not staged. Factors such as age at diagnosis and initial white blood cell count are primary in the identification of risk level in ALL [6]. Improvements in survival rates for pediatric cancers have been led by increased tailoring of therapies, often determined by risk factors. Risk-adapted therapies have resulted in reduced toxicity for lower-risk patients and improved cure rates for higher-risk patients [32].

Advances in treatment for leukemia and lymphoma are associated with a recent trend in evaluating genetic contributions to individual treatment response factors. Gene expression profiling can successfully be used to classify subtypes of leukemia for treatment consideration [33]. Brouwers has suggested that research initiatives should also be concentrated on investigating the polymorphisms that affect current therapies and the study of genetic factors which may increase or decrease vulnerability to hematological malignancies and their treatments [34]. As an example of this, a genetic polymorphism for folate metabolism (i.e., 5,10-methylenetetrahydrofolate reductase; MTHFR) has been tied to medical outcome following treatment for leukemia [35]. This same polymorphism has been linked to differential neurocognitive outcomes following chemotherapy [36].

Although multiple biological mechanisms may be responsible for the neurocognitive impairment after cancer therapy, free oxygen radical-mediated damage with increased homocysteine and depleted folate may be a potential cause [37]. As stated earlier, MTX and its metabolites inhibit folate pathway enzymes (dihydrofolate reductase, thymidilate synthase, and MTHFR) and cause folate depletion in tumor and normal cells [17]. MTHFR plays a key role in determining the available levels of folate for DNA synthesis and methylation. The MTHFR enzyme has two single nucleotide polymorphisms (i.e. C677T and A1298C)

that alter the function of the enzymes, leading to reduced folate and increased homocysteine [38]. Homocysteine in turn may lead to neuronal injury through excessive excitation in amino acid pathways [39].

Other factors that may have mediating/moderating effects on treatment intensity and/or outcome include neurotoxicity (i.e. leukoencephalopathy), cardiovascular toxicity, and hepatic toxicity. Chemotherapeutic agents are cytotoxic and often result in secondary adverse systemic toxicities to organ systems. MTX has been associated with acute leukoencephalopathy and hepatic toxicity, while anthracyclines have been associated with cardiotoxicity [20]. If these toxicities become overly troublesome, modifications to the treatment regimens may be made. Furthermore, in addition to the clear connection to leukoencephalopathy, hepatic and cardiovascular toxicities may contribute to the adverse neurocognitive outcomes following chemotherapeutic treatment.

Neurocognitive outcomes

Pediatric leukemia and lymphoma survivors may suffer from neurocognitive impairment on a transient (i.e. acute) or lasting (i.e. late effects) basis in one or more domains that impede learning new information along with maintaining previously learned information, ultimately leading to declines in intelligence and academic and vocational success, as well as lowered self-esteem and behavioral disorders. Adult survivors of pediatric ALL treated with chemotherapy were 1.6 and 2.0 times as likely to report problems with mental health and functional impairment, respectively, compared to sibling controls [40]. Table 13a.2 presents a summary of the neurocognitive effects related to various treatment agents.

Higher cumulative doses of cranial radiation and young age at the time of radiation are associated with general intellectual dysfunction and reduced academic performance [41]. Schatz and colleagues demonstrated that underlying the deficits in intelligence in patients treated for ALL with cranial radiation are specific deficits in working memory and processing speed [42]. It is also well established that the decline in intelligence test performance after cranial radiation continues progressively for at least 6 years [43].

Although numerous chemotherapeutic agents may also play a role in the development of these negative consequences, most attention has been focused on MTX. MTX in children has been linked to reduced

Table 13a.2. Treatment exposure types and anatomical correlates and neurocognitive outcomes of leukemia and lymphoma treatment.

Treatment exposure	Anatomical correlates	Neurocognitive outcomes
Cranial radiation	Demyelination of white matter in the frontal lobes and basal ganglia	Intellectual functioning Academic functioning (e.g. mathematics) Attention (i.e. focusing, shifting, and sustaining) Processing speed Verbal and nonverbal memory
Involved-field radiation therapy	Cardiovascular Pulmonary Endocrine	Fatigue and sleep disturbance Potential cognitive deficits
Antimetabolites (e.g. methotrexate)	Demyelination of frontal lobe white matter	Attention Processing speed Executive functions
Corticosteroids (e.g. prednisone and dexamethasone)	Hippocampal	Short- and long-term memory
Anthracyclines (e.g. adriamycin, daunomycin)	Cardiovascular	Potential cognitive deficits
Vinca alkaloids (e.g. vincristine)	Peripheral nervous system	Fine motor speed and dexterity
Bacterial enzymes (e.g. asparaginase)	Cerebrovascular	Potential cognitive deficits based upon location of cerebrovascular insult (e.g. language, motor, executive functions)
Nonspecific chemotherapy effects		Adaptive behaviors (e.g. social skills) Psychosocial (e.g. anxiety/depression) Fatigue and sleep disturbance

intelligence, visual-motor decline, and academic problems, particularly in mathematics [44, 45]. Attention deficits in these children appear to be particularly common. The amount or intensity of MTX has been correlated with the degree of neurocognitive problems [46]. Furthermore, as indicated above, intensive MTX therapy has been associated with white matter changes in the frontal lobes, a brain region often associated with attention processes [47].

There are relatively few reported studies of neurocognitive changes during active therapy for pediatric leukemia or lymphoma. In a feasibility study with a small sample of ALL patients, Jansen and colleagues reported no changes in IQ, language, memory, or attention when patients were evaluated within 2 weeks of starting therapy [48]. However, in a prospective longitudinal study with a larger sample size, declines in both fine motor functions and attention have been reported [46, 49].

Children diagnosed with ALL demonstrate acute changes in neurocognitive functions during the first 2 years of chemotherapeutic treatment [46]. In this study, attention skills were assessed during the first and second year of active treatment. Children treated with lower doses of IV MTX improved in performance from the first to the second year, while children treated with higher doses declined in performance over time. By the end of the second year of therapy,

10.5% of the children treated with low doses fell more than one standard deviation below the mean, while 38.5% of the children treated with high dose IV MTX fell more than one standard deviation below the mean.

The relationship between initial processing speed and the development of higher-level cognitive abilities has also been examined over the 3-year course of chemotherapy for ALL [49]. In a sample of 84 newly diagnosed patients, significant slowing in processing speed was noted during the initial 6 months of chemotherapy treatment, with a mean decrease of 0.8 standard deviations. As therapy continued into the second and third years of treatment, visual-motor integration and perceptual problem-solving skills steadily declined. Significant positive correlations were found between initial performance on processing speed and subsequent visual-motor integration ($r = 0.54$, $P < 0.001$), as well as between the initial processing speed and subsequent perceptual problem-solving ($r = 0.33$, $P < 0.007$).

Long-term survivors of pediatric ALL (i.e. ≥ 5 years post-diagnosis) appear to be at increased risk for brain abnormalities. In a large retrospective multicenter study, pathological brain magnetic resonance imaging (MRI) scans were reported in 52% of ALL survivors [50]. Although rates of MRI abnormality were higher in children who received cranial irradiation, 39% of the children who received only chemotherapy also displayed abnormal MRI. In a prospective study of brain MRI in pediatric ALL survivors, 16.7% of those treated with chemotherapy only were identified as having white matter changes, which were predominantly in the frontal lobes [22].

Neurocognitive impairment is one of the most common late effects in long-term survivors of pediatric leukemia, with 20% to 40% of all patients demonstrating deficits in one or more domains of function [51, 52]. Children who survive leukemia are more likely to need special education services and are rated lower on academic skills when compared with referenced controls [53]. Deficits in mathematics calculation and applied arithmetic problem-solving are frequently noted, though reading difficulties have also been reported [45]. This impact on academic as well as global cognitive abilities may not fully emerge until at least 5 years after diagnosis, with a steady decline in functions over time [54].

Although neurocognitive problems were often attributed to cranial radiation effects, high-dose chemotherapy has also been implicated. In a study of pediatric ALL patients treated at St. Jude Children's Research Hospital, children who received IV or IT MTX had neurotoxic effects similar to those experienced by patients who received 18 Gy of cranial radiation [55]. Neurocognitive problems included impairment in intelligence as well as arithmetic achievement. In fact, roughly 25% of the children who received no radiation experienced clinically apparent deficits in neurocognitive function during the follow-up period (median 7.4 years) [51].

Intellectual and academic functions have been a common focus for studies of long-term problems. In a recent meta-analysis of 13 studies examining ALL survivors treated with chemotherapy only, moderate to large effect sizes were consistently identified for intelligence and academic achievement [45]. Performance-based intelligence appears more impacted by chemotherapy treatment, with significant relationships reported between cumulative IT MTX and Performance IQ (PIQ) [44]. Mathematical skills also appear to be particularly vulnerable, though impairment in reading has also been reported [45]. In a recent report of children treated with CRT and IT chemotherapy compared to a chemotherapy-only group, reduced academic fluency was identified, though overall intellect and academic knowledge was reportedly intact [56].

In addition to intellectual functioning and academics, abnormalities in specific neurocognitive skills are reported, particularly processing speed, attention, and memory functions. Behavioral attention problems are common, and these problems correspond to reduced school performance and teacher-rated math difficulties [36, 57]. In a recent survey of 2979 parents of adolescent survivors, both children with leukemia and those with lymphoma (HD and NHD) were identified as having significantly higher rates of attention problems compared to sibling controls [58]. Early-onset attention deficits can have a major impact on the development of functional academic skills, as well as higher-level cognitive functions. Chemotherapy intensity, younger age at treatment and female sex have all been reported to be risk factors for these attention problems [59].

Reddick and colleagues have examined the relationship between neurocognitive problems and the occurrence of white matter abnormalities [47]. Specifically, 112 ALL survivors were compared to 33 healthy siblings who participated as a control group. Within the ALL group, 84 patients received chemotherapy treatment only, while 28 also received cranial irradiation. Neurocognitive measures of sustained attention, intelligence, and academic achievement were performed. MRI was obtained and subsequently segmented for tissue volume measurement. Those patients treated with CRT displayed reduced development of academic functions, including mathematics and reading skills, as well as problems with sustained attention. For the chemotherapy-only group, sustained attention was the single task that was significantly reduced (i.e. more than 1.0 standard deviation below national norms). Furthermore, in both groups, smaller white matter volumes were significantly associated with impaired sustained attention.

Executive dysfunction may also contribute to the problems with academics and aspects of intelligence [42]. Common areas of impaired executive function in long-term survivors include mental flexibility and verbal fluency [60]. In a recent report by Waber and colleagues, roughly 30% of ALL survivors scored below the 10th percentile on indices of the Rey-Osterrieth Complex Figure. However, these deficits in executive functions do not necessarily appear related to treatment intensity. In an examination of survivors 1 year off chemotherapy, basic sustained attention problems were identified more often in children exposed to high-dose IV MTX compared to those on a standard dose [59]. However, both the high-dose and standard-dose groups demonstrated reduced mental flexibility, suggesting a potentially lower threshold for impact on executive functions. Recent meta-analyses of studies examining neurocognitive outcomes in pediatric leukemia support this finding. Of the studies reviewed, attention problems were most common, with moderate to large effect sizes, though problems in executive functions were also consistently reported, with moderate effect sizes [45, 61]. These deficits in executive functions may contribute to the finding that young adult survivors of childhood cancer tend to be underemployed and have lower incomes [62].

Recent research has also raised concern over the neurotoxic effects of corticosteroids. Clinical treatment with dexamethasone has been linked to memory impairment in survivors of chronic illness (e.g. asthma, systemic lupus erythematosus) [63]. Memory problems and reduced visual-spatial organization have been reported in children with ALL treated with dexamethasone compared with prednisone [64]. However, this study employed historical controls, treated in different decades and, as a result, direct comparison is difficult.

Neurocognitive complications following bone marrow transplantation have also been reported; however, it is unclear as to whether the impact is from the pre-existing radiation and chemotherapy versus a unique contribution from the transplant process. Shah and colleagues compared patients scheduled for HSCT to their sibling controls [65]. Reduced intellect was identified in the patient group both before and after the transplant, with no discernible change following transplantation. Similarly, Harder and colleagues found 25% of transplant patients impaired on several domains of functioning prior to HSCT, with a slight improvement in memory within the year following the procedure [66].

The impact of chemotherapeutic agents on neurocognitive function is not universal, and most investigations have found significant individual variability in outcomes. Using a prospective-longitudinal design, Kingma and colleagues reported few cognitive problems in children exposed to chemotherapy alone, with only one measure demonstrating impairment several years following the end of therapy [67]. However, the one impaired measure was sustained attention, and no measures of executive functions were administered. In addition, some children displayed large declines in functioning, while others appeared relatively

unaffected. Other investigators have reported no neurocognitive deficits in children treated only with chemotherapy and have questioned whether chemotherapy truly impacts brain functions. In a recent examination of patients treated with CRT, high-dose IV MTX, or standard-dose IV MTX, Spiegler and colleagues reported few neurocognitive deficits by 5 years post-diagnosis [68]. Of the many measures included, again only a measure of sustained attention demonstrated reduction in the non-CRT group. Other measures focused on long-term memory and intellectual and academic functions, which may demonstrate an increased threshold for chemotherapeutic impact or a more gradual decline in function. No measures of executive function were included. Waber and colleagues have also reported fewer problems associated with chemotherapy treatment [56]. In comparing patients treated with 18 Gy CRT to a chemotherapy-only group, no impact of treatment on standard measures of intelligence, academic knowledge, or memory storage and retrieval was reported in either group when compared to national norms.

These differences in outcome studies raise questions of sample representation and individual variability. Recruitment strategies focused on samples of convenience (e.g. patients who show up in the long-term survivor clinic) may result in over-representation of pathology. Those patients lost to follow-up may not experience the same degree of problems as those seeking medical evaluations. Unfortunately, many studies do not include sufficient data to determine whether the results can generalize to the patient population. When more representative samples are included, the impact of chemotherapy-only treatment is often more localized to specific processes (i.e. sustained attention, cognitive fluency) or to a specific subset of patients at higher risk due to treatment intensity or genetic predispositions. For example, we recently reported data suggesting that the elevated rates of ADHD in long-term survivors of pediatric leukemia are related to individual genetic polymorphisms [36]. In a sample of 120 long-term survivors of pediatric leukemia, ADHD was identified in 22.9% of the patients, and all patients who met criteria had attention problems. Polymorphisms in the MTHFR enzyme were related to ADHD diagnosis, with 35% found to meet the criteria for the inattentive type of ADHD. This resulted in a 7.4-fold increase (95% confidence interval = 1.3 to 42.5; $P < 0.025$) in risk of inattentive ADHD diagnosis after adjustment for age at diagnosis and sex. This investigation illustrates the need to consider intra-group variability in outcome studies.

Evaluation and management

The Children's Oncology Group (COG) is a multi-disciplinary organization funded by the National Cancer Institute to organize and implement clinical trials in pediatric cancer. COG has established guidelines for the standard of care in monitoring the late effects of long-term survivors of pediatric cancer (www.survivorshipguidelines.org) [8]. These guidelines call for neurocognitive evaluation of all patients treated with CRT or antimetabolite chemotherapy. A recent extension to this recommendation calls for such testing to include assessment of intellectual, academic, and specific neurocognitive processes [69]. It was further recommended that such testing occur as a baseline when the patient enters the phase of long-term follow-up, with re-evaluations conducted at times of life transition and when academic difficulties occur.

For a variety of reasons, including costs, time restraints, health insurance, and access to professional resources, these guidelines are often difficult to implement. As such, systematic screening for deficits may be a more practical approach. The reliability and validity of such a brief neurocognitive screening method have recently been reported [70]. In this study, 240 consecutive patients were screened during their annual visits to a long-term survivor clinic using standard neurocognitive measures and a brief parent-rating scale. The measures focused on assessment of attention, processing speed, and working memory, skills that have been identified as being sensitive to the effects of cancer treatment. From the total sample, 48 patients had a second screening and 52 patients had a comprehensive follow-up evaluation. Good test–retest reliability was demonstrated, with an overall $r = 0.72$ and all individual subtest correlations above $r = 0.40$. The screen accurately predicted follow-up performance on measures of global intellect (sensitivity = 94%, specificity = 63%), reading skills (sensitivity = 87%, specificity = 57%), and mathematics (sensitivity = 100%, specificity = 50%). The parent rating was a marginal indicator of global intellect only (sensitivity = 53%, specificity = 46%). This brief measure, which can be completed in 30 minutes, was concluded to be a practical and reliable method to identify cancer survivors in need of further neurocognitive follow-up.

Recent attempts at intervention for neurocognitive consequences of cancer therapy have focused on psychostimulant medication (i.e. methylphenidate). Initial studies show promise in the treatment of primary attention problems, based on performance on the Conners' Continuous Performance Test (CPT) [71]. Similar improvement was noted on parent and teacher rating scales [72]. In addition, the results of a large-scale double-blind cross-over study using a single trial of methylphenidate also reported improvement on measures of interference control (i.e. Stroop) [73]. However, none of these trials to date has demonstrated long-term efficacy or an impact on higher-level cognitive skills. Furthermore, improvement seen during medication may not be maintained following discontinuation of the drug.

Direct cognitive rehabilitation of deficits in long-term survivors has also been conducted. Intensive attention training has recently been reported to improve primary attention skills in ALL survivors experiencing attention problems [74]. However, in this study no improvement in higher-level cognitive abilities was demonstrated and no indication was given that improvement in daily activities occurred (i.e. school performance). Furthermore, those skills that demonstrated improvement following rehabilitation were similar in nature to the tasks practiced during the rehabilitation training.

Perhaps such rehabilitation attempts begin too late in the process of development of neurocognitive problems. With the identification of an "at risk" population, it may be feasible to implement preventative training approaches to reduce the eventual decline during long-term survivorship. For example, training of the attention network in typically developing children as young as 4 years old has been demonstrated to improve basic attention skills, as well as increase reasoning and problem-solving abilities [75]. Similarly, we have found initial improvement in cognitive skills following preventative training in pediatric leukemia survivors. In conjunction with colleagues at the University of Arizona (I. M. Moore and K. Kaemingk), we examined the efficacy of a preventative intervention trial in a small group of pediatric leukemia patients. In this study, we enrolled newly diagnosed patients and prospectively assessed neurocognitive function. The primary aim of the study was to determine whether a teacher-assisted math intervention could prevent a decline in math achievement in children with ALL. Fifty-seven children with ALL (32 females and 25 males) were enrolled during the beginning of their second year of chemotherapy. Mean age at the time of ALL diagnosis was 85.6 months (SD = 37.7); slightly higher than incidence data given the need to engage in mathematical education during the intervention. Patients were randomized to either a math intervention (n = 24) or standard care (n = 33) group; no group differences were evident in age at diagnosis, sex, mothers' education, or total dose of MTX received. Healthy siblings (n = 16) were also included to obtain an estimate of practice effects associated with the repeated measures design. It was hypothesized that there would be less of a decline in math achievement scores in the math intervention group compared to the standard care group. After correcting for minor practice effects (with estimates obtained from the sibling controls), children in the math intervention group had a mean increase of 11.6 points on a standardized measure of math achievement by the end of the intervention, while the control group had a mean decline of 8.5 points on the same measure. Subjects in the intervention group demonstrated improvement in their ability to analyze and solve practical mathematics problems presented visually or verbally. We also found the intervention group to demonstrate increased performance on neurocognitive measures of attention skills and visual-motor integration.

Future directions

As evident in the preceding discussion, the specific type and extent of impairment experienced by survivors of pediatric leukemia is dependent upon a variety of factors. One factor in particular is the type and intensity of chemotherapy treatment. Anti-metabolite therapy, in particular MTX, has been a focus of much neurocognitive investigation. However, this focus has concentrated on pediatric leukemia survivors, in spite of the fact that many other forms of pediatric cancer are treated with MTX (e.g. HL, NHL, soft tissue sarcomas, and bone cancers). Research efforts need to expand their focus to include specificity of treatment agents rather than just clusters of cancer diagnoses. As base rates for these cancer diagnoses are slightly lower than ALL, multi-site studies will be required. In addition, pooling children across diagnoses based on treatment agents may be necessary.

Often only one aspect of the treatment is the focus of investigation. However, treatments rarely occur in isolation. For example, most current leukemia protocols include IT and IV MTX, as well as corticosteroids, enzymes, etc. Due to relatively low base rates and the variety of protocols, few studies have sufficient power to control for all of these other treatment factors. As such, many questions about specificity of the interaction of neurotoxic agents remain. Multisite studies examining the interaction of chemotherapeutic agents on neurocognitive outcomes are needed. However, such investigations have frequently been limited in recruitment, with few neuropsychological evaluations conducted according to protocol. Although it is easy to blame the neuropsychologists for limited involvement in collaborative trials, the problem is more systemic than individual. Such collaborative trials often have limited or no funds specifically designated to cover neuropsychological evaluations, and medical insurance coverage is highly variable for clinical services. Thus, most trials are funded through local institutions or costs are absorbed by the neuropsychologist. Financial commitment from collaborative trials will be needed to further this line of investigation.

In addition to examining individual agent and interactive chemotherapy regimens at the group level, an examination of individual variability is needed. As evident from the discussion above, outcomes are not purely dictated by disease or treatment agent. Within most recent studies, subsets of patients can be identified that experience more significant impairment, regardless of risk stratification or treatment intensity. Age at diagnosis, sex, and genetic predispositions are just a few of the factors that have been associated with poor outcomes. Similarly, cognitive stimulation and access to educational resources may be a couple of the protective factors that buffer children against negative impacts. In order to better identify risk and protective factors, sub-group clustering based on outcomes rather than risk stratification or treatment intensity is necessary. Refocusing the question to understand why 20–40% of patients experience neurocognitive impairment, rather than whether a specific treatment agent impacts an entire group, may shed light on these individual risk factors.

An additional need for future research, probably related to the discussion of individual risk, is the understanding of the contribution of the health status of the patient. Systemic chemotherapy agents are not only neurotoxic, but also have toxic impact on multiple other organ systems (e.g. hepatic, cardiovascular, pulmonary, endocrine, etc.). To date, little attention has been given to the potential for these other organ impacts to mediate neurocognitive outcomes.

Summary

Improvements in treatment have led to substantially increased survival rates for children and adolescents diagnosed with ALL, AML, HL, and NHL, with overall rates exceeding 80%. This success, combined with gradually increasing incidence rates, has resulted in a substantial population of pediatric cancer survivors. As long-term care for these survivors has gained increased focus, recognition of substantial neurocognitive and psychosocial sequelae of treatment has occurred. The long-term sequelae, commonly referred to as late effects, can be particularly problematic and may vary in severity, duration, and manifestation over time. The pattern of problems may be specific at onset (i.e. sustained attention or processing speed), though evolving into more expansive deficits (i.e. academic learning, executive functioning) as the child ages.

Although many children may escape cancer therapy with relatively few problems, a subset of children appears to be particularly affected. Current estimates suggest that 20–40% of children and adolescent survivors may experience potentially long-lasting effects of their cancer with respect to physiological, neuropsychological, and psychosocial outcomes following treatment. Relevant risk factors for neurocognitive late effects include the specific type and intensity of treatment, age at treatment, sex, genetic predispositions, and health of organ systems. Given current COG guidelines, it is incumbent upon healthcare providers to be familiar with these risk factors and various deficits associated with treatment for pediatric cancer. As further progress is made in tailoring treatments to individuals or targeting treatments to specific groups (e.g. based on risk or genetic polymorphisms), it will be important to continue to evaluate neurocognitive and psychosocial outcomes with the goal of developing rehabilitative strategies for these survivors to achieve educational and vocational success and to promote the best quality of life possible. Given the gradual onset of significant impairment, treatment approaches should encompass preventative strategies, particularly when increased risk has been determined.

References

1. Ries LAG, et al. *SEER Cancer Statistics Review, 1975–2004*. 2007, National Cancer Institute: Bethesda, MD. http://seer.cancer.gov/csr/1975_2004/.

2. Pui CH, and Evans WE. Treatment of acute lymphoblastic leukemia. *N Engl J Med* 2006;**354**(2):166–78.

3. Jemal A, et al. Cancer statistics, 2006. *CA Cancer J Clin* 2006;**56**(2):106–30.

4. Oeffinger KC, et al. Grading of late effects in young adult survivors of childhood cancer followed in an ambulatory adult setting. *Cancer* 2000;**88**(7):1687–95.

5. Hewitt M, Weiner SL, Simone JV. *Childhood Cancer Survivorship: Improving Care and Quality of Life*. Washington DC: National Academy of Sciences; 2003; 224.

6. Margolin JF, Steuber CP, Poplack DG. Acute lymphoblastic leukemia. In Pizzo PA, Poplack DG, eds. *Principles and Practice of Pediatric Oncology*. Philadelphia, PA: Lippincott, Williams, & Wilkins; 2006: 538–590.

7. Golub TR, Arceci RJ. Acute myelogenous leukemia. In Pizzo PA, Poplack DG, eds. *Principles and Practice of Pediatric Oncology*. Philadelphia, PA: Lippincott, Williams, & Wilkins; 2006: 591–644.

8. Children's Oncology Group. *Long-term follow-up guidelines*. 2006. Available from: www.survivorshipguidelines.org.

9. Hodgson DC, Hudson MM, Constine LS. Pediatric hodgkin lymphoma: maximizing efficacy and minimizing toxicity. *Semin Radiat Oncol* 2007;**17**(3):230–42.

10. Link MP, Weinstein HJ. Malignant non-Hodgkin lymphomas in children. In Pizzo PA, Poplack DG, eds. *Principles and Practice of Pediatric Oncology*. Philadelphia, PA: Lippincott, Williams, & Wilkins; 2006: 722–747.

11. Geenen MM, et al. Medical assessment of adverse health outcomes in long-term survivors of childhood cancer. *J Am Med Assoc* 2007;**297**(24):2705–15.

12. Kondoh T, et al. Moyamoya syndrome after prophylactic cranial irradiation for acute lymphocytic leukemia. *Pediatr Neurosurg* 2003;**39**(5):264–9.

13. Duhem R, et al. Cavernous malformations after cerebral irradiation during childhood: report of nine cases. *Childs Nerv Syst* 2005;**21**(10):922–5.

14. Hudson MM. Achieving cure for early stage pediatric Hodgkin disease with minimal morbidity: are we there yet? *Pediatr Blood Cancer* 2006;**46**(2):122–6.

15. Pui CH, Robison LL, Look AT. Acute lymphoblastic leukaemia. *Lancet* 2008;**371**(9617):1030–43.

16. Bleyer WA, et al. Reduction in central nervous system leukemia with a pharmacokinetically derived intrathecal methotrexate dosage regimen. *J Clin Oncol* 1983;**1**(5):317–25.

17. Goldman ID, Matherly LH. The cellular pharmacology of methotrexate. *Pharmacol Ther* 1985;**28**(1):77–102.

18. Robien K, Ulrich CM. 5,10-Methylenetetrahydrofolate reductase polymorphisms and leukemia risk: a HuGE minireview. *Am J Epidemiol* 2003;**157**(7):571–82.

19. Robien K, Boynton A, Ulrich CM. Pharmacogenetics of folate-related drug targets in cancer treatment. *Pharmacogenomics* 2005;**6**(7):673–689.

20. Adamson PC, et al. General principles of chemotherapy. In Pizzo PA, Poplack DG, eds. *Principles and Practice of Pediatric Oncology*. Philadelphia, PA: Lippincott, Williams, & Wilkins; 2006: 290–365.

21. Reddick WE, et al. Prevalence of leukoencephalopathy in children treated for acute lymphoblastic leukemia with high-dose methotrexate. *AJNR Am J Neuroradiol* 2005;**26**(5):1263–9.

22. Paakko E, et al. White matter changes on MRI during treatment in children with acute lymphoblastic leukemia: correlation with neuropsychological findings. *Med Pediatr Oncol* 2000;**35**(5):456–61.

23. Sapolsky RM. The possibility of neurotoxicity in the hippocampus in major depression: a primer on neuron death. *Biol Psychiatry* 2000;**48**(8):755–65.

24. Hoschl C, Hajek T. Hippocampal damage mediated by corticosteroids – a neuropsychiatric research challenge. *Eur Arch Psychiatry Clin Neurosci* 2001;**251** Suppl 2:II81–8.

25. Mitchell CD, et al. Benefit of dexamethasone compared with prednisolone for childhood acute lymphoblastic leukaemia: results of the UK Medical Research Council ALL97 randomized trial. *Br J Haematol* 2005;**129**(6):734–45.

26. Doroshow JH. Anthracyclines and anthracenediones. In Chabner BA, Longo DL, eds. *Cancer Chemotherapy and Biotherapy Principles and Practice*. Philadelphia, PA: Lippincott-Raven; 1996: 409–34.

27. Kremer LC, et al. Frequency and risk factors of subclinical cardiotoxicity after anthracycline therapy in children: a systematic review. *Ann Oncol* 2002;**13**(6):819–29.

28. Reinders-Messelink HA, et al. Analysis of handwriting of children during treatment for acute lymphoblastic leukemia. *Med Pediatr Oncol* 2001;**37**(4):393–9.

29. Kieslich M, et al. Cerebrovascular complications of L-asparaginase in the therapy of acute lymphoblastic leukemia. *J Pediatr Hematol Oncol* 2003;**25**(6):484–7.

30. Bollard CM, Krance RA, Heslop HE. Hematopoietic stem cell transplantation in pediatric oncology. In Pizzo PA, Poplack DG, eds. *Principles and Practice of Pediatric Oncology*. Philadelphia, PA: Lippincott, Williams, & Wilkins; 2006: 476–500.

31. Morrison VA, Peterson BA. High-dose therapy and transplantation in non-Hodgkin's lymphoma. *Semin Oncol* 1999;**26**(1):84–98.

32. Meshinchi S and Arceci RJ. Prognostic factors and risk-based therapy in pediatric acute myeloid leukemia. *Oncologist* 2007;**12**(3):341–55.

33. Mullighan CG, Flotho C, Downing JR. Genomic assessment of pediatric acute leukemia. *Cancer J* 2005;**11**(4):268–82.

34. Brouwers P. Commentary: study of the neurobehavioral consequences of childhood cancer: entering the genomic era? *J Pediatr Psychol* 2005;**30**(1):79–84.

35. Kishi S, et al. Homocysteine, pharmacogenetics, and neurotoxicity in children with leukemia. *J Clin Oncol* 2003;**21**(16):3084–91.

36. Krull KR, et al. Folate pathway genetic polymorphisms are related to attention disorders in childhood leukemia survivors. *J Pediatr* 2008;**152**(1):101–5.

37. Miketova P, et al. Oxidative changes in cerebral spinal fluid phosphatidylcholine during treatment for acute lymphoblastic leukemia. *Biol Res Nurs* 2005;**6**(3):187–95.

38. Ogino S, Wilson RB. Genotype and haplotype distributions of MTHFR677C>T and 1298A>C single nucleotide polymorphisms: a meta-analysis. *J Hum Genet* 2003;**48**(1):1–7.

39. Lipton SA, Rosenberg PA. Excitatory amino acids as a final common pathway for neurologic disorders. *N Engl J Med* 1994;**330**(9):613–22.

40. Thornton KE, Carmody DP. Electroencephalogram biofeedback for reading disability and traumatic brain injury. *Child Adolesc Psychiatr Clin N Am* 2005;**14**(1):137–62, vii.

41. Hoppe-Hirsch E, et al. Malignant hemispheric tumors in childhood. *Childs Nerv Syst* 1993;**9**(3):131–5.

42. Schatz J, et al. Processing speed, working memory, and IQ: A developmental model of cognitive deficits following cranial radiation therapy. *Neuropsychology* 2000;**14**(2):189–200.

43. Mulhern RK, et al. Neurocognitive consequences of risk-adapted therapy for childhood medulloblastoma. *J Clin Oncol* 2005;**23**(24):5511–9.

44. Montour-Proulx I, et al. Cognitive changes in children treated for acute lymphoblastic leukemia with chemotherapy only according to the Pediatric Oncology Group 9605 protocol. *J Child Neurol* 2005;**20**(2):129–33.

45. Peterson CC, et al. A meta-analysis of the neuropsychological sequelae of chemotherapy-only treatment for pediatric acute lymphoblastic leukemia. *Pediatr Blood Cancer*, 2008;**51**:99–104.

46. Carey ME, et al. Brief report: effect of intravenous methotrexate dose and infusion rate on neuropsychological function one year after diagnosis

of acute lymphoblastic leukemia. *J Pediatr Psychol* 2007;**32**(2):189–93.

47. Reddick WE, et al. Smaller white-matter volumes are associated with larger deficits in attention and learning among long-term survivors of acute lymphoblastic leukemia. *Cancer* 2006;**106**(4):941–9.

48. Jansen NC, et al. Feasibility of neuropsychological assessment in leukaemia patients shortly after diagnosis: directions for future prospective research. *Arch Dis Child* 2005;**90**(3):301–4.

49. Hockenberry M, et al. Longitudinal evaluation of fine motor skills in children with leukemia. *J Pediatr Hematol Oncol* 2007;**29**(8):535–9.

50. Hertzberg H, et al. CNS late effects after ALL therapy in childhood. Part I: Neuroradiological findings in long-term survivors of childhood ALL – an evaluation of the interferences between morphology and neuropsychological performance. The German Late Effects Working Group. *Med Pediatr Oncol* 1997;**28**(6):387–400.

51. Mulhern RK, Fairclough D, Ochs J. A prospective comparison of neuropsychologic performance of children surviving leukemia who received 18-Gy, 24-Gy, or no cranial irradiation. *J Clin Oncol* 1991;**9**(8):1348–56.

52. Moleski M. Neuropsychological, neuroanatomical, and neurophysiological consequences of CNS chemotherapy for acute lymphoblastic leukemia. *Arch Clin Neuropsychol* 2000;**15**(7):603–30.

53. Christie D, et al. Intellectual performance after presymptomatic cranial radiotherapy for leukaemia: effects of age and sex. *Arch Dis Child* 1995;**73**(2):136–40.

54. Brown RT, Madan-Swain A. Cognitive, neuropsychological, and academic sequelae in children with leukemia. *J Learn Disabil* 1993;**26**(2):74–90.

55. Ochs J, et al. Comparison of neuropsychologic functioning and clinical indicators of neurotoxicity in long-term survivors of childhood leukemia given cranial radiation or parenteral methotrexate: a prospective study. *J Clin Oncol* 1991;**9**(1):145–51.

56. Waber DP, et al. Neuropsychological outcomes from a randomized trial of triple intrathecal chemotherapy compared with 18 Gy cranial radiation as CNS treatment in acute lymphoblastic leukemia: findings from Dana-Farber Cancer Institute ALL Consortium Protocol 95-01. *J Clin Oncol* 2007;**25**(31):4914–21.

57. Buizer AI, et al. Behavioral and educational limitations after chemotherapy for childhood acute lymphoblastic leukemia or Wilms tumor. *Cancer* 2006;**106**(9):2067–75.

58. Schultz KA, et al. Behavioral and social outcomes in adolescent survivors of childhood cancer: a report from the childhood cancer survivor study. *J Clin Oncol* 2007;**25**(24):3649–56.

59. Buizer AI, et al. Chemotherapy and attentional dysfunction in survivors of childhood acute lymphoblastic leukemia: effect of treatment intensity. *Pediatr Blood Cancer* 2005;**45**(3):281–90.

60. Anderson V, et al. Neurobehavioural sequelae following cranial irradiation and chemotherapy in children: an analysis of risk factors. *Pediatr Rehabil* 1997;**1**(2):63–76.

61. Campbell LK, et al. A meta-analysis of the neurocognitive sequelae of treatment for childhood acute lymphocytic leukemia. *Pediatr Blood Cancer* 2007;**49**(1):65–73.

62. Hudson MM, et al. Health status of adult long-term survivors of childhood cancer: a report from the Childhood Cancer Survivor Study. *J Am Med Assoc* 2003;**290**(12):1583–92.

63. Wolkowitz OM, et al. The 'steroid dementia syndrome': an unrecognized complication of glucocorticoid treatment. *Ann N Y Acad Sci* 2004;**1032**:191–4.

64. Waber DP, et al. Cognitive sequelae in children treated for acute lymphoblastic leukemia with dexamethasone or prednisone. *J Pediatr Hematol Oncol* 2000;**22**(3):206–13.

65. Shah AJ, et al. Busulfan and cyclophosphamide as a conditioning regimen for pediatric acute lymphoblastic leukemia patients undergoing bone marrow transplantation. *J Pediatr Hematol Oncol* 2004;**26**(2):91–7.

66. Harder H, et al. Neurocognitive functions and quality of life in haematological patients receiving haematopoietic stem cell grafts: a one-year follow-up pilot study. *J Clin Exp Neuropsychol* 2006;**28**(3):283–93.

67. Kingma A, et al. No major cognitive impairment in young children with acute lymphoblastic leukemia using chemotherapy only: a prospective longitudinal study. *J Pediatr Hematol Oncol* 2002;**24**(2):106–14.

68. Spiegler BJ, et al. Comparison of long-term neurocognitive outcomes in young children with acute lymphoblastic leukemia treated with cranial radiation or high-dose or very high-dose intravenous methotrexate. *J Clin Oncol* 2006;**24**(24):3858–64.

69. Nathan PC, et al. Guidelines for identification of, advocacy for, and intervention in neurocognitive problems in survivors of childhood cancer: a report from the Children's Oncology Group. *Arch Pediatr Adolesc Med* 2007;**161**(8):798–806.

70. Krull KR, et al. Screening for neurocognitive impairment in pediatric cancer long-term survivors. *J Clin Oncol* 2008;**26**:4138–43.

71. Thompson SJ, et al. Immediate neurocognitive effects of methylphenidate on learning-impaired survivors of childhood cancer. *J Clin Oncol* 2001;**19**(6):1802–8.

72. Mulhern RK, et al. Short-term efficacy of methylphenidate: a randomized, double-blind, placebo-controlled trial among survivors of childhood cancer. *J Clin Oncol* 2004;**22**(23):4795–803.

73. Conklin HM, et al. Acute neurocognitive response to methylphenidate among survivors of childhood cancer: a randomized, double-blind, cross-over trial. *J Pediatr Psychol* 2007;**32**(9):1127–39.

74. Butler RW, Copeland DR. Attentional processes and their remediation in children treated for cancer: a literature review and the development of a therapeutic approach. *J Int Neuropsychol Soc* 2002;**8**(1):115–24.

75. Rueda MR, et al. Training, maturation, and genetic influences on the development of executive attention. *Proc Natl Acad Sci USA* 2005;**102**(41):14931–6.

Lifespan aspects of brain tumors

Celiane Rey-Casserly

Introduction

This chapter will focus on brain tumors across the lifespan with an emphasis on the contribution of developmental factors to incidence, presentation, treatment, and outcome. The epidemiology, classification, signs and symptoms, and major types of treatment of brain tumors are reviewed for children and adults. Neuropsychological outcomes and management strategies are then described for each of these populations separately.

Epidemiology

It is estimated that over 51 000 new cases of primary brain tumors were diagnosed in the USA in 2007, including over 3700 new cases of childhood primary brain tumors [1]. Brain tumors are the most common solid tumor of childhood and a leading cause of cancer-related death; in adults, they constitute the sixth most common neoplasm [2, 3]. The incidence of different types of tumors varies by age group, histology, and location. Survival rates also vary significantly among age groups [Table 13b.1]. Primary brain tumors develop as a consequence of genetic, molecular, or cytogenetic errors that allow cells to proliferate and turn off mechanisms that regulate cell growth [4]. Investigation into the molecular basis of tumorigenesis is an active area of neuroscience research though identification of specific causes of brain tumors has remained elusive, particularly in the case of childhood tumors. Primary risk factors for brain tumors include certain hereditary syndromes associated with mutations of tumor suppressor genes (neurofibromatosis Type 1 and Type 2, Turcot syndrome, nevoid basal cell carcinoma (Gorlin) syndrome, tuberous sclerosis, and Li-Fraumeni syndrome) and exposure to ionizing radiation. Other environmental risk factors have been more difficult to confirm [5, 6].

Classification of brain tumors

Tumors of the central nervous system are classified according to the presumed cell of origin and location; the most recent revision of the World Health Organization classification scheme includes new variants and incorporates genetic profiles [7, 8]. The WHO classification also provides a grading scheme based on histology that ranges from benign (grade I) to malignant (grade IV) based on proliferative potential and invasiveness. Major categories of brain tumors include neuroepitheleal tumors, tumors of the peripheral nerves, tumors of the meninges, lymphomas and hemopoietic neoplasms, germ cell tumors, tumors of the sellar region, and metastatic tumors. A listing of the types of brain tumors and most common sites is provided in Table 13b.2 according to these major categories.

Brain tumors in children differ from adult brain tumors with respect to types of tumors, locations, and survival rates. In adults, tumors occur more often in the supratentorial compartment of the brain (cerebrum, basal ganglia, thalamus, hypothalamus, optic chiasm/suprasellar region) whereas in children almost half of tumors occur in infratentorial sites (cerebellum, fourth ventricle, brainstem) [1]. Over the course of development, the incidence of different tumor types changes. With advances in molecular genetics, specific developmental pathways have been identified for the same tumor for different age groups comparing younger children, older children, and adults [9]. These age-related variations in distribution and behavior of brain tumors suggest fundamental differences in biology and etiology across development. Childhood tumors, particularly embryonal types, emerge as a result of disruptions in brain mechanisms of normal development, since they arise from rapidly dividing progenitor cells that are active in developmental processes [10]. Astrocytomas are most common in children, with low-grade types predominating, whereas

Table 13b.1. Frequency of tumor types and survival rates across age groups.

Frequency of tumor types

	Age at diagnosis (years)					
	Childhood 0–14	Adolescence 15–19	Young adult 20–29	Adult		Older adult ≥ 60
				30–39	40–59	
Most common tumor types[a]	Pilocytic astrocytoma 20.5%	Pilocytic astrocytoma 14.6%	Pituitary 17.3%	Meningioma 20.8%	Meningioma 33.3%	Meningioma 41.2%
	Embryonal 15.6%	Pituitary 13.9%	Meningioma 13.5%	Pituitary 14.8%	Glioblastoma 18.6%	Glioblastoma 25%

Survival rates

	Age at diagnosis (years)								
	Child					Adult			
	<1	1–4	5–9	10–14	15–19	20–45	45–54	55–64	≥ 65
Five-year survival rate (percent)[b]	47.8	72.5	69.4	77.9	73.8	49.2	28.4	13.0	5.9

[a] From CBTRUS [1] and McCarthy [99].
[b] From Ries et al. [100].

Table 13b.2. Brain tumors – classification and site.

Histology	Common sites
Neuroepithelial tumors	
Glial tumors	
Astrocytic	Posterior fossa (children), supratentorial (adults), midline
Glioma, glioblastoma	Optic pathway, brainstem, supratentorial
Oligodendroglial/mixed gliomas	Cerebral hemispheres (frontal, temporal lobes)
Ependymoma	Posterior fossa, spinal cord, cerebrum
Embryonal/neuronal tumors	
Medulloblastoma	Posterior fossa
Primitive neuroectodermal tumor	Supratentorial
Pineoblastoma	Pineal region
Atypical teratoid rhabdoid tumor	Posterior fossa (cerebello-pontine angle), supratentiorial
Choroid plexus tumors	Lateral ventricle, fourth ventricle
Tumors of cranial and peripheral nerves	
Schwannoma	Vestibular nerve
Malignant peripheral nerve sheath tumor	Medium or large nerves (sciatic nerve common)
Germ cell tumors	Midline structures (pineal, third ventricle, suprasellar)
Tumors of the sellar region	
Craniopharyngioma	Suprasellar region
Pituitary	Sellar region
Tumors of the meninges	Cerebral convexity, falx cerebri, olfactory groove
Metastatic tumors	Cerebral hemispheres (cortical/subcortical border)

From CBTRUS [1] and Riefenberger et al. [13].

meningiomas and glioblastomas are more common in adults. In the case of gliomas, pilocytic astrocytomas (grade I) predominate in childhood, low-grade astrocytomas and oligodendrogliomas are more common in young adults, whereas more highly malignant variants (glioblastoma multiforme and anaplastic astrocytoma) are typical in older adults [11]. Diffuse pontine gliomas are malignant brainstem tumors that comprise 8% to 10% of pediatric tumors and little progress has been made in improving the dismal prognosis for this disease [12]. The incidence of brain tumors varies with gender and ethnicity: for neuroepithelial and germ cell tumors there is a male predominance whereas meningiomas are more than twice as frequent in females than males. Germ cell tumors, though rare, occur most often in older children/adolescents, in males, and in Asian populations (3% of brain tumors in Japan compared to 0.5% in the US) [13].

Types of brain tumors

An extensive description of types of brain tumors is beyond the scope of this chapter; excellent summaries are available in several recent books and chapters [5, 14]. Tumors of neuroepithelial tissue include *gliomas* and *embryonal tumors*. Gliomas comprise 70% of brain tumors and most of these are astrocytic; the specific types of gliomas are distinguished by morphological and molecular criteria, as well as infiltrative and proliferative capacity (grades I to IV) [15]. Low-grade gliomas, particularly pilocytic astrocytomas in children, are typically treated successfully with resection only. Adjuvant treatment (chemotherapy, radiation) can be necessary with incomplete resection or tumor recurrence. In adults, gliomas are more often grade III (anaplastic astrocytoma) or IV (glioblastoma multiforme); lower-grade tumors can undergo transformation to become more infiltrative. Embryonal tumors (medulloblastoma, primitive neuroectodermal tumor) arise from transformations of immature neuroepithelial cells and are classified as malignant. These tumors have the capacity to seed through the neuroaxis and require intensive multimodality treatment (surgery, radiation, chemotherapy). *Ependymomas* are more common in children than adults and arise from ependymal remnant cells; they are locally invasive tumors and can invade adjacent areas of the brain [5]. Treatment typically includes surgery and extent of resection is strongly associated with prognosis [12]. Radiation therapy is often required as well, though it can be deferred in patients with gross total resection. Chemotherapy can be used, particularly in very young children to delay radiation treatment or in cases of incomplete resection or progression [16]. *Germ cell tumors* arise from precursor cells that give rise to the gonads and are homologous to germ cell tumors that occur in other parts of the body [13]. It is hypothesized that these tumors arise from germ cells that have failed to migrate as expected in development. Pure germinomas are treated with radiation therapy; pre-radiation chemotherapy is used to reduce tumor bulk such that a more limited field of radiation (whole ventricular field instead of whole brain) can be used to minimize toxicity. Survival rates approximate 95% in pure germinomas [16]. Tumors of the sellar region include *craniopharyngiomas* and *pituitary adenomas*. Pituitary adenomas are derived from secretory cells of the pituitary and occur preferentially in younger adults. Craniopharyngioma is believed to arise from epithelial embryonic remnants of the craniopharyngeal duct (Rathke's pouch). Craniopharyngiomas are treated with surgery; there is considerable controversy regarding the role of aggressive surgery given that the tumor tends to invade critical structures (hypothalamus, optic chiasm and visual pathways, third ventricle, carotid arteries, undersurface of frontal lobe), making surgery very challenging. Radiation is often used in the context of subtotal resection or recurrence and survival rates are high [16]. *Meningiomas* are typically slow-growing tumors that arise from arachnoidal cells. Presenting symptoms vary depending on site and size of tumor; affective disorders, seizures, speech deficits, hemiparesis, or memory problems can be associated with cortical convexity tumors; seizures or motor/sensory deficits are more common with parasagittal tumors. Prognosis for survival is very good with complete resection [17]. *Brain metastases* are the most common intracranial tumor in adults, occurring in 20% to 40% of adults with cancer; these most often occur in the cerebral hemispheres [6].

Signs and symptoms of brain tumors

Presentation in adults

Adults can present with a range of symptoms related to overall mass effect or specific location as a consequence of destruction of tissue in a specific area or parenchymal infiltration. In general, symptoms can be grouped into four clinical syndromes: raised intracranial pressure, progressive neurological deficit, seizures, or cognitive or behavioral changes [3] .The most common presenting symptom is headaches, which can be associated with early morning wakening and nausea/vomiting [6]. Since cortical locations are common in adult malignant tumors, new onset of seizures can be a frequent presenting sign [18]. Other symptoms include focal neurological deficits, personality changes, and cognitive dysfunction (memory, attention, confusion). Meningiomas may not cause symptoms or symptoms may be mistaken for or attributed to other conditions, including depression, menopause, and vascular problems [19].

Signs and symptoms in children

In children, symptoms can often be fairly diffuse. Presenting symptoms can reflect increased intracranial pressure due to hydrocephalus, edema, or tumor mass effects, or more focal symptoms can be related to the location of the tumor and associated neurological dysfunction (Table 13b.3). The triad of symptoms of early-morning vomiting, eye-movement abnormalities, and ataxia occur more often in children diagnosed with infratentorial tumors; seizures, vision deficits, and focal neurological signs are more commonly associated with supratentorial tumors [20]. Obstruction of cerebral spinal fluid (CSF) flow is frequent in childhood brain tumors due to the more common midline location of these tumors; obstruction can occur at the level of the lateral, third, or fourth ventricle. Children can sustain severe neurological damage from the hydrocephalus including blindness and cognitive deficits. Hydrocephalus has been identified as a significant risk factor for neuropsychological deficits, apart from effects of the tumor itself and its treatment [21].

Treatments for brain tumors

There are three basic modalities of treatment for brain tumors: surgery, radiation, and chemotherapy. Therapeutic protocols vary as a function of type of

Table 13b.3. Signs and symptoms of childhood brain tumors.

Symptoms of increased intracranial pressure	
Headaches, vomiting	
Diffuse symptoms – irritability, loss of milestones	
Increased head circumference	
Mental status/behavioral changes	
Gait problems	
More severe ICP:	
Neck pain, stiffness	
Altered consciousness	
Status epilepticus	
Focal symptoms related to location	Typical site
Seizures	Cortical
Focal neurological signs (hemiparesis)	Cortical
Vision changes	Optic pathway
Cranial nerve deficits, gait changes, swallowing problems, long tract signs (upper motor neuron signs)	Brainstem
Truncal or limb ataxia, nystagmus	Posterior fossa, cerebellum
Failure to thrive, endocrine dysfunction, behavioral changes	Hypothalamic-pituitary, suprasellar region
Abnormal eye movements, Perinaud's syndrome (gaze palsy, loss of upgaze, convergence nystagmus)	Pineal

From Punt [101] and Ullrich and Pomeroy [102].

tumor, location, degree of malignancy, age of the patient, and genetic factors. Current treatment regimens are beginning to incorporate molecular markers which can help with stratification of risk and identification of tumors that are more likely to respond to treatment, thus allowing for individualization of therapy and reductions in toxicity [16, 22].

Surgery

Surgical resection is typically the front-line intervention for tumors that are accessible to surgery; biopsies provide tumor tissue to determine pathological diagnosis and guide the treatment plan. Extent of resection is associated with more favorable prognosis in many tumor types. Advances in surgical techniques and technology such as stereotactic guidance and intraoperative MRI have allowed for more precise tailoring of surgery to minimize damage to normal tissues [5]. Complications of surgery include neurological deficits and endocrine dysfunction, as well as changes in physical appearance. Location of the tumor can be critical. For example, surgical approaches to reach tumors in the sellar region may damage critical structures

(hypothalamus, optic chiasm, orbital frontal region) and cause significant morbidity [23]. Cerebellar mutism or posterior fossa syndrome is a complication of surgery to the posterior fossa. This syndrome occurs after surgery (12 hours to 6 days post-surgery) and involves significant reduction in expressive language, pseudobulbar deficits, mood lability, and ataxia [24]. The incidence of posterior fossa syndrome is controversial but estimates suggest that approximately one-fourth of patients who undergo surgery for medulloblastoma experience some of the symptoms of this disorder [25]. Children typically recover their speech and demonstrate improvements in balance and coordination over time, though the course of recovery can be quite variable. The long-term consequences of the disorder are not well understood and it seems likely that residual deficits in the areas of emotional functioning and language expression persist [26].

Radiation

Radiation therapy is essential in the management of brain tumors in adults and children. Radiation affects cells by damaging DNA in tumor cells. Unfortunately, normal brain cells are also damaged. Most importantly, cells undergoing rapid development are particularly vulnerable. Normal tissue has the potential to repair radiation damage whereas rapidly dividing tumor cells are preferentially involved in replication. Consequently, radiation doses are given in fractions (total dose is divided into fractions and fractions are delivered over the course of approximately 6 weeks) to allow for normal tissue repair. Radiation can also be delivered in one high dose through the use of stereotactic radiosurgery (SRS), which deposits the dose in a region with small margins, sparing normal tissue. However, this type of treatment is limited to very small tumors. Other innovations in radiation therapy include intensity-modulated radiation therapy (IMRT) and particle beam therapy. IMRT provides for very sophisticated three-dimensional planning and delivery of dose based on algorithms that modify radiation intensity of individual beams to prioritize optimal dose to the tumor and minimal dose to surrounding normal tissue [27]. Proton beam radiation therapy employs technology that essentially eliminates the exit dose, thereby reducing toxicity to surrounding normal tissue. It is expected that use of proton beam radiotherapy will reduce complications from treatment [28]. Indeed, predictive models based on dose distributions expected through the use of proton beam radiation suggest some amelioration of radiation-induced cognitive deficits for medulloblastoma, craniopharyngioma and optic glioma [29].

Radiation to the developing brain is particularly toxic to the development of white matter. The pathophysiology of radiation injury to the developing brain and consequent compromise of intellectual development are being elucidated. It is hypothesized that radiation causes white matter abnormalities and disrupts myelination by damaging oligodendrocyte precursor cells or endothelial microvasculature, which disrupts the blood–brain barrier [30]. This injury to the vessel walls is presumed to precede white matter damage (leukoencephalopathy) and specific growth factors involved in the process are being identified. The damage caused by radiation is believed to be progressive, in that effects can continue to emerge over time, rather than be related to a one-time acute insult [31]. Another parallel mechanism underlying the neuropsychological effects of cranial radiation is related to damage to the hippocampus. Animal models have demonstrated that cranial irradiation alters basic biological functions of hippocampal progenitor cells: neurogenesis is ablated and precursor proliferation is significantly reduced through disruption of the stem cell pool and alterations in signaling in the local environment. In addition, the inflammatory response to irradiation contributes to changes in microvasculature which ultimately can inhibit neurogenesis as well [32]. Radiation can have differential effects related to the developmental status of the organism. Very young patients as well as elderly patients can be more susceptible to the impact of radiation, including brain atrophy and dementia due to pre-existing vascular and other medical conditions [33]. Late effects of radiation include neuropsychological deficits and decline in intelligence, growth deficits affecting the brain, bone, and soft tissue, endocrine dysfunction, hearing loss, vascular changes, and second tumors.

Chemotherapy

The role of chemotherapy in the management of brain tumors has expanded in recent years. In adults, chemotherapy has been demonstrated to extend survival in malignant brain tumors when added to radiation; the introduction of oral temozolomide is seen as a significant advance [6, 34]. In the treatment of childhood brain tumors, the addition of chemotherapy has led to reductions in radiation dose without changes in survival rates [35]. High-dose myeloablative chemotherapy followed by peripheral blood stem cell support allows for the delay of, or provides alternatives to, radiation, which is critical for very young children diagnosed with malignant tumors [36].

Most chemotherapy agents are cytoxans, agents developed to incite cell death directly; recently, novel therapies are targeting cell signaling pathways and tumor angiogenesis [37]. Cancer chemotherapy is associated with adverse neurological events including changes in white matter integrity, leukoencephalopathy, seizures, hearing loss, cerebellar symptoms, and cognitive impairment; these effects have been found in systemic as well as direct CNS chemotherapy [38, 39]. The cellular basis for chemotherapy toxicity to the CNS has been linked to damage to normal neural progenitor cells and oligodendrocytes [39]. Increased neurotoxicity is associated with intrathecal administration as opposed to intravenous delivery, as well as higher doses. In addition, corticosteroids, which are often used in cancer treatment, can exacerbate neurotoxic effects of chemotherapeutic agents [40].

Neuropsychological and adaptive outcomes in children

The literature documenting neuropsychological late effects in children treated for brain tumors is extensive [23, 41–43]. In survivors of childhood brain tumors, studies have consistently identified younger age at diagnosis and higher intensity of treatment as contributors to increased risk of developing neurocognitive deficits and learning disabilities. Recent studies document the added contribution of hydrocephalus and other medical complications as well as tumor location [44, 45]. For adults, neurological complications and associated cognitive impairments vary depending on the location, size, and degree of invasiveness of the tumor.

Understanding late effects of tumors and their treatment (Table 13b.4) requires an appreciation of developmental factors. Brain development is a dynamic, interactive and adaptive process that unfolds over time [46]. Children who sustain a brain injury continue to develop in the context of the effects of that injury, which can affect multiple systems and processes over time. Skills that are yet to be developed can be compromised by early injury and processes undergoing rapid development are more vulnerable [23]. Late effects of injury can emerge over time as specific developmental stages and contexts demand mastery of more complex tasks and behaviors. Brain-related factors such as location of tumor, treatments, associated complications, and genetic differences need to be considered along with developmental factors such as age at diagnosis/treatment and time since treatment, as well as contextual factors including family functioning, educational resources, social/cultural influences, and community supports. There is an additional factor that needs to be integrated into this complex equation when dealing with children with medical disorders. As a result of medical advances, treatment protocols have changed substantially over time such that survivors of childhood brain tumors who are now adults were exposed to very different treatments with different long-term toxicity implications. Consequently, the additional time factor related to the epoch of treatment is highly relevant. For example, radiation is now avoided in the treatment of brain tumors in children with neurofibromatosis-1, due to their genetic predisposition for developing tumors which is exacerbated by ionizing radiation, as well as because of their increased risk of vascular

Table 13b.4. Late effects of brain tumor treatments.

Treatment	Late effects
Neurosurgery	Neurological/sensory deficits Endocrine dysfunction Changes to physical appearance Cerebellar mutism syndrome Neuropsychological deficits Psychological adjustment issues
Radiation	Cerebral white matter damage – leukoencephalopathy Vascular changes (Moyamoya syndrome) Endocrine dysfunction Hearing loss Bone growth abnormality Infertility Vision problems (cataracts) Secondary malignancy Neuropsychological deficits Psychosocial problems
Chemotherapy	Cerebral white matter damage – leukoencephalopathy Endocrine dysfunction Seizures Hearing loss (particularly with platinum agents) Neuropathy/encephalopathy Cerebellar symptoms Neuropsychological deficits

abnormalities such as Moyamoya syndrome [47]. Furthermore, newer chemotherapy treatment protocols have been shown to be effective in the management of low-grade gliomas, thus reducing the need for radiation therapy. This consideration is critical in evaluating the research literature on the long-term neuropsychological sequelae of childhood brain tumors. Survivors treated with more aggressive treatments and higher radiation doses will show more adverse outcomes. For example, in a follow-up study of children treated for medulloblastoma between 1980 and 1989, survivors were evaluated 10 years after treatment. These children were treated with higher doses of radiation than used in current protocols. Significant neuropsychological impairments were found in the areas of intellectual ability, executive functions, visual spatial ability, motor skills, and memory. Long-term adaptive outcomes were also compromised: limited independence and social difficulties were noted as well [48]. Neuropsychological outcomes for very young children (under age 3 years) diagnosed with brain tumors have been documented to be poor; almost 75% of these patients treated with craniospinal radiation had IQ scores less than 70 on follow up [49]. However, these data need to be interpreted cautiously when considering outcomes of children being treated currently due to treatment innovations that avoid or defer radiation.

Brain tumor location is an important factor in outcome, in addition to age and type of treatment. Supratentorial tumors are associated with more significant compromise in neurocognitive functions and overall IQ [50]. There is some evidence that tumors in the third ventricle region are associated with memory deficits [51] secondary to possible involvement of the medial temporal lobe, fornix, and mammillary bodies in this particular location. Studies of children treated for craniopharyngioma have demonstrated problems with memory, organizational skills, and behavioral regulation [52, 53]. Deficits in cognitive and adaptive skills are reported in children with cerebellar tumors who were treated with only surgery [54]. The role of the cerebellum in cognitive processing is beginning to be elucidated as sophisticated techniques have documented pathways between the cerebellum and the frontal lobes [55, 56]. This work has particular relevance in childhood brain tumors given that a substantial proportion occur in the posterior fossa. The cerebellum begins to form early on in embryonic development, but its development is protracted, continuing to some months after birth; consequently, it is more vulnerable to abnormalities in development, including abnormal cell proliferation [57].

Children treated for posterior fossa tumors with craniospinal radiation demonstrate decrease in intelligence over time as well as relative compromise of specific functions in the areas of attention, working memory, speed of processing, academic achievement, and memory [58, 59]. Differences in pattern of deficits noted in children treated for cerebellar tumors can be related to tumor location within the cerebellum, with nonverbal deficits more commonly noted with left cerebellar hemisphere location. Affective disturbance and language problems have been associated with location in the vermis [60]. However, lateralizing findings are not always found [54], perhaps because lesion specificity can be difficult to ascertain, particularly in children with more invasive tumors who require extensive treatment. Although there is good evidence that the decline in IQ scores is related to effects of radiation therapy through damage to developing white matter, deficits in specific cognitive domains have been linked to direct effects of tumor or treatment on cerebellar pathways. Schmahman and Sherman have proposed that the cerebellum integrates and modulates behaviors through circuits and feedback loops linking the cerebellum, frontal lobe, temporal lobe and limbic system [61]. In a recent review of neurocognitive late effects of posterior fossa tumors, Cantelmi et al. argue that studies have attributed these late effects almost exclusively to the impact of radiation, even though in some studies children who do not receive radiation also demonstrate some cognitive deficits [62]. They note that the neurocognitive late effects experienced by children treated for posterior fossa tumors are not exclusively attributable to cortical damage from radiation therapy but are also related to disruption of cerebellar circuits which can have a significant effect on neurocognitive function.

Characteristic deficits

As in many areas of pediatric neuropsychology, the focus has turned from assessment of only IQ to identifying underlying cognitive deficits, specific neuropathological underpinnings, and effects of development. In addition, current studies are driven more by theory, seeking to identify the impact of brain tumors and treatment on brain development and specific functions. Impairments in fundamental cognitive processes of *working memory*, *attention*, and *processing speed* have consistently emerged in studies of children treated for brain tumors such that the concept of a core set of deficits has been proposed [63]. It is hypothesized that it is the compromise of these basic processes secondary to tumor and treatment (particularly at a young age) that constrains development of intellectual ability and academic achievement over time. The underlying pathophysiology is not well understood although the effects of radiation have received a great deal of study. As stated above, systems undergoing rapid change or those with a more protracted developmental course are most vulnerable to insult. Therefore, it is not unexpected that functions supported by tertiary, multi-modal association cortical areas (frontal, parietal-temporal regions) would be more affected in children. A recent diffusion tensor imaging study of children treated for medulloblastoma with radiation (whole brain dose delivered ranging from 23.4 to 40 Gy) found that white matter fractional anisotropy was more severely reduced in the frontal than in the parietal lobes [64]. These findings suggest that radiosensitivity of brain structures may vary by location and stage of development, as well as by dose.

Attention

Attention deficits in children treated for brain tumors differ from some of the classic symptoms of attention deficit disorder in that problems with sustained attention and slow reaction times seem more prevalent, as opposed to fundamental deficits in inhibitory control [65]. The children who demonstrate attention problems tend to encounter social difficulties as well [66]. Researchers at St. Jude Children's Research Hospital have focused on identifying the specific impact of radiation therapy on attentional processes. They demonstrate that radiation affects the development of normal white matter and that decreases in white matter volume are associated with neurocognitve decline and impairment in fundamental processes of attention [67]. Other factors contributing to attentional impairment in addition to radiation include tumor location and radiation of central structures [68]. Attention deficits are associated with lower adaptive functioning overall [69].

Working memory

Working memory deficits have been consistently identified in children treated for brain tumors, with more severe deficits found in children treated at a younger age [44, 58]. In a recent study of memory function in survivors of childhood brain tumors, verbal learning was noted to be slower but retention was less affected and working memory was more compromised than long-term memory [50]. Over the course of development, working memory capacity expands in concert with stages in brain maturation and more complex working memory skills continue to develop in adolescence, whereas less change is seen in recognition memory [70]. It is likely that the impact of early insult will become more salient in adolescence as demands for more efficient and higher-order processing of information expand.

Speed of information processing

Processing speed encompasses concepts of speed and efficiency of the use of information in cognitive and motor output tasks. It is supported by a complex, distributed frontal subcortical network [38]. Deficits in speed and efficiency of information processing are common in children and adults with any kind of brain lesion, and have been consistently documented in the case of brain tumors [71, 72]. In many studies, this construct is typically assessed by the Processing Speed subtests of the Wechsler scales, though the concept encompasses a much broader set of skills from the quite basic (inspection time, simple reaction time) to the more complex (speed of decision-making on multi-faceted, multi-dimensional tasks). In a cohort of children treated for posterior fossa tumors, Mabbot and collaborators compared performance on tests of sustained attention, processing speed and working memory of children with posterior fossa tumors treated with surgery and radiation and report that information-processing speed appears to be compromised by both cranial radiation and surgical complications [71]. It is not surprising that processing speed would be highly vulnerable to brain insult because disruptions at any level of this complex frontal subcortical network can lead to cognitive deficits. The issue of processing speed is quite critical for the developing brain and children's ability to acquire new information. Deficits in speed of processing can interfere with the ability to link information across modalities, integrate material in a timely manner and keep pace with rate of presentation of material. Consequently, it is not unexpected that early deficits in speed of processing can interfere with learning required to maintain level of intelligence over the course of development.

Psychosocial and adaptive function

Children treated for brain tumors can encounter significant psychosocial adjustment issues. Similar to children who have to deal with chronic or other life-threatening illness, families face complex challenges in coping with medical procedures and extended treatment, disruption to family life, and absence from school. Specific psychological problems can arise and these are more likely to be in the domain of internalizing disorders and social skills [73]. As compared to survivors of other childhood cancers, survivors of CNS tumors encounter not only more educational problems, but also more difficulties establishing or maintaining friendships [74, 75]. The quality of social relationships in children surviving brain tumors is receiving increased attention as it is recognized that friendships and social support are critical for positive adjustment and overall health. An ongoing multi-site study of peer relationships in children with brain tumors indicates that these children are at particular risk for social isolation and peer victimization [76].

Role of neuropsychological assessment

Comprehensive neuropsychological evaluation and follow-up is a critical component of care for the child diagnosed with a brain tumor. Monitoring of the effects of the illness on development over the short and long term is needed to assist with ongoing medical management and to develop targeted intervention plans. The current standard of care includes comprehensive assessment of long-term effects [77]. Periodic assessments, particularly at times of significant transition in development, are important given that neuropsychological issues emerge over time in response to specific environmental and developmental challenges. Neuropsychological evaluation needs to include assessment of specific cognitive processes as well as overall intellectual ability and academic achievement. In many instances, IQ and basic scores in academic skills may be in the average range, yet the child can have major deficits functioning in the classroom or keeping up with academic challenges. Even subtle deficits can compromise academic performance and adaptive function. A whole-child approach that includes attention to the family and social context is needed to generate a risk-responsive intervention plan.

Management and interventions

The goal of the management plan is to optimize neuropsychological and adaptive outcomes by modifying the match between the child's needs and the developmental challenges being faced. The intervention plan needs to be risk-responsive and address the multiple systems and contexts. Interventions for children treated for brain tumors are developed for the educational and home setting; plans also need to consider the long term and provide recommendations to manage future challenges, such as the transition to adulthood. Interventions for children are implemented primarily in the educational setting. Consequently, consultation with educators and ongoing monitoring of implementation of services are critical in fostering understanding of the individual child's needs and consistent provision of required supports. Teachers benefit from education related to the impact of brain tumors and treatment such that they can adapt their classroom and teaching methods effectively. School consultation programs, such as Hospital Education Advocacy Liaisons (HEAL) at Lucile Packard Children's Hospital or the School Liaison Program at the Dana-Farber Cancer

Institute, provide valuable services in this regard. An intervention plan can include direct services, such as physical, occupational, and speech/language therapy as well as services to manage sensory impairments. Recommendations to address specific neurobehavioral deficits can vary from supportive tutoring to major redesign of the curriculum, learning goals, and progress benchmarks. Strategies and techniques that support executive function skills can be very useful and need to be adapted to the developmental status of the child as well as contextual demands [78]. Treatment plans also need to include interventions to manage social and psychological late effects. Individual and family therapy focusing on enhancing coping skills and teaching effective strategies for psychological symptoms is often recommended. The importance of supporting social networks and social skills is more widely recognized. Social skills groups as well as participation in structured group activities such as camps for childhood cancer survivors can serve to address some of the social problems experienced by survivors of brain tumors. The effectiveness of social skills interventions is being evaluated [79].

Psychopharmacological interventions are important in the management of attentional dysfunction and other neurobehavioral symptoms. Stimulant medication has been used with good effect in children and adolescents treated for brain tumors [80–83]. Fatigue, arousal deficits, or mood problems can be treated with psychopharmacological interventions as well.

Cognitive remediation approaches developed from rehabilitation programs for traumatic brain injury can be useful. Behavioral techniques that focus on teaching skills, remediating specific functions, and modifying the context can all be components of an intervention plan. The Cognitive Remediation Program (CRP) developed by Butler and colleagues is currently undergoing Phase III studies across seven centers [84, 85]. The CRP has three components: an adaptation of techniques used for brain injury rehabilitation to address attentional processes, special educational supports to teach metacognitive strategies, and cognitive behavioral methods to manage problems with distractibility. Findings from a clinical trial assessing the efficacy of the intervention noted improvements in academic functioning. In addition, children participating in the training learned metacognitive strategies and their parents reported improvements in attention. Improvements were not found on tests of neurocognitive processes, however. The investigators plan further work on examining factors that contribute to improvements in specific cohorts of participants. The program involves a time-intensive intervention that presents challenges for implementation across sites due to issues of compliance and the significant investment required on the part of families and therapists. Further work is needed in this area and this research highlights the need to develop assessment tools that integrate findings from cognitive neuroscience in the areas of executive functions and attention that reliably and validly assess these constructs in clinical trials. There is also a need for developmentally tailored programs of intervention that address multiple contexts within an overall comprehensive plan.

Adult brain tumors

The incidence of malignant gliomas increases with age, with the median age of diagnosis for glioblastoma of 64 years. There has been progress recently in understanding molecular pathogenesis of malignant gliomas and in the ability to classify these tumors using gene expression profiling. Advancements in these areas have contributed to innovations in the area of treatment such as the development of targeted molecular therapies. Tumors with the same morphology and pathological classification can have different gene-expression profiles and these genetic differences can provide clues as to responsiveness to different treatment modalities and other behaviors [18].

Treatment for brain tumors in adults is similar to that in children. The three major treatment approaches of surgery, radiation and chemotherapy are used to prolong survival. Benign tumors in adults (meningiomas) are treated with surgery if the tumor is in an accessible site. In some cases, meningiomas are found in the course of work-ups for other issues and, if not associated with symptoms, these may not require intervention beyond periodic surveillance. Radiotherapy is used when resection is not feasible. Most brain tumors in adults are metatastatic, occurring ten times more often than primary brain tumors. These tumors occur primarily in the context of lung and breast cancer and melanoma. Patients are treated with surgery and often whole brain radiation in addition [86]. A substantial proportion of these tumors are not surgically resectable [6]. Overall survival is poor, with life expectancy of 1 year or less [86, 87]. Survival rates for primary neuroepithelial tumors in adults vary with respect to tumor histology and age of the patient. Younger patients with low-grade tumors, small tumor size, and greater extent of tumor resection have a more favorable prognosis. Higher-grade tumors, older age, and neurological impairments are associated with poor prognosis. Glioblastoma multiforme is the most common neuroepithelial tumor in adults and survival is 12 to 15 months with optimal treatment [18]. Current treatment regimens include maximal surgical resection, radiation therapy, and adjuvant chemotherapy with temozolomide [34] or carmustine wafers [18]. New therapies for malignant gliomas such as molecular therapies and antiangiogenic agents are currently under investigation.

Neuropsychological issues in adult brain tumors

Evidence of cognitive dysfunction is seen in most patients diagnosed with brain tumors [88]. The types of deficits seen are similar to those encountered in patients who suffer strokes or traumatic brain injury though tend to be less severe and more diffuse than those associated with these sudden-onset events. Neurological and neuropsychological deficits can occur due to direct effects of the tumor or tumor progression on brain function, damage from surgery, toxicities of treatment (radiation therapy, chemotherapy), effects of other medications (anti-epileptic drugs, steroids), impact of associated complications (seizures, vascular events, metabolic disturbances), and psychological factors [89]. Cognitive deficits can be related to the site and volume of the tumor as well as its degree of malignancy. In addition to focal neurological deficits, patients experience problems with working memory, focused and divided attention, mental flexibility, and memory. Higher frequency of seizures and use of anti-epileptic medications are associated with increased deficits in information-processing speed, psychomotor functioning, executive functions, and working memory capacity [90]. Fatigue, pain, and sensorimotor deficits contribute to cognitive dysfunction since patients need to expend more effort to sustain cognitive tasks, while at the same time they have limited energy and stamina.

Neuropsychological assessment plays an important role in the evaluation of adult patients with brain tumors. Decline in cognitive functioning can be an early sign of progression of tumor [91, 92], whereas improvements in neurocognitive status can hallmark response to therapy and improved survival [90, 93]. Consequently, reason for referral for neuropsychological assessment can include evaluation of cognitive functioning to ascertain effects of tumor and treatments, to document improvements or decline in response to treatment, to direct rehabilitation strategies and patient/family counseling, to assess adaptive function, psychological adjustment, and quality of life, and to document response to interventions/rehabilitation. For patients with lower-grade tumors with more favorable prognoses, assessment of neuropsychological status can help guide ongoing medical management and cognitive, psychiatric, and psychosocial interventions that can promote optimal quality of life and adjustment. For patients with malignant tumors, functional gains, particularly in motor independence, can be achieved with individualized rehabilitation programs and these gains are associated with improved survival [87]. Adult studies of multidisciplinary cognitive rehabilitation demonstrate that issues are complex and treatments need to be individualized.

A recent review of the evidence supporting different methods to improve cognitive function or prevent decline in adult patients with brain tumors notes that the literature has focused primarily on documenting cognitive deficits, with few studies devoted to prevention or rehabilitation. Most studies have not used randomized clinical trial designs but some degree of efficacy is reported. Small sample size, unsophisticated and underpowered statistical designs, less sensitive assessment tools, and inability to assess practice effects compromise findings from these studies. A large-scale clinical trial of a cognitive rehabilitation program is under way [94].

Problems with fatigue and concentration are frequent in adults with brain tumors and treatment with stimulants can be useful [95]. In addition, preliminary evidence for improvements in memory and concentration as well as mood have been reported with donepezil, although randomized, double-blinded, placebo-controlled clinical trials are still needed [96]. Patients can also suffer from depression and benefit from psychiatric intervention and antidepressants [18].

Future research directions

Efforts to reduce the toxicity of treatments continue to evolve and prevention of late effects remains a most important goal, in conjunction with the development of effective cures. Current advances in diagnosis and treatment include new techniques for drug delivery, more fine-tuned stratification of risk based on molecular biology, enhancement of tumor response to treatment, reduction of toxicity to specific cells in the brain with anti-inflammatory agents, and use of novel therapies such as antiangiogenic agents, immunotherapy and gene therapy [32, 97]. The impact of these advances on the developing brain will need to be carefully studied. It will be important to include evaluation of neuropsychological and adaptive outcomes as these new techniques are incorporated into treatment protocols. In addition, continued long-term follow-up of survivors of childhood brain tumors is indicated given that these survivors will be facing the developmental challenges of adulthood with neuropsychological and medical vulnerabilities that can have an effect on overall functioning over the lifespan. Future research will need to employ more sophisticated methodology as the complex interactions among multiple factors in outcomes become clear. Neuropsychological outcomes vary widely, especially in children, and future investigations will need to identify factors promoting resilience in particular individuals to help guide development of intervention strategies. Advances in the understanding of genetic polymorphisms and individual host factors as well as of the impact of social/family influences will contribute significantly to the design of studies and interventions of the future [98].

Acknowledgement

Supported in part by the Stop and Shop Pediatric Brain Tumor Program.

References

1. CBTRUS. Statistical Report: Primary Brain Tumors in the United States, 2000–2004: Central Brain Tumor Registry of the United States; 2008.

2. Baldwin RT, Preston-Martin S. Epidemiology of brain tumors in childhood – a review. *Toxicol Appl Pharmacol* 2004;**199**(2):118–31.

3. Rees J. Neurological oncology. *Medicine (Baltimore)* 2004;**32**(10):75–9.

4. Wrensch M, Minn Y, Chew T, Bondy M, Berger MS. Epidemiology of primary brain tumors: current concepts and review of the literature. *Neuro Oncol* 2002;**4**(4): 278–99.

5. Blaney SM, Kun LE, Hunter J, Rorke-Adams LB, Lau C, Strother D, et al. Tumors of the central nervous system. In Pizzo PA, Poplack DG, eds. *Principles and Practice of Pediatric Oncology*, 5th edn. Philadelphia: Lippincott Williams & Wilkins; 2006: 787–863.

6. Buckner JC, Brown PD, O'Neill BP, Meyer FB, Wetmore CJ, Uhm JH. Central nervous system tumors. *Mayo Clin Proc* 2007;**82**(10):1271–86.

7. Louis DN, Ohgaki H, Wiestler OD, Cavenee WK, eds. *WHO Classification of tumours of the central nervous system.* Lyon: IARC; 2007.

8. Louis DN, Ohgaki H, Wiestler OD, Cavenee WK, Burger PC, Jouvet A, et al. The 2007 WHO classification of tumours of the central nervous system. *Acta Neuropathol* 2007;**114**(2):97–109.

9. Nakamura M, Shimada K, Ishida E, Higuchi T, Nakase H, Sakaki T, et al. Molecular pathogenesis of pediatric astrocytic tumors. *Neuro Oncol* 2007;**9**(2):113–23.

10. Grimmer MR, Weiss WA. Childhood tumors of the nervous system as disorders of normal development. *Curr Opin Pediatr* 2006;**18**(6):634–8.

11. Bannykh S. Pathology and classification of tumors of the nervous system. In Baehring JM, Peipmeier JM, eds. *Brain Tumors: Practical Guide to Diagnosis and Treatment.* New York: Informa Health Care; 2007: 133–58.

12. Partap S, Fisher PG. Update on new treatments and developments in childhood brain tumors. *Curr Opin Pediatr* 2007;**19**(6):670–4.

13. Riefenberger G, Blumcke I, Pietsch T, Paulus W. Pathology and classification of tumors of the nervous system. In Tonn JC, Westphal M, Rutka JT, Grossman SA, eds. *Neuro-Oncology of CNS Tumors.* Berlin: Springer; 2006: 3–72.

14. Tonn JC, Westphal M, Rutka JT, Grossman SA, eds. *Neuro-Oncology of CNS Tumors.* Berlin: Springer; 2006.

15. Van den Bent M. Astrocytic tumors. In Baehring JM, Piepmeier JM, eds. *Brain Tumors: Practical Guide to Diagnosis and Treatment.* New York: Informa Health Care; 2007: 159–92.

16. Packer RJ, MacDonald T, Vezina G. Central nervous system tumors. *Pediatr Clin North Am* 2008;**55**(1):121.

17. Westphal M, Lamszus K, Tonn JC. Meningiomas and meningeal tumors. In Tonn JC, Westphal M, Rutka JT, Grossman SA, eds. *Neuro-Oncology of CNS Tumors.* Berlin: Springer; 2006: 82–101.

18. Wen PY, Kesari S. Malignant gliomas in adults. *N Engl J Med.* 2008;**359**(5):492–507.

19. Black P, Hogan SH. *Living with a Brain Tumor.* New York: Henry Holt; 2006.

20. Reulecke BC, Erker CG, Fiedler BJ, Niederstadt T-U, Kurlemann G. Brain tumors in children: Initial symptoms and their influence on the time span between symptom onset and diagnosis. *J Child Neurol* 2008;**23**(2):178–83.

21. von Hoff K, Kieffer V, Habrand JL, Kalifa C, Dellatolas G, Grill J. Impairment of intellectual functions after surgery and posterior fossa irradiation in children with ependymoma is related to age and neurologic complications. *BMC Cancer* 2008;**8**:15.

22. Crawford JR, MacDonald TJ, Packer RJ. Medulloblastoma in childhood: new biological advances. *Lancet Neurol* 2007;**6**(12):1073–85.

23. Dennis M, Spiegler BJ, Riva D, MacGregor DL. Neuropsychological outcome. In Walker D, Perilongo G, Punt CJA, Taylor RE, eds. *Brain and Spinal Tumors of Childhood.* London: Arnold; 2004: 213–27.

24. Pollack IF. Neurobehavioral abnormalities after posterior fossa surgery in children. *Int Rev Psychiatry* 2001;**13**(4):302–12.

25. Robertson PL, Muraszko KM, Holmes EJ, Sposto R, Packer RJ, Gajjar A, et al. Incidence and severity of postoperative cerebellar mutism syndrome in children with medulloblastoma: a prospective study by the Children's Oncology Group. *J Neurosurg* 2006;**105**(6 Suppl):444–51.

26. Huber JF, Bradley K, Spiegler BJ, Dennis M. Long-term effects of transient cerebellar mutism after cerebellar astrocytoma or medulloblastoma tumor resection in childhood. *Childs Nerv Syst* 2006;**22**(2 (Print)):132–8.

27. Knisely JPS. Principles of radiation therapy. In Baehring JM, Piepmeier JM, eds. *Brain Tumors: Practical Guide to Diagnosis and Treatment.* New York: Informa Health Care; 2007: 17–42.

28. Yock TI, Tarbell NJ. Technology insight: proton beam radiotherapy for treatment in pediatric brain tumors. *Nat Clin Pract Oncol.* 2004;**1**(2):97–103.

29. Merchant TE, Hua C, Shukla H, Ying X, Nill S, Oelfke U. Proton versus photon radiotherapy for common pediatric brain tumors: comparison of models of dose characteristics and their relationship to cognitive function. *Pediatr Blood Cancer* 2008;**51**(1):110–7.

30. Kaye DL. Pediatric brain tumors. In Coffey CE, Brumback RA, eds. *Pediatric Neuropsychiatry.* Philadelphia: Lippincott Williams & Wilkins; 2006:565–86.

31. Sarkissian V. The sequelae of cranial irradiation on human cognition. *Neurosci Lett* 2005;**382**(1–2):118–23.

32. Monje ML, Mizumatsu S, Fike JR, Palmer TD. Irradiation induces neural precursor-cell dysfunction. *Nat Med* 2002;**8**(9):955–62.

33. Brandes AA, Compostella A, Blatt V, Tosoni A. Glioblastoma in the elderly: current and future trends. *Crit Rev Oncol Hematol* 2006;**60**(3):256–66.

34. Gilbert MR, Armstrong TS. Management of patients with newly diagnosed malignant primary brain tumors with a focus on the evolving role of temozolomide. *Ther Clin Risk Manag* 2007;**3**(6):1027–33.

35. Packer RJ, Goldwein J, Nicholson HS, Vezina LG, Allen JC, Ris MD, et al. Treatment of children with medulloblastomas with reduced-dose craniospinal

radiation therapy and adjuvant chemotherapy: a Children's Cancer Group Study. *J Clin Oncol* 1999;**17**(7): 2127–36.

36. Marachelian A, Butturini A, Finlay J. Myeloablative chemotherapy with autologous hematopoietic progenitor cell rescue for childhood central nervous system tumors. *Bone Marrow Transplant* 2008;**41**(2): 167–72.

37. Ali-Osman F, Friedman HS, Antoun GR, Reardon D, Bigner DD, Buolamwini JK. Rational design and development of targeted brain tumor therapeutics. In Ail-Osman F, ed. *Contemporary Cancer Research: Brain Tumors*. Totowa, NJ: Humana Press; 2005: 359–81.

38. Ahles TA, Saykin AJ. Candidate mechanisms for chemotherapy-induced cognitive changes. *Nat Rev Cancer* 2007;**7**(3):192–201.

39. Dietrich J, Han R, Yang Y, Mayer-Proschel M, Noble M. CNS progenitor cells and oligodendrocytes are targets of chemotherapeutic agents in vitro and in vivo. *J Biol* 2006;**5**(7):22.

40. Mrakotsky C, Waber D. Chemotherapy agents for treatment of acute lymphoblastic leukemia. In Bellinger D, ed. *Human Developmental Neurotoxicology*. New York: Taylor and Francis; 2006: 131–47.

41. Butler RW, Haser JK. Neurocognitive effects of treatment for childhood cancer. *Ment Retard Dev Disabil Res Rev* 2006;**12**(3):184–91.

42. Hoppe-Hirsch E, Renier D, Lellouch-Tubiana A, Sainte-Rose C, Pierre-Kahn A, Hirsch JF. Medulloblastoma in childhood: progressive intellectual deterioration. *Childs Nerv Syst* 1990;**6**(2):60–5.

43. Mulhern RK, Merchant TE, Gajjar A, Reddick WE, Kun LE. Late neurocognitive sequelae in survivors of brain tumours in childhood. *Lancet Oncol* 2004;**5**(7 (Print)):399–408.

44. Reimers TS, Ehrenfels S, Mortensen EL, Schmiegelow M, Sonderkaer S, Carstensen H, et al. Cognitive deficits in long-term survivors of childhood brain tumors: Identification of predictive factors. *Med Pediatr Oncol* 2003;**40**(1):26–34.

45. Roncadin C, Dennis M, Greenberg ML, Spiegler BJ. Adverse medical events associated with childhood cerebellar astrocytomas and medulloblastomas: natural history and relation to very long-term neurobehavioral outcome. *Childs Nerv Syst* 2008;**24**(9):995–1002.

46. Stiles J. *The Fundamentals of Brain Development: Integrating Nature and Nurture*. Cambridge, MA: Harvard University Press; 2008.

47. Ullrich NJ. Inherited disorders as a risk factor and predictor of neurodevelopmental outcome in pediatric cancer. *Dev Disabil Res Rev* 2008;**14**(3):229–37.

48. Maddrey AM, Bergeron JA, Lombardo ER, McDonald NK, Mulne AF, Barenberg PD, et al. Neuropsychological performance and quality of life of 10 year survivors of childhood medulloblastoma. *J Neurooncol* 2005;**72**(3): 245–53.

49. Fouladi M, Gilger E, Kocak M, Wallace D, Buchanan G, Reeves C, et al. Intellectual and functional outcome of children 3 years old or younger who have CNS malignancies. *J Clin Oncol* 2005;**23**(28):7152–60.

50. Reimers TS, Mortensen EL, Schmiegelow K. Memory deficits in long-term survivors of childhood brain tumors may primarily reflect general cognitive dysfunctions. *Pediatr Blood Cancer* 2007;**48**(2):205–12.

51. King TZ, Fennell EB, Williams L, Algina J, Boggs S, Crosson B, et al. Verbal memory abilities of children with brain tumors. *Child Neuropsychol* 2004;**10**(2): 76–88.

52. Carpentieri SC, Waber DP, Scott RM, Goumnerova LC, Kieran MW, Cohen LE, et al. Memory deficits among children with craniopharyngiomas. *Neurosurgery* 2001;**49**(5):1053–7; discussion 7–8.

53. Sands SA, Milner JS, Goldberg J, Mukhi V, Moliterno JA, Maxfield C, et al. Quality of life and behavioral follow-up study of pediatric survivors of craniopharyngioma. *J Neurosurg* 2005;**103**(4 Suppl): 302–11.

54. Beebe DW, Ris MD, Armstrong FD, Fontanesi J, Mulhern RK, Holmes E, et al. Cognitive and adaptive outcome in low-grade pediatric cerebellar astrocytomas: evidence of diminished cognitive and adaptive functioning in National Collaborative Research Studies (CCG 9891/POG 9130). *J Clin Oncol* 2005;**23**(22): 5198–204.

55. Dum RP, Strick PL. An unfolded map of the cerebellar dentate nucleus and its projections to the cerebral cortex. *J Neurophysiol* 2003;**89**(1):634–9.

56. Middleton FA, Strick PL. The cerebellum: an overview. *Trends Neurosci* 1998;**21**(9):367–9.

57. Scotting PJ, Appleby VJ. Neuroembryology. In Walker DA, Perilongo G, Punt JAG, Taylor RE, eds. *Brain and Spinal Turmors of Childhood*. London: Arnold; 2004: 50–66.

58. Ris MD, Packer RJ, Goldwein J, Jones-Wallace D, Boyett JM. Intellectual outcome after reduced-dose radiation therapy plus adjuvant chemotherapy for medulloblastoma: a Children's Cancer Group study. *J Clin Oncol* 2001;**19**(15):3470–6.

59. Spiegler BJ, Bouffet E, Greenberg ML, Rutka JT, Mabbott DJ. Change in neurocognitive functioning after treatment with cranial radiation in childhood. *J Clin Oncol* 2004;**22**(4):706–13.

60. Riva D, Pantaleoni C, Devoti M, Saletti V, Nichelli F, Giorgi C. Late neuropsychological and behavioural outcome of children surgically treated for craniopharyngioma. *Childs Nerv Syst* 1998;**14**:170–84.

61. Schmahmann JD, Sherman JC. The cerebellar cognitive affective syndrome. *Brain* 1998;**121** (Pt 4):561–79.

62. Cantelmi D, Schweizer TA, Cusimano MD. Role of the cerebellum in the neurocognitive sequelae of treatment of tumours of the posterior fossa: an update. *Lancet Oncol* 2008;**9**(6):569–76.

63. Mulhern RK, White HA, Glass JO, Kun LE, Leigh L, Thompson SJ, et al. Attentional functioning and white matter integrity among survivors of malignant brain tumors of childhood. *J Int Neuropsychol Soc* 2004;**10**(2): 180–9.

64. Qiu D, Kwong DL, Chan GC, Leung LH, Khong PL. Diffusion tensor magnetic resonance imaging finding of discrepant fractional anisotropy between the frontal and parietal lobes after whole-brain irradiation in childhood medulloblastoma survivors: reflection of regional white matter radiosensitivity? *Int J Radiat Oncol Biol Phys* 2007;**69**(3):846–51.

65. Merchant TE, Kiehna EN, Miles MA, Zhu J, Xiong X, Mulhern RK. Acute effects of irradiation on cognition: changes in attention on a computerized continuous performance test during radiotherapy in pediatric patients with localized primary brain tumors. *Int J Radiat Oncol Biol Phys* 2002;**53**(5):1271–8.

66. Patel SK, Lai-Yates JJ, Anderson JW, Katz ER. Attention dysfunction and parent reporting in children with brain tumors. *Pediatr Blood Cancer* 2007;**49**(7):970–4.

67. Reddick WE, White HA, Glass JO, Wheeler GC, Thompson SJ, Gajjar A, et al. Developmental model relating white matter volume to neurocognitive deficits in pediatric brain tumor survivors. *Cancer* 2003;**97**(10):2512–9.

68. Kiehna EN, Mulhern RK, Li C, Xiong X, Merchant TE. Changes in attentional performance of children and young adults with localized primary brain tumors after conformal radiation therapy. *J Clin Oncol* 2006;**24**(33):5283–90.

69. Papazoglou A, King TZ, Morris RD, Morris MK, Krawiecki NS. Attention mediates radiation's impact on daily living skills in children treated for brain tumors. *Pediatr Blood Cancer* 2008;**50**(6):1253–7.

70. Conklin HM, Luciana M, Hooper CJ, Yarger RS. Working memory performance in typically developing children and adolescents. *Dev Neuropsychol* 2007;**31**(1):103–28.

71. Mabbott DJ, Penkman L, Witol A, Strother D, Bouffet E. Core neurocognitive functions in children treated for posterior fossa tumors. *Neuropsychology* 2008;**22**(2):159–68.

72. Stargatt R, Rosenfeld JV, Maixner W, Ashley D. Multiple factors contribute to neuropsychological outcome in children with posterior fossa tumors. *Dev Neuropsychol* 2007;**32**(2):729–48.

73. Fuemmeler BF, Elkin TD, Mullins LL. Survivors of childhood brain tumors: Behavioral, emotional, and social adjustment. *Clin Psychol Rev* 2002;**22**(4):547–86.

74. Vannatta K, Gerhardt CA, Wells RJ, Noll RB. Intensity of CNS treatment for pediatric cancer: prediction of social outcomes in survivors. *Pediatr Blood Cancer* 2007;**49**(5):716–22.

75. Barrera M, Shaw AK, Speechley KN, Maunsell E, Pogany L. Educational and social late effects of childhood cancer and related clinical, personal, and familial characteristics. *Cancer* 2005;**104**(8):1751–60.

76. Vannatta K, Fairclough F, Farkas-Patenaude A, Gerhardt C, Kupst M, Olshefski R, et al. Peer relationships of pediatric brain tumor survivors. Paper presented at *13th International Symposium on Pediatric Neuro-Oncology* 2008.

77. Duffner PK. Long-term effects of radiation therapy on cognitive and endocrine function in children with leukemia and brain tumors. *Neurologist* 2004;**10**(6): 293–310.

78. Mahone EM, Slomine B. Managing dysexecutive disorders. In Hunter SJ, Donders J, eds. *Pediatric Neuropsychological Intervention: A Critical Review of Science and Practice.* Cambridge: Cambridge University Press; 2007:314–37.

79. Barakat LP, Hetzke JD, Foley B, Carey ME, Gyato K, Phillips PC. Evaluation of a Social-Skills Training Group Intervention With Children Treated for Brain Tumors: A Pilot Study. *J Pediatr Psychol* 2003;**28**(5):299–307.

80. Conklin HM, Khan R, Reddick WE, Lawford J, Howard SC, Morris B, et al. Medication for learning-impaired survivors of childhood cancer. Paper presented at *13th International Symposium on Pediatric Neuro-Oncology.* 2008.

81. Conklin HM, Khan RB, Reddick WE, Helton S, Brown R, Howard SC, et al. Acute neurocognitive response to methylphenidate among survivors of childhood cancer: a randomized, double-blind, cross-over trial. *J Pediat Psychol* 2007;**32**(9):1127–39.

82. Daly BP, Brown RT. Scholarly literature review: management of neurocognitive late effects with stimulant medication. *J Pediatr Psychol* 2007;**32**(9): 1111–26.

83. Thompson SJ, Leigh L, Christensen R, Xiong X, Kun LE, Heideman RL, et al. Immediate neurocognitive effects of methylphenidate on learning-impaired survivors of childhood cancer. *J Clin Oncol* 2001;**19**(6):1802–8.

84. Butler RW, Copeland DR. Attentional processes and their remediation in children treated for cancer: a literature review and the development of a therapeutic approach. *J Int Neuropsychol Soc* 2002;**8**(1):115–24.

85. Butler RW, Copeland DR, Fairclough DL, Mulhern RK, Katz ER, Kazak AE, et al. A multicenter, randomized clinical trial of a cognitive remediation program for childhood survivors of a pediatric malignancy. *J Consult Clin Psychol* 2008;**76**(3):367–78.

86. Richards GM, Khuntia D, Mehta MP. Therapeutic management of metastatic brain tumors. *Crit Rev Oncol Hematol* 2007;**61**(1):70–8.

87. Tang V, Rathbone M, Park Dorsay J, Jiang S, Harvey D. Rehabilitation in primary and metastatic brain tumours: impact of functional outcomes on survival. *J Neurol* 2008;**255**(6):820–7.

88. Tucha O, Smely C, Preier M, Lange KW. Cognitive deficits before treatment among patients with brain tumors. *Neurosurgery* 2000;**47**(2):324.

89. Taphoorn MJ, Klein M. Cognitive deficits in adult patients with brain tumours. *Lancet Neurol* 2004;**3**(3):159–68.

90. Klein M, Engelberts NH, van der Ploeg HM, Kasteleijn-Nolst Trenite DG, Aaronson NK, Taphoorn MJ, et al. Epilepsy in low-grade gliomas: the impact on cognitive function and quality of life. *Ann Neurol* 2003;**54**(4):514–20.

91. Armstrong CL, Goldstein B, Shera D, Ledakis GE, Tallent EM. The predictive value of longitudinal neuropsychologic assessment in the early detection of brain tumor recurrence. *Cancer* 2003;**97**(3):649–56.

92. Meyers CA, Hess KR. Multifaceted end points in brain tumor clinical trials: cognitive deterioration precedes MRI progression. *Neuro-Oncology* 2003;**5**(2):89–95.

93. Meyers CA, Hess KR, Yung WK, Levin VA. Cognitive function as a predictor of survival in patients with recurrent malignant glioma. *J Clin Oncol* 2000;**18**(3): 646–50.

94. Gehring K, Sitskoorn MM, Aaronson NK, Taphoorn MJ. Interventions for cognitive deficits in adults with brain tumours. *Lancet Neurol* 2008;**7**(6):548–60.

95. Meyers CA, Weitzner MA, Valentine AD, Levin VA. Methylphenidate therapy improves cognition, mood, and function of brain tumor patients. *J Clin Oncol* 1998;**16**(7):2522–7.

96. Shaw EG, Rosdhal R, D'Agostino RB, Jr., Lovato J, Naughton MJ, Robbins ME, et al. Phase II study of donepezil in irradiated brain tumor patients: effect on cognitive function, mood, and quality of life. *J Clin Oncol* 2006;**24**(9):1415–20.

97. Robertson PL. Advances in treatment of pediatric brain tumors. *NeuroRx* 2006;**3**(2):276–91.

98. Brouwers P. Commentary: study of the neurobehavioral consequences of childhood cancer: entering the genomic era? *J Pediatr Psychol* 2005;**30**(1):79–84.

99. McCarthy BJ (Principal Investigator) CBTRUS. Specific Requested Analysis, 2000–2004 Data. Central Brain Tumor Registry of the United States, July 2008.

100. Ries LAG, Melbert D, Krapcho M, Stinchcomb DG, Howlader N, Horner MJ, et al. SEER Cancer Statistics Review, 1975–2005. 2008 (cited based on November 2007 SEER data submission posted to the SEER web site, 2008); Available from: http://seer.cancer.gov/csr/1975_2005.

101. Punt JAG. Clinical syndromes. In Walker DA, Perilongo G, Punt JAG, Taylor RE, eds. *Brain and Spinal Tumors of Childhood.* London: Arnold; 2004: 99–106.

102. Ullrich NJ, Pomeroy SL. Pediatric brain tumors. *Neurol Clin* 2003;**21**(4):897–913.

Lifespan aspects of endocrine disorders

Geoffrey Tremont, Jennifer Duncan Davis and Christine Trask

Endocrine disorders across the lifespan

Endocrine disorders are a complex set of conditions resulting in abnormal hormonal release and regulation that can negatively impact growth and development, metabolism, and sexual functioning/reproduction. These disorders can arise at almost any point throughout the lifespan, from the prenatal period to old age. The effect of these conditions on the central nervous system may also vary from profound developmental disorders to subtle and possibly reversible cognitive impairments. In many cases, the mechanisms for cognitive and neurobehavioral effects of endocrine disorders are poorly understood.

Overview of the endocrine system

Table 14.1 presents the major anatomical structures of the endocrine system, their general function, and associated hormones. These structures regulate and release hormones in the body. The system is responsible for growth and development, reproduction, metabolism (energy production and storage), homeostasis, and responding to internal and external environmental changes. There are strong interactions between the endocrine, nervous, and immune systems. The pituitary gland and the hypothalamus are particularly important because they are involved in a feedback regulation of hormone production across the thyroid, adrenal, and gonadal axes. In general, a neural signal of imbalance in one of these endocrine systems leads to secretion of releasing factor from the hypothalamus, which triggers the pituitary gland to release a tropic hormone. The tropic hormone stimulates production and release of hormones from the specified endocrine gland. As a result, levels of circulating hormones normalize. This information feeds back to the hypothalamus and pituitary, which in turn inhibit further production of releasing factor and/or the tropic hormone. Disorders of the endocrine system typically result in hormone deficiency or excess and can involve lesion, injury, or dysfunction of any organ in the axis (e.g. hypothalamus-pituitary-thyroid). As will be seen in the following review, the most common cause of hormone deficiency is an autoimmune condition involving the endocrine gland (e.g. Hashimoto's thyroiditis, type I diabetes mellitus).

Thyroid disease

Hypothyroidism

Primary hypothyroidism is defined as elevated thyroid stimulating hormone (TSH) and low serum thyroid hormone concentrations, including thyroxine (T4) and triiodothyronine (T3; see Box 1). Subclinical, or mild, hypothyroidism is defined by an elevated serum TSH in the presence of normal serum thyroid hormone levels. Congenital hypothyroidism (CH) occurs in infancy and is generally identified and treated at birth. The disorder is relatively uncommon in young children and adolescence and becomes steadily more common with aging. In adults, the most common cause of hypothyroidism is Hashimoto's thyroiditis, an autoimmune form of thyroid disease. Antithyroglobulin antibodies are useful in evaluating autoimmune-related thyroid disease.

In early childhood, the prevalence of CH is approximately 1 in 3650 [1]. Very extreme forms of CH can lead to cretinism, which is manifested by failure of skeletal growth and development, and marked delays in intelligence [2]. In most cases, the disorder is detected at birth and immediately treated. Despite this, CH can have long-term cognitive effects. CH has been associated with lower scores on measures of intellectual functioning and motor skills. Risk factors for cognitive delay include severity of disease, as reflected by high serum TSH levels and pretreatment T4 levels [3]. Research has generally supported a positive correlation between aggressive treatment, particularly during the first year of life, and later intellectual abilities [4]. Moreover, severity of CH continues to be associated

Table 14.1. Primary endocrine structures, their functions, and associated hormones.

Endocrine structure	Primary function	Hormones
Anterior pituitary	Stimulate and inhibit hormone release from endocrine glands; works in conjunction with hypothalamus	Stimulating hormones – growth hormone, prolactin, follicle-stimulating; luteinizing hormone, adrenocorticotropin, thyroid-stimulating hormone
Posterior pituitary	Regulate blood vessels, childbirth and lactation	Vasopressin, oxytocin
Thyroid gland	Metabolism	Triiodothyronine (T3); thyroxine (T4)
Adrenal cortex	Response to stressors	Cortisol, aldosterone, DHEA
Pancreas	Regulate blood glucose level, digestion	Insulin, glucagon
Parathyroid glands	Calcium regulation	Parathyroid hormone
Ovaries and testes	Reproduction, growth of sex organs and secondary sex characteristics	Testosterone, estrogen, progesterone
Pineal	Circadian rhythms	Melatonin

with intellectual abilities and motor skills in young adulthood [5]. Rovet and Hepworth [6] and Alvarez et al. [7] also reported an association between attention deficits and higher circulating free T4 concentrations at the time of testing and with late normalization of T4 concentrations after the start of therapy. Behaviorally, CH has been associated with higher parent reports of inattention and aggression [4].

In adulthood, hypothyroidism is more common in women than in men, and the prevalence steadily increases with age [8]. Physical signs and symptoms of hypothyroidism include excessive fatigue, cold intolerance, dry skin, hair loss, menstrual irregularities, constipation, and weight loss. Psychiatric symptoms are often the presenting complaint in hypothyroidism, and there is significant symptom overlap between depression and hypothyroidism. For example, dysphoric mood, apathy, fatigue, diminished libido, and psychomotor retardation are commonly reported and may be misdiagnosed as depression. As such, laboratory data are essential to avoid misdiagnosis.

The most common neuropsychological deficits observed in hypothyroidism include mental slowing and long response latencies, diminished attention and concentration, impairments in learning and memory, and executive dysfunction [9]. Global cognitive deficits (i.e. dementia) may be seen in severe hypothyroidism. Language and motor skills are generally unaffected. Older adults may be more vulnerable to the cognitive effects of hypothyroidism, including delirium. Subclinical hypothyroidism may also be associated with mild cognitive deficits (see Davis and Tremont [10] for review) and may be a possible risk factor for age-related cognitive decline [11].

Despite the widely held belief that significant cognitive disturbance is associated with hypothyroidism, there are few comprehensive neuropsychological investigations of large groups of patients with this condition. Therefore, a clear neuropsychological profile and description of specific, associated neurological substrates/systems are relatively undefined at this time. Positron emission tomography (PET) techniques have shown relatively global, diffuse changes in blood flow and metabolism that appear to reverse with treatment [12]. There is some suggestion that the deficits in hypothyroidism occur secondary to frontal systems dysfunction. For example, Smith and Ain [13] demonstrated increased oxidative metabolism in the frontal lobes in patients with hypothyroidism that normalized following T4 treatment using P nuclear magnetic-resonance spectroscopy (MRS). Similarly, a functional MRI study showed deficits on a working memory task (N-Back task) that is mediated by frontoparietal regions. In that paradigm, patients with subclinical hypothyroidism performed more poorly than healthy controls, and their deficits reversed with thyroid hormone replacement [14]. There is some indication that there may be more central nervous system involvement with the autoimmune form of the disease as patients with Hashimoto's thyroiditis have been shown to have greater abnormalities in the frontal lobes on SPECT imaging than those without autoimmune etiologies to their thyroid disease [15]. Taken together, both cognitive and functional neuroimaging studies suggest that the cognitive deficits in hypothyroidism could be associated with frontal systems dysfunction, but the neural substrates/systems that underlie cognitive deficits in hypothyroidism remain poorly characterized.

Box 1: Hypothyroidism

- Signs and symptoms: fatigue, cold intolerance, dry skin, hair loss, menstrual irregularities, constipation, weight loss
- Neurobehavioral findings: slowed processing speed, decreased attention and concentration, executive dysfunction, and reduced learning and memory (non-amnestic profile); considerable overlap with depression; symptoms present in both overt and subclinical hypothyroidism
- Neuroimaging/neuroanatomical: relatively global, diffuse changes on functional neuroimaging (PET and SPECT); possibly frontal involvement (fMRI)
- Treatment and reversibility: improvement with treatment, but full reversibility uncommon
- Developmental variations: common endocrine disorder usually detected at birth and can be associated with lower IQ scores and poor motor skills despite treatment; more common with aging, and may be a contributor or risk factor to cognitive decline; rarely a cause of reversible dementia

Cognitive and mood symptoms tend to improve with treatment and normalization to a euthyroid state [10], although a few studies have produced negative treatment results or lack of significant improvement on a number of cognitive tests following stabilization of thyroid levels [16, 17]. In addition, in an analysis of 2781 cases of hypothyroidism, 14 individuals showed hypothyroidism-associated dementia, but only one case showed complete reversibility of cognitive deficits [18]. Despite the lack of complete reversibility, it appears that aspects of cognition respond to treatment [19] in younger and older adults, with improvements in mood and quality of life being less robust. The pattern of recovery is inconsistent, however, and complete recovery is uncertain.

Hyperthyroidism

Hyperthyroidism is a condition in which there is sustained overproduction of thyroid hormone by the thyroid gland, resulting in elevated levels of the circulating thyroid hormones (i.e. elevated T3 and T4; see Box 2). The most common underlying cause of hyperthyroidism is Graves' disease, an autoimmune disorder, which typically presents in the third to fourth decades. Although quite rare, the primary presentation of hyperthyroidism in childhood is also most commonly related to Graves' disease. The condition predominantly affects women (70–80%), who may experience weight loss despite increased appetite, heart palpitations/arrhythmias, tremor, excessive perspiration and heat intolerance, hyperactive reflexes, dyspnea, and warm, moist skin. Ophthalmic involvement is also associated with Graves' disease, presenting

as exophthalmos (i.e. bulging eyes). An important feature of the ophthalmopathy (i.e. eye disease) is that it can have a course that is independent of the thyroid gland dysfunction, probably reflecting the separate effects of the autoimmune disorder. The most common treatment of Graves' hyperthyroidism is radioactive iodine, which typically results in the individual initially becoming hypothyroid. Hypothyroidism is associated with a different set of physical, emotional, and cognitive symptoms (see section above).

Diagnosing Graves' disease is complicated by the behavioral nature of the symptoms. There is considerable overlap between the phenomenology of primary anxiety and hyperthyroidism. Because Graves' disease most commonly presents in young women who are otherwise quite healthy and who may be managing careers and family responsibilities, the condition is frequently misdiagnosed as stress-related. Therefore, many of these patients initially present to psychiatrists, psychologists, or other mental health professionals.

The majority of individuals with hyperthyroidism meet formal diagnostic criteria for anxiety disorders or major depressive episodes [20]. Some of the psychiatric symptoms associated with Graves' disease may be due to increased peripheral sympathetic tone that can frequently be relieved by beta-blockers. Survey studies of individuals with Graves' disease reveal cognitive and emotional changes associated with the acute hyperthyroid state as well as residual cognitive complaints and functional disability following treatment [21]. In addition, these studies show evidence of delay of diagnosis and treatment in over one-third of patients.

411

- Signs and symptoms: weight loss despite increased appetite, heart palpitations/arrhythmias, tremor, excessive perspiration and heat intolerance, hyperactive reflexes, dyspnea, and warm, moist skin, eye disease
- Neurobehavioral findings: decreased concentration, slowed reaction time, impaired complex visual processing and spatial organization abilities, and poor conceptual skills, considerable overlap with anxiety
- Neuroimaging/neuroanatomical: possibly frontal involvement
- Treatment and reversibility: most cases improve following treatment; may become hypothyroid
- Developmental variations: Rare in children and older adults; apathetic presentation possible in older adults

Individuals with hyperthyroidism often complain of cognitive impairments, such as memory and attentional difficulties. Objective evidence of cognitive problems is not consistently seen, although research on the topic is plagued by a variety of methodological problems. In addition, thyroid hormone levels are not consistently found to be associated with neuropsychological test performance in Graves' disease [22]. These inconsistencies are not surprising, given frequent symptom variability seen in autoimmune disorders. Studies that report cognitive deficits typically refer to decreased concentration, slowed reaction time, impaired complex visual processing and spatial organization abilities, and poor conceptual skills [20]. These deficits are not necessarily attributable to psychiatric symptomatology. There is some evidence of persisting cognitive impairment once individuals are euthyroid [23]. Very limited research with magnetic-resonance spectroscopy reveals prefrontal cortex abnormalities that normalize following treatment and return to euthyroidism [24].

Although relatively rare in older adults, hyperthyroidism in elderly individuals often presents with fewer overt symptoms or with apathy and decreased motivation as the prominent symptoms [25]. There is also evidence of dementia associated with hyperthyroidism that reverses following achievement of euthyroidism [26]. Mild or subclinical hyperthyroidism is associated with an increased risk of dementia, particularly in those with positive thyroid peroxidase antibodies [27].

Hashimoto's encephalopathy

Hashimoto's encephalopathy is a rare condition involving alteration in mental state, fluctuating level of consciousness, impaired attention, and behavior and personality changes (see Box 3). The condition can occur at any age, although the mean age of onset is between 45 and 55 years. For adults, females are approximately 5-times more likely to be affected than males. In the pediatric population, gender distribution is equivalent. There is no specific cognitive profile associated with Hashimoto's encephalopathy, although deficits can include memory and language impairment. The course of the condition often follows a relapsing and remitting or progressive pattern [28]. Stroke-like episodes and seizures are common. Hallucinations, delusions, and mood disturbance also frequently occur. Other autoimmune conditions can be associated with Hashimoto's encephalopathy, although interestingly overt thyroid disease is quite rare. Instead, individuals show abnormal elevations of anti-thyroid antibodies. Neuroimaging can show nonspecific findings of generalized atrophy and periventricular white matter changes, although they may be normal in up to 50% of patients [29]. EEG can show characteristic slowing typically seen in delirium. In most cases, improvement is seen with corticosteroid treatment, although no studies have addressed neuropsychological functioning post-treatment [29].

Parathyroid disease

Hypoparathyroidism

Hypoparathyroidism is a disorder in which there is deficient parathyroid hormone secretion (see Box 4). The condition can occur at any age and appears equally prevalent in males and females. Parathyroid hormone is responsible for maintaining calcium homeostasis in the body as well as regulating other ions, such as phosphate. The most common cause of hypoparathyroidism is surgical removal or damage to the parathyroid glands. The damage is typically linked to thyroidectomy, neck surgery for laryngeal or esophageal cancers, or irradiation of the neck. Other etiologies include autoimmune disorder and developmental conditions. Hypoparathyroidism is common

Box 3: Hashimoto's encephalopathy

- Signs and symptoms: alteration in mental state, fluctuating level of consciousness, impaired attention, and behavior and personality changes, abnormal anti-thyroid antibodies, seizures
- Neurobehavioral findings: not well-characterized, but may include memory and language impairment, hallucinations
- Neuroimaging/neuroanatomical: generalized atrophy, periventricular white matter changes
- Treatment and reversibility: most cases improve following treatment
- Developmental variations: unknown variations – quite rare in young children

Box 4: Hypoparathryoidism

- Signs and symptoms: paresthesias, muscle cramps, seizures, decreased or absent deep tendon reflexes, alopecia, and dry and pigmented skin
- Neurobehavioral findings: intellectual deficits and delirium; 50% have cognitive deficits; anxiety and psychosis common
- Neuroimaging/neuroanatomical: unknown
- Treatment and reversibility: 80% improve with treatment
- Developmental variations: children with 22q11.2 Deletion syndrome (velocardiofacial syndrome)

in the 22q11.2 Deletion syndrome (i.e. velocardiofacial syndrome), which is a complex congenital defect. Common symptoms of hypoparathyroidism include paresthesias, muscle cramps, seizures, decreased or absent deep tendon reflexes, alopecia, and dry and pigmented skin. Approximately 50% of cases experience cognitive impairment that can include intellectual deficits and delirium [30]. Anxiety appears to be the most common psychiatric symptom, although psychosis has also been reported. In a large case series, almost 80% of patients improved following treatment with calcium and vitamin D replacement [30].

Hyperparathyroidism

Hyperparathyroidism is a condition in which there are elevated parathyroid hormone levels and an associated elevation in serum calcium (see Box 5). The most common etiology of primary hyperparathyroidism is dysfunction in parathyroid glands, such as an adenoma or hyperplasia of the glands. The condition can occur at any age, although it is quite rare under the age of 10. Two-thirds of cases are females and the prevalence of the condition increases with age

(particularly in females), with a peak between the ages of 50 and 70. Many individuals with hyperparathyroidism are asymptomatic or report nonspecific complaints of fatigue and cognitive inefficiencies [31]. Other common symptoms include renal stones, weakness and bone pain in extremities, and weight loss. Given the variability in symptom presentation and often nonspecific signs, there is typically considerable delay in making the diagnosis. The most effective treatment of the condition is parathyroidectomy, although there is debate about whether to surgically treat individuals with mild disease. It is possible that, in the future, neuropsychological evaluation of these patients may play an important role in surgery decision-making. Case reports have described a variety of psychiatric and cognitive symptoms in individuals with hyperparathyroidism, including delirium, psychosis, and depression [32]. There also appears to be a positive association between severity of psychiatric symptoms and elevated serum calcium. Many of the neuropsychological studies have addressed the issue of whether surgical treatment improves cognitive functioning. Three of the six studies demonstrated improvement in attention, memory, and reasoning

---

Box 5: Hyperparathryoidism

- Signs and symptoms: asymptomatic, nonspecific complaints (fatigue and cognitive inefficiencies), renal stones, weakness and bone pain in extremities, and weight loss
- Neurobehavioral findings: variety of cognitive impairments, psychosis, depression
- Neuroimaging/neuroanatomical: global SPECT abnormality, possible medial prefrontal
- Treatment and reversibility: improvements in attention, memory, and reasoning following treatment
- Developmental variations: prevalence increases with age; rare in children younger than 10

---

following parathyroidectomy [33]. Despite finding correlations between serum calcium levels and motor speed, novel problem-solving, and memory, Brown et al. [34] did not find improvement in cognition 6 months post-parathyroidectomy. Very limited imaging data suggest abnormalities on brain SPECT that typically normalize following parathyroidectomy [35]. Preliminary fMRI findings in patients with hyperparathyroidism found post-surgery changes in medial prefrontal cortex during Stroop tasks along with a neuropsychological finding of improvement on the Trail Making Test [36].

Diabetes

Diabetes mellitus is a term applied to a group of metabolic disorders that result in chronic elevations in blood glucose levels, or hyperglycemia. Physical symptoms can include thirst, polyuria, fatigue, weight loss, and blurred vision. The most common forms of diabetes are type 1 and type 2 diabetes, but a transient form of diabetes can also be associated with pregnancy. Type 1 diabetes is caused by the autoimmune destruction of pancreatic beta cells where insulin is produced, resulting in insulin deficiency and hyperglycemia. Type 1 diabetes has also been referred to as insulin-dependent diabetes mellitus (IDDM), as patients require insulin to live. In contrast, type 2 diabetes is characterized by resistance to insulin and relative insulin deficiency.

Of note, diabetes insipidus is not to be confused with diabetes mellitus. Diabetes insipidus refers to acute onset of polydipsia and polyuria, caused by inadequate secretion of antidiuretic hormone from the hypothalamus or anterior pituitary. In many cases, the etiology is unknown, but this can be a consequence of brain trauma or pituitary tumor. This condition is easily controlled by vasopressin replacement therapy or treatment of the underlying cause (i.e. tumor resection).

Normal brain function is dependent on sufficient levels of circulating glucose, and deprivation can affect brain functions. As such, the acute effects of hypoglycemia on cognition are well recognized and include slowed reaction time and psychomotor speed, reduced verbal fluency, and poor naming. Hypoglycemic episodes are common in type 1 diabetes, but these acute effects on cognition are usually reversible. Importantly, recurrent episodes do not appear to have long-term consequences on cognition [37]. Short-term episodes of hyperglycemia are more common in type 2 diabetes. Acute hyperglycemia appears to have minimal effects on cognition. The longer-term effects of recurrent hyperglycemia are unclear, but it may be an important risk factor for cognitive decline in both type I and type 2 diabetes [38]. The relationship between glycemic control and long-term cognitive effects remains controversial and will need to be addressed in large-scale, longitudinal studies.

Pregestational and gestational diabetes

Approximately 10% of pregnancies are complicated by maternal pre-existing diabetes mellitus or gestational diabetes [39] (see Box 6). Historically, there has been an association between diabetes during pregnancy and increased risk of miscarriage and congenital anomalies [40]; however, this has declined as glycemic control in early pregnancy has been improved [41]. Macrosomia is a common risk associated with maternal diabetes, particular with poor glycemic control during the last trimester. Children who were large for gestational age and born to mothers with diabetes are also at increased risk for metabolic syndrome and the development of type 2 diabetes [42].

In addition, there is a small body of literature exploring the relationship between maternal hyperglycemia and the child's motor and cognitive development. For example, weaknesses in attention and motor functioning were noted for children of mothers

Box 6: Pregestational and gestational diabetes

- Signs and symptoms: large birth weight, associated with maternal glycemic control
- Neurobehavioral findings: decreased attention, motor coordination deficits
- Neuroimaging/neuroanatomical: N/A
- Treatment and reversibility: N/A

with diabetes or gestational diabetes in comparison to normal controls matched for age, socioeconomic status, and birth order [43]. Moreover, there was an association between maternal blood glycosylated hemoglobin levels and acetonuria with attentional and motor performance in the children. In children born to mothers with pregestational diabetes with nephropathy, there is a high risk for premature birth with low birth weight (e.g. small for gestational age [44]), which can impact development of intellectual, attentional, and motor functioning. In general, however, children born to mothers with pregestational or gestational diabetes do not typically exhibit significant intellectual delays, unless the mother's diabetes is complicated by nephropathy or hypertension [44]. In addition, longitudinal studies and studies with larger and more diverse participants are needed to confirm the reported association between attentional and motor development in children and maternal glycemic control.

Type 1 diabetes

Type 1 diabetes accounts for 5–10% of patients with diabetes and typically develops in childhood or early adulthood (i.e. younger than 30 years of age) [45] (see Box 7). With severe hyperglycemia, diabetic ketoacidosis (DKA) may occur, and children are at particular risk for DKA-related cerebral edema [46]. Intensive insulin treatment is recommended to prevent microvascular complications of type 1 diabetes, but it is associated with increased risk of hypoglycemia [47]. Although adults may be resilient to effects of hypoglycemia, neuropsychological deficits in children have been associated with episodes of severe hypoglycemia, particularly in young children [48]. Increased cognitive deficits associated with type 1 diabetes in childhood may reflect a "critical period" of vulnerability to hypoglycemia in the developing brain, particularly before age 5.

Children with type 1 diabetes have lower intellectual scores, reduced attention and mental efficiency, psychomotor retardation, and lower school performance [49]. In general, cognitive deficits are most often seen in children who developed type 1 diabetes before age 5 and children who had frequent periods of hypoglycemia [50], although some studies have failed to find a relationship between cognitive functions and episodes of hypoglycemia [51]. Desrocher and Rovet [52] developed a hypothetical model relating disease factors to neuropsychological outcomes in children. They noted that early-onset type 1 diabetes before age 5, as well as episodes of hypoglycemia before age 12, is associated with motor and visual-spatial impairments. In contrast, episodes of hyperglycemia are suggested to be more related to hormonal effects of puberty and are related to executive dysfunction. Factors associated with severe episodes of hypoglycemia in children with type 1 diabetes include earlier age of onset of diabetes, longer duration of diabetes, and higher cumulative hyperglycemia levels (standardized median A1C level plus standardized duration of diabetes) [53].

With regard to brain imaging studies, children with one or more episodes of severe hypoglycemia were reported to have smaller gray matter volume at the left temporal-occipital junction, in relationship to peers with diabetes who have not had any severe episodes of hypoglycemia [53]. Children with high cumulative hyperglycemia levels were also more likely to show smaller gray matter volume in the posterior cortical areas [53].

In adults, type 1 diabetes can be associated with mild deficits in mental processing speed and aspects of executive functioning. Memory functions are generally spared [54]. Cognitive deficits in younger to middle-aged adults who had childhood-onset type 1 diabetes are clearly linked to the development of microvascular disease, a common complication of

415

Box 7: Type 1 diabetes

- Signs and symptoms: excessive thirst, polyuria, fatigue, weight loss, blurred vision
- Neurobehavioral findings: mildly reduced processing speed and aspects of executive functioning
- Neuroimaging/neuroanatomical: microvascular changes common after 40 years of age, though can occur earlier with poor glycemic control; risk for large vessel stroke
- Treatment and reversibility: cognitive deficits related to vascular changes may improve following acute recovery, but residual deficits possible; may show deficits when acutely hypoglycemic or hyperglycemic that may improve with normalization of glucose level
- Developmental variations: in childhood, early onset is associated with poorer cognitive outcome; children are at risk for diabetic ketoacidosis related cerebral edema; associated with greater cognitive effects in children than type 2 diabetes

type 1 diabetes. Microvascular changes typically do not occur in adults younger than 40 years of age. Lower density of cortical gray matter and a greater frequency of white matter lesions are commonly seen on structural brain imaging as individuals with type 1 diabetes age [55]. The degree to which these neuroimaging findings correlate with cognition remains somewhat controversial, although some studies have demonstrated a relationship between subcortical white matter disease and both cortical and subcortical volume loss [56]. In contrast, frequency of hypoglycemic episodes and poor metabolic control seem less related to cognitive functioning in large longitudinal studies [47, 54, 55, 57, 58]. Few studies have investigated the interaction between type 1 diabetes and aging in individuals over 60 years of age, though there is some suggestion that the effects on cognition are minimal and very similar to the mild cognitive deficits seen in younger and middle-aged adults [57]. In general, cognitive deficits secondary to type 1 diabetes typically occur in patients with substantial diabetes-related comorbidities, particularly microvascular disease, and this applies to both younger and older adults.

Type 2 diabetes

Although there is a genetic component for type 2 diabetes, lifestyle factors, such as obesity and sedentary habits, may trigger the development of type 2 diabetes (see Box 8). The progression to type 2 diabetes is gradual, developing over several years. The incidence of type 2 diabetes increases with age, from less than 0.1% in people younger than 30 years to 1% in

individuals around 70 years of age [59, 60]. Notably, the rate of type 2 diabetes is steadily increasing in adolescence as a consequence of the rising rates of childhood obesity. For example, in the National Health and Nutrition Examination Survey (NHANES) of 1999 to 2002, 16.0% of children between the ages of 6 and 19 years were considered to be overweight [60] and the increase in childhood obesity has also been associated with an increase in the incidence of type 2 diabetes in adolescents [61]. There is minimal research, however, addressing the possible cognitive deficits associated with type 2 diabetes with onset in adolescence. These individuals are at risk for microvascular complications, as well as the development of metabolic syndrome, which refers to the co-occurrence of multiple cardiac risk factors, including dyslipidemia and hypertension [62]. All of these factors would place an adolescent at risk for cognitive deficits.

The cognitive deficits in adults with type 2 diabetes are generally more pronounced than the cognitive deficits associated with type 1 diabetes and include deficits in verbal list-learning and processing speed [63]. In fact, structural neuroimaging studies show greater deep white matter disease and cortical atrophy in individuals with type 2 diabetes than those with type 1 diabetes who have a longer history of illness [64]. In individuals younger than 70 years of age with good diabetic control, cognitive deficits are generally mild, and some deficits may be attenuated with treatment and subsequent glycemic control as measured by HbA_{1c} [63].

The aging brain may be more susceptible to the deleterious consequences of poor glycemic control, as

Box 8: Type 2 diabetes

- Signs and symptoms: excessive thirst, polyuria, fatigue, weight loss, blurred vision
- Neurobehavioral findings: cognitive deficits more pronounced compared to type I diabetes and include deficits in processing speed and verbal list learning
- Neuroimaging/neuroanatomical: deep white matter disease and cortical atrophy
- Treatment and reversibility: cognitive deficits related to vascular changes may improve following acute recovery, but residual deficits possible; may show deficits when acutely hypoglycemic or hyperglycemic that may improve with normalization of glucose level
- Developmental variations: incidence increases with age; older adults more susceptible to the cognitive effects of poor glycemic control; may be a risk factor for conversion from mild cognitive impairment to Alzheimer's disease; although occurring more frequently in adolescents, there is little information about any immediate cognitive impact

there is a stronger relationship between indices of glycemic control and cognition in individuals with type 2 diabetes who are greater than 70 years of age [65]. In addition, in older adults, diabetes may interact with cerebrovascular disease and Alzheimer's disease to accelerate cognitive decline [66]. Diabetes may also be a possible prognostic indicator for conversion, in individuals with mild cognitive impairment, to Alzheimer's disease [67].

Disorders of the adrenal gland

Hypercortisolism

Cortisol is produced by the adrenal glands and is responsible for a number of functions throughout the body, including regulation of blood pressure, response to stress, and effects on protein, carbohydrate, and lipid metabolism. Hypercortisolism, also known as Cushing's syndrome, refers to the clinical syndrome associated with prolonged exposure to glucosteroids (see Box 9). The most common cause of Cushing's syndrome is associated with the use of corticosteroid medications (e.g. prednisone). The condition is most common in women (5 to 1) and typical age of onset is 25–40. Cushing's syndrome is quite rare in children. Other causes include overproduction of cortisol by the adrenal glands, pituitary adenoma, primary adrenal tumor, or other neoplasms that secrete adrenocorticotropic hormone (ACTH). When caused by a pituitary adenoma, the condition is referred to as Cushing's disease. Common symptoms include truncal obesity, plethoric (full) facies, hirsutism and baldness, osteoporosis, impotence or amenorrhea, hypertension, and generalized muscular weakness.

In children, there is evidence of reduced cerebral and amygdala volumes while cortisol levels are high. Following normalization of cortisol levels, brain volumes normalized, but there is evidence of persisting intellectual and academic deficiencies [68].

Depression, anxiety, emotional lability, decreased libido, and psychosis can occur in up to 50% of patients with hypercortisolism. Cognitive impairment is present in the majority of patients with hypercortisolism, particularly deficits in attention, executive, and memory functions [69]. Glucosteroid receptors are highly concentrated in the medial prefrontal cortex and hippocampus. Hippocampal volumes have been shown to decrease when cortisol levels are high and increase following normalization of cortisol [70]. Similar to neuroanatomical changes, cognitive improvement typically occurs following normalization of cortisol levels, although may be delayed in older adults [70].

In older adults, there is evidence of associations between high cortisol levels and poor performance on measures of language, processing speed, eye–hand coordination, executive functioning, verbal memory and learning, and visual memory [71].

Hypocortisolism

The most common cause of hypocortisolism is Addison's disease (75–80% of cases), which is a rare autoimmune disorder (destruction of the adrenal cortex; see Box 10). The prevalence of the disease is approximately 39–60 cases per million people. Most cases are diagnosed in individuals between the ages of 30 and 50, although there are familial autoimmune conditions involving onset in childhood and

---

Box 9: Hypercortisolism (Cushing's syndrome)

- Signs and symptoms: truncal obesity, plethoric (full) facies, hirsutism and baldness, osteoporosis, impotence or amenorrhea, hypertension, and generalized muscular weakness
- Neurobehavioral findings: attention, executive, and memory, depression, anxiety, emotional lability, decreased libido, and psychosis
- Neuroimaging/neuroanatomical: medial prefrontal cortex and hippocampus
- Treatment and reversibility: improvement in brain volumes and cognition following treatment; may be persisting intellectual and academic deficiencies in children
- Developmental variations: rare in children, but show same symptom profile as adults; older adults show deficits in language, processing speed, eye–hand coordination, executive functioning, verbal memory and learning, and visual memory

---

Box 10: Hypocortisolism (Addison's disease)

- Signs and symptoms: hyperpigmentation of the skin and mucous membranes, nausea, vomiting, weight loss, hypotension, muscle weakness, fatigue, and dizziness
- Neurobehavioral findings: memory impairment, disorientation, and delirium, delusions, hallucinations, depression, irritability, anxiety, and mania
- Neuroimaging/neuroanatomical: unknown, slowing on EEG
- Treatment and reversibility: improvement in cognition and psychiatric symptoms following treatment
- Developmental variations: familial autoimmune conditions can affect children and adolescents

---

adolescence. Low levels of cortisol trigger increased production of ACTH by the hypothalamus and anterior pituitary. Pituitary or hypothalamic dysfunction can also result in reduced CRH and ACTH production resulting in low levels of cortisol. Common symptoms of hypocortisolism include hyperpigmentation of the skin and mucous membranes, nausea, vomiting, weight loss, hypotension, muscle weakness, fatigue, and dizziness. The disorder is very commonly associated with other endocrine and non-endocrine autoimmune conditions.

In a recent review of published case reports of Addison's disease, Anglin et al. [72] indicate that the frequency of psychiatric symptoms associated with Addison's disease ranges from 64 to 84%. These symptoms can include delusions, hallucinations, depression, irritability, anxiety, and mania. Memory impairment, disorientation, and delirium have also been noted with the disease. Psychiatric and cognitive symptoms are typically seen prior to diagnosis and treatment, arguing against treatment-induced symptoms. In general, the active phase of hypocortisolism is associated with confusion, memory deficits, and attentional dysfunction. Once cortisol levels normalize following replacement therapy, cognitive functioning typically improves. Unlike Cushing's syndrome, little is known about structural CNS effects of hypocortisolism, although there is typical slowing seen on EEG. Mechanisms for psychiatric and cognitive symptoms of Addison's disease are unknown, but could be due to electrophysiological abnormalities, glucocorticoid deficiency (which is important for memory and frontal functions), associated metabolic changes (e.g. hyponatremia, hypoglycemia), direct autoimmune effects on the brain (i.e. Hashimoto's encephalopathy), and associated increases in endorphins.

Congenital adrenal hyperplasia

Congenital adrenal hyperplasia (CAH) is a genetic condition (autosomal recessive) in which there is prenatal exposure to high levels of androgens (see Box 11). The most common form of the disorder involves deficiency in the enzyme 21-hydroxylase, which prevents formation of cortisol and results in increased levels of ACTH, CRH, and androgens. The exposure

Box 11: Congenital adrenal hyperplasia

- Signs and symptoms: masculinization of the genitalia and clitoral hypertrophy in females and enlarged phallus in males
- Neurobehavioral findings: females: increased risk of left-handedness, enhanced spatial skills, and PIQ>VIQ, learning disabilities; males: less is known
- Neuroimaging/neuroanatomical: atypical symmetry of right and left perisylvian regions
- Treatment and reversibility: iatrogenic effects of glucosteroids
- Developmental variations: typically detected at birth

has known effects on development of genitalia, including masculinization of the genitalia and clitoral hypertrophy in females and enlarged phallus in males. Overall prevalence of the disorder is 1 case per 60, although may be much higher in select subpopulations. Both sexes are equally affected. The condition is typically detected at birth and treated with glucosteroids. CAH can involve two subtypes: (1) salt-wasters who experience high-level prenatal androgen exposure and severe episodes of hyponatremia and hypotension; and (2) simple virilizers who only experience high-level prenatal androgen exposure. Much of the research has explored whether exposure to testosterone and other androgens impedes development of the left hemisphere and enhances development of the right hemisphere. Although there are some contradictory findings, females with CAH show increased incidence of left-handedness, evidence of enhanced spatial skills, and more frequent pattern of PIQ>VIQ [73]. The relationship between early androgen overexposure and brain development in males is more complex, although some studies show increased likelihood of left-handedness. There appears to be a higher incidence of language-based learning disabilities in individuals with CAH and more frequent findings of atypical symmetry of right and left perisylvian regions [74]. Iatrogenic effects of glucosteroids on brain development are also potential contributors to cognitive changes in individuals with CAH. Individuals classified as salt-wasters have lower IQ scores than simple virilizers (probably reflecting more severe disease), but simple virilizers are more likely to have learning disabilities [75].

Androgen insensitivity

Androgen insensitivity is a rare disorder, in which individuals have a 46,XY karyotype and a varying degree of female or partially masculinized genitalia (i.e. pseudohermaphroditism). These individuals have a decreased response to normal levels of androgens. The degree of feminization of the genitalia typically influences the decision to raise the child as a girl or boy. Given the potential role of androgens in right-hemisphere development, it is not surprising that individuals with androgen insensitivity show poorer performance on the perceptual organization factor of the Wechsler Intelligence Scale compared to healthy sibling controls [76].

Hormones and aging

Testosterone

Testosterone generally declines with age, and is associated with loss of muscle and bone mass, sexual dysfunction, lethargy, depression, irritability, and changes in cognitive functioning. Research has suggested an association between prenatal exposure to high levels of testosterone and increased vulnerability to autism (e.g. Knickmeyer et al. [77]). Similarly, the Geschwind–Galaburda theory of brain development postulates that in utero testosterone exposure causes dyslexia, which has had some mixed empirical support [78]. There is considerable evidence to show that males have better visuospatial skills than females (especially mental rotation [79]). Sex steroid receptors are located throughout the brain, particularly in the hippocampus and frontal regions. Evidence from animal research suggests that testosterone may have neuroprotective effects, including protection against oxidative stress [80]. Studies of older adult males reveal mixed findings, although most large epidemiological studies demonstrate an association between high endogenous testosterone (especially free testosterone rather than total testosterone) and better cognitive functioning [81]. Similar findings with positron emission tomography show that individuals with high free testosterone show increased relative blood flow in the hippocampus bilaterally compared to those with lower testosterone levels [82]. Men with Alzheimer's disease have lower testosterone levels than age-matched controls [83], although it is unclear whether higher levels of testosterone are associated with a lower risk for Alzheimer's disease. There is evidence of an interaction between testosterone levels and apolipoprotein ε4 allele. High levels of testosterone are associated with poor cognitive peformance in ε4-positive individuals and good cognitive functioning in non-carriers [84]. There are conflicting findings about whether testosterone supplementation can improve cognitive functioning in healthy elderly and in those with mild cognitive impairment or early Alzheimer's disease [80].

Estrogens and progesterone

There is limited empirical research on the effects of estrogen or progesterone on cognitive functioning in childhood. Based on animal models, high levels of estrogen are associated with increased sensitivity to stress [85] and may lower the threshold for stress-induced prefrontal cortical dysfunction in adolescence [86]. Children with premature adrenarche have also been reported to have higher levels of estrogen (E_2), as well as more symptoms of depression, more behavior problems, and lower cognitive functioning in comparison to peers with on-time adrenarche [87].

Significant age-related changes in estrogens and progesterone occur in women at the time of menopause. Despite the fact that women experiencing menopause often have memory complaints, there is little empirical support for an association between endogenous estrogen levels and cognition prior to, during, or after menopause [88]. Hormone replacement therapy (HRT) has been utilized for many years to treat the physical symptoms of menopause, but the effects of HRT on cognition have yielded conflicting results. Some reports have shown enhanced verbal and nonverbal memory in younger women with HRT and estrogen replacement therapy (ERT), possibly due to enhanced activation of frontal lobe functioning, [89]. In older women without dementia, estrogen supplementation has been associated with enhanced cognitive performance [90].

The wide-spread use of HRT following menopause has been the source of significant controversy in recent years due to findings of an increased incidence of breast cancer and cardiovascular disease associated with HRT [91]. As such, the utility of HRT for reducing health risks remains somewhat controversial. Post hoc analyses of those data and newer studies suggest that the timing of estrogen replacement and health risk may be related. For example, the risk for stroke seems far less in women under the age of 60 who begin HRT closer to the onset of menopause [92].

Interestingly, the effects of HRT on cognition and risk for dementia may also be age-dependent. Early initiation of HRT around the time of menopause appears to have cognitive benefits, and later initiation of HRT may have a detrimental effect on cognition [90, 93]. A review of randomized placebo-controlled trials that do not necessarily factor in the age at which HRT was initiated concluded that there is minimal evidence to support cognitive enhancement with HRT or ERT in postmenopausal women [94]. Other factors need to be considered, however, to determine the potential risks and benefits of HRT for an individual.

Estrogen may also play a role in the development of Alzheimer's disease (AD). Postmenopausal women have a greater risk of developing AD than men [95], and it has been hypothesized that declines in endogenous estrogen levels following menopause may explain this finding [96]. Furthermore, prospective studies report a lower risk of dementia in women taking postmenopausal estrogen compared to those who do not [96, 97]. Trials of ERT to improve cognition and slow cognitive decline in women diagnosed with Alzheimer's disease, however, have been negative with only modest, positive short-term effects on memory [83]. In fact, recent evidence suggests that there may be an increased risk for dementia in women 65 years of age and older who are taking combination hormone therapy compared to placebo [98].

Growth hormone

Over the last 10–15 years, there has been growing interest in the use of human growth hormone (GH) to potentially reverse the physical and cognitive effects of aging. GH replacement significantly improves attention and memory and other cognitive functions in adults and children with GH deficiency [99]. Considerable controversy is associated with the use of GH in healthy individuals, and there are concerns about negative physical effects, including soft tissue edema, arthralgias, carpal tunnel syndrome, and gynecomastia. One significant area of concern for both adults and children is the possibility that GH increases the risk of cancer. Most studies in healthy older adults show improved cognition after a trial of GH or GH-releasing hormone [100]. There are no studies to date investigating the use of GH for dementia.

Melatonin

Melatonin is the principal hormone secreted by the pineal gland. Melatonin regulates the sleep–wake cycle, as well as sleep, sexual behavior, and immunological function. With aging melatonin levels decline. Across the lifespan, melatonin is typically prescribed for treatment of insomnia, including for sleep disturbance in children with attention-deficit hyperactivity disorder. Melatonin is also sold to treat jet lag. Slowed reaction time has been associated with melatonin, but the direct effects of melatonin on cognition appear minimal. Rather, any cognitive effects are likely to be secondary to the indirect effects of melatonin's hypothermic properties and disruption in the sleep–wake cycle. Several studies have shown a relationship between decline of melatonin and symptoms of dementia. However, trials of melatonin for sleep disturbance [101] and cognitive impairment in Alzheimer's disease [102] have been negative.

Conditions associated with neuroendocrine disorders

Klinefelter's syndrome

One of the most common sex chromosome disorders is Klinefelter's syndrome, a condition in which boys are born with one or more extra X chromosomes. The syndrome includes signs such as small firm testes, infertility, varying degrees of impaired sexual maturation, sparse body hair, and gynecomastia, with elevated gonadotropin levels and above average height. Research has suggested a strong tendency for deficits in language-processing, with verbal intellectual scores being relatively weaker than visual reasoning abilities (e.g. Netley and Rovet [103]) with specific learning difficulties in reading and spelling (e.g. Rovet et al. [104]).

Turner syndrome

Turner Syndrome (TS) is a sex chromosome disorder characterized by loss of some X chromosome material. Originally, Dr. Henry Turner identified characteristics of short stature, sexual infantilism, abnormality of elbow formation, and webbing of the neck in five women. Cognitively, TS has been associated with deficits in visual-analytic abilities, in contrast to relatively preserved verbal-language skills (e.g. Rovet [105]). Academically, difficulty with math has been prominent [105] and difficulties with social cognition are common [106].

Cancer

Endocrine dysfunction is a common occurrence with neoplastic disorders. This may be a direct result of a tumor, or a secondary effect from treatment. A variety of brain tumors, including craniopharyngiomas, pituitary adenomas, pineal gland tumors, and hypothalamic hamartomas, can impact endocrine functioning. In addition, when treatment for cancer includes cranial radiation, a radiation-induced endocrinopathy can occur. (See chapters by Krull et al. and Rey-Casserly for further information.)

Summary and implications for assessment

Endocrine disorders are a complex set of conditions that interact with multiple organ systems including the brain. These disorders can arise at any time during the lifespan. Endocrine dysfunction can influence neuronal organization and development and impact intellectual and academic skills. The goal of a neuropsychological evaluation of an individual with an endocrine disorder may vary, based on age at presentation. In children, it is more common that an endocrine disorder prompts a neuropsychological referral. At this stage, it is important to establish intellectual level and academic achievement to address implications for cognitive development and school functioning. In contrast, adults with endocrine disorders are not routinely referred for neuropsychological evaluation. During this developmental period, endocrine disorders may be misdiagnosed as psychiatric conditions and often present with subtle emotional and cognitive complaints. The neuropsychological evaluation may be helpful in distinguishing between endocrine, psychiatric, and cognitive symptoms. Often patients have multiple risks for cognitive impairment. In these cases, the evaluation should address the contribution of endocrine dysfunction to any notable deficits or emotional changes. Because many endocrine conditions increase in prevalence with age, evaluations for older adults with endocrine disorders frequently involve questions of differential diagnosis and identification of delirium and/or reversible cognitive impairments. Cognitive and neurobehavioral symptoms typically improve following treatment of endocrine disorders, although a subset of individuals may have persisting symptoms. Therefore, neuropsychology may play a role in identifying symptom improvement. Subtle cognitive complaints associated with endocrine disorders can significantly reduce one's quality of life and perception of functioning. As such, inclusion of mood and quality-of-life measures is important for the comprehensive neuropsychological evaluation of endocrine disorders.

References

1. Jones JH, Mackenzie J, Croft GA, et al. Improvement in screening performance and diagnosis of congenital hypothyroidism in Scotland 1979–2003. *Arch Dis Child* 2006;**91**:680–5.

2. Hadley M, Levine JE. *Endocrinology*, 6th edn. Upper Saddle River, NJ: Prentice Hall; 2007.

3. Selva KA, Harper A, Downs A, et al. Neurodevelopmental outcomes in congenital hypothyroidism: Comparison of initial T4 dose and time to reach target T4 and TSH. *J Pediatr* 2005;**147**:775–80.

4. Bongers-Schokking JJ, de Muinck Keizer-Schrama SMPF. Influence of timing and dose of thyroid hormone replacement on mental, psychomotor, and behavioral development in children with congenital hypothyroidism. *J Pediatr* 2005;**147**:768–74.

5. Kempers MJE, van der Sluijs Veer L, Nijhuis-van der Sanden RWG, et al. Intellectual and motor development of young adults with congenital hypothyroidism diagnosed by neonatal screening. *J Clin Endocrinol Metab* 2006;**91**:418–24.

6. Rovet J, Hepworth S. Attention problems in adolescents with congenital hypothyroidism: A multicomponential analysis. *J Int Neuropsychol Soc* 2001;**7**:734–44.

7. Alvarez M, Guell R, Chong D, et al. Attention processing in hyperthyroid children before and after treatment. *J Pediatr Endocrinol Metab* 1996;**9**:447–54.

8. Tunbridge WMG, Evered DC, Hall R, et al. The spectrum of thyroid disease in the community: The Whickham Survey. *Clin Endocrinol* 1977;**7**:481–93.

9. Whybrow PC, Prange AJ, Treadway CR. Mental changes accompanying thyroid gland dysfunction. A reappraisal using objective psychological measurement. *Arch Gen Psychiat* 1969;**20**:48–63.

10. Davis JD, Tremont G. Neuropsychatric aspects of hypothyroidism and treatment reversibility. *Minerva Endocrinol* 2007;**32**:49–65.

11. Ganguli M, Burmeister LA, Seaberg EC, et al. Association between dementia and elevated TSH: a community-based study. *Biol Psychiat* 1996;**40**:714–25.

12. Constant EL, De Volder AG, Ivanoiu A, et al. Cerebral blood flow and glucose metabolism in hypothyroidism: a positron emission tomography study. *J Clin Endocrinol Metab* 2001;**86**:3864–70.

13. Smith CD, Ain KB. Brain metabolism in hypothyroidism studies with ^{31}P magnetic-resonance spectroscopy. *Lancet* 1993;**345**:619–20.

14. Zhu D-F, Wang Z-X, Zhang D-R, et al. fMRI revealed neural substrate for reversible working memory dysfunction in subclinical hypothyroidism. *Brain* 2006;**129**:2923–30.

15. Piga M, Serra A, Deiana L, et al. Brain perfusion abnormalities in patients with euthyroid autoimmune thyroiditis. *Eur J Nucl Med Mol I* 2004;**31**:1639–44.

16. Osterweil D, Syndulko K, Cohen SN, et al. Cognitive function in non-demented older adults with hypothyroidism. *J Am Geriatr Soc* 1992;**40**:325–35.

17. Jorde R, Waterloo K, Storhaug H, et al. Neuropsychological function and symptoms in subjects with subclinical hypothyroidism and the effect of thyroxine treatment. *J Clin Endocrinol Metab* 2006;**91**:145–53.

18. Clarnette RM, Patterson CJ. Hypothyroidism: Does treatment cure dementia? *J Geriatr Psychiatry Neurol* 1994;**6**:23–7.

19. Haupt M, Kurz A. Reversibility of dementia in hypothyroidism. *J Neurol* 1993;**240**:333–5.

20. Trzepacz PT, McCue M, Klein I, Greenhouse J, Levey GS. Psychiatric and neuropsychological response to propanolol in Graves' disease. *Biol Psychiat* 1988;**23**:678–88.

21. Fahrenfort JJ, Wilterdink AM, van der Veen EA. Long-term residual complaints and psychosocial sequelae after remission of hyperthyroidism. *Psychoneuroendocrinology* 2000;**25**:201–11.

22. Vogel A, Elberling TV, Hording M, Dock J, et al. Affective symptoms and cognitive functions in the acute phase of Graves' thyrotoxicosis. *Psychoneuroendocrinology* 2007;**32**:36–43.

23. Bommer M, Eversemann T, Pickardt R, et al. Psychopathological and neuropsychological symptoms in patients with subclinical and remitted hyperthyroidism. *Klin Wochenschrift* 1990;**68**:552–8.

24. Bhatara VS, Tripathi RP, Sankar R et al. Frontal lobe proton magnetic-resonance spectroscopy in Graves' disease: a pilot study. *Psychoneuroendoncrinology* 1998;**23**:605–12.

25. Trivalle C, Doucet J, Chassagne P, et al. Differences in the signs and symptoms of hyperthyroidism in older and younger patients. *J Am Geriatr Soc* 1996;**44**:50–3.

26. Fukui T, Hasegawa Y, Takenaka H. Hyperthyroidism dementia: Clinicoradiological findings and response to treatment. *J Neurol Sci* 2001;**184**:81–8.

27. Kalmijn S, Mehta KM, Pois HA, et al. Subclinical hyperthyroidism and the risk of dementia. The Rotterdam study. *Clin Endocrinol* 2000;**53**:733–7.

28. Mocellin R, Walterfang M, Velakoulis D. Hashimoto's encephalopathy: epidemiology, pathogenesis, and management. *CNS Drugs* 2007;**21**:799–11.

29. Chong JY, Rowland LP, Utiger RD. Hashimoto encephalopathy: syndrome or myth. *Arch Neurol* 2003;**60**:164–71.

30. Denko J, Kaelbling R. The psychiatric aspects of hypoparathyroidism. *Acta Psychiatr Scand* 1962;**164**:1–70.

31. Coker LH, Rorie K, Cantley L, et al. Primary hyperparathyroidism, cognition, and quality of life. *Ann Surg* 2005;**242**:642–50.

32. Okamoto T, Gerstein HC, Obara T. Psychiatric symptoms, bone density and non-specific symptoms in patients with mild hypercalcemia due to primary hyperparathyroidism: a systematic overview of the literature. *Endocr J* 1997;**44**:367–74.

33. Numann PJ, Torppa AJ, Blumetti AE. Neuropsychologic deficits associated with primary hyperparathyroidism. *Surgery* 1984;**96**:1119–23.

34. Brown GG, Preisman RC, Kleerekoper M. Neurobehavioral symptoms in mild primary hyperparathyroidism: Related to hypercalcemia but not improved by parathyroidectomy. *Henry Ford Hosp Med J* 1987;**35**:211–15.

35. Mjaland O, Normann E, Halvorsen E, et al. Regional cerebral blood flow in patients with primary hyperparathyroidism before and after successful parathyroidectomy. *Br J Surg* 2003;**134**:732–7.

36. Perrier ND, Coker LH, Rorie KD, et al. Preliminary Report: Functional MRI of the brain may be the ideal tool for evaluating neuropsychologic and sleep complaints of patients with primary hyperparathyroidism. *World J Surg* 2006;**30**:686–96.

37. Heller SR, Macdonald IA. The measurement of cognitive function during acute hypoglycaemia: experimental limitations and their effect on the study of hypoglycaemia unawareness. *Diabet Med* 1996;**13**:607–15.

38. Cox DJ, Kovatchev BP, Gonder-Frederice LA, et al. Relationships between hyperglycemia and cognitive performance among adults with type 1 and type 2 diabetes. *Diabetes Care* 2005;**28**:71–7.

39. Nold J, Georgieff MK. Infants of diabetic mothers. In Rademacher R, Kliegman R, eds. *Pediatric Clinics of North America*. Philadelphia, PA: WB Saunders; 2004: 619–37.

40. Miller E, Hare JW, Cloherty JP, et al. Elevated maternal hemoglobin A1C in early pregnancy and major congenital anomalies in infants of diabetic mothers. *N Engl J Med* 1981;**304**:1331–4.

41. Mills JL, Simpson JL, Driscoll SG, et al. Incidence of spontaneous abortion among normal women and insulin-dependent diabetic women whose pregnancies were identified within 21 days of conception. *N Engl J Med* 1988;**319**:1617–23.

42. Boney CM, Verma A, Tucker R, et al. Metabolic syndrome in childhood: association with birth weight, maternal obesity and gestational diabetes mellitus. *Pediatrics* 2005;**115**:e290–6.

43. Ornoy A, Ratzon N, Greenbaum C, et al. School-age children born to diabetic mothers and to mothers with gestational diabetes exhibit a high rate of inattention and fine and gross motor impairment. *J Pediatr Endocrinol Metab* 2001;**14** S1:681–9.

44. Ornoy A. Growth and neurodevelopmental outcome of children born to mothers with pregestational and gestational diabetes. *Pediatr Endocrinol Rev* 2005;**3**:104–13.

45. Bruno G, Runzo C, Vavallo-Perin P, et al. Incidence of type 1 and type 2 diabetes in adults aged 30–49 years: the population-based registry in province of Turin, Italy. *Diabetes Care* 2005;**28**:2613–19.

46. Rosenbloom AL. Intracerebral crises during treatment of diabetic ketoacidosis. *Diabetes Care* 1990;**13**:22–33.

47. The Diabetes Control and Complications Trial: Effects of intensive diabetes therapy on neuropsychological function in adults in the diabetes control and complications trial. *Ann Intern Med* 1996;**124**:379–88.

48. Ryan C, Becker D. Hypoglycemia in children with type 1 diabetes mellitus: risk factors, cognitive function, and management. *Endocrinol Metab Clin North Am* 1999;**28**:883–900.

49. Northam EA, Anderson PJ, Jacobs R, et al. Neuropsychological profiles of children with type 1

diabetes 6 years after disease onset. *Diabetes Care* 2001;**24**:1541–6.

50. Ferguson SC, Blane A, Wardlaw J et al. Influence of an early-onset age of type 1 diabetes on cerebral structure and cognitive function. *Diabetes Care* 2005;**28**:1431–7.

51. Strudwick SK, Carne C, Gardner J, et al. Cognitive functioning in children with early onset type 1 diabetes and severe hypoglycemia. *J Pediatr* 2005;**147**:680–5.

52. Desrocher M, Rovet J. Neurocognitive correlates of Type 1 diabetes mellitus in childhood. *Child Neuropsychol* 2004;**10**:36–52.

53. Perantie DC, Wu J, Koller JM, et al. *Diabetes Care* 2007;**30**:2331–7.

54. Brands AM, Biessels GJ, DeHaan EH, et al. The effects of type 1 diabetes on cognitive performance; a meta-analysis. *Diabetes Care* 2005;**28**:726–35.

55. Musen G, Lyoo IK, Sparks CR, et al. Effects of type 1 diabetes on gray matter density as measured by voxel-based morphometry. *Diabetes* 2006;**55**:326–33.

56. Ferguson SC, Blane A, Perros P, et al. Cognitive ability and brain structure in type 1 diabetes: relation to microangiopathy preceding severe hypoglycemia. *Diabetes* 2003;**52**:149–56.

57. Brands AMA, Kessels RPC, Hoogma RPLM, et al. Cognitive performance, psychological well-being, and brain magnetic resonance imaging in older patients with type 1 diabetes. *Diabetes* 2006;**55**:1800–6.

58. The Diabetes Control and Complications Trial Research Group. Long-term effect of diabetes and its treatment on cognitive function. *N Engl J Med* 2007;**356**:1842–52.

59. Berger B, Stenstrom G, Sundkvist G. Incidence, prevalence, and mortality of diabetes in a large population. A report from the Skaraborg Diabetes Registry. *Diabetes Care* 1999;**22**:773–8.

60. Hedley AA, Ogden CL, Johnson CL, et al. Prevalence of overweight and obesity among US children, adolescents and adults, 1999–2002. *J Am Med Assoc* 2004;**291**:2847–50.

61. Kaufman F. Type 2 diabetes mellitus in children and youth: a new epidemic. *J Pediatr Endocrinol Metab* 2002;**15**:737–44.

62. Peterson K, Silverstein J, Kaufman F, et al. Management of type 2 diabetes in youth: an update. *Am Fam Physician* 2007;**76**:658–64.

63. Awad N, Gagnon M, Messier C. The relationship between impaired glucose tolerance, type 2 diabetes, and cognitive function. *J Clin Exper Neuropsychol* 2004;**26**:1044–80.

64. Brands AM, Biessels GJ, Kappelle LJ, et al. Cognitive functioning and brain MRI in patients with type 1 and type 2 diabetes mellitus: a comparative study. *Dement Geriatr Cogn Disord* 2007;**23**:343–50.

65. Ryan CM, Geckle MO. Why is learning and memory dysfunction in Type 2 diabetes limited to older adults? *Diabetes Metab Res* 2000;**16**:308–15.

66. Peila R, Rodriguez BL, Launer LJ. Type 2 diabetes, APOE gene, and the risk for dementia and related pathologies – the Honolulu-Asia aging study. *Diabetes* 2002;**51**:1256–62.

67. Luchsinger JA, Reitz C, Patel B, et al. Relation of diabetes to mild cognitive impairment. *Arch Neurol* 2007;**64**:570–75.

68. Merke DP, Giedd JN, Keil MF, et al. Children experience cognitive decline despite reversal of brain atrophy one year after resolution of Cushing syndrome. *J Clin Endocrinol Metab* 2005;**90**:2531–6.

69. Starkman MN, Giordani B, Gebarski SS, et al. Improvement in learning associated with increase in hippocampal formation volume. *Biol Psychiat* 2003;**53**:233–8.

70. Hook JN, Giordani B, Schteingardt DE, et al. Patterns of cognitive change over time and relationship to age following successful treatment of Cushing's disease. *J Int Neuropsychological Soc* 2007;**13**:21–9.

71. Lee BK, Glass TA, McAtee MJ, et al. Associations of salivary cortisol with cognitive function in the Baltimore memory study. *Arch Gen Psychiatr* 2007;**64**:810–18.

72. Anglin RE, Rosebush PI, Mazurek MF. The neuropsychiatric profile of Addison's disease: Revisiting a forgotten phenomenon. *J Neuropsych Clin N* 2006;**18**:450–9.

73. Kelso WM, Nicholls MER, Warne GL, et al. Cerebral lateralization and cognitive functioning in patients with congenital adrenal hyperplasia. *Neuropsychology* 2000;**14**:370–8.

74. Plante E, Boliek C, Binkiewicz A, et al. Elevated androgen, brain development and language/learning disabilities in children with congenital adrenal hyperlplasia. *Dev Med Child Neurol* 1996;**38**:423–37.

75. Johannsen TH, Ripa CPL, Reinisch JM, et al. Impaired cognitive function in women with congenital adrenal hyperpasia. *J Clin Endocrinol Metab* 2006;**91**:1376–81.

76. Imperato-McGinley J, Pichardo M, Gautier T, et al. Cognitive abilities in androgen-insensitive subjects: Comparison with control males and females from the same kindred. *Clin Endocrinol* 1991;**34**:341–7.

77. Knickmeyer R, Baron-Cohen S, Fane BA, et al. Androgens and autistic traits: a study of individuals with

congenital adrenal hyperplasia. *Horm Behav* 2006;**50**:148–53.

78. Geschwind N, Galaburda AM. *Cerebral Lateralization: Biological Mechanisms, Associations and Pathology.* Cambridge, MA: MIT Press; 1987.

79. Hooven CK, Chabris CF, Ellsion, PT, et al. The relationship of male testosterone to components of mental rotation. *Neuropsychologia* 2004;**42**:782–90.

80. Driscoll I, Resnick, SM. Testosterone and cognition in normal aging and Alzheimer's disease: An update. *Curr Alzheimer Res* 2007;**4**:33–45.

81. Yaffe K, Lui L-Y, Zmuda J, Cauley J. Sex hormones and cognitive function in older men. *J Am Geriatrics Soc* 2002;**50**:707–12.

82. Moffat SD. Effects of testosterone on cognitive and brain aging in elderly men. *Ann N Y Acad Sci* 2005;**1055**:80–92.

83. Hogervorst E, Williams J, Budge M, et al. Serum total testosterone is lower in men with Alzheimer's disease. *Neuroendocrinol Lett* 2001;**22**:163–8.

84. Burkhardt MS, Foster JK, Clarnette RM, et al. Interaction between testosterone and epsilon 4 status on cognition in healthy older men. *J Clin Endocrinol Metab* 2006;**91**:1168–72.

85. Hodes GE, Shors TJ. Distinctive stress effects on learning during puberty. *Horm Behav* 2005;**48**:163–71.

86. Arnsten AF, Shansky RM. Adolescence: vulnerable period for stress-induced prefrontal cortical function? Introduction to part IV. *Ann N Y Acad Sci* 2004;**1021**:143–7.

87. Dorn LD, Hitt SF, Rotenstein D. Biopsychological and cognitive difference in children with premature vs on-time adrenarche. *Arch Pediatr Adolesc Med* 1999;**153**:137–46.

88. Herlitz A, Thilers P, Habib R. Endogenous estrogen is not associated with cognitive performance before, during, or after menopause. *Menopause* 2007;**14**:425–31.

89. Joffe H, Hall JE, Gurber S, et al. Estrogen therapy selectively enhances prefrontal cognitive processes: a randomized, double-blind, placebo-controlled study with functional magnetic resonance imaging in perimenopausal and recently postmenopausal women. *Menopause* 2006;**13**:411–22.

90. Rapp SR, Espeland MA, Shumaker SA, et al. Effect of estrogen plus progestin on global cognitive function in postmenopausal women: the Women's Health Initiative Memory Study: a randomized controlled trial. *J Am Med Assoc* 2003;**28**:2663–72.

91. Writing Group for the Women's Health Initiative Investigators. Risks and benefits of estrogen plus progestin in healthy postmenopausal women. Principal results from the Women's Health Initiative Randomized Controlled Trial. *J Am Med Assoc* 2002;**288**:321–33.

92. Rossouw JE, Prentice RL, Manson JE, et al. Postmenopausal hormone therapy and risk of cardiovascular disease by age and years since menopause. *J Am Med Assoc* 2007;**297**:1465–77.

93. MacLennan AH, Henderson VW, Paine BJ, et al. Hormone therapy, timing of initiation, and cognition in women aged older than 60 years: the REMEMBER pilot study. *Menopause* 2006;**13**:28–36.

94. Hogervorst E, Yaffe K, Richards M, et al. Hormone replacement therapy for cognitive function in postmenopausal women. *Cochrane Db Syst Rev* 2002;**3**:CD003122.

95. Jorm AF, Korten AE, Henderson AS. The prevalence of dementia: A quantitative integration of the literature. *Acta Psychiatr Scand* 1987;**76**:475–9.

96. Paganini-Hill A, Henderson VW. Estrogen deficiency and risk of Alzheimer disease in women. *Am J Epidemiol* 1994;**140**:256–61.

97. Kawas C, Resnick S, Morrison A, et al. A prospective study of estrogen replacement therapy and the risk of developing Alzheimer's disease: the Baltimore Longitudinal study of Aging. *Neurol* 1997;**48**:1517–21.

98. Shumaker SA, Legault C, Rapp SR, et al. for the Women's Health Initiative Memory Study. Estrogen plus progestin and the incidence of dementia and mild cognitive impairment in postmenopausal women. *J Am Med Assoc* 2003;**20**:2651–62.

99. Falleti MG, Maruff P, Burman P, et al. The effects of growth hormone (GH) deficiency and GH replacement on cognitive performance in adults: a meta-analysis of the current literature. *Psychoneuroendocrinology* 2006;**31**:681–91.

100. Vitiello MV, Moe KE, Merriam GR, et al. Growth hormone releasing hormone improves the cognition of healthy older adults. *Neurobiol Aging* 2006;**27**:318–23.

101. Singer C, Tractenberg RE, Kaye J, et al. for the Alzheimer's Disease Cooperative Study. A multicenter, placebo-controlled trial of melatonin for sleep disturbance in Alzheimer's disease. *Sleep* 2003;**26**:893–901.

102. Jansen SL, Forbes DA, Duncan V, et al. Melatonin for cognitive impairment. *Cochrane Db Syst Rev* 2006;**25**:CD003802.

103. Netley C, Rovet J. Verbal deficits in children with 47, XXY and 47, XXX karyotypes: A descriptive and experimental study. *Brain Cogn* 1982;**17**:58–72.

104. Rovet J, Netley C, Bailey J, et al. Intelligence and achievement in children with extra X aneuoploidy: a longitudinal perspective. *Am J Med Genet* 1995;**60**:356–63.

105. Rovet J. The cognitive and neuropsychological characteristics of females with Turner syndrome. In Berch DB, Bender BD, eds. *Sex Chromosome Abnormalities and Human Behavior*. Boulder, CO: Westview Press; 1990: 38–77.

106. Rovet J. Turner syndrome: a review of genetic and hormonal influences on neuropsychological functioning. *Child Neuropsychol* 2004;**4**:262–79.

Metabolic and neurodegenerative disorders across the lifespan

Richard Ziegler and Elsa Shapiro

Introduction

This chapter is about the effects on the central nervous system (CNS) of inborn errors of metabolism (IEM). IEM are a large number of rare genetic disorders caused by biochemical errors. The genes that code for enzymes that convert substances (substrates) into specific products are defective. Disease is caused either by the defect/absence of a specific enzyme that disrupts a metabolic pathway causing abnormal build-up of substrate in cells or by the defect/absence of important proteins or enzymes that help in the synthesis of essential compounds.

Inborn errors of metabolism can be categorized into disorders of carbohydrate metabolism (e.g. galactosemia), amino acid metabolism (e.g. phenylketonuria and maple syrup urine disease), lysosomal storage, peroxisomal function, and a myriad of others not covered in this chapter. Although the majority of IEM have some CNS effects, this chapter will concentrate on *lysosomal storage disorders* and *peroxisomal disorders* because of the known CNS effects on neuropsychological function and development in both untreated and treated individuals and because of the advances in diagnosis and treatment with improved outcomes for these categories of diseases.

In the past 25 years, inborn errors of metabolism that affect the CNS have been the first genetic diseases to have effective treatments. The first treatments for these disorders were alterations in diet for a number of these diseases such as phenylketonuria and maple syrup urine disease, resulting in prevention of mental retardation. Subsequently, bone marrow transplantation, cord blood transplantation, and enzyme replacement have become the standard of care for a number of lysosomal and peroxisomal diseases. More recently medical treatments such as substrate reduction, chaperone therapies, and antioxidants have had some positive benefits, and clinical trials of gene therapy are under way for some diseases. For more information

about these diseases the reader is referred to Scriver et al.'s [1] comprehensive book.

Why should these diseases be interesting to the neuropsychologist? First, many of these diseases have specific behavioral and cognitive profiles that reflect the neuropathology of the disease. Consequently, neurobehavioral and neurocognitive data can often provide hypotheses about the specific neural substrate affected by the disease. In addition, these diseases provide a "natural laboratory" to study the effects of both disease and treatment on the function related to specific parts of the brain. Such information can inform about specific brain–behavioral relationships in general, and specifically can provide information about functional changes related to neural pathways as the disease progresses and is treated. In addition, many of these disorders have different effects at different ages; the same brain abnormality produces different phenotypes at different ages, which provides important information about neurodevelopmental processes. Finally, neuropsychological outcomes can be crucial for treatment monitoring and predictive of treatment response; the neuropsychologist can provide functional monitoring of treatment effects. As a result of such monitoring, we have been able to document that early diagnosis (as indicated by more intact cognitive ability), treated at an earlier stage of disease, has led to better functional outcomes for the individual patient [2, 3].

One key issue in IEMs is the rarity of these diseases. In order to learn about the natural history of these disorders and then to determine the effectiveness of treatments, obtaining larger *N*s for research, multicenter and network projects are necessary. Each of these diseases has been studied in one or two centers in the USA and one or two centers in Europe. Expertise develops with familiarity with the disorder. Thus a pyramid of centers is being developed with those with the most expertise setting up protocols in collaboration with other centers less familiar with the disorder.

In neuropsychology, there are only a few centers around the country that can carry out research on any one disease primarily because of their contacts with other centers and networks that collaborate in pooling patient subjects. However, neuropsychologists also need to provide clinical services for these patients and become familiar enough with them in order that they do not overlook a diagnosis and they understand the needs of these patients for the provision of local clinical service. This chapter is directed at those neuropsychologists who may see a handful of these patients in their entire career.

Neuropsychological evaluation in neurodegenerative disease

The goals of neuropsychological assessment are to help in clinical management, to provide educational recommendations, and to identify the need for rehabilitative therapies targeted to specific deficits. Some children with IEMs have serious behavioral problems that are a challenge for parents, some have significant motor and sensory problems that require adaptations and therapies, and most have learning difficulties that are a challenge for schools in providing appropriate services. Importantly, such evaluations can document the stage of disease to determine whether medical interventions may be helpful or whether they can be detrimental. For example, in adrenoleukodystrophy, transplant of hematopoietic stem cells can stabilize the disease in less advanced cases but, if the disease is advanced, such treatment can accelerate the downhill course [4] and leave the child partially or completely disabled.

While comprehensive assessments that include adaptive functioning, cognition, behavior, language, motor, memory, visual spatial and executive functions are standard, knowledge of the disease phenotype provides guidelines for a more focused evaluation. For example, sensitivity to the high incidence of visual spatial problems in a given disease would lead the clinician to develop more intense evaluation of that domain. Even if no complaints are made about a function that is usually impaired in a specific disease, it is important to establish a baseline and to continue to monitor these functions because they may decline at a later time as the disease progresses.

Practically all children with IEMs require special education services. The neuropsychologist should generate specific recommendations for such children based on both the child's individual needs and knowledge of the natural history of the disease. Teachers and school-based therapists are often at a loss to know what to do with such children; they are often frustrated because they do not know how to provide targeted services. It is often difficult to provide a service for children whose only benefit is to slow the rate of decline rather than improve in function. Concrete suggestions for curriculum and behavioral management are often welcomed; better yet, a telephone or face-to-face conference can be beneficial. Outlining the type of rehabilitative services such as physical, occupational, and speech/language therapy with specific therapeutic goals will be helpful.

Another important function of the neuropsychological evaluation is baseline determination of eligibility or prognosis for medical treatments that will be helpful in counseling parents. Quantitative measurement of CNS function can be accomplished by a neuropsychological assessment. Guidelines for application of medical treatment can often be informed by neuropsychological research. For example: for those who may be undergoing stem cell transplant, children with Hurler syndrome who are under 2 years of age with a developmental quotient over 70 do better [5, 6]; boys with IQ under 80 do very poorly in adrenoleukodystrophy [4]. Treatment monitoring after the application of treatment is also very important.

Repeated testing and practice effects

If a child is going to be followed regularly for neuropsychological assessment of treatment response several factors are important. In very young children unless the sessions are very close in time, the item set administered, for example 6 months apart, will be very different as development is very rapid and the item set from one testing to another is likely to overlap only minimally. In older children who are on a rapid course of dementia, we are always delighted to see practice effects because it implies memory from previous testing. The problem of practice effects lies in conditions with slow progression or at an older age where cognitive development is slower. In such cases, the existence of practice effects (not seen in all functions) needs to be considered. Use of tests with alternative forms (examples: Hopkins Verbal Learning Test [7], Brief Visual Spatial Learning Test [8]) is warranted despite sparse normative data.

Neuropsychologists worry considerably about practice effects. As mentioned above, practice effects are not a big concern with very young children. In addition, some measures assess developmental level through ratings by parents, who presumably will provide information as they see it in the child. In older children who are not very impaired, repetition of IQ tests is a consideration. However, Sirois et al. [9] found no practice effects on the WISC-R and WAIS-R in consecutive yearly testing in children with hemophilia and their siblings.

A related issue is lack of valid results due to intra-individual variation. Salthouse and Berish [10] have found in demented adults that "within-person" variability may increase with neurological compromise and that repeated measurements may be necessary to obtain a "true" measurement of ability. Intra-individual variation in adult patients is an important characteristic in conditions as diverse as chronic fatigue syndrome [11], malingering [12], and dementia [13]. Further work has indicated that intra-individual variability may be an indicator of neurological integrity [14]. However, little work has been done in this area with children. It has been noted that children with ADHD show marked intra-individual variation [15]; however, no work could be found in children with neurological disease. In children with neurodegenerative diseases, intra-individual variability may pose a significant problem as the confounding effects of physical illness and declining mental ability may render a single testing inaccurate. For this reason, whenever possible we divide our assessment into two sessions.

When repeating testing, some tests show some effects of novelty at the first administration and then familiarity may occur, and the examiner may mistakenly think that the child's performance has declined. These effects of novelty and familiarity probably have more impact than practice and on the first and second testing session only. In a repeated measures research design, building in a "pre-test" to familiarize the child with the testing situation may alleviate this effect.

Test selection

In young children, measurements are global. As the child grows older, more specific functions can be measured mirroring the neural differentiation of those functions. It is also likely that cerebral pathways that subserve a specific neuropsychological function change with age. In young children, some already emerged characteristics can be very difficult to measure. However, we have had some success in developing measures for attention and memory to substitute for observational data. New quantitative measurements of attention and memory have been developed in our laboratory and may provide help in quantifying early neuropsychological functions in children who will be followed longitudinally [16, 17].

Test consistency

For many reasons, it is important to use the same tests over a period. The advantage of using the Stanford Binet [18] in contrast to the Wechsler [19] tests or the Mullen [20] in contrast to the Bayley [21] is to allow monitoring of the same functions over a longer time because the test does not substantially change. When tests administered change because of age, overlapping of test administrations is extremely important as the functions and scores may differ from one test to another. A very important reason for test consistency is the ability to track a child using raw scores or age-equivalent scores to examine rate of growth of various functions measured by the test. Although age-equivalent scores have psychometric limitations, they are often the only way to track the development of young children across tests if the same test cannot be administered.

Importance of developmental growth curves and use of age-equivalent or raw scores for monitoring

As we have said in previous work [22, 23], the process of decline (or childhood dementia) in childhood is an alteration in the normal course of development of mental functions due to disease, and this alteration can be characterized as slowing of development, "plateauing" or lack of new learning, or loss of skills. Standardized age scores do not inform about which of these are taking place in the context of declining IQ. Use of raw scores or age-equivalent scores (note limitations mentioned above) can produce a growth curve that allows the neuropsychologist to trace the growth of each mental function over time and to examine how interventions may alter the slope of development for that child. In neurodegenerative disease the opposing vectors of development and deterioration often mask effects of disease and thus early dementia (or disease effect) often mimics developmental disability. The premorbid level then should be viewed as a rate of development, not a level of performance [22].

Many factors affect the neuropsychological phenotype at the time of assessment. Some of these include the disease process, the locus of the process, the age of the child at onset and the stage of the disease at evaluation. In addition, intra-individual variation as mentioned above may affect performance. Each disease has a characteristic natural history; however, there are biological factors, many of which are unknown, which affect the expression of disease. For example, in MPS I several mutations are known to be associated with severe disease.

Importance of the physical condition of the child

Individuals with neurodegenerative disorders often have physical handicaps that interfere with their cognitive, language, spatial, and motor development, which interferes with their capacity to demonstrate their abilities in formal neuropsychological testing. Hearing loss, visual capacity, attention span, and motor skills need "preassessment" to ensure that the performance is not due to a sensory or motor deficit [24–26]. For example, a majority of very young children with Hurler syndrome have hearing loss [27], and most have corneal clouding and other visual problems [28]. Boys with adrenoleukodystrophy develop visual agnosia [29] and patients with metachromatic leukodystrophy have poor motor function [30, 31]. All such characteristics contribute to the phenotype, but also are known to interfere with a "true" measure of intelligence.

Testing demented adults and children

For children and adults who have declined there are several tips in testing that are important: (a) waiting for an answer is important; do not accept silence or "don't know"; often processing is immensely delayed, and it may take the patient considerable time to give a correct response; (b) increase structure so expectations are clear; (c) do not be afraid to set limits and be strict in the testing session; it will not hurt the child; (d) initiative may be a problem in older patients, especially those with frontal lobe problems; help the patient start to respond; (e) testing the limits is extremely important; under what conditions can the child respond correctly? Although scores are very important, a process-focused assessment will be helpful to understand the child's performance and assist with recommendations; (f) have the parents in the room with younger children; it is often helpful in explaining what kinds of deficits children may have and enhances their performance; and (g) be aware of sensory and motor problems that may interfere with test performance.

Examining predictors of outcome

One goal of research in children with neurodegenerative disorders is to determine what factors predict the child's developmental trajectory. For example in a study of language development in children with Hurler syndrome factors [32] were studied that include severity of hearing loss, early cognition, enlarged ventricular size on MRI, white matter changes on MRI, atrophy on MRI, amount of speech and language therapy, neurological events, and success of the transplant. Such studies help focus on interventions (e.g. monitoring hearing, providing adequate rehabilitation therapies, and monitoring for hydrocephalus) and thus improve outcomes. Confounding factors, both biological and environmental, are likely to be problematic when samples are small. Socioeconomic and family environment as well as co-existing biological factors need to be accounted for. As an example, in our sample of 150 children with Hurler syndrome, we have one child on the autistic spectrum as one might expect from base rates. Children diagnosed late in the course of their disease due to less up-to-date medical care are more likely to be disadvantaged than children diagnosed early, who are more likely to be seen in high-quality medical centers.

Correlations with neuroimaging and biological markers (imaging, genetic information, enzyme levels, etc.)

Cross-validation of neuropsychological test results with neuroimaging and biological markers provides additional information and confirmation of results. Current neuroimaging techniques in use for patients with neurodegenerative diseases are qualitative and use clinical diagnostic protocols designed to reach a diagnosis rather than attempt to understand the disease process. Standardized neuroimaging protocols using quantified imaging analysis will produce better understanding of changes in brain structure and function with disease progression and can serve as a sensitive biomarker for treatment efficacy. A move from qualitative to quantitative methodologies such as volumetric analysis, magnetic resonance spectroscopy (MRS) and diffusion tensor imaging (DTI) will help to develop combined imaging and neuropsychological markers to delineate natural history and to monitor treatment. An example of such a study is the correlation of MRS with neuropsychological test results in adrenoleukodystrophy [33] and DTI in adrenoleukodystrophy as a marker of early disease [34]. Unfortunately to date these new quantitative imaging procedures have little pediatric normative data. Gathering normative data will be essential for these measures to have sufficient predictive power.

Clinical recommendations

The neuropsychologist is a key member of the team in managing these diseases. Their role is to help in the decision-making process regarding whether a patient may be a good candidate for a therapy and to help in the counseling of parents regarding what to expect during and after treatment. As such, the neuropsychologist must know the neuropsychological natural history of the disease and whether the treatment has the potential to benefit the patient. Knowing the course of the disease will help in the counseling of parents who may be uncertain about making a decision regarding a new treatment or what expectations for the future might be with a disease, treated or untreated. While the literature is sparse about treatment outcomes for these diseases and many of the treatments are new and untested, the natural history is known for many of these diseases. Counseling the parents about what the potential is for altering the course of the disease is crucial for parental treatment decision-making. Parents are often more focused on saving a child's life than on the consequent disabilities that may result. If the prognosis is for significant disability, the neuropsychologist must be sensitive to the effects on family functioning and psychosocial and economic stressors that may ensue.

Treatment outcome monitoring

After a treatment is applied, the neuropsychologist can also help the physicians in measuring how effective the treatment is and what other rehabilitative, palliative, and symptomatic treatments may be necessary. Regular neuropsychological follow-up of these patients during a treatment period will aid the physician in knowing what is happening to the cognitive and behavioral status of the patient.

We have found that it is the neuropsychologist who focuses on the rehabilitative, symptomatic, and palliative interventions. Identifying whether interventions such as speech/language, occupational therapy, physical therapy, and educational interventions are required will depend on the comprehensiveness of the neuropsychological battery and knowledge of the course of the disease. Children with IEMs often have specific disabilities that rehabilitation specialists may not be aware of and require specific attention. For example, children with mucopolysaccharidoses have serious orthopedic problems that require avoidance of high-impact activities as well as restricted range of motion that is unlikely to be responsive to therapy. In contrast, our studies have indicated in the long run that speech/language therapy improves outcomes in MPS I. Boys with adrenoleukodystrophy frequently present with visual agnosia, a difficult to understand abnormality that requires explanation and adaptations in interventions. Assessing areas of adaptive skills that may be amenable to rehabilitation is crucially important in both maintaining and improving abilities in children at risk of losing such skills. Repeated yearly assessments can yield important information about the effectiveness of these interventions and need for change or augmentation of such therapies.

Lysosomal and peroxisomal disease

Lysosomal diseases are caused by accumulation of substrate within a cell due to a genetic malfunction of an enzyme of the lysosome. The lysosome is an organelle in the cytoplasm of the cell surrounded by a membrane which contains a variety of enzymes that digest large molecules taken up by the cell by endocytosis. This degradation is hydrolytic (using water to break down a compound). If an enzyme that breaks down a particular substrate is absent or malfunctions, the substrate builds up in the cell, which is the basis of various "lysosomal storage" diseases. More than 60 lysosomal diseases are known with various outcomes and effects on the central nervous system. A listing of the more common disorders with links to the National Library of Medicine OMIM website can be found at the website of the Lysosomal Disease Network (www.lysosomaldiseasenetwork.org).

Adrenoleukodystrophy is the only disease we shall discuss in the category of peroxisomal diseases. The peroxisome is an organelle in the cell which contains enzymes necessary to oxidize toxic substances such as very-long-chain fatty acids. In this disease, it is not the enzymes that are absent but rather there is a defect in the gene that codes for a group of transporter proteins that transfer fatty acids into the peroxisomes. How this happens is still not known.

In this chapter we will discuss two lysosomal disease categories in detail: (1) mucopolysaccharidoses

431

(MPS), (2) the leukodystrophies, metachromatic and globoid cell leukodystrophies (MLD and GLD); and we will address a peroxisomal disease, adrenoleukodystrophy (ALD). Finally, we will cover Batten disease, Gaucher disease, Fabry disease, Neimann Pick A, B, and C disease, and the gangliosidoses (Sandhoff and Tay-Sachs diseases) by presenting information in tabular format (Table 15.1).

Mucopolysaccharidoses

The mucopolysaccharidoses are caused by the absence of enzymes that break down glycosaminoglycans (GAGs) (mucopolysaccharides – long chains of sugars) which as a result collect in cells throughout the body and are not broken down into simpler molecules. Accumulation of GAGs damages cells in various parts of the body depending on which enzyme is absent, causing physical and mental disability. Damage to the cells affects many parts of the body, depending on the absent enzyme. Generally, bone, cartilage, corneas, skin, connective tissue, soft tissue and brain can be affected. Diagnosis is usually made by urine tests measuring excretion of GAGs, by enzyme analysis, and by clinical examination. Definitive analysis can be made by examining white blood cells and searching for the mutation. The incidence in Australia is 1:22 500 births [35] for all MPS disorders. Estimates for the USA have been made around 1 in 26 000 but no studies have been done [36].

Children with MPS disorders generally appear normal at birth but the first signs can occur any time depending on the form of MPS disorder. MPS disorders are progressive and worsen over time, but the severity varies. Generally, the more severe the disorder, the earlier is the onset of signs and symptoms. All but one MPS disorder are autosomal recessive; MPS II (Hunter syndrome) is an X-linked disorder, transmitted through the X chromosome from mother to son. These syndromes are found across all races although mutations vary from one ethnic group to another. Generally the severity of the disease is concordant within a family. For example, if one child has a severe form of the disease, other siblings with the disease will show a similar natural history.

The most common forms of MPS disorders are MPS I (Hurler, Hurler-Scheie, and Scheie syndromes in order of lessening severity) and MPS III (Sanfilippo A, B, C or D). MPS II (Hunter syndrome, mild and severe form) and MPS VI (Maroteaux Lamy syndrome)) follow in frequency, and MPS IV (Morquio

syndrome) and VII (Sly syndrome) are extremely rare and will not be extensively discussed here. Of these disorders, MPS III is the only one that is primarily a neurological disease; the others are multi-organ diseases. MPS I and MPS II in their severe forms affect the CNS, while MPS VI has the fewest effects on the CNS. A general review of the MPS disorders can be found in Neufeld and Muenzer [37], Whitley [38], and Muenzer [39].

Mucopolysaccharidosis Type I

MPS I is due to the deficiency of alpha-L-iduronidase. As a result of this deficiency, heparan sulfate and dermatan sulfate, two mucopolysaccharides or GAGs, build up in the body and gradually cause organ damage. The first symptoms are enlargement of the liver and spleen, inguinal hernias, and chronic otitis media. Later the cardiac and respiratory function are affected, corneal clouding develops, and conductive hearing loss occurs. Orthopedic problems develop later and become quite severe. During the first and second year of life, facial features coarsen and airway problems become more severe.

The defective gene in MPS I has been mapped to 4p16.3. The two most common severe mutations are W402X and Q70X. Of the three forms of MPS I, Hurler syndrome, the most severe, has an onset in the first 2 years of life and is characterized by gradual cognitive involvement. Early in the severe disease, while no abnormalities of reflexes are found, large head and peripheral nerve involvement does occur. Communicating hydrocephalus is a common occurrence; seizures are not seen until end-stage disease. MRI scans indicate increased ventricular size, occasional T2 white matter periventricular hyperintensities, and Virchow-Robin space (perivascular inclusions). Figure 15.1 demonstrates these abnormalities. The median age of death is 5 years for untreated children with Hurler syndrome.

Hurler syndrome

Most children with Hurler syndrome show normal developmental milestones during the first year of life. During the second year, development slows, and in the third year plateaus followed by decline. Because of new treatments, data are sparse regarding the untreated natural history of cognitive development. However, our database yields cross-sectional information about 137 untreated or not yet treated children suggesting

Table 15.1. Table of lysosomal diseases.

Disease	Phenotypes	Description	Cognitive/behavioral	MR findings	Treatment
Gaucher disease (glucocerebrosidase deficiency) lipid storage disease	1. Non-neuronopathic type; any age onset; no CNS involvement 2. Neuronopathic type; any age onset with CNS involvement; early childhood onset usually die by age 2	Enlarged spleen and liver, destruction of red/white blood cells and platelets, osteoporosis, oculomotor apraxia and supranuclear gaze palsy	Homozygotes and heterozygotes of non-neuronopathic types, the neuronopathic predisposed to Parkinsons; neuronopathic: dementia; learning, speech, auditory, visual problems found in children; IQ diminishes but neuropsychological profile not yet defined	Although most MRIs are normal even in non-neuronopathic types, the most common abnormalities are those in the basal ganglia	ERT for both types; substrate reduction
Fabry disease X-linked disorder (alpha-galactosidase-A deficiency) lipid storage disease	Males and female carriers; females have a wider range of symptoms from none to severe; age of onset in males is often in childhood	Male homozygotes; affects kidneys, autonomic nervous system, cardiovascular system; risk heart attack, stroke, kidney failure; skin lesions	No studies done but the risk of stroke is high; neuropsychological profiles are those related to location of stroke and white matter changes; pain and peripheral neuropathy cause poor quality of life	White matter findings are common in Fabry typical of small vessel disease; MRS findings implicate deep white matter changes.	ERT
Niemann Pick A and B (sphingomyelinase deficiency)	A. Presents in infancy around 6 months of age B. Any age of onset. Spleen, liver and lungs – free of neurological disease; possibly A and B are opposite ends of a spectrum of neurological involvement	A. Hepatospleno-megaly, lose milestones, hypotonia, cherry red spot, diagnosis to death mean is 21 months	Normal development to 6 months, then stops progressing and regresses	Delayed myelination	No treatment. HSCT has been tried with little success. Gene therapy trials in animals
Niemann Pick C (acid sphingomyelinase deficiency secondary to problem in cellular cholesterol metabolism)	Spectrum of onset from infancy to adulthood	Average age of diagnosis 10 years but can start much earlier. Ataxia, dystonia, spasticity, myoclonic jerks, vertical supranuclear gaze palsy, dementia, and psychiatric illness in adults Neurofibrillary tangles on autopsy	Motor and cognitive decline in children. In adults psychiatric symptoms of psychosis predominate and may be the initial presenting symptom; decreased executive (trailmaking, verbal fluency), and verbal memory are seen in early disease; visual spatial memory intact	Normal at first; cerebellar atrophy and cortical atrophy in late stages; sometimes thinning of the corpus callosum and white matter changes	Substrate reduction is in clinical trials

Table 15.1. (cont.)

Disease	Phenotypes	Description	Cognitive/behavioral	MR findings	Treatment
Pompe disease (alpha-glucosidase deficiency) glycogen storage disease	1. Early onset, die in the first yr of life 2. Late onset, any age from childhood on	1. Hypotonia, weakness, cardiomyopathy 2. Highly variable age of onset with muscle weakness; respiratory insufficiency	1. Question of neurological abnormality in treated children who now survive longer 2. No known cognitive abnormalities; motor problems	Myelination defect in infants; ERT associated with improved myelin development	ERT improved survival in early onset and relief of symptoms in late onset
Batten disease (neuronal ceroid lipofuscinosis; protein for CLN3 not yet identified)	CLN1: infantile onset 6 mos to 2 yrs of age (Santavuori-Haltia disease) CLN2: late infantile onset 2–4 yrs of age (Jansky-Bielschowsky disease) CLN3: juvenile onset 5–8 yrs of age (Batten disease)	1. Microcephaly, myoclonic jerks, mental deterioration, seizures 2. Ataxia, seizures, mental deterioration 3. Insidious onset of seizures, cognitive decline, loss of vision and motor skills	1. Rapid visual and cognitive decline, little acquisition of skills 2. Loss of motor and visual function, cognitive decline 3. Visual processing difficulties; memory loss, IQ decline, motor difficulties, psychiatric problems in a subset (depression/anxiety)	Abnormal basal ganglia, thalamus, and atrophy.	No treatment except symptomatic treatment of seizures
GM1 gangliosidosis (beta-galactosidase deficiency)	1. Early infantile 2. Late infantile 3. Adult	1. Neurodegeneration, seizures, liver and spleen enlargement, facial coarsening, exaggerated startle, motor problems; deaf/blind by age 1 year 2. Same as above but with speech problems and ataxia 3. Muscle atrophy, slow cognitive decline, and dystonia	1. and 2. Failure to thrive; speech and motor development absent or loss; loss of milestones 3. Severe speech dysarthria, dystonia and motor incapability, but dementia if exists is very slow	Abnormal myelin development; basal ganglia, specifically putamen abnormality	Substrate reduction is being tried
GM2 gangliosidosis Tay-Sachs (alpha subunit of hexosaminidase A deficiency) **Sandhoff** (beta subunit of hexosaminidase A and B deficiency)	1. Infantile 2. Late onset (LOTS)	1. Deterioration of brain with seizures, blindness, deafness, unable to swallow; death by 4 years 2. Speech and gait difficulties, cognitive decline, psychosis	1. Normal development to 6 months, then stops progressing and regresses 2. Problems in executive functioning, memory; cerebellar dysfunction; impairment in specific domains, but no dementia	1. Abnormality of basal ganglia and thalamus extending to cortex. MRS shows demyelination, gliosis, neuronal loss 2. Marked cerebellar atrophy	Substrate reduction in LOTS seems to slow disease progress; gene therapy is research goal

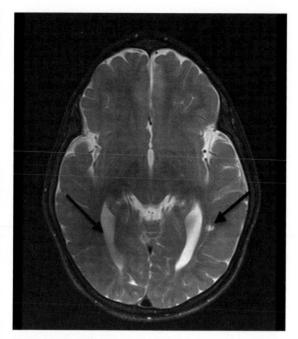

Figure 15.1. MPS I with enlarged ventricles and Virchow-Robin spaces; T2 weighted image.

that a loss occurs of about 20 points per year in developmental quotient. For example, between 1 and 2 years of age the mean developmental quotient declines from 100 to 80. Thus a child who has Hurler syndrome without treatment is likely to make slower progress month-to-month, with a mental age equivalent beginning at an average 12 months, but at 24 months the child with Hurler syndrome on average will have an age equivalent of 19 months on standardized measures. After hematopoietic stem cell transplant treatment, the slowing is diminished by half of that, with an average age equivalent of 22 months at 2 years. We have examined both cognition and language but not motor development in this fashion.

Language development appears to be most severely affected, due to a variety of causes including (1) hearing difficulties, (2) enlarged tongue preventing fluent speech, and (3) inability to encode verbal information. Motor function is impaired because of enlarged fingers and developing carpal tunnel syndrome. Visual perceptual and spatial ability is impaired due to both corneal clouding and lack of adequate motor feedback due to mobility problems early on. Behavior is normal; we have reported that in blind ratings of videotaped play behavior, no difference was found in temperament or behavior [22].

Our standard neurodevelopmental battery at first visit for children includes the Mullen Scales of Early Development [20], and the following parent-administered scales: the Vineland Adaptive Behavior Scales [40], the Bzoch League Receptive Expressive Emergent Language Scale [41], and the Child Development Inventory (if over 12 months of age) [42]. The Preschool Language Scale [43] is optional, depending on whether the child has enough reserve as these are usually 3-hour-long appointments. When the child is 18 months we add the Color Object Association Test, a measure of declarative memory [17].

At this time standard of care for treatment for severe disease is hematopoietic stem cell transplant (HSCT – bone marrow or cord blood transplant), which apparently delivers enzyme to the brain through manufacture of donor-derived microglia in the bone marrow [44]. HSCT corrects soft-tissue abnormalities and generally improves mortality. The oldest living individual in the USA with MPS I, who is alive and well, is in the mid-20s, having had a bone marrow transplant during the first year of life. Once engraftment is established and rejection by the donor cells is overcome, life expectancy improves dramatically. It has been established that the earlier the transplant the better the outcome, with children under 2 and with cognitive quotients over 70 doing better [5, 6, 45, 46]. During the first year post-transplant, the disease continues to progress but by 1 year stabilization occurs and development resumes. Thus, developmental quotients continue to decline until 1 year after transplant and then stabilize at the 1-year post-transplant level.

Initially, bone marrow transplant was a dangerous treatment when introduced by Dr. William Krivit at the University of Minnesota in the early 1980s. Since then, with the introduction of umbilical cord transplants and better transplant regimens, mortality has improved, with about a 90% survival rate. With the development of recombinant enzyme (Aldurazyme™) which does not cross the blood–brain barrier, pre-treatment prior to transplant with enzyme replacement therapy (ERT) to improve the physical health of children undergoing transplant has decreased the mortality risk much further [47]. Although treatment with enzyme improves the physical health of children [48], since enzyme does not cross the blood–brain barrier, it is not a sufficient treatment for the cognitive decline, thus retaining transplant as a necessary treatment for neurological disease.

435

Despite these successes, the underlying mechanism of the cognitive decline is not certain. As noted above, perivascular Virchow-Robin spaces are frequent but we have found that the size and number of these spaces are not related to cognitive ability. Matheus et al. [49] also found that MRI findings did not correlate with disease severity except when atrophy or white matter abnormalities were present. Animal work [50] has indicated secondary storage of gangliosides which are neurotoxic agents. One of these gangliosides, GM2, correlates with abnormal formation of dendrites on the axon hillock during development and results in sparse synaptic connections. In a study by Karachunski [51], nine brains of children who died as a result of transplant before any treatment could take effect were examined and storage material was found distributed around all of the cortex, but the dentate gyrus and CA4 of the hippocampus were the only parts of the brain that were universally affected.

Long-term follow-up after transplant: in the examination of children 5 to 20 years post-transplant, preliminary data from our laboratory indicate low normal IQ, language skills, and memory, and no behavioral or emotional problems. However, poor vigilance, slow reaction time, and deficits in visual perceptual/spatial skills (possibly secondary to corneal clouding) were prevalent. Most children had severe corneal clouding impairing vision of low-contrast stimuli. On imaging, no difference was found in the hippocampus compared to controls (suggesting HSCT has a protective effect on the hippocampus), but significant effects on white matter were found on diffusion tensor imaging (DTI) with decreased fractional anisotropy using sagittal sections of the corpus callosum as the region of interest. This preliminary finding suggests poor white matter connectivity. Furthermore, significant correlations with fractional anisotropy were found on both reaction time and measures of vigilance on the TOVA (Test of Variables of Attention) [52], suggesting poor visual processing and attention related to white matter compromise. From other related findings of late effects in children undergoing chemotherapy for leukemia (Anderson, unpublished data), these findings are probably secondary to the late effects of the chemotherapy and in some cases radiation preparatory to the transplant.

Attenuated MPS I

Forms of MPS I with later onset and less CNS disease are rarer than the severe form, and the mortality and morbidity are less. There is great variability in the presentation of attenuated MPS disease [53].

However, recent literature has indicated that the moderate form of the disease called Hurler-Scheie syndrome may also be associated with decline [54]. Onset of physical symptoms, similar to those of Hurler syndrome, occurs in early to middle childhood, and learning disabilities have been reported in these patients. We reported three siblings who over a period of more then 10 years showed considerable decline in IQ but even more dramatic loss of ability to encode new information and declarative memory [55]. Another patient with Hurler-Scheie and a mild patient with early adult onset of symptoms (Scheie syndrome) also showed significant difficulties in encoding. All of these patients were on enzyme replacement therapy with Aldurazyme™. We compared six IQ-matched attenuated MPS patients with post-transplant Hurler patients and found while IQ was the same, encoding and visual spatial ability was significantly more impaired in the attenuated patients, suggesting that transplant may protect from later memory/visual spatial loss. Preliminary results of an ongoing study using quantitative imaging and neuropsychological testing of seven patients with attenuated MPS I and seven post-transplant Hurler patients indicated memory encoding on the CVLT to be inversely related to the size of the head of the hippocampus such that the larger the head the poorer the total CVLT score [56]. This finding is completely different from the relationship reported in normals and also from the Hurler transplanted patients, in whom larger hippocampal head is positively correlated with memory. This suggests that an affinity to the hippocampus for storage material may both interfere with encoding and result in larger than normal hippocampus heads.

Neuropsychological profiles in attenuated MPS I indicate poor visual spatial ability, poor encoding of both verbal and visual spatial material, but retained problem-solving and executive functioning. Some patients demonstrate significant decline over time. With respect to emotional/behavioral symptoms, we have seen onset of internalizing difficulties in some patients especially during adolescence, but it appears to be secondary to their physical symptoms. Depression and anxiety may be present in a proportion of children. This may in part be related to their physical difficulties; frequent pain related to connective tissue and orthopedic problems which are not well resolved with ERT. Future treatments are likely to involve intrathecal enzyme replacement (injected into spinal fluid), which is feasible because data from animal work indicate that the enzyme reduces storage material in the brain and persists for 3 months, which would make it feasible in humans [57].

Mucopolysaccharidosis Type II

Hunter syndrome is an X-linked disorder which has a similar presentation to MPS I. Hunter syndrome has two forms, a severe form with onset in early childhood with significant neurological involvement, and a late-onset form with presumably normal intellectual development.

The severe form starts later than the severe form of MPS I, after 2 years of age. Early on these children often have multiple surgeries for hernia, tube placement, and tonsillectomies/adenoidectomies, often before the diagnosis is made. The pattern of organ difficulties is the same as MPS I, although the airway disease may be more severe. Major airway problems during anesthesia, sleep apnea, and decreased lung capacity are life-threatening problems. Orthopedic problems and sensory problems are similar to MPS I. The onset of problems is later and much more variable than MPS I, thus it becomes difficult early in the course of the disease to determine whether a child has a mild or severe form [58].

The CNS problems include diminishing cognitive capacity, seizures, and significant behavioral abnormalities. However, no studies have been done of the neuropsychological, neurological, or behavioral phenotypes and their progression. The lack of good neuropsychological longitudinal studies in untreated children will no doubt hamper research on treatments that can affect the CNS. Currently, a recombinant enzyme replacement, Elaprase™, has been approved by the FDA, and is effective in improving somatic manifestations [59]; however, it is unlikely to cross the blood–brain barrier. HSCT has been tried, but results are not definitive. It probably helps in the somatic disease, but no evidence exists for effectiveness on CNS disease.

The mild phenotype is associated with normal intelligence, but with many orthopedic, airway, and cardiac problems, similar to young children with the severe form. Again no data are available on the natural history of this form of MPS II.

Mucopolysaccharidosis Type III

Sanfilippo syndrome has been ignored, despite its being the most common of the MPS disorders, because no treatment has been found to be effective.

Four different subtypes have been identified, A, B, C, and D, each with a different enzymatic deficiency, but all four deposit heparan sulfate in cells. Sanfilippo A is the most common and most severe. The somatic manifestations of MPS III are few; primarily it is a neurodegenerative disease. Although atrophy on the MRI sometimes precedes dementia in these patients, no correlation between severity of MRI findings and phenotypic severity has been found [60]. Characteristic of MPS III are severe cognitive and behavioral problems. Neither the cognitive nor behavioral decline has been carefully tracked or studied. Cognitive decline includes major loss of language function and mental ability beginning in early childhood. Unless they are diagnosed very early in the course of their disease, these children are often too impaired for direct neuropsychological testing because of both language and behavioral abnormalities. Sleep problems are found in 78% of children with MPS III [61], which may also contribute to the behavioral difficulties. In older literature, aggressive, hyperactive, and increasingly demented behaviors are noted with no specific pattern defined. However, a recent questionnaire study in its pilot phase has determined a pattern of behaviors (hyperorality, masturbation, hyperlocomotion, poor visual and social recognition) that may be consistent with a Klüver-Bucy syndrome [62]. Further studies are under way to further define the nature of the problem, and determine whether amygdala/bilateral temporal lobe abnormalities are present. No treatment exists for Sanfilippo; HSCT has not been found to work [63]. Enzyme therapy is being developed, but it will need to be administered to the brain either intrathecally (spinal fluid) or directly into brain parenchyma. Gene therapies are also being developed. However, in this very interesting disease, collection of basic longitudinal data and phenotype characterization are yet to be done.

Mucopolysaccharidosis Type VI

Maroteaux Lamy syndrome has severe somatic abnormalities similar to MPS I and II, but no cognitive component. However, as in all of these diseases, sleep apnea, cardiac insufficiency, hydrocephalus, and poor quality of life as a result of orthopedic and other somatic problems contribute to poor neuropsychological function in some children. These children are not significantly impaired and have no consistent neuropsychological findings, with the exception of a subset who appear to have attention problems, but are not hyperactive. It is unclear whether this is secondary to physical illness or reflects the baseline in the population. Enzyme replacement therapy for this disease is effective [64] and now approved by the FDA. This treatment is likely to provide sufficient symptomatic relief as there is no CNS involvement.

Leukodystrophies

The leukodystrophies are a group of rare progressive genetic disorders causing demyelination with resultant dementia and death when left untreated. While all the leukodystrophies by definition are diseases of the white matter primarily, each disease has it own pathophysiological mechanism, and characteristic neurological and neuropsychological profile. Adrenoleukodystrophy is a peroxisomal disease and metachromatic leukodystrophy and globoid cell leukodystrophy are lysosomal disorders [22].

Adrenoleukodystrophy

Adrenoleukodystrophy (ALD) is a peroxisomal disease that is X-linked and maps to Xq28. Its approximate incidence is 1 in 17 900. Several phenotypes are known in ALD. The mildest phenotype is that of children and adults who have a biochemical defect only with Addison's disease. Addison's disease is adrenal insufficiency caused by pathology of the adrenal cortex. Many adults with Addison's disease are likely to progress to adrenomyeloneuropathy (AMN). This demyelinating disease affects long fiber tracts of the spinal cord and peripheral nerves only. The most devastating phenotype is the cerebral phenotype, which can occur at any time of life, but the vast majority of males who have cerebral symptoms have onset between the ages of 4 and 10. Cerebral disease occurs in 40% of cases of ALD. While family members may have the same genetic defect, phenotypic concordance is rare, with a range of phenotypes within a family [65]. Mutation analysis shows no correlation with phenotype or predicts which individuals will convert from the biochemical abnormality to cerebral disease. In addition, it is known that female carriers also have symptoms of AMN and in rare instances also can have cerebral disease manifestations [66].

Laboratory diagnosis

ALD is diagnosed by the presence of elevated plasma very-long-chain fatty acids (VLCFAs). Accumulation of VLCFAs in the plasma, adrenal cortex and brain is the result of defective beta-oxidation. Resultant pathology of the adrenal cortex causes adrenal insufficiency (Addison's disease) in 90% of patients with the biochemical abnormality. Adrenal insufficiency along with behavioral and learning problems are usually the first clinical manifestation of ALD in childhood. We have reported that the VLCFAs do not correlate with phenotype, disease progression, or neurocognitive status [27].

Cerebral ALD

It is not known what triggers the cerebral form of ALD (C-ALD). An inflammatory process has been implicated partly evidenced by the enhancement of lesions on MRI when gadolinium is infused. The role of cytokines and other neuroimmunological processes have been implicated in the inflammatory process [65]. In a case of adult-onset C-ALD, CNS trauma may have precipitated or accelerated demyelination [67].

C-ALD is characterized by rapid and devastating demyelination of the brain. If left untreated, boys with C-ALD demonstrate a downhill course affecting all aspects of higher cortical and motor functions, leading to death. The age of the child correlates with the rapidity of deterioration such that younger children have a more rapid downhill course. Approximately 80% of children with C-ALD present with characteristic demyelination of the posterior white matter on MRI with concomitant signs on neuropsychological testing. Early signs of the disease consist of diminished visual processing skills with progression to visual agnosia and eventually cortical blindness. Children with these visual symptoms are often first identified by deteriorating visual motor skills; the "visual", not the motor, is impaired. In approximately 15–20% of cases, demyelination is frontal (anterior presentation). These children have behavioral dysregulation and executive dysfunction in association with damaged frontal lobe circuits [68]. Their behaviors are similar to those typically seen in ADHD and other externalizing behavior disorders, and therefore early diagnosis may be missed due to failure to rule out an organic etiology of the child's behavioral dysregulation. New onset of ADHD during the school age years should always raise suspicions of frontal C-ALD. Figures 15.2 and 15.3 demonstrate posterior and anterior demyelination in ALD.

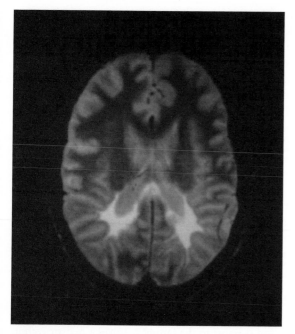

Figure 15.2. ALD with posterior increased signal; T2 weighted image.

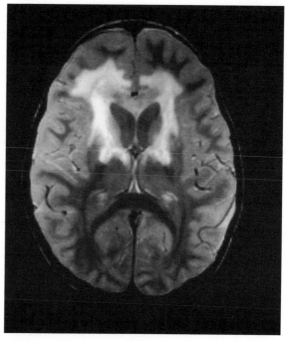

Figure 15.3. ALD with anterior increased signal; T2 weighted image.

Treatment and management

The only effective treatment of C-ALD and now the standard of care is hematopoietic stem cell transplantation (HSCT), using either bone marrow or umbilical cord blood. It usually takes 6 months before the disease is halted in children who become fully engrafted. For boys who are early in the course of their disease, HSCT appears to be effective and the mortality rate is about 10–15% [4]. Unfortunately HSCT is a very high-risk procedure due to the need to ablate the recipient's marrow, leaving the child in an immuno-compromised state. Further, continued disease progression while waiting for the full effect of transplantation, graft failure, partial engraftment, or complications of transplant including graft-versus-host disease and infection result in a high level of morbidity and a 30% mortality rate when boys with severe disease are included in the statistics. This mortality rate is high because in severe disease, HSCT appears to accelerate the course of the disease, presumably because the transplant regimen has a negative effect on boys with severe demyelination. It is known that some agents used in the pre-transplant regimens (e.g. busulfan) are neurotoxic and potentially enhance disease progression during the time between transplant, engraftment, and remission. For these reasons, an agent with antioxidant and radical scavenger

capabilities, N-acetyl-L-cysteine (NAC), has been used and found to stabilize the disease during the transplant process (NAC is known as Mucomyst™). NAC has been hypothesized to provide neuroprotective capacity. Along with this treatment, a less neurotoxic transplant regimen has been put in place. In three boys with advanced disease, treatment with NAC pre- and post-transplant resulted in survival. Prior to the use of NAC no patient survived with disease as severe as these three patients. Unfortunately, these boys were left with severe disability [69].

Evidence is strong that the earlier the child comes to transplant, the better are the physical and neurocognitive outcomes. Previous neuropsychological research suggested that a Performance IQ below 80 was a marker for poorer neurocognitive outcome and continued disease progression, suggesting that there is a point of separation where the risks of continued disease progression outstrip the potential neurocognitive and quality-of-life benefits of HSCT [3, 22].

For children with the biochemical abnormality, longitudinal monitoring with biannual MRIs utilizing a standardized scoring method (Loes Scale) [70] and repeatable neuropsychological assessment battery is essential for detecting the earliest signs and symptoms of onset of cerebral disease. Early detection is critical for positive transplant prognosis. Neuropsychological functioning is the primary yardstick for disease severity.

Neuropsychological functioning

Profiles of neuropsychological test results in ALD were characterized in the 1990s using a sample of boys being evaluated for HSCT. As a group they tended to show early signs of the disease including early MRI white matter changes and emerging visual processing deficits. The Performance IQ (PIQ) from the Wechsler Intelligence Scale for Children, Third Edition (WISC-III) was a particularly sensitive measure of disease progression and a robust predictor of outcome following HSCT. Children with posterior disease with PIQs below 80 often showed persistent disease progression even in the context of engraftment. Statistically PIQ accounted for 83% of the variance in clinical status [71]. Since the revision of the Wechsler Scale to the Fourth Edition (WISC-IV), the Perceptual Reasoning Index as a replacement of Performance IQ has not shown similar sensitivity. It is likely that the dropping of the Picture Completion and Picture Arrangement subtests from the composite score in the WISC-IV made the PRI insensitive to disease status, progress, and outcome. We had previously found that these three subtests taken together along with the Block Design were exquisitely sensitive to the disease state in ALD (posterior presentation). We had previously determined that the Raven progressive matrices (similar to Matrices) as well as object identification measures (similar to Picture Reasoning) were not sensitive to ALD disease status. Thus the change in make-up of the nonverbal measures on the WISC altered the sensitivity of the test to the disease.

In boys with the anterior presentation, measures of attention/executive functioning and verbal/language skills are a better clinical indicator of disease status and progression. Unfortunately, given the limited number of boys with anterior disease no test composite predicted outcome. However, measures of attention such as the TOVA [52] and working memory from the WISC-III were abnormal.

While neuropsychological measures and structural MRI are sensitive indicators of cerebral disease, no imaging paradigm, biomarker or neuropsychological assessment procedures have been able to predict which boys will convert from biochemical abnormality to cerebral disease or identify these boys prior to the emergence of clinical or MRI signs. Early trials using MRS held some promise in cerebral disease prediction. In a small sample MRS metabolite abnormalities were found to correlate with impairment on neuropsychological testing before the presence of demyelination on MRI [72]. While this finding held promise, in a follow-up study we were unable to predict progression to cerebral disease even with high-field (4 tesla) magnetic resonance spectroscopy [33]. In a series of three patients diffusion tensor imaging (DTI) showed sensitivity to demyelination, and in one case DTI abnormality preceded white matter lesions [73]. This technology holds promise in predicting cerebral onset prior to appearance of structural MRI abnormalities.

The neuropsychologist is critical in the management of ALD. Monitoring asymptomatic patients, measuring disease severity prior to transplant, and monitoring treatment outcomes are crucial activities. In addition, helping parents obtain appropriate services, interpreting unusual behavioral manifestations such as visual agnosia and executive dysfunction in the context of the school environment, suggesting educational and rehabilitative interventions, and providing support to the family requires a neuropsychologist who will be willing to see such children on a regular basis and is familiar with the disease course.

Metachromatic leukodystrophy

Metachromatic leukodystrophy (MLD) is a lysosomal storage disease due to the enzyme deficiency of arylsulfatase A. Progressive demyelination results from an accumulation of sulfatides (cerebroside sulfate) stored in the brain, peripheral nervous system and other tissues. Left untreated the disease results in death. MLD is an autosomal recessive disorder mapping to 22q13. Its incidence is approximately 1 in 100 000 births [67, 74].

Diagnosis

Arylsulfatase A enzyme activity may be decreased in leukocytes or in cultured skin fibroblasts. It is important that it is distinguished from arylsulfatase A pseudodeficiency by obtaining urine sulfatide levels and DNA mutation analysis [75]. Structural MRI scan abnormalities are often the indication for further diagnostic testing. MLD is characterized by increased signal in the white matter, greater in the anterior than posterior regions.

Phenotypic variability

There are at least three phenotypes associated with age of disease onset, a late infantile form (2 to 6 years), a juvenile form (6 to 12 years), and a late-onset form in adolescents and adults. The concordance of pheno-types within a family is tight. Children and adults show onset of disease generally within the same age group and with similar rate of decline and disease course.

Disease onset of late infantile MLD is character-ized by rapid motor deterioration with tremor and weakness. This is often misdiagnosed as cerebral palsy. Soon after motor symptoms, neurocognitive impairments appear and the children are often bed-ridden within months after diagnosis. The children can survive for years in a vegetative state. Juvenile and adult phenotypes differ from early-onset forms by the first indicator being neurobehavioral symptoms. The disease then shows variable progression of motor disability. In the juvenile form children often show symptoms of ADHD and are treated for years with psychostimulants with poor results. In adolescents and adults, neurobehavioral symptoms are depres-sion, psychosis, and conduct difficulties [76, 77]. In particular, signs of executive dysfunction are prom-inent with symptoms such as trouble with the law, promiscuous behavior, and credit-card debt. In others, depression and psychotic symptoms are man-ifest. These psychiatric presentations usually lead to misdiagnosis. Eventually the signs and symptoms of frontal dementia and loss of cognition results in an MRI identified as indicative of demyelination with subsequent biochemical diagnosis. An MRI in a late-onset MLD patient with frontal demyelination can be seen in Figure 15.4.

Treatment

While HSCT is often used to treat MLD, its effec-tiveness is variable. In the late infantile form in which motor disease is present, motor decline con-tinues. In children who were identified based on sibling diagnosis before the onset of CNS symptoms, HSCT can arrest or slow cerebral disease progression [78], but it does not halt peripheral demyelination and severe motor disability. Such children are in wheel chairs and are unable to physically perform any physical tasks; even though they may have pre-served cognitive functions, their quality of life is poor [79].

In adults, HSCT has been found to halt disease pro-gression and the motor disease is less salient. However, given that many patients are diagnosed late, due to misdiagnoses associated with the neuropsychiatric pre-sentation, their pre-transplant disease is advanced and

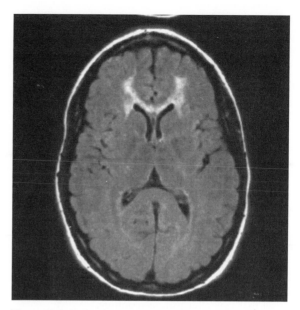

Figure 15.4. MLD with anterior increased signal; diffusion weighted image.

their quality of life may be poor. Adults are left with a considerable frontal lobe syndrome, characterized by behavioral and emotional dysregulation, poor initiation, and need for full-time care [80].

At this time HSCT is generally recommended for late-onset patients who are early in their disease course. Although asymptomatic cases are still being transplanted, HSCT is not recommended for sympto-matic early-onset cases. As HSCT is an imperfect treat-ment for MLD, novel treatments such as enzyme replacement and gene therapy are in development. However, ERT will need to be delivered to the brain directly, which as discussed above is problematic.

Neuropsychological functioning

In late infantile MLD, Shapiro et al. reported findings on 21 untreated patients, ages 2.3 to 7.2 years [68]. Motor symptoms appear first, followed quickly by visual perceptual and verbal learning deficits. Language, reading and behavioral and emotional func-tioning appear spared until later in the disease. The pattern of deficit somewhat resembles nonverbal learning disability without social and emotional prob-lems. This may be due to the fact that social skills were acquired prior to disease onset [81].

In late-onset disease, frontal dementia is identified after diagnosis with psychiatric disorders ranging from ADHD to schizophrenia. In 11 patients, ages 10 to 35 years, very poor attention skills were documented on continuous performance testing. Verbal learning was also deficient. There was moderate impairment on formal measures of executive functioning and visual memory. Auditory processing, language and reading skills were preserved. Motor impairments were variable [68, 76].

From a neuropsychological standpoint, this disease illustrates a point that the timing of disease onset in development alters the phenotype. While all patients have the same biochemical abnormality, and most show frontal demyelination, the phenotype varies from age to age; motor symptoms predominate in young children, ADHD symptoms in older children, and psychiatric disorders in adolescents and adults. We do not know whether this relates to the particular pathways that are functional at different ages or the particular mutations associated with early and late onset that may alter pathophysiology.

Globoid cell leukodystrophy

Global cell leukodystrophy (GLD), also called Krabbé disease, is a lysosomal storage disease caused by deficiency of galactocerebrosidase (GALC) activity. GALC degrades psychosine. Increased psychosine levels lead to destruction of oligodendrocytes, resulting in demyelination. GLD is an autosomal recessive disease caused by a mutation in the GALC gene at 14q31 [82]. GLD can be diagnosed by testing a sample of blood or skin cells to measure activity levels of galactocerebrocidase. Patients with GLD show very low or absent activity levels.

Phenotypic variability

GLD has two phenotypes; the infantile and late-onset forms. The most common form of GLD is the rapidly progressing infantile form, usually called Krabbé disease. Symptoms that appear before 6 months of age and include irritability, dysphagia, progressive spasticity, mental deterioration, blindness, deafness, seizures, and death, usually before 2 years of age. The late-onset form typically begins later from childhood through adulthood, has a more insidious onset, and progresses variably over a period of several years slowly to death. The late-onset form is not concordant. First symptoms are usually motor, but not always, as demyelination can occur in any areas of the brain. Rate of disease progression, effect on neuropsychological function, and age of onset also can vary enormously. MRIs show patchy demyelination in any area of the brain but more likely in posterior white matter [68, 83].

Treatment

HSCT using cord blood is the only treatment that has had any success in treating Krabbé disease. Disease progression at the time of transplant is highly predictive of developmental outcomes. Thus, children must be treated before the onset of neurological symptoms for a favorable outcome. Transplantation after neurological symptoms does not halt disease progression [84, 85]. A newborn screening program has been put into place in the state of New York for Krabbé disease. Several infants have been detected in this fashion and early transplant has occurred. However, outcomes are yet to be studied due to slow accrual of patients in this rare disease.

In late-onset GLD, patients treated with HSCT show generally positive outcomes. Again this depends on the disease stage and extent of demyelination [86].

Neuropsychological functioning

In Krabbé disease, an HSCT treatment outcome study found that most children gained cognitive, language, fine and adaptive skills at a normal rate in those treated before the onset of significant neurological symptoms. Most, however, had some degree of gross motor delay [84].

In a small sample of treated late-onset GLD patients, most present with progressive motor involvement. However, visual perceptual and visual spatial problems are found with associated math, visual processing, and executive functioning deficits. Language and auditory processing skills remain preserved [86]. Generally, this is concordant with MRI data showing increased signal in any area of the white matter, but more likely in posterior than anterior regions. Pathology in GLD is demonstrated in Figure 15.5.

Future directions

Newborn screening

This has been a controversial topic. One question is whether screening is ethical for diseases for which we have no effective treatment. What constitutes an effective treatment is also debatable. One problem is that we cannot identify whether a child will have an early severe or a late mild disease from newborn screening.

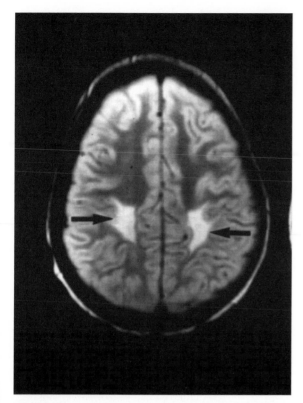

Figure 15.5. GLD (Krabbé) with posterior increased signal; T2 weighted image.

Many of the treatments are expensive and pose risks in themselves. On the other hand, very early diagnosis may have beneficial effects for both brain and bone [87]. However, most current treatments are not effective to ensure cognitive normality and absence of orthopedic problems. Due to passage and signing of a newborn screening bill in April 2008, funds will be available to states in the USA to increase their efforts to carry out newborn screening. More children with these diseases will be identified earlier.

Early diagnosis

Most studies have determined that earlier treatment is better for prevention of cognitive abnormality. The role of the neuropsychologist in tracking children who have been identified at birth requires knowledge of infant testing and the development of better measures of neuropsychological function for very young children. In addition to our usual armamentarium of measures, we need to incorporate experimental measures such as evoked responses and EEG and imaging techniques to monitor outcomes.

New treatments

Hematopoietic stem cell treatment was the first effective treatment for several diseases (Hurler syndrome, and late-onset metachromatic and globoid cell leukodystrophy, adrenoleukodystrophy). It continues to be the only effective way to get enzyme into the brain. Enzyme replacement therapy is now an important way of treating somatic features of these diseases, but because these large molecules cannot cross the blood–brain barrier, ERT does not change cognitive function except indirectly. However, efforts are now under way to develop methods of directly infusing enzyme either into the spinal fluid or directly into the brain parenchyma. Here neuropsychological measurement is going to be crucial to monitor outcome. There are other new treatments as well, including substrate reduction, chaperone therapies, and anti-inflammatory/antioxidant agents. Gene therapy trials are now beginning in a few diseases. In addition, combinations of these treatments are likely to be the future of effective treatments; two examples discussed above are ERT and HSCT and anti-inflammatories and HSCT, both creating better outcomes.

Neuropsychologists have been involved from the beginning in tracking the outcomes of these disorders after treatment and play a key role not only in providing a necessary clinical service but also in developing research designs that answer important questions of treatment outcome. However, in order to do that, delineating the natural history and the specific localization of disruption of neural development is necessary in order to know what functions need tracking over time. All of the new treatment approaches will require neuropsychological approaches to measuring outcome. However, ever-changing technology in diagnosis and treatment will have an impact on neuropsychological outcomes, requiring the neuropsychologist to keep up with these innovations and rapidly adjust their methods and research goals. Neuropsychologists will need to work in innovative ways to measure outcomes using tools such as imaging, experimental techniques, and longitudinal methods as well as develop a knowledge base that includes the genetics, biochemistry, and neurodevelopmental characteristics of these diseases.

Resources for the clinician:
www.lysosomaldiseasenetwork.org
www.mpssociety.org

www.ulf.org

www.rarediseases.org

http://www.lysosomaldiseasenetwork.org/resources.shtml

(this last web site lists many patient advocacy groups/resources)

References

1. Scriver CR, Beaudet AL, Sly WS, Valle D, eds. *The Metabolic and Molecular Bases of Inherited Disease.* New York: McGraw-Hill; 2001.

2. Bjoraker K, Delaney K, Peters C, Krivit W, Shapiro E. Long term outcomes of adaptive functions for children with MPS I. *J Dev Behav Pediatr* 2006;**27**:290–6.

3. Shapiro E, Krivit W, Lockman L, Jambaqué I, Peters C, Cowan M, et al. Long-term beneficial effect of bone marrow transplantation for childhood onset cerebral X-linked adrenoleukodystrophy. *Lancet* 2000;**356**:713–18.

4. Peters C, Charnas L, Tan Y, Ziegler R, Shapiro E, DeFor T, et al. Cerebral X-linked adrenoleukodystrophy: the international hematopoietic cell transplantation experience from 1982 to 1999. *Blood* 2004;**104**:881–8.

5. Peters C, Shapiro E, Anderson J, Henslee-Downey J, Klemperer M, Cowan M, et al. Hurler Syndrome: II. Outcome of HLA-genotypically identical sibling and HLA-haploidentical related donor bone marrow transplantation in fifty-four children. *Blood* 1998;**91**:2601–8.

6. Peters C, Balthazor M, Shapiro E, King R, Kollman C, Hegland J, et al. Outcome of unrelated donor bone marrow transplantation in forty children with Hurler syndrome. *Blood* 1996;**87**:4894–902.

7. Brandt J. The Hopkins Verbal Learning Test: development of a new memory test with six equivalent forms. *Clin Neuropsychol* 1991;**5**:125–42.

8. Benedict RHB, Schretlen D, Groninger L, Dobraski M, Shpritz, B. Revision of the Brief Visuospatial Memory Test: studies of normal performance, reliability, and validity. *Psychol Assess* 1996;**8**:145–53.

9. Sirois P, Posner M, Stehbens JA, Loveland KA, Nichols S, Donfield SM, et al. Hemophilia Growth and Development Study. Quantifying practice effects in longitudinal research with the WISC-R and WAIS-R: A study of children and adolescents with hemophilia and male siblings without hemophilia. *J Ped Psychol* 2002;**27**:121–31.

10. Salthouse TA, Berish DE. Correlates of within-person (across-occasion) variability in reaction time. *Neuropsychology* 2005;**19**:77–87.

11. Fuentes K, Hunter MA, Strauss E, Hultsch DF. Intraindividual variability in cognitive performance in persons with chronic fatigue syndrome. *Clin Neuropsychol* 2001;**15**:210–27.

12. Strauss E, Hultsch DF, Hunter M, Slick DJ, Patry B, Levy-Bencheton J. Using intraindividual variability to detect malingering in cognitive performance. *Clin Neuropsychol* 1999;**13**:420–32.

13. Strauss E, MacDonald S, Hunter M, Moll A, Hultsch DF. Intraindividual variability in cognitive performance in three groups of older adults: cross-domain links to physical status and self-perceived affect and beliefs. *J Int Neuropsych Soc* 2002;**8**:893–906.

14. Macdonald S, Hultsch DF, Bunce D. Intraindividual variability in vigilance performance: does degrading visual stimuli mimic age-related "neural noise"?' *J Clin Exp Neuropsychol* 2006;**28**:655–75.

15. Russell VA, Oades, RD, Tannock R, Killeen PR, Auerbach JG, Johansen EB, Sagvolden T. Response variability in Attention-Deficit/Hyperactivity Disorder: a neuronal and glial energetics hypothesis. *Behav Brain Funct* 2006;**2**:30.

16. Goldman D, Shapiro E, Nelson CA. Measurement of vigilance in 2-year old children. *Dev Neuropsychol* 2004;**25**:227–50.

17. Jordan C, Hughes S, Johnson A, Shapiro E. The Color Object Association Test (COAT): the development of a new measure of declarative memory for 18 to 36 month-old toddlers. *Child Neuropsychol* 2008;**14**:21–41.

18. Roid, Gale H. *Stanford Binet Intelligence Scale, 5th edn.*, Rolling Meadows, IL: Riverside; 2003.

19. Wechsler D. *Wechsler Intelligence Scale for Children. Fourth Edition.* San Antonio, TX: Harcourt Assessments; 2003.

20. Mullen E. *The Mullen Scales of Early Learning.* Bloomington, MN: Pearson Assessments; 1995.

21. Bayley N. *Bayley Scales of Infant Development II.* San Antonio, TX: Harcourt Assessments; 1993.

22. Shapiro E, Balthazor M. Metabolic and neurodegenerative disorders of childhood. In Taylor G. Ris D, Yeates K, eds. *Pediatric Neuropsychology: Research, Theory and Practice.* New York: Guilford Press; 2001: 171–205.

23. Charnas L, Ziegler R, Shapiro E. Pediatric chronic disease. In Rizzo M, Eslinger P, eds. *Principles and Practice of Behavioral Neurology and Neuropsychology.* Philadelphia, PA: Saunders; 2004: 983–99.

24. Martin HR, Poe MD, Reinhartsen D, Pretzel RE, Roush J, Rosenberg A, Dusing SC, Escolar, M. Methods for assessing neurodevelopment in lysosomal storage diseases and related

disorders: a multidisciplinary perspective. *Acta Pædiatr* 2008;**97**:69–75.

25. Kempen J, Kritchevsky M, Feldman ST. Effect of visual impairment on neuropsychological test performance. *J Clin Exp Neuropsychol* 1994;**16**:223–31.

26. Das JP, Ojile E. Cognitive processing of students with and without hearing loss. *J Spec Educ* 1995;**29**:323–36.

27. Krivit W, Lockman L, Watkins P.A, Hirsch J, Shapiro E. The future for treatment by bone marrow transplantation for adrenoleukodystrophy, metachromatic leukodystrophy, globoid cell leukodystrophy and Hurler syndrome. *J Inher Metab Dis* 1995;**18**:398–412.

28. Ashworth JL, Biswas S, Wraith E, Lloyd IC. Mucopolysaccharidoses and the eye. *Survey Ophthal* 2006;**51**:1–17.

29. Sakai S, Hirayama K, Ogura K, Sakai N, Sudoh M, Murata N, Iwasaki S. Visual function of a patient with advanced adrenoleukodystrophy: comparison of luminance and color contrast sensitivities. *Brain Dev* 2008;**30**:68–72.

30. Baumann N, Turpin J-C, Lefevre M, Colsch B. Motor and psycho-cognitive clinical types in adult metachromatic leukodystrophy: genotype/phenotype relationships. *J Physiol Paris* 2002;**96**:301–6.

31. Shapiro E, Lipton M, Krivit W. White matter dysfunction and its neuropsychological correlates: a longitudinal study of a case of metachromatic leukodystrophy treated with bone marrow transplant. *J Clin Exp Neuropsychol* 1992;**14**:610–24.

32. Shapiro E, Thrall M, Peters C, Krivit W. Language, hearing loss, and mental development in Hurler syndrome. *J Int Neuropsychol Soc* 2000;**6**:161(Abstract).

33. Öz G, Tkác I, Charnas L, Choi I-Y, Bjoraker K. Shapiro E, Gruetter R. Assessment of adrenoleukodystrophy lesions by high field *MRS* in non-sedated pediatric patients. *Neurology* 2005;**64**:434–41.

34. Schneider JFL, Il'yansov KA, Boltshauser E, Henniga J, Martin E. Diffusion tensor imaging in cases of adrenoleukodystrophy: preliminary experience as a marker for early demyelination? *Am J Neuroradiol* 2003;**24**:819–24.

35. Nelson J, Crowhurst J, Carey B, Greed L. Incidence of the mucopolysaccharidoses in Western Australia. *Am J Med Genet* 2003;**123A**:310–13.

36. Whitley C, Draper KA, Dutton CM, Brown PA, Severson SL, France LA. Diagnostic test for mucopolysaccharidosis. II. Rapid quantification of glycosaminoglycan in urine samples collected on a paper matrix. *Clin Chem* 1989;**35**:2074–81.

37. Neufeld EF, Muenzer J. The mucopolysaccharidoses. In Scriver CR, Beaudet AL, Sly WS, Valle D, eds. *The Metabolic and Molecular Bases of Inherited Disease.* New York: McGraw-Hill; 2001: 3421–52.

38. Whitley CB. The mucopolysaccharidoses. In Moser HW, ed. *Neurodystrophies and Neurolipidoses*, vol. 22 of *Handbook of Clinical Neurology.* Amsterdam: Elsevier; 1996: 281–328.

39. Muenzer J. The mucopolysaccharidoses: a heterogeneous group of disorders with variable pediatric presentations. *J Pediatr* 2004;**144**:S27–34.

40. Sparrow S, Cicchetti D, Balla D. *Vineland Adaptive Behavior Scales*, 2nd edn. Bloomington, MN: Pearson Assessments; 1984.

41. Bzoch K, League R, Brown V. *Receptive–Expressive Emergent Language Scale*, 3rd edn. Austin, TX: Pro-Ed; 2003.

42. Ireton, H. *Child Development Inventory (CDI).* Minneapolis, MN: Behavior Science Systems; 1992.

43. Zimmerman I, Steiner V, Pond R. *Preschool Language Scale*, 4th edn. San Antonio, TX: Harcourt Assessment; 2002.

44. Krivit W, Sung J, Shapiro E, Lockman L. Microglia: the effector cell for reconstitution of the central nervous system following bone marrow transplantation for lysosomal and peroxisomal storage diseases. *Cell Transpl* 1995;**4**:385–92.

45. Staba SL, Escolar ML, Poe M, Kim Y, Martin PL, Szabolcs P, et al. Cord-blood transplants from unrelated donors in patients with Hurler's syndrome. *N Engl J Med* 2004;**350**:1960–9.

46. Souillet G, Guffon N, Maire I, Pujol M, Taylor P, Sevin F, et al. Outcome of 27 patients with Hurler's syndrome transplanted from either related or unrelated haematopoietic stem cell sources. *Bone Marrow Transpl* 2003;**31**:1105–17.

47. Tolar J, Grewal S, Bjoraker K, Whitley C, Shapiro E, Charnas L, Orchard P. Combination of enzyme replacement and hematopoietic stem cell transplantation as therapy for Hurler syndrome. *Bone Marrow Transpl* 2007;**41**:531–5.

48. Wraith JE, Beck M, Lane R, vander Ploeg A, Shapiro E, Guffon, N. Enzyme replacement therapy for mucopolysaccharidosis I patients less than 5 years old: results of a multinational study of recombinant human alpha-L-iduronidase (laronidase). *Pediatrics* 2007;**120**: e37–46.

49. Matheus G, Castillo M, Smith JK, Armao D, Towle D, Muenzer J. Brain MRI findings in patients with mucopolysaccharidosis types I and II and mild clinical presentation. *Neuroradiology* 2004;**46**:666–72.

50. Walkley SU. Secondary accumulation of gangliosides in lysosomal storage disorders. *Semin Cell Dev Biol* 2004;**15**:433–44.

51. Karachunski P, Clark B, Shapiro E. Distribution of lysosomal storage in the CNS neurons in patients with Mucopolysaccharidosis Type I. In *Proceedings of the 1st annual WORLD symposium of the Lysosomal Disease Network*, Minneapolis, MN: May 2004: 33.

52. Greenberg L. *The Test of Variables of Attention (T.O.V.A.).* Los Alamitos, CA: The TOVA Company; 1996.

53. Vijay S, Wraith JE. Clinical presentation and follow-up of patients with the attenuated phenotype of mucopolysaccharidosis type I. *Acta Paediatr* 2005;**94**:872–7.

54. Elkin TD, Megason G, Robinson A, Bock H-GO, Schrimsher G, Muenzer J. Longitudinal neurocognitive outcome in an adolescent with Hurler-Scheie syndrome. *Neuropsychiatr Dis Treat* 2006;**2**:381–6.

55. Bjoraker K, Charnas L, Whitley CB, Delaney K, Shapiro E. Neuropsychological function in attenuated MPS I: possible decline of memory and visual spatial function. In *Proceedings of the International Neuropsychological Society meetings*; Boston, MA: February 2006: 144.

56. Shapiro E, Thomas K, Guler E, Delaney K, Bjoraker K, Whitley C, Charnas L. Neuroimaging and neuropsychological function and neuroimaging in severe and attenuated mucopolysaccharidosis I. In *Proceedings of the 4th WORLD symposium of the Lysosomal Disease Network, Mol Gen Metab XX*; Las Vegas, NV: Feb 2008; 32.

57. Kakkis E, McEntee M, Vogler C, Le S, Levy B, Belichenko P, Passage M. et al. Intrathecal enzyme replacement therapy reduces lysosomal storage in the brain and meninges of the canine model of MPS I. *Mol Gen Metab* 2004;**83**:163–74.

58. Martin R, Beck M, Eng C, Giugliani R, Harmatz P, Muñoz V, Muenzer J. Recognition and diagnosis of mucopolysaccharidosis II (Hunter syndrome). *Pediatrics* 2008;**121**:e377–86.

59. Muenzer J, Wraith JE, Beck M, Giugliani R, Harmatz P, Eng C, et al. A phase II/III clinical study of enzyme replacement therapy with idursulfase in mucopolysaccharidosis II (Hunter syndrome). *Gen Med* 2006;**8**:465–73.

60. Barone R, Nigro F, Triulzi F, Musumeci S, Fiumara A, Pavone L. Clinical and neuroradiological follow-up in mucopolysaccharidosis type III (Sanfilippo syndrome). *Neuropediatrics* 1999;**30**:270–4.

61. Colville GA, Watters JP, Yule W, Bax M. Sleep problems in children with Sanfilippo syndrome. *Dev Med Child Neurol* 1996;**38**:538–44.

62. Potegal M, Shapiro E. Delineation of the MPS III behavioral phenotype. In *Proceedings of the 4th annual WORLD symposium of the Lysosomal Disease Network, Mol Gen Metab XX*; Las Vegas, NV: Feb 2008;11.

63. Klein K, Krivit W, Whitley C, Peters C, Cool VA, Fuhrman M, et al. Poor cognitive outcome of nine children with Sanfilippo Syndrome following after bone marrow transplantation and successful engraftment. *Bone Marrow Transpl* 1995;**15**:S17681.

64. Harmatz P, Giugliani R, Schwartz I, Guffon N, Teles EL, Miranda MC, et al. Enzyme replacement therapy for mucopolysaccharidosis VI: a phase 3, randomized, double-blind, placebo-controlled, multinational study of recombinant human N-acetylgalactosamine 4-sulfatase (recombinant human arylsulfatase B or rhASB) and follow-on, open-label extension study. MPS VI Phase 3 Study Group. *J Pediatr* 2006;**148**:533–9.

65. Moser HW. Adrenoleukodystrophy: phenotype, genetics, pathogenesis and therapy. *Brain* 1997;**120**:1485–508.

66. Moser HW, Moser AB, Smith KD, Bergin A, Borel J, Shankroff J. Adrenoleukodystrophy: phenotypic variability and implications. *J Inherit Metab Dis* 1992;**15**:645–64.

67. Weller M, Liedtke W, Petersen D, Opitz H, Poremba M. Very-late-onset adrenoleukodystrophy: possible precipitation of demyelination by cerebral contusion. *Neurology* 1992;**42**:367–70.

68. Shapiro E, Lockman L, Balthazor M, Krivit W. Neuropsychological outcomes in several storage diseases with and without bone marrow transplantation. *J Inherit Metab Dis* 1995;**18**:413–29.

69. Tolar J, Orchard PJ, Bjoraker KJ, Ziegler RS, Shapiro EG, Charnas L. N-acetyl-L-cysteine improves outcome of advanced cerebral adrenoleukodystrophy. *Bone Marrow Transpl* 2007;**39**:211–15.

70. Loes DJ, Hite S, Moser H, Stillman AE, Shapiro E, Lockman, L, el al. Adrenoleukodystrophy: a scoring method for brain MR observation. *Am J Neuroradiol* 1994;**15**:1761–6.

71. Balthazor M, Rajanayagam V, Shapiro, E, Loes D, Stillman, A, Lockman, L et al. Predicting dementia in white matter disease: magnetic resonance imaging, magnetic resonance spectroscopy, and neuropsychology (Abstract). *Ann Neurol* 1995;**40**:290.

72. Rajanayagam V, Grad J, Krivit W, Loes, DJ, Lockman L, Balthazor M, et al. Proton MR spectroscopy of childhood adrenoleukodystrophy. *Am J Neuroradiol* 1996;**17**:1013–24.

73. Schneider JF, Il'yansov KA, Boltshauser E, Hennig J, Martin E. Diffusion tensor imaging in cases of adrenoleukodystrophy: preliminary experience as a

marker for early demyelination? *Am J Neuroradiol* 2003;**24**:819–24.

74. Gieselmann V, Zlotogora J, Harris A, Wenger D, Morris CP. Molecular genetics of metachromatic leukodystrophy. *Hum Mutat* 1994;**4**:233–43.

75. Wenger DA, Coppola S, Liu, S-L Insights into the diagnosis and treatment of lysosomal storage diseases. *Arch Neurol* 2003;**60**:322–8.

76. Shapiro E, Lockman, LA, Knopman D, Krivit, W. Characteristics of the dementia in late-onset metachromatic leukodystrophy. *Neurology* 1994;**44**;662–5.

77. Hyde TM, Ziegler JC, Weinberger DR. Psychiatric disturbances in metachromatic leukodystrophy. *Arch Neurol* 1992;**49**:401–6.

78. Krivit W, Shapiro E, Kennedy W, Lipton M, Lockman L, Smith S, Summers C, Wenger D, Ramsey N, Kersey J, Yao JK, Kaye E. Effective treatment of late infantile metachromatic leukodystrophy by bone marrow transplantation. *N Engl J Med* 1992;**322**:28–32.

79. Pridjian G, Humbert J, Willis J, Shapiro E. Presymptomatic late-infantile metachromatic leukodystrophy treated with bone marrow transplantation. *J Pediatr* 1994;**12J**:755–8.

80. Navarro C, Fernandez JM, Dominguez C, Fachal C, Alvarez M. Late juvenile metachromatic leukodystrophy treated with bone marrow transplantation; a 4-year follow-up study. *Neurology* 1996;**46**:254–6.

81. Shapiro E, Lipton M, Krivit W. White matter dysfunction and its neuropsychological correlates: a longitudinal study of a case of metachromatic leukodystrophy treated with bone marrow transplant. *J Clin Exp Neuropsychol* 1992;**14**:610–24.

82. Wenger DA. Krabbe disease (globoid cell leukodystrophy). In Rosenberg RN, Prusiner SB, DiMauro S, Barchi RL, eds. *The Molecular and Genetic Basis of Neurological Disease*. Boston, MA: Butterworth–Heinemann; 1997: 421–31.

83. Kolodny EH. Globoid leukodystrophy. In Moser HW, ed. *Neurodystrophies and Neurolipidoses, vol. 66 of Handbook of Clinical Neurology*. Amsterdam: Elsevier; 1996: 187–210.

84. Escolar ML, Poe MD, Provenzale JM, et al. Transplantation of umbilical-cord blood in babies with infantile Krabbe's disease. *N Engl J Med* 2005;**352**:2069–81.

85. Escolar ML, Poe MD, Martin HR, Kurtzberg J. A staging system for infantile Krabbe disease to predict outcome after unrelated umbilical cord blood transplantation. *Pediatrics* 2006;**118**:e879–89.

86. Krivit W, Shapiro EG, Peters C, Wagner J, Cornu G, Kurtzberg J, et al. Hematopoietic stem-cell transplantation in globoid-cell leukodystrophy. *N Engl J Med* 1998;**338**:1119–26.

87. Meikle PJ, Hopwood JJ, Clague AE, Carey, WF Prevalence of lysosomal storage disorders. *J Am Med Assoc* 1999;**281**:249–54.

Psychopathological conditions in children and adolescents

Abigail B. Sivan

Imagine the following scenario: a parent calls a neuropsychologist asking for an appointment because her latency-age child, a son, has been talking about not wanting to go to school. When queried, the parent reports that the child has never really liked school and over the last year has become more vocal about how bad a setting school is. When asked about other difficulties the child has, the parent answers that her son has difficulties with concentration, poor sleep, and states that he often appears restless and "on-edge". A referral such as this is routine for and the "bread and butter" of the practices of most child and adolescent neuropsychologists. Typically, the neuropsychologist next plans for an assessment that will include an examination of learning difficulties and attention and, for good measure, she might add a behavior-rating scale. Her considerations are "primarily neuropsychological", as the neuropsychologist probably hypothesizes that the school refusal behavior and somatic complaints are "secondary responses" to the child's learning and attentional concerns.

One might ask the question, however, is there anything wrong with this approach? After all, learning disabilities and attentional problems are common childhood conditions. According to the CDC (Centers for Disease Control and Prevention) [1], 7.8% of school-aged children are reported by their parents to have an attention deficit hyperactivity disorder (ADHD) diagnosis. The LDA (Learning Disabilities Association) [2] reports that 4–6% of all students in the public schools are classified as having specific learning disabilities. Yet, making a diagnosis of ADHD in this situation is not so simple. The DSM-IV [3] specifies in the Criteria E of Attention-Deficit/Hyperactivity Disorder that to make a diagnosis of ADHD, the presenting symptoms

> … do not occur exclusively during the course of a Pervasive Developmental Disorder, Schizophrenia, or other Psychotic Disorder and are not better accounted for by another mental disorder (e.g. Mood Disorder, Anxiety Disorder, Dissociative Disorder, or a Personality Disorder).

It is the neuropsychological characteristics of these other mental disorders that are the purview of this chapter. Where is it that clinicians can find guidance and useful strategies for differentiating among all these common conditions? Or are these common conditions? SAMHSA estimated that about 13% of children and adolescents ages 9 to 17 experience some kind of anxiety disorder [4]. NAMI, the National Alliance on Mental Illness [5], reports that 1 in 8 or 12.5% of adolescents may have depression, and according to the AACAP (American Academy of Child and Adolescent Psychiatry) [6] at any given point in time, 5% of children and adolescents in the general population suffer from depression. Given these epidemiological findings, why then do pediatric neuropsychologists begin by examining a less prevalent condition? How is it that we make the diagnosis of ADHD when we have no tools for differentiating a diagnosis of ADHD from more prevalent conditions such as depression and anxiety?

When I began to develop this chapter, I had thought that reviewing the literature on neuropsychological testing and psychopathological conditions in children and adolescents would be straightforward. My first pass at a literature search, however, yielded nothing. I was sure I had made a mistake and tried again. And again, I had no success. I had to contrast this with the adult neuropsychological literature (summarized by Ruocco et al., in this book), where there is a seemingly voluminous set of studies addressing the neuropsychological features of such psychopathological conditions as schizophrenia, depression, and even bipolar disorder. Unlike the adult neuropsychologist, the child and adolescent neuropsychologist has almost no clear, available research to draw on directly that can help him or her understand and then offer differential diagnoses between learning problems, processing-speed difficulties, and conditions such as depression or anxiety in pre-adult clients.

Was I missing something or are there no answers? It is not unusual to hear an adult psychiatrist report that many, if not most, of their cases were diagnosed as having ADHD as children. Still other clinicians, including ones who work with children and adolescents, often assume that depression and low self-esteem are reflections of a child or adolescent's reaction to his or her impaired performances, rather than a causal factor. But do we know whether this is true? Is it not also the case, using what we know about the potential for mood disorders in children and adolescents, that the primary concerns presenting in a referral may in fact be emotional or behavioral, and the learning difficulties secondary?

Baron [7], in her book on assessment of children, addresses this question in an early chapter. She notes that measures of attention and concentration as well as of motor speed are particularly susceptible to the effects of depression and other mood disorders. Much of her discussion focuses on the 2001 study by Ready and colleagues [8] that examines the ecological validity of two types of measures of executive functions (neuropsychological and personality) and real-world behaviors in a sample ($n = 61$) of undergraduate college students. These researchers highlighted the need for including personality measures in a standard neuropsychological assessment, and reported finding ecological validity for both personality and neuropsychological measures, noting that their associations differ. Specifically, their research found that the neuropsychological measures were significant predictors of achievement and work-related behavior, while personality measures were more strongly associated with behavioral difficulties such as disinhibition, risk-taking, and aggression.

This study offers a window into how one might begin to disentangle the relative influences of neuropsychological and mental health difficulties, particularly with regard to child and adolescent development. Yet for the pediatric neuropsychologist, this study cannot be easily generalized because the research subjects considered by Ready and colleagues were very different from those children and adolescents who generally present in the neuropsychologist's office. Specifically, the youngest subjects in the study were not only 17-year-olds, but these subjects had experienced enough academic success to enter college. Seventeen-year-olds with some academic success are not the usual population of children who present in a typical child and adolescent psychiatry or clinical psychology clinic and they are surely not the children who are being seen first by their

pediatricians or other health providers for mood or behavioral concerns.

In their recently updated book, Ellison and Semrud-Clikeman [9] devote an entire chapter to the neuropsychological correlates of psychiatric disorders in children and adolescents. In their chapter, they review a myriad of research studies from the 1980s and 90s that examined the neuropsychological factors related to diagnosed internalizing psychiatric conditions, such as anxiety and depression. With respect to depression, the authors concluded (p. 140) that

> … clients with depression may present in much the same manner as those with organic problems. The astute clinician will recognize such overlap and seek to differentiate, *if at all possible*, between the two types of disorders. Clues for differentiation may be found in specific areas of the child's social functioning/relationships (e.g. isolation, rejection, withdrawal, etc.) and emotional adjustment/ well-being (e.g. overwhelming feelings of sadness, prolonged/chronic feelings of sadness/depression, etc.). In such cases where such a distinction is not possible, retesting should be pursued after a trial of medication and/or therapy is attempted.

Their conclusions with respect to anxiety are similar (p. 145):

> It is important to note that anxious children rarely pose significant overt behavioral difficulties in school and often are not referred for assessment by their teachers. … However, such anxiety has been found to impair the child's social and academic functioning … As with depression, it is important to utilize a multi-method approach to the diagnosis of anxiety disorders. Semistructured interview, rating scales, self-report scales, and observations are important pieces of an assessment. … Children have been found to report more anxiety symptoms than parents, possibly indicating that because of the internal nature of these signs, children are more aware of these difficulties than their caregivers [10].

As we seek clues to how to differentiate between difficulties such as mood disorders, learning concerns, and ADHD, recent research on developmental psychopathology may offer some help. Specifically, research on depression and anxiety, as well as other significant psychopathology in children, has focused more on the comorbidities among and on the developmental trajectories of common psychopathological conditions. For example, Ross and colleagues [11] found that in a sample of 82 children, ages 4–15 years, with diagnoses of schizophrenia or schizoaffective disorder, all but one had at least one comorbid psychiatric illness (ADHD 84%, ODD 43%, depression 30%, and SAD 25%) and these comorbid conditions were untreated pharmacologically. It is possible that the lack of treatment itself is one source of underlying difficulty for the affected child, particularly as it relates to managing learning and adaptive tasks, and the latter may also be reflected in neuropsychological deficits.

Bitter and colleagues [12] completed a prospective, community-based, population study of over 3000 children who were followed from ages 9, 11 and 13 until age 19 years. Their data showed that more than 16% of their participants met criteria for an anxiety disorder of some type during the study period and found that the anxiety disorders, more than other conditions (depression, ODD, CD, ADHD, and substance use), were predictors not only of anxiety in adolescence but of other psychiatric disorders as well. Interestingly, in their conclusion, these authors questioned the advisability of substituting special childhood and adolescent rules for Generalized Anxiety Disorder in DSM-IV-TR, rather than keeping what they consider the more predictive diagnosis of Overanxious Disorder of Childhood from DSM-III (p. 1180), with its emphasis on aspects of anxiety that are more commonly observed in children.

Rutter and his colleagues [13] use two overarching concepts to explore the observation that behavior at an early age is predictive of behavior of a different type at a later age. One of these concepts is "heterotypic continuity" such as that found in the association between reading difficulties in childhood and spelling problems later in adult life. The second concept is that of "psychopathological progressions", as represented by the example of the progression from early conduct disorder to later substance abuse. In this case, the progression is conceived of as different representations, demonstrated at different times in the lifespan, of an underlying difficulty with disinhibition. In their discussion of possible mediators of these continuities and discontinuities, Rutter and colleagues offer a list that includes: genetic liabilities, kindling effects, environmental exposures in adulthood, adverse experiences in childhood, and an individual's behavioral or cognitive responses to the presence of psychopathology. Specifically, they emphasize the likely multidimensional impact psychopathology can have, across time and environments, on functioning. In the end, these authors conclude that in studies of the trajectories of psychopathology from childhood to adulthood,

> there needs to be a focus on competing alternatives with respect to mediating mechanisms, and this requires attention to measurement, research design, and data analysis. (p. 290)

Among the factors that they consider important is "basic research into brain development during adolescence" with particular focus on "individual differences and their implications for psychological functioning". This discussion highlights the complex relationship that exists between neuropsychological development and factors that impact trajectories of that development, including difficulties with behavioral and emotional regulation. Alternatively, it also highlights the vulnerability that exists for individuals with neuropsychological disorders, with regard to developing comorbid psychopathology.

For more than a decade, Biederman and his colleagues [14] have been carefully studying the overlapping symptomatology of severe ADHD and disruptive behavior disorders such as bipolar disorder, oppositional defiant disorder, and substance use disorder. In their attempts to disentangle the overlapping symptomatology, they carefully consider the contribution of familial risk patterns, of clinical correlates of each condition, and of the individual therapeutic responses. The authors conclude a summary of their research with the following observations (pp. 1167–8):

> The symptomatic overlap and co-occurrence of mania with disruptive behavior disorders has produced debate as to whether these children have disruptive behavior disorders, mania, or both. Because the existence of disruptive behavior disorders is atypical in adult-onset mania, there has been intense resistance to considering bipolarity in these children. This question is of high public heath relevance. Considering the full diagnostic spectrum in these complex children creates important advantages provided by diagnostic precision. Such advantages include a scientific understanding of symptoms, their prognoses, and course and likely treatment options.
>
> Although the presence of comorbidity denotes a combination of separate clinical entities, it is possible that these disorders are not etiologically distinct, just as infectious pathogens may affect many body organs despite sharing a common pathophysiology.

... [R]ecognition of potential mood disorders in disruptive disordered children provides a paradigm shift that allows a new set of therapeutic options in these often refractory conditions. What was previously considered refractory ADHD, ODD, or CD may respond after mood stabilization. ... Unraveling the pathophysiology of childhood mania will require careful attention and analytic correction by comorbid status.

More recently, Biederman's team has explored the neuropsychological functioning of children with bipolar disorder. In two papers [15, 16], the team attempted to parse out the relative effect of BPD on neuropsychological test performances taking into consideration the high comorbidity of this disorder with ADHD. Doyle and her colleagues [15] found impairments in sustained attention, working memory, and processing speed on a variety of neuropsychological measures and lower arithmetic achievement, requiring more tutoring and special education placements in the children affected with BPD, after controlling for comorbid ADHD.

Henin and associates [16] further refined this analysis by differentiating the performances of unmedicated outpatient children with BPD and comorbid ADHD, children with ADHD alone, and control children with neither disorder. This group found that children with comorbid ADHD/BPD performed in a manner similar to those children with ADHD alone. Namely, when compared to control subjects, both diagnosed groups showed deficits in verbal learning (CVLT) and in interference control (Stroop) but did not differ from each other. Sarkis and her colleagues [17] used the Tower of London task to examine the relative contribution of conditions that were comorbid in a group of children diagnosed with ADHD. Their findings suggested no additive or subtractive effect of the comorbid disorder on the performances of their group of ADHD subjects.

Careful research like that of Sarkis's and Biederman's groups is not plentiful. As one example, Ostrander and his colleagues [18] used path analysis to examine the mediating effects of comorbid depression on the social competence of older and younger children with ADHD. Although their study did not use neuropsychological measures, the methodology would be one that could be applied to neuropsychological research.

As noted earlier, there have been few research studies that have explored the overlapping symptomatology of depression and anxiety with the most common neuropsychological conditions such as learning difficulties or problems with executive functioning. The paucity of available research has contributed to a "large hole" in the field regarding differential diagnosis, and how to best work with children and their families when current psychopathology is contributing to difficulties with daily activities such as learning in school, making friends, and keeping up with chores and expectations at home.

The National Institutes of Mental Health (NIMH) [19] remind us that

unlike most physical diseases, mental illness begins very early in life. Half of all lifetime cases begin by age 14; three quarters have begun by age 24. Thus, mental disorders are really the chronic diseases of the young. ... Unlike heart disease or most cancers, young people with mental disorders suffer disability when they are in the prime of life, when they would normally be the most productive.

Clearly, mental disorders in childhood can lead to long-term disability; thus it is critical that we reach a better level of understanding regarding the potential influences developing psychopathology may have on neuropsychological functioning. Currently, we are left floundering as we "downwardly adapt" findings from the adult research. This approach is particularly problematic given our understanding of the course of developing cognitive and behavioral capacities. For the younger child, a course of depression may serve to move the trajectory of cognitive development quite significantly; problems with learning can lead to increased struggles with mood and behavioral management. Thus, for the affected child or adolescent, it is quite difficult to meet the demands of day-to-day development; in the long run, independence and adaptability are the likely losers.

This chapter was intended to challenge pediatric neuropsychologists, child psychiatrists, pediatric neurologists, and other health professionals, and their students. Clearly the direction of pediatric neuropsychological research in the future should be on clarifying the differential diagnosis of these treatable, yet often undiagnosed, conditions that overlap in their presentation with so many common neuropsychological conditions. To do so is likely to advance the field far further, and support our understanding of comorbidities and risk, as well as resilience. As Pennington [20] has recently discussed, the better we come to understand the underlying brain mechanisms of many of the disorders that impact children and adolescents – the disorders of motivation, action, and engagement – the more effectively we will be able to identify and then intervene to modify the impact on negative effects of these disorders.

References

1. Centers for Disease Control. *Attention-Deficit / Hyperactivity Disorder*, http://www.cdc.gov/ncbddd/ADHD/ [Accessed on May 1, 2008].

2. Learning Disability Association. *About LD*, http://www.ldanatl.org/about ld/teachers/index.asp, [Accessed on May 1, 2008].

3. American Psychiatric Association. *DSM-IV*. 1994, Washington DC.

4. Substance Abuse and Mental Health Services Administration (SAMHSA). National Mental Health Information Center, Anxiety Disorders in Children and Adolescents, http://mentalhealth.samhsa.gov/publications/allpubs/CA-0007/default.asp, [Accessed on Jan 2, 2008].

5. National Alliance on Mental Illness. *Early-onset Depression*, http://www.nami.org/helpline/depression-child.html, [Accessed on Jan 2, 2008].

6. American Academy of Child and Adolescent Psychiatry. *Facts for families, The Depressed Child*, http://www.aacap.org/cs/root/facts_for_families /the_depressed_child, [Accessed on Jan 2, 2008].

7. Baron IS. *Neuropsychological Evaluation of the Child*. Oxford University Press; 2004.

8. Ready RE, Stierman S, Paulsen JS. Ecological validity of neuropsychological and personality measures of executive functions. *Clin Neuropsychol* 2001;**15**(3):314–32.

9. Ellison PAT, Semrud-Clikeman M. *Child Neuropsychology: Assessment and Interventions for Neurodevelopmental Disorders*. Springer; 2007.

10. Edelbrock C, Costello AJ, Dulcan MK, Conover, NC, Kala R. Parent-Child agreement on child psychiatric symptoms assessed via structured interview. *J. Child Psychol Psychiatry* 1986;**27**(2):181–90.

11. Ross RG, Heinlein S, Tregellas H. High rates of comorbidity found in childhood-onset schizophrenia. *J. Schizophr Res* 2006;**88**:90–95.

12. Bitter A, Egger HL, Erkanli A, Costello EJ, Foley DL, Angold A. What do childhood anxiety disorders predict? *J Child Psychol Psychiatry* 2007;**48**(12):1174–83.

13. Rutter M, Kim-Cohen J, Maughan B. Continuities and discontinuities in psychopathology between childhood and adult life. *J Child Psychol Psychiatry* 2006;**47**(3):276–95.

14. Spencer TJ, Biederman J, Wozniak J, Faraone SV, Wilens TE, Mick E. Parsing pediatric bipolar disorder from its associated comorbidity with the disruptive behavior disorders. *Biol Psychiatry* 2001;**49**:1062–70.

15. Doyle AE, Wilens TE, Kwon A, Seidman LJ, Faraone SV, Fried R, Swezey A, Snyder L, Biederman J. Neuropsychological functioning in youth with bipolar disorder. *Biol Psychiatry* 2005;**58**:540–8.

16. Henin A, Mick E, Biederman J, Fried R, Wozniak, Faraone SV, Harrington K, Davis S, Doyle AE. Can bipolar disorder-specific neuropsychological impairments in children be identified? *J Consult Clin Psychol* 2007;**75**(2):210–20.

17. Sarkis SM, Sarkis EH, Marshall D, Archer J. Self-regulation and inhibition in comorbid ADHD children: an evaluation of executive functions. *J Attent Disord* 2005;**8**(3):96–108.

18. Ostrander R, Crystal DS, August G. Attention deficit-hyperactivity disorder, depression, and self- and other-assessments of social competence: a developmental study. *J Abnorm Child Psychol* 2006;**34**:773–87.

19. National Institutes of Mental Health. *Mental illness exacts heavy toll, beginning in youth*, http://nimh.nih.gov/science-news/2005/mental-illness-exacts-heavy-toll-beginning-in-youth.shtml, [Accessed on Jan 16, 2008].

20. Pennington BF. *The Development of Psychopathology*. New York: Guilford Press; 2002.

Chapter 16b

Psychopathological conditions in adults

Anthony C. Ruocco, Elizabeth Kunchandy and Maureen Lacy

Introduction

With psychiatric disorders affecting nearly one-half of American adults at some point in their lifetime, it is important to consider the impact psychopathological conditions may have on neuropsychological function; this is particularly true as individuals entering adulthood and later, old age, are often at greater risk for the development of psychopathological conditions. Whereas several adult psychopathological conditions may present with some form of cognitive inefficiency, the present discussion focuses on three disorders with relatively well-characterized neuropsychological profiles in adulthood and old age: schizophrenia, bipolar disorder, and major depression. What follows is a description of the pathophysiological mechanisms of these conditions, their most salient cognitive manifestations during adulthood and old age, assessment issues which may arise in neuropsychological evaluation of individuals with these disorders, and a review of the effects of treatment of these conditions on cognitive function.

Schizophrenia

Adulthood-onset schizophrenia is a psychiatric illness characterized by a constellation of symptoms that may include psychosis, thought disorder, disorganized behavior, and some form of negative symptomatology (e.g. alogia, affective flattening, or avolition). The prevalence of schizophrenia after 15 years of age is estimated to be between 2.7 and 8.3 per 1000 [1]. Whereas the peak incidence for males and females occurs between 15 and 24 years of age, females appear to have a second peak during the decade between the ages of 55 and 64 years. This later peak appears to counterbalance the higher prevalence of early-onset schizophrenia among males.

Subtypes of schizophrenia may be distinguished based on age of illness onset [2]. Early-adulthood-onset schizophrenia (EAOS) identifies a group of patients whose illness first appeared in adolescence through early adulthood (ages 15 through 24 years). These patients can be distinguished from middle-age-onset schizophrenia (MAOS), for whom illness appears after 40 years of age. There is some debate about the onset of schizophrenia later in life. The preponderance of the evidence, however, supports the face validity and clinical utility of a very-late-onset schizophrenia-like psychosis (VLOS) (onset after age 60 years). Several clinical distinctions can be made between EOS and MAOS, the latter representing a higher proportion of females, presenting with lower severity of negative symptoms, and demonstrating a positive response to lower daily doses of antipsychotic medication.

The pathophysiology of schizophrenia is such that multiple neural systems may go awry during various stages of development. Molecular mechanisms underlying the disorder have been posited and include dysfunction of dopaminergic, glutamatergic, and GABAergic systems, which may act in concert with genes implicating immune, signaling and networking deficits [3]. Neuropathological studies over the past 20 years converge in remarkable findings across most areas of the brain, with reports of temporal and frontal lobe abnormalities most frequent. Quantitative volume abnormalities of frontal and temporal brain regions have been reported, along with neuronal cytoarchitectural irregularities involving the entorhinal cortex [4]. Box 1 summarizes the major clinical features of schizophrenia and their neuroanatomic correlates. Whereas neuropathological aberrations appear diffuse, most histological studies highlight the absence of any progressive neurodegeneration in schizophrenia. Nevertheless, there are clear cognitive deficits associated with the disorder which may, for at least a subset of patients, show progressive deterioration with advancing age.

Box 1: Neuroanatomic correlates of major clinical features of adulthood schizophrenia

Clinical feature	Neuroanatomic correlate
Auditory hallucinations	Greater activation of Broca's area, left superior temporal gyrus, and Heschl's gyrus
Visual hallucinations	Greater activation of bilateral inferior temporal and middle occipital gyri, superior parietal lobule, precuneus, posterior cingulate, and hippocampus
Paranoid delusions	Less activation of medial temporal lobe
Persecutory delusions	Less rostral-ventral anterior cingulate activation and greater posterior cingulate gyrus activation
Positive formal thought disorder	Less activation of left and middle temporal gyri
Negative symptoms	Less activation of frontal and temporal lobes, and greater activation of deep cerebellar nuclei

Schizophrenia in early and middle adulthood

Neuropsychological function

Several assessment batteries have been developed for the assessment of cognitive function in schizophrenia (See Table 16b.1). For a detailed review and description of these batteries, refer to Kraus and Keefe [5]. Using these batteries and more traditional assessment instruments, a voluminous literature has accumulated regarding cognitive function in schizophrenia. The first-episode illness which tends to occur in young adulthood is represented by generalized neuropsychological deficits as observed in studies of patients following initial stabilization of psychosis [6]. Whereas episodic memory and executive function deficits predominate the neuropsychological profiles of these patients, tests of orbitofrontal functions may show relative preservation. Over the first 2–3 years of illness, patients tend to recover in their intellectual and verbal memory performances while demonstrating significant gray matter abnormalities on magnetic resonance imaging (MRI) [7].

Perhaps the most comprehensive quantitative review of the neuropsychological literature for schizophrenia patients in the 18 to 56 year age range (mean age of illness onset 21.9 years) revealed significant deficits (Cohen's $d > 0.60$) across several cognitive domains to include general intelligence, verbal and visual memory, auditory and visual attention, executive function, spatial abilities, language, and motor functions [8]. Indices of verbal memory demonstrated the greatest magnitude of difference between schizophrenia patients and healthy controls, followed by

Table 16.1. Cognitive batteries for schizophrenia.

Brief Assessment of Cognition in Schizophrenia
Brief Cognitive Assessment
Clinical Antipsychotic Trials of Intervention Effectiveness
MATRICS Consensus Cognitive Battery
Schizophrenia Cognition Rating Scale
UCSD Performance-Based Skills Assessment

bilateral motor skill and performance IQ. Of note, no single test or cognitive domain completely discriminated patients from healthy controls. A more recent review of this literature supports findings of marked impairments in verbal episodic memory and executive control processes superimposed on a generalized cognitive inefficiency [9]. The "deficit syndrome", thought to characterize patients with predominantly negative symptoms, is associated with less efficient performances on tests of olfaction, global cognition, and language compared with non-deficit schizophrenia patients.

Assessment issues

Adult patients with schizophrenia frequently present with comorbid substance use disorders which makes differential diagnosis difficult, with upwards of 80% of schizophrenia patients meeting criteria for a substance use disorder at some point during their lifetime [10]. Substance misuse may have deleterious effects on cognitive function in schizophrenia, potentially exacerbating existing cognitive vulnerabilities. Alcohol, cannabis, and cocaine use disorders are associated with decrements in cognitive function for adults with comorbid schizophrenia [11]. Interestingly, nicotine may have a beneficial effect on cognitive function, with cigarette-smoking possibly serving as a form of self-medication to remedy mild cognitive disturbances experienced by these patients.

Neuropsychologists may be called upon to characterize the cognitive strengths and weaknesses of schizophrenia patients with comorbid substance use disorders, often to determine the functional capacities of these patients and to design appropriate treatment plans. Studies show that improved social and vocational function in adults with schizophrenia is associated with stronger cognitive performances across the domains of attention (vigilance), auditory memory, executive function, and processing speed [12], suggesting that comorbid substance use problems may have additional consequences for social and vocational functions by way of their effects on cognitive function. Patients with less efficient cognitive abilities may also experience greater difficulty in benefiting from or complying with prescribed treatments. The prognosis for patients with comorbid substance use problems may be particularly poor, with only minimal improvements in cognitive function (e.g. motor speed) associated with symptomatic recovery.

Treatment

As previously mentioned, cognitive function is a potent predictor of functional impairment in schizophrenia. It is perhaps not surprising that cognition often serves as a primary outcome measure in medication trials for these patients. Atypical and conventional antipsychotic medications show slight to modest improvements in cognitive function in adults with schizophrenia, with no clear advantage of one medication over another [13]. Attention, verbal memory, and executive functions tend to demonstrate the bulk of the gains following treatment. Cognitive remediation produces substantial improvements in cognitive function for patients with schizophrenia, even for programs of relatively short duration (e.g. 5–15 hours) [14]. While improvements tend to be particularly strong for the domains of verbal learning and memory, there also tend to be beneficial impacts on psychosocial function, especially when adjunctive psychiatric rehabilitation is provided. Programs which emphasize drill and practice as well as strategy coaching tend to witness stronger effects on cognition than either

component alone. Evidence for long-term gains is not well confirmed but appears promising.

Schizophrenia in older adults

Neuropsychological function

The neuropsychological profile of schizophrenia is remarkably stable as patients enter late life. There is, however, strong cross-sectional evidence for an association between poorer cognitive function and worse overall functional outcome for elderly schizophrenia patients [15]. Indeed, patients with very poor baseline cognitive function witness the greatest declines in basic activities of daily living in old age. With regard to cognitive profiles, some useful distinctions may be drawn between deficit (i.e. primary negative symptoms) and non-deficit elderly patients with schizophrenia. The latter category may also be meaningfully grouped based on primarily disorganized versus delusional symptoms. The evidence suggests a decline in cognitive function over a 6-year period for deficit and non-deficit delusional elderly patients, but no change in cognitive function for non-deficit patients with primarily disorganized symptoms [16]. These findings underscore the practical significance of delineating subtypes of schizophrenia to aid in the prediction of patients who are most likely to experience cognitive decline in old age.

For patients with VLOS, most patients do not appear to suffer cognitive decline over time; however, there is a significant minority of patients who may show some cognitive and functional declines. Compared with elderly schizophrenia patients, those with VLOS are characterized by higher levels of education, higher percentage married, more pronounced cerebellar atrophy, and better response to treatment [17]. Less is known about their neuropsychological profiles, although there is the suggestion that they may not differ from EAOS patients who, as reviewed above, tend to show deficits on measures of executive function, learning and memory, verbal abilities, and motor skills. Diffusion tensor imaging results bolster these neuropsychological findings in detecting no appreciable frontal cortex white matter tract abnormalities in VLOS patients compared with healthy age-matched controls [18]. Nevertheless, functional impairments may be more diffuse in these patients, with males more likely to be admitted to hospital and lost to follow-up than female patients.

Assessment issues

Differential diagnosis of late-onset schizophrenia may be complicated by conditions which may have similar presentations during old age, such as Alzheimer's disease (AD) and other dementias. Some researchers have even suggested that late-onset schizophrenia may be a prodrome of AD. Certainly, neuropsychological testing may be critical for older schizophrenia patients given that persons presenting with both psychotic symptoms and late-life dementia have a greater likelihood of mortality as compared to patients with psychotic or mood disorder alone.

The differential diagnosis of late-onset schizophrenia and AD may be difficult because the latter may present with neuropsychiatric disturbances such as psychosis, hyperactivity, affective symptoms, and apathy. Neuropsychological testing, however, can assist in the differentiation of late-onset schizophrenia and AD. Overall, elderly patients with schizophrenia tend to outperform AD patients across most neuropsychological tests, albeit with significant variability in their performances [19]. Specifically, AD patients have been shown to perform more poorly than late-onset schizophrenia patients on measures of attention (Trail Making Test Part A), executive function (Trail Making Test Part B), and delayed auditory memory (Wechsler Memory Scale Logical Memory delayed recall, California Verbal Learning Test [CVLT] long-delay free recall). Those tests which best discriminate AD from late-onset schizophrenia include the short- and long-delay free recall from the CVLT, and the Similarities subtest of the Wechsler Adult Intelligence Scale, with AD patients performing more poorly than elderly schizophrenia patients solely on the CVLT long-delay free recall. It is important to note that these findings may be impacted by duration of illness and medication effects, which were not controlled in the Zakzanis and colleagues [19] investigation. Whereas these findings provide clinically useful data for distinguishing late-onset schizophrenia from AD, more studies are needed to assist in the differential diagnosis of schizophrenia from similarly presenting conditions which tend to occur with greater frequency in older adulthood.

Treatment

Unfortunately, little is known regarding treatment of late-onset schizophrenia. In general, conventional neuroleptics show a moderate therapeutic response in these patients, while atypical antipsychotics may also show a beneficial behavioral response with perhaps a more favorable side-effects profile [20]. It is important to note, however, that there is a black box warning for the use of atypical antipsychotics with demented older adults because of an increased risk of mortality. The effects of these pharmacological treatments on cognition in elderly schizophrenia patients are by and large unknown, although some evidence suggests some improvement in attention, memory, executive function, and verbal fluency associated with atypical antipsychotic treatment [21]. Adjunctive anticonvulsant medications appear efficacious for non-demented late-onset schizophrenia patients, demonstrating no apparent effects, beneficial or otherwise, on cognitive function. A comprehensive review of considerations for the use of antipsychotic medications in older adults, including those with schizophrenia, is provided elsewhere [22]. Nevertheless, there is a clear need to establish a more complete understanding of the effects of antipsychotic medication on cognition in elderly schizophrenia patients, particularly given that these patients may be at a higher risk for cognitive impairment.

Bipolar disorder

Bipolar disorder (BD) is characterized by a distinct change in mood whereby a person experiences feelings of elation and expansiveness or anger and irritability, accompanied by additional symptoms such as inflated self-esteem or decreased need for sleep. Two subtypes of BD can be differentiated: bipolar I (BD I) and bipolar II disorder (BD II), distinguished by the presence of manic and hypomanic episodes, respectively. The lifetime prevalence rate for BD I is greater than for BD II, estimated at 1.1 and 0.6%, respectively [23].

Some individuals may experience a single episode of illness while others will encounter multiple episodes, frequent hospitalizations, and greater functional impairment. Research suggests that the latter is a more common experience for individuals with BD, whereby fewer than 10% remain symptom-free for more than 1 year [24]. The impact of repeated relapses on cognitive functioning is great, with more episodes associated with more impaired cognitive functioning. Repeated relapses also lead to greater disruption of social and occupational functioning.

A comprehensive understanding of the pathophysiology of BD has only recently emerged [25]. Manic and depressive episodes appear to be linked to abnormal levels of intrasynaptic monoamines.

Neuroendocrine dysfunction and signaling network abnormalities for important circuits mediating cognitive, behavioral, and emotional functions appear commonplace in BD and other mood disorders. There is also evidence for impaired neurogenesis, brain lesions, and dysfunction of the circadian rhythm in association with BD. Finally, these pathophysiological abnormalities occur in the context of multiple genes which increase one's vulnerability for BD.

Structural and functional neuroimaging studies provide additional evidence regarding the pathophysiology of BD [26]. Several studies suggest abnormalities involving right frontal cortex, including white matter hyperintensities in areas of the frontal lobe, periventricular region, amygdala, and basal ganglia. Postmortem studies have shown decreased glial density of the subgenual and dorsolateral prefrontal cortex. There are also emerging data which suggest state-related abnormalities in caudal ventral prefrontal cortex and trait-related abnormalities in rostral ventral prefrontal cortex for patients in depressed, manic, or euthymic states. Patients with a history of multiple manic episodes and a strong genetic vulnerability to BD may also have larger lateral ventricular volumes compared with healthy individuals. The widespread neuroanatomic abnormalities associated with BD may best be characterized as involving diffuse pathology of the fronto-striatal system. Box 2 summarizes the major clinical features of BD and their neuroanatomic correlates.

Adult bipolar disorder

Neuropsychological function

Review of the neuropsychological literature of BD reveals a generalized pattern of neurocognitive deficits. Factors which seem to moderate the neurocognitive deficits associated with BD include mood state (depressed versus manic), number of manic and depressive episodes, and course of illness. Whereas a single BD neuropsychological profile has not been clearly delineated, there is evidence which suggests that distinct state- and subtype-specific neuropsychological profiles can be distinguished.

Patients with BD I demonstrate a varied neuropsychological profile with a relatively distinct pattern of cognitive strengths and weaknesses, although the findings may be difficult to interpret given the patient's mood state at the time of testing [27]. While in a manic or hypomanic state, BD I patients most commonly demonstrate deficits involving verbal memory and executive functions. Studies of verbal (auditory) and visual memory for patients in manic or hypomanic states provide evidence for difficulties with encoding and retention of information. The executive functions typically affected include planning, problem-solving, and decision-making, although findings of executive deficits in these patients certainly are not unequivocal. Overall, impairments in executive function and verbal memory increase proportionately with severity of the manic state. Attentional fluctuations are also common in manic or hypomanic patients as demonstrated on continuous performance tests which require sustained attention to visual and/or auditory stimuli over protracted periods. In euthymic states, difficulties with encoding of verbal information into memory appear more prevalent than during manic states, which may suggest abnormalities in brain regions associated with learning (i.e. prefrontal cortex, hippocampus).

Neuropsychological studies of BD II have compared patients' performances on cognitive measures with healthy persons or patients with unipolar depression [27]. In comparison with healthy individuals, patients with BD II exhibit deficits in set-shifting, planning, problem-solving, nonverbal intellectual abilities, and visual memory. Unipolar and bipolar depressive disorders are associated with remarkably

Box 2: Neuroanatomic correlates of major clinical features of adulthood bipolar disorder

Clinical feature	Neuroanatomic correlate
Manic state	Greater activation of right basal ganglia, insula, amygdala, and subcortical limbic regions; less activation in right ventral prefrontal cortex
Depressed mood	Greater activation of left ventral prefrontal cortex
Transient sadness	Less blood flow in medial prefrontal cortex
History of more affective episodes	Greater white matter hyperintensities in periventricular and frontal areas, and larger lateral ventricle volume

similar cognitive profiles, both exhibiting deficits in verbal memory and executive function. Greater deficits in sustained attention and immediate and delayed verbal memory may also characterize patients with BD II. Whereas both unipolar and bipolar depressed patients exhibit deficits in verbal fluency, only patients with bipolar depression tend to show greater deficits in semantic (i.e. category) fluency.

Individuals with BD suffer inter-episode difficulties with cognitive, occupational, and social functioning. Whereas no consensus has emerged regarding cognitive deficits in euthymic BD patients, some persons may exhibit residual cognitive deficits in working memory, executive control, and verbal learning. The perhaps more rigorous studies implicate impaired executive function with additional deficits in verbal memory and response latency. Persistent sustained attentional deficits may also be present during manic and euthymic states in BD patients, possibly representing a trait marker for the disorder. Interestingly, length of time between episodes of illness does not appear to affect cognitive test performance.

Assessment issues

There is great variability in the neuropsychological profile of patients with BD. Some of this variability may be attributed to the use of different assessment measures across studies, differences in demographic and clinical features of participants (e.g. age, community versus inpatient), and treatment status. An often overlooked variable in neuropsychological studies of BD is the influence of comorbid personality disorder on cognitive test findings with these patients. Epidemiologic data indicate that the lifetime prevalence of comorbid BD I and personality disorder may be as high as 70% [28].

The differential diagnosis of BD and borderline personality disorder (BPD) is an issue faced by many clinicians, including neuropsychologists, who frequently encounter patients with complex psychiatric presentations which may be additionally complicated by some form of neurological insult. Whereas much attention has been given to a BD–BPD spectrum, the preponderance of the evidence supports a robust distinction between the clinical features of these conditions. Neuropsychological testing may additionally aid in the differential diagnosis of BD and BPD. Although their cognitive profiles share a generalized cognitive deficit, BPD is characterized by more marked impairments in visual memory and executive planning

abilities [29]. As reviewed above, BD tends to show a different pattern of deficits, namely, verbal memory difficulties and a constellation of executive function deficits. Overall, neuropsychological testing may be useful in distinguishing between these sometimes comorbid conditions which may share important clinical features.

Treatment

Pharmacological treatment of BD I and BD II typically entails mood stabilizers such as lithium, olanzapine, lamotrigine, imipramine, and valproate [30]. Pharmacological agents targeting dopamine and glutamate receptors tend to offer the best outcome for improvement of cognitive deficit in adults with BD, while traditional antidepressant medications tend to exacerbate manic symptoms. Psychotherapeutic interventions include psychoeducation, family-focused therapy, cognitive-behavioral therapy, and interpersonal therapy. Although psychological treatments demonstrate efficacy in improving both the subsyndromal interepisode symptoms of BD and overall psychosocial functioning of patients, studies typically have not examined treatment effects on neurocognitive function. One might suspect that improved mood regulation may lead to improved efficiency on cognitive testing; however, this speculation requires empirical testing.

Bipolar disorder in older adulthood

Neuropsychological function

BD patients seem to experience an amelioration of symptoms with age, while a small subset of these individuals go on to develop dementia. The 1-year prevalence of BD is estimated at 0.1% among adults aged 65 and older living in the community, compared with approximately 8–10% for psychiatric inpatients aged 55–60 [31]. Compared with their younger-aged counterparts, older patients with BD exhibit more psychotic features (primarily paranoia), have a longer latency period between the first episode of depression and onset of mania (17 versus 3 years), are more likely to relapse into depression following a manic episode, and are less likely to achieve full functional recovery. Older patients who report a later onset of their first manic episode tend to have a consistently higher rate of cerebrovascular risk factors, with possible consequences for neurological dysfunction.

Box 3: Neuroanatomic correlates of major clinical features of adulthood major depression

Clinical feature	Neuroanatomic correlate
Transient sadness	Greater activation of medial and inferior prefrontal cortices, middle temporal cortex, cerebellum, and caudate
Anhedonia	Greater activity in ventromedial prefrontal cortex and less activity in amygdala and ventral striatum
Melancholia	Decreased gray matter density in subgenual prefrontal cortex
Longer duration of illness	Smaller hippocampal volume
Earlier age of illness onset	Smaller volumes of the caudate and putamen

Neuroimaging studies of older adults with BD reveal increased signs of cerebrovascular lesions and atrophy compared with age-matched peers [31]. For late-onset manic patients, 65% show silent cerebral infarctions, a rate which is higher than that found in patients with late-onset unipolar depression and early-onset affective disorders. Compared with age-matched controls, patients with BD have higher levels of atrophy in the cortical sulci and lateral ventricle [32]. There are limited data regarding the performance of older BD patients on neuropsychological measures, although some studies report poorer performances on measures of complex problem-solving (i.e. Halstead Category Test) [33]. Unfortunately, little is known regarding other neuropsychological features of BD in older adults. These data may have important implications for determining the likelihood of disability in this population, such as determining which cognitive factors might predict a patient's ability to maintain residence in the community or necessitate higher levels of care.

Major depression

Major depressive disorder (MDD) is a mood disorder typified by depressed mood or loss of interest or pleasure in life activities. These symptoms may be accompanied by disturbances of weight, appetite, sleep, psychomotor speed, energy, self-esteem, concentration, and decision-making. Recurrent thoughts of death may also be present whether or not in combination with suicidal thoughts or behaviors. MDD has a 12-month prevalence rate estimated at 6.6% in the USA and it is associated with significant impairment of work, household, relationship, and social roles [34]. Cases of MDD tend to emerge during teenage years

and the risk for MDD generally increases progressively throughout adulthood.

Attempts have been made over the past several decades to identify the pathophysiological underpinnings of MDD. The most robust biological markers of MDD include decreased platelet imipramine binding, decreased 5-HT1A receptor expression, increased soluble interleukin-2 receptor and interleukin-6 in serum, decreased brain-derived neurotrophic factor in serum, hypocholesterolemia, low blood folate levels, and impaired suppression on the dexamethasone suppression test [35]. None of these markers, however, has shown sufficient specificity to warrant inclusion in diagnostic criteria sets. Neuroanatomic features of the condition include smaller volumes of the hippocampus and subgenual cingulate. In particular, there is converging evidence of cellular death in the hippocampus in response to stress-related glucocorticoid secretion, possibly contributing to the pathophysiology of MDD and associated cognitive disturbances [36]. Additionally, functional hyper-activation of the amygdala may occur in tandem with dysfunction of prefrontal regions which modulate emotion and stress-response systems. Box 3 presents the neuroanatomic correlates of the clinical features of adulthood major depression.

Major depression in early and middle adulthood

Neuropsychological function

A review of the neuropsychological literature reveals several factors which may obfuscate the cognitive profile of MDD. These include comorbidity of MDD with other psychiatric disorders (e.g. anxiety and personality disorders), clinical features of the depression (e.g. psychosis, melancholia), unipolar versus bipolar depression, variability in neuropsychological measures, and other potentially complicating factors (e.g. phase of menstrual cycle, medication effects, premorbid function). Reports of neuropsychological function in adult patients with MDD range from minimal or no cognitive deficit to severe dysfunction in several domains [37]. The preponderance of the evidence, however, implicates inefficiencies on tests of psychomotor speed and executive function in patients with MDD.

Executive function has received perhaps the greatest attention of all cognitive domains with regard to its association with depression. Deficits in various executive functions have been identified in MDD to include planning, initiating, and completing goal-directed activities, with more severe forms of depression (e.g. psychotic, melancholic) associated with greater executive function deficits [38]. Executive dysfunction, when present, may also be associated with poorer treatment response and vocational disability. Tests of verbal fluency, which rely on executive processes in addition to speed and language-related functions, show some inefficiency in MDD patients. A quantitative literature review of studies of verbal fluency in MDD patients revealed relative deficits more likely attributable to a generalized cognitive impairment, including slowed processing speed, rather than a specific executive dysfunction [39].

Several theories have been put forth to explain the mechanisms by which cognitive deficits arise in MDD. Such theories include poor effortful processing on tests of attention and executive function, catastrophic responses to perceived failure on cognitive tasks, mood-related attentional and memory biases, and disruption of frontostriatal-limbic systems (for a review, see Porter et al. [40]). With regard to frontal systems dysfunction, emerging functional MRI evidence suggests increased hemodynamic activity in rostral anterior cingulate and other medial prefrontal structures during the performance of effortful cognitive activities [41]. This increased engagement of frontal regions is thought to reflect compensatory mechanisms to maintain task performance, lending support to theories involving effortful processing difficulties and disruption of frontal circuitry in MDD.

Assessment Issues

It is not uncommon for neuropsychologists to be asked to evaluate patients in early and middle adulthood who carry a diagnosis of MDD for the purpose of determining the presence and, if present, the nature and extent of cognitive difficulties. Sometimes the referral will occur within a medicolegal context (e.g. worker's compensation) or the situation is one which calls into question the validity of the patient's cognitive and emotional complaints. These situations necessitate the use of symptom validity tests which span neuropsychological and psychiatric domains as part of the neuropsychological evaluation. As previously mentioned, the nature of depression is such that effortful cognitive processes are less efficient. When patients are placed in situations where there are incentives to perform below their actual abilities, the question of effort takes on particular importance and requires that neuropsychologists have valid and reliable measures to quantify effortful performance.

Preliminary evidence indicates that individuals evaluated in a neuropsychological context, should they magnify cognitive or psychiatric complaints, tend to do so in one domain to the exclusion of the other [42]. This is supported by findings of a limited relationship between depression and neuropsychological symptom validity tests, although attention should be given to the potential for symptom validity test failure when evaluating severely depressed patients [43]. Thus, neuropsychologists should be aware of the demand characteristics of the evaluation setting and be attuned to the selective presentation of cognitive and psychiatric symptom complaints for situations in which there are grounds to suspect the veracity of patients' complaints.

Treatment

A handful of studies have examined cognitive function in remitted MDD patients in euthymic states. The speculation is that MDD patients may have chronic neurocognitive vulnerabilities which persist despite improved clinical status. Overall, findings from studies of remitted MDD patients highlight executive function and verbal memory deficits, which appear to persist even in euthymic states [44]. For currently depressed patients, aerobic exercise may exert positive influences on executive function in MDD, with even a 30-minute exercise program demonstrating significant gains on tests of selective attention and inhibition of a prepotent response [45]. Also focusing on remediation of cognitive deficits in MDD, a study of a 10-week course of computerized cognitive rehabilitation for adults with chronic MDD showed significant improvements in the domains of attention, verbal learning and memory, psychomotor speed, and executive function [46].

Patients treated with antidepressant medication show some improvement in cognitive function. Treatment with selective serotonin reuptake inhibitors, for instance, may have beneficial effects on memory function with no detectable structural changes in hippocampus [47]. Baseline neuropsychological function may also be predictive of therapeutic response to some antidepressant agents. Repetitive transcranial magnetic stimulation over dorsolateral prefrontal cortex as an adjunct to antidepressant treatment does not appear to have deleterious effects on cognitive function in patients experiencing a major depressive episode, although it may have mild beneficial effects on verbal memory functions [48]. Conversely, electroconvulsive therapy for depression has well-documented adverse effects on several aspects of cognition. Most notable are memory disturbances for information learned prior to the treatment course (i.e. retrograde amnesia), as well as poor memory for subsequently learned information (i.e. anterograde amnesia) which tends to resolve within several weeks. Objective cognitive disruptions are more common with bilateral stimulation using high-intensity electrical dosage and sine wave forms, although subjective cognitive complaints may be more strongly influenced by mood state [49].

Major depression in older adulthood

The 12-month prevalence of MDD among older adults (≥ 65 years) is less than that of their younger adult counterparts, estimated at 2.7% [50]. This number is higher in elderly nursing-home patients, where the prevalence reaches 8.1%, although subclinical depressive symptomatology may affect nearly one-quarter of these patients [51]. The presence of depression in late life increases the risk for mortality and physical illness, although depression management in older adulthood may reduce this risk. Depression also has consequences for cognitive function in old age, with neuropsychologists often playing a crucial role in the management and treatment of these patients.

Neuropsychological function

The prevalence of depression tends to increase in tandem with age-related cognitive declines in older adulthood. When the stage of cognitive decline becomes more severe, however, depressive symptoms tend to subside. Persons who go on to develop AD show the lowest levels of depression, presumably due to lack of insight for patients with this condition [52]. Depression in old age is associated with several structural abnormalities on neuroimaging which may be more pronounced when the onset of depression occurs later in life. These findings include ventricular enlargement, sulcal widening, white matter lesions, and smaller volumes of frontal lobes, hippocampus, and caudate nucleus [53].

The pattern of neuropsychological function in older adults with MDD, as with younger adults, varies across individuals depending upon several factors (e.g. comorbid Axis I and Axis II disorders, physical illness and disability). A quantitative review of the literature comparing early- and late-onset depression suggests that there are minimal differences in the pattern of neuropsychological function between younger and older adults with major depression [54]. Significant deficits can be seen across most cognitive domains, including executive function, processing speed, and episodic and semantic memory. The extent of neuropsychological deficit, however, tends to distinguish between early- and late-onset depression. Patients with late-onset depression demonstrate more severe deficits with regard to executive function and processing speed, although these differences tend to be moderate in magnitude relative to healthy older adults. Depression may actually increase the risk for subsequent declines in executive function during old age [55], although the pathophysiological mechanism for this possible decline is unclear.

The evidence for cognitive dysfunction among elderly individuals with MDD is not firmly established. There are several factors which may moderate the impact of MDD on cognitive function in older adults. A large-scale study of community-dwelling persons aged 65 years or older discovered that MDD, whether past or current, is not associated with poorer cognitive performance when current depressive symptoms are taken into account [56]. Further complicating matters is an apparent interaction between depression and subjective cognitive complaints. In one study, older adults carrying a diagnosis of MDD reported more subjective complaints of memory, language, and other cognitive complaints compared with patients who were not depressed [57]. Neuropsychological evaluation revealed no difference between these groups on measures of memory and learning, attention, processing speed, verbal fluency, and fine motor

463

dexterity. The results from this study and several others suggest that depression may increase the propensity for some older adults to report cognitive disturbance in the absence of objective neuropsychological deficit.

Assessment issues

One issue commonly faced by neuropsychologists in the assessment of older adults is the differential diagnosis of depression and early dementia. The question is a difficult one given that depression may often occur during the initial stages of a dementing condition. Neuropsychological testing can assist in differentiating a depressive disorder in older adulthood, sometimes called pseudodementia, from a dementing illness, such as Alzheimer's disease.

As reviewed above, depression may present with a broad set of cognitive deficits which may masquerade as dementia. However, there are several neuropsychological features which can distinguish these cognitive deficits from those seen in dementia (for a review, see Pfennig et al. [58]). Patients with depression and dementia often demonstrate significant episodic memory deficits. Memory is typically the first affected cognitive domain among patients with early dementia, while those with depression tend to present with more pronounced deficits in executive function and processing speed. The episodic memory deficit in depression is one which is characterized by intact encoding and consolidation of information as evidenced by improved performances on tests of recognition memory, suggesting a primary difficulty with the retrieval of information from long-term store [59]. Early dementia, on the other hand, is characterized by rapid forgetting of information with reduced recognition memory capacity. Language problems (e.g. word-finding difficulty, confabulation) are common in dementia but relatively infrequent in depression. Clinical features may also be helpful in distinguishing depression and early dementia, the former often presenting with disrupted sleep, apathy, poor motivation, and magnification of cognitive complaints. Accurate diagnosis of depression and dementia, especially when the two co-occur, is crucial for appropriate treatment of these often disabling conditions.

Treatment

Depression in late life has shown a favorable response to psychotherapeutic and pharmacological treatment [60]. Most treatment studies of MDD which examine impacts on cognitive function, however, involve trials of antidepressant medications. Some of these medications have shown improvements in verbal memory and executive function along with alleviation of depressive symptoms, while other agents have demonstrated no significant impacts on cognitive function. Of note, the presence of dementia at follow-up for depressed older patients with existing cognitive impairment may reduce the beneficial effects of antidepressant treatment on cognitive function. More research is needed to investigate the effects of psychotherapeutic treatment on cognitive deficits in older adults with MDD, as well as the possibility of additional benefit from adjunctive cognitive rehabilitation.

Conclusions

Psychopathological conditions may present with a range of neuropsychological inefficiencies. Patterns of cognitive deficit for older adults may depart from those of their younger adult counterparts, with neurocognitive function often serving as a potent predictor of disability in old age. Treatments targeted at ameliorating the psychiatric symptomatology of psychopathological conditions tend to be associated with subtle improvements in cognitive function, whereas more research is needed to understand the effect of cognitive rehabilitation for more severely affected patients. While neuropsychological testing may provide important information regarding cognitive strengths and weaknesses, functional capacity, and treatment planning for these patients, there exists no single neuropsychological profile which can serve as an identifying marker of a particular condition. Thus, the prudent neuropsychologist should consider the context in which specific behavioral and neurocognitive manifestations of a psychopathological condition occur, such that appropriate treatment strategies may be designed to improve the patient's quality of life and to make accommodations which are tailored to the individual's cognitive and functional capacities. Finally, further research is needed to understand the etiology of neuropsychological disturbance associated with psychopathological conditions. Most notably, prospective studies seem necessary to determine the differential and interactive influences of developmental insult, premorbid ability, mood state, comorbid medical and psychiatric disorder, and treatment effects on neurocognitive deficit associated with a range of psychopathological conditions.

References

1. Messias EL, Chen CY, Eaton WW. Epidemiology of schizophrenia: review of findings and myths. *Psychiatr Clin North Am* 2007;**30**:323–38.

2. Howard R, Rabins PV, Seeman MV, et al. Late-onset schizophrenia and very-late-onset schizophrenia-like psychosis: an international consensus. The International Late-Onset Schizophrenia Group. *Am J Psychiatry* 2000;**157**:172–8.

3. Iritani S. Neuropathology of schizophrenia: a mini review. *Neuropathology* 2007;**27**:604–8.

4. Jakob H, Beckmann H. Circumscribed malformation and nerve cell alterations in the entorhinal cortex of schizophrenics. Pathogenetic and clinical aspects. *J Neural Transm Gen Sect* 1994;**98**:83–106.

5. Kraus MS, Keefe RS. Cognition as an outcome measure in schizophrenia. *Br J Psychiatry Suppl* 2007;**50**:s46–51.

6. Bilder RM, Goldman RS, Robinson D, et al. Neuropsychology of first-episode schizophrenia: initial characterization and clinical correlates. *Am J Psychiatry* 2000;**157**:549–59.

7. Zipparo L, Whitford TJ, Redoblado Hodge MA, et al. Investigating the neuropsychological and neuroanatomical changes that occur over the first 2–3 years of illness in patients with first-episode schizophrenia. *Prog Neuropsychopharmacol Biol Psychiatry* 2008;**32**:531–8.

8. Heinrichs RW, Zakzanis KK. Neurocognitive deficit in schizophrenia: a quantitative review of the evidence. *Neuropsychology* 1998;**12**:426–45.

9. Reichenberg A, Harvey PD. Neuropsychological impairments in schizophrenia: Integration of performance-based and brain imaging findings. *Psychol Bull* 2007;**133**:833–58.

10. Westermeyer J. Comorbid schizophrenia and substance abuse: a review of epidemiology and course. *Am J Addict* 2006;**15**:345–55.

11. Coulston CM, Perdices M, Tennant CC. The neuropsychology of cannabis and other substance use in schizophrenia: review of the literature and critical evaluation of methodological issues. *Aust N Z J Psychiatry* 2007;**41**:869–84.

12. Helldin L, Kane JM, Karilampi U, et al. Remission and cognitive ability in a cohort of patients with schizophrenia. *J Psychiatr Res* 2006;**40**:738–45.

13. Wittorf A, Sickinger S, Wiedemann G, et al. Neurocognitive effects of atypical and conventional antipsychotic drugs in schizophrenia: A naturalistic 6-month follow-up study. *Arch Clin Neuropsychol* 2008;**23**:271–82.

14. McGurk SR, Twamley EW, Sitzer DI, et al. A meta-analysis of cognitive remediation in schizophrenia. *Am J Psychiatry* 2007;**164**:1791–802.

15. Friedman JI, Harvey PD, McGurk SR, et al. Correlates of change in functional status of institutionalized geriatric schizophrenic patients: focus on medical comorbidity. *Am J Psychiatry* 2002;**159**:1388–94.

16. Chemerinski E, Reichenberg A, Kirkpatrick B, et al. Three dimensions of clinical symptoms in elderly patients with schizophrenia: prediction of six-year cognitive and functional status. *Schizophr Res* 2006;**85**:12–19.

17. Barak Y, Aizenberg D, Mirecki I, et al. Very late-onset schizophrenia-like psychosis: clinical and imaging characteristics in comparison with elderly patients with schizophrenia. *J Nerv Ment Dis* 2002;**190**:733–6.

18. Jones DK, Catani M, Pierpaoli C, et al. A diffusion tensor magnetic resonance imaging study of frontal cortex connections in very-late-onset schizophrenia-like psychosis. *Am J Geriatr Psychiatry* 2005;**13**:1092–9.

19. Zakzanis KK, Andrikopoulos J, Young DA, et al. Neuropsychological differentiation of late-onset schizophrenia and dementia of the Alzheimer's type. *Appl Neuropsychol* 2003;**10**:105–14.

20. Salzman C, Tune L. Neuroleptic treatment of late-life schizophrenia. *Harv Rev Psychiatry* 2001;**9**:77–83.

21. Harvey PD, Napolitano JA, Mao L, et al. Comparative effects of risperidone and olanzapine on cognition in elderly patients with schizophrenia or schizoaffective disorder. *Int J Geriatr Psychiatry* 2003;**18**:820–9.

22. Alexopoulos GS, Streim J, Carpenter D, et al. Using antipsychotic agents in older patients. *J Clin Psychiatry* 2004;**65** Suppl 2:5,99; discussion 100–102; quiz 103–4.

23. National Institutes of Mental Health. *Bipolar disorder*. 1995. http://www.nimh.nih.gov/health/publications/bipolar-disorder/introduction.shtml [Accessed Mar 10, 2008].

24. Johnson SL. Defining bipolar disorder. In Johnson SL, Leahy RL, eds. *Psychological Treatment of Bipolar Disorder*. New York: Guilford; 2000: 3–16.

25. Newberg AR, Catapano LA, Zarate CA, et al. Neurobiology of bipolar disorder. *Expert Rev Neurother* 2008;**8**:93–110.

26. Clark L, Sahakian BJ. Cognitive neuroscience and brain imaging in bipolar disorder. *Dialogues Clin Neurosci* 2008;**10**:153–63.

27. Malhi GS, Ivanovski B, Hadzi-Pavlovic D, et al. Neuropsychological deficits and functional impairment

in bipolar depression, hypomania and euthymia. *Bipolar Disord* 2007;**9**:114–25.

28. Grant BF, Stinson FS, Hasin DS, et al. Prevalence, correlates, and comorbidity of bipolar I disorder and axis I and II disorders: results from the National Epidemiologic Survey on Alcohol and Related Conditions. *J Clin Psychiatry* 2005;**66**:1205–15.

29. Ruocco AC. The neuropsychology of borderline personality disorder: a meta-analysis and review. *Psychiatry Res* 2005;**137**:191–202.

30. Burdick KE, Braga RJ, Goldberg JF, et al. Cognitive dysfunction in bipolar disorder: future place of pharmacotherapy. *CNS Drugs* 2007;**21**:971–81.

31. Depp CA, Jeste DV. Bipolar disorder in older adults: a critical review. *Bipolar Disord* 2004;**6**:343–67.

32. Rabins PV, Aylward E, Holroyd S, et al. MRI findings differentiate between late-onset schizophrenia and late-life mood disorder. *Int J Geriatr Psychiatry* 2000;**15**:954–60.

33. Savard RJ, Rey AC, Post RM. Halstead-Reitan Category Test in bipolar and unipolar affective disorders. Relationship to age and phase of illness. *J Nerv Ment Dis* 1980;**168**:297–304.

34. Kessler RC, Berglund P, Demler O, et al. The epidemiology of major depressive disorder: results from the National Comorbidity Survey Replication (NCS-R). *J Am Med Assoc* 2003;**289**:3095–105.

35. Mossner R, Mikova O, Koutsilieri E, et al. Consensus paper of the WFSBP Task Force on Biological Markers: biological markers in depression. *World J Biol Psychiatry* 2007;**8**:141–74.

36. Campbell S, Macqueen G. The role of the hippocampus in the pathophysiology of major depression. *J Psychiatry Neurosci* 2004;**29**:417–26.

37. Castaneda AE, Tuulio-Henriksson A, Marttunen M, et al. A review on cognitive impairments in depressive and anxiety disorders with a focus on young adults. *J Affect Disord* 2008;**106**:1–27.

38. DeBattista C. Executive dysfunction in major depressive disorder. *Expert Rev Neurother* 2005;**5**:79–83.

39. Henry J, Crawford JR. A meta-analytic review of verbal fluency deficits in depression. *J Clin Exp Neuropsychol* 2005;**27**:78–101.

40. Porter RJ, Bourke C, Gallagher P. Neuropsychological impairment in major depression: its nature, origin and clinical significance. *Aust N Z J Psychiatry* 2007;**41**:115–28.

41. Ebmeier K, Rose E, Steele D. Cognitive impairment and fMRI in major depression. *Neurotox Res* 2006;**10**:87–92.

42. Ruocco AC, Swirsky-Sacchetti T, Chute DL, et al. Distinguishing between neuropsychological malingering and exaggerated psychiatric symptoms in a neuropsychological setting. *Clin Neuropsychol* 2008;**22**:547–64.

43. Yanez YT, Fremouw W, Tennant J, et al. Effects of severe depression on TOMM performance among disability-seeking outpatients. *Arch Clin Neuropsychol* 2006;**21**:161–5.

44. Smith DJ, Muir WJ, Blackwood DH. Neurocognitive impairment in euthymic young adults with bipolar spectrum disorder and recurrent major depressive disorder. *Bipolar Disord* 2006;**8**:40–6.

45. Kubesch S, Bretschneider V, Freudenmann R, et al. Aerobic endurance exercise improves executive functions in depressed patients. *J Clin Psychiatry* 2003;**64**:1005–12.

46. Elgamal S, McKinnon MC, Ramakrishnan K, et al. Successful computer-assisted cognitive remediation therapy in patients with unipolar depression: a proof of principle study. *Psychol Med* 2007;**37**:1229–38.

47. Vythilingam M, Vermetten E, Anderson GM, et al. Hippocampal volume, memory, and cortisol status in major depressive disorder: effects of treatment. *Biol Psychiatry* 2004;**56**:101–12.

48. Hausmann A, Pascual-Leone A, Kemmler G, et al. No deterioration of cognitive performance in an aggressive unilateral and bilateral antidepressant rTMS add-on trial. *J Clin Psychiatry* 2004;**65**:772–82.

49. Prudic J, Peyser S, Sackeim HA. Subjective memory complaints: a review of patient self-assessment of memory after electroconvulsive therapy. *J ECT* 2000;**16**:121–32.

50. Hasin DS, Goodwin RD, Stinson FS, et al. Epidemiology of major depressive disorder: results from the National Epidemiologic Survey on Alcoholism and Related Conditions. *Arch Gen Psychiatry* 2005;**62**:1097–106.

51. Jongenelis K, Pot AM, Eisses AM, et al. Prevalence and risk indicators of depression in elderly nursing home patients: the AGED study. *J Affect Disord* 2004;**83**:135–42.

52. Bierman EJ, Comijs HC, Jonker C, et al. Symptoms of anxiety and depression in the course of cognitive decline. *Dement Geriatr Cogn Disord* 2007;**24**:213–19.

53. Schweitzer I, Tuckwell V, Ames D, et al. Structural neuroimaging studies in late-life depression: a review. *World J Biol Psychiatry* 2001;**2**:83–8.

54. Herrmann LL, Goodwin GM, Ebmeier KP. The cognitive neuropsychology of depression in the elderly. *Psychol Med* 2007;**37**:1693–702.

55. Cui X, Lyness JM, Tu X, et al. Does depression precede or follow executive dysfunction? Outcomes in older primary care patients. *Am J Psychiatry* 2007;**164**:1221–8.

56. Godin O, Dufouil C, Ritchie K, et al. Depressive symptoms, major depressive episode and cognition in the elderly: the three-city study. *Neuroepidemiology* 2007;**28**:101–8.

57. Fischer C, Schweizer TA, Atkins JH, et al. Neurocognitive profiles in older adults with and without major depression. *Int J Geriatr Psychiatry* 2008;**23**:851–6.

58. Pfennig A, Littmann E, Bauer M. Neurocognitive impairment and dementia in mood disorders. *J Neuropsychiatry Clin Neurosci* 2007;**19**:373–82.

59. Dierckx E, Engelborghs S, De Raedt R, et al. Differentiation between mild cognitive impairment, Alzheimer's disease and depression by means of cued recall. *Psychol Med* 2007;**37**:747–55.

60. Butters MA, Becker JT, Nebes RD, et al. Changes in cognitive functioning following treatment of late-life depression. *Am J Psychiatry* 2000;**157**:1949–54.

Neuropsychological aspects of psychopathology across the lifespan: a synthesis

Alexandra Zagoloff and Scott J. Hunter

As evident in the previous two chapters, the understanding of psychopathology and its associated neuropsychological deficits across the lifespan is complicated by the uneven investigation of pediatric and adult disorders [1, 2]. In particular, as Sivan [2] emphasizes, while select disorders that impact developmental functioning are considered in the pediatric neuropsychology literature (i.e. the comorbidity of attention deficit hyperactivity disorder (ADHD) with other mood and behavioral disorders [3]; also see Marks et al. and Halperin et al., this volume), examination of mood disorders and other forms of developmental psychopathology, and their associated neuropsychological markers, is less frequent. This has led to these disorders being less clearly understood with regard to their neuropsychological profiles and impact across childhood. At the same time, this situation contrasts significantly with our understanding of adult psychopathology. Schizophrenia, bipolar disorder, and the depressive disorders, among other psychopathologies, have been extensively examined with regard to their neurocognitive impact; and in the case of schizophrenia in particular, well characterized as a neuropsychological disorder.

There is evidence that this situation is changing with regard to developmental psychopathology. There have been an increased number of recent studies published that have examined the neurocognitive and behavioral markers of such mood and regulatory disorders that occur during childhood as pediatric bipolar disorder [3, 4]. Descriptions of early underlying neuropsychological vulnerabilities to psychopathology are also being more fully considered, specifically with disorders such as schizophrenia (e.g. see work of Walker and colleagues [5]), or depression and mood dysregulation, particularly following early maltreatment (see work by Cicchetti and colleagues [6]).

Still, while research on specific pediatric neuropsychological profiles and markers has increased, in response to the recognition that adult models cannot reliably be applied to childhood disorders (see Bernstein's chapter in this volume), there remains infrequent consideration within clinical neuropsychology of the lifespan impact of developmental psychopathology. This has contributed to a paucity of available data in the literature for review and consideration. As a result, clinicians working with either population, adult or child, encounter a similar set of problems: how to think longitudinally about the potential effects a mood or behavioral disorder might engender; how to know what the base rates of mood and behavioral disorders are across development, and how that can influence diagnosis; and correspondingly, how to address comorbidity, which is a frequently observed diagnostic phenomenon. In particular, it has been difficult for practitioners in clinical neuropsychology to

> resolve the predicament of the conflictual relationship between two or more disorders [in order to] enable meaningful interpretations that are most likely to result in application of appropriate intervention. (Stefanatos and Baron [7], p. 15)

The goal of this chapter is to synthesize what we know about psychopathology and its impact on lifespan neuropsychological development, as has been cogently discussed in the prior two chapters, and to highlight important issues these authors have raised when considering and attempting to resolve the relationship between co-occurring disorders in adult and pediatric patients. In order to do so, this chapter starts with a discussion of diagnosis, and in particular, information gathering, by emphasizing the importance of collateral informants and the validity of their reports when considering psychopathology and its comorbidity. Next, we summarize what has been shared about neuropsychological impairments associated with different types of psychopathology seen across the lifespan, in order to highlight the prominent issues that need to be considered with potential diagnoses and intervention. Finally, the chapter concludes with a consideration of issues related to treatment of psychopathology and its impact on neuropsychological functioning and status.

Information gathering in neuropsychology

As discussed by Bernstein in her chapter on models, neuropsychological assessment is based on a structured approach to information gathering that emphasizes the integration of multiple, often multidisciplinary sources of information regarding a patient and his or her concerns. Through a comprehensive review of medical records, school reports, self and parent reports for children, and in adults, self, spouse, and family reports, and following the completion of a series of standardized tests by the patient, the neuropsychologist coalesces data from these multiple sources and procedures, to obtain a descriptive understanding of the patient's difficulties, concerns, and strengths, and develops and presents a diagnosis and set of recommendations. As a result, it is very important for the clinician or researcher interested in understanding the relationship between psychopathology and neuropsychological status to identify, have available, and make use of well-developed, valid tools for ascertaining the degree of distress and disorder present in a particular patient. This has commonly led to a reliance on standardized rating scales, which provide a description of symptoms experienced, and foster diagnostic considerations.

Stefanatos and Baron [7] have described several important issues to consider when utilizing mood and behavior rating scales when conducting neuropsychological evaluations. They emphasize that while rating scales are popular for their convenience, they are often insufficient for objectively forming or even confirming a diagnosis. The modest correlations observed between multiple informants across the majority of the commonly used mood and behavior rating scales are one reason for this caution. Yet, these tools are still quite helpful in assisting the clinician, as well as the researcher, in detailing potential diagnostic influences, specifically with regard to comorbidity. The development of clinical impressions can and

does benefit from the use of multiple informant reports when gathering data; these data both assist the interview process, by highlighting areas of concern that may be easily overlooked by the clinician during the interview or assessment, and objectively support the process of hypothesis generation.

Through the completion of parent and teacher report measures for children, or the addition of spouse and even parent reports when working with an adult, the consideration of developmental psychopathology is enhanced, and differential diagnosis is often improved. This is due to the fact that each person queried may provide unique information [8, 9], as well as support and extend what is being reported by the patient, as well as observed during the evaluation. This is crucial, as has been noted by Sivan [2], with regard to thinking critically about the direction of influence a form of psychopathology may have when developing a diagnostic understanding of the patient. For example, both anxiety and depression have been shown to impact aspects of such neuropsychological processes in adults as memory, attention, and executive control [1]. As a result, the prevailing wisdom is that the adult presenting with a concern about memory or attentional difficulties benefits by being closely screened for potential or ongoing mood concerns that may extend or influence neurological difficulties. Similarly, in children, irritability and restlessness, in addition to inattention and poor organization are common symptoms underlying the presentation of ADHD; however, clinical observations and some research have strongly indicated that ongoing anxiety or mood dysfunction in a child can contribute to these neuropsychological difficulties independently [2]. This argues strongly, as both Sivan and Ruocco et al. have observed, for careful and comprehensive assessment of behavioral and mood presentation when conducting differential diagnosis.

The validity of self- and observer-report is crucial whether the patient is a child or an adult. Additionally, information about psychopathology frequently comes from behavioral observation and clinical interviews. As such, clinical interviews are considered an invaluable component of adult assessment, particularly given that adults are generally considered to be reliable reporters [10]. Clinicians who work with children include parent and teacher reports in part because children provide less reliable information [10], and it is important to gain a broad understanding of the pattern of concerns across environments.

Cross-informant correlations regarding children's behavior tend to be low, though, so while it is helpful to obtain perspectives from various people associated with the patient, there is often significant variability to be considered with such reports. Such discrepancies can result from a variety of factors, including differences in the child behavior across environments and conditions, whether problems are observed or inferred, and the type of the problematic behavior that is under consideration. Fewer studies have been conducted evaluating inter-rater reliability between adult self-report measures and information provided by their collaterals. Results suggest that correlations are highest regarding substance use behavior; however, the validity and reliability of reports regarding other types of behavior warrant further investigation. This argues for a multidimensional, progressive integration of information being collected across environments and sources.

The possibility of conducting behavioral observations provides one potential solution to the problem. While observations of children may be instructive, though, such opportunities may be impractical for adults. This is where aspects of the evaluation become important tools for gaining clarification, although the nature of the testing situation limits generalizability.

Biological measures provide another avenue for research and clinical data gathering. This has been particularly emphasized with regard to understanding and classifying pediatric bipolar disorder [3], and remains an avenue of intense exploration with schizophrenia [6]. However, to date such measures have not provided information superior to that provided by collaterals, or even from adult patients during a diagnostic interview. Similarly, data from physiological measures, such as MRI, SPECT, or PET, seldom inform us about individual markers of behavior or mood dysfunction. Research findings are descriptive of group but not individual neurological variabilities in psychopathology.

One encouraging finding regarding the obtaining of broad-based information about symptom presentation and impact is that the majority of adults provide consent to have collaterals contacted and collaterals typically respond to such requests [9, 10]. This suggests that it is practical and useful to collect such information. Despite low correlations between self- and other-reports, both sources provide important information to be considered and can guide and direct hypothesis generation, particularly with regard to the question of a specific disorder being the sole reason for a set of neuropsychological concerns, or whether comorbidities need to be considered. When the two reports concur, a clinician can be more confident that the behavior at hand occurs as is reported, and is a source of the variance attempting to be explained. When the reports disagree, the clinician is alerted to behavior that warrants further investigation. For example, if a teacher reports externalizing behavior but a parent does not, the clinician can investigate contextual factors that might influence the child's behavior [11].

Studies of individuals with substance abuse often include information provided by collaterals. Weiss et al. [9] investigated comorbid substance abuse and bipolar disorder in adult patients, using self-reports of substance use, urine toxicology screenings, and reports from collateral informants. The authors combined self-report and urine screens in the following way: the combination was considered negative if both reports were negative, but was considered positive if one was positive. Overall, there was 75% agreement between collateral report and the combination. Of these, 65% agreed with a negative report, while 35% agreed with a positive one. There were few instances of false positives as reported by the collateral, but 23% of the collaterals reported false negatives. There were only seven instances (5%) in which the patient denied use but their urine screen was positive. Spouses and significant others were significantly more likely than other informants to agree with the patient. This relationship was attenuated when the authors controlled for frequency of contact. Even though collaterals were generally confident in their report, their confidence ratings were not correlated with accuracy.

In this study, collateral informants provided little additional information compared to that from the patient or urine screen. The authors noted that the investigators were well-known to the patients, which may have resulted in more honest reporting than is typical. Consequently, they note that collaterals may provide useful information when patients are more distrustful of the researchers or clinicians. The finding regarding frequency of contact can guide clinicians when deciding which collateral informants to contact. Nonetheless, the authors mentioned that it is time-consuming to collect collateral information and the results of their study indicated that the benefit may not always be worth the cost in certain populations. This indicates a need for continued investigation of when collateral data are most informative clinically.

Another avenue of research has compared self-report with established objective measures. Muris and colleagues [12] administered the Attention Control Scale (ACS), Effortful Control Scale (ECS), Revised Child Anxiety and Depression Scale, the Child Rating of Aggression, and five subtests of the Test of Everyday Attention for Children (TEA-Ch) to 207 boys and girls. Scores from the ACS and the ECS were significantly, positively correlated. The ACS was correlated with some subtests of the TEA-Ch, but the ECS was not correlated at all. The authors suggest this may be a result of insufficient psychometric properties of the self-report measures. However, this presupposes that the TEA-Ch is the more valid assessment tool. Alternatively, they mention that five subtests from the TEA-Ch may be an insufficient way to evaluate a concept as complex as attention. This indicates a need to explore the cumulative reliability of these data when considering the interactions between mood and attention. In support of this, anxiety and depression were both significantly, negatively correlated with the ACS, ECS, and TEA-Ch, although the associations were stronger with the self-report measures than the objective assessment. Self-reported aggression scores were significantly correlated with self-reported executive function. After controlling for gender and age, the correlations between self-reported attention and pathology remained significant, but the correlations with the TEA-Ch did not.

Types of psychopathology

As addressed by Ruocco et al. [1], adult psychopathology is commonly associated with neuropsychological impairments. Sivan [2] suggests similarly, but emphasizes that the paucity of comprehensive research regarding neuropsychological aspects of psychopathology in children limits our understanding of the potential vulnerabilities that may be present and influential, and decreases generalizability of the few findings available. Yet, as emphasized by both chapters, we require, as neuropsychologists, ongoing consideration of and a continued emphasis on our training background as clinical psychopathologists. Consideration of base rates for disorders, an ability to think conceptually and critically about what particular patterns of symptoms may represent, and an ability to approach data from an objective standpoint are required when attempting to ascertain whether difficulties seen with a given patient reflect neurocognitive dysfunction that is secondary to a specific neurodevelopmental or acquired insult, or are representative of neurocognitive difficulties secondary to a mood or behavioral concern. In line with this, what follows is a discussion of additional issues not raised by those authors.

Memory has been identified as a particular area of interest, and concern, with regard to considerations of neuropsychological dysfunction in psychopathology. This is one of the more common complaints expressed by individuals where mood difficulties are of concern. Airaksinen and colleagues [13] investigated episodic memory dysfunction in a population-based sample of individuals with anxiety disorders. Their sample included 112 individuals who met criteria for one or more anxiety disorder based on the Schedules for Clinical Assessments in Neuropsychiatry. They further divided their group into individuals with panic disorder (PD, with and without agoraphobia), social phobia, specific phobia (SP), obsessive compulsive disorder (OCD), and generalized anxiety disorder. Slightly less than half also met criteria for other psychiatric disorders and several were taking prescription medication.

Episodic memory dysfunction was revealed among participants with PD, SP, and OCD. Executive functioning, measured by the Trail Making Tests, was also impaired in individuals with PD and OCD. Individuals with SP also demonstrated impairments in verbal fluency on the Word Association Test. In general, these results held after removal of participants with comorbid conditions. Removing individuals with substance abuse, though, decreased observed differences in executive function. Results held when comparing medicated and unmedicated individuals with two exceptions. Medicated individuals performed slightly better on verbal fluency and took more time to complete Trails B. The magnitude of gain from free to cued recall was similar for the anxiety and control groups.

The authors suggest that this reveals an encoding, but not retrieval, impairment in anxiety disorders. For this sample, executive dysfunction may be more a result of substance abuse rather than anxiety. Interestingly, the authors note that only 53% of randomly selected individuals participated. They argue that individuals suffering from more severe pathology would be less inclined to participate. They also noted demographic differences between participants and non-participants that might suggest higher than average functioning among their participants. As a result, they argue that "true" effects of anxiety on cognition may be stronger than their results indicate.

With regard to studies considering whether differential classification can be made based on neuropsychological factors, ascertained through self- and teacher-reports, Kusche et al. [14] classified a community-based population of children into one of four groups based on self- and teacher-reports: anxious, externalizing, comorbid anxious/externalizing, and unaffected controls. Groups were created using individual and combined reports. Children from each of the groups were assessed across multiple variables, including intellectual functioning, academic skill development, performances on select verbal and nonverbal tasks, executive functioning, classroom behavior, and emotional functioning. Results revealed that the control group obtained the highest scores with regard to status and functioning, while the comorbid anxious/externalizing group obtained the lowest. The singularly classified anxious and externalizing groups obtained scores that fell in between the other two groups. This was true for IQ, academic achievement, verbal and nonverbal tasks, emotional understanding, executive functioning, and classroom functioning. Interestingly, the anxious group was elevated on externalizing symptoms, and the reverse was true for the externalizing group. The authors suggested that their results indicate that a mild overlap exists between the groups. However, this lack of difference may speak to the frequent comorbidity of psychopathology under consideration (co-occurring symptoms of anxiety and externalizing behavior), and may call into question the validity of results regarding differences between the two groups.

The authors conducted discriminant analyses and found that IQ, academic achievement, nonverbal functioning, and executive functioning contributed unique variance in terms of distinguishing the controls from children with psychopathology. Statistics were re-analyzed excluding children with IQ scores below 85. One-fourth of the previously significant findings no longer remained so primarily because the Auxious/Externalizing group had a significantly higher percentage of children with low IQ. The comparisons between the control group and the pathological groups remained similar.

With regard to neurocognitive findings, the authors argue that observed patterns of dysfunction for the anxious group suggest that early identification of children with affective symptoms is important given the broad range of deficits and the tendency for these problems to go undetected. The authors also highlighted the high rate of comorbid depression, and the value of dividing externalizers into more specific groups

(e.g. aggressive, impulsive), in addition to differential identification based on teacher and self-reports.

Davis [15] has reviewed studies of the neuropsychological basis of childhood psychopathology, in order to help school psychologists understand the range and presentation of behavior problems and learning concerns frequently encountered in academic settings. While primarily studies of older adolescents and adults, his review of selective findings highlights that depression can interfere with processing speed, attention, and aspects of memory. Davis suggests that differential structural findings in individuals with psychopathology, such as amygdala volume abnormalities seen in adults with depression, may relate to the variabilities in memory performance seen with mood disorder earlier in life. Davis observes, correctly, that a combination of biological, neuropsychological, and observational approaches are coalescing to tie difficulties with executive functions, memory, and emotional dysregulation with psychopathology. Data from a broad range of studies also suggest that with appropriate intervention, either pharmacological or behavioral, improvements in cognitive and neuropsychological profiles may be observed.

Treatment of psychopathology and its impact on neuropsychological status

Pharmacological treatment of psychopathology is not neurocognitively benign. Accumulating evidence indicates that many of the pharmacological agents used to treat psychiatric disorders impact aspects of cognitive functioning. Given the prevalence of pharmacological interventions and their continued emphasis as a first-line approach to treatment, ongoing research concerning their cognitive effects is strongly needed.

Barker and colleagues [16] conducted a meta-analysis of 13 studies that investigated the effects of benzodiazepine use on 12 cognitive domains. Across the studies, 60% of the participants were female, the average age was 47.6 years, the mean duration of use was 9.9 years, and a variety of benzodiazepines were investigated (most commonly lorazepam and diazepam). The extent to which results can be generalized is complicated by the wide age range (21–75) of the participants as well as the length of time the medication was used (1–34 years). The most frequently measured abilities were verbal memory, working memory, and attention/concentration. Effect sizes ranged from

−0.42 for verbal reasoning to −1.30 for sensory processing, indicating that long-term benzodiazepine users were significantly impaired on a variety of neuropsychological measures. Time since last dose was the only moderator that reached significance with respect to its effect on psychomotor speed.

Based on their results, the authors expressed concern that long-term effects of benzodiazepine use are a potential source of neurocognitive disruption, specifically in adults. This has provided additional support to the concern that use of these medications to treat psychopathology, over time, may intensify or exacerbate already subtle to more significant neuropsychological concerns. Neuropsychologists working with patients complaining of long-term anxiety and increased memory difficulties are warranted to examine the potential for cumulative effects given medication management of the disorder.

A similar concern has long been standing regarding the potential impact of selective antiepilepsy medications, including more recently developed compounds such as levetiracetam. Children with partial seizure disorders treated with levetiracetam have shown an increased vulnerability to behavioral and mood disruption [17]. Because these compounds are more commonly being explored for the treatment of mood difficulties, both in adults and pediatric populations over time, it is imperative that we gain an understanding of the potential impact these drugs may have on functioning, in order to effectively parse what is associated with the disorder, and what is likely to be a medication effect.

Conclusion

Across the chapters in this volume an emphasis has been placed on how both individually, and comorbidly, neuropsychological and psychopathological conditions impact functioning, both at the level of the disorder itself, and with regard to treatments utilized. What is also clear is that there remains a significant need to continue to study these relationships, in order to more effectively parse the variety of influences illness and disorder may have on functioning. Regardless of the patient's age, it is important that the information gathered regarding an individual and her or his difficulties, as well as capabilities, be reliable and valid. While adults and children often present quite differently, the range of presenting problems across time is similar in its ability to disrupt and affect developmental processes, with a potential for doing so quite dramatically. Assessment and treatment of impairments related to psychopathology, both independently and comorbid with known brain pathology, require a careful process of parceling out effects, and involve a broad consideration of what difficulties are at play. Taking a hypothesis-driven approach will continue to provide an appropriate avenue for investigating the impact of psychopathology across the lifespan.

Currently, far more research has been conducted that addresses disorder and treatment effects in adults with psychopathology, as opposed to children. This is changing, but at a slow pace. As a result, avenues for improved understanding across the lifespan, of both the range of developmental comorbidities that exist, and the more general impact mood and behavioral disorders can have on neuropsychological functioning, requires an increased emphasis in research. Utilizing multidisciplinary approaches to investigation, taking advantage of multiple sources of data, and taking into account the variable impact treatments may have on status are all important guidelines for advancing our knowledge. By better defining the impact psychopathology may have on functioning, as well as potential treatment effects that exist, neuropsychology will be better situated to guide future avenues of etiological theorization and intervention.

References

1. Ruocco AC, Kunchandy E, Lacy M. Psychopathological conditions in adults. In Donders J, Hunter SJ, eds. *Principles and Practice of Lifespan Developmental Neuropsychology*. Cambridge: Cambridge University Press; 2010.

2. Sivan A. Psychopathological conditions in children and adolescents. In Donders J, Hunter SJ, eds. *Principles and Practice of Lifespan Developmental Neuropsychology*. Cambridge: Cambridge University Press; 2010.

3. Leibenluft E, Rich BA. Pediatric bipolar disorder. *Annu Rev Clin Psychology* 2008;**4**:163–87.

4. Pavuluri M, West A, Hill SK, Jindal K, Sweeney, JA. Neurocognitive function in pediatric bipolar disorder: 3-year follow-up shows cognitive developmental lagging behind healthy youths. *J Am Acad Child Adolesc Psychiatry* 2009;**48**:299–307.

5. Walker E, Kestler L, Bollini A, Hochman, K. Schizophrenia: etiology and course. *Annu Rev Psychol* 2004;**55**:401–30.

6. Cicchetti D, Walker EF, eds. *Neurodevelopmental Mechanisms in Psychopathology*. Cambridge: Cambridge University Press; 2004.

7. Stefanatos GA, Baron IS. Attention-deficit/hyperactivity disorder: a neuropsychological perspective towards DSM-V. *Neuropsych Rev* 2007;**17**:5–38.

8. Boonstra AM, Kooij JJS, Oosterlaan J, Sergeant JA, Buitelaar JK. Does methylphenidate improve inhibition and other cognitive abilities in adults with childhood-onset ADHD? *J Clin Exp Neuropsychol* 2005;**27**:278–98.

9. Weiss RD, Greenfield SF, Griffin ML, Najavits LM, Fucito LM. The use of collateral reports for patients with bipolar and substance use disorders. *Am J Drug Alchocol Abuse* 2000;**26**(3):369–78.

10. Achenbach TM. As others see us: clinical and research implications of cross-informant correlations for psychopathology. *Curr Dir Psychol Sci* 2006;**15**(2):94–8.

11. Havey JM, Olson JM, McCormick C, Cates GL. Teachers' perceptions of the incidence and management of Attention-Deficit/Hyperactivity Disorder. *Appl Neuropsychol* 2005;**12**(2):120–7.

12. Muris P, van der Pennen E, Sigmond R, Mayer B. Symptoms of anxiety, depression, and aggression in non-clinical children: Relationships with self-report and performance-based measures of attention and effortful control. *Child Psychiatry Hum Dev* 2008;**39**:455–67.

13. Airaksinen E, Larsson M, Forsell Y. Neuropsychological functions in anxiety disorders in population-based samples: evidence of episodic memory dysfunction. *J Psychiatric Res* 2005;**39**:207–14.

14. Kusche CA, Cook ET, Greenberg MT. Neuropsychological and cognitive functioning in children with anxiety, externalizing, and comorbid psychopathol. *J Clin Child Psychol* 1993;**22**(2):172–95.

15. Davis AS. The neuropsychological basis of childhood psychopathology. *Psychol Schools* 2006;**43**(4):503–12.

16. Barker MJ, Greenwood KM, Jackson M, Crowe SF. Cognitive effects of long-term benzodiazepine use. *CNS Drugs* 2004;**18**(1):37–48.

17. De la Loge C, Hunter S, Schiemann J, Yang H, LEV N01103 Pediatric Study Group. *Adjunctive levetiracetam for partial onset seizures: assessment of behavioral and emotional function in children and adolescents in a randomized placebo-controlled study.* Presentation to the 60th Annual Meeting of the American Academy of Neurology, Chicago, IL: 2008.

Index